| | | |
|---|---|---|
| **E5-1A** | 1. | $650,000 |
| | 2. | $1,050,000 |
| **E5-2A** | 1. | $700,000 |
| | 2. | $1,000,000 |
| **E5-3A** | 1. | Land, $640,000; Goodwill, $160,000 |
| | 2. | Land, $700,000; Goodwill, $200,000 |
| **E6-2** | 1. | Independence is met—5% |
| | 2. | Independence not met—15% |
| **E6-3** | 1. | Independence not met—13% |
| | 2. | 12:1 |
| **E6-4** | 1. | Independence not met—12% |
| **E6-5** | 1. | Credit add'l. paid-in capital, $500,000 |
| **E6-6** | 1d. | Credit retained earnings, $35,000 |
| **E6-7** | 1d. | Credit retained earnings, $34,000 |
| **E6-8** | 1. | Credit add'l. paid-in capital, $80,000 |
| **E6-9** | 1. | Credit add'l. paid-in capital, $72,000 |
| **E6-10** | 1. | $45,000 |
| | 2. | c. |
| **E6-11** | | $1,700,000 |
| **E6-12** | d. | $127,000 |
| **E6-13** | | $21,200,000 |
| **E6-14** | c. | |
| **P6-1** | 1. | Carrying value of investment at date of pooling, $128,000 |
| **P6-2** | 5. | Consolidated net income, $80,000; Consolidated assets, $1,000,000 |
| **P6-3** | 3. | Carrying value of investment at Dec. 31, 19X2, $144,000 |
| | 5. | Consolidated net income, $77,000; Consolidated assets, $1,000,000 |
| **P6-4** | 3. | Consolidated net income, $1,620,000; Consolidated retained earnings, $2,130,000 |
| **P6-5** | 3. | Consolidated net income, $1,600,000; Consolidated retained earnings, $2,079,000 |
| **P6-6** | 5. | Consolidated net income, $102,000; Consolidated retained earnings, $156,000 |
| **P6-7** | 1. | $909,000 |
| | 2. | $744,000 |
| **P6-8** | 1. | Combined assets, $37,700,000; Combined net income, $7,800,000; Retained earnings at Dec. 31, 19X3, $14,700,000 |
| | 2. | Combined assets, $42,270,000; Combined net income, $6,050,000; Retained earnings at Dec. 31, 19X3, $8,950,000 |
| **E7-1** | | Adjusted balances, $84,000 |
| **E7-3** | 2. | Defer $9,000 |
| **E7-6** | 1a. | $24,000 |
| | 1b. | $22,000 |
| **E7-7** | 1. | Defer $20,000 |
| | 2. | Reduce equity in net income by $14,000 |
| **P7-1** | 3. | Consolidated net income, $41,000 Consolidated assets, $694,000 |
| **P7-2** | 3. | Consolidated net income, $85,000 Consolidated retained earnings, $992,000 |
| **P7-3** | 4. | Consolidated net income, $57,000; Consolidated assets, $950,000 |
| **P7-4** | 4. | Consolidated net income, $124,000; |

| | | |
|---|---|---|
| | | Conso... interes... |
| **P7-5** | 3. | Consolidated retained earnings, $4,317,000; Consolidated assets, $15,129,000 |
| **P7-6** | 2. | Adjusted balances, $38,000 |
| | 6. | Consolidated net income, $227,000; Consolidated assets, $6,652,000 |
| **E8-3** | 1. | Net book value, $500,000 |
| | 2. | Net book value, $525,000 |
| **P8-1** | 3. | Consolidated net income, $168,000; Consolidated assets, $860,000 |
| **P8-2** | 3. | Consolidated net income, $257,800; Consolidated assets, $534,000 |
| **P8-3** | 4. | Consolidated net income, $82,000; Consolidated assets, $459,000; Minority interest in net assets, $18,000 |
| **P8-4** | 4. | Consolidated net income, $80,000; Consolidated assets, $792,000; Minority interest in net assets, $39,000 |
| **P8-5** | 4. | Consolidated net income, $83,200; Consolidated assets, $1,113,000 |
| **E9-1** | 1. | Gain of $19,000 |
| **E9-2** | 1. | Loss of $14,000 |
| **E9-3** | 1. | Gain of $44,000 |
| **E9-4** | 1. | Loss of $29,500 |
| **E9-5** | 1. | Gain of $10,000 |
| **P9-1** | | MODULE 1 |
| | 1. | Parent's net income, $1,899,000; Subsidiary's net income, $305,000 |
| | | MODULE 2 |
| | 1. | Parent's net income, $1,899,000; Subsidiary's net income, $319,000 |
| | | MODULE 3 |
| | 1. | Parent's net income, $1,850,000; Subsidiary's net income, $305,000 |
| **P9-2** | 1. | Loss of $96,000 |
| **P9-3** | 1. | Loss of $120,000 |
| **P9-4** | 1. | Gain of $3,500 |
| | 5. | Consolidated net income, $170,500; Consolidated assets, $1,134,500 |
| **P9-5** | 1. | Loss of $20,000 |
| | 5. | Consolidated net income, $207,100; Consolidated assets, $1,146,000 |
| **P9-6** | 1. | Gain of $21,000 |
| | 3. | Dec. 31, 19X3 investment balance: MODULE 1, $373,000; MODULE 2, $353,000; MODULE 3, $361,000; |
| | 5. | Consolidated net income, $213,000; Consolidated assets, $1,948,500 |
| **E10-1** | | Goodwill, $35,500 |
| **E10-2** | | Parent's equity interest decrease, $52,941; Minority interest equity decrease, $7,059 |
| **E10-3** | | Retained earnings; decrease of $160,000 |
| **E10-4** | | No changes. |
| **E10-5** | | Goodwill, $16,000; Minority interest, $176,000 |
| **E10-6** | | Goodwill, $228,000; Minority interest, $608,000 |

*(continued on p. 1311)*

# ADVANCED ACCOUNTING

## CONCEPTS AND PRACTICE

FOURTH EDITION

## THE HBJ ACCOUNTING SERIES

Bischoff, *Introduction to College Accounting,* Chs. 1–14
Bischoff, *Introduction to College Accounting,* Chs. 1–28
Lee, *Accounting: An Introduction,* Part I, Revised Edition
Lee and Kelley, *Accounting: An Introduction,* Part II
Hillman, Kochanek, and Reynolds, *Principles of Accounting,* Fifth Edition
Walgenbach, Hanson, and Hamre, *Principles of Accounting,* Fifth Edition
Wanlass, *Computer Resource Guide: Principles of Accounting,* Third Edition
Backer, Elgers, and Asebrook, *Financial Accounting*
Beirne and Dauderis, *Financial Accounting: An Introduction to Decision Making*
Brigham and Knechel, *Financial Accounting with Lotus 1-2-3*
Hoskin and Hughes, *Financial Accounting Cases*
Kochanek and Hillman, *Financial Accounting*
Stickney, Weil, and Davidson, *Financial Accounting,* Sixth Edition
Walgenbach and Hanson, *Financial Accounting,* Sixth Edition
Ketz, Campbell, and Baxendale, *Management Accounting*
Maher, Stickney, Weil, and Davidson, *Managerial Accounting,* Fourth Edition
Williams, Stanga, and Holder, *Intermediate Accounting,* Third Edition
Huefner and Largay, *Advanced Financial Accounting,* Second Edition
Pahler and Mori, *Advanced Accounting,* Fourth Edition
Stickney, *Financial Statement Analysis*
Guy, Alderman, and Winters, *Auditing,* Second Edition
Douglas, *Government and Nonprofit Accounting*
Ziebell and DeCoster, *Management Control Systems in Nonprofit Organizations*
Bloom and Elgers, *Accounting Theory and Policy,* Second Edition
Everett, Boley, Duncan, and Jamison, *HBJ Federal Tax Course,* Vol. I
Sommerfeld, Madeo, and Milliron, *An Introduction to Taxation*
Miller, *GAAP Guide,* College Edition
Miller and Bailey, *GAAS Guide,* College Edition

# ADVANCED ACCOUNTING

## CONCEPTS AND PRACTICE

FOURTH EDITION

**ARNOLD J. PAHLER**
San Jose State University

**JOSEPH E. MORI**
San Jose State University

**HARCOURT BRACE JOVANOVICH, PUBLISHERS**

San Diego   New York   Chicago   Austin   Washington, D.C.
London   Sydney   Tokyo   Toronto

To my family, Anne, Laura, and Brett
Arnold J. Pahler

To my family, Carol Ann, David, and Julie
Joseph E. Mori

# PREFACE

The Fourth Edition of *Advanced Accounting: Concepts and Practice* is noticeably different from the Third Edition in many respects. Aside from updating the book for new technical pronouncements throughout, the changes fall into two categories: general changes and topical coverage changes.

## GENERAL CHANGES

**Advanced Level Assignment Material.** Advanced cases and problems have been added to eight of the consolidation chapters (Chapters 1–6, 10, and 13) and one of the foreign currency translation chapters (Chapter 16). This material consists of (1) cases from *The Trueblood Professors' Seminar;* (2) other cases from actual practice; (3) problems dealing with issues involving leveraged buyouts; (4) problems dealing with accounting theory; and (5) problems requiring financial analysis.

The primary purpose of including these cases and problems is to provide materials that conveniently enable instructors to give greater emphasis to intellectual development as opposed to learning and memorization of current accounting principles and practices (for which there is a never-ending proliferation of pronouncements of increasing complexity). This goal is consistent with the mission of the Accounting Education Change Commission, which was created by the American Accounting Association in 1989, to promote improvements in accounting education.

These advanced cases and problems are designed to challenge students to either: (1) evaluate economic events and transactions as to substance versus form, or (2) think across disciplinary lines by applying basic finance concepts to advanced accounting situations. In gradually introducing these cases and problems during the preceding two years, we found that they not only added depth to the course but also provoked a much greater interest from students. Virtually all of these cases and problems can either be assigned as: (1) written assignments—forcing students to develop their writing skills (the Instructor's Resource Manual suggests how to require numerous written assignments without burdening the instructor); or (2) group projects with four or five students working together to arrive at a group solution, which can be presented in class—forcing students to develop their oral communication skills.

**Multiple-choice Self-study Questions.** Students can readily assess their comprehension with these questions (approximately 10 per chapter), which serve as a study guide. Answers are provided at the end of the chapter.

**Demonstration Problems.** Demonstration problems with solutions have been added for the four key consolidation chapters (Chapters 3–6).

## TOPICAL COVERAGE CHANGES

**Expanded Discussion of Leveraged Buyouts (Chapter 2).** The material on leveraged buyouts (formerly in Chapter 13) has been greatly expanded in light of the increased use of these transactions. Two new problems (one in Chapter 2 and one in Chapter 5) now deal with the basis of accounting issue inherent in leveraged buyouts.

**Push-down Accounting Moved to the Chapter Appendix (Chapter 3).** Comments from users of the Third Edition clearly reflect that opinion is evenly divided over whether push-down accounting should be covered before or after non-push-down accounting. In addition, time constraints may allow only for the coverage of non-push-down accounting. Accordingly, to provide greater flexibility to instructors, push-down accounting (formerly covered in Chapter 3 before non-push-down accounting) is now presented in the appendix to Chapter 3 in a manner that gives instructors the option of covering this material before non-push-down accounting.

**Adoption of Modular Format for Covering Deferral and Recognition of Intercompany Profits and Losses (Chapters 7–9).** In the chapters dealing with intercompany inventory, fixed assets, and bond transactions, we offer three procedures for deferring and recognizing intercompany profit. Each procedure is **presented in a self-contained module, enabling instructors to assign the particular module they choose to cover.** These modules are as follows for all three chapters:

Module 1: **The Complete Equity Method—Using Investment Account Adjustment Procedures** (adjustments made through the Equity in Net Income of Subsidiary account).

Module 2: **The Complete Equity Method—Using Noninvestment Account Adjustment Procedures** (adjustments made using deferral accounts). (These procedures were used in the Third Edition.)

Module 3: **The Partial Equity Method,** (These procedures were presented in appendices to these chapters in the Third Edition.)

Three sets of solutions are provided for all exercises and problems in these three chapters.

**Internationalizing the Foreign Currency Material (Chapters 14—16).**
To enable students to have a better grasp of the "globalization" phenomenon, we have added discussions of: (1) the various alternative means of
generating sales abroad; (2) the reasons why so many U.S. companies
have foreign subsidiaries; (3) the foreign trade deficit and the related foreign investment deficit; and, more importantly, (4) how inflation affects
the exchange rates.

Additionally, we have resequenced the material to discuss foreign currency transactions in Chapter 14 (rather than in Chapter 16). This gives
students a basic familiarity with foreign currency transactions before
delving into the much greater conceptual area of translating foreign currency financial statements.

**Governmental Accounting Extensively Revised (Chapters 20 and 21).**
The material in these chapters has been substantially revised to: (1) place
greater emphasis on combined financial statements and the comprehensive annual financial report (which are now extensively tested on the CPA
examination); (2) allow for a step-by-step development of the governmental financial reporting process; and (3) incorporate the new terminology
used in the 1988 edition of *Governmental Accounting, Auditing, and
Financial Reporting,* as published by the Government Finance Officers
Association. In addition, we summarize the major changes mandated in
*GASB Statement No. 11,* "Measurement Focus and Basis of Accounting:
Governmental Fund Operating Statements," which was issued in 1990
but is not effective until 1994.

**Hospital Accounting in Nonprofit Organizations Revised (Chapter
22).** The material in this chapter covering hospitals has been revised
based on the AICPA's 1990 audit guide *Audits of Providers of Health Care
Services,* which is substantially changed from the previous hospital audit
guide and is effective for audits of financial statements for periods beginning after June 15, 1990.

## STUDENT-ORIENTED FEATURES

The following is a list of Fourth Edition features designed to heighten students' interest and make the text easy to read and use:

1. **Topic outlines** preceding each chapter.
2. **Chapter overviews** beginning each chapter.
3. Inclusion of **numerous relevant articles** from *The Wall Street Journal,
   Forbes,* and *Business Week* so that students can better relate the material to current events.
4. Extensive use of **boldface type for key terms and key concepts.**

5. Convenient **vertical format for consolidating statement worksheets** that uses a **plus-and-minus scheme that is consistent with Lotus 1-2-3®  spreadsheet software.**
6. Clearly marked **review points** for major illustrations.
7. **End-of-chapter review sections** for each chapter that include: (a) a **summary of key points;** (b) a **glossary of new terms;** (c) **demonstration problems and solutions** in key consolidation chapters (Chapters 3–6); and (d) **multiple-choice self-study questions.**
8. **Descriptive overviews of discussion cases, exercises, and problems.**
9. **Checklist of key figures** for both **exercises and problems** on the inside covers for easy reference.
10. Placement of advanced level assignment material separately after the regular assignment material.
11. Placement of chapter appendix material after all chapter assignment material.
12. Placement of the student manual for electronic spreadsheet software in the Appendix for convenient reference.

## MAJOR CONSOLIDATIONS FEATURE

For preparing consolidated financial statements, we continue the technique of **analyzing the investment account by its conceptual elements, updating the analysis using the equity method of accounting, and then preparing the basic consolidation elimination entry from this updated analysis. This is a simple and understandable approach for handling all aspects of preparing consolidated financial statements**—including keeping track of and reporting of any minority interest, as well as accommodating block acquistions, partial disposals, and the issuance of additional common stock by a subsidiary. As shown in Chapters 7, 8, and 9, the conceptual analysis can be modified to keep track of unrealized intercompany profit on asset transfers and imputed gains or losses resulting from intercompany bond purchases when the complete equity method using investment account adjustment procedures is used (Module 1 in Chapters 7, 8, and 9). Finally, this conceptual analysis readily lends itself to dealing with the change in basis issue in leveraged buyouts.

## ELECTRONIC SPREADSHEET SOFTWARE AND RELATED STUDENT MANUAL

The Appendix to the book is a student manual for using the Electronic Spreadsheet Templates that are available free to adopting instructors on a master diskette. These templates are designed for use on IBM® personal computers and compatibles with Lotus 1-2-3® electronic spreadsheet software (Release 2.0 or later). Other spreadsheet programs can be used, although the user may encounter subtle differences in menu or command routines. The templates are also available for use on Apple Macintosh® computers with spreadsheet software such as Microsoft Excel®.

The templates diskette contains 12 class-tested models individually tailored and customized for the following text chapters:

| | |
|---|---|
| Chapter 1 | Model 1 |
| Chapter 3 | Model 3 |
| Chapter 4 | Model 4 |
| Chapter 5 | Model 5 |
| Chapter 6 | Model 6 |
| Chapter 7 | Model 7 |
| Chapter 8 | Model 8 |
| Chapters 9–10 | Model 9 |
| Chapter 16 | Model 16T (translation) |
| Chapter 16 | Model 16R (remeasurement) |
| Chapter 23 | Model 23 |
| Chapter 25 | Model 25 |

Ten of the models have problem data from the text stored in an out-of-the-way section of the model. At the touch of a key, this data can be loaded into the worksheet section of the model using a macro command (a pre-programmed stored instruction). Models 3, 4, 5, 6, 7, 8, 9, and 16T also contain a conceptual analysis of the investment account, from which the primary elimination entry for consolidation can be readily prepared and then, using a macro command, posted to the worksheet. Approximately 60 problems from the text can be worked on the computer.

The templates have been designed so that students must perform a limited amount of spreadsheet programming. **No prior computer experience is required.** Furthermore, using the manual in the Appendix, students can work problems on their own, **without instructor involvement.** Using the templates diskette and the step-by-step instructions in the Appendix, a student with no prior computer experience should be able to complete the first problem in about two hours. Later problems require from 15 to 30 minutes of computer time, depending on complexity. These software files are fully usable on student and modified versions of Lotus 1-2-3®.

For this edition, the following enhancements were made to the consolidation models for Chapters 3 through 10 so that students can perform consolidations in a much more efficient manner:

1. The conceptual analysis of the investment account now precedes the consolidation worksheet.

2. The conceptual analysis of the investment account now appears in a continuous format (rather than split into two sections as in the Third Edition).

3. More formulas are used in the later consolidation models (after students have mastered certain basic procedures) for (a) cross-totaling within the conceptual analysis of the investment account, and (b) deriving amounts used in the primary elimination entry (as obtained from the conceptual analysis of the investment account).

## ANCILLARIES

The following updated ancillaries are available with this edition.

**Solutions Manual.**   To assist instructors in evaluating and selecting problem materials, the Solutions Manual contains a description of each discussion case, exercise, and problem. The **relative difficulty** and **estimated time** for completion of problem materials are also included. (The manual is perforated to facilitate the preparation of additional transparencies.)

**Instructor's Resource Manual and Testbook.**   For this edition the manual is divided into four parts. Part I consists of course coverage considerations. Part II is an instructor's introduction to the enhanced Electronic Spreadsheet Templates diskette and student manual Appendix to this book. Part III contains teaching suggestions and additional items of current interest to students. Part IV is a test bank for each chapter of the text. The test bank contains approximately 300 true-or-false statements, 200 multiple-choice questions, 240 completion statements (fill-ins), and 140 short problems. Because CPA examinations consistently contain excellent questions pertaining to theory, we have obtained or adapted many of the multiple-choice questions from recent examinations. The test bank is also available in microcomputer software form.

**Transparencies.**   For all problems involving consolidation or translation worksheets, a transparency is available of that worksheet and, for the more involved consolidation problems, of the related conceptual analysis of the parent's investment account (Chapters 1, 3–10, and 16). In addition, selected solutions are provided for the other key chapters (Chapters 13, 20, 21, 23, 24, and 25).

**Working Papers.**   Working Papers are provided, where appropriate, for problems in Chapters 1, 3–11, 14, 16, and 23. The time saved using the Working Papers in these chapters can be considerable.

# ACKNOWLEDGEMENTS

We are indebted to the following instructors who gave generously of their time and provided many fine suggestions in reviewing material for the Fourth Edition before publication:

| | |
|---|---|
| Sara A. Reiter | University of Illinois, Urbana |
| Marilynn Collins | John Carroll University |
| Martha J. Marshall | University of North Carolina at Asheville |
| James S. H. Chiu | California State University, Northridge |
| Stewart S. Karlinsky | San Jose State University |
| Charles F. Vincent | San Jose State University |
| Joseph H. Black | San Jose State University |

We also thank the following users of the Third Edition who responded to a questionnaire relating to that edition: Dan Acton, Alfred University; Jack Armitage, University of Nebraska at Omaha; Ruth Bloom, Augustana College; Wayne Burkowski, St. Martin's College; Wagih Dafashy, College of William & Mary; John Davis, King's College; James Dear, University of Southern Mississippi; David Dibblee, Illinois Benedictine College; Orapin Duangploy, University of Houston; David Durkee, University of Delaware; Mike Emerson, Harding University; John Gehman, Moravian College; W. Neil Gentry, Georgia State University; Harold Gey, Colorado State University; Al Hannan, College of Notre Dame; Coby Harmon, University of California, Santa Barbara; Kenneth Hiltebeitel, Villanova University; Sharron Hoffmans, University of Texas at El Paso; Rohit Jain, Drexel University; Richard Jones, Lamar University; Floyd Kirby, Jacksonville State University; Gregory Kordecki, Clayton State College; Fraser MacHaffie, Marietta College; Joseph Marcheggiani, Butler University; Robert Maurer, Central College; Randall Newell, Adams State College; Tim O'Keefe, Emory University; Larry Ozzello, University of Wisconsin—Eau Claire; Alfred Roberts, Georgia State University; Jacci Rodgers, University of Oklahoma; Barbara Shiarappa, Trenton State College; William Stevens, De Paul University; Frederic Stiner, Jr., University of Delaware; Neal Ushman, Santa Clara University; Barry Vallee, Northwood Institute; G. Lee Willinger, University of Oklahoma; Dwight Zulauf, Humboldt State University; Robert Yahr, Marquette University.

We thank Arthur Andersen & Co., for allowing us to use its professional libraries and materials. We express appreciation to the American Institute of Certified Public Accountants, the Financial Accounting Standards Board, and the Government Finance Officers Association for their permission to quote material from their respective pronouncements and various other publications. We also thank the American Institute of

Certified Public Accountants for their permission to use and adapt material from the CPA examinations.

Finally, we express our appreciation to Ken Rethmeier, Bill Teague, and Paul Raymond, our editors at Harcourt Brace Jovanovich; Craig Avery and Jon Preimesberger, manuscript editors; Mary Allen and David Hill, production editors; Cathy Reynolds, designer; and Sarah Randall and Mary Kay Yearin, production managers. Their diligence was greatly appreciated.

We welcome all comments from users of the Fourth Edition.

Arnold J. Pahler

Joseph E. Mori

# CONTENTS

## 4 THE PURCHASE METHOD OF ACCOUNTING: SUBSEQUENT TO DATE OF ACQUISITION 156

## 5 THE PURCHASE METHOD OF ACCOUNTING: PARTIALLY OWNED SUBSIDIARIES AND BLOCK ACQUISITIONS 208

## 6 THE POOLING OF INTERESTS METHOD OF ACCOUNTING 265

## 22 ACCOUNTING FOR NONPROFIT ORGANIZATIONS 999

## PART V PARTNERSHIPS 1105

## 23 PARTNERSHIPS: FORMATION AND OPERATION 1106

# ADVANCED ACCOUNTING

## CONCEPTS AND PRACTICE

FOURTH EDITION

# I

# CONSOLIDATED FINANCIAL STATEMENTS: FUNDAMENTALS

■ ■ ■ ■ ■

# 1
# BRANCH ACCOUNTING

## TOPIC OUTLINE

## CHAPTER OVERVIEW

**A** substantial portion of the subject matter of advanced accounting concerns businesses that increase the number of their outlying manufacturing, retailing, or service locations to increase sales and profits. A business may establish additional outlying locations in one of the following two ways: internal expansion and external expansion. **Internal expansion** means that a business constructs or leases additional outlying facilities. In most instances, the additional facilities increase the company's manufacturing, retailing, or service capacities in the same line of business in which it currently operates. Much of the growth of International Business Machines Corp., Sears, Roebuck and Co., and Bank of America occurred through such internal expansion. **External expansion** takes place when two existing businesses combine into a unified larger business. Although many business combinations enable companies to increase their operations in the same line of business, an increasing proportion of business combinations occur among companies in unrelated fields. Such combinations enable companies to diversify their product lines. Much of the growth of International Telephone and Telegraph, Gulf and Western Industries, and Litton Industries came about through external expansion.

This chapter deals exclusively with the internal expansion of businesses. Subsequent chapters deal with external expansion. By discussing internal expansion first, we establish some fundamental principles of accounting for multilocation operations that will benefit us in later chapters. Accounting for outlying locations established in foreign countries through internal expansion involves special considerations; accordingly, we discuss these situations in Chapters 14–16, which deal with foreign operations and transactions.

## GENERAL MATTERS

### Terminology

A business's outlying location established through internal expansion is not a separate legal entity but merely an extension of a legal entity. Accordingly, it cannot be referred to as a company, because it is only part of a company. Because the professional accounting pronouncements do not specify how outlying locations should be referred to, many terms have evolved over the years. Banks commonly refer to their outlying locations as *branches*; insurance companies commonly refer to them as *sales offices*; and manufacturing companies use the terms *division* and *plant*. Some companies, however, use *division* to refer to geographical area; for example, all outlying manufacturing plants in a designated eastern location might be called the East Coast Division. Some companies use *division* to refer to a particular product line. General Motors Corp., for example, has five automobile divisions, and each division has several manufacturing plants. An outlying location of a retail establishment is a *store.* Companies in the computer-manufacturing industry often establish outlying locations to service computers; these locations may be referred to as *field engineering offices.* In some companies, the outlying locations carry only demonstration units and sales brochures—any sales that they generate are approved and filled by the home office; such outlying locations are called *sales offices* or *agencies.* In all these instances, the headquarters location of the legal entity that established the outlying location is referred to as the **home office.**

## Delegation of Decision-making Authority

When an outlying location is established, the home office must decide the extent to which it will grant decision-making authority to management at its outlying location. Although companywide policies are established by the home office, many day-to-day operating decisions can be delegated to the outlying management. The extent of delegation is part of the broad topic of centralized versus decentralized management decision making. For example, varying degrees of delegation are found in the retail industry. At one extreme are some home offices that decide all the merchandise to be carried by each outlying retail outlet, and each retail outlet must purchase all such merchandise from the home office. At the other extreme are home offices that grant managements at the outlying retail outlets complete discretion over the merchandise they may carry and from where they may buy it. Between these extremes are situations in which outlying retail outlets must carry certain merchandise specified by the home office (which often must be purchased from the home office), but local managers have complete discretion over other merchandise and where they buy it. In the banking industry, branches usually are assigned dollar limits on the amount of money they may loan to a given customer; any loan requests above the designated limits must then be approved by a higher regional office or the home office. Some home offices handle national and regional advertising, allowing outlying locations to do only limited local advertising. Other home offices make each outlying location responsible for its own local advertising.

## Accounting Systems

The home office must decide how to account for the activities and transactions of the outlying location. This decision is based on what is most practical and economical in a given situation. Accounting systems can be categorized as either centralized or decentralized.

**Centralized Accounting.** Under a **centralized accounting** system, an outlying location does not maintain a separate general ledger in which to record its transactions. Instead, it sends source documents on sales, purchases, and payroll to the home office. Outlying locations usually deposit cash receipts in local bank accounts, which only the home office can draw upon. When the home office receives source documents, it reconciles sales information with bank deposits, reviews and processes invoices for payment, and prepares payroll checks and related payroll records. Inventory and fixed assets at each outlying location also are recorded in the home office general ledger, appropriately coded to signify the location to which they belong. Journal entries pertaining to each outlying location's transactions are then prepared and posted to the home office general ledger. These entries are usually coded so that accountants at the home office can readily prepare operating statements for each outlying location. Centralized accounting systems commonly use computers at the home office to minimize the clerical aspects of keeping records and preparing financial statements. The home office reviews operating statements for each outlying location and provides copies to outlying management. Centralized accounting systems are usually practical when the operations of the outlying location do not involve complex manufacturing operations or extensive retailing or service activities. Grocery, drug, and shoe store chains usually use centralized accounting systems. Because they present no unusual accounting issues, centralized accounting systems are not discussed any further.

**Decentralized Accounting.** Under a **decentralized accounting** system, an outlying location maintains a separate general ledger in which to record its transactions. Thus, the outlying location is a separate **accounting entity,** even though it is not a separate legal entity. It prepares its own journal entries and financial statements, submitting the latter to the home office, usually on a monthly basis. Decentralized accounting systems are common for outlying locations that have complex manufacturing operations or extensive retailing operations involving significant credit sales. The following two accounting issues must be resolved in a decentralized accounting system:

1. The manner in which transactions between the home office and the outlying locations are recorded.
2. The procedures by which the revenues, costs, and expenses of the outlying locations are reported for financial and income tax reporting purposes.

The remainder of this chapter deals with these two issues. As mentioned previously, many industries create outlying locations through internal expansion. We use the retail industry to illustrate the fundamental accounting principles for multilocation operations using a decentralized accounting system because retailing activities allow a complete discussion of the issues. In discussing and illustrating such issues, the outlying locations are referred to hereafter as **branches.**

# BRANCH GENERAL LEDGER ACCOUNTS

## Intracompany Accounts

A branch is established when a home office transfers cash, inventory, or other assets to an outlying location. Because the home office views the assets transferred to the branch as an investment, it makes the following entry:

| | | |
|---|---|---|
| Investment in Branch | xxx | |
| Asset(s) | | xxx |

This investment in Branch account (sometimes called *Branch Current*) is used to keep track of and maintain control over (1) the assets transferred to the branch and (2) the increase or decrease in the branch's net assets as a result of the branch's operations.

On receipt of the assets from the home office, the branch makes the following entry:

| | | |
|---|---|---|
| Asset(s) | xxx | |
| Home Office Equity | | xxx |

The Home Office Equity account represents the equity interest of the home office in the branch. The use of such an account allows double-entry bookkeeping procedures to be used at the branch level. (Remember that branches are not separate legal entities and do not have Common Stock, Additional Paid-in Capital, and Retained Earnings accounts.)

The balance in the Investment in Branch account on the books of the home office always equals the balance in the Home Office Equity account on the books of the branch. In practice, these accounts are referred to as the **intracompany** or **reciprocal accounts.** At the end of each accounting period, the branch closes its income or loss to its Home Office Equity account. Upon receipt of the branch's financial statements, the home office adjusts its Investment in Branch account to reflect the branch's income or loss and makes the offsetting credit or debit to an income statement account called **Branch Income** or **Branch Loss.** As a result of this entry and upon closing the Branch Income or Branch Loss account to retained earnings, the branch's income or loss is included in the home office's Retained Earnings account.

Branches are usually financed entirely by the home office and typically do not establish relations with local banks. Therefore, they do not incur interest expense. If a branch has cash in excess of its immediate needs, it usually transfers it to the home office, which is responsible for investing excess cash on a companywide basis. Thus, branches do not have interest income from investments.

## Income Tax Accounts and Reporting

Because branches are not separate legal entities, they do not file their own income tax returns. The home office must include the income or loss from its branches along with its own income or loss from operations for federal income tax reporting purposes. If the home office has operations in states that impose income taxes, the home office must file branch income tax returns in those states. Federal and state income taxes are almost always computed at the home office and recorded exclusively in the home office's general ledger. Few companies attempt to allocate or transfer income tax expense from the home office general ledger to branch general ledgers. This not only simplifies the tax recording procedures but also eliminates the need to make arbitrary allocation assumptions. Furthermore, the potential benefits, if any, from allocating income tax expense to the branches would be minimal in most instances.

Because branches do not have interest income, interest expense, or income tax expense, the income or loss from their operations is an **operating income** or **loss,** not a net income or loss. Hereafter, all references to a branch's income or loss are in this context.

## Home Office Allocations

The home office usually arranges and pays for certain expenses that benefit the branches. The most common example is insurance. In theory, some portion of the insurance expense should be allocated to the various branches, so that the home office may determine the true operating income or loss of each branch. In practice, however, allocations of home office expenses vary widely. Numerous home offices allocate only those expenses that relate directly to the branch operations, such as insurance and national advertising costs. Some home offices without any revenue-producing operations of their own allocate all of their expenses (including salaries of home office executives, facilities costs, legal fees, audit fees, and interest expense) to the branches. Branch managers are therefore continually aware that branch operations must cover these costs. Some home offices do not allocate any home office expenses to the branches on the theory that because the branches have no control over them, arbitrary allocations serve no useful purpose. The home office records allocations by debiting the Investment in Branch account and crediting the applicable expense accounts. The branch debits the applicable expense accounts and credits its Home Office Equity account. The end result is the same as though the home office had transferred cash to the branch and the branch had arranged for and incurred the expenses.

## Inventory Transfer Accounts

When inventory is transferred from the home office to a branch, all that has really happened is that the inventory has physically moved from one location in the company to another. A sale has not occurred, because sales take place only between the company and outside customers. To measure the profitability of a branch, however, an **intracompany billing** must be prepared. The purpose of the intracompany billing is to transfer purchases from the books of the home office to the books of the branch. The branch uses a special purchases account called Shipments from Home Office to record these inventory transfers and makes the following entry:

| | | |
|---|---|---|
| Shipments from Home Office.................. | xxx | |
|     Home Office Equity...................... | | xxx |

The home office uses a special contra purchases account called Shipments to Branch to record inventory transfers. If the inventory is transferred and billed at the home office's cost, the home office makes the following entry:

| | | |
|---|---|---|
| Investment in Branch........................ | xxx | |
|     Shipments to Branch................... | | xxx |

The branch's ending inventory, cost of goods sold, gross margin, and operating profit or loss depend on the amounts of these intracompany billings. If the intracompany billing is made at the home office's cost, then these special accounts should always agree. By using these special accounts, the home office can strengthen control over branch operations. If these special accounts do not agree, then at least one of the accounting entities has made an error or a shipment is in transit. Before the month-end closing can be properly completed, an adjusting entry must be made to bring the two special accounts into agreement. Using the home office's cost in pricing intracompany inventory transfers is quite common, primarily because it does not require any special considerations in the preparation of month-end combined financial statements for the home office and its branches.

Although the use of the Shipments to Branch and Shipments from Home Office accounts strengthen control over branch operations, the period-end closing procedures and the preparation of combined financial statements are more understandable and simpler if these accounts are closed to respective Cost of Goods Sold accounts at month-end. (The inventory accounts are also adjusted in this closing entry to arrive at cost of goods sold.) These closing entries and the preparation of combined financial statements are discussed and illustrated later in the chapter, as are situations in which inventory transfers are made at above the home office's cost.

## Fixed Asset Accounts

Some home offices require their branches' fixed assets to be recorded on the books of the home office instead of on the books of the branches. Such a procedure automatically ensures that uniform depreciation methods and asset lives are used for all branches. The home office usually charges the branch for the depreciation expense of its fixed assets. It does this by crediting Accumulated Depreciation and debiting the Investment in Branch account instead of debiting Depreciation Expense. The branch debits Depreciation Expense and credits the Home Office Equity account instead of crediting Accumulated Depreciation. When fixed assets are recorded on the home office's books, the fixed assets pertaining to the branch must be added to the Investment in Branch account to evaluate the profitability of branch operations in relation to the total assets actually invested in the branch.

## Other General Ledger Accounts

The branch maintains the balance sheet and income statement accounts necessary to record transactions that take place between (1) the home office and the branch, and (2) the branch and its customers, creditors, and employees. The extent of the accounts required depends on the scope of the branch's operations.

## Typical Transactions for a Branch

Assume that Searbuck Company, which prepares financial reports at the end of the calendar year, established a branch on July 1, 19X1. The following transactions occurred during the formation of the branch and its first six months of operations, ending December 31, 19X1.

1. The home office sent $28,000 cash to the branch to begin operations.
2. The home office shipped inventory to the branch. Intracompany billings totaled $60,000, which was the home office's cost. (Both the home office and the branch use a periodic inventory system.)
3. The branch acquired merchandise display equipment which cost $12,000 on July 1, 19X1. (Assume that branch fixed assets are not carried on the home office books.)

4. The branch purchased inventory costing $43,000 from outside vendors on account.
5. The branch had credit sales of $85,000 and cash sales of $35,000.
6. The branch collected $44,000 on accounts receivable.
7. The branch paid outside vendors $28,000.
8. The branch incurred selling expenses of $15,000 and general and administrative expenses of $12,000. These expenses were paid in cash when they were incurred and include the expense of leasing the branch's facilities.
9. The home office charged the branch $2,000 for its share of insurance.
10. Depreciation expense on the merchandise display equipment acquired by the branch is $1,000 for the six-month period. (Depreciation expense is classified as a selling expense.)
11. The branch remitted $10,000 cash to the home office.
12. The branch's physical inventory on December 31, 19X1, is $33,000, of which $25,000 was acquired from the home office (there was no beginning inventory). The home office's physical inventory on December 31, 19X1, is $150,000 (the beginning inventory was $135,000). (Home office purchases were $285,000.) Cost of goods sold is determined and recorded in a separate account for each accounting entity. (Note that the year-end inventory accounts are adjusted in this entry to the year-end physical inventory balances.)
13. The branch closes its income statement accounts.
14. The home office prepares its adjusting entry to reflect the increase in the branch's net assets resulting from the branch's operations.

The journal entries for these transactions as they would be recorded by the home office and the branch are presented in Illustration 1-1.

# COMBINED FINANCIAL STATEMENTS: INVENTORY TRANSFERS AT HOME OFFICE COST

## Month-end Verification of Intracompany Account Balances

Before the branch prepares its closing entries and submits financial statements to the home office, it must verify that its Home Office Equity account and Shipments from Home Office account agree with the corresponding reciprocal accounts maintained by the home office. If the accounts do not agree, there are two possible explanations:

1. A transaction initiated by one of the accounting entities has been improperly recorded by the other accounting entity. The accounting entity that made the error must make the appropriate adjusting entry.

# ■ ILLUSTRATION 1-1
## Typical Transactions for a Branch

| Home Office Books | | | Branch Books | | |
|---|---|---|---|---|---|
| 1. Investment in Branch | 28,000 | | 1. Cash | 28,000 | |
| Cash | | 28,000 | Home Office Equity | | 28,000 |
| 2. Investment in Branch | 60,000 | | 2. Shipments from | | |
| Shipments to | | | Home Office | 60,000 | |
| Branch | | 60,000 | Home Office Equity | | 60,000 |
| | | | 3. Equipment | 12,000 | |
| | | | Cash | | 12,000 |
| | | | 4. Purchases | 43,000 | |
| | | | Accounts Payable | | 43,000 |
| | | | 5. Cash | 35,000 | |
| | | | Accounts Receivable | 85,000 | |
| | | | Sales | | 120,000 |
| | | | 6. Cash | 44,000 | |
| | | | Accounts | | |
| | | | Receivable | | 44,000 |
| | | | 7. Accounts Payable | 28,000 | |
| | | | Cash | | 28,000 |
| | | | 8. Selling Expenses | 15,000 | |
| | | | Administrative | | |
| | | | Expenses | 12,000 | |
| | | | Cash | | 27,000 |
| 9. Investment in Branch | 2,000 | | 9. Administrative | | |
| Administrative | | | Expenses | 2,000 | |
| Expenses | | 2,000 | Home Office Equity | | 2,000 |
| | | | 10. Selling Expenses | 1,000 | |
| | | | Accumulated | | |
| | | | Depreciation | | 1,000 |
| 11. Cash | 10,000 | | 11. Home Office Equity | 10,000 | |
| Investment in | | | Cash | | 10,000 |
| Branch | | 10,000 | | | |
| 12. Inventory | 15,000 | | 12. Inventory Acquired | | |
| Shipments to Branch | 60,000 | | from Vendors | 8,000 | |
| Cost of Goods Sold | 210,000 | | Inventory Acquired | | |
| Purchases | | 285,000 | from Home Office | 25,000 | |
| | | | Cost of Goods Sold | 70,000 | |
| | | | Shipments from | | |
| | | | Home Office | | 60,000 |
| | | | Purchases | | 43,000 |
| | | | 13. Sales | 120,000 | |
| | | | Cost of Goods Sold | | 70,000 |
| | | | Selling Expenses | | 16,000 |
| | | | Administrative | | |
| | | | Expenses | | 14,000 |
| | | | Home Office Equity | | 20,000 |
| 14. Investment in Branch | 20,000 | | | | |
| Branch Income | | 20,000 | | | |

2. A transaction initiated by one of the accounting entities has been recorded by the initiating entity but not yet by the receiving entity—for example, cash transfers in transit, inventory shipments in transit, and intracompany charges. Normally, the receiving accounting entity prepares the adjusting entry as though it has completed the transaction before the end of the accounting period. (It would be more disruptive to have the initiating accounting entity reverse the transaction.)

These adjusting entries to bring the intracompany accounts into agreement are absolutely necessary for the proper preparation of combined financial statements. After making any necessary adjustments, the branch submits an income statement and a balance sheet to the home office.

## The Primary Elimination Entry

After the home office general ledger is adjusted for the branch's income or loss, it reflects the overall net income earned by the home office and the branch. Generally accepted accounting principles require, however, that in reporting the results of operations to its shareholders, the home office combine the detail of the branch's income or loss with the detail of the accounts making up the net income or loss from the home office's own operations. In other words, the home office cannot report a one-line item amount called "branch income" or "loss for the branch's operations"; it must combine the sales, the cost of goods sold, and the operating expenses of both accounting entities and report the combined amounts. This is accomplished by substituting the branch's income statement for the Branch Income or Loss account in the home office general ledger. Likewise, generally accepted accounting principles require that in reporting the balance sheet amounts to its shareholders, the home office combine the individual assets and liabilities of both accounting entities and report the combined amounts. This is accomplished by substituting the individual assets and liabilities of the branch for the Investment in Branch account (which, by its nature, always equals the branch's net assets).

This substitution takes place on a worksheet used to eliminate the appropriate accounts so that the assets, liabilities, sales, cost of goods sold, and operating expenses of each accounting entity can be combined. Such a worksheet, called a **combining statement worksheet,** is shown in Illustration 1-2. A journal entry, which for instructional purposes and ease of reference, we call the **primary elimination entry,** is posted to the worksheet to eliminate (1) the Investment in Branch account in the home office column, (2) the Branch Income account in the home office column, and (3) the preclosing balance of the Home Office Equity account in the branch column of the statement of retained earnings/analysis of home office equity section.

# ■ ILLUSTRATION 1-2
## Inventory Transferred at Cost

| | Home Office | Branch[a] | Eliminations Dr. | Eliminations Cr. | Combined |
|---|---|---|---|---|---|
| **SEARBUCK COMPANY** Combining Statement Worksheet for the Year Ended December 31, 19X1 | | | | | |
| **Income Statement** | | | | | |
| Sales . . . . . . . . . . . . . . . . . . . . . . . . . . . | 380,000 | 120,000 | | | 500,000 |
| Cost of goods sold . . . . . . . . . . . . . . . | (210,000) | (70,000) | | | (280,000) |
| Selling expenses . . . . . . . . . . . . . . . . . | (52,000) | (16,000) | | | (68,000) |
| Administrative expenses . . . . . . . . . . | (59,000) | (14,000) | | | (73,000) |
| Interest expense . . . . . . . . . . . . . . . . . | (19,000) | | | | (19,000) |
| Branch income . . . . . . . . . . . . . . . . . | 20,000 | | 20,000(1) | | –0– |
| Income before Income Taxes . . . . . . | 60,000 | 20,000 | 20,000 | | 60,000 |
| Income tax expense @ 40% . . . . . . . . | (24,000) | | | | (24,000) |
| Net Income . . . . . . . . . . . . . . . . . . . . | 36,000 | 20,000 | 20,000 | | 36,000 |
| **Statement of Retained Earnings/ Analysis of Home Office Equity** | | | | | |
| Retained earnings, Jan. 1, 19X1 . . . | 114,000 | | | | 114,000 |
| Home office equity (preclosing) . . . . . | | 80,000 | 80,000(1) | | –0– |
| + Net income . . . . . . . . . . . . . . . . . . . | 36,000 | 20,000 | 20,000 | | 36,000 |
| – Dividends declared . . . . . . . . . . . . . | (10,000) | | | | (10,000) |
| Balances, Dec. 31, 19X1 . . . . . . . . . . | 140,000 | 100,000 | 100,000 | | 140,000 |
| **Balance Sheet** | | | | | |
| Cash . . . . . . . . . . . . . . . . . . . . . . . . . . | 50,000 | 30,000 | | | 80,000 |
| Accounts receivable, net . . . . . . . . . . | 60,000 | 41,000 | | | 101,000 |
| Inventory:[b] | | | | | |
| Acquired from vendors . . . . . . . . . . | 150,000 | 8,000 | | | 158,000 |
| Acquired from home office . . . . . . . | | 25,000 | | | 25,000 |
| Land . . . . . . . . . . . . . . . . . . . . . . . . . . . | 22,000 | | | | 22,000 |
| Buildings and equipment, net . . . . . | 118,000 | 11,000 | | | 129,000 |
| Investment in branch . . . . . . . . . . . . | 100,000 | | | 100,000(1) | –0– |
| Total Assets . . . . . . . . . . . . . . . . . . | 500,000 | 115,000 | | 100,000 | 515,000 |
| Accounts payable and accruals . . . . . | 60,000 | 15,000 | | | 75,000 |
| Long-term debt . . . . . . . . . . . . . . . . . . | 200,000 | | | | 200,000 |
| Common stock . . . . . . . . . . . . . . . . . . | 100,000 | | | | 100,000 |
| Retained earnings . . . . . . . . . . . . . . . | 140,000 | | | | 140,000 |
| Home office equity . . . . . . . . . . . . . . . | | 100,000 | 100,000 | | –0– |
| Total Liabilities and Equity . . . . . | 500,000 | 115,000 | 100,000 | | 515,000 |
| Proof of debit and credit postings . . . . . . . . . . . . . . . . . . . . . . . . . . . . . . | | | 100,000 | 100,000 | |

Explanation of entry:
(1) The primary elimination entry.

[a]The amounts in this column reflect the activity shown in Illustration 1-1.
[b]The separation of the inventory into these two categories is not necessary if transfers are made at cost. It is shown here only for later comparison with Illustration 1-4, where transfers are made above cost.

All worksheet entries in this book are shaded to differentiate them from general ledger entries. The worksheet entry is as follows:

| | | |
|---|---|---|
| Branch Income . . . . . . . . . . . . . . . . . . . . . . . . . . . . . . | xxx | |
| Home Office Equity (preclosing balance) . . . . . . | xxx | |
|     Investment in Branch . . . . . . . . . . . . . . . . . . | | xxx |

The debit to Branch Income in the income statement section of the worksheet is totaled at the net income line and then carried forward to the net income line in the statement of Retained Earnings/Analysis of Home Office Equity section of the worksheet. Each account on the worksheet is then cross-totaled to arrive at the combined amounts. The amounts in the combined column are used to prepare the financial statements that are distributed to the company's stockholders.

## ILLUSTRATION  A Combining Statement Worksheet

The worksheet in Illustration 1-2 combines the financial statements of a home office with those of its branch. The financial statement amounts for the branch reflect the transactions shown in Illustration 1-1. The primary elimination entry is:

| | | |
|---|---|---|
| Branch Income . . . . . . . . . . . . . . . . . . . . . . . . . . . . | 20,000 | |
| Home Office Equity . . . . . . . . . . . . . . . . . . . . . . . | 80,000 | |
|     Investment in Branch . . . . . . . . . . . . . . . . . . | | 100,000 |

**Review Points for Illustration 1-2.**  Note the following:

1. The combining worksheet is started *after* the home office has made its adjusting entry concerning the branch's income and after it has provided for income taxes on the branch's income.
2. The balance in the Retained Earnings account in the home office column includes the branch's income net of applicable income taxes. This retained earnings amount is the combined retained earnings.
3. The debit balance in the eliminations column of the worksheet at the net income line of the income statement is carried forward to the net income line in the statement of retained earnings/analysis of home office equity section.
4. The net income in the home office column is the same as the net income in the combined column.
5. The combining worksheet is not distributed to the home office's stockholders; only the financial statements, which can be readily prepared from the combined column of the worksheet, are distributed to them. (The formal balance sheet and the income statement are not shown.)

6. The primary elimination entry is posted only to the worksheet, not to the general ledger.
7. The primary elimination entry is the same each time the combination is performed; only the amounts differ.

## COMBINED FINANCIAL STATEMENTS: INVENTORY TRANSFERS ABOVE HOME OFFICE COST

Some home offices transfer inventory to their branches at costs above their own cost. In some instances, the mark-up is designed to absorb the costs of central purchasing, warehousing, and handling, or to have those operations show a profit. In other instances, the transfer costs reflect prices that the branches would pay if they acquired the merchandise directly from the manufacturers and distributors. In theory, large volume discounts generated by the central purchasing department of the home office should not be reflected in the branch income statements. In other instances, the mark-up is designed to achieve greater companywide profits because branch personnel base the mark-up to their customers on the inflated billing prices from the home office. (Often branch personnel are not informed of the extent of the home office's mark-up).

In situations involving inventory transfers at above cost, it is necessary to distinguish carefully between a mark-up expressed in relation to cost and one expressed in relation to the transfer price. For example, inventory costing $800 and transferred at $1,000 has a 25% mark-up based on cost ($200 ÷ $800) but a 20% mark-up based on the transfer price ($200 ÷ $1,000).

### Procedures for Transferring Inventory above Home Office Cost

Any time transfers are made at above cost, the home office must defer recognition of the mark-up until the branch sells the inventory to its customers. To do otherwise would result in the recognition of profit merely from transferring inventory from one location to another within the company. When inventory is transferred to the branch, the home office (1) credits the Shipments to Branch account at the home office's cost, (2) credits an account called Deferred Profit for the amount of the mark-up, and (3) debits the Investment in Branch account for the total intracompany billing amount. The proper journal entry is as follows:

| | | |
|---|---|---|
| Investment in Branch | xxx | |
| Shipments to Branch | | xxx |
| Deferred Profit | | xxx |

The branch makes the same entry as it does when inventory transfers are made at the home office's cost. Thus, the branch debits the Shipments from Home Office account for the total intracompany billing amount and credits the Home Office Equity account. In Illustration 1-3, journal entry 2 records an inventory transfer above cost.

When the branch submits its month-end financial statements to the home office, it must show separately that portion of its ending inventory that was acquired from the home office. The home office can then (1) determine the amount of mark-up in the ending branch inventory, (2) adjust the Deferred Profit account to this amount, and (3) credit the Branch Income account for the recognizable mark-up. This procedure still keeps the Investment in Branch account on the home office books and the Home Office Equity account on the branch books in agreement. However, the Shipments to Branch account on the books of the home office is always less than the Shipments from Home Office account on the books of the branch by the amount of the mark-up. As a result of the

■ **ILLUSTRATION 1-3**
**Inventory Transfers above Cost**

| Home Office Books | | | Branch Books | | |
|---|---|---|---|---|---|
| 2. Investment in Branch.. | 72,000 | | 2. Shipments from | | |
|    Shipments to | | |    Home Office......... | 72,000 | |
|       Branch........ | | 60,000 |      Home Office Equity | | 72,000 |
|       Deferred Profit ... | | 12,000 | | | |
| 12. Inventory............ | 15,000[a] | | 12. Inventory Acquired | | |
|    Shipments to Branch.. | 60,000 | |     from Vendors........ | 8,000[b] | |
|    Cost of Goods Sold.... | 210,000 | |     Inventory Acquired | | |
|       Purchases....... | | 285,000 |      from Home Office..... | 30,000[c] | |
| | | |     Cost of Goods Sold..... | 77,000 | |
| | | |       Shipments from | | |
| | | |         Home Office...... | | 72,000 |
| | | |       Purchases....... | | 43,000 |
| | | | 13. Sales................ | 120,000 | |
| | | |     Cost of Goods Sold. | | 77,000 |
| | | |     Selling Expenses.. | | 16,000 |
| | | |     Administrative | | |
| | | |       Expenses........ | | 14,000 |
| | | |     Home Office Equity | | 13,000 |
| 14. Investment in Branch.. | 13,000 | | | | |
|      Branch Income ... | | 13,000 | | | |
|    Deferred Profit ....... | 7,000[d] | | | | |
|      Branch Income ... | | 7,000 | | | |

[a]This is the increase in the inventory ($150,000 − $135,000).
[b]This is the increase in the inventory acquired from vendors ($8,000 − $0). (There was no beginning inventory.)
[c]This is the increase in the inventory acquired from the home office ($30,000 − $0). (There was no beginning inventory.)
[d]Adjusts the Deferred Profit account to the $5,000 mark-up in the ending inventory (total mark-up of $12,000 − $5,000 = $7,000).

mark-up, the branch's cost of goods sold is greater and the branch reports a lower operating profit than if the transfer had been billed at the home office's cost. The lower profit reported by the branch is offset by the recognition of the deferred profit by the home office. This procedure results in the same net income being reported on companywide basis, just as though the inventory had been transferred at cost.

ILLUSTRATIVE
ENTRIES

## Inventory Transfers above Cost

Assume that the inventory transferred to the branch from the home office in Illustration 1-1 was marked up 20% over the home office's cost of $60,000. In Illustration 1-2, we assumed that the branch had a $33,000 ending inventory, of which $8,000 represented purchases from outside vendors and $25,000 represented inventory obtained from the home office. In this case, the branch's ending inventory acquired from the home office is $30,000 ($25,000 + $5,000 mark-up). Thus, the branch's total ending inventory is $38,000 ($30,000 + $8,000 acquired from outside vendors). Illustration 1-3 shows the journal entries for the transfer of this inventory above cost, along with the appropriate year-end closing and adjusting entries. The journal entries are numbered to correspond to Illustration 1-1, which shows inventory transfers made at the home office's cost.

In practice, the mark-up must be calculated from the amount of home office–acquired inventory reported by the branch at month-end. (The branch keeps track of and accounts for its inventory based on the transfer price—not the home office's cost.) Using the same facts as in the preceding paragraph, the branch would report home office–acquired inventory of $30,000. (This could be determined from perpetual inventory records or from a physical count.) Knowing that the mark-up is 20% of the home office's cost, the home office would calculate the mark-up in the branch's ending inventory as follows:

$$\frac{\$30,000}{1.20} = \$25,000 \text{ (the home office's cost)}$$

$$\$30,000 - \$25,000 = \$5,000 \text{ (the mark-up)}$$

## The Secondary Elimination Entry

When inventory transfers are made above the home office's cost, an additional elimination entry must be used to prepare combined financial statements. For instructional purposes and ease of reference, we call this the **secondary elimination entry.** It adjusts the branch's cost of goods sold downward to the amount that it would be if the inventory were transferred from the home office at cost. The overstatement of the branch's cost of goods sold equals the amount of the deferred profit that was earned during the year and recognized by the home office. Accordingly, that portion of the credit balance in the Branch Income account pertaining to the recognition of profit from the Deferred Profit account must be reclassified to the Cost of Goods Sold account in the income statement. Because this entry takes place entirely within the income statement section of the worksheet, it is merely a reclassification entry.

| ILLUSTRATION | ## Combining Statement Worksheet: Inventory Transferred above Cost |

Illustration 1-4 shows a worksheet that combines the financial statements of a home office with those of a branch when inventory transfers were made above cost. The financial statement amounts for the home office and the branch are taken from those in Illustration 1-2. They have been adjusted to reflect inventory transfers at 20% above cost, as in Illustration 1-3.

The following elimination entries are made:

1. The primary elimination entry:

**WORKSHEET ENTRY ONLY**

| | | |
|---|---|---|
| Branch Income...................................... | 13,000 | |
| Home Office Equity (preclosing balance)...... | 92,000 | |
| Investment in Branch................... | | 105,000 |

2. The secondary elimination entry:

**WORKSHEET ENTRY ONLY**

| | | |
|---|---|---|
| Branch Income...................................... | 7,000 | |
| Cost of Goods Sold...................... | | 7,000 |

3. The deferred profit elimination entry:

**WORKSHEET ENTRY ONLY**

| | | |
|---|---|---|
| Deferred Profit...................................... | 5,000 | |
| Inventory...................................... | | 5,000 |

The following analysis proves that the branch's cost of goods sold is $7,000 more than if the transfers had been made at the home office's cost:

| | Transfers above Cost | Transfers at Cost | Mark-up |
|---|---|---|---|
| Purchases (from vendors)............. | $ 43,000 | $ 43,000 | $ –0– |
| Shipments from home office ......... | 72,000 | 60,000 | 12,000 |
| Total Inventory Available for Sale .. | $115,000 | $103,000 | $12,000 |
| Less—Ending Inventory: | | | |
| Acquired from vendors.............. | 8,000 | 8,000 | |
| Acquired from home office ......... | 30,000 | 25,000 | 5,000 |
| Cost of Goods Sold.................. | $ 77,000 | $ 70,000 | $ 7,000 |

■ **ILLUSTRATION 1-4**
Inventory Transferred above Cost

| | Home Office | Branch | Eliminations Dr. | Eliminations Cr. | Combined |
|---|---|---|---|---|---|
| **SEARBUCK COMPANY** | | | | | |
| **Combining Statement Worksheet for the Year Ended December 31, 19X1** | | | | | |
| **Income Statement** | | | | | |
| Sales . . . . . . . . . . . . . . . . . . . . . . . . . . | 380,000 | 120,000 | | | 500,000 |
| Cost of goods sold . . . . . . . . . . . . . . . | (210,000) | (77,000) | | 7,000(2) | (280,000) |
| Selling expenses . . . . . . . . . . . . . . . . | (52,000) | (16,000) | | | (68,000) |
| Administrative expenses . . . . . . . . . . | (59,000) | (14,000) | | | (73,000) |
| Interest expense . . . . . . . . . . . . . . . . . | (19,000) | | | | (19,000) |
| Branch income . . . . . . . . . . . . . . . | 20,000 | | 13,000(1)⎫ 7,000(2)⎭ | | –0– |
| Income before Income Taxes . . . . . . | 60,000 | 13,000 | 20,000 | 7,000 | 60,000 |
| Income tax expense @ 40% . . . . . . . . | (24,000) | | | | (24,000) |
| Net Income . . . . . . . . . . . . . . . . . . . . . | 36,000 | 13,000 | ⌐ 20,000 | ⌐ 7,000 | 36,000 |
| **Statement of Retained Earnings/ Analysis of Home Office Equity** | | | | | |
| Retained earnings—Jan. 1, 19X1 . . | 114,000 | | | | 114,000 |
| Home office equity (preclosing) . . . . . | | 92,000 | 92,000(1) | | –0– |
| + Net income . . . . . . . . . . . . . . . . . . . . | 36,000 | 13,000 | 20,000 | 7,000 | 36,000 |
| – Dividends declared . . . . . . . . . . . . . | (10,000) | | | | (10,000) |
| Balances, Dec. 31, 19X1 . . . . . . . . . . | 140,000 | 105,000 | 112,000 | 7,000 | 140,000 |
| **Balance Sheet** | | | | | |
| Cash . . . . . . . . . . . . . . . . . . . . . . . . . . | 50,000 | 30,000 | | | 80,000 |
| Accounts receivable, net . . . . . . . . . . | 60,000 | 41,000 | | | 101,000 |
| Inventory: | | | | | |
| Acquired from vendors . . . . . . . . . . | 150,000 | 8,000 | | | 158,000 |
| Acquired from home office . . . . . . . | | 30,000 | | 5,000(3) | 25,000 |
| Deferred profit . . . . . . . . . . . . . . . . | (5,000) | | 5,000(3) | | –0– |
| Land . . . . . . . . . . . . . . . . . . . . . . . . . . | 22,000 | | | | 22,000 |
| Buildings and equipment, net . . . . . | 118,000 | 11,000 | | | 129,000 |
| Investment in branch . . . . . . . . . . . . . | 105,000 | | | 105,000(1) | –0– |
| Total Assets . . . . . . . . . . . . . . . . . | 500,000 | 120,000 | 5,000 | 110,000 | 515,000 |
| Accounts payable and accruals . . . . . | 60,000 | 15,000 | | | 75,000 |
| Long-term debt . . . . . . . . . . . . . . . . . | 200,000 | | | | 200,000 |
| Common stock . . . . . . . . . . . . . . . | 100,000 | | | | 100,000 |
| Retained earnings . . . . . . . . . . . . . . | 140,000 | | | | 140,000 |
| Home office equity . . . . . . . . . . . . . . | | 105,000 | 112,000 | 7,000 | –0– |
| Total Liabilities and Equity . . . . . | 500,000 | 120,000 | 112,000 | 7,000 | 515,000 |
| Proof of debit and credit postings . . . . . . . . . . . . . . . . . . . . . . . . . . . . . . . . . . . . . | | | 117,000 | 117,000 | |

Explanation of entries:
 (1) The primary elimination entry.    (3) The deferred profit elimination entry.
 (2) The secondary elimination entry.

### Review Points for Illustration 1-4.   Note the following:

1. The only change from Illustration 1-2 is that the merchandise shipments from the home office were billed at $72,000 instead of $60,000, with the $12,000 mark-up initially credited to the Deferred Profit account.
2. The combined balances are the same in Illustrations 1-2 and 1-4.
3. Regardless of the transfer price for intracompany billing, the combined financial statements are the same for financial reporting purposes.
4. In whichever subsequent accounting period the branch sells the remaining portion of the inventory acquired from the home office, a reclassification entry is required within the income statement section of the combining worksheet:

| | | |
|---|---|---|
| Branch Income............................. | 5,000 | |
| Cost of Goods Sold.................... | | 5,000 |

This entry reduces the branch's reported cost of goods sold to agree with the home office's cost.

## MISCELLANEOUS AREAS

### Perpetual Inventory Systems

When the home office and the branch both use perpetual inventory systems, the respective general ledger Inventory accounts are used instead of the Shipments to Branch and Shipments from Home Office accounts, as shown below:

| | Transfers at Cost | | Transfers above Cost | |
|---|---|---|---|---|
| **Home Office Books** | | | | |
| Investment in Branch..... | 60,000 | | 72,000 | |
| Inventory.............. | | 60,000 | | 60,000 |
| Deferred Profit ......... | | | | 12,000 |
| **Branch Books** | | | | |
| Inventory................ | 60,000 | | 72,000 | |
| Home Office Equity..... | | 60,000 | | 72,000 |

As sales occur, each entity relieves inventory directly to its Cost of Goods Sold account. The primary and secondary elimination entries are the same as those shown previously.

## Interbranch Transactions

Branches often transfer inventory to one another. Each branch records the transfer using an Interbranch Receivable or Payable account and a Shipments to or from Branch account. For example, assume Branch A transfers inventory costing $4,000 to Branch B. The entry to Branch A's books would be:

| | | |
|---|---|---|
| Interbranch Receivable | 4,000 | |
|     Shipments to Branch B | | 4,000 |

Correspondingly, the entry to Branch B's books would be:

| | | |
|---|---|---|
| Shipments from Branch A | 4,000 | |
|     Interbranch Payable | | 4,000 |

The Shipments to Branch B account offsets the Shipments from Branch A account when combined financial statements are prepared. Any unpaid interbranch receivables and payables at month-end also offset each other when combined financial statements are prepared. Some home offices do not require branches to make cash payments to one another for interbranch transfers, because this is not sound cash management on a companywide basis. Instead, company policy may require each branch to close its Interbranch Receivable or Payable accounts to its respective Home Office Equity account at month-end. Assuming no other transactions occurred between branches A and B for the month, the entries to close these accounts would be as follows, for Branch A:

| | | |
|---|---|---|
| Home Office Equity | 4,000 | |
|     Interbranch Receivable | | 4,000 |

for Branch B:

| | | |
|---|---|---|
| Interbranch Payable | 4,000 | |
|     Home Office Equity | | 4,000 |

The branch must inform the home office of the amounts that have been charged or credited to the Home Office Equity accounts. The home office would then make the following entry:

| | | |
|---|---|---|
| Investment in Branch B | 4,000 | |
|     Investment in Branch A | | 4,000 |

## Freight

Freight charges incurred in acquiring inventory from the home office or from outside sources are inventoriable. When a branch acquires inventory from another branch rather than from the normal source of supply, sound accounting theory dictates that any freight charges in excess of normal should be expensed currently. If the home office is responsible for a branch having to use another branch as a supply source, then such incremental freight charges should be borne by the home office, regardless of which accounting entity makes the cash payment for the freight charges.

## Start-up Costs

Expenses incurred by a branch *before* it formally opens for business are start-up costs. An operating loss incurred for a period of time after the formal opening is not considered a start-up cost.

Start-up costs may be expensed as incurred, or they may be capitalized for subsequent amortization over a reasonably short period of time (usually no more than a 3- to 5-year amortization period). Most companies expense start-up costs as incurred.

## Agencies

Some companies open outlying sales offices that carry only product samples, demonstration units, and brochures, all of which are used in obtaining sales orders. These offices are commonly referred to as *agencies*. Sales orders are forwarded to the home office for approval and filling.

Agency personnel are almost always paid from the home office. The home office may establish a nominal imprest cash fund for each of these outlying locations. The imprest funds, which may be in the form of petty cash or a local bank account, are used to pay for miscellaneous expenses incurred. As imprest funds are depleted, the outlying location sends invoices and receipts to the home office, which reviews them and sends a check to replenish the fund. The home office records these expenses in its general ledger, usually in accounts specially coded to signify the outlying location to which they pertain. This manner of accounting for sales offices is a predominantly centralized system.

# END-OF-CHAPTER REVIEW

## Summary of Key Points

1. Branch locations can be accounted for using a centralized or decentralized accounting system.

2. Under a centralized accounting system, the assets, liabilities, revenues, and expenses of the branch are recorded on the books of the home office.
3. Under a decentralized accounting system, each branch uses its own general ledger to reflect its assets, liabilities, revenues, costs, and expenses.
4. A decentralized accounting system requires the home office to use accounting procedures that effectively treat the outlying locations as investments to maintain control over their net assets and operations.
5. Management must evaluate the profitability of branch operations carefully when inventory is acquired from the home office, because intracompany billing prices set by the home office directly affect the income or loss reported by the branch.
6. The treatment of home office expenses—none, some, or all of which may be allocated to the branches—complicates the process of evaluating the profitability of branch operations.
7. In preparing financial statements for stockholders, the company must combine the financial statements of the branches with those of the home office.
8. Combined financial statement amounts are the same regardless of the transfer price used for home office inventory transfers to branches.
9. Combined financial statements reflect only those transactions that occur between the company and outside parties.

## Glossary of New Terms

**Agency**   An outlying location that carries product samples, demonstration units, and brochures for the purpose of obtaining sales orders, which are approved and filled by the home office.

**Branch**   An outlying manufacturing, service, or retailing location of a legal business entity.

**Centralized accounting**   A system whereby the accounting for outlying locations is performed at the home office; the outlying locations do not maintain general ledgers.

**Decentralized accounting**   A system whereby outlying locations maintain their own general ledgers and submit financial reports periodically to the home office.

**External expansion**   The expansion of a business by combining two existing businesses into a unified larger business.

**Home office**   The headquarters location of a legal business entity that establishes a branch.

**Intracompany accounts (or reciprocal accounts)**   Two accounts each in a different general ledger for which the debit balance in one account is to equal the credit balance in the other account. In branch accounting, the Investment in Branch account on the home office's books and the Home Office Equity account on the branch's books.

**Internal expansion**   The expansion of a business through the construction or leasing of additional facilities at an existing or outlying location.

**Primary elimination entry**   A worksheet entry that enables the separate financial statements of a home office and its branch to be combined by eliminating the reciprocal accounts (Investment in Branch and Home Office Equity) and the Branch Income account recorded on the home office's books.

**Secondary elimination entry**    A worksheet entry that reclassifies the realized intracompany profit in the Branch Income account to the Cost of Goods Sold account.

## Self-Study Questions

*(Answers are at the end of this chapter.)*

1. The net income amount in the combined income statement is:
   a. Dependent on whether or not inventory transfers from the home office to the branch are at cost or above cost.
   b. Always the same as if centralized accounting had been used instead of decentralized accounting.
   c. Dependent on the extent of home office overhead allocations made to the branch.
   d. None of the above.
2. Which of the following sets of accounts must always be kept in agreement?
   a. Investment in Branch and Equity in Home Office.
   b. Shipments to Branch and Shipments from Home Office.
   c. Branch Income and Equity in Branch Income.
   d. None of the above.
3. Which of the following is the only reason why a home office cannot report inventory shipments to a branch as sales?
   a. The inventory transfer is a transaction with a related party.
   b. There is no practicable means of determining whether the transfer prices approximate those that would occur in an arms length transaction between independent parties.
   c. Only inventory transactions between the company and outside third parties can be considered sales.
   d. The principle of conservatism.

## ASSIGNMENT MATERIAL

### Review Questions

1. What is the difference between a centralized accounting system and a decentralized accounting system?
2. Why is the branch's operating income or loss not a net income or loss?
3. What is the function of the Shipments to Branch and Shipments from Home Office accounts?
4. If the intracompany accounts do not agree, what are some possible explanations? Which accounting entity must make the adjustments?
5. Why are the elimination entries not posted to any general ledger?
6. What does the primary elimination entry accomplish? The secondary elimination entry?
7. When is the secondary elimination entry necessary?

8. Why is the shipment of inventory to a branch not considered a reportable sale for combined financial reporting purposes?
9. Why does the intracompany inventory transfer price have no effect on the combined amounts for financial reporting purposes?
10. Define *start-up costs*.

## Discussion Cases

### DC 1-1

### Mark-up of Intracompany Inventory Transfers

You are the controller of a company that is establishing its first branch, which will use a decentralized accounting system. A substantial portion of the branch's inventory will be purchased from the home office to take advantage of the additional volume discounts that the home office can obtain. You must advise top management on the billing prices of intracompany inventory shipments to the branch. This decision is important, because the billing prices selected will directly affect the branch's operating income or loss. The branch manager has told you that all of the company's additional savings on volume discounts resulting from the formation of the branch should be passed on to the branch, since without the branch, they would not have been realized.

#### Required:

What considerations should be taken into account in determining the intracompany transfer pricing policy?

### DC 1-2

### Determination and Treatment of Start-up Costs

Trunkley Company has numerous branch outlets, which operate from leased facilities. A new branch outlet historically has taken approximately two months from inception of its facility lease until it starts to generate sales, and another four months before its monthly operations start showing a profit. The typical new branch incurs a loss of $80,000 during this six-month period. Near the beginning of the current year, Lemcoe established the Jadeville and Rubysville branches:

|  | Jadeville Branch | Rubysville Branch |
|---|---|---|
| Number of months from lease inception until operations showed a profit. . . . . . . . . . . . . . . . . . . . | 5 | 11 |
| Excess of costs and expenses over revenues until monthly operations showed a profit . . . . . . . | $(65,000) | $(130,000) |

Management intends to treat as a deferred charge $160,000 of the combined $195,000 excess of costs and expenses over revenues for the two new branches. Any amount in excess of $80,000 is considered an unfavorable start-up variance, which should be expensed as a period cost.

#### Required:

Evaluate the treatment proposed by the company.

## Exercises

<table>
<tr><td>E<br>1-1</td></tr>
</table>

### Journal Entry Preparation: Periodic Inventory System—Inventory Transfers at Cost

The following transactions pertain to a branch's first month's operations:

1. The home office sent $9,000 cash to the branch.
2. The home office shipped inventory costing $40,000 to the branch; the intra-company billing is at cost.
3. The branch purchased inventory from outside vendors for $30,000.
4. The branch had sales of $80,000 on account.
5. The home office allocated $2,000 in advertising expenses to the branch.
6. The branch collected $45,000 on accounts receivable.
7. The branch incurred operating expenses of $14,000, none of which were paid at month-end.
8. The branch remitted $17,000 to the home office.
9. The branch's ending inventory is $28,000.

**Required:**
1. Prepare the home office and branch journal entries for these transactions, assuming a periodic inventory system is used.
2. Prepare the month-end closing entries for the branch.
3. Prepare the month-end adjusting entry for the home office relating to the branch's operations for the month.

<table>
<tr><td>E<br>1-2</td></tr>
</table>

### Journal Entry Preparation: Periodic Inventory System—Inventory Transfers above Cost

The following transactions pertain to a branch's first month's operations:

1. The home office sent $9,000 cash to the branch.
2. The home office shipped inventory costing $40,000 to the branch; the intra-company billing was for $50,000.
3. Branch inventory purchases from outside vendors totaled $30,000.
4. Branch sales on account were $80,000.
5. The home office allocated $2,000 in advertising expenses to the branch.
6. Branch collections on accounts receivable were $45,000.
7. Branch operating expenses of $14,000 were incurred, none of which were paid at month-end.
8. The branch remitted $17,000 to the home office.
9. The branch's ending inventory (as reported in its balance sheet) is composed of:

| | |
|---|---:|
| Acquired from outside vendors................................... | $12,000 |
| Acquired from home office (at billing price)..................... | 20,000 |
| Total........................................................ | $32,000 |

**Required:**

1. Prepare the home office and branch journal entries for these transactions, assuming a periodic inventory system is used.
2. Prepare the month-end closing entries for the branch.
3. Prepare the month-end adjusting entries for the home office relating to the branch's operations for the month.

| E |
|---|
| **1-3** |

## Reconciliation of Intracompany Accounts

On December 31, 19X1, the Home Office Equity account on the branch's books has a balance of $44,000 and the Investment in Branch account on the home office's books has a balance of $85,000. In analyzing the activity in each of these accounts for December, you find the following differences:

1. A $10,000 branch remittance to the home office initiated on December 27, 19X1, was recorded on the home office books on January 3, 19X2.
2. A home office inventory shipment to the branch on December 28, 19X1, was recorded by the branch on January 4, 19X2; the billing of $20,000 was at cost.
3. The home office incurred $12,000 of advertising expenses and allocated $5,000 of this amount to the branch on December 15, 19X1. The branch has not recorded this transaction.
4. A branch customer erroneously remitted $3,000 to the home office. The home office recorded this cash collection on December 23, 19X1. Meanwhile, back at the branch, no entry has been made yet.
5. Inventory costing $43,000 was sent to the branch by the home office on December 10, 19X1. The billing was at cost, but the branch recorded the transaction at $34,000.

**Required:**

Prepare the entries to bring the intracompany accounts into balance as of December 31, 19X1. Assume that a periodic inventory system is in use. (Use T accounts.)

| E |
|---|
| **1-4** |

## Reconciliation of Intracompany Accounts

The following entries are reflected in the intracompany accounts of a home office and its lone branch for June 19X2:

**Home Office Equity**

| | | | | | |
|---|---|---|---|---|---|
| | | | 6/1 | Balance | 50,000 |
| 6/2 | Remittance | 10,000 | 6/8 | Inventory shipment | 30,000 |
| 6/24 | Purchase of equipment (carried on home office books) | 7,000 | 6/10 | Collection of home office receivable | 2,000 |
| | | | 6/16 | Inventory shipment | 12,000 |
| 6/29 | Remittance | 15,000 | 6/24 | Inventory shipment | 17,000 |
| 6/30 | Inventory returned to home office | 1,000 | 6/28 | Advertising allocation | 400 |
| 6/30 | Depreciation allocation | 2,000 | | | |
| | | | 6/30 | Balance | 76,400 |

**Investment in Branch**

| | | | | |
|---|---|---|---|---|
| 6/1 | Balance ............. | 50,000 | | |
| 6/5 | Inventory shipment .... | 30,000 | 6/2 Remittance.......... | 10,000 |
| 6/12 | Inventory shipment .... | 12,000 | 6/8 Collection of branch | |
| 6/20 | Inventory shipment .... | 17,000 | receivable ......... | 1,000 |
| 6/25 | Advertising allocation to | | 6/27 Equipment purchase by | |
| | branch (50% of $8,000 | | branch ............ | 7,000 |
| | incurred) .......... | 4,000 | | |
| 6/28 | Inventory shipment .... | 14,000 | | |
| 6/30 | Depreciation allocation . | 2,000 | | |
| 6/30 | Balance ............. | 111,000 | | |

### Required:

1. Prepare a schedule to reconcile the intracompany accounts. Assume that inventory shipments to the branch are billed at 25% above the home office's cost.
2. Prepare the adjusting journal entries to bring the intracompany accounts into balance.

## E 1-5   Analysis of Branch Inventory and Deferred Profit

A home office shipped inventory to its branch during the year. The following information has been obtained from the records of the home office and the branch at the end of the current year:

| | Total | Resold | On Hand |
|---|---|---|---|
| Shipments from home office............ | $90,000 | | $18,000 |
| Shipments to branch ................. | 75,000 | | |
| Mark-up......................... | $15,000 | | |

### Required:

1. Complete the analysis.
2. Prepare the branch's entry to record cost of goods sold, assuming the branch purchases all of its inventory from the home office and reported a beginning inventory of $12,000, all of which had been sold by the end of the current year. (Assume the same mark-up percentage for last year as for this year.)
3. Prepare an analysis of the Deferred Profit account for the year.

## E 1-6   Adjusting the Deferred Profit Account

A home office ships inventory to its branch at 125% of cost. The Deferred Profit account balance at the beginning of the year was $4,000. During the year, the branch was billed $70,000 for inventory transfers from the home office. At year-end, the branch's balance sheet shows $16,000 of inventory on hand that was acquired from the home office.

### Required:

1. Determine the amount of the branch's beginning inventory (as shown in its prior year-end financial statements).
2. Prepare the branch's entry to record cost of goods sold.
3. Calculate the year-end adjustment to the Deferred Profit account and show the adjusting journal entry.

## E 1-7 Journal Entry Preparation: Periodic Inventory System—Inventory Transfers above Cost

The following transactions pertain to branch operations:

1. The branch purchased and paid for equipment costing $3,000. All fixed assets are recorded on the home office books.
2. The branch received and deposited a $1,000 remittance from a customer of a nearby branch.
3. The home office paid the monthly lease expense of $4,000 on the branch's facilities. Company policy is to allocate such expenses to the branch.
4. A branch customer made a payment of $2,000 directly to the home office. The home office notified the branch, which then made the appropriate entry.
5. The branch remitted $15,000 to the home office.
6. The home office computed the monthly depreciation expense pertaining to the branch's fixed assets, which are recorded on the home office books. The depreciation expense of $4,500 was charged to the branch.
7. The home office allocated overhead expenses of $8,000 to the branch.
8. The home office shipped inventory to the branch. The home office's cost was $55,000, and it billed the branch $66,000.
9. With respect to the inventory purchased from the home office in transaction 8, assume the branch had $3,600 of this inventory on hand at month-end, as reflected in its financial statements submitted to the home office. Assume the branch reported a beginning inventory of items purchased from the home office of $6,000, all of which was sold during the current year.
10. The home office received the branch's monthly financial statements, which showed the branch had operating income of $25,000.

### Required:

Prepare the home office and branch journal entries for these transactions, assuming a periodic inventory system is used. For transaction 9, prepare the branch's entry to record cost of goods sold.

## E 1-8 Calculating Beginning Inventory from Selected Data

A home office transfers inventory to its branch at a 20% mark-up. During the current year, inventory costing the home office $80,000 was transferred to the branch. At year-end, the home office adjusted its Deferred Profit account downward by $18,200. The branch's year-end balance sheet shows $4,800 of inventory acquired from the home office.

**Required:**

Calculate the home office's cost of the branch's beginning inventory.

## Problems

### Combining Statement Worksheet: Inventory Transfers at Cost

The December 31, 19X1, financial statements of Kringle Company and its 34th Street branch (which was established in 19X1) are given as follows:

| | Home Office | Branch |
|---|---|---|
| **Income Statement** | | |
| Sales. . . . . . . . . . . . . . . . . . . . . . . . . . . . . . . . . . . . . . . | $ 700,000 | $200,000 |
| Cost of goods sold . . . . . . . . . . . . . . . . . . . . . . . . | (390,000) | (135,000) |
| Selling expenses. . . . . . . . . . . . . . . . . . . . . . . . . . | (42,000) | (11,000) |
| Administrative expenses. . . . . . . . . . . . . . . . . . . | (28,000) | (4,000) |
| Interest expense. . . . . . . . . . . . . . . . . . . . . . . . . . | (40,000) | |
| Branch income . . . . . . . . . . . . . . . . . . . . . . . . . . | 50,000 | |
| Income before Income Taxes . . . . . . . . . . . . . . . | $ 250,000 | $ 50,000 |
| Income tax expense @ 40%. . . . . . . . . . . . . . . . . | (100,000) | |
| Net Income. . . . . . . . . . . . . . . . . . . . . . . . . . . . | $ 150,000 | $ 50,000 |
| **Balance Sheet** | | |
| Cash . . . . . . . . . . . . . . . . . . . . . . . . . . . . . . . . . . . | $ 90,000 | $ 10,000 |
| Accounts receivable, net . . . . . . . . . . . . . . . . . . . | 80,000 | 20,000 |
| Inventory: | | |
| Acquired from vendors. . . . . . . . . . . . . . . . . . . | 180,000 | 10,000 |
| Acquired from home office . . . . . . . . . . . . . . . . | | 30,000 |
| Fixed assets, net. . . . . . . . . . . . . . . . . . . . . . . . . | 770,000 | 140,000 |
| Investment in branch. . . . . . . . . . . . . . . . . . . . . | 170,000 | |
| Total Assets. . . . . . . . . . . . . . . . . . . . . . . . . . . | $1,290,000 | $210,000 |
| Accounts payable and accruals . . . . . . . . . . . . . . | $ 200,000 | $ 40,000 |
| Long-term debt. . . . . . . . . . . . . . . . . . . . . . . . . . | 350,000 | |
| Common stock . . . . . . . . . . . . . . . . . . . . . . . . . . | 500,000 | |
| Retained earnings . . . . . . . . . . . . . . . . . . . . . . | 240,000 | |
| Home office equity . . . . . . . . . . . . . . . . . . . . . . . | | 170,000 |
| Total Liabilities and Equity. . . . . . . . . . . . . . . | $1,290,000 | $210,000 |
| Dividends declared during 19X1 . . . . . . . . . . . . . | $110,000 | |

**Required:**

Prepare a combining statement worksheet as of December 31, 19X1, assuming inventory transfers to the branch from the home office are at cost.

*The financial statement information presented for problems accompanied by asterisks is also provided on Model 1 (filename: Model1) of the software file disk that is available for use with the text, enabling the problem to be worked on the computer.

P
1-2*

## Combining Statement Worksheet: Problem 1-1 Revised to Reflect Inventory Transfers above Cost

The December 31, 19X1, financial statements of Kringle Company and its 34th Street branch are as follows:

|  | Home Office | Branch |
|---|---|---|
| **Income Statement** | | |
| Sales | $ 700,000 | $200,000 |
| Cost of goods sold | (390,000) | (149,000) |
| Selling expenses | (42,000) | (11,000) |
| Administrative expenses | (28,000) | (4,000) |
| Interest expense | (40,000) | |
| Branch income | 50,000 | |
| Income before Income Taxes | $ 250,000 | $ 36,000 |
| Income tax expense @ 40% | (100,000) | |
| Net Income | $ 150,000 | $ 36,000 |
| **Balance Sheet** | | |
| Cash | $ 90,000 | $ 10,000 |
| Accounts receivable, net | 80,000 | 20,000 |
| Inventory: | | |
| Acquired from vendors | 180,000 | 10,000 |
| Acquired from home office | | 36,000 |
| Deferred profit | (6,000) | |
| Fixed assets, net | 770,000 | 140,000 |
| Investment in branch | 176,000 | |
| Total Assets | $1,290,000 | $216,000 |
| Accounts payable and accruals | $ 200,000 | $ 40,000 |
| Long-term debt | 350,000 | |
| Common stock | 500,000 | |
| Retained earnings | 240,000 | |
| Home office equity | | 176,000 |
| Total Liabilities and Equity | $1,290,000 | $216,000 |
| Dividends declared during 19X1 | $110,000 | |

## Required:

1. Prepare a combining statement worksheet as of December 31, 19X1.
2. Complete the following analysis of the branch's inventory:

|  | Transfers above Cost | Transfers at Cost | Mark-up |
|---|---|---|---|
| Purchases (from vendors) | $75,000 | $75,000 | $ –0– |
| Shipments from home office | | | |
| Total Inventory Available for Sale | | | |
| Less—Ending Inventory: | | | |
| Acquired from vendors | | | |
| Acquired from home office | | | |
| Cost of Goods Sold | $ | $ | $ |

3. Prepare the entry that the branch made to record cost of goods sold.

4. Calculate the mark-up percentage.

## COMPREHENSIVE  Year-end Adjusting and Closing Entries; Combining Statement Worksheet: Inventory Transfers above Cost

**P 1-3***

The preclosing trial balances Wrigley Company and its State Street branch for the year ended December 31, 19X3, prior to adjusting and closing entries are as follows:

| Accounts | Home Office Dr. | Home Office Cr. | Branch Dr. | Branch Cr. |
|---|---|---|---|---|
| Cash................... | $  35,000 | | $  10,000 | |
| Accounts receivable, net... | 80,000 | | 50,000 | |
| Inventory, January 1, 19X3: | | | | |
|  Acquired from vendors .. | 230,000 | | 50,000 | |
|  Acquired from home office | | | 20,000 | |
| Deferred profit .......... | | $  25,000 | | |
| Fixed assets, net......... | 870,000 | | 90,000 | |
| Investment in branch...... | 155,000 | | | |
| Accounts payable and accruals.............. | | 221,000 | | $  45,000 |
| Long-term debt.......... | | 400,000 | | |
| Common stock.......... | | 300,000 | | |
| Retained earnings, January 1, 19X3........ | | 350,000 | | |
| Home office equity....... | | | | 115,000 |
| Sales ................ | | 960,000 | | 320,000 |
| Purchases............. | 800,000 | | 120,000 | |
| Shipments from home office | | | 90,000 | |
| Shipments to branch...... | | 84,000 | | |
| Selling expenses ........ | 81,000 | | 34,000 | |
| Administrative expenses .. | 54,000 | | 16,000 | |
| Interest expense......... | 35,000 | | | |
| | $2,340,000 | $2,340,000 | $480,000 | $480,000 |
| Inventory per physical count on December 31, 19X3: | | | | |
|  Acquired from vendors. | $180,000 | | $20,000 | |
|  Acquired from home office | | | $30,000 | |

## Additional Information:

1. Inventory transferred to the branch from the home office is billed at 125% of cost.

2. The home office billed the branch $15,000 for inventory it shipped to the branch on December 28, 19X3; the branch received and recorded this shipment on January 2, 19X4.

3. The branch remitted $25,000 cash to the home office on December 31, 19X3; the home office received and recorded this remittance on January 4, 19X4.
4. The Deferred Profit account is normally adjusted at the end of the year.
5. Income taxes are to be recorded at 40%.
6. No dividends were declared during the year.

### Required:

1. Prepare the year-end adjusting entries to:
    a. Bring the intracompany accounts into agreement. (Be sure to adjust the other accounts in the trial balance as appropriate.)
    b. Adjust the inventory accounts and record cost of goods sold.
2. Complete the following analysis of the branch's inventory:

| | Transfers above Cost | Transfers at Cost | Mark-up |
|---|---|---|---|
| Beginning inventory: | $ | $ | $ |
|   Acquired from vendors . . . . . . . . . . . . . . | | | |
|   Acquired from home office . . . . . . . . . . | | | |
|   +Purchases (from vendors) . . . . . . . . . | | | |
|   +Shipments from home office . . . . . . . | | | |
| Total Inventory Available for Sale . . . . . | | | |
| Less—Ending Inventory: | | | |
|   Acquired from vendors . . . . . . . . . . . . . . | | | |
|   Acquired from home office . . . . . . . . . . | | | |
| Cost of Goods Sold. . . . . . . . . . . . . . . . . . | | | |

3. Prepare the following year-end adjusting entries to:
    a. Record the branch's income on the home office's books.
    b. Adjust the Deferred Profit account to the proper balance.
    c. Provide for income taxes.
4. Prepare the year-end closing entries for the home office and the branch.
5. Prepare a combining statement worksheet as of December 31, 19X3, after completing requirements 1–4.

### COMPREHENSIVE   Year-end Adjusting and Closing Entries; Combining Statement Worksheet: Inventory Transfers above Cost

The preclosing trial balances of Mart Company and its K Street branch for the year ended December 31, 19X4, are as follows:

| | Home Office | | Branch | |
|---|---|---|---|---|
| Accounts | Dr. | Cr. | Dr. | Cr. |
| Cash. . . . . . . . . . . . . . . . . . . . . | $ 36,000 | | $  5,000 | |
| Accounts receivable, net. . . . . | 35,000 | | 12,000 | |
| Inventory, January 1, 19X4 . . | 70,000 | | 18,000 | |
| Inventory, deferred profit . . . . | | $  11,000 | | |

| Accounts | Home Office Dr. | Home Office Cr. | Branch Dr. | Branch Cr. |
|---|---|---|---|---|
| Fixed assets, net............ | 90,000 | | | |
| Investment in branch........ | 20,000 | | | |
| Accounts payable and accruals................ | | 50,000 | | $ 16,000 |
| Common stock............. | | 50,000 | | |
| Retained earnings, January 1, 19X4.......... | | 53,000 | | |
| Dividends declared ........ | 12,000 | | | |
| Home office equity.......... | | | | 9,000 |
| Sales .................... | | 392,000 | | 95,000 |
| Purchases................. | 290,000 | | 21,000 | |
| Shipments to branch........ | | 40,000 | | |
| Shipments from home office . | | | 45,000 | |
| Expenses................. | 43,000 | | 19,000 | |
| | $596,000 | $596,000 | $120,000 | $120,000 |

## Additional Information:

1. On December 23, the branch manager purchased $4,000 of furniture and fixtures but failed to notify the home office. The bookkeeper, knowing that all fixed assets are carried on the home office books, recorded the proper entry on the branch records. It is the company's policy not to take any depreciation on assets acquired in the last half of the year.
2. On December 27, a branch customer erroneously paid his $2,000 account to the home office. The bookkeeper made the correct entry on the home office books but did not notify the branch.
3. On December 30, the branch remitted $5,000 cash, which the home office received in January 19X5.
4. On December 31, the branch erroneously recorded the December allocated expenses from the home office as $500 instead of $1,500.
5. On December 31, the home office shipped merchandise billed at $3,000 to the branch. The branch received this shipment in January 19X5.
6. The entire beginning inventory of the branch was purchased from the home office. The physical inventories on December 31, 19X4, excluding the shipment in transit, are:

| | |
|---|---|
| Home office.................................................... | $55,000 |
| Branch (composed of $21,000 from home office and $2,000 from outside vendors)..................................... | 23,000 |

7. The home office consistently bills shipments to the branch at 20% above cost.
8. The Deferred Profit account is adjusted at year-end.

## Required:

1. Prepare December 31, 19X4, adjusting entries to:
   a. Bring the intracompany accounts into agreement. (Be sure to adjust the other accounts in the trial balance as appropriate.)

b. Adjust the inventory accounts and record cost of goods sold.
2. Complete the following analysis of the branch's inventory:

|  | Transfers above Cost | Transfers at Cost | Mark-up |
|---|---|---|---|
| Beginning inventory . . . . . . . . . . . . . . . . . | $ | $ | $ |
| +Purchases (from vendors) . . . . . . . . . | | | |
| +Shipments from home office . . . . . . . | | | |
| Total Inventory Available for Sale . . . . . . | | | |
| Less—Ending Inventory: | | | |
|   Acquired from vendors . . . . . . . . . . . . | | | |
|   Acquired from home office . . . . . . . . . . | | | |
| Cost of Goods Sold. . . . . . . . . . . . . . . . . . | | | |

3. Prepare the following year-end adjusting entries to:
   a. Record the branch income on the home office books.
   b. Adjust the Deferred Profit account to the proper balance.
   c. Provide income tax expense at 40%.
4. Prepare the year-end closing entries for the home office and the branch.
5. Prepare a combining statement worksheet as of December 31, 19X4, after completing requirements 1–4.

# ADVANCED LEVEL ASSIGNMENT MATERIAL

## Advanced Problems

| AP 1-1 |
|---|

### Evaluating Profitability: Branch Performance and Return on Investment

Data for Pinesburg Company for the year ended December 31, 19X1, follow:

| | |
|---|---|
| Operating income . . . . . . . . . . . . . . . . . . . . . . . . . . . . . . . . . . . . . | $ 160,000 |
| Interest expense. . . . . . . . . . . . . . . . . . . . . . . . . . . . . . . . . . . . . . . | (60,000) |
|   Income before Income Taxes . . . . . . . . . . . . . . . . . . . . . . . . . | 100,000 |
| Income tax expense @ 40% . . . . . . . . . . . . . . . . . . . . . . . . . . . . . | (40,000) |
|   Net Income . . . . . . . . . . . . . . . . . . . . . . . . . . . . . . . . . . . . . . . | $ 60,000 |
| | |
| Current liabilities (average balance) . . . . . . . . . . . . . . . . . . . . . . | $ 250,000 |
| Long-term debt, 10% (average balance). . . . . . . . . . . . . . . . . . . . | 600,000 |
| Stockholders' equity (average balance). . . . . . . . . . . . . . . . . . . . . | 400,000 |
|   Total Liabilities and Equity . . . . . . . . . . . . . . . . . . . . . . . . . . . | $1,250,000 |
| Revenues. . . . . . . . . . . . . . . . . . . . . . . . . . . . . . . . . . . . . . . . . . . . | $1,600,000 |

During the fourth quarter of 19X1, steps were taken for the opening of a branch in Sappsville. This branch opened for business on January 1, 19X2. Data for the Sappsville branch for the quarter ended March 31, 19X2, follow:

| | |
|---|---|
| Income for the quarter, as reported to the home office . . . . . . . . . . . . | $ 48,000 |
| Average balance in the Home Office Equity account. . . . . . . . . . . . . . | 300,000 |
| Total assets (average balance, per the branch records) . . . . . . . . . . . | 500,000 |
| Revenues. . . . . . . . . . . . . . . . . . . . . . . . . . . . . . . . . . . . . . . . . . . . . . . . . | 400,000 |

## Additional Information:

1. To finance the new branch, on January 1, 19X2, the home office (a) issued 10,000 shares of its common stock, which raised $200,000; and (b) borrowed $800,000 at 12% interest, due in five years. (This debt is recorded on the home office's books).
2. The $1,000,000 of capital raised was used to acquire fixed assets ($700,000), acquire inventory ($250,000), and provide working capital ($50,000) for the branch. (The fixed assets of the branch are recorded on the home office's books and are pledged as collateral on the $800,000 loan.)
3. All inventory shipments to the branch were billed at the home office's cost.
4. The branch has the same square footage of retail space as the home office.
5. The only expenses allocated to the branch were for insurance, advertising, and depreciation, all of which were directly traceable to the branch.
6. For 19X1, the annual audit by the company's independent auditors cost $20,000. For 19X2, the cost of the audit will be approximately $24,000. The $4,000 increase is entirely attributable to having an additional location. The company's interim reporting policy is to spread the annual cost of the audit over the four quarters. Accordingly, the home office has expensed $6,000 on its books for the first quarter of 19X2. Disregard this information in completing requirements 1, 2, and 3.

## Required:

1. Make appropriate rate-of-return calculations for 19X1 that will be useful in serving as a standard for evaluating the profitability of the branch.
2. Make appropriate rate of return calculations for the branch for the first quarter of 19X2. (One of the objectives here is to enable the home office to evaluate its investment in the branch from the perspective of an investor in the same manner that stockholders evaluate a company's performance from their unique perspective.)
3. Compare the percentages in requirements 1 and 2 and evaluate whether investing in the branch was worthwhile. Can you think of other items that should be considered in this evaluation?
4. How should the cost of the annual audit be dealt with in comparing the profitability of the two locations?

## ANSWERS TO SELF-STUDY QUESTIONS

1. b
2. d
3. c

# 2

■■■■■

# INTRODUCTION TO BUSINESS COMBINATIONS

## TOPIC OUTLINE

## CHAPTER OVERVIEW

**S**tockholders expect management to increase a company's sales and profitability each year. Consequently, growth of sales and profit is one of the major objectives of corporate management. Many companies can attain this growth either by expanding their existing line of business or by entering into a new line of business through internal expansion. Internal expansion can be a lengthy and involved process, considering the problems of choosing a site location, designing facilities, preparing environmental impact reports, obtaining governmental permits, dealing with architects and contractors, hiring qualified employees, developing new channels of distribution and markets, and the likely prospect of incurring operating losses for some time before revenues reach expected levels. Furthermore, entering into a new line of business through internal expansion generally is considered much riskier than expanding in the same line of business. This is simply because, initially at least, management's degree of expertise in the new line of business is less than that of existing competitors. Also, becoming an additional competitor in the field is bound to be risky.

The alternative to internal expansion is **external expansion,** whereby all or a segment of an existing business combines with the business seeking growth. Bringing together two separate businesses under common ownership is known as a **business combination.** Most of the problems of internal expansion are not encountered in external expansion; only the assessment of the prospects of an existing business is involved. If the assessment is favorable, then efforts can be made to combine the businesses. Most business combinations are completed in far less time than it would take to develop a new product, build manufacturing facilities to produce it, and then successfully market it. Often the newly acquired business produces a profit from the start. The management of the newly acquired business may be retained, and no new competitor is introduced into the field.

## THE DESIRE TO MERGE

### Terminology

In the business community, business combinations are referred to as mergers and acquisitions. The company whose business is being sought is often called the **target company.** The company attempting to acquire the target company's business is referred to as the **acquiring company.** The legal agreement that specifies the terms and provisions of the business combination is known as the *acquisition, purchase,* or *merger agree-*

*ment.* For simplicity, we refer to this legal agreement as the **acquisition agreement.** The process of trying to acquire a target company's business is often called a **takeover attempt.** Business combinations can be categorized as vertical, horizontal, or conglomerate. **Vertical combinations** take place between companies involved in the same industry but at different levels—for example, a tire manufacturer and a tire distributor. **Horizontal combinations** take place between companies that are competitors at the same level in a given industry—two tire manufacturers, for example. **Conglomerate combinations** involve companies in totally unrelated industries—such as a tire manufacturer and an insurance company. In recent years, conglomerate combinations have become much more prevalent as businesses seek to diversify their product lines and minimize the effects of cyclical sales and earnings patterns in their businesses. These categories of business combination have no bearing on how the combination is recorded for financial reporting purposes.

## Legal Restrictions on Business Combinations

Before discussing business combinations any further, we should note that certain combinations are prohibited. Section 7 of the Clayton Act (1914) prohibits any business combination in which "the effect of such acquisition may be substantially to lessen competition or tend to create a monopoly." The Justice Department and the Federal Trade Commission, the two federal agencies with antitrust jurisdiction, enforce this law. These agencies have issued certain precombination notification regulations: A company with assets or sales of at least $10 million that plans to acquire a manufacturing company with assets or sales of at least $10 million must file a detailed 21-page form 30 days before the planned date of consummation. (If the target company is not a manufacturing company, notification is required only if one company has at least $100 million in sales or assets and the other company has sales or assets of at least $10 million.) Such regulations enable the regulatory agencies to review proposed business combinations before they occur and, if necessary, to obtain preliminary court injunctions to block proposed combinations. The most recent example of an injunction involving widely known companies was in 1986 when the Federal Trade Commission sought a preliminary court injunction against the proposed sale by Philip Morris Co. of Seven-Up Co., its subsidiary, to PepsiCo Inc., and against the proposed purchase of Dr. Pepper Co. by Coca-Cola Co., because the transactions would give Coke and Pepsi nearly 80% of the soft drink market in the United States. Shortly thereafter, Philip Morris announced it would seek another buyer.[1]

[1]"Philip Morris Ends Plan to Sell Seven-Up to Pepsi, but Coke Still Seeks Dr. Pepper," *The Wall Street Journal*, June 25, 1986, p. 3.

Even when a proposed business combination is not challenged by the government before it is consummated, the government can later issue a *divestiture order* requiring the acquiring company to dispose of its acquired business. If the acquiring company appeals the order, the courts may or may not uphold it.

Although the Clayton Act apparently applies only to horizontal and vertical combinations, the regulatory agencies have challenged certain conglomerate combinations too. For the most part, these challenges have not been successful, and companies expanding externally into unrelated fields generally have no problem complying with the Clayton Act. Many companies obtain a legal opinion on the application of this law to each contemplated business combination before taking steps that lead to consummation.

**Are Large Mergers Bad by Definition?**   Many observers feel that certain mergers should be prohibited simply because of their size, even though the merger would not have the effect of reducing competition or creating a monopoly. Their concern is that huge combinations concentrate economic power in fewer hands, which is deemed undesirable. However, the courts and the governmental agencies have taken the position in recent years that mergers are not bad merely because they are large. As a result, virtually all of the 25 largest business combinations in U.S. history have occurred in the 1980s.

**Which Party Is in Power?**   The zeal with which antitrust laws are interpreted and enforced by the governmental agencies is greatly influenced by which political party is in the White House. In the 1980s, for example, under the Republican administrations, governmental agencies generally restricted their challenges to proposed mergers between competing companies. Even in these cases, however, the agencies have increasingly taken into consideration foreign (rather than simply domestic) competition in assessing market concentration. The result has been that fewer combinations between competing companies are challenged.

Allowing more mergers between competing companies, and allowing large mergers, has resulted in a substantial shrinkage in the size of the antitrust division of the Justice Department, which has lost over a hundred lawyers since 1981. Further, this policy has necessitated sharp reductions in the staffs of many law firms that specialize in antitrust law; even some leading firms have gone out of business.

## The Prevalence of Business Combinations

External expansion is a major vehicle of corporate growth. The number of business expansions occurring in a given year is largely a function of the state of the economy: Merger activity is usually low during recessionary periods and high during boom periods, when companies tend to accumulate healthy amounts of cash. Excess cash not used for dividends must be invested. Stock market prices tend to rise during a boom, which enables an acquiring company, using stock as consideration instead of cash, to issue fewer shares of its stock to acquire another company. In recent years, approximately 3,000 business combinations have occurred each year. In most cases a large company combines with a significantly smaller company. Often such combinations enable a small company to expand more rapidly than would be possible with existing resources. Recently, however, an increasing number of business combinations have involved large companies combining with other large companies, in which the consideration given to effect the combination is in the billions of dollars.

Much of the impetus for business combinations comes from the belief that high asset returns and growth rates exist in other businesses—what could be called the "greener pastures syndrome." As a result, capital is redeployed; the less desirable companies are sold and the presumed emerging "stars" are bought. In fact, some companies have made hundreds of acquisitions and divestitures—with the result that they are no longer in their original businesses or their main lines of business turn over (or *churn*) every 10 to 15 years.

## When Combinations Subsequently Become Unworkable

Bringing together two companies through a business combination is not without risks. Unfortunately, managements often find they cannot manage a new business that they know nothing about any better than the businesses with which they are familiar. As high as 40% of all acquired businesses do not achieve their projected sales and profit growth, and in such circumstances the acquiring companies find that they have grossly overpaid for these poorly performing firms. In numerous other cases, unanticipated organizational problems and changing market conditions have proved disastrous to the combined companies.

**The New Bureaucracy.**  Often the target company's top management and key employees become both frustrated at having to work within the acquiring company's newly imposed rigid operating procedures and resentful of the unwanted involvement in daily operations. Many of them simply leave the firm rather than continue under the new management—draining the company of leadership and talent needed to remain competitive. Often major operating losses result. (This is most notable in the electronics industry, in which over 500 companies have been acquired since 1980.)

**Attempts at Diversification—and Retrenchment.** When the U.S.'s major oil companies became flush with cash in the 1970s as a result of rising oil prices, many of them became fearful of the day when the world's oil reserves would run out and they began diversifying into other industries. For example, Mobil Corp. purchased retailer Montgomery Ward, Exxon Corp. acquired a premier electric motor manufacturer for $1.2 billion in cash, and Atlantic Richfield Co. and Standard Oil Co. acquired mining companies. By 1990 most of the diversified operations had been written down in value, shut down, sold, or placed on the selling block.

Because their vast operations simply became unmanageable, conglomerates that were created in the 1960s and 1970s have now disposed of great numbers of the companies they so eagerly acquired. One example of this is General Electric Co., which has disposed of approximately 200 subsidiaries since 1981.

A Harvard Business School study released in 1987 that examined the diversification undertakings of 33 large companies from 1950 to 1986 revealed that over half of the nearly 3,400 diversifications through acquisitions, joint ventures, or start-ups ended in failure.

Many of the takeover attempts in the 1980s began when a bidder recognized that a company's stock was selling at a depressed level (in relation to the value of the business) precisely because of management's inability to effectively oversee diversified operations. In this common scenario, discussed in the next section, one segment of the company begins to experience operating losses, and this leads to a significant drop in the price of the stock as investors begin to lose confidence in the company overall. This situation makes the company a potential takeover candidate. After buying up the company's stock at a fraction of its value, thus gaining management control, the acquirer can then sell off the various divisions at a substantial profit (called a *breakup*).

# THE ATTEMPTED TAKEOVER

## Preventing a Takeover Attempt

Because business combinations are so prevalent, managements in fear of a potential takeover have in the last few years taken defensive steps (colloquially known as "shark repellant") to make it more difficult for an acquiring company to effect a takeover. Some of the more routine steps involve requesting stockholders to approve such articles of incorporation, charter, and bylaw provisions as the following:

1. **Elimination of cumulative voting.** Under cumulative voting, each stockholder has as many votes as the number of shares owned multiplied by the number of directors up for election. Thus, a potential

acquiring company with a relatively small holding of common stock could get representation on the board of directors. Many companies have reincorporated in Delaware, which does not require cumulative voting.

2. **Use of staggered terms for directors.** If directors have staggered terms, changes in the composition of the board of directors occur more slowly, making it impossible for a successful suitor to gain control of the board upon either consummation of the business combination or winning a proxy contest.

3. **Adoption of supermajority provisions.** For votes on statutory mergers and acquisitions of assets (specific types of business combinations that are discussed in detail later in the chapter), imposing a stipulated percentage in excess of a simple majority (80% is commonly used) makes it more difficult to be taken over by either of these types of business combinations.

4. **Authorization of blank check preferred stock.** Such authorization enables management to place the preferred stock privately in friendly hands. Typically, the owners of the preferred stock have either (1) the right to approve any proposed merger or sale of assets, or (2) multiple voting rights (such as three votes for each vote of common stock).

Such actions by management that tend to insulate a company from acquisition have not gone unnoticed by the Securities and Exchange Commission (SEC). In recognition of the possibility that the interests of management to stay in power may conflict with the interests of the stockholders (who might be receptive to an acquisition), the staff of the SEC has indicated that it intends to review proxy materials in detail to ensure that management has made adequate disclosure to shareholders regarding its proposals. Specifically, the staff has indicated that appropriate disclosures in proxy materials regarding such proposals should include the following:

1. The reason(s) for the proposal and the bases of such reason(s).
2. Whether the corporation's charter or bylaws presently contain other provisions having an anti-takeover effect, whether the . . . proposal is part of a plan by management to adopt a series of such amendments, and whether management presently intends to propose other anti-takeover measures in future proxy solicitations.
3. The overall effects of the proposal, if adopted.
4. The advantages and disadvantages of the proposal . . . both to incumbent management and to shareholders generally.
5. Disclosure of how the proposal will operate.[2]

---

[2]Release No. 34-15230, Disclosure in Proxy and Information Statements, "Anti-takeover or Similar Proposals" (Washington, D.C.: Securities and Exchange Commission, October 13, 1978), pp. 7–10.

**A Continuous State of Readiness.**    In recent years, scores of companies that considered themselves potential takeover candidates started operating in a state of continuous readiness to fend off takeover attempts. Such steps include the following:

1. Arranging in advance for investment bankers and lawyers who specialize in takeover attempts to assist them in the event of a "hostile" offer.
2. Lining up extensive credit resources in case funds are needed.
3. Contracting with "stock watch" companies that closely monitor purchases of its stock to see if a "raider" is accumulating its stock.
4. Entering into management contracts known as "golden parachutes," whereby top executives are to receive substantial cash and other benefits (millions of dollars, in numerous instances) in the event of an unfriendly takeover or their dismissal after a takeover. These companies justify such contracts on the grounds that an executive with a secure financial future can more objectively evaluate a takeover offer without regard to the impact on his or her job. Others contend that it assures management stability in a troubled time and prevents a drain of talent during an attempted takeover. Critics charge that these contracts merely allow executives to walk away rich and also make the acquisition more expensive for the acquiring company, which effectively must pay for these costs if the takeover is successful.

## Steps Leading to a Business Combination

Few business activities match the excitement that can be generated by an attempt to acquire a target company's business. Often an acquiring company must operate in strict secrecy until the last possible moment, in order to avoid attracting the attention of other companies that might be interested in acquiring the business. Such secrecy minimizes the possibility of a bidding war. (Some companies, as a matter of policy, immediately cease their takeover efforts if a bidding war starts; the presumption here is that the successful bidder would probably wind up paying too much.) The acquiring company may start purchasing the common stock of the target company slowly, over a period of time, until it owns just under 5% of the target company's common stock (5% ownership requires public disclosure). Such secrecy also affects the target company: If it is opposed to the takeover, its management has less time in which to take defensive actions.

**The Friendly Approach.**    In theory, a business combination should involve only the acquiring company and the stockholders of the target company. In its simplest terms, the stockholders of the target company must decide whether or not to accept the acquiring company's offer. In evaluating the offer, the stockholders consider the recommendation of their directors and management. Because of this, most acquiring companies attempt to obtain a favorable recommendation from the directors and management of the target company before they present the offer to the target company's stockholders. The usual procedure for this involves negotiating an acquisition agreement with the target company's management. If successful, and the agreement is also approved by the target company's directors, the offer is then submitted to the target company's stockholders for their approval or rejection. This sequence of events is characterized as a "friendly" takeover attempt.

### The Refusal to Be Friendly.
Less friendly situations occur when (1) the approval of the target company's directors and its management is not sought; (2) the target company's directors and management refuse to negotiate an acquisition agreement; and (3) negotiations do not result in an offer that the target company's directors and management feel is in the best interests of the target company's stockholders. The acquiring company must then present its offer directly to the stockholders of the target company without the approval of its directors and management. These cases are characterized as "unfriendly" takeover attempts. Some companies have a policy of pursuing a target company only if it can be done on a friendly basis.

### Resorting to the Tender Offer.
An offer made by an acquiring company directly to the target company's stockholders is known as a **tender offer,** commonly known as a *takeover bid.* Under a tender offer, the stockholders of the target company are requested to give up their shares in exchange for cash or securities offered by the acquiring company. The usual features of a tender offer are the following:

1. The offer is made in newspapers.
2. The offering price substantially exceeds the current market price of the target company's common stock.
3. The offer must be accepted by a certain specified date, usually in the near future (such as 30 days).
4. The acquiring company reserves the right to withdraw the offer if a specified number of shares are not tendered. (If more than the specified number of shares are tendered, the acquiring company reserves the right to reject such excess shares.)

Because the stockholders send their shares to a financial institution, which holds the shares in a fiduciary capacity until the expiration date of the offer, the shares are said to have been *tendered*—not sold. At the expiration date, and provided the minimum number of shares have been tendered, the acquiring company then pays for the tendered shares.

## Statutes Governing Tender Offers

**Federal Statutes.**   In 1968, in response to that decade's wave of takeovers, Congress passed the Williams Act, which provides for federal regulation of tender offers. The avowed purpose of the law, which is enforced by the SEC, is to protect the target company's shareholders by requiring the bidder to furnish detailed disclosures to the target company and its stockholders, including the following:

1. The number of shares being sought.
2. Background information about the bidder.
3. The source and amount of funds or other consideration for the acquisition of the securities for which the tender is made.
4. The purpose of the tender offer and any plans for the target company.
5. Recent financial statements.

The main provision of the law requires potential acquirers to disclose their plans for a tender offer within 10 days after purchasing 5% of the target company's stock. The impact of the law has been to:

1. Prevent potential acquirers from offering to pay a premium in the open market and obtain control within a few days.
2. Enable incumbent managements to have additional time to take defensive actions designed to defeat the takeover attempt.
3. Allow inside information of an impending takeover to be known to more people. (This was an unanticipated result that led to the much publicized insider trading scandals of 1987.)
4. Create the field of takeover arbitrage. (Trading specialists, commonly referred to as *arbs*, now commonly buy up shares that the potential acquirer is forbidden to buy—buying as much as 80% of the shares in some takeovers—and then selling them back to the highest bidder.)

Some feel the Williams Act should be abolished in its entirety, allowing a return to the pre-1968 open-market takeover environment. Others feel the act should be toughened.

**State Statutes.**   Since 1968, almost all states have passed legislation ostensibly to provide further protection to stockholders of the target company. For the most part, these statutes require more detailed disclosures than the federal statutes. Furthermore, most of them do not permit a tender offer to be made until 20 days after the initial public disclosure, whereas the federal requirement is only five days. A great controversy has developed over whether these state laws are really essential to protect the stockholders or whether they merely favor the in-state targets over out-of-state bidders, since the additional disclosures and waiting period give the target company extra time to thwart the takeover bid if it desires. The constitutionality of these laws may be questioned on the grounds that they interfere with interstate commerce and that federal statutes preempt state statutes. Until 1987, the courts have generally declined to enforce these laws for these reasons. As a result, bidding companies routinely filed suits (at the public announcement of their takeover bids) seeking injunctions against the enforcement of these laws. In 1987, the United States Supreme Court for the first time upheld a state law (Indiana) regulating corporate takeovers. Since that decision, over 30 states have modified their takeover statutes, primarily by adopting provisions similar to those in the Indiana statute.

## Defensive Tactics during Takeover Attempts

The board of directors of a target company may authorize management to take aggressive action to try to prevent a takeover. A common defensive action is the filing of lawsuits against the acquiring company on various grounds relating to probable violation of antitrust laws, violation of state takeover laws, and violation of securities laws pertaining to public disclosures. Even if a lawsuit by itself is not successful, it entangles the acquiring company in legal proceedings and usually gives management more time to fight the takeover attempt.

Prior to the 1980s, these **legalistic defenses** were reasonably successful and were often referred to as "show-stoppers" (a defense that stops a bidder dead in its tracks). Beginning in the 1980s, however, legalistic defenses lost much of their effectiveness as courts began taking the position that the stockholders must decide on such attempts. As a result, other types of defensive tactics emerged, most of which are considered **financial defenses.** The following list summarizes the major financial defenses, along with selected examples of their use in certain large takeover attempts of the 1980s involving widely known companies. (Some of these attempts became titanic struggles between the bidder and the target company.)

1. **Seeking a "white knight."** When the bidder is unlikely to need the management of the target company after the takeover, management may seek a bidder (the "white knight") that *will* need management. For example, after Mobil Corp. sought to acquire Marathon Oil Co. in 1984 for $5.1 billion, Marathon attracted U.S. Steel Corp., which won the bidding war with a $6.4 billion offer. This tactic is also used when the management of the bidder is not to the liking of the target company's management, even though management is likely to be retained.

2. **The "scorched earth" (or "selling the crown jewels") defense.** When a bidder's primary interest in a target company is one or more prized segments, management may sell those segments to make itself less

attractive as a target. For example, after GAF Corp. sought to acquire Union Carbide Corp. in 1986 for $4.1 billion, Union Carbide sold its cherished consumer products lines (which included Eveready batteries and Glad plastic bags) to other companies, causing GAF to abandon its takeover efforts. A variation of this tactic is the **lock-up option,** whereby a friendly company is granted the option to acquire the prized segment in the event the takeover succeeds.

3. **Adding a fair price amendment to the corporate charter.** Some tender offers are two-tiered offers, whereby cash—for example, $100 per share—is offered for just over 50% of the target company's outstanding common stock, but a lesser amount—worth, for example, $80 per share—is offered for the remaining shares. Individuals who tender their shares early receive an extra premium of $20 per share. Fair price amendments are designed to ensure that all stockholders receive an equivalent price for their shares. Sometimes the second tier of the offer will consist of noncash consideration, such as common or preferred stock and notes making the first tier of the offer even more attractive.

   Critics of two-tiered offers claim that such offers are coercive and place enormous pressure on stockholders to tender their shares promptly to avoid a lower price on the second tier.

4. **Making a self-tender offer.** When the bidder's offer is deemed unfairly low, the target company may make a higher tender offer to a large percentage of its shareholders, called a **self-tender offer.** This tactic is usually paired with the "selling the crown jewels" defense, which raises money from which to pay for the shares acquired in the self-tender offer.

   Many self-tender offers are two-tiered tender offers, thus having the same supposed coercive effect as hostile tender offers that are two-tiered. (Of course, fair price amendments are worded so that they do not apply to two-tiered self-tender offers.)

5. **The recapitalization defense.** When an increased debt load is likely to make the acquisition unattractive to the acquiring company, the target may try to boost its debt and use the proceeds to pay a huge one-time dividend to its shareholders, thereby shrinking its equity drastically. (This tactic has the same effect on the debt-to-equity ratio as the self-tender offer.)

6. **The Pac-Man defense.** When the target company is fairly large relative to the acquiring company, it may attempt to acquire the acquiring company. For example, when Bendix Corp. sought to acquire Martin-Marietta Corp. in 1982 for $1.5 billion, Martin-Marietta then sought to acquire Bendix. Considered the most bizarre and spectacular takeover attempt to date, the two companies exhausted their liquid assets trying to gain control of each other and be the first to oust the other's

management and directors. As it became evident that the two companies would end up owning each other and the result would be a unified but financially ailing enterprise, Bendix sought refuge by being acquired by Allied Chemical Corp. Martin-Marietta successfully resisted the takeover attempt.

7. **The mudslinging defense.** When the acquiring company offers stock instead of cash, the target company's management may try to convince the stockholders that the stock would be a bad investment. In several recent takeover attempts, the fierce attacks on the integrity and ability of the acquiring company's management (in light of certain past transactions and recent performance) put the acquiring company on the defensive to such a degree that it abandoned its takeover attempts. In many cases, private investigators are hired to discover information that would be embarrassing and discrediting to the management of the hostile bidder. For example, immediately after receiving a $2.1 billion offer from Amway Corp. in 1989, Avon Products, Inc., hired the well-known New York private detective firm of Kroll Associates, Inc., which shortly thereafter unearthed allegations about Amway's chief operating officer that threatened to embarrass the company. Shortly after making Amway aware that it had this information, Amway dropped its offer (which was made only eight days earlier).[3]

8. **The defensive acquisition tactic.** When a major reason for an attempted takeover is the target company's favorable cash position, the target company may try to rid itself of this excess cash by attempting a takeover of its own. Such an action may also result in a combined business that the initial acquiring company is not interested in acquiring. For example, acquiring a competitor of the initial acquiring company creates antitrust issues that would probably derail the takeover attempt with prospective litigation.

9. **The leveraged buyout defense.** When management desires to own the business, it may arrange to buy out the stockholders using the company's assets to finance the deal. (This increasingly common tactic is discussed in detail later in the chapter.)

10. **Adopting a "poison pill" provision.** Although many variations exist, the common procedure is to grant the company's stockholders—excluding shares owned by the acquiring company—the right to purchase additional common shares of the company (or of an acquiring company) at bargain prices (typically at 50% of the market price of the stock). The rights usually become exercisable (or *triggered*) when an "unfriendly" acquiring company acquires 20% of the common stock or makes a bid to acquire 30% of the common stock. The purpose

---

[3]"Did Avon's Digging for Amway Skeletons Scuttle Takeover Bid?" *The Wall Street Journal*, May 25, 1989, p. 1.

of the provision is to make the acquisition prohibitively expensive to the unfriendly company (or make it suffer unwanted dilution of its own shares if the rights pertain to its own common stock). The provision customarily enables the company to redeem the rights if it chooses to complete a friendly merger. A Delaware Supreme Court decision of 1985 upheld the right of managements to use the "poison pill" defenses without shareholder approval. Since then, this tactic has become widely used (both during takeover attempts and to prevent future takeover attempts). Approximately 200 of the Fortune 500 companies have adopted poison pill provisions.

11. **Paying "greenmail."** When a bidder acquires perhaps 10–20% of the target company's stock, the company may agree to purchase these stockholdings at a premium, allowing the bidder (most commonly called a **corporate raider**) to walk away with a hefty profit (on the condition that it not buy any stock in the future). For example, Walt Disney Productions paid a $60 million premium in 1984 to a bidder that had acquired 11% of Disney's stock (a total buyback of $325 million). (Over 20 antigreenmail stockholder lawsuits were subsequently filed against Disney alleging mismanagement, breach of fiduciary duty, and waste of corporate assets.)

The article reprinted in this section reflects the extent to which one company used defensive tactics in an unsuccessful attempt to prevent being taken over.

## Defensive Tactics: Whose Interest Is Served?

Sometimes turning down an offer or even refusing to negotiate results in the acquiring company's making a higher offer. This is clearly in the best interest of the target company's stockholders. In some cases, however, such actions by management are self-serving; managers oppose the takeover because they want to remain top executives of an independent company rather than become top executives of a small part of a much larger company—or they fear the loss of their jobs. In some instances, management's actions in defending against takeover attempts are irresponsible, especially when their stockholders are overwhelmingly tendering their shares and thereby accepting the offer.

As evident by preceding examples, more and more stockholders of target companies file lawsuits against their managers and directors alleging one of two things: (a) misuse of corporate resources in resisting takeover attempts (in a great number of instances, millions have been spent fighting the takeover attempt); or (b) violation of their fiduciary duty to stockholders by refusing to negotiate for the highest price possible. For the most part, the courts have been reluctant to find managements and

## PERSPECTIVE

### An Anti-Takeover Arsenal That Failed

How far will managers go to prevent an outsider from buying their company? How far *can* they go? The case of Macmillan Inc. may provide some answers.

Few management groups have thrown up as many takeover defenses as the one running Macmillan, a publishing and information-services company based in New York. Although many of the strategies Macmillan used have become commonplace in recent years, it tried more of them—and pushed them further—than almost any company in recent memory.

Macmillan granted its managers hundreds of thousands of restricted shares for which they paid nothing; it borrowed millions of dollars to buy shares for an employee stock-ownership plan, then made management the plan's trustees; and it funded a mammoth "golden parachute" plan for executives. Most audacious of all was the company's restructuring plan, which would have preserved Macmillan's independence by giving management ownership of the company's best assets at very little cost to themselves.

Although Macmillan rejected several bids that would have profited shareholders handsomely, investors who held on to their shares will be richly rewarded for management's recalcitrance.

Yesterday, Macmillan's board finally surrendered, recommending to shareholders that they tender their stock to Maxwell Communication Corp. Meanwhile, Kohlberg Kravis Roberts & Co. withdrew its rival offer. Maxwell last night completed its tender offer, and will pay $90.25 a share, or $2.62 billion. That price is 80% higher than when Macmillan's six-month-long battle to retain independence began.

Harbir Singh, an associate professor of management at the University of Pennsylvania's Wharton School, says one of the only restraints on a management's defensive excesses is the company's board of directors, who are vulnerable to shareholder lawsuits. Macmillan's board, however, approved almost every plan management devised to remain independent, even when those plans could have been costly to shareholders.

The board also voted itself two raises, to $30,000 a year from $20,000, and granted itself a retirement plan guaranteeing $30,000 a year for life for most of its outside members—as well as benefits for their spouses. The board eventually asked the final two bidders for the company to indemnify the members against shareholder suits.

Edward P. Evans, Macmillan's proud and stubborn chairman and chief executive officer, contends that the maneuvers were meant only to protect shareholders. He also maintains that he has been more a hapless victim than an active player in the struggle. "I didn't mean to do it," he says. "It was more or less done to me."

Even critics who say Mr. Evans's efforts were excessive concede that he deserved more than a gold watch for his work at Macmillan. When he took over in 1980, it was an overly diversified concern whose earnings and stock price were sagging. Mr. Evans cut expenses and refocused the company on three core businesses—publishing, information services and instruction. The company's per-share earnings and stock price soared.

Mr. Evans has been well compensated for this. In addition to a respectable salary— $420,000 in 1987—he now controls at least 739,000 Macmillan shares. Many came through option plans, but at least 230,000 shares were an outright gift from a grateful board of directors. His stock is now valued at more than $65 million.

Though Macmillan's stock price was rising, Mr. Evans was acutely aware that the company

**An Anti-Takeover Arsenal That Failed** (continued)

was takeover bait, a prosperous and growing company in a glamour industry. Macmillan had already put its board of directors on staggered terms, which made the board much less vulnerable to a change of control instituted by an outsider. It also had a by-law provision prohibiting the calling of a special meeting without a 75% shareholder vote.

But in May 1987, another publishing company, Harcourt Brace Jovanovich Inc., narrowly escaped a takeover by Robert Maxwell. Fearful of being the British press baron's next target, Macmillan launched its unprecedented campaign to ward off trespassers.

**Golden parachutes:** In July 1987, Macmillan's board approved golden-parachute severance agreements for 21 executives, backed by a $60 million letter of credit. If the executives actually received any golden-parachute payments—some of which could be triggered if anyone acquired as little as 20% of the company—Macmillan agreed to pay all income or other taxes on the payments.

**Poison pill:** The company also adopted a shareholder-rights, or "poison pill," plan. Under the plan, if anyone acquired 30% of Macmillan's stock, the other stockholders could exchange their rights for the common stock at half price. The effect would be to dilute severely the investment of the potential acquirer, thus deterring all stock acquisitions above the 30% "trigger" level.

**Voting rights:** A $60 million loan was approved for the company's employee stock-ownership plan, which was to be used to buy a million Macmillan shares. The company ousted the ESOP's trustee, replacing it with management members, who would have had voting control of all unallocated shares deposited in the plan. The company was also authorized to issue up to 50 million new "blank check" preferred shares with potentially disproportionate voting rights to be set by the board.

**Restructuring:** Of all the company's defenses, the most extreme was its restructuring plan. Although management weighed several approaches, all shared one aspect: They would leave Mr. Evans and a few other top managers owning a sizable chunk of the revamped company. Management would acquire that stake not by investing new capital at prevailing market prices, but by trading in previously granted restricted shares and stock options.

Under the chosen plan, Macmillan would be split into two companies, one containing the publishing businesses, the other the information-services businesses, considered the crown jewels of the company. At first, management, which just a year earlier owned only 1.2% of Macmillan, decided to trade its restricted shares and stock options for a 55% stake in the information-services business. But the company's advisers pointed out that such a hefty stake would be considered a change of corporate control from public stockholders to management. So management's stake in the information businesses was reduced to 39%.

The restructuring not only thwarted unwanted suitors and gave a huge share of the company to management, but it also avoided the necessity of a shareholder vote because, management argued, control of the company wasn't changing. In fact, shareholders first heard of the restructuring on May 31, the day after the board approved it—and just 10 days before it was to be consummated. There was no time for shareholders to organize a protest.

Only a legal challenge filed by Robert M. Bass Group, which was trying to acquire Macmillan, stood between management and its plan. A Delaware court stopped the restructuring cold. In a stinging opinion, the court ruled that not only did the plan "offer inferior value to shareholders, it also forced them to accept it."

With its restructuring plans quashed—and both Bass Group and Maxwell vying for the company—investors hoped that management would stop fighting to stay independent

*(continued)*

and start looking for a buyer willing to pay a premium price. Management did neither, and refused to negotiate terms, disclose financial information or discuss price with either bidder.

**White knight:** Meanwhile, management thought it had found a way to sell the company while keeping a large stake. It struck a deal with Kohlberg Kravis Roberts, the leveraged buy-out specialists, in which management would end up with 20% equity in the company. Macmillan's board quickly endorsed KKR's first offer without giving either Bass Group or Maxwell a chance to top it.

Maxwell was not deterred. It topped KKR's bid, ultimately forcing management to do what it had been resisting: hold an auction. But when the auction was over, KKR had won even though Maxwell was prepared to pay more. Furthermore, Macmillan took steps to prevent anyone else from getting the company, granting KKR the right to buy four of its best assets if the KKR merger fell through.

Once again, a suitor—Maxwell, in this case—took Macmillan to court, and once again the suitor won. The Delaware Supreme Court ruled that the auction was "neither evenhanded nor neutral," and that management had tainted the process by getting involved even though it had a personal interest in the outcome.

Now that Maxwell has succeeded in buying Macmillan, it appears that the company's elaborate defenses, which cost almost an entire quarter's profits for fees and expenses, only delayed the inevitable. "No takeover defense is impenetrable," says Wharton's Mr. Singh. But as fast as they're knocked down, he adds, managements will find new ones to take their place.

Source: Cynthia Crossen and Karen Blumenthal, "An Anti-Takeover Arsenal That Failed," *The Wall Street Journal,* November 4, 1988, p. B-1. Reprinted by permission of *The Wall Street Journal.* © Dow Jones & Company, Inc. 1988. All rights reserved worldwide.

directors guilty of these charges. Some companies attempt to protect their directors from such potential actions by dissatisfied stockholders by having the stockholders require the board of directors (through an amendment to the articles of incorporation) to consider factors other than the value and type of consideration offered when determining whether or not to accept an offer. Such factors might include the economic effects the takeover would have on employees and communities in which the target company has its operations.

In recent years, it has been debated in financial circles and by congressional committees whether these widespread defensive tactics are: (1) really necessary to protect stockholders (presumably from voluntarily selling their stock at a higher price), or (2) nothing more than self-serving management entrenchment devices that should be legally banned or at least voted on annually by the stockholders because of the changing composition of the stockholders from year to year.

## Waging a Proxy Contest

In recent years, several factors (poison pills, increased state anti-takeover legislation, and the lessening availability of financing since the 198' stock market crash) have weakened the case for making tender offers. As a result, many acquiring companies have turned to **proxy contests** (often called "proxy wars") to obtain control instead of making a direct purchase. In a proxy contest, both management and the acquirer solicit votes from the target company's stockholders for their respective proposed slates of directors.

In theory, the proxy system appears to be a superior way to obtain control of a target company, inasmuch as the insurgents can have their people placed on the board (who will approve a proposed merger) without having to buy over 50% of the company to obtain control. In practice, however, the proxy system is extremely inefficient and gives management several built-in advantages over challengers. For example, management has full access to the corporate treasury to pay for its proxy solicitation effort (which can cost up to $10 million), while the acquirer must use its own funds. Obtaining lists of shareholders, while easy for management, is quite difficult for challengers (who often have to go through the courts). Tracking down stockholders is often impossible when the stock is held in street name by their brokers. In most cases, managements win these proxy contests. The most famous recent proxy contest was in 1988 when Carl Icahn (often referred to as the most feared corporate raider in America) sought control of Texaco, Inc., in which incumbent management narrowly won.

## The Debate over Takeovers Resurfaces

The years 1982 through 1989 saw mergers and acquisitions, divestitures, breakups, leveraged buyouts, buybacks, and recapitalizations (collectively called restructurings) reach a record high in terms of the value of the transactions (mergers and acquisitions alone approached $200 billion per year). The sheer magnitude of the restructurings during this period has raised questions as to whether all this restructuring is good or bad for the country.

Some observers contend that it results in: (1) many companies becoming overleveraged; (2) substantial disruption of the job market, with a consequent major adverse social impact on the communities affected; and (3) inordinate enrichment of the investment bankers and lawyers who are paid seemingly huge sums for their services ($100 million on a $2 billion deal is not uncommon) and who, therefore, are highly motivated to continually "put companies into play."

Others contend that it is revitalizing our industry in response to fierce foreign competition by simplifying or "streamlining" corporations that have become too large and too complicated to be efficient, enabling managers to be in closer touch with production workers, customers, and stockholders.

**The Debate from a Historical Perspective.** Four distinct periods of financial restructurings have occurred in the last 100 years: (1) the horizontal combinations near the turn of the century; (2) the vertical combinations of the 1920s; (3) the conglomerate combinations of the 1960s; and (4) the current one in which many of the conglomerate combinations of the 1960s are being undone using leveraged reorganizations. Why do financial restructurings occur so frequently? Many contend that periodic waves of restructurings are necessary in an economy based on capitalism, as they force the business sector to adapt to economic and technological change (the invisible hand of Adam Smith at work that makes for a more productive and competitive economy).

## LEVERAGED BUYOUTS

A **leveraged buyout (LBO)** is the acquisition of a target company's assets or common stock in which the acquirer uses an extremely high percentage of debt and thus a very low percentage of equity—typically 10%, but sometimes as low as 1% of the purchase price—to pay for the acquisition. The target company's assets are used as collateral to secure the loans. Thus the debt structure of the target company is refinanced simultaneously with the acquisition, making an LBO nothing more than a combination of an acquisition and a refinancing.

### Historical Development

Pioneered in the 1960s, LBOs became immensely popular and widespread in the early 1980s when large conglomerates began their drive to divest marginal subsidiaries. Because of the recession and resultant depressed stock market from 1980 to 1982, numerous subsidiaries were purchased at bargain prices. As the technique grew in popularity it also began to be used widely in acquiring privately and publicly owned companies.

In the early days of LBOs, the ideal LBO candidate was in a recession-resistant industry and had abundant hard assets. Currently, however, investors place substantial emphasis on projected cash flows.

Since 1981, over 1,600 companies have gone private in LBO transactions (the approximate number of companies listed on the New York Stock Exchange), including RJR Nabisco in 1988, the tenth largest company in the country based on stock market valuation. The LBO phenomenon can be likened to a roaring freight train that is restructuring companies, reshaping management's way of thinking, and challenging the status quo of the professionally managed public corporation.

### The Motivation behind Leveraged Buyouts

The phenomenal surge in the use of LBOs results primarily from recognizing and eliminating the inherent conflicts of interest that exist between stockholders and management in publicly owned companies. In a public company, management typically must devote an enormous amount of time to managing the market price of its stock. Recall that if the price of the stock falls to a depressed level in relation to the value of the firm, the company can quickly become a takeover candidate. If the company becomes the object of a takeover attempt, management is forced to spend still less time running the business while it concentrates on fighting the takeover attempt. Accordingly, a short-term focus on quarterly profits takes hold. When given a choice between acting in the best interest of the business and doing what will look good to the public, all too often management chooses the latter. Underlying all of this is the natural conflict of interest between the stockholders (whose desire is wealth maximization) and management (who wish to keep their jobs). These divergent interests become more pronounced when managements have very little of their own personal wealth invested in the companies they run. A contributing factor is the corporate culture, which fosters incentives to build empires. Managements of mature companies that generate more than sufficient cash flow from operations are reluctant to distribute excess cash to stockholders. Instead, in far too many instances, it is used to expand the company (often by diversification) beyond the size that maximizes shareholders' wealth. (The oil industry is the prime example of this; according to *Fortune* magazine, it made seven of the worst large acquisitions of the 1970s.) Thus management goes through the motions of acting as though their own money were at stake. Being accountable to a largely anonymous group of stockholders, management is acountable more in theory than in practice and ends up doing what it pleases with the corporation's assets.

### The LBO's Solution: Aligning the Interests.

In the typical LBO transaction, the buyer is a group of investors—including management of the target company. In most cases, this investment group forms a corporation that acquires the target company's assets or common stock. Because management is included in the investment group, LBOs are sometimes referred to as "management buyouts." Participating managers are required to invest a substantial portion of their own money, which results in their having as much as a 50% equity position. Thus, these managers are given an enormous incentive to manage effectively. And because they answer to only a handful of co-owners—who want exactly what the managers want—nearly perfect alignment of interests is formed, which makes a tremendous difference that is hard to overstate.

### LBO-Generated Debt as Disciplinarian.

By saddling the acquired business with a mountain of debt, the early fear of disaster focuses mangement's attention and forces it to be more aggressive in making tough decisions.

In most cases, virtually all of the cash flow from operations is needed to service the debt. Consequently, a discipline is imposed on management that denies it the opportunity to overexpand the existing business or diversify into new businesses by acquiring other companies. With a re-dedicated management, the expectation is that: (1) the business's operations will substantially improve; (2) the huge debt load will be paid down reasonably fast; and (3) the business (which may have been acquired at 4–10 times earnings) may be taken public in a few years at 20–30 times earnings or sold to another company.

Nevertheless, LBOs are often criticized on the grounds that (1) financial institutions make excessively risky loans to companies effecting take-overs, and (2) the large cash flow required to service the debt may deprive a company of cash needed to stay competitive (such as for research and development or reinvestment in fixed assets). Later we discuss some LBOs that encountered financial difficulty.

**Other Changes That Affect Cash Flows.** The annual direct costs of public ownership generally range between $75,000 and $300,000, depending on the size of the company (excluding management time). Taking the company private eliminates this cost. Because the purchase of the target company is a taxable transaction, the target company's assets are reval-ued to their current values (based on the purchase price). This allows greater depreciation charges for tax reporting purposes. The combination of increased depreciation expense and increased interest expense often re-sults in the target company not having to pay income taxes for several years.

**Some Spectacular Results of LBOs.** For most leveraged buyouts, the yearly returns on equity have been in the 50–120% range. The most spectacular LBO success story of all is the $1 million equity investment made in 1981 in Gibson Greetings, Inc. (owners of the Garfield the Cat cartoon charac-ter). The investors, who were leveraged to the amount of $79 million, later sold their equity interest for $290 million, a phenomenal return on their investment. However, a few LBOs have gone into bankruptcy (among them Revco in 1988) or troubled debt restructurings. LBOs leave little room for error, but the rewards for management—if they are successful—are sensational.

## ACCOUNTING METHODS

The two basic methods of accounting for business combinations are the **pooling of interests method** and the **purchase method.** They are dis-cussed in detail in *APB Opinion No. 16,* "Accounting for Business Combi-nations," which became effective in November 1970. When the value of the consideration given by the acquiring company is above or below the book value of the target company's net assets, these two methods produce dramatically different reporting of results of operations and financial position. Acquiring companies are fully aware of these consequences and often attempt to use the method that maximizes future earnings and earnings per share amounts. A major result of this pronouncement, however, was to eliminate the considerable latitude that previously existed in the use of either the purchase method or the pooling of interests method. If one of these methods is desired, then the terms and provisions of the acquisition agreement must be structured accordingly. This is a key point because **for a given set of terms and provisions only one accounting method will apply.** The methods used in a given set of circumstances are no longer elective.

In this respect, company accountants must be thoroughly familiar with *APB Opinion No. 16,* so they can properly advise top management during the negotiations. Many corporate controllers routinely obtain an opinion from their certified public accountants concerning whether or not a proposed set of terms and conditions will allow the use of the desired accounting method. This is practically essential, considering the complexity of the pronouncement. The objective of this practice is to prevent a situation in which a combination is completed under the assumption that it will be accounted for under a desired method only to have the certified public accountants later uncover something in the acquisition agreement that disallows the use of that method.

## The Pooling of Interests Method

The theory underlying pooling of interests accounting is that **a sale and purchase of a business have not occurred.** Two companies have simply pooled their financial resources and managerial talents in such a manner that the owners of each of the separate businesses are now the owners of an enlarged business. This fusion of equity interests is the foundation of the pooling of interests concept, and it occurs only if the target company's shareholders receive common stock of the acquiring company as consideration for their business. This is the most important condition of the pooling of interests method. Specifically, twelve conditions must be met for pooling of interests accounting to be allowed. These conditions involve the attributes of the combining companies, the mechanics of the exchange, and transactions that are prohibited in periods subsequent to the exchange. **If any one of these twelve rules is not met, then the pooling of interests method cannot be used. If all twelve rules are complied with, then the pooling of interests method** *must* be used. These twelve rules are discussed in detail in Chapter 6, which discusses and illustrates the application of this method in detail.

When a combination qualifies for the pooling of interests treatment, the recorded assets and liabilities of the separate companies are carried forward to the combined corporation at their historically recorded amounts. Goodwill is never created, and future income statements of the combined, enlarged business never include goodwill amortization expense. Furthermore, in the event future income statements are presented for periods before the combination date, the separate income statements of each constituent company are combined, restated, and then reported as income of the combined corporation.

## The Purchase Method

If the transaction does not qualify for pooling of interests treatment, then the purchase method must be used. The underlying concept of the purchase method is that **one company has acquired the business of another company and a sale has occurred.** Under this method, the acquiring company's cost (essentially the value of the consideration given for the acquired business) must be allocated to the individual assets acquired. In most situations, the acquired assets are valued at their current values. To the extent that the acquiring company's cost exceeds the current value of the identifiable assets, then goodwill arises, which must be amortized to income over a period not to exceed 40 years. In an economy that has experienced inflation, the acquiring company usually pays in excess of the book value of the net assets of the acquired business. If this excess relates to assets other than land (a nondepreciable asset), greater depreciation and amortization charges are reflected in future income statements than if the pooling of interests method had been used. Accordingly, future earnings are lower under the purchase method. This upward revaluation of the acquired business's assets and the possible creation of goodwill are the major disadvantages of the purchase method compared with the pooling of interests method from the viewpoint of future earnings and earnings per share.

## Criticism of *APB Opinion No. 16*

*APB Opinion No. 16* received barely the required two-thirds majority vote. Since its issuance, it has been widely criticized for not being a sound or logical solution to the issues associated with business conbinations. The main criticism is that the results produced under the pooling of interests method often do not accurately portray the underlying economics of the business combination. For example, a company that has sales and assets of $100,000 could "pool" its resources and management with a company having sales and assets of $100 million. Many accountants feel that to treat such a combination as a pooling is just not sensible. In this situation, the substance of the combination is obviously the acquisition of the small business by the large business—a reality that is ignored under the pooling of interests method.

Most accountants agree with the fundamental concept of the purchase method, except for the treatment of goodwill. Many accountants and corporate executives think that goodwill should not be shown as an asset of the acquiring company but should be charged to the equity section of the acquiring company at the acquisition. Their reasoning is that the acquiring entity has, in substance, given up some of its equity with the hope of recouping it in subsequent years through the acquired company's superior earnings (which may or may not materialize). Also criticized are the arbitrary rules relating to the amortization of goodwill, as set forth in *APB Opinion No. 17*, "Intangible Assets." Goodwill created before November 1, 1970, does not have to be amortized at all, whereas goodwill created after October 31, 1970, must be amortized over a period no longer than 40 years.

About three years after these two controversial pronouncements were issued, the rule-making authority for the accounting profession was transferred to the Financial Accounting Standards Board (FASB), with the hope that a more independent organization (whose members are not tied to the public accounting profession that serves the public corporations) would be more effective in resolving current accounting issues.

### Reevaluation of Issues by the FASB

In 1975, the FASB considered the possibility of completely reevaluating the pooling of interests criteria set forth in *APB Opinion No. 16.* The board later decided to reexamine the entire issue of business combinations, and in August 1976 it issued a discussion memorandum. In 1978 the FASB removed this project from its active agenda because of its low priority in relation to other projects. As this book goes to print, the project remains off the active agenda.

## TERMS AND PROVISIONS OF THE ACQUISITION AGREEMENT

### Types of Consideration Given

The consideration given by the acquiring company can be the same as that used to pay for or finance internal expansions—namely, cash, other assets, or issuance of debt, preferred stock, or common stock. Under the purchase method, the consideration may consist of various combinations of cash, debt, and common stock. As stated earlier, the consideration given in a transaction that qualifies for pooling of interests treatment is the acquiring company's common stock.

## Types of Assets Acquired

A business may be acquired in one of two ways: the acquisition of assets or the acquisition of common stock.

1. The **acquisition of assets.** Assume the agreed-upon value of the target company's assets is $7 million and the current value of the target company's liabilities is $5 million. When the target company's assets are acquired, the acquiring company has the option of either (1) giving consideration of $7 million, or (2) giving consideration of $2 million and assuming responsibility for paying the target company's $5 million of liabilities. (The latter option is most common.) If the pooling of interests treatment is desired, 100% of the assets must be acquired; no such requirement exists for the purchase method.

2. The **acquisition of common stock.** The acquiring company must purchase more than 50% of the target company's outstanding common stock for a business combination to have occurred. With an ownership interest greater than 50%, the acquiring company can control the target company. If the pooling of interests treatment is desired, at least 90% of the common stock must be acquired; no such requirement exists for the purchase method.

## Acquiring Assets versus Common Stock

Many circumstances affect the determination of whether the acquiring company should acquire assets or common stock of the target company. Here are some of the more common considerations:

1. **Unrecorded liabilities.** A major concern of the buyer of a business is whether the seller has unrecorded liabilities. Accordingly, it is common procedure in a purchase investigation to search for unrecorded liabilities and make requests to the seller's legal counsel about litigation and unasserted claims that could be assserted later to pose a serious risk to the new owner. If common stock is acquired, the buyer inherits responsibility for the unrecorded liabilities. (Some buyers of common stock either obtain costly liability insurance or include a clause in the purchase agreement making the former owners responsible for subsequent events that had their origin prior to the closing date of the transaction.) By acquiring assets, however, the acquiring company can best insulate itself from responsiblity for these contingencies, inasmuch as a well-drafted acquisition agreement will clearly specify those liabilities for which it assumes responsibility. One of the major pitfalls for acquirers in the 1980s was unrecorded other postretirement benefits (primarily obligations to pay for medical costs not covered by Medicare), which were being accounted for on the cash basis and were estimated to be between $300 billion and $1 trillion for all U.S. corporations. Probably the most unfortunate omission of this unrecorded liability in an acquisition was the 1987 acquisition

of Uniroyal for $1 billion, in which the buyer was stuck with benefits estimated to be as high as $600 million. Acquiring assets instead of common stock, however, is not always a foolproof way of avoiding all potential unrecorded liabilities. For example, the buyer would inherit liabilities for toxic waste cleanup (estimated to be $500 billion for the 10,000 identified toxic waste sites, as disucssed in the accompanying article) regardless of whether assets or common stock is acquired.

2. **Nontransferability of contracts.** If the target company's contracts, leases, franchises, or operating rights cannot be transferred through the sale of assets, common stock must be acquired.

3. **Ease of transfer.** Transferring stock certificates is easier than transferring assets. The transfer of assets may require the preparation of separate bills of sale for each asset or class of asset: also, state laws concerning bulk sales must be observed.

4. **Unwanted facilities or segments.** If the acquiring company does not wish to acquire all of the target company's assets, the acquisition of assets allows the acquiring company to obtain only those assets it desires. (To arrange for the acquisition of its common stock, the target company could dispose of the unwanted assets, but it may not always be feasible to do so in the time specified in the acquisition agreement.)

5. **Access to target company's cash.** If the acquiring company offers cash as consideration and the target company has substantial cash and short-term investment assets, the acquisition of assets makes the target company's cash and short-term investment assets available to the acquiring company to either help replenish its cash or repay loans obtained to finance the acquisition. In effect, the acquisition can be partially paid for using the funds of the target company. If common stock were acquired, then the target company's cash and short-term investment assets would not be available to the acquiring company, except to the extent that the target company (as a subsidiary and a separate legal entity) could pay dividends to the acquiring company (as the parent).

## THE RESULTING ORGANIZATIONAL FORM OF THE ACQUIRED BUSINESS

Accounting for business combinations focuses on **how the acquiring company initially records the transaction that brings about the combination.** The detailed accounting entries for the acquiring company require substantial explanation under both the purchase method and the pooling of interests method; these are discussed and illustrated in detail in Chapters 3 and 6, respectively. The entries made by the target company, on the other hand, are quite simple. The following discussion is general in nature, so that an overall understanding can be grasped of the organizational effects of business combinations.

# PERSPECTIVE

## Deals That Smell Bad

Robert Santoski could almost smell victory as he closed in on a $660 million deal to buy Koppers Co.'s chemical operations last summer. But then Santoski, a partner in Houston's Sterling Group, caught a whiff of something else: Koppers' toxic waste dumps. He walked away from the deal.

Santoski isn't alone. More and more deals are being torpedoed by toxic waste liabilities. "Five or six years ago environmental liability was a technical point people dealt through. Now it's a major consideration," says Robert O'Brien, head of leveraged buyout lending for Bankers Trust Corp., who has seen toxic waste problems ruin several deals.

Even when toxic waste doesn't kill a deal, it can force sellers to slash their asking price. "I've seen prices cut 30% because of environmental liabilities," says Maynard Toll Jr., a managing director at First Boston Corp.

The new awareness of toxic waste is changing the way businesses are bought and sold, and corroding stock prices in chemicals and other manufacturing industries. Wall Street is scrambling to figure out which companies are sitting on hidden toxic liabilities and who will pay. The estimated cost of cleaning up the nation's 10,000-plus toxic waste dumps: a staggering $500 billion over the next 50 years. And just about any company—from car manufacturers to silicon chip makers to food processors—can have a toxic waste liability.

Investment bankers at firms like Kohlberg Kravis Roberts, the Blackstone Group and Bankers Trust are hiring environmental experts to comb company records and inspect waste sites before they put their money into a deal. Environmental lawyers are suddenly in great demand. Skadden, Arps, Slate, Meagher & Flom, the New York City-based firm known for its takeover work, now employs 23 environmental attorneys who spend as much as 40% of their time vetting corporate deals.

Scampering to keep up are federal securities regulators and credit-rating outfits. Moody's Investors Service is now asking companies it rates for more detailed information on their potential environmental liabilities. "We're starting to see the leading edge of investor consciousness," says Robert Buhr, a senior Moody's analyst who is currently assembling a review on environmental credit risks. "It's not yet affecting credit quality, but it absolutely could."

The Securities & Exchange Commission has sent letters to a number of corporations asking for more information on their environmental liabilities. And in the next few months the SEC will provide more guidance on how some of its disclosure requirements should apply to companies with toxic waste problems.

Everybody involved is watching something called the Federal Superfund National Priorities List, a roster of the nation's roughly 1,200 nastiest toxic dump sites. Typical estimated cleanup cost: anywhere between $10 million and $30 million per site. And much of America's oozing goop isn't even chronicled on the Superfund list. Excluded are thousands of toxic dumps on company-owned sites still used for waste disposal and an even larger number that haven't yet made the Superfund list because they have not yet been fully evaluated.

Just as the cost of asbestos litigation bankrupted some previously solid companies, so could the cost of cleaning up toxic wastes. James Kirk is chairman of OHM Corp., a Findlay, Ohio hazardous waste cleanup company. Says he, "We see large companies that tell us they have six sites that will cost a total of $600 million to $900 million to clean up." Sums like that could easily put into Chapter 11 some thinly capitalized or overleveraged companies.

For stock pickers and investment bankers alike, getting good information on companies' toxic liabilities is extremely difficult—if for no

**Deals That Smell Bad** (continued)

other reason than some companies them-selves don't know. Cleanup costs can run any-where from $100,000 to $500 million or more per site, depending on the type of waste and the extent of the problem, and how it is cleaned up. And many sites involve multiple companies.

Adding to the uncertainty is the sweeping nature of the Superfund law. A company can be required to pay cleanup costs, even if its actions were lawful at the time the waste was dumped. Banks can be held responsible if they foreclose on an offending company or get involved in its management. And a company that contributes just a fraction of the waste at a Superfund site could be forced to pick up as much as 100% of the cleanup cost.

"It's really the harshest liability scheme around," says Margaret Murphy, a partner at the New York law firm White & Case, who advises dealmakers on environmental risks. Little wonder that takeover agreements today frequently hold the seller responsible for the cost of cleaning up any identified waste sites.

As happens all too often these days, lawyers have been among the chief beneficiaries to date of the legislation against toxic waste. For example, Southland Corp. is suing Ashland Oil and its Ashland Chemical unit in a dispute over cleanup costs at a Southland chemical plant in New Jersey, once owned by Ashland. Toxic chemicals were dumped there over the course of three decades.

Dozens of companies, including Westing-house, SCM and United Technologies, have flooded state courts with lawsuits alleging that insurance companies are liable for cleanup bills. So far only a handful of these cases have been decided, and the results are mixed.

In two recent decisions, companies with cleanup problems lost out. In December, a Ca-lifornia jury said Shell Oil—not its insurers—must pay to clean up contaminated ground-water at the Rocky Mountain Arsenal. That

### In the Dumps

The companies below rank among those with the largest number of toxic waste sites in the U.S. desig-nated by the EPA as requiring urgent attention. EPA data on these so-called Superfund sites are incom-plete, so we asked these companies for their own estimates. B.F. Goodrich, Mobil and Ford refused to cooperate. Cleaning up a Superfund site costs on average $10 million to $30 million, but you can't estimate a company's liability simply by multiplying that average by its number of sites. Many sites involve multiple companies.

| Company | Number of Sites | Company | Number of Sites |
|---|---|---|---|
| General Motors | 140 | Texaco | 40 |
| Westinghouse | 80 | PPG Industries | 37 |
| Union Carbide | 75 | BASF | 35 |
| Chrysler | 64 | Ciba-Geigy | 33 |
| Du Pont | 64 | ICI | 32 |
| Shell Oil | 59 | Dow | 31 |
| Ashland Oil | 45 | Mobil | 25* |
| Allied-Signal | 44 | B.F. Goodrich | 25† |
| Monsanto | 42 | Rohm & Haas | 24 |
| General Electric | 41 | Ford | 21* |

*EPA estimates, based on incomplete data.
†*Forbes* estimates.          Source: Company estimates.

means Shell and the U.S. government will split costs, which could exceed $1 billion. Then, in April, a New Jersey court held Diamond Shamrock responsible for the $10 million to $20 million it will cost to clean up a chemical plant contaminated with dioxin, a toxic sub-stance created when making Agent Orange. Diamond Shamrock's insurers won't have to pay a penny for the cleanup.

But insurers are by no means off the hook. In April, for example, a California appeals court ruled that insurers would have to pay some $100 million to clean up contaminated groundwater near an Aerojet-General rocket

## Acquisition of Assets

**Centralized Accounting.** One manner of accounting for the operations of the acquired business is called **centralized accounting,** whereby the assets acquired and the liabilities assumed are recorded in the existing general ledger of the acquiring company. This is common, however, only when the acquiring company already has similar operations that are accounted for on a centralized basis. Thus, this method would most likely be found only in a horizontal combination. When centralized accounting is used, only two general ledgers are involved in the transaction—the acquiring company's and the target company's. (Assets and liabilities are simply transferred from the target company's general ledger to the acquiring company's general ledger.) For example, assume Punn Company acquired all of the assets and assumed all of the liabilities of Sunn Company by giving cash as the consideration. The following entries (in condensed format) would be made by each company:

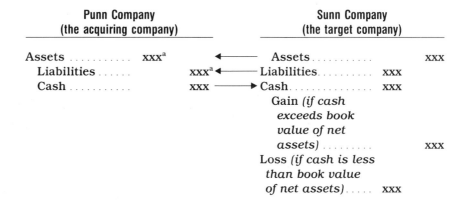

[a]Because cash is the consideration given, the transaction must be accounted for as a purchase. Accordingly, the assets acquired and liabilities assumed are recorded at their current values based on the purchase price. (This is discussed further in Chapter 3.)

**Decentralized Accounting.** Another manner of accounting for the operations of the acquired business is called **decentralized accounting,** whereby the assets acquired and the liabilities assumed are recorded in a new general ledger maintained at the location of the newly acquired business. The newly acquired business is normally referred to as a **division** of the acquiring company. The difference between the assets acquired and the liabilities assumed are reflected in the division's Home Office account. The balance in this account always equals the balance in the Investment in Division account in the general ledger maintained at the acquiring company's headquarters. (At this point, the division refers to the acquiring company as the "home office.") Note that under this approach, three general ledgers are involved in the transaction—the two general ledgers of the acquiring company (one maintained at the home office and one maintained at the division) and the general ledger of the target company (which is still a separate legal entity). (Assets and liabilities merely are transferred from the target company's general ledger to the newly formed division's general ledger.)

Continuing with the preceding example, the following entries (in condensed format) would be made by the acquiring company, its newly established division, and the target company.

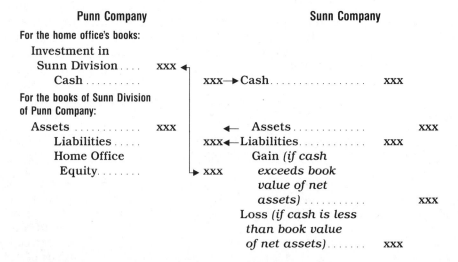

**Forming a Wholly Owned Subsidiary to Acquire the Assets.** In some cases, the acquiring company forms a wholly owned subsidiary to effect the acquisition of the target company's assets. This is done in situations in which it is not possible, practicable, or desirable to acquire the target company's common stock, but it is desirable to operate the acquired business as a separate legal entity insulated from the existing operations of the acquiring company.

**Removal of Records.** The target company must pack up its records (including its general ledger) and remove them from the location of the business that was sold.

**Subsequent Courses of Action for the Target Company.** If all its assets are disposed of and all its liabilities are assumed, the target company's remaining assets consist solely of the consideration received from the acquiring company. At this point, the target company (still a separate legal entity) is referred to as a **nonoperating company,** because it has no operating business—only passive assets. The following three courses of action are then available:

1. Continue as a nonoperating company.
2. Use the assets to enter a new line of business.
3. Distribute the assets to its shareholders. (This option is the most common one selected.)

If it chooses option 3, the target company becomes a **"shell" company** because it has no operating business and no assets. However, it still is a separate legal entity until steps are taken to have its charter withdrawn (which is usually done).

**Acquiring Rights to the Target Company's Name.** In acquiring assets, the acquiring company usually specifies in the acquisition agreement that it also is acquiring the exclusive right to the target company's corporate name. Accordingly, if the target company intends to remain in business (either as a nonoperating company or as an operating company in a new line of business), it must make a corporate name change. This avoids any future confusion that might arise between having, as in the example shown earlier, a Sunn Division and a Sunn Company.

**Tax Treatment on Any Gain by the Target Company.** The target company is taxed on any gain resulting from the sale of its assets only if the transaction is a taxable combination. (Taxable versus nontaxable combinations are discussed later in the chapter.)

## Acquisition of Common Stock

A company owning more than 50% of the outstanding common stock of another company is referred to as the **parent** of that company. Conversely, a company whose outstanding common stock is more than 50% owned by another company is referred to as a **subsidiary** of that company. A subsidiary (as opposed to a division) is a separate legal entity that must maintain its own general ledger. Accordingly, the subsidiary's operations must be accounted for on a decentralized basis. The acquisition of the outstanding common stock of the acquired company is a personal transaction involving the acquiring company and the acquired company's shareholders. For the target company, all that has happened is that the company's ownership is concentrated in the hands of significantly fewer stockholders, or even one stockholder if 100% of the outstanding common stock has been acquired. Consequently, only the acquiring company (the parent) must make an entry relating to the business combination.

Assuming that Punn Company acquired more than 50% of the outstanding common stock of Sunn Company, the relationship would be depicted as follows:

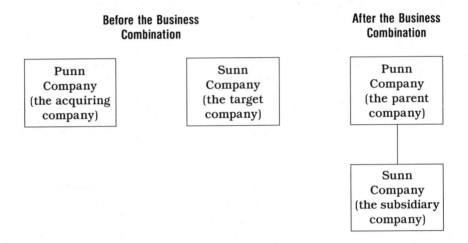

**Cash-for-Stock Exchange.**   If the acquiring company gives cash as consideration for the target company's outstanding common stock (which would automatically disqualify the transaction for pooling of interests treatment), it makes the following entry:

Investment in Subsidiary . . . . . . . . . . . . . . . . . . . . . .       xxx
    Cash . . . . . . . . . . . . . . . . . . . . . . . . . . . . . . . . . . . .            xxx

**Stock-for-Stock Exchange.**   If the acquiring company gives common stock as consideration (a necessary condition for pooling of interests treatment) for the target company's outstanding common stock, it is necessary to understand what is known as the exchange ratio. The **exchange ratio** is the number of common shares to be issued by the acquiring company for each outstanding common share of the target company to be surrendered. Say the acquiring company will issue 30,000 shares and the target company has 10,000 shares outstanding, all of which are to be exchanged. This produces a 3:1 exchange ratio. Note that the number of shares to be issued by the acquiring company first has to be calculated by dividing the price the acquiring company is willing to pay for the target company (say, $1,200,000) by the market price per share of the acquiring company's common stock (say, $40 per share), producing the number of shares to be issued (30,000). The exchange ratio is usually set forth in the acquisition agreement.

Assuming the acquiring company issues 30,000 shares of common stock to effect the business combination, the following entry would be made by the acquiring company:

| | | |
|---|---|---|
| Investment in Subsidiary............................... | xxx | |
|     Common Stock (30,000 × the par value). | | xxx |
|     Additional Paid-in Capital ................. | | xxx |

This entry is slightly more involved if pooling of interests treatment applies (more about this in Chapter 6).

## Statutory Mergers

A third common way of effecting a business combination is the **statutory merger,** in which the target company's equity securities are retired and the corporate existence of the target company is terminated. This can be depicted as follows:

The assets and liabilities of the target company are transferred to the acquiring company. Because the acquiring company is the only surviving legal entity, the target company is said to have been "merged" into the acquiring company. Because these combinations take place pursuant to state laws, they are called statutory mergers. There are two primary requirements of the state statutory merger laws:

1. The board of directors of each company must approve the plan of proposed merger before the plan can be submitted to the shareholders of each company.
2. The required percentage (usually a simple majority to 80%) of the voting power of each company must approve the plan of proposed merger.

The end result of a statutory merger is the same as though the acquiring company had acquired directly the target company's assets and the target company had then ceased its legal existence. The reasons for using this roundabout manner of acquiring a target company's assets are explained in the following paragraphs.

**Forcing out Dissenting Shareholders.**   In most cases in which the acquiring company acquires common stock, it desires 100% of the outstanding common stock of the target company. In some of these situations, this outcome may be unlikely because some shareholders of the target company object to the business combination and refuse to sell their shares. However, if the acquiring company acquires the required percentage of outstanding shares to approve a statutory merger, it can force out the dissenting shareholders by taking the necessary steps to liquidate the target company. (In some tender offers, the acquiring company clearly specifies that if all of the target company's shareholders do not accept the offer, the acquiring company intends to effect a statutory merger of the target company into the acquiring company, once the required ownership percentage is attained. This message means, "Tender your shares now or get forced out later.")

In these cases, the business combination technically occurs when the acquiring company acquires more than 50% of the target company's outstanding common stock, which creates a parent–subsidiary relationship. Thus, the statutory merger takes place after the business combination date, a process that normally can be completed within 30 to 60 days after approval of the plan of merger.

When the statutory merger subsequently becomes effective, entries are made (1) to transfer the target company's assets and liabilities to the acquiring company, and (2) to close out the equity accounts in the target company's general ledger. In addition, it is necessary to make a settlement with the dissenting shareholders of the target company (who did not tender their shares). State laws pertaining to statutory mergers generally provide that dissenting shareholders have the right to receive (in cash) the fair value of their shares as of the day before shareholder approval of the merger. Such value may have to be established through a judicial determination as provided under state law if the dissenting shareholders and the acquiring company cannot agree on the value of these shares.

**Forcing out Shareholders Who Cannot Be Located.**   The company acquiring common stock in a takeover cannot always locate all of the target company's shareholders; in most publicly held companies, a small number of shareholders simply cannot be found. When the acquiring company desires 100% ownership notwithstanding, it may take the statutory merger route in order to liquidate these interests in the target company.

**Acquiring Assets Indirectly.**   In unfriendly takeover attempts, the acquiring company is prevented from acquiring the assets directly from the target company, because the directors' refusal of the offer prevents the shareholders of the target company from voting on it. The acquiring company must then make a tender offer to the shareholders. If the acquiring company acquires the required percentage of outstanding shares through the tender offer and it does not wish to maintain a parent–subsidiary relationship, the acquiring company can then take the necessary steps to liquidate the target company via a statutory merger.

## Formation of a Holding Company

Infrequently, two companies (generally of comparable size) combine in such a manner that a new corporate entity is established that controls the operations of both combining companies. This is done when the existing name of each corporation would not indicate the scope of operations of the combined business or it is desired to have the top-level corporation operate as a **holding company.** (A holding company has no revenue-producing operations of its own, only investments in subsidiaries.) To illustrate, assume Punn Company and Sunn Company wish to combine. They form Integrated Technology Company, which issues its stock for the stock of Punn Company and Sunn Company. Punn Company and Sunn Company are now subsidiaries of Integrated Technology Company. This would be depicted as follows:

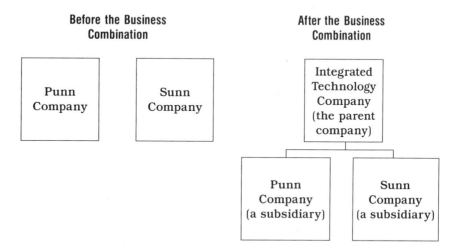

## Statutory Consolidation

More infrequent than forming a holding company is statutory consolidation. A **statutory consolidation** results in a new legal entity that takes over the assets and assumes the liabilities of each of the combining companies. The combining companies simultaneously cease their separate corporate existences. Because the new legal entity is the only surviving legal entity, the combining companies are said to have been "consolidated" into the new corporation. Because these combinations take place pursuant to state laws, they are called statutory consolidations. The primary requirements of the state statutory consolidation laws are the same as for statutory mergers.

For example, assume Punn Company and Sunn Company agree to combine using a statutory consolidation. The surviving company is called Integrated Technology Company. This would be depicted as follows:

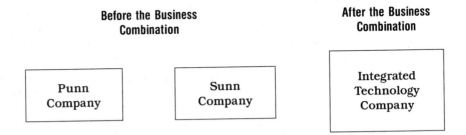

**Before the Business Combination**

| Punn Company | Sunn Company |

**After the Business Combination**

| Integrated Technology Company |

---

**ILLUSTRATION** ## Summary of Business Combinations

Illustration 2-1 presents the interrelationships of the various topics discussed up to this point.

## TAX CONSIDERATIONS

The income tax rules for business combinations are quite complex and thus more properly the topic of an advanced income tax course. However, it is important at this point to understand the relationship and similarities between the accounting rules and the income tax rules—an understanding that does not always result when the tax rules are dealt with solely in an advanced tax course. Accordingly, the following discussion is limited, general in nature, and designed to accomplish this purpose.

For financial reporting purposes, the terms and provisions in the acquisition agreement (along with some other factors discussed in Chapter 6) determine whether the purchase method or the pooling of interests method is used to record the combination. For income tax reporting purposes, the same terms and provisions in the acquisition agreement determine whether the combination is treated as a **taxable combination** or as a **tax-deferrable combination.** The latter is commonly referred to as a **tax-free combination.**

**■ ILLUSTRATION 2-1**
**Summary of Business Combinations**

| | Business Combinations | | | |
|---|---|---|---|---|
| | **Purchase** | | **Pooling of interests**[a] | |
| 1. Accounting method | | | | |
| 2. Type of consideration given | Cash, other assets, debt, preferred stock, common stock—in any combination | | Common stock | |
| 3. Type of asset acquired | Common stock | Assets | Common stock | Assets |
| 4. Resulting organizational form of the acquired business | Subsidiary | Division | Subsidiary | Division |
| 5. Type of accounting system used—centralized or decentralized | Decentralized | Either | Decentralized | Either |

[a]The discussion in this chapter focuses on the general concept of pooling of interests. Chapter 6 explores in detail this method's finer points.

## Taxable Combinations

**The Underlying Concept: A Sale Has Occurred.** The underlying concept of purchase accounting—that one company has acquired the business of another company—is essentially the same as that embodied in the Internal Revenue Code with respect to taxable combinations. For income tax reporting purposes, **a taxable combination is a completed and closed transaction in that a sale is deemed to have occurred.** Accordingly, an acquired business reports, or its shareholders report, a gain or loss in the year of the transaction. The fair value of the consideration received by the acquired business or its shareholders is compared with the tax basis of the assets sold to the acquiring business to compute the taxable gain or tax-deductible loss.

**The Resulting Change in Basis.** The acquiring company's tax basis for the acquired property (whether assets or common stock) is the purchase price paid. If assets are acquired for more than their carrying value as of the acquisition date, the acquired assets are stepped up in basis for tax depreciation and amortization purposes. If common stock is acquired, the assets of the acquired business can be stepped up in basis only if the acquiring company elects to treat the acquisition of the target company's common stock as an asset purchase (called a *Section 338 election*). Accordingly, if it elects to do so, the basis of the common stock is effectively transferred to the assets of the acquired business. (A more detailed discussion of this election is contained in Chapter 12.) This allows the acquirer to be in the same position as it would be if assets had been acquired rather than common stock.

**Accounting and Tax Rules Compared.**  Although the underlying concept of the purchase method for financial reporting purposes is the same as that embodied in the Internal Revenue Code for taxable combinations, it is important to recognize that the specific rules of *APB Opinion No. 16* regarding the purchase method are different from the specific rules of the Internal Revenue Code regarding taxable combinations. In other words, each set of rules is independent; the treatment for financial reporting purposes does not determine the treatment for tax reporting purposes and vice versa. Accordingly, some combinations that are accounted for under the purchase method for financial reporting purposes are treated as taxable combinations for income tax reporting purposes, whereas other combinations that are accounted for under the purchase method of accounting for financial reporting purposes are treated as tax-free combinations for income tax reporting purposes. Because of this similarity of the concepts but the difference in their specific rules, the only generalization that can be made is that **combinations accounted for under the purchase method for financial reporting purposes are more likely to be taxable combinations than tax-free combinations.**

## Tax-free Combinations

**The Underlying Concept: *No Sale Has Occurred.***  The underlying concept of pooling of interests accounting—that the two equity interests of the combining companies pool together in such a manner that there is a continuity of interest in the new, enlarged business—is essentially the same concept as that embodied in the Internal Revenue Code with respect to **tax-free combinations** (referred to as *tax-free reorganizations* in the Internal Revenue Code). **For income tax reporting purposes, a tax-free reorganization is not a completed or closed transaction in that a sale is not deemed to have occurred.** Accordingly for tax-reporting purposes, the acquired business (or its shareholders) does not report a gain or loss in the year of the transaction. Only the form of the investment has changed; the investment in the business itself is maintained even though such business is now part of a larger business. (This is the same principle used in "like-kind" real estate exchanges, which also are not taxable because the owners are continuing their investment in real estate.) At some later time, when the property that was received in the combination (typically the acquiring company's common stock) is disposed of in a completed taxable transaction, a gain or loss is reportable for income tax reporting purposes. Accordingly, in a tax-free reorganization income taxes are merely deferred or postponed until a later date.

**No Resulting Change in Basis.** With respect to the continuing enlarged business, the basis of the property acquired is not changed for income tax reporting purposes, regardless of whether assets or common stock is received in the exchange. The tax rules relating to tax-free reorganizations can accommodate acquisitions of assets and acquisitions of common stock. Section 368a of the Internal Revenue Code describes the various procedures by which tax-free combinations may be attained. Three specific procedures for accomplishing this are set forth in subsections a1A, a1B, and a1C. In practice, these are referred to as "A," "B," and "C" reorganizations. *Type A reorganizations* pertain to statutory mergers and statutory consolidations that take place under a specific state statute. *Type B reorganizations* pertain to stock for stock exchanges. *Type C reorganizations* pertain to an exchange of stock for assets. If the combining companies agree on a tax-free reorganization, the terms and provisions of the acquisition agreement must be structured carefully around one of these three specific procedures. The requirements of the Internal Revenue Code must be fully complied with before tax-free treatment is allowed. The safest course of action is to secure a specific ruling in advance from the Internal Revenue Service. Because this is a highly specialized area of tax practice, competent tax advice should be obtained.

As this book goes to print, congressional tax committees in search of additional tax revenues are considering proposals to make many "like-kind" real estate exchanges taxable. This raises a larger question of whether Congress will make changes to stock-for-stock exchanges, inasmuch as the provisions are identical in purpose to "like-kind" exchanges and substantial tax revenues could be raised by limiting the use of non-taxable stock-for-stock exchanges.

**Accounting and Tax Rules Compared.** The underlying concept of the pooling of interests method for financial reporting purposes is the same as that embodied in the Internal Revenue Code with respect to tax-free reorganizations. The same independent relationship exists between the pooling of interests method (for financial reporting) and tax-free reorganizations (for income tax reporting) as was explained for purchase accounting (for financial reporting) in relation to taxable combinations (for income tax reporting). The pooling of interests requirements, however, are much more stringent than the tax-free reorganization rules. Accordingly, combinations accounted for under the pooling of interests method for financial reporting purposes almost always qualify for tax-free reorganization treatment.

## Disincentive for Acquiring a Company for Its Net Operating Loss Carryforward

Many companies with significantly high net operating loss carryforwards (NOLs) have dim prospects of ever using their NOLs on a stand-alone basis to offset taxable income for tax purposes, which means that the NOLs will expire. (The carryover period for NOLs is 3 years back and 15 years forward.) Accordingly, such companies (usually having minimal net worth) are in the position of seeking a buyer that can use the NOL to offset its own income. Although it would appear logical that the purchaser must acquire common stock in order to inherit the NOL, the purchaser could also inherit the NOL by acquiring assets in a tax-free transaction. Such transactions, in substance, are merely the "buying and selling of NOLs." Prior to the enactment of the Tax Reform Act of 1986, many corporations having significant net operating loss carryforwards were acquired primarily with the intent of using their NOLs by the acquiring company. For example, an acquiring company pays $2 million for a corporation with a $10 million NOL. Assuming the purchaser is in the 34% tax bracket, it will save $3.4 million in taxes by using the NOL to offset its taxable income, thereby being ahead $1.4 million. In spite of enacted limitations prior to the Tax Reform Act of 1986, continued buying and selling of NOLs (and their subsequent use by acquiring companies) was a tax loophole waiting to be closed.

In 1986, congressional concern over the NOL "market" resulted in the passage of major additional limitations as Section 382 of the Internal Revenue Code. An annual limitation is now imposed on the amount of taxable income that may be offset by any NOL of an acquired company (whether or not the acquired company is liquidated into the parent company in a common stock purchase). Specifically, the value of the NOL corporation immediately before the ownership change is multiplied by a special rate of return (as determined from yields of long-term tax-exempt securities), which is published by the Treasury Department. For example, assume the value of the NOL corporation is $1 million and the special rate of return is 10%. The annual taxable income that the NOL may offset is limited to $100,000 ($1,000,000 × 10%). The result of the new limitations is to neutralize the impact of NOLs as a factor in planning acquisitions. The new limitations have been so effective that corporations with NOL carryforwards no longer offer to sell at 15–20 cents on the dollar but instead now offer to sell at 1–2 cents on the dollar (typically in advertisements in *The Wall Street Journal*).

## NEGOTIATING POSITIONS AND CONFLICTING INTERESTS

### Factors Determining the Positions of the Parties

It is useful at this point to look at the factors that shape the negotiating or posturing positions of each of the parties in an acquisition. Structuring the transaction entails the financial reporting treatment, the tax reporting treatment, and the use of specific types of consideration. We may then discuss conflicts that can arise between the parties.

**The Perspective of the Owners of the Target Company.**    The position of the owners of the business for sale is usually shaped by income tax considerations. Sometimes tax considerations are of primary importance. In such cases, the owners do not insist on a specific type of consideration for nontax reasons (such as desiring cash because of financial need or desiring common stock so as to have a continuing equity participation in the combined businesses). However, the owners do insist on a specific type of consideration for tax reasons, so as to minimize taxes and maximize their wealth. Sometimes this manifests itself in a preference for receiving stock or notes, so that income taxes that otherwise would be paid in a cash deal can be deferred to a later date (using a nontaxable exchange if stock is received and using the installment basis for reporting the gain if notes are received).[4] This is particularly useful for an elderly owner whose death before either the sale of the stock or the collection of the installment notes would totally eliminate the reporting of the untaxed gain inasmuch as the estate is entitled to a step-up in tax basis. Sometimes tax considerations motivate the target's owners to prefer cash, such as when they expect future income tax rates to be significantly higher,[5] or when they have capital losses that they would like to offset with capital gains from the purchaser's cash.[6]

At other times, tax considerations are of secondary importance, as when the owners insist on receiving cash (either out of financial need or from an unwillingness to assume the risk of owning notes or stock in the acquiring company). But even in cash deals, the owners can wind up with much greater after-tax proceeds by selling stock to the purchaser instead of assets (as explained in detail later).

In summary, the owners of the target company are very motivated by tax consequences and the specific type of consideration. How the transaction is reported for financial reporting purposes by the target company (if it relinquishes its assets) or by the owners individually (if they relinquish their stock) is of no importance to the owners in negotiations.

---

[4]The installment basis is available only when the target company is a nonpublic company.

[5]This occurred in 1986 when the individual capital gains tax of 20% was eliminated, with future rates on capital gains to be 28% or 33%.

[6]The October 19, 1987, stock market crash resulted in many corporate and private investors incurring capital losses.

**The Perspective of the Acquiring Company.** The acquiring company's position may or may not be shaped by tax considerations, depending on the focus of its management. Some managements focus solely on *maximizing net income:* for them, financial reporting considerations prevail, and tax considerations are secondary. (Financial reporting considerations would include whether to structure the transaction as a purchase or a pooling of interests so as to minimize any future depreciation and amortization charges.) At the other extreme are managements that focus solely on *minimizing cash outflows.* In these cases, tax considerations prevail and financial reporting considerations are secondary. Such tax considerations would include whether to structure the transaction as a taxable or a nontaxable transaction, so as to obtain the highest possible basis in the target company's assets for depreciation purposes and thus minimize cash outflows for income taxes.

## Financial Reporting Conflicts

The most common financial reporting conflict occurs when the acquiring company desires to use pooling of interests accounting (which requires that it issue common stock to the target company or to its shareholders), whereas the owners of the target company want cash or other nonstock consideration. (Recall that the reporting of goodwill and the related amortization charges to future income statements are avoided in a pooling of interests.) Because of the enormous importance that many acquiring companies place on obtaining pooling of interests treatment for financial reporting, we consider this a financial reporting conflict even though the target company (or its shareholders) has only one financial reporting method available to it. Technically from the target's perspective, the issue is merely which type of consideration should be used—not a financial reporting conflict.

## Tax Reporting Conflicts

The tax reporting conflicts center around two issues: (1) whether the acquiring company desires to change the tax basis of the property received in the combination (assets or common stock) to its current value based on the consideration given by the acquiring company; and (2) whether the acquired company or its shareholders want a tax-free treatment. The position of each party usually depends on whether the value of the consideration is above or below the tax basis of the target company's property, as discussed more fully below.

**The Value of Consideration Exceeds the Tax Basis.** In an economy that has experienced inflation, the acquiring company usually gives consideration that is greater in value than the tax basis of the property it is to receive.

The acquiring company would prefer a taxable treatment so that it can step up the basis of the property it is to receive. Thus, it will have greater depreciation and amortization deductions for income tax reporting purposes (or a higher basis in the acquired company's stock if a parent–subsidiary relationship is to be maintained). The acquired company or its shareholders, however, may prefer a tax-free treatment to defer or postpone the recognition of a gain for income tax reporting purposes.

**The Value of Consideration Is below the Tax Basis.**  The roles are usually reversed when the acquiring company gives consideration that is lower in value than the tax basis of the property it is to receive. In such a situation, the acquiring company would prefer a tax-free treatment, so that the higher basis of the property it is to receive will carry over. Thus, it would have greater depreciation and amortization deductions for income tax reporting purposes (or a higher basis in the acquired company's stock if a parent–subsidiary relationship is to be maintained). The acquired company or its shareholders, however, may prefer a taxable treatment to immediately recognize a loss for income tax reporting purposes.

**Conflicts Arising from Double Taxation.**   When a corporation sells its assets in a taxable transaction, it must pay taxes at the corporate level on any gain resulting from the sale (that is, when the value of the consideration exceeds the tax basis). Assuming the corporation then distributes the net proceeds (the sales price less taxes) to its stockholders, the stockholders themselves then must pay taxes on any gain they realize. From the perspective of these stockholders, they are incurring a double tax—once before distribution and once after distribution. One way for the stockholders to avoid taxes at the corporate level is for the seller to stipulate that the purchaser must acquire common stock instead of assets. However, this merely shifts the burden of paying the corporate-level tax from the seller to the buyer, because the buyer has now inherited (some might say "is stuck with") the low carryover adjusted basis of the underlying property. The buyer pays this tax under either of the following two options:

1. **Make a Section 338 Election.** By making a Section 338 election, the basis of the common stock is effectively transferred to the underlying assets of the acquired business. However, the acquired business (now a subsidiary) would have to report a taxable gain in order to achieve a step-up in basis. This option, in most cases, makes no sense inasmuch as the subsidiary pays taxes now merely to have greater tax deductions in future years (through higher depreciation charges, inventory costs, and so on).
2. **Do Not Make a Section 338 Election.** By not making a Section 338 election, no taxes are payable at the corporate level at the acquisition

date. However, as the underlying assets are either disposed of or used and depreciated, the acquired business (now a subsidiary) will pay greater taxes. Thus, the corporate-level tax is deferred and paid in future periods.

As we have seen, in taxable transactions there is a built-in conflict of interest over whether the transaction should be structured as a purchase of assets or of common stock, with the real issue which party should pay the corporate-level tax. With the problem of the corporate-level tax looming in a taxable transaction, clearly the tax-deferred treatment becomes doubly attractive because it enables taxes at the corporate level (as well as taxes at the individual stockholder level) to be deferred. Also, taxable stock purchases without a Section 338 election are more attractive because the corporate-level tax is deferred.

## Concluding Comments on Conflicting Interests

The ultimate resolution of the conflicting financial reporting interests (pooling of interests versus purchase) and the conflicting tax interests (taxable versus tax-free, and which party should be responsible for taxes at the corporate level in a taxable transaction) depends on the relative bargaining strengths and positions of each party.

## SELECTED REFERENCES

Anderson, Charles M. "1 + 1 = 3." *Management Accounting* (April 1987), pp. 28–31.

Gorman, Jerry. "M&As: The CPA as Acquisition Adviser." *Journal of Accountancy* (August 1988), pp. 37–42.

————. "LBO Accounting: Consensus at Last." *Journal of Accountancy* (August 1989), pp. 68–78.

Maupin, Rebekah J., and Wayne A. Label. "Profiting from a Management Buyout." *Management Accounting* (April 1987), pp. 32–34.

Rock, Milton L., and Martin Sikora. "Accounting for Merger Mania." *Management Accounting* (April 1987), pp. 20–26.

Willens, Robert. "M&As: The CPA as Tax Adviser." *Journal of Accountancy* (August 1988), pp. 44–52.

## END-OF-CHAPTER REVIEW

## Summary of Key Points

1. The acquiring company may structure a business combination to be either a purchase or a pooling of interests.

2. The purchase method treats the combination as a purchase of the target company's business, whereby the assets of the target company are to be reported at the acquiring company's cost, which is based essentially on the fair value of the consideration given.

3. In contrast, the pooling of interests method treats the combination as a fusion of equity interests, whereby the assets of the target company are to be reported at the target company's historical book values as of the acquisition date.

4. This fusion of equity interests is accomplished through the issuance of the acquiring company's common stock as consideration.

5. If the twelve conditions for a pooling of interests are not met, the combination must be accounted for as a purchase.

6. Many important factors must be considered in deciding whether to acquire the target company's assets or its outstanding common stock.

7. Whether assets or common stock shares are acquired has no bearing on the accounting treatment; only the resulting organizational form of the acquired business is different.

8. Business combinations are treated as either taxable or tax-free transactions.

9. In a taxable transaction, the acquiring company establishes a new tax basis for the acquired assets.

10. In a tax-free transaction, the tax basis of the target company's assets as of the combination date carries over to the acquiring company.

11. The desired financial reporting treatment for the acquirer, the type of consideration to be used, and tax considerations are important issues that often lead to conflicts between the parties in negotiating the terms of the acquisition agreement.

## Glossary of New Terms

**Acquiring company**  A company attempting to acquire the business of another company.

**Acquisition agreement**  The legal agreement that specifies the terms and provisions of a business combination.

**Conglomerate combination**  A business combination that takes place between companies in unrelated industries.

**Division**  In this chapter, a newly acquired business that does not maintain its separate legal existence.

**Exchange ratio**  The number of common shares issued by the acquiring company in exchange for each outstanding common share of the target company.

**Holding company**  A company that has no revenue-producing operations of its own, only investments in subsidiaries.

**Horizontal combination**  A business combination that takes place between companies involved as competitors at the same level in a given industry.

**Leveraged buyout (LBO)**  Investors and management buy a controlling interest in a company, financing the purchase by borrowing from a financial institution and using the company's own assets as collateral.

**Parent**  A company that owns more than 50% of the outstanding common stock of another company.

**Pooling of interests method**  A method of accounting for a business combination whereby the assets of the acquired business are carried forward to the combined corporation at their historically recorded amounts. A fusion of equity interests is deemed to have occurred as opposed to a sale.

**Proxy contest**   A system whereby management and an opposing group each solicit votes from the stockholders concerning proposed slates of directors or another issue such as a proposed change to the company's charter.

**Purchase method**   A method of accounting for a business combination whereby the assets and liabilities of the acquired business are valued at their current values based on the consideration given by the acquiring company. A sale is deemed to have occurred.

**Shell company**   A corporation that has no assets or liabilities.

**Statutory consolidation**   A legal term referring to a specific type of business combination in which a new corporation is formed to carry on the businesses of two predecessor corporations that are liquidated.

**Statutory merger**   A legal term referring to a specific type of business combination in which a newly acquired target company is liquidated into a division at the time of the business combination.

**Subsidiary**   A company whose outstanding common stock is more than 50% owned by another company.

**Takeover attempt**   The process of trying to acquire the business of a target company.

**Target company**   The company whose business a company is seeking to acquire.

**Tax-free combination**   A specific type of business combination in which the acquired business or its shareholders do not report a gain or loss at the time of the business combination for income tax reporting purposes.

**Tender offer**   An offer made by an acquiring company directly to the stockholders of the target company, whereby the stockholders of the target company are requested to give up their common shares in exchange for the consideration offered by the acquiring company.

**Vertical combination**   A business combination that takes place between companies involved at different levels in a given industry.

## Self-Study Questions
*(Answers are at the end of this chapter.)*

The nine choices listed A through I pertain to how a business combination can be structured. From these choices, select the appropriate answer for the multiple-choice questions that follow the choices.

A. Acquisition of assets.
B. Acquisition of common stock.
C. Statutory merger.
D. Statutory consolidation.
E. Purchase accounting.
F. Pooling of interests accounting.
G. Taxable transaction.
H. Nontaxable (tax-deferred) transaction.
I . None of the above.

More than one choice may be appropriate for some of the questions.

1. The acquiring company does not want to report any goodwill.
2. The acquiring company does not want to be responsible for the target company's unrecorded post-retirement benefit obligations.
3. The acquiring company does not want to be responsible for the target company's potential unrecorded liabilities pertaining to toxic waste site cleanups.
4. The target company's contracts and leases are not transferable.
5. The legal existence of the target company is to be terminated.
6. The legal existence of the acquiring company and the target company is to be terminated.
7. The target company desires to continue in business as a nonoperating company.
8. The target company's directors have turned down the acquiring company's offer.
9. The acquiring company will have to force out a small minority of dissenting stockholders of the target company.
10. A holding company is to be formed.
11. The acquiring company desires to issue preferred stock as consideration.
12. The acquiring company does not want to change the basis of accounting for the target company's assets.
13. The target company's stockholders desire a cash deal that maximizes the after-tax dollars they will receive.
14. The acquiring company does not want to be responsible for taxes at the corporate level.
15. The value of the consideration exceeds the tax basis of the target company's underlying property.

## ASSIGNMENT MATERIAL

### Review Questions

1. What is the difference between horizontal, vertical, and conglomerate combinations?
2. Contrast the purchase method with the pooling of interests method of accounting.
3. Why is the acquisition agreement so important in determining the ultimate accounting method used in recording a business combination?
4. On what grounds has *APB Opinion No. 16* been criticized?
5. What types of consideration can be given under purchase accounting and under pooling of interests accounting?
6. What types of assets can the acquiring company obtain in business combinations?
7. What various organizational forms can result from a business combination?
8. What is the difference between centralized and decentralized accounting systems?
9. How is the selling entity's gain or loss computed on the disposition of its assets?
10. Explain the relationship between *APB Opinion No. 16* and the income tax rules relating to business combinations.

11. What is meant by a tax-free combination?
12. Why does a conflict often exist between the acquiring company and the target company or its stockholders with respect to whether the combination should be treated in a taxable or nontaxable manner?
13. For the acquiring company, what is "the best of both worlds" from the standpoint of financial reporting and tax reporting?
14. Does a target company that sells its assets have to pay taxes if there is a gain?

# Discussion Cases

<table>
<tr><td>DC<br>2-1</td><td>

## Purchase versus Pooling of Interests

On July 1, 19X1, Plodder Company acquired all of the outstanding common stock of Sharp Company by issuing 80,000 shares of common stock as consideration (valued at $4,000,000). Plodder's controller informed you of the business combination in August 19X1 and indicated that management has not yet decided whether to use the purchase method or the pooling of interests method to account for this business combination. The controller has asked you to assist him in evaluating the alternative accounting treatments between now and December 31, 19X1, Plodder's year-end.

### Required:
How would you advise the controller?

</td></tr>
</table>

<table>
<tr><td>DC<br>2-2</td><td>

## Accounting versus Tax Treatment

Pioneer Company plans to embark on a business acquisition program to diversify its product lines. The controller is unclear about whether the tax treatment determines the accounting treatment or whether the accounting treatment determines the tax treatment.

### Required:
How would you advise the controller?

</td></tr>
</table>

<table>
<tr><td>DC<br>2-3</td><td>

## Limiting Legal Liability and Consistency

Putnam Company is having merger discussions with Sentry Company. All of Putnam's business acquisitions to date have been acquisitions of common stock resulting in parent–subsidiary relationships. Putnam prefers to legally insulate each of its acquired businesses from all other operations. Sentry has been and still is involved as a defendant in several lawsuits. As a result, Putnam plans to acquire Sentry's assets to insulate itself from any current or potential legal entanglements.

Further, the controller indicates to you that if the merger is consummated in this manner, the company will not be accounting for its acquisitions consistently, which will violate a fundamental accounting principle. All businesses acquired to date have been consistently recorded as poolings of interests; the acquisition of Sentry will not qualify for pooling of interests treatment, which means an additional inconsistency will be created.

</td></tr>
</table>

**Required:**

1. How could Putnam achieve the objective of insulating the business of Sentry?
2. Is the consistency principle violated as a result of acquiring assets? Why or why not?
3. Is the consistency principle violated as a result of the combination not qualifying for pooling of interests treatment? Why or why not?

# Exercises

E
2-1

## Terminology

Indicate the appropriate term or terms for each of the following:

1. The expansion of a business by constructing a manufacturing facility.
2. A business combination in which a company acquires one of its suppliers.
3. A business combination in which a company acquires one of its competitors.
4. A business combination in which a company acquires businesses to diversify its product lines.
5. The broad terms used to refer to business combinations.
6. A business combination in which the target company's corporate existence is terminated in conjunction with the transfer of its assets and liabilities to the acquiring company.
7. A business combination in which a new corporation is formed to acquire the businesses of two existing corporations.
8. The two methods of accounting for business combinations as set forth in *APB Opinion No. 16.*
9. The two types of assets that can be acquired in a business combination.
10. The expansion of a business by the acquisition of an existing business.
11. An acquired business that maintains its separate legal existence.
12. An acquiring business that acquires common stock of the acquired business, the latter maintaining its separate legal existence.
13. An acquired business that ceases to be a separate legal entity but continues to use a separate general ledger.
14. The primary type of consideration given in a business combination that is accounted for as a pooling of interests.
15. The allowable types of consideration that can be given in a business combination accounted for as a purchase.

E
2-2

## Pooling of Interests Method: Acquisition of Assets

Perez Company acquired all of the assets of Serna Company in a business combination that qualified for pooling of interests treatment. The current value of the common stock issued by Perez exceeded the book value of Serna's net assets by $300,000.

**Required:**

Explain the general accounting procedures to be followed by Perez in recording the acquisition of the assets.

<table>
<tr><td>E<br>2-3</td><td></td></tr>
</table>

### Purchase Method: Acquisition of Assets

Perry Company acquired all of the assets of Sparkle Company in a business combination that did not qualify for pooling of interests treatment. Perry paid $800,000 cash. The book value of Sparkle's net assets is $600,000, and their current value is $750,000.

#### Required:

Explain the general accounting procedures to be followed by Perry in recording the acquisition of the assets.

<table>
<tr><td>E<br>2-4</td><td></td></tr>
</table>

### Divestiture Accounting: Sale of Common Stock

Phu Company acquired all of the outstanding common stock of Smiley Company from its shareholders by issuing common stock.

#### Required:

Explain in general how Smiley should account for this change in ownership of its outstanding common stock.

<table>
<tr><td>E<br>2-5</td><td></td></tr>
</table>

### Divestiture Accounting: Sale of Assets

Photem Company acquired all of the assets of Santos Company by issuing common stock (and assuming Santos's liabilities).

#### Required:

Explain in general how Santos Company should account for this transaction.

<table>
<tr><td>E<br>2-6</td><td></td></tr>
</table>

### Statutory Merger and Statutory Consolidation

Printex Corporation is considering a merger or consolidation with Segal Corporation. Both methods of acquisition are being considered under applicable corporate statutory law. Printex is the larger of the two corporations and is in reality acquiring Segal Corporation.

#### Required:

Discuss the meaning of the terms *merger* and *consolidation* as used in corporate law with particular emphasis on the legal difference between the two.

(AICPA adapted)

## Problems

<table>
<tr><td>P<br>2-1</td><td></td></tr>
</table>

### COMPREHENSIVE  Acquisition of Assets for Cash

PBX Company acquired all of the assets of Sprint Company by assuming responsibility for all of its liabilities and paying $1,500,000 cash. Information with respect to Sprint at the date of combination follows:

| | Book Value | Current Value |
|---|---|---|
| Cash ..................................... | $   10,000 | $   10,000 |
| Accounts receivable, net (including | | |
|     $30,000 due from PBX Company) ........... | 90,000 | 90,000 |
| Inventory ................................ | 200,000 | 200,000 |
| Land ..................................... | 400,000 | 500,000 |
| Building and equipment ................... | 2,500,000 | 1,600,000 |
| Accumulated depreciation ................. | (1,200,000) | |
|     Total Assets ...................... | $2,000,000 | $2,400,000 |
| Accounts payable and accruals ............. | $  300,000 | $  300,000 |
| Long-term debt .......................... | 800,000 | 800,000 |
|     Total Liabilities..................... | $1,100,000 | $1,100,000 |
| Common stock, $1 par value ............... | $  100,000 | |
| Additional paid-in capital ................. | 500,000 | |
| Retained earnings ........................ | 300,000 | |
|     Total Stockholders' Equity ............ | $  900,000 | $1,300,000 |
|     Total Liabilities and Equity ........... | $2,000,000 | $2,400,000 |

## Required:

1. Does the acquisition appear to be a horizontal, vertical, or conglomerate type of combination?
2. Would the transaction be accounted for as a purchase or a pooling of interests?
3. Is PBX Company the parent company of Sprint Company? Why or why not?
4. Is Sprint a subsidiary? Why or why not?
5. Is Sprint a separate legal entity after the transaction has been consummated?
6. Can the acquired business be accounted for on a centralized or a decentralized basis?
7. Prepare the journal entry that would be made by Sprint on the date of the combination. Assume a 40% income tax rate.
8. Prepare a balance sheet for Sprint after recording the entry in requirement 7.
9. What options are available to Sprint after the business combination?
10. What is Sprint's book value in total and per share after the business combination?
11. What is the most likely market price of Sprint's common stock immediately after the transaction? (How would your answer change if Sprint planned to liquidate and cash would be distributed to its stockholders one year from now?)
12. Prepare the entry—in condensed form—that PBX would make, assuming that centralized accounting is to be used.
13. Why did PBX pay $1,500,000 for a company whose net assets are worth only $1,300,000?
14. How could PBX have determined the current value of Sprint's assets and liabilities?
15. Tax questions (optional):
    a. What is the treatment for income tax reporting purposes?
    b. From your answer in requirement 15a, what is PBX's tax basis of the land, buildings, and equipment it obtained?

## COMPREHENSIVE   Acquisition of Assets for Common Stock

Assume the same information as in Problem 2-1, except that PBX Company gave as consideration 50,000 shares of its $10 par value common stock (of which 950,000 shares are already outstanding) having a market value of $30 per share. Assume that all conditions for pooling of interests are met.

### Required:

Respond to requirements 2–11 in Problem 2-1. Then continue with the following requirements:

12. At what amount would PBX record the assets acquired from Sprint? (Do not prepare PBX's entry to record the combination; doing so requires an understanding of material in Chapter 6.)
13. Reevaluate your answer to requirement 7 in light of your answer to requirement 12. (Hint: Does PBX's accounting treatment affect Sprint's accounting treatment—that is, is symmetry required?)
14. How will Sprint account for its 5% interest in PBX?
15. Tax questions (optional):
    a. What is the probable treatment for income tax reporting purposes?
    b. From your answer in requirement 15a, what is PBX's tax basis of the land, buildings, and equipment it obtained?
    c. What is Sprint's tax basis in the PBX common stock it received?

## COMPREHENSIVE   Acquistion of Common Stock for Cash

Assume the same information as in Problem 2-1, except that PBX Company acquired all of the outstanding common stock of Sprint Company rather than acquiring all of Sprint's assets and assuming all of Sprint's liabilities.

### Required:

Respond to requirements 2–10 in Problem 2-1. Then continue with the following requirements:

11. Prepare the entry that PBX would make to record the combination.
12. Where is the goodwill recorded that PBX paid for?
13. Tax questions (optional):
    a. What is the treatment for income tax reporting purposes?
    b. If the combination is taxable, taxable to whom?
    c. Do the selling shareholders have a taxable gain or a taxable loss?
    d. Assuming the selling shareholders were all initial founders of Sprint, calculate their taxable gain or loss in total.
    e. In what asset does PBX have a tax basis?
    f. How much is its tax basis in this asset?
    g. Does the tax basis of Sprint's land, buildings, and equipment change?

## P 2-4

### COMPREHENSIVE    Acquisition of Common Stock for Common Stock

Assume the same information as provided in Problem 2-1, except that PBX Company gave as consideration 50,000 shares of its $10 par value common stock (of which 950,000 shares are already outstanding) having a market value of $30 per share for all of the outstanding common stock of Sprint Company. Assume all conditions for pooling of interests are met.

### Required:

Respond to requirements 2–10 in Problem 2-1. Then continue with the following requirements:

11. At what amount would PBX record the Sprint common stock it obtained? (Do not prepare PBX's entry to record the combination; doing so requires an understanding of material in Chapter 6.)
12. What is the exchange ratio used in the transaction?
13. Tax questions (optional):
    a. What is the probable tax treatment?
    b. In what asset does PBX have a tax basis?
    c. How much is its tax basis in this asset?
    d. Nick Tymer acquired 3,000 shares of Sprint's common stock for $34,000 (shortly before the announcement of the business combination). What is his tax basis of the PBX shares he received in the exchange?
    e. Did Tymer gain from his investment?

## P 2-5

### COMPREHENSIVE    Acquisition of Common Stock for Common Stock

Assume the same information as provided in Problem 2-1, except that PBX Company gave as consideration 50,000 shares of its $10 par value common stock (of which 950,000 shares are already outstanding) having a market value of $30 per share for all of the outstanding common stock of Sprint company. Also, one of the remaining eleven conditions for pooling of interests was *not* met.

### Required:

Respond to requirements 2–10 in Problem 2-1. Then continue with the following requirements:

11. Prepare the entry that PBX would make to record the combination.
12. What is the exchange ratio used in the transaction?
13. Tax questions (optional):
    a. What is the probable treatment for income tax reporting purposes?
    b. In what asset does PBX Company have a tax basis?
    c. How much is its tax basis in this asset?
    d. Nick Tymer acquired 3,000 shares of Sprint's common stock for $34,000 (shortly before the announcement of the business combination). What is his tax basis of the PBX shares he received in the exchange?
    e. Did Tymer gain from his investment?

**P 2-6**

## Comparing Reporting Results of Pooling of Interests Method versus Purchase Method

Supresso Company's assets consist of undervalued land holdings that were acquired many years ago for $4,000,000. The fair value of these holdings at various dates follows:

|  | Fair Value |
|---|---|
| January 1, 19X1 | $7,000,000 |
| January 1, 19X4 | 8,000,000 |
| January 1, 19X7 | 9,000,000 |

On January 1, 19X1, Pal Company acquired all of the assets of Supresso by issuing common stock having a market value of $7,000,000. (None of Supresso's liabilities were assumed.) On January 1, 19X4, Penn Company acquired all of the assets of Pal Company by issuing common stock having a market value of $20,000,000. Of this amount, assume that $8,000,000 was for the real estate holdings of Pal Company that it had acquired from Supresso in 19X1. On January 1, 19X7, Penn Company sold for $9,000,000 cash all of the real estate holdings initially owned by Supresso.

### Required:
1. Determine the gain to be reported by Supresso, Pal, and Penn upon the disposal of the land assuming the 19X1 and 19X4 business combinations are recorded under purchase accounting. (Assume that the proceeds received in these transactions is properly recordable at its current value.) Add up the total reportable gain by the three companies and compare to the difference between Supresso's cost of the land and Penn's proceeds. Evaluate the soundness of these reporting results.
2. Repeat requirement 1, but assume that the 19X1 and 19X4 business combinations qualified for pooling of interests accounting treatment.

# ADVANCED LEVEL ASSIGNMENT MATERIAL

## Technical Research Question

Answers to technical research questions that appear here and elsewhere in the book may be found by consulting the pronouncements of the Financial Accounting Standards Board, the Accounting Principles Board, and the Securities and Exchange Commission.

Pickens Company acquired 15% of the outstanding common stock of Selno Company. In a defensive move to prevent being taken over, Selno entered into an agreement with Pickens to purchase the stock acquired by Pickens at a 20% premium above market value. As part of this agreement, Pickens agrees to not acquire any more common stock of Selno for the next ten years. How should the premium be accounted for and classified?

## Advanced Problem

| AP |
| 2-1 |

### Leveraged Buyout: Determining the Change in Basis—The Continuing Ownership Percentage Increases

Oldco is a publicly owned company having 10,000 shares of common stock outstanding. In November 19X1, Oldco's upper management, which owns 500 common shares (5%) of Oldco, approached an independent investment firm concerning a leveraged buyout of Oldco. The investment company has strong relationships with lending institutions. In December 19X1, a new corporation (Newco) was formed to serve as a holding company to acquire all of Oldco's outstanding common stock. Newco issued 200 shares of common stock as follows:

1. 100 shares to the investment firm for $25,000 cash.
2. 100 shares to Oldco's upper management in exchange for the 500 shares of Oldco common stock it held.

In December 19X1, Newco borrowed $450,000 from a lending institution, which loan is secured by Oldco's assets. On December 31, 19X1, Newco acquired the remaining 9,500 outstanding common shares of Oldco by paying cash of $475,000 ($50 per share). Information concerning Oldco at December 31, 19X1, follows:

|  | Book Value | Current Value |
|---|---|---|
| Assets | $600,000 | $850,000 |
| Liabilities | $400,000 | $400,000 |
| Stockholder's Equity | 200,000 | 450,000 |
|  | $600,000 | $850,000 |

Assume that management's basis in Oldco is equal to its share of the book value of the net assets.

### Required:
1. At what amount should the 100 shares of Newco common stock issued to upper management be recorded?
2. Determine the extent to which Oldco's assets would be revalued upward.
3. Determine the amount of goodwill to be reported.
4. Would your answers to requirements 2 and 3 be different if the transaction had been structured as follows: (a) Oldco borrowed $450,000 from the lending institution; (b) Oldco issued 500 shares of its common stock to the investment

firm for $25,000 cash; and (c) Oldco acquired the 9,500 shares of its outstanding common stock held by the outside investors for $475,000 cash through a self-tender offer?

## ANSWERS TO SELF-STUDY QUESTIONS

| | | | |
|------|------|--------|------------------------------|
| 1. F | 5. C | 9. C | 13. E, B, G |
| 2. A | 6. D | 10. I | 14. A |
| 3. I | 7. A | 11. E | 15. G (from buyer's perspective) |
| 4. B | 8. B | 12. F | H (from seller's perspective) |

# 3

....

# THE PURCHASE METHOD OF ACCOUNTING: DATE OF ACQUISITION

## *TOPIC OUTLINE*

# CHAPTER OVERVIEW

Chapter 2 introduced the purchase method and the pooling of interests method of accounting for business combinations. Because these two methods are conceptual opposites, they are best discussed and illustrated separately. Consequently, this chapter and Chapters 4 and 5 cover the purchase method; Chapter 6 focuses on the pooling of interests method.

The purchase method, like the pooling of interests method, can be applied to either form of business combination, the acquisition of assets and the acquisition of common stock; with either, the results of reporting operations and the financial position of the combined businesses are the same. To make this point, we discuss and illustrate each form of business combination. In the illustrations we must compare a situation in which all of the assets are acquired with one in which all of the common stock is acquired; otherwise, a comparison is not possible. Acquisition of less than 100% of the common stock requires some additional considerations that are not relevant in situations in which all of the common stock is acquired. Discussion of these more involved situations is delayed until Chapter 5.

The procedures for preparing combined and consolidated balance sheets at the acquisition date are dealt with in this chapter. The preparation of combined and consolidated income statements for periods subsequent to the acquisition date are dealt with in Chapter 4.

# THE ESSENCE OF THE PURCHASE METHOD

The underlying concept of the purchase method of accounting is that one entity has purchased the business of another entity—that is, a sale has been consummated. The acquiring company records at its cost the assets or the common stock acquired. The cost is based essentially on the value of the consideration given. If the cost is above the current value of the target company's net assets, then goodwill exists, which must be amortized over a period not to exceed 40 years. Thus, **goodwill is determined in a residual manner.** (Value is determined by valuing its tangible assets, identifiable intangible assets, and liabilities at their current values, which may involve qualified appraisers.) In the far less frequent circumstances in which the acquiring company's cost is below the current value of the target company's net assets, a **bargain purchase element** exists, which must be allocated against the current value of certain noncurrent assets. If the bargain purchase element is so great that it reduces the applicable noncurrent assets to zero, the remaining amount is recorded as a **deferred credit** and amortized over a period not to exceed 40 years.

The purchase method parallels accounting for the acquisition of individual assets—that is, historical cost is used. Consequently, some assets and liabilities of the enlarged business are recorded at their historical cost (the assets and liabilities of the acquiring company), whereas some assets and liabilities of the enlarged business (the assets and liabilities of the acquired business) are reported at their current values as of the acquisition date. These current values become the acquiring company's historical cost. From the date of acquisition, the income of the acquired business is combined with the income of the acquiring company. **The acquired business's preacquisition earnings are never combined with the preacquisition earnings of the acquiring company.**

The purchase method can be neatly divided into two questions:

1. What is the total cost of the acquired business to the acquiring business?
2. What specifically is acquired for the total cost incurred?

The rest of the chapter discusses the procedures for answering these questions, in addition to the procedures for presenting the financial position of the enlarged business as of the acquisition date.

## DETERMINING THE TOTAL COST OF THE ACQUIRED BUSINESS

The total cost of the acquired business equals the sum of the following:

1. The **fair value of the consideration given.**
2. The **direct costs** incurred in connection with the acquisition, excluding costs of registering with the Securities and Exchange Commission any securities given as consideration by the acquiring company.
3. The **fair value of any contingent consideration** that is given subsequent to the acquisition date.

Each of these areas is discussed below.

### The Fair Value of the Consideration Given

The following three types of consideration may be given in any business combination:

1. **Cash or other assets.** Cost is the amount of cash or the fair value of other assets given.
2. **Debt.** Cost is the present value of the debt issued, determined by applying the provisions of *APB Opinion No. 21*, "Interest on Receivables and Payables."
3. **Equity securities.** Cost is the fair value of the equity securities issued. However, if the fair value of the property acquired is more

clearly evident than the fair value of the equity securities issued, then the fair value of the property acquired is used to determine cost.

As a practical matter, when equity securities issued are identical with the acquiring company's outstanding publicly traded securities, the fair value of the equity securities given is readily determinable and is almost always used to determine cost. If the acquiring company's equity securities are not publicly traded or a new class of stock is issued, it is usually necessary to obtain either (a) an appraisal of the fair value of the equity securities issued (usually obtainable from an investment banker) or (b) an appraisal of the property acquired, the latter alternative being preferable.

## Direct Costs

Acquiring companies commonly use outside lawyers and accountants in various capacities throughout the course of events leading to a completed acquisition. Travel costs are common during acquisition negotiations, as are finders' fees. Such **costs and fees**, as well as any other direct costs, **that pertain to the acquisition are added to the cost of the acquired business.** In situations in which the consideration given is equity securities, **costs and fees that pertain to the issuance or registration of the equity securities are not added to the cost of the acquired business.** Instead, they are charged to additional paid-in capital. (Recall from intermediate accounting that the costs incurred to issue and register equity securities in nonbusiness combinations are treated in this manner because they are considered a reduction of the fair value of the securities issued.) Indirect and general expenses, including salary and overhead costs of an internal acquisitions department, are not direct costs of an acquisition and are expensed as incurred.

## Contingent Consideration

**Contingent consideration** is often used as a compromise when the buyer and seller disagree on the purchase price or the form of consideration to be given, or both. Contingent consideration may be divided into two mutually exclusive categories: (1) contingencies whose outcomes are currently determinable, and (2) contingencies whose outcomes are not currently determinable.

**Contingencies Whose Outcomes Are Currently Determinable.**   If it can be determined beyond a reasonable doubt at the acquisition date that the outcome of the contingency will be such that the contingent consideration will have to be paid, then the fair value of the additional consideration should be recorded at that time as part of the cost of the acquired business. Relatively few contingencies fall into this category.

**Contingencies Whose Outcomes Are Not Currently Determinable.** If it cannot be determined beyond a reasonable doubt at the acquisition date that the contingent consideration will have to be paid, the contingent consideration should be disclosed but not recorded as a liability or shown as outstanding securities until it is determinable beyond a reasonable doubt. An example of an appropriate disclosure is given later in the chapter in the section on disclosures. (This **"determinable beyond a reasonable doubt" criterion** of *APB Opinion No. 16* is more demanding than the "probable" criterion set forth in *FASB Statement No. 5*, "Accounting for Contingencies," which applies only to loss and gain contingencies. Contingencies that are not currently determinable can be divided into two categories:

1. **Contingencies based on other than security prices.** This type of contingency is often based on sales or earnings goals for the acquired business. It is commonly used when the target company or its shareholders want to protect themselves from selling out too cheaply in the event that the acquired business later realizes the potential they feel it possesses and the buyer wants to protect itself from paying too much in the event that the acquired business does not realize such potential. Contingent consideration is the compromise whereby an additional amount of consideration is given to the seller(s) at a later date if the acquired business achieves certain agreed-upon sales or earnings levels within a specified period of time. Later, when the contingency is resolved and any additional consideration is distributable, **the current value of the additional consideration is added to the acquiring company's cost of the acquired business.** (Usually this increases the amount of goodwill.)

2. **Contingencies based on security prices.** This type of contingency is common when the target company or its shareholders receive as consideration the acquiring company's equity securities, which must be held for a certain period of time. In this situation, the target company or its shareholders want protection in the event the market price of the securities at the expiration of the holding period is below the market price of the securities at the acquisition date. The acquiring company must issue an additional number of securities if the market price at the end of the holding period is below the market price that existed on the acquisition date. The result is to bring the total value of the holdings of the target company or its shareholders at that time up to the total value existing on the acquisition date. If additional securities are later issued, the current value of the additional consideration is added to the acquiring company's cost of the acquired business. However, the amount previously recorded for securities issued at the date of acquisition should simultaneously be reduced to the lower current

value of those securities. **The net effect of this procedure is not to increase the cost of the acquired business above what was recorded at the acquisition date.** The rationale is that the initial recorded cost represents the amount that would have been paid for the business in a straight cash transaction. Illustration 3-1 gives an example of the accounting entries for this type of contingency.

## ■ ILLUSTRATION 3-1
### An Example of Contingent Consideration Based on Security Prices

Pine Company acquires the business of Spruce Company. (Whether it acquires assets or common stock is irrelevant.) The total consideration Pine pays is $1,000,000 worth of its $5 par value common stock. The market price of Pine's common stock on the acquisition date is $50 per share; thus, 20,000 shares are issued at that time. A condition of the purchase is that the common stock issued be held by the seller for two years. If, at the end of two years, the market price of the common stock is below $50 per share, then an appropriate additional number of shares must be issued so that the total value of the issued shares equals $1,000,000. Two years later, the market price of Pine's common stock is $40 per share. Thus, $1,000,000 divided by $40 per share equals 25,000 shares. Because 20,000 shares have already been issued, an additional 5,000 shares are issued at that time.

Entry at the acquisition date:

| | | |
|---|---:|---:|
| Cost of Acquired Business[a] | 1,000,000 | |
| Common Stock | | 100,000 |
| Additional Paid-in Capital | | 900,000 |
| To record the issuance of 20,000 shares of $5 par value common stock. | | |

Entries required two years later:

| | | |
|---|---:|---:|
| Cost of Acquired Business[a] | 200,000 | |
| Common Stock | | 25,000 |
| Additional Paid-in Capital | | 175,000 |
| To record the issuance of 5,000 shares of $5 par value common stock as additional consideration. | | |
| Additional Paid-in Capital | 200,000 | |
| Cost of Acquired Business[a] | | 200,000 |
| To reflect the reduction in value of the previously issued shares from $50 per share to $40 per share. | | |

Note that the effect of the entries recorded two years after acquisition is to debit Additional Paid-in Capital for $25,000 and credit Common Stock for $25,000. Thus, there is no effect on the cost of the acquired business, as initially recorded on the acquisition date.

[a]Later in the chapter, more descriptive account titles are used: "Investment in Subsidiary" when common stock is acquired and "Investment in Division" when assets are acquired.

# THE RELATIONSHIP OF TOTAL COST TO CURRENT VALUE OF THE ACQUIRED BUSINESS'S NET ASSETS

Once the total cost of the acquired business is determined, the next step in purchase accounting is to determine the current value of its assets and liabilities. Assume the assets have a current value of $270,000 and the liabilities have a current value of $190,000. The $80,000 difference between the two is the current value of the net assets ($80,000). This current value is then multiplied by the acquiring company's ownership interest in the acquired business (always 100% when assets are acquired or when all of the outstanding common stock is acquired) to obtain the acquiring company's ownership interest in the current value of the net assets. This amount is then compared to the total cost of the acquisition to determine if goodwill exists (the most common situation) or a bargain purchase element is present. This process can be expressed in a formula applicable to all combinations, as well as the above example, as shown in Illustration 3-2.

**Review Points for Illustration 3-2.**   Note the following:

1. When the total cost is above the acquiring company's ownership interest in the current value of the acquired business's net assets, the assets and liabilities of the acquired business will be reported at their full current values in the financial statements of the enlarged combined business. (The same is true when total cost equals the ownership interest in the current value of the net assets.)

2. When a bargain purchase element is present, the amount of the bargain purchase element must be allocated to certain noncurrent assets (reducing their current values) to the extent possible. The adjusted amounts then become the current values for financial reporting purposes.

■ **ILLUSTRATION 3-2**
**Relationship of Total Cost to Current Value of the Acquired Business's Net Assets**

|  | Total Cost | − | Acquiring Company's Ownership Interest in Current Value of Net Assets | = | Goodwill or Bargain Purchase Element |
|---|---|---|---|---|---|
| Goodwill Situation: | $90,000 | — | $80,000[a] | = | $10,000 |
| Bargain Purchase Element Situation: | $75,000 | — | $80,000[a] | = | $(5,000) |

[a]Assume assets have a current value of $270,000, liabilities have a current value of $190,000, and either assets were acquired or all of the outstanding common stock was acquired.

## Accounting for Goodwill

When the acquiring company's total cost is greater than its ownership interest in the current value of the acquired business's net assets, the excess amount is considered **goodwill.** Note that goodwill is a residually determined amount. Goodwill is reported in the financial statements as an asset of the enlarged, combined business. It must be amortized over no more than 40 years. Its value and remaining life must be reassessed in each subsequent period (discussed more fully in Chapter 4). Accounting for goodwill is controversial, as indicated in the accompanying article. A capsule history of accounting for goodwill is on page 125.

**Goodwill versus Covenants Not to Compete.** Because goodwill is not deductible for income tax reporting purposes, acquiring companies often try to include in the acquisition agreement a tax-deductible feature known as a **covenant not to compete.** Covenants not to compete are intangible assets similar to goodwill. Such a covenant prevents the target company from reentering the same line of business for a specified period of time.

**Tax Rules for Determining Goodwill.** In allocating the purchase price of a business between depreciable and nondepreciable assets for tax reporting purposes, the amount allocated to goodwill must be calculated in a residual manner (termed the residual method of allocation). Thus goodwill is determined in the same manner for both financial reporting and tax reporting.

## Accounting for Bargain Purchase Elements

When the acquiring company's total cost is below its ownership interest in the current value of the acquired business's net assets, then a **bargain purchase element** exists. Bargain purchase elements are treated arbitrarily under the provisions of *APB Opinion No. 16*, "Accounting for Business Combinations." First, the bargain purchase element must be treated as a reduction of the current values assigned to any noncurrent assets acquired other than long-term investments in marketable securities. If the bargain purchase element is so large that the applicable noncurrent assets are reduced to zero (which rarely, if ever, happens), any remaining credit is recorded as a deferred credit and amortized to income over a period not more than 40 years. The rationale for attempting to eliminate the bargain purchase element is that the values assigned to the net assets as a whole should not exceed the purchase price paid. Under historical cost–based accounting, the purchase price constitutes cost. Were it not for this requirement, managements would have the opportunity to seek or use the highest possible appraisals for the assets to obtain the highest

## PERSPECTIVE

### The Unlevel Accounting Field

As an article in the *Wall Street Journal* recently pointed out, foreign companies have a walloping advantage over U.S. companies in playing the takeover game in this country. The advantage is intangible, but it's a big advantage all the same. Whereas U.S. companies must amortize, which is to say, write off, the goodwill that results for paying more than book value for a company that it acquires, foreign companies need not do so at all.

Take the case of British-based Grand Metropolitan's $5.2 billion bid for Pillsbury Co. The Grand Met bid amounts to an almost $4 billion premium over Pillsbury's balance sheet book value. No U.S. white knight is likely to match that stunning offer since that would mean an unavoidable $100 million annual reduction in earnings for the next 40 years. That's a large and incredibly difficult pill for any public company to swallow, since doing so would offset much if not most of any synergy or savings that might result from the takeover itself. Says Peter Berger, a partner at Arthur Andersen, "Chief executives are compensated based on earnings per share. That makes them very wary about taking a big bite of goodwill."

By contrast, under British rules the whole notion of goodwill is handled differently, with the result that premiums over book value can be charged off against shareholder equity instead of earnings. By reducing the book value of the equity capital, the charging off of the goodwill makes the earnings look even more impressive as a return on equity.

In case they don't want to see the book value of their shareholder's equity shrink too much, the foreign companies have further flexibility to use, further cards to play. Instead of simply writing the premium off against equity, British firms, including Grand Met, can choose to spread the goodwill over the various brand names they've acquired in the takeover. Those

brands, in effect assigned a value for accounting purposes, then go on the acquiring firm's balance sheet as assets. This in turn offsets much of the hit to shareholder's equity. By contrast, any brands treated as assets on a U.S. balance sheet must be amortized over 40 years just as if their value consisted of nothing beyond goodwill.

British firms are not alone in this. West German, Canadian and Japanese accounting and tax rules also allow more favorable treatment of goodwill than is permitted under the tight constrictions of U.S. rules.

Let's look at Philip Morris' $12.9 billion offer to acquire Kraft Inc. Of that purchase price, $11 billion is for goodwill—that is, it is a premium over book value of that amount. Amortizing that goodwill will result in an annual $275 million earnings reduction for Philip Morris for the next 40 years. "Even Philip Morris will find it tough to earn its way out of that," says Robert Willens, a tax expert at Shearson Lehman Hutton.

Many U.S. accountants have long argued that the whole concept of goodwill accounting needs some serious rethinking. They say that goodwill should really be treated as a balance sheet item, and have nothing to do with earnings. In other words, it should be left as is and not depreciated the way tangible assets are.

"The 40-year amortization period is arbitrary," points out Shearson's Willens. Says he, "Some brands, like Coke, have actually increased in value dramatically over the years. Why shouldn't we be able to write up these assets?"

With business becoming increasingly globalized and transnational in nature, what's obviously needed here is some uniform international accounting standards. But the International Accounting Standards Committee, a London-based organization working possible bargain purchase element. The high (artificial) bargain purchase element could then be amortized to income over a relatively short period of time in comparison with time periods assigned to the noncurrent assets. Thus, substantial opportunity for manipulating income would exist.

Because bargain purchase elements arise most frequently when the acquired business has recently experienced operating losses, this treatment results in a conservative valuation of the noncurrent assets other than long-term investments in marketable securities. This makes sense; such noncurrent assets acquired from a company experiencing operating losses are subject to greater realization risks than if the target company had not experienced operating losses.

To illustrate the manner of allocating a bargain purchase to the appropriate assets, assume a $5,000 bargain purchase element. Assume further that the only noncurrent assets of the acquired business are land, buildings, and equipment. The $5,000 bargain purchase element is allocated to these accounts based on their relative current values as follows:

*based on relative CV's*

| Appropriate Noncurrent Assets | Current Value | Percentage to Total (Rounded) | Bargain Purchase Element | Percentage Times Bargain Purchase Element | Adjusted Current Value |
|---|---|---|---|---|---|
| Land | $ 42,000 | 20% | $5,000 | $1,000 | $ 41,000 |
| Buildings and Equipment | 156,000 | 80 | 5,000 | 4,000 | 152,000 |
| | $198,000 | 100% | | $5,000 | $193,000 |

**Key Review Point.** When a bargain purchase element is present, it clearly suggests that the assets are worth more individually than as part of a going business. If this were true, the previous owners of the acquired business would have been better off to liquidate the company by selling its individual assets than by selling the business as a whole. Because they did not do this, the initially determined current values must be overstated to the extent of the bargain purchase element.

**"Negative Goodwill."** Some accountants incorrectly refer to an excess of current value over cost as *negative goodwill* rather than as a bargain purchase element. The use of this term is unfortunate and improper. Goodwill either does or does not exist; there is no such thing as a company having negative goodwill. We point this term out only because you may encounter it in practice.

## THE IRRELEVANCE OF BOOK VALUE FOR REPORTING PURPOSES

For future reporting purposes, the book values of the acquired business's various assets and liabilities as of the combination date become irrelevant to the acquiring company, inasmuch as a new basis of accounting occurs under the purchase method. By comparing the current value of the net assets to the book value of the net assets, however, we determine by how much the net assets are under- or overvalued. For example, assume the acquiring company's total cost is $90,000 and the net assets of the acquired business have a current value of $80,000 and a book value of $60,000. The formula shown in Illustration 3-2 can be modified slightly to display this information by separating the acquiring company's ownership interest in the current value of the net assets into its interest in (a) the book value of the net assets and (b) the amount of the under- or overvaluation of the net assets:

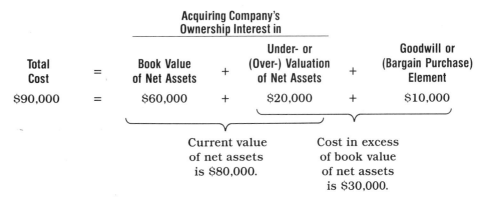

This additional information concerning the amount by which the net assets are under- or overvalued is not necessary in order to record the combination, regardless of whether the combination takes the form of acquiring assets or common stock. When common stock is acquired, however, we must have this additional information to prepare consolidated financial statements. The rest of this chapter deals with recording business combinations and preparing combined and consolidated financial statements as of the date of the business combination. In an economy that has experienced inflation over many years, the net assets of an acquired business are usually undervalued. Accordingly, we will continue under this assumption.

## Acquisition of Assets

When assets are acquired, the procedures to record the business combination and to prepare financial statements reflecting the enlarged, combined operations are not complicated. This is because **the assets acquired and liabilities assumed are recorded directly by the acquiring company in its own general ledger** (or in the general ledger of a newly established division) **at their current values.**

## Acquisition of Common Stock

When common stock is acquired, the procedures used to record the business combination are also relatively simple. However, the procedures to prepare financial statements reflecting the enlarged, combined operations *are* somewhat involved, because **the acquired subsidiary continues to account for its assets and liabilities using its recorded book values.** Stated differently, the parent does not directly record the assets and liabilities of the acquired business in its own general ledger. The only account in which the parent records the cost of the acquired business is called Investment in Subsidiary. As a result, the parent must deal with the **amount of the under- or overvaluation in preparing financial statements that reflect the enlarged, combined operations.**

# THE ACQUISITION OF ASSETS

The acquisition of assets is merely the purchase of the target company's assets. Part of the purchase price takes the form of assuming responsibility for the target company's existing liabilities. Before the acquiring company can record the acquisition of assets, it must determine whether the operations of the acquired business will be accounted for on a centralized or a decentralized basis. This decision is based on what is most practical and economical.

## Centralized Accounting

Under a centralized accounting system, the acquiring company records the assets acquired and liabilities assumed at their current values directly in the general ledger maintained at its own headquarters. Thus the combined businesses are accounted for entirely in one general ledger, eliminating the need to combine financial statements produced from multiple general ledgers (as is necessary in decentralized accounting). In practice, centralized accounting is used infrequently.

## Decentralized Accounting

Under a decentralized accounting system, the individual assets acquired and liabilities assumed are recorded at their current values in a new general ledger maintained at the location of the acquired business. This location is usually referred to as a *division* of the acquiring company. The acquiring company, referred to as the *home office,* charges the cost of the acquired business to an account called Investment in Division.

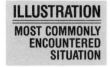

## Acquisition of Assets Where:

- Assets Are Undervalued
- Goodwill Exists

To illustrate recording the acqusition and preparing combined financial statements as of the acquisition date, we assume in this basic example that the net assets of the acquired business are undervalued and the purchase price includes an amount for goodwill (the most commonly encountered situation).

Assume that P Company acquired all of S Company's assets on January 1, 19X1, by assuming responsibility for all of its liabilities and paying $90,000 cash. The balance sheets for each company as of January 1, 19X1—immediately prior to the business combination—are as follows:

|  | P Company | S Company |
|---|---|---|
| **Assets** | | |
| Cash | $108,000 | $ 15,000 |
| Accounts receivable, net | 52,000 | 23,000 |
| Inventory | 100,000 | 32,000 |
| Land | 220,000 | 30,000 |
| Buildings and equipment | 500,000 | 200,000 |
| Accumulated depreciation | (280,000) | (50,000) |
|  | $700,000 | $250,000 |
| **Liabilities and Stockholders' Equity** | | |
| Liabilities | $300,000 | $190,000 |
| Common stock | 300,000 | 40,000 |
| Retained earnings | 100,000 | 20,000 |
|  | $700,000 | $250,000 |

Additional assumed information follows:

| | |
|---|---|
| 1. Total cost | $90,000 |
| 2. Current value of net assets | $80,000 |
| 3. Book value of net assets | $60,000 |

4. The current values of S Company's assets and liabilities are assumed to equal their book values, except for the following assets:

| | Book Value | Current Value | Current Value over Book Value |
|---|---|---|---|
| Inventory | $ 32,000 | $ 34,000 | $ 2,000 |
| Land | 30,000 | 42,000 | 12,000 |
| Buildings and equipment | 150,000[a] | 156,000 | 6,000[b] |
| | | | $20,000 |

[a]Net of $50,000 accumulated depreciation.

[b]For simplicity, we have combined buildings and equipment. (Also for simplicity, we will later assume that the entire $6,000 pertains to equipment.)

Accordingly, $20,000 of the cost in excess of the book value of the net assets is attributable to these assets. The remaining $10,000 of cost in excess of the book value of the net assets represents goodwill.

**Centralized Accounting.**    The entries to record the combination using centralized accounting follow:

| | | |
|---|---|---|
| Accounts Receivable | 23,000 | |
| Inventory | 34,000 | |
| Land | 42,000 | |
| Buildings and Equipment | 156,000 | |
| Goodwill | 10,000 | |
| Liabilities | | 190,000 |
| Cash ($90,000 − $15,000) | | 75,000 |

**Decentralized Accounting.**    The entries to record the combination using decentralized accounting follow:

### Home Office's Books

| | | |
|---|---|---|
| Investment in Division S | 90,000 | |
| Cash | | 90,000 |

### Division's Books

| | | |
|---|---|---|
| Cash | 15,000 | |
| Accounts Receivable | 23,000 | |
| Inventory | 34,000 | |
| Land | 42,000 | |
| Buildings and Equipment | 156,000 | |
| Goodwill | 10,000 | |
| Liabilities | | 190,000 |
| Home Office Equity | | 90,000 |

**Review Points.** Note the following for these entries:

1. Each asset and liability is recorded at its current value.
2. The accumulated depreciation accounts relating to the fixed assets recorded on S Company's books do not carry over to the acquiring company. The current values of these assets are the new cost basis for P Company.
3. After S Company records the receipt of the cash and the sale of its assets, its sole asset is $90,000 cash, which most likely will be distributed to its stockholders. S Company will then end its legal existence.

**Combined Financial Statements.** For financial reporting purposes, the financial statements of the home office and the division must be combined. This is done outside the general ledger on a worksheet. An entry is made on the worksheet to eliminate the Investment in Division and Home Office Equity accounts (the two accounts that were created to enable decentralized accounting to be done on a double-entry bookkeeping basis). All worksheet entries are so labeled and shown in shading to differentiate them from general ledger entries. The elimination entry to combine the two balance sheets as of the acquisition date is as follows:

| | | |
|---|---|---|
| Home Office Equity........................... | 90,000 | |
|     Investment in Division S ................. | | 90,000 |

Illustration 3-3 shows a combining statement worksheet, which combines the balance sheets of the home office and the newly established division as of the acquisition date.

# THE ACQUISITION OF COMMON STOCK (WHOLLY OWNED SUBSIDIARY)

When common stock is acquired, the acquiring company charges its total cost to an account called Investment in Subsidiary. Assuming that the value of the consideration given by the acquiring company (hereafter referred to as the parent company) is $85,000 and direct costs incurred are $5,000 (that may be properly added to the cost of the acquisition), the entry to record the acquisition would be as follows, assuming that $85,000 cash is the consideration given:

| | | |
|---|---|---|
| Investment in Subsidiary...................... | 90,000 | |
|     Cash ....................................... | | 90,000 |

The following entry assumes that 1,000 shares of $1 par value common stock (having a market value of $85,000) is the consideration given:

# ■ ILLUSTRATION 3-3
## The Acquisition of Assets Where Assets Are Undervalued and Goodwill Exists

**P COMPANY**
**Combining Statement Worksheet**
**As of January 1, 19X1**

| | Home Office | S Division | Eliminations Dr. | Eliminations Cr. | Combined |
|---|---|---|---|---|---|
| **Balance Sheet** | | | | | |
| Cash............................. | 18,000 | 15,000 | | | 33,000 |
| Accounts receivable, net.......... | 52,000 | 23,000 | | | 75,000 |
| Inventory ....................... | 100,000 | 34,000 | | | 134,000 |
| Investment in Division S......... | 90,000 | | | 90,000(1) | –0– |
| Land............................ | 220,000 | 42,000 | | | 262,000 |
| Buildings and equipment ........ | 500,000 | 156,000 | | | 656,000 |
| Accumulated depreciation........ | (280,000) | –0– | | | (280,000) |
| Goodwill........................ | | 10,000 | | | 10,000 |
| | 700,000 | 280,000 | | 90,000 | 890,000 |
| Liabilities....................... | 300,000 | 190,000 | | | 490,000 |
| Home office equity............... | | 90,000 | 90,000(1) | | –0– |
| Common stock.................... | 300,000 | | | | 300,000 |
| Retained earnings ............... | 100,000 | | | | 100,000 |
| | 700,000 | 280,000 | 90,000 | | 890,000 |

Proof of debit and credit postings........................... 90,000   90,000

Explanation of entry:
(1) The elimination entry.

| | | | |
|---|---|---|---|
| Investment in Subsidiary...................... | 90,000 | | |
| Common Stock ......................... | | 1,000 | |
| Additional Paid-in Capital.............. | | 84,000 | |
| Cash..................................... | | 5,000 | |

Note that if the common stock issued is registered with the Securities and Exchange Commission (SEC), the following additional entry would be made for the additional direct costs incurred to register the common stock:

| | | |
|---|---|---|
| Additional Paid-in Capital..................... | xxx | |
| Cash..................................... | | xxx |

For reporting to the parent's stockholders, it is nearly always necessary to combine the financial statements of the parent and the subsidiary, a process called **consolidation.** This is essentially the same as combining the financial statements of a home office and a division. However, because the subsidiary retains its status as a separate legal entity (thus retaining ownership of its assets and responsibilities for its liabilities), there are several conceptual issues for subsidiaries that do not exist for divisions. Before discussing the preparation of consolidated financial statements, we focus on these issues and on professional pronouncements that cover when a subsidiary must be consolidated.

## CONSOLIDATED FINANCIAL STATEMENTS: CONCEPTUAL ISSUES AND PROFESSIONAL PRONOUNCEMENTS

### Conceptual Issues

The following conceptual issues exist when a parent–subsidiary relationship is formed:

1. **Appropriateness of consolidating.** Is it appropriate to present consolidated financial statements in view of the fact that each company is a separate legal entity? (The alternative is to present the separate company financial statements of the parent and the subsidiary.)
2. **Minimum ownership level and conditions.** What level of ownership or other conditions must be met to permit consolidation?
3. **Appropriateness of consolidating a subsidiary in a different line of business.** Would consolidated financial statements be understandable and meaningful if the subsidiary is in an entirely different industry than the parent, thereby having a radically different (a) asset composition, (b) debt–equity structure, and (c) income statement format? Imagine consolidated financial statements for a parent having several manufacturing subsidiaries, one finance subsidiary, one insurance subsidiary, and one savings and loan subsidiary. The ability of financial statement users to analyze such a company's conditions, trends, and ratios—and, therefore, to predict the company's finance performance—would be greatly limited.
4. **Appropriateness of consolidating foreign subsidiaries.** Should subsidiaries located in foreign countries be consolidated even though they are exposed to several unique risks not faced by domestic companies? Such risks include (a) the seizure or confiscation of assets following political upheaval and (b) currency exchange restrictions (the subsidiary's inability to pay dividends to the parent).
5. **Potentially misleading inferences.** Does it make sense to show one combined amount for cash when restrictions exist on the transferability of cash within the consolidated group? (Most states have laws preventing or limiting a subsidiary's making loans to the parent or other subsidiaries.) Would the bondholders of the parent be misled

into thinking all of the cash is available for liquidation of the bond indebtedness? Similarly, the consolidated retained earnings amount is not fully available for dividends to the extent subsidiaries have not remitted all of their postcombination earnings to the parent.

6. **Manner of revaluing the assets and liabilities of a subsidiary acquired in a purchase transaction.** An internal issue, concerning solely the mechanics of preparing consolidated statements, is whether the assets and liabilities of a subsidiary acquired in a purchase transaction should be revalued to their current values in (a) the subsidiary's general ledger, or (b) the consolidation process (on the consolidating statement worksheet).

7. **Manner of presenting subsidiary's separate financial statements.** If a subsidiary that was acquired in a purchase transaction issues separate financial statements (perhaps because of a loan agreement requirement), on what basis should its assets and liabilities be reported—the subsidiary's historical cost or current values based on the parent's cost?

## Requirements of Professional Pronouncements

The preceding issues are dealt with in the professional pronouncements discussed in the remainder of this section.

**The Purpose of Consolidated Statements.**   The purpose of consolidated financial statements is best expressed in *ARB No. 51:*

> The purpose of consolidated statements is to present, primarily for the benefit of the shareholders and creditors of the parent company, the results of operations and the financial position of a parent company and its subsidiaries essentially as if the group were a single company with one or more branches or divisions. There is a presumption that consolidated statements are more meaningful than separate statements and that they are usually necessary for a fair presentation when one of the companies in the group directly or indirectly has a controlling financial interest in the other companies.[1]

**The Conditions for Consolidation.**   The decision whether or not a subsidiary should be consolidated is governed by the policy set forth in *FASB Statement No. 94*, "Consolidation of All Majority-owned Subsidiaries" (an amendment of *ARB No. 51*), which states:

> The usual condition for a controlling financial interest is ownership of a majority voting interest, and therefore, as a general rule ownership by

---

[1]*Accounting Research Bulletin No. 51*, "Consolidated Financial Statements" (New York: American Institute of Certified Public Accountants, 1959), par. 1.

one company, directly or indirectly, of over fifty percent of the outstanding voting shares of another company is a condition pointing toward consolidation. However, there are exceptions to this general rule. A majority-owned subsidiary shall not be consolidated if control is likely to be temporary or if it does not rest with the majority owners (as, for instance, if the subsidiary is in legal reorganization or in bankruptcy or operates under foreign exchange restrictions, controls, or other governmentally imposed uncertainties so severe that they cast significant doubt on the parent's ability to control the subsidiary).[2]

Thus, consolidation of subsidiaries is the general rule, not the exception. **The only exception allowed is when the parent does not control the subsidiary;** that is, it cannot freely transfer or do what it pleases with the subsidiary's assets. One of the effects of the above policy is to make **consolidated statements the general-purpose financial statements of companies having one or more majority-owned subsidiaries** (this is clearly stated in *FASB Statement No. 94*).

The accounting to be followed for unconsolidated subsidiaries is discussed in Chapter 4.

**Elimination of the Nonhomogeneity Exception.** The purpose of issuing *FASB Statement No. 94* was to eliminate the practice allowed under *ARB No. 51* of not consolidating a subsidiary in a different line of business (commonly referred to as the *nonhomogeneity exception*). Since the issuance of *ARB No. 51* in 1959, businesses have become more diverse and complex. For example, many companies previously considered nonfinancial in the scope of their operations have diversified into financial services (financing, insurance, leasing, investment banking, and real estate). The liabilities carried by unconsolidated financial subsidiaries had become enormous, contributing greatly to the growing off-balance-sheet financing controversy. Practice had become quite diverse. Some companies would consolidate such subsidiaries; others would not. The requirement to consolidate these subsidiaries has drastically changed the reported assets and liabilities of many companies. For example, Ford Motor Co. reported $45 billion in assets and $27 billion in liabilities for 1987. For 1988, under the new rules, it reported $143 billion in assets and $122 billion in liabilities; its debt—equity ratio went from 1.43:1 to 5.65:1.

**The Rules of the Securities and Exchange Commission.** The consolidation rules of the Securities and Exchange Commission (SEC), which apply only to publicly owned companies, are slightly broader than the policy in the amended *ARB No. 51*. The reason for this is that the SEC discovered

---

[2]*Statement of Financial Accounting Standards No. 94*, "Consolidation of All Majority-owned Subsidiaries" (Stamford: Financial Accounting Standards Board, 1987), par. 13.

the emerging practice of companies forming "nonsubsidiary subsidiaries." Such entities were formed to perform marketing or research and development. The entities were controlled not by majority voting interest, which would require consolidation, but through loan agreements and stock-option purchase agreements. The purpose was to exclude the operating expenses of these entities from the consolidated income statement of the parent. To end this emerging practice, the SEC broadened its consolidation rules to require the following:

1. Ownership of a majority voting interest should not be the sole way of determining whether control of an entity exists.
2. Facts and circumstances of the relationship between entities should be carefully analyzed when majority voting interest does not exist.
3. **Substance versus form** should be evaluated in deciding if consolidated financial statements are appropriate.

Therefore, an entity that is less than majority owned may be deemed to be a subsidiary for which consolidation is appropriate. (The FASB is currently addressing this issue as part of its project involving a reexamination of all remaining consolidation issues.)

**A Subsidiary Having a Different Year-end.**   The subsidiary's fiscal year-end should be within three months of the parent's year-end. If not, the subsidiary (or possibly even the parent) must change its fiscal year-end.

**Disclosure of Consolidation Policy.**   The parent must disclose its consolidation policy. A typical example of such disclosure in a note to the financial statements is as follows:

> The consolidated financial statements include the accounts of the company and its domestic and foreign subsidiaries. Significant intercompany accounts and transactions have been eliminated.

**Required Segment Reporting.**   Consolidated financial statements have limited usefulness in assessing the future prospects of companies with significant diversified operations in more than one industry or significant foreign operations. In recognition of this fact, *FASB Statement No. 14,* "Financial Reporting for Segments of a Business Enterprise," was issued in 1976. It requires specified information on industry segments and foreign operations to be presented as supplementary information to the consolidated financial statements. This pronouncement, which is discussed at length in Chapter 13, imposes extensive reporting requirements on companies with diversified or foreign operations.

**Push-down Accounting.**   In 1983, the staff of the SEC issued *Staff Accounting Bulletin No. 54.* This bulletin requires that **when a subsidiary acquired**

**in purchase transaction issues separate financial statements, such statements shall reflect the new basis of accounting.** In other words, the assets and liabilities must be revalued to their current values. Thus the new basis of accounting is "pushed down" to the subsidiary. **This pronouncement applies only to publicly owned companies.** The manner of implementing push-down accounting is examined in the appendix to this chapter.

## CONSOLIDATED FINANCIAL STATEMENTS: PREPARATION AS OF THE ACQUISITION DATE

### The Consolidating Statement Worksheet

Unless the business combination occurs on the last day of the parent's reporting year (which rarely happens), there is no need to prepare consolidated financial statements as of the acquisition date. They are illustrated in the worksheets in this chapter for instructional purposes only.

The balance sheet is the only financial statement of the subsidiary that can be consolidated with the parent's financial statement as of the acquisition date. This follows from a fundamental concept of the purchase method: **the parent company can report to its stockholders only the operations of the subsidiary that occur subsequent to the acquisition date.** (Combining the future income statements of a parent and a subsidiary is discussed in Chapter 4.)

The consolidation worksheets are much more important than other types of working papers. They are just as much part of the books and records of the company as the general ledgers are—especially since consolidated statements are the general-purpose financial statements of companies having one or more majority-owned subsidiaries.

### The Primary Elimination Entry

The consolidation is prepared by posting a *primary elimination entry* to the consolidating statement worksheet. The entry eliminates the Investment in Subsidiary account and the subsidiary's capital accounts, thus affecting accounts in both the parent column and the subsidiary column. The purpose of the entry is to substitute the asset and liability accounts of the subsidiary for the Investment in Subsidiary account. This substitution prevents double counting the subsidiary's net assets in arriving at the consolidated amounts. **The entry is posted only to the worksheet, not to any general ledger accounts.** (We call this entry the primary elimination entry for instructional and reference purposes only. In later chapters, other types of eliminations are encountered in preparing consolidated financial statements.)

## The Non-push-down Basis of Accounting: The Subsidiary Retains the Historical Cost Basis of Its Assets and Liabilities

The **non-push-down basis of accounting** holds that the subsidiary cannot revalue its assets and liabilities to their current values merely because its outstanding common stock has changed hands and has become concentrated in the hands of significantly fewer or even a single stockholder.

The obvious question, then, is this: How are the subsidiary's assets and liabilities revalued to their current values as required under the purchase method of accounting? The answer requires an understanding of the major conceptual elements of the parent's total cost of the investment as reflected in its Investment in Subsidiary account.

## The Major Conceptual Elements of Total Investment Cost

The total cost of the investment as recorded on the parent's books must be separated into its major conceptual elements. We do this by analyzing the relationship among the total cost, the current value of the subsidiary's net assets, and the book value of the subsidiary's net assets as shown earlier in the chapter. For clarity, we repeat the information and data as in the discussion on pages 105–106 involving the acquisition of assets, except we assume that common stock was acquired instead of assets. All of the assumed information is as follows:

1. P Company acquired all of S Company's outstanding common stock on January 1, 19X1, by paying $90,000 cash.
2. Total cost . . . . . . . . . . . . . . . . . . . . . . . . . . . . . . . . . . . . . . . . . . . .    $90,000
3. Current value of net assets . . . . . . . . . . . . . . . . . . . . . . . . . . . .    $80,000
4. Book value of net assets . . . . . . . . . . . . . . . . . . . . . . . . . . . . . .    $60,000
5. The current values of S Company's assets and liabilities are assumed to equal their book values, except for the following assets:

|  | Book Value | Current Value | Current Value over Book Value |
|---|---|---|---|
| Inventory. . . . . . . . . . . . . . . . . . . . . . . . | $ 32,000 | $ 34,000 | $ 2,000 |
| Land . . . . . . . . . . . . . . . . . . . . . . . . . . . . | 30,000 | 42,000 | 12,000 |
| Buildings and equipment. . . . . . . . | 150,000[a] | 156,000 | 6,000 |
|  |  |  | $20,000 |

[a]Net of $50,000 accumulated depreciation.

Accordingly, $20,000 of the cost in excess of the book value of the net assets is attributable to these assets. The remaining $10,000 of cost in excess of the book value represents goodwill.

Thus, the total cost of the investment may be considered to comprise three major elements:

1. **The book value element.** The parent's ownership interest in the subsidiary's recorded net assets at their book value (100% of $60,000) . . . . . . . . . . . . . . . . . . . . . . . . . . . . . . . . . . . . . . . . . $60,000
2. **The current value over book value element.** The parent's ownership interest in the subsidiary's excess of the current value of its net assets over their book value (100% of $20,000) . . . . . . . . . . . . . . . . . . . . . . . . . . . . . . . . . . . . . . . . . . . 20,000
3. **The goodwill element.** The parent's total cost in excess of the current value of the subsidiary's net assets ($90,000 − $80,000) . . . . . . . . . . . . . . . . . . . . . . . . . . . . . . . . . . . . . . . . . . . . . . . . 10,000

Total cost of the investment . . . . . . . . . . . . . . . . . . . . . . . . . . . . $90,000

The $20,000 difference between the current value of the subsidiary's net assets and their book value is included in the parent's investment account. When the subsidiary's financial statements are consolidated with its parent's financial statements, this $20,000 difference is reclassified from the investment account to the specific assets with which it has been identified. (In this situation, $2,000 is identified with undervalued inventories, $12,000 is identified with undervalued land, $6,000 is identified with undervalued equipment.) The parent accounts for the individual items that make up this difference in the same manner that the subsidiary accounts for the specific assets that are undervalued. Specifically, the following occurs:

1. The subsidiary continues to depreciate its assets at their historical cost as though the business combination had never occurred.
2. The parent amortizes to its future income that portion of its cost in excess of book value that is attributable to depreciable or amortizable assets (in this example, $2,000 pertaining to the inventory and $6,000 pertaining to the equipment). The $2,000 amount relating to inventory is amortized to income as the subsidiary sells its inventory. The $6,000 amount relating to the equipment is amortized to income using the same remaining life that the subsidiary uses to depreciate its historical cost.
3. The parent also amortizes that portion of its investment account that represents goodwill ($10,000 in this example).

In other words, depreciation and amortization of the subsidiary's assets take place on two sets of books instead of just one set, as when assets are acquired. These amortization procedures on the books of the parent company are necessary to charge the combined operations with the current value of the assets acquired, because the assets were not revalued on the subsidiary's books. In substance, the net effect on the enlarged business as a whole is the same as though the subsidiary had revalued its assets to their current values (push-down accounting).

ILLUSTRATION

## Separating the Total Cost of the Investment into its Major Conceptual Elements

Separating the total cost of the investment into its major conceptual elements is possible for all common stock investments, regardless of the price paid by the parent, the current value of the net assets, or the book value of the net assets. Many possible combinations of relationship between these three items can be shown. To show how the total cost is separated into its major conceptual elements for various possible combinations of date, four such combinations are shown in Illustration 3-4.

**Review Points for Illustration 3-4.** Note the following:

1. In situation A, only one major conceptual element exists because total cost equals current value and current value equals book value.
2. In situation B, all three major conceptual elements exist. If the total cost of the investment had been $10,000 less, no goodwill element and only two major conceptual elements would have existed.
3. In situation C, all three major conceptual elements exist, but the parent has a negative balance instead of a positive balance for its current value under book value element. This negative balance is identified with depreciable assets and is amortized in future periods to the parent's income statement, as are the positive balances in situations B and D, which are identified with depreciable assets.

## ■ ILLUSTRATION 3-4
### The Major Conceptual Elements of the Total Cost of the Investment

| | Net Assets of Subsidiary | | Current Value over (under) Book Value | | Separation of Total Cost into Its Major Conceptual Elements | | |
| | Current Value (1) | Book Value (2) | (3) | Total Cost = (4) | Book Value Element + (5) | Current Value over (under) Book Value Element + (6) | Goodwill (Bargain Purchase) Element (7) |
|---|---|---|---|---|---|---|---|
| Situation | (Given) | (Given) | (1) – (2) | (Given) | (2) | (3) | (Residual) |
| A | $60,000 | $60,000 | | $60,000 = $60,000 | | | |
| B | 80,000 | 60,000 | $20,000 | 90,000 = 60,000 | + $20,000 | + $10,000 | |
| C | 50,000 | 60,000 | (10,000) | 55,000 = 60,000 | (10,000) | 5,000 | |
| D | 80,000 | 60,000 | 20,000 | 75,000 = 60,000 | + 20,000 | + (5,000)[a] | |

[a]This bargain purchase element must be allocated to the extent possible to noncurrent assets other than long-term investments. If all of it is allocated thus, then the amounts in the column to the left decrease by $5,000, and no deferred credit remains. (See Illustration 3-5, in which all of it is allocated to the appropriate noncurrent assets.)

## Displaying the Major Conceptual Elements by Their Components

The analysis of the parent's total cost by its major conceptual elements can be expanded so that the *components* of book value and of the current value over book value are displayed. This expanded analysis can be used as the source of an elimination entry that consolidates the financial statements of the parent with those of the subsidiary. The preparation of consolidated financial statements has always been an involved process. However, the use of this expanded analysis of the total cost of the investment, which displays the components of the major conceptual elements, substantially simplifies the consolidation procedures. The procedures for expanding the analysis are explained below using situation B of Illustration 3-4, in which total cost is above current value and current value is above book value.

**Separating the Book Value Element.**   The book value element is easily separated into its components by multiplying the parent's ownership interest by the balance in each of the subsidiary's individual capital accounts—Common Stock, Additional Paid-in Capital, and Retained Earnings—as of the acquisition date. The capital accounts of S Company as of the acquisition date are as follows:

| | |
|---|---:|
| Common stock | $40,000 |
| Retained earnings | 20,000 |
| Total stockholders' equity | $60,000 |

Because we assume P Company acquires 100% of S Company's outstanding common stock, the $60,000 book value element comprises these two components.

**Separating the Current Value over (under) the Book Value Element.**   As stated previously, the parent accounts for the components of the current value over (under) book value element—not for the total difference as a lump sum. Thus, the current value over (under) book value element can be thought of as comprising the following three components:

| | |
|---|---:|
| Inventory | $ 2,000 |
| Land | 12,000 |
| Equipment | 6,000 |
| Total current value over book value | $20,000 |

**The Goodwill Element and the Bargain Purchase Element.**   No separation is needed for goodwill, which is a residual amount accounted for as a lump sum. When a bargain purchase element exists, the initial credit must be allocated as much as possible to noncurrent assets other than long-term investments in marketable securities. Any remaining bargain purchase element is amortized to income in future periods.

**Recapping the Conceptual Elements.**  The analysis of the total investment cost in situation B of Illustration 3-4 is shown below by the major conceptual elements and their components:

|  | Analysis of Total Investment Cost | |
|---|---|---|
|  | By the Major Conceptual Elements | By the Components of the Major Conceptual Elements |
| Book value element: | | |
|     Common stock . . . . . . . . . . . |  | $40,000 |
|     Retained earnings . . . . . . . . |  | 20,000 |
|         Total . . . . . . . . . . . . . . . . . | $60,000 | $60,000 |
| Current value over book value element: | | |
|     Inventory . . . . . . . . . . . . . . . . . |  | $ 2,000 |
|     Land . . . . . . . . . . . . . . . . . . . . |  | 12,000 |
|     Equipment . . . . . . . . . . . . . . |  | 6,000 |
|         Total . . . . . . . . . . . . . . . . . | 20,000 | $20,000 |
| Goodwill element . . . . . . . . . . . . | 10,000 | $10,000 |
|         Total cost . . . . . . . . . . . . . . | $90,000 | $90,000 |

Illustration 3-5 displays the major conceptual elements for the situations in Illustration 3-4 by their components.

## ■ ILLUSTRATION 3-5
### The Major Conceptual Elements and Their Components

| Situation from Illustration 3-4 | Total Cost = | Book Value Element | | + | Current Value over (under) Book Value Element | | | + | Goodwill (Bargain Purchase) Element |
|---|---|---|---|---|---|---|---|---|---|
|  |  | Common Stock + | Retained Earnings | + Inventory + | Land | + Equipment + | | | |
| A | $60,000 = | $40,000 + | $20,000 | | | | | | |
| B | 90,000 = | 40,000 + | 20,000 | + $2,000 + | $12,000 + | $ 6,000 + | | | $10,000 |
| C | 55,000 = | 40,000 + | 20,000 | | + | (10,000) + | | | 5,000 |
| D | $75,000 = | $40,000 + | $20,000 | + $2,000 + | $12,000 + | $ 6,000 + | | | $ (5,000) |
|  |  |  |  | | (1,000)[a] | (4,000)[a] | | | 5,000[a] |
|  | $75,000 | $40,000 | $20,000 | $2,000 | $11,000 | $ 2,000 | | | $ –0– |

[a]This allocation is the same as that illustrated on page 102.

**Review Points for Illustration 3-5.**   Note the following:

1. In situation A, in which only the book value element exists, the parent has completed accounting for its investment under the purchase method of accounting. No additional accounting procedures are necessary because no other major conceptual elements exist.
2. In situations B and D, in which the current value of the net assets exceeds their book value and the parent pays more than the book value of the net assets, the amount applicable to the equipment is amortized to the parent's future income over the remaining life of these assets, using the same remaining life that the subsidiary uses to depreciate these items. The amount determined for inventory is amortized in the following year, assuming the subsidiary sells its inventory. The amount determined for the land is not amortized because land is never depreciated. When the land is ever sold, the amount determined for land is charged to income at that time. In summary, the parent accounts for each individual component in a manner consistent with the way the subsidiary accounts for its historical cost. Goodwill is amortized over its expected life, up to 40 years.
3. In situation C, in which the current value of the net assets is below their book value, the parent has credit amounts instead of debit amounts to amortize to its subsequent income statements. Otherwise, the procedures are the same as in point 2 above. The amortization partially offsets the depreciation expense recorded on the subsidiary's books from the viewpoint of combined operations.
4. The expanded analysis of the investment account is maintained in a supporting schedule to the Investment in Subsidiary general ledger account.

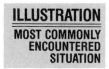
**ILLUSTRATION**
MOST COMMONLY
ENCOUNTERED
SITUATION

## Acquisition of Common Stock Where:
- Assets Are Undervalued
- Goodwill Exists

Using the information from situation B in Illustration 3-5 (in which the net assets are undervalued and goodwill exists), the following primary elimination entry as of the acquisition date is obtained directly from the expanded analysis of the total investment cost:

WORKSHEET
ENTRY ONLY

| | | |
|---|---|---|
| Common Stock | 40,000 | |
| Retained Earnings | 20,000 | |
| Inventory | 2,000 | |
| Land | 12,000 | |
| Equipment | 6,000 | |
| Goodwill | 10,000 | |
| Investment in Subsidiary | | 90,000 |

Illustration 3-6 shows the preparation of the consolidating statement worksheet as of the acquisition date using the above primary elimination entry. In addition, the following accumulated depreciation entry is needed to recognize that a new cost basis has been established for the subsidiary's fixed assets for consolidated reporting purposes:

**WORKSHEET ENTRY ONLY**

| | | |
|---|---|---|
| Accumulated Depreciation | 50,000 | |
| Buildings and Equipment | | 50,000 |

**Review Points for Illustration 3-6.** Note the following:

1. The parent's investment cost in excess of the book value of the subsidiary's net assets becomes clear in the consolidation process. The

## ■ ILLUSTRATION 3-6
### The Acquisition of Common Stock (Non-push-down Accounting Used by Subsidiary)

**P COMPANY AND SUBSIDIARY (S COMPANY)**
**Consolidating Statement Worksheet**
**As of January 1, 19X1**

| | P Company | S Company | Eliminations Dr. | Eliminations Cr. | Consolidated |
|---|---|---|---|---|---|
| **Balance Sheet** | | | | | |
| Cash | 18,000 | 15,000 | | | 33,000 |
| Accounts receivable, net | 52,000 | 23,000 | | | 75,000 |
| Inventory | 100,000 | 32,000 | 2,000(1) | | 134,000 |
| Investment in S Company | 90,000 | | | 90,000(1) | –0– |
| Land | 220,000 | 30,000 | 12,000(1) | | 262,000 |
| Buildings and equipment | 500,000 | 200,000 | 6,000(1) | 50,000(2) | 656,000 |
| Accumulated depreciation | (280,000) | (50,000) | 50,000(2) | | (280,000) |
| Goodwill | | | 10,000(1) | | 10,000 |
| | 700,000 | 250,000 | 80,000 | 140,000 | 890,000 |
| Liabilities | 300,000 | 190,000 | | | 490,000 |
| P Company: | | | | | |
| Common stock | 300,000 | | | | 300,000 |
| Retained earnings | 100,000 | | | | 100,000 |
| S Company: | | | | | |
| Common stock | | 40,000 | 40,000(1) | | –0– |
| Retained earnings | | 20,000 | 20,000(1) | | –0– |
| | 700,000 | 250,000 | 60,000 | | 890,000 |
| Proof of debit and credit postings | | | 140,000 | 140,000 | |

Explanation of entries:
(1) The primary elimination entry.
(2) The accumulated depreciation elimination entry.

excess is effectively reclassified to the balance sheet accounts with which it has been identified.

2. The amounts in the consolidated column are composed of (a) the parent's items based on book values, and (b) the subsidiary's items based on the current value of those items as of the acquisition date.
3. The amounts shown in the consolidated column are the same as those in the combined column of Illustration 3-3—in which assets were acquired.
4. The Investment in Subsidiary account and the subsidiary's equity accounts are eliminated in consolidation and have a zero balance in the consolidated column.

## Preparing Consolidating Statement Worksheets in All Other Situations

The procedures for preparing consolidated financial statements in all situations are identical to those shown in the preceding illustration. The primary elimination entry is always derived from the expanded analysis of the investment account. In some cases, assets may be overvalued as of the acquisition date. Accordingly, they are written down in the consolidation process to their current values. Such is the case for situation C in Illustration 3-5, in which equipment is overvalued by $10,000. The primary elimination entry would be as follows:

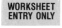

| | | |
|---|---:|---:|
| Common Stock | 40,000 | |
| Retained Earnings | 20,000 | |
| Goodwill | 5,000 | |
| Equipment | | 10,000 |
| Investment in Subsidiary | | 55,000 |

The preparation of consolidated financial statements for this situation is not shown, because the procedures are the same as for situations in which the current value is above the book value of the net assets.

## Over- or Undervalued Liabilities

For simplicity, the previous discussions and illustrations dealt only with certain over- and undervalued assets. The current values of accounts payable and accrued liabilities (using present value procedures) are usually so close to their book values—because of the relatively short period until payment of the obligation—that the difference is often ignored in the interest of practicality. The current value of borrowings that have a floating interest rate always equals the book value. If the borrowings have a fixed interest rate that is different from the interest rate existing at the acquisition date, however, the present value of the debt does not equal its book value. Thus, the difference must be reflected as one of the components of the current value over (under) book value element in the conceptual analysis of the Investment in Subsidiary account. (For liabilities, however, the description "current value over (under) book value element" is changed so that the description becomes "current value under (over) book value element.") For example, assume that a subsidiary has 8% bonds payable outstanding at the acquisition date. If the current interest rate is 12%, the present value of the debt is below the book value. (The low fixed interest rate of 8% in relation to the current interest rate of 12% means that the debt appears larger than it really is.)

### Reporting the Debt at Its Present Value.

To illustrate, assume that on the acquisition date of January 1, 19X1, the subsidiary has 8% bonds outstanding having a face amount of $100,000 and a maturity date of December 31, 19X2 (two years from now). If the current interest rate is 12%, the present value of the bonds would be calculated as follows:

Present value of $100,000 principal payment due
December 31, 19X2 ($100,000 × 0.79719) . . . . . . . . . . . . . . . . . $79,719
Present value of two $8,000 interest payments due
at the end of 19X1 and 19X2 ($8,000 × 1.69005) . . . . . . . . . .   13,520
Total . . . . . . . . . . . . . . . . . . . . . . . . . . . . . . $93,239

Accordingly, the $6,761 difference between the book value of the bonds ($100,000) and their present value ($93,239) would be reflected as an individual component of the current value under (over) book value element. If consolidated financial statements were prepared as of the acquisition date, the bonds would be reported in the consolidated column at their present value of $93,239 because the $6,761 amount would be debited to the Bonds Payable account in consolidation:

| | P Company | S Company | Eliminations Dr. | Cr. | Consolidated |
|---|---|---|---|---|---|
| Bonds payable | | 100,000 | 6,761 | | 93,239 |

### Subsequent Treatment of the Difference.

The $6,761 amount is analogous to a discount and would be amortized to interest expense over the next two years using the interest method of amortization. Over the next two years, interest expense would be reported at 12% of the debt's carrying value (rather than at 8% of the book value of $100,000). For 19X1, interest expense of $11,190 would be reported (12% × $93,239), and the $3,190 difference between the $11,190 and the $8,000 cash payment would be amortized out of the Investment account. At December 31, 19X1, this component of the Investment account would have an unamortized balance of $3,571, which results in a $96,429 carrying value of the debt in consolidation at that date. For 19X2, interest expense of $11,571 would be reported (12% × $96,429), which is made up of the $8,000 cash payment and $3,571 amortized out of the Investment account. In the following chapter, we show in detail how to amortize amounts out of the Investment account.

**"Old Goodwill."**   Sometimes an acquired business has unamortized good-will on its books at the acquisition date. In determining the current value of the net assets, this "old goodwill" is assumed to always have a zero value under the requirements of *APB Opinion No. 16.* In the conceptual analysis of the investment account, old goodwill is treated as an overvalued asset in the current value over (under) book value element. This allows the goodwill the parent was willing to pay for to be properly shown as a single amount for which a single amortization period will be used. Otherwise, goodwill would be considered to comprise two amounts, each with a different life. Assuming old goodwill of $3,000 exists at the acquisition date and new goodwill is calculated to be $10,000, the consolidation worksheet section pertaining to these accounts would appear as follows:

|  | P Company | S Company | Eliminations Dr. | Eliminations Cr. | Consolidated |
|---|---|---|---|---|---|
| Goodwill (old) . . . |  | 3,000 |  | 3,000 (1) | –0– |
| Goodwill (new) . . |  |  | 10,000 (1) |  | 10,000 |

## REQUIRED DISCLOSURES

The acquiring company must make the following disclosures for each period in which a business combination is accounted for under the purchase method:

1. The name and brief description of the acquired business.
2. A statement that the purchase method has been used to record the combination.
3. The period for which the results of operations of the acquired business are included in the acquiring company's income statement. (This period is from the acquisition date to the acquiring entity's reporting year-end.)
4. The cost of the acquired business, including information about the number of shares issued, issuable, and their assigned value.
5. The life and method of amortizing any goodwill.
6. Contingent consideration, if any, and the related proposed accounting treatment.

Here is an example of this basic disclosure for an acquiring company having a calendar year-end:

> On July 1, 19X1, the Pana Company acquired all of the outstanding common stock of Sonic Corporation, a manufacturer of small computers. The acquisition has been accounted for as a purchase; therefore, the results of operations of the acquired business for the period from July 1, 19X1, through December 31, 19X1, are included in the consolidated income statement of the Pana Company. The recorded cost of the acquisition was $5,200,000 (50,000 common shares issued times their then fair market value of $100 per share, plus legal and finders' fees of $200,000). Goodwill of $1,000,000 is being amortized over 40 years using the straight-line method. Additional common shares are issuable (a maximum of 100,000 shares), depending on the cumulative sales level of the acquired business for the three years subsequent to the acquisition date. If and when any of all of these contingent shares are distributable (June 30, 19X4), the current value of the shares issuable will be recorded as an additional cost of the acquired business, which will increase goodwill. As of December 31, 19X1, no additional shares would be issuable based on the sales level of the acquired business for the six months then ended.

## Supplemental Disclosures for Publicly Owned Companies

In addition to basic footnote disclosures, certain supplemental information related to income statements (including revenues, net income and earnings per share, among other items) must be disclosed by publicly owned companies for the following periods:

1. Income statement–related information that would have resulted had the combination occurred at the beginning of the current reporting period.
2. Income statement–related information that would have resulted had the combination occurred at the beginning of the preceding reporting period.

This supplemental disclosure notifies readers of the financial statements that some percentage of the change in revenues and net income is the result of external expansion, not just the result of internal expansion.

Here is an example of a supplemental disclosure that relates to the preceding basic disclosure:

> Results of operations of the Pana Company combined on a pro forma basis with the operating results of Sonic Corporation for the years ended December 31, 19X1, and 19X0, as if the companies had been combined at January 1, 19X0, are as follows (see page 128):

## PERSPECTIVE

## A Capsule History of Accounting for Goodwill

Accounting for goodwill has been studied and debated since about 1880. Through the years, it has evolved from a state of "anything goes" to the restrictive, arbitrary, and uniform accounting requirements of *APB Opinion Nos. 16* and *17*, issued in 1970. No accounting topic has inspired more diversely held views (and fiercely strong ones) than goodwill. Consequently, students must not simply memorize the rules of the current pronouncements; they must also understand how and why we have arrived at the present rules from what was tried in the past and rejected. And as their predecessors have done, they must continually question the logic and practicality of these rules and their current application.

Prior to 1917    The entire cost of an acquisition in excess of book value is treated as goodwill. Accountants favor charging goodwill to stockholders' equity at the acquisition date. There is no support for charging goodwill to income, either through amortization or in a lump sum.

1917    The American Institute of Accountants, the predecessor to the AICPA, "recommends" that goodwill be shown as a reduction to stockholders' equity (if it is not already charged to capital).

1918–1929    Companies begin capitalizing internally generated goodwill. (Amounts range from advertising costs to arbitrary estimates of the value of the goodwill.) Many abuses result.

1930–1944    Recording as goodwill only purchased goodwill becomes the prevalent thinking. Permanent retention of goodwill as an asset and periodically amortizing it to income, retained earnings, or additional paid-in capital become acceptable practice (in addition to immediately charging these to capital). Accounting writers begin advocating the analysis of the cost in excess of book value.

1944    *Accounting Research Bulletin No. 24* is issued. It states that only historical cost should be used to value goodwill. Arbitrary write-ups and capitalization of start-up costs as goodwill is thus banned. The door is left open for companies to capitalize advertising costs as goodwill.

1945    The Securities and Exchange Commission (SEC) begins encouraging companies to amortize goodwill if they have been using the permanent retention treatment.

1953    *Accounting Research Bulletin No. 43* is issued. It prohibits charging goodwill to stockholders' equity immediately after acquisition. The discretionary write-downs of goodwill are banned—a loss of value must take place for a write-down or write-off.

1968    *Accounting Research Study No. 5*, "Accounting for Goodwill" (written by two senior partners of Arthur Andersen and Co.) is issued. The study concludes that goodwill is not an asset

**A Capsule History of Accounting for Goodwill** (continued)

and should be charged to stock-holders' equity at the time of the acquisition.

**1968–1970**    A fierce and heated debate takes place within the accounting profession concerning accounting for business combinations and the related issue of goodwill.

**1970**    *ABP Opinion Nos. 16* and *17* are issued, the first by a vote of 12 to 6 and the second by a vote of 13 to 5. As a result: (1) goodwill can arise only from a business combination; (2) the cost in excess of book value must be analyzed; (3) goodwill existing as of October 31, 1970, need not be amortized to income; (4) goodwill arising after that date must be amortized to income over no more than 40 years; and (5) if goodwill loses its value, it must be written off to income as an extraordinary charge. (The positions of the various opposing factions of the APB are so strongly held that, with a two-thirds majority required for passage, many members cannot talk to one another for three months after the voting. One of the largest CPA firms seriously considers not supporting these pronouncements in its practice but decides to continue to work within the profession to bring about needed changes.)

**1971**    The handling of the business combinations and goodwill issues by the APB (in which strong positions were taken only to be withdrawn because of pressure from client companies) ulti-mately leads to the demise of the APB and the establishment of the FASB in 1973.

**1971–1980**    Goodwill becomes a dead issue.

**1981**    A crisis develops in the savings and loan industry because of high interest rates. Over a thousand savings and loan associations become financially distressed—many actually exhausting their net worths and thus facing bankruptcy—and are forced to merge with stronger savings and loans. Seeking ways to report higher earnings, the acquiring firms take advantage of a quirk in *APB Opinion No. 16* and account for these arranged, regulatory mergers as purchases (rather than as poolings of interests, the usual practice for such mergers). Consequently, billions of dollars of goodwill are reported as being amortized over 30 to 40 years. (The offsetting loan discount is credited to income over 10 to 12 years.)

Undaunted by the peculiarity (some would say absurdity) that companies facing bankruptcy could possibly possess goodwill, auditors of these acquiring companies allow this reporting of artificial income without exception. Form prevails over substance.

**1983**    In response to public criticism of the reporting of artificial income in the savings and loan industry, the FASB amends *APB Opinion No. 17* in *FASB Statement No. 72*, "Accounting for

*(continued)*

Certain Acquisitions of Banking or Thrift Institutions." It requires much shorter lives for goodwill (10 to 12 years)—but only for that portion of goodwill attributable to the acquired financial institution having an excess of liabilities over assets on a fair value basis.

Some savings and loans rush through their mergers to beat the effective date of the pronouncement, which is retroactive only to September 30, 1982. The auditors of these firms give unqualified ("clean") opinions on the financial statements presented under the old rules as well as those presented under the new rules—deeming all the statements to "present fairly."

Analyzing and understanding the financial statements of such savings and loans becomes quite difficult. (Perplexed investors ask their stockbrokers, "What are the 'real' earnings?")

**1983–1985** Scores of companies that went on acquisition binges in the 1970s begin disposing of hundreds of previously acquired companies due to their operating problems and unprofitability. Billions of dollars of unamortized goodwill (most companies were choosing a 40-year life) must be written off.

**1985** The staff of the SEC issues *Staff Accounting Bulletin No. 42A*, which states that the maximum amortization life for goodwill that it will accept for financial institutions is 25 years.

**1985–1986** A congressional committee headed by Rep. John Dingell holds hearings on the conduct of the accounting profession because of the rising number of collapses, corporate failures and abuses, and alleged auditing failures among large financial institutions.

**1986–1987** The accounting profession explores ways to enhance public confidence in itself.

**1989** The savings and loans industry, which reported a $12.1 billion loss for 1988, continues to report approximately $38 billion of goodwill (about 75% of its net worth at book value).

Congress passes the most expensive taxpayer bailout in U.S. history by approving a $306 billion rescue bill for the savings and loan industry. The bill requires savings and loans to maintain "real capital" equal to at least 3% of total assets—with goodwill to be excluded from capital after 1994. (Goodwill may be considered part of capital up to 1.5% until then.) Prior to the bill's passage, the savings and loan industry attempted to have goodwill counted as part of capital to its fullest extent.

Source: A major portion of the capsule history prior to 1970 is based on Research Monograph No. 80, *Goodwill in Accounting: A History of the Issues and Problems,* by Hugh P. Hughes (Atlanta: Georgia State University, 1982).

| | 19X1 | 19X0 |
|---|---|---|
| Revenues. . . . . . . . . . . . . . . . . . . . . . . . . . . . . | $53,500,000 | $26,750,000 |
| Net income . . . . . . . . . . . . . . . . . . . . . . . . . . . | 2,400,000 | 1,400,000 |
| Net income per common and common equivalent share. . . . . . . . . . . . . . . . . . . . . . | $2.47 | $1.27 |

## SELECTED REFERENCES

Holley, Charles L., and Michael C. Chester. "The Push-Down Accounting Controversy." *Management Accounting*, (January 1987), pp. 39–42.

Hughes, Hugh P. *Goodwill in Accounting: A History of the Issues and Problems.* Research Monograph No. 80. Atlanta: Business Publishing Division, College of Business Administration, Georgia State University, 1982.

Key, Stephen L., and Simon S. Straus. "Allocating Purchase Price in an Acquisition: A Practical Guide." *Journal of Accountancy* (November 1987), pp. 32–37.

Sorter, George H. "Accounting for Baseball." *Journal of Accountancy* (June 1986), pp. 126–133.

Thomas, Paula B., and J. Larry Hagler. "Push-Down Accounting: A Descriptive Assessment." *Accounting Horizons* (September 1988), pp. 26–31.

## END-OF-CHAPTER REVIEW

### Summary of Key Points

1. The acquisition of either assets or common stock results in a revaluation of the assets and liabilities of the acquired business to their current values.
2. When assets are acquired, the acquired assets and assumed liabilities are recorded at their current values directly in the books of the acquiring company (which may require the creation of a new general ledger at the division level if decentralized accounting is used).
3. When common stock is acquired, the revaluation to current values is done by making adjustments to the subsidiary's book values in the consolidation process (non-push-down accounting). The alternative is to have the subsidiary adjust its general ledger accounts (push-down accounting).
4. All majority-owned subsidiaries must be consolidated unless control is lacking, in which case they cannot be consolidated.
5. The total cost of an acquisition is the sum of (a) the fair value of the consideration given, (b) any direct costs clearly traceable to the acquisition, and (c) the fair value of any contingent consideration.

### Glossary of New Terms

**Bargain purchase element**   The amount by which the total cost of the investment is below the current value of an acquired business's net assets.

**Consolidation** The process of combining the financial statements of a parent and one or more subsidiaries, so that results of operations and financial position are presented as though the separate companies were a single company with one or more divisions or branches.

**Contingent consideration** Consideration that must be paid if certain future conditions are satisfied.

**Controlling interest** In general, a controlling interest exists when one company owns, either directly or indirectly, more than 50% of the outstanding voting shares of another company. However, in some cases, control may exist even though a majority voting interest does not exist.

**Goodwill** The amount by which the total cost of the investment is above the current value of an acquired business's net assets.

**Non-push-down basis of accounting** The subsidiary retains its historical cost basis in accounting for its assets and liabilities. (Adjustments to current values are made in the consolidation process.)

**Push-down basis of accounting** The subsidiary's assets and liabilities are adjusted to their current values in the general ledger based on the parent's cost.

## Self-Study Questions

*(Answers are at the end of this chapter, preceding the appendix.)*

1. In a business combination accounted for as a purchase, costs of registering equity securities to be issued by the acquiring company are a (an)
   a. Expense of the combined company for the period of which the costs were incurred.
   b. Direct addition to stockholders' equity of the combined company.
   c. Reduction of the otherwise determinable fair value of the securities.
   d. Addition to goodwill.

2. A business combination is accounted for appropriately as a purchase. Which of the following should be deducted in determining the combined corporation's net income for the current period?

|  | Direct Costs of Acquisition | General Expenses Related to Acquisition |
|---|---|---|
| a. | Yes | No |
| b. | Yes | Yes |
| c. | No | Yes |
| d. | No | No |

3. Which of the following is the appropriate basis for valuing fixed assets acquired in a business combination accounted for as a purchase carried out by exchanging cash for common stock?
   a. Historic cost.
   b. Book value.
   c. Cost plus any excess of purchase price over book value of asset acquired.
   d. Fair value.

4. Pax Company acquired all of the outstanding common stock of Sax Company in exchange for cash. The acquisition price exceeds the fair value of the net

assets. How should Pax determine the amounts to be reported for the inventories and long-term debt of Sax in its consolidated statements?

| Inventories | Long-term Debt |
|---|---|
| a. Fair value | Sax's carrying amount |
| b. Fair value | Fair value |
| c. Sax's carrying amount | Fair value |
| d. Sax's carrying amount | Sax's carrying amount |

5. On April 1, 19X6, Place Company paid $400,000 for all the issued and outstanding common stock of Show Corporation in a transaction properly accounted for as a purchase. Show's assets and liabilities on April 1, 19X6, are as follows:

| | |
|---|---:|
| Cash ...................................................... | $ 40,000 |
| Inventory................................................ | 120,000 |
| Property and equipment (net of accumulated depreciation | |
| of $160,000)........................................ | 240,000 |
| Liabilities .............................................. | (90,000) |

On April 1, 19X6, the current value of Show's inventory was $95,000, and its property and equipment (net) had a current value of $280,000.

**Required:**
What is the amount of goodwill as a result of the business combination?
a. $–0–
b. $25,000
c. $75,000
d. $90,000

6. Page Company acquired all of the outstanding common stock of Sage Company at a total cost of $100,000. Sage Company's net assets have a book value of $60,000 and a current value of $90,000. In the parent's general ledger, how much would be shown in the Goodwill account?
a. $–0–
b. $10,000
c. $30,000
d. $40,000

7. Patron Company acquired all of the outstanding common stock of Saint Company at a total cost of $200,000. Saint Company's net assets have a book value of $160,000 and a current value of $210,000. In the consolidated financial statements, which of the following would be reported?
a. Goodwill of $10,000.
b. A deferred credit of $10,000.
c. Goodwill of $40,000.
d. None of the above.

8. What is a valid reason for Pax Company (a publicly owned company) to not consolidate an entity in which Pax owns common stock?

   a. The entity is a finance subsidiary of Pax, which is a manufacturing company.
   b. The entity is a foreign subsidiary of Pax.
   c. The entity is a subsidiary that has a different year-end than Pax.
   d. Pax does not own over 50% of the entity's outstanding common stock.
   e. None of the above.

9. Pitt Company acquired all of the assets of Seed Company by (1) giving cash of $200,000, (2) issuing 3,000 shares of common stock that had a market value of $100 per share, and (3) assuming responsibility for all of Seed Company's liabilities totaling $400,000 (at book value and current value). Seed Company's assets have a book value of $800,000 and a current appraised value of $1,100,000. For financial reporting purposes, each company has or reports:

| Pitt Company | Seed Company |
|---|---|
| a. Goodwill | Negative goodwill |
| b. Gain on acquisition | Loss on disposal |
| c. Negative goodwill | Bargain purchase element |
| d. Bargain purchase element | Gain on disposal |
| e. None of the above. | |

10. Assume the information in question 9. In recording the acquisition, each company would:

| Pitt Company | Seed Company |
|---|---|
| a. Debit investment in Seed Company | Debit common stock |
| b. Credit common stock | Debit investment in Pitt Company |
| c. Credit common stock | Make no entry. |
| d. Credit bargain purchase element | Debit investment in Pitt Company. |
| e. None of the above. | |

(AICPA adapted, nos. 1–5)

## Demonstration Problems

## 1. Acquisition of Common Stock

Pane Company acquired all of the outstanding common stock of Sill Company on June 30, 19X3, by issuing 20,000 shares of its $1 par value common stock (having a market price of $30 per share). Pane incurred legal and accounting fees of $75,000, of which $25,000 pertained to registering the shares issued with the SEC. If Sill's sales for the two years ended June 30, 19X5, exceed $8 million, then Pane must issue an additional 4,000 shares of common stock to Sill's former owners. The balances in the capital accounts of the subsidiary as of the acquisition date are as follows:

| | |
|---|---|
| Common Stock | $ 40,000 |
| Retained Earnings | 360,000 |
| | $400,000 |

All the assets and liabilities of the subsidiary have a current value equal to their book value, except the following:

|  | Book Value | Current Value |
|---|---|---|
| Land | $150,000 | $270,000 |
| Long-term debt, 8% | 200,000 | 230,000 |

The subsidiary has $20,000 of goodwill on its books as of the acquisition date that Sill's management feels is fully realizable. Of the $75,000 incurred for legal and accounting fees, $33,000 was paid by June 30, 19X3, and charged to a Deferred Charges account pending consummation of the acquisition. The remaining $42,000 has not been paid or accrued.

## Required:
1. Prepare the entry to record the acquisition.
2. Prepare an expanded analysis of the investment account.
3. Prepare the primary elimination entry for consolidation at June 30, 19X3.

### SOLUTION TO DEMONSTRATION PROBLEM 1

1. 
| | | |
|---|---|---|
| Investment in Sill Company (20,000 shares × $30 market price) | 600,000 | |
| Common Stock (20,000 shares × $1 par) | | 20,000 |
| Additional Paid-in Capital | | 580,000 |
| To record issuance of common stock. | | |

| | | |
|---|---|---|
| Investment in Sill Company | 50,000 | |
| Additional Paid-in Capital | 25,000 | |
| Deferred Charges | | 33,000 |
| Accrued Liabilities | | 42,000 |
| To record direct acquisition costs of $50,000 and $25,000 cost of registering common stock. | | |

No entry would be made pertaining to the contingent consideration at this time. Disclosure would be made in the notes to the financial statements.

2.

| | | Book Value Element | | Current Value over (under) Book Value Element | | | | |
|---|---|---|---|---|---|---|---|---|
| Total Cost | = | Common Stock | + Retained Earnings | + Land | + Old Goodwill | + Long-term Debt | + | Goodwill Element |
| $650,000 | | $40,000 | $360,000 | $120,000 | $(20,000) | $(30,000) | | $180,000 |

3. 
| | | |
|---|---|---|
| Common Stock | 40,000 | |
| Retained Earnings | 360,000 | |
| Land | 120,000 | |
| Goodwill (new) | 180,000 | |
| Goodwill (old) | | 20,000 |
| Long-term Debt | | 30,000 |
| Investment in Sill Company | | 650,000 |

## 2. Acquisition of Assets

Pitt Company acquired all of the assets of Seed Company by: (1) giving cash of $100,000; (2) issuing 2,000 shares of its $5 par value common stock that had a market value of $150 per share; and (3) assuming responsibility for all of Seed Company's liabilities having a book value and current value of $500,000. Seed Company's assets have a book value of $840,000 and a current value of $950,000. Assume centralized accounting is to be used by Pitt Company.

### Required:

Prepare the entries to be recorded by both companies as a result of this business combination.

### SOLUTION TO DEMONSTRATION PROBLEM 2

#### Pitt Company

| | | |
|---|---:|---:|
| Assets (net of $50,000 bargain purchase element) | 900,000 | |
| Cash | | 100,000 |
| Common Stock (2,000 shares × $5 par) | | 10,000 |
| Additional Paid-in Capital | | 290,000 |
| Liabilities | | 500,000 |
| To record acquisition of Seed Company's assets. | | |

#### Seed Company

| | | |
|---|---:|---:|
| Cash | 100,000 | |
| Liabilities | 500,000 | |
| Investment in Pitt Company (2,000 shares @ $150/share) | 300,000 | |
| Assets | | 840,000 |
| Gain on Sale of Assets | | 60,000 |
| To record sale of assets. | | |

## ASSIGNMENT MATERIAL

## Review Questions

1. What is the essence of the purchase method of accounting?
2. What two basic questions must be answered with respect to the purchase method of accounting?
3. What types of consideration can the acquiring entity give in a business combination?
4. When is it preferable in recording a business combination to use the fair value of the equity securities issued instead of the current value of the net assets of the acquired business?
5. How should direct costs incurred in a business combination be treated?

6. What is contingent consideration and how should it be accounted for?
7. What are the three major conceptual elements into which the total cost of an investment could possibly be separated?
8. In which situations would only one major conceptual element exist? In which situation would only two major conceptual elements exist?
9. What is the purpose of separating the total cost of the investment into the individual components of the major conceptual elements?
10. Why is there no separate account for goodwill on the parent company's books (under non-push-down accounting)?
11. Why are consolidated financial statements necessary?
12. What is the usual condition for a controlling interest?
13. What is the distinction between the basic disclosures and the supplemental disclosures required for business combinations accounted for under the purchase method of accounting?
14. How are preacquisition earnings of an acquired business treated under the purchase method of accounting?

# Discussion Cases

| DC |
| 3-1 |

## Manner of Reporting "Cost in Excess of Net Assets"

The December 31, 19X1, consolidated balance sheet of Hyde Company has the following described asset:

**Excess of cost over related net assets**
of businesses acquired . . . . . . . . . . . . . . . . . . . . . . . . . . . . . . . . . . . $75,000,000

The related footnote reads as follows:

> The excess of cost over related net assets applicable to businesses acquired prior to November 1, 1970, amounts to $11,000,000 and is not amortized, as it is believed to have continuing value; the balance applicable to businesses acquired after October 31, 1970, is being amortized on a straight-line basis over 40 years.

### Required:
1. Is the title of the asset accurate?
2. Is the title of the asset informative?
3. What does the asset represent?
4. What is the theoretical justification for amortizing only part of this amount?

| DC |
| 3-2 |

## Treatment of Goodwill

You are the controller of a company that has recently acquired a business having substantial goodwill. While determining whether the treatment prescribed by *APB Opinion No. 17,* "Intangible Assets," presents your company's financial statements fairly, you discover that the APB considered the following alternatives before it issued *No. 17:*

1. Allow goodwill to be reported as a "permanent" asset, with no amortization required unless impairment occurred.
2. Require goodwill to be amortized.
3. Require goodwill to be charged to stockholders' equity of the acquiring company at the acquisition date.

### Required:

1. Briefly evaluate the soundness of each of these alternatives.
2. For alternative 2, evaluate the soundness of allowing up to 40 years to amortize goodwill.

## DC 3-3 Treatment of Bargain Purchase Element

You are the CPA for a company that has recently acquired all of the assets of another company at an amount below their current value. The controller has indicated to you that the bargain purchase element will be accounted for in one of the following ways:

1. Credit it to income in the year of the acquisition, possibly classified as an extraordinary item.
2. Amortize it to income over the two-year period needed to turn the acquired operation into a profit-making operation.
3. Allocate it to the acquired assets based on relative current values, thereby lowering the recorded values of these items.
4. Credit it to contributed capital.

### Required:

How would you respond to these proposed treatments? Be sure to evaluate the theoretical soundness of each alternative regardless of the requirements of *APB Opinion No. 16*.

## DC 3-4 Determining Whether Consolidation Is Appropriate

Patentex Company and its head engineer, Dee Ziner, form Secretex Company, which will perform research and development. Secretex issues 5,000 shares of common stock to Ziner. Patentex lends $450,000 to Secretex for initial working capital in return for a note receivable that can be converted at will into 95,000 shares of Secretex common stock. Patentex also grants Secretex a line of credit of $2,500,000. If Ziner wants to sell the 5,000 shares, Patentex has the right of first refusal.

### Required:

Determine if consolidation of Secretex's financial statements is appropriate.

## DC 3-5 Treatment of Cost in Excess of Book Value of Acquired Subsidiary's Net Assets

Pomglomerate Company, a highly diversified company, acquired all of the outstanding common stock of three companies during the current year. In each case,

Pomglomerate's total cost was $500,000 in excess of book value of the net assets. The reason it paid more than the book value of the net assets of each company is stated below:

1. **Acquisition of Ironex Company.** Ironex mines iron ore from land it owns. Pomglomerate acquired Ironex to assure itself a continual supply of iron ore for its steel-making operation.

2. **Acquisition of Memco Company.** Memco manufactures high-quality memory chips for computers. Few companies can manufacture high-quality chips of this type. Pomglomerate acquired Memco to assure itself of a continual supply of high-quality memory chips for its computer manufacturing operation.

3. **Acquisition of Farmco Company.** Farmco manufactures farm machinery. Farmco earns a return on investment that is average for its industry. On this basis, Farmco was not worth acquiring. Pomglomerate, however, feels it can bring about substantial efficiencies by integrating Farmco's operations with those of another subsidiary, which manufactures farm machinery. The combined results are expected to increase substantially the overall return on investment of each previously separate operation.

### Required:
For each of these acquisitions, determine how you would classify Pomglomerate's cost in excess of book value and how you would account for it in future-period consolidated financial statements.

## Exercises

<table>
<tr><td>E<br>3-1</td><td></td></tr>
</table>

### Recording Acquisition of Assets for Cash

Pomeroy Company acquired all of the assets (except cash) and assumed all of the liabilities of Stiles Company for $1,100,000 cash. The acquired business is to be accounted for as a division with a decentralized accounting system. The assets and liabilities of Stiles Company as of the acquisition date are as follows:

|  | Book Value | Current Value |
|---|---|---|
| Cash.................................... | $ 30,000 | $ 30,000 |
| Accounts receivable, net ..................... | 80,000 | 80,000 |
| Inventory.................................... | 90,000 | 80,000 |
| Land........................................ | 100,000 | 150,000 |
| Buildings and equipment..................... | 1,200,000 | 870,000 |
| Accumulated depreciation.................... | (500,000) |  |
|  | $1,000,000 | $1,210,000 |
| Accounts payable and accruals ............... | $ 100,000 | $ 100,000 |
| Long-term debt ............................. | 200,000 | 200,000 |
|  | $ 300,000 | $ 300,000 |
| Net Assets................................. | $ 700,000 | $ 910,000 |

**Required:**

1. Prepare the entry to record the acquisition on the books of the home office and on the books of the newly formed division.
2. How would the entries be different if the accounting for the acquired business were centralized?

## Recording Acquisition of Assets for Stock

**E
3-2**

Assume the same information as in Exercise 3-1, except that Pomeroy Company issued 10,000 shares of its common stock ($5 par value), which was selling for $110 per share at the acquisition date, instead of giving cash to effect the business combination.

**Required:**

1. Prepare the entry to record the acquisition on the books of the home office and on the newly formed division.
2. How would the entries be different if the accounting for the acquired business were centralized?

## Recording Acquisition of Common Stock for Cash and Stock

**E
3-3**

Party Time acquired 100% of the outstanding common stock of Streamers for $2,300,000 cash and 10,000 shares of its common stock ($2 par value), which was traded at $40 per share at the acquisition date.

**Required:**

Prepare the entry to record the business combination on Party Time's books.

## Recording Direct Costs

**E
3-4**

Assume the same information provided in Exercise 3-3. In addition, assume that Party Time incurred the following direct costs:

| | |
|---|---:|
| Legal fees for preparing the acquisition agreement | $ 47,000 |
| Accounting fees for the purchase investigation | 17,000 |
| Travel expenses for meetings held with management of Streamers | 8,000 |
| Legal fees for registering the common stock issued with the SEC | 32,000 |
| Accounting fees for the review of unaudited financial statements and other data included in the registration statement | 16,000 |
| SEC filing fees | 4,000 |
| | $124,000 |

Prior to the consummation date, $103,000 had been paid and charged to a Deferred Charges suspense account, pending consummation of the acquisition. The remaining $21,000 has not been paid or accrued.

**Required:**

Prepare the journal entry to record the business combination and the direct costs.

## E 3-5    Contingent Consideration Based on Future Sales

Polychrome acquired all of the outstanding common stock of Spectrum Company for $1,000,000 cash. If the cumulative sales of Spectrum for the three years subsequent to the acquisition date exceed $10,000,000, then additional cash of $200,000 is to be paid to the former shareholders of Spectrum.

**Required:**

Prepare the entry to record the business combination. Explain the accounting treatment of the contingent consideration.

## E 3-6    Contingent Consideration Based on Future Security Prices: Existing Security Price to Be Maintained

Pratt Company acquired all of the outstanding common stock of Switney Company by issuing 80,000 shares of its common stock ($10 par value), which had a market value of $40 per share at the acquisition date. If the market value of Pratt's common stock is below $40 per share two years after the acquisition date, then Pratt must issue additional shares at that time to Switney's former shareholders so that the total value of the shares issued equals $3,200,000.

**Required:**

Note: You may want to review paragraphs 81 and 82 of *APB Opinion No. 16* before solving.

1. Prepare the entry to record the business combination. Explain the accounting treatment of the contingent consideration.
2. Assume the market value of Pratt Company's common stock is $32 per share two years later. Prepare the entry to record the additional shares issued.

## E 3-7    Contingent Consideration Based on Future Security Prices: Higher Security Price to be Attained

Photo Company acquired all of the outstanding common stock of Snapco Company by issuing 60,000 shares of its common stock ($5 par value), which had a market value of $50 per share as of the acquisition date. If the market value of Photo's common stock is not at least $70 per share two years after the acquisition date, then additional shares must be issued to Snapco's former shareholders so that the total value of the shares issued equals $4,200,000.

**Required:**

Note: You may want to review paragraphs 81 and 82 of *APB Opinion No. 16* before solving.

1. Prepare the entry to record the business combination. Explain the accounting treatment of the contingent consideration.
2. Assume the market value of Photo Company's common stock is $60 per share two years later. Prepare the entry to record the additional shares issued.

| E 3-8 |
|---|

## Separating Total Cost into Major Conceptual Elements

Potasha Company acquired all of the outstanding common stock of Sulpha Company at a total cost of $1,000,000. Sulpha Company's net assets have a book value of $600,000 and a current value of $880,000 as of the acquisition date.

### Required:
Separate the total cost of the investment into its major conceptual elements as of the acquisition date.

| E 3-9 |
|---|

## Separating Total Cost into Major Conceptual Elements

Pomona Company acquired 100% of the outstanding common stock of Sonora Company, a manufacturing company with extensive manufacturing facilities, at a total cost of $2,000,000. Sonora's net assets have a book value of $1,800,000 and a current value of $2,100,000 as of the acquisition date.

### Required:
Separate the total cost of the investment into its major conceptual elements as of the acquisition date.

| E 3-10 |
|---|

## Separating Total Cost into Components of the Major Conceptual Elements

Pending Company acquired all of the outstanding common stock of Sheb Company for $800,000 cash. (Assume there were no direct costs or contingent consideration.) Information about Sheb Company as of the acquisition date is as follows:

| | Book Value | Current Value |
|---|---|---|
| Cash | $ 50,000 | $ 50,000 |
| Accounts receivable, net | 100,000 | 100,000 |
| Inventory | 200,000 | 210,000 |
| Land | 300,000 | 420,000 |
| Buildings and equipment | 670,000 | 680,000 |
| Accumulated depreciation | (120,000) | |
| Total Assets | $1,200,000 | $1,460,000 |
| Accounts payable and accruals | $ 100,000 | $ 100,000 |
| Long-term debt | 600,000 | 625,000 |
| Total Liabilities | $ 700,000 | $ 725,000 |
| Common stock | $ 50,000 | |
| Additional paid-in capital | 300,000 | |
| Retained earnings | 150,000 | |

*(continued)*

| | Book Value | Current Value |
|---|---|---|
| Total Stockholders' Equity | $ 500,000 | 735,000 |
| Total Liabilities and Equity | $1,200,000 | $1,460,000 |

**Required:**

1. Separate the total cost of the investment into the individual components of the major conceptual elements as of the acquisition date.
2. Explain why the current value of the long-term debt is greater than its book value.

## Problems

**P 3-1**

### Analyzing Total Cost: Cost Is above Current Value of Net Assets and Current Value Is above Book Value

Perusal Company acquired all of the outstanding stock of Scanner Company for $2,500,000 cash. Information with respect to Scanner Company as of the acquisition date is as follows:

| | Book Value | Current Value |
|---|---|---|
| Cash | $ 55,000 | $ 55,000 |
| Accounts receivable, net | 180,000 | 180,000 |
| Notes receivable | 100,000 | 60,000 |
| Inventory | 300,000 | 330,000 |
| Land | 500,000 | 600,000 |
| Buildings and equipment | 600,000[a] | 750,000 |
| Patent | 45,000 | 105,000 |
| Goodwill, net of amortization to date | 120,000 | See note. |
| Total Assets | $1,900,000 | |
| Accounts payable and accruals | $ 300,000 | $300,000 |
| Long-term debt (10% bonds) | 700,000 | 650,000 |
| Total liabilities | $1,000,000 | |
| Common stock | $ 100,000 | |
| Additional paid-in capital | 500,000 | |
| Retained earnings | 300,000 | |
| Total Stockholders' Equity | $ 900,000 | |
| Total Liabilities and Equity | $1,900,000 | |

[a]Net of accumulated depreciation of $123,000.

**Note:**

The $120,000 of unamortized goodwill arose from Scanner's acquisition two years ago of the net assets of a local competitor. The goodwill is being amortized over 10 years. During the negotiations with Perusal Company, the management of

④ write off old GW ←

new GW = 1370

① BV = 900
② CV - BV = 250
③ GW = 1370

Scanner Company indicated that these acquired operations have produced superior earnings since acquisition, which are expected to continue for at least another eight years.

### Required:

1. For other than existing goodwill, what procedures and guidelines are used to determine current values of assets acquired and liabilities assumed? (Refer to paragraphs 87 and 88 of *APB Opinion No. 16.*)
2. As to the 10% bonds payable, is the current rate of interest more or less than 10%? Will future interest expense be at a rate more or less than 10%?
3. Separate the total investment cost into the individual components of the major conceptual elements.
4. Prepare the elimination entries required in consolidation as of the acquisition date.

---

**P 3-2**

## Analyzing Total Cost: Cost Is below Current Value of Net Assets and Current Value Is above Book Value

Pladd Company acquired all of the outstanding common stock of Stripes Company for $310,000 cash. Information about Stripes as of the acquisition date is as follows:

| | Book Value | Current Value |
|---|---|---|
| Cash. . . . . . . . . . . . . . . . . . . . . . . . . . . . . . . . . . | $ 20,000 | $ 20,000 |
| Accounts receivable, net . . . . . . . . . . . . . . . . . . . . . | 40,000 | 40,000 |
| Inventory. . . . . . . . . . . . . . . . . . . . . . . . . . . . . . . | 200,000 | 140,000 |
| Land. . . . . . . . . . . . . . . . . . . . . . . . . . . . . . . . . . | 90,000 | 300,000 |
| Buildings, net. . . . . . . . . . . . . . . . . . . . . . . . . . . . | 130,000[a] | 180,000 |
| Equipment, net. . . . . . . . . . . . . . . . . . . . . . . . . . . | 100,000[b] | 120,000 |
| Total Assets . . . . . . . . . . . . . . . . . . . . . . . . | $580,000 | $800,000 |
| Accounts payable and accruals . . . . . . . . . . . . . . . . | $100,000 | $100,000 |
| Long-term debt . . . . . . . . . . . . . . . . . . . . . . . . . . | 280,000 | 280,000 |
| Total Liabilities. . . . . . . . . . . . . . . . . . . . . . . | $380,000 | $380,000 |
| Common stock. . . . . . . . . . . . . . . . . . . . . . . . . . . | $ 30,000 | |
| Additional paid-in capital . . . . . . . . . . . . . . . . . . . . | 270,000 | |
| Accumulated deficit . . . . . . . . . . . . . . . . . . . . . . . . | (100,000) | |
| Total Stockholders' Equity. . . . . . . . . . . . . . | $200,000 | 420,000 |
| Total Liabilities and Equity . . . . . . . . . . . . . . . | $580,000 | $800,000 |

[a]Net of accumulated depreciation of $55,000.
[b]Net of accumulated depreciation of $44,000.

### Required:

1. Separate the total investment cost into the components of the major conceptual elements.
2. Prepare the elimination entries required in consolidation as of the acquisition date.

## Analyzing Total Cost: Cost Is below Current Value of Net Assets and Current Value Is below Book Value

Plugg Company acquired all of the outstanding common stock of Sparks Company for $150,000 cash. Information about Sparks, which leases its manufacturing facilities and is in poor financial condition as of the acquisition date, is as follows:

| | Book Value | Current Value |
|---|---|---|
| Cash............................................ | $ 20,000 | $ 20,000 |
| Accounts receivable, net ...................... | 380,000 | 380,000 |
| Inventory....................................... | 300,000 | 270,000 |
| Equipment, net................................. | 100,000[a] | 60,000 |
|     Total Assets........................ | $800,000 | $730,000 |
| Accounts payable and accruals ................ | $450,000 | $450,000 |
| Long-term debt................................. | 50,000 | 50,000 |
|     Total Liabilities...................... | $500,000 | $500,000 |
| Common stock.................................. | $210,000 | |
| Additional paid-in capital...................... | 340,000 | |
| Accumulated deficit ........................... | (250,000) | |
|     Total Stockholders' Equity............. | $300,000 | 230,000 |
|     Total Liabilities and Equity ........... | $800,000 | $730,000 |

[a]Net of accumulated depreciation of $77,000.

### Required:

1. Separate the total investment cost into the components of the major conceptual elements.
2. Prepare the elimination entries required in consolidation as of the acquisition date.

## Preparing a Consolidation Worksheet: Cost Equals Current Value of Net Assets and Current Value Equals Book Value

Payles Company, which is a calendar-year reporting company, acquired all of the outstanding common stock of Selmore Company at a total cost of $600,000 (an amount equal to the current value and book value of Selmore's net assets) on December 31, 19X1. The financial statements of each company for the year ended on that date immediately after the acquisition are as follows:

| | Payles Company | Selmore Company |
|---|---|---|
| **Income Statement (19X1)** | | |
| Sales......................................... | $8,000,000 | $ 700,000 |
| Cost of goods sold............................ | (5,000,000) | (300,000) |
| Expenses..................................... | (2,100,000) | (280,000) |
|     Net Income............................. | $ 900,000 | $ 120,000 |

| | Payles Company | Selmore Company |
|---|---|---|
| **Balance Sheet (as of December 31, 19X1)** | | |
| Cash . . . . . . . . . . . . . . . . . . . . . . . . . . . . . . . . . . . . . . . . . . . . | $ 500,000 | $ 100,000 |
| Accounts receivable, net . . . . . . . . . . . . . . . . . . . . . | 900,000 | 400,000 |
| Inventory . . . . . . . . . . . . . . . . . . . . . . . . . . . . . . . . . . . . | 1,200,000 | 700,000 |
| Investment in Selmore Company . . . . . . . . . . . . . . . | 600,000 | |
| Land . . . . . . . . . . . . . . . . . . . . . . . . . . . . . . . . . . . . . . . . . | 800,000 | 300,000 |
| Buildings and equipment . . . . . . . . . . . . . . . . . . . . . . | 5,000,000 | 900,000 |
| Accumulated depreciation . . . . . . . . . . . . . . . . . . . . . | (1,000,000) | (200,000) |
| | $8,000,000 | $2,200,000 |
| | | |
| Accounts payable and accruals . . . . . . . . . . . . . . . . | $1,000,000 | $ 500,000 |
| Long-term debt . . . . . . . . . . . . . . . . . . . . . . . . . . . . . . . | 2,000,000 | 1,100,000 |
| Common stock . . . . . . . . . . . . . . . . . . . . . . . . . . . . . . . | 1,000,000 | 100,000 |
| Additional paid-in capital . . . . . . . . . . . . . . . . . . . . . | 2,000,000 | 200,000 |
| Retained earnings . . . . . . . . . . . . . . . . . . . . . . . . . . . | 2,000,000 | 300,000 |
| | $8,000,000 | $2,200,000 |

### Required:

1. Prepare the elimination entries required in consolidation as of December 31, 19X1.
2. Prepare a consolidating statement worksheet as of December 31, 19X1.
3. What amount of income does the parent company report to its stockholders for 19X1?

## Preparing a Consolidation Worksheet: Cost Is above Current Value of Net Assets and Current Value Is above Book Value

P 3-5*

Peanut Company, which is a calendar-year reporting company, acquired all of the outstanding common stock of Shell Company at a total cost of $300,000 on December 31, 19X1. The analysis of the parent company's investment account by the individual components of the major conceptual elements as of the acquisition date is as follows:

| | |
|---|---|
| Book value element: | |
| Common stock . . . . . . . . . . . . . . . . . . . . . . . . . . . . . . . . . . . . . . . . . . . . | $100,000 |
| Retained earnings . . . . . . . . . . . . . . . . . . . . . . . . . . . . . . . . . . . . | 90,000 |
| Current value over (under) book value element: | |
| Inventory . . . . . . . . . . . . . . . . . . . . . . . . . . . . . . . . . . . . . . . . . . . . . | 5,000 |
| Land . . . . . . . . . . . . . . . . . . . . . . . . . . . . . . . . . . . . . . . . . . . . . . . . . | 30,000 |
| Equipment . . . . . . . . . . . . . . . . . . . . . . . . . . . . . . . . . . . . . . . . . . . | 50,000 |
| Patent . . . . . . . . . . . . . . . . . . . . . . . . . . . . . . . . . . . . . . . . . . . . . . . | (15,000) |
| Goodwill element . . . . . . . . . . . . . . . . . . . . . . . . . . . . . . . . . . . . . . . | 40,000 |
| Total cost . . . . . . . . . . . . . . . . . . . . . . . . . . . . . . . . . . . . . . . . . . . | $300,000 |

*The financial statement information presented for problems accompanied by asterisks is also provided on Model 3 (filename: Model3) of the software file disk that is available for use with the text, enabling the problem to be worked on the computer.

The financial statements of each company for the year ended December 31, 19X1, immediately after the acquisition are as follows:

|  | Peanut Company | Shell Company |
|---|---|---|
| **Income Statement (19X1)** | | |
| Sales. . . . . . . . . . . . . . . . . . . . . . . . . . . . . . . . | $2,500,000 | $500,000 |
| Cost of goods sold. . . . . . . . . . . . . . . . . . . . . . . | (1,400,000) | (250,000) |
| Expenses. . . . . . . . . . . . . . . . . . . . . . . . . . . . . | (860,000) | (202,000) |
| Net Income. . . . . . . . . . . . . . . . . . . . . . . . | $ 240,000 | $ 48,000 |
| **Balance Sheet (as of December 31, 19X1)** | | |
| Cash. . . . . . . . . . . . . . . . . . . . . . . . . . . . . . . . | $ 100,000 | $ 20,000 |
| Accounts receivable, net. . . . . . . . . . . . . . . . . . | 200,000 | 55,000 |
| Inventory. . . . . . . . . . . . . . . . . . . . . . . . . . . . . | 350,000 | 80,000 |
| Investment in Shell Co.. . . . . . . . . . . . . . . . . . . | 300,000 | |
| Land. . . . . . . . . . . . . . . . . . . . . . . . . . . . . . . . | 400,000 | 70,000 |
| Buildings and equipment. . . . . . . . . . . . . . . . . . | 800,000 | 200,000 |
| Accumulated depreciation . . . . . . . . . . . . . . . . . | (150,000) | (40,000) |
| Patent. . . . . . . . . . . . . . . . . . . . . . . . . . . . . . | | 15,000 |
| | $2,000,000 | $400,000 |
| Accounts payable and accruals . . . . . . . . . . . . . . | $ 250,000 | $ 60,000 |
| Long-term debt. . . . . . . . . . . . . . . . . . . . . . . . . | 1,000,000 | 150,000 |
| Common stock. . . . . . . . . . . . . . . . . . . . . . . . . | 300,000 | 100,000 |
| Retained earnings . . . . . . . . . . . . . . . . . . . . . . | 450,000 | 90,000 |
| | $2,000,000 | $400,000 |

## Required:

1. Prepare the elimination entries required in consolidation as of December 31, 19X1.
2. Prepare a consolidating statement worksheet as of December 31, 19X1.

## Preparing a Consolidation Worksheet: Cost Is Equal to Current Value of Net Assets and Current Value Is below Book Value

Post Company, which is a calendar-year reporting company, acquired all of the outstanding common stock of Script Company, at a total cost of $400,000 on December 31, 19X1. The analysis of the parent company's investment account by the individual components of the major conceptual elements as of the acquisition date is as follows:

| Book value element: | |
|---|---|
| Common stock. . . . . . . . . . . . . . . . . . . . . . . . . . . . . . . . . | $ 50,000 |
| Additional paid-in capital. . . . . . . . . . . . . . . . . . . . . . . . . . . | 200,000 |
| Retained earnings . . . . . . . . . . . . . . . . . . . . . . . . . . . . . . . | 250,000 |

Current value over (under) book value element:

| | |
|---|---:|
| Inventory | (70,000) |
| Land | 30,000 |
| Building | (100,000) |
| Long-term debt | 40,000[a] |
| Total Cost | $400,000 |

[a]Recall that for liabilities, the "over (under)" description is reversed to "under (over)."

The financial statements of each company for the year ended December 31, 19X1, immediately after the acquisition are as follows:

| | Post Company | Script Company |
|---|---:|---:|
| **Income Statement (19X1)** | | |
| Sales | $6,000,000 | $800,000 |
| Cost of goods sold | (3,300,000) | (600,000) |
| Expenses | (1,500,000) | (250,000) |
| Net Income | $1,200,000 | $ (50,000) |
| **Balance Sheet (as of December 31, 19X1)** | | |
| Cash | $ 240,000 | $ 30,000 |
| Accounts receivable, net | 360,000 | 50,000 |
| Inventory | 800,000 | 220,000 |
| Investment in Script Company | 400,000 | |
| Land | 500,000 | 100,000 |
| Buildings and equipment | 2,600,000 | 550,000 |
| Accumulated depreciation | (400,000) | (50,000) |
| | $4,500,000 | $900,000 |
| | | |
| Accounts payable and accruals | $ 800,000 | $100,000 |
| Long-term debt | 2,100,000 | 300,000 |
| Common stock | 20,000 | 50,000 |
| Additional paid-in capital | 480,000 | 200,000 |
| Retained earnings | 1,100,000 | 250,000 |
| | $4,500,000 | $900,000 |

## Required:

1. Prepare the elimination entries required in consolidation as of December 31, 19X1.
2. Prepare a consolidating statement worksheet as of December 31, 19X1.

## COMPREHENSIVE   Analyzing the Investment and Preparing Consolidated Financial Statements

P 3-7*

Pinnacle acquired all of the outstanding common stock of Summit for $900,000 cash on January 1, 19X1. Pinnacle also incurred $55,000 of costs in connection with the acquisition. Of this amount, $15,000 was a finder's fee, $12,000 was an allocation of overhead from the mergers and acquisition department, and $8,000 was an allocated portion of the president's salary (the president had devoted approximately 20% of his time during 19X0 to the merger). The remaining $20,000 was for legal and accounting fees and travel costs.

Financial data for each company immediately **before** the acquisition are as follows:

| | Pinnacle Company | Summit Company | |
| --- | --- | --- | --- |
| | Book Value | Book Value | Current Value |
| Cash......................... | $1,345,000 | $ 100,000 | $ 100,000 |
| Accounts receivable, net ........ | 900,000 | 140,000 | 140,000 |
| Notes receivable............... | | 80,000 | 60,000 |
| Inventory...................... | 1,100,000 | 310,000 | 330,000 |
| Land.......................... | 500,000 | 250,000 | 410,000 |
| Buildings and equipment........ | 4,500,000 | 800,000 | 620,000 |
| Accumulated depreciation....... | (1,400,000) | (300,000) | |
| Patent, net.................... | 200,000 | 40,000 | 100,000 |
| Goodwill, net of amortization .... | | 80,000 | |
| Deferred acquisition costs....... | 55,000 | | |
| | $7,200,000 | $1,500,000 | $1,760,000 |
| | | | |
| Accounts payable and accrued liabilities ............ | $1,800,000 | $ 250,000 | $ 250,000 |
| Long-term debt ............... | 4,000,000 | 600,000 | 660,000 |
| Common stock................. | 600,000 | 150,000 | |
| Retained earnings ............. | 800,000 | 500,000 | |
| | $7,200,000 | $1,500,000 | |

*(handwritten note in margin: AC = 900 + 15 + 20)*

If Summit's sales for 19X2 exceed $850,000, then Pinnacle must pay an additional $60,000 cash to Summit's stockholders. Management feels optimistic that this sales level can be attained.

### Required:

1. Analyze the investment account by the components of the major conceptual elements as of the acquisition date.

*(handwritten note in margin: non-push down)*

2. Prepare the elimination entries required in consolidation as of the acquisition date.
3. Prepare a consolidating statement worksheet as of the acquisition date.

### P 3-8* COMPREHENSIVE   Acquisition of Assets: Recording the Acquisition and Preparing Combined Financial Statements

Use the same information provided in Problem 3-7, except that (a) all of the assets were acquired instead of all of the common stock, and (b) all of the liabilities of Summit Company were assumed by Pinnacle Company.

### Required:

1. Prepare the entries made by Pinnacle to record the acquisition, assuming a decentralized accounting system is used.

2. Prepare the primary elimination entry as of the acquisition date.
3. Prepare a combining statement worksheet as of the acquisition date.

# ADVANCED LEVEL ASSIGNMENT MATERIAL

## Technical Research Questions

Here and elsewhere in the book, answers to technical research questions may be found by consulting the pronouncements of the FASB, the APB, and the SEC.

1. Pert Products purchases Sprig & Sons and immediately incurs costs to close Sprig's duplicate facilities. Should those costs be added to the cost of the acquisition?
2. Should the costs Pert incurs in question 1 be added to the cost of the acquisition if it closes its own duplicate facilities instead?

## Advanced Problems

| AP 3-1 | ### Case Study from Actual Practice: A Bargain Purchase |
|---|---|

Case 9 from The Trueblood Professors' Seminar, The Touche Ross Foundation and American Accounting Association. Copyright © 1988, reprinted by special permission.

Matrix Manufacturing Company has purchased 100% of West Taxicab Company, which owns operating permits issued by three major cities for fleets of taxicabs. This was a stock-for-stock transaction in which Matrix exchanged nonvoting, cumulative preferred stock for all of the West common. The market price of Matrix shares issued in the purchase was $5 million. West was a subsidiary of a large corporation prior to being acquired by Matrix. The accounting Matrix proposes for the purchase is as follows:

**($000s Omitted)**

| | West's Net Book Value | Fair Value of West's Identifiable Assets | Proposed Accounting Allocation of Excess | Proposed Accounting Matrix's New "Cost" For West |
|---|---|---|---|---|
| **Balance Sheet Accounts** | | | | |
| Taxicabs | $ 3,000 | $ 1,500 | $ (600) | $ 900 |
| Garages and Equipment | 1,000 | 2,500 | (1,000) | 1,500 |
| Permits | — | 6,000 | (2,400) | 3,600 |
| Goodwill | 1,000 | — | — | — |
| Liabilities | (1,000) | (1,000) | — | (1,000) |
| Total | $ 4,000 | | | $ 5,000 |
| Fair Value of "Purchased Assets" | | 9,000 | | |

*(continued)*

**($000s Omitted)**

| Balance Sheet Accounts | West's Net Book Value | Fair Value of West's Identifiable Assets | Proposed Accounting | |
|---|---|---|---|---|
| | | | Allocation of Excess | Matrix's New "Cost" For West |
| Cost of Purchase | | 5,000 | | |
| Excess of Fair Value Over Cost | | $ 4,000 | $(4,000) | |

The valuation of the permits is based on bona fide offers made by three other taxicab operators within the last two months. The permits probably can be said to have an indefinite life, but they will be amortized over 40 years. The fair values of the other assets are based on sound appraisals. The average useful remaining life of the taxicabs is three years and of the garages and equipment, 15 years.

West's operations have suffered recenty due to fuel difficulties and related economic dislocations. As a result current profits are depressed.

### Required:

1. Discuss why this transaction should be accounted for as a purchase.
2. Comment upon the economics of this transaction.
3. Critique the accounting which Matrix has proposed for this purchase. Be sure to consider the following aspects:
   a. Determination of the cost of the acquisition
   b. Allocation of the negative goodwill
   c. Valuation and amortization of the permits
4. How would the accounting be different if this had been a tax-free exchange?

## Financial Analysis of Financial Statements

AP 3-2

In an actual acquisition in late 1983, Financial Corporation of America (FCA) acquired all of American Savings and Loan. FCA paid cash of $290,000,000 and issued common and preferred stock valued at $625,000,000. At the acquisition date, American had a net worth at book value of $600,000,000. In valuing American's loans at their current values (using current interest rates, which were higher than contractual rates), the current value was found to be $793,000,000 lower than the book value.

The consolidated balance sheet and certain income statement data for the two years ended December 31, 1984, and December 31, 1987, follow in condensed form:

| | 1987 | 1984 |
|---|---|---|
| | (in millions) | |
| **Assets** | | |
| Cash and security investments................... | $20,962 | $ 7,249 |
| Loans receivable ............................... | 10,326 | 18,020 |
| Property acquired through foreclosure............ | 417 | 733 |

|  | 1987 | 1984 |
|---|---|---|
|  | (in millions) | |
| Real estate investments . . . . . . . . . . . . . . . . . . . . . . . . | 714 | 934 |
| Intangible assets arising from acquisition . . . . . . . . . | 995 | 1,105 |
| Premises and equipment, net . . . . . . . . . . . . . . . . . . . | 229 | 258 |
| Deferred charges and other assets . . . . . . . . . . . . . . | 221 | 219 |
| Total Assets . . . . . . . . . . . . . . . . . . . . . . . . . . . | $33,864 | $28,518 |
| **Liabilities** | | |
| Deposits . . . . . . . . . . . . . . . . . . . . . . . . . . . . . . . . . . . . | $16,683 | $20,308 |
| All other liabilities . . . . . . . . . . . . . . . . . . . . . . . . . . . . | 17,344 | 8,017 |
| Total Liabilities . . . . . . . . . . . . . . . . . . . . . . . . . . | $34,027 | $28,325 |
| **Stockholders' Equity** | | |
| Common stock and paid-in capital . . . . . . . . . . . . . . | $    635 | $    634 |
| Accumulated deficit . . . . . . . . . . . . . . . . . . . . . . . . . . . | (798) | (441) |
| Total Stockholders' Equity . . . . . . . . . . . . . . . . . . | (163) | 193 |
| Total Liabilities and Equity . . . . . . . . . . . . . . . . . . | $33,864 | $28,518 |
| **Income Statement Data** | | |
| Net loss . . . . . . . . . . . . . . . . . . . . . . . . . . . . . . . . . . . . | (468) | (590) |
| Amortization of intangibles . . . . . . . . . . . . . . . . . . . . | (62) | (55) |

## Required:
1. Calculate the goodwill paid for by FCA.
2. As a potential depositor of FCA, evaluate the financial soundness of FCA. (Ignore the fact of deposit insurance.) Hint: Do you notice anything that does not make sense?

## ANSWERS TO SELF-STUDY QUESTIONS
1. c    6. a ($10,000 of goodwill is in the Investment in Subsidiary account.)
2. c    7. d (The $10,000 bargain purchase element normally would be ex-
3. d        tinguished.)
4. b    8. e
5. c    9. d
      10. b

## Appendix  THE PUSH-DOWN BASIS OF ACCOUNTING

## THE PARENT HAS THE SUBSIDIARY REVALUE ITS ASSETS AND LIABILITIES TO THEIR CURRENT VALUES IN ITS GENERAL LEDGER

Under the push-down basis of accounting, the subsidiary does the following as of the acquisition date:

1. Adjusts its assets and liabilities to their current values and records goodwill, if there is any. This makes the subsidiary's adjusted net assets equal the parent company's Investment in Subsidiary account.
2. Eliminates the balance(s) in its Accumulated Depreciation account(s). This recognizes that a new basis of accounting has been established for its fixed assets.
3. Closes its Retained Earnings account balance to Additional Paid-in Capital.
4. Uses this new basis of accounting in its separate financial statements. Retained earnings should be dated.

## The Rationale for Using the Push-down Basis of Accounting

The rationale for having the subsidiary adjust its assets and liabilities to their current values as of the acquisition date rests on an argument of substance over form. Advocates of push-down accounting contend that **the relevant factor is the acquisition itself, not the form of consummating the acquisition.** In their view, whether the parent company acquires assets or common stock is irrelevant. Recall that when assets are acquired, the individual assets and liabilities are revalued to their current values when they are recorded in the acquiring company's general ledger (or in the division's general ledger if decentralized accounting is used). As the acquisition itself is the relevant factor, a new basis of accounting has been established for the assets and liabilities. Merely because common stock is acquired instead of assets should not prevent this new basis of accounting from being reflected at the subsidiary level. Furthermore, in most cases **the parent controls the form of the ownership.** That is, **it has the legal power to liquidate the subsidiary into a division.** The fact that the parent chooses to maintain the acquired business as a separate legal entity should not have a bearing on whether a new cost basis should be established at the subsidiary level.

## The SEC Leads the Way

Push-down accounting had not gained significant acceptance or use until 1983, when the Securities and Exchange Commission issued *Staff Accounting Bulletin No. 54.* **This bulletin requires push-down accounting in the separate financial statements of a subsidiary acquired in a purchase transaction.** (Exceptions to this policy are discussed later.)

The SEC was convinced about the soundness of its position and concerned by the potentially misleading results from the many subsidiaries that had recently issued common stock based on historical cost-based financial statements using non-push-down accounting. The result of this practice was that these subsidiaries did not report their true cost of doing business and thus overstated their earnings. The SEC concluded that the time for substance over form had come.

**General Motors Tests the Waters.**   Perhaps to test the conviction of the SEC, General Motors Corp. argued before the commission that it should not have to apply push-down accounting to its $5 billion acquisition of all of Hughes Aircraft Co. in 1985 (in which there was $4 billion of cost in excess of book value). The SEC stood its ground.

| | |
|---|---|
| **ILLUSTRATION** | ## Acquisition of Common Stock Where: |
| MOST COMMONLY ENCOUNTERED SITUATION | ■ Assets Are Undervalued<br>■ Goodwill Exists |

To illustrate the entries that would be made under the push-down basis of accounting and the elimination entry made in preparing consolidated financial statements as of the acquisition date, we use the same information used earlier in the chapter to illustrate the non-push-down basis of accounting (page 114), in which the assets of the acquired business were undervalued and the purchase price includes an amount for goodwill (the most commonly encountered situation). Recall that P Company acquired all of the outstanding common stock of S Company on January 1, 19X1, by paying $90,000 cash. For convenience, we repeat the rest of the assumed information used earlier:

1. Total cost ................................................. $90,000
2. Current value of net assets ................................. $80,000
3. Book value of net assets .................................. $60,000
4. The current values of S Company's assets and liabilities are assumed to equal their book values, except for the following assets:

| | Book Value | Current Value | Current Value over Book Value |
|---|---|---|---|
| Inventory ..................... | $ 32,000 | $ 34,000 | $ 2,000 |
| Land ......................... | 30,000 | 42,000 | 12,000 |
| Buildings and Equipment ....... | 150,000 | 156,000 | 6,000 |
| | | | $20,000 |

[a]Net of $50,000 accumulated depreciation.

5. Goodwill of $10,000 ($90,000 − $80,000) exists.

Additionally, S Company's retained earnings balance at the acquisition date is $20,000.

The subsidiary would make the following entries as of the acquisition date.

1. To adjust assets to their current values and record goodwill:

| | | |
|---|---|---|
| Inventory | 2,000 | |
| Land | 12,000 | |
| Equipment | 6,000 | |
| Goodwill | 10,000 | |
| Additional Paid-in Capital[a] | | 30,000 |

2. To eliminate the balance in the Accumulated Depreciation account:

| | | |
|---|---|---|
| Accumulated Depreciation | 50,000 | |
| Buildings and Equipment | | 50,000 |

3. To close out the balance in Retained Earnings:

| | | |
|---|---|---|
| Retained Earnings | 20,000 | |
| Additional Paid-in Capital[a] | | 20,000 |

[a]For simplicity, we used this common capital account. A good case could be made for using an account called Revaluation Capital.

| | | |
|---|---|---|
| Common Stock | 40,000 | |
| Additional Paid-in Capital | 50,000 | |
| Investment in Subsidiary | | 90,000 |

Illustration 3-7 shows the consolidating statement worksheet, which consolidates the balance sheets of the parent company and the subsidiary as of the acquisition date (the subsidiary having already applied push-down accounting), for this illustration.

**Review Points for Illustration 3-7.** Note the following:

1. Except for the equity accounts, the amounts in Illustration 3-7 are identical to the amounts in Illustration 3-3, when assets were acquired and recorded directly in the division's general ledger at their current values.
2. The consolidation process could not be any simpler than it is in Illustration 3-7. In contrast, the consolidation process under the non-push-down basis of accounting (as shown in Illustration 3-6 for the same set of assumptions) is much more involved in arriving at the same consolidated amounts.
3. The only difference between Illustrations 3-6 and 3-7 is that here we are doing in the general ledger what was done on the worksheet: revaluing assets to their current values and eliminating the accumulated depreciation as of the acquisition date.

■ **ILLUSTRATION 3-7**

**The Acquisition of Common Stock (Push-down Accounting Applied by Subsidiary)**

| | P Company | S Company | Eliminations Dr. | Eliminations Cr. | Consolidated |
|---|---|---|---|---|---|
| **P COMPANY AND SUBSIDIARY (S COMPANY)** Consolidating Statement Worksheet As of January 1, 19X1 | | | | | |
| **Balance Sheet** | | | | | |
| Cash......................... | 18,000 | 15,000 | | | 33,000 |
| Accounts receivable, net......... | 52,000 | 23,000 | | | 75,000 |
| Inventory..................... | 100,000 | 34,000 | | | 134,000 |
| Investment in S Company........ | 90,000 | | | 90,000(1) | –0– |
| Land......................... | 220,000 | 42,000 | | | 262,000 |
| Buildings and equipment........ | 500,000 | 156,000 | | | 656,000 |
| Accumulated depreciation....... | (280,000) | –0– | | | (280,000) |
| Goodwill..................... | | 10,000 | | | 10,000 |
| | 700,000 | 280,000 | | 90,000 | 890,000 |
| Liabilities.................... | 300,000 | 190,000 | | | 490,000 |
| P Company: | | | | | |
|   Common stock.............. | 300,000 | | | | 300,000 |
|   Retained earnings........... | 100,000 | | | | 100,000 |
| S Company: | | | | | |
|   Common stock.............. | | 40,000 | 40,000(1) | | –0– |
|   Additional paid-in capital...... | | 50,000 | 50,000(1) | | –0– |
|   Retained earnings........... | | –0– | | | –0– |
| | 700,000 | 280,000 | 90,000 | | 890,000 |

Proof of debit and credit postings.......................... 90,000    90,000

Explanation of entry:
(1) The primary elimination entry.

## Allowable Exceptions to Push-down Accounting

Despite its hard line in the matter, the SEC does not require the use of push-down accounting when the parent does not control the form of ownership in its subsidiary. When a subsidiary has preferred stock outstanding, public debt outstanding, or a substantial minority interest (the parent owns less than 100% of the subsidiary's outstanding common stock), the parent is presumed to be unable to control the form of its ownership in the acquired business. In other words, it probably could not legally liquidate the subsidiary into a division if it desired. In such cases, *SEC Staff Accounting Bulletin No. 54* does not require the push-down basis of accounting to be used.

In the absence of preferred stock or public debt outstanding, the SEC staff uses the following guidelines for determining when a firm should use push-down accounting:

| Parent's Ownership Percentage | Guidelines |
|---|---|
| 90% or more | Substantially owned. Push-down accounting is required. |
| 80–89% | Push-down accounting is encouraged but not required. |
| Below 80% | Push-down accounting may not be appropriate. |

When a subsidiary is partially owned and push-down accounting is applied, it is done so in the same manner as illustrated earlier except that the revaluation of the subsidiary's assets and liabilities is made only to the extent of the parent's cost in excess of book value using the parent company theory (discussed in Chapter 5).

## Pushing Down Certain Parent Company Debt

In *Staff Accounting Bulletin No. 73* (issued in 1987), the staff of the SEC imposed the pushing down of certain debt of the parent company (including related interest expense and debt issuance costs) to the separate financial statements of a subsidiary when the subsidiary's financial statements are included in a registration statement for (a) a public offering of its stock or debt under the Securities Act of 1933, or (b) trading under the Securities and Exchange Act of 1934. (For a discussion of these acts, see Chapter 18.) The parent company debt to be pushed down is that debt incurred in connection with or otherwise related to the acquisition of the common stock of a company in a purchase transaction. The debt should be "pushed down" to the separate financial statements of the subsidiary if: (1) the subsidiary is to assume the debt of the parent, either presently or in a planned transaction in the future; (2) the proceeds of a debt or equity offering of the subsidiary will be used to retire all or a part of the parent's debt; or (3) the subsidiary guarantees or pledges its assets as collateral for the parent's debt.

## Concluding Comments

The push-down accounting issue is a debate between relevancy and historical cost. In 1989, the FASB's project on consolidations was reactivated to address the remaining issues under consideration, one of which is push-down accounting. Accordingly, an FASB pronouncement on this topic is expected in the near future.

## APPENDIX ASSIGNMENT MATERIAL

## Discussion Case for Appendix

### Evaluating the Push-down Basis of Accounting

Press Company acquired all of the outstanding common stock of Search Company by issuing a new class of common stock (Class B) valued at $700,000,000. The terms of the issuance call for dividends to be based on Search's audited net income using Search's historical cost basis. Search will remain a separate legal entity under the terms of the acquisition and will continue to use its own auditors.

For the year following the acquisition, assume that Search expected to do the following:

1. It will have net income of $100,000,000.
2. It will pay cash dividends of $80,000,000 to the Class B stockholders.
3. It will have net income of only $60,000,000 if push-down accounting is used.

#### Required:

1. Evaluate whether the push-down basis of accounting makes sense in this situation.
2. If push-down accounting were used, could the dividends still be based on the earnings excluding the additional depreciation and amortization of $40,000,000 resulting from push-down accounting?

## Exercise for Appendix

### E 3-1A    Applying Push-down Accounting

Use the information provided in Exercise 3-10 (page 139).

#### Required:

1. Prepare the entries the subsidiary would make under the push-down basis of accounting.
2. Prepare the primary elimination entry as of the acquisition date.

## Problems for Appendix

### P 3-1A to P 3-7A

For Problems 3-1 to 3-7, the following requirements can be used for implementing push-down accounting.

#### Required under Push-down Accounting:

1. Prepare the general ledger entries the subsidiary would make under the push-down basis of accounting.
2. Prepare the primary elimination entry as of the acquisition date.

# 4
# ·····

# THE PURCHASE METHOD OF ACCOUNTING: SUBSEQUENT TO DATE OF ACQUISITION

*TOPIC OUTLINE*

## CHAPTER OVERVIEW

**C**hapter 3 explained recording initially, under the purchase method of accounting, an investment in an acquired business, and preparing consolidated financial statements as of the acquisition date. This chapter focuses on how to account for such investments for periods subsequent to the combination date, and how to prepare consolidated financial statements in such subsequent periods.

The chapter deals only with accounting for investments in common stock in which the non-push-down basis of accounting is used. We do not illustrate the preparation of consolidated financial statements when push-down accounting is applied, as that process is substantively identical to when assets are acquired and decentralized accounting is used (home office–division accounting), which is illustrated in Appendix B.

Two methods are available for valuing investments in common stock: the equity method and the cost method. These methods are at the opposite ends of the conceptual spectrum. We emphasize the equity method when discussing investments in common stock, because it is the predominant method in use. Further, when push-down accounting is not used (*SEC Staff Accounting Bulletin No. 54* applies only to publicly owned companies), the equity method allows the analysis of the investment account to be updated for all later activity by each component of the major conceptual elements in a manner that simplifies the preparation of consolidated financial statements.

The reporting of financial position and results of operations on a consolidated basis for periods subsequent to the acquisition date are the same, however, regardless of whether (a) the equity or cost method is used in accounting for a common stock investment, (b) the acquisition takes the form of common stock or assets, and (c) the subsidiary's assets and liabilities are revalued to their current values in the subsidiary's general ledger (push-down accounting).

## ACCOUNTING FOR INVESTMENTS IN COMMON STOCK: THE EQUITY METHOD AND THE COST METHOD

Accounting for long-term investments, as covered in intermediate accounting texts, requires that investments in common stocks be accounted for as follows:

1. **Ownership interest is below 20%:** Apply the rule of lower of cost or market in accordance with the provisions of *FASB Statement No. 12*, "Accounting for Certain Marketable Securities."

2. **Ownership interest is at least 20% but not over 50%:** Apply the equity method of accounting in accordance with the provisions of *APB Opinion No. 18*, "The Equity Method of Accounting for Investments in Common Stock." (Note: The equity method applies here only if the investor's interest is in *voting stock.*)

3. **Ownership interest is above 50%:** Use either the equity method or the cost method, with the following stipulation for **unconsolidated subsidiaries:** Under *FASB Statement No. 94*, "Consolidation of All Majority-owned Subsidiaries," when a parent no longer controls the subsidiary (making consolidation inappropriate), the parent would have to be able to exert significant influence over the subsidiary to use the equity method. Lacking such influence, the cost method would be used. Even when significant influence exists, however, the cost method may be used instead of the equity method. In practice, the cost method is used in most instances in which a subsidiary is no longer consolidated.

## The Equity Method

The **equity method** of valuing an investment in a subsidiary is similar to the accrual method of accounting in that it reflects the substance of the economic activity that has occurred. Under the equity method, the parent's interest in the subsidiary's earnings and losses is reflected as upward and downward adjustments, respectively, to the Investment in Subsidiary account. The offsetting credit or debit is recorded in the parent's income statement. Any dividends on common stock declared by the subsidiary are credited to the Investment in Subsidiary account at their declaration, and an offsetting debit is made to Dividends Receivable. Thus, **all dividends (except stock dividends) declared by the subsidiary are treated as a liquidation of the investment.**

**The "One-line Consolidation" Concept.**   When a subsidiary is not consolidated and is reported under the equity method, the equity method is viewed as a "one-line consolidation." This is because the subsidiary's earnings are reported on one line in the parent's income statement (using an account called Equity in Net Income of Subsidiary) instead of the subsidiary's sales, cost of goods sold, and expenses. Likewise in the parent's balance sheet, one account is reported (the Investment in Subsidiary account) instead of the individual assets and liabilities of the subsidiary. Thus the difference between the equity method and consolidation is the amount of detail reported in the statements.

## The Cost Method

Under the cost method, **dividends declared by the subsidiary are recorded as dividend income by the parent at their declaration,** with the offsetting debit to Dividends Receivable. (When dividends subsequently declared by the subsidiary exceed **postacquisition earnings,** the parent treats such excess dividends as a **liquidating dividend** and, accordingly, credits the investment account instead of Dividend Income.) The parent's interest in the subsidiary's earnings and losses is completely ignored unless the magnitude of the subsidiary's losses is such that realization of the parent's cost is in serious doubt. In such instances, a write-down of the investment may be necessary. If such a write-down is made and, subsequently, the subsidiary's operations improve to such a degree that, in retrospect, the original write-down was not required, no adjustment is made to write up the investment to its original cost.

The cost method is conceptually unsound. When a subsidiary continues to have profitable operations, this method can result in an overly conservative valuation of the investment, unless the subsidiary declares dividends equal to earnings each year. Furthermore, the parent's dividend income can be easily manipulated, because the parent controls the subsidiary's dividend policy.

| ILLUSTRATION | ## The Equity Method and the Cost Method Compared |

In this section we compare the equity method and the cost method for a period of two years subsequent to the acquisition date. We assume that all of the common stock of a target company was acquired on January 1, 19X1, and that the earnings, losses, and dividends of the subsidiary for the following two years are as shown below:

|  | 19X1 | 19X2 |
|---|---|---|
| Net income | $15,000 | $25,000 |
| Dividends (Declared December 15, 19X1, and paid January 15, 19X2) | 5,000 | –0– |

Before the equity method and the cost method can be illustrated, the amount of any amortization of cost over or under the book value of the subsidiary's net asset must be determined. Based on situation B of Illustration 3-5 (the parent's total cost of $90,000 was $30,000 in excess of the $60,000 book value of the subsidiary's net assets), the amortization for the two years subsequent to January 1, 19X1, is calculated as follows:

| | Current Value over Book Value Element | | | Goodwill Element | Total |
|---|---|---|---|---|---|
| | Inventory | Land | Equipment | | |
| Remaining life | (3 months) | (Indefinite) | (6 years) | (10 years) | |
| Balance, January 1, 19X1 | $2,000 | $12,000 | $6,000 | $10,000 | $30,000 |
| Amortization—19X1 | (2,000) | | (1,000) | (1,000) | (4,000) |

*(continued)*

| | Current Value over Book Value | | | Goodwill | |
| | Element | | | | |
| | Inventory | Land | Equipment | Element | Total |
|---|---|---|---|---|---|
| Balance, December 31, 19X1 | $ –0– | $12,000 | $5,000 | $ 9,000 | $26,000 |
| Amortization—19X2 ...... | | | (1,000) | (1,000) | (2,000) |
| Balance, December 31, 19X2 | $ –0– | $12,000 | $4,000 | $ 8,000 | $24,000 |

The entries that would be made under the equity method and the cost method are presented in Illustration 4-1.

## Income Statement Classification of Parent's Amortization of Cost in Excess of (or below) Book Value

Note that in Illustration 4-1 the parent's amortization of cost in excess of (or below) book value of the subsidiary's net assets is charged directly to

■ **ILLUSTRATION 4-1**
**The Equity Method and the Cost Method Compared**

| Equity Method | Cost Method |
|---|---|
| **Entries for 19X1** | |
| 1. Subsidiary has $15,000 of earnings:<br>Investment in Subsidiary .... 15,000<br>    Equity in Net Income of<br>        Subsidiary ............ 15,000 | No entry. |
| 2. Subsidiary declares $5,000 of dividends:<br>Dividends Receivable ........ 5,000<br>    Investment in Subsidiary        5,000 | Dividends Receivable....... 5,000<br>    Dividend Income.......        5,000 |
| 3. Parent amortizes cost in excess of book value:<br>Equity in Net Income<br>    of Subsidiary ............. 4,000<br>        Investment in Subsidiary        4,000 | No entry. |
| **Entries for 19X2** | |
| 1. Subsidiary pays dividend declared in 19X1:<br>Cash ...................... 5,000<br>    Dividends Receivable ....        5,000 | Cash ..................... 5,000<br>    Dividends Receivable ...        5,000 |
| 2. Subsidiary has $25,000 of earnings:<br>Investment in Subsidiary .... 25,000<br>    Equity in Net Income of<br>        Subsidiary ............        25,000 | No entry. |
| 3. Parent amortizes cost in excess of book value:<br>Equity in Net Income of<br>    Subsidiary ............... 2,000<br>        Investment in Subsidiary        2,000 | No entry. |

Note: If the subsidiary had a net loss instead of a net income, the entry under the equity method would be:

Equity in Net Loss of Subsidiary ......................... xxx
    Investment in Subsidiary ........................... xxx

the Equity in Net Income of Subsidiary account. Therefore, the true earnings of the subsidiary—using the new basis of accounting that results from the purchase transaction—are obtained ($11,000 for 19X1 and $23,000 for 19X2). **Under the non-push-down basis of accounting, no revaluation to current values is made in the subsidiary's general ledger. Accordingly, the financial statement amounts reported by the subsidiary reflect its old basis of accounting. From the parent's perspective, such amounts are wholly irrelevant.** Under the push-down basis of accounting discussed in the Appendix after Chapter 3, adjustments are made in the subsidiary's general ledger to revalue the subsidiary's assets and liabilities to their current values as of the acquisition date. If push-down accounting had been applied by S Company, then the amortization relating to the undervalued assets and goodwill ($4,000 for 19X1) would have been recorded on S Company's books. As a result, its reported net income for 19X1 would have been $11,000—not $15,000.

**The Secondary Elimination Entry.** Charging the amortization recorded by the parent to the Equity in Net Income of Subsidiary account adds a minor extra step to the consolidation effort. An additional elimination entry must be made **to reclassify this amortization to the appropriate traditional cost and expense accounts.** For example, that portion of the amortization relating to inventory should be shown as part of cost of goods sold. That portion of the amortization relating to the building should be allocated among all departments that use the building—such as manufacturing, marketing, and administration. This elimination entry could be avoided if the parent initially charged the appropriate traditional cost and expense accounts when it recorded the amortization. Doing so would not be proper, however, because the amortization account relates solely to the parent's investment in the subsidiary and not to any of its own separate operations. The entry does not affect net income, because it takes place entirely within the income statement section of the worksheet. For instructional purposes and ease of reference, we find it convenient to label this entry; accordingly, we call it the **secondary elimination entry.**

To illustrate the reclassification nature of this entry, the secondary elimination entry for 19X1, assuming all of the amortization is properly classifiable in Cost of Goods Sold, would be:

| | | |
|---|---|---|
| Cost of Goods Sold. . . . . . . . . . . . . . . . . . . . . . . | 4,000 | |
| Equity in Net Income of Subsidiary . . . . . | | 4,000 |

## The Merits of the Equity Method

The equity method of accounting is a marvelous valuation technique that is unique in accounting. It has become the dominant practice for the following reasons:

1. **It reflects economic substance.** Only the equity method consistently reflects the economic substance of whether the parent's investment has increased or decreased in value as a result of the subsidiary's economic activity. (Under the cost method, the investment is never increased and can be reduced only for liquidating dividends and impairments of value.)

2. **It keeps track of the amount invested.** The equity method automatically keeps track of how much the parent has invested in the subsidiary (including the reinvestment of a subsidiary's undistributed earnings), enabling calculations of return on investment to be made more readily. (Under the cost method, analyses or tracking the investment must be made on working papers outside the general ledger to arrive at the denominator in such calculations.)

3. **It enables parent company financial statements to be used meaningfully internally.** A parent company's financial statements (unconsolidated) are usually meaningful only if investments in subsidiaries are accounted for under the equity method. (Under the cost method, such statements can become of limited usefulness.)

4. **It provides a built-in self-checking feature.** Under the equity method, the parent's net income and retained earnings are identical to the respective consolidated amounts. Thus, a useful self-checking feature exists. This makes the consolidation effort easier. (Under the cost method, no such feature exists.)

5. **It provides a better means of keeping records.** Under the equity method, amortization entries are made in the general ledger. (Under the cost method, such entries are made in consolidation.) General ledger entries provide a better means of keeping records than do worksheet elimination entries.

6. **It is a more logical method for pooled subsidiaries.** To record an investment in a pooled subsidiary at the parent's underlying equity in the subsidiary's net assets and then use the cost method does not make as much sense as maintaining the investment at the parent's underlying equity in the net assets using the equity method.

The remainder of this chapter discusses the preparation of consolidated financial statements for periods subsequent to the acquisition date when the parent uses the equity method of accounting. Appendix A following this chapter focuses on the preparation of consolidated financial statements for periods subsequent to the acquisition date when the parent uses the cost method of accounting for its investment.

We should point out that regardless of the general use of the cost method for unconsolidated subsidiaries (as discussed earlier), *FASB Statement No. 94* did not address in any way whatsoever how investments in consolidated subsidiaries should be carried on the books of parent companies. From our inquiries to numerous high-ranking Fortune 500 companies and practicing certified public accountants, *FASB Statement No. 94* has not resulted in any shift away from the equity method to the cost method.

## Tax Matters

For income tax reporting purposes, the Internal Revenue Service (IRS) rules are based on the cash basis, not the equity method. Accordingly, a parent company is not taxed on its subsidiary's earnings until the parent receives dividends. Even then, if certain ownership conditions are met, a consolidated federal income tax return can be filed whereby no taxes need be paid on the subsidiary's dividends. Income tax matters are discussed in more detail in Chapter 12.

# PREPARING CONSOLIDATED FINANCIAL STATEMENTS

## Updating the Expanded Analysis of the Investment Account Using the Equity Method to Obtain the Source of the Primary Elimination Entry

To prepare consolidated financial statements for periods subsequent to the acquisition date, we must first update the analysis of the investment account by the components of the major conceptual elements for the entries recorded under the equity method. Certain changes in format and assumptions are made to make the preparation of the consolidated financial statements easier. Two additional retained earnings columns are used: one column to isolate the parent company's interest in the subsidiary's current earnings, and one column to isolate the parent company's share of dividends declared by the subsidiary during the current year.

Updating the analysis of the investment account in this manner allows the balances at a given date to be the source of the primary elimination entry that effects the consolidation. This technique greatly simplifies the preparation of the consolidated financial statements. After the statements are prepared, the balances in the two additional retained earnings columns are reclassified to the "Prior Years" retained earnings column to facilitate the preparation of the consolidated financial statements in the following year.

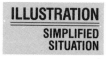

**ILLUSTRATION**
SIMPLIFIED
SITUATION

## Purchase Price Is Equal to Book Value of Net Assets: No Over- or Undervalued Assets

Before approaching a consolidation of normal complexity, we first focus on a simple (although somewhat unrealistic) situation in which: (1) none

of the subsidiary's assets or liabilities are over- or undervalued (thus eliminating the need for the current value over (or under) book value element
of the conceptual analysis of the investment account); and (2) the parent's
cost of acquiring the subsidiary is 100% of the book value of the subsidiary's net assets (thus eliminating the need for the goodwill or bargain
purchase element). Accordingly, only the book value element exists.

Assume P Company acquired all of the outstanding common stock of
S Company at a total cost of $60,000 and S Company's net assets have a
current value and a book value of $60,000. Also assume that the sub-
sidiary had the same net income and dividends declared as in Illustration
4-1 (net income of $15,000 for 19X1 and $25,000 for 19X2; dividends
declared of $5,000 for 19X1 and no dividends declared for 19X2). The
expanded analysis of the investment account for the two years subsequent to the acquisition date, using the equity method of accounting, is
updated in Illustration 4-2.

### Preparing the Primary Elimination Entry from the Updated Analysis of the Investment Account.
The primary elimination entries that would be obtained
from the preceding analysis to prepare consolidated financial statements
as of December 31, 19X1, (one year after the acquisition date), and
December 31, 19X2 (two years after the acquisition date), are as follows:

■ ILLUSTRATION 4-2
**Updating the Expanded Analysis of the Investment Account Using the Equity Method: Total Cost Equals Book Value of Net Assets (No Over- or Undervalued Assets)**

| | Total Cost | = | Common Stock | + | Prior Years | + | Earnings | − | Dividends |
|---|---|---|---|---|---|---|---|---|---|
| | | | | | | | Book Value Element — Retained Earnings — Current Year | | |
| Balance, Jan. 1, 19X1 . . . . . . | $60,000 | | $40,000 | | $20,000 | | | | |
| Equity in net income . . . . . | 15,000 | | | | | | $15,000 | | |
| Dividends . . . . . . . . . . . . . . . | (5,000) | | | | | | | | $(5,000) |
| Subtotal . . . . . . . . . . . . . . . . . | $70,000 | | $40,000 | | $20,000 | | $15,000 | | $(5,000) |
| Reclassification[a] . . . . . . . . . | | | | | 10,000 | | (15,000) | | 5,000 |
| Balance, Dec. 31, 19X1 . . . . . | $70,000 | | $40,000 | | $30,000 | | $ –0– | | $ –0– |
| Equity in net income . . . . . | 25,000 | | | | | | 25,000 | | |
| Subtotal . . . . . . . . . . . . . . . . | $95,000 | | $40,000 | | $30,000 | | $25,000 | | $ –0– |
| Reclassification[a] . . . . . . . . | | | | | 25,000 | | (25,000) | | |
| Balance, Dec. 31, 19X2 . . . . . | $95,000 | | $40,000 | | $55,000 | | $ –0– | | $ –0– |

Note: The amounts used to update the analysis are from Illustration 4-1.

[a]This reclassification is made after the primary elimination is prepared and is analogous to a closing entry. No formal journal entry is
recorded because the analysis of the total cost of the investment is maintained in a schedule outside the general ledger.

WORKSHEET
ENTRIES ONLY

|  | Consolidation Date | |
| --- | --- | --- |
|  | December 31, 19X1 | December 31, 19X2 |
| Common Stock ............. | 40,000 | 40,000 |
| Retained Earnings (beginning of year)......... | 20,000 | 30,000 |
| Equity in Net Income of Subsidiary................ | 15,000 | 25,000 |
| Dividends Declared ..... | 5,000 | –0– |
| Investment in Subsidiary............. | 70,000 | 95,000 |

The following points are important for understanding this entry:

1. **The debit to Equity in Net Income of Subsidiary:** Isolating the subsidiary's current-year earnings or losses in a separate column enables us to eliminate the Equity in Net Income or Loss of Subsidiary account balance in the parent's column of the consolidating statement worksheet by posting the balance in the current-year column directly to this account on the worksheet. (The posting is then totaled at the net income line and carried forward to the net income line in the analysis of retained earnings section of the worksheet.)

2. **The credit to Dividends Declared:** The dividends declared by the subsidiary are posted directly to the dividends declared line in the analysis of retained earnings section of the worksheet. This prevents the subsidiary's dividends from being added to the parent's dividends in arriving at the dividends to be reported for consolidated purposes. Any dividends declared by the wholly owned subsidiary are intercompany transactions that cannot be considered dividends from the consolidated group to stockholders. The only dividends to stockholders are the dividends declared by the parent.

3. **The effect on the subsidiary's retained earnings:** The direct postings to the analysis of retained earnings (for the beginning balance and dividends declared), and the carryforward from the income statement to the net income line in the analysis of retained earnings, combine to eliminate the subsidiary's retained earnings in consolidation.

Illustration 4-3 shows a consolidating statement worksheet as of December 31, 19X1 (one year after the acquisition date), using the primary elimination entry for that date in the previous section. An elimination entry is also needed for the subsidiary's accumulated depreciation balances as of the acquisition date. That entry is for the same amount as that used in the worksheet illustrations in Chapter 3. The entry follows:

WORKSHEET
ENTRY ONLY

| Accumulated Depreciation .................... | 50,000 | |
| --- | --- | --- |
| Buildings and Equipment ............... | | 50,000 |

## ■ ILLUSTRATION 4-3
### First Year Subsequent to Acquisition Date

**P COMPANY AND SUBSIDIARY (S COMPANY)**
**Consolidating Statement Worksheet for the Year Ended December 31, 19X1**

| | P Company | S Company | Eliminations Dr. | Eliminations Cr. | Consolidated |
|---|---|---|---|---|---|
| **Income Statement** | | | | | |
| Sales .......................... | 600,000 | 225,000 | | | 825,000 |
| Cost of goods sold .............. | (360,000) | (110,000) | | | (470,000) |
| Expenses ...................... | (190,000) | (100,000) | | | (290,000) |
| Intercompany Account: | | | | | |
| Equity in net income of S Company ............... | 15,000 | | 15,000(1) | | –0– |
| Net Income .................... | 65,000 | 15,000 | 15,000 | | 65,000 |
| **Statement of Retained Earnings** | | | | | |
| Balances, January 1, 19X1 ...... | 100,000ᵃ | 20,000 | 20,000(1) | | 100,000 |
| +Net income ................... | 65,000 | 15,000 | 15,000 | | 65,000 |
| −Dividends declared ........... | (45,000) | (5,000) | | 5,000(1) | (45,000) |
| Balances, December 31, 19X1 ... | 120,000 | 30,000 | 35,000 | 5,000 | 120,000 |
| **Balance Sheet** | | | | | |
| Cash .......................... | 55,000 | 11,000 | | | 66,000 |
| Accounts receivable, net ........ | 75,000 | 37,000 | | | 112,000 |
| Inventory ..................... | 110,000 | 55,000 | | | 165,000 |
| Investment in S Company ....... | 70,000 | | | 70,000(1) | –0– |
| Land.......................... | 220,000 | 30,000 | | | 250,000 |
| Buildings and equipment ....... | 500,000 | 200,000 | | 50,000(2) | 650,000 |
| Accumulated depreciation ....... | (320,000) | (63,000) | 50,000(2) | | (333,000) |
| Total Assets ................ | 710,000 | 270,000 | 50,000 | 120,000 | 910,000 |
| Liabilities ...................... | 290,000 | 200,000 | | | 490,000 |
| P Company: | | | | | |
| Common stock ............... | 300,000 | | | | 300,000 |
| Retained earnings ........... | 120,000 | | | | 120,000 |
| S Company: | | | | | |
| Common stock ............... | | 40,000 | 40,000(1) | | –0– |
| Retained earnings ........... | | 30,000 | 35,000 | 5,000 | –0– |
| Total Liabilities and Equity .... | 710,000 | 270,000 | 75,000 | 5,000 | 910,000 |
| Proof of debit and credit postings ................... | | | 125,000 | 125,000 | |

Explanation of entries:
(1) The primary elimination entry.
(2) The accumulated depreciation elimination entry. (Note that this is the amount at the acquisition date—not the subsidiary's accumulated depreciation at this consolidation date.

ᵃThis amount is the parent's retained earnings as of the acquisition date as shown in Illustration 3-6.

### Review Points for Illustration 4-3.    Note the following:

1. P Company's net income is the same as the consolidated net income.
2. P Company's retained earnings is the same as the consolidated retained earnings.
3. All of the subsidiary's equity accounts have been eliminated.
4. The Equity in Net Income of S Company account has been eliminated.

**ILLUSTRATION**
**MORE COMPLEX**
**SITUATION**

## Purchase Price Is More Than Book Value of Net Assets: Assets Are Undervalued and Goodwill Exists

We now concentrate on a consolidation of normal complexity in which the subsidiary's assets are undervalued and the parent's purchase price includes an amount for goodwill. We use the information provided on page 159 earlier in the chapter for Illustration 4-1, in which the $90,000 purchase price is $30,000 in excess of the $60,000 book value of the net assets. The net income and dividends declared amounts for the subsidiary are taken from the preceding simplified situation. The expanded analysis of the investment account for the two years subsequent to the acquisition, using the equity method of accounting, is updated as shown in Illustration 4-4.

### Review Points for Illustration 4-4.    Note the following:

1. The entries pertaining to the amortization of the current value over book value element actually expense a portion of the total cost of the investment on the parent company's books. These entries bring the investment's total carrying value closer to the book value of the subsidiary's net assets.
2. The inventory component of the current value over book value element was completely expensed in 19X1. Therefore, this component does not exist after 19X1.
3. The land component of the current value over book value element is part of that element until the land is disposed of, at which time it is charged to income.
4. The equipment component of the current value over book value element is amortized to expense over 6 years. At the end of 6 years, the amount in the accumulated depreciation column will equal the amount in the equipment cost column. Thereafter, these offsetting amounts are part of the current value over book value element until the asset is disposed of.
5. The goodwill element is amortized to expense over 10 years. At the end of 10 years, the goodwill element will no longer exist.

**Preparing the Primary Elimination Entry from the Updated Analysis of the Investment Account.**    The primary elimination entries as of December 31, 19X1

# ■ ILLUSTRATION 4-4
## Updating the Expanded Analysis of the Investment Account Using the Equity Method
(Wholly owned subsidiary — Total cost is above current value of subsidiary's net assets [Current value is above book value])

| | | Book Value Element | | | | Current Value over Book Value Element | | | | |
| | | | | Retained Earnings | | | | | Equipment | | |
| | Total Cost | = Common Stock | + Prior Years | + Current Year Earnings | − Dividends | + Inventory | + Land | + Cost | + Accum. Depr. | + Goodwill Element |
|---|---|---|---|---|---|---|---|---|---|---|
| Balance, Jan. 1, 19X1 | $ 90,000 | $40,000 | $20,000 | | | $2,000 | $12,000 | $6,000 | | $10,000 |
| Equity in net income | 15,000 | | | $15,000 | | | | | | |
| Dividends | (5,000) | | | | $(5,000) | | | | | |
| Amortization | (4,000) | | | | | (2,000) | | | $(1,000) | (1,000) |
| Subtotal | $ 96,000 | $40,000 | $20,000 | $15,000 | $(5,000) | $ –0– | $12,000 | $6,000 | $(1,000) | $ 9,000 |
| Reclassification[a] | | | 10,000 | (15,000) | 5,000 | | | | | |
| Balance, Dec. 31, 19X1 | $ 96,000 | $40,000 | $30,000 | $ –0– | $ –0– | $ –0– | $12,000 | $6,000 | $(1,000) | $9,000 |
| Equity in net income | 25,000 | | | 25,000 | | | | | | |
| Amortization | (2,000) | | | | | | | | (1,000) | (1,000) |
| Subtotal | 119,000 | $40,000 | $30,000 | $25,000 | $ –0– | $ –0– | $12,000 | $6,000 | $(2,000) | $8,000 |
| Reclassification[a] | | | 25,000 | (25,000) | | | | | | |
| Balance, Dec. 31, 19X2 | $119,000 | $40,000 | $55,000 | $ –0– | $ –0– | $ –0– | $12,000 | $6,000 | $(2,000) | $8,000 |

Note: The beginning balances are taken from situation B of Illustration 3-5. The amounts used to update the analysis are from Illustration 4-1.

[a]This reclassification is made after the primary elimination entry is prepared and is analogous to a closing entry. No formal journal entry is recorded because the analysis of the total cost of the investment is maintained in a schedule outside the general ledger.

(one year after the acquisition date), and December 31, 19X2 (two years after the acquisition date), are as follows:

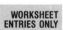

|  | Consolidation Date | |
|---|---|---|
|  | December 31, 19X1 | December 31, 19X2 |
| Common Stock . . . . . . . . . . . . . | 40,000 | 40,000 |
| Retained Earnings (beginning of year) . . . . . . . . | 20,000 | 30,000 |
| Equity in Net Income of Subsidiary . . . . . . . . . . . . . . . | 15,000 | 25,000 |
| Land . . . . . . . . . . . . . . . . . . . . | 12,000 | 12,000 |
| Equipment . . . . . . . . . . . . . . . | 6,000 | 6,000 |
| Goodwill . . . . . . . . . . . . . . . . . | 9,000 | 8,000 |
| Dividends Declared . . . . . | 5,000 | –0– |
| Accumulated Depreciation . . . . . . . . . . . | 1,000 | 2,000 |
| Investment in Subsidiary . . . . . . . . . . . . . | 96,000 | 119,000 |

### Preparing the Secondary Elimination Entry from the Updated Analysis of the Investment Account.

The secondary elimination entries as of December 31, 19X1 (one year after the acquisition date), and December 31, 19X2 (two years after the acquisition date), are as follows:

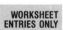

|  | Consolidation Date | |
|---|---|---|
|  | December 31, 19X1 | December 31, 19X2 |
| Cost of Goods Sold . . . . . . . . . | 4,000 | 2,000 |
| Equity in Net Income of Subsidiary . . . . . . . . . . . . | 4,000 | 2,000 |

For simplicity, we arbitrarily assumed that all of the goodwill amortization and all of the amortization relating to the building should be classified as part of Cost of Goods Sold. The amortization relating to the inventory belongs in Cost of Goods Sold.

### Preparation of Worksheets.

Using the primary and secondary elimination entries at December 31, 19X1 and 19X2 (shown in the preceding sections), consolidating statement worksheets at these dates are shown in Illustrations 4-5 and 4-6. The same accumulated depreciation elimination for $50,000 used in the earlier simplified situation is used.

### Review Points for Illustrations 4-5 and 4-6.

Note the following:

1. As was the case in Illustration 4-3, (the simplified situation), the net income and retained earnings amounts in the P Company column

## ILLUSTRATION 4-5
### First Year Subsequent to Acquisition Date

| | P Company | S Company | Eliminations Dr. | Eliminations Cr. | Consolidated |
|---|---|---|---|---|---|
| **Income Statement** | | | | | |
| Sales......................... | 600,000 | 225,000 | | | 825,000 |
| Cost of goods sold............. | (360,000) | (110,000) | 4,000(2) | | (474,000) |
| Expenses...................... | (190,000) | (100,000) | | | (290,000) |
| Intercompany Account: | | | | | |
| Equity in net income of | | | | | |
| S Company................ | 11,000[a] | | 15,000(1) | 4,000(2) | –0– |
| Net Income................... | 61,000 | 15,000 | 19,000 | 4,000 | 61,000 |
| **Statement of Retained Earnings** | | | | | |
| Balances, January 1, 19X1...... | 100,000 | 20,000 | 20,000(1) | | 100,000 |
| +Net income.................. | 61,000 | 15,000 | 19,000 | 4,000 | 61,000 |
| –Dividends declared........... | (45,000) | (5,000) | | 5,000(1) | (45,000) |
| Balances, December 31, 19X1... | 116,000 | 30,000 | 39,000 | 9,000 | 116,000 |
| **Balance Sheet** | | | | | |
| Cash......................... | 25,000 | 11,000 | | | 36,000 |
| Accounts receivable, net......... | 75,000 | 37,000 | | | 112,000 |
| Inventory..................... | 110,000 | 55,000 | | | 165,000 |
| Investment in S Company....... | 96,000 | | | 96,000(1) | –0– |
| Land......................... | 220,000 | 30,000 | 12,000(1) | | 262,000 |
| Buildings and equipment....... | 500,000 | 200,000 | 6,000(1) | 50,000(3) | 656,000 |
| Accumulated depreciation....... | (320,000) | (63,000) | 50,000(3) | 1,000(1) | (334,000) |
| Goodwill...................... | | | 9,000(1) | | 9,000 |
| Total Assets.................. | 706,000 | 270,000 | 77,000 | 147,000 | 906,000 |
| Liabilities..................... | 290,000 | 200,000 | | | 490,000 |
| P Company: | | | | | |
| Common stock............... | 300,000 | | | | 300,000 |
| Retained earnings ............ | 116,000 | | | | 116,000 |
| S Company: | | | | | |
| Common stock............... | | 40,000 | 40,000(1) | | –0– |
| Retained earnings ............ | | 30,000 | 39,000 | 9,000 | –0– |
| Total Liabilities and Equity.... | 706,000 | 270,000 | 79,000 | 9,000 | 906,000 |
| Proof of debit and credit postings......................... | | | 156,000 | 156,000 | |

Explanation of entries:
(1) The primary elimination entry.
(2) The secondary elimination entry.
(3) The accumulated depreciation elimination entry.

[a] S Company's $15,000 of reported net income less $4,000 of amortization of cost in excess of book value.

## ■ ILLUSTRATION 4-6
### Second Year Subsequent to Acquisition Date

**P COMPANY AND SUBSIDIARY (S COMPANY)**
**Consolidating Statement Worksheet for the Year Ended December 31, 19X2**

| | P Company | S Company | Eliminations Dr. | Eliminations Cr. | Consolidated |
|---|---|---|---|---|---|
| **Income Statement** | | | | | |
| Sales . . . . . . . . . . . . . . . . . . . . . . . . . | 650,000 | 250,000 | | | 900,000 |
| Cost of goods sold. . . . . . . . . . . . . . | (398,000) | (120,000) | 2,000(2) | | (520,000) |
| Expenses . . . . . . . . . . . . . . . . . . . . . . | (185,000) | (105,000) | | | (290,000) |
| Intercompany Account: | | | | | |
| Equity in net income of | | | | | |
| S Company. . . . . . . . . . . . . . . . | 23,000ᵃ | | 25,000(1) | 2,000(2) | –0– |
| Net Income . . . . . . . . . . . . . . . . . . . | 90,000 | 25,000 | 27,000 | 2,000 | 90,000 |
| **Statement of Retained Earnings** | | | | | |
| Balances, January 1, 19X1. . . . . . . | 116,000 | 30,000 | 30,000(1) | | 116,000 |
| + Net income . . . . . . . . . . . . . . . . . . . | 90,000 | 25,000 | 27,000 | 2,000 | 90,000 |
| – Dividends declared. . . . . . . . . . . . | (61,000) | –0– | | | (61,000) |
| Balances, December 31, 19X1 . . . . | 145,000 | 55,000 | 57,000 | 2,000 | 145,000 |
| **Balance Sheet** | | | | | |
| Cash . . . . . . . . . . . . . . . . . . . . . . . . . . | 41,000 | 31,000 | | | 72,000 |
| Accounts receivable, net. . . . . . . . . | 95,000 | 45,000 | | | 140,000 |
| Inventory . . . . . . . . . . . . . . . . . . . . . . | 130,000 | 80,000 | | | 210,000 |
| Investment in S Company. . . . . . . . | 119,000 | | | 119,000(1) | –0– |
| Land . . . . . . . . . . . . . . . . . . . . . . . . . . | 220,000 | 30,000 | 12,000(1) | | 262,000 |
| Buildings and equipment . . . . . . . . | 540,000 | 200,000 | 6,000(1) | 50,000(3) | 696,000 |
| Accumulated depreciation . . . . . . . . | (360,000) | (76,000) | 50,000(3) | 2,000(1) | (388,000) |
| Goodwill. . . . . . . . . . . . . . . . . . . . . . . | | | 8,000(1) | | 8,000 |
| Total Assets . . . . . . . . . . . . . . . . | 785,000 | 310,000 | 76,000 | 171,000 | 1,000,000 |
| Liabilities. . . . . . . . . . . . . . . . . . . . . . | 340,000 | 215,000 | | | 555,000 |
| P Company: | | | | | |
| Common stock. . . . . . . . . . . . . . . | 300,000 | | | | 300,000 |
| Retained earnings . . . . . . . . . . . . | 145,000 | | | | 145,000 |
| S Company: | | | | | |
| Common stock. . . . . . . . . . . . . . . | | 40,000 | 40,000(1) | | –0– |
| Retained earnings . . . . . . . . . . . . | | 55,000 | 57,000 | 2,000 | –0– |
| Total Liabilities and Equity. . . . . | 785,000 | 310,000 | 97,000 | 2,000 | 1,000,000 |
| Proof of debit and credit postings . . . . . . . . . . . . . . . . . . . . . . . . | | | 173,000 | 173,000 | |

Explanation of entries:
(1) The primary elimination entry.   (3) The accumulated depreciation elimination entry.
(2) The secondary elimination entry.

ᵃ$25,000 of income recorded under the equity method, net of $2,000 of amortization of cost in excess of book value.

are the same as in the consolidated column. This equality always exists under the equity method of accounting.

2. On full amortization of the excess relating to the equipment and the goodwill, the Investment in Subsidiary account balance will then be $12,000 over the subsidiary's net assets at book value. This amount pertains to the land component.

3. If the subsidiary's land is sold, this $12,000 would be amortized in full at that time, and the investment account balance would then equal the book value of the subsidiary's net assets.

4. **Key Review Point:** The amounts reported in the financial statements prepared by the subsidiary are wholly irrelevant amounts. Under the non-push-down basis of accounting, such amounts do not reflect the new basis of accounting that takes place as a result of the acquisition being accounted for as a purchase (as opposed to a pooling of interests). Accordingly, the true earnings of the subsidiary from the parent's perspective are not $15,000. The parent earned only $11,000 on its investment in 19X1 (the $15,000 of "irrelevant income" recorded under the equity method of accounting, less the $4,000 of amortization of cost in excess of book value) and $23,000 for 19X2 ($25,000 − $2,000).

## All Other Possible Situations

Many other possible situations may exist. For instance, assets may be overvalued, a bargain purchase element may be present, or the purchase price may be below the book value of the net assets. The conceptual analysis of the investment account can be used for any situation. For example, when the current value of the subsidiary's net assets is below their book value, the net overvaluation produces a negative amount in the second major conceptual element—the current value over (or under) book value element. Separating this major conceptual element into its individual components may reveal that certain assets are overvalued and certain assets are undervalued. For those depreciable and amortizable assets that are overvalued, a credit balance is amortized instead of a debit balance. Therefore, the secondary elimination entry involves reclassifying the *credit* made to the Equity in Net Income of Subsidiary account.

The procedures for preparing consolidated financial statements for these situations are the same as when the current value of the subsidiary's net assets is above their book value.

## Mid-year Acquisitions

The preceding examples used an acquisition date as of the beginning of the parent's reporting year (January 1, 19X1). Most business combinations occur at various times during a year. **Regardless of the acquisition date, only the postacquisition income statement of the subsidiary is con-**

**solidated.** For example, assume the acquisition date is April 1, 19X1, and S Company had the following income statement amounts for 19X1:

|  | Jan. 1–Mar. 31 | April 1–Dec. 31 | Total |
|---|---|---|---|
| Revenues............ | $ 55,000 | $170,000 | $225,000 |
| Cost of goods sold.... | (23,000) | (87,000) | (110,000) |
| Expenses............ | (30,000) | (70,000) | (100,000) |
| Net Income......... | $ 2,000 | $ 13,000 | $ 15,000 |
| Relevance of above amounts: | Disregard | Use | Disregard |

Accordingly, the parent would apply the equity method of accounting to the $13,000 of earnings occurring after the acquisition date, and only the income statement amounts for this period would be consolidated.

## THE ONGOING ASSESSMENT OF THE VALUE OF GOODWILL

*Accounting Principles Board Opinion No. 17*, "Intangible Assets," requires that a continual assessment be made to determine whether subsequent events and circumstances warrant either (a) a change in the estimated remaining life (it can never exceed 40 years in total), or (b) a write-down or write-off of the unamortized amount of goodwill. This is one of the most judgmental areas in all of accounting, primarily because guidance from professional pronouncements is virtually nonexistent.

### Revising the Estimated Remaining Life

In practice, changes in the estimated remaining life are rarely made, mostly because the majority of companies initially assign the maximum 40-year life to goodwill so as to minimize the annual charge to each year's earnings. With goodwill generally viewed as the amount paid for the projected or anticipated superior earnings stream of a business, managements that are audacious enough to assert that the superior earnings stream will last for at least 40 years in this day and age of rapid technological change are very reluctant to shorten the remaining life. Recall from Chapter 2 that a high percentage of acquired businesses are later sold because management was unable to successfully run the business as initially had been planned. In fact, the number and percentage of acquired businesses for which the 40-year life was assigned for goodwill and that were later sold long before the 40-year amortization period expired is extremely high. This tends to make a mockery of the allowable 40-year life.

### Taking a Major Write-down or Write-off

A major problem in practice is how to value goodwill when a business begins experiencing operating or financial difficulties. The *APB Opinion*

*No. 17* suggests that if the business has a loss for one year or possibly a few years in a row, serious consideration should be given to lowering the carrying value of goodwill. This guidance focuses entirely on **recoverability.** When a company is reporting losses, obviously the goodwill is not being recovered—that is, not being converted back into cash. As long as the business is profitable or breaking even, the goodwill *is* being recovered. **Unfortunately, by focusing solely on recoverability, accountants lose sight of the real issue, which is whether the value of the goodwill has diminished.** A company does not have to incur losses for goodwill to have diminished in value. Goodwill can lose its value when a company becomes marginally profitable, operates at a breakeven point, or operates at a level far below that anticipated when the business was acquired. Far too often, goodwill is carried on the books long after its value has diminished as a result of poor (but still profitable) operating results.

Perhaps the most glaring example of the 1980s (and possibly of all time) of reporting goodwill as an asset long after it should have been cleared off the balance sheet is of Financial Corporation of America (FCA), the parent company of American Savings and Loan (American), the largest savings and loan in the country. FCA acquired American in 1983, paying $1.1 billion for goodwill, which it chose to amortize over 30 years. In 1984, American incurred a loss of approximately $600 million, wiping out approximately 75% of its net worth. The company was so financially distressed that the federal regulators imposed stringent operating restrictions (a common procedure whenever the net worth of a federal savings and loan drops below the minimum 3% of total assets). American was barely profitable in 1985 and 1986. In 1987, it reported another huge loss (approximately $470 million), which lowered stockholders' equity to approximately $170 million negative. From 1984 through 1988, American (with over $30 billion in assets) was the number one problem institution of the federal regulators. After numerous attempts to sell American failed, it was finally sold at the end of 1988, with federal agencies to provide aid of $1.7 billion. During these five years of troubled times, the company's independent auditors did not insist on, nor did management make, a write-down or write-off of goodwill. Approximately $950 million of goodwill was written off at the time of the disposal.

## SELECTED REFERENCES

Colley, J. Ron, and Ara G. Volkan. "Accounting for Goodwill." *Accounting Horizons* (March 1988), pp. 35–41. (This article deals with the impact of goodwill on earnings.)

Rue, Joseph C., and David E. Tosh. "Should We Consolidate Finance Subsidiaries?" *Management Accounting* (April 1987), pp. 45–50. (This article refers to the equity method of accounting in detail.)

## END-OF-CHAPTER REVIEW

### Summary of Key Points

1. Parent companies may account for investments in subsidiaries using the equity method or the cost method.
2. Under the equity method, the carrying value of the investment is automatically adjusted for the economic activity of the subsidiary.
3. Under the cost method, the carrying value of the investment is not adjusted unless the subsidiary (a) pays dividends in excess of postacquisition earnings (liquidating dividends) or (b) incurs losses to such an extent that the carrying value of the investment is impaired.
4. The consolidated financial statement amounts are the same regardless of whether the parent uses the equity method or the cost method.
5. Amortization of the parent's cost in excess of book value is recorded (a) in the parent's general ledger under the equity method and (b) in the consolidation worksheet under the cost method.
6. Only postacquisition income statements can be consolidated.
7. If a subsidiary is not consolidated (this is only possible when control no longer exists), the general method of accounting for the investment is the cost method (although the equity method may be used providing the parent can exert significant influence).

### Glossary of New Terms

**Cost method**   A method of accounting for an investment in a subsidiary whereby the carrying value of the investment is never changed unless it is permanently impaired.

**Equity method (as applied to subsidiaries)**   A method of accounting for an investment in a subsidiary whereby the carrying value of the investment is (1) increased as a result of the subsidiary's earnings, (2) decreased as a result of the subsidiary's losses (3) decreased as a result of the dividends declared on the subsidiary's common stock, and (4) adjusted for the amortization of cost over or under the book value of the subsidiary's net assets.

**Liquidating dividend**   Dividends declared by a subsidiary that are in excess of the subsidiary's earnings subsequent to the acquisition date.

**Postacquisition earnings**   Earnings of a subsidiary that occur subsequent to the acquisition date.

### Self-Study Questions
*(Answers are at the end of this chapter, preceding the appendices.)*

1. What would be the effect on the financial statements if an unconsolidated subsidiary is accounted for by the equity method but consolidated statements are prepared with other subsidiaries?
   a. All of the unconsolidated subsidiary's account are included individually in the consolidated statements.
   b. The consolidated retained earnings amount does not reflect the earnings of the unconsolidated subsidiary.

c. The consolidated retained earnings amount is the same as it would be if the subsidiary had been included in the consolidation.

d. Dividend revenue, from the unconsolidated subsidiary is reflected in consolidated net income.

e. None of the above.

2. A parent accounts for its investment in its subsidiary in its general ledger using the cost method. In the parent's unconsolidated financial statements, which accounts other than Cash are affected as a result of the subsidiary reporting profits and paying dividends?

a. Dividends Revenue, Equity in Earnings of Subsidiary, and Retained Earnings.

b. Dividend Revenue and Retained Earnings.

c. Investment in Subsidiary, Equity in Earnings of Subsidiary, Dividend Revenue, and Retained Earnings.

d. Investment in Subsidiary, Equity in Earnings of Subsidiary, and Retained Earnings.

e. None of the above.

3. Cash dividends declared out of current earnings are distributed to an investor. How will the investor's investment account be affected by those dividends under each of the following accounting methods?

| | **Cost Method** | **Equity Method** |
|---|---|---|
| a. | Decrease | No effect |
| b. | Decrease | Decrease |
| c. | No effect | Decrease |
| d. | No effect | No effect |

4. How will the investor's investment account be affected by the investor's share of the earnings of the investee after the date of acquisition under each of the following accounting methods?

| | **Cost Method** | **Equity Method** |
|---|---|---|
| a. | No effect | Increase |
| b. | Increase | Increase |
| c. | Increase | No effect |
| d. | No effect | No effect |

5. On April 1, 19X1, Pax Company acquired 100% of the outstanding common stock of Sax Company for cash of $500,000. For 19X1, Sax had net income of $20,000 each quarter. Also for 19X1, Sax declared and paid cash dividends of $12,000 for each of the first three quarters and $40,000 for the fourth quarter. Amortization of cost in excess of book value for 19X1 is $10,000. What is Pax's carrying value of its investment in Sax at December 31, 19X1, under the equity method?

a. $486,000

b. $494,000

c. $496,000

d. $504,000

e. $546,000

6. Assume the same information as in question 5. What is the carrying value of the investment in Sax at December 31, 19X1, under the cost method?
   a. $486,000
   b. $494,000
   c. $496,000
   d. $500,000
   e. $504,000

7. Assume the same information in question 5. What amount appears in Pax's 19X1 income statement if Pax accounts for its investment in Sax under the equity method?
   a. $(6,000)
   b. $4,000
   c. $46,000
   d. $50,000
   e. $70,000

8. Assume the same information in question 5. What amount appears in Pax's 19X1 income statement if Pax accounts for its investment in Sax under the cost method?
   a. $50,000
   b. $54,000
   c. $60,000
   d. $64,000
   e. $76,000

9. Consolidated financial statements are typically prepared when one company has
   a. Accounted for its investment in another company by the equity method.
   b. Accounted for its investment in another company by the cost method.
   c. Significant influence over the operating and financial policies of another company.
   d. The controlling financial interest in another company.

10. A parent cannot consolidate a subsidiary when:
   a. The parent uses the equity method of accounting.
   b. The parent has changed from the equity method to the cost method.
   c. The parent will present the subsidiary's separate financial statements along with its own separate financial statements.
   d. The parent has definitive plans to sell its entire ownership interest in the subsidiary.
   e. None of the above.

11. Which of the choices below is an *incorrect* completion of the sentence: Consolidated financial statement amounts are always the same regardless of whether
   a. The acquisition is of common stock or assets.
   b. The equity method or the cost method is used.
   c. The non-push-down basis of accounting or the push-down basis of accounting is used.
   d. The acquisition occurs at the beginning of the parent's reporting year or later in the year.
   e. None of the above.

(AICPA adapted, Nos. 1–4, 9)

# Demonstration Problem

Poda Company acquired all of the outstanding common stock of Suda Company on April 1, 19X4, at a total cost of $540,000. Suda's capital accounts at the acquisition date were:

| | |
|---|---:|
| Common stock | $ 90,000 |
| Retained earnings | 310,000 |

The only assets and liabilities of Suda that were over- or undervalued at the acquisition date were as follows:

Patent—overvalued by $40,000 (10-year remaining life)
Land—undervalued by $120,000

For 19X4, Suda had the following earnings and dividends:

| | First Quarter | Remainder of Year | Total |
|---|---:|---:|---:|
| Net Income | $30,000 | $70,000 | $100,000 |
| Dividends declared | 20,000 | 60,000 | 80,000 |

Poda has chosen to use: (a) the equity method of accounting and (b) a five-year life for goodwill.

## Required:

1. Prepare the journal entries Poda would make for the year ended December 31, 19X4, under the equity method.
2. Prepare an expanded analysis of the investment account as of the acquisition date, and update it for the entries developed in requirement 1.
3. Prepare the primary and secondary elimination entries for consolidation at December 31, 19X4.

### SOLUTION TO DEMONSTRATION PROBLEM

| | | |
|---|---:|---:|
| 1. Investment in Suda Company | 70,000 | |
|     Equity in Net Income of Subsidiary | | 70,000 |
|     To record share of subsidiary's earnings from April 1, 19X4, to December 31, 19X4. | | |
| Dividends Receivable | 60,000 | |
|     Investment in Suda Company | | 60,000 |
|     To record dividends from subsidiary for period April 1, 19X4, to December 31, 19X4. | | |
| Equity in Net Income of Subsidiary | 6,000 | |
|     Investment in Suda Company | | 6,000 |
|     To amortize cost in excess of book value. | | |

2.

| Total Cost = | Common Stock + | Book Value Element | | | Current Value over (under) Book Value Element | | Goodwill Element |
|---|---|---|---|---|---|---|---|
| | | | Retained Earnings | | | | |
| | | Prior Periods + | Current Year | | | | |
| | | | Earnings − | Dividends + | Land + | Patent + | |
| $540,000 | $90,000 | $310,000 | | | $120,000 | $(40,000) | $60,000 |
| 70,000 | | | $70,000 | | | | |
| (60,000) | | | | $(60,000) | | | |
| (6,000) | | | | | | 3,000[a] | (9,000)[b] |
| $544,000 | $90,000 | $310,000 | $70,000 | $(60,000) | $120,000 | $(37,000) | $51,000 |
| | | 10,000 | (70,000) | 60,000 | | | |
| $544,000 | $90,000 | $320,000 | $ –0– | $ –0– | $120,000 | $(37,000) | $51,000 |

[a]$40,000 ÷ 10 years × ¾ year
[b]$60,000 ÷ 5 years × ¾ year

3. The primary elimination entry:

| | | |
|---|---|---|
| Common Stock . . . . . . . . . . . . . . . . . . . . . . . . . . . . . . . . . . | 90,000 | |
| Retained Earnings (beginning of year) . . . . . . . . . . . . . . | 310,000 | |
| Equity in Net Income of Subsidiary. . . . . . . . . . . . . . . . . | 70,000 | |
| Land. . . . . . . . . . . . . . . . . . . . . . . . . . . . . . . . . . . . . . . . . . | 120,000 | |
| Goodwill . . . . . . . . . . . . . . . . . . . . . . . . . . . . . . . . . . . . . . | 51,000 | |
| Patent . . . . . . . . . . . . . . . . . . . . . . . . . . . . . . . . . . . | | 37,000 |
| Dividends Declared . . . . . . . . . . . . . . . . . . . . . . . . | | 60,000 |
| Investment in Suda Company. . . . . . . . . . . . . . . . . | | 544,000 |

The secondary elimination entry:

| | | |
|---|---|---|
| Cost of Goods Sold . . . . . . . . . . . . . . . . . . . . . . . . . . . . . . | 6,000 | |
| Equity in Net Income of Subsidiary . . . . . . . . . . . . | | 6,000 |

# ASSIGNMENT MATERIAL

## Review Questions

1. Contrast the equity method of accounting with the cost method.
2. When it is inappropriate to consolidate a subsidiary's financial statements with those of its parent, how must the parent company account for its investment in the subsidiary?
3. What are liquidating dividends? How are they treated under the equity method? Under the cost method?
4. Why must the consolidated amounts be the same regardless of whether the parent company uses the equity method or the cost method to account for its investment in a subsidiary?
5. In the expanded analysis of the investment account, why is a separate column used for the parent company's share of the subsidiary's current-year net income or loss?

6. What is the source of the primary elimination entry when the parent uses the equity method?
7. What is the purpose of the secondary elimination entry?

# Discussion Cases

### DC 4-1

## Selecting the Accounting Method for Measuring Return on Investment

Presto Company acquired all of the outstanding common stock of Speedley Company on January 1, 19X1, for $1,000,000 cash. Presto views the Speedley operation as an investment and wants to account for its investment in a manner that will enable it to evaluate readily the profitability of the investment each year, using a return-on-investment approach. Assume that Speedley expects net income of $200,000 for 19X1 and $300,000 for 19X2, and that no dividends will be paid to the parent company during these two years.

### Required:
1. Calculate the expected return on investment for 19X1 and 19X2 assuming the parent company uses (a) the equity method and (b) the cost method.
2. Which method allows the correct return on investment to be calculated?

### DC 4-2

## Treatment of Amortization of Cost in Excess of Book Value in Calculating Return on Investment under the Equity Method

Pinnex Company acquired all of the outstanding common stock of Stickles Company on January 1, 19X1, for $1,000,000 cash. For 19X1, Stickles reported net income of $150,000. On December 31, 19X1, Stickles paid a $100,000 dividend to Pinnex. Pinnex amortized $30,000 of cost in excess of book value during 19X1, which it recorded under the equity method of accounting.

### Required:
1. Calculate the parent company's 19X1 return on investment.
2. Calculate the parent company's 19X1 return on investment assuming that the dividend was paid on January 3, 19X1. For simplicity assume the declaration date of the dividend is the same as the payment date.

### DC 4-3

## Treatment of Subsidiary Dividends in Preparing the Consolidated Statement of Retained Earnings

The controller of Plumex Company is preparing the consolidated statement of retained earnings. Plumex declared dividends of $100,000 on its common stock during the year. Plumex's wholly owned subsidiary, which was acquired at the beginning of the year, declared dividends of $20,000 on its common stock during the year ($10,000 of which was declared on the last day of the year and has not been paid). The controller wants to know whether the consolidated statement of retained earnings for the year should reflect dividends of $100,000, $110,000, or $120,000.

**Required:**

How would you advise the controller?

| DC 4-4 |
|---|

## Subsequent Accounting for "Cost in Excess of Net Assets"

Payton Company acquired the business of Simpson Company on January 1, 19X1, at a cost of $800,000 in excess of the current value of Simpson's net assets. Simpson's operations had been unprofitable for the two years preceding the business combination and thus did not possess superior earning power. Payton paid the $800,000 so that it could readily establish itself in this high-risk industry. Payton expects Simpson's operations to report profits within three years. The cost in excess of current value is being amortized over 10 years.

**Required:**

Assume that at December 31, 19X4, Simpson's operations are still unprofitable. Management is uncertain whether Simpson's operations will ever be profitable. What are the implications of this situation?

## Exercises

| E 4-1 |
|---|

## Preparation of Comparative Entries under the Equity Method and the Cost Method

Pidgeon Company acquired 100% of the outstanding common stock of Seagull Company at a total cost of $550,000 on January 1, 19X1. Assume the current value of Seagull's net assets equals their book value of $510,000. Also assume goodwill is assigned a 40-year life. The net income (loss) and dividends declared by Seagull for 19X1 and 19X2 are as follows:

|  | Net Income (Loss) | Dividends Declared (and Paid) |
|---|---|---|
| 19X1 | 30,000 | 10,000 |
| 19X2 | (12,000) | 5,000 |

**Required:**

Prepare in comparative form the parent company's entries for 19X1 and 19X2 under the equity method and the cost method.

| E 4-2 |
|---|

## Applying the Equity Method and Preparing the Primary Elimination Entry

On January 1, 19X1, Planet Company acquired 100% of the outstanding common stock of Solar Company at a total cost of $750,000. The general ledger balances of Solar's capital accounts on the acquisition date were as follows:

| | |
|---|---|
| Common stock | $100,000 |
| Additional paid-in capital | 400,000 |
| Retained earnings | 250,000 |
| | $750,000 |

Assume the current value of Solar's net assets equals their book value. The net income (loss) and dividends declared by Solar for 19X1 and 19X2 are as follows:

| | Net Income (Loss) | Dividends Declared (and Paid) |
|---|---|---|
| 19X1 | $80,000 | $25,000 |
| 19X2 | (40,000) | 10,000 |

### Required:

1. Assuming that the parent company uses the equity method of accounting, prepare the journal entries it would make for 19X1 and 19X2 for its investment in the subsidiary.
2. Prepare an expanded analysis of the investment account as of the acquisition date and update it for the entries developed in requirement 1.
3. Prepare the primary elimination entry as of December 31, 19X1, and December 31, 19X2.
4. Explain why there is no secondary elimination entry.

**E 4-3**

## Applying the Equity Method and Preparing the Primary and Secondary Elimination Entries

On January 1, 19X1, Pele Company acquired 100% of the outstanding common stock of Soccerex Company at a total cost of $400,000. The analysis of Pele's investment in Soccerex by the individual components of the major conceptual elements as of the acquisition date is as follows:

| | | Remaining Life |
|---|---|---|
| Book value element: | | |
| Common stock | $100,000 | |
| Retained earnings | 60,000 | |
| Current value over book value element: | | |
| Inventory | 5,000 | 3 months |
| Land | 105,000 | Indefinite |
| Building | 90,000 | 15 years |
| Goodwill element | 40,000 | 40 years |
| Total cost | $400,000 | |

The net income (loss) and dividends declared by Soccerex for 19X1 and 19X2 are as follows:

| | Net Income (Loss) | Dividends Declared (and Paid) |
|---|---|---|
| 19X1 | $35,000 | $5,000 |
| 19X2 | (10,000) | 5,000 |

**Required:**

1. Assuming that the parent company uses the equity method of accounting, prepare the journal entries it would make for 19X1 and 19X2 for its investment in the subsidiary.
2. Prepare an analysis of the investment account by the components of the major conceptual elements as of the acquisition date, and update it for the entries developed in requirement 1.
3. Prepare the primary and secondary elimination entries as of December 31, 19X1, and December 31, 19X2.

## Applying the Equity Method and Preparing the Primary and Secondary Elimination Entries

Pitt Company acquired 100% of the outstanding common stock of Sitters Company at a total cost of $310,000 on January 1, 19X1. The analysis of Pitt's investment in Sitters by the components of the major conceptual elements as of the acquisition date (after appropriate allocation of the bargain purchase element) is as follows:

|  |  | Remaining Life |
|---|---:|---|
| Book value element: | | |
| Common stock . . . . . . . . . . . . . . . . . . . . . . . . . . . . . . . . . . | $250,000 | |
| Retained earnings . . . . . . . . . . . . . . . . . . . . . . . . . . . . | 100,000 | |
| Current value over (under) book value element: | | |
| Inventory . . . . . . . . . . . . . . . . . . . . . . . . . . . . . . . . . . . . . | 5,000 | 3 months |
| Land . . . . . . . . . . . . . . . . . . . . . . . . . . . . . . . . . . . . . . . . . . | 30,000 | Indefinite |
| Building . . . . . . . . . . . . . . . . . . . . . . . . . . . . . . . . . . . . . | (75,000) | 25 years |
| Total cost . . . . . . . . . . . . . . . . . . . . . . . . . . . . . . . . . | $310,000 | |

The net income (loss) and dividends declared by Sitters for 19X1 and 19X2 are as follows:

|  | Net Income (Loss) | Dividends Declared (and Paid) |
|---|---:|---:|
| 19X1 . . . . . . . . . . . . . . . . . . . . . . . . . . . . . . . . . . . | $(15,000) | $1,000 |
| 19X2 . . . . . . . . . . . . . . . . . . . . . . . . . . . . . . . . . . . | 30,000 | 5,000 |

**Required:**

1. Assuming the parent company uses the equity method of accounting, prepare the journal entries it would make for 19X1 and 19X2 with respect to its investment in the subsidiary.
2. Prepare an analysis of the investment account by the individual components of the major conceptual elements as of the acquisition date and update it for the entries developed in situation 1.

3. Prepare the primary and secondary elimination entries as of December 31, 19X1, and December 31, 19X2.

## Problems

P
4-1*

### Preparing a Consolidation Worksheet (Continuation of Problem 3-4)

On December 31, 19X1, Payles Company, a calendar-year reporting company, acquired all of the outstanding common stock of Selmore Company at a total cost of $600,000 (an amount equal to the current value and book value of Selmore's net assets). The analysis of the investment account as of the acquisition date is as follows:

Book value element:
| | |
|---|---|
| Common stock | $100,000 |
| Additional paid-in capital | 200,000 |
| Retained earnings | 300,000 |
| Total cost | $600,000 |

The financial statements of each company for the year ended December 31, 19X2, are as follows:

| | Payles Company | Selmore Company |
|---|---|---|
| **Income Statement (19X2)** | | |
| Sales | $8,500,000 | $ 900,000 |
| Cost of goods sold | (5,500,000) | (400,000) |
| Expenses | (2,400,000) | (320,000) |
| Equity in net income of subsidiary | 180,000 | |
| Net Income | $ 780,000 | $ 180,000 |
| **Balance Sheet (December 31, 19X2)** | | |
| Cash | $ 220,000 | $ 140,000 |
| Accounts receivable, net | 1,000,000 | 500,000 |
| Inventory | 1,500,000 | 800,000 |
| Investment in Selmore Company | 680,000 | |
| Land | 800,000 | 300,000 |
| Buildings and equipment | 5,200,000 | 900,000 |
| Accumulated depreciation | (1,200,000) | (240,000) |
| | $8,200,000 | $2,400,000 |
| Accounts payable and accruals | $ 700,000 | $ 620,000 |
| Long-term debt | 2,100,000 | 1,100,000 |
| Common stock | 1,000,000 | 100,000 |

*The financial statement information presented for problems accompanied by asterisks is also provided on Model 4 (filename: Model4) of the software file disk that is available for use with the text, enabling the problem to be worked on the computer.

|  | Payles Company | Selmore Company |
|---|---|---|
| Additional paid-in capital.................... | 2,000,000 | 200,000 |
| Retained earnings ......................... | 2,400,000 | 380,000 |
|  | $8,200,000 | $2,400,000 |
| Dividends declared during 19X2.............. | $380,000 | $100,000 |

### Required:

1. Update the analysis of the investment account through December 31, 19X2.
2. Prepare the consolidation elimination entries as of December 31, 19X2.
3. Prepare a consolidating statement worksheet at December 31, 19X2. (The parent's retained earnings as of January 1, 19X2, was $2,000,000.)

## Preparing a Consolidation Worksheet (Continuation of Problem 3-5)

**P 4-2***

Peanut Company, a calendar-year reporting company, acquired all of the outstanding common stock of Shell Company at a total cost of $300,000 on December 31, 19X1. The analysis of the parent company's investment account as of the acquisition date is as follows:

|  |  | Remaining Life |
|---|---|---|
| Book value element: |  |  |
| Common stock ............................... | $100,000 |  |
| Retained earnings ........................... | 90,000 |  |
| Current value over (under) book value element: |  |  |
| Inventory...................................... | 5,000 | 2 months |
| Land........................................... | 30,000 | Indefinite |
| Equipment..................................... | 50,000 | 10 years |
| Patent......................................... | (15,000) | 3 years |
| Goodwill element.............................. | 40,000 | 4 years |
| Total cost................................. | $300,000 |  |

The financial statements of each company for the year ended December 31, 19X2, are as follows:

|  | Peanut Company | Shell Company |
|---|---|---|
| **Income Statement (19X2)** |  |  |
| Sales........................................ | $2,800,000 | $600,000 |
| Cost of goods sold .......................... | (1,500,000) | (300,000) |
| Expenses.................................... | (1,000,000) | (240,000) |
| Equity in net income of subsidiary............ | 45,000 |  |
| Net Income............................... | $ 345,000 | $ 60,000 |

*(continued)*

| Balance Sheet (December 31, 19X2) | Peanut Company | Shell Company |
|---|---:|---:|
| Cash | $ 120,000 | $ 25,000 |
| Accounts receivable, net | 300,000 | 50,000 |
| Inventory | 500,000 | 120,000 |
| Investment in Shell Company | 290,000 | |
| Land | 400,000 | 70,000 |
| Buildings and equipment | 1,100,000 | 220,000 |
| Accumulated depreciation | (210,000) | (65,000) |
| Patent | | 10,000 |
| | $2,500,000 | $430,000 |
| | | |
| Accounts payable and accruals | $ 320,000 | $ 85,000 |
| Long-term debt | 1,300,000 | 150,000 |
| Common stock | 300,000 | 100,000 |
| Retained earnings | 580,000 | 95,000 |
| | $2,500,000 | $430,000 |
| | | |
| Dividends declared during 19X2 | $215,000 | $55,000 |

## Required:

1. Update the analysis of the investment account through December 31, 19X2.
2. Prepare the consolidation elimination entries as of December 31, 19X2.
3. Prepare a consolidating statement worksheet at December 31, 19X2. (The parent's retained earnings as of January 1, 19X2, was $450,000.)

## Preparing a Consolidation Worksheet (Continuation of Problem 3-6)

**P 4-3\***

Post Company, a calendar-year reporting company, acquired all of the outstanding common stock of Script Company at a total cost of $400,000 on December 31, 19X1. The analysis of Post's investment account as of the acquisition date is as follows:

| | | Remaining Life |
|---|---:|---|
| Book value element: | | |
| Common stock | $ 50,000 | |
| Additional paid-in capital | 200,000 | |
| Retained earnings | 250,000 | |
| Current value over (under) book value element: | | |
| Inventory | (70,000) | 6 months |
| Land | 30,000 | Indefinite |
| Building | (100,000) | 20 years |
| Long-term debt | 40,000 | 4 years |
| Total cost | $400,000 | |

The financial statements of each company for the year ended December 31, 19X2, are as follows:

| | Post Company | Script Company |
|---|---|---|
| **Income Statement (19X2)** | | |
| Sales. . . . . . . . . . . . . . . . . . . . . . . . . . . . . . | $7,000,000 | $850,000 |
| Cost of goods sold . . . . . . . . . . . . . . . . . . . . | (3,800,000) | (600,000) |
| Expenses. . . . . . . . . . . . . . . . . . . . . . . . . . . | (1,700,000) | (310,000) |
| Equity in net income of subsidiary. . . . . . . . . . . | 5,000 | |
| Net Income (Loss). . . . . . . . . . . . . . . . . . . . | $1,505,000 | $ (60,000) |
| | | |
| **Balance Sheet (December 31, 19X2)** | | |
| Cash . . . . . . . . . . . . . . . . . . . . . . . . . . . . . . | $ 295,000 | $ 20,000 |
| Accounts receivable, net. . . . . . . . . . . . . . . . . | 400,000 | 80,000 |
| Inventory . . . . . . . . . . . . . . . . . . . . . . . . . . . | 700,000 | 130,000 |
| Investment in Script Company . . . . . . . . . . . . . | 405,000 | |
| Land . . . . . . . . . . . . . . . . . . . . . . . . . . . . . . | 500,000 | 100,000 |
| Buildings and equipment . . . . . . . . . . . . . . . . . | 3,100,000 | 550,000 |
| Accumulated depreciation . . . . . . . . . . . . . . . . | (600,000) | (80,000) |
| | $4,800,000 | $800,000 |
| | | |
| Accounts payable and accruals. . . . . . . . . . . . . | $ 495,000 | $ 60,000 |
| Long-term debt. . . . . . . . . . . . . . . . . . . . . . . | 2,000,000 | 300,000 |
| Common stock . . . . . . . . . . . . . . . . . . . . . . . | 20,000 | 50,000 |
| Additional paid-in capital. . . . . . . . . . . . . . . . . | 480,000 | 200,000 |
| Retained earnings . . . . . . . . . . . . . . . . . . . . . | 1,805,000 | 190,000 |
| | $4,800,000 | $800,000 |
| | | |
| Dividends declared during 19X2. . . . . . . . . . . . | $800,000 | $–0– |

## Required:

1. Update the analysis of the investment account through December 31, 19X2.
2. Prepare the consolidation elimination entries as of December 31, 19X2.
3. Prepare a consolidating statement worksheet at December 31, 19X2. (The parent's retained earnings as of January 1, 19X2, was $1,100,000.)

## COMPREHENSIVE   Recording the Acquisition, Analyzing the Investment Account, Applying the Equity Method, and Preparing a Consolidation Worksheet

On January 1, 19X1, Pinchnell Company acquired 100% of the outstanding common stock of Squeezers Company by issuing 7,000 shares of $10 par value common stock (which was trading at $60 per share on that date). In addition, Pinchnell incurred direct costs of $95,000 relating to the acquisition, $25,000 of which was for the registration of the shares issued with the SEC. (All these direct costs were charged to the investment account.) The balances in the capital accounts of the subsidiary as of the acquisition date are as follows:

| | |
|---|---|
| Common stock. . . . . . . . . . . . . . . . . . . . . . . . . . . . . . . . . . . . . . | $100,000 |
| Retained earnings . . . . . . . . . . . . . . . . . . . . . . . . . . . . . . . . . . . . | 402,000 |
| | $502,000 |

All the assets and liabilities of the subsidiary have a current value equal to their book value, except for the following:

|  | Book Value | Current Value | Remaining Life |
|---|---|---|---|
| Land held for development............ | $600,000 | $710,000 | Indefinite |
| Deferred charges.................... | 42,000 | –0– | 3 years |
| Long-term debt, 10%................. | 200,000 | 230,000 | 6 years |

## Additional Information:

1. The subsidiary is a real estate development company, which owns several parcels of land. None of the land owned was developed during 19X1. However, one parcel acquired eight years ago was sold in its undeveloped stage. This was the only sale for 19X1.
2. The parent company is privately owned and chose to use non-push-down accounting.
3. The parent's accounting policy is to amortize goodwill over 10 years.
4. The only entry the parent made in its books relating to the subsidiary was at the acquisition date.
5. The combination did not qualify for pooling of interests treatment.
6. The subsidiary's buildings and equipment were fully depreciated at the acquisition date.

The financial statements of each company for the year ended December 31, 19X1, are as follows:

|  | Pinchnell Company | Squeezers Company |
|---|---|---|
| **Income Statement (19X1)** |  |  |
| Sales...................................... | $ 950,000 | $330,000 |
| Cost of goods sold....................... | (520,000) | (200,000) |
| Expenses.................................. | (204,000) | (45,000) |
| Net Income............................. | $ 226,000 | $ 85,000 |
| **Balance Sheet (December 31, 19X1)** |  |  |
| Cash...................................... | $ 200,000 | $ 22,000 |
| Accounts receivable, net.................... | 300,000 |  |
| Notes receivable........................... |  | 350,000 |
| Inventory.................................. | 600,000 |  |
| Investment in Squeezers Company ........... | 515,000 |  |
| Land...................................... | 500,000 |  |
| Buildings and equipment................... | 2,700,000 | 5,000 |
| Accumulated depreciation.................. | (600,000) | (5,000) |
| Land held for development................. |  | 400,000 |
| Deferred charges ......................... |  | 28,000 |
|  | $4,215,000 | $800,000 |
| Accounts payable/accruals ................ | $ 160,000 | $ 13,000 |
| Dividends payable ....................... |  | 35,000 |
| Long-term debt.......................... | 1,600,000 | 200,000 |
| Common stock ........................... | 700,000 | 100,000 |

|  | Pinchnell Company | Squeezers Company |
|---|---|---|
| Additional paid-in capital. . . . . . . . . . . . . . . . . . | 1,015,000 | |
| Retained earnings . . . . . . . . . . . . . . . . . . . . . | 740,000 | 452,000 |
| | $4,215,000 | $800,000 |
| Dividends declared during 19X1. . . . . . . . . . . . . | $100,000 | $35,000 |

### Required:

1. Analyze the investment account by the components of the major conceptual elements as of the acquisition date. Make any appropriate adjusting entries.
2. Update the analysis of the investment account to reflect activity under the equity method through December 31, 19X1.
3. Prepare the consolidation elimination entries as of December 31, 19X1.
4. Adjust the parent company's financial statements as shown above to reflect the equity method, and then prepare a consolidating statement worksheet at December 31, 19X1.

## COMPREHENSIVE CHALLENGER  Converting to the Equity Method from the Cost Method Two Years after the Acquisition Date: Analyzing the Investment Account and Preparing a Consolidation Worksheet

Phonetics Company acquired all of the outstanding common stock of Sounder Company for $820,000 cash on January 1, 19X1. Phonetics also incurred $47,000 of direct costs in connection with the acquisition. Selected information on Sounder as of the acquisition date is as follows:

|  | Book Value | Current Value | Remaining Life |
|---|---|---|---|
| Inventory. . . . . . . . . . . . . . . . . . . . . . . . . | $ 303,000 | $ 310,000 | 4 months |
| Buildings and equipment. . . . . . . . . . . . . | 1,400,000[a] | 1,490,000 | 15 years |
| Patent. . . . . . . . . . . . . . . . . . . . . . . . . . | 20,000 | 60,000 | 5 years |
| Goodwill . . . . . . . . . . . . . . . . . . . . . . . | 60,000 | –0– | 6 years |
| 10% bonds payable . . . . . . . . . . . . . . . . | 1,200,000 | 1,000,000 | 10 years |

[a]Net of $300,000 of accumulated depreciation.

### Additional Information:

1. The parent company is privately owned and chose to use non-push-down accounting.
2. The parent company has used the cost method since the acquisition date and has decided to change to the equity method to account for its investment in the subsidiary.
3. Assume a 40-year life for any goodwill paid in the transaction.

The financial statements of each company for the year ended December 31, 19X2 (two years after the acquisition date), are as follows:

|  | Phonetics Company | Sounder Company |
|---|---:|---:|
| **Income Statement (19X2)** | | |
| Sales...................................... | $8,500,000 | $ 980,000 |
| Cost of goods sold......................... | (4,500,000) | (530,000) |
| Expenses................................... | (3,640,000) | (310,000) |
| Dividend income ........................... | 50,000 | |
| Net Income................................. | $ 410,000 | $ 140,000 |
| **Balance Sheet (December 31, 19X2)** | | |
| Cash....................................... | $ 458,000 | $ 118,000 |
| Accounts receivable, net................... | 750,000 | 190,000 |
| Inventory.................................. | 820,000 | 380,000 |
| Investment in Sounder Company............. | 867,000 | |
| Land....................................... | 760,000 | 240,000 |
| Buildings and equipment................... | 6,260,000 | 1,720,000 |
| Accumulated depreciation.................. | (2,465,000) | (480,000) |
| Patent..................................... | 100,000 | 12,000 |
| Goodwill .................................. | | 40,000 |
| | $7,550,000 | $2,220,000 |
| Accounts payable and accruals ............. | $1,600,000 | $ 370,000 |
| Long-term debt............................. | 3,000,000 | 1,200,000 |
| Common stock.............................. | 2,000,000 | 250,000 |
| Retained earnings ......................... | 950,000 | 400,000 |
| | $7,550,000 | $2,220,000 |
| Dividends declared during 19X2............. | $100,000 | $50,000 |
| Dividends declared during 19X1............. | 80,000 | 40,000 |
| Reported net income for 19X1.............. | 200,000 | 90,000 |

## Required:

1. Analyze the investment account by the components of the major conceptual elements as of the acquisition date.
2. Update the analysis of the investment account to reflect activity under the equity method of accounting through December 31, 19X2 (a two-year period).
3. Prepare the journal entry to convert to the equity method from the cost method.
4. Prepare the consolidation elimination entries as of December 31, 19X2.
5. Adjust the parent company's financial statements to reflect the equity method, and then prepare a consolidating statement worksheet at December 31, 19X2.
6. Would the parent's independent auditors have to mention the change to the equity method in their audit report?

## COMPREHENSIVE (Chapters 3 and 4)   Recording the Acquisition, Selecting Relevant Data, and Preparing a Consolidation Worksheet

On July 1, 19X1, in a business combination that did not qualify as a pooling of interests, PBM Company acquired 100% of the outstanding common stock of Sapple Company by issuing 6,000 shares of its $10 par value common stock (which was trading at $70 per share on that date). In addition, PBM incurred direct costs of $90,000 relating to the acquisition, $40,000 of which was for the registration of the shares issued with the SEC. Selected relevant data follows:

| | | June 30, 19X1 | |
|---|---|---|---|
| | Book Value | Current Value | Remaining Life |
| **Sapple Company** | | | |
| Inventory. . . . . . . . . . . . . . . . . . . . . . . . . | $ 66,000 | $ 70,000 | 3 months |
| Buildings and equipment . . . . . . . . . . . | 310,000[a] | 382,000 | 12 years |
| Goodwill . . . . . . . . . . . . . . . . . . . . . . . | 20,000 | | 5 years |
| Long-term debt. . . . . . . . . . . . . . . . . . | 400,000 | 384,000 | 8 years |
| Common stock . . . . . . . . . . . . . . . . . . . | 200,000 | | |
| Retained earnings . . . . . . . . . . . . . . . . | 138,000 | | |
| **PBM Company** | | | |
| Common stock . . . . . . . . . . . . . . . . . . | 100,000 | | |
| Additional paid-in capital. . . . . . . . . . . | 500,000 | | |
| Retained earnings . . . . . . . . . . . . . . . . | 800,000 | | |

[a]Net of $140,000 accumulated depreciation.

## Additional Information:

1. Assume any goodwill arising from the combination has a 10-year life from the acquisition date of July 1, 19X1.
2. The non-push-down basis of accounting was selected.
3. The equity method of accounting is to be used.
4. For 19X1, Sapple had the following earnings and dividends:

| | Jan. 1– June 30, 19X1 | July 1– Dec. 31, 19X1 | Total |
|---|---|---|---|
| Sales . . . . . . . . . . . . . . . . . . . . . . | $400,000 | $500,000 | $900,000 |
| Cost of goods sold. . . . . . . . . . . | (220,000) | (260,000) | (480,000) |
| Expenses. . . . . . . . . . . . . . . . . . | (130,000) | (180,000) | (310,000) |
| Net Income . . . . . . . . . . . . . . | $ 50,000 | $ 60,000 | $110,000 |
| Dividends declared and paid . . | $15,000 | $20,000 | $35,000 |

5. During 19X1, PBM declared and paid $75,000 of dividends each quarter. Also, PBM reported a net income of $200,000 for the six months ended June 30, 19X1.

## Required:

1. Prepare the entry to record the business combination on July 1, 19X1.
2. Complete the PBM Company and Sapple Company financial statements that follow:

| | PBM Company | Sapple Company |
|---|---|---|
| **Income Statement** | | |
| Sales. . . . . . . . . . . . . . . . . . . . . . . . . . . . . . . . . . . . . | $2,600,000 | |
| Cost of goods sold . . . . . . . . . . . . . . . . . . . . . . . | (1,300,000) | |
| Expenses. . . . . . . . . . . . . . . . . . . . . . . . . . . . . . . | (800,000) | |

*(continued)*

|  | PBM Company | Sapple Company |
|---|---|---|
| Net Income.................................... | | |
| **Statement of Retained Earnings** | | |
| Balances, beginning ........................ | $ 750,000 | |
| + Net income .............................. | | |
| − Dividends declared........................ | (300,000) | |
| Balances, Dec. 31, 19X1 .................... | | |
| **Balance Sheet** | | |
| Current assets ............................. | $ 700,000 | $400,000 |
| Land....................................... | 943,000 | 202,000 |
| Buildings and equipment .................... | 2,200,000 | 450,000 |
| Accumulated depreciation ................... | (330,000) | (170,000) |
| Investment in Sapple Company................ | | |
| Goodwill .................................. | | 18,000 |
| Total Assets............................... | | $900,000 |
| Accounts payable........................... | $ 433,000 | $122,000 |
| Long-term debt............................. | 1,600,000 | 400,000 |
| PBM Company: | | |
| Common stock ........................... | | |
| Additional paid-in capital ................ | | |
| Retained earnings ....................... | | |
| Sapple Company: | | |
| Common stock ........................... | | 200,000 |
| Retained earnings ....................... | | 178,000 |
| Total Liabilities and Equity............... | | $900,000 |

3. Prepare the consolidation elimination entries.
4. Prepare a consolidating statement worksheet.

# ADVANCED LEVEL ASSIGNMENT MATERIAL

| AP 4-1 | **Evaluating Future Results under the Purchase Method in a Business Combination with a Troubled Savings and Loan** |
|---|---|

You are the auditor for Pyramid Savings and Loan Association, which recently acquired all of the outstanding common stock of Sham Savings and Loan Association. The combination was structured so that the transaction did not qualify for pooling-of-interests treatment. Sham had incurred losses for approximately two years prior to the combination as a result of paying a higher interest rate to its depositors than it was earning on its loan portfolio. The combination was arranged by the Federal regulators to prevent Sham's liquidation, as Sham had exhausted its net worth. Selected data for Sham as of the combination date are as follows:

|  | Book Value | Current Value |
|---|---|---|
| Assets | $300,000,000 | $260,000,000 |
| Liabilities | 300,000,000 | 300,000,000 |
| Common stock | 12,000,000 | |
| Accumulated deficit | (12,000,000) | |

The current value of the assets is lower than the book value because the current lending rate on home mortgages is 12%, whereas the yield on the loan portfolio (which has an average remaining life of 10 years) is only 10%. Pyramid did not have to pay any consideration; it merely took title to all of Sham's outstanding common stock. Management intends to amortize goodwill over 40 years.

### Required:

1. Prepare an analysis of the investment account at the acquisition date.
2. Prepare the primary elimination entry as of the acquisition date. (Assume non-push-down accounting was used.)
3. For years 1–10 (in total) and for years 11–40 (in total), determine the effect on income of amortizations made from the parent company's investment account.
4. Evaluate the soundness of the results that are reported under the purchase method at the acquisition date and for future periods.
5. What, if anything, should be done differently?

## Case Study from Actual Practice: How to Account for Unrecorded Liabilities Found after the Combination Date

On June 30, 19X1, Primex Company acquired all of the outstanding common stock of Sumex Company for consideration of approximately $300 million. Of this purchase price, $70 million was assigned to goodwill. In September 19X1, Primex discovered that Sumex's liabilities at the acquisition date were understated by $40 million.

### Required:
How should the $40 million be accounted for?

## Applying Finance Concepts to Evaluate Profitability: Accounting for Goodwill

The Cork City Batters is a minor league baseball team that was formed eleven years ago. Operations quickly reached expected levels. For years 8, 9, and 10, the team reported net income of approximately $1,000,000 each year. (For simplicity, ignore income taxes.)

At the end of year 10, the team was sold to a partnership that was formed with capital of $5,000,000. The purchase price was $4,000,000. The remaining $1,000,000 is needed for working capital purposes. For simplicity, assume that: (1) the initial capital of the team, when formed, was $1; (2) all earnings for the ten years had been distributed to the owners by the end of the tenth year; (3) assets therefore equaled liabilities at the time of sale; and (4) none of the recorded assets or liabilities are over- or under-valued.

As the partnership's accountant, you assigned the $4,000,000 to goodwill having a four-year life. The income statement for year 11 follows:

| | |
|---|---:|
| Revenues. . . . . . . . . . . . . . . . . . . . . . . . . . . . . . . . . . . . . . . . . . . . | $8,600,000 |
| Expenses. . . . . . . . . . . . . . . . . . . . . . . . . . . . . . . . . . . . . . . . . . . . | (7,000,000) |
| Operating income. . . . . . . . . . . . . . . . . . . . . . . . . . . . . . . . . . | $1,600,000 |
| Goodwill amortization . . . . . . . . . . . . . . . . . . . . . . . . . . . . . . . | (1,000,000) |
| Net Income . . . . . . . . . . . . . . . . . . . . . . . . . . . . . . . . . . . . . . . | $  600,000 |

The players' union and management are currently negotiating a new contract for year 12. Management and the players' union are in wide disagreement as to the true profitability of the team. At issue is the validity of the goodwill amortization. Management contends that the 12% return on investment for year 11 ($600,000 ÷ 5,000,000) is not excessive, and, therefore, no pay raises are appropriate.

### Additional Information and Assumptions:

1. The decision to form the partnership and acquire the baseball team was based on the high rate of return calculated using the internal rate of return method. The calculation produced an estimated annual return on capital exceeding 30% for the six years that the partnership expected to be in existence. (In the calculation, it was estimated that the team would be sold for a minimum of $4,000,000 at the end of year 16.)
2. Revenues and income from operations are expected to remain constant through year 16.
3. Cash is to be distributed to partners at the end of each year equal to net income.
4. For years 11 through 14, an additional $1,000,000 cash is to be distributed to partners at the end of each year as a return of capital.
5. The partnership sells the team at the end of year 16 for $4,000,000. (At the end of years 11, 12, 13, and 14, a group of outside investors had offered to buy the team for $4,500,000.)
6. All cash on hand at the end of year 16 was distributed to the partners, and the partnership was dissolved.

### Required:

1. Before completing requirements 2 through 6, assess whether management's position is reasonable.
2. Using the reported or assumed net income for years 12 through 16, calculate the partners' return on investment. (For simplicity, ignore the impact of each year's earnings in determining the capital balances to be used in the denominator. In other words, use the beginning capital balances for the denominator for each year rather than an average capital balance.)
3. Assuming revenues and income from operations occurred as expected through the end of year 16 when the team was sold for $4,000,000, how accu-

rately did the calculations for return on investment (ROI) in requirement 2 portray the economics of what transpired? Why or why not?

**Guidance Questions:**
As the partnership's accountant, you should be able to explain the following to the partners:

a. Why the ROI for year 11 (and almost every year thereafter) is so greatly different from the over 30% initial projected return on capital.

b. Whether the partners really earned twice as much on their capital in year 14, in terms of return on investment, as in year 12.

4. Calculate the internal rate of return (IRR) from the perspective of the partners from the time the partnership was formed until it was dissolved. (Use $5,000,000 as the initial cash outflow.)

**Note:** You may readily obtain this answer using the IRR function available in Lotus 1-2-3® spreadsheet program. (You merely need to set up a cash flow table *and then* program the IRR function with the cell cursor located in the cell in which you want your answer to appear.)

5. Explain why the internal rate of return in requirement 4 differs from the return on investment calculations in requirement 2. Which is correct?

6. Given that none of the team's recorded assets or liabilities were under- or overvalued at the acquisition date, what else might the $4,000,000 (or some portion of it) be assigned to? (Hint: Refer to paragraph 88 of *APB Opinion No. 16*, which discusses "assigning" cost in excess of book value.)

## Advanced Problem 4-3 with Changed Assumption

Use the information in Advanced Problem 4-3 except assume that the value of the team is zero at the end of year 16; that is, the team is disbanded, cash on hand is distributed to the partners and the partnership is dissolved. This resulted from the city closing its ballpark at the end of year 16 to make room for a new freeway, which was voted upon and passed in year 15. Through the end of year 14, the team could have been sold at any time for the partnership's purchase price of $4,000,000. Once the decision to build the new freeway was made, no other investors were interested in buying the team.

### Required:

1. Repeat requirement 4 of Advanced Problem 4-3 under the new assumption. (State your answer to two decimal points, for example 12.75%).

2. Explain why the internal rate of return (IRR) calculated in requirement 1 differs from the calculations for return on investment (ROI) in requirement 2 of Advanced Problem 4-3. (The calculation in requirement 2 of Advanced Problem 4-3 for year 16 must be redone because of the changed assumption regarding the value of the team at the end of year 16.)

3. Starting with both the IRR percentage calculated in requirement 1 and the $5,000,000 beginning capital balance of the partners, determine for year 11 how much of the $1,600,000 cash distribution to the partners is assumed to be:

a. Net income under the internal rate of return method (a return *on* capital).

b. Return of the initial capital investment of $5,000,000 (a recovery *of* capital).

Repeat for years 12 through 16 using: (a) the same internal rate of return percentage and (b) the beginning of year capital balance, as reduced by the prior year's return *of* capital. (Round all amounts to the nearest thousand and include any rounding error in year 16.) Use the following format:

| Year | Internal Rate of Return | Beginning (Unrecovered) Capital Balance | Cash Flow Returned to Partners | Cash Flow Deemed to Be | |
|------|------|------|------|------|------|
| | | | | A Return On Investment (Net Income) | A Return Of Investment (Recovery of Capital) |
| | | (Omit 000s) | | | |
| 11 | | $5,000 | $1,600 | | |

**Note:** You can simplify the above calculations by putting the above format on an electronic spreadsheet, programming three simple formulas, and duplicating these formulas for subsequent years.

4. Using the net income amounts calculated in requirement 3 (and the cash distributions to the partners), prepare a T-account analysis of the partners' capital account by year from inception through dissolution of the partnership. (Omit 000s.)

5. Supply the missing amounts for the following tables:

a. As reported by the partnership's accountant:

| | 11 | 12 | 13 | 14 | 15 | 16 |
|------|------|------|------|------|------|------|
| Operating income | $1,600 | | | | | |
| Goodwill expense | (1,000) | | | | | |
| Net Income | $ 600 | | | | | |
| Beginning Capital | $5,000 | | | | | |
| Return on Equity | 12% | | | | | |

b. As assumed in the internal rate of return method:

| | 11 | 12 | 13 | 14 | 15 | 16 |
|------|------|------|------|------|------|------|
| Operating income | $1,600 | | | | | |
| Goodwill expense | | | | | | |
| Net Income | | | | | | |
| Beginning capital | $5,000 | | | | | |
| Return on equity | | | | | | |

6. Which section in requirement 5 reflects the economic reality? Explain the reasoning behind your answer.

**ANSWERS TO SELF-STUDY QUESTIONS**

| | | | |
|------|------|------|------|
| 1. c | 4. a | 7. d | 10. e |
| 2. b | 5. a | 8. c | 11. d |
| 3. c | 6. c | 9. d | |

## Appendix A   PREPARATION OF CONSOLIDATED FINANCIAL STATEMENTS WHEN THE PARENT ACCOUNTS FOR ITS INVESTMENT UNDER THE COST METHOD

Under the cost method of accounting for an investment in a subsidiary, the parent never changes the original cost of the investment unless either a liquidating dividend or a permanent impairment of the investment's value occurs. If the same consolidated amounts are to be obtained as when the equity method is used, the consolidation elimination entries must be different from those used when the equity method is used.

Whether the parent uses the equity method or the cost method, the consolidated amounts are identical—only the procedures of preparing the consolidating statement worksheet are different. The cost method has two main conceptual points:

1. To arrive at consolidated net income each year, the net income of the parent must be reduced for any dividend income of the subsidiary that is included. This adjusted net income is then added to the subsidiary's net income to arrive at consolidated net income.
2. To arrive at consolidated retained earnings, the parent's retained earnings (which includes only those earnings of the subsidiary that have been remitted to the parent in the form of dividends since the acquisition date) must be added to the postacquisition earnings of the subsidiary that have not been remitted to the parent.

### The Primary Elimination Entry

The primary elimination entry is always exactly the same as the primary elimination entry made on the acquisition date. Using the assumptions of Illustration 4-4, in which the parent's cost of $90,000 exceeded both the current value ($80,000) and the book value ($60,000) of the subsidiary's net assets, we determine the primary elimination for all future consolidation dates as follows:

| | | |
|---|---|---|
| Common Stock | 40,000 | |
| Retained Earnings (beginning of year) | 20,000 | |
| Inventory | 2,000 | |
| Land | 12,000 | |
| Equipment | 6,000 | |
| Goodwill | 10,000 | |
| Investment in Subsidiary | | 90,000 |

If this entry is used for all future consolidation dates, the secondary entry must be revised so that the consolidated financial statements reflect subsequent, appropriate amortization of cost over the book value of the net assets.

## The Secondary Elimination Entry

The secondary elimination entry reflects the amortization of cost over the book value of the net assets directly in the appropriate, traditional cost and expense accounts. Under the cost method, therefore, the secondary elimination entry is an *adjusting* entry (rather than a reclassifying entry as under the equity method). This accomplishes on the consolidating statement worksheet what is otherwise done in the parent's general ledger under the equity method.

For all periods after the year following the acquisition date, the credits are made to the individual components on a cumulative basis. The beginning-of-period cumulative amortization is charged to Retained Earnings. For the two years subsequent to the acquisition date, the secondary elimination entries are as follows:

|  | Consolidation Date | | | |
|---|---|---|---|---|
|  | December 31, 19X1 | | December 31, 19X2 | |
| Cost of Goods Sold......... | 4,000 | | 2,000 | |
| Inventory .............. | | 2,000 | | 2,000 |
| Accumulated | | | | |
| Depreciation.......... | | 1,000 | | 2,000 |
| Goodwill............... | | 1,000 | | 2,000 |
| Retained Earnings ......... | | | 4,000 | |

**WORKSHEET ENTRIES ONLY**

## The Dividend Income Elimination Entry

A third elimination entry is necessary to eliminate any dividend income recorded on the parent's books that results from dividends received from the subsidiary. This entry is necessary only in years in which the subsidiary declares a dividend. The entry is as follows:

|  | Consolidation Date | | |
|---|---|---|---|
|  | December 31, 19X1 | | December 31, 19X2 |
| Dividend Income ........... | 5,000 | | No entry |
| Dividends Declared ..... | | 5,000 | |

**WORKSHEET ENTRIES ONLY**

This entry does not affect the balance sheet because the debit is carried forward from the income statement to the net income line in the analysis of retained earnings section of the worksheet. The sole purpose of the entry is to eliminate the dividend income from the parent's income statement.

**ILLUSTRATION**

## Consolidating Statement Worksheets When the Parent Company uses the Cost Method

Illustrations 4-7 and 4-8 show the consolidation worksheets as of December 31, 19X1 (the year subsequent to acquisition) and December 31, 19X2 (two years subsequent to acquisition), prepared using the cost method.

**■ ILLUSTRATION 4-7**

**Cost Method Used by Parent Company: First Year Subsequent to Acquisition Date**

| | | | | | | |
|---|---|---|---|---|---|---|
| | **P COMPANY AND SUBSIDIARY (S COMPANY)** | | | | | |
| | **Consolidating Statement Worksheet for the Year Ended December 31, 19X1** | | | | | |
| | P Company | S Company | Eliminations | | Consolidated |
| | | | Dr. | Cr. | |
| **Income Statement** | | | | | |
| Sales . . . . . . . . . . . . . . . . . . . . . . . . | 600,000 | 225,000 | | | 825,000 |
| Cost of goods sold. . . . . . . . . . . . . | (360,000) | (110,000) | 4,000(2) | | (474,000) |
| Expenses . . . . . . . . . . . . . . . . . . . . . | (190,000) | (100,000) | | | (290,000) |
| Intercompany Account: | | | | | |
| Dividend income. . . . . . . . . . . . . | 5,000 | | 5,000(3) | | –0– |
| Net Income. . . . . . . . . . . . . . . . . . . | 55,000 | 15,000 | ⌐ 9,000 | | 61,000 |
| **Statement of Retained Earnings** | | | | | |
| Balances, January 1, 19X1 . . . . . . | 100,000 | 20,000 | 20,000(1) | | 100,000 |
| +Net income . . . . . . . . . . . . . . . . . | 55,000 | 15,000 | ↳ 9,000 | | 61,000 |
| –Dividends declared. . . . . . . . . . . . | (45,000) | (5,000) | | 5,000(3) | (45,000) |
| Balances, December 31, 19X1. . . . | 110,000 | 30,000 | ⌐29,000 | ⌐5,000 | 116,000 |
| **Balance Sheet** | | | | | |
| Cash. . . . . . . . . . . . . . . . . . . . . . . . . | 25,000 | 11,000 | | | 36,000 |
| Accounts receivable, net . . . . . . . . | 75,000 | 37,000 | | | 112,000 |
| Inventory . . . . . . . . . . . . . . . . . . . . . | 110,000 | 55,000 | 2,000(1) | 2,000(2) | 165,000 |
| Investment in S Company. . . . . . . . | 90,000 | | | 90,000(1) | –0– |
| Land. . . . . . . . . . . . . . . . . . . . . . . . . | 220,000 | 30,000 | 12,000(1) | | 262,000 |
| Buildings and equipment . . . . . . . . | 500,000 | 200,000 | 6,000(1) | 50,000(4) | 656,000 |
| Accumulated depreciation. . . . . . . . | (320,000) | (63,000) | 50,000(4) | 1,000(2) | (334,000) |
| Goodwill. . . . . . . . . . . . . . . . . . . . . . | | | 10,000(1) | 1,000(2) | 9,000 |
| Total Assets. . . . . . . . . . . . . . . . . | 700,000 | 270,000 | 80,000 | 144,000 | 906,000 |
| Liabilities. . . . . . . . . . . . . . . . . . . . . | 290,000 | 200,000 | | | 490,000 |
| P Company: | | | | | |
| Common stock. . . . . . . . . . . . . . . . | 300,000 | | | | 300,000 |
| Retained earnings . . . . . . . . . . . . | 110,000 | | | | 110,000 |
| S Company: | | | | | |
| Common stock. . . . . . . . . . . . . . . . | | 40,000 | 40,000(1) | | –0– |
| Retained earnings . . . . . . . . . . . . | | 30,000 | ↳29,000 | ↳ 5,000 | 6,000 |
| Total Liabilities and Equity . . . . | 700,000 | 270,000 | 69,000 | 5,000 | 906,000 |
| Proof of debit and credit postings . . . . . . . . . . . . . . . . . . . . . . . . . | | | 149,000 | 149,000 | |

Explanation of entries:
  (1) The primary elimination entry.
  (2) The secondary elimination entry.
  (3) The dividend income elimination entry.
  (4) The accumulated depreciation elimination entry.

Recap of Retained Earnings:
  P Company . . . . . . . .   $110,000
  S Company . . . . . . . .      6,000
      Total . . . . . . . . . .   $116,000

■ **ILLUSTRATION 4-8**

**Cost Method Used by Parent Company: Second Year Subsequent to Acquisition Date**

| | P Company | S Company | Eliminations Dr. | Eliminations Cr. | Consolidated |
|---|---|---|---|---|---|
| **P COMPANY AND SUBSIDIARY (S COMPANY)** Consolidating Statement Worksheet for the Year Ended December 31, 19X2 | | | | | |
| **Income Statement** | | | | | |
| Sales | 650,000 | 250,000 | | | 900,000 |
| Cost of goods sold | (398,000) | (120,000) | 2,000(2) | | (520,000) |
| Expenses | (185,000) | (105,000) | | | (290,000) |
| Intercompany Account: | | | | | |
| Dividend income | –0– | | | | –0– |
| Net Income | 67,000 | 25,000 | 2,000 | | 90,000 |
| **Statement of Retained Earnings** | | | | | |
| Balances, January 1, 19X1 | 110,000 | 30,000 | 4,000(2) 20,000(1) | | 116,000 |
| +Net income | 67,000 | 25,000 | 2,000 | | 90,000 |
| –Dividends declared | (61,000) | –0– | | | (61,000) |
| Balances, December 31, 19X1 | 116,000 | 55,000 | 26,000 | | 145,000 |
| **Balance Sheet** | | | | | |
| Cash | 41,000 | 31,000 | | | 72,000 |
| Accounts receivable, net | 95,000 | 45,000 | | | 140,000 |
| Inventory | 130,000 | 80,000 | 2,000(1) | 2,000(2) | 210,000 |
| Investment in S Company | 90,000 | | | 90,000(1) | –0– |
| Land | 220,000 | 30,000 | 12,000(1) | | 262,000 |
| Buildings and equipment | 540,000 | 200,000 | 6,000(1) | 50,000(3) | 696,000 |
| Accumulated depreciation | (360,000) | (76,000) | 50,000(3) | 2,000(2) | (388,000) |
| Goodwill | | | 10,000(1) | 2,000(2) | 8,000 |
| Total Assets | 756,000 | 310,000 | 80,000 | 146,000 | 1,000,000 |
| Liabilities | 340,000 | 215,000 | | | 555,000 |
| P Company: | | | | | |
| Common stock | 300,000 | | | | 300,000 |
| Retained earnings | 116,000 | | | | 116,000 |
| S Company: | | | | | |
| Common stock | | 40,000 | 40,000(1) | | –0– |
| Retained earnings | | 55,000 | 26,000 | | 29,000 |
| Total Liabilities and Equity | 756,000 | 310,000 | 66,000 | | 1,000,000 |
| Proof of debit and credit postings | | | 146,000 | 146,000 | |

Explanation of entries:
(1) The primary elimination entry.
(2) The secondary elimination entry.
(3) The accumulated depreciation elimination entry.

Recap of Retained Earnings:
| | | |
|---|---|---|
| P Company | | $116,000 |
| S Company | | 29,000 |
| Total | | $145,000 |

**Review Points for Illustrations 4-7 and 4-8.**   Note the following:

1. The amounts in the parent's column are different from the amounts in Illustrations 4-5 (page 170) and 4-6 (page 171) (the comparable consolidation worksheets as of these dates when the equity method is used), whereas the amounts in the subsidiary's column and the consolidated column are the same.
2. The parent's Retained Earnings account under the cost method includes only those postacquisition earnings that have been remitted to the parent through dividends, whereas the parent's Retained Earnings account under the equity method includes all postacquisition earnings of the subsidiary.
3. The retained earnings of the subsidiary that did not get eliminated are added to the parent's retained earnings to obtain consolidated retained earnings.

## Exercise for Appendix A

| | |
|---|---|
| **E 4-1A** | **Applying the Cost Method and Preparing the Primary, Secondary, and Dividend Income Elimination Entries** |

On January 1, 19X1, Psi Company acquired all of the outstanding common stock of Seta Company at a total cost of $200,000. The analysis of Psi's investment in Seta by the individual components of the major conceptual elements as of the acquisition date is as follows:

|  |  | Remaining Life |
|---|---:|---|
| Book value element: | | |
| Common stock | $ 50,000 | |
| Retained earnings | 25,000 | |
| Current value over book value element: | | |
| Inventory | 5,000 | 1 month |
| Land | 45,000 | Indefinite |
| Building | 25,000 | 25 years |
| Equipment | 10,000 | 5 years |
| Goodwill element | 40,000 | 10 years |
| Total cost | $200,000 | |

The net income (loss) and dividends declared by Seta for 19X1 and 19X2 are as follows:

|  | Net Income (Loss) | Dividends Declared (and Paid) |
|---|---|---|
| 19X1 | $10,000 | $6,000 |
| 19X2 | (2,000) | 2,000 |

**Required:**

1. Assuming that the parent company uses the cost method of accounting for its investment in the subsidiary, prepare the entries it would make for 19X1 and 19X2.
2. Prepare the primary, secondary, and dividend income elimination entries, as appropriate, as of December 31, 19X1, and December 31, 19X2.
3. Explain how your answer would change for 19X2 if $5,000 of dividends were declared and paid instead of $2,000.

## Problems for Appendix A

### Preparing a Consolidation Worksheet (Problem 4-1 Revised to Reflect the Cost Method)

On December 31, 19X1, Payles Company acquired all of the outstanding common stock of Selmore Company at a total cost of $600,000 (an amount equal to the book value of Selmore's net assets). The financial statements of each company for the year ended December 31, 19X2, are as follows:

|  | Payles Company | Selmore Company |
|---|---|---|
| **Income Statement (19X2)** | | |
| Sales. | $8,500,000 | $ 900,000 |
| Cost of goods sold | (5,500,000) | (400,000) |
| Expenses. | (2,400,000) | (320,000) |
| Dividend income. | 100,000 | |
| Net Income. | $ 700,000 | $ 180,000 |
| **Balance Sheet (December 31, 19X2)** | | |
| Cash. | $ 220,000 | $ 140,000 |
| Accounts receivable, net. | 1,000,000 | 500,000 |
| Inventory. | 1,500,000 | 800,000 |
| Investment in Selmore Company | 600,000 | |
| Land. | 800,000 | 300,000 |
| Buildings and equipment. | 5,200,000 | 900,000 |
| Accumulated depreciation | (1,200,000) | (240,000) |
| | $8,120,000 | $2,400,000 |
| Accounts payable and accruals. | $ 700,000 | $ 620,000 |
| Long-term debt. | 2,100,000 | 1,100,000 |
| Common stock. | 1,000,000 | 100,000 |
| Additional paid-in capital. | 2,000,000 | 200,000 |
| Retained earnings | 2,320,000 | 380,000 |
| | $8,120,000 | $2,400,000 |
| Dividends declared during 19X2. | $380,000 | $100,000 |

*The financial statement information presented for problems accompanied by asterisks is also provided on Model 4 (filename: Model4) of the software file disk that is available for use with the text, enabling the problem to be worked on the computer.

### Required:

1. Prepare the consolidation elimination entries at December 31, 19X2.
2. Why is there no secondary elimination entry at December 31, 19X2?
3. Prepare a consolidating statement worksheet at December 31, 19X2. (The parent's retained earnings on January 1, 19X2, was $2,000,000.)

## Preparing a Consolidation Worksheet (Problem 4-2 Revised to Reflect the Cost Method)

Peanut Company acquired all of the outstanding common stock of Shell Company at a total cost of $300,000 on December 31, 19X1. The analysis of the parent company's investment account as of the acquisition date is as follows:

|  |  | Remaining Life |
|---|---|---|
| Book value element: |  |  |
| Common stock | $100,000 |  |
| Retained earnings | 90,000 |  |
| Current value over book value element: |  |  |
| Inventory | 5,000 | 2 months |
| Land | 30,000 | Indefinite |
| Equipment | 50,000 | 10 years |
| Patent | (15,000) | 3 years |
| Goodwill element | 40,000 | 4 years |
| Total cost | $300,000 |  |

The financial statements of each company for the year ended December 31, 19X2, are as follows:

|  | Peanut Company | Shell Company |
|---|---|---|
| **Income Statement (19X2)** |  |  |
| Sales | $2,800,000 | $600,000 |
| Cost of goods sold | (1,500,000) | (300,000) |
| Expenses | (1,000,000) | (240,000) |
| Dividend income | 55,000 |  |
| Net Income | $ 355,000 | $ 60,000 |
| **Balance Sheet (December 31, 19X2)** |  |  |
| Cash | $ 120,000 | $ 25,000 |
| Accounts receivable, net | 300,000 | 50,000 |
| Inventory | 500,000 | 120,000 |
| Investment in Shell Company | 300,000 |  |
| Land | 400,000 | 70,000 |
| Buildings and equipment | 1,100,000 | 220,000 |
| Accumulated depreciation | (210,000) | (65,000) |
| Patent |  | 10,000 |
|  | $2,510,000 | $430,000 |
| Accounts payable and accruals | $ 320,000 | $ 85,000 |

*(continued)*

|  | Peanut Company | Shell Company |
|---|---|---|
| Long-term debt. . . . . . . . . . . . . . . . . . . . . . . . . . . | 1,300,000 | 150,000 |
| Common stock . . . . . . . . . . . . . . . . . . . . . . . . . . | 300,000 | 100,000 |
| Retained earnings . . . . . . . . . . . . . . . . . . . . . . . | 590,000 | 95,000 |
|  | $2,510,000 | $430,000 |
| Dividends declared during 19X2. . . . . . . . . . . . . | $215,000 | $55,000 |

### Required:

1. Prepare the consolidation elimination entries at December 31, 19X2.
2. Prepare a consolidating statement worksheet at December 31, 19X2. (The parent's retained earnings on January 1, 19X2, was $450,000.)

## Preparing a Consolidation Worksheet (Problem 4-3 Revised to Reflect the Cost Method)

**P 4-3A***

Post Company acquired all of the outstanding common stock of Script Company at a total cost of $400,000 on December 31, 19X1. The analysis of the parent company's investment account as of the acquisition date is as follows:

|  |  | Remaining Life |
|---|---|---|
| Book value element: |  |  |
| Common stock . . . . . . . . . . . . . . . . . . . . . . . . . . . . | $ 50,000 |  |
| Additional paid-in capital. . . . . . . . . . . . . . . . . . . . | 200,000 |  |
| Retained earnings . . . . . . . . . . . . . . . . . . . . . . . | 250,000 |  |
| Current value over (under) book value element: |  |  |
| Inventory. . . . . . . . . . . . . . . . . . . . . . . . . . . . . . . . | (70,000) | 6 months |
| Land. . . . . . . . . . . . . . . . . . . . . . . . . . . . . . . . . . . . | 30,000 | Indefinite |
| Building. . . . . . . . . . . . . . . . . . . . . . . . . . . . . . . . . | (100,000) | 20 years |
| Long-term debt. . . . . . . . . . . . . . . . . . . . . . . . . . . | 40,000 | 4 years |
| Total cost. . . . . . . . . . . . . . . . . . . . . . . . . . . . . | $400,000 |  |

The financial statements of each company for the year ended December 31, 19X2, are as follows:

|  | Post Company | Script Company |
|---|---|---|
| **Income Statement (19X2)** |  |  |
| Sales. . . . . . . . . . . . . . . . . . . . . . . . . . . . . . . . . . . | $7,000,000 | $850,000 |
| Cost of goods sold . . . . . . . . . . . . . . . . . . . . . . . . | (3,800,000) | (600,000) |
| Expenses . . . . . . . . . . . . . . . . . . . . . . . . . . . . . . . | (1,700,000) | (310,000) |
| Net Income (Loss). . . . . . . . . . . . . . . . . . . . . . | $1,500,000 | $ (60,000) |
| **Balance Sheet (December 31, 19X2)** |  |  |
| Cash. . . . . . . . . . . . . . . . . . . . . . . . . . . . . . . . . . . | $ 295,000 | $ 20,000 |
| Accounts receivable, net. . . . . . . . . . . . . . . . . . . | 400,000 | 80,000 |
| Inventory. . . . . . . . . . . . . . . . . . . . . . . . . . . . . . . | 700,000 | 130,000 |
| Investment in Script Company . . . . . . . . . . . . . | 400,000 |  |

|  | Post Company | Script Company |
|---|---|---|
| Land . . . . . . . . . . . . . . . . . . . . . . . . . . . . . . . . . . . . . . | 500,000 | 100,000 |
| Buildings and equipment . . . . . . . . . . . . . . . . . . | 3,100,000 | 550,000 |
| Accumulated depreciation . . . . . . . . . . . . . . . . . | (600,000) | (80,000) |
|  | $4,795,000 | $800,000 |
| Accounts payable and accruals. . . . . . . . . . . . . | $ 495,000 | $ 60,000 |
| Long-term debt. . . . . . . . . . . . . . . . . . . . . . . . . . | 2,000,000 | 300,000 |
| Common stock . . . . . . . . . . . . . . . . . . . . . . . . . . | 20,000 | 50,000 |
| Additional paid-in capital. . . . . . . . . . . . . . . . . . | 480,000 | 200,000 |
| Retained earnings . . . . . . . . . . . . . . . . . . . . . . . | 1,800,000 | 190,000 |
|  | $4,795,000 | $800,000 |
| Dividends declared during 19X2. . . . . . . . . . . . . | $800,000 | $-0- |

### Required:
1. Prepare the consolidation elimination entries at December 31, 19X2.
2. Prepare a consolidating statement worksheet at December 31, 19X2. (The parent's retained earnings as of January 1, 19X2, was $1,100,000.)

## Appendix B  INVESTMENTS IN ASSETS

Recall from Chapter 3 that in acquisitions of assets, (a) the division always records the assets acquired and liabilities assumed at their current values, and (b) the home office's Investment in Division account always equals the net assets of the division. To maintain this equality in subsequent periods, the home office must adjust its Investment in Division account for the income or loss of the division. For example, assume that the division reported $11,000 of income for the year following the acquisition. The home office's entry would be:

| | | |
|---|---|---|
| Investment in Division. . . . . . . . . . . . . . . . . . . . . . . | 11,000 | |
| Division Income . . . . . . . . . . . . . . . . . . . . . . . | | 11,000 |

The debit side of the entry maintains the Investment in Division account equal to the division's net assets. The credit side of the entry allows the division's income to be included in the home office's Retained Earnings account. (Recall from Chapter 3 that a division is not a separate legal entity and thus has no Retained Earnings account—only the lone equity account, Home Office Equity.)

## Preparing Combined Financial Statements

The process of combining home office and division financial statements after the acquisition is the same as it is at the acquisition date, except that the home office's income statement must be combined with the division's income statement. A combined statement of retained earnings must also be prepared.

### Combining the Income Statements.

In combining the details of the two income statements, we must eliminate the Division Income or Loss account balance in the home office column of the worksheet. The effect of eliminating this account is to substitute for this account balance the revenue, cost, and expense accounts of the division.

### The Combined Statement of Retained Earnings.

The combining worksheets in this chapter incorporate analyses of the home office's Retained Earnings account and of the division's Home Office Equity account between the income statement and the balance sheet. Because the company must issue a combined statement of retained earnings, the analysis of the home office's retained earnings in the worksheet readily provides the amounts for this statement. Because the home office records the division's income or loss on its books, the home office's Retained Earnings account contains all the information necessary to prepare this statement.

## Combined Financial Statements for a Home Office and Division

To illustrate the preparation of combined financial statements, we can use the same information and assumptions used in Illustration 4-4 (the acquiring company paid $90,000 cash and the acquired business's net assets had a book value of $60,000 and a current value of $80,000). The only change is that assets were acquired instead of all the outstanding common stock. For simplicity, we assume that the home office and its division had no intracompany transactions during the year following the acquisition, and that the division had $11,000 in income. The following worksheet elimination entry would be made:

**WORKSHEET ENTRY ONLY**

| | | |
|---|---|---|
| Division Income........................... | 11,000 | |
| Home Office Equity (preclosing balance) ....... | 90,000 | |
| Investment in Division .................. | | 101,000 |

Illustration 4-9 is a combining statement worksheet for this company at December 31, 19X1.

### Review Points for Illustration 4-9.

Note the following:

1. The elimination entry substitutes the division's individual income statement accounts for the Division Income account; this prevents double-counting the division's income in the combined column.
2. The debit balance in the eliminations column at the net income line (of the income statement) is carried forward to the net income line in the statement of retained earnings/analysis of home office equity section.

■ **ILLUSTRATION 4-9**

**Combining Statement Worksheet for a Home Office and Division**

| | Home Office | Division | Eliminations Dr. | Eliminations Cr. | Combined |
|---|---|---|---|---|---|
| **P COMPANY** Combining Statement Worksheet for the Year Ended December 31, 19X1 | | | | | |
| **Income Statement** | | | | | |
| Sales......................... | 600,000 | 225,000 | | | 825,000 |
| Cost of goods sold............. | (360,000) | (114,000) | | | (474,000) |
| Expenses...................... | (190,000) | (100,000) | | | (290,000) |
| Division income............... | 11,000 | | 11,000(1) | | –0– |
| Net Income.................. | 61,000 | 11,000 | 11,000 | | 61,000 |
| **Statement of Retained Earnings/ Analysis of Home Office Equity** | | | | | |
| Retained earnings—Beginning . | 100,000 | | | | 100,000 |
| Home office equity (pre-closing) | | 90,000 | 90,000(1) | | –0– |
| +Net income.................. | 61,000 | 11,000 | 11,000 | | 61,000 |
| −Dividends declared.......... | (45,000) | | | | (45,000) |
| Balances, December 31, 19X1.. | 116,000 | 101,000 | 101,000 | | 116,000 |
| **Balance Sheet** | | | | | |
| Cash......................... | 20,000 | 16,000 | | | 36,000 |
| Accounts receivable, net........ | 75,000 | 37,000 | | | 112,000 |
| Inventory...................... | 110,000 | 55,000 | | | 165,000 |
| Investment in Division ......... | 101,000 | | | 101,000(1) | –0– |
| Land.......................... | 220,000 | 42,000 | | | 262,000 |
| Buildings and equipment ...... | 500,000 | 156,000 | | | 656,000 |
| Accumulated depreciation...... | (320,000) | (14,000) | | | (334,000) |
| Goodwill ...................... | | 9,000 | | | 9,000 |
| Total Assets................. | 706,000 | 301,000 | | 101,000 | 906,000 |
| Liabilities...................... | 290,000 | 200,000 | | | 490,000 |
| Common stock ................. | 300,000 | | | | 300,000 |
| Retained earnings ............. | 116,000 | | | | 116,000 |
| Home office equity ............ | | 101,000 | 101,000 | | –0– |
| Total Liabilities and Equity... | 706,000 | 301,000 | 101,000 | | 906,000 |
| Proof of debit and credit postings........................ | | | 101,000 | 101,000 | |

3. The amounts in the combined column are identical to the amounts in the consolidated column of Illustration 4-5 (in which common stock was acquired instead of assets).

# 5

# THE PURCHASE METHOD OF ACCOUNTING: PARTIALLY OWNED SUBSIDIARIES AND BLOCK ACQUISITIONS

*TOPIC OUTLINE*

## CHAPTER OVERVIEW

**M**ost subsidiaries are wholly owned. However, there are numerous partially owned subsidiaries, for the following reasons: (1) the parent has chosen not to purchase all of the outstanding common stock; (2) the parent is unable to locate a small number of stockholders; (3) some stockholders refuse to sell their shares to the parent company at its offering price; and (4) the parent sells a portion of its holdings in a wholly owned subsidiary to raise cash or merely to reduce its holdings (the accounting for this is discussed in Chapter 10).

When the parent owns less than 100% of the subsidiary's common stock, the consolidation process outlined in Chapter 4 becomes more complicated because special procedures are required to account for the interest of the subsidiary's other stockholders, hereafter called **minority interest.** This chapter uses examples from Chapters 3 and 4, adjusted to reflect only partial ownership, to illustrate accounting for partially owned subsidiaries.

## CONCEPTUAL ISSUES

Many conceptual issues arise when a subsidiary is less than 100% owned. Some of these issues are discussed in Chapters 10 and 11. The remaining issues are:

1. Whether to use proportional or full consolidation.
2. How to present the minority interest in the consolidated financial statements (an issue that arises only under full consolidation).
3. Whether the subsidiary's assets and liabilities should be revalued to 100% of their current values or only to the extent of the parent's ownership interest (not an issue in poolings of interests).

### Conceptual Issue 1: Proportional or Full Consolidation?

**Proportional Consolidation.** Under *proportional consolidation*, the parent consolidates only its ownership in each of the items in the subsidiary's financial statements. In other words, for an 80%-owned subsidiary we would multiply the subsidiary's cash, accounts receivable, sales, and so forth by 80% to arrive at the amounts to be included in the consolidation. Under this method, accounting for the minority interest in the consolidated financial statements is not necessary because it is not reported there. The rationale underlying proportional consolidation is as follows:

1. The consolidated financial statements should be merely an extension of the parent's financial statements.

2. In substance (although not as a legality), the parent has a percentage interest in each of the subsidiary's assets, liabilities, revenues, and expenses.
3. The consolidated financial statements should be the same whether the acquiring company purchases 80% of the assets or 80% of the common stock.

In recent years, proportional consolidation has become one of several methods of accounting for investments in real estate partnerships and construction joint ventures. Moreover, it has been advocated increasingly for consolidated financial statements. Currently however, the requirements of *ARB No. 51* (presently under reconsideration by the Financial Standards Accounting Board [FASB]) allow only full consolidation.

 **Full Consolidation.**    Under *full consolidation,* the parent consolidates the entire amount of each of the subsidiary's individual assets, liability, and income statement accounts with those of the parent company. Because the subsidiary is only partially owned, however, the additional amounts consolidated constitute the minority interest. Therefore, the minority interest in the subsidiary's net assets and net income are reported as separate items in the consolidated financial statements. The rationale underlying full consolidation is as follows:

1. The parent does not have a separable percentage interest in each individual asset, liability, and income statement account of the subsidiary. Its ownership interest is a percentage of the net assets and net income as a whole.
2. The parent controls all of the subsidiary even though its ownership is less than 100%.
3. The purpose of consolidated statements is to combine the operations of the parent and the subsidiary as though they were a single company.

## Conceptual Issue 2: Classification of Minority Interest under Full Consolidation

Two theories have evolved concerning the treatment of the minority interest under full consolidation in consolidated financial statements: (1) the parent company theory and (2) the entity theory. Both methods of treatment are discussed below.

**The Parent Company Theory.**    The **parent company theory** assumes that the reporting entity does not change as a result of the consolidation process. Consolidated reporting merely represents a different manner of reporting the parent's financial position and the results of its operations. Thus, **the parent company is still considered the reporting entity.** As a result, (1) the interest of the minority shareholders is not considered an equity interest of the consolidated reporting entity, and (2) consolidated net income equals the parent's net income (which includes its share of the subsidiary's net income through application of the equity method of accounting). Therefore, the minority interest is presented in the consolidated financial statements as follows:

1. **In the consolidated balance sheet:** The minority interest in the subsidiary's net assets is treated as an outside interest and is shown outside the stockholders' equity section in one of the following two ways:
   a. **Between liabilities and stockholders' equity:** This presentation reflects the unique nature of the minority interest. It is an equity interest, but not of the parent company, which is the reporting entity.
   b. **Among liabilities:** This presentation has little or no supporting theory. However, if the minority interest is insignificant and a separate classification is unwarranted, companies commonly classify it among liabilities.
2. **In the consolidated income statement:** The minority interest in the subsidiary's net income is shown as a deduction in the consolidated income statement in arriving at the consolidated net income. For example, assuming that an 80%-owned subsidiary had net income of $15,000 for the year, the minority interest deduction would be $3,000 (20% of $15,000) and would be presented as follows:

|  | Consolidated Income Statement |
|---|---:|
| Revenues | $800,000 |
| Cost of goods sold | (476,000) |
| Expenses | (273,000) |
| Minority interest in net income of subsidiary | (3,000) |
| Net Income | $ 48,000 |

**The Entity Theory.** The **entity theory** assumes that the reporting entity has changed as a result of the consolidation process. **A new reporting entity is deemed to exist.** This new reporting entity has two classes of equity interests—the controlling interest (the parent's shareholders) and the minority interest. Because the nature of these interests is the same, they must be treated the same way in consolidated financial statements. As a result, (1) the interest of the minority shareholders is treated as an equity interest of the consolidated reporting entity, and (2) consolidated net income equals the combined net incomes of both companies (without the application of the equity method of accounting). The minority interest is presented in the consolidated financial statements as follows:

1. **In the consolidated balance sheet,** the minority interest in the subsidiary's net assets is shown as a separate category within the stockholders' equity section.
2. **In the consolidated income statement,** the minority interest in the subsidiary's net income is shown as a portion of the total net income of the consolidated entity. Using the same amounts as in the above example, we can present the consolidated income statement as follows:

|  | Consolidated Income Statement |
|---|---|
| Revenues | $800,000 |
| Cost of goods sold | (476,000) |
| Expenses | (273,000) |
| Net Income | $ 51,000 |
| Division of net income: | |
| To controlling interest | $ 48,000 |
| To minority interest | 3,000 |
| Total Net Income | $ 51,000 |

**Which Theory Is Correct?**    Whether the parent company theory or the entity theory is correct depends on whether the reporting entity is considered to have changed as a result of the consolidation process—a purely subjective evaluation. The minority shareholders do not influence the parent's operating policies. Thus, the consolidated financial statements are usually of no benefit whatsoever to the minority shareholders. This group is entitled only to the financial statements of the partially owned subsidiary.

**Guidance from *ARB No. 51.***    How minority interests should be presented in consolidated financial statements is not specifically addressed in *ARB No. 51*. However, *ARB No. 51* does state that consolidated financial statements are prepared primarily for the benefit of the parent's shareholders and creditors. This provision is consistent with the parent company theory but not with the entity theory. **In practice, the minority interest is presented in consolidated financial statements almost exclusively in accordance with the parent company theory.** For these reasons, the income statement sections of the consolidating statement worksheets presented later in this chapter are consistent with the parent company theory, under which the minority interest in the subsidiary's net income is shown as a deduction in arriving at the consolidated net income. Likewise, the balance sheets shown later are presented consistent with the parent company theory (with the minority interest in the subsidiary's net assets being shown between liabilities and stockholders' equity).

A later section focuses on how the conceptual analysis of the investment account can be slightly modified so that the minority interest can be

parent company theory

easily dealt with in preparing consolidated financial statements under the parent company theory.

**Manner of Reporting Dividends Paid to Minority Shareholders.**  Under both the entity theory and the parent company theory, **dividends paid to the minority shareholders reduce the amount reported in the balance sheet as Minority Interest in Net Assets of Subsidiary.** Such dividends cannot be added to those declared by the parent in preparing the consolidated statement of retained earnings. The reason is obvious. The consolidated retained earnings include only the earnings of the subsidiary that accrue to the parent. Including dividends paid to minority shareholders with dividends paid to the parent's shareholders would be inconsistent. This holds true regardless of the fact that such dividends (unlike dividends paid to the parent) leave the consolidated group. Recall from Chapter 4 that dividends paid to the parent are also not reported as dividends in the consolidated statement of retained earnings. Thus none of a subsidiary's dividends are reported as dividends declared in the consolidated statement of retained earnings.

### Conceptual Issue 3: Partial or Full Revaluation of the Subsidiary's Assets and Liabilities

When the subsidiary has over- or undervalued assets or liabilities at the acquisition date, to what extent should these items be revalued to their current values? Some accountants advocate revaluing to 100% of current values. This approach is part of the entity theory, and we demonstrate this manner of valuation in Chapter Appendix A. Others advocate revaluing only to the extent of the parent's ownership interest. For example, an asset that is undervalued by $10,000 would be revalued upward by only $8,000 if the parent's ownership percentage was 80%. This approach is part of the parent company theory, and we demonstrate this manner of valuation later in the chapter.

Both methods of revaluation are found in practice inasmuch as the governing pronouncement on this issue, *APB Opinion No. 16*, is interpreted both ways. However, the partial revaluation method under the parent company theory is much more widely used in practice.

### The New Basis of Accounting Concept

Recall from Chapter 3 that under the purchase method, a new basis of accounting is established for the acquired business's assets and liabilities. Recall also that this new basis of accounting can be implemented by either: (a) the push-down basis of accounting (discussed in the Appendix to Chapter 3), whereby the subsidiary's general ledger amounts are adjusted; or (b) revaluation in consolidation when the non-push-down basis of accounting is used. In this chapter we illustrate the non-push-down basis of accounting because: (a) the push-down basis of accounting has much more limited application when subsidiaries are partially owned; and (b) the preparation of consolidated statements when push-down accounting is used is much less involved than under non-push-down accounting.

# PREPARING CONSOLIDATED FINANCIAL STATEMENTS

## Including Minority Interest in the Conceptual Analysis of the Investment Account

When a minority interest exists, the conceptual analysis of the investment account can be easily modified so that the minority interest can be reported properly in the consolidated statements with a minimum of extra effort. Specifically, an extra column (called "minority interest") is added to the conceptual analysis of the investment account. The column is placed to the left of the total cost column. The initial amount appearing in this column is the minority interest in the subsidiary's net assets at their book value. All subsequent amounts appearing in the column to update the analysis are based on the changes in the subsidiary's book value.

There are advantages to this format change:

1. It reinforces the fact that the minority ownership interest in the net assets of the subsidiary is always equal to the minority ownership percentage times the book value of the subsidiary (under parent company theory).
2. It readily provides the entry needed in consolidation to establish the minority interest deduction in the consolidated income statement.
3. It illustrates the parallel treatment of the parent's and the minority shareholders' interest in the subsidiary's income and dividends.
4. It provides the check figure for the minority interest reported in the consolidated balance sheet.
5. It shows how the current value over (under) book value element and the goodwill element are associated only with the parent.

The following illustrations demonstate how to account for the minority interest in the above manner.

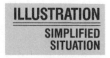

ILLUSTRATION
SIMPLIFIED
SITUATION

## Acquisition of 80% of Common Stock; Purchase Price Is 80% of Book Value of Net Assets; No Over- or Undervalued Assets

Before discussing a consolidation of normal complexity, we first turn to a simple (although somewhat unrealistic) situation in which (1) none of the subsidiary's assets or liabilities are over- or undervalued (thus eliminating the need for the current value over (or under) book value element of the conceptual analysis of the investment account), and (2) the parent's cost of acquiring an 80% interest is 80% of the current value of the subsidiary's net assets (thus eliminating the need for the goodwill or bargain purchase element). Accordingly, only the book value element exists.

Assume the same information for P Company and S Company as provided in situation A of Illustration 3-4 (in which total cost was $60,000 and the book value and current value were also $60,000), except assume that P Company acquired only 80% of S Company's outstanding common stock at a cost of $48,000 (rather than 100% at a cost of $60,000).

### Expanding the Conceptual Analysis of the Investment Account to Include the Minority Interest.  The minority interest is added to the conceptual analysis:

|  |  |  | Book Value Element | | |
| --- | --- | --- | --- | --- | --- |
| Date | Total Cost | = | Common Stock | + | Retained Earnings |
| Balances, Jan. 1, 19X1 | $48,000 | | $32,000 (80% of $40,000) | | $16,000 (80% of $20,000) |

Format modification for minority interest

|  | Minority Interest (20% of $60,000) |  |  |  |  |  |
| --- | --- | --- | --- | --- | --- | --- |
| Add minority interest | $12,000 | | | 8,000 (20% of $40,000) | | 4,000 (20% of $20,000) |
| Modified balances | $12,000 | + | $48,000 | = | $40,000 | + | $20,000 |

### Consolidation for the First Year Subsequent to the Acquisition Date.  From this analysis of the investment account, the primary elimination entry as of the acquisition date is as follows:

**WORKSHEET ENTRY ONLY**

| | | |
| --- | --- | --- |
| Common Stock | 40,000 | |
| Retained Earnings | 20,000 | |
|     Investment in Subsidiary | | 48,000 |
|     Minority Interest in Net Assets of | | |
|        S Company | | 12,000 |

Reformatting the conceptual analysis of the investment account as shown above allows the minority interest to be established as one amount. This amount is always equal to the minority interest ownership percentage times the book value of the subsidiary's net assets (20% of $60,000 in this example).

Illustration 5-1 shows a consolidating statement worksheet as of January 1, 19X1 (the acquisition date), using the above information.

In addition to making the primary elimination entry, it is necessary to eliminate the subsidiary's accumulated depreciation as of the acquisition date to reflect that a new basis of accounting has been established. Even though only 80% of the common stock was acquired, the elimination is made at 100% of the accumulated depreciation balance of $50,000.[1]

| WORKSHEET ENTRY ONLY | | |
|---|---|---|
| Accumulated Depreciation | 50,000 | |
| Buildings and Equipment | | 50,000 |

# ■ ILLUSTRATION 5-1
## Consolidating Statement Worksheet as of the Acquisition Date

### P COMPANY AND SUBSIDIARY (S COMPANY)
### Consolidating Statement Worksheet as of January 1, 19X1

| | P Company | S Company | Eliminations Dr. | Eliminations Cr. | Consolidated |
|---|---|---|---|---|---|
| **Balance Sheet** | | | | | |
| Cash | 60,000 | 15,000 | | | 75,000 |
| Accounts receivable, net | 52,000 | 23,000 | | | 75,000 |
| Inventory | 100,000 | 32,000 | | | 132,000 |
| Investment in S Company | 48,000 | | | 48,000(1) | –0– |
| Land | 220,000 | 30,000 | | | 250,000 |
| Buildings and equipment | 500,000 | 200,000 | | 50,000(2) | 650,000 |
| Accumulated depreciation | (280,000) | (50,000) | 50,000(2) | | (280,000) |
| Total Assets | 700,000 | 250,000 | 50,000 | 98,000 | 902,000 |
| Liabilities | 300,000 | 190,000 | | | 490,000 |
| Minority interest in net assets of | | | | | |
| S Company | | | | 12,000(1) | 12,000 |
| P Company: | | | | | |
| Common stock | 300,000 | | | | 300,000 |
| Retained earnings | 100,000 | | | | 100,000 |
| S Company: | | | | | |
| Common stock | | 40,000 | 40,000(1) | | –0– |
| Retained earnings | | 20,000 | 20,000(1) | | –0– |
| Total Liabilities and Equity | 700,000 | 250,000 | 60,000 | 12,000 | 902,000 |
| Proof of debit and credit postings | | | 110,000 | 110,000 | |

Explanation of entries:
(1) The primary elimination entry.    (2) The accumulated depreciation elimination entry.

**Updating the Expanded Analysis of the Investment Account.** Assume the subsidiary in the preceding illustration had a net income of $15,000 in 19X1 and declared dividends of $5,000 in that year. Under the equity method of accounting, the parent would record its share of these amounts. The expanded analysis of the investment account would be updated as follows:

| | Minority Interest (20%) | + | Total Cost | = | Common Stock | + | Book Value Element Retained Earnings Prior Years | + | Current Year Earnings | − | Dividends |
|---|---|---|---|---|---|---|---|---|---|---|---|
| Balances, January 1, 19X1 | $12,000 | | $48,000 | | $40,000 | | $20,000 | | | | |
| Equity in net income: | | | | | | | | | | | |
| To parent | | | 12,000 | | | | | | $12,000 | | |
| To minority interest | 3,000 | | | | | | | | 3,000 | | |
| Dividends declared: | | | | | | | | | | | |
| To parent | | | (4,000) | | | | | | | | $ (4,000) |
| To minority interest | (1,000) | | | | | | | | | | (1,000) |
| Subtotal | $14,000 | | $56,000 | | $40,000 | | $20,000 | | $15,000 | | $(5,000) |
| Reclassification | | | | | | | | 10,000 | (15,000) | | 5,000 |
| Balances, December 31, 19X1 | $14,000 | | $56,000 | | $40,000 | | $30,000 | | $ –0– | | $ –0– |

**Consolidation for First Year Subsequent to the Acquisition Date.** Consolidated financial statements as of December 31, 19X1, would be prepared using the following primary elimination entry:

| WORKSHEET ENTRY ONLY | | |
|---|---|---|
| Common Stock | 40,000 | |
| Retained Earnings | 20,000 | |
| Equity in Net Income of Subsidiary | 12,000 | |
| Minority Interest in Net Income of S Company | 3,000 | |
|     Dividends Declared | | 5,000 |
|     Investment in Subsidiary | | 56,000 |
|     Minority Interest in Net Assets of | | |
|       S Company | | 14,000 |

The above entry is posted to the consolidating statement worksheet as of December 31, 19X1, in Illustration 5-2. (Also posted is the accumulated depreciation elimination entry for $50,000.)

---

[1]The authors discussed with the staff of the Securities and Exchange Commission whether all of the accumulated depreciation should be eliminated or only a portion based on the parent's ownership percentage. The staff's unofficial position was that it makes the most sense to eliminate 100% of the accumulated depreciation.

## ■ ILLUSTRATION 5-2
### First Year Subsequent to Acquisition Date

**P COMPANY AND SUBSIDIARY (S COMPANY)**
**Consolidating Statement Worksheet for the Year Ended December 31, 19X1**

| | P Company | S Company | Eliminations Dr. | Eliminations Cr. | Consolidated |
|---|---|---|---|---|---|
| **Income Statement** | | | | | |
| Sales.......................... | 600,000 | 225,000 | | | 825,000 |
| Cost of goods sold.............. | (360,000) | (110,000) | | | (470,000) |
| Expenses ...................... | (190,000) | (100,000) | | | (290,000) |
| Intercompany Account: | | | | | |
| Equity in net income of S Company ................ | 12,000 | | 12,000(1) | | –0– |
| Income before Minority Interest . | 62,000 | 15,000 | 12,000 | | 65,000 |
| Minority interest .............. | | | 3,000(1) | | (3,000) |
| Net Income.................... | 62,000 | 15,000 | 15,000 | | 62,000 |
| **Statement of Retained Earnings** | | | | | |
| Balances, January 1, 19X1 ..... | 100,000 | 20,000 | 20,000(1) | | 100,000 |
| + Net income................... | 62,000 | 15,000 | 15,000 | | 62,000 |
| − Dividends declared........... | (45,000) | (5,000) | | 5,000(1) | (45,000) |
| Balances, December 31, 19X1... | 117,000 | 30,000 | 35,000 | 5,000 | 117,000 |
| **Balance Sheet** | | | | | |
| Cash.......................... | 66,000 | 11,000 | | | 77,000 |
| Accounts receivable, net......... | 75,000 | 37,000 | | | 112,000 |
| Inventory...................... | 110,000 | 55,000 | | | 165,000 |
| Investment in S Company....... | 56,000 | | | 56,000(1) | –0– |
| Land.......................... | 220,000 | 30,000 | | | 250,000 |
| Buildings and equipment ....... | 500,000 | 200,000 | | 50,000(2) | 650,000 |
| Accumulated depreciation....... | (320,000) | (63,000) | 50,000(2) | | (333,000) |
| Total Assets.................. | 707,000 | 270,000 | 50,000 | 106,000 | 921,000 |
| Liabilities...................... | 290,000 | 200,000 | | | 490,000 |
| Minority interest in net assets of S Company.......... | | | | 14,000(1) | 14,000 |
| P Company: | | | | | |
| Common stock................ | 300,000 | | | | 300,000 |
| Retained earnings ............ | 117,000 | | | | 117,000 |
| S Company: | | | | | |
| Common stock................ | | 40,000 | 40,000(1) | | –0– |
| Retained earnings ............ | | 30,000 | 35,000(1) | 5,000 | –0– |
| Total Liabilities and Equity ... | 707,000 | 270,000 | 75,000 | 19,000 | 921,000 |
| Proof of debit and credit postings ........................ | | | 125,000 | 125,000 | |

Explanation of entries:
(1) The primary elimination entry.    (2) The accumulated depreciation elimination entry.

**Review Points for Illustration 5-2.**   Note the following:

1. The same equalities and control features that existed for wholly owned subsidiaries exist for partially owned subsidiaries. That is, the net income and retained earnings amounts in the P Company column are the same as the comparable items in the consolidated column.
2. The minority interest in the net assets of the subsidiary ($14,000) can be proved by multiplying the minority interest ownership percentage (20%) by the total stockholders' equity of the subsidiary ($70,000).

## Acquisition of 80% of Common Stock; Purchase Price Is More than 80% of Book Value of Net Assets; Assets Are Undervalued and Goodwill Exists

We now turn to a consolidation of normal complexity in which the subsidiary's assets are undervalued and the parent's purchase price includes an amount for goodwill. When the subsidiary has undervalued assets or goodwill, or both, the parent's cost in excess of its ownership interest in the book value of the subsidiary's net assets logically depends on the parent's ownership interest. For example, assume that the subsidiary has undervalued assets worth $20,000. If the acquiring company is willing to pay $20,000 in excess of the book value of the net assets for all of the outstanding common stock, then for an 80% ownership interest the acquiring company should be willing to pay only $16,000 in excess of its ownership interest in the book value of the net assets. Similarly, if the acquiring company is willing to pay $10,000 for goodwill in acquiring all of the common stock, then it should be willing to pay only $8,000 for goodwill if it acquired only an 80% ownership interest.

**Separating Total Cost into the Major Conceptual Elements.**   Knowing the factors that determine how much the acquiring company is willing to pay in partial ownership situations, we separate the total cost into its major conceptual elements using the following procedures:

1. **The book value element:** Multiply the book value of the subsidiary's stockholders' equity by the parent's ownership percentage.
2. **The current value over (under) book value element:** Multiply the total amount of undervaluation of the subsidiary's net assets times the parent's ownership percentage.
3. **The goodwill element:** Add the amounts determined in elements 1 and 2 above to arrive at the parent's interest in the current value of the subsidiary's net assets. Subtract this total from the parent's cost to obtain goodwill. (Note that as in Chapter 4, goodwill is calculated in a residual manner.)

Once these steps are completed, we can include the minority interest in the conceptual analysis.

In situation B of Illustration 3-4, P Company acquired 100% of the outstanding common stock of S Company at a cost of $90,000, which was

$30,000 in excess of the book value of the subsidiary's net assets. The $30,000 excess payment was identified as undervalued assets ($20,000) and goodwill ($10,000). Assume instead that P Company purchased only 80% of the outstanding common stock for $72,000 (80% of $90,000). The separation of the total cost into its major conceptual elements is shown as follows:

| Minority Interest (20% of $60,000) | + | Total Cost | = | Book Value Element (100% of $60,000) | + | Current Value over Book Value Element (80% of $20,000) | + | Goodwill Element (Residual) |
|---|---|---|---|---|---|---|---|---|
| | | $72,000 | | $48,000 (80%) | | $16,000 | | $8,000 |
| $12,000 | | | | 12,000 (20%) | | | | |
| $12,000 | + | $72,000 | = | $60,000 | + | $16,000 | + | $8,000 |

### Separating the Major Conceptual Elements into Their Components.
We separate the current value over book value element into its components by multiplying the parent's ownership percentages by the amount that each asset is undervalued. In Illustration 3-5, the $20,000 undervaluation was attributed to Inventory, Land, and Equipment accounts. This $20,000 is separated into its components as follows:

| Asset | Total Current Value over Book Value | Parent's Ownership Percentage | Parent's Interest in Current Value over Book Value |
|---|---|---|---|
| Inventory............. | $ 2,000 | 80% | $ 1,600 |
| Land................ | 12,000 | 80% | 9,600 |
| Equipment.......... | 6,000 | 80% | 4,800 |
| | $20,000 | | $16,000 |

The expanded analysis of the investment account by the components of the major conceptual elements is as follows:

| | | |
|---|---|---|
| Book value element: | | |
|   Common stock ........................... | $40,000 | |
|   Retained earnings ....................... | 20,000 | $60,000 |
| Current value over book value element: | | |
|   Inventory................................ | $ 1,600 | |
|   Land.................................... | 9,600 | |
|   Equipment............................... | 4,800 | 16,000 |
| Goodwill element............................ | | 8,000 |
|     Total of major elements ................ | | $84,000 |
| Total cost (the parent's cost)................. | | $72,000 |
| Minority interest ........................... | | 12,000 |
| | | $84,000 |

The primary elimination entry obtained with this procedure (which would be used only if non-push-down accounting were used) revalues the subsidiary's assets to their current values **only to the extent that such undervaluation is paid for by the parent company** ($16,000 in this example). Likewise, goodwill is reflected in the consolidated financial statements only to the extent that it is paid for by the parent company ($8,000 in this example). This approach results in **partial revaluation** of the subsidiary's assets, which is consistent with the parent company theory.

A different revaluation result occurs under the entity theory, which is discussed in Chapter Appendix A. We now illustrate the preparation of consolidated financial statements (as of the acquisition date and in years subsequent to the acquisition date) using the partial revaluation results that occur under the parent company theory.

### Consolidation as of the Acquisition Date.

For this example, the primary elimination entry as of the acquisition date, taken from the expanded analysis of the investment account, is as follows:

| | | |
|---|---|---|
| Common Stock | 40,000 | |
| Retained Earnings | 20,000 | |
| Inventory | 1,600 | |
| Land | 9,600 | |
| Equipment | 4,800 | |
| Goodwill | 8,000 | |
|     Investment in Subsidiary | | 72,000 |
|     Minority Interest in Net Assets of | | |
|       S Company | | 12,000 |

This primary elimination entry is used in Illustration 5-3 to prepare a consolidating statement worksheet as of January 1, 19X1 (the acquisition date), for P Company and S Company.

### Major Review Point for Illustration 5-3.

The amount reported in consolidation for each of the subsidiary's undervalued assets is the book value of the asset plus 80% of the undervaluation—not 80% of the current value. For example, note the following for land:

| | |
|---|---|
| Current value | $42,000 |
| Amount reported in consolidation (100% of book value of | |
|   $30,000 plus 80% of the undervaluation of $12,000) | $39,600 |
| Book value | $30,000 |

Land is not reported in consolidation at 80% of the current value of $42,000 (or $33,600).

### Updating the Expanded Analysis of the Investment Account Using the Equity Method.

Assume that S Company had the following earnings, losses, dividends

# ■ ILLUSTRATION 5-3
## Consolidating Statement Worksheet as of the Acquisition Date

| P COMPANY AND SUBSIDIARY (S COMPANY) Consolidating Statement Worksheet as of January 1, 19X1 | | | | | |
|---|---|---|---|---|---|
| | P Company | S Company | Eliminations Dr. | Cr. | Consolidated |
| **Balance Sheet** | | | | | |
| Cash .......................... | 36,000 | 15,000 | | | 51,000 |
| Accounts receivable, net ......... | 52,000 | 23,000 | | | 75,000 |
| Inventory ..................... | 100,000 | 32,000 | 1,600(1) | | 133,600 |
| Investment in S Company ....... | 72,000 | | | 72,000(1) | –0– |
| Land .......................... | 220,000 | 30,000 | 9,600(1) | | 259,600 |
| Buildings and equipment ....... | 500,000 | 200,000 | 4,800(1) | 50,000(2) | 654,800 |
| Accumulated depreciation ....... | (280,000) | (50,000) | 50,000(2) | | (280,000) |
| Goodwill....................... | | | 8,000(1) | | 8,000 |
| Total Assets .................. | 700,000 | 250,000 | 74,000 | 122,000 | 902,000 |
| Liabilities...................... | 300,000 | 190,000 | | | 490,000 |
| Minority interest in net assets of S Company .................. | | | | 12,000(1) | 12,000 |
| P Company: | | | | | |
| Common stock ............... | 300,000 | | | | 300,000 |
| Retained earnings ........... | 100,000 | | | | 100,000 |
| S Company: | | | | | |
| Common stock ............... | | 40,000 | 40,000(1) | | –0– |
| Retained earnings ........... | | 20,000 | 20,000(1) | | –0– |
| Total Liabilities and Equity .... | 700,000 | 250,000 | 60,000 | 12,000 | 902,000 |
| Proof of debit and credit postings ................ | | | 134,000 | 134,000 | |

Explanation of entries:
  (1) The primary elimination entry.
  (2) The accumulated depreciation elimination entry.

and amortization of cost over book value for the two years subsequent to the acquisition date:

| | 19X1 | 19X2 |
|---|---|---|
| Net income......................................... | $15,000 | $21,000 |
| Dividends.......................................... | 5,000 | –0– |
| Amortization of cost in excess of book value... | 3,200 | 1,600 |

Illustration 5-4 shows an expanded analysis of the investment account for two years following the acquisition date, using the above information.

# ■ ILLUSTRATION 5-4
## Updating the Expanded Analysis of the Investment Account Using the Equity Method: 80%-owned Subsidiary

| | Book Value Element | | | | | | Current Value over Book Value Element | | | | |
| | | | | | Retained Earnings | | | | | Equipment | | |
| | | | | | | Current Year | | | | | | |
| | Minority Interest (20%) | + Total Cost | = Common Stock | + Prior Years | + Earnings | − Dividends | + Inven- tory (3 Mo.) | + Land (Inde- finite) | + Cost (6 Yrs.) | + Accum. Depr. (6 Yrs.) | + Goodwill Element (10 Yrs.) |
|---|---|---|---|---|---|---|---|---|---|---|---|
| Remaining life | | | | | | | (3 Mo.) | (finite) | (6 Yrs.) | (6 Yrs.) | (10 Yrs.) |
| Balances, Jan. 1, 19X1 | $12,000 | $72,000 | $40,000 | $20,000 | | | $1,600 | $9,600 | $4,800 | | $8,000 |
| Equity in net income: | | | | | | | | | | | |
| To parent | | 12,000 | | | $12,000 | | | | | | |
| To minority interest | 3,000ᵃ | | | | 3,000 | | | | | | |
| Dividends: | | | | | | | | | | | |
| To parent | | (4,000) | | | | $(4,000) | | | | | |
| To minority interest | (1,000)ᵃ | | | | | $(1,000) | | | | | |
| Amortization | | (3,200) | | | | | (1,600) | | | (800) | (800) |
| Subtotal | $14,000 | $76,800 | $40,000 | $20,000 | $15,000 | $(5,000) | $ –0– | $9,600 | $4,800 | $ (800) | $7,200 |
| Reclassification | | | | 10,000 | (15,000) | 5,000 | | | | | |
| Balances, Dec. 31, 19X1 | $14,000 | $76,800 | $40,000 | $30,000 | $ –0– | $ –0– | $ –0– | $9,600 | $4,800 | $ (800) | $7,200 |
| Equity in net income: | | | | | | | | | | | |
| To parent | | 16,800 | | | 16,800 | | | | | | |
| To minority interest | 4,200ᵃ | | | | 4,200 | | | | | | |
| Amortization | | (1,600) | | | | | | | | (800) | (800) |
| Subtotal | $18,200 | $92,000 | $40,000 | $30,000 | $21,000 | $ –0– | $ –0– | $9,600 | $4,800 | $(1,600) | $6,400 |
| Reclassification | | | | 21,000 | (21,000) | | | | | | |
| Balances, Dec. 31, 19X2 | $18,200 | $92,000 | $40,000 | $51,000 | $ –0– | $ –0– | $ –0– | $9,600 | $4,800 | $(1,600) | $6,400 |

ᵃNo general ledger entry is necessary in the parent's books.

## Consolidation for the First and Second Years Subsequent to the Acquisition Date.

The consolidated financial statements as of December 31, 19X1 (one year after the acquisition date), and December 31, 19X2 (two years after the acquisition date), are prepared using the following primary, secondary, and accumulated depreciation elimination entries.

1. The primary elimination entry:

**WORKSHEET ENTRIES ONLY**

| | Consolidation Date | |
| --- | --- | --- |
| | December 31, 19X1 | December 31, 19X2 |
| Common Stock | 40,000 | 40,000 |
| Retained Earnings (beginning-of-year balance) | 20,000 | 30,000 |
| Equity in Net Income of S Company | 12,000 | 16,800 |
| Minority Interest in Net Income of S Company | 3,000 | 4,200 |
| Land | 9,600 | 9,600 |
| Equipment | 4,800 | 4,800 |
| Goodwill | 7,200 | 6,400 |
|     Dividends Declared | 5,000 | –0– |
|     Accumulated Depreciation | 800 | 1,600 |
|     Investment in S Company | 76,800 | 92,000 |
|     Minority Interest in Net Assets of S Company | 14,000 | 18,200 |

2. The secondary elimination entry:

**WORKSHEET ENTRIES ONLY**

| | | |
| --- | --- | --- |
| Cost of Goods Sold | 3,200 | 1,600 |
|     Equity in Net Income of S Company | 3,200 | 1,600 |

3. The accumulated depreciation elimination entry:

**WORKSHEET ENTRIES ONLY**

| | | |
| --- | --- | --- |
| Accumulated Depreciation | 50,000 | 50,000 |
|     Buildings and Equipment | 50,000 | 50,000 |

Illustration 5-5 shows the consolidating statement worksheet as of December 31, 19X1. (Consolidating statement worksheet illustrations under push-down accounting are not shown, as their preparation is less involved than earlier illustrations under non-push-down accounting.)

**Major Review Point for Illustration 5-5.** It is extremely important to realize that from the parent's perspective—but not from that of the minority

■ **ILLUSTRATION 5-5**
**First Year Subsequent to Acquisition Date**

| | P COMPANY AND SUBSIDIARY (S COMPANY) | | | | | |
|---|---|---|---|---|---|
| | Consolidating Statement Worksheet for the Year Ended December 31, 19X1 | | | | | |
| | P Company | S Company | Eliminations | | Consolidated |
| | | | Dr. | Cr. | |
| **Income Statement** | | | | | |
| Sales ........................... | 600,000 | 225,000 | | | 825,000 |
| Cost of goods sold.............. | (360,000) | (110,000) | 3,200(2) | | (473,200) |
| Expenses ...................... | (190,000) | (100,000) | | | (290,000) |
| Intercompany Accounts: | | | | | |
| Equity in net income of | | | | | |
| S Company ................. | 8,800[a] | | 12,000(1) | 3,200(2) | –0– |
| Income before Minority Interest .. | 58,800 | 15,000 | 15,200 | 3,200 | 61,800 |
| Minority interest.............. | | | | 3,000(1) | (3,000) |
| Net Income..................... | 58,800 | 15,000 | 18,200 | 3,200 | 58,800 |
| **Statement of Retained Earnings** | | | | | |
| Balances, January 1, 19X1 ...... | 100,000 | 20,000 | 20,000(1) | | 100,000 |
| + Net income................... | 58,800 | 15,000 | 18,200 | 3,200 | 58,800 |
| – Dividends declared........... | (45,000) | (5,000) | | 5,000(1) | (45,000) |
| Balances, December 31, 19X1.... | 113,800 | 30,000 | 38,200 | 8,200 | 113,800 |
| **Balance Sheet** | | | | | |
| Cash.......................... | 42,000 | 11,000 | | | 53,000 |
| Accounts receivable, net ......... | 75,000 | 37,000 | | | 112,000 |
| Inventory ...................... | 110,000 | 55,000 | | | 165,000 |
| Investment in S Company........ | 76,800 | | | 76,800(1) | –0– |
| Land.......................... | 220,000 | 30,000 | 9,600(1) | | 259,600 |
| Buildings and equipment........ | 500,000 | 200,000 | 4,800(1) | 50,000(3) | 654,800 |
| Accumulated depreciation........ | (320,000) | (63,000) | 50,000(3) | 800(1) | (333,800) |
| Goodwill....................... | | | 7,200(1) | | 7,200 |
| Total Assets.................. | 703,800 | 270,000 | 71,600 | 127,600 | 917,800 |
| Liabilities..................... | 290,000 | 200,000 | | | 490,000 |
| Minority interest in net | | | | | |
| assets of S Company........... | | | | 14,000(1) | 14,000 |
| P Company: | | | | | |
| Common stock................. | 300,000 | | | | 300,000 |
| Retained earnings ............. | 113,800 | | | | 113,800 |
| S Company: | | | | | |
| Common stock................. | | 40,000 | 40,000(1) | | –0– |
| Retained earnings ............. | | 30,000 | 38,200 | 8,200 | –0– |
| Total Liabilities and Equity .... | 703,800 | 270,000 | 78,200 | 22,200 | 917,800 |
| Proof of debit and credit postings ........................ | | | 149,800 | 149,800 | |

Explanation of entries:
(1) The primary elimination entry.       (3) The accumulated depreciation elimination entry.
(2) The secondary elimination entry.

[a]$12,000 share of S Company's reported net income, net of $3,200 of amortization of cost in excess of book value.

shareholders—**the amounts reported in the financial statements prepared by the subsidiary are wholly irrelevant amounts.** Under the non-push-down basis of accounting, such amounts do not reflect the new basis of accounting that takes place as a result of the acquisition being accounted for as a purchase (as opposed to a pooling of interests). Accordingly, the true earnings of the subsidiary from the parent's perspective are not $15,000. The parent earned only $8,800 on its investment in 19X1 (the $12,000 of "irrelevant income" recorded under the equity method of accounting, less the $3,200 of amortization of cost in excess of book value).

## All Other Possible Situations

Of course, many other possible situations may exist, such as when assets are overvalued, a bargain purchase element is present, or the purchase price is below the parent's share of the net assets at book value. For all situations, the conceptual analysis of the investment account is always prepared in the same manner as shown for the preceding situation.

# BLOCK ACQUISITIONS

All the business combinations illustrated so far (in which a parent–subsidiary relationship was formed) were assumed to result from a single acquisition of the acquired company's outstanding common stock. But in many cases companies gain control over an entity by acquiring blocks of its common stock over a period of time. When the acquiring company attains more than 50% ownership, the acquired company becomes a subsidiary and consolidation procedures are appropriate. Until then, the investor must account for the investment as follows:

1. For **less than 20% ownership,** use the lower of cost or market, as prescribed in *FASB Statement No. 12*, "Accounting for Certain Marketable Securities."
2. For **20% through 50% ownership,** use the equity method of accounting, as prescribed in *APB Opinion No. 18*, "The Equity Method of Accounting for Investments in Common Stock."

When blocks of stock are acquired, *ARB No. 51* governs the determination of the individual components as of the control date so that consolidated financial statements can be prepared:

When one company purchases two or more blocks of stock of another company at various dates and eventually obtains control of the other company, the date of acquisition (for the purpose of preparing consolidated statements) depends on the circumstances. If two or more purchases are made over a period of time, the earned surplus [current terminology is "retained earnings"] of the subsidiary at acquisition should generally be determined on a step-by-step basis; however, if small purchases are made over a period of time and then a purchase is made which results in control, the date of the latest purchase, as a matter of convenience, may be considered as the date of acquisition.[2]

## The Date of Latest Purchase Method

The **date of latest purchase method** makes the practical (although artificial) assumption that all of the acquired shares were purchased on the date control was obtained. Accordingly, the total carrying value of the investment, as of the control date, is separated into the components of the major conceptual elements **using data that apply only to the date control is obtained.** It is identical with the procedures discussed earlier in the chapter when control was achieved in a single purchase. Therefore, it is not illustrated in this section. For the date of the latest purchase method to be used, the investor would have to make several small purchases that, cumulatively, do not exceed the 20% ownership level, and then make a large purchase that gives more than 50% ownership—for example, 5%, 5%, 5%, and 40%. In other words, the 20–50% ownership range would have to be bypassed. (If this range is entered into, the step-by-step method must be used, as discussed below.)

## The Step-by-step Method

In the **step-by-step method,** the cost of each block of stock acquired is separated into its components of the major conceptual elements **using data that apply to the date the block was purchased.** Cumulative amounts are then determined for each of the components as of the control date, using the analysis of each block's cost by component. The procedures for analyzing the cost of each block of stock in this way are identical with those discussed earlier in the chapter when the purchase of a single (although large) block of stock resulted in control. Recall from intermediate accounting that whenever the 20–50% ownership level exists, *APB Opinion No. 18* requires the investor to:

1. Separate its cost into the components of the major conceptual elements using step-by-step procedures.
2. Adjust the investment account retroactively using step-by-step procedures whenever less than 20% ownership exists and an additional purchase results in attaining the 20–50% ownership range.

The procedures for determining the cumulative amounts in each component of the major conceptual elements as of the control date using the step-by-step method are the same whether the investor attains the

---

[2]*ARB No. 51,* par. 10.

20–50% range from the initial block purchase or from several block purchases. Accordingly, only the former situation must be illustrated.

## Preparing the Expanded Analysis of the Investment Account as of the Control Date Using the Step-by-step Method

Assume the following block acquisition information:

| Date of Block Acquisition | Ownership Percentage Acquired | Cost | Information Relating to Investee | | Net Assets Current Value over Book Value[a] |
|---|---|---|---|---|---|
| | | | Common Stock | Retained Earnings | |
| January 1, 19X1 | 30% | $ 73,000 | $80,000 | $ 60,000 | $50,000 |
| 19X1 net income | | | | 40,000 | |
| 19X1 dividends declared | | | | (10,000) | |
| January 1, 19X2 | 10% | $ 28,000 | $80,000 | $ 90,000 | $50,000 |
| 19X2 net income (6 mo.) | | | | 20,000 | |
| July 1, 19X2 | 50%[b] | $149,000 | $80,000 | $110,000 | $50,000 |

[a]For simplicity, we assume that the entire undervaluation of net assets relates to a parcel of land held by the subsidiary.
[b]If any additional shares are acquired after July 1, 19X2, the date control is established, the transaction would be considered the acquisition of some or all of the minority interest. The accounting for this is discussed in Chapter 10.

**Review Points for Illustration 5-6.**   Illustration 5-6 separates the cost of each block of stock into its components using the above information. The following points are important for understanding this illustration:

1. *APB Opinion No. 18* requires investors to amortize the excess of cost over book value to the extent such excess relates to depreciable or amortizable tangible and intangible assets.
2. The information given assumes that the investor can obtain information on the current value of the subsidiary's assets as of each block acquisition date. Often this is not possible or practicable. In such situations, the entire excess of cost over the investor's interest in the investee's net assets at book value must be assigned to goodwill.
3. The July 1, 19X2, balances (after the acquisition of the last block) are the starting point for the procedures the parent must use to account for its investment in the subsidiary.
4. The primary elimination entry that would be used in preparing consolidated financial statements as of July 1, 19X2, is as follows:

**WORKSHEET ENTRY ONLY**

| | | |
|---|---|---|
| Common Stock | 80,000 | |
| Retained Earnings | 110,000 | |
| Land | 45,000 | |
| Goodwill | 44,000 | |
| Investment in Subsidiary | | 260,000 |
| Minority Interest in Net Assets | | 19,000 |

# ILLUSTRATION 5-6

## Preparing the Expanded Analysis of the Investment Account as of the Control Date Using the Step-by-step Method

| Ownership Percentage Acquired | Date | Total Cost | = | Common Stock | + | Book Value Element Retained Earnings | + | Current Value over Book Value Element Land | + | Goodwill Element[d] |
|---|---|---|---|---|---|---|---|---|---|---|
| 30 | Block purchase, January 1, 19X1 | $ 73,000 | | $24,000[a] | | $18,000[b] | | $15,000[c] | | $16,000 |
| | Equity in 19X1 net income (30% × $40,000) | 12,000 | | | | 12,000 | | | | |
| | Dividends (30% × $10,000) | (3,000) | | | | (3,000) | | | | |
| | Amortize cost in excess of book value | (4,000) | | | | | | | | (4,000) |
| 30 | Balance, December 31, 19X1 | $ 78,000 | | $24,000 | | $27,000 | | $15,000 | | $12,000 |
| 10 | Block purchase, January 1, 19X2 | 28,000 | | 8,000 | | 9,000 | | 5,000[e] | | 6,000 |
| | Equity in net income (6 mo.) (40% × $20,000) | 8,000 | | | | 8,000 | | | | |
| | Amortize cost in excess of book value: | | | | | | | | | |
| | Block 1 ($16,000 × ¼ × ½ yr.) | (2,000) | | | | | | | | (2,000) |
| | Block 2 ($ 6,000 × ⅓ × ½ yr.) | (1,000) | | | | | | | | (1,000) |
| 40 | Balance, June 30, 19X2 | $111,000 | | $32,000 | | $44,000 | | $20,000 | | $15,000 |
| +50 | Block purchase, July 1, 19X2 | 149,000 | | 40,000 | | 55,000 | | 25,000[f] | | 29,000 |
| 90 | Balance, July 1, 19X2 | $260,000 | | $72,000 | | $99,000 | | $45,000 | | $44,000 |

**Format modification for minority interest**

| | | Minority Interest (10%) |
|---|---|---|
| | | $19,000 |
| | | 8,000 |
| | | 11,000 |
| Adjusted Balances, July 1, 19X2 | $19,000 | $260,000 |

| | Total Cost | Common Stock | Retained Earnings | Land | Goodwill |
|---|---|---|---|---|---|
| Adjusted Balances, July 1, 19X2 | $260,000 | $80,000 | $110,000 | $45,000 | $44,000 |

*See 228*

[a]Calculated at 30% of $80,000. (Subsequent additions to this column are based on ownership percentages and book values.)
[b]Calculated at 30% of $60,000. (Subsequent additions to this column are based on ownership percentages and book values.)
[c]Calculated at 30% of $50,000.
[d]A remaining life of four years from the initial acquisition date is used to amortize goodwill. Thus, the $6,000 of goodwill from the second block purchase has a three-year life.
[e]Calculated at 10% of $50,000.
[f]Calculated at 50% of $50,000.

5. For all subsequent periods, the two additional separate retained earnings columns must be used in the analysis of the investment account to isolate the subsidiary's future earnings and dividends. These additional columns were not necessary in prior periods, because consolidated financial statements could not be prepared (the ownership was not more than 50%).

## SELECTED REFERENCES

Rosenfield, Paul, and Steven Rubin. "Minority Interest: Opposing Views." *Journal of Accountancy* (March 1986) pp. 78–89. As evident by this single article listed here, the issues associated with minority interests are not burning controversies.

## END-OF-CHAPTER REVIEW

### Summary of Key Points

1. Partially owned subsidiaries must be fully consolidated—proportional consolidation is not allowed.
2. The parent company theory is the predominant practice in presenting minority interest in the consolidated statements.
3. Under parent company theory: (a) the minority interest in the subsidiary's net income is shown as a deduction in arriving at consolidated net income; (b) the minority interest in the subsidiary's net assets is shown outside stockholders' equity; and (c) the subsidiary's assets and liabilities are revalued to their current values only to the extent that the undervaluation is bought and paid for (likewise for goodwill).
4. Dividends paid to minority shareholders are always treated as a reduction of the minority interest in the subsidiary's net assets—never as dividends of the consolidated group.
5. Under the non-push-down basis of accounting, the amounts reported by the subsidiary are wholly irrelevant amounts from the perspective of the parent.

### Glossary of New Terms

**Block acquisitions**   Acquisitions in which blocks of an investee company's outstanding common stock are acquired over time until the ownership level exceeds 50%.

**Date of latest purchase method**   When control over a company is achieved as a result of block acquisitions, the carrying value of the investment as of the control date is separated into the components of the major conceptual elements, using the current values of the subsidiary's assets and liabilities at the date control is obtained.

**Entity theory**   A theory pertaining to how the assets and liabilities of partially owned subsidiaries and the related minority shareholders' interests in the subsidiary's earnings and net assets should be valued and presented in consolidated financial statements. The foundation of the theory is that a new reporting entity (other than the parent) is deemed to exist as a result of consolidation. Minority interest, therefore, is treated as an equity interest of the new consolidated reporting entity. Assets and liabilities of partially owned subsidiaries are revalued to their full current values as of the date of the business combination. Goodwill value is based on total goodwill implicit in the purchase price.

**Minority interest**   The interest of the shareholders of a partially owned subsidiary, other than the parent, in the subsidiary's earnings, losses, and net assets.

**Parent company theory**   A theory pertaining to how the assets and liabilities of partially owned subsidiaries and the related minority shareholders' interests in the subsidiary's earnings and net assets should be valued and presented in consolidated financial statements. The foundation of the theory is that the parent company is the consolidated reporting entity. Minority interest, therefore, is not treated as an equity interest of the consolidated reporting entity. Assets and liabilities of partially owned subsidiaries are revalued to their current values as of the business combination date only to the extent of the parent's cost over or under its ownership interest in the book value of the subsidiaries' net assets. Goodwill is reported only to the extent that it is paid for by the parent.

**Step-by-step method**   When control over a company is achieved as a result of block acquisitions, the total carrying value of the investment as of the control date is separated into the individual components of the major conceptual elements by analyzing the cost of each separate block of stock.

## Self-Study Questions

*(Answers are at the end of this chapter, preceding the appendices.)*

1. How are dividends paid to minority shareholders reported in the consolidated statements?
   a. They reduce the amount reported as "minority interest in net income of subsidiary" in the consolidated income statement.
   b. They reduce the amount reported as "minority interest in net assets of subsidiary" in the consolidated balance sheet.
   c. They are included in the dividends declared line in the consolidated statement of retained earnings.
   d. They are combined with expenses in the consolidated income statement.
   e. None of the above.
2. Pale Company acquired 60% of the outstanding common stock of Sanguine Company for $156,000 cash. The book value of Sanguine Company's net assets is $200,000. Sanguine Company's only over- or undervalued asset or liability is land that has a book value of $100,000 and a current value of $50,000. Under the parent company theory, at what amount would the land, the minority interest, and goodwill be reported in the consolidated statements?

| | Land | Goodwill | Minority Interest |
|---|---|---|---|
| a. | $130,000 | $6,000 | $80,000 |
| b. | $130,000 | $10,000 | $100,000 |
| c. | $130,000 | $44,000 | $104,000 |
| d. | $150,000 | $6,000 | $80,000 |
| e. | $150,000 | $10,000 | $100,000 |
| f. | $150,000 | $44,000 | $104,000 |

3. Plummet Company acquired 75% of Soarex Company's outstanding common stock on April 1, 19X1. For 19X1, Soarex Company reported $80,000 of net income, all of which was earned evenly throughout the year. In 19X1, Plummet Company recorded $4,000 of amortization of cost in excess of book value. Plummet Company's share of Soarex Company's true earnings (from Plummet Company's perspective) are:

a. $60,000.    d. $42,000.

b. $56,000.    e. $41,000.

c. $45,000.    f. None of the above.

## Demonstration Problem

Parr Company acquired 60% of the outstanding common stock of Subb Company on May 1, 19X5, at a total cost of $273,000. Subb's capital accounts at the acquisition date were:

| | |
|---|---|
| Common stock. . . . . . . . . . . . . . . . . . . . . . . . . . . . . . . . . . . . . . . . . | $  10,000 |
| Retained earnings . . . . . . . . . . . . . . . . . . . . . . . . . . . . . . . . . . . . | 240,000 |

All of Subb's assets and liabilities had current values equal to book values as of the acquisition date, except copyrights, which had a current value of $90,000 and a book value of $20,000. The copyrights have a remaining life of 14 years. Goodwill was assigned a nine-year life.

For 19X5, Subb had the following earnings and dividends:

| | Jan. 1–<br>April 30, 19X1 | May 1–<br>Dec. 31, 19X1 | Total |
|---|---|---|---|
| Net income . . . . . . . . . . . . . . . . . . . . . | $25,000 | $55,000 | $80,000 |
| Dividends declared . . . . . . . . . . . . . . | 15,000 | 60,000 | 75,000 |

## Required:

1. Prepare the journal entries Parr would make for the year ended December 31, 19X5, under the equity method.

2. Prepare an expanded analysis of the investment account as of the acquisition date and update it through December 31, 19X5.

3. Prepare the primary and secondary elimination entries for consolidation at December 31, 19X5.

### SOLUTION TO DEMONSTRATION PROBLEM

1. Investment in Subb Company................    33,000
       Equity in Net Income of Subsidiary......         33,000
   To record share of earnings of subsidiary
       from May 1, 19X5, to December 31, 19X5
       ($55,000 × 60%).

   Dividends Receivable.......................    36,000
       Investment in Subb Company............         36,000
   To record dividends from subsidiary from
       May 1, 19X5, to December 31, 19X5
       ($60,000 × 60%).

   Equity in Net Income of Subsidiary...........    8,000
       Investment in Subb Company...........         8,000
   To amortize cost in excess of book value
       ($2,000 for copyrights and $6,000
       for goodwill).

2.

| Minority Interest | + | Total Cost | = | Common Stock | + | Book Value Element Prior Periods | + | Current Year Earnings | Current Year Dividends | + | Current Value over Book Value Element Copyrights | + | Goodwill Element |
|---|---|---|---|---|---|---|---|---|---|---|---|---|---|
| | | $273,000 | | $ 6,000 | | $144,000 | | | | | $42,000 | | $81,000 |
| $100,000 | | | | 4,000 | | 96,000 | | | | | | | |
| $100,000 | | $273,000 | | $10,000 | | $240,000 | | | | | $42,000 | | $81,000 |
| | | 33,000 | | | | | | $33,000 | | | | | |
| 22,000 | | | | | | | | $22,000 | | | | | |
| (24,000) | | (36,000) | | | | | | | $(36,000) | | | | |
| | | | | | | | | | (24,000) | | | | |
| | | (8,000) | | | | | | | | | (2,000)[a] | | (6,000)[b] |
| $ 98,000 | | $262,000 | | $10,000 | | $240,000 | | $55,000 | $(60,000) | | $40,000 | | $75,000 |
| | | | | | | (5,000) | | (55,000) | 60,000 | | | | |
| $ 98,000 | | $262,000 | | $10,000 | | $235,000 | | $ –0– | $ –0– | | $40,000 | | $75,000 |

[a]$42,000 ÷ 14 yrs. × 2/3 yr.
[b]$81,000 ÷ 9 yrs. × 2/3 yr.

3. The primary elimination entry:

|  | Dr. | Cr. |
|---|---|---|
| Common Stock ........................... | 10,000 | |
| Retained Earnings—(beginning)................. | 240,000 | |
| Equity in Net Income of Subsidiary............... | 33,000 | |
| Minority Interest in Net Income of Subsidiary....... | 22,000 | |

|  | Dr. | Cr. |
|---|---|---|
| Copyrights . . . . . . . . . . . . . . . . . . . . . . . . . . . . . . . . . . . . | 40,000 | |
| Goodwill . . . . . . . . . . . . . . . . . . . . . . . . . . . . . . . . . . . . . | 75,000 | |
|     Dividends Declared . . . . . . . . . . . . . . . . . . . . . . . | | 60,000 |
|     Minority Interest in Net Assets of Subsidiary. . | | 98,000 |
|     Investment in Subb Company. . . . . . . . . . . . . . | | 262,000 |

The secondary elimination entry:

|  | Dr. | Cr. |
|---|---|---|
| Cost of Goods Sold . . . . . . . . . . . . . . . . . . . . . . . . . . . . | 8,000 | |
|     Equity in Net Income of Subsidiary . . . . . . . . . | | 8,000 |

## ASSIGNMENT MATERIAL

### Review Questions

1. Explain what proportional consolidation is.
2. What are the arguments for full consolidation?
3. What are the three possible ways of classifying minority interest in the balance sheet? Which way is used most often?
4. How are dividends that are paid to minority shareholders treated for consolidated reporting purposes?
5. Explain the difference between the parent company theory and the entity theory.
6. Under which theory is the minority interest reported in the consolidated financial statements based on the subsidiary's book value of the net assets?
7. How does the step-by-step method work when control is achieved after several block purchases?
8. When control is achieved after several block acquisitions, in which situations is the date of latest purchase method appropriate?

### Exercises

### Calculation of Consolidated Net Income

Pushco Company owns 75% of the outstanding common stock of Shovex Company. Each company's 19X1 net income from its own separate operations, exclusive of earnings and amortization recorded under the equity method, is as follows:

| | |
|---|---|
| Pushco Company. . . . . . . . . . . . . . . . . . . . . . . . . . . . . . . . . . . . . . . . . . . . . . . . . . | $1,000,000 |
| Shovex Company . . . . . . . . . . . . . . . . . . . . . . . . . . . . . . . . . . . . . . . . . . . . . . . . | 200,000 |

During 19X1, Pushco had $20,000 of amortization cost in excess of book value.

#### Required:

1. Determine the amount of consolidated net income.
2. Determine the amount of the minority interest in the subsidiary's net income.

## Calculation of Consolidated Net Income

E 5-2

Potter Company owns 80% of the outstanding common stock of Stainless Company and 90% of the outstanding common stock of Steele Company. Each company's 19X1 net income from its own separate operations, exclusive of earnings recorded under the equity method and amortization of cost over book value of net assets, is as follows:

| | |
|---|---:|
| Potter Company.......................................... | $1,000,000 |
| Stainless Company....................................... | 100,000 |
| Steele Company.......................................... | 10,000 |

Amortization of cost over book value of net assets on a full-year basis is $4,000 and $2,000 for Stainless and Steele, respectively.

### Required:
1. Calculate the minority interest in each subsidiary's net income and the consolidated net income for 19X1, assuming the subsidiaries were owned during the entire year.
2. Calculate the minority interest in each subsidiary's net income and the consolidated net income for 19X1, assuming Stainless was acquired on April 1, 19X1, and Steele was acquired on July 1, 19X1. (Assume earnings occurred evenly throughout the year.)

## Determining Amounts for the Consolidated Income Statement without Using a Consolidation Worksheet

E 5-3

On January 1, 19X1, Palmer Company acquired 75% of the outstanding common stock of Snead Company at an amount equal to 75% of Snead's net assets at carrying value. Each company's 19X1 income statement, exclusive of earnings recorded under the equity method, is as follows:

| | Palmer Company | Snead Company |
|---|---:|---:|
| Sales ...................................... | $800,000 | $200,000 |
| Cost of goods sold ......................... | (400,000) | (100,000) |
| Expenses................................... | (150,000) | (40,000) |
| Net Income................................. | $250,000 | $ 60,000 |

Balance sheet amounts for each company at December 31, 19X1, are purposely not furnished; therefore, a formal consolidating statement worksheet cannot be prepared. However, the consolidated amounts still can be determined if the main concept of the chapter is understood.

### Required:
1. Determine the consolidated income statement amounts.
2. Determine the consolidated income statement amounts assuming Palmer amortized $2,000 of cost in excess of book value of net assets that pertains to goodwill.

<table>
<tr><td>E<br>5-4</td></tr>
</table>

## Separating Total Cost into Components of the Major Conceptual Elements

On January 1, 19X6, Prima Company acquired 70% of the outstanding common stock of Seconde Company at a total cost of $180,000. Seconde's capital account balances at December 31, 19X5, are as follows:

| | |
|---|---:|
| Common stock | $100,000 |
| Additional paid-in capital | 50,000 |
| Retained earnings | 60,000 |
| | $210,000 |

Each of Seconde's assets and liabilities has a current value equal to its book value, except for the following items:

| | Book Value | Current Value |
|---|---:|---:|
| Land | $170,000 | $240,000 |
| Goodwill | 50,000 | –0– |
| 10% Bonds payable | 160,000 | 140,000 |

### Required:

Prepare an expanded analysis of the investment account as of the acquisition date. (Be sure to include the minority interest.)

<table>
<tr><td>E<br>5-5</td></tr>
</table>

## Determining Subsidiary's Equity from Consolidated Data

Popp Company acquired 70% of the outstanding common stock of Soda Corporation. Popp's separate balance sheet immediately after the acquisition and the consolidated balance sheet are as follows:

| | Popp Company | Consolidated |
|---|---:|---:|
| Current assets | $106,000 | $148,000 |
| Investment in Soda (cost) | 100,000 | — |
| Goodwill | — | 8,100 |
| Fixed assets (net) | 270,000 | 370,000 |
| | $476,000 | $526,100 |
| | | |
| Current liabilities | $ 15,000 | $ 30,000 |
| Minority interest | — | 35,100 |
| Capital stock | 350,000 | 350,000 |
| Retained earnings | 111,000 | 111,000 |
| | $476,000 | $526,100 |

Of the excess payment for the investment in Soda, $10,000 was attributed to undervaluation of its fixed assets; the balance was attributed to goodwill.

**Required:**

1. Calculate the total stockholders' equity of the subsidiary when it was acquired.
2. Prepare a conceptual analysis of the investment account at the acquisition date.

(AICPA adapted)

# Problems

P
5-1

## Preparing a Consolidation Worksheet as of the Acquisition Date

On December 31, 19X1, Payles Company, a calendar-year reporting company, acquired 75% of the outstanding common stock of Selmore Company at a total cost of $450,000. Each of Selmore's assets and liabilities has a current value equal to its book value. Each company's financial statements for the year ended December 31, 19X1, immediately after the acquisition date, are as follows:

|  | Payles Company | Selmore Company |
|---|---|---|
| **Income Statement (19X1)** | | |
| Sales. . . . . . . . . . . . . . . . . . . . . . . . . . . . . . . . . . . . . . | $8,000,000 | $ 700,000 |
| Cost of goods sold . . . . . . . . . . . . . . . . . . . . . . . . | (5,000,000) | (300,000) |
| Expenses. . . . . . . . . . . . . . . . . . . . . . . . . . . . . . . . . | (2,100,000) | (280,000) |
| Net Income. . . . . . . . . . . . . . . . . . . . . . . . . . . . . . | $ 900,000 | $ 120,000 |
| **Balance Sheet (as of December 31, 19X1)** | | |
| Cash . . . . . . . . . . . . . . . . . . . . . . . . . . . . . . . . . . . . . | $ 650,000 | $ 100,000 |
| Accounts receivable, net . . . . . . . . . . . . . . . . . . . | 900,000 | 400,000 |
| Inventory . . . . . . . . . . . . . . . . . . . . . . . . . . . . . . . . | 1,200,000 | 700,000 |
| Investment in Selmore Company . . . . . . . . . . . . | 450,000 | |
| Land . . . . . . . . . . . . . . . . . . . . . . . . . . . . . . . . . . . . | 800,000 | 300,000 |
| Buildings and equipment . . . . . . . . . . . . . . . . . . | 5,000,000 | 900,000 |
| Accumulated depreciation . . . . . . . . . . . . . . . . . | (1,000,000) | (200,000) |
| | $8,000,000 | $2,200,000 |
| Accounts payable and accruals . . . . . . . . . . . . . | $1,000,000 | $ 500,000 |
| Long-term debt . . . . . . . . . . . . . . . . . . . . . . . . . . | 2,000,000 | 1,100,000 |
| Common stock . . . . . . . . . . . . . . . . . . . . . . . . . . . | 1,000,000 | 100,000 |
| Additional paid-in capital . . . . . . . . . . . . . . . . . . | 2,000,000 | 200,000 |
| Retained earnings . . . . . . . . . . . . . . . . . . . . . . . . | 2,000,000 | 300,000 |
| | $8,000,000 | $2,200,000 |

**Required:**

1. Prepare the elimination entries required in consolidation as of December 31, 19X1.
2. Prepare a consolidating statement worksheet at December 31, 19X1.
3. What amount of income does the parent company report to its stockholders for the year 19X1?

| | P 5-2* | **Preparing a Consolidation Worksheet Subsequent to the Acquisition Date (Continuation of Problem 5-1)** |

As described in Problem 5-1, Payles Company acquired 75% of Selmore Company for $450,000 on December 31, 19X1. Each company's financial statements as of December 31, 19X2 (one year after the acquisition date) are as follows:

| | Payles Company | Selmore Company |
|---|---|---|
| **Income Statement (19X2)** | | |
| Sales................................... | $8,500,000 | $900,000 |
| Cost of goods sold ....................... | (5,500,000) | (400,000) |
| Expenses................................. | (2,400,000) | (320,000) |
| Equity in net income of subsidiary ........... | 135,000 | |
| Net Income............................. | $ 735,000 | $ 180,000 |
| **Balance Sheet (as of December 31, 19X2)** | | |
| Cash..................................... | $ 345,000 | $ 140,000 |
| Accounts receivable, net................... | 1,000,000 | 500,000 |
| Inventory .............................. | 1,500,000 | 800,000 |
| Investment in Selmore Company ............. | 510,000 | |
| Land .................................. | 800,000 | 300,000 |
| Buildings and equipment ................... | 5,200,000 | 900,000 |
| Accumulated depreciation .................. | (1,200,000) | (240,000) |
| | $8,155,000 | $2,400,000 |
| Accounts payable and accruals.............. | $ 700,000 | $ 620,000 |
| Long-term debt ......................... | 2,100,000 | 1,100,000 |
| Common stock .......................... | 1,000,000 | 100,000 |
| Additional paid-in capital.................. | 2,000,000 | 200,000 |
| Retained earnings ....................... | 2,355,000 | 380,000 |
| | $8,155,000 | $2,400,000 |
| Dividends declared during 19X2 ............. | $380,000 | $100,000 |

### Required:

1. Prepare and update the expanded analysis of the investment account through December 31, 19X2.
2. Prepare the consolidation elimination entries at December 31, 19X2.
3. Prepare a consolidating statement worksheet at December 31, 19X2. (The parent's retained earnings at December 31, 19X1, was $2,000,000.)
4. Prepare a formal consolidated balance sheet and income statement to be included in the annual report to the stockholders.

| | P 5-3 | **Preparing a Consolidation Worksheet as of the Acquisition Date** |

On December 31, 19X1, Peanut Company, a calendar-year reporting company, acquired 80% of the outstanding common stock of Shell Company at a total cost of

---

*The financial statement information presented for problems accompanied by asterisks is also provided on Model 5 (filename: Model5) of the software file disk that is available for use with the text, enabling the problem to be worked on the computer.

$240,000. Selected information on Shell Company as of the acquisition date is as follows:

|  | Book Value | Current Value | Remaining Life |
|---|---|---|---|
| Inventory | $80,000 | $ 85,000 | 2 months |
| Land | 70,000 | 100,000 | Indefinite |
| Equipment | 40,000 | 90,000 | 10 years |
| Patent | 15,000 | –0– | 3 years |

Assume a four-year life for any goodwill paid in the transaction.

Each company's financial statements for the year ended December 31, 19X1, immediately after the acquisition date, are as follows:

|  | Peanut Company | Shell Company |
|---|---|---|
| **Income Statement (19X1)** | | |
| Sales | $2,500,000 | $500,000 |
| Cost of goods sold | (1,400,000) | (250,000) |
| Expenses | (860,000) | (202,000) |
| Net Income | $ 240,000 | $ 48,000 |
| **Balance Sheet (as of December 31, 19X1)** | | |
| Cash | $ 160,000 | $ 20,000 |
| Accounts receivable, net | 200,000 | 55,000 |
| Inventory | 350,000 | 80,000 |
| Investment in Shell Company | 240,000 | |
| Land | 400,000 | 70,000 |
| Buildings and equipment | 800,000 | 200,000 |
| Accumulated depreciation | (150,000) | (40,000) |
| Patent | | 15,000 |
|  | $2,000,000 | $400,000 |
| Accounts payable and accruals | $ 250,000 | $ 60,000 |
| Long-term debt | 1,000,000 | 150,000 |
| Common stock | 300,000 | 100,000 |
| Retained earnings | 450,000 | 90,000 |
|  | $2,000,000 | $400,000 |

## Required:

1. Prepare an analysis of the investment account by the components of the major conceptual elements as of the acquisition.
2. Prepare the elimination entries required in consolidation as of December 31, 19X1.
3. Prepare a consolidating statement worksheet at December 31, 19X1.
4. What amount of income does the parent company report to its stockholders for the year 19X1?

<table>
<tr><td>P<br>5-4*</td><td>Preparing a Consolidation Worksheet Subsequent to the Acquisition Date<br>(Continuation of Problem 5-3)</td></tr>
</table>

As described in Problem 5-3, Peanut Company acquired 80% of Shell Company for $240,000 on December 31, 19X1. Each company's financial statements as of December 31, 19X2, one year after the acquisition date, are as follows:

|  | Peanut<br>Company | Shell<br>Company |
|---|---|---|
| **Income Statement (19X2)** | | |
| Sales | $2,800,000 | $600,000 |
| Cost of goods sold | (1,500,000) | (300,000) |
| Expenses | (1,000,000) | (240,000) |
| Equity in net income of subsidiary | 36,000 | |
| Net Income | $ 336,000 | $ 60,000 |
| **Balance Sheet (as of December 31, 19X2)** | | |
| Cash | $ 169,000 | $ 25,000 |
| Accounts receivable, net | 300,000 | 50,000 |
| Inventory | 500,000 | 120,000 |
| Investment in Shell Company | 232,000 | |
| Land | 400,000 | 70,000 |
| Buildings and equipment | 1,100,000 | 220,000 |
| Accumulated depreciation | (210,000) | (65,000) |
| Patent | | 10,000 |
|  | $2,491,000 | $430,000 |
| Accounts payable and accruals | $ 320,000 | $ 85,000 |
| Long-term debt | 1,300,000 | 150,000 |
| Common stock | 300,000 | 100,000 |
| Retained earnings | 571,000 | 95,000 |
|  | $2,491,000 | $430,000 |
| Dividends declared during 19X2 | $215,000 | $55,000 |

### Required:

1. Update the expanded analysis of the investment account through December 31, 19X2.
2. Prepare the consolidation elimination entries at December 31, 19X2.
3. Prepare a consolidating statement worksheet at December 31, 19X2. (The parent's retained earnings at December 31, 19X1, was $450,000.)
4. Prepare a formal consolidated balance sheet and income statement to be included in the annual report to the stockholders.

<table>
<tr><td>P<br>5-5</td><td>Preparing a Consolidation Worksheet as of the Acquisition Date</td></tr>
</table>

Post Company, a calendar-year reporting company, acquired 80% of the outstanding common stock of Script Company at a total cost of $320,000 on December 31, 19X1. Selected information on Script Company as of the acquisition date is as follows:

|  | Book Value | Current Value | Remaining Life |
|---|---|---|---|
| Inventory | $220,000 | $150,000 | 6 months |
| Land | 100,000 | 130,000 | Indefinite |
| Building | 410,000 | 310,000 | 20 years |
| Long-term debt | 300,000 | 260,000 | 4 years |

Each company's financial statements for the year ended December 31, 19X1, immediately after the acquisition date, are as follows:

|  | Post Company | Script Company |
|---|---|---|
| **Income Statement (19X1)** | | |
| Sales | $6,000,000 | $800,000 |
| Cost of goods sold | (3,300,000) | (600,000) |
| Expenses | (1,500,000) | (250,000) |
| Net Income (Loss) | $1,200,000 | $ (50,000) |
| **Balance Sheet (as of December 31, 19X1)** | | |
| Cash | $ 320,000 | $ 30,000 |
| Accounts receivable, net | 360,000 | 50,000 |
| Inventory | 800,000 | 220,000 |
| Investment in Script Company | 320,000 | |
| Land | 500,000 | 100,000 |
| Buildings and equipment | 2,600,000 | 550,000 |
| Accumulated depreciation | (400,000) | (50,000) |
|  | $4,500,000 | $900,000 |
| Accounts payable and accruals | $ 800,000 | $100,000 |
| Long-term debt | 2,100,000 | 300,000 |
| Common stock | 20,000 | 50,000 |
| Additional paid-in capital | 480,000 | 200,000 |
| Retained earnings | 1,100,000 | 250,000 |
|  | $4,500,000 | $900,000 |

## Required:

1. Prepare an analysis of the investment account by the components of the major conceptual elements as of the acquisition date.
2. Prepare the consolidation elimination entries at December 31, 19X1.
3. Prepare a consolidating statement worksheet at December 31, 19X1.
4. What amount of income does the parent company report to its stockholders for 19X1?

## Preparing a Consolidation Worksheet Subsequent to the Acquisition Date (Continuation of Problem 5-5)

As described in Problem 5-5, Post Company acquired 80% of Script Company for $320,000 on December 31, 19X1. Each company's financial statements as of December 31, 19X2, one year after the acquisition date, are as follows:

| | Post Company | Script Company |
|---|---|---|
| **Income Statement (19X2)** | | |
| Sales | $7,000,000 | $850,000 |
| Cost of goods sold | (3,800,000) | (600,000) |
| Expenses | (1,700,000) | (310,000) |
| Equity in net income of subsidiary | 4,000 | |
| Net Income (Loss) | $1,504,000 | $ (60,000) |
| **Balance Sheet (as of December 31, 19X2)** | | |
| Cash | $ 375,000 | $ 20,000 |
| Accounts receivable, net | 400,000 | 80,000 |
| Inventory | 700,000 | 130,000 |
| Investment in Script Company | 324,000 | |
| Land | 500,000 | 100,000 |
| Buildings and equipment | 3,100,000 | 550,000 |
| Accumulated depreciation | (600,000) | (80,000) |
| | $4,799,000 | $800,000 |
| | | |
| Accounts payable and accruals | $ 495,000 | $ 60,000 |
| Long-term debt | 2,000,000 | 300,000 |
| Common stock | 20,000 | 50,000 |
| Additional paid-in capital | 480,000 | 200,000 |
| Retained earnings | 1,804,000 | 190,000 |
| | $4,799,000 | $800,000 |
| | | |
| Dividends declared during 19X2 | $800,000 | |

### Required:

1. Update the expanded analysis of the investment account through December 31, 19X2.
2. Prepare the consolidation elimination entries at December 31, 19X2.
3. Prepare a consolidating statement worksheet at December 31, 19X2. (The parent's retained earnings at December 31, 19X1 was $1,100,000.)
4. Prepare a formal consolidated balance sheet and income statement to be included in the annual report to the stockholders.

**P 5-7\***

### COMPREHENSIVE   Analyzing the Investment; Applying the Equity Method; Preparing a Consolidation Worksheet Subsequent to the Acquisition Date

Poor Company acquired 60% of the outstanding common stock of Stands Company for cash of $503,000 on January 1, 19X1. Poor also incurred $37,000 of direct out-of-pocket costs in connection with the acquisition. Information with respect to Stands as of the acquisition date is as follows:

| | Book Value | Current Value | Remaining Life |
|---|---|---|---|
| Cash | $ 74,000 | $ 74,000 | |
| Accounts receivable, net | 266,000 | 266,000 | |
| Inventory | 280,000 | 260,000 | 6 months |

|  | Book Value | Current Value | Remaining Life |
|---|---|---|---|
| Land. . . . . . . . . . . . . . . . . . . . . . | 780,000 | 780,000 | Indefinite |
| Buildings and equipment. . . . . . . | 900,000 | 675,000 | 15 years |
| Accumulated depreciation. . . . . . . | (300,000) | | |
| Patent. . . . . . . . . . . . . . . . . . . . . | 40,000 | 165,000 | 5 years |
| Goodwill . . . . . . . . . . . . . . . . . . | 60,000 | | 2 years |
| | $2,100,000 | $2,220,000 | |
| | | | |
| Accounts payable and accruals . . . | $  380,000 | $  380,000 | |
| Long-term debt . . . . . . . . . . . . . . | 1,200,000 | 1,040,000 | 4 years |
| Common stock. . . . . . . . . . . . . . . | 200,000 | 800,000 | |
| Retained earnings. . . . . . . . . . . . | 320,000 | | |
| | $2,100,000 | $2,220,000 | |

The parent company intends to use the equity method to account for its investment. The only entry it has made to the investment account since the acquisition date, however, is to reflect the receipt of its share of $55,000 of dividends declared and paid during 19X1 by the subsidiary. The parent assigned a six-year life to goodwill that it paid for.

The financial statements of each company for the year ended December 31, 19X1, one year after the acquisition date, are as follows:

|  | Poor Company | Stands Company |
|---|---|---|
| **Income Statement (19X1)** | | |
| Sales. . . . . . . . . . . . . . . . . . . . . . . . . . . . | $9,000,000 | $  870,000 |
| Cost of goods sold. . . . . . . . . . . . . . . . . . . . | (5,000,000) | (470,000) |
| Expenses. . . . . . . . . . . . . . . . . . . . . . . . . | (2,800,000) | (190,000) |
| Net Income. . . . . . . . . . . . . . . . . . . . . | $1,200,000 | $  210,000 |
| **Balance Sheet (as of December 31, 19X1)** | | |
| Cash. . . . . . . . . . . . . . . . . . . . . . . . . . . | $  653,000 | $  168,000 |
| Accounts receivable, net. . . . . . . . . . . . . . . . | 840,000 | 270,000 |
| Inventory. . . . . . . . . . . . . . . . . . . . . . . . . | 1,200,000 | 560,000 |
| Investment in Stands Company . . . . . . . . . . . . | 507,000 | |
| Land. . . . . . . . . . . . . . . . . . . . . . . . . . . . | 1,000,000 | 780,000 |
| Buildings and equipment. . . . . . . . . . . . . . . . | 4,800,000 | 1,050,000 |
| Accumulated depreciation . . . . . . . . . . . . . . . | (1,700,000) | (390,000) |
| Patent. . . . . . . . . . . . . . . . . . . . . . . . . . | 300,000 | 32,000 |
| Goodwill . . . . . . . . . . . . . . . . . . . . . | | 30,000 |
| | $7,600,000 | $2,500,000 |
| Accounts payable and accruals . . . . . . . . . . . . | $1,100,000 | $  625,000 |
| Long-term debt. . . . . . . . . . . . . . . . . . . . . | 2,600,000 | 1,200,000 |
| Common stock . . . . . . . . . . . . . . . . . . . . . | 2,000,000 | 200,000 |
| Retained earnings . . . . . . . . . . . . . . . . . . . | 1,900,000 | 475,000 |
| | $7,600,000 | $2,500,000 |
| Dividends declared during 19X1. . . . . . . . . . . . | $900,000 | $55,000 |

### Required:

1. Prepare an expanded analysis of the investment account as of the acquisition date.
2. Update the expanded analysis of the investment account to reflect activity under the equity method of accounting for the investment through December 31, 19X1.
3. Adjust the parent company's financial statements as of December 31, 19X1, to reflect the equity method of accounting.
4. Prepare the consolidation elimination entries at December 31, 19X1.
5. Prepare a consolidating statement worksheet at December 31, 19X1.

---

**P 5-8**

### REVIEW (Chapters 4 and 5)  Analyzing the Investment; Applying the Equity Method; Computing Minority Interest and Consolidated Retained Earnings

On January 1, 19X6, Puttnam Corporation made the following investments:

1. It acquired 75% of the outstanding common stock of Shaft Corporation for $14 cash per share. The stockholders' equity of Shaft on January 1, 19X1, consisted of the following:

| | |
|---|---|
| Common stock, $10 par value . . . . . . . . . . . . . . . . . . . . . . . . . . . . . . . . . . | $100,000 |
| Retained earnings . . . . . . . . . . . . . . . . . . . . . . . . . . . . . . . . . . . . . . . . . . | 20,000 |

2. It acquired 60% of the outstanding common stock of Tee Corporation for $40 cash per share. The stockholders' equity of Tee on January 1, 19X1, consisted of the following:

| | |
|---|---|
| Common stock, $20 par value . . . . . . . . . . . . . . . . . . . . . . . . . . . . . . . . . | $60,000 |
| Paid-in capital in excess of par value . . . . . . . . . . . . . . . . . . . . . . . . . . | 10,000 |
| Retained earnings . . . . . . . . . . . . . . . . . . . . . . . . . . . . . . . . . . . . . . . . . . | 50,000 |

The current values of each subsidiary's net assets equal their book values except for a parcel of land owned by Shaft that has a current value of $40,000 *less* than its book value. At the time of these acquisitions, Puttnam expected both companies to have superior earnings for the next five years. Puttnam has accounted for these investments using the cost method. An analysis of each company's retained earnings for 19X1 is as follows:

| | Puttnam | Shaft | Tee |
|---|---|---|---|
| Balance, January 1, 19X1 . . . . . . . . . . . . . | $300,000 | $20,000 | $50,000 |
| Net income (loss) . . . . . . . . . . . . . . . . . . . . | 190,000 | 36,000 | (15,000) |
| Cash dividends declared and paid . . . . . . | (110,000) | (24,000) | (10,000) |
| Balance, December 31, 19X1 . . . . . . . . . . | $380,000 | $32,000 | $25,000 |

### Required:

1. Under the equity method, what entries should have been made on the books of the parent during 19X1 to record the following:

      a. Investments in subsidiaries.

      b. Parent's share of subsidiary income or loss.

      c. Subsidiary dividends received.

      d. Amortization of cost in excess of (under) book value, if any.

2. Compute the amount of minority interest in each subsidiary's stockholders' equity at December 31, 19X1.

3. What were the parent's earnings from its own operations for 19X1, excluding accounts relating to its ownership in these subsidiaries?

4. What amount should be reported as consolidated retained earnings as of December 31, 19X1?

(AICPA adapted)

## COMPREHENSIVE (Chapters 3–5)  Recording the Acquisition; Selecting Relevant Data; Preparing a Consolidation Worksheet

On July 1, 19X2, in a business combination that did *not* qualify as a pooling of interests, Pepsi acquired 80% of the outstanding common stock of Sprite Company by issuing 8,000 shares of its $5 par value common stock (which was trading at $60 per share on that date). In addition, Pepsi incurred direct costs of $100,000 relating to the acquisition, $60,000 of which was for the registration of the shares issued with the Securities and Exchange Commission. Selected relevant data follow:

|  | June 30, 19X2 | | |
|---|---|---|---|
|  | Book Value | Current Value | Remaining Life |
| **Sprite Company** |  |  |  |
| Inventory | $110,000 | $120,000 | 2 months |
| Buildings and equipment | 700,000[a] | 770,000 | 14 years |
| Patents | 90,000 | 60,000 | 3 years |
| Long-term debt | 500,000 | 475,000 | 2 years |
| Common stock | 300,000 |  |  |
| Retained earnings | 225,000 |  |  |
| **Pepsi Company** |  |  |  |
| Common stock | $500,000 |  |  |
| Additional paid-in capital | 500,000 |  |  |
| Retained earnings | 400,000 |  |  |

[a]Net of $200,000 of accumulated depreciation.

### Additional Information:

1. Assume any goodwill arising from the combination has a five-year life.

2. The equity method of accounting is to be used.

3. For 19X2, Sprite had the following earnings and dividends:

|  | Jan. 1– June 30, 19X2 | July 1– Dec. 31, 19X2 | Total |
|---|---|---|---|
| Sales | $ 600,000 | $ 800,000 | $1,400,000 |
| Cost of goods sold | (320,000) | (430,000) | (750,000) |

*(continued)*

|  | Jan. 1–<br>June 30, 19X2 | July 1–<br>Dec. 31, 19X2 | Total |
|---|---|---|---|
| Expenses............. | (240,000) | (310,000) | (550,000) |
| Net Income ......... | $ 40,000 | $ 60,000 | $ 100,000 |
| Dividends declared .... | $25,000 | $45,000[a] | $70,000 |
| Dividends paid......... | 25,000 | –0– | 25,000 |

[a]This dividend was paid January 5, 19X3.

4. During 19X2, Pepsi declared and paid $80,000 of dividends each quarter. Also, Pepsi reported a net income of $200,000 for the six months ended June 30, 19X2.

## Required:

1. Prepare the entry to record the business combination on July 1, 19X2.
2. Complete the Pepsi Company and Sprite Company financial statements that follow:

|  | Pepsi<br>Company | Sprite<br>Company |
|---|---|---|
| **Income Statement** |  |  |
| Sales.................................. | $2,200,000 |  |
| Cost of goods sold.................... | (1,100,000) |  |
| Expenses............................. | (600,000) |  |
| | | |
| Income before Minority Interest.......... |  |  |
| Minority interest...................... |  |  |
| Net Income .......................... |  |  |
| | | |
| **Statement of Retained Earnings** |  |  |
| Balances, beginning ................... |  |  |
| + Net income......................... |  |  |
| – Dividends declared.................. |  |  |
| Balances, Dec. 31, 19X2............... |  |  |
| **Balance Sheet** |  |  |
| Current assets ....................... | 1,383,000 | $ 475,000 |
| Land................................. | 700,000 | 200,000 |
| Buildings and equipment.............. | 3,000,000 | 900,000 |
| Accumulated depreciation ............. | (600,000) | (250,000) |
| Investment in Sprite Company .......... |  |  |
| Patents.............................. | –0– | 75,000 |
| | | |
| Total Assets ....................... |  | 1,400,000 |
| Accounts payable..................... | 907,000 | 360,000 |
| Long-term debt....................... | 2,100,000 | 500,000 |

|  | Pepsi Company | Sprite Company |
|---|---|---|
| _____ . . . . . . . . . . . . . . . . |  |  |
| _____ . . . . . . . . . . . . . . . . |  |  |
| _____ . . . . . . . . . . . . . . . . |  |  |
| Pepsi Company |  |  |
|    Common stock . . . . . . . . . . . . . . . . . . . . . . |  |  |
|    Additional paid-in capital . . . . . . . . . . . . . |  |  |
|    Retained earnings . . . . . . . . . . . . . . . . . . . |  |  |
| Sprite Company |  |  |
|    Common stock . . . . . . . . . . . . . . . . . . . . . |  | 300,000 |
|    Retained earnings . . . . . . . . . . . . . . . . . . . |  | 240,000 |
|       Total Liabilities and Equity . . . . . . . . . . . |  | 1,400,000 |

3. Prepare the consolidation elimination entries.
4. Prepare a consolidating statement worksheet.

## Problems for Block Acquisitions

### Block Acquisitions: The Step-by-step Method

Pommel Company acquired blocks of stock of Sorse Company over a period of several years. Information regarding such purchases along with pertinent information relating to the investee as of each purchase date is as follows:

| Date of Block Acquisition | Ownership Percentage Acquired | Cost | Common Stock | Retained Earnings[a] | Net Assets Current Value over Book Value[b] |
|---|---|---|---|---|---|
| | | | | | *Information on Investee* |
| January 1, 19X1 | 20 | $ 35,000 | $100,000 | $25,000 | [c] |
| January 1, 19X2 | 20 | 56,000 | 100,000 | 55,000 | [c] |
| December 31, 19X2 | 50 | 132,000 | 100,000 | 90,000 | $40,000[d] |

[a]Sorse Company declared cash dividends on common stock of $10,000 per year during 19X1 and 19X2.
[b]Assume Pommel Company uses a 10-year life for any goodwill acquired; also, assume that goodwill associated with each block acquisition has its own separate life.
[c]It was impractical to obtain specific information from the investee as to the current value of its individual assets and liabilities at the time of this block purchase.
[d]This amount is identified entirely with land.

### Required:

1. Using the step-by-step method, determine the balances that should exist in the investment account by the individual components of the major conceptual elements as of the control date (December 31, 19X2). *Hint:* Refer to paragraph 19n of *APB Opinion No. 18* for treatment of cost over investor's share of the investee's net assets at book value that cannot be identified with specific assets of liabilities.
2. Prepare the primary elimination entry at December 31, 19X2.

## Block Acquisitions: The Step-by-step Method

**P 5-11**

On January 1, 19X8, Plaza Company acquired 30% of the outstanding common stock of Storelle Company at a total cost of $380,000. At that time, Storelle's capital accounts were as follows:

| | |
|---|---:|
| Common stock | $ 600,000 |
| Retained earnings | 400,000 |
| | $1,000,000 |

On April 1, 19X8, Plaza acquired 40% of Storelle's outstanding common stock at a cost of $604,000. Earnings and dividend information for Storelle for 19X8 is as follows:

| | First Quarter | Remainder of Year |
|---|---|---|
| Net income | $60,000 | $200,000 |
| Dividends declared | 50,000 | 140,000 |

Assume that Plaza uses a 10-year life for goodwill associated with each block of stock. Assume also that none of Storelle's recorded assets or liabilities is over- or undervalued at either block acquisition date.

### Required:

1. Using the step-by-step method, determine the balances that should exist in the investment account by the individual components of the major conceptual elements as of the control date (April 1, 19X8).
2. Update the analysis of the investment account through December 31, 19X8, assuming the parent intends to include only the revenue and expense items of the subsidiary for the period April 1, 19X8, to December 31, 19X8, in preparing the consolidated income statement for 19X8.
3. Prepare the primary elimination entry at April 1, 19X8.
4. Prepare all the elimination entries required at December 31, 19X8.
5. Explain the two methods available to the parent in reporting the subsidiary's earnings for 19X8. Specifically, explain how the earnings recorded under the equity method of accounting for the first quarter are presented.

## Block Acquisitions: Comparison of the Date of Latest Purchase Method with the Step-by-step Method

**P 5-12**

Pestex Company acquired two blocks of stock of Sprayco Company. Information regarding each purchase along with pertinent information about the investee as of each purchase date is as follows:

| | | | | Information on Investee | | |
| --- | --- | --- | --- | --- | --- | --- |
| Date of Block Acquisition | Ownership Percentage Acquired | Cost | Common Stock | Retained Earnings[a] | | Net Assets Current Value over Book Value |
| January 1, 19X4 | 10 | $100,000[b] | $400,000 | $300,000 | | $50,000[c] |
| December 31, 19X6 | 60 | 800,000 | 400,000 | 640,000 | | 70,000[c] |

[a]Sprayco Company declared cash dividends on common stock of $90,000 per year in 19X4, 19X5, and 19X6.
[b]The carrying value of this block on Pestex Company's books has never been below cost from the date it was acquired.
[c]This amount is identified entirely with land.

### Required:

1. Using the date of latest purchase method, determine the balances that should exist in the investment account by the individual components of the major conceptual elements as of the control date (December 31, 19X6).
2. Using the step-by-step method, determine the balances that should exist in the investment account by the individual components of the major conceptual elements as of the control date (December 31, 19X6).

# ADVANCED LEVEL ASSIGNMENT MATERIAL

## Advanced Problems

**AP 5-1**

### Applying Finance Concepts to Evaluate the Profitability of the Parent's Investment in the Subsidiary

PTA Company acquired 80% of the outstanding common stock of Scoolex Company on January 1, 19X1, for $400,000 cash. Selected financial information follows:

| | PTA Company | Scoolex Company | |
| --- | --- | --- | --- |
| | Amortization of Cost in Excess | Reported Net | Dividends |
| Year | of Book Value | Income (Loss) | Declared |
| 19X1 | $20,000 | $150,000 | |
| 19X2 | 20,000 | 275,000 | $125,000 |
| 19X3 | 20,000 | 100,000 | 200,000 |
| 19X4 | 10,000 | (75,000) | –0– |

### Additional Information:

1. The decision to acquire Scoolex was based on cash flow projections, which showed an estimated internal rate of return of approximately 30%.
2. Of the $400,000 purchase price, $150,000 was assigned to goodwill having a 15-year life. (Scoolex's book value was $250,000 on 1/1/X1.)

3. The parent chose to use (a) non-push-down accounting and (b) the equity method of accounting.
4. The subsidiary's reported net income or loss amounts occurred evenly throughout the year.
5. The subsidiary declared its dividends on December 20 of each year and paid them 10 days later.
6. In early 19X4, the subsidiary's major competitor announced a startling patented improvement to its main product, whereby the subsidiary was placed at a major competitive disadvantage.
7. On December 31, 19X4, the parent (in light of its assessment that the subsidiary would be only marginally profitable in the future because of the competitor's announcement) sold its entire interest in the subsidiary for $288,640 cash.

### Required:

1. Prepare a T-account analysis of the Investment in Subsidiary account over the life of the investment.
2. Calculate the parent's return on its investment (ROI) for each year.
3. Explain whether it is correct to use the beginning of year investment balance or the average investment balance for the year in the denominator in requirement 2.
4. Repeat requirement 2 for 19X2 under each of the following changed assumptions concerning the $125,000 of dividends declared in 19X2:

| Assumption | Date Declared | Date Paid |
|---|---|---|
| A | January 1, 19X2 | January 5, 19X2 |
| B | July 1, 19X2 | July 5, 19X2 |

5. Calculate the internal rate of return (IRR) over the life of the investment. State your answer to the nearest whole percent (for example, 15%).

   *Note:* You may readily obtain this answer using the IRR function available in Lotus 1-2-3®. (You merely need to set up a cash flow table and *then* program the IRR function with the cell cursor located in the cell in which you want your answer to appear.)
6. Repeat requirement 5 under each of the following changed assumptions concerning the $125,000 of dividends declared in 19X2:

| Assumption | Date Declared | Date Paid |
|---|---|---|
| A | December 20, 19X2 | January 3, 19X3 |
| B | January 1, 19X2 | January 5, 19X2 |
| C | June 25, 19X2 | July 1, 19X2 |

7. Prepare a T-account analysis of the Investment in Subsidiary account by year over the life of the investment using (a) the dividend information provided and (b) the net income amounts assumed under the IRR method. (Use the percentage you calculated in requirement 5 to calculate each year's assumed net income.)

8. Compare the ROI calculations in requirement 2 with the IRR calculation in requirement 5. Which is best suited for evaluating the profitability of this investment? Why?
9. If the subsidiary had been sold on January 3, 19X5 (instead of on December 31, 19X4), would the parent's ROI for 19X4 be any different? Why or why not?

---

**AP 5-2**

## Leveraged Buyout: Determining the Change in Basis—The Continuing Ownership Percentage Decreases

Oldco is a privately owned company having 1,000 shares of common stock outstanding, 100% of which is owned by Ralph and Ruth Richy, the founders of the company. The Richys retired several years ago and are no longer active in the management of the business. In November 19X1, upper management proposed a leveraged buyout to the Richys. The Richys were agreeable to this, and management approached an independent investment firm that has strong relationships with lending institutions. In December 19X1, a new corporation (Newco) was formed to serve as a holding company to acquire all of the outstanding common stock of Oldco. Newco borrowed $350,000 from a lending institution, which loan is secured by Oldco's assets. On December 31, 19X1, Newco issued 1,000 shares of common stock as follows:

1. 350 shares to the investment firm for $35,000 cash.
2. 350 shares to upper management for $35,000 cash.
3. 300 shares to the Richys for $30,000 cash.

Also on that date, Newco paid $450,000 cash to the Richys for the entire 1,000 shares of Oldco common stock held by them.

Information concerning Oldco at December 31, 19X1, follows:

|  | Book Value | Current Value |
|---|---|---|
| Assets | $500,000 | $800,000 |
| Liabilities | $300,000 | $300,000 |
| Stockholders' equity | 200,000 | 500,000 |
|  | $500,000 | $800,000 |

### Required:

1. Prepare a conceptual analysis of the Investment in Oldco account by the major conceptual elements (showing the extent to which Oldco's assets would be revalued upward in consolidation and the amount to be reported for goodwill in consolidation).
2. Would your answer to requirement 1 be different if the transaction had been structured as follows: (a) Oldco borrowed $350,000 from the financial institution; (b) Oldco paid a special dividend of $350,000 cash to the Richys; (c) the investment firm acquired 350 shares of Oldco common stock directly from the Richys for $35,000 cash; and (d) upper management acquired 350 shares of Oldco common stock directly from the Richys for $35,000 cash?

3. Would your answer in requirement 1 be different if the Richys had been issued only 100 shares of Newco common stock (with the remaining 900 shares having been issued to upper management and the investment firm for cash of $90,000)?

## Creating a Consolidation Template and Two Keystroke Macros (Stored Instructions)

**AP 5-3**

The purpose of this assignment is to give you programming experience in: (1) creating a template and (2) creating two specific keystroke macros (stored instructions that can be automatically executed instantaneously at the touch of a key). These two macros are highly useful in reviewing a newly created template to see if errors were made in the programmed formulas.

### Required:

1. Prepare a consolidation template (complete with formulas) for the trial balance consolidation approach on pages 262–63 in Appendix B. Use the Comma format with zero decimal places. (Do not use the Range command to format—you might unintentionally prevent your macro from changing column widths.)
2. Program a keystroke macro (a stored instruction) to convert your model from Comma format to Text format (which displays formulas). Include in this macro instructions to change column widths as necessary for full display of the formulas. (Use Macro Y in the templates provided for Chapters 1–10 as a guide.)
   **Specific Instructions and Cautions:**
   a. Be sure to leave a blank row between your stored macros (Lotus 1-2-3®'s method of indicating the end of a macro).
   b. Be sure to use the ' (apostrophe) key before trying to store any command instruction that begins with the / (slash) key. This allows the command to be stored as a label; otherwise, the computer will start executing the command you merely are trying to store.
   c. Use the / Range Name Create command of Lotus 1-2-3® as explained below:
      (1) Place the cell cursor on the top row of your stored instructions.
      (2) Strike the keys /RNC. You will then be prompted to enter the letter of the alphabet you wish to assign to this macro. Strike the appropriate key.
      (3) You will then be prompted to indicate the range in which you have stored the instructions that constitute this macro. Indicate this range either by (a) typing in the coordinates (such as C20.C24) or (b) using the down arrow key to enlarge the cell cursor over each row of instructions. Then strike the ENTER key.
   d. Once you individually have changed a column width, that column is no longer under the control of the Global command. To bring it back under the control of the Global command, use the /Worksheet Column Reset command.
3. Program a macro to reverse the macro you programmed in requirement 2 (to go back to the Comma format). (Use Macro Z in the templates provided for Chapters 1–10 as a guide.)

ANSWERS TO SELF-STUDY QUESTIONS:
 1. b
 2. a
 3. e

**Appendix A**

# PREPARATION OF CONSOLIDATED FINANCIAL STATEMENTS USING THE COMBINATION ENTITY–PARENT COMPANY APPROACH AND THE ENTITY THEORY

## The Entity Theory

In the example used earlier in the discussions of the parent company theory, the subsidiary's assets were undervalued by $20,000 at the acquisition date, and the undervalued assets were revalued upward by $16,000 (80% × $20,000) in consolidation. Some accountants believe that the **subsidiary's identifiable assets and liabilities should be fully revalued in consolidation to 100% of their current values, regardless of the parent's ownership interest.** They would revalue the subsidiary's assets upward by $20,000 instead of $16,000. The additional $4,000 valuation would be reflected as an increase in the minority interest in the balance sheet. Such additional valuation results in additional amortization charges in future consolidated income statements. However, a corresponding reduction in the amount of consolidated net income is allocated to the minority shareholders. Thus, the amount of consolidated net income allocated to the controlling interests (the parent's shareholders) is not affected. This approach comes under the entity theory, which was discussed earlier in the chapter. Theoretically, the approach has merit in that a partial revaluation of the subsidiary's assets and liabilities results in a hybrid valuation of such items somewhere between their historical costs and their current values. The proponents of this theory feel that it makes more sense to revalue the assets and liabilities to their current values, as this would be more informative. However, because most business combinations involve large companies acquiring significantly smaller companies, the consolidated financial statements would not be that much more meaningful under the full revaluation approach.

Under the entity theory, the value of goodwill in consolidation is based on the amount of goodwill implicit in the transaction. For example, if the parent paid $8,000 for goodwill in acquiring an 80% ownership interest, then the goodwill implicit in the transaction would be $10,000 ($8,000 ÷ 80%). Thus, goodwill would be valued at $10,000 instead of $8,000, and the additional $2,000 valuation would be reflected as an increase to the minority interest in the balance sheet. As in the case of undervalued assets, this additional goodwill results in additional amortization expense in future consolidated income statements. However, a corresponding reduction in the amount of consolidated net income is allocated to the minority shareholders. Therefore, the amount of consolidated net income allocated to the controlling interests (the parent's shareholders) is not affected.

## The Combination Entity–Parent Company Approach

A third alternative adopts certain features of both the parent company theory and the entity theory. We refer to this as the **combination entity– parent company approach.** Under this approach, the subsidiary's identifiable assets and liabilities are fully revalued in consolidation to 100% of their current values, as is done under the entity theory. However, goodwill is valued in consolidation only to the extent that it is paid for by the parent company, as is done under the parent company theory.

Whether the minority interest should be presented in the consolidated financial statements in accordance with the entity theory or the parent company theory is an arbitrary decision, because the approach is a combination of the two theories. The minority interest is rarely presented under the entity theory; apparently companies that use this combination approach present the minority interest in accordance with the parent company theory.

## The Selection of a Valuation Method

### The Requirements of the Official Pronouncements.

Neither *ARB No. 51* nor *Accounting Principles Board Opinion No. 16* provides explicit guidance on which of the three valuation methods to use. A survey by the staff of the Financial Accounting Standards Board (FASB) in 1976 (seven years before the SEC's *Staff Accounting Bulletin No. 54*) found overwhelming use of the parent company theory and negligible use of the other two valuation theories.[3]

Regardless of the theoretical soundness of the entity theory, we believe that it produces results that are not consistent with the historical cost basis of accounting (which underlies the purchase method) because values are imputed above and beyond cost. The answers to the CPA examination problems from the American Institute for Certified Public Accountants in this area support this position; they show assets and liabilities revalued and goodwill valued only to the extent of the parent company's cost over its ownership interest in the book value of the subsidiary's net assets.

The entity theory and the combination entity–parent company approach make the preparation of consolidated financial statements somewhat more involved. When the parent's ownership interest is close to

---

[3]The survey results may be found in an FASB discussion memorandum, "Accounting for Business Combinations and Purchased Intangibles," pp. 107, E-8, and E-17.

100%, using the entity theory or the combination entity–parent company approach usually has no appreciable effect on the balance sheet. (In most business combinations in which common stock is acquired, the parent's ownership is more than 90%.)

For these reasons, we used the parent company theory instead of the entity theory or the combination entity–parent company approach to illustrate the preparation of consolidated financial statements earlier in the chapter. Consequently, the minority interest presented in the consolidated balance sheet always equals the ownership percentage of the minority shareholders multiplied by the book value of the subsidiary's stockholders' equity. Likewise, the minority interest presented in the consolidated income statement (which is shown as a deduction in arriving at consolidated net income under the parent company theory) is always based on the subsidiary's net income as shown in its separate income statement.

**The FASB Looks into the Issue.** The FASB is addressing the valuation method issue for minority interest situations in its project on consolidations and the equity method of accounting. It may choose any one of the three valuation methods. Accordingly, in this appendix we focus on how to deal with the additional values reported in consolidation under the entity theory and the combination entity–parent company approach.

ILLUSTRATION

## The Combination Entity–Parent Company Approach

Recall that under the combination entity–parent approach:

1. The subsidiary's assets are revalued in consolidation to 100% of their current values as of the acquisition date.
2. Goodwill is reported in consolidation only to the extent that it is paid for by the parent company.

In the chapter example that examined the parent company theory, the subsidiary's assets were undervalued by $20,000. In consolidation, these assets were revalued upward by $16,000 (80% of $20,000). Thus an additional $4,000 of undervaluation must be dealt with under the combination entity–parent company approach. This $4,000 is analyzed as follows:

| Asset | Total Current Value over Book Value | Parent's Interest in Undervaluation (80%) | Minority Interest in Undervaluation (20%) |
|---|---|---|---|
| Inventory........ | $ 2,000 | $ 1,600 | $ 400 |
| Land ........... | 12,000 | 9,600 | 2,400 |
| Building......... | 6,000 | 4,800 | 1,200 |
| | $20,000 | $16,000 | $4,000 |

One way to deal with the $4,000 in consolidation is to add these values into the conceptual analysis of the investment account. Illustration 5-7 shows how this is done. Because the entire additional valuation of $4,000 is added to the minority interest column, no entry is made in the parent company's general ledger.

ILLUSTRATION

## Preparing Consolidated Financial Statements For the First and Second Years Subsequent to the Acquisition Date

For the two years following the acquisition date, the following entries would be made in consolidation.

The primary elimination entry:

| | Consolidation Date | | | |
|---|---|---|---|---|
| | December 31,19X1 | | December 31, 19X2 | |
| Common Stock . . . . . . . . . . . . . | 40,000 | | 40,000 | |
| Retained Earnings (beginning-of-year balance). . . . . . | 20,000 | | 30,000 | |
| Equity in Net Income of Subsidiary . . . . . . . . . . . . . . . | 12,000 | | 16,800 | |
| Minority Interest in Net Income of S Company . . . . . . | 3,000 | | 4,200 | |
| Land . . . . . . . . . . . . . . . . . . . . . | 12,000 | | 12,000 | |
| Equipment . . . . . . . . . . . . . . . . | 6,000 | | 6,000 | |
| Goodwill . . . . . . . . . . . . . . . . . | 7,200 | | 6,400 | |
| Dividends Declared . . . . | | 5,000 | | –0– |
| Accumulated Depreciation . . . . . . . . . | | 1,000 | | 2,000 |
| Investment in Subsidiary . . . . . . . . . . | | 76,800 | | 92,000 |
| Minority Interest in Net Assets of S Company | | 17,400 | | 21,400 |

*Worksheet entries only*

The secondary elimination entry:

| | | | | |
|---|---|---|---|---|
| Cost of Goods Sold. . . . . . . . . | 3,200 | | 1,600 | |
| Equity in Net Income of S Company. . . . . . . | | 3,200 | | 1,600 |

*Worksheet entries only*

The minority interest additional amortization entry:

| | | | | |
|---|---|---|---|---|
| Cost of Goods Sold. . . . . . . . . . . | 600 | | 200 | |
| Minority Interest in Net Income of S Company | | 600 | | 200 |

*Worksheet entries only*

# ■ ILLUSTRATION 5-7
## Additional Valuation under the Combination Entity—Parent Company Approach

| | Book Value Element | | | | | | Current Value over Book Value Element | | | | |
| --- | --- | --- | --- | --- | --- | --- | --- | --- | --- | --- | --- |
| | Minority Interest (20%) | Total Cost | = Common Stock | + Retained Earnings Prior Years | + Current Year Earnings | − Dividends | + Inventory (3 Mo.) | + Land (Indefinite) | + Equipment Cost (6 Yrs.) | + Accum. Depr. | + Goodwill Element (10 Yrs.) |
| Remaining life | | | | | | | (3 Mo.) | (Indefinite) | (6 Yrs.) | | (10 Yrs.) |
| Balances, Jan. 1, 19X1 (per Illustration 5-4) | $12,000 | $72,000 | $40,000 | $20,000 | | | $1,600 | $9,600 | $4,800 | | $8,000 |
| Additional valuation | 4,000[a] | | | | | | 400[a] | 2,400[a] | 1,200[a] | | |
| Adjusted Balances, Jan. 1, 19X1 | $16,000 | $72,000 | $40,000 | $20,000 | | | $2,000 | $12,000 | $6,000 | | $8,000 |
| Equity in net income: | | | | | | | | | | | |
| To parent | | 12,000 | | | $12,000 | | | | | | |
| To minority interest | 3,000[a] | | | | 3,000 | | | | | | |
| Dividends: | | | | | | | | | | | |
| To parent | | (4,000) | | | | $(4,000) | | | | | |
| To minority interest | (1,000)[a] | | | | | (1,000) | | | | | |
| Amortization: | | | | | | | | | | | |
| Parent's share | | (3,200) | | | | | (1,600) | | | (800) | (800) |
| Minority interest's share | (600)[a] | | | | | | (400) | | | (200) | |
| Subtotal | $17,400 | $76,800 | $40,000 | $20,000 | $15,000 | $(5,000) | $ –0– | $12,000 | $6,000 | $(1,000) | $7,200 |
| Reclassification | | | | 10,000 | (15,000) | 5,000 | | | | | |
| Balances, Dec. 31, 19X1 | $17,400 | $76,800 | $40,000 | $30,000 | $ –0– | $ –0– | $ –0– | $12,000 | $6,000 | $(1,000) | $7,200 |
| Equity in net income: | | | | | | | | | | | |
| To parent | | 16,800 | | | 16,800 | | | | | | |
| To minority interest | 4,200[a] | | | | 4,200[a] | | | | | | |
| Amortization: | | | | | | | | | | | |
| Parent's share | | (1,600) | | | | | | | | (800) | (800) |
| Minority interest's share | (200)[a] | | | | | | | | | (200)[a] | |
| Subtotal | $21,400 | $92,000 | $40,000 | $30,000 | $21,000 | $ –0– | $ –0– | $12,000 | $6,000 | $(2,000) | $6,400 |
| Reclassification | | | | 21,000 | (21,000) | | | | | | |
| Balances, Dec. 31, 19X2 | $21,400 | $92,000 | $40,000 | $51,000 | $ –0– | $ –0– | $ –0– | $12,000 | $6,000 | $(2,000) | $6,400 |

[a]No general ledger entry is necessary in the parent's books in keeping track of the minority interest.

The accumulated depreciation elimination entry:

| | | | |
|---|---|---|---|
| Accumulated Depreciation | 50,000 | | 50,000 |
| Buildings and | | | |
| Equipment | | 50,000 | 50,000 |

**Review Points for Illustration 5-8.**   Illustration 5-8 shows a consolidating statement worksheet as of December 31, 19X1. The following points are important for understanding the illustration:

1. The primary elimination entry was obtained from the conceptual analysis of the investment as usually done.
2. Entries 2 and 4 are exactly the same as entries 2 and 3, respectively, used in Illustration 5-5, which demonstrates the parent company approach.
3. Entry 3 is a new entry necessary because of the additional values reported under the combination entity—parent company approach. The entry has no effect on the parent's net income or the consolidated net income. An additional $600 is reported for cost of goods sold. However, exactly $600 less is reported for the minority interest deduction in the income statement.
4. The parent company's net income and the consolidated net income are the same as in Illustration 5-5.
5. Consolidated assets and the minority interest in the consolidated balance sheet are $3,400 greater than in Illustration 5-5. The difference relates entirely to the additional values being accounted for ($4,000), net of amortization to date of $600.
6. Illustration 5-8 shows that a minority interest deduction of $2,400 is reported in consolidation. The proof of this amount is shown in the following calculations:

| | |
|---|---|
| Subsidiary's reported net income | $15,000 |
| Less: Total amortization on undervalued assets: | |
| Parent company's portion | (2,400) |
| Minority interest portion | (600) |
| Subtotal | $12,000 |
| Minority ownership percentage | 20% |
| Minority interest in net income | $ 2,400 |

# The Entity Theory

Recall that under the entity theory:

1. The subsidiary's net assets are revalued in consolidation to 100% of their current values as of the acquisition date.

## ■ ILLUSTRATION 5-8
### Combination Entity–Parent Company Approach

**P COMPANY AND SUBSIDIARY (S COMPANY)**
**Consolidating Statement Worksheet for the Year Ended December 31, 19X1**

| | P Company | S Company | Eliminations Dr. | Eliminations Cr. | Consoli-dated |
|---|---|---|---|---|---|
| **Income Statement** | | | | | |
| Sales | 600,000 | 225,000 | | | 825,000 |
| Cost of goods sold | (360,000) | (110,000) | 3,200(2) | | (473,800) |
| Expenses | (190,000) | (100,000) | 600(3) | | (290,000) |
| Intercompany Accounts: | | | | | |
| Equity in net income of S Company | 8,800 | | 12,000(1) | 3,200(2) | –0– |
| Income before Minority Interest | 58,800 | 15,000 | 15,800 | 3,200 | 61,200 |
| Minority interest | | | 3,000(1) | 600(3) | (2,400) |
| Net Income | 58,800 | 15,000 | 18,800 | 3,800 | 58,800 |
| **Statement of Retained Earnings** | | | | | |
| Balances, January 1, 19X1 | 100,000 | 20,000 | 20,000(1) | | 100,000 |
| + Net income | 58,800 | 15,000 | 18,800 | 3,800 | 58,800 |
| − Dividends declared | (45,000) | (5,000) | | 5,000(1) | (45,000) |
| Balances, December 31, 19X1 | 113,800 | 30,000 | 38,800 | 8,800 | 113,800 |
| **Balance Sheet** | | | | | |
| Cash | 42,000 | 11,000 | | | 53,000 |
| Accounts receivable, net | 75,000 | 37,000 | | | 112,000 |
| Inventory | 110,000 | 55,000 | | | 165,000 |
| Investment in S Company | 76,800 | | | 76,800(1) | –0– |
| Land | 220,000 | 30,000 | 12,000(1) | | 262,000 |
| Buildings and equipment | 500,000 | 200,000 | 6,000(1) | 50,000(4) | 656,000 |
| Accumulated depreciation | (320,000) | (63,000) | 50,000(4) | 1,000(1) | (334,000) |
| Goodwill | | | 7,200(1) | | 7,200 |
| Total Assets | 703,800 | 270,000 | 66,200 | 118,800 | 921,200 |
| Liabilities | 290,000 | 200,000 | | | 490,000 |
| Minority interest in net assets of S Company | | | | 17,400(1) | 17,400 |
| P Company: | | | | | |
| Common stock | 300,000 | | | | 300,000 |
| Retained earnings | 113,800 | | | | 113,800 |
| S Company: | | | | | |
| Common stock | | 40,000 | 40,000(1) | | –0– |
| Retained earnings | | 30,000 | 38,800 | 8,800 | –0– |
| Total Liabilities and Equity | 703,800 | 270,000 | 78,800 | 26,200 | 921,200 |
| Proof of debit and credit postings | | | 145,000 | 145,000 | |

Explanation of entries:
(1) The primary elimination entry.
(2) The secondary elimination entry.
(3) The minority interest additional amortization entry.
(4) The accumulated depreciation elimination entry.

2. Goodwill is reported in consolidation based on the amount of goodwill implicit in the transaction.

The only difference between the combination entity–parent company approach and the entity theory is that additional goodwill must be accounted for under the entity theory. In the chapter example of the parent company theory, goodwill of $8,000 was determined. We also demonstrated in the discussion of the entity theory, at the beginning of this appendix, that $10,000 is the total goodwill implicit in the transaction ($8,000 ÷ 80% ownership interest). Thus, an additional $2,000 of goodwill is reported under the entity theory. Accounting for this additional goodwill presents no difficulty. We would merely add the $2,000 to the conceptual analysis of the investment account in the same manner that the $4,000 of additional value was added for the undervalued assets. Consolidated financial statements would be prepared in the same manner as shown for the combination entity–parent company approach.

## Exercises for Appendix A

| E 5-1A |
|---|

### Comparison of the Parent Company Theory and the Entity Theory for Treatment of Tangible Assets

On January 1, 19X1, Placido Company acquired 60% of the outstanding common stock of Scotto Company for $2,400,000. All cost in excess of Placido's share of net assets at carrying value is entirely attributable to a parcel of land owned by Scotto. Scotto acquired this land many years ago for $50,000; its current value is $1,050,000. (The book value of Scotto's net assets is $3,000,000.)

#### Required:
1. Under the parent company theory, at what amount would the land be reported in the consolidated balance sheet?
2. Under the entity theory, at what amount would the land be reported in the consolidated balance sheet?
3. Compare the results in requirement 1 with those in requirement 2. What is the effect on the stockholders' equity section and the minority interest in the subsidiary's net assets as reported in the consolidated balance sheet?

| E 5-2A |
|---|

### Comparison of the Parent Company Theory and the Entity Theory for Treatment of Goodwill

Poem Company acquired 70% of the outstanding common stock of Sonnet Company on January 1, 19X3, for $4,200,000. The cost in excess of its share of book value is entirely attributable to Sonnet's expected superior earnings ability. (The book value of Sonnet's net assets is $5,000,000.)

**Required:**

1. Under the parent company theory at what amount would goodwill be reported in the consolidated balance sheet?
2. Under the entity theory, at what amount would the goodwill be reported in the consolidated balance sheet?
3. Compare the results in requirement 1 with those in requirement 2. What is the effect on the stockholders' equity section and the minority interest in the net assets of the subsidiary as reported in the consolidated balance sheet?

| E 5-3A |
|---|

## Comparison of the Parent Company Theory and the Entity Theory for Treatment of Tangible Assets and Goodwill

Pocahontas Company purchased 80% of the outstanding common stock of Smith Company for $6,400,000. All of Smith's assets and liabilities have book values equal to current values, except that land has a book value of $400,000 and a current value of $700,000. (The book value of Smith's net assets is $7,500,000.)

**Required:**

1. Under the parent company theory, at what amount would the land and goodwill be reported in the consolidated balance sheet?
2. Under the entity theory, at what amount would the land and goodwill be reported in the consolidated balance sheet?
3. Compare the results in requirement 1 with those in requirement 2. What is the effect on the stockholders' equity section and the minority interest in the net assets of the subsidiary as reported in the consolidated balance sheet?

## Appendix B    PREPARATION OF CONSOLIDATED FINANCIAL STATEMENTS USING THE TRIAL BALANCE APPROACH

To demonstrate the preparation of the worksheet using the trial balance approach when a subsidiary is partially owned, we have reformatted the financial statements used in Illustration 5-5 (page 225) into the trial balance approach shown in Illustration 5-9. The elimination entries used in Illustration 5-5 are repeated below for convenience.

The primary elimination entry:

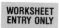

| | Dr. | Cr. |
|---|---|---|
| Common Stock | 40,000 | |
| Retained Earnings (beginning of year) | 20,000 | |
| Equity in Net Income of S Company | 12,000 | |
| Minority Interest in Net Income of S Company | 3,000 | |
| Land | 9,600 | |
| Equipment | 4,800 | |
| Goodwill | 7,200 | |

*(continued)*

# ■ ILLUSTRATION 5-9
## The Trial Balance Approach (Illustration 5-5 Reformatted)

### P COMPANY AND SUBSIDIARY (S COMPANY)
### Consolidating Statement Worksheet for the Year Ended December 31, 19X1

| | P Company Dr. | P Company Cr. | S Company Dr. | S Company Cr. |
|---|---|---|---|---|
| Cash .................... | 42,000 | | 11,000 | |
| Accounts receivable, net ........ | 75,000 | | 37,000 | |
| Inventory .................... | 110,000 | | 55,000 | |
| Investment in S Company ........ | 76,800 | | | |
| Land.................... | 220,000 | | 30,000 | |
| Buildings and equipment ........ | 500,000 | | 200,000 | |
| Accumulated depreciation ....... | | 320,000 | | 63,000 |
| Goodwill .................... | | | | |
| | | | | |
| Liabilities .................... | | 290,000 | | 200,000 |
| Minority interest in net assets of S Company | | | | |
| P Company: | | | | |
| Common stock ................ | | 300,000 | | |
| Retained earnings, January 1, 19X1 .......... | | 100,000 | | |
| Dividends declared ........... | 45,000 | | | |
| S Company: | | | | |
| Common stock ................ | | | | 40,000 |
| Retained earnings, January 1, 19X1 ............ | | | | 20,000 |
| Dividends declared ........... | | | 5,000 | |
| Sales .................... | | 600,000 | | 225,000 |
| Cost of goods sold .............. | 360,000 | | 110,000 | |
| Expenses .................... | 190,000 | | 100,000 | |
| Intercompany accounts: | | | | |
| Equity in net income of S Company ................ | | 8,800 | | |
| Minority interest in net income of S Company .................... | | | | |
| | 1,618,800 | 1,618,800 | 548,000 | 548,000 |

Consolidated Net Income ............................................................

Consolidated Retained Earnings ......................................................

Explanation of entries:
(1) The primary elimination entry.
(2) The secondary elimination entry.
(3) The accumulated depreciation elimination entry.

| | Eliminations | | Consolidated Income Statement | | Retained Earnings | Balance Sheet |
| | Dr. | Cr. | Dr. | Cr. | (Dr.) Cr. | |
|---|---|---|---|---|---|---|
| | | | | | | 53,000 |
| | | | | | | 112,000 |
| | | 76,800(1) | | | | 165,000 |
| | 9,600(1) | | | | | −0− |
| | 4,800(1) | 50,000(3) | | | | 259,600 |
| | 50,000(3) | 800(1) | | | | 654,800 |
| | 7,200(1) | | | | | (333,800) |
| | | | | | | 7,200 |
| | | | | | | 917,800 |
| | | 14,000(1) | | | | 490,000 |
| | | | | | | 14,000 |
| | | | | | | 300,000 |
| | | | | | 100,000 | |
| | | | | | (45,000) | |
| | 40,000(1) | | | | | −0− |
| | 20,000(1) | | | | | −0− |
| | | 5,000(1) | | | | −0− |
| | | | | 825,000 | | |
| | 3,200(2) | | 473,200 | | | |
| | | | 290,000 | | | |
| | 12,000(1) | 3,200(2) | | −0− | | |
| | 3,000(1) | | 3,000 | | | |
| | 149,800 | 149,800 | 766,200 | 825,000 | | |
| | | | 58,800 | | 58,800 | |
| | | | 825,000 | 825,000 | 113,800 | 113,800 |
| | | | | | | 917,800 |

|  | Dr. | Cr. |
|---|---|---|
| Dividends Declared | | 5,000 |
| Accumulated Depreciation (building) | | 800 |
| Investment in S Company | | 76,800 |
| Minority Interest in Net Assets of S Company | | 14,000 |

The secondary elimination entry:

**WORKSHEET ENTRY ONLY**

| | Dr. | Cr. |
|---|---|---|
| Cost of Goods Sold | 3,200 | |
| Equity in Net Income of S Company | | 3,200 |

The accumulated depreciation elimination entry:

**WORKSHEET ENTRY ONLY**

| | Dr. | Cr. |
|---|---|---|
| Accumulated Depreciation | 50,000 | |
| Buildings and Equipment | | 50,000 |

# 6

..... 

# THE POOLING
# OF INTERESTS
# METHOD
# OF ACCOUNTING

## TOPIC OUTLINE

# CHAPTER OVERVIEW

In this chapter, the pooling of interests method of accounting for a business combination is discussed, illustrated, and contrasted with the purchase method. Recall from Chapter 2 that the terms of the combination agreement and certain other conditions determine whether the purchase method or the pooling of interests method is used to record a business combination. The terms and provisions that qualify a business combination as a pooling of interests are reviewed in general and then in detail.

Paragraphs 27–65 of *APB Opinion No. 16* cover the pooling of interests method. Throughout these paragraphs, the terms *acquiring company* and *acquired company* are purposely not used because the word *acquiring* describes the purchase method of accounting in paragraphs 66 to 96. Instead, the discussion uses the terms **combining company, combined company,** and **company issuing stock to effect the combination.**[1] This language is consistent with the underlying concept of pooling of interests accounting, which is that a combining, or pooling, of the equity interests occurs rather than an acquisition. The latter term refers to a situation in which one company acquires the business of another company, for which purchase accounting is appropriate.

However, it is more convenient in some instances to refer to a company that gives up its assets (or whose stockholders give up their common stock) as the target company (which is how that company is commonly referred to by the parties involved).

# THE "NO CHANGE IN BASIS OF ACCOUNTING" CONCEPT

## The Essence of a Pooling of Interests

Under the pooling of interests method, **each company's stockholders are presumed to have combined or fused their ownership interests in such a manner that each group becomes an owner of the combined, enlarged business.** To accomplish this fusing of ownership interests, the target company or its stockholders must receive common stock as consideration from the other company.

**The Relevance of the Negotiated Value.** Of course the number of common shares to be issued to consummate the transaction will be based on the negotiated agreed-upon value of the target company, regardless of either

---

[1]*Opinions of the Accounting Principles Board, No. 16,* "Accounting for Business Combinations" (New York: American Institute of Certified Public Accountants, 1970).

the book value or current value of the target company's net assets. For example, if the target company's net assets have a book value of $60,000, a current value of $80,000, but an agreed-upon value of $90,000, the other combining company would issue common shares having a market value of $90,000. Assuming the market price of the other combining company's common stock is $30 per share, then it would issue 3,000 shares of its common stock ($90,000 ÷ $30 per share). If the target company has 5,000 shares outstanding, for instance, and all of these shares are exchanged for the 3,000 shares being issued by the other combining company (a stock-for-stock exchange), the exchange ratio (discussed in Chapter 2) would be 3:5.

**The Relevance of the Book Value.**   Because a fusing of the ownership interests is deemed to occur in a pooling of interests (as opposed to a buyout of one business by the other business, the concept in purchase accounting), the fair value of the consideration given ($90,000 in the preceding example) and the current value of the target company's net assets ($80,000 in the preceding example) are completely irrelevant. Instead, the book value of the target company's net assets ($60,000 in the preceding example) is used as the basis for recording the "cost" of the investment to the company issuing common stock. As a result, the assets and liabilities of the target company are reported at their historical costs in the consolidated financial statements. Furthermore, goodwill is never created. In an economy in which inflation has occurred over many years, the assets of companies are usually undervalued. Thus, the pooling of interests method is popular because the acquired company's assets do not have to be reflected at their current values, along with any goodwill, in the future financial statements. Future charges to income are thereby avoided. The disadvantage—an understatement of the consolidated stockholders' equity—is almost always of secondary importance compared with the advantages that result in the income statement. This manner of accounting—in which there is no change in the basis of accounting for financial reporting purposes—is completely the opposite of that under the purchase method.

**Presenting Precombination Earnings and Dividends.**   When financial statements are presented for periods prior to the combination date, **the earnings and dividends of each company are combined as though the combination had occurred at the beginning of the earliest period presented—but only to the extent of the ownership interest combined.** This is just the opposite of the purchase method, which disallows presenting the two companies' operations results and dividend information together for preacquisition periods.

# THE GROWTH OF POOLING OF INTERESTS: FROM CONCEPT TO COMMON PRACTICE

When the pooling of interests concept emerged in the early 1940s, its implementation was limited to businesses of comparable size. Here are simple examples of such poolings, one for similarly sized professional businesses and one for equally matched corporations:

1. Two CPAs practice as sole proprietorships. One CPA specializes in taxes, the other in auditing. Each realizes that by joining together as a partnership they would both achieve certain advantages, among them (a) economics related to overhead, (b) better servicing of clients, and (c) greater attractiveness to prospective clients. Because each CPA continues as an owner in the partnership, it is obvious that no buy-out of the other has occurred. The combination is one of association, not acquisition.

2. Two companies of approximately the same size are in the same industry. One company has an excellent research and development department; the other company has excellent manufacturing and marketing organizations. The owners of each company realize that their firm, on its own, will have a difficult time becoming a major force in the industry. By combining the strengths of the two companies, however, the unified firm could have a better chance of success. Accordingly, one of the combining companies issues common stock to the stockholders of the other company. Each owner in the formerly separate businesses is now a fellow owner in the same company, sharing the risks and rewards of common ownership with the others. None of the owners sells his or her stock as a result of the combination. Thus, neither group has bought out the other group.

Because of the favorable effects on the income statement that often result in a pooling of interests compared to a purchase transaction, companies have tried over the years to broaden (and thereby alter) the original concept of a pooling of interests so that many other types of business combinations can be classified as poolings of interests and thereby obtain the more desirable accounting treatment. (Examples would be industrial giants combining with start-up companies and companies combining from unrelated industries.) These efforts have been so successful that pooling of interests is no longer considered in the abstract by business people (and probably to most accountants as well) but instead is simply another useful accounting method.

In fact, because most business combinations that are accounted for under the pooling of interests method involve companies of dispropor- tionate sizes, they are viewed by the parties involved as acquisitions—in the sense that one entity acquires the business of another entity, and the acquiring entity is completely dominant. In other words, the transaction is viewed as an acquisition (from other than an accounting viewpoint) that is merely recorded as a pooling of interests.

## CONCEPTUAL ISSUES

Although accounting authorities agree that a pooling of interests cannot take place without the equity interests of the two companies joining together, they differ widely and strongly over the relevance of several other factors, among them (1) the relative size of the combining interests, (2) the ready negotiability of each interest's common stock, (3) the similarity or complementary nature of the two lines of business, (4) possible lack of continuity of interests, and (5) interests in one or the other company that dissent from the combination.

1. **Relative size:** *Should the equity interests be approximately the same size for a pooling of interests to take place?* For example, could an eight-partner partnership have a pooling of interests with one having two partners? What about forty-eight partners and two? Could a combination between IBM Corporation, which has revenues approaching $60 billion, and an electronics company having revenues of only $100 million—a 600:1 ratio—be considered a pooling of interests? Or should this be considered a buy-out? Should a line be drawn? If so, where?

2. **Ready negotiability of common stock:** Assume that each group of former owners now holds common stock that is negotiable and readily exchangeable into cash. Does this mean that there is no real significance to the fact that common stock was given to one of the equity interests instead of cash? In other words, *does a true pooling of interests occur just because common stock is given?*

3. **Similar or complementary lines of business:** *Should there be a compelling economic relationship (similar or complementary lines of business) between the combining companies to have a pooling of interests?* For example, in 1986 Burroughs Corp., which had the third largest revenues in its industry, and Sperry Corp., with the seventh largest revenues, combined to create Unisys Corp., the world's second largest computer company. The reason these firms gave for their combination was to be able to compete aggressively with IBM, the world's largest, in the $7 billion mainframe market. Could a business combination between Burroughs and Ford Motor Co., for example, be considered a pooling of interests?

4. **Continuity of interests:** Suppose some or all of one of the former businesses sell their newly received common stock holdings shortly after the combination, effectively "cashing out" rather than continuing as owners in the combined business. *Should there be continuity of interests for a reasonable period after the consummation date? If so, for how long?*

5. **Dissenting interests:** Suppose some members of one of the equity interests choose not to be a party to the combination. For example, two partnerships of ten partners each contemplate combining, but two of the ten from one firm choose to withdraw their capital from the partnership and not be parties to the combination. *Should dissenting interests in one firm prevent the remaining partners from having a pooling of interests with the other partnership?*

## Grounds for Difference

At one end of the spectrum are accountants who would disregard all five of these factors. For them, as long as a fusion of equity interests occurs (through the issuance of common stock by one of the combining companies in exchange for the assets or common stock of the other combining company), a pooling of interests occurs. In general, *APB Opinion No. 16* takes this approach.

Critics of *Opinion No. 16* contend that for most combinations treated as poolings of interests, the fusion of the equity interests is irrelevant. They maintain that what is relevant is whether or not one company has acquired or obtained *control* over the business of another company. If this control is the substance of the transaction, then purchase accounting is appropriate, regardless of the type of consideration given. This is the primary conclusion of *Accounting Research Study No. 5*, "A Critical Study of Accounting for Business Combinations," by Arthur R. Wyatt, which the American Institute of Certified Public Accountants published in 1963. (Research studies do not constitute the official position of the AICPA; they are for discussion purposes only.) This group would allow poolings of interests only when the companies involved are of comparable size and it is evident that a buy out is not occurring. Because most transactions accounted for as poolings of interests involve companies of significantly disproportionate sizes, few business combinations would be treated as poolings of interests with this approach.

In summary, each group views the economic substance of a business combination involving the issuance of common stock differently. As mentioned in Chapter 2, *APB Opinion No. 16* is a controversial pronouncement that has received such substantial criticism since its issuance that the Financial Accounting Standards Board is expected to reexamine the accounting issues involved in business combinations in the future.

# CRITERIA FOR POOLING OF INTERESTS: A BRIEF OVERVIEW

Before *APB Opinion No. 16* was issued, only general guidelines determined when a business combination should be treated as a pooling of interests. Because the guidelines could not be logically supported for the most part, in practice they were often ignored or broadly interpreted. The relative looseness of accounting principles in this area resulted in substantial criticism of the accounting profession, which led to the issuance of a pronouncement that contained specific pooling of interests criteria. In addition, *Opinion No. 16* eliminated management's ability to choose between accounting alternatives for a given set of terms and conditions:

1. It specifically defines the criteria under which a business combination is treated as a pooling of interests.
2. It requires all business combinations meeting each of these specific criteria to be accounted for as a pooling of interests.
3. It requires all business combinations failing to meet any one of the specific criteria to be accounted for using purchase accounting.

*APB Opinion No. 16* outlines twelve specific conditions that the combining firms must meet before pooling of interests accounting is permitted. In many respects, the conditions are arbitrary and not totally clear or comprehensive. As a result, the AICPA and the FASB have issued numerous interpretations. With the possible exception of accounting for leases, more interpretations have been issued for this pronouncement than for any other professional pronouncement. In practice, it has been one of the most difficult professional pronouncements with which to work. Many large public accounting firms have prepared lengthy booklets for internal use that explain how certain areas of the pronouncement are to be interpreted for uniform application within their firms.

The twelve conditions generally allow pooling of interests treatment only when a combination of independent equity interests occurs rather than a buy out of one of the common shareholder equity interests. As a result, most of the emphasis is placed on the form and manner of accomplishing the combination so that the two stockholder groups fuse their ownership interests. Most of the conditions pertain to the manner of effecting the combination. The more salient points of the criteria are as follows:

1. Common stock must be the sole consideration given for the pooled interest.
   a. **Common stock exchanged for assets:** In this type of transaction, the target company must transfer **100% of its assets** to the issuing company solely for common stock of the issuing company.
   b. **Common stock exchanged for common stock:** In this type of transaction, **at least 90% of the outstanding common stock** of the target

company must be exchanged solely for common stock of the issuing company. (Cash or other consideration may be given to dissenting stockholders of the target company so long as this group does not hold more than 10% of the target company's outstanding common stock.)

2. The common stock issued **must have the same rights and privileges** as the already issued and outstanding common stock of the issuing company. In other words, the issuing company's new stockholders must be full-fledged stockholders of the enlarged business.

3. **Neither combining company may alter its own equity interest or the equity interest of the other combining company in contemplation of a pooling of interests.**

4. There can be **no arrangements to reacquire the common stock issued** as consideration for the assets or common stock exchanged.

Interestingly, the stockholders receiving common stock from the issuing company can sell the stock immediately after the combination is consummated, if they do not want to continue as owners in the combined business. No "continuity of ownership interest" is required whereby the new stockholders must remain shareholders of the combined business for any specified period of time. Thus, the "fusion" of equity interests may take place for only an instant.

## SPECIFIC CONDITIONS FOR POOLING OF INTERESTS

The twelve conditions for the pooling of interests method in *APB Opinion No. 16* fit into three broad categories:

1. The attributes of the combining companies.
2. The manner of combining equity interests.
3. The absence of planned transactions.

Each condition is quoted below under the appropriate category and discussed in detail. Because all the conditions are found in *Opinion No. 16*, only paragraph references to that pronouncement are given. Note that many of the conditions are designed to prevent companies from circumventing the basic concept of having to combine substantially all common shareholder equity interests.

### 1. Attributes of the Combining Companies

Two conditions pertain to the necessary attributes of the combining companies:

A. "Each of the combining companies is autonomous and has not been a subsidiary or division of another corporation within two years before the plan of combination is initiated" (Paragraph 46a).

This condition presumes that the pooling of interests concept applies only to independent companies. For the most part, this condition is sound; most divestitures of subsidiaries or divisions are intended disposals of interests as opposed to intended poolings of equity interests.

A subsidiary that is spun off pursuant of a governmental divestiture order or a new company that acquires assets it must dispose of is an arbitrary exception to this condition and is deemed an "autonomous company." This exception does not appear to be based on logic, and its inclusion is apparently an accommodation to the disposing company for purposes of facilitating the disposal.

When a portion of a business is spun off to certain stockholders in exchange for some or all of their stock, the stockholders of the newly established corporation may wish to combine their equity interests with another company in the true sense of the pooling of interests concept. Such a combining of equity interests could not be accounted for as a pooling of interests unless two years had elapsed from the spin-off date. Thus, a portion of a business cannot be spun off in this manner and then pooled with another company shortly thereafter. This is because the spinning off and subsequent combination are viewed as mere steps of a single transaction, the substance of which is a disposal of an interest.

B. "Each of the combining companies is independent of the other combining companies" (Paragraph 46b).

This condition means that at the initiation date and until the business combination is consummated, the combining companies cannot hold more than 10% of the outstanding voting common stock of any combining company. Voting common stock that is acquired during this time interval in exchange for voting common stock issued in connection with the terms of the business combination agreement is excluded in the percentage computation.

This condition is intended to prevent a combining company from altering the equity interests of the other combining company. (Paragraph 47c, which is discussed later in the chapter, prohibits each combining company from altering the equity interest of its own voting common stock in contemplation of a pooling.) If this condition were not imposed, a combining company could circumvent the intended purpose of paragraph 47c by buying out a large group of dissenting shareholders of the other combining company and then effecting a pooling of interests with its remaining shareholders.

**Independence Based on Net Worth Invested.**    Usually, each combining company is independent of the other if neither company owns more than 10%

of the outstanding voting common stock of the other. Occasionally, however, neither company owns more than 10% of the outstanding common stock of the other and independence still does not exist. This can occur when the smaller company has a significant investment—**in terms of its own net worth**—in the larger company. For example, assume that Mini-Computer Company (the target company) owns 6% of IBMM Company's outstanding common stock. If this investment constitutes more than 10% of Mini-Computer's net worth, then the companies are not independent. The calculation to determine if the 10% figure is exceeded uses the following facts:

1. IBMM has 600,000 common shares outstanding.
2. Mini-Computer has 100,000 common shares outstanding.
3. IBMM will issue two shares of its common stock for each share of Mini-Computer's outstanding common stock—in other words, a 2-for-1 exchange ratio. Recall that before this 2:1 exchange ratio could have been calculated, it first would have been necessary to calculate the number of shares to be issued by IBMM Company (200,000 shares in this example) by dividing the negotiated agreed-upon value of Mini-Computer Company (say, $10 million) by the market price of IBMM's common stock (say, $50 per share).
4. Mini-Computer owns 24,000 IBMM common shares, which is 4% of IBMM's outstanding common shares.

Because Mini-Computer's shareholders will receive 200,000 shares of IBMM common stock, Mini-Computer's net worth can be considered the equivalent of 200,000 shares of IBMM common stock. The following calculation is then made:

$$\frac{\text{Shares of IBMM common stock held by Mini-Computer}}{\substack{\text{Shares of IBMM common stock to be issued} \\ \text{(100,000 shares of Mini-Computer} \times 2)}} = \frac{24,000}{200,000} = 12\%$$

In an alternate approach, the 24,000 shares of IBMM owned by Mini-Computer are considered the equivalent of 12,000 shares of Mini-Computer common stock. The following calculation is then made:

$$\frac{\substack{\text{Equivalent number of Mini-Computer's} \\ \text{shares invested in IBMM (24,000} \div 2)}}{\text{Shares of Mini-Computer common stock outstanding}} = \frac{12,000}{100,000} = 12\%$$

In this example, the companies are not independent because the 10% level has been exceeded.

Accordingly, independence is evaluated not only from the perspective of how much of the other combining company's outstanding common stock is owned but also from the perspective of how much of a company's own net worth is invested in the other combining company.

**Smaller Company Issues the Common Stock.**  In the preceding situation, the larger of the two companies issued common stock to bring about the combination (the typical case). In a stock-for-stock exchange, the relative holdings of each group of stockholders can be the same regardless of which company issues the common stock to effect the pooling of interests. In that situation, the relative holdings of each group of stockholders was 3:1 (IBMM's shareholders owning 600,000 shares and Mini-Computer's shareholders receiving 200,000 shares of IBMM common stock). Let us change the facts of the situation to make Mini-Computer the issuing company. The same relative holdings of each group of stockholders is maintained if Mini-Computer issues one share for each two shares of IBMM outstanding common stock (a 1-for-2 exchange ratio). This still gives IBMM's shareholders three times as many shares (300,000 shares) in Mini-Computer as those held by Mini-Computer's stockholder group just prior to the combination (100,000 shares). In this case, the issuing company has the intercorporate investment. However, the companies are still not independent, for the reasons discussed in the preceding paragraph. The smaller of the two companies issues the common stock (and thereby becomes the parent company) when it is more desirable to use the smaller company's name than the larger company's name. For example, the larger company may have an unfavorable public image, or the smaller company may have a wider investor following.

**Dual Intercorporate Investments.**  The 10% independence test must be performed in a cumulative manner when each company has an investment in the other. To illustrate, assume the following facts:

1. IBMM Company has 600,000 common shares outstanding.
2. Mini-Computer Company has 100,000 common shares outstanding.
3. IBMM will issue two shares of its common stock for each share of Mini-Computer's outstanding common shares—a 2-for-1 exchange ratio.
4. Mini-Computer owns 18,000 IBMM outstanding common shares, which is 3% of IBMM's outstanding common shares.
5. IBMM owns 2,000 shares of Mini-Computer's outstanding common shares, which is 2% of Mini-Computer's outstanding common shares.

Although neither company owns more than 10% of the other company's outstanding common stock and neither company has more than 10% of its own net worth invested in the other company, the *combination* of intercorporate investments exceeds the 10% level, as shown by the following calculation:

Percent of Mini-Computer's common stock owned by IBMM . .           2%

Percent of Mini-Computer's net worth invested in IBMM
[18,000 shares ÷ 200,000 common shares to be received
in the exchange, or alternately, 9,000 shares (adjusted for
the 2-for-1 exchange ratio) ÷ 100,000 outstanding shares] .     <u>9%</u>

                                                   <u>11%</u>

The manner of dealing with an investment in the company issuing the common stock is explained in connection with paragraph 47b of *APB Opinion No. 16.* The approach treats shares owned in the issuing company (adjusted for the exchange ratio) as a reduction of the target company's outstanding shares to determine if 90% of the target company's outstanding common stock has been acquired in exchange for the issuing company's common stock:

| | |
|---|---:|
| Mini-Computer's outstanding common shares . . . . . . . . . . . . . . . | 100,000 |
| Less: Shares owned by IBMM . . . . . . . . . . . . . . . . . . . . . . . . . . . . | (2,000) |
| Equivalent number of shares invested in IBMM by Mini-Computer (18,000 ÷ 2) . . . . . . . . . . . . . . . . . . . . . . . . . | (9,000) |
| | 89,000 |
| Shares needed to reach the 90% level . . . . . . . . . . . . . . . . . . . . . | 90,000 |

Thus, the 90% level has not been reached. This analysis is difficult to understand. Because the issue is *independence,* we presented the discussion of dealing with investments in the issuing company from paragraph 46b rather than paragraph 47b.

## 2. Manner of Combining Equity Interests

Seven conditions pertain to the manner of effecting the combination, as follows:

> A. "The combination is effected in a single transaction or is completed in accordance with a specific plan within the year after the plan is initiated" (Paragraph 47a).

Evidently the APB felt that the transaction should be consummated within a reasonable period of time—one year.

> B. "A corporation offers and issues only common stock with rights identical to those of its outstanding voting common stock in exchange for substantially all of the voting common stock interest of another company at the date the plan of combination is consummated" (Paragraph 47b).

This condition is the fundamental requirement for effecting a pooling of interests. It means that the company issuing common stock must acquire at least 90% of the other combining company's outstanding common stock **subsequent to the initiation date** in exchange for its own common stock. **Thus, shares acquired prior to the initiation date—no matter how acquired—cannot be used to determine if the 90% requirement has been met.** To illustrate how the 90% rule is applied, assume the following facts:

1. P is the company issuing common stock.
2. S has 102,000 common shares issued, of which 2,000 shares are held in treasury. Thus, S has 100,000 common shares outstanding.
3. P acquires common shares of S as follows:
   a. Prior to the initiation date . . . . . . . . . . . . . . . . . . . . . . . . . . . . . . . . .   3,000
   b. Between the initiation date and the consummation date:
      For cash . . . . . . . . . . . . . . . . . . . . . . . . . . . . . . . . . . . . . . . . . . . . . .   4,000
      For its common stock pursuant to the terms of the
          combination agreement . . . . . . . . . . . . . . . . . . . . . . . . . . . . . . . .   5,000
   c. At the consummation date by exchanging its own
      common stock pursuant to the terms of the combination
      agreement . . . . . . . . . . . . . . . . . . . . . . . . . . . . . . . . . . . . . . . . . . . .   84,000
          Total shares owned . . . . . . . . . . . . . . . . . . . . . . . . . . . . . . . . . .   96,000

Although P Company owns more than 90% of S Company's outstanding common shares, it did not obtain at least 90,000 shares (90% of S's 100,000 outstanding shares) after the initiation date by exchanging common stock. Only 89,000 were obtained after the initiation date through an exchange of common stock (5,000+84,000). Therefore, the combination must be accounted for as a purchase instead of a pooling of interests.

**The 90% rule does not allow the issuing company to give any cash to the 90% group of shareholders. (An exception pertains to cash given for fractional shares.)** Dissenting shareholders, which as a group cannot hold more than 10% of the target company's outstanding common shares, may be given cash or other consideration in obtaining their shares.

This condition implies a stock-for-stock exchange. However, assets of a target company can be exchanged, providing 100% of the assets are exchanged. In these situations, the target company can retain assets to settle liabilities, contingencies, or disputed items that are not assumed by the acquiring company, providing any assets remaining after settlement are transferred to the issuing company.

C. "None of the combining companies changes the equity interest of the voting common stock in contemplation of effecting the combination either within two years before the plan of combination is initiated or between the dates the combination is initiated and consummated; changes in contemplation of effecting the combination may include distributions to stockholders and additional issuances, exchanges, and retirements of securities" (Paragraph 47c).

The concept of a pooling of interests does not allow a change in or alteration of the equity interests of the voting common stock of either combining company; only a fusing of the existing ownership interests occurs. Thus, this condition is necessary so that the fundamental concept is not violated. Above-normal dividend distributions to common shareholders would be considered a "change in the equity interest." The spin-off of a subsidiary or division to certain existing shareholders in exchange for some or all of their common stock (technically called a *split-off* for tax purposes) is an example of a distribution and retirement of outstanding securities. (This condition does not pertain to the disposal of a subsidiary or division by other means, such as an outright sale to an unrelated party.)

> D. "Each of the combining companies reacquires shares of voting common stock only for purposes other than business combinations [to be accounted for as poolings of interests], and no company reacquires more than a normal number of shares between the dates the plan of combination is initiated and consummated" (Paragraph 47d).

This condition has a twofold purpose **designed to prevent treasury stock manipulation:**

1. It prevents a target company from buying out a large group of its own dissenting shareholders (more than 10%) so that its remaining shareholders can effect a combination as a pooling of interests in the manner set forth in paragraph 47b.
2. Sometimes an issuing company desires to effect a combination as a pooling of interests and yet does not want to increase the number of its outstanding common shares at all or beyond a certain number. This condition prevents the issuing company from using cash or other assets or incurring liabilities to reacquire common shares, and then using such reacquired shares to effect a combination as a pooling of interests. This would clearly be an alteration of the equity interest, which is prohibited by paragraph 47c.

The phrase "for purposes other than business combinations" as used in paragraph 47d seems to allow substantial subjective interpretation of the company's purpose for acquiring shares. For example, an issuing company could assert that it reacquired some of its shares because the company was overcapitalized or the price of its stock was at an attractive level. On the surface, such reacquisitions would not appear to be for purposes of business combinations. Thus, the intended purpose of the condition could be easily circumvented. As a result, the AICPA issued the following interpretation to this condition:

> In the absence of persuasive evidence to the contrary . . . it should be presumed that all acquisitions of treasury stock during the two years pre-

ceding the date a plan of combination is initiated . . . and between the initiation and consummation were made in contemplation of effecting business combinations to be accounted for as a pooling of interests. Thus, lacking such evidence, this combination would be accounted for by the purchase method regardless of whether treasury stock or unissued shares or both are issued in the combination.

The specific purposes for which treasury shares may be reacquired prior to consummation of a "pooling" include shares granted under stock option or compensation plans, stock dividends declared (or to be declared as a recurring distribution), and recurring distributions as provided in paragraph 47d. Likewise, treasury shares reacquired for issuance in a specific "purchase" or to resolve an existing contingent share agreement from a prior business combination would not invalidate a concurrent "pooling." Treasury shares reacquired for these purposes should be either reissued prior to consummation or specifically reserved for these purposes existing at consummation.[2]

Assessing the purpose of the reacquisition of treasury shares by an issuing company generally involves evaluating the subsequent distribution of such shares. In most instances, a systematic pattern of reacquisitions for specified distribution purposes must be established at least two years before the combination plan is initiated to constitute "persuasive evidence to the contrary." "Systematic" does not necessarily require a precise program that operates like a monthly investment plan. A definable plan such as buying shares from employees who resign, or from the estate of deceased shareholders, or when the market price is at a predetermined level should suffice.

E. **"The ratio of the interest of an individual common stockholder to those of other common stockholders in a combining company remains the same as a result of the exchange of stock to effect the combination" (Paragraph 47e).**

Each shareholder of the target company who exchanges common stock for voting common stock of the issuing company must receive that voting common stock in exact proportion to his or her relative common stock interest in the target company before the combination is effected. Thus, a shareholder who owns 20% of the target company's outstanding common stock must receive 20% of the voting common shares that the issuing company issues to effect the combination. If a shareholder owning 20% of the target company were to receive more or less than 20% of the common stock issued by the issuing company, then a reshuffling of the target company's equity interests would result, which was deemed contrary to a pure combining of the equity interests.

---

[2]*Accounting Interpretation No. 20 to APB Opinion No. 16,* "Accounting for Business Combinations" (New York: American Institute of Certified Public Accountants, 1971).

This also means that the 20% shareholder cannot pool part of his or her holdings and be a dissenter, or a minority, for the remaining shares. **Thus an individual shareholder cannot at the same time be both an assenter and a dissenter or minority interest.**

F. "The voting rights to which the common stock ownership interests in the resulting combined corporation are entitled are exercisable by the stockholders; the stockholders are neither deprived of nor restricted in exercising those rights for a period" (Paragraph 47f).

Any limitations on voting rights would obviously be inconsistent with the pooling of interests concept.

G. "The combination is resolved at the date the plan is consummated and no provisions of the plan relating to the issue of securities or other considerations are pending" (Paragraph 47g).

This condition is intended primarily to prohibit poolings of interests when contingent consideration is issuable based on future sales, earnings, or market prices. Such contingencies are incompatible with the mutual sharing of risks and rewards, which underlies the pooling of interests concept. An interpretation says the following:

> The only contingent arrangement permitted under paragraph 47g is for settlement of a contingency pending at consummation, such as the later settlement of a lawsuit. A contingent arrangement would also be permitted for an additional income tax liability resulting from the examination of "open" income tax returns.[3]

## 3. Absence of Planned Transactions

Three conditions pertain to certain types of postcombination transactions that cannot be included either explicitly or implicitly in either the negotiations or the terms of the combination agreement. The conditions are as follows:

A. "The combining corporation does not agree directly or indirectly to retire or reacquire all or part of the common stock issued to effect the combination" (Paragraph 48a).

This condition prevents an issuing company from circumventing the intended purpose of paragraph 47b. Obviously, issuing common shares to effect a combination and subsequently repurchasing the shares issued would not be, in substance, a combining of equity interests.

*APB Opinion No. 16* does not prohibit an issuing company from reacquiring shares issued in a pooling of interests (or an equivalent number

---

[3]*Accounting Interpretation No. 14 to APB Opinion No. 16,* "Accounting for Business Combinations" (New York: American Institute for Certified Public Accountants, 1971).

of shares issued). It is prohibited only from making an agreement to repurchase the shares issued. In this area, the Securities and Exchange Commission (SEC) has taken the following position:

> In specific fact situations, subsequent reacquisitions may be so closely related to the prior combination that they should be considered part of the combination plan. Thus, significant reacquisitions closely following a plan of combination which otherwise qualified as a pooling of interests may invalidate the applicability of that method. . . . [4]

> The Commission does not intend to establish an additional criterion for determining the accounting treatment of a business combination. Rather it intended simply to caution registrants and auditors that the substance of reacquisitions closely following consummation of a combination should not be ignored. . . . [5]

**B.** **"The combined corporation does not enter into other financial arrangements for the benefit of the former stockholders of a combining company, such as a guaranty of loans secured by stock issued in the combination, which in effect negates the exchange of securities"** (Paragraph 48b).

Arrangements of this nature are considered "bailouts" of former stockholders of the target company. Such provisions are inconsistent with the pooling of interests concept.

**C.** **"The combined corporation does not intend or plan to dispose of a significant part of the assets of the combining companies within two years after the combination other than disposals in the ordinary course of business of the formerly separate companies and to eliminate duplicate facilities or excess capacity"** (Paragraph 48c).

The apparent purpose of this condition is to prohibit companies from effecting pooling of interests with companies having substantially undervalued assets, when the intent is to sell the undervalued assets shortly after consummation and thereby report immediate profits from the sale. (Such widely criticized practices existed before *APB Opinion No. 16* was issued.)

If a significant portion of the assets of either combining company is disposed of within two years after the combination is consummated, any material profit or loss is to be classified as an extraordinary item.

---

[4]*Accounting Series Release No. 146*, "Effect of Treasury Stock Transactions on Accounting for Business Combinations" (Washington, D.C.: Securities and Exchange Commission, 1973), par. 10. This release is now part of *Financial Reporting Release No. 1* (Section 201.02), which was issued in 1982 and is a codification of all accounting-related releases in effect at that time.

[5]*Accounting Series Release No. 146-A*, "Statement of Policy and Interpretations in Regard to *Accounting Series Release No. 146*" (Washington, D.C.: Securities and Exchange Commission, 1974), par. 3. (Section 201.02 of *Financial Reporting Release No. 1*.)

# VIEWS OF THE DISSENTING MEMBERS OF THE ACCOUNTING PRINCIPLES BOARD

Six of the eighteen members of the Accounting Principles Board dissented to the issuance of *APB Opinion No. 16*. The following is a summary of their views:

1. *APB Opinion No. 16* will curtail some abuses in pooling of interests accounting; however, the real abuse is pooling of interests itself.
2. The form of the consideration (cash or common stock) is irrelevant; the value of the consideration is what is relevant. Substance should prevail over form.
3. The value of the consideration is determined in a bargained exchange. To ignore this value (the buyer's true cost) and record the combination based on the wholly irrelevant amount of the seller's financial reporting cost basis (the seller's cost), is an aberration from historical-cost reporting which should be abolished.
4. The abuse of acquiring other companies having substantially undervalued assets and then reporting profits on the subsequent sale of those assets (allowing the same gain to be reported by both corporations) continues, even though the second company did not actually earn anything and should not report a profit on such subsequent sale (except to the extent that assets appreciated in value after the combination date).
5. Pooling of interests should not be kept alive because some fear its demise would discourage mergers (which occurred for many decades before pooling was concocted). The purpose of accounting is to account for transactions fairly—not to aid or discourage certain types of transactions (here, mergers).

## RECORDING A POOLING OF INTERESTS

Assume the following information:

1. P Company and S Company have agreed to combine under terms that provide for P Company to issue common stock (in exchange for either the assets or the outstanding common stock of S Company).
2. Information with respect to each company as of the combination date (January 1, 19X1) is as follows:

|  | P Company | S Company |
|---|---|---|
| Common stock, $10 par value (30,000 shares outstanding) | $300,000 | |
| Common stock, $3 par value (5,000 shares outstanding) | | $ 15,000 |

| | P Company | S Company |
|---|---|---|
| Additional paid-in capital | 12,000 | 5,000 |
| Retained earnings | 100,000 | 40,000 |
| Total Stockholders' Equity | $412,000 | $ 60,000 |
| Book value of assets | Irrelevant | $250,000 |
| Book value of liabilities | Irrelevant | $190,000 |
| Current value of net assets | Irrelevant | $ 80,000[a] |
| Market price of stock on combination date | $90[a] | Irrelevant |

[a]This amount is relevant only under the purchase method.

3. All conditions for pooling of interests have been met.
4. P Company issues 1,000 shares of its common stock.

The next two sections show the entries to record the pooling of interests assuming, first, that the assets are exchanged and, second, that the common stock is exchanged. In showing the entry when common stock is exchanged, we also present the entry under the purchase method to emphasize the conceptual difference between the two methods. (To make this comparison, we must assume that the combination does not qualify for pooling in one minor respect, but that the terms and conditions relating to the exchange of stock are the same.)

## Common Stock Exchanged for Assets

When assets are exchanged, the issuing company records these assets and the liabilities assumed at their book values as shown on the target business's books. As in purchase accounting, a centralized or a decentralized accounting system may be used subsequently to account for the target business. Assuming a centralized accounting system, the entry is as follows:

| | | |
|---|---|---|
| Assets (record at book value)[a] | 250,000 | |
| Liabilities (record at book value) | | 190,000 |
| Common stock (1,000 shares issued × $10 par value) | | 10,000 |
| Retained Earnings (100% of the target company's retained earnings) | | 40,000 |
| Additional Paid-in Capital (residual amount to balance) | | 10,000 |

[a]Recall that 100% of the assets must be exchanged.

The preceding entry would also be made if the combination were made pursuant to a **statutory merger,** in which the target company's legal existence is terminated (discussed in Chapter 2).

## Common Stock Exchanged for Common Stock

The entry when common stock is exchanged is nearly the same as when assets are exchanged. The only difference is that rather than recording assets and liabilities at their book values, the Investment in Subsidiary account is debited an amount equal to the book value of the net assets ($60,000 in the preceding example).

The residual balancing amount in the preceding example, is a credit to Additional Paid-in Capital. This is not always the case. The following illustration shows, among other things, what to debit when a debit is needed to balance the entry.

**ILLUSTRATION**

### Comparison of Entries under the Pooling of Interests Method and the Purchase Method—100% of Outstanding Common Stock Acquired

Illustration 6-1 shows the entries when 1,000, 2,000, 3,000, and 4,000 shares of common stock are issued by P Company in exchange for all of the 5,000 outstanding shares of S Company (the latter two situations resulting in debit entries to balance the entry). In addition, for comparison we present the entries that would be made under the purchase method (for this illustration, we assume the market price of P Company's common stock is $30 per share rather than the $90 per share used in the earlier example).

**Review Points for Illustration 6-1.**   Note the following:

1. The pooling of interests method ignores both the fair value of the consideration given and the current value of the subsidiary's net assets in determining the "cost" of the investment.
2. The purchase method uses the fair value of the consideration given—the number of shares issued multiplied by the market price on the date of the combination—to determine the cost of the investment.
3. Under the pooling of interests method, the investment account has only one major element—the book value element. Thus, there is no cost above or below book value to amortize against the combined income of future periods.
4. Under the purchase method, the current value over or under the book value element exists in all four situations in Illustration 6-1, the goodwill element existing only in situations C and D and a bargain purchase element existing in situation A.
5. The given information purposely used a low amount for P Company's additional paid-in capital to show the extreme situation of reducing P Company's Additional Paid-in Capital account to zero. In practice, this would rarely occur because companies usually assign a very low par value to their common stock.

**ILLUSTRATION** **Comparison of Entries under the Pooling of Interest Method and the Purchase Method—90% of Outstanding Common Stock Acquired**

Illustration 6-2 compares the recording of a business combination under both methods using the information given above, but assuming only 90% of the outstanding common stock is obtained in exchange for 10% fewer shares issued by P Company. Note that the manner of determining the amounts recorded is the same as that used in Illustration 6-1, except 90%

## ■ ILLUSTRATION 6-1
### Comparison of the Pooling of Interests Method with the Purchase Method—100% of Common Stock Acquired

| | Situation A 1,000 Shares | | Situation B 2,000 Shares | | Situation C 3,000 Shares | | Situation D 4,000 Shares | |
|---|---|---|---|---|---|---|---|---|
| | Dr. | Cr. | Dr. | Cr. | Dr. | Cr. | Dr. | Cr. |
| **Pooling of Interests** | | | | | | | | |
| (1) Investment in S Company..... | 60,000 | | 60,000 | | 60,000 | | 60,000 | |
| (4) Additional Paid-in Capital .. | | | | | 10,000 | | 12,000 | |
| (2) Common Stock ($10 par value) | | 10,000 | | 20,000 | | 30,000 | | 40,000 |
| (4) Additional Paid-in Capital | | 10,000 | | | | | | |
| (3) Retained Earnings ... | | 40,000 | | 40,000 | | 40,000 | | 32,000[a] |
| **Purchase Method** | | | | | | | | |
| (5) Investment in S Company..... | 30,000 | | 60,000 | | 90,000 | | 120,000 | |
| (2) Common Stock....... | | 10,000 | | 20,000 | | 30,000 | | 40,000 |
| (6) Additional Paid-in Capital | | 20,000 | | 40,000 | | 60,000 | | 80,000 |

Explanation of entries:
(1) This amount always equals the parent's ownership interest in the subsidiary's net assets at book value.
(2) This amount always equals the number of shares issued multiplied by the par value of the issuing company's common stock ($10 in this example).
(3) This amount always equals (a) the parent's ownership interest in the subsidiary's Retained Earnings account less (b) any amount that cannot be charged to the parent's Additional Paid-in Capital account, inasmuch as a debit balance would be created in Additional Paid-in Capital.
(4) This is a residual amount to balance the entry: a debit plug cannot be greater than the Additional Paid-in Capital account balance on the parent's books. (Any additional debit is charged to Retained Earnings.)
(5) This amount always equals the number of shares issued multiplied by the market price on the date of the combination.
(6) This amount is always the difference between the amounts determined in entries 5 and 2.

Note: Shares are assumed to be issued.

[a]$40,000 − $8,000 that could not be charged to the parent's Additional Paid-in Capital account.

# ■ ILLUSTRATION 6-2
## Comparison of the Pooling of Interests Method with the Purchase Method—90% of Common Stock Acquired

| | Situation A | | Situation B | | Situation C | | Situation D | |
| --- | --- | --- | --- | --- | --- | --- | --- | --- |
| | 900 Shares | | 1,800 Shares | | 2,700 Shares | | 3,600 Shares | |
| | Dr. | Cr. | Dr. | Cr. | Dr. | Cr. | Dr. | Cr. |
| **Pooling of Interests** | | | | | | | | |
| (1) Investment in S Company..... | 54,000 | | 54,000 | | 54,000 | | 54,000 | |
| (4) Additional Paid-in Capital .. | | | | | 9,000 | | 12,000 | |
| (2) Common Stock ($10 par value) | | 9,000 | | 18,000 | | 27,000 | | 36,000 |
| (4) Additional Paid in Capital | | 9,000 | | | | | | |
| (3) Retained Earnings ... | | 36,000 | | 36,000 | | 36,000 | | 30,000[a] |
| **Purchase Method** | | | | | | | | |
| (5) Investment in S Company..... | 27,000 | | 54,000 | | 81,000 | | 108,000 | |
| (2) Common Stock....... | | 9,000 | | 18,000 | | 27,000 | | 36,000 |
| (6) Additional Paid-in Capital | | 18,000 | | 36,000 | | 54,000 | | 72,000 |

Explanation of entries:
  (1) This amount always equals the parent's ownership interest in the subsidiary's net assets at book value.
  (2) This amount always equals the number of shares issued multiplied by the par value of the issuing company's common stock ($10 in this example).
  (3) This amount always equals (a) the parent's ownership interest in the subsidiary's Retained Earnings account less (b) any amount that cannot be charged to the parent's Additional Paid-in Capital account, inasmuch as a debit balance would be created in Additional Paid-in Capital.
  (4) This is a residual amount to balance the entry; a debit plug cannot be greater than the Additional Paid-in Capital account balance on the parent's books. (Any additional debit is charged to Retained Earnings.)
  (5) This amount always equals the number of shares issued multiplied by the market price on the date of the combination.
  (6) This amount is always the difference between the amounts determined in entries 5 and 2.

Note: Shares are assumed to be issued.

[a]$36,000 − $6,000 that could not be charged to the parent's Additional Paid-in Capital account.

instead of 100% is used to determine the amount of the investment in S Company and the credit to retained earnings.

## Purchase of Shares from Dissenting Shareholders

Occasionally, some shareholders of the target company refuse to take common stock of the issuing company as consideration. These shareholders are known as **dissenting shareholders.** To obtain these shares, the issuing company must usually offer other types of consideration—cash is the most common. **So long as the dissenting shareholders do not hold**

**more than 10% of the target company's outstanding shares, consideration other than the issuing company's common stock may be given to dissenting shareholders, and pooling of interests treatment is allowed.**

The purchase of these shares is similar to the purchase of a block of stock as discussed and illustrated in the preceding chapter. Accordingly, the manner of acquiring these shares seems to dictate that purchase accounting be used to account for their acquisition. However, *APB Opinion No. 16* provides that when shares are acquired from dissenting shareholders at the same time the business combination is consummated, "a single method should be applied to an entire combination."[6] Thus, the purchase method cannot be used to account for the cost of acquiring these shares from the dissenting shareholders; the pooling of interests method is used to account for all of the shares acquired. In other words, **the combination cannot be recorded as part pooling, part purchase.**

**ILLUSTRATION**

### Dissenting Shareholders Bought Out with Cash at Combination Date

In situation B of Illustration 6-2, we assumed that P Company issued 1,800 shares of its common stock in exchange for 4,500 shares of S Company's outstanding common stock (90% of the outstanding shares). Let us assume that P Company acquired the remaining 500 shares from the dissenting shareholders at the combination date by paying $10,000 cash. The entry to record the entire transaction as a pooling of interests is as follows:

| | | |
|---|---|---|
| Investment in S Company (100% of $60,000). . | 60,000 | |
| Additional Paid-in Capital (residual amount). . | 8,000 | |
| Cash (to dissenting shareholders) . . . . . . | | 10,000 |
| Common Stock (1,800 shares × $10). . . . | | 18,000 |
| Retained Earnings (100% of $40,000) . . . | | 40,000 |

## Treatment of Direct Costs and Registration Expenses

**Financial Accounting Treatment.**   Under the purchase method of accounting, direct costs relating to the acquisition of the common stock or the assets are included in the cost of the investment. In contrast, **under the pooling of interests method, direct costs are charged to income in the period in which they are incurred. In addition, the costs of registering equity shares issued by the issuing company are charged to income as incurred** instead of being charged to Additional Paid-in Capital as under the purchase method. The rationale is that no new capital is raised—only a "pooling" of the existing capital occurs.[7] In practice, these costs and expenses are customarily deferred until the combination is consummated, so that the costs and expenses are charged against the first period

[6]*APB Opinion No. 16*, par. 43.
[7]*APB Opinion No. 16*, par. 58.

in which income from the newly combined business is included in net income.

**Income Tax Accounting Treatment.**   Recall from Chapter 2 that a combination that qualifies for pooling of interests treatment for financial reporting purposes is almost always treated as a tax-free reorganization for income tax reporting purposes. In almost all instances, direct costs are not currently deductible for income tax reporting purposes. The obtaining of assets is treated as a capital expenditure that results in the creation of a capital asset with an indeterminable useful life. This asset remains intact until it is totally worthless or is disposed of, at which time a tax deduction may be obtained. When common stock is obtained, direct costs are treated as an upward adjustment to the basis of the common stock received by the acquiring company. If the subsidiary is ever sold, these costs are effectively deducted against the proceeds from the sale.

# PREPARING CONSOLIDATED FINANCIAL STATEMENTS

| ILLUSTRATION |

## Combination Date and First Year Subsequent—Wholly Owned Subsidiary

Assume that for 19X1, S Company had net income of $15,000 and declared dividends of $5,000. Using the information given earlier as to S Company's capital account balances as of the combination date (pages 282–83), we analyze P Company's investment account by the individual components of the book value element as of the combination date (January 1, 19X1), and then update the analysis for the subsequent year's activity (under the equity method of accounting) as follows:

| | Total Cost | = | Common Stock | + | Additional Paid-in Capital | + | Prior Years | + | Current Year Earnings | Current Year Dividends |
|---|---|---|---|---|---|---|---|---|---|---|
| | | | | | | | Retained Earnings | | | |
| Balance, Jan. 1, 19X1 | $60,000 | | $15,000 | | $5,000 | | $40,000 | | | |
| Equity in net income | 15,000 | | | | | | | | $15,000 | |
| Dividends | (5,000) | | | | | | | | | $(5,000) |
| Subtotal | $70,000 | | $15,000 | | $5,000 | | $40,000 | | $15,000 | $(5,000) |
| Reclassification | | | | | | | 10,000 | | (15,000) | 5,000 |
| Balance, Dec. 31, 19X1 | $70,000 | | $15,000 | | $5,000 | | $50,000 | | $ –0– | $ –0– |

Note that this analysis is the same regardless of the number of shares issued by P Company.

The primary elimination entries as of January 1, 19X1 (the combination date), and December 31, 19X1 (one year subsequent to the combination date), are as follows:

**WORKSHEET ENTRY ONLY**

|  | Consolidation Date | |
| --- | --- | --- |
|  | January 1, 19X1 | December 31, 19X1 |
| Common Stock | 15,000 | 15,000 |
| Additional Paid-in Capital | 5,000 | 5,000 |
| Retained Earnings (beginning of year) | 40,000 | 40,000 |
| Equity in Net Income of Subsidiary |  | 15,000 |
| Dividends Declared |  | 5,000 |
| Investment in S Company | 60,000 | 70,000 |

Because the book value element is the only major element under pooling of interests accounting, there is no cost over or under book value to amortize, and thus no secondary elimination entry is necessary.

Illustrations 6-3 and 6-4 show consolidating statement worksheets as of the above dates, assuming that 3,000 shares were issued (situation C in Illustration 6-1) to effect the combination.

### Review Points for Illustrations 6-3 and 6-4.   Note the following:

1. The primary elimination entry is developed in exactly the same way as in purchase accounting, except that the updating of the expanded analysis of the investment account is simpler because only the book value element is involved.
2. The amounts in the consolidated column are composed of (a) the parent's items based on book values and (b) the subsidiary's items based on book values. No revaluation to current values has been made.
3. A secondary elimination entry is not needed when pooling of interests accounting is used.
4. The use of the equity method to account subsequently for the parent's investment maintains the investment account balance equal to the subsidiary's net assets at book value, which simplifies the consolidation process.
5. When ownership of the subsidiary is less than 100% (it must be at least 90% to qualify for pooling of interests treatment), the necessary minority interest deduction is determined and derived in the same manner as shown in the preceding chapter for situations in which purchase accounting is used.
6. The formal consolidated statement of retained earnings would be presented as follows:

| | |
| --- | --- |
| Balance, December 31, 19X0, as previously reported | $100,000 |
| Effect of pooling of interests with S Company | 40,000 |
| Balance, December 31, 19X0, as restated | $140,000 |

*(continued)*

# ■ ILLUSTRATION 6-3
## Date of Combination

| | P COMPANY AND SUBSIDIARY (S COMPANY) | | | | |
|---|---|---|---|---|---|
| | Consolidating Statement Worksheet as of January 1, 19X1 | | | | |
| | P | S | Eliminations | | |
| | Company | Company | Dr. | Cr. | Consolidated |
| **Balance Sheet** | | | | | |
| Cash . . . . . . . . . . . . . . . . . . . . . . . . | 90,000 | 15,000 | | | 105,000 |
| Accounts receivable, net . . . . . . . . . | 70,000 | 23,000 | | | 93,000 |
| Inventory. . . . . . . . . . . . . . . . . . . . . . | 100,000 | 32,000 | | | 132,000 |
| Investment in S Company. . . . . . . . | 60,000 | | | 60,000(1) | –0– |
| Land . . . . . . . . . . . . . . . . . . . . . . . . . | 220,000 | 30,000 | | | 250,000 |
| Buildings and equipment. . . . . . . . | 500,000 | 200,000 | | | 700,000 |
| Accumulated depreciation . . . . . . . | (280,000) | (50,000) | | | (330,000) |
| Total Assets . . . . . . . . . . . . . . . . . . | 760,000 | 250,000 | | 60,000 | 950,000 |
| Liabilities . . . . . . . . . . . . . . . . . . . . . | 288,000 | 190,000 | | | 478,000 |
| P Company: | | | | | |
| Common stock . . . . . . . . . . . . . . . | 330,000 | | | | 330,000 |
| Additional paid-in capital. . . . . . | 2,000 | | | | 2,000 |
| Retained earnings. . . . . . . . . . . . | 140,000 | | | | 140,000 |
| S Company: | | | | | |
| Common stock . . . . . . . . . . . . . . . | | 15,000 | 15,000(1) | | –0– |
| Additional paid-in capital. . . . . . | | 5,000 | 5,000(1) | | –0– |
| Retained earnings. . . . . . . . . . . . | | 40,000 | 40,000(1) | | –0– |
| Total Liabilities and Equity . . . . | 760,000 | 250,000 | 60,000 | | 950,000 |

Proof of debit and credit postings. . . . . . . . . . . . . . . . . . . . . . . .   60,000   60,000

Explanation of entry:
  (1) The primary elimination entry.

Note: The journal entry recorded by the parent for the pooling (which effect is included in the P Company column) is:

| | | |
|---|---|---|
| Investment in S Company (100% of $60,000) . . . | 60,000 | |
| Additional Paid-in Capital (residual amount). . . . | 10,000 | |
|    Common Stock (3,000 shares × $10). . . . . . | | 30,000 |
|    Retained Earnings (100% of $40,000). . . . . . | | 40,000 |

Prior to the combination, the parent's Additional Paid-in Capital account had a balance of $12,000.

| | |
|---|---|
| Net income for the year. . . . . . . . . . . . . . . . . . . . . . . . . . . . . . . . | 65,000 |
| Subtotal . . . . . . . . . . . . . . . . . . . . . . . . . . . . . . . . . . | $205,000 |
| Dividends. . . . . . . . . . . . . . . . . . . . . . . . . . . . . . . . . . . | (45,000) |
| Balance, December 31, 19X1 . . . . . . . . . . . . . . . . . . . . . . . . . . . . | $160,000 |

## Key Points:
   a. **Effect of pooling:** The retained earnings of S Company on January 1, 19X1 when multiplied by the parent's ownership percentage

## ■ ILLUSTRATION 6-4
### First Year Subsequent to Combination Date

**P COMPANY AND SUBSIDIARY (S COMPANY)**
**Consolidating Statement Worksheet for the Year Ended December 31, 19X1**

| | P Company | S Company | Eliminations Dr. | Eliminations Cr. | Consolidated |
|---|---|---|---|---|---|
| **Income Statement** | | | | | |
| Sales......................... | 600,000 | 225,000 | | | 825,000 |
| Cost of goods sold.............. | (360,000) | (110,000) | | | (470,000) |
| Expenses...................... | (190,000) | (100,000) | | | (290,000) |
| Intercompany Account: | | | | | |
| Equity in net income of | | | | | |
| S Company ............... | 15,000 | | 15,000(1) | | –0– |
| Net Income.................. | 65,000 | 15,000 | ⌐ 15,000 | | 65,000 |
| **Statement of Retained Earnings** | | | | | |
| Balances, January 1, 19X1...... | 100,000 | 40,000 | 40,000(1) | | 100,000 |
| + Effect of pooling............. | 40,000 | | | | 40,000 |
| + Net income ................... | 65,000 | 15,000 | ⌐→ 15,000 | | 65,000 |
| – Dividends declared .......... | (45,000) | (5,000) | | 5,000(1) | (45,000) |
| Balances, December 31, 19X1... | 160,000 | 50,000 | ⌐ 55,000 | ⌐ 5,000 | 160,000 |
| **Balance Sheet** | | | | | |
| Cash.......................... | 115,000 | 11,000 | | | 126,000 |
| Accounts receivable, net......... | 75,000 | 37,000 | | | 112,000 |
| Inventory...................... | 110,000 | 55,000 | | | 165,000 |
| Investment in S Company ....... | 70,000 | | | 70,000(1) | –0– |
| Land.......................... | 220,000 | 30,000 | | | 250,000 |
| Buildings and equipment ....... | 500,000 | 200,000 | | | 700,000 |
| Accumulated depreciation....... | (320,000) | (63,000) | | | (383,000) |
| Total Assets................... | 770,000 | 270,000 | | 70,000 | 970,000 |
| Liabilities....................... | 278,000 | 200,000 | | | 478,000 |
| P Company: | | | | | |
| Common stock................ | 330,000 | | | | 330,000 |
| Additional paid-in capital ..... | 2,000 | | | | 2,000 |
| Retained earnings ............ | 160,000 | | | | 160,000 |
| S Company: | | | | | |
| Common stock................ | | 15,000 | 15,000(1) | | –0– |
| Additional paid-in capital ..... | | 5,000 | 5,000(1) | | –0– |
| Retained earnings ............. | | 50,000 | ⌐→ 55,000 | ⌐→ 5,000 | –0– |
| Total Liabilities and Equity.... | 770,000 | 270,000 | 75,000 | 5,000 | 970,000 |
| Proof of debit and credit postings....................... | | | 75,000 | 75,000 | |

Explanation of entry:
(1) The primary elimination entry.

($40,000 × 100% in this case) always equals the "effect of pooling" amount, regardless of the actual business combination date.

b. **Earnings:** The rationale for the preceding statement stems from the fact that in a pooling of interests the subsidiary's earnings for the entire year are combined with those of the parent, no matter when during the year the combination occurs.

c. **Dividends:** Dividends declared by the subsidiary prior to the combination date—none in this case—that went to those stockholders who pooled (thus excluding dividends to minority shareholders) would be combined with the parent's dividends in this statement. Accordingly, the amount shown for dividends declared in the consolidated column always includes dividends paid to persons who no longer own the pooled subsidiary.

The preceding illustration assumed that the parent company used the equity method to account for its investment in the subsidiary. The parent may, however, account for its investment in the subsidiary using the cost method. The cost method is not illustrated, because the procedures are the same as those shown in Appendix A to Chapter 4.

## Mid-year Pooling of Interests

For poolings of interests that occur other than at the beginning of the year, the simplest manner of both recording the pooling of interests and preparing the consolidation worksheet is to (1) record the pooling of interests as though it had been consummated at the beginning of the year (using the book value of the net assets at that date), and (2) apply the equity method of accounting for the full year (using the parent's ownership percentage). However, one slight variation from normal equity procedures must be made: **For dividends declared by the subsidiary prior to the consummation date (which dividends were paid to S Company's former shareholders), debit the Dividends Declared account instead of Dividends Receivable or Cash.** This allows dividends paid to shareholders who pooled their equity interest to be combined with dividends declared by the parent, which combined amount must be reported in the consolidated statement of retained earnings.

Let us change the consummation date from January 1, 19X1 (the beginning of the year), to April 1, 19X1. Assume further that S Company's earnings and dividends for 19X1 were as follows:

| | Jan. 1–Mar. 31 | April 1–Dec. 31 | Total |
|---|---|---|---|
| Net income | $3,000 | $12,000 | $15,000 |
| Dividends | 1,000 | 4,000 | 5,000 |

Accordingly, the entries under the equity method of accounting for 19X1 would be as follows:

| | | |
|---|---:|---:|
| Investment in Subsidiary . . . . . . . . . . . . . . . . . . . . . . . | 15,000 | |
|     Equity in Net Income of Subsidiary . . . . . . | | 15,000 |
|   To record equity in net income. | | |

| | | |
|---|---:|---:|
| Dividends Declared . . . . . . . . . . . . . . . . . . . . . . . . . . | 1,000 | |
|     Investment in Subsidiary . . . . . . . . . . . . . . . | | 1,000 |
|   To reflect dividends declared | | |
|     prior to the consummation date | | |
|     as dividends to be reported | | |
|     in consolidation along with | | |
|     the parent's dividends. | | |

| | | |
|---|---:|---:|
| Dividends Receivable . . . . . . . . . . . . . . . . . . . . . . . . | 4,000 | |
|     Investment in Subsidiary . . . . . . . . . . . . . . . | | 4,000 |
|   To record dividends declared | | |
|     after the consummation | | |
|     date of April 1, 19X1. | | |

Illustration 6-5 shows the retained earnings section of the consolidating statement worksheet assuming the pooling of interests was consummated on April 1, 19X1, and the preceding entries had been made. Comparing this illustration to Illustration 6-4 (consummation at the beginning of the year), note that here dividends declared are $1,000 greater in both the parent's column and the consolidated column. The income statement is not presented because it is identical to the one in Illustration 6-4. The balance sheet is not presented either because it also is identical to the one in Illustration 6-4 except that both Cash and

## ■ ILLUSTRATION 6-5
### Combination Occurs in Mid-year

| P COMPANY AND SUBSIDIARY (S COMPANY) | | | | | |
|---|---|---|---|---|---|
| Consolidating Statement Worksheet (Retained Earnings Section Only) | | | | | |
| For the Year Ended December 31, 19X1 | | | | | |
| | **P**<br>Company | **S**<br>Company | **Eliminations** | | **Consolidated** |
| | | | **Dr.** | **Cr.** | |
| **Statement of Retained Earnings** | | | | | |
|   Balances, January 1, 19X1 . . . . . . | 100,000 | 40,000 | 40,000(1) | | 100,000 |
|   + Effect of pooling . . . . . . . . . . . . . | 40,000 | | | | 40,000 |
|   + Net income . . . . . . . . . . . . . . . . . | 65,000 | 15,000 | 15,000 | | 65,000 |
|   − Dividends declared . . . . . . . . . . | (46,000) | (5,000) | | 5,000(1) | (46,000) |
|   Balances, December 31, 19X1 . . . . | 159,000 | 50,000 | 55,000 | 5,000 | 159,000 |

Retained Earnings in both the parent's column and the consolidated column would be $1,000 less.

## Comparative Income Statements: Pooling of Interests versus Purchase Accounting

We assumed in Illustration 6-4 that 3,000 shares of common stock were issued to effect the combination (Situation C in Illustration 6-1). The fair value of the consideration given was $90,000. If the combination did not qualify for pooling of interests treatment, then under purchase accounting the $90,000 total cost would consist of the following major conceptual elements:

| | |
|---|---:|
| 1. The book value element (100% of $60,000) . . . . . . . . . . . . | $60,000 |
| 2. The current value over book value element ($80,000 − $60,000). . . . . . . . . . . . . . . . . . . . . . . . . . . . . . . . . . . . | 20,000 |
| 3. The goodwill element ($90,000 − $80,000) . . . . . . . . . . . . | 10,000 |
| | $90,000 |

Assume that $4,000 of amortization of cost in excess of book value would be recorded in 19X1 under the purchase method. Income statements for 19X1 are shown under both methods for comparison:

| | Pooling of Interests[a] | Purchase Method |
|---|---:|---:|
| Revenues. . . . . . . . . . . . . . . . . . . . . . . . . . . . . . . | $825,000 | $ 825,000 |
| Cost of goods sold. . . . . . . . . . . . . . . . . . . . . | (470,000) | (474,000) |
| Expenses. . . . . . . . . . . . . . . . . . . . . . . . . . . . . . | (290,000) | (290,000) |
| Net Income . . . . . . . . . . . . . . . . . . . . . . . . . . . | $ 65,000 | $ 61,000 |

[a]From Illustration 6-4.

# DISCLOSURES

The acquiring entity must make the following disclosures for each period in which a business combination accounted for under the pooling of interests method occurs.

## Disclosure in the Financial Statements

The financial statements must indicate that a business combination accounted for under the pooling of interests method has occurred. This indication may be either by captions or by references to notes to the financial statements.[8]

[8]APB Opinion No. 16, par 63.

## PERSPECTIVE

### A Capsule History of Pooling of Interests Accounting

Early 1940s   The term *pooling of interests* emerges. In rate-base cases brought before it involving business combinations, the Federal Power Commission (FPC) prohibits companies from revaluing their assets upward to their current values when the separate parties have merely pooled their interests. This policy is applied to both related parties and unrelated parties. For revaluation to be allowed, the FPC requires that a sale must occur—one party must dispose of an interest and the other party must acquire that interest.

1945   The Committee on Accounting Procedure of the American Institute for Certified Public Accountants (AICPA) begins to address poolings of interests. Internal memos show that only combinations of two or more interests of comparable size are considered to be poolings of interests.

1950   *ARB No. 40*, "Business Combinations," is issued. It lists four factors to be considered in determining whether the transaction is a purchase or pooling of interests: (1) The **continuity of the former ownership:** Eliminating one of the ownerships or altering the equity interests of either interest immediately before or after the combination indicates a purchase transaction. (2) The **relative size:** One party that is "quite minor" in size compared to the other suggests a purchase transaction. (3) **Continuity of management:** If the management of one of the interests is eliminated or has little influence after the combination, a purchase transaction is indicated. (4) **Similar or complementary lines of business:** If the businesses are in similar or complementary lines of business, a presumption of a pooling of interests is strengthened.

No single factor is the deciding one—the presence or absence of each of the factors is to be considered cumulatively.

OBSERVATION: After *ARB No. 40* was issued, it was possible in most cases to have the assets reported at the same values regardless of whether purchase accounting or pooling of interests accounting were used. This occurred because it was acceptable practice to immediately charge to retained earnings the cost in excess of book value that arose under the purchase method. As a result, there was no major controversy at this time.

---

**A Capsule History of Pooling of Interests Accounting** *(continued)*

1953   *ARB No. 43*, a restatement and revision of *ARB Nos. 1 to 42*, is issued. No substantive changes are made concerning business combinations. Of great importance, however, is the prohibition of immediately charging intangibles arising from acquisition to retained earnings (or to additional paid-in capital). Capitalization as an asset is required and amortization to income is encouraged.

OBSERVATIONS: The effect of *ARB No. 43* was to make pooling of interests much more desirable because the cost in excess of book value can be eliminated from accountability only under pooling of interests. Thus the stage was set for the explosive shift to the pooling of interests method that would occur during the 1950s and 1960s.

At this time, the accounting profession did not have detailed rules concerning pooling of interests—only factors to be evaluated. The burden of determining whether or not pooling of interests should be applied was placed squarely on the auditors' judgment and integrity.

1950–1956   Because of the manner in which *ARB Nos. 40* and *43* are written—no single factor

determines the need for pooling of interests—companies and their auditors interpret them loosely. The result in most cases is that companies have almost complete discretion to account for a combination as a purchase or as a pooling of interests.

1957   *ARB No. 48*, "Business Combinations," is issued, superseding the business combinations section of *ARB No. 43*. The "similar or complementary" lines of business factor is dropped. Concerning the relative size of the combining interests, the wording "quite minor" is replaced by a range of percentages: if one of the combining interests ends up with 90–95% of the stock, purchase accounting is indicated.

OBSERVATIONS: The fast-growing trend toward diversification most likely played a role in the deletion of the similar or complementary business factor. Thus, one of the major reasons why companies might want to pool their interests was deemed nonessential. It was now considered perfectly reasonable for the shareholders of a medical equipment manufacturer and a toy manufacturer to pool their interests.

The insertion of the 90–95% wording removed

*(continued)*

the intent of *ARB No. 40* that the combining companies be of comparable size. Now, companies of greatly disproportionate size could have a pooling of interests.

1958–1962   The relative-size factor having been already weakened, it becomes virtually ignored in practice. Companies begin to use preferred stock to maintain the "continuity of ownership." An abuse known as "retroactive poolings" becomes widespread and is severely criticized.[a]

1963   *Accounting Research Study No. 5*, "A Critical Study of Accounting for Business Combinations," by Arthur R. Wyatt and sponsored by the American Institute of Certified Public Accountants, is issued.[b] It recommends the following: (a) The pooling of interests accounting treatment should be abolished unless the parties are related. (b) When the parties are unrelated and approximately the same size, a fresh start (termed "fair value pooling of interests") should be made by revaluing the assets of both companies to their current values.

1965   The Accounting Principles Board issues *APB Opinion No. 6*, "Status of Accounting Research Bulletins." Commenting on *ARB No. 48*, it states that the factors set forth therein are guidelines rather than literal requirements.

1966–1968   New abuses crop up, such as the part-purchase, part-pooling method. Finding a company with undervalued assets, recording a combination with it as a pooling of interests, and then later selling off the undervalued assets to report phenomenal gains becomes a popular practice. Many companies call upon their auditors to teach them the intricacies of pooling of interests accounting.

The profession comes under mounting criticism for not having adequate standards by which to judge pooling of interests, especially in light of the largest wave of business combinations in history. One of the most scathing articles during this period is "Dirty Pooling" by Abraham J. Briloff of Baruch College.[c] Briloff subsequently becomes one of the leading critics of the accounting profession and is often referred to as its conscience.

February 1969   The chairman of the Securities and Exchange Commission, testifying before a congressional committee, states that unless the accounting profession takes prompt action to resolve the business combinations controversy,

**A Capsule History of Pooling of Interests Accounting** *(continued)*

the SEC would establish rules in this area.

June 1969    The AICPA holds a symposium on accounting for business combinations.

September 1969    The AICPA's executive vice president, Leonard Savoie, states in an address that a forthcoming exposure draft will propose abolishing pooling of interests method of accounting. He also states: "Anything less than this solution will mean simply a 'repositioning' of the abuses which have become so rampant in recent years."[d]

November 1969    The Accounting Principles Board tentatively decides to abolish pooling of interests accounting. A Federal Trade Commission study (authorized by a Senate antitrust committee) released about the same time recommends that the SEC eliminate pooling of interests accounting when stock is given as consideration.

December 1969    The APB reverses itself and tentatively decides pooling of interests accounting should be allowed but not as an alternative that can be freely chosen if desired. For a given set of circumstances and conditions, only one method will apply.

February 1970    The APB issues an exposure draft. The detailed conditions set forth to be met for a pooling of interests will severely limit its use. A three-one comparable size test is included. Lawsuits are subsequently threatened over this condition.

June 1970    The APB reduces the size test to nine to one (about what it was under *ARB No. 48*).

August 1970    *APB Opinion No. 16* is issued; it barely passes on a 12-to-6 vote. The requirement that the combining companies effect a continuity of interests becomes the cornerstone for pooling of interests treatment; the size test is dropped entirely, and there are no requirements for continuity of management or similar or complementary lines of business. The combining interests must meet twelve detailed conditions in order to effect a pooling of interests. If they do not meet any one of the twelve conditions, they must use purchase accounting in their combination.

OBSERVATION: The fact that the conditions for pooling of interests treatment are spelled out in such detail clearly shows that setting guidelines requiring the use of professional judgment and integrity does not work very well. This may be because the judgment of so many is either questionable or compromised as a result of concern over loss of clients to other CPAs who are more willing to liberally interpret the guidelines.

*(continued)*

1970–1973  *APB Opinion No. 16* proves to be difficult to apply. Because of its complexity and in order to close loopholes, the AICPA issues 30 interpretations and the SEC issues four Accounting Series Releases. (Later, from 1974 to 1987, the FASB will issue three interpretations and three technical bulletins.)

1973  The FASB replaces the APB and immediately requests views on previous APB pronouncements. The responses show that *APB Opinion Nos. 16* and *17* are of greatest concerns.

1974  The FASB decides to reevaluate the twelve conditions for pooling of interests in *APB Opinion No. 16.*

1975  The FASB expands the scope of the project to encompass all issues associated with business combinations and goodwill.

1976  The FASB issues a discussion memorandum on the topic, "Accounting for Business Combinations and Purchased Intangibles."

1981  The FASB removes the project from its active agenda because of its "low priority in relation to other existing and potential projects."

1990  Business combinations and purchased intangibles continue to be low in priority for the FASB, even though 17 years have passed since respondents indicated that they were most concerned with these issues.

[a]Retroactive poolings is a technique in which poolings of interests consummated after the year-end but before the issuance of the year-end annual report are given effect in the current year's financial statements rather than in the year of the combination.

[b]Wyatt was then a professor of accountancy at the University of Illinois. A short time later, he became a senior partner in the home office of Arthur Andersen & Co. and subsequently becomes one of the most respected accountants in the profession. In 1985 he became a member of the Financial Accounting Standards Board.

[c]*The Accounting Review* (July 1967), p. 489.

[d]The Accounting Profession at the Hump of the Decades." By Abraham J. Briloff, *Financial Analysts Journal* (May–June 1970), p. 61.

Sources: A good portion of the history prior to 1971 was based on information contained in:

*A Critical Study of Accounting for Business Combinations,* by Arthur R. Wyatt (New York: American Institute of Certified Public Accountants, 1963).

*Goodwill in Accounting: A History of the Issues and Problems,* by Hugh P. Hughes. Research Monograph No. 80. (Atlanta: Georgia State University, 1982. Because of the close relationship of the goodwill issue with pooling of interests accounting, this publication devotes considerable attention to the pooling of interests issue.

## Disclosure in the Notes to the Financial Statements

The following footnote disclosures, among others, are required:

1. The name and description of the business combined.
2. The fact that the pooling of interests method is used to account for the combination.
3. The number of shares issued and a description thereof.
4. Income information (including revenues and net income) for preacquisition periods of the acquired business that are included in the current combined income statement.

5. Reconciliations of revenues and earnings to amounts previously reported by the acquiring entity.[9]

# END-OF-CHAPTER REVIEW

## Summary of Key Points

1. A pooling of interests is a fusing together of ownership interests.
2. This fusion occurs only when one of the combining companies issues voting common stock in exchange for either (a) 100% of the target company's assets or (b) at least 90% of the outstanding common stock of the target company.
3. In addition, numerous other conditions grouped into three broad areas (attributes of the combining companies, the manner of combining, and the absence of planned transactions) must be met.
4. If any one of the twelve conditions is not met, then purchase accounting must be used.
5. The basis of accounting for the target company's assets and liabilities is not changed in a pooling of interests. Nor is goodwill ever reported.
6. Precombination earnings and dividends of the target company are always combined with those of the issuing company—but only to the extent of the ownership interest exchanged—whenever periods prior to the combination date are presented.

## Glossary of New Terms

**Dissenting shareholders**   Target company shareholders who refuse to exchange their common shares for only common stock of the acquiring company.

**Spin-off**   A divestiture of a portion of a business whereby certain assets, liabilities, or common stock holdings of a subsidiary are given to certain shareholders of a company in exchange for some or all of their outstanding common stock holdings in the company.

## Self-Study Questions

*(Answers are at the end of this chapter.)*

1. One of the conditions or requirements for pooling of interests treatment is:
   a. A common-stock-for-common-stock exchange must take place.
   b. The companies must be in similar or complementary lines of business.
   c. The target company cannot own any stock of the company issuing common stock between the initiation date and the consummation date.
   d. The common stock issued must be voting common stock.
   e. None of the above.
2. One of the conditions or requirements for pooling of interests treatment is:
   a. Holders of at least 90% of the target company's common stock agree not to sell the shares they receive from the issuing company for two years.
   b. Dissenting shareholders may not receive cash for their interest.

---

[9]*APB Opinion No. 16*, par 64.

c. The issuing company cannot agree to buy back (as a purchase of treasury stock) any of the shares issued to effect the combination.

d. The smaller of the two combining companies cannot be the company that issues common stock to effect the pooling of interests.

e. None of the above.

3. One of the conditions or requirements for pooling of interests treatment is:

a. Each company must have been audited by independent outside auditors for at least two years prior to the initiation date.

b. Treasury stock, no matter why or when acquired, cannot be used to effect a pooling of interests.

c. Shares of the target company acquired prior to the consummation date—no matter whether acquired for cash or common stock—are disregarded in calculating whether the 90% test has been satisfied.

d. The companies must be of comparable size.

e. None of the above.

4. One of the conditions or requirements for pooling of interests treatment is:

a. Shares of the target company acquired prior to the initiation date—no matter whether acquired for cash or common stock—are disregarded in calculating whether the 90% test has been satisfied.

b. The 90% group of shareholders cannot receive any cash whatsoever from the issuing company.

c. Neither combining company can have been involved in a business combination accounted for as a pooling of interests within the preceding two years.

d. No more than 10% of the common stock issued to effect the pooling of interests can be required to be purchased back for cash.

e. None of the above.

5. One of the conditions or requirements for a pooling of interests is:

a. Treasury stock may be used by the issuing company to effect a pooling of interests so long as the specific shares used were acquired at least two years prior to the initiation date.

b. Restrictions must be placed on the negotiability of the common stock issued.

c. Continuity of management must be expected.

d. The stock issued cannot be voting preferred stock that is convertible into common stock.

e. None of the above.

6. One of the conditions or requirements for a pooling of interests is:

a. If each combining company has an ownership interest in the other combining company, the cumulative ownership percentage cannot exceed 20%.

b. Neither combining company has been a subsidiary or division of another corporation for two years prior to the initiation date.

c. Purchases of treasury stock are not deemed to be alterations of the equity interests—even when made within two years before the initiation date.

d. Financial arrangements made for the benefit of former stockholders of a combining company cannot extend beyond two years after the consummation date.

e. None of the above.

7. A supporting argument for the pooling of interests method of accounting for a business combination is that:

   a. One company is clearly the dominant and continuing entity.

   b. Goodwill is generally a part of any acquisition.

   c. It was developed within the boundaries of the historical cost system and is compatible with it.

   d. A portion of the total cost is assigned to individual assets acquired on the basis of their current value.

8. A subsidiary may be acquired by issuing common stock in a pooling of interests transaction or by paying cash in a purchase transaction. Which of the following items would be reported in the consolidated financial statements at the same amount regardless of the accounting method used?

   a. Minority interest.

   b. Goodwill.

   c. Retained earnings.

   d. Capital stock accounts (in total).

9. In a business combination, how should the acquired corporation's plant and equipment be reported under each of the following methods?

   | Pooling of Interests | Purchase Method |
   |---|---|
   | a. At current value | At recorded value |
   | b. At current value | At current value |
   | c. At recorded value | At recorded value |
   | d. At recorded value | At current value |

10. How would the retained earnings of a subsidiary acquired in a business combination usually be treated in a consolidated balance sheet prepared immediately after the acquisition under each of the following methods?

    | Pooling of Interests | Purchase Method |
    |---|---|
    | a. Excluded | Excluded |
    | b. Excluded | Included |
    | c. Included | Included |
    | d. Included | Excluded |

11. If all other conditions for consolidation are met, how should subsidiaries acquired in a business combination be shown under each of the following methods?

    | Pooling of Interests | Purchase Method |
    |---|---|
    | a. Consolidated | Not consolidated |
    | b. Consolidated | Consolidated |
    | c. Not consolidated | Consolidated |
    | d. Not consolidated | Not consolidated |

12. Ownership of 51% of the outstanding voting stock of a company would usually result in:
    a. The use of the cost method.
    b. The use of the lower of cost or market method.
    c. A pooling of interests.
    d. A consolidation.

13. Perkins Company incurred a $20,000 finder's and consultation fee and $7,000 of SEC registration costs in acquiring Sayco Company. Of these costs, how much should be reported in the income statement as business combination expenses in the year of the acquisition under each of the following methods?
    a. Pooling of interests.
    b. Purchase method.

14. Using the information in the preceding question, how much would be capitalized as part of the acquisition cost?
    a. Under pooling of interests.
    b. Under the purchase method.

15. A business combination between Plata Company and Silver Company occurs September 30, 19X1. During 19X1, Plata Company declares dividends of $25,000 per quarter, except for the fourth quarter when it declares $30,000. Silver Company declares dividends of $10,000 each quarter. Assume that Silver Company is 100% owned (10% of Silver Company's shareholders dissented and were bought out with cash). From the choices available as shown below, what amount would appear in the consolidated statement of retained earnings as dividends declared for the year ended December 31, 19X1, under (a) the pooling of interests method and (b) the purchase method.
    a. $105,000
    b.  114,000
    c.  132,000
    d.  135,000
    e.  145,000

16. Using the information in question 15, but assuming that Silver Company is only 90% owned, answer the same questions.

(AICPA adapted, Nos. 7–12)

## Demonstration Problem

On October 1, 19X6, Pak Company combined with Shipp Company. Pak issued 19,000 shares of its common stock in exchange for 45,000 outstanding shares of Shipp. Pak paid $50,000 cash for the remaining 5,000 outstanding shares of Shipp. Pak's common stock had a market price of $40 at the combination date. The capital accounts of each company on September 30, 19X6, follow:

|  | Pak | Shipp |
| --- | --- | --- |
| Common stock, $5 par value | $150,000 | |
| Common stock, $2 par value | | $100,000 |
| Additional paid-in capital | 20,000 | 15,000 |
| Retained earnings | 720,000 | 485,000 |

For 19X6, each company—on a stand-alone basis—had the following earnings and dividends:

| | Jan. 1 – Sept. 30, 19X6 | Oct. 1– Dec. 31, 19X6 | Total |
|---|---|---|---|
| **Pak Company** | | | |
| Net income | $120,000 | $50,000 | $170,000 |
| Dividends declared | 90,000 | 49,000 | 139,000 |
| **Shipp Company** | | | |
| Net income | $70,000 | $20,000 | $90,000 |
| Dividends declared | 30,000 | 10,000 | 40,000 |

Pak incurred $35,000 of costs directly related to the combination and $25,000 of costs in registering the shares issued with the SEC.

## Required:

1. Prepare the entries required at the combination date.
2. Prepare the entries required under the equity method of accounting for 19X6.
3. Prepare an analysis of the Investment account as updated through December 31, 19X6.
4. Prepare the primary elimination entry for consolidation at December 31, 19X6.
5. Prepare a consolidated statement of retained earnings for 19X6.

## SOLUTION TO DEMONSTRATION PROBLEM

1. Entry to record the combination as if it occurred as of the beginning of the year:

| | | |
|---|---|---|
| Investment in Shipp Company (100% of Shipp's total stockholders' equity at December 31, 19X5) | 560,000 | |
| Common Stock (19,000 shares × $5 par value) | | 95,000 |
| Cash (to dissenting shareholders) | | 50,000 |
| Retained Earnings (100% of Shipp's Dec. 31, 19X5, retained earnings balance) | | 445,000 |

At this point a $30,000 debit is needed to balance the entry:

| | | |
|---|---|---|
| Additional Paid-in Capital (a $20,000 debit brings this account to a –0– balance) | 20,000 | |
| Retained Earnings (residual) | 10,000 | |

Note: The effect of the pooling is $435,000 ($445,000 – $10,000), and this amount is reported in the consolidated statement of retained earnings for the year 19X6.

Entry to account for costs incurred:

| | | |
|---|---|---|
| Expenses. . . . . . . . . . . . . . . . . . . . . . . . . . . . . . . . . . . . . . . . . . . . . . | 60,000 | |
| Accrued Liabilities. . . . . . . . . . . . . . . . . . . . . . . . . . . | | 60,000 |

2. 

| | | |
|---|---|---|
| Investment in Shipp Company . . . . . . . . . . . . . . . . . . . . . | 90,000 | |
| Equity in Net Income of Subsidiary . . . . . . . . . . . | | 90,000 |

To record equity in earnings of subsidiary
for 19X6 (100% of $90,000).

| | | |
|---|---|---|
| Dividends Declared. . . . . . . . . . . . . . . . . . . . . . . . . . . . . . | 30,000 | |
| Investment in Shipp Company. . . . . . . . . . . . . . . | | 30,000 |

To reflect dividends paid prior to the
combination date (to Shipp shareholders who
surrendered their stock) as dividends to be
reported in the consolidated statement of
retained earnings.

| | | |
|---|---|---|
| Dividends Receivable . . . . . . . . . . . . . . . . . . . . . . . . . . . . | 10,000 | |
| Investment in Shipp Company. . . . . . . . . . . . . . . | | 10,000 |

To record dividends declared after the combination date.

3.

| | Total Cost | = | Common Stock | + | Additional Paid-in Capital | + | Book Value Element | | | |
|---|---|---|---|---|---|---|---|---|---|---|
| | | | | | | | Retained Earnings | | | |
| | | | | | | | Prior Year | + | Current Year | |
| | | | | | | | | | Earnings | Dividends |
| Jan. 1, 19X6 . . . . . . . . | $560,000 | | $100,000 | | $15,000 | | $445,000 | | | |
| Net income. . . . . . . . | 90,000 | | | | | | | | $90,000 | |
| Dividends. . . . . . . . . | (30,000) | | | | | | | | | $(30,000) |
| Dividends. . . . . . . . . | (10,000) | | | | | | | | | (10,000) |
| Dec. 31, 19X6 . . . . . . . | $610,000 | | $100,000 | | $15,000 | | $445,000 | | $90,000 | $(40,000) |
| Reclassify. . . . . . . . . | | | | | | | 50,000 | | (90,000) | 40,000 |
| Dec. 31, 19X6 . . . . . . . | $610,000 | | $100,000 | | $15,000 | | $495,000 | | $ –0– | $ –0– |

4. The primary elimination entry:

| | | |
|---|---|---|
| Common Stock . . . . . . . . . . . . . . . . . . . . . . . . . . . . . . . . . | 100,000 | |
| Additional Paid-in Capital . . . . . . . . . . . . . . . . . . . . . . . . | 15,000 | |
| Retained Earnings (beginning of year) . . . . . . . . . . . . . . | 445,000 | |
| Equity in Net Income of Subsidiary. . . . . . . . . . . . . . . . . | 90,000 | |
| Dividends Declared . . . . . . . . . . . . . . . . . . . . . . . . . | | 40,000 |
| Investment in Shipp Company. . . . . . . . . . . . . . . . | | 610,000 |

5.

**Pak Company**
**Statement of Retained Earnings**
**For the Year Ended December 31, 19X6**

| | | |
|---|---|---|
| Balance, December 31, 19X5, as previously reported. . . . . . . . . . . . . | $ | 690,000 |
| Effect of pooling of interests with Shipp Company . . . . . . . . . . . . . | | 435,000 |

*(continued)*

| | |
|---|---|
| Balance, December 31, 19X5, as restated............................ | $1,125,000 |
| Net income for the year............................................. | 200,000[a] |
| Subtotal.................................................... | $1,325,000 |
| Dividends declared ...................................... | (169,000)[b] |
| Balance, December 31, 19X6................................ | $1,156,000 |

[a]Comprised of $170,000 from Pak, $90,000 from Shipp, and less $60,000 of expenses incurred.
[b]Comprised of $139,000 for Pak plus $30,000 for Shipp that was paid to Shipp's shareholders prior to the combination date. (The entire $30,000 is reported even though 5% of Shipp's shareholders dissented—Pak obtained a 100% interest in Shipp.)

# ASSIGNMENT MATERIAL

## Review Questions

1. Why is the term *acquired business* not used in the discussion of pooling of interests accounting in *APB Opinion No. 16?*
2. What is the essence of a pooling of interests?
3. What accounts for the popularity of the pooling of interests method?
4. How has the original concept of a pooling of interests changed over the years?
5. Distinguish between a joining together of the equity interests and a continuity of ownership of the separate equity interests.
6. What are the major conceptual issues pertaining to pooling of interests?
7. What criteria determine whether a business combination is treated as a pooling of interests?
8. What is the major criticism of the pooling of interests criteria in *APB Opinion No. 16?*
9. How is the value of the consideration given by the acquiring company accounted for in a business combination that qualifies as a pooling of interests?
10. Can cash be given to the shareholders of the target company in a business combination that is accounted for as a pooling of interests?
11. How are preacquisition earnings of the target business treated in income statements for periods before the combination date when the combination has been accounted for as a pooling of interests?
12. Why might pooling of interests be considered the lesser of two evils by some accountants?

## Discussion Cases

### A Lawsuit Alleging Deception via a Pooling of Interests

DC
6-1

In January 19X5, Planner Company entered into a business combination transaction with Supresso Company. Planner issued the common stock to effect the transaction. The twelve conditions for pooling of interests treatment were met, so the transaction was recorded as a pooling of interests. Supresso had a substantial amount of undervalued assets as of the combination date.

Through December 31, 19X7, Planner had reported six consecutive years of increased profits and had attracted a wide following on Wall Street. In 19X8, its earnings from operations were down slightly from 19X7. To show a continued trend of higher profits, management sold Supresso's undervalued assets throughout 19X8 at a substantial profit. In 19X9, Planner's earnings from operations were the same as in 19X8, but the company had no undervalued assets to sell. Accordingly, 19X9 earnings were substantially below those of 19X8 and 19X7.

As a result of its reporting lower profits in 19X9, the price of the company's common stock dropped sharply, and many investors lost substantial amounts of money. A class-action lawsuit was filed against the company shortly after earnings were reported for 19X9, alleging that the company had conspired to issue false and misleading financial statements for 19X8. The focal point of the lawsuit was that the use of the pooling of interests method in 19X5 resulted in deceptive financial reporting in 19X8 and that the purchase method of accounting should have been used instead. (Only a nominal gain would have been reported on the sale of the assets in 19X8 if the purchase method had been used.)

The parties named in the lawsuit are Planner's top management, including the controller, and its certified public accountants.

### Required:

1. Does the company have an adequate defense that it used generally accepted accounting principles?
2. To use the pooling of interests method, did Planner's controller have to believe personally that it results in a fair presentation?
3. How might the lawyer for the plaintiffs use *Accounting Research Study No. 5*? What impact might its use have on the jury?
4. In reading *APB Opinion No. 16*, the lawyer for the plaintiffs found that one of the dissenting members of the Accounting Principles Board was a partner in the CPA firm named in the lawsuit. Further research revealed that this CPA firm was vehemently against the pooling of interests concept prior to the issuance of *APB Opinion No. 16*. Of what use might this information be?

| DC |
| 6-2 |

## Review of Conditions for Pooling of Interests

The boards of directors of Paterno Corporation, Sata Company, Seta Company, and Sita Company are meeting jointly to discuss plans for a business combination. Each corporation has one class of common stock outstanding; Sata also has one class of preferred stock outstanding. Although terms have not been settled, Paterno will be the acquiring or issuing corporation.

### Required:

For question 1, determine which position is correct. For the remaining questions, determine how these facts affect the accounting method to the used. (Consider each question independently of the others.)

1. Some of the directors believe that the terms of the combination should be settled immediately and that the method of accounting to be used (whether pooling of interests, purchase, or a mixture) may be chosen at some later date.

Others believe that the terms of the combination and the accounting method are closely related.

2. Paterno and Sata are comparable in size; Seta and Sita are much smaller.
3. Seta was formerly a subsidiary of Spinner Corporation, which is not related to any of the four companies discussing combination. Eighteen months ago, Spinner voluntarily spun off Seta.
4. Don Dissento, who holds 5% of Sita's common stock, will almost certainly object to the combination. Assume that Paterno can acquire only 95% (rather than 100%) of Sita's stock, issuing Paterno common stock in exchange. (If Paterno can acquire the remaining 5% at some future time—in five years, for instance—in exchange for its own common stock, which accounting method will be applicable to this second acquisition?)
5. Because the directors feel that one of Sita's major divisions will not be compatible with the combined company's operations, they expect to sell it as soon as possible after the combination is consummated. They expect to have no trouble finding a buyer.
6. Twenty months ago, Sata acquired 12% of its common stock because the price of the stock was attractively low. Fourteen months ago, Sata retired this treasury stock.
7. Sata is in the same industry as Paterno. Seta is in a complementary industry; and Sita is in a totally unrelated industry.

(AICPA adapted)

## Exercises

### Review of Conditions for Pooling of Interests

Indicate whether each of the following conditions or terms disqualifies the pooling of interests accounting treatment:

1. Issuing common stock in exchange for 90% of the target company's assets.
2. Issuing common stock in exchange for 90% of the target company's outstanding shares.
3. Distribution of common stock and cash—on a pro rata basis—to the target company's shareholders.
4. Additional common stock to be issued by the issuing company if its common stock has a fair market value below $50 per share two years after the combination date.
5. After a common-stock-for-common-stock exchange, the subsidiary is to be liquidated into a division. (No sell-off of assets will take place.)
6. The issuing company plans to use treasury shares it acquired three years ago rather than issue new shares of common stock.
7. The only dissenting shareholder of the target company (a 15% owner holding 15,000 shares) agrees to (a) exchange 10,000 of the shares for common stock of the issuing company using the same exchange ratio that other shareholders have agreed to, and (b) exchange the remaining 5,000 shares for cash.
8. The common stock issued to the target company's shareholders has certain limited voting restrictions.

9. Additional common shares are to be issued by the issuing company, depending on the subsequent sales level of the target business for three years after the combination date.
10. The issuing company agrees to purchase for cash less than 10% of the shares issued within three years of the combination date.

## E 6-2  Testing for Independence

Paine Company and Swebber Company are contemplating a business combination structured to qualify as a pooling of interests. Common stock information is as follows:

|  | Paine Company | Swebber Company |
|---|---|---|
| Outstanding common shares . . . . . . . . . . . . . . . . . . | 300,000 | 100,000 |
| Paine Company common stock owned by Swebber Company . . . . . . . . . . . . . . . . . |  | 15,000 |
| Market price of stock . . . . . . . . . . . . . . . . . . . . . . . . | $20 |  |

### Required:

1. Determine whether the companies are independent. Assume Paine will issue three shares for every one outstanding share of Swebber Company.
2. Determine whether the companies are independent, but assume that Paine will issue one share for every one outstanding share of Swebber Company.
3. Explain why the answers in requirements 1 and 2 are different.

## E 6-3  Testing for Independence: Dual Intercorporate Investments

Pecos Company and Slimm Company are contemplating a business combination structured to qualify as a pooling of interests. Common stock information is as follows:

|  | Pecos Company | Slimm Company |
|---|---|---|
| Outstanding common shares . . . . . . . . . . . . . . . . . . | 600,000 | 100,000 |
| Slimm Company common stock owned by Pecos Company . . . . . . . . . . . . . . . . . | 5,000 |  |
| Pecos Company common stock owned by Slimm Company. . . . . . . . . . . . . . . . . |  | 4,000 |
| Market price of stock . . . . . . . . . . . . . . . . . . . . . . . . | $25 |  |

Pecos will issue one common share for each two outstanding common shares of Slimm.

### Required:

1. Determine whether the companies are independent.
2. If Slimm were the company issuing the common stock, what exchange ratio would it use to maintain the relative holdings between the two stockholder groups?

<table>
<tr><td>E<br>6-4</td></tr>
</table>

## CHALLENGER   Testing for Independence: Dual Intercorporate Investments

Pigital Company and Sterry Company are contemplating a business combination structured to qualify as a pooling of interests. Common stock information is as follows:

|  | Pigital<br>Company | Sterry<br>Company |
|---|---|---|
| Outstanding common stock . . . . . . . . . . . . . . . . . . | 900,000 | 200,000 |
| Pigital Company common stock<br>    owned by Sterry Company . . . . . . . . . . . . . . . . . . |  | 9,000 |
| Sterry Company common stock<br>    owned by Pigital Company . . . . . . . . . . . . . . . . . . | 18,000 |  |
| Market price of stock . . . . . . . . . . . . . . . . . . . . . . . | $10 |  |

Pigital will issue three common shares for every two common shares of Sterry.

### Required:

1. Determine whether the companies are independent.
2. Determine whether the companies are independent, but assume that Sterry will be the issuing company and will issue 600,000 shares to Pigital's stockholders. (These shares maintain the same relationship as when Pigital was the issuing company.)
3. Explain why the answers in requirements 1 and 2 are different even though the relative holdings between the two stockholder groups was held constant. Which answer must be used to determine independence?

<table>
<tr><td>E<br>6-5</td></tr>
</table>

## Recording a Pooling of Interests (100% Ownership)

On January 1, 19X1, Panhandle Company obtained 100% of the outstanding common stock of Stover Company by issuing 20,000 shares of its $5 par value common stock. Selected information as of the combination date is as follows:

|  | Panhandle<br>Company | Stover<br>Company |
|---|---|---|
| Common stock, $5 par value . . . . . . . . . . . . . . . . . . | $1,000,000 |  |
| Common stock, $1 par value . . . . . . . . . . . . . . . . . . |  | $200,000 |
| Additional paid-in capital . . . . . . . . . . . . . . . . . . . . | 3,000,000 | 400,000 |
| Retained earnings . . . . . . . . . . . . . . . . . . . . . . . . . . | 2,000,000 | 250,000 |
|  | $6,000,000 | $850,000 |
| Fair market value per share . . . . . . . . . . . . . . . . . . | $50 | $25 |
| Net assets at current value . . . . . . . . . . . . . . . . . . | $7,000,000 | $900,000 |

Assume the business combination qualifies for pooling of interests treatment.

### Required:

1. Prepare the entry to record the business combination.
2. Prepare an expanded analysis of the investment account as of the combination date.

3. Prepare the primary elimination entry at January 1, 19X1.
4. What amount should be reported as the consolidated retained earnings at the combination date?

## Recording a Pooling of Interests (100% Ownership)

E
6-6

On January 1, 19X1, Pinkert Company obtained 100% of the outstanding common stock of Security Company by issuing shares of its common stock. Each company's equity accounts as of the combination date are as follows:

|  | Pinkert Company | Security Company |
|---|---|---|
| Common stock, $10 par value | $1,000,000 | |
| Common stock, $5 par value | | $ 80,000 |
| Additional paid-in capital | 25,000 | 20,000 |
| Retained earnings | 200,000 | 50,000 |
|  | $1,225,000 | $150,000 |

Assume the business combination qualifies for pooling of interest accounting.

**Required:**

1. Prepare the entry to record the business combination, assuming Pinkert issued:
   a. 8,000 shares.
   b. 10,000 shares.
   c. 12,000 shares.
   d. 14,000 shares.
2. Prepare the primary elimination entry as of the combination date for each situation in requirement 1.
3. What amount should be reported as the consolidated retained earnings at the combination date?

## Recording a Pooling of Interests (90% Ownership)

E
6-7

Assume the information provided in Exercise 6-6, except that Pinkert Company obtained only 90% of the outstanding common stock of Security Company.

**Required:**

1. Prepare the entry to record the business combination, assuming Pinkert issued:
   a. 7,200 shares.
   b. 9,000 shares.
   c. 10,800 shares.
   d. 12,600 shares.
2. Prepare the primary elimination entry as of the combination date for each situation in requirement 1.
3. What amount should be reported as the consolidated retained earnings at the combination date?

| | E 6-8 | **COMPREHENSIVE** Recording a Pooling of Interests (100% Ownership); Preparing the Elimination Entry One Year Later |

On January 1, 19X1, Platter Company obtained 100% of the outstanding common stock of Singer Company by issuing 20,000 shares of its common stock. Each company's equity accounts as of the combination date are as follows:

| | Platter Company | Singer Company |
|---|---|---|
| Common stock, $1 par value................... | $ 100,000 | |
| Common stock, $5 par value................... | | $ 5,000 |
| Additional paid-in capital..................... | 900,000 | 95,000 |
| Retained earnings............................ | 500,000 | 60,000 |
| | $1,500,000 | $160,000 |

For the year ended December 31, 19X1, Singer had net income of $40,000 and declared cash dividends of $10,000. Assume the business combination qualifies for pooling of interests accounting.

**Required:**
1. Prepare the entry to record the business combination.
2. Prepare the primary elimination entry as of the combination date.
3. Prepare the entries for 19X1 required under the equity method of accounting.
4. Update the analysis of the investment account for 19X1, and prepare the primary elimination entry as of December 31, 19X1.

| | E 6-9 | **COMPREHENSIVE** Recording a Pooling of Interests (90% Ownership); Preparing the Elimination Entry One Year Later |

Assume the information provided in Exercise 6-8, except that Platter Company obtained only 90% of the outstanding common stock of Singer Company on January 1, 19X1, by issuing 18,000 shares of its common stock.

**Required:**
The requirements are the same as those in Exercise 6-8.

| | E 6-10 | **Determining Consolidated Retained Earnings and Consolidated Net Income in Year of Combination** |

On June 30, 19X5, Prospero Company merged with Success, Inc., in a business combination properly accounted for as a pooling of interests. Prospero exchanged six of its shares of common stock for each share of Success's outstanding common stock. June 30 was the fiscal year-end for both companies. No intercompany transactions occurred during the year. The balance sheets immediately before the combination are as follows:

|  | Prospero Company Book Value | Success, Inc. | |
| --- | --- | --- | --- |
|  |  | Book Value | Fair Value |
| Current assets . . . . . . . . . . . . . . . . . . . . . | $ 40,000 | $ 30,000 | $ 45,000 |
| Equipment (net) . . . . . . . . . . . . . . . . . . . | 150,000 | 120,000 | 140,000 |
| Land . . . . . . . . . . . . . . . . . . . . . . . . . . . . . | 30,000 | | |
|  | $220,000 | $150,000 | $185,000 |
| Current liabilities . . . . . . . . . . . . . . . . . | $ 35,000 | $ 15,000 | $ 15,000 |
| Notes payable . . . . . . . . . . . . . . . . . . . . . | 40,000 | | |
| Bonds payable . . . . . . . . . . . . . . . . . . . . . | | 100,000 | 100,000 |
| Common stock ($1 par value) . . . . . . . . . | 75,000 | | |
| Common stock ($5 par value) . . . . . . . . . | | 50,000 | |
| Retained earnings . . . . . . . . . . . . . . . . . . | 70,000 | (15,000) | |
|  | $220,000 | $150,000 | |

### Required:

1. What was the Retained Earnings account balance on the combined balance sheet at June 30, 19X5?
   a. $45,000
   b. $55,000
   c. $70,000
   d. $80,000
2. How should the combined net income for the year be computed?
   a. Use only Prospero's income because the combination occurred on the last day of the fiscal year.
   b. Use only Success's income because the combination occurred on the last day of the fiscal year.
   c. Add together both companies' incomes even though the combination occurred on the last day of the fiscal year.
   d. Add together both companies' incomes and subtract the annual amortization of goodwill.

(AICPA adapted)

---

**E 6-11**

## Determining Consolidated Net Income in Acquisition Year

On January 1, 19X7, Preserve, Inc., issued 100,000 additional shares of $10 par value voting common stock in exchange for all of Stuckers Company's voting common stock in a business combination appropriately accounted for as a pooling of interests. Net income for the year ended December 31, 19X7, was $400,000 for Stuckers and $1,300,000 for Preserve, exclusive of any consideration of Stuckers. During 19X7, Preserve paid $900,000 dividends to its stockholders, and Stuckers paid $250,000 dividends to Preserve.

### Required:

Determine the consolidated net income for the year ended December 31, 19X1.

(AICPA adapted)

| E 6-12 |
|---|

## Determining the Effect of Pooling on Parent's Stockholders' Equity

Panda Corporation issued voting common stock with a $90,000 stated value in exchange for all of the outstanding common stock of Soo-Soo Company. The combination was properly accounted for as a pooling of interests.

The stockholders' equity section in Soo-Soo's balance sheet at the combination date was as follows.

| | |
|---|---:|
| Common stock. . . . . . . . . . . . . . . . . . . . . . . . . . . . . . . . . . . . . . . . . . . . . . . . | $ 70,000 |
| Capital contributed in excess of stated value. . . . . . . . . . . . . . . . . . . . | 7,000 |
| Retained earnings . . . . . . . . . . . . . . . . . . . . . . . . . . . . . . . . . . . . . . . . . . . . | 50,000 |
| | $127,000 |

### Required:

What should be the increase in Panda's stockholders' equity at the acquisition date as a result of this business combination?

a. $–0–
b. $37,000
c. $90,000
d. $127,000

(AICPA adapted)

| E 6-13 |
|---|

## Determining Consolidated Stockholders' Equity

On January 1, 19X1, Platt Company issued 200,000 shares of $5 par value common stock in exchange for all of Slatter Company's common stock in a business combination that qualified as a pooling of interests. Immediately before the business combination, Platt's total stockholders' equity was $16,000,000 and of Slatter was $4,000,000. Other data for 19X1 are as follows:

| | Platt Company | Slatter Company |
|---|---:|---:|
| Net income (excluding income recorded under the equity method). . . . . . . . . . . . . . . . . . . | $1,500,000 | $450,000 |
| Dividends declared . . . . . . . . . . . . . . . . . . . . . . . . . | $ 750,000 | $200,000 |

### Required:

What is the consolidated stockholders' equity at December 31, 19X1?

(AICPA adapted)

| E 6-14 |
|---|

## Determining the Effect of Pooling of Interest on Parent's Equity

In a business combination accounted for as a pooling of interests, the combined corporation's retained earnings usually equals the sum of the retained earnings of the individual combining corporations.

**Required:**

Assuming there is no contributed capital other than capital stock at par value on each company's books, which of the following describes a situation in which the combined retained earnings must be increased or decreased?

a. Increased if the par value dollar amount of the outstanding shares of the combined corporation exceeds the total capital stock of the separate combining companies.

b. Increased if the par value dollar amount of the outstanding shares of the combined corporation is less than the total capital stock of the separate combining companies.

c. Decreased if the par value dollar amount of the outstanding shares of the combined corporation exceeds the total capital stock of the separate combining companies.

d. Decreased if the par value dollar amount of the outstanding shares of the combined corporation is less than the total capital stock of the separate combining companies.

(AICPA adapted)

# Problems

**P 6-1***

## Recording a Beginning of Year Pooling of Interests (100% Ownership); Preparing a Consolidation Worksheet at Year-end

On January 1, 19X4, Poca Company issued 4,000 shares of its common stock in exchange for 100% of the outstanding common stock of Shontus Company. The financial statements of each company for the year ended December 31, 19X4, are as follows:

|  | Poca Company | Shontus Company |
|---|---|---|
| **Income Statement (19X4)** | | |
| Sales | $ 800,000 | $100,000 |
| Cost of goods sold | (500,000) | (50,000) |
| Expenses | (270,000) | (44,000) |
| Equity in net income of subsidiary | 6,000 | |
| Net Income | $ 36,000 | $ 6,000 |
| **Balance Sheet (as of December 31, 19X4)** | | |
| Cash | $ 60,000 | $ 10,000 |
| Accounts receivable, net | 90,000 | 20,000 |
| Inventory | 150,000 | 60,000 |
| Investment in subsidiary | 133,000 | |
| Fixed assets, net | 567,000 | 110,000 |
|  | $1,000,000 | $200,000 |

(continued)

*The financial statement information presented for problems accompanied by asterisks is also provided on Model 6 (filename: Model6) of the software file disk that is available for use with the text, enabling the problem to be worked on the computer.

|  | Poca Company | Shontus Company |
|---|---|---|
| Accounts payable and accruals............... | $ 76,000 | $ 17,000 |
| Long-term debt........................... | 300,000 | 50,000 |
| Common stock, $10 par value............... | 100,000 | |
| Common stock, $1 par value................ | | 20,000 |
| Additional paid-in capital................... | 400,000 | 80,000 |
| Retained earnings ........................ | 124,000 | 33,000 |
| | $1,000,000 | $200,000 |
| Dividends declared in 19X4................. | $10,000 | $1,000 |

Assume the business combination qualifies for pooling of interests accounting.

**Required:**
1. Prepare an expanded and updated analysis of the investment account for 19X4, using the equity method of accounting.
2. Determine the entry made on January 1, 19X4, to record the business combination.
3. Prepare the primary elimination entry at December 31, 19X4.
4. Prepare a consolidating statement worksheet at December 31, 19X4.
5. Prepare a formal consolidated statement of retained earnings for 19X4.

| P 6-2* | ## Recording a Year-end Pooling of Interests (100% Ownership); Preparing a Consolidation Worksheet |
|---|---|

On December 31, 19X2, Patter Company issued 1,000 shares of its common stock in exchange for 100% of the outstanding common stock of Sprinkles Company. The financial statements of each company for the year ended December 31, 19X2, *before the business combination,* are as follows:

|  | Patter Company | Sprinkles Company |
|---|---|---|
| **Income Statement (19X2)** | | |
| Sales..................................... | $400,000 | $140,000 |
| Cost of goods sold ....................... | (200,000) | (70,000) |
| Expenses................................ | (150,000) | (40,000) |
| Net Income ............................. | $ 50,000 | $ 30,000 |
| **Balance Sheet (as of December 31, 19X2)** | | |
| Cash..................................... | $ 50,000 | $ 33,000 |
| Accounts receivable, net.................. | 60,000 | 20,000 |
| Inventory................................ | 80,000 | 27,000 |
| Fixed assets, net......................... | 610,000 | 120,000 |
| | $800,000 | $200,000 |
| Accounts payable and accruals............. | $ 90,000 | $ 25,000 |
| Long-term debt.......................... | 260,000 | 15,000 |

| | Patter Company | Sprinkles Company |
|---|---|---|
| Common stock, $10 par value | 200,000 | |
| Common stock, $2 par value | | 100,000 |
| Additional paid-in capital | 130,000 | |
| Retained earnings | 120,000 | 60,000 |
| | $800,000 | $200,000 |
| Dividends declared in 19X2 | $20,000 | $10,000 |

Assume that the business combination qualifies for pooling of interests treatment.

### Required:

1. Prepare the entry to record the business combination.
2. Prepare the entries that would be recorded under the equity method of accounting for 19X2.
3. Prepare and update the analysis of the investment account through December 31, 19X2.
4. Prepare the primary elimination entry at December 31, 19X2.
5. Adjust the parent company's financial statements as shown above to reflect the equity method, and then prepare a consolidating statement worksheet at December 31, 19X2.
6. Prepare a formal consolidated statement of retained earnings for 19X2.

---

**P 6-3\***

### Recording a Year-end Pooling of Interests (90% Ownership); Preparing a Consolidation Worksheet

Assume the information provided in Problem 6-2, except that Patter Company issued 900 shares of its common stock in exchange for 90% of the outstanding common stock of Sprinkles Company on December 31, 19X2.

### Required:

The requirements are the same as for Problem 6-2.

---

**P 6-4\***

### COMPREHENSIVE   Recording a Mid-year Pooling of Interests (100% Ownership—Dissenting Shareholders Bought Out for Cash); Direct Costs Incurred; Preparing a Consolidation Worksheet at Year-end.

On September 30, 19X2, Pace Company issued 270,000 shares of its common stock to holders of 18,000 shares of Strider Company common stock and also gave $140,000 cash to dissenting holders of 2,000 shares of Strider common stock. Direct costs incurred in connection with the business combination were $20,000. An additional $60,000 cost was incurred in registering the common stock issued with the SEC. Each company's financial statements for the year ended December 31, 19X2, are as follows:

| | Pace Company | Strider Company |
|---|---|---|
| **Income Statement (19X2)** | | |
| Sales. . . . . . . . . . . . . . . . . . . . . . . . . . . . . . . . . . . . . . | $9,000,000 | $ 900,000 |
| Cost of goods sold . . . . . . . . . . . . . . . . . . . . . . . . . | (5,000,000) | (400,000) |
| Marketing expenses . . . . . . . . . . . . . . . . . . . . . . . | (2,500,000) | (300,000) |
| Net Income. . . . . . . . . . . . . . . . . . . . . . . . . . . . | $1,500,000 | $ 200,000 |
| **Balance Sheet (as of December 31, 19X2)** | | |
| Cash . . . . . . . . . . . . . . . . . . . . . . . . . . . . . . . . . . . . | $ 410,000 | $100,000 |
| Accounts receivable, net. . . . . . . . . . . . . . . . . . . . | 900,000 | 200,000 |
| Inventory. . . . . . . . . . . . . . . . . . . . . . . . . . . . . . . . | 2,000,000 | 300,000 |
| Investment in subsidiary . . . . . . . . . . . . . . . . . . . | 110,000 | |
| Fixed assets, net. . . . . . . . . . . . . . . . . . . . . . . . . . | 3,500,000 | 1,400,000 |
| Deferred charges . . . . . . . . . . . . . . . . . . . . . . . . . | 80,000 | |
| | $7,000,000 | $2,000,000 |
| Accounts payable and accruals. . . . . . . . . . . . . . | $1,800,000 | $ 280,000 |
| Long-term debt. . . . . . . . . . . . . . . . . . . . . . . . . . . | 2,000,000 | 800,000 |
| Common stock, $2 par value . . . . . . . . . . . . . . . . | 700,000 | |
| Common stock, $5 par value . . . . . . . . . . . . . . . . | | 100,000 |
| Additional paid-in capital. . . . . . . . . . . . . . . . . . . | 800,000 | 340,000 |
| Retained earnings . . . . . . . . . . . . . . . . . . . . . . . . | 1,700,000 | 480,000 |
| | $7,000,000 | $2,000,000 |
| Dividends declared and paid in 19X2. . . . . . . . . . | $800,000 | $120,000 |

### Additional Information:

1. Strider's income was earned evenly throughout the year.
2. Strider declared and paid dividends of $30,000 each quarter.
3. The $80,000 of out-of-pocket costs were paid and charged to a Deferred Charges suspense account.
4. No entry has been made to record the combination (which qualifies as a pooling of interests) other than for the amount paid to the dissenting shareholders. (The parent desires to use the equity method.)

### Required:

1. Prepare the entry to record the business combination and any necessary year-end adjusting entries.
2. Prepare the primary elimination entry at December 31, 19X2. (Hint: Prepare an updated conceptual analysis of the investment account.)
3. Prepare a consolidating statement worksheet at December 31, 19X2.
4. Prepare a formal consolidated statement of retained earnings for 19X2.

---

| P 6-5* |
|---|

### COMPREHENSIVE   Recording a Mid-year Pooling of Interests (90% Ownership); Direct Costs Incurred; Preparing a Consolidation Worksheet at Year-end

Assume the information provided in Problem 6-4, except that Pace Company issued 270,000 shares of its common stock for 90% of the outstanding common stock of Strider Company. Pace did not acquire the shares of the dissenting share-holders. (Adjust the parent's financial statements for (a) the $140,000 that was not paid to the dissenting shareholders, and (b) the $30,000 of dividends received from the subsidiary in the last quarter that instead would have been paid to the minority interests.)

### Required:
The requirements are the same as those for Problem 6-4.

---

**P 6-6\***

### COMPREHENSIVE  Recording a Mid-year Pooling of Interests (100% Ownership); Analytical Development of Key Amounts; Preparing a Consolidation Worksheet at Year-end.

On September 30, 19X4, Pana Company obtained a 100% interest in Sonic Company through an exchange of its common stock for Sonic common stock on a 1-for-4 basis. Pana's common stock was selling on the market for $8 per share at the time, and the investment was recorded on this basis using the following journal entry:

| | | |
|---|---|---|
| Investment in Sonic | 80,000 | |
| Common Stock | | 50,000 |
| Additional Paid-in Capital | | 30,000 |

The transaction qualified for pooling of interests treatment.

No market price was available for Sonic's common stock when Pana acquired it. Its book value was $1.60 per share at the combination date. Pana's board of directors justified the premium paid for the Sonic stock on the grounds that the fixed assets and inventory were undervalued.

Each company's financial statements for the year ended December 31, 19X4, are as follows:

| | Pana Company | Sonic Company |
|---|---|---|
| **Income Statement (19X4)** | | |
| Sales | $450,000 | $200,000 |
| Cost of goods sold | (250,000) | (110,000) |
| Expenses | (130,000) | (58,000) |
| Net Income | $ 70,000 | $ 32,000 |
| **Balance Sheet (as of December 31, 19X4)** | | |
| Cash | $ 50,000 | $ 12,000 |
| Accounts receivable, net | 110,000 | 68,000 |
| Inventory | 177,000 | 22,000 |
| Investment in subsidiary | 80,000 | |
| Fixed assets, net | 318,000 | 180,000 |
| | $735,000 | $282,000 |
| Accounts payable and accruals | $117,000 | $ 98,000 |

*(continued)*

| | Pana Company | Sonic Company |
|---|---|---|
| Long-term debt. . . . . . . . . . . . . . . . . . . . . . . . . . . | 140,000 | 106,000 |
| Common stock, $5 par value . . . . . . . . . . . . . . . | 200,000 | |
| Common stock, $1 par value . . . . . . . . . . . . . . . | | 40,000 |
| Additional paid-in capital . . . . . . . . . . . . . . . . . | 160,000 | |
| Retained earnings . . . . . . . . . . . . . . . . . . . . . . . | 118,000 | 38,000 |
| | $735,000 | $282,000 |
| Dividends declared in 19X4 . . . . . . . . . . . . . . . . | $55,000 | $ –0– |

### Required:

1. Prepare the entry that should have been made to record the combination as a pooling of interests. Then make the appropriate correcting entry.
2. Prepare the entries resulting from the application of the equity method of accounting through December 31, 19X4.
3. Prepare an expanded analysis of the investment account, and update it through December 31, 19X4.
4. Prepare the primary elimination entry at December 31, 19X4.
5. Prepare a consolidating statement worksheet for 19X4 (after adjusting the financial statements for entries in requirements 1 and 2).
6. Prepare a formal consolidated statement of retained earnings for 19X4.

(AICPA adapted)

## Problems Comparing the Pooling of Interests Method with Purchase Method

### Calculation of Consolidated Net Income: Pooling of Interests Method versus Purchase Method

Pomglomerates Company acquired several businesses during 19X1. Information relating to each business is as follows:

| Company | Combination Date | Ownership Percentage | Net Income (Loss) for 19X1 |
|---|---|---|---|
| Able Company . . . . . . . . . . . . | 1/1/X1 | 100 | $100,000 |
| Baker Company . . . . . . . . . . . . | 4/1/X1 | 90 | 200,000 |
| Charley Company . . . . . . . . . | 7/1/X1 | 100 | 60,000 |
| Delta Company. . . . . . . . . . . . | 11/1/X1 | 95 | 120,000 |
| Echo Company. . . . . . . . . . . . | 12/31/X1 | 90 | (50,000) |

Assume all earnings and losses occurred evenly throughout the year. Assume Pomglomerates had net income of $500,000 from its own separate operations, exclusive of earnings or losses recorded under the equity method of accounting.

### Required:

1. Determine the amount of consolidated net income for 19X1, assuming all business combinations qualified for pooling of interests accounting.

2. Determine the amount of consolidated net income for 19X1, assuming none of the business combinations qualified for pooling of interests accounting. Assume Pomglomerates amortized $40,000 cost in excess of book value, which is not reflected in the $500,000 amount given above.

## P 6-8    COMPREHENSIVE (Chapters 3, 4, and 6)    Comparing the Purchase Method with the Pooling of Interests Method: Preparing Consolidated Financial Statements

Sparrow Company merged into Plover Company on June 30, 19X3, and Sparrow ceased to exist. Both companies report on a calendar year-end basis.

### Additional Information:

As of the date of the merger:

1. The fair value of each corporation's assets and liabilities on June 30, 19X3, was as follows:

|  | Plover Company | Sparrow Company |
| --- | --- | --- |
| Current assets | $ 4,900,000 | $ 3,400,000 |
| Land | 3,000,000 | 1,000,000 |
| Buildings and equipment | 19,000,000 | 13,000,000 |
| Patents | 700,000 | 400,000 |
| Total Assets | $27,600,000 | $17,800,000 |
| Liabilities | (2,500,000) | (2,100,000) |
| Net Assets | $25,100,000 | $15,700,000 |

2. Plover has charged $70,000 of direct out-of-pocket costs relating to the merger and $30,000 of internally generated general expenses of the acquisitions department to the Prepaid Expenses account (part of current assets) pending the recording of the combination.
3. Revaluing Plover's and Sparrow's assets to their current values results in additional amortization and depreciation of $240,000 and $80,000 for the six months ended December 31, 19X3.
4. Dividends declared and paid for 19X3 were:

|  | Plover Company | Sparrow Company |
| --- | --- | --- |
| First six months | $800,000 | $400,000 |
| Last six months | 900,000 | |

The balance sheets immediately before the merger date and net income data for all of 19X3 are as follows:

|  | Plover Company | Sparrow Company |
|---|---|---|
| **Balance Sheet (as of June 30, 19X3)** | | |
| Current assets . . . . . . . . . . . . . . . . . . . . . . . . . . . . | $ 4,200,000 | $ 3,000,000 |
| Land . . . . . . . . . . . . . . . . . . . . . . . . . . . . . . . . . . | 2,000,000 | 1,000,000 |
| Building and equipment . . . . . . . . . . . . . . . . . . . . | 20,500,000 | 12,300,000 |
| Accumulated depreciation . . . . . . . . . . . . . . . . . . | (4,000,000) | (2,000,000) |
| Patents . . . . . . . . . . . . . . . . . . . . . . . . . . . . . . . . | 600,000 | 200,000 |
|  | $23,300,000 | $14,500,000 |
|  | | |
| Liabilities . . . . . . . . . . . . . . . . . . . . . . . . . . . . . . | $ 2,500,000 | $ 2,000,000 |
| Common stock, $10 par value . . . . . . . . . . . . . . . . | 12,000,000 | — |
| Common stock, $5 par value . . . . . . . . . . . . . . . . . | — | 3,800,000 |
| Paid-in capital in excess of par value . . . . . . . . . . | 4,200,000 | 3,200,000 |
| Retained earnings . . . . . . . . . . . . . . . . . . . . . . . . | 6,000,000 | 5,500,000 |
|  | $24,700,000 | $14,500,000 |
| Less treasury stock, at cost 100,000 shares . . . . . | (1,400,000) | — |
|  | $23,300,000 | $14,500,000 |
|  | | |
| **Net Income** | | |
| January 1, 19X3 to June 30, 19X3 . . . . . . . . . . . . | $2,200,000 | $1,500,000 |
| July 1, 19X3 to December 31, 19X3 | | |
|    (excluding amounts that would be | | |
|    recorded as a result of the merger) . . . . . . . . . . | 2,400,000 | 1,800,000 |
|  | $4,600,000 | $3,300,000 |

## Required:

Do the following for each of the independent situations given below: (a) prepare a combined balance sheet as of June 30, 19X3; (b) determine the combined net income to be reported for 19X3 (12 months); and (c) prepare a formal combined statement of retained earnings for 19X3 (12 months).

1. Plover Company exchanged 400,000 shares of previously unissued common stock and 100,000 shares of treasury stock for all the assets and liabilities (which were assumed) of Sparrow Company. All the conditions for pooling of interests accounting were met.
2. Plover purchased the assets and assumed Sparrow's liabilities of Sparrow by paying $3,100,000 cash and issuing debentures of $16,900,000 at face value.

(AICPA adapted)

# ADVANCED LEVEL ASSIGNMENT MATERIAL

# Technical Research Questions

1. Immediately after a business combination, a third party buys all or a portion of the common stock issued to effect the combination. Would such an arrangement disqualify the use of the pooling of interests method?

2. Would the accounting for a business combination be affected if the consummation is contingent upon the purchase by a third party or parties of all or part of the common stock issued in the combination?

3. Could the common stock issued in a business combination to be accounted for as a pooling of interests be designated as a class of stock different from the majority class (for example, Class A if the majority class has no designation)?

4. A company issues some maximum number of shares to stockholders of the target company under an agreement that part of the shares are to be returned if future earnings are below a certain amount or the future market price of the stock is above a stipulated price. Would this invalidate pooling of interests treatment?

5. Would the granting of an employment contract or a deferred compensation plan by the combined enterprise to former stockholders of the combining company invalidate pooling of interests treatment?

---

## AP 6-1

## Case Study from Actual Practice Pooling of Interests: A Question of Intent

> Case 10 from *The Trueblood Professors' Seminar* The Touche Ross Foundation and American Accounting Association, Copyright © 1988, reprinted by special permission.

Your client is Mega, Inc., a New York Stock Exchange company that has acquired several profitable businesses in recent years. It has subsidiaries in lines such as home computers, seismographic operations, agricultural chemicals, and solar energy. Its earnings have shown steady growth, and the stock market has valued the company with a high price-earnings ratio.

One month ago, you and Mega's treasurer discussed the proposed acquisition of Sellum, Inc., a southwestern real estate brokerage operation with subsidiaries that own and operate apartment houses. Because of the region's depressed real estate market and flat earnings, the stock of Sellum was trading at less than book value. The acquisition was to be made by a straightforward exchange of common stock for common stock using market prices. After reviewing the criteria for business combinations, the treasurer and you agreed that the accounting would follow the pooling-of-interests method.

But now the treasurer has suggested a complication. He tells you, "It looks like the deal for Sellum will go through. As I see it, if we intend to sell off some of the apartment house subsidiaries, or any of our other assets, we have to use the purchase method of accounting. Then we'll have a minimum of $20,000,000 negative goodwill to take into income over the next three years. We can discuss whether three is the right number of years later, but I just wanted to check and be sure that purchase accounting is OK before we close the deal." You say, "Yes, that's what the accounting standards say, provided it's a significant part of the assets and not a disposal in the ordinary course of business." The treasurer responds, "That's great; you can tell us later what is significant and that's the amount we intend to sell."

Your hesitations center around the thought that Mega may be able to "manipulate" $20,000,000 or more into its future earnings stream by expressing an intention to sell off some properties. Six months earlier you were confronted with a similar situation. Another client had acquired a ladies' apparel manufacturing complex in a pooling-of-interests transaction with no intention (represented in writing) of selling off any assets. But 16 months after the acquisition, it had sold off a significant, unprofitable manufacturing subsidiary.

**Required:**

1. Discuss how the auditor can determine a client's "intent."
2. Consider the form versus substance of a pooling-of-interests versus purchase transaction.
3. Was the right answer given to Mega?
4. What should you tell the treasurer is a "significant part of the assets"?
5. If the purchase method of accounting is followed, what should be done if Mega does not sell off a significant amount of assets?

---

**AP 6-2**

## Case Study from Actual Practice
## Pooling of Interests: A Question of Substance

Plotter Company recently issued common stock in exchange for all of the assets of Sleeper Company in a transaction structured to qualify as a pooling of interests. Sleeper has been in various stages of the timber business since the company's inception 60 years ago. Sleeper had approximately 100 shareholders at the combination date. Many years ago, its sawmills had been closed. Since that time, its only revenues have been contract sales of timber. In recent years, a lack of mature trees has resulted in significantly reduced cutting operations, and income from operations had been nominal. Virtually all of its forest land holdings are now in a regrowth stage. The fair value of the common stock issued by Plotter is $25,000,000. The book value of Sleeper's assets is $3,000,000. The current value of Sleeper's land holdings is $25,000,000. The common stock issued was treasury stock that was acquired in a block purchase six years ago when the price of the company's stock was at a very depressed level.

**Required:**

Using only the information provided, assess whether the transaction should be recorded as a pooling of interests. Explain your reasoning.

---

**AP 6-3**

## Financial Analysis: Determining Financial Reporting Impact of a Merger under Pooling of Interests versus Purchase Method (Debt Ratios and Returns on Investment)

PDQ Company is contemplating a business combination with Sprint Company on January 1, 19X1. Selected information follows:

1. PDQ will issue 10,000 shares of its $1 par value common stock to Sprint Company in exchange for 100% of Sprint's assets.
2. PDQ will assume all of the liabilities of Sprint.
3. PDQ will account for Sprint's operations as a decentralized division to be evaluated as a profit center.
4. Other financial information:

| | PDQ Company | Sprint Company |
|---|---|---|
| **Book Values** | | |
| Assets ....................................... | $3,000,000 | $1,300,000 |
| Liabilities ................................. | 2,000,000 | 1,000,000 |
| **Current Values** | | |
| Assets ....................................... | 4,000,000 | 1,500,000 |
| Liabilities ................................. | 2,000,000 | 1,000,000 |
| Current market price of common stock ........ | $80 | $35 |
| Common stock shares outstanding ........... | 40,000 | 20,000 |

5. The terms of the combination are being negotiated. Accordingly, it is not known whether all conditions for pooling of interests accounting treatment will be satisified. The expected future annual net income of the acquired business is:

| | |
|---|---|
| Under pooling of interests accounting............................. | $90,000 |
| Under purchase accounting...................................... | 80,000 |

6. For 19X0, PDQ reported $150,000 of net income, all of which was distributed as dividends at the end of 19X0.

## Required:

1. Calculate the issuing company's debt–equity ratio:
   a. Before the combination.
   b. After the combination on a consolidated basis, assuming pooling of interests treatment.
   c. After the combination on a consolidated basis, assuming purchase method treatment.
2. Calculate PDQ's return on equity for 19X0.
3. Calculate the issuing company's expected return on investment for 19X1 assuming the combination qualifies for pooling of interests treatment.
4. Calculate the issuing company's expected return on investment for 19X1 assuming the combination does *not* qualify for pooling of interests treatment.
5. Comment on the impact of each alternative. Which method reflects economic reality?

## ANSWERS TO SELF-STUDY QUESTIONS

| | | | | |
|---|---|---|---|---|
| 1. d | 5. d | 9. d | 13. a. $27,000 | 15. a. d |
| 2. c | 6. b | 10. d | b. –0– | b. a |
| 3. e | 7. c | 11. b | 14. a. –0– | 16. a. c |
| 4. a | 8. a | 12. d | b. $20,000 | b. a |

# II

# CONSOLIDATED FINANCIAL STATEMENTS: SPECIALIZED SUBJECTS

■ ■ ■ ■ ■

# 7

......

# INTERCOMPANY INVENTORY TRANSFERS

*TOPIC OUTLINE*

# CHAPTER OVERVIEW

C ompanies within a consolidated group often have numerous types of intercompany transactions. Because such transactions take place between companies that are separate legal entities (rather than between various divisions and the home office of a single company), several conceptual issues are created. In preparing consolidated financial statements, entries (called *elimination entries*) are made on the consolidation worksheet to undo these transactions. As a result, the consolidated financial statements are presented as though these transactions had never occurred.

## Selection of Module

Some intercompany transactions (discussed later) require minimal effort to eliminate in consolidation. However, intercompany transactions pertaining to inventory transfers, fixed asset transfers, and bond investments require more involved procedures. Three equally acceptable methods can be used to accomplish the desired elimination in consolidation for these more involved transactions. Each of these methods is presented in this textbook as a self-contained, independent module. **Each module is written in such a manner that it may be covered independently of the other two modules.** Furthermore, if more than one module is assigned by your instructor, **the modules may be covered in any order whatsoever. Accordingly, the order in which the modules are presented is arbitrary and completely irrelevant.** The three modules are:

Module 1: The Complete Equity Method: Investment Account Adjustment Procedures

Module 2: The Complete Equity Method: Noninvestment Account Adjustment Procedures

Module 3: The Partial Equity Method

**In most instances, only one of the modules will be assigned, with other modules assigned if time permits.**

The remainder of this chapter covers (1) conceptual issues pertaining to intercompany transactions and (2) the manner of accomplishing eliminations in the consolidating statement worksheets for intercompany inventory transfers. Chapter 8 deals with fixed-asset transfers, and Chapter 9 deals with intercompany bond investments.

# TYPES OF INTERCOMPANY TRANSACTIONS

Intercompany transactions among parent companies and subsidiaries consist of the following types:

1. **Sales of inventory.** Sales of inventory are most common in vertically integrated operations in which a customer–supplier relationship exists. Because the selling and buying entities are legally separate, the transfer prices almost always approximate outside market prices. Consequently, the selling entity usually records a gross profit at the time of sale.

   Inventory sales from a parent to one of its subsidiaries are referred to as **downstream sales.** Inventory sales from a subsidiary to its parent are referred to as **upstream sales.** Inventory sales between subsidiaries of a common parent are referred to as **lateral sales.** Because lateral sales are less frequent than upstream or downstream sales, they are not illustrated. The principles and procedures of eliminating intercompany transactions in lateral sales, however, are the same as those in downstream and upstream sales, which are discussed and illustrated.

2. **Transfers of long-lived assets.** Far less common than inventory transfers are transfers of long-lived assets. This type of transaction most often occurs when one entity has surplus assets or when one entity manufactures assets usable by another. In the latter situation, the consolidated group has widely diverse operations. The procedures to account for intercompany fixed-asset transfers are discussed in Chapter 8.

3. **Leasing of long-lived assets. Sales-type leases** are dealt with using the principles and procedures discussed in Chapter 8. **Operating leases** merely require some offsetting in the income statement, as shown later in this chapter.

4. **Bond investments.** Infrequently, an entity within a consolidated group purchases bonds of another entity within the group. The procedures to account for these intercompany bond holdings in consolidation are discussed in Chapter 9.

5. **Loans.** Subsidiaries often do not have local banking relationships, because treasury functions are usually centralized at the parent's headquarters. This allows the parent to monitor closely the cash positions of its subsidiaries, which obtain needed cash from the parent in the form of **loans.** Practice varies widely as to the charging of interest on loans to subsidiaries.

6. **Services.** A parent may charge its subsidiaries for top management services, including centralized research and development services, central computer services, and legal and advertising expenses.

7. **Dividends.** When a parent uses the equity method to account for its investment in a subsidiary, no elimination entry is necessary because the dividend reduces the Investment account. However, when a parent uses the cost method, the dividend is recorded as dividend income, which must be eliminated in preparing consolidated financial statements, as shown in Appendix A to Chapter 4.

## Using Separate Intercompany Accounts

In practice, intercompany transactions are normally recorded in separate general ledger accounts to make the consolidation process easier. The income statement usually has several intercompany accounts, such as Intercompany Sales, Intercompany Cost of Goods Sold, Intercompany Interest Income, Intercompany Interest Expense, and Intercompany Gain on Long-lived Asset Transfer. For the balance sheet, however, most intercompany transactions can be dealt with using one account, Intercompany Receivable/Payable, the balance of which can be either a debit or a credit.

Before the consolidation process begins, all intercompany accounts that are to have reciprocal balances (both in the income statement and the balance sheet) must be reconciled and adjusted, if necessary, to bring them into agreement. Only by being in agreement will they completely eliminate each other in consolidation.

# CONCEPTUAL ISSUES

Although there are several conceptual issues regarding intercompany transactions, none of them are considered highly controversial, as was the case for goodwill and poolings of interests.

## Conceptual Issue 1: Should Intercompany Transactions Be Eliminated?

If intercompany transactions are not eliminated, the consolidated financial statements include transactions and balances outstanding that are of no value to users of the financial statements. Thus, the criterion of relevance, as discussed in the Financial Accounting Standards Board's *Statement of Financial Accounting Concepts No. 2,* "Qualitative Characteristics of Accounting Information," is not met. Further, management would have virtually unlimited opportunity to influence or manipulate reported sales and earnings, which would violate the criterion of reliability in *SFAC No. 2.*

**Requirements of Professional Pronouncements.** The governing pronouncement in this area is *Accounting Research Bulletin No. 51:*

> In the preparation of consolidated statements, intercompany balances and transactions should be eliminated. This includes intercompany open account balances, security holdings, sales and purchases, interest, dividends, etc. As consolidated statements are based on the assumption that they represent the financial position and operating results of a single business enterprise, such statements should not include gain or loss on transactions among the companies in the group. Accordingly, any

intercompany profit or loss on assets remaining with the group should be eliminated; the concept usually applied for this purpose is gross profit or loss.[1]

To show how the reporting results would include meaningless amounts or how the reported amounts could be manipulated if intercompany transactions and open balances are not eliminated, we use some common types of intercompany transactions as discussion examples.

**Intercompany Loan.**   Assume that on January 1, 19X1, P Company made a $100,000 three-year loan bearing interest at 8% to its subsidiary, S Company. If no elimination entries are made in consolidation at December 31, 19X1 (the assumed reporting year-end), the following amounts would be reported in the consolidated financial statements:

**Income Statement**

| | |
|---|---:|
| Intercompany interest income | $8,000 |
| Intercompany interest expense | (8,000) |

**Balance Sheet**

| | |
|---|---:|
| Intercompany note receivable | $100,000 |
| Intercompany note payable | (100,000) |

Reporting these offsetting amounts clearly serves no useful purpose to users of consolidated financial statements.

**Intercompany Inventory Transfer at Cost.**   Assume that P Company sold inventory costing $40,000 to its wholly owned subsidiary, S Company, in 19X1 for $40,000 (no intercompany mark-up). Assume also that by year-end, S Company had resold all of the inventory for $90,000. If no elimination entry is made in consolidation at December 31, 19X1, the following amounts would be reported in the consolidated income statement:

| | |
|---|---:|
| Sales | $90,000 |
| Cost of goods sold | (40,000) |
| Intercompany sales | $40,000 |
| Intercompany cost of goods sold | (40,000) |
| Gross Profit | $50,000 |

From a consolidated perspective, the only useful reported amounts are the $90,000 of sales to outside third parties and the related consolidated entity's $40,000 cost of goods sold pertaining to that sale. The fact that the inventory had been transferred between companies within the consolidated group prior to the sale to the third party is irrelevant. It

[1]*Accounting Research Bulletin No. 51*, "Consolidated Financial Statements" (New York: American Institute of Certified Public Accountants, 1959), par. 6.

would be misleading to report total sales of $130,000 and total cost of goods sold of $80,000. Clearly, there is double-counting taking place. Note also that if such intercompany sales were not eliminated in consolidation, management would be able to influence the amounts reported for total sales and total cost of goods sold by merely transferring inventory excessively between the entities within the consolidated group.

**Intercompany Inventory Transfer at above Cost.** Assume P Company sold inventory costing $40,000 to its wholly owned subsidiary, S Company, in 19X1 for $70,000 (a $30,000 intercompany mark-up). Also assume that by year-end, S Company had resold all of the inventory for $90,000. If no elimination entry is made in consolidation at December 31, 19X1, the following amounts would be reported in the consolidated income statement:

**Income Statement**

| | |
|---|---|
| Sales | $90,000 |
| Cost of goods sold | (70,000) |
| Intercompany sales | 70,000 |
| Intercompany cost of goods sold | (40,000) |
| Gross Profit | $50,000 |

As in the preceding example, the only useful reported amounts are the $90,000 of sales to outside third parties and the related consolidated entity's $40,000 cost of goods sold pertaining to those sales. To achieve this meaningful reporting result, the two intercompany accounts must be eliminated and a downward adjustment of $30,000 to the Cost of Goods Sold account must be made.

Note that as long as the entire intercompany-acquired inventory is resold in the same period in which the intercompany transfer occurs, the consolidated gross profit is always $50,000—regardless whether the intercompany transfer price is more or less than $70,000.

An even more compelling reason for eliminating intercompany transactions can be seen if the intercompany-acquired inventory is still on hand at year-end. In this case, the following amounts would be reported in the consolidated statements if no elimination entry were made:

**Income Statement**

| | |
|---|---|
| Intercompsany sales | $70,000 |
| Intercompany cost of goods sold | (40,000) |
| Gross Profit | $30,000 |

**Balance Sheet**

| | |
|---|---|
| Inventory | $70,000 |
| Retained earnings | 30,000 |

In this case, management is able to report profits by merely transferring inventory within the consolidated group. This is clearly an artificial profit from a consolidated perspective, and the intercompany profit must be deferred and not recognized until the subsidiary resells the inventory. In accounting parlance, the $30,000 of intercompany gross profit is unrealized, and realization does not occur until sale to a third party.

Thus from a consolidated viewpoint, the sale of inventory among entities within a consolidated group is considered merely the physical movement of inventory from one location to another (similar to the movement of inventory from one division to another division), and a bona fide transaction does not occur. This holds true regardless of the reasonableness of the transfer price. For instance, even though the transfer prices may be equal to the prices the acquiring entity would have paid had it acquired the inventory directly from an unrelated vendor, the transaction must be nullified for consolidated reporting purposes. Only from a separate company perspective are such transactions considered to be bona fide and reportable.

### Conceptual Issue 2: Should Intercompany Gross Profit, Operating Profit, or Profit before Income Taxes Be Eliminated?

As stated in the previously quoted section of *ARB No. 51*, when inventory and fixed assets are transferred from one company to another within a consolidated group, *ARB No. 51* designates the amount of profit to be eliminated in consolidation as the selling entity's gross profit. In selecting gross profit as the amount to be eliminated, other measures of profit—such as operating profit and profit before income taxes—were rejected *to prevent the effect of capitalizing the selling entity's marketing, administrative, and borrowing expenses.* Such expenses are period costs on a separate-company basis, and there is no justification for treating them otherwise on a consolidated basis.

### Conceptual Issue 3: Should Income Taxes Provided on Gross Profit Eliminated in Consolidation Also Be Eliminated?

*ARB No. 51* requires elimination of any income taxes that have been provided on gross profit eliminated in consolidation. For simplicity, however, we assume in our illustrations for Chapters 7–9 that this year-end elimination entry has already been recorded in the general ledger of the parent or the subsidiary. Thus, a separate entry dealing with the tax effects of gross profit deferred in consolidation is not required on the consolidating statement worksheet. Chapter 12 discusses income tax considerations for consolidated entities as a separate topic. That chapter discusses the manner of eliminating income taxes on intercompany transfers and shows how this is accomplished.

## Conceptual Issue 4: Should Intercompany Profit on Downstream Sales to Partially Owned Subsidiaries Be Considered Realized to the Extent of the Minority Interest?

Assume a parent company has downstream inventory sales to its 70%-owned subsidiary and the subsidiary has on hand at year-end $60,000 of intercompany acquired inventory, which cost the parent company $40,000. Thus, total intercompany gross profit is $20,000. There are two schools of thought regarding the amount of gross profit to be deferred in consolidation:

1. **Complete elimination.** Under this approach, all of the $20,000 of intercompany profit is considered unrealized.
2. **Fractional elimination.** By following this approach, $6,000 ($20,000 × 30%) is considered realized due to the 30% minority interest ownership in the subsidiary. Accordingly, only $14,000 would be deferred in consolidation.

**Requirements of *ARB No. 51*.**    In *ARB No. 51*, the American Institute of Certified Public Accountants chose the first alternative, whereby all of the gross profit is eliminated:

> The amount of intercompany profit or loss to be eliminated . . . is not affected by the existence of a minority interest. The complete elimination of the intercompany profit or loss is consistent with the underlying assumption that the consolidated statements represent the financial position and operating results of a single business enterprise.[2]

## Conceptual Issue 5: When a Partially Owned Subsidiary Has Upstream Sales, Should the Intercompany Profit Accruing to the Minority Shareholders Be Deferred in Consolidation?

Assume that an 80%-owned subsidiary has upstream inventory sales to its parent company and the parent has on hand at year-end $15,000 of intercompany-acquired inventory, which cost the subsidiary $10,000. Thus total intercompany gross profit is $5,000, of which $4,000 accrues to the parent company and $1,000 accrues to the minority interest. Again, there are two schools of thought regarding the amount of gross profit to be deferred in consolidation:

1. **Complete elimination.** Under this approach, the entire $5,000 of gross profit is eliminated on the grounds that to do otherwise would be inconsistent with the underlying purpose of consolidated financial statements, which is to report activities as though a single entity

[2]*ARB No. 51*, par. 14.

existed. As a result, consolidated net income and consolidated retained earnings would be reduced $4,000, and the minority interest would be reduced $1,000. (Allocating a portion of the $5,000 gross profit to the minority interest is the theoretically correct procedure.)

2. **Fractional elimination.** Under this approach, only the portion of the gross profit that accrues to the parent is eliminated. The portion of the profit that accrues to the minority interest is not eliminated on the grounds that it has been realized from the viewpoint of the minority interest shareholders. It is irrelevant to whom the subsidiary sells as far as the subsidiary's minority shareholders are concerned. As a result, consolidated net income and consolidated retained earnings would be reduced $4,000. The minority interest would not be reduced $1,000.

**Requirements of *ARB No. 51.*** In *ARB No. 51,* the first alternative, complete elimination, is required. Thus the entire $5,000 would be deferred. However, concerning whether or not the amount to be deferred should be shared, the pronouncement states that

> the elimination of the intercompany profit or loss may be allocated proportionately between the majority and minority interests.[3]

When the minority interest ownership percentage is quite low and the dollar amounts are not significant, it is usually more expedient, in practice, to reduce consolidated net income and consolidated retained earnings by the full amount of the gross profit associated with the ending inventory, rather than to take the additional step of allocating a portion to the minority interest.

# INTERCOMPANY LOANS, MANAGEMENT FEES, AND OPERATING LEASES

## Intercompany Loans

When interest is charged on intercompany loans, the interest income on the parent's books equals the interest expense on the subsidiary's books. The following elimination entry is made on the consolidating statement worksheet:

| | | |
|---|---|---|
| Intercompany Interest Income ............... | xxx | |
|     Intercompany Interest Expense ......... | | xxx |

[3]*ARB No. 51,* par. 14.

When a loan remains unpaid as of the consolidation date, the intercompany loan receivable on the parent's books equals the intercompany loan payable on the subsidiary's books. The following elimination entry is made on the consolidating statement worksheet:

| | | |
|---|---|---|
| Intercompany Loan Payable................... | xxx | |
| Intercompany Loan Receivable.......... | | xxx |

## Intercompany Management Charges

When the parent has charged management fees to the subsidiary, the intercompany management fee income on the parent's books equals the intercompany management fee expense on the subsidiary's books. The following elimination entry is made on the consolidating statement worksheet:

| | | |
|---|---|---|
| Intercompany Management Fee Income ....... | xxx | |
| Intercompany Management Fee Expense............................... | | xxx |

## Intercompany Operating Leases

When an operating lease exists between entities within the consolidated group, the Intercompany Lease Expense account on the lessee's books equals the Intercompany Lease Revenue account on the lessor's book. The following elimination entry is made on the consolidating statement worksheet:

| | | |
|---|---|---|
| Intercompany Lease Revenues ................ | xxx | |
| Intercompany Lease Expense.......... | | xxx |

## Elimination by Rearrangement

Each of the above elimination entries takes place entirely within one of the financial statements. Most companies arrange the individual accounts on the consolidating statement worksheet so that these entries do not have to be made there. It is only necessary to show in parentheses the intercompany accounts of one of the entities in the corresponding section of the worksheet. For example, by putting the subsidiary's intercompany loan payable amount in parentheses on the same line as the parent's intercompany loan receivable in the asset section of the balance sheet, the balances add across to zero in the consolidated column. (The intercompany accounts should agree before the consolidation process.) Elimination by rearrangement reduces the number of required elimination entries. An example of this procedure follows:

| | P Company | S Company | Eliminations Dr. Cr. | Consol- idated |
|---|---|---|---|---|
| Intercompany interest income (expense)...... | 1,000 | (1,000) | | –0– |
| Intercompany receivable (payable) .............. | 10,000 | (10,000) | | –0– |

## INVENTORY TRANSFERS AT COST

When intercompany inventory transfers are made at the selling entity's cost, the only entry needed in consolidation in the year of the transfer is to eliminate the Intercompany Sales account and the Intercompany Cost of Goods Sold account—both of which have the same dollar amount. For example, assume P Company sold inventory costing $50,000 to its 80%-owned subsidiary, S Company, in 19X1 for $50,000. The entry required in consolidation at year-end is as follows:

| | | |
|---|---|---|
| Intercompany Sales............................ | 50,000 | |
| Intercompany Cost of Goods Sold........ | | 50,000 |

The elimination entry is the same regardless of whether: (1) the sale is upstream or downstream; (2) the subsidiary is wholly owned or partially owned; and (3) all, some, or none of the inventory remains on hand at the consolidation date. Note also that the decision whether to use the partial equity method or the complete equity method does not apply—that decision must be made only when an intercompany profit is recorded as a result of the transfer being made at above cost. In practice, intercompany inventory transfers are usually recorded at amounts approximating outside market prices; thus, the selling entity records a profit at the time of sale. This is usually necessary to aid management's review of the operating performance of the individual companies.

## INVENTORY TRANSFERS ABOVE COST: GENERAL METHODOLOGY

When inventory transfers are made at above the selling entity's cost, the most important thing is to determine how much of the inventory remains on hand at the consolidation date. The amount of the mark-up pertaining to this inventory is then calculated. This profit is then deferred until the acquiring entity sells the inventory to a third party customer. A universal elimination entry can be used, regardless of the percentage of inventory that remains unsold. This entry is as follows:

| | | |
|---|---|---|
| Intercompany Sales ........................... | xxx | |
|     Intercompany Cost of Goods Sold ........ | | xxx |
|     Cost of Goods Sold .................... | | xxx |
|     Inventory ............................ | | xxx |

The first two lines of the entry undo the reporting of the intercompany sale and the related cost of that sale. The difference between these two amounts is then analyzed to determine how much of this gross profit pertains to inventory that has been resold versus how much pertains to inventory that remains within the consolidated group, enabling the entry to be completed.

Assume that in 19X1 P Company sells inventory costing $50,000 to its wholly owned subsidiary for $75,000 and $15,000 of the inventory is reported in the subsidiary's balance sheet at December 31, 19X1. Thus the subsidiary has charged to Cost of Goods Sold $60,000 of the $75,000 of inventory acquired from the parent. Accordingly, the financial statements of each company at December 31, 19X1, would appear as follows:

| | P Company | S Company |
|---|---|---|
| **Income Statement** | | |
|   Cost of goods sold......................... | | $(60,000) |
|   Intercompany sales........................ | $75,000 | |
|   Intercompany cost of goods sold........... | (50,000) | |
| **Balance Sheet** | | |
|   Inventory—intercompany acquired ........ | | 15,000 |

Usually a formal analysis, such as the one shown below, is prepared to show how much of the total intercompany gross profit is associated with the remaining inventory and the inventory that has been sold.

| | Total (Given) | Resold | On Hand |
|---|---|---|---|
| Intercompany sales.................. | $75,000 | $60,000 | $15,000 |
| Intercompany cost of goods sold.... | (50,000) | (40,000) | (10,000) |
|     Gross Profit.................. | $25,000 | $20,000 | $ 5,000 |

The first line of the analysis, intercompany sales, shows what portion of the year's total intercompany purchases have been charged to Cost of Goods Sold by the subsidiary and what portion remains on hand at year-end. This separation is made by determining the amount of intercompany inventory purchases on hand at year-end ($15,000) and then subtracting this amount from the total intercompany sales for the year ($75,000) to arrive at the amount charged to cost of goods sold ($60,000).

The second line of the analysis, intercompany cost of goods sold, shows what amount would have been charged to Cost of Goods Sold and at what amount the ending inventory would be stated had the intercompany transfer been at the selling entity's cost. The percentage of inventory resold and the percentage of inventory still on hand (determined using the amounts on the first line) are applied to the total intercompany cost of goods sold ($50,000) to determine the amounts in the resold and on hand columns.

Gross profit, the difference between the first and second lines, is the amount by which cost of goods sold and ending inventory are overstated, as to the consolidated entity, because the inventory transfer was made above cost. From the preceding analysis, the following elimination entry would be prepared:

**WORKSHEET ENTRY ONLY**

| | | |
|---|---|---|
| Intercompany Sales............................. | 75,000 | |
| Intercompany Cost of Goods Sold........ | | 50,000 |
| Cost of Goods Sold ...................... | | 20,000 |
| Inventory ................................ | | 5,000 |

**The Deferral of Profit Effect of This Entry.**   This entry accomplishes substantially more than (1) eliminating the two intercompany accounts and (2) adjusting the Cost of Goods Sold account downward so as to report the correct cost of goods sold (that is, without the intercompany mark-up). The key point is that the effect of the entry is to defer the recognition of $5,000 of unrealized intercompany profit (the debit posting to the income statement is $5,000 more than the sum of the two credit postings to the income statement). As a result, consolidated net income and consolidated retained earnings are both $5,000 lower than would be reported otherwise.

This universal entry is the same in each of the three modules that follow. Additional entries are necessary in certain of the modules, and these entries are discussed in those particular modules. This example, involving $75,000 of intercompany sales, is used in each of the three modules.

---

**MODULE 1    The Complete Equity Method: Investment Account Adjustment Procedures**

## INVENTORY TRANSFERS ABOVE COST: MECHANICAL PROCEDURES TO DEFER UNREALIZED PROFIT

**Module Overview.**   In a complete application of the equity method of accounting in situations involving unrealized intercompany profit, certain adjustments are made so that the parent's net income and retained earnings are the same as consolidated net income and consolidated retained earnings, respectively. Consequently, the highly desirable built-in checking feature characteristic of the equity method, discussed in Chapters 4 and 5, is retained. In this module, these adjustments are made in applying the equity method of accounting to the subsidiary's reported net income.

## Harmony of *APB Opinion No. 18* and *ARB No. 51*

In applying the equity method of accounting in the parent's financial statements, it should be noted that the requirements of *APB Opinion No. 18,* "The Equity Method of Accounting for Investments in Common Stock," are in harmony with the requirements of *ARB No. 51* concerning the preparation of consolidated financial statements. That is, both pronouncements require all unrealized intercompany profit to be deferred until realized in a transaction with a third party—regardless of the existence of a minority interest. *Accounting Interpretation No. 1* to *APB Opinion No. 18* states:

> When an investor controls an investee through majority voting interest and enters into a transaction with an investee which is not on an "arm's length" basis,[4] none of the intercompany profit or loss from the transaction should be recognized in income by the investor until it has been realized through transactions with third parties.[5]

## DOWNSTREAM TRANSFERS ABOVE COST
## Deferring Profit on Downstream Transfers

In this module, we use the example discussed on pages 339–40 in which the parent sold inventory costing $50,000 to its wholly owned subsidiary for $75,000 in 19X1 and $15,000 of the $75,000 of inventory is reported in the subsidiary's balance sheet at December 31, 19X1. In that example, we demonstrated that of the $25,000 total intercompany profit ($75,000 − $50,000), $20,000 is associated with inventory the subsidiary has resold and $5,000 is associated with inventory remaining on hand at year-end.

To defer the recognition of the $5,000 of unrealized intercompany profit at December 31, 19X1, the parent would make the following adjustment to its share of the subsidiary's reported net income before applying the equity method of accounting:

---

[4]That is, a transaction between completely independent parties. (All transactions with controlled companies are considered to be on less than an "arms length" basis.)

[5]*Accounting Interpretation No. 1* to *APB Opinion No. 18* (New York: American Institute of Certified Public Accountants, 1971), par. 4.

## MODULE 1    The Complete Equity Method: Investment Account Adjustment Procedures *(continued)*

| | |
|---|---:|
| Subsidiary's reported net income for 19X1 . . . . . . . . . . . . . . . . . | $15,000 |
| Parent's ownership percentage . . . . . . . . . . . . . . . . . . . . . . . . . . . | 100% |
| Parent's share of subsidiary's reported net income . . . . . . . . | $15,000 |
| Less—Unrealized intercompany profit at | |
|    December 31, 19X1 . . . . . . . . . . . . . . . . . . . . . . . . . . . . . . . . . . | (5,000) |
| Parent's share of subsidiary's reported net income, | |
|    as adjusted for unrealized profit . . . . . . . . . . . . . . . . . . . . . . . | $10,000 |

The following general ledger entry is then made:

| | | |
|---|---:|---:|
| Investment in Subsidiary . . . . . . . . . . . . . . . . . . . . . | 10,000 | |
|    Equity in Net Income of Subsidiary . . . . . | | 10,000 |
|    To record the equity in the subsidiary's | | |
|    net income. | | |

The rationale for treating the unrealized intercompany profit in this manner is as follows:

1. The subsidiary's net assets are overstated by $5,000 based on the parent's cost of the inventory. By debiting the Investment in Subsidiary account for $10,000 instead of $15,000, the carrying value of the investment is maintained at amounts based on the parent's historical cost. (This may be understood more readily by assuming that at the time this remaining inventory was shipped to the subsidiary, the subsidiary's only asset was $15,000 cash and it had no liabilities. If it paid the parent $15,000 cash upon taking delivery of the inventory, then it would report $15,000 of inventory, and its net assets of $15,000 would be overstated by $5,000 from the parent's perspective.)

2. By crediting the Equity in Net Income of Subsidiary account for $10,000 instead of $15,000, the deferral of $5,000 of unrealized profit is conveniently handled as part of the routine entry applying the equity method of accounting. Technically, the Intercompany Sales account on the parent's books is overstated by $5,000; however, it would be more inconvenient to debit this account for $5,000, as this would result in an oddball type of entry whereby the Investment in Subsidiary account is debited for $10,000, the Intercompany Sales account is debited for $5,000, and the Equity in Net Income of Subsidiary account is credited for $15,000.

## ILLUSTRATION    Preparing Consolidated Financial Statements

- The Complete Equity Method—Investment Account Adjustment Procedures
- Downstream Transfers above Cost

MODULE 1    **The Complete Equity Method: Investment Account Adjustment Procedures** (continued)

In preparing consolidated financial statements at December 31, 19X1, the following universal intercompany transaction elimination entry would be made on the worksheet:

**WORKSHEET ENTRY ONLY**

| | | |
|---|---|---|
| Intercompany Sales | 75,000 | |
| Intercompany Cost of Goods Sold | | 50,000 |
| Cost of Goods Sold (to third parties) | | 20,000 |
| Inventory | | 5,000 |
| To eliminate current-year intercompany transactions. | | |

Illustration 7-1 shows a consolidating statement worksheet for the year ended December 31, 19X1. The P Company and S Company financial statement amounts presented in worksheet Illustration 4-5, along with the primary, secondary, and accumulated depreciation elimination entries used in that illustration, are used in Illustration 7-1. (Of course, we had to modify the primary elimination entry by showing $5,000 less income recorded under the equity method of accounting.) The P Company and S Company columns were modified to reflect the $75,000 of downstream intercompany inventory transactions. For convenience, all of the elimination entries used in Illustration 7-1 are shown below in sequence:

1. The primary elimination entry:

**WORKSHEET ENTRY ONLY**

| | | |
|---|---|---|
| Common Stock | 40,000 | |
| Retained Earnings (beginning of year) | 20,000 | |
| Equity in Net Income of Subsidiary ($15,000 − $5,000) | 10,000 | |
| Land | 12,000 | |
| Equipment | 6,000 | |
| Goodwill | 9,000 | |
| Dividends Declared | | 5,000 |
| Accumulated Depreciation | | 1,000 |
| Investment in Subsidiary ($96,000 − $5,000) | | 91,000 |

2. The secondary elimination entry:

**WORKSHEET ENTRY ONLY**

| | | |
|---|---|---|
| Cost of Goods Sold (to third parties) | 4,000 | |
| Equity in Net Income of Subsidiary | | 4,000 |

3. The accumulated depreciation elimination entry:

**WORKSHEET ENTRY ONLY**

| | | |
|---|---|---|
| Accumulated Depreciation | 50,000 | |
| Buildings and Equipment | | 50,000 |

■ **ILLUSTRATION 7-1**

**The Complete Equity Method: Investment Account Adjustment Procedures—Downstream Transfers above Cost**

| P COMPANY AND SUBSIDIARY (S COMPANY) Consolidating Statement Worksheet for the Year Ended December 31, 19X1 | | | | | |
|---|---|---|---|---|---|
| | P Company | S Company | Eliminations Dr. | Eliminations Cr. | Consoli-dated |
| **Income Statement** | | | | | |
| Sales | 525,000 | 225,000 | | | 750,000 |
| Cost of goods sold | (310,000) | (110,000) | 4,000(2) | 20,000(4) | (404,000) |
| Expenses | (190,000) | (100,000) | | | (290,000) |
| Intercompany Accounts: | | | | | |
| Equity in net income of subsidiary | 6,000[a] | | 10,000(1) | 4,000(2) | –0– |
| Sales | 75,000 | | 75,000(4) | | –0– |
| Cost of goods sold | (50,000) | | | 50,000(4) | –0– |
| Net Income | 56,000 | 15,000 | 89,000 | 74,000 | 56,000 |
| **Statement of Retained Earnings** | | | | | |
| Balances, January 1, 19X1 | 100,000 | 20,000 | 20,000(1) | | 100,000 |
| +Net income | 56,000 | 15,000 | 89,000 | 74,000 | 56,000 |
| −Dividends declared | (45,000) | (5,000) | | 5,000(1) | (45,000) |
| Balances, December 31, 19X1 | 111,000 | 30,000 | 109,000 | 79,000 | 111,000 |
| **Balance Sheet** | | | | | |
| Cash | 25,000 | 11,000 | | | 36,000 |
| Accounts receivable, net | 75,000 | 37,000 | | | 112,000 |
| Inventory: | | | | | |
| From vendors | 110,000 | 40,000 | | | 150,000 |
| Intercompany | | 15,000 | | 5,000(4) | 10,000 |
| Investment in S Company | 91,000 | | | 91,000(1) | –0– |
| Land | 220,000 | 30,000 | 12,000(1) | | 262,000 |
| Buildings and equipment | 500,000 | 200,000 | 6,000(1) | 50,000(3) | 656,000 |
| Accumulated depreciation | (320,000) | (63,000) | 50,000(3) | 1,000(1) | (334,000) |
| Goodwill | | | 9,000(1) | | 9,000 |
| Total Assets | 701,000 | 270,000 | 77,000 | 147,000 | 901,000 |
| Liabilities | 290,000 | 200,000 | | | 490,000 |
| Common stock | 300,000 | 40,000 | 40,000(1) | | 300,000 |
| Retained earnings | 111,000 | 30,000 | 109,000 | 79,000 | 111,000 |
| Total Liabilities and Equity | 701,000 | 270,000 | 149,000 | 79,000 | 901,000 |
| Proof of debit and credit postings | | | 226,000 | 226,000 | |

Explanation of entries:
(1) The primary elimination entry.        (3) The accumulated depreciation elimination entry.
(2) The secondary elimination entry.      (4) The current-year intercompany transactions elimination entry.

[a]Comprised of $15,000 of subsidiary's reported net income, net of $5,000 of unrealized intercompany profit and $4,000 of amortization of cost in excess of book value.

---

**MODULE 1    The Complete Equity Method: Investment Account Adjustment Procedures** (continued)

---

4. The current-year intercompany transactions elimination entry:

| | | |
|---|---|---|
| Intercompany Sales | 75,000 | |
| Intercompany Cost of Goods Sold | | 50,000 |
| Cost of Goods Sold (to third parties) | | 20,000 |
| Inventory | | 5,000 |

## Subsequent-year Treatment of Unsold Inventory

This section explains the treatment of the $5,000 of unrealized intercompany profit at December 31, 19X1, in preparing consolidated financial statements subsequent to that date. If this intercompany-acquired inventory is still on hand at December 31, 19X2, it will be necessary in consolidation to make a credit to the Inventory account for $5,000 (so as to bring the subsidiary's reported carrying value of $15,000 down to the parent's cost of $10,000, just as was done in 19X1). In the year in which the inventory is resold by the subsidiary, it will be necessary in consolidation to make a credit to the Cost of Goods Sold account (so as to bring the subsidiary's reported cost of goods sold of $15,000 for this inventory down to the parent's cost of $10,000). By making a slight modification to the conceptual analysis of the investment account, this $5,000 of unrealized intercompany profit at December 31, 19X1, can be kept track of easily so that the appropriate credit is made in subsequent years. Specifically, an additional column is added to the book value element (labeled unrealized profit). This allows the prior years retained earnings column (after reclassification for current year activity at year-end) to always equal the subsidiary's reported retained earnings. Amounts are added to and subtracted from this unrealized profit column by making reclassifications at year-end (on the line below the line used for the source of the primary elimination entry).

Illustration 7-2 shows how the $5,000 of unrealized intercompany profit at December 31, 19X1, is accounted for in the modified conceptual analysis of the investment account. We assume this inventory remains unsold at December 31, 19X2 (one year later), but that it is resold in 19X3. Only the book value element is shown, inasmuch as the current value over (under) book value element and the goodwill element are not relevant to the procedures involved. For simplicity we assumed the subsidiary reported $25,000 of net income in 19X2 and 19X3 and declared no dividends in either year, and that the parent had $2,000 amortization of cost in excess of book value for both years.

Note that for 19X3 the parent would apply the equity method of accounting as follows:

**MODULE 1   The Complete Equity Method: Investment Account Adjustment Procedures** (continued)

## ■ ILLUSTRATION 7-2
### Updating the Book Value Element of the Conceptual Analysis When Unrealized Intercompany Profit Exists at Year-end on Downstream Sales

| | Total Cost = | Common Stock + | Prior Years + | Current Year Earnings − | Current Year Dividends | Unrealized − Profit |
|---|---|---|---|---|---|---|
| | | | | **Book Value Element** | | |
| | | | | **Retained Earnings** | | |
| Balance, Jan. 1, 19X1 | $90,000 | $40,000 | $20,000 | | | |
| Equity in net income ($15,000 of reported net income less $5,000 of unrealized profit) | 10,000 | | | $10,000 | | |
| Dividends . . . . . . . . . . | (5,000) | | | | $(5,000) | |
| Amortization . . . . . . . . | (4,000) | | | | | |
| Subtotal . . . . . . . . . . . . . | $91,000 | $40,000 | $20,000 | $10,000 | $(5,000) | |
| Reclassification . . . . . . | | | | 5,000 | | $(5,000) |
| Reclassification . . . . . . | | | 10,000 | (15,000) | 5,000 | |
| Balance, Dec. 31, 19X1 | $91,000 | $40,000 | $30,000 | $ −0− | $ −0− | $(5,000) |
| Equity in net income | 25,000 | | | 25,000 | | |
| Amortization . . . . . . . . | (2,000) | | | | | |
| Subtotal . . . . . . . . . . . . . | $114,000 | $40,000 | $30,000 | $25,000 | $ −0− | $(5,000)[a] |
| Reclassification . . . . . . | | | 25,000 | (25,000) | | |
| Balance, Dec. 31, 19X2 | $114,000 | $40,000 | $55,000 | $ −0− | $ −0− | $(5,000) |
| Equity in net income ($25,000 of reported net income plus $5,000 of previously deferred profit now realized) | 30,000 | | | 30,000 | | |
| Amortization . . . . . . . . | (2,000) | | | | | |
| Subtotal . . . . . . . . . . . . . | $142,000 | $40,000 | $55,000 | $30,000 | $ −0− | $(5,000)[b] |
| Reclassification . . . . . . | | | | (5,000) | | 5,000 |
| Reclassification . . . . . . | | | 25,000 | (25,000) | | |
| Balance, Dec. 31, 19X3 | $142,000 | $40,000 | $80,000 | $ −0− | $ −0− | $ −0− |

[a]Because the intercompany-acquired inventory is still on hand at this consolidation date, this amount is posted as a credit to the Inventory account in the primary elimination entry prepared from this line.

[b]Because the intercompany-acquired inventory is assumed to have been resold by the subsidiary at this consolidation date, this amount is posted as a credit to Cost of Goods Sold in the primary elimination entry prepared from this line.

Note: The amounts do not cross-total to the total cost column at the beginning and end of each year because the current value over (under) book value element and the goodwill element are not shown as they are not relevant to the procedure in this illustration.

---

**MODULE 1    The Complete Equity Method: Investment Account Adjustment Procedures** (continued)

| | |
|---|---|
| Subsidiary's reported net income for 19X3............... | $25,000 |
| Parent's ownership percentage........................... | 100% |
| Parent's share of subsidiary's reported net income for 19X3 ....................................... | $25,000 |
| Add—Realized intercompany gross profit previously deferred...................................... | 5,000 |
| Parent's share of subsidiary's reported net income, as adjusted for realized profit.................. | $30,000 |

The following general ledger entry is made for 19X3:

| | | |
|---|---|---|
| Investment in Subsidiary...................... | 30,000 | |
|     Equity in Net Income of Subsidiary ..... | | 30,000 |
|     To record the equity in the subsidiary's net income. | | |

## Dealing with Beginning Inventory and Current-year Transfers

In a normal consolidation involving intercompany inventory transactions, intercompany sales of inventory usually occur each year. Accordingly, entries are required both (1) to recognize the profit on the beginning intercompany inventory, and (2) to eliminate the current-year intercompany transactions. In this regard, it is simpler to account for the unrealized profit at the beginning of the year separately from the current-year intercompany transactions in updating the book value element of the conceptual analysis. In other words, we use a separate reclassification line for the unrealized profit at the beginning of the year and a separate reclassification line for the year-end unrealized profit.

Some of the beginning inventory may be physically part of the ending inventory. However, the consolidation effort is simplified if it is assumed that the beginning inventory has been sold and that all of the ending inventory came from the current-year intercompany inventory transactions. So long as the gross profit rates are the same (or very close) from year to year, the assumption is a safe one.

## Downstream Sales to a Partially Owned Subsidiary

When the intercompany transfers are downstream to a partially owned subsidiary, the procedures are the same as those shown for downstream transfers to a wholly owned subsidiary. In updating the conceptual analysis of the investment account, however, the minority interest column is updated using the subsidiary's reported earnings times the minority interest ownership percentage. In other words, the unrealized intercompany profit is always treated as an adjustment to the parent's share of the subsidiary's reported earnings.

## UPSTREAM TRANSFERS ABOVE COST FROM PARTIALLY OWNED SUBSIDIARY

## Deferring Profit on Upstream Transfers

We use the same example discussed in the previous section that covered downstream sales. However, we assume here that the $75,000 of intercompany sales for 19X1 are upstream from S Company, an 80%-owned subsidiary of P Company. To defer the recognition of the $5,000 of unrealized intercompany profit at December 31, 19X1, the parent would make the following adjustment to the subsidiary's reported net income before applying the equity method of accounting:

| | |
|---|---:|
| Subsidiary's reported net income for 19X1.................. | $15,000 |
| Less—Unrealized intercompany profit at year-end......... | (5,000) |
| Subsidiary's reported net income, as adjusted for unrealized profit........................................ | $10,000 |
| Parent's ownership percentage............................ | 80% |
| Parent's share of subsidiary's reported net income, as adjusted for unrealized profit .......................... | $ 8,000 |

The following general ledger entry is then made:

| | | |
|---|---:|---:|
| Investment in Subsidiary...................... | 8,000 | |
| Equity in Net Income of Subsidiary ..... | | 8,000 |
| ($10,000×80% ownership percentage) | | |

In updating the conceptual analysis of the investment account, the minority interest column would be increased by $2,000 ($10,000×20%). Note that in this situation, the unrealized profit is subtracted from the subsidiary's total reported net income, whereas in the example involving downstream sales, the unrealized profit was subtracted from the parent's share of the subsidiary's net income. Other than this procedural difference, the manner of dealing with unrealized intercompany profit in upstream situations from partially owned subsidiaries is the same as in downstream situations.

**Subsidiary's Reporting to Its Minority Shareholders.**    Under existing generally accepted accounting principles, the subsidiary need not defer any of its intercompany profit in reporting to its minority shareholders. Insofar as the minority shareholders are concerned, such intercompany profit has been realized.

**ILLUSTRATION**

## Preparing Consolidated Financial Statements

- The Complete Equity Method: Investment Account Adjustment Procedures
- Upstream Sales above Cost from 80%-owned Subsidiary

Illustration 7-3 shows a consolidating statement worksheet involving upstream inventory sales. The worksheet adapts the P Company and S Company financial statements presented in Illustration 5-5 so that S Company has upstream sales. P Company's financial statements have been adjusted for its $4,000 share of unrealized intercompany profit at year-end (80% of $5,000). The intercompany transaction elimination entries are the same as those used in Illustration 7-1.

**Review Points for Illustration 7-3.**   Note the following:

1. The parent's net income and retained earnings equals the consolidated net income and retained earnings, respectively.
2. No additional adjustment is required to the minority interest in dealing with the intercompany transaction eliminations.

## Subsequent-year Treatment of Unrealized Profit

The accounting to be followed in subsequent years is basically the same as that shown earlier for downstream transfers (page 345). The only difference is how the equity method of accounting is applied in the year in which the deferred intercompany gross profit becomes realized as a result of the parent reselling the intercompany acquired inventory to a third party. Assuming the parent resells this inventory in 19X3 and the subsidiary's reported net income for 19X3 is $25,000, the parent would make the following adjustment before applying the equity method of accounting:

| | |
|---|---:|
| Subsidiary's reported net income for 19X3 | $25,000 |
| Add—Realized intercompany gross profit previously deferred | 5,000 |
| Subsidiary's reported net income, as adjusted for realized intercompany profit | $30,000 |
| Parent's ownership percentage | 80% |
| Parent's share of subsidiary's net income, as adjusted for realized gross profit | $24,000 |

The following general ledger entry is then made:

| | | |
|---|---:|---:|
| Investment in Subsidiary | 24,000 | |
| Equity in Net Income of Subsidiary | | 24,000 |
| ($30,000 × 80% ownership interest) | | |

■ **ILLUSTRATION 7-3**

The Complete Equity Method: Investment Account Adjustment Procedures—Upstream Transfers above Cost (80%-owned Subsidiary)

| | P Company | S Company | Eliminations Dr. | Eliminations Cr. | Consolidated |
|---|---|---|---|---|---|
| **P COMPANY AND SUBSIDIARY (S COMPANY)** Consolidating Statement Worksheet for the Year Ended December 31, 19X1 | | | | | |
| **Income Statement** | | | | | |
| Sales. . . . . . . . . . | 600,000 | 150,000 | | | 750,000 |
| Cost of goods sold . . . . . . . . . . . . . . | (360,000) | (60,000) | 3,200(2) | 20,000(4) | (403,200) |
| Expenses. . . . . . . . . . . . . . . . . . | (190,000) | (100,000) | | | (290,000) |
| Intercompany Accounts: | | | | | |
| Equity in net income. . . . . . . . . | 4,800[a] | | 8,000(1) | 3,200(2) | –0– |
| Sales. . . . . . . . . . . . . . . . . . . | | 75,000 | 75,000(4) | | –0– |
| Cost of goods sold . . . . . . . . . . . | | (50,000) | | 50,000(4) | –0– |
| Income before Minority Interest. . | 54,800 | 15,000 | 86,200 | 73,200 | 56,800 |
| Minority interest . . . . . . . . . . . . | | | 2,000(1) | | (2,000) |
| Net Income. . . . . . . . . . . . . . . . . | 54,800 | 15,000 | 88,200 | 73,200 | 54,800 |
| **Statement of Retained Earnings** | | | | | |
| Balances, January 1, 19X1. . . . . . | 100,000 | 20,000 | 20,000(1) | | 100,000 |
| + Net income . . . . . . . . . . . . . . . | 54,800 | 15,000 | 88,200 | 73,200 | 54,800 |
| – Dividends declared . . . . . . . . . | (45,000) | (5,000) | | 5,000(1) | (45,000) |
| Balances, December 31, 19X1 . . . | 109,800 | 30,000 | 108,200 | 78,200 | 109,800 |
| **Balance Sheet** | | | | | |
| Cash . . . . . . . . . . . . . . . . . . . . . . | 42,000 | 11,000 | | | 53,000 |
| Accounts receivable, net . . . . . . . . | 75,000 | 37,000 | | | 112,000 |
| Inventory: | | | | | |
| From vendors . . . . . . . . . . . . . . | 95,000 | 55,000 | | | 150,000 |
| Intercompany . . . . . . . . . . . . . . | 15,000 | | | 5,000(4) | 10,000 |
| Investment in S Company . . . . . . . | 72,800 | | | 72,800(1) | –0– |
| Land . . . . . . . . . . . . . . . . . . . . . . | 220,000 | 30,000 | 9,600(1) | | 259,600 |
| Buildings and equipment . . . . . . . | 500,000 | 200,000 | 4,800(1) | 50,000(3) | 654,800 |
| Accumulated depreciation . . . . . . . | (320,000) | (63,000) | 50,000(3) | 800(1) | (333,800) |
| Goodwill . . . . . . . . . . . . . . . . . . . | | | 7,200(1) | | 7,200 |
| Total Assets . . . . . . . . . . . . . . . | 699,800 | 270,000 | 71,600 | 128,600 | 912,800 |
| Liabilities . . . . . . . . . . . . . . . . . . | 290,000 | 200,000 | | | 490,000 |
| Minority interest in net assets . . . | | | | 13,000(1) | 13,000 |
| Common stock . . . . . . . . . . . . . . . | 300,000 | 40,000 | 40,000(1) | | 300,000 |
| Retained earnings . . . . . . . . . . . . | 109,800 | 30,000 | 108,200 | 78,200 | 109,800 |
| Total Liabilities and Equity . . . . | 699,800 | 270,000 | 148,200 | 91,200 | 912,800 |
| Proof of debit and credit postings. . . . . . . . . . . . . . . . . . . . . . | | | 219,800 | 219,800 | |

Explanation of entries:

(1) The primary elimination entry.    (3) The accumulated depreciation elimination entry.

(2) The secondary elimination entry.    (4) The current-year intercompany transactions elimination entry.

[a]Comprised of 80% share of subsidiary's reported earnings of $15,000 as adjusted for $5,000 of unrealized profit (80% of $10,000 = $8,000), net of $3,200 of amortization of cost in excess of book value.

**MODULE 1**   The Complete Equity Method: Investment Account Adjustment Procedures *(continued)*

The procedures for updating the conceptual analysis of the investment account parallel those demonstrated for downstream sales in Illustration 7-2.

**MODULE 2**   The Complete Equity Method: Noninvestment Account Adjustment Procedures

## INVENTORY TRANSFERS ABOVE COST: MECHANICAL PROCEDURES TO DEFER UNREALIZED PROFIT

**Module Overview.** In a complete application of the equity method of accounting in situations involving unrealized intercompany profit, certain adjustments are made so that the parent's net income and retained earnings are the same as consolidated net income and consolidated retained earnings, respectively. Consequently, the highly desirable built-in checking feature characteristic of the equity method, discussed in Chapters 4 and 5, is retained. In this module, these adjustments are made to each of the parent's financial statements (for downstream sales) or each of the subsidiary's financial statements (for upstream sales) using the following two accounts: a Deferred Profit account (a contra asset account) and a Deferral or Recognition of Intercompany Gross Profit account (for the income statement).

### Harmony of *APB Opinion No. 18* and *ARB No. 51*

In applying the equity method of accounting in the parent's financial statements, it should be noted that the requirements of *APB Opinion No. 18*, "The Equity Method of Accounting for Investments in Common Stock," are in harmony with the requirements of *ARB No. 51* concerning the preparation of consolidated financial statements. That is, both pronouncements require all unrealized intercompany profit to be deferred until realized in a transaction with a third party—regardless of the existence of a minority interest. *Accounting Interpretation No. 1* to *APB Opinion No. 18* states:

> When an investor controls an investee through majority voting interest and enters into a transaction with an investee which is not on an "arm's length" basis,[6] none of the intercompany profit or loss from the transaction should

---

[6]That is, a transaction between completely independent parties. (All transactions with controlled companies are considered to be on less than an "arms length" basis.)

be recognized in income by the investor until it has been realized through transactions with third parties.[7]

## DOWNSTREAM TRANSFERS ABOVE COST
### Deferring Profit on Downstream Transfers

In this module, we use the example discussed on pages 339–40 in which the parent sold inventory costing $50,000 to its wholly owned subsidiary for $75,000 in 19X1 and $15,000 of the $75,000 of inventory is reported in the subsidiary's balance sheet at December 31, 19X1. In that example, we showed that of the $25,000 total intercompany profit ($75,000 − $50,000), $20,000 is associated with inventory the subsidiary has resold and $5,000 is associated with inventory remaining on hand at year-end. To defer the recognition of the $5,000 of unrealized intercompany profit at December 31, 19X1, **the parent would make the following general ledger entry** at December 31, 19X1:

Deferral of Gross Profit on Intercompany
    Sales (income statement). . . . . . . . . . . . . . . . . .    5,000
        Deferred Gross Profit (balance sheet). . .               5,000
    To defer the reporting of unrealized
      intercompany gross profit on
      inventory transfers.

**ILLUSTRATION**

### Preparing Consolidated Financial Statements

- The Complete Equity Method: Noninvestment Account Adjustment Procedures
- Downstream Transfers above Cost

In preparing consolidated financial statements at December 31, 19X1, the preceding general ledger entry would be reversed on the consolidation worksheet and the universal intercompany transaction elimination entry also would be made on the worksheet. The entries are:

**WORKSHEET
ENTRY ONLY**

Deferred Gross Profit (balance sheet). . . . . . . .    5,000
    Deferral of Gross Profit on
      Intercompany Sales (income
      statement). . . . . . . . . . . . . . . . . . . . . . . . . . . .               5,000
    To reverse in consolidation the year-end
      general ledger entry deferring
      intercompany gross profit.

[7]*Accounting Interpretation No. 1* to *APB Opinion No. 18* (New York: American Institute of Certified Public Accountants, 1971), par. 4.

| MODULE 2 | The Complete Equity Method: Noninvestment Account Adjustment Procedures *(continued)* |

**WORKSHEET ENTRY ONLY**

| Intercompany Sales | 75,000 | |
| Intercompany Cost of Goods Sold | | 50,000 |
| Cost of Goods Sold (to third parties) | | 20,000 |
| Inventory | | 5,000 |
| To eliminate current-year intercompany transactions. | | |

Illustration 7-4 shows a consolidating statement worksheet for the year ended December 31, 19X1. The P Company and S Company financial statement amounts presented in worksheet Illustration 4-5, along with the primary, secondary, and accumulated depreciation elimination entries used in that illustration, are used in Illustration 7-4. The P Company and S Company columns were modified, however, to reflect the $75,000 of downstream intercompany inventory transactions.

For convenience, all of the elimination entries used in Illustration 7-4 are shown below in sequence:

1. The primary elimination entry: (same entry as on page 169):

**WORKSHEET ENTRY ONLY**

| Common Stock | 40,000 | |
| Retained Earnings (beginning of year) | 20,000 | |
| Equity in Net Income of Subsidiary | 15,000 | |
| Land | 12,000 | |
| Equipment | 6,000 | |
| Goodwill | 9,000 | |
| Dividends Declared | | 5,000 |
| Accumulated Depreciation | | 1,000 |
| Investment in Subsidiary | | 96,000 |

2. The secondary elimination entry:

**WORKSHEET ENTRY ONLY**

| Cost of Goods Sold (to third parties) | 4,000 | |
| Equity in Net Income of Subsidiary | | 4,000 |

3. The accumulated depreciation elimination entry:

**WORKSHEET ENTRY ONLY**

| Accumulated Depreciation | 50,000 | |
| Buildings and Equipment | | 50,000 |

4. The reversal of the general ledger deferral entry:

### ■ ILLUSTRATION 7-4

The Complete Equity Method: Noninvestment Account Adjustment Procedures—Downstream Transfer above Cost

**P COMPANY AND SUBSIDIARY (S COMPANY)**
Consolidating Statement Worksheet for the Year Ended December 31, 19X1

| | P Company | S Company | Eliminations Dr. | Eliminations Cr. | Consolidated |
|---|---|---|---|---|---|
| **Income Statement** | | | | | |
| Sales | 525,000 | 225,000 | | | 750,000 |
| Cost of goods sold | (310,000) | (110,000) | 4,000(2) | 20,000(5) | (404,000) |
| Expenses | (190,000) | (100,000) | | | (290,000) |
| Intercompany Accounts: | | | | | |
| Equity in net income | 11,000[a] | | 15,000(1) | 4,000(2) | –0– |
| Sales | 75,000 | | | 75,000(5) | –0– |
| Cost of goods sold | (50,000) | | | 50,000(5) | –0– |
| Deferral of gross profit | (5,000) | | | 5,000(4) | –0– |
| Net Income | 56,000 | 15,000 | 94,000 | 79,000 | 56,000 |
| **Statement of Retained Earnings** | | | | | |
| Balances, January 1, 19X1 | 100,000 | 20,000 | 20,000(1) | | 100,000 |
| + Net income | 56,000 | 15,000 | 94,000 | 79,000 | 56,000 |
| − Dividends declared | (45,000) | (5,000) | | 5,000(1) | (45,000) |
| Balances, December 31, 19X1 | 111,000 | 30,000 | 114,000 | 84,000 | 111,000 |
| **Balance Sheet** | | | | | |
| Cash | 25,000 | 11,000 | | | 36,000 |
| Accounts receivable, net | 75,000 | 37,000 | | | 112,000 |
| Inventory: | | | | | |
| From vendors | 110,000 | 40,000 | | | 150,000 |
| Intercompany | | 15,000 | | 5,000(5) | 10,000 |
| Deferred profit | (5,000) | | 5,000(4) | | –0– |
| Investment in S Company | 96,000 | | | 96,000(1) | –0– |
| Land | 220,000 | 30,000 | 12,000(1) | | 262,000 |
| Buildings and equipment | 500,000 | 200,000 | 6,000(1) | 50,000(3) | 656,000 |
| Accumulated depreciation | (320,000) | (63,000) | 50,000(3) | 1,000(1) | (334,000) |
| Goodwill | | | 9,000(1) | | 9,000 |
| Total Assets | 701,000 | 270,000 | 82,000 | 152,000 | 901,000 |
| Liabilities | 290,000 | 200,000 | | | 490,000 |
| Common stock | 300,000 | 40,000 | 40,000(1) | | 300,000 |
| Retained earnings | 111,000 | 30,000 | 114,000 | 84,000 | 111,000 |
| Total Liabilities and Equity | 701,000 | 270,000 | 154,000 | 84,000 | 901,000 |

Proof of debit and credit postings.......................... 236,000    236,000

Explanation of entries:
(1) The primary elimination entry.
(2) The secondary elimination entry.
(3) The accumulated depreciation elimination entry.
(4) The reversal of the general ledger deferral entry.
(5) The current-year intercompany transactions elimination entry.

[a]Comprised of $15,000 of subsidiary's reported net income, net of $4,000 of amortization of cost in excess of book value.

| | MODULE 2 | The Complete Equity Method: Noninvestment Account Adjustment Procedures *(continued)* |

**WORKSHEET ENTRY ONLY**

| Deferred Gross Profit (balance sheet) . . . . . . . . . | 5,000 | |
| Deferral of Gross Profit on | | |
| Intercompany Sales | | |
| (income statement) . . . . . . . . . . . . . . . . . . | | 5,000 |

5. The current-year intercompany inventory transactions elimination entry:

**WORKSHEET ENTRY ONLY**

| Intercompany Sales . . . . . . . . . . . . . . . . . . . . . . | 75,000 | |
| Intercompany Cost of Goods Sold . . . . . . . | | 50,000 |
| Cost of Goods Sold (to third parties) . . . . | | 20,000 |
| Inventory . . . . . . . . . . . . . . . . . . . . . . . . . . . . . | | 5,000 |

## Subsequent-year Treatment of Unrealized Profit

**Inventory Not Resold in 19X2.** If the inventory is still on hand at the end of 19X2, the only entry needed in consolidation relating to the unrealized intercompany gross profit is to reclassify the balance in the Deferred Gross Profit account to the Inventory account (strictly a balance sheet reclassification). The entry is:

**WORKSHEET ENTRY ONLY**

| Deferred Profit . . . . . . . . . . . . . . . . . . . . . . . . . . | 5,000 | |
| Inventory . . . . . . . . . . . . . . . . . . . . . . . . . . | | 5,000 |

This entry is made at every consolidation date after December 31, 19X1 until the inventory is resold by the parent.

**Inventory Resold in 19X3.** If the inventory has been resold by the end of 19X3, the following entry would be made **in the parent's general ledger** at the time of the sale:

| Deferred Gross Profit (balance sheet) . . . . . . . . . | 5,000 | |
| Recognition of Gross Profit on | | |
| Intercompany Inventory Sales | | |
| (income statement) . . . . . . . . . . . . . . . . . . | | 5,000 |
| To recognize the gross profit on prior year's | | |
| intercompany sales deferred in 19X1. | | |

In consolidation at December 31, 19X3, the following elimination entry would be made on the worksheet:

**WORKSHEET ENTRY ONLY**

| Recognition of Gross Profit on Intercompany Inventory Sales (income statement)......... | 5,000 | |
|---|---|---|
|     Cost of Goods Sold (to third parties).... | | 5,000 |

To reclassify the credit balance in the Recognition of Gross Profit account to Cost of Goods Sold (to third parties).

Note that in consolidation this entry posts an equal debit and credit to the income statement ($5,000). As a result, a zero net effect is carried forward to retained earnings. The $5,000 of gross profit being reported has already been reflected in the general ledger Retained Earnings account.

## Dealing with Beginning Inventory and Current-year Transfers

In a normal consolidation involving intercompany inventory transactions, intercompany sales of inventory usually occur each year. Accordingly, entries are required both (1) to recognize the profit on the beginning intercompany inventory, and (2) to eliminate the current-year intercompany transactions. In this regard, it is simpler to separate these entries rather than to handle them as a single, combined elimination entry.

Some of the beginning inventory may be physically part of the ending inventory. However, the consolidation effort is simplified if it is assumed that the beginning inventory has been sold and that all of the ending inventory came from the current-year intercompany inventory transactions. So long as the gross profit rates are the same (or very close) from year to year, the assumption is a safe one.

### UPSTREAM TRANSFERS ABOVE COST FROM PARTIALLY OWNED SUBSIDIARY

## Deferring Profit on Upstream Transfers

We use the same example discussed in the previous section that covered downstream sales. However, we assume here that the $75,000 of intercompany sales are upstream from S Company, an 80%-owned subsidiary of P Company.

A strict application of the equity method (as described in paragraph 6b of *APB Opinion No. 18*) calls for the investor to adjust the investee's reported net income to eliminate any unrealized intercompany gross profit before applying the equity method. This adjustment can be made by requiring the **subsidiary to adjust its general ledger** as follows:

---

**MODULE 2**    **The Complete Equity Method: Noninvestment Account Adjustment Procedures** *(continued)*

---

| | | |
|---|---:|---:|
| Deferral of Gross Profit on Intercompany | | |
| Sales (income statement)...................... | 5,000 | |
| Deferred Gross Profit (balance sheet)..... | | 5,000 |
| To defer the reporting of unrealized | | |
| intercompany gross profit on | | |
| inventory transfers. | | |

(The parent booked the same entry in its general ledger when the intercompany transfer was downstream.) Thus, the subsidiary's net income and retained earnings would be $5,000 lower. Accordingly, the equity method of accounting would then be applied to the lower net income amount. In consolidation at year-end, this entry would be reversed and the universal intercompany inventory transaction elimination entry would be made. These entries are not shown here, as they are identical to the entries shown for a downstream inventory transfer.

In summary, the procedures for upstream transfers are identical to those for downstream transfers, except that the adjusting entry to defer the reporting of the unrealized intercompany gross profit at year-end is made to the subsidiary's general ledger instead of in the parent's general ledger.

**Subsidiary's Reporting to Its Minority Shareholders.**   Under existing generally accepted accounting principles, the subsidiary need not defer any of its intercompany profit in reporting to its minority shareholders. Insofar as the minority shareholders are concerned, such intercompany profit has been realized. Accordingly, for reporting to the minority shareholders, the subsidiary would make a "financial statement adjusting entry" to reverse the intercompany profit deferral entry.

The consolidation effort is greatly simplified when the subsidiary is required to maintain its general ledger for reporting to the parent rather than to the minority shareholders. If the subsidiary's general ledger were kept the opposite way, the parent would have to make a financial statement adjusting entry to the subsidiary's financial statements prior to the start of the consolidation process. Some companies have hundreds of subsidiaries and large numbers of intercompany inventory transfers; making such an entry for each subsidiary would put a substantial burden on the parent's accounting department. It is best to have the subsidiaries maintain their general ledgers for reporting to the parent.

**ILLUSTRATION**    ## Preparing Consolidated Financial Statements

- The Complete Equity Method: Noninvestment Account Adjustment Procedures
- Upstream Sales above Cost from 80%-owned Subsidiary

*Ơ∕ʍⱮT*

## ■ ILLUSTRATION 7-5

### The Complete Equity Method: Noninvestment Account Adjustment Procedures—Upstream Transfer above Cost (80%-owned Subsidiary)

| | P Company | S Company | Eliminations Dr. | Eliminations Cr. | Consolidated |
|---|---|---|---|---|---|
| **P COMPANY AND SUBSIDIARY (S COMPANY)** | | | | | |
| **Consolidating Statement Worksheet for the Year Ended December 31, 19X1** | | | | | |
| **Income Statement** | | | | | |
| Sales | 600,000 | 150,000 | | | 750,000 |
| Cost of goods sold | (360,000) | (60,000) | 3,200(2) | 20,000(5) | (403,200) |
| Expenses | (190,000) | (100,000) | | | (290,000) |
| Intercompany Accounts: | | | | | |
| Equity in net income | 4,800[a] | | 8,000(1) | 3,200(2) | –0– |
| Sales | | 75,000 | 75,000(5) | | –0– |
| Cost of goods sold | | (50,000) | | 50,000(5) | –0– |
| Deferral of gross profit | | (5,000) | | 5,000(4) | –0– |
| Income before Minority Interest | 54,800 | 10,000 | 86,200 | 78,200 | 56,800 |
| Minority interest | | | | 2,000(1) | (2,000) |
| Net Income | 54,800 | 10,000 | 88,200 | 78,200 | 54,800 |
| **Statement of Retained Earnings** | | | | | |
| Balances, January 1, 19X1 | 100,000 | 20,000 | 20,000(1) | | 100,000 |
| + Net income | 54,800 | 10,000 | 88,200 | 78,200 | 54,800 |
| − Dividends declared | (45,000) | (5,000) | | 5,000(1) | (45,000) |
| Balances, December 31, 19X1 | 109,800 | 25,000 | 108,200 | 83,200 | 109,800 |
| **Balance Sheet** | | | | | |
| Cash | 42,000 | 11,000 | | | 53,000 |
| Accounts receivable | 75,000 | 37,000 | | | 112,000 |
| Inventory: | | | | | |
| From vendors | 95,000 | 55,000 | | | 150,000 |
| Intercompany | 15,000 | | | 5,000(5) | 10,000 |
| Deferred profit | | (5,000) | 5,000(4) | | –0– |
| Investment in subsidiary | 72,800 | | | 72,800(1) | –0– |
| Land | 220,000 | 30,000 | 9,600(1) | | 259,600 |
| Buildings and equipment | 500,000 | 200,000 | 4,800(1) | 50,000(3) | 654,800 |
| Accumulated depreciation | (320,000) | (63,000) | 50,000(3) | 800(1) | (333,800) |
| Goodwill | | | 7,200(1) | | 7,200 |
| Total Assets | 699,800 | 265,000 | 76,600 | 128,600 | 912,800 |
| Liabilities | 290,000 | 200,000 | | | 490,000 |
| Minority interest in net assets | | | | 13,000(1) | 13,000 |
| Common stock | 300,000 | 40,000 | 40,000(1) | | 300,000 |
| Retained earnings | 109,800 | 25,000 | 108,200 | 83,200 | 109,800 |
| Total Liabilities and Equity | 699,800 | 265,000 | 148,200 | 96,200 | 912,800 |
| Proof of debit and credit postings | | | 224,800 | 224,800 | |

Explanation of entries:
(1) The primary elimination entry.
(2) The secondary elimination entry.
(3) The accumulated depreciation elimination entry.
(4) The reversal of the general ledger deferral entry.
(5) The current-year intercompany transactions elimination entry.

[a]Comprised of $8,000 (80% share of subsidiary's reported net income of $10,000), net of $3,200 of amortization of cost in excess of book value.

Illustration 7-5 shows a consolidating statement worksheet involving upstream inventory sales. The worksheet adapts the P Company and S Company financial statements presented in Illustration 5-5 so that S Company has upstream sales and its financial statements have been adjusted for $5,000 of unrealized intercompany profit at year-end. The intercompany transaction elimination entries are the same as those used in Illustration 7-4.

### Review Points for Illustration 7-5.   Note the following:

1. The parent's net income and retained earnings equals the consolidated net income and retained earnings, respectively.
2. No additional adjustment is required to the minority interest in dealing with the intercompany transaction eliminations.

## Subsequent-year Treatment of Unrealized Profit

The accounting to be followed for subsequent years is the same as that shown earlier for downstream transfers (page 355). The only difference is that the subsidiary, not the parent, would make a general ledger entry to recognize the intercompany profit upon resale of the inventory.

## INVENTORY TRANSFERS ABOVE COST: MECHANICAL PROCEDURES TO DEFER UNREALIZED PROFIT

**Module Overview.**   Under the partial equity method, the deferral of unrealized intercompany gross profit is accomplished entirely on the consolidation worksheet. Accordingly, the parent's net income and retained earnings do not agree with the consolidated net income and consolidated retained earnings, respectively. Thus the built-in checking feature characteristic of the equity method in going from the parent's column to the consolidated column, discussed in Chapters 4 and 5, no longer exists.

### DOWNSTREAM TRANSFERS ABOVE COST

In this module, we use the example discussed on pages 339–40 in which the parent sold inventory costing $50,000 to its wholly owned subsidiary for $75,000 in 19X1 and $15,000 of the $75,000 of inventory is reported in the subsidiary's balance sheet at December 31, 19X1. In that example,

---

**MODULE 3**   **The Partial Equity Method** *(continued)*

---

we demonstrated that of the $25,000 total intercompany profit ($75,000 – $50,000), $20,000 is associated with inventory the subsidiary has resold and $5,000 is associated with inventory remaining on hand at year-end.

## Preparing Consolidated Financial Statements

- The Partial Equity Method
- Downstream Transfers above Cost

In preparing consolidated financial statements at December 31, 19X1, the following universal elimination entry would be made:

| | | |
|---|---|---|
| **WORKSHEET ENTRY ONLY** | | |

| | | |
|---|---|---|
| Intercompany Sales | 75,000 | |
| Intercompany Cost of Goods Sold | | 50,000 |
| Cost of Goods Sold (to third parties) | | 20,000 |
| Inventory | | 5,000 |

Illustration 7-6 shows a consolidating statement worksheet for the year ended December 31, 19X1. The P Company and S Company financial statements presented in Illustration 4-5, along with the primary, secondary, and accumulated depreciation elimination entries used in that Illustration, are used in Illustration 7-6. The P Company and S Company columns were modified to reflect the intercompany inventory transactions discussed above. For convenience, all of the elimination entries used in Illustration 7-6 are shown below in sequence:

1. The primary elimination entry:

| | | |
|---|---|---|
| **WORKSHEET ENTRY ONLY** | | |

| | | |
|---|---|---|
| Common Stock | 40,000 | |
| Retained Earnings (beginning of year) | 20,000 | |
| Equity in Net Income of Subsidiary | 15,000 | |
| Land | 12,000 | |
| Equipment | 6,000 | |
| Goodwill | 9,000 | |
| Dividends Declared | | 5,000 |
| Accumulated Depreciation | | 1,000 |
| Investment in Subsidiary | | 96,000 |

2. The secondary elimination entry:

| | | |
|---|---|---|
| **WORKSHEET ENTRY ONLY** | | |

| | | |
|---|---|---|
| Cost of Goods Sold (to third parties) | 4,000 | |
| Equity in Net Income of Subsidiary | | 4,000 |

3. The accumulated depreciation elimination entry:

## MODULE 3  The Partial Equity Method *(continued)*

| WORKSHEET ENTRY ONLY | | | |
|---|---|---|---|
| Accumulated Depreciation | | 50,000 | |
| Buildings and Equipment | | | 50,000 |

4. The current-year intercompany transactions elimination entry:

| WORKSHEET ENTRY ONLY | | | |
|---|---|---|---|
| Intercompany Sales | | 75,000 | |
| Intercompany Cost of Goods Sold | | | 50,000 |
| Cost of Goods Sold (to third parties) | | | 20,000 |
| Inventory | | | 5,000 |

**Review Points for Illustration 7-6.**   Note the following:

1. Consolidated net income and consolidated retained earnings are both $5,000 lower than the comparable amounts in the parent's column.
2. If P Company were to issue **"parent company" financial statements** in addition to consolidated statements, the parent's net income of $61,000 first would have to be adjusted downward by $5,000. It would not make sense for a parent company that has intercompany transactions to report a greater profit by not consolidating a subsidiary. Accordingly, the parent would make the following adjustment to its financial statements:

| | | | |
|---|---|---|---|
| Deferral of Gross Profit on Intercompany Sales (income statement) | | 5,000 | |
| Deferred Gross Profit (balance sheet) | | | 5,000 |
| To defer the recognition of unrealized gross profit on intercompany inventory sales. | | | |

## Subsequent-year Treatment of Unrealized Profit

This section explains the accounting treatment in 19X2 of the 20% of the intercompany inventory transfer that was unsold at December 31, 19X1. We assume this intercompany acquired inventory remains unsold at December 31, 19X2 (one year later), but that it is resold in 19X3.

**Not Resold at the End of 19X2.**   If the inventory is still on hand at the end of 19X2, the following elimination entry is required in consolidation at December 31, 19X2:

| WORKSHEET ENTRY ONLY | | | |
|---|---|---|---|
| Retained Earnings—P Company (beginning of year) | | 5,000 | |
| Inventory | | | 5,000 |

## MODULE 3   The Partial Equity Method (continued)

■ ILLUSTRATION 7-6
### The Partial Equity Method: Downstream Transfers above Cost

| P COMPANY AND SUBSIDIARY (S COMPANY) | | | | | |
|---|---|---|---|---|---|
| Consolidating Statement Worksheet for the Year Ended December 31, 19X1 | | | | | |
| | P Company | S Company | Eliminations Dr. | Eliminations Cr. | Consolidated |
| **Income Statement** | | | | | |
| Sales. . . . . . . . . . . . . . . . . . . . . . . . | 525,000 | 225,000 | | | 750,000 |
| Cost of goods sold . . . . . . . . . . . . . | (310,000) | (110,000) | 4,000(2) | 20,000(4) | (404,000) |
| Expenses. . . . . . . . . . . . . . . . . . . . . | (190,000) | (100,000) | | | (290,000) |
| Intercompany Accounts: | | | | | |
| Equity in net income | | | | | |
| of subsidiary . . . . . . . . . . . . . . | 11,000[a] | | 15,000(1) | 4,000(2) | –0– |
| Sales. . . . . . . . . . . . . . . . . . . . . . | 75,000 | | 75,000(4) | | –0– |
| Cost of goods sold . . . . . . . . . . . | (50,000) | | | 50,000(4) | –0– |
| Net Income . . . . . . . . . . . . . . . . . . . . | 61,000 | 15,000 | ⌐ 94,000 | ⌐ 74,000 | 56,000 |
| **Statement of Retained Earnings** | | | | | |
| Balances, January 1, 19X1. . . . . . | 100,000 | 20,000 | 20,000(1) | | 100,000 |
| + Net income . . . . . . . . . . . . . . . . . | 61,000 | 15,000 | ➧ 94,000 | ➧ 74,000 | 56,000 |
| – Dividends declared . . . . . . . . . . | (45,000) | (5,000) | | 5,000(1) | (45,000) |
| Balances, December 31, 19X1 . . . | 116,000 | 30,000 | ⌐114,000 | ⌐ 79,000 | 111,000 |
| **Balance Sheet** | | | | | |
| Cash . . . . . . . . . . . . . . . . . . . . . . . . | 25,000 | 11,000 | | | 36,000 |
| Accounts receivable, net . . . . . . . . | 75,000 | 37,000 | | | 112,000 |
| Inventory: | | | | | |
| From vendors. . . . . . . . . . . . . . . . | 110,000 | 40,000 | | | 150,000 |
| Intercompany . . . . . . . . . . . . . . . | | 15,000 | | 5,000(3) | 10,000 |
| Investment in S Company . . . . . . . | 96,000 | | | 96,000(1) | –0– |
| Land . . . . . . . . . . . . . . . . . . . . . . . . | 220,000 | 30,000 | 12,000(1) | | 262,000 |
| Buildings and equipment. . . . . . . . | 500,000 | 200,000 | 6,000(1) | 50,000(4) | 656,000 |
| Accumulated depreciation . . . . . . . | (320,000) | (63,000) | 50,000(3) | 1,000(1) | (334,000) |
| Goodwill . . . . . . . . . . . . . . . . . . . . . | | | 9,000(1) | | 9,000 |
| Total Assets . . . . . . . . . . . . . . . . . | 706,000 | 270,000 | 77,000 | 152,000 | 901,000 |
| Liabilities . . . . . . . . . . . . . . . . . . . . | 290,000 | 200,000 | | | 490,000 |
| Common stock . . . . . . . . . . . . . . . . | 300,000 | 40,000 | 40,000(1) | | 300,000 |
| Retained earnings. . . . . . . . . . . . . . | 116,000 | 30,000 | ➧114,000 | ➧ 79,000 | 111,000 |
| Total Liabilities and Equity. . . . | 706,000 | 270,000 | 154,000 | 79,000 | 901,000 |
| Proof of debit and credit postings. . . . . . . . . . . . . . . . . . . . . . . . | | | 231,000 | 231,000 | |

Explanation of entries:
(1) The primary elimination entry.       (3) The accumulated depreciation elimination entry.
(2) The secondary elimination entry.     (4) The current-year intercompany transactions elimination entry.

[a]Comprised of $15,000 of subsidiary's reported net income, net of $4,000 of amortization of cost in excess of book value.

**MODULE 3**   **The Partial Equity Method** (continued)

The credit brings S Company's $15,000 inventory down to $10,000 in consolidation, just as the $5,000 credit did in consolidation at December 31, 19X1 ($10,000 is the parent's cost). The $5,000 debit to retained earnings eliminates the gross profit recorded in the general ledger in 19X1 that is still not reportable from a consolidated viewpoint. (This entry is made at every consolidation date after December 31, 19X1, until the inventory is resold by the subsidiary.) Note that this entry does not involve the Intercompany Sales or Intercompany Cost of Goods Sold accounts. The Intercompany Sales related to this inventory took place in 19X1, and those accounts were eliminated in consolidation in 19X1.

**Resold by the End of 19X3.**   If the inventory has been resold by the end of 19X3, then the gross profit deferred at the end of 19X1 is now reportable. In consolidation at December 31, 19X3, the following entry would be made:

**WORKSHEET ENTRY ONLY**

| | | |
|---|---|---|
| Retained Earnings—P Company (beginning of year) . . . . . . . . . . . . . . . . . . . . . . . . . . . . . . . . . . . . . | 5,000 | |
| Cost of Goods Sold (to third parties) . . . . . | | 5,000 |

After this elimination entry is posted, the appropriate worksheet accounts (assuming the inventory is resold for $18,000) would appear as follows:

| | P Company | S Company | Eliminations Dr. | Eliminations Cr. | Consolidated |
|---|---|---|---|---|---|
| **Income Statement (19X3)** | | | | | |
| Sales . . . . . . . . . . . . . . . . . . . . . . . . . . . . . . | | 18,000 | | | 18,000 |
| Cost of goods sold . . . . . . . . . . . . . . . . . . . | | (15,000) | | 5,000(2) | (10,000) |
| Intercompany Accounts: | | | | | |
| Equity in net income . . . . . . . . . . . . . . | 3,000 | | 3,000(1) | | –0– |
| Net Income . . . . . . . . . . . . . . . . . . . . . . . . | 3,000 | 3,000 | 3,000 | 5,000 | 8,000 |
| **Statement of Retained Earnings (19X3)** | | | 5,000(2) | | |
| Beginning of year . . . . . . . . . . . . . . . . . . . | 166,000 | 55,000 | 55,000(1) | | 161,000 |
| + Net income . . . . . . . . . . . . . . . . . . . . . | 3,000 | 3,000 | 3,000 | 5,000 | 8,000 |
| End of year . . . . . . . . . . . . . . . . . . . . . . . . | 169,000 | 58,000 | 63,000 | 5,000 | 169,000 |

Explanation of entries:
  (1) The primary elimination entry.
  (2) The entry to recognize gross profit previously deferred.

Note: The beginning retained earnings balances for both companies are the December 31, 19X1, balances in Illustration 7-6 plus assumed net increases for 19X2 of $50,000 for P Company and $25,000 for S Company.

Note that this elimination entry has a "wash" effect on retained earnings. This allows the $5,000 of gross profit recorded in the general ledger in 19X1 to flow across and be reported in the consolidated column.

## Dealing with Beginning Inventory and Current-year Transfers

In a normal consolidation involving intercompany inventory transactions, intercompany sales of inventory usually occur each year. Accordingly, entries are required both (1) to recognize the profit on the beginning intercompany inventory, and (2) to eliminate the current-year intercompany transactions. In this regard, it is simpler to separate these entries rather than to handle them as a single, combined elimination entry.

Some of the beginning inventory may be physically part of the ending inventory. However, the consolidation effort is simplifed if it is assumed that the beginning inventory has been sold and that all of the ending inventory came from the current-year intercompany inventory transactions. So long as the gross profit rates are the same (or very close) from year to year, the assumption is a safe one.

### UPSTREAM TRANSFERS ABOVE COST FROM PARTIALLY OWNED SUBSIDIARY

Because the elimination of all of the gross profit in consolidation is required regardless of whether or not a minority interest exists, the only difference between upstream and downstream inventory transfers is that an additional worksheet adjustment is made to the minority interest in an upstream transfer to allocate a portion of the deferred intercompany gross profit to the minority interest. Without this adjustment, the consolidated net income and consolidated retained earnings would be reduced by the total amount of the deferred intercompany gross profit (rather than just the portion that accrues to the parent company).

Based on the intercompany inventory transaction information given for Illustration 7-6, but assuming that the intercompany sales are upstream and the subsidiary is 80% owned, the appropriate elimination entries are as follows:

| | | |
|---|---|---|
| Intercompany Sales . . . . . . . . . . . . . . . . . . . . . . . . . . . | 75,000 | |
|     Intercompany Cost of Goods Sold . . . . . . . | | 50,000 |
|     Cost of Goods Sold (to third parties) . . . . | | 20,000 |
|     Inventory (balance sheet) . . . . . . . . . . . . . . | | 5,000 |

To eliminate the intercompany transactions and defer the recognition of $5,000 of intercompany gross profit.

**MODULE 3** **The Partial Equity Method** (continued)

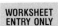

| | | |
|---|---|---|
| Minority Interest in Net Assets of Subsidiary. | 1,000 | |
| Minority Interest in Net Income of Subsidiary. . . . . . . . . . . . . . . . . . . . . | | 1,000 |
| To allocate to the minority interest $1,000 of the $5,000 deferred intercompany gross profit. | | |

In the latter entry, the credit to the minority interest deduction in the income statement reduces that deduction and thereby results in consolidated net income being reduced by $4,000 ($5,000 from the first entry less the $1,000 in the second entry) rather than by $5,000.

ILLUSTRATION

## Preparing Consolidated Financial Statements

- The Partial Equity Method
- Upstream Transfers above Cost from 80%-owned Subsidiary

Illustration 7-7 shows a consolidating statement worksheet for the year ended December 31, 19X1. The P Company and S Company financial statements presented in Illustration 5-5, along with the primary, secondary, and accumulated depreciation elimination entry are used. The P Company and S Company columns were modified to reflect the intercompany upstream transactions discussed above. For convenience, all of the elimination entries used in Illustration 7-7 are shown below in sequence:

1. The primary elimination entry:

**WORKSHEET ENTRY ONLY**

| | | |
|---|---|---|
| Common Stock . . . . . . . . . . : . . . . . . . . . . . . . . . . . . . . | 40,000 | |
| Retained Earnings (beginning of year). . . . . . . . | 20,000 | |
| Equity in Net Income of Subsidiary (80% of $15,000) . . . . . . . . . . . . . . . . . . . . . | 12,000 | |
| Minority Interest in Net Income of S Company. . . . . . . . . . . . . . . . . . . . . . . . . . . . | 3,000 | |
| Land. . . . . . . . . | 9,600 | |
| Equipment. . . . . . . . . . . . . . . . . . . . . . . . . . . . . . . . . . . . . | 4,800 | |
| Goodwill. . . . . . . . . . . . . . . . . . . . . . . . . . . . . . . . . . . . . . | 7,200 | |
| Dividends Declared . . . . . . . . . . . . . . . . . . . . | | 5,000 |
| Accumulated Depreciation . . . . . . . . . . . . . . | | 800 |
| Investment in Subsidiary . . . . . . . . . . . . . | | 76,800 |
| Minority Interest in Net Assets of S Company . . . . . . . . . . . . . . . . . . . . . . . . . | | 14,000 |

2. The secondary elimination entry:

**MODULE 3   The Partial Equity Method** (continued)

■ ILLUSTRATION 7-7

### The Partial Equity Method: Upstream Transfer above Cost (80%-owned Subsidiary)

| | P Company | S Company | Eliminations Dr. | Eliminations Cr. | Consoli-dated |
|---|---|---|---|---|---|
| **P COMPANY AND SUBSIDIARY (S COMPANY)** Consolidating Statement Worksheet for the Year Ended December 31, 19X1 | | | | | |
| **Income Statement** | | | | | |
| Sales | 600,000 | 150,000 | | | 750,000 |
| Cost of goods sold | (360,000) | (60,000) | 3,200(2) | 20,000(4) | (403,200) |
| Expenses | (190,000) | (100,000) | | | (290,000) |
| Intercompany Accounts: | | | | | |
| Equity in net income | 8,800ᵃ | | 12,000(1) | 3,200(2) | –0– |
| Sales | | 75,000 | 75,000(4) | | –0– |
| Cost of goods sold | | (50,000) | | 50,000(4) | –0– |
| Income before Minority Interest | 58,800 | 15,000 | 90,200 | 73,200 | 56,800 |
| Minority interest | | | 3,000(1) | 1,000(5) | (2,000) |
| Net Income | 58,800 | 15,000 | 93,200 | 74,200 | 54,800 |
| **Statement of Retained Earnings** | | | | | |
| Balances, January 1, 19X1 | 100,000 | 20,000 | 20,000 | | 100,000 |
| + Net income | 58,800 | 15,000 | 93,200 | 74,200 | 54,800 |
| – Dividends declared | (45,000) | (5,000) | | 5,000(1) | (45,000) |
| Balances, December 31, 19X1 | 113,800 | 30,000 | 113,200 | 79,200 | 109,800 |
| **Balance Sheet** | | | | | |
| Cash | 42,000 | 11,000 | | | 53,000 |
| Accounts receivable, net | 75,000 | 37,000 | | | 112,000 |
| Inventory: | | | | | |
| From vendors | 95,000 | 55,000 | | | 150,000 |
| Intercompany | 15,000 | | | 5,000(4) | 10,000 |
| Deferred profit | | | | | |
| Investment in S Company | 76,800 | | | 76,800(1) | –0– |
| Land | 220,000 | 30,000 | 9,600(1) | | 259,600 |
| Buildings and equipment | 500,000 | 200,000 | 4,800(1) | 50,000(3) | 654,800 |
| Accumulated depreciation | (320,000) | (63,000) | 50,000(3) | 800(1) | (333,800) |
| Goodwill | | | 7,200(1) | | 7,200 |
| Total Assets | 703,800 | 270,000 | 71,600 | 132,600 | 912,800 |
| Liabilities | 290,000 | 200,000 | | | 490,000 |
| Minority interest in net assets | | | 1,000(5) | 14,000(1) | 13,000 |
| Common stock | 300,000 | 40,000 | 40,000(1) | | 300,000 |
| Retained earnings | 113,800 | 30,000 | 113,200 | 79,200 | 109,800 |
| Total Liabilities and Equity | 703,800 | 270,000 | 154,200 | 93,200 | 912,800 |
| Proof of debit and credit postings | | | 225,800 | 225,800 | |

Explanation of entries:
(1) The primary elimination entry.
(2) The secondary elimination entry.
(3) The accumulated depreciation elimination entry.
(4) The current-year intercompany transactions elimination entry.
(5) The adjustment to the minority interest to share deferral of profit.

ᵃComprised of $12,000 (80% share of subsidiary's reported net income of $15,000), net of $3,200 of amortization of cost in excess of book value.

**MODULE 3   The Partial Equity Method** (continued)

| WORKSHEET ENTRY ONLY | Cost of Goods Sold (to third parties)......... | 3,200 | |
|---|---|---|---|
| | Equity in Net Income of Subsidiary..... | | 3,200 |
| | (80% of the $4,000 used in Illustration 7-1) | | |

3. The accumulated depreciation entry:

| WORKSHEET ENTRY ONLY | Accumulated Depreciation.................... | 50,000 | |
|---|---|---|---|
| | Buildings and Equipment.............. | | 50,000 |

4. The current-year intercompany transactions elimination entry:

| WORKSHEET ENTRY ONLY | Intercompany Sales........................... | 75,000 | |
|---|---|---|---|
| | Intercompany Cost of Goods Sold....... | | 50,000 |
| | Cost of Goods Sold (to third parties).... | | 20,000 |
| | Inventory................................ | | 5,000 |

5. The adjustment to the minority interest to share the deferral of profit:

| WORKSHEET ENTRY ONLY | Minority Interest in Net Assets of Subsidiary................................. | 1,000 | |
|---|---|---|---|
| | Minority Interest in Net Income of Subsidiary ........................... | | 1,000 |

**Review Points for Illustration 7-7.**   Note the following:

1. From the parent column to the consolidated column, net income and retained earnings have been reduced by $4,000 (80% of $5,000).
2. The $2,000 minority interest deduction in the consolidated column is equal to 20% of $10,000, which is the subsidiary's recorded net income of $15,000 less the $5,000 intercompany gross profit deferred in consolidation.
3. If the parent were to issue **"parent company" financial statements,** in addition to consolidated financial statements (which rarely occurs), it first would have to make the following financial statement adjusting entry to reflect that the subsidiary's book net income includes unrealized intercompany profit:

| | | | |
|---|---|---|---|
| Equity in Net Income of Subsidiary ........... | 4,000 | |
| Investment in Subsidiary................ | | 4,000 |
| (80% of $5,000) | | |

**MODULE 3** **The Partial Equity Method** *(continued)*

## Subsequent-year Treatment of Unrealized Profit

**Not Resold at the End of 19X2.** If the intercompany-acquired inventory is still on hand at the end of 19X2, the following elimination entry is required in consolidation at December 31, 19X2:

| | | |
|---|---|---|
| Retained Earnings—P Company (beginning of year) | 4,000 | |
| Minority Interest in Net Assets of S Company | 1,000 | |
| Inventory | | 5,000 |

This entry is made at every consolidation date after December 31, 19X1, until the inventory is resold by the parent.

**Resold by the End of 19X3.** If the intercompany-acquired inventory has been resold by the end of 19X3, then the gross profit deferred at the end of 19X1 is now reportable. In consolidation at December 31, 19X3, the following entry would be made:

| | | |
|---|---|---|
| Retained Earnings—P Company (beginning of year) | 4,000 | |
| Minority Interest (income statement) | 1,000 | |
| Cost of Goods Sold (to third parties) | | 5,000 |

The postings to the income statement effectively report $4,000 more consolidated net income ($5,000−$1,000). The $1,000 debit and the $5,000 credit are subtotaled at the net income line and carried forward to the net income line in the analysis of the retained earnings section of the worksheet. These carryforward amounts offset the $4,000 direct posting to the parent's Retained Earnings account, resulting in a wash effect. This allows the $4,000 in the parent's Retained Earnings account—in the general ledger—to flow across the consolidated column and be reported for consolidated reporting purposes.

## MISCELLANEOUS AREAS

## Transportation Costs

*ARB No. 51* does not specifically address the consolidation treatment of transportation costs incurred in transferring inventory among entities of a consolidated group. Because normal transportation costs are inventoriable costs, there is no sound reason to treat them otherwise in consolidated financial statements.

When the buying entity incurs the transportation costs and treats them as inventoriable costs, the elimination of all the selling entity's gross profit makes the transportation costs part of inventory cost on a consolidated basis. (Thus, no special procedures or elimination entries relating to transportation costs are needed in consolidation.) However, when the selling entity incurs the transportation costs—which it considers marketing costs—the elimination of its gross profit results in the expensing of the transportation costs on a consolidated basis. Accordingly, in consolidation an additional elimination entry must be made in these latter cases to (1) eliminate the transportation costs being reported as marketing expenses and (2) charge the transportation costs to inventory.

For the sake of simplicity, the illustrations pertaining to inventory transfers assumed transportation costs were insignificant. Such costs are therefore treated as period costs on a separate company and on a consolidated basis.

## Lower of Cost or Market Adjustments

Occasionally, the buying entity makes an adjustment for intercompany-acquired inventory in its general ledger that is based on its own cost or the market value, whichever is less. For purposes of consolidated reporting, the appropriate valuation is the lower of the *selling* entity's cost or the market value.

## END-OF-CHAPTER REVIEW

### Summary of Key Points

1. In consolidation, all intercompany transactions must be eliminated, so that the consolidated financial statements reflect only transactions between the consolidated group and outside parties.
2. From a consolidated viewpoint, intercompany profit on inventory transfers within the consolidated group is not considered realized until the acquiring entity has disposed of the inventory.
3. In deferring the recognition of intercompany profit, gross profit is the concept of profit used. Income taxes provided on such gross profit must also be deferred for consolidated reporting purposes.
4. The existence of a minority interest does not affect the amount of gross profit to be deferred. For upstream intercompany sales from partially owned subsidiaries, the gross profit deferred may be shared with the minority interest.

### Glossary of New Terms

**Arm's length transaction**   Transactions that take place between completely independent parties.

Downstream sale   The sale of an asset from a parent to one of its subsidiaries.
Lateral sale   The sale of an asset between subsidiaries of a common parent.
Upstream sale   The sale of an asset from a subsidiary to its parent.

## Self-Study Questions

*(Answers are at the end of this chapter.)*

1. P Company sold inventory costing $100,000 to its 60%-owned subsidiary, S Company, for $140,000 in 19X1. At the end of 19X1, S Company reported $35,000 of intercompany-acquired inventory in its balance sheet. The amount of unrealized intercompany profit at the end of 19X1 that accrues to the parent's stockholders is:
   a. $6,000.
   b. $10,000.
   c. $24,000.
   d. $40,000.
   e. None of the above.

2. Assume the information in question 1, except assume that the sale is upstream from S Company to P Company.
   a. $6,000.
   b. $10,000.
   c. $24,000.
   d. $40,000.
   e. None of the above.

3. In 19X2, P Company resold for $70,000 inventory that it had acquired from S Company in 19X1 for $50,000. S Company's cost was $36,000. In preparing consolidated financial statements for 19X2, which of the following entries will be made on the worksheet?
   a. Credit Intercompany Cost of Goods Sold.
   b. Credit Equity in Net Income of Subsidiary.
   c. Credit Minority Interest in Net Income of Subsidiary.
   d. Credit Inventory.
   e. None of the above.

4. In 19X2, S Company resold for $40,000 inventory that it had acquired from P Company in 19X1 for $32,000. P Company's cost was $25,000. In preparing consolidated financial statements for 19X2, which of the following entries will be made on the worksheet?
   a. Credit Intercompany Cost of Goods Sold for $32,000.
   b. Credit Inventory for $32,000.
   c. Credit Cost of Goods Sold for $7,000.
   d. Credit Cost of Goods Sold for $8,000.
   e. None of the above.

5. At the end of 19X2, P Company reports in its balance sheet $80,000 for inventory acquired in 19X1 (the preceding year) from S Company, its 75%-owned subsidiary. S Company's cost was $60,000. In preparing consolidated financial statements for 19X2, which of the following entries should be made on the worksheet?
   a. Credit Cost of Goods Sold.
   b. Credit Intercompany Cost of Goods Sold.

      c. Credit Retained Earnings.

      d. Credit Inventory.

      e. None of the above.

6. P Company sold inventory costing $200,000 to its 90%-owned subsidiary, S Company, in 19X1 for $250,000. At the end of 19X1, S Company reported $30,000 of this inventory in its balance sheet. S Company also reported net income of $100,000 for 19X1. In the consolidated income statement for 19X1, the minority interest deduction would be reported as:

      a. $7,000.

      b. $9,250.

      c. $9,400.

      d. $10,000.

      e. None of the above.

7. S Company, an 80%-owned subsidiary of P Company, sold inventory costing $300,000 to its parent for $400,000 in 19X1. P Company resold $340,000 of this inventory in 19X1 for $510,000. S Company reported a net income of $200,000 for 19X1 disregarding any unrealized intercompany profit at the end of 19X1. In the consolidated income statement for 19X1, the minority interest deduction would be reported at:

      a. $28,000.

      b. $36,000.

      c. $37,000.

      d. $40,000.

      e. None of the above.

# ASSIGNMENT MATERIAL

## Review Questions

1. List five types of intercompany transactions.
2. Why are intercompany transactions usually recorded in separate general ledger accounts?
3. Why are intercompany sales not considered arm's length transactions?
4. Why must intercompany transactions be eliminated?
5. Which intercompany accounts can be eliminated by the rearrangement process?
6. How much profit on an intercompany sale of inventory must be eliminated in consolidation?
7. If intercompany profit is deferred in consolidation, must income taxes that have been provided on that profit be deferred also? Why or why not?
8. What is a downstream sale? an upstream sale?
9. Why are intercompany inventory transfers usually recorded at amounts in excess of cost?
10. When may the profit on an intercompany inventory sale be recognized for financial reporting purposes?
11. Are elimination entries relating to intercompany inventory transactions recorded in the general ledger?
12. If a parent company sells inventory to a subsidiary at prices equal to competitive market prices, has a bona fide sale occurred? Why or why not?

# Discussion Cases

| DC 7-1 |
|---|

## Evaluation of the Manner of Determining Intercompany Transfer Prices and Accounting Ramifications of Pricing Disparities

Porta Company manufactures a standard line of minicomputers. A substantial portion of the domestic manufacturing output is marketed in numerous foreign countries through wholly owned foreign subsidiaries. The subsidiaries purchase the minicomputers from the domestic parent, which has only a single subsidiary in any one foreign country. You have recently been assigned the task of preparing the monthly consolidating statement worksheet, and you notice that the parent's gross profit rates are quite high for intercompany sales to foreign subsidiaries with high income tax rates (higher than the U.S. income tax rate) and quite low to foreign subsidiaries with low income tax rates (lower than the U.S. income tax rate). Considering that the product is highly standardized, this seems unusual. You query the vice president of marketing, who informs you of the following facts:

1. The transfer prices are negotiated by the marketing personnel at the parent's location and the individual managements of the foreign subsidiaries.
2. The parent could impose transfer prices, but company policy is to negotiate transfer prices so that meaningful evaluations of each separate company can be made.

### Required:
1. What other reason might account for this disparity?
2. What are the potential ramifications, if any, of this disparity?

| DC 7-2 |
|---|

## Treatment of Expenses Incurred by Parent on Behalf of Subsidiary

Sadler Company is a wholly owned subsidiary of Painter Company. Sadler files a registration statement with the SEC in connection with a proposed sale of bonds. In the past, certain expenses incurred by the parent on behalf of the subsidiary have not been charged to the subsidiary.

### Required:
1. Should the subsidiary's historical income statements reflect all of the expenses that the parent incurred on behalf of the subsidiary?
2. If yes, how should the amount of expenses incurred on the subsidiary's behalf by the parent be determined?

# Exercises

| E 7-1 |
|---|

## Reconciling Intercompany Accounts

During 19X1, Pontos Company and Santini Company (a wholly owned subsidiary) had the following intercompany transactions:

1. The parent advanced the subsidiary $50,000 on a noninterest-bearing basis.
2. The parent charged the subsidiary management fees of $36,000.
3. The subsidiary sold inventory costing $128,000 to the parent for $160,000. Of this inventory, $145,000 was resold by the parent by the end of 19X1.)
4. The subsidiary declared dividends of $25,000.
5. The subsidiary paid dividends of $20,000. (The remaining $5,000 was paid on January 7, 19X2.)
6. The parent charged the subsidiary $15,000 for legal expenses incurred on behalf of the subsidiary.
7. On December 31, 19X1, inventory costing $24,000 was shipped to the parent at a billing price of $30,000. The parent received this inventory on January 2, 19X2.

### Required:
1. Prepare T-account analyses of the intercompany receivable and payable accounts for 19X1.
2. Calculate the unrealized intercompany inventory profit at December 31, 19X1.

## E 7-2

## Downstream Transfers at Cost

In 19X1, Passer Company sold inventory costing $40,000 to its wholly owned subsidiary, Selkirk Company for $40,000.

### Required:
Prepare the elimination entry required in consolidation at the end of 19X1, 19X2, and 19X3 relating to this intercompany inventory transfer under each of the following assumptions:
a. All of the inventory was resold by the subsidiary in 19X3 for $60,000.
b. All of the inventory was resold by the subsidiary in 19X1 for $60,000.
c. In 19X1, 75% of the inventory was sold for $45,000, and the remaining 25% was sold in 19X3 for $15,000.

## E 7-3

## Downstream Transfers above Cost

A parent company and its subsidiary had intercompany inventory transactions in 19X1. The following information has been obtained from the individual financial statements of each company:

| | Total | Resold | On Hand |
|---|---|---|---|
| Intercompany sales | $240,000 | _204_ | $36,000 |
| Intercompany cost of goods sold | – 180,000 | _–153_ | _–27_ |
| Gross Profit | $ 60,000 | _51_ | _9_ |

### Required:
1. Complete the analysis.
2. Prepare the universal elimination entry required in consolidation at the end of the year 19X1.

*100%*

## E 7-4 Downstream Transfers above Cost to 75%-owned Subsidiary *100%*

In 19X1, Probe Company sold inventory costing $50,000 to its 75%-owned subsidiary, Search Company, for $70,000. (Search resold a portion of the inventory for $65,000 in 19X1.) As of December 31, 19X1, Search's balance sheet showed $21,000 of intercompany-acquired inventory. It resold this remaining inventory in 19X3 for $28,000. Assume Search reported $80,000 of net income for 19X1, 19X2, and 19X3.

*70 - 21*
*49 sold*
*16k NI*

### Required for Modules 1 and 2:
1. Prepare the general ledger entry required for 19X1, 19X2, and 19X3 under the complete equity method.
2. Prepare the elimination entry or entries required in consolidation at the end of 19X1, 19X2, and 19X3 relating to this intercompany inventory transfer.
3. Determine the amount at which the inventory is reported in consolidation at the end of 19X1 and 19X2.

### Required for Module 3:
Complete requirements 2 and 3 above.

*Intercomp. Analysis Matrix*

| | total | resold | on hand |
|---|---|---|---|
| Sales | (70) | (49) | (21) |
| COGS | 50 | 35 | 15 |
| | (20) | (14) | (6) |

## E 7-5 Upstream Transfers above Cost from 75%-owned Subsidiary

In 19X1, Potash Company acquired inventory from Saline Company, its 75%-owned subsidiary, for $100,000. Saline's cost was $80,000. At December 31, 19X1, Potash's balance sheet showed $40,000 of intercompany-acquired inventory on hand. (A portion of the inventory was resold during 19X1 for $90,000.) The remaining inventory was resold in 19X3 for $52,000. Assume Saline reported $100,000 of net income for 19X1, 19X2, and 19X3.

### Required for Modules 1 and 2:
1. Prepare the general ledger entry required for 19X1, 19X2, and 19X3 under the complete equity method.
2. Prepare the elimination entry or entries required in consolidation at the end of 19X1, 19X2, and 19X3 relating to this intercompany inventory transfer.
3. Determine the amount at which the inventory is reported in consolidation at the end of 19X1 and 19X2.

### Required for Module 3:
Complete requirements 2 and 3 above.

## E 7-6 Lower of Cost or Market Adjustment

In 19X1, Ponderosa Company sold inventory costing $60,000 to its subsidiary Saguaro Company, for $70,000. At the end of 19X1, the subsidiary recorded a lower of cost or market adjustment relating to this inventory, 60% of which had been sold during 19X1.

**Required:**
Determine the amount at which the inventory should be reported in consolidation assuming the adjustment was:
a. $3,000.
b. $6,000.

---

| | |
|---|---|
| **E** | |
| **7-7** | |

### Issuing "Parent Company" Financial Statements (Module 3 only)

Polymeric Company and Solarus Company, a 70%-owned subsidiary, had intercompany inventory transfers during 19X5. At the end of 19X5, $20,000 of unrealized intercompany profit was deferred in consolidation. (The partial equity method is used.) Pursuant to a loan agreement, the parent also issues "parent company" financial statements.

**Required:**

1. Prepare the financial statement entry the parent must make before issuing "parent company only" financial statements assuming the transfers are downstream.
2. Prepare the financial statement entry as in requirement 1, but assume that the transfers are upstream.

## Problems

| | |
|---|---|
| **P** | |
| **7-1\*** | |

### Preparing the Consolidation Worksheet: Downstream Transfers above Cost to 100%-owned Subsidiary—Profit in Ending Inventory    *formed*

On January 1, 19X1, Pillow Company ~~acquired all of the outstanding common stock of~~ Sandman Company ~~for $104,000~~ cash. The following information concerns the subsidiary at that date:  *95,000*

| | |
|---|---|
| Common stock | ~~$10,000~~ *95,000* |
| Retained earnings | ~~85,000~~ *0* |

~~The entire cost in excess of book value was assigned to goodwill, which was deemed to have a 9-year life.~~ Financial statements for 19X1 and at December 31, 19X1, follow.

| | Pillow Company | Sandman Company |
|---|---|---|
| **Income Statement (19X1)** | | |
| Sales | $200,000 | $147,000 |
| Cost of goods sold | (110,000) | (82,000) |
| Expenses | (84,000) | (53,000) |
| Intercompany Accounts: | | |
| Equity in net income | ~~11,000~~  *$12,000* | *(continued)* |

\*The financial statement information presented for problems accompanied by asterisks is also provided on Model 7 (filename: Model7) of the software file disk that is available for use with the text, enabling the problem to be worked on the computer.

|  | Pillow Company | Sandman Company |
|---|---|---|
| Sales...................................... | 70,000 | |
| Cost of goods sold ........................ | ( 40,000) | |
| Net Income ............................... | $ ~~47,000~~ | $ 12,000 |

*handwritten: $48,000*

**Balance Sheet (December 31, 19X1)**

| | | |
|---|---|---|
| Inventory: | | |
| From vendors............................ | $ 55,000 | |
| Intercompany ........................... | | $ 14,000 |
| Investment in Sandman Company ....... | $100,000 ~~108,000~~ | |
| Other assets .............................. | 346,000 ~~337,000~~ | 286,000 |
|    Total Assets....................... | $501,000 ~~$500,000~~ | $300,000 |
| Liabilities ................................ | $170,000 | $200,000 |
| Common stock............................. | 150,000 | ~~10,000~~ 95,000 |
| Retained earnings ........................ | 181,000 ~~180,000~~ | 90,000  5,000 |
|    Total Liabilities and Equity......... | $501,000 ~~$500,000~~ | $300,000 |
| Dividends declared—19X1 ................. | $23,000 | $7,000 |

*handwritten left margin: Need to change in computer*

## Additional Information:

In applying the equity method of accounting to the subsidiary's earnings for 19X1, the accountant recorded $12,000 ($12,000 × 100% ownership interest).

## Required:

1. For Modules 1 and 2 only: make any necessary year-end adjusting entries that are appropriate to the module you are using to work this problem. (Then adjust the financial statements accordingly.)
2. Prepare the worksheet elimination entries required in consolidation at December 31, 19X1.
3. Prepare a consolidating statement worksheet at December 31, 19X1.
4. How would the elimination entry or entries pertaining to the intercompany transfers be different if the acquisition of the subsidiary had qualified for pooling of interests treatment?

**P 7-2***

## Preparing a Consolidation Worksheet: Upstream Transfer above Cost from 90%-owned Subsidiary—Profit in Ending Inventory

On January 1, 19X1, Planeco Company acquired 90% of the outstanding common stock of Sanders Company for $310,000 cash. Information regarding Sanders on that date is:

| | |
|---|---|
| Common stock........................................... | $120,000 |
| Retained earnings ....................................... | 80,000 |
| Land—Book value......................................... | 85,000 |
|    —Current value......................................... | 185,000 |

Goodwill was assigned a 20-year life. Separate company financial statements follow for 19X1 and at December 31, 19X1:

|  | Planeco Company | Sanders Company |
|---|---|---|
| **Income Statement (19X1)** |  |  |
| Sales | $330,000 | $ 70,000 |
| Cost of goods sold | (175,000) | (35,000) |
| Expenses | (95,000) | (45,000) |
| Intercompany Accounts: |  |  |
| Equity in net income | 34,000 |  |
| Sales |  | 250,000 |
| Cost of goods sold |  | (200,000) |
| Net Income | $ 94,000 | $ 40,000 |
| **Balance Sheet (December 31, 19X1)** |  |  |
| Inventory: |  |  |
| From vendors | $ 65,000 | $ 60,000 |
| Intercompany | 50,000 |  |
| Land | 200,000 | 85,000 |
| Other assets | 159,000 | 255,000 |
| Investment in Sanders Company | 326,000 |  |
| Total Assets | $800,000 | $400,000 |
| Liabilities | $155,000 | $180,000 |
| Common stock | 400,000 | 120,000 |
| Retained earnings | 245,000 | 100,000 |
| Total Liabilities and Equity | $800,000 | $400,000 |
| Dividends declared in 19X1 | $60,000 | $20,000 |

## Additional Information:

In applying the equity method of accounting to the subsidiary's earnings for 19X1, the accountant recorded $36,000 ($40,000×90%).

## Required:

1. For Modules 1 and 2 only: make any necessary year-end adjusting entries that are appropriate for the module you are using to work this problem. (Then adjust the financial statements accordingly.)
2. Prepare the worksheet elimination entries required in consolidation at December 31, 19X1.
3. Prepare a consolidating statement worksheet at December 31, 19X1.
4. How would the elimination entry or entries pertaining to the intercompany inventory transfer be different if the acquisition of the subsidiary had qualified for pooling of interests treatment?

## Preparing a Consolidation Worksheet: Downstream Transfers above Cost to 90%-owned Subsidiary—Profit in Beginning and Ending Inventory

The financial statements of Plateau Company and its 90%-owned subsidiary, Sundance Company, for the year ended December 31, 19X2, are as follows:

| | Plateau Company | Sundance Company |
|---|---|---|
| **Income Statement (19X2)** | | |
| Sales. . . . . . . . . . . . . . . . . . . . . . . . . . . . . . . . . . . . . | $502,000 | $200,000 |
| Cost of goods sold . . . . . . . . . . . . . . . . . . . . . . . | (290,000) | (110,000) |
| Expenses . . . . . . . . . . . . . . . . . . . . . . . . . . . . . . . . | (215,000) | (70,000) |
| Intercompany accounts: | | |
|   Equity in net income . . . . . . . . . . . . . . . . . . . | 18,000 | |
|   Sales. . . . . . . . . . . . . . . . . . . . . . . . . . . . . . . . | 100,000 | |
|   Cost of goods sold . . . . . . . . . . . . . . . . . . . . | (60,000) | |
| Net Income . . . . . . . . . . . . . . . . . . . . . . . . . . . . | $ 55,000 | $ 20,000 |
| | | |
| **Statement of Retained Earnings (19X2)** | | |
| Beginning of year. . . . . . . . . . . . . . . . . . . . . . . . | $210,000 | $ 50,000 |
| +Net income. . . . . . . . . . . . . . . . . . . . . . . . . . . . | 55,000 | 20,000 |
| −Dividends declared. . . . . . . . . . . . . . . . . . . . . | (25,000) | (10,000) |
| End of year . . . . . . . . . . . . . . . . . . . . . . . . . . . . | $240,000 | $ 60,000 |
| | | |
| **Balance Sheet (December 31, 19X2)** | | |
| Cash. . . . . . . . . . . . . . . . . . . . . . . . . . . . . . . . . . . | $90,000 | $ 30,000 |
| Accounts receivable, net. . . . . . . . . . . . . . . . . . | 164,000 | 40,000 |
| Inventory: | | |
|   From vendors. . . . . . . . . . . . . . . . . . . . . . . . . | 200,000 | 70,000 |
|   Intercompany . . . . . . . . . . . . . . . . . . . . . . . . | | 10,000 |
| Investment in Sundance Company . . . . . . . . . . . | 126,000 | |
| Fixed assets, net. . . . . . . . . . . . . . . . . . . . . . . . . | 260,000 | 90,000 |
|   Total Assets. . . . . . . . . . . . . . . . . . . . . . . | $840,000 | $240,000 |
| Liabilities . . . . . . . . . . . . . . . . . . . . . . . . . . . . . . | $300,000 | $100,000 |
| Common stock . . . . . . . . . . . . . . . . . . . . . . . . . . | 300,000 | 80,000 |
| Retained earnings . . . . . . . . . . . . . . . . . . . . . . . | 240,000 | 60,000 |
|   Total Liabilities and Equity. . . . . . . . . . . . . | $840,000 | $240,000 |

## Additional Information:

1. Plateau and Sundance combined in May 19X1 in a combination that qualified as a pooling of interests.
2. At December 31, 19X1 (the preceding year-end), Sundance's inventory included inventory it had acquired in 19X1 from its parent at a cost of $15,000. The parent's cost was $9,000. Sundance resold all of this inventory in 19X2 for $26,000.
3. The investment account has not been adjusted for any intercompany transactions in 19X1 or 19X2.

## Required:

1. For Modules 1 and 2 only: make any necessary year-end and beginning of year adjusting entries that are appropriate for the module you are using to work this problem. (Then adjust the financial statements accordingly.)
2. Prepare a conceptual analysis of the investment account as of December 31, 19X1, and update it through December 31, 19X2.

3. Prepare all elimination entries required in consolidation at December 31, 19X2.

4. Prepare a consolidation worksheet at December 31, 19X2.

**P 7-4***

## Preparing a Consolidation Worksheet; Upstream Transfers above Cost from 80%-owned Subsidiary—Profit in Beginning and Ending Inventory

The financial statements of Pebble Company and its 80%-owned subsidiary, Stoner Company, for the year ended December 31, 19X2, are as follows:

| | Pebble Company | Stoner Company |
|---|---|---|
| **Income Statement (19X2)** | | |
| Sales. . . . . . . . . . . . . . . . . . . . . . . . . . . . . . . . . | $600,000 | $ 80,000 |
| Cost of goods sold . . . . . . . . . . . . . . . . . . . . . | (350,000) | (50,000) |
| Expenses. . . . . . . . . . . . . . . . . . . . . . . . . . . . . | (150,000) | (40,000) |
| Intercompany Accounts: | | |
| Equity in net income . . . . . . . . . . . . . . . . . . | 16,000 | |
| Sales. . . . . . . . . . . . . . . . . . . . . . . . . . . . . . . | | 90,000 |
| Cost of goods sold . . . . . . . . . . . . . . . . . . . | | (60,000) |
| Net Income . . . . . . . . . . . . . . . . . . . . . . . . . . . | $116,000 | $ 20,000 |
| **Statement of Retained Earnings (19X2)** | | |
| Beginning of year. . . . . . . . . . . . . . . . . . . . . . . | $150,000 | $ 35,000 |
| + Net income. . . . . . . . . . . . . . . . . . . . . . . . . . | 116,000 | 20,000 |
| − Dividends declared. . . . . . . . . . . . . . . . . . . . | (50,000) | (15,000) |
| End of year . . . . . . . . . . . . . . . . . . . . . . . . . . . | $216,000 | $ 40,000 |
| **Balance Sheet (December 31, 19X2)** | | |
| Cash. . . . . . . . . . . . . . . . . . . . . . . . . . . . . . . . . | $ 63,000 | $15,000 |
| Accounts receivable, net. . . . . . . . . . . . . . . . . | 110,000 | 45,000 |
| Inventory: | | |
| From vendors. . . . . . . . . . . . . . . . . . . . . . . . | 150,000 | 50,000 |
| Intercompany . . . . . . . . . . . . . . . . . . . . . . . | 15,000 | |
| Investment in Stoner Company. . . . . . . . . . . . | 88,000 | |
| Fixed assets, net. . . . . . . . . . . . . . . . . . . . . . . | 390,000 | 100,000 |
| Total Assets. . . . . . . . . . . . . . . . . . . . . . | $816,000 | $210,000 |
| Liabilities . . . . . . . . . . . . . . . . . . . . . . . . . . . . | $200,000 | $100,000 |
| Common stock . . . . . . . . . . . . . . . . . . . . . . . . | 400,000 | 70,000 |
| Retained earnings . . . . . . . . . . . . . . . . . . . . . | 216,000 | 40,000 |
| Total Liabilities and Equity. . . . . . . . . . . . | $816,000 | $210,000 |

## Additional Information:

1. Pebble Company and Stoner Company combined seven years ago in a pooling of interests. Immediately after the combination, Pebble owned all of the outstanding common stock of Stoner. Three years ago, Pebble sold 20% of its interest in Stoner and properly reduced the carrying value of the investment by 20% at that time.

2. At December 31, 19X1 (the preceding year-end), Pebble's inventory included inventory it had acquired in 19X1 from Stoner at a cost of $25,000. Stoner's cost was $10,000. In 19X2, Pebble resold this inventory for $33,000.
3. The investment account has not been adjusted for any intercompany transactions in any year that intercompany sales occurred.

### Required:

1. For Modules 1 and 2 only: make any necessary year-end and beginning-of-year adjusting entries that are appropriate for the module you are using to work this problem. (Then adjust the financial statements accordingly.)
2. Prepare a conceptual analysis of the investment account as of December 31, 19X1, and update it through December 31, 19X2.
3. Prepare all elimination entries required in consolidation at December 31, 19X2.
4. Prepare a consolidation worksheet at December 31, 19X2.

---

| P 7-5* |
|---|

### COMPREHENSIVE (Chapters 3–7)  Preparing Consolidated Statements; Downstream Transfers above Cost to 100%-owned Subsidiary. Intercompany Loans; Mid-year Pooling of Interests

Pearl, Inc., acquired all of the outstanding $25 par common stock of Sapphire, Inc., on June 30, 19X4, in exchange for 40,000 shares of its $25 par common stock. The business combination meets all conditions for a pooling of interests. On June 30, 19X4, Pearl's common stock closed at $65 per share on a national stock exchange. Both corporations continued to operate as separate businesses maintaining separate accounting records with years ending December 31.

On December 31, 19X4, after year-end adjustments and closing nominal accounts, the companies had condensed balance sheet accounts as follows:

|  | Pearl, Inc. | Sapphire, Inc. |
|---|---|---|
| **Assets** | | |
| Cash | $   825,000 | $   330,000 |
| Accounts and other receivables | 2,140,000 | 835,000 |
| Inventories | 2,310,000 | 1,045,000 |
| Land | 650,000 | 300,000 |
| Buildings and equipment | 5,575,000 | 2,380,000 |
| Accumulated depreciation | (1,000,000) | (400,000) |
| Investment in Sapphire, Inc. | 2,430,000 | — |
| Long-term investments and other assets | 865,000 | 385,000 |
|  | $13,795,000 | $4,875,000 |
| **Liabilities and Stockholders' Equity** | | |
| Accounts payable and other current liabilities | $ 2,465,000 | $1,145,000 |
| Long-term debt | 1,900,000 | 1,300,000 |
| Common stock, $25 par value | 3,200,000 | 1,000,000 |

|  | Pearl,<br>Inc. | Sapphire,<br>Inc. |
|---|---|---|
| Additional paid-in capital | 1,850,000 | 190,000 |
| Retained earnings | 4,380,000 | 1,240,000 |
|  | $13,795,000 | $4,875,000 |

## Additional Information:

1. Pearl uses the equity method of accounting for its investment in Sapphire. The investment in Sapphire has not been adjusted for any intercompany transactions.
2. On June 30, 19X4, Sapphire's assets and liabilities had fair values equal to the book balances with the exception of Land, which had a fair value of $550,000.
3. On June 15, 19X4, Sapphire paid a cash dividend of $4 per share on its common stock.
4. On December 10, 19X4, Pearl paid a cash dividend totaling $256,000 on its common stock.
5. On June 30, 19X4, immediately before the combination, the stockholders' equities were:

|  | Pearl,<br>Inc. | Sapphire,<br>Inc. |
|---|---|---|
| Common stock | $2,200,000 | $1,000,000 |
| Additional paid-in capital | 1,660,000 | 190,000 |
| Retained earnings | 3,036,000 | 980,000 |
|  | $6,896,000 | $2,170,000 |

6. Sapphire's long-term debt consisted of 10% 10-year bonds issued at face value on March 31, 19X1. Interest is payable semiannually on March 31 and September 30. Pearl had purchased Sapphire's bonds at face value of $320,000 in 19X1, and there was no change in ownership through December 31, 19X4. Note: Even though intercompany bond holdings are not discussed until Chapter 9, the facts given are such that you need to know only that intercompany bond holdings are the equivalent of an intercompany loan.
7. During October 19X4, Pearl sold merchandise to Sapphire at an aggregate invoice price of $720,000, which included a profit of $180,000. At December 31, 19X4, $252,000 of the merchandise was reported in Sapphire's inventory, and Sapphire had not paid Pearl for the merchandise purchased.
8. The 19X4 net income amounts per the separate books of Pearl and Sapphire were $890,000 (exclusive of equity in Sapphire's earnings) and $580,000, respectively.
9. The balances in retained earnings at December 31, 19X3, were $2,506,000 and $820,000 for Pearl and Sapphire, respectively.

## Required:

1. For Modules 1 and 2 only: make any necessary year-end adjusting entries that are appropriate for the module you are using to work this problem. (Then adjust the financial statements accordingly.)

2. Prepare all elimination entries required to prepare a consolidated balance sheet. (Because a consolidated income statement is not called for, prepare the entries in a manner so that they will be posted only to the balance sheet.)
3. Prepare a consolidated balance sheet as of December 31, 19X4.
4. Prepare a formal consolidated statement of retained earnings for the year ended December 31, 19X4. (Determine the proper balances from the information given and your elimination entries, rather than from using a formal consolidating statement worksheet.)

(AICPA adapted)

**P 7-6\***

## COMPREHENSIVE (Chapters 3–5, 7)    Preparing a Consolidation Worksheet: Upstream Transfers above Cost from 75%-owned Subsidiary—Profit in Ending Inventory; Intercompany Loans and Management Fees; Adjustment of Statements to the Equity Method at the End of the Acquisition Year

On June 30, 19X3, Puntt Company acquired 75% of the outstanding common stock of Shank Company for $533,000 cash. At the purchase date, each of Shank's recorded assets and liabilities had a current value equal to its book value, except for the following items:

|  | Book Value | Current Value |
|---|---|---|
| Inventory | $ 90,000 | $ 70,000 |
| Equipment—Cost | 400,000 | 320,000 |
| —Accumulated depreciation | (160,000) | |

As of June 30, 19X3, Shank's equipment had an estimated remaining life of 5 years. (Shank uses straight-line depreciation.) Puntt's policy is to amortize intangibles over 10 years. By December 31, 19X3, Shank's inventory on hand at June 30, 19X3, had been charged to cost of goods sold.

No intercompany transactions had occurred between Puntt and Shank prior to the acquisition date. During the six months ended December 31, 19X3, the following intercompany transactions occurred:

1. Shank sold inventory to Puntt for $150,000, $80,000 of which has been paid for at December 31, 19X3.
2. On October 1, 19X3, Puntt loaned Shank $200,000 for internal expansion. The borrowing is in the form of a note bearing interest at 10%. (No interest or principal payments have been made to Puntt.)
3. Certain of Shank's management functions are now performed by Puntt. As a result, Puntt charges Shank a management fee of $4,000 per month. (All intercompany management fees for the six months were paid by Shank on December 27, 19X3, and received by Puntt on December 29, 19X3.)
4. On December 28, 19X3, Shank declared a $36,000 dividend payable on January 15, 19X4. The only entry Puntt has made with respect to the dividend is to record the receipt of its share of the dividend on January 17, 19X4.

Puntt's financial statements for the year ended December 31, 19X3, and Shank's financial statements for the six months ended December 31, 19X3, are as follows:

| | Puntt Company | Shank Company July 1, 19X3– Dec. 31, 19X3 |
|---|---|---|
| **Income Statement (19X3)** | | |
| Sales. | $3,500,000 | $730,000 |
| Cost of goods sold | (2,100,000) | (450,000) |
| Expenses | (1,249,000) | (259,000) |
| Intercompany Accounts: | | |
| Sales | | 150,000 |
| Cost of goods sold | | (90,000) |
| Interest income | 5,000 | |
| Interest expense | | (5,000) |
| Management fees | 24,000 | |
| Net Income | $ 180,000 | $ 76,000 |
| **Balance Sheet (December 31, 19X3)** | | |
| Cash | $ 365,000 | $ 115,000 |
| Accounts receivable, net | 290,000 | 160,000 |
| Intercompany receivables | | 38,000 |
| Intercompany note receivable | 200,000 | |
| Inventory: | | |
| From vendors | 402,000 | 205,000 |
| Intercompany | 50,000 | |
| Investment in Shank Company | 533,000 | |
| Land | 900,000 | 125,000 |
| Buildings and equipment | 4,680,000 | 900,000 |
| Accumulated depreciation | (1,270,000) | (380,000) |
| Total Assets | $6,150,000 | $1,163,000 |
| Accounts payable | $ 705,000 | $ 370,000 |
| Dividend payable | | 9,000 |
| Intercompany payables | 65,000 | |
| Intercompany note payable | | 200,000 |
| Long-term debt | 2,500,000 | |
| Common stock | 2,000,000 | 400,000 |
| Retained earnings | 880,000 | 184,000 |
| Total Liabilities and Equity | $6,150,000 | $1,163,000 |
| Dividends declared in 19X3 | $110,000 | $36,000 |

## Additional Information:

1. Shank's depreciation expense for the six months ended December 31, 19X3, was $40,000. There were no retirements.
2. The parent desires to account for its investment in the subsidiary using the equity method; however it has not made any entries to the investment account since the acquisition date.

3. Except for the intercompany loan, each company is to maintain one Intercompany Receivable/Payable account.

### Required:

1. For Modules 1 and 2 only: prepare any necessary year-end adjusting entries that are appropriate for the module you are using to work this problem. (Then adjust the financial statements accordingly.)
2. Prepare T-account analyses of the activity that should be recorded in the Intercompany Receivable/Payable accounts for the six months. Make sure the accounts have the correct balances before you prepare the consolidating statement worksheet. (Also, make sure all income statement intercompany reciprocal accounts agree.)
3. Prepare an expanded analysis of the investment account as of the acquisition date. Update it through December 31, 19X3, using the equity method. (Adjust the parent's and subsidiary's financial statements as necessary to reflect the equity method of accounting.)
4. Prepare the primary, secondary, and accumulated depreciation elimination entries at December 31, 19X3.
5. Prepare the elimination entries relating to intercompany transactions.
6. Prepare a consolidating statement worksheet.

### ANSWERS TO SELF-STUDY QUESTIONS

1. b    3. e    5. d    7. c
2. a    4. c    6. d

# 8

■ ■ ■ ■ ■

# INTERCOMPANY TRANSFERS OF FIXED ASSETS

## *TOPIC OUTLINE*

# CHAPTER OVERVIEW

**F**ixed assets are occasionally transferred among entities of a consolidated group. If the transfers are made at the carrying values of the assets, then no entries are necessary in consolidation because no intercompany gain or loss is recorded. If transfers are made above or below the carrying value, special procedures are required to defer recognition of the gain or loss. The reason for deferring the gain or loss is the same as in the case of inventory transfers—no gain or loss is reportable on intercompany transactions from a consolidated viewpoint.

Because the intercompany gain or loss is deferred, fixed assets are reported at the cost to the selling entity. Likewise, depreciation (for depreciable assets) is reported in consolidation based on this cost to the selling entity. From a consolidated viewpoint, the reported amount for a fixed asset cannot change merely because the asset has been moved to a different location within the consolidated group or because legal ownership within that group has changed.

As was done in Chapter 7, the discussion of income taxes is delayed until Chapter 12. For current purposes, note that if an intercompany gain or loss is deferred, then the tax (or tax benefit) pertaining to the gain or loss must also be deferred.

## Selection of Module

As was the case with inventory transfers in Chapter 7, three equally acceptable methods can be used to accomplish the desired elimination of intercompany transfers of fixed assets in consolidation. Each of these methods is presented as a self-contained, independent module. **Each module is written in such a manner that it may be covered independently of the other two modules. Furthermore, if more than one module is assigned by your instructor, the modules may be covered in any order whatsoever. Accordingly, the order in which the modules are presented is arbitrary and completely irrelevant.** The three modules are:

Module 1:   The Complete Equity Method—Investment Account Adjustment Procedures

Module 2:   The Complete Equity Method—Noninvestment Account Adjustment Procedures

Module 3:   The Partial Equity Method

**In most instances, only one of the modules will be assigned, with other modules being assigned only if time permits.**

| **MODULE 1** | The Complete Equity Method: Investment Account Adjustment Procedures |

## FIXED ASSET TRANSFERS: MECHANICAL PROCEDURES TO DEFER UNREALIZED GAIN OR LOSS

**Module Overview.** Recall from Chapter 7 that under the complete equity method using investment account adjustment procedures, the parent's share of any unrealized intercompany profit (intercompany gain in this chapter) is deferred in the parent's general ledger by making an adjustment in applying the equity method of accounting to the subsidiary's reported net income.

### TRANSFERS OF NONDEPRECIABLE ASSETS

### Downstream Transfers above Carrying Value

For the example that follows, assume that land costing $20,000 is sold by a parent to its wholly owned subsidiary for $30,000 on January 1, 19X1.

**Consolidation at January 1, 19X1.** If a consolidation is done as of January 1, 19X1—the transfer date is our example—the parent would make the following **general ledger entry:**

| | | |
|---|---|---|
| Equity in Net Income of Subsidiary ........... | 10,000 | |
| Investment in Subsidiary................ | | 10,000 |
| To apply the equity method of accounting. | | |

In consolidation, the Equity in Net Income of Subsidiary account would be eliminated by the primary elimination entry. The Intercompany Gain account would be eliminated in consolidation as follows:

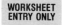

| | | |
|---|---|---|
| Intercompany Gain.......................... | 10,000 | |
| Land........................................ | | 10,000 |
| To defer recognition of unrealized intercompany gain. | | |

The preceding worksheet entry would be made at any other consolidation date in 19X1 providing the land is still owned by the subsidiary at that consolidation date.

### Subsequent-year Treatment of Unrealized Gain

This section explains the manner of dealing with the $10,000 of unrealized intercompany gain at December 31, 19X1, in preparing consolidated financial statements subsequent to that date. If the subsidiary still owns the land at December 31, 19X2, it will be necessary in consolidation to make a credit to the Land account for $10,000 (so as to bring the subsidiary's reported carrying value of $30,000 down to the parent's cost of $20,000, just as was done in 19X1). In the year in which the land is resold by the subsidiary, it will be necessary in consolidation to make a credit to the Gain on Sale of Land account (so as to report the $10,000 gain that has now been realized).

By making a slight modification to the conceptual analysis of the investment account, this $10,000 of unrealized intercompany gain at December 31, 19X1, can be kept track of easily so that the appropriate credit is made in subsequent years. As was done in Chapter 7, an additional column is added to the book value element (labeled Unrealized Gain). Amounts are added to and subtracted from this unrealized gain column by making reclassifications at year end (on the line below the line used for the source of the primary elimination entry).

**Land Not Resold at the End of 19X2.**    If the subsidiary still owns the land at the end of 19X2, the $10,000 negative balance in the unrealized gain column of the conceptual analysis is posted as a credit to the Land account in consolidation.

**Land Resold by the End of 19X3.**    If the subsidiary subsequently sells the land in 19X3 for $32,000, it would then report a gain of $2,000 ($32,000 − $30,000). However, the previously deferred gain of $10,000 has now been realized, making the reportable gain for consolidated reporting purposes $12,000. The parent would make the following **general ledger entry:**

| | | |
|---|---|---|
| Investment in Subsidiary...................... | 10,000 | |
|     Equity in Net Income of Subsidiary ..... | | 10,000 |
|   To apply the equity method of accounting. | | |
|   (This is a reversal of the entry made | | |
|   in 19X1.) | | |

In consolidation, the Equity in Net Income of Subsidiary account would be eliminated by the primary elimination entry. The $10,000 negative balance in the unrealized gain column of the conceptual analysis would be posted as a credit to the Gain on Sale of Land account. After the consolidation procedures have been performed at December 31, 19X3, the $10,000 balance in the unrealized gain column of the conceptual analysis would be eliminated by reclassifying the balance to the current year earnings column. (These procedures are identical to those shown in Illustration 7-2, which dealt with unrealized intercompany profit resulting from inventory transfers.)

## Transfers below Carrying Value and Upstream Transfers

When land is transferred at below its carrying value, the loss must be deferred. The principle is the same as that for a transfer above its carrying value; only the debits and credits are reversed.

When the transfer is upstream, the procedures are exactly the same as for a downstream sale. Upstream transfers are discussed and illustrated in the next section on transfers of depreciable assets.

## TRANSFERS OF DEPRECIABLE FIXED ASSETS

## Downstream Equipment Transfer above Carrying Value

When a depreciable asset is transferred at above its carrying value, the gain recorded by the selling entity must be deferred in the same manner that a gain on the transfer of a nondepreciable asset is deferred.

Because the buying entity uses the transfer price as its cost, its depreciation expense in future periods is greater than it would have been had the selling entity transferred the asset at its carrying value. This additional depreciation expense in future periods must be eliminated, because from a consolidated viewpoint, depreciation expense must be based on the selling entity's carrying value at the transfer date. This additional depreciation expense on the buying entity's books eventually offsets the initial gain recorded on the selling entity's books.

After the elimination entries, the selling entity's cost and accumulated depreciation (based on that cost) are reported in consolidation in the fixed assets section of the balance sheet.

**ILLUSTRATION**    ## Downstream Equipment Transfer above Carrying Value

Assume the following facts:

|  | P Company | S Company |
|---|---|---|
| Sales price of equipment sold to subsidiary on January 1, 19X1 . . . . . . . . . . |  | $18,000 |
| Carrying value on parent's books: |  |  |
| Cost . . . . . . . . . . . . . . . . . . . . . . . . . . . . . . . . . . . . . . | $40,000 |  |
| Accumulated depreciation . . . . . . . . . . . . . . . . | (25,000) | 15,000 |

(continued)

|  | P<br>Company | S<br>Company |
| --- | --- | --- |
| Gain recorded by parent...................... |  | $ 3,000 |
| Remaining life............................. |  | 3 years |

Note: For simplicity, we assumed that the equipment is used by an administrative department of the subsidiary. Thus, the acquiring entity's depreciation expense on this equipment is included in its administrative expenses.

The subsidiary bases its periodic depreciation expense on the $18,000 transfer price. As a result, the subsidiary records $6,000 of depreciation expense per year over the next three years rather than $5,000 per year (which is based on the parent company's $15,000 carrying value).

**Master Analysis.** For intercompany depreciable asset transfers at above (or below) carrying value, a company often prepares an overall analysis that readily develops the elimination entries necessary over the asset's remaining life. Such an analysis is shown in Illustration 8-1.

Section 1 of the analysis (the pro forma part) shows the balances and activity that would have existed if the asset had been transferred at its $15,000 carrying value. In preparing this part of the analysis, companies assume that the subsidiary recorded the asset at the parent's cost ($40,000) less the related accumulated depreciation on the parent's books at the transfer date ($25,000).

Section 2 shows the balances and activity that will occur in the subsidiary's general ledger as a result of the transfer at $18,000. In preparing sections 1 and 2, companies must use the assets' **new remaining assigned life,** if different from the old remaining life. The old remaining life is no longer relevant.

Section 3 is merely the differences between the amounts in sections 1 and 2. The balances produced in this section are the amounts used in the elimination entries at each consolidation date. Section 4 shows these elimination entries for each consolidation date (as well as the parent's general ledger adjusting entries under the equity method of accounting at each consolidation date).

**Effect on Parent's Retained Earnings at the End of 19X3.** In reviewing Illustration 8-1, you should realize that at December 31, 19X3 (the date the equipment is fully depreciated by the subsidiary), there will be no net effect on the parent's general ledger Retained Earnings account as a result of the intercompany equipment transfer at above carrying value. The $3,000 gain recorded by the parent has been completely offset by the $3,000 incremental depreciation expense recorded on the subsidiary's

## MODULE 1     The Complete Equity Method: Investment Account Adjustment Procedures (continued)

### ■ ILLUSTRATION 8-1
## Analysis of Equipment Sold to Subsidiary at above Carrying Value

| | Assets | | Annual Depreciation Expense | Gain to Be Deferred |
|---|---|---|---|---|
| | Cost | Accum. Depr. | | |
| **1. Balances that would have existed if transferred at carrying value:** | | | | |
| January 1, 19X1 | $40,000 | $25,000 | | |
| 19X1 | | 5,000 | $5,000 | |
| December 31, 19X1 | $40,000 | $30,000 | | |
| 19X2 | | 5,000 | 5,000 | |
| December 31, 19X2 | $40,000 | $35,000 | | |
| 19X3 | | 5,000 | 5,000 | |
| December 31, 19X3 | $40,000 | $40,000 | | |
| **2. Balances that will exist since transferred at above carrying value:** | | | | |
| January 1, 19X1 | $18,000 | | | |
| 19X1 | | $ 6,000 | $6,000 | |
| December 31, 19X1 | $18,000 | $ 6,000 | | |
| 19X2 | | 6,000 | 6,000 | |
| December 31, 19X2 | $18,000 | $12,000 | | |
| 19X3 | | 6,000 | 6,000 | |
| December 31, 19X3 | $18,000 | $18,000 | | |
| **3. Differences between 1 and 2 (basis for intercompany elimination entries):** | | | | |
| January 1, 19X1 | $22,000 | $25,000 | | $3,000 |
| 19X1 | | | $1,000 | |
| December 31, 19X1 | 22,000 | 24,000 | | 2,000 |
| 19X2 | | | 1,000 | |
| December 31, 19X2 | 22,000 | 23,000 | | 1,000 |
| 19X3 | | | 1,000 | |
| December 31, 19X3 | 22,000 | 22,000 | | –0– |

**4. Entries required:**

| | Consolidation Date | | | | | | | |
|---|---|---|---|---|---|---|---|---|
| | Jan. 1, 19X1 | | Dec. 31, 19X1 | | Dec. 31, 19X2 | | Dec. 31, 19X3 | |
| | Dr. | Cr. | Dr. | Cr. | Dr. | Cr. | Dr. | Cr. |
| **Parent's General Ledger Entries:** | | | | | | | | |
| Equity in Net Income | 3,000 | | | | | | | |
|    Investment in Subsidiary | | 3,000 | | | | | | |
| Investment in Subsidiary | | | 1,000 | | 1,000 | | 1,000 | |
|    Equity in Net Income | | | | 1,000 | | 1,000 | | 1,000 |
| **Consolidation Entries (per 3. above):** | | | | | | | | |
| Intercompany Gain | | | | | | | | |
|   (Income statement) | 3,000 | | 3,000 | | | | | |
|    Depreciation Expense | | | | 1,000 | | 1,000[a] | | 1,000[a] |
| Equipment | | | | | | | | |
|   ($40,000 – $18,000) | 22,000 | | 22,000 | | 22,000 | | 22,000 | |
|    Accumulated | | | | | | | | |
|     Depreciation | | 25,000 | | 24,000 | | 23,000[b] | | 22,000 |

Note: The entry after December 31, 19X3 (until the asset is sold or retired), is as follows:

| | | |
|---|---|---|
| Equipment | 22,000 | |
|   Accumulated | | |
|    Depreciation | | 22,000 |

[a]As explained later, this credit posting comes from the primary elimination entry.
[b]As explained later, $1,000 of this credit posting comes from the primary elimination entry.

books, which under the equity method of accounting the parent has recorded as a reduction to its retained earnings.

**Concluding Comments.**   An illustration of the full consolidation process for financial statements is not presented for downstream equipment transfers. In the following section, which deals with an upstream transfer, the full consolidation process for financial statements is illustrated.

## Upstream Equipment Transfers above Carrying Value

**Consolidation Entries.**   When depreciable assets are transferred from the subsidiary to the parent (upstream), the consolidation entries shown in Illustration 8-1 for downstream equipment transfers are used—regardless of whether the subsidiary is wholly or partially owned.

**General Ledger Entries under the Equity Method of Accounting.**   If the subsidiary is partially owned, then the parent's general ledger adjusting entries under the equity method of accounting as shown in Illustration 8-1 would be reduced by the minority interest ownership percentage.

**Updating the Minority Interest Column of the Conceptual Analysis of the Investment Account.**   When a minority interest exists, the minority interest column of the conceptual analysis is updated based on the same net income amount that the parent uses in applying the equity method of accounting. (This easily enables the minority interest to be properly reported in the consolidated financial statements without having to make any adjustment to the minority interest in the consolidation process.) For example, assume the intercompany equipment transfer in Illustration 8-1 is upstream from S Company, which is 80% owned by P Company. Assume further that S Company reports $23,000 of net income for 19X1, $3,000 of which is the intercompany gain ($2,000 of which is unrealized at December 31, 19X1). In applying the equity method of accounting for 19X1, the parent would record $16,800 (80% of $21,000). In updating the minority interest column of the conceptual analysis of the investment account, $4,200 should be used as the minority interest share of the 19X1 earnings (20% of $21,000).

ILLUSTRATION ## Preparing Consolidated Financial Statements

- The Complete Equity Method: Investment Account Adjustment Procedures
- Upstream Equipment Transfer above Carrying Value from 80%-owned Subsidiary

---

**MODULE 1** **The Complete Equity Method Investment Account Adjustment Procedures** (continued)

The elimination entries at December 31, 19X1, in Illustration 8-1 are used in preparing a consolidating statement worksheet at December 31, 19X1, shown in Illustration 8-2. The worksheet begins with the P Company and S Company financial statements presented in Illustration 5-5. These financial statements were modified as follows:

1. The subsidiary's financial statements reflect a $3,000 gain on the equipment transfer (as well as $5,000 less depreciation expense since it did not use this equipment during 19X1).
2. The parent's financial statements reflect the $6,000 of additional depreciation expense ($1,000 of which is the incremental depreciation resulting from the subsidiary's $3,000 intercompany gain).
3. The parent's financial statements reflect an additional $4,800 recorded under the equity method of accounting (80% of $6,000). The $6,000 results from:

| | |
|---|---:|
| Additional reportable income by subsidiary: | |
| Reduced depreciation expense | $5,000 |
| Intercompany gain | 3,000 |
| Subtotal | $8,000 |
| Less—Unrealized intercompany gain at | |
| December 31, 19X1 | 2,000 |
| | $6,000 |

The primary elimination entry (modified for the upstream transfer) along with the other elimination entries follow:

1. The primary elimination entry:

**WORKSHEET ENTRY ONLY**

| | | |
|---|---:|---:|
| Common Stock | 40,000 | |
| Retained Earnings (beginning of year) | 20,000 | |
| Equity in Net Income of Subsidiary (80% of $21,000) | 16,800 | |
| Minority Interest in Net Income of S Company (20% of $21,000) | 4,200 | |
| Land | 9,600 | |
| Equipment | 4,800 | |
| Goodwill | 7,200 | |
| Dividends Declared | | 5,000 |
| Accumulated Depreciation | | 800 |
| Investment in S Company | | 81,600 |
| Minority Interest in Net Assets of S Company | | 15,200 |

## ■ ILLUSTRATION 8-2

**The Complete Equity Method—Investment Account Adjustment Procedures: Upstream Equipment Transfer above Carrying Value from 80%-owned Subsidiary**

### P COMPANY AND SUBSIDIARY (S COMPANY)
#### Consolidating Statement Worksheet for the Year Ended December 31, 19X1

| | P Company | S Company | Eliminations Dr. | Eliminations Cr. | Consolidated |
|---|---|---|---|---|---|
| **Income Statement** | | | | | |
| Sales.......................... | 600,000 | 225,000 | | | 825,000 |
| Cost of sales.................... | (360,000) | (110,000) | 3,200(2) | | (473,200) |
| Expenses...................... | (196,000) | (95,000) | | 1,000(4) | (290,000) |
| Intercompany Accounts: | | | | | |
| Equity in net income............ | 13,600ᵃ | | 16,800(1) | 3,200(2) | –0– |
| Gain ....................... | | 3,000 | 3,000(4) | | –0– |
| Income before Minority Interest..... | 57,600 | 23,000 | 23,000 | 4,200 | 61,800 |
| Minority interest ............... | | | 4,200(1) | | (4,200) |
| Net Income ...................... | 57,600 | 23,000 | 27,200 | 4,200 | 57,600 |
| **Statement of Retained Earnings** | | | | | |
| Balances, January 1, 19X1......... | 100,000 | 20,000 | 20,000(1) | | 100,000 |
| +Net income .................... | 57,600 | 23,000 | 27,200 | 4,200 | 57,600 |
| −Dividends declared ............. | (45,000) | (5,000) | | 5,000(1) | (45,000) |
| Balances, December 31, 19X1 ...... | 112,600 | 38,000 | 47,200 | 9,200 | 112,600 |
| **Balance Sheet** | | | | | |
| Cash.......................... | 24,000 | 29,000 | | | 53,000 |
| Accounts receivable, net........... | 75,000 | 37,000 | | | 112,000 |
| Inventory....................... | 110,000 | 55,000 | | | 165,000 |
| Investment in S Company.......... | 81,600 | | | 81,600(1) | –0– |
| Land........................... | 220,000 | 30,000 | 9,600(1) | | 259,600 |
| Buildings and equipment .......... | 518,000 | 160,000 | 4,800(1) 22,000(4) | 50,000(3) | 654,800 |
| Accumulated depreciation.......... | (326,000) | (33,000) | 50,000(3) | 800(1) 24,000(4) | (333,800) |
| Goodwill ....................... | | | 7,200(1) | | 7,200 |
| Total Assets..................... | 702,600 | 278,000 | 93,600 | 156,400 | 917,800 |
| Liabilities ...................... | 290,000 | 200,000 | | | 490,000 |
| Minority interest in net assets ...... | | | | 15,200(1) | 15,200 |
| Common stock................... | 300,000 | 40,000 | 40,000(1) | | 300,000 |
| Retained earnings................ | 112,600 | 38,000 | 47,200 | 9,200 | 112,600 |
| Total Liabilities and Equity....... | 702,600 | 278,000 | 87,200 | 24,400 | 917,800 |

Proof of debit and credit postings ............................. 180,800    180,800

Explanation of entries:
(1) The primary elimination entry.
(2) The secondary elimination entry.
(3) The accumulated depreciation elimination entry.
(4) The incremental depreciation expense elimination entry.
(5) The change in carrying value elimination entry.

ᵃComprised of $16,800 (80% of $21,000) less $3,200 of amortization.

2. The secondary elimination entry:

| WORKSHEET ENTRY ONLY | | | |
|---|---|---|---|
| Cost of Goods Sold | | 3,200 | |
| Equity in Net Income of Subsidiary | | | 3,200 |

3. The accumulated depreciation elimination entry:

| WORKSHEET ENTRY ONLY | | | |
|---|---|---|---|
| Accumulated Depreciation | | 50,000 | |
| Buildings and Equipment | | | 50,000 |

4. The intercompany gain elimination entry:

| WORKSHEET ENTRY ONLY | | | |
|---|---|---|---|
| Intercompany Gain | | 3,000 | |
| Equipment | | 22,000 | |
| Accumulated Depreciation | | | 24,000 |
| Depreciation Expense | | | 1,000 |

## Subsequent-year Treatment of Unrealized Gain

This section explains the manner of dealing with the $2,000 of unrealized intercompany gain at December 31, 19X1 in preparing consolidated financial statements subsequent to that date. The procedures are the same as those explained in Chapter 7 for unrealized intercompany profit on inventory transfers (as shown in Illustration 7-2) and those explained earlier in the chapter for nondepreciable asset transfers. Specifically, an extra column (labeled Unrealized Gain) is added to the book value element of the conceptual analysis. Amounts are added to and subtracted from this unrealized gain column by making reclassifications at year end (on the line below the line used for the source of the primary elimination entry). Illustration 8-3 shows how the $2,000 of unrealized intercompany gain at December 31, 19X1 is accounted for in the modified conceptual analysis of the investment account. For simplicity, we assume the subsidiary reported $25,000 of net income in 19X2 and 19X3, declared no dividends in either year, and the parent had $1,600 of amortization of cost in excess of book value each year.

■ **ILLUSTRATION 8-3**

**Updating the Book Value Element of the Conceptual Analysis When Unrealized Intercompany Gain Exists at Year-end on Upstream Sales**

| | Minority Interest + | Total Cost = | Common Stock + | Prior Years + | Current Year Earnings − | Dividends − | Unrealized Gain |
|---|---|---|---|---|---|---|---|
| | | | | | | **Book-Value Element** | |
| | | | | | | **Retained Earnings** | |
| Balance, January 1, 19X1 | $12,000 | $72,000 | $40,000 | $20,000 | | | |
| Equity in net income ($23,000 − $2,000): | | | | | | | |
| To parent . . . . . . . . . . . | | 16,800 | | | $16,800 | | |
| To minority int. . . . . . . | 4,200 | | | | 4,200 | | |
| Dividends: | | | | | | | |
| To parent . . . . . . . . . . . | | (4,000) | | | | $(4,000) | |
| To minority int. . . . . . . | (1,000) | | | | | (1,000) | |
| Amortization . . . . . . . . . . | | (3,200) | | | | | |
| Subtotal . . . . . . . . . . . . . . | $15,200 | $81,600 | $40,000 | $20,000 | $21,000 | $(5,000) | |
| Reclassification . . . . . . . . | | | | | 2,000 | | $(2,000) |
| Reclassification . . . . . . . . | | | | 18,000 | (23,000) | 5,000 | |
| Balance, December 31, 19X1 | $15,200 | $81,600 | $40,000 | $38,000 | $ −0− | $ −0− | $(2,000) |
| Equity in net income ($25,000 + $1,000): | | | | | | | |
| To parent . . . . . . . . . . . | | 20,800 | | | 20,800 | | |
| To minority int. . . . . . . | 5,200 | | | | 5,200 | | |
| Amortization . . . . . . . . . . | | (1,600) | | | | | |
| Subtotal . . . . . . . . . . . . . . | $20,400 | $100,800 | $40,000 | $38,000 | $26,000 | $ −0− | $(2,000)[a] |
| Reclassification . . . . . . . . | | | | | (1,000) | | 1,000 |
| Reclassification . . . . . . . . | | | | 25,000 | (25,000) | | |
| Balance, December 31, 19X2 | $20,400 | $100,800 | $40,000 | $63,000 | $ −0− | $ −0− | $(1,000) |
| Equity in net income ($25,000 + $1,000): | | | | | | | |
| To parent . . . . . . . . . . . | | 20,800 | | | 20,800 | | |
| To minority int. . . . . . . | 5,200 | | | | 5,200 | | |
| Amortization . . . . . . . . . . | | (1,600) | | | | | |
| Subtotal . . . . . . . . . . . . . . | $25,600 | $120,000 | $40,000 | $63,000 | $26,000 | $ −0− | $(1,000)[b] |
| Reclassification . . . . . . . . | | | | | (1,000) | | 1,000 |
| Reclassification . . . . . . . . | | | | 25,000 | (25,000) | | |
| Balance, December 31, 19X3 | $25,600 | $120,000 | $40,000 | $88,000 | $ −0− | $ −0− | $ −0− |

[a]Because only $1,000 of this amount is unrealized at this consolidation date, $1,000 is posted as a credit to the asset account (specifically the Accumulated Depreciation account) and the other $1,000 is posted as a credit to the Depreciation Expense account.

[b]Because none of the intercompany gain is unrealized at this consolidation date, this $1,000 is posted as a credit to the Depreciation Expense account.

Note: The amounts do not cross total to the amounts in the Total Cost column at the beginning and end of each year because the current value over (under) book value element and the goodwill element are not shown as they are not relevant to the procedure being illustrated.

**MODULE 2**    The Complete Equity Method: Noninvestment Account Adjustment Procedures

## FIXED ASSET TRANSFERS: MECHANICAL PROCEDURES TO DEFER UNREALIZED GAIN OR LOSS

**Module Overview.**    Recall from Chapter 7 that under the complete equity method using noninvestment account adjustment procedures, any unrealized intercompany profit at year-end was deferred in the general ledger of the parent for downstream transfers or in the general ledger of the subsidiary for upstream transfers (using a Deferred Profit account). Unlike intercompany inventory transfers, which involve accounts for both intercompany sales and intercompany cost of goods sold, transfers of fixed assets use only one income statement account, called Intercompany Gain. Accordingly, it is not necessary to use a Deferral of Profit account (as in Chapter 7). The general ledger entry to defer the intercompany gain is made by directly debiting the Intercompany Gain account and crediting a Deferred Gain account.

### TRANSFERS OF NONDEPRECIABLE FIXED ASSETS
### Downstream Transfers above Carrying Value

For the following example, assume that land costing $20,000 is sold by a parent to its wholly owned subsidiary for $30,000 on January 1, 19X1.

**Consolidation at January 1, 19X1.**    If a consolidation is done as of January 1, 19X1—the transfer date in our example—the parent would make the following **general ledger entry:**

| | | |
|---|---|---|
| Intercompany Gain (income statement) ....... | 10,000 | |
|     Deferred Gain (balance sheet)........... | | 10,000 |
|   To defer the intercompany gain. | | |

In consolidation, the following entry would be made:

| | | |
|---|---|---|
| Deferred Gain (balance sheet)............... | 10,000 | |
|     Land..................................... | | 10,000 |
|   To lower the carrying value of the land. | | |

This worksheet entry would be made at any other consolidation date in 19X1 providing the land is still owned by the subsidiary at that consolidation date(s).

**Land Not Resold at the End of 19X2.**    If the subsidiary still owns the land at the end of 19X2, the following entry would be made in consolidation:

## MODULE 2    The Complete Equity Method: Noninvestment Account Adjustment **Procedures** (continued)

| WORKSHEET ENTRY ONLY | | |
|---|---|---|
| Deferred Gain (balance sheet)............... | 10,000 | |
|     Land................................... | | 10,000 |
| To lower the reported carrying value of the land. | | |

**Land Resold by the End of 19X3.**  If the subsidiary subsequently sells the land in 19X3 for $32,000, it would then report a gain of $2,000 ($32,000 − $30,000). However, the reportable gain in the consolidated income statement is $12,000 ($32,000 − $20,000). Accordingly, the following general ledger entry would be made by the parent:

| | | |
|---|---|---|
| Deferred Gain (balance sheet)............... | 10,000 | |
|     Gain on Sale of Land (income statement)........................... | | 10,000 |
| To recognize intercompany gain on the 19X1 land transfer. | | |

No elimination entry or entries are necessary in consolidation, as the two gain accounts would be lumped together so that a $12,000 gain is reported.

## Transfers below Carrying Value and Upstream Transfers

When the transfer is upstream, the procedures are exactly the same as for a downstream transfer, except that the adjusting entry to defer the intercompany profit is made to the subsidiary's general ledger rather than to the parent's general ledger.

When land is transferred below the carrying value, the loss must be deferred. The principle is the same as that for a transfer above cost; only the debits and credits are reversed.

## TRANSFERS OF DEPRECIABLE FIXED ASSETS

## Downstream Equipment Transfer above Carrying Value

When a depreciable asset is transferred at above its carrying value, the gain recorded by the selling entity must be deferred in the same manner that a gain on the transfer of a nondepreciable asset is deferred.

Because the buying entity uses the transfer price as its cost, its depreciation expense in future periods is greater than it would have been had the selling entity transferred the asset at its carrying value. This additional depreciation expense in future periods must be eliminated, because from a consolidated viewpoint, depreciation expense must be based on the selling entity's carrying value at the transfer date. This additional depreciation expense on the buying entity's books eventually offsets the initial gain recorded on the selling entity's books.

After the elimination entries, the selling entity's cost and accumulated depreciation (based on that cost) are reported in consolidation in the fixed assets section of the balance sheet.

**ILLUSTRATION** ## Downstream Equipment Transfer above Carrying Value

Assume the following facts:

| | P Company | S Company |
|---|---|---|
| Sales price of equipment sold to subsidiary on January 1, 19X1 . . . . . . . . . . | | $18,000 |
| Carrying value on parent's books: | | |
| Cost . . . . . . . . . . . . . . . . . . . . . . . . . . . . . . . . . . | $40,000 | |
| Accumulated depreciation . . . . . . . . . . . . . . . | (25,000) | 15,000 |
| Gain recorded by parent . . . . . . . . . . . . . . . . . . | | $ 3,000 |
| Remaining life . . . . . . . . . . . . . . . . . . . . . . . . . . | | 3 years |

Note: For simplicity, we assumed that the equipment is used by an administrative department of the subsidiary. Thus, the acquiring entity's depreciation expense on this equipment is included in its administrative expenses.

The subsidiary bases its periodic depreciation expense on the $18,000 transfer price. As a result, the subsidiary records $6,000 of depreciation expense per year over the next three years rather than $5,000 per year (which is based on the parent company's $15,000 carrying value).

**Consolidation at January 1, 19X1.** Immediately after the transfer, the appropriate accounts of the parent and the subsidiary would be as follows:

| | P Company | S Company |
|---|---|---|
| Intercompany gain . . . . . . . . . . . . . . . . . . . . . . . | 3,000 | |
| Retained earnings—P Company (net income line) . . . . . . . . . . . . . . . . . . . . . . | 3,000 | |
| Equipment . . . . . . . . . . . . . . . . . . . . . . . . . . . . . . | | 18,000 |
| Accumulated depreciation . . . . . . . . . . . . . . . . | | –0– |

Under the complete equity method using noninvestment account adjustment procedures, however, the $3,000 gain would be deferred in the parent's **general ledger** as follows:

**MODULE 2   The Complete Equity Method: Noninvestment Account Adjustment Procedures** (continued)

| | | |
|---|---|---|
| Intercompany Gain............................ | 3,000 | |
| Deferred Gain (balance sheet)........... | | 3,000 |
| To defer the unrealized intercompany gain. | | |

If a consolidating statement worksheet is prepared on January 1, 19X1 (the transfer date), the following worksheet elimination entry is made to report the equipment at the parent's cost, along with the related accumulated depreciation based on this cost:

**WORKSHEET ENTRY ONLY**

| | | |
|---|---|---|
| Deferred Gain (balance sheet)................ | 3,000 | |
| Equipment ($40,000 – $18,000)............... | 22,000 | |
| Accumulated Depreciation.............. | | 25,000 |

After this entry is posted, the appropriate worksheet accounts would appear as follows:

| | P Company | S Company | Eliminations Dr. | Eliminations Cr. | Consolidated |
|---|---|---|---|---|---|
| **Income Statement (for January 1, 19X1)** | | | | | |
| Intercompany gain............ | –0– | | | | –0– |
| Net income.............. | –0– | | | | –0– |
| **Statement of Retained Earnings** | | | | | |
| Beginning of year............. | | | | | |
| + Net income ................. | –0– | | | | –0– |
| **Balance Sheet (January 1, 19X1)** | | | | | |
| Equipment.................... | | 18,000 | 22,000 | | 40,000 |
| Accumulated depreciation.... | | –0– | | 25,000 | (25,000) |
| Deferred gain ................ | 3,000 | | | 3,000 | –0– |

Note that the equipment is reported in consolidation as though it had been transferred at the parent's $15,000 carrying value and the subsidiary had recorded $40,000 and $25,000 as its cost and accumulated depreciation, respectively, rather than $18,000 and $–0–.

**Consolidation at December 31, 19X1.**   At the end of 19X1, the appropriate accounts of the parent (prior to adjustment) and subsidiary would be as follows:

| | P Company | S Company |
|---|---|---|
| Intercompany Accounts: | | |
| Equity in net income ..................... | (6,000) | |

**MODULE 2    The Complete Equity Method: Noninvestment Account Adjustment Procedures** (continued)

| | P Company | S Company |
|---|---|---|
| Gain | –0– | |
| Depreciation expense | | (6,000) |
| Retained earnings—P Company | | |
| (net income line) | (6,000) | |
| Equipment | | 18,000 |
| Accumulated depreciation | | (6,000) |
| Deferred gain | (3,000) | |

However, because the subsidiary has recorded $1,000 of incremental depreciation expense as a result of the transfer price being $18,000 instead of the parent's cost of $15,000, only $2,000 of the intercompany gain need be deferred at December 31, 19X1. Accordingly, the parent would make the following **general ledger** adjusting entry:

| | | |
|---|---|---|
| Deferred Gain (balance sheet) | 1,000 | |
|     Intercompany Gain (income statement) | | 1,000 |
|     To reduce the deferred gain account to a | | |
|       $2,000 balance at December 31, 19X1 | | |
|       as a result of $1,000 of incremental | | |
|       depreciation expense having been | | |
|       recorded by the subsidiary. | | |

If a consolidating statement worksheet is prepared at December 31, 19X1, the following two elimination entries would be made:

**WORKSHEET ENTRY ONLY**

| | | |
|---|---|---|
| Intercompany Gain (income statement) | 1,000 | |
|     Depreciation Expense | | 1,000 |
|     To eliminate the intercompany gain and | | |
|     the incremental depreciation expense. | | |

**WORKSHEET ENTRY ONLY**

| | | |
|---|---|---|
| Deferred Gain (balance sheet) | 2,000 | |
| Equipment ($40,000 – $18,000) | 22,000 | |
|     Accumulated Depreciation | | |
|       ($25,000 + $5,000 = $30,000; | | |
|       $30,000 – $6,000 = $24,000) | | 24,000 |
|     To report the equipment at the parent's | | |
|     cost, along with the related accumulated | | |
|     depreciation based on this cost. | | |

On posting this entry, the appropriate worksheet accounts would appear as follows:

**MODULE 2   The Complete Equity Method: Noninvestment Account Adjustment Procedures** (continued)

| | P Company | S Company | Eliminations Dr. | Eliminations Cr. | Consolidated |
|---|---|---|---|---|---|
| **Income Statement (19X1)** | | | | | |
| Intercompany Accounts: | | | | | |
| Equity in net income (loss) . | (6,000) | | | 6,000[a] | –0– |
| Gain. . . . . . . . . . . . . . . . . . . . . | 1,000 | | 1,000 | | –0– |
| Depreciation expense. . . . . . . . | | (6,000) | | 1,000 | (5,000) |
| Net income. . . . . . . . . . . . . . . | (5,000) | (6,000) | 1,000 | 7,000 | (5,000) |
| **Statement of Retained Earnings (19X1)** | | | | | |
| Beginning of year . . . . . . . . . . . . | | | | | |
| +Net income . . . . . . . . . . . . . . . | (5,000) | (6,000) | 1,000 | 7,000 | (5,000) |
| **Balance Sheet (December 31, 19X1)** | | | | | |
| Equipment. . . . . . . . . . . . . . . . . . . | | 18,000 | 22,000 | | 40,000 |
| Accumulated depreciation . . . . | | (6,000) | | 24,000 | (30,000) |
| Deferred gain . . . . . . . . . . . . . . . | (2,000) | | 2,000 | | –0– |

[a]This debit posting would come from the primary elimination entry.

Note that consolidated depreciation expense is $5,000, which is the $15,000 carrying value of the equipment at the transfer date divided by the three-year remaining life.

**Master Analysis.**   For intercompany depreciable asset transfers at above (or below) carrying value, a company often prepares an overall analysis that readily develops the elimination entries necessary over the asset's remaining life. Such an analysis is shown in Illustration 8-4.

Section 1 of the analysis (the pro forma part) shows the balances and activity that would have existed if the asset had been transferred at its $15,000 carrying value. In preparing this part of the analysis, companies assume that the subsidiary recorded the asset at the parent's cost ($40,000) less the related accumulated depreciation on the parent's books at the transfer date ($25,000).

Section 2 shows the balances and activity that will occur in the subsidiary's general ledger as a result of the transfer at $18,000. In preparing sections 1 and 2, companies must use the assets' **new remaining assigned life,** if different from the old remaining life. The old remaining life is no longer relevant.

Section 3 is merely the differences between the amounts in sections 1 and 2. The balances produced in this section are the amounts used in the elimination entries at each consolidation date. Section 4 shows these elimination entries for each consolidation date (as well as the transferring entity's general ledger adjusting entries at each consolidation date).

**MODULE 2    The Complete Equity Method: Noninvestment Account Adjustment Procedures** (continued)

### ■ ILLUSTRATION 8-4
### Analysis of Equipment Sold to Subsidiary at above Carrying Value

| | Asset Cost | Asset Accum. Depr. | Annual Depreciation Expense | Gain to Be Deferred |
|---|---|---|---|---|
| **1. Balances that would have existed if transferred at carrying value:** | | | | |
| January 1, 19X1 | $40,000 | $25,000 | | |
| 19X1 | | 5,000 | $5,000 | |
| December 31, 19X1 | $40,000 | $30,000 | | |
| 19X2 | | 5,000 | 5,000 | |
| December 31, 19X2 | $40,000 | $35,000 | | |
| 19X3 | | 5,000 | 5,000 | |
| December 31, 19X3 | $40,000 | $40,000 | | |
| **2. Balances that will exist since transferred at above carrying value:** | | | | |
| January 1, 19X1 | $18,000 | | | |
| 19X1 | | $ 6,000 | $6,000 | |
| December 31, 19X1 | $18,000 | $ 6,000 | | |
| 19X2 | | 6,000 | 6,000 | |
| December 31, 19X2 | $18,000 | $12,000 | | |
| 19X3 | | 6,000 | 6,000 | |
| December 31, 19X3 | $18,000 | $18,000 | | |
| **3. Differences between 1 and 2 (basis for intercompany elimination entries):** | | | | |
| January 1, 19X1 | $22,000 | $25,000 | | $3,000 |
| 19X1 | | | $1,000 | |
| December 31, 19X1 | 22,000 | 24,000 | | 2,000 |
| 19X2 | | | 1,000 | |
| December 31, 19X2 | 22,000 | 23,000 | | 1,000 |
| 19X3 | | | 1,000 | |
| December 31, 19X3 | 22,000 | 22,000 | | —0— |

**4. Entries required:**

| | Jan. 1, 19X1 Dr. | Jan. 1, 19X1 Cr. | Dec. 31, 19X1 Dr. | Dec. 31, 19X1 Cr. | Dec. 31, 19X2 Dr. | Dec. 31, 19X2 Cr. | Dec. 31, 19X3 Dr. | Dec. 31, 19X3 Cr. |
|---|---|---|---|---|---|---|---|---|
| **Parent's General Ledger Entries:** | | | | | | | | |
| Intercompany Gain (income statement) | 3,000 | | | | | | | |
| Deferred Gain (balance sheet) | | 3,000 | | | | | | |
| Deferred Gain (balance sheet) | | | 1,000 | | 1,000 | | 1,000 | |
| Intercompany Gain (income statement) | | | | 1,000 | | 1,000 | | 1,000 |
| **Consolidation Entries (per 3. above):** | | | | | | | | |
| Intercompany Gain (income statement) | | | 1,000 | | 1,000 | | 1,000 | |
| Depreciation Expense | | | | 1,000 | | 1,000 | | 1,000 |
| Deferred Gain (balance sheet) | 3,000 | | 2,000 | | 1,000 | | —0— | |
| Equipment ($40,000 – $18,000) | 22,000 | | 22,000 | | 22,000 | | 22,000 | |
| Accumulated Depreciation | | 25,000 | | 24,000 | | 23,000 | | 22,000 |

Note: The entry after December 31, 19X3 (until the asset is sold or retired), is as follows:

| | | |
|---|---|---|
| Equipment | 22,000 | |
| Accumulated Depreciation | | 22,000 |

**Effect on Parent's Retained Earnings at the End of 19X3.** In reviewing Illustration 8-4, you should realize that at December 31, 19X3 (the date the equipment is fully depreciated by the subsidiary), there will be no net effect on the parent's general ledger Retained Earnings account as a result of the intercompany equipment transfer at above carrying value. The $3,000 gain recorded by the parent has been completely offset by the $3,000 incremental depreciation expense recorded on the subsidiary's books, which under the equity method of accounting the parent has recorded as a reduction to its retained earnings.

**Concluding Comments.** An illustration of the full consolidation process for financial statements is not presented for downstream equipment transfers. In the following section, which deals with an upstream transfer, the full consolidation process for financial statements is illustrated.

## Upstream Transfers above Carrying Value

When depreciable assets are transferred from the subsidiary to the parent (upstream), the general ledger entries and consolidation entries shown earlier for downstream transfers are used except that the general ledger deferral entries take place on the subsidiary's books rather than on the parent's books.

**ILLUSTRATION** **Preparing Consolidated Financial Statements**

- The Complete Equity Method: Noninvestment Account Adjustment Procedures
- Upstream Equipment Transfer above Carrying Value from 80%-owned Subsidiary

The December 31, 19X1, elimination entries in Illustration 8-4 are used in Illustration 8-5. The worksheet begins with the P Company and S Company financial statements presented in Illustration 5-5. These financial statements were modified as follows:

1. The subsidiary's financial statements reflect a $3,000 gain on the equipment transfer, $2,000 of which has been deferred in its general ledger.
2. The parent's financial statements reflect the $6,000 of additional depreciation expense ($1,000 of which is the incremental depreciation resulting from the subsidiary's $3,000 intercompany gain).
3. The subsidiary's financial statements reflect $5,000 less depreciation expense.

**MODULE 2    The Complete Equity Method: Noninvestment Account Adjustment Procedures** (continued)

■ **ILLUSTRATION 8-5**

**The Complete Equity Method—Noninvestment Account Adjustment Procedures: Upstream Equipment Transfer above Carrying Value from 80%-owned Subsidiary**

| P COMPANY AND SUBSIDIARY (S COMPANY) Consolidating Statement Worksheet for the Year Ended December 31, 19X1 | | | | | |
|---|---|---|---|---|---|
| | P Company | S Company | Eliminations Dr. | Eliminations Cr. | Consolidated |
| **Income Statement** | | | | | |
| Sales. . . . . . . . . . . . | 600,000 | 225,000 | | | 825,000 |
| Cost of sales . . . . . . . . . . . . | (360,000) | (110,000) | 3,200(2) | | (473,200) |
| Expenses. . . . . . . . . . | (196,000) | (95,000) | | 1,000(4) | (290,000) |
| Intercompany Accounts: | | | | | |
| Equity in net income. . . . . . . . | 13,600[a] | | 16,800(1) | 3,200(2) | –0– |
| Gain . . . . . . . . . . . | | 1,000 | 1,000(4) | | –0– |
| Income before Minority Interest . . . . | 57,600 | 21,000 | 21,000 | 4,200 | 61,800 |
| Minority interest . . . . . . . . . . | | | 4,200(1) | | (4,200) |
| Net Income . . . . . . . . . . | 57,600 | 21,000 | 25,200 | 4,200 | 57,600 |
| **Statement of Retained Earnings** | | | | | |
| Balances, January 1, 19X1 . . . . . . | 100,000 | 20,000 | 20,000(1) | | 100,000 |
| +Net income | 57,600 | 21,000 | 25,200 | 4,200 | 57,600 |
| –Dividends declared . . . . . . . . . | (45,000) | (5,000) | | 5,000(1) | (45,000) |
| Balances, December 31, 19X1 . . . . . | 112,600 | 36,000 | 45,200 | 9,200 | 112,600 |
| **Balance Sheet** | | | | | |
| Cash. . . . . . . . . . . . | 24,000 | 29,000 | | | 53,000 |
| Accounts receivable, net. . . . . . . . | 75,000 | 37,000 | | | 112,000 |
| Inventory. . . . . . . . . . | 110,000 | 55,000 | | | 165,000 |
| Investment in S Company . . . . . . . | 81,600 | | | 81,600(1) | –0– |
| Land. . . . . . . . . . . . | 220,000 | 30,000 | 9,600(1) | | 259,600 |
| Buildings and equipment . . . . . . . | 518,000 | 160,000 | 4,800(1) 22,000(5) | 50,000(3) | 654,800 |
| Accumulated depreciation . . . . . . . | (326,000) | (33,000) | 50,000(3) | 800(1) 24,000(5) | (333,800) |
| Goodwill . . . . . . . . . . | | | 7,200(1) | | 7,200 |
| Total Assets. . . . . . . . . . | 702,600 | 278,000 | 93,600 | 156,400 | 917,800 |
| Liabilities . . . . . . . . . . | 290,000 | 200,000 | | | 490,000 |
| Deferred Gain. . . . . . . . . . | | 2,000 | 2,000(5) | | –0– |
| Minority interest in net assets . . . . . | | | | 15,200(1) | 15,200 |
| Common stock . . . . . . . . . . | 300,000 | 40,000 | 40,000(1) | | 300,000 |
| Retained earnings. . . . . . . . . . | 112,600 | 36,000 | 45,200 | 9,200 | 112,600 |
| Total Liabilities and Equity . . . . . . | 702,600 | 278,000 | 87,200 | 24,400 | 917,800 |
| Proof of debit and credit postings . . . . . . . . . . . . . . . . . . . . . . | | | 180,800 | 180,800 | |

Explanation of entries:
(1) The primary elimination entry.
(2) The secondary elimination entry.
(3) The accumulated depreciation elimination entry.
(4) The incremental depreciation expense elimination entry.
(5) The change in carrying value elimination entry.

[a]Comprised of $16,800 (80% of $21,000) less $3,200 of amortization.

---

4. The parent's financial statements reflect an additional $4,800 recorded under the equity method of accounting ($6,000 × 80%) because the subsidiary's reported net income is $6,000 greater ($1,000 of gain and $5,000 of less depreciation expense).

The primary elimination entry (modified for the upstream transfer) along with the other elimination entries follow.

1. The primary elimination entry:

| WORKSHEET ENTRY ONLY | | |
|---|---|---|
| Common Stock | 40,000 | |
| Retained Earnings (beginning of year) | 20,000 | |
| Equity in Net Income of Subsidiary (80% of $21,000) | 16,800 | |
| Minority Interest in Net Income of S Company (20% of $21,000) | 4,200 | |
| Land | 9,600 | |
| Equipment | 4,800 | |
| Goodwill | 7,200 | |
|     Dividends Declared | | 5,000 |
|     Accumulated Depreciation | | 800 |
|     Investment in S Company | | 81,600 |
|     Minority Interest in Net Assets of S Company | | 15,200 |

2. The secondary elimination entry:

| WORKSHEET ENTRY ONLY | | |
|---|---|---|
| Cost of Goods Sold | 3,200 | |
|     Equity in Net Income of Subsidiary | | 3,200 |

3. The accumulated depreciation elimination entry:

| WORKSHEET ENTRY ONLY | | |
|---|---|---|
| Accumulated Depreciation | 50,000 | |
|     Buildings and Equipment | | 50,000 |

4. The incremental depreciation expense elimination entry:

| WORKSHEET ENTRY ONLY | | |
|---|---|---|
| Intercompany Gain | 1,000 | |
|     Depreciation Expense | | 1,000 |

5. The change in carrying value elimination entry:

| MODULE 2 | The Complete Equity Method: Noninvestment Account Adjustment Procedures *(continued)* |
|----------|---------------------------------------------------------------------------------------|

| | | |
|---|---|---|
| Deferred Gain (balance sheet)................. | 2,000 | |
| Buildings and Equipment..................... | 22,000 | |
| Accumulated Depreciation............... | | 24,000 |

---

| MODULE 3 | The Partial Equity Method |
|----------|---------------------------|

# FIXED ASSET TRANSFERS: MECHANICAL PROCEDURES TO DEFER UNREALIZED GAIN OR LOSS

**Module Overview.** Recall from Chapter 7 that under the partial equity method the deferral of the unrealized intercompany profit (gain in this chapter) is accomplished entirely on the consolidation worksheet. As a result, the consolidated net income and consolidated retained earnings are less than the parent's net income and retained earnings, respectively.

## TRANSFERS OF NONDEPRECIABLE FIXED ASSETS

### Downstream Transfers above Carrying Value

When land is transferred at above its carrying value, the selling entity records a gain. In preparing the consolidated financial statements, the gain is not reportable and must be deferred until the acquiring entity resells the land. For example, assume land costing $20,000 is sold in 19X1 by a parent to its wholly owned subsidiary for $30,000.

**Consolidation at January 1, 19X1.** In consolidation, the entry necessary to eliminate the gain and reduce the land to the parent's carrying value at the transfer date is as follows:

| | | |
|---|---|---|
| Intercompany Gain........................... | 10,000 | |
| Land.................................... | | 10,000 |
| To defer recognition of unrealized intercompany gain. | | |

On posting this entry to the worksheet, the appropriate worksheet accounts would appear as follows:

## MODULE 3    The Partial Equity Method *(continued)*

|  | P Company | S Company | Eliminations Dr. | Cr. | Consolidated |
|---|---|---|---|---|---|
| **Income Statement (for January 1, 19X1)** | | | | | |
| Intercompany gain . . . . . . . . . . . . | 10,000 | | 10,000 | | –0– |
| Net income . . . . . . . . . . . . . . | 10,000 | | 10,000 | | –0– |
| **Statement of Retained Earnings** | | | | | |
| Beginning of year . . . . . . . . . . . | | | | | |
| + Net income . . . . . . . . . . . . . . | 10,000 | | 10,000 | | –0– |
| **Balance Sheet (January 1, 19X1)** | | | | | |
| Land . . . . . . . . . . . . . . . . . . . . . | | 30,000 | | 10,000 | 20,000 |

The preceding worksheet entry would be made at any other consolidation date in 19X1 providing the subsidiary still owns the land at that consolidation date(s).

Note that if the parent were to issue **"parent company" financial statements,** it first would have to make the following financial statement adjusting entry:

| | | |
|---|---|---|
| Intercompany Gain (income statement) . . . . . . . | 10,000 | |
| Deferred Gain (balance sheet) . . . . . . . . . . | | 10,000 |

**Land Not Resold at the End of 19X2.**    If the subsidiary still owns the land at the end of 19X2, the following elimination entry would be necessary:

| WORKSHEET ENTRY ONLY | | |
|---|---|---|
| Retained Earnings—P Company (beginning of year) . . . . . . . . . . . . . . . . . . . . . . . | 10,000 | |
| Land . . . . . . . . . . . . . . . . . . . . . . . . . . . . . . . . . | | 10,000 |
| To defer recognition of unrealized intercompany gain. | | |

On posting this entry, the appropriate worksheet accounts would appear as follows:

|  | P Company | S Company | Eliminations Dr. | Cr. | Consolidated |
|---|---|---|---|---|---|
| **Statement of Retained Earnings (19X2)** | | | | | |
| Beginning of year . . . . . . . . . . . . | 10,000 | | 10,000 | | –0– |
| + Net income . . . . . . . . . . . . . . | | | | | |
| **Balance Sheet (December 31, 19X2)** | | | | | |
| Land . . . . . . . . . . . . . . . . . . . . . | | 30,000 | | 10,000 | 20,000 |

The entry does not involve the income statement accounts because the income statement activity occurred in 19X1. This entry would be made in all periods after 19X1 until the land is sold by the subsidiary.

**Land Resold by the End of 19X3.**  If the subsidiary subsequently sells the land in 19X3 for $32,000, it would then report a $2,000 gain ($32,000 − $30,000). However, the reportable gain in the consolidated income statement is $12,000 ($32,000 − $20,000). Accordingly, the entry required in consolidation to recognize the previously deferred gain of $10,000 is as follows:

| | | | |
|---|---|---|---|
| **WORKSHEET ENTRY ONLY** | Retained Earnings—P Company (beginning of year).......................... | 10,000 | |
| | Gain on Sale of Land................... | | 10,000 |
| | To recognize intercompany gain previously deferred. | | |

On posting this entry, the appropriate worksheet accounts would appear as follows:

| | P Company | S Company | Eliminations Dr. | Eliminations Cr. | Consolidated |
|---|---|---|---|---|---|
| **Income Statement (19X3)** | | | | | |
| Gain on sale of land........... | | 2,000 | | 10,000 | 12,000 |
| Intercompany Accounts: | | | | | |
| Equity in net income........ | 2,000 | | 2,000[a] | | –0– |
| Net income............... | 2,000 | 2,000 | 2,000 | 10,000 | 12,000 |
| **Statement of Retained Earnings (19X3)** | | | | | |
| Beginning of year............. | 10,000 | | 10,000 | | –0– |
| +Net income................. | 2,000 | 2,000 | 2,000 | 10,000 | 12,000 |
| End of year.................. | 12,000 | 2,000 | 12,000 | 10,000 | 12,000 |

[a]This debit posting would come from the primary elimination entry.

## Transfers below Carrying Value and Upstream Transfers

When land is transferred at below its carrying value, the loss must be deferred. The principle is the same as that for a transfer above its carrying value; only the debits and credits are reversed.

When the transfer is upstream, the procedures are exactly the same as for a downstream sale only if the subsidiary is wholly owned. If the subsidiary is partially owned, then an additional adjustment is necessary for the minority interest. Upstream transfers are discussed and illustrated in the next section on transfers of depreciable assets.

## TRANSFERS OF DEPRECIABLE FIXED ASSETS

## Downstream Equipment Transfer above Carrying Value

When a depreciable asset is transferred at above its carrying value, the gain recorded by the selling entity must be deferred in the same manner that a gain on the transfer on a nondepreciable asset is deferred.

Because the buying entity uses the transfer price as its cost, its depreciation expense in future periods is greater than it would have been had the selling entity transferred the asset at its carrying value. This additional depreciation expense in future periods must be eliminated, because from a consolidated viewpoint, depreciation expense must be based on the selling entity's carrying value at the transfer date. This additional depreciation expense on the buying entity's books eventually offsets the initial gain recorded on the selling entity's books.

After the elimination entries, the selling entity's cost and accumulated depreciation (based on that cost) are reported in consolidation in the fixed assets section of the balance sheet.

 **ILLUSTRATION**   ## Downstream Equipment Transfer above Carrying Value

Assume the following facts:

|  | P Company | S Company |
|---|---|---|
| Sales price of equipment sold to subsidiary on January 1, 19X1 | | $18,000 |
| Carrying value on parent's books: | | |
| Cost | $40,000 | |
| Accumulated depreciation | (25,000) | 15,000 |
| Gain recorded by parent | | $ 3,000 |
| Remaining life | | 3 years |

Note: For simplicity, we assumed that the equipment is used by an administrative department of the subsidiary. Thus, the acquiring entity's depreciation expense on this equipment is included in its administrative expenses.

The subsidiary bases its periodic depreciation expense on the $18,000 transfer price. As a result, the subsidiary records $6,000 of depreciation expense per year over the next three years rather than $5,000 per year (which is based on the parent company's $15,000 carrying value).

**Master Analysis.**   For intercompany depreciable asset transfers at above (or below) carrying value, a company often prepares an overall analysis that readily develops the elimination entries necessary over the asset's remaining life. Such an analysis is shown in Illustration 8-6.

Section 1 of the analysis (the pro forma part) shows the balances and activity that would have existed if the asset had been transferred at its $15,000 carrying value. In preparing this part of the analysis, companies assume that the subsidiary recorded the asset at the parent's cost ($40,000) less the related accumulated depreciation on the parent's books at the transfer date ($25,000).

Section 2 shows the balances and activity that will occur in the subsidiary's general ledger as a result of the transfer at $18,000. In preparing sections 1 and 2, companies must use the assets' **new remaining assigned life,** if different from the old remaining life. The old remaining life is no longer relevant.

Section 3 is merely the differences between the amounts in sections 1 and 2. The balances produced in this section are the amounts used in the elimination entries at each consolidation date. Section 4 shows these elimination entries for each consolidation date.

**Effect on Parent's Retained Earnings at the End of 19X3.**   In reviewing Illustration 8-6, you should realize that at December 31, 19X3, (the date the equipment is fully depreciated by the subsidiary), there will be no net effect on the parent's general ledger Retained Earnings account as a result of the intercompany equipment transfer at above carrying value. The $3,000 gain recorded by the parent has been completely offset by the $3,000 incremental depreciation expense recorded on the subsidiary's books, which under the equity method of accounting the parent has recorded as a reduction to its retained earnings.

**Concluding Comments.**   An illustration of the full consolidation process for financial statements is not presented for downstream equipment transfers. In the following section, which deals with an upstream transfer, the full consolidation process for financial statements is illustrated.

## Upstream Transfers above Carrying Value

When depreciable assets are transferred from the subsidiary to the parent (upstream), the entries required in consolidation are the same as those previously shown for a downstream transfer, but only if the subsidiary is wholly owned. When the subsidiary is partially owned, the entries are modified so that the deferral of the gain can be shared with the minority

**MODULE 3   The Partial Equity Method** (continued)

## ■ ILLUSTRATION 8-6
### Analysis of Equipment Sold to Subsidiary at above Carrying Value

| | Asset | | Annual | Gain |
| | Cost | Accum. Depr. | Depreciation Expense | to Be Deferred |
|---|---|---|---|---|
| **1. Balances that would have existed if transferred at carrying value:** | | | | |
| January 1, 19X1 | $40,000 | $25,000 | | |
| 19X1 | | 5,000 | $5,000 | |
| December 31, 19X1 | $40,000 | $30,000 | | |
| 19X2 | | 5,000 | 5,000 | |
| December 31, 19X2 | $40,000 | $35,000 | | |
| 19X3 | | 5,000 | 5,000 | |
| December 31, 19X3 | $40,000 | $40,000 | | |
| **2. Balances that will exist since transferred at above carrying value:** | | | | |
| January 1, 19X1 | $18,000 | | | |
| 19X1 | | $ 6,000 | $6,000 | |
| December 31, 19X1 | $18,000 | $ 6,000 | | |
| 19X2 | | 6,000 | 6,000 | |
| December 31, 19X2 | $18,000 | $12,000 | | |
| 19X3 | | 6,000 | 6,000 | |
| December 31, 19X3 | $18,000 | $18,000 | | |
| **3. Differences between 1 and 2 (basis for intercompany elimination entries):** | | | | |
| January 1, 19X1 | $22,000 | $25,000 | | $3,000 |
| 19X1 | | | $1,000 | |
| December 31, 19X1 | 22,000 | 24,000 | | 2,000 |
| 19X2 | | | 1,000 | |
| December 31, 19X2 | 22,000 | 23,000 | | 1,000 |
| 19X3 | | | 1,000 | |
| December 31, 19X3 | 22,000 | 22,000 | | –0– |

**4. Entries required in consolidation:**

| | Consolidation Date | | | | | | | |
| | Jan. 1, 19X1 | | Dec. 31, 19X1 | | Dec. 31, 19X2 | | Dec. 31, 19X3 | |
| | Dr. | Cr. | Dr. | Cr. | Dr. | Cr. | Dr. | Cr. |
|---|---|---|---|---|---|---|---|---|
| Intercompany Gain | 3,000 | | 3,000 | | | | | |
| Equipment | 22,000 | | 22,000 | | 22,000 | | 22,000 | |
| Accumulated Depreciation | | 25,000 | | 24,000 | | 23,000 | | 22,000 |
| Depreciation Expense | | | | 1,000 | | 1,000 | | 1,000 |
| Retained Earnings—P Company (beginning of year) | | | | | 2,000[a] | | 1,000[a] | |

[a]The unreportable retained earnings at the beginning of the year.

interests if the parent chooses. This requires either modifying the previously shown entries or adding an additional entry. For instructional purposes, we have chosen to do the latter.

Using the facts in Illustration 8-6, except that the sale is upstream from an 80%-owned subsidiary, we determine the minority interest in the subsidiary's gain as $600 (20% of $3,000). This amount is reportable as an increase to the minority interest, but not at the transfer date. Instead, it is reported over the period that the parent depreciates the equipment. (Note that the net effect of the upstream transfer on the parent's general ledger Retained Earnings account is a decrease of $600, which is the total incremental depreciation expense of $3,000 recorded by the parent less its $2,400 share of the subsidiary's reported gain of $3,000 (80% of $3,000) that the parent records under the equity method of accounting.)

Illustration 8-7 shows the entries presented in Illustration 8-6, plus the additional entries needed to share the deferral of the gain with the minority interest. The entries assume that the minority interest—based on the subsidiary's reported net income—has already been established from the primary elimination entry.

## ILLUSTRATION

## Preparing Consolidated Financial Statements

- ■ The Partial Equity Method
- ■ Upstream Equipment Transfer above Carrying Value from 80%-owned Subsidiary

The elimination entries at December 31, 19X1, in Illustration 8-7 are used in preparing a consolidating statement worksheet at December 31, 19X1, shown in Illustration 8-8. The worksheet begins with the P Company and S Company financial statements presented in Illustration 5-5. These financial statements were modified as follows:

1. The subsidiary's financial statements reflect a $3,000 intercompany gain on the equipment transfer (as well as $5,000 less depreciation expense since it did not use this equipment during 19X1).
2. The parent's financial statements reflect the $6,000 of additional depreciation expense ($1,000 of which is the incremental depreciation resulting from the subsidiary's $3,000 intercompany gain).
3. The parent's financial statements reflect an additional $6,400 recorded under the equity method of accounting ($8,000 × 80%) because the subsidiary's reported net income is $8,000 higher ($3,000 of intercompany gain and $5,000 of less depreciation expense).

The primary elimination entry (modified for the upstream transfer) along with the other elimination entries follow:

## MODULE 3   The Partial Equity Method *(continued)*

### ■ ILLUSTRATION 8-7
### Consolidation Entries for Upstream Transfer from 80%-owned Subsidiary

| | Consolidation Date | | | | | | | |
|---|---|---|---|---|---|---|---|---|
| | Jan. 1, 19X1 | | Dec. 31, 19X1 | | Dec. 31, 19X2 | | Dec. 31, 19X3 | |
| | Dr. | Cr. | Dr. | Cr. | Dr. | Cr. | Dr. | Cr. |
| **To Negate Equipment Transfer:**[a] | | | | | | | | |
| Intercompany Gain . . . . . . . . . | 3,000 | | 3,000 | | | | | |
| Equipment . . . . . . . . . . . . . . | 22,000 | | 22,000 | | 22,000 | | 22,000 | |
| Accumulated | | | | | | | | |
| Depreciation . . . . . . . . | | 25,000 | | 24,000 | | 23,000 | | 22,000 |
| Depreciation Expense . . . | | | | 1,000 | | 1,000 | | 1,000 |
| Retained Earnings— | | | | | | | | |
| P Company | | | | | | | | |
| (beginning of year) | | | | | 2,000 | | 1,000 | |
| **To Share Deferral with the Minority Interest:** | | | | | | | | |
| Minority Interest | | | | | | | | |
| in Net Assets . . . . . . . . . . . | 600[b] | | 400[b] | | 200[b] | | –0– | |
| Minority Interest | | | | | | | | |
| in Net Income . . . . . . . . | | 600 | | 400 | 200 | | 200 | |
| Retained Earnings— | | | | | | | | |
| P Company | | | | | | | | |
| (beginning of year) . . | | | | | | 400[c] | | 200[c] |

[a]The amounts in this entry at each consolidation date are the same as those in Illustration 8-6.
[b]The unreportable minority interest at this consolidation date.
[c]The unreportable minority interest at the beginning of the year. (Note that this credit posting partially offsets the debit posting to this account in the preceding entry; if the two entries were combined, a net debit posting would be made to P Company's Retained Earnings account.)

1. The primary elimination entry:

**WORKSHEET ENTRY ONLY**

| | | |
|---|---|---|
| Common Stock . . . . . . . . . . . . . . . . . . . . . . . . . . . . | 40,000 | |
| Retained Earnings (beginning of year) . . . . . . . . . . | 20,000 | |
| Equity in Net Income of Subsidiary | | |
| (80% of $23,000) . . . . . . . . . . . . . . . . . . . . . . . . . | 18,400 | |
| Minority Interest in Net Income of | | |
| S Company (20% of $23,000) . . . . . . . . . . . . . . . . | 4,600 | |
| Land . . . . . . . . . . . . . . . . . . . . . . . . . . . . . . . . . . . . | 9,600 | |
| Equipment . . . . . . . . . . . . . . . . . . . . . . . . . . . . . . . | 4,800 | |
| Goodwill . . . . . . . . . . . . . . . . . . . . . . . . . . . . . . . . . | 7,200 | |
| Dividends Declared . . . . . . . . . . . . . . . . . . . . . | | 5,000 |
| Accumulated Depreciation . . . . . . . . . . . . . . . . | | 800 |
| Investment in S Company . . . . . . . . . . . . . . . . . | | 83,200 |
| Minority Interest in Net Assets of | | |
| S Company . . . . . . . . . . . . . . . . . . . . . . . . . . . | | 15,600 |

**MODULE 3** **The Partial Equity Method** (continued)

2. The secondary elimination entry:

WORKSHEET
ENTRY ONLY

| | | |
|---|---|---|
| Cost of Goods Sold | 3,200 | |
| Equity in Net Income of Subsidiary | | 3,200 |

3. The accumulated depreciation elimination entry:

WORKSHEET
ENTRY ONLY

| | | |
|---|---|---|
| Accumulated Depreciation | 50,000 | |
| Buildings and Equipment | | 50,000 |

4. The intercompany gain elimination entry:

WORKSHEET
ENTRY ONLY

| | | |
|---|---|---|
| Intercompany Gain | 3,000 | |
| Equipment | 22,000 | |
| Accumulated Depreciation | | 24,000 |
| Depreciation Expense | | 1,000 |

5. The adjustment to the minority interest to share deferral of gain entry:

WORKSHEET
ENTRY ONLY

| | | |
|---|---|---|
| Minority Interest in Net Assets of Subsidiary | 400 | |
| Minority Interest in Net Income of Subsidiary | | 400 |

**Review Points for Illustration 8-8.** Note the following:

1. The consolidated net income and consolidated retained earnings are both $1,600 lower than the parent's net income and retained earnings, respectively. The correctness of this amount can be proven as follows:

| | |
|---|---|
| Total intercompany gain | $3,000 |
| Less—Incremental depreciation recorded through December 31, 19X1 | (1,000) |
| Unreportable gain at December 31, 19X1 | $2,000 |
| Less—Minority interest in unrealized gain (20% of $2,000) | (400) |
| Unreportable retained earnings at December 31, 19X1 | $1,600 |

## ■ ILLUSTRATION 8-8

### The Partial Equity Method: Upstream Equipment Transfer above Cost from 80%-owned Subsidiary

| | P Company | S Company | Eliminations Dr. | Eliminations Cr. | Consolidated |
|---|---|---|---|---|---|
| **P COMPANY AND SUBSIDIARY (S COMPANY)** Consolidating Statement Worksheet for the Year Ended December 31, 19X1 | | | | | |
| **Income Statement** | | | | | |
| Sales | 600,000 | 225,000 | | | 825,000 |
| Cost of sales | (360,000) | (110,000) | 3,200(2) | | (473,200) |
| Expenses | (196,000) | (95,000) | | 1,000(4) | (290,000) |
| Intercompany Accounts: | | | | | |
| Equity in net income | 15,200[a] | | 18,400(1) | 3,200(2) | —0— |
| Gain | | 3,000 | 3,000(4) | | —0— |
| Income before Minority Interest | 59,200 | 23,000 | 24,600 | 4,200 | 61,800 |
| Minority interest | | | 4,600(1) | 400(5) | (4,200) |
| Net Income | 59,200 | 23,000 | 29,200 | 4,600 | 57,600 |
| **Statement of Retained Earnings** | | | | | |
| Balances, January 1, 19X1 | 100,000 | 20,000 | 20,000(1) | | 100,000 |
| +Net income | 59,200 | 23,000 | 29,200 | 4,600 | 57,600 |
| −Dividends declared | (45,000) | (5,000) | | 5,000(1) | (45,000) |
| Balances, December 31, 19X1 | 114,200 | 38,000 | 49,200 | 9,600 | 112,600 |
| **Balance Sheet** | | | | | |
| Cash | 24,000 | 29,000 | | | 53,000 |
| Accounts receivable, net | 75,000 | 37,000 | | | 112,000 |
| Inventory | 110,000 | 55,000 | | | 165,000 |
| Investment in S Company | 83,200 | | | 83,200(1) | —0— |
| Land | 220,000 | 30,000 | 9,600(1) | | 259,600 |
| Buildings and equipment | 518,000 | 160,000 | 4,800(1) 22,000(4) | 50,000(3) | 654,800 |
| Accumulated depreciation | (326,000) | (33,000) | 50,000(3) | 800(1) 24,000(4) | (333,800) |
| Goodwill | | | 7,200(1) | | 7,200 |
| Total Assets | 704,200 | 278,000 | 93,600 | 158,000 | 917,800 |
| Liabilities | 290,000 | 200,000 | | | 490,000 |
| Minority interest in net assets | | | 400(5) | 15,600(1) | 15,200 |
| Common stock | 300,000 | 40,000 | 40,000(1) | | 300,000 |
| Retained earnings | 114,200 | 38,000 | 49,200 | 9,600 | 112,600 |
| Total Liabilities and Equity | 704,200 | 278,000 | 89,600 | 25,200 | 917,800 |
| Proof of debit and credit postings | | | 183,200 | 183,200 | |

Explanation of entries:
 (1) The primary elimination entry.
 (2) The secondary elimination entry.
 (3) The accumulated depreciation elimination entry.
 (4) The intercompany gain elimination entry.
 (5) The adjustment to the minority interest to share deferral of gain entry.
 [a]Comprised of $18,400 (80% of $23,000) less $3,200 of amortization.

2. The $4,200 minority interest deduction in the consolidated column can be determined as follows:

| | |
|---|---:|
| Subsidiary's reported net income. . . . . . . . . . . . . . . . . . . . . . . . . . | $23,000 |
| Less—Intercompany gain not deemed realized as far as the minority interest is concerned ($3,000 total gain − $1,000 deemed realized in 19X1). . . . . . . . . | (2,000) |
| | $21,000 |
| Minority ownership percentage. . . . . . . . . . . . . . . . . . . . . . . . . . . | 20% |
| Reportable minority interest deduction. . . . . . . . . . . . . . . . . . . | $ 4,200 |

**Consolidation at December 31, 19X2.**   The entries in Illustration 8-7 for periods after the year of transfer are slightly harder to visualize and understand. To show how the appropriate accounts would be dealt with on the worksheet at December 31, 19X2, assume that: (1) the subsidiary reported $25,000 of net income for 19X2 and declared no dividends, and (2) the parent has $50,000 of net income for 19X2, exclusive of its share of S Company's net income for 19X2, and declared no dividends. The 19X2 beginning of year retained earnings balances are taken from Illustration 8-8, which shows the balances at the end of 19X1. The following illustration portrays the consolidation process at December 31, 19X2 (see table on page 418).

**Review Points for 19X2 Entries.**   Note the following:

1. During the year 19X2, $800 of the parent's $2,400 share of the $3,000 intercompany gain is recognized in consolidation. This results from the $1,000 credit posted to depreciation expense and the $200 debit posted to the minority interest in the net income of the subsidiary.

2. At the beginning of 19X2, $1,600 of the parent's general ledger retained earnings balance was not reportable. (The $2,000 debit posted to the beginning balance and the $400 credit posted to the beginning balance result in the correct beginning consolidated balance for 19X2.)

3. At the end of 19X2, $800 of the parent's general ledger retained earnings balance is deferred.

**MODULE 3   The Partial Equity Method** *(continued)*

| | P Company | S Company | Eliminations Dr. | Eliminations Cr. | Consolidated |
|---|---|---|---|---|---|
| **Income Statement (19X2)** | | | | | |
| Depreciation expense ........... | (6,000) | | | 1,000(2) | (5,000) |
| Subtotal .................... | 50,000 | 25,000 | | 1,000 | 76,000 |
| Equity in net income ........... | 20,000 | | 20,000(1) | | –0– |
| Income before Minority Interest | 70,000 | 25,000 | 20,000 | 1,000 | 76,000 |
| Minority interest ............... | | | 5,000(1) 200(3) | | (5,200) |
| Net Income .................... | 70,000 | 25,000 | 25,200 | 1,000 | 70,800 |
| **Statement of Retained Earnings (19X2)** | | | | | |
| Beginning of year .............. | 114,200 | 38,000 | 38,000(1) 2,000(2) | 400(3) | 112,600 |
| +Net income ................... | 70,000 | 25,000 | 25,200 | 1,000 | 70,800 |
| End of year .................... | 184,200 | 63,000 | 65,200 | 1,400 | 183,400 |
| **Balance Sheet (Dec. 31, 19X2)** | | | | | |
| Equipment .................... | 18,000 | | 22,000(2) | | 40,000 |
| Accumulated depreciation ....... | (12,000) | | | 23,000(2) | (35,000) |
| Minority interest in net assets of S Company .......... | | | 200(3) | 20,600(1)[a] | 20,400 |

Explanation of entries:
(1)  The primary elimination entry.
(2)  To negate the equipment transfer.
(3)  To share the deferral with the minority interest.

[a]This $20,600 amount is 20% of the subsidiary's reported book value of $103,000 ($78,000 at December 31, 19X1 as shown in Illustration 8-8 plus the $25,000 increase in book value in 19X2 from earnings).

# HISTORICAL NOTE

During the Great Depression, many parent companies had companies within the consolidated group sell assets to one another in order to report profits in an attempt to increase the price of the parent's common stock. (At that time, such intercompany gains were not required to be deferred for consolidated reporting purposes.)

# END-OF-CHAPTER REVIEW

## Summary of Key Points

1. Transfer of fixed assets between companies within a consolidated group cannot result in a reportable gain or loss from a consolidated viewpoint.
2. Where a depreciable asset is involved, the recorded depreciation expense must be adjusted in consolidation to obtain an amount based on the selling entity's carrying value at the transfer date (using the new remaining life assigned to the asset).

## Glossary of New Terms

**Downstream transfer**   The transfer of a fixed asset from a parent to one of its subsidiaries.

**Upstream transfer**   The transfer of a fixed asset from a subsidiary to its parent.

## Self-Study Questions
*(Answers are at the end of this chapter.)*

1. On April 1, 19X1, Prism Company sold equipment costing $105,000 to its 80%-owned subsidiary, Spectrum Company, for $96,000. At the time of the sale, the equipment had been 20% depreciated (using the straight-line method and an assigned life of five years) Spectrum continued depreciating the equipment by using the straight-line method but assigned a remaining life of six years.

   What are the cost and accumulated depreciation, respectively, of this equipment in the December 31, 19X2 (not 19X1) consolidated balance sheet?
   a. $96,000 and $28,000.
   b. $96,000 and $42,000.
   c. $105,000 and $45,500.
   d. $105,000 and $49,000.
   e. $105,000 and $57,750.
   f. None of the above.

2. Assume the same information in question 1. What is the amount of the intercompany gain or loss that must be deferred at December 31, 19X2 (not 19X1)?
   a. $12,000.
   b. $8,500.
   c. $8,400.
   d. $6,800.
   e. $6,750.
   f. None of the above.

3. On January 2, 19X1, Soot Company, a 60%-owned subsidiary of Poot Company, sold equipment having a cost of $500,000 and accumulated depreciation of $200,000 to Poot Company for $240,000. Soot had been using a five-year life. Poot estimated the equipment would last four years. Each company uses the straight-line depreciation method. On January 4, 19X2, Poot sold the equipment to an outside third party for $250,000.

What is the amount of the gain or loss to be reported in the 19X2 consolidated income statement?

a. $10,000.
b. $15,000.
c. $25,000.
d. $70,000.
e. $(35,000).

# ASSIGNMENT MATERIAL

## Discussion Cases

| DC 8-1 |
|---|

### Review of Procedures for Consolidation: An Upstream Sale of Equipment

Shadd Company, a wholly owned subsidiary of Pike Company, manufactures and installs air conditioning systems. Shadd's sales are normally to outside parties, but during the current year Shadd sold Pike an air conditioning system for its new corporate headquarters. Shadd charged Pike $600,000 for the system and a fee of $90,000 for its installation. (Shadd's manufacturing cost was $400,000 and its installation costs were $65,000.)

**Required:**

Explain the procedures for preparing consolidated financial statements for the current year and in future years with respect to this transaction.

## Exercises

| E 8-1 |
|---|

### Downstream Land Transfer above Cost

On January 1, 19X1, Pastoral Company sold land costing $40,000 to its wholly owned subsidiary, Shepherd Company, for $100,000.

**Required:**
1. Prepare the consolidation elimination entries as of January 1, 19X1, December 31, 19X1, and December 31, 19X2. (For Modules 1 and 2 only: first prepare the general ledger adjusting entries at these dates.)
2. Prepare the necessary consolidation entry or entries at December 31, 19X3, assuming that Shepherd Company subsequently sold the land for $120,000. For Modules 1 and 2 only: first prepare the general ledger adjusting entries at these dates.)

| E 8-2 |
|---|

### Upstream Land Transfer above Cost from 80%-owned Subsidiary

On June 30, 19X1, Praline Company purchased land from Saints Company, its 80%-owned subsidiary, for $90,000. Saints' cost was $60,000.

**Required:**

1. Prepare the consolidation elimination entries as of June 30, 19X1, December 31, 19X1, and December 31, 19X2. (For Modules 1 and 2 only: first prepare the general ledger adjusting entries at these dates.)
2. Prepare the necessary consolidation entry or entries at December 31, 19X3, assuming that P Company subsequently sells the land for $85,000. For Modules 1 and 2 only: first prepare the general ledger adjusting entries at these dates.

---

**E 8-3**

## Calculating Consolidated Amounts: Downstream Equipment Transfer above Carrying Value

On January 1, 19X1, Pacific Company sold equipment to its wholly owned subsidiary, Southern Company for $800,000. The equipment cost Pacific $1,000,000; accumulated depreciation at the time of the sale was $400,000. Pacific has depreciated the equipment over 10 years using the straight-line method and no salvage value.

**Required:**

Determine the amounts at which the cost and accumulated depreciation should be reported in the consolidated balance sheet at December 31, 19X1, under each of the following assumptions:

1. The subsidiary does not revise the estimated remaining life.
2. The subsidiary estimates the remaining life as eight years.

---

**E 8-4**

## Downstream Equipment Transfer above Carrying Value

On January 1, 19X1, Placid Company sold machinery to its wholly owned subsidiary, Sereno Company. Information related to the sale is as follows:

| | | |
|---|---:|---:|
| Sales price | | $16,000 |
| Cost | $40,000 | |
| Less—Accumulated depreciation | (30,000) | 10,000 |
| Gain | | $ 6,000 |
| Original life used by Placid Company | | 8 years |
| Remaining life assigned by Sereno Company | | 3 years |

**Required:**

1. Prepare sections I, II, and III of a master analysis for the period January 1, 19X1 through December 31, 19X3.
2. Prepare the appropriate consolidation elimination entries at January 1, 19X1, December 31, 19X1, December 31, 19X2, and December 31, 19X3. (For Modules 1 and 2 only: first prepare the general ledger adjusting entries at these dates.)

| E 8-5 |
|---|

## Upstream Equipment Transfer above Carrying Value from 90%-owned Subsidiary

On January 1, 19X1, Prawn Company purchased equipment from its 90%-owned subsidiary Shrimp Company. Information related to the sale is as follows:

| | | |
|---|---:|---:|
| Sales price | | $42,000 |
| Cost | $75,000 | |
| Less—Accumulated depreciation | (60,000) | 15,000 |
| Gain | | $27,000 |
| Original life used by subsidiary | | 5 years |
| Remaining life assigned by parent | | 3 years |

### Required:

1. Prepare sections I, II, and III of a master analysis for the period January 1, 19X1 through December 31, 19X3.
2. Prepare the appropriate consolidation elimination entries at January 1, 19X1, December 31, 19X1, December 31, 19X2, and December 31, 19X3. (For Modules 1 and 2 only: first prepare the general ledger adjusting entries at these dates.)

## Problems

| P 8-1* |
|---|

## MINI-COMPREHENSIVE (Chapters 3, 4, and 8)   Full Consolidation: Downstream Equipment Transfer above Carrying Value

On January 1, 19X1, Paton Company acquired all of the outstanding common stock of Seaver Company for $90,000 cash. Seaver's book value was $70,000 at that date ($45,000 common stock + $25,000 retained earnings). The entire cost in excess of book value was assigned to goodwill, which was deemed to have a four-year life. On January 2, 19X1, Paton sold equipment to Seaver. Information related to the sale is as follows:

| | | |
|---|---:|---:|
| Sales price | | $35,000 |
| Cost | $50,000 | |
| Less—Accumulated depreciation | (30,000) | 20,000 |
| Gain | | $15,000 |
| Original life used by Paton Company | | 10 years |
| Remaining life assigned by Seaver Company | | 5 years |

Condensed financial statement information for 19X1 and at December 31, 19X1, follows:

*The financial statement information presented for problems accompanied by asterisks is also provided on Model 8 (filename: Model8) of the software file disk that is available for use with the text, enabling the problem to be worked on the computer.

|  | Paton Company | Seaver Company |
|---|---|---|
| **Income Statement (19X1)** | | |
| Sales | $440,000 | $150,000 |
| Cost of goods sold | (230,000) | (80,000) |
| Expenses | (70,000) | (40,000) |
| Intercompany Accounts: | | |
| Equity in net income of subsidiary | 25,000 | |
| Gain on sale of equipment | 15,000 | |
| Net Income | $180,000 | $ 30,000 |
| **Balance Sheet (December 31, 19X1)** | | |
| Investment in Seaver Company | $103,000 | |
| Buildings and equipment | 250,000 | $ 75,000 |
| Accumulated depreciation | (100,000) | (24,000)* |
| Other assets | 597,000 | 59,000 |
| Total Assets | $850,000 | $110,000 |
| Liabilities | $110,000 | $ 22,000 |
| Common stock | 300,000 | 45,000 |
| Retained earnings | 440,000 | 43,000 |
| Total Liabilities and Equity | $850,000 | $110,000 |
| Dividends declared | $ 80,000 | $ 12,000 |

*The balance was $10,000 at the acquisition date.

Neither company has made any general ledger adjustment for any unrealized intercompany gain at December 31, 19X1, on the equipment transfer.

### Required:

1. For Modules 1 and 2 only: make any necessary year-end general ledger adjusting entry(s). Then adjust the financial statements accordingly.
2. Prepare the elimination entries required in consolidation at December 31, 19X1.
3. Prepare a consolidation worksheet at December 31, 19X1.

## MINI-COMPREHENSIVE (Chapters 3, 4, 5, and 8)   Full Consolidation: Upstream Equipment Transfer above Carrying Value from an 80%-owned Subsidiary

**P 8-2***

On January 1, 19X1, Pak Company purchased 80% of the outstanding common stock of Shipp company for $143,000 cash. At that date, Shipp Company had (1) a book value of $150,000 ($100,000 common stock + $50,000 retained earnings) and (2) land that was undervalued by $10,000. Goodwill in the transaction was assigned a five-year life. On January 3, 19X1, Shipp sold equipment to Pak. Information related to the sale is as follows:

| | |
|---|---|
| Sales price | $22,000 |
| Cost | $25,000 |

*(continued)*

| | | |
|---|---|---|
| Less—Accumulated depreciation............... | (15,000) | 10,000 |
| Gain...................................... | | $12,000 |
| Original life used by Shipp Company............ | | 5 years |
| Remaining life assigned by Pak Company........ | | 4 years |

Condensed financial statements for the year ended December 31, 19X1, follow:

| | Pak Company | Shipp Company |
|---|---|---|
| **Income Statement (19X1)** | | |
| Sales..................................... | $520,000 | $168,000 |
| Cost of goods sold......................... | (210,000) | (80,000) |
| Expenses.................................. | (90,000) | (40,000) |
| Intercompany Accounts: | | |
| Equity in net income of subsidiary........... | 45,000 | |
| Gain on sale of equipment.................. | | 12,000 |
| Net Income............................... | $265,000 | $ 60,000 |
| **Balance Sheet (December 31, 19X1)** | | |
| Investment in Shipp Company................ | $172,000 | |
| Buildings and equipment.................... | 130,000 | $ 44,000 |
| Accumulated depreciation................... | (40,000) | (14,000)* |
| Other assets.............................. | 238,000 | 165,000 |
| Total Assets.......................... | $500,000 | $195,000 |
| Liabilities................................ | $ 75,000 | $ 5,000 |
| Common stock............................ | 200,000 | 100,000 |
| Retained earnings......................... | 225,000 | 90,000 |
| Total Liabilities and Equity.............. | $500,000 | $195,000 |
| Dividends declared........................ | $135,000 | $ 20,000 |

*The balance was $10,000 at the acquisition date.

Neither company has made any general ledger adjustment for the unrealized intercompany gain at December 31, 19X1, on the equipment transfer.

### Required:

1. For Modules 1 and 2 only: make any necessary year-end general ledger adjusting entry(s). Then adjust the financial statements accordingly.
2. Prepare the elimination entries required in consolidation at December 31, 19X1.
3. Prepare a consolidation worksheet at December 31, 19X1.

P 8-3*

### Consolidation Worksheet: Downstream Equipment Transfer to 80%-owned Subsidiary—Unrealized Gain at Beginning and End of Current Year

The financial statements of Prop Company and its 80%-owned subsidiary. Stage Company, for the year ended December 31, 19X2, are as follows:

|  | Prop Company | Stage Company |
|---|---|---|
| **Income Statement (19X2)** | | |
| Sales | $310,000 | $145,000 |
| Cost of goods sold | (140,000) | (70,000) |
| Expenses | (110,000) | (50,000) |
| Net Income | $ 60,000 | $ 25,000 |
| **Statement of Retained Earnings (19X2)** | | |
| Beginning of year | $ 55,000 | $ 30,000 |
| + Net income | 60,000 | 25,000 |
| − Dividends declared | (20,000) | (15,000) |
| End of year | $ 95,000 | $ 40,000 |
| **Balance Sheet (December 31, 19X2)** | | |
| Investment in subsidiary | $ 52,000 | |
| Buildings and equipment | 160,000 | $ 86,000 |
| Accumulated depreciation | (40,000) | (26,000)[a] |
| Other assets | 190,000 | 90,000 |
| Total Assets | $362,000 | $150,000 |
| Liabilities | $167,000 | $ 60,000 |
| Common stock | 100,000 | 50,000 |
| Retained earnings | 95,000 | 40,000 |
| Total Liabilities and Equity | $362,000 | $150,000 |

[a]The balance was $7,000 at the acquisition date.

On July 1, 19X1 (the previous year), Prop sold a piece of office equipment to Stage. Information pertaining to this transfer follows:

| | | |
|---|---|---|
| Sales price | | $12,000 |
| Carrying value: | | |
| Cost | $30,000 | |
| Accumulated depreciation through July 1, 19X1 | (22,000) | (8,000) |
| Gain recorded by parent | | $ 4,000 |
| Remaining life | | 2 years |

## Additional information:

1. Prop Company acquired 80% of the outstanding common stock of Stage Company on May 1, 19X1 at a cost equal to 80% of the book value of Stage's net assets at that date. None of Stage's assets or liabilities was over- or undervalued at that date.
2. Prop has not made any adjustment in its general ledger for unrealized intercompany gain at the end of 19X1 and 19X2.
3. Prop maintains its investment in the subsidiary using the equity method; however, it has not yet applied the equity method for 19X2 other than to record its share of dividends declared by the subsidiary.

**Required:**

1. Make any necessary year-end and beginning of year general ledger adjusting entries. Then adjust the financial statements accordingly.
2. Prepare a conceptual analysis of the investment account as of December 31, 19X1, and update it through December 31, 19X2.
3. Prepare all elimination entries required in consolidation at December 31, 19X2.
4. Prepare a consolidation worksheet at December 31, 19X2.

## P 8-4* Consolidation Worksheet: Upstream Equipment Transfer from 75%-owned Subsidiary—Unrealized Gain at Beginning and End of Current Year

The financial statements of Pert Company and its 75%-owned subsidiary, Savvy Company, for the year ended December 31, 19X2, are as follows:

| | Pert Company | Savvy Company |
|---|---|---|
| **Income Statement (19X2)** | | |
| Sales | $240,000 | $156,000 |
| Cost of goods sold | (120,000) | (80,000) |
| Expenses | (70,000) | (40,000) |
| Equity in net income of subsidiary | 27,000 | |
| Net Income | $ 77,000 | $ 36,000 |
| **Statement of Retained Earnings (19X2)** | | |
| Beginning of year | $100,000 | $ 44,000 |
| +Net income | 77,000 | 36,000 |
| −Dividends declared | (45,000) | (16,000) |
| End of year | $132,000 | $ 64,000 |
| **Balance Sheet (December 31, 19X2)** | | |
| Investment in subsidiary | $123,000 | |
| Buildings and equipment | 300,000 | $140,000 |
| Accumulated depreciation | (90,000) | (50,000)[a] |
| Other assets | 290,000 | 210,000 |
| Total Assets | $623,000 | $300,000 |
| Liabilities | $291,000 | $136,000 |
| Common stock | 200,000 | 100,000 |
| Retained earnings | 132,000 | 64,000 |
| Total Liabilities and Equity | $623,000 | $300,000 |

[a]The balance was $20,000 at the acquisition date.

On January 4, 19X1 (the previous year), Savvy sold office equipment to Pert. Information pertaining to this transfer follows:

| | | |
|---|---|---|
| Sales price | | $31,000 |
| Carrying value: | | |
| Cost | $25,000 | |

| | | |
|---|---:|---:|
| Accumulated depreciation through | | |
| January 1, 19X1 | (10,000) | (15,000) |
| Gain recorded by subsidiary | | $16,000 |
| Original life used by subsidiary | | 5 years |
| Remaining life assigned by parent | | 4 years |

## Additional information:

1. Pert Company acquired 75% of the outstanding common stock of Savvy Company on January 1, 19X1, at a cost equal to 75% of the book value of Savvy's net assets at that date. None of Savvy's assets or liabilities was over- or undervalued at that date.
2. Neither company has made any general ledger adjustment for unrealized intercompany gain at the end of 19X1 or 19X2.

## Required:

1. For Modules 1 and 2 only: make any necessary year-end and beginning of year general ledger adjusting entries. Then adjust the financial statements accordingly.
2. Prepare a conceptual analysis of the investment account as of December 31, 19X1, and update it through December 31, 19X2.
3. Prepare all elimination entries required in consolidation at December 31, 19X2.
4. Prepare a consolidation worksheet at December 31, 19X2.

---

**P 8-5\***

## COMPREHENSIVE (Chapters 3–8)  Consolidation Worksheet: Downstream Inventory Transfers above Cost—Profit in Beginning and Ending Inventory; Upstream Equipment Transfers above Carrying Value from 60%-owned Subsidiary—Unrealized Gain at Year-end

On January 1, 19X1, Park Company acquired 60% of the outstanding common stock of Stall Company for $160,000 cash. An additional $12,000 of direct costs were incurred. At the time, Stall's common stock had a book value of $36 per share. Also, Stall's land was undervalued by $50,000, and its 5% long-term debt (due December 31, 19X4) had a current value of $40,000 less than its book value. Park assigned a 10-year life to goodwill.

Many of the management functions of the two companies have been consolidated since the acquisition date. Park charges Stall a management fee of $1,000 per month.

On January 3, 19X2, Stall sold office equipment to Park. Information related to this transfer is as follows:

| | | |
|---|---:|---:|
| Sales price | | $25,000 |
| Cost | $45,000 | |
| Accumulated depreciation | (30,000) | 15,000 |
| Gain | | 10,000 |
| Original life used by Stall Company | | 9 years |
| Remaining life assigned by Park Company | | 5 years |

The financial statements of each company for the year ended December 31, 19X2 (two years after the acquisition), are as follows:

| | Park Company | Stall Company |
|---|---|---|
| **Income Statement (19X2)** | | |
| Sales. | $910,000 | $400,000 |
| Cost of goods sold | (570,000) | (200,000) |
| Expenses. | (302,000) | (158,000) |
| Intercompany Accounts: | | |
| Equity in net income of subsidiary. | 17,000 | |
| Sales. | 50,000 | |
| Cost of goods sold | (30,000) | |
| Management fee income | 12,000 | |
| Management fee expense | | (12,000) |
| Gain on equipment sale | | 10,000 |
| Net Income | $ 87,000 | $ 40,000 |
| | | |
| **Balance Sheet (December 31, 19X2)** | | |
| Cash. | $ 40,000 | $ 20,000 |
| Accounts receivable, net. | 112,000 | 60,000 |
| Intercompany receivable. | 70,000 | |
| Inventory: | | |
| From vendors. | 247,000 | 90,000 |
| Intercompany | | 10,000 |
| Investment in Stall Company. | 173,000 | |
| Land. | 123,000 | 95,000 |
| Buildings and equipment | 355,000 | 140,000 |
| Accumulated depreciation | (150,000) | (55,000)[c] |
| Total Assets. | $970,000 | $360,000 |
| | | |
| Accounts payable and accruals. | $130,000 | $ 15,500 |
| Intercompany payable. | | 70,000 |
| Long-term debt. | 200,000 | 90,000 |
| Common stock, $10 par value | 400,000 | |
| Common stock, $20 par value | | 100,000 |
| Retained earnings | 240,000 | 105,000 |
| Less—Treasury stock (at cost) (500 shares). | | (20,500)[a] |
| Total Liabilities and Equity | $970,000 | $360,000 |
| | | |
| Dividends declared:[b] | | |
| 19X1. | $ 30,000 | $ 5,000 |
| 19X2. | 41,000 | 25,000 |

[a]The treasury stock was purchased at a very favorable price on December 31, 19X2.
[b]Assume all dividends were declared on December 10 and paid ten days later.
[c]The balance was $40,000 at the acquisition date.

## Additional Information:

1. Stall's December 31, 19X1, inventory included inventory costing $15,000 that had been acquired from Park in 19X1. Park's cost was $10,000. Assume that all of this inventory was resold by the subsidiary in 19X2.

2. Neither company has made any general ledger adjustment for unrealized inter-company gain and profit at the end of 19X1 and 19X2.
3. In applying the equity method of accounting for 19X2, Park recorded $24,000 (60% of $40,000).

## Required:

1. For Modules 1 and 2 only: make any necessary year-end and beginning of year general ledger adjusting entries. Then adjust the financial statements accordingly.)
2. Prepare a conceptual analysis of the investment account from inception through December 31, 19X2.
3. Prepare all elimination entries required in consolidation at December 31, 19X2.
4. Prepare a consolidation worksheet at December 31, 19X2.

## ANSWERS TO SELF-STUDY QUESTIONS:

1. c
2. b, gain
3. c, gain

# 9

**......**

# INTERCOMPANY BOND HOLDINGS

# CHAPTER OVERVIEW

**A** parent or a subsidiary that has outstanding bonds may want to retire some or all of the bonds before their maturity dates. This is common when interest rates have declined significantly since the original issue date and new bonds can be issued at a lower interest rate, or when excess cash has accumulated beyond foreseeable needs. The entity that issues the bonds (referred to as the **issuing entity**) may not have the cash available to retire the bonds, or it may be impractical to issue new bonds to retire the old ones. In these situations, another company within the consolidated group that has available cash or the ability to issue debt can purchase some or all of the outstanding bonds in the open market. Although it is not unusual for a parent to purchase a subsidiary's bonds, a subsidiary purchases a parent's bonds only if directed to do so by the parent.

When bonds are acquired within a consolidated group, no amounts are owed to any party outside the group. Therefore, the purchase by one entity within the group of any or all of the outstanding bonds of another entity represents a constructive retirement of the bonds. Any imputed gain or loss on this deemed retirement must be reported in the consolidated income statement in the period of the purchase, as required by *APB Opinion No. 26*, "Early Extinguishment of Debt." If the gain or loss is material, it must be reported as an extraordinary item, as required by *FASB Statement No. 4*, "Reporting Gains and Losses from Extinguishment of Debt."

The accounting in consolidation is complicated by the fact that the issuing entity continues to account for the bonds as though they were outstanding, which they are from its viewpoint. The acquiring entity continues to account for the bonds as an investment until the issuing entity actually retires them. Accordingly, the objective of the consolidation procedures is to make the necessary adjustments on the consolidating statement worksheets to reflect, in the consolidated financial statements, amounts that would have existed if the issuing entity, rather than the acquiring entity, had acquired the bonds. These adjustments must be made from the acquisition date of the bonds to the date that they are actually retired.

As in Chapters 7 and 8, three equally acceptable mechanical procedures can be used to deal with intercompany bond holdings:

Module 1: The Complete Equity Method—Investment Account Adjustment Procedures
Module 2: The Complete Equity Method—Noninvestment Account Adjustment Procedures
Module 3: The Partial Equity Method

**Your instructor will assign the module to be read.**

# DETERMINING THE GAIN OR LOSS ON THE EXTINGUISHMENT OF DEBT

The procedure for calculating the gain or loss on the extinguishment of debt is the same regardless of which particular module is used. The amount of the *imputed* gain or loss on the extinguishment of debt that is reported in the period in which the affiliate's bonds are purchased is determined by comparing the acquisition cost to the applicable percentage of the carrying value of the bonds payable as of the bond purchase date. For example, assume that P Company acquired in the open market 40% of the outstanding 10% bonds of its wholly owned subsidiary, S Company, for $19,400 on January 1, 19X4. (The assumed maturity date of the bonds is December 31, 19X6, which is three years later.) Interest is payable on July 1 and January 1. Thus, none of the purchase cost relates to interest. The gain or loss is calculated at that date as follows:

|  | Face Amount | Unamortized Premium (S Co.) | Unamortized Discount (P Co.) | Carrying Value |
|---|---|---|---|---|
| Bonds payable . . . . . . . . . . . | $50,000 | $3,750 |  | $53,750 |
| Percent acquired . . . . . . . | 40% | 40% |  | 40% |
| Amount deemed retired . . | $20,000 | $1,500 |  | $21,500 |
| Investment in bonds . . . . . . | 20,000 |  | $600 | 19,400 |
| Unrecorded gain on extinguishment of debt |  | $1,500 | $600 | $ 2,100 |

The gain is attributable to the applicable percentage (40%) of the unamortized premium on the subsidiary's books and all of the discount on the parent's books. At the bond purchase date, the subsidiary would make the following **general ledger entry** to reflect the fact that the parent company now holds a portion of the bonds:

| Bonds Payable. . . . . . . . . . . . . . . . . . . . . . . . . . . . . . . . . | 20,000 | |
| Bond Premium . . . . . . . . . . . . . . . . . . . . . . . . . . . . . . . . | 1,500 | |
|     Intercompany Bonds Payable. . . . . . . . . . . . | | 20,000 |
|     Intercompany Bond Premium . . . . . . . . . . . . | | 1,500 |

The preceding example involved a premium on the issuing company's books and a discount on the acquiring company's books. This combination always results in a gain. If the issuing company has the discount and the acquiring company has the premium, a loss on early extinguishment of debt always results. When each company has a discount or each company has a premium, the net effect is a gain or a loss, depending on which company has the greater discount or premium. In all of these situations, the correct procedures for preparing consolidated financial statements can be determined through careful application of the principles discussed and illustrated in this chapter.

## Purchase between Interest Payment Dates

In the preceding example, we assumed for simplicity that the bond purchase occurred on an interest payment date. When an affiliate's bonds are acquired between interest dates, the only other item to account for is the additional amount that would be paid by the acquiring entity for interest from the last interest payment date to the purchase date. This additional amount is charged to interest receivable at the purchase date. The procedures to determine and account for the gains and losses do not change.

## Reissuance of Intercompany Bond Holdings

Infrequently, an acquiring entity sells some or all of the intercompany bonds to an outside party instead of holding them until their maturity date. In these cases, the bonds sold by the acquiring entity are considered to be reissued from a consolidated viewpoint. Any difference between the face value of the bonds and the proceeds (excluding amounts for interest) is treated in the same manner as a premium or discount on the issuance of bonds.

---

**MODULE 1**    The Complete Equity Method: Investment Account Adjustment Procedures

---

## MECHANICAL PROCEDURES FOR REPORTING GAIN OR LOSS ON THE EXTINGUISHMENT OF DEBT

**Module Overview.**    Under this approach to having the parent's net income equal consolidated net income, the gain or loss on extinguishment of debt is recorded by the parent as an adjustment to the income it records under the equity method of accounting. Subsequent to the bond acquisition date, the intercompany bond premium and discount are amortized to income in the general ledgers. In applying the equity method of accounting, however, the parent uses the subsidiary's net income adjusted to exclude the amortizations of the intercompany bond premium and discount. In consolidation, the amortizations are eliminated from the income statement.

In this module, we use the example given on page 432 in which a $2,100 gain on extinguishment resulted ($1,500 from the subsidiary's premium and $600 from the parent's discount).

## Consolidation in the Year in Which the Bonds Are Acquired

**Consolidation at the Bond Acquisition Date.**    If consolidated financial statements are prepared on January 1, 19X4 (the bond acquisition date), the parent would make the following **general ledger adjusting entry** under the equity method of accounting:

| | | |
|---|---|---|
| Investment in Common Stock of S Company.... | 2,100 | |
| Equity in Net Income of S Company ...... | | 2,100 |

On the consolidation worksheet, the following elimination entry is made to (1) reflect the deemed retirement of the bonds and (2) report the gain on extinguishment:

**WORKSHEET ENTRY ONLY**

| | | |
|---|---|---|
| Intercompany Bonds Payable.................. | 20,000 | |
| Intercompany Bond Premium ................ | 1,500 | |
| Investment in S Company Bonds......... | | 19,400 |
| Gain on Extinguishment................ | | 2,100 |

This entry produces the same results as though the subsidiary had acquired and retired the bonds.

### Consolidation at the End of the Bond Acquisition Year.

At December 31, 19X4, the parent would make the following **general ledger adjusting entry** under the equity method of accounting:

| | | |
|---|---|---|
| Equity in Net Income of S Company ............ | 700 | |
| Investment in Common Stock of | | |
| S Company............................. | | 700 |

This entry reverses $700 of the $2,100 recorded under the equity method of accounting on January 1, 19X4, inasmuch as $700 has been amortized into income in the general ledgers during 19X4 ($500 on the subsidiary's books and $200 on the parent's books). On the consolidation worksheet, the following elimination entries are made to (1) reflect the deemed retirement of the bonds, (2) report the gain on extinguishment, and (3) eliminate the intercompany interest income and intercompany interest expense:

**WORKSHEET ENTRY ONLY**

| | | |
|---|---|---|
| Intercompany Bonds Payable................... | 20,000 | |
| Intercompany Bond Premium ($1,500 − $500 | | |
| of premium amortization in 19X4) ........... | 1,000 | |
| Investment in S Company Bonds | | |
| ($19,400 + $200 of discount | | |
| amortization in 19X4)................. | | 19,600 |
| Gain on Extinguishment................ | | 1,400 |

| | | |
|---|---|---|
| **MODULE 1** | **The Complete Equity Method: Investment Account Adjustment Procedures** *(continued)* | |

| WORKSHEET ENTRY ONLY | Intercompany Interest Income ($2,000 + $200 of discount amortization in 19X4) . . . . . . . . . . . . . | 2,200 | |
|---|---|---|---|
| | Intercompany Interest Expense ($2,000 − $500 of premium amortization in 19X4) . . . . . . . . . . . . . . . | | 1,500 |
| | Gain on Extinguishment . . . . . . . . . . . . . . . . | | 700 |

## ILLUSTRATION

### Preparing Consolidated Financial Statements

- The Complete Equity Method: Investment Account Adjustment Procedures
- At the End of the Bond Acquisition Year—100%-owned Subsidiary

Illustration 9-1 shows a consolidation worksheet at December 31, 19X4. The preceding two elimination entries are used along with the following primary elimination entry:

| WORKSHEET ENTRY ONLY | Common Stock . . . . . . . . . . . . . . . . . . . . . . . . . | 40,000 | |
|---|---|---|---|
| | Retained Earnings (beginning of year) . . . . . . . . . | 65,000 | |
| | Equity in Net Income of Subsidiary ($30,000 plus $1,400) . . . . . . . . . . . . . . . . . . . | 31,400 | |
| | Dividends Declared . . . . . . . . . . . . . . . . . . . . | | 5,000 |
| | Investment in Common Stock of S Company . . . . . . . . . . . . . . . . . . . . . . . . | | 131,400 |

## Consolidation in Years Subsequent to the Year in Which the Bonds Are Acquired

For consolidations in years subsequent to the bond acquisition year, the amounts that are reported in the separate company income statements resulting from amortization of the premium and discount in the general ledgers are eliminated by postings from the primary elimination. Likewise, the unamortized premium and unamortized discount amounts are eliminated by postings from the primary elimination entry. Accordingly, the only other entries required in consolidation are as follows (assume a consolidation date of December 31, 19X5):

| WORKSHEET ENTRY ONLY | Intercompany Bonds Payable . . . . . . . . . . . . . . . . . . | 20,000 | |
|---|---|---|---|
| | Investment in S Company Bonds . . . . . . . . . | | 20,000 |

| WORKSHEET ENTRY ONLY | Intercompany Interest Income . . . . . . . . . . . . . . . | 2,000 | |
|---|---|---|---|
| | Intercompany Interest Expense . . . . . . . . . | | 2,000 |

The appropriate postings from the primary elimination entry are obtained by modifying the book value element of the conceptual analysis

■ **ILLUSTRATION 9-1**

**The Complete Equity Method: Investment Account Adjustment Procedures;**
**Consolidation at Year-end of Bond Acquisition Year—100%-owned Subsidiary**

**P COMPANY AND SUBSIDIARY (S COMPANY)**
**Consolidating Statement Worksheet for the Year Ended December 31, 19X4**

| | P Company | S Company | Eliminations Dr. | Eliminations Cr. | Consolidated |
|---|---|---|---|---|---|
| **Income Statement** | | | | | |
| Sales | 680,000 | 280,000 | | | 960,000 |
| Cost of goods sold | (380,000) | (120,000) | | | (500,000) |
| Expenses | (242,200) | (128,500) | | | (370,700) |
| Intercompany Accounts: | | | | | |
| Equity in net income | 31,400[a] | | 31,400(1) | | –0– |
| Interest expense | | (1,500) | | 1,500(2) | –0– |
| Interest income | 2,200 | | 2,200(2) | | –0– |
| Gain on extinguishment of debt | | | | 700(2) 1,400(3) | 2,100 |
| Net Income | 91,400 | 30,000 | 33,600 | 3,600 | 91,400 |
| **Statement of Retained Earnings** | | | | | |
| Balances, January 1, 19X1 | 163,000 | 65,000 | 65,000(1) | | 163,000 |
| + Net income | 91,400 | 30,000 | 33,600 | 3,600 | 91,400 |
| – Dividends declared | (51,000) | (5,000) | | 5,000(1) | (51,000) |
| Balances, December 31, 19X1 | 203,400 | 90,000 | 98,600 | 8,600 | 203,400 |
| **Balance Sheet** | | | | | |
| Investment in S Company: | | | | | |
| Common stock | 131,400 | | | 131,400(1) | –0– |
| Bonds | 19,600 | | | 19,600(3) | –0– |
| Intercompany interest receivable (payable) | 1,000 | (1,000) | | | –0– |
| Other assets | 600,400 | 311,000 | | | 911,400 |
| Total Assets | 752,400 | 310,000 | | 151,000 | 911,400 |
| Accounts payable and accruals | 249,000 | 127,500 | | | 376,500 |
| Bonds payable | | 30,000 | | | 30,000 |
| Bond premium | | 1,500 | | | 1,500 |
| Intercompany bonds payable | | 20,000 | 20,000(3) | | –0– |
| Intercompany bond premium | | 1,000 | 1,000(3) | | –0– |
| Common stock | 300,000 | 40,000 | 40,000(1) | | 300,000 |
| Retained earnings | 203,400 | 90,000 | 98,600 | 8,600 | 203,400 |
| Total Liabilities and Equity | 752,400 | 310,000 | 159,600 | 8,600 | 911,400 |
| Proof of debit and credit postings | | | 159,600 | 159,600 | |

Explanation of entries:
(1) The primary elimination entry.
(2) The intercompany interest income and intercompany interest expense elimination entry.
(3) The elimination of the bond investment and related intercompany bond payable.

[a]Comprised of $30,000 of reported net income plus $1,400 (which amount equals the $1,000 of unamortized intercompany bond premium and $400 of the parent's unamortized discount).

so that two additional columns are added (labeled "Parent's Bond Discount" and "Subsidiary's Bond Premium").

**ILLUSTRATION**

## Updating the Book Value Element of the Conceptual Analysis When Imputed Gain Has Been Recognized on Intercompany Bond Transaction

Illustration 9-2 shows how the modified conceptual analysis of the investment account would be maintained from the bond acquisition date (January 1, 19X4 through December 31, 19X6 (the maturity date). For simplicity, we assume the subsidiary reported $30,000 of net income in 19X4, 19X5, and 19X6; the subsidiary declared dividends of $5,000 in 19X4, and the parent had no amortization of cost in excess of book value.

## Minority Interest Considerations

When a subsidiary is partially owned, the conceptual analysis of the investment account must be updated in such a manner that none of the parent's discount is treated as accruing to the minority interest. To illustrate, assume the information in Illustration 9-2, except that the subsidiary is 80% owned. The $30,000 of net income reported by the subsidiary for 19X4 would be dealt with as follows:

| | |
|---|---:|
| Subsidiary's reported net income for 19X4 . . . . . . . . . . . . . . . . . | $30,000 |
| Plus—Subsidiary's unamortized intercompany bond premium at December 31, 19X4 . . . . . . . . . . . . . . . . . . . | 1,000 |
| Subsidiary's adjusted net income . . . . . . . . . . . . . . . . . . . . . . . | $31,000 |
| Parent's ownership percentage . . . . . . . . . . . . . . . . . . . . . . . | 80% |
| Parent's Share of Subsidiary's adjusted net income . . . . . . . . | $24,800 |
| Plus—Parent's unamortized bond discount at December 31, 19X4 . . . . . . . . . . . . . . . . . . . . . . . . . . . . . . . . . | 400 |
| Parent's equity in 19X4 net income of subsidiary . . . . . . . . . | $25,200 |
| Minority interest in 19X4 net income of subsidiary (20% of $31,000) . . . . . . . . . . . . . . . . . . . . . . . . . . | $6,200 |

Note that the sum of the $25,200 and $6,200 equal $31,400, which is the subsidiary's reported net income for 19X4 of $30,000 plus the $1,400 of unamortized intercompany premium and discount at December 31, 19X4. The minority interest column of the conceptual analysis of the investment account would be updated using the $6,200 amount. Reclassifications would be made for the parent's unamortized discount of $400 and the subsidiary's unamortized intercompany premium of $1,000.

## ■ ILLUSTRATION 9-2
### Updating the Book Value Element of the Conceptual Analysis When Imputed Gain Has Been Recognized on Intercompany Bond Transaction

| | Total Cost | Common Stock | Prior Years | Book Value Element | | | |
| --- | --- | --- | --- | --- | --- | --- | --- |
| | | | | Retained Earnings | | | |
| | | | | Current Year | | Parent's Bond Discount | Sub's Bond Premium |
| | | | | Earnings | Dividends | | |
| Balance, January 1, 19X4 | $105,000 | $40,000 | $ 65,000 | | | | |
| Equity in net income ($30,000 + $1,400) | 31,400 | | | $31,400 | | | |
| Dividends declared | (5,000) | | | | $(5,000) | | |
| Subtotal | $131,400 | $40,000 | $ 65,000 | $31,400 | $(5,000) | | |
| Reclassification | | | | (400) | | $400 | |
| Reclassification | | | | (1,000) | | | $1,000 |
| Reclassification | | | 25,000 | (30,000) | 5,000 | | |
| Balance, December 31, 19X4 | $131,400 | $40,000 | $ 90,000 | $ -0- | $ -0- | $400 | $1,000 |
| Equity in net income ($30,000 − $700) | 29,300 | | | 29,300 | | | |
| Subtotal | $160,700 | $40,000 | $ 90,000 | $29,300 | $ -0- | $400[a] | $1,000[b] |
| Reclassification | | | | 200 | | (200) | |
| Reclassification | | | | 500 | | | (500) |
| Reclassification | | | 30,000 | (30,000) | | | |
| Balance, December 31, 19X5 | $160,700 | $40,000 | $120,000 | $ -0- | $ -0- | $200 | $500 |
| Equity in net income ($30,000 − $700) | 29,300 | | | 29,300 | | | |
| Subtotal | $190,000 | $40,000 | $120,000 | $29,300 | $ -0- | $200[c] | $500[d] |
| Reclassification | | | | 200 | | (200) | |
| Reclassification | | | | 500 | | | (500) |
| Reclassification | | | 30,000 | (30,000) | | | |
| Balance, December 31, 19X6 | $190,000 | $40,000 | $150,000 | $ -0- | $ -0- | $ -0- | $ -0- |

[a]Because the parent amortized $200 of its discount to income during 19X5. $200 of this balance is posted as a debit to Intercompany Interest Income (so as to eliminate the parent's amortization). The remaining $200 is posted as a debit to the Investment in Bonds of S Company account (so as to eliminate the unamortized discount).

[b]Because the subsidiary amortized $500 of its premium to income during 19X5. $500 of this balance is posted as a debit to Intercompany Interest Expense (so as to eliminate the subsidiary's amortization). The remaining $500 is posted as a debit to the Intercompany Bond Premium account (so as to eliminate the unamortized premium).

[c]Posted as a debit to Intercompany Interest Income (so as to eliminate the parent's 19X6 amortization of its discount).

[d]Posted as a debit to Intercompany Interest Expense (so as to eliminate the subsidiary's 19X6 amortization of its premium).

## MODULE 2  The Complete Equity Method: Noninvestment Account Adjustment Procedures

# MECHANICAL PROCEDURES FOR REPORTING GAIN OR LOSS ON THE EXTINGUISHMENT OF DEBT

**Module Overview.**   Recall that under the complete equity method, the parent company's net income and retained earnings always equal the consolidated net income and consolidated retained earnings, respectively. For this to occur, the gain or loss on the deemed extinguishment of intercompany bonds must be reflected in the parent's income statement. This is accomplished by adjusting the general ledgers of each company so as to eliminate the premium(s) or discount(s) that give rise to the imputed gain or loss.

In this module, we use the example given on page 432 in which a $2,100 gain on extinguishment resulted ($1,500 from the subsidiary's premium and $600 from the parent's discount). Using this example, the following **general ledger entries** would be made on the bond acquisition date:

|  | P Company | S Company |
|---|---|---|
| **Subsidiary's Entry** | | |
| Intercompany Bond Premium .. | | 1,500 |
| Gain on Extinguishment of Debt. . . . . . . . . . . . . . . . . . . | | 1,500 |
| **Parent's Entries** | | |
| Investment in Bonds of S Company . . . . . . . . . . . . . . . . . | 600 | |
| Gain on Extinguishment of Subsidiary's Debt. . . . . . . | | 600 |
| Investment in Common Stock of S Company. . . . . . . . . . | 1,500 | |
| Equity in Net Income of S Company. . . . . . . . . . . . . | | 1,500 |
| To apply the equity method of accounting. | | |

Note that the parent's income statement now reports $2,100 of income, which is equal to the gain on the extinguishment of debt that would be reported in consolidation.

**The Rationale for Making the General Ledger Entries.**   The rationale for eliminating the discount on the parent's books and the intercompany bond premium on the subsidiary's books is that the accounting treatment should be no different than if the parent had formally exchanged $20,000 checks with the subsidiary. That is, the parent advances $20,000 to the subsidiary with the stipulation that the subsidiary retire the $20,000 face value of bonds held by the parent. Using this procedure, the parent would record a $600 gain on the extinguishment of the debt and the subsidiary would record a $1,500 gain. Thus, the parent has two means of accomplishing the same end result. The accounting should reflect the substance of the end result—not the form of the particular alternative selected to achieve the end result.

**Entries Required in Consolidation.**   After the general ledger entries shown earlier have been recorded, the parent's Investment in Bonds of S Company account has a balance of $20,000. Likewise, the subsidiary's intercompany bond accounts show only the $20,000 balance in the Intercompany Bonds Payable account. As a result, no amortization is necessary by either company in their general ledgers in subsequent periods. At each future year-end consolidation date (preceding the actual retirement of the bonds), the following two entries would be made in consolidation:

| WORKSHEET ENTRY ONLY | Intercompany Bonds Payable | 20,000 | |
|---|---|---|---|
| | Investment in Bonds of S Company | | 20,000 |

| WORKSHEET ENTRY ONLY | Intercompany Interest Income | 2,000 | |
|---|---|---|---|
| | Intercompany Interest Expense | | 2,000 |

**Preparing Consolidated Financial Statements**

- The Complete Equity Method: Noninvestment Account Adjustment Procedures
- At Year-end of Bond Acquisition Year—100%-owned Subsidiary

Illustration 9-3 presents a consolidating statement worksheet as of December 31, 19X4.

**Partially Owned Subsidiaries.**   Even when the subsidiary is partially owned, the procedures are the same as those for wholly owned subsidiaries. The parent would use its percentage of ownership (rather than 100%) when applying the equity method.

**How the Subsidiary Reports to Minority Shareholders.**   If the subsidiary is partially owned, the income or loss it records as a result of eliminating its intercompany premium or discount is not realized insofar as the minority shareholders are concerned. Accordingly, in reporting to them the subsidiary would make an adjusting entry to the financial statements to

**MODULE 2    The Complete Equity Method: Noninvestment Account Adjustment Procedures** (continued)

## ■ ILLUSTRATION 9-3

**The Complete Equity Method: Noninvestment Account Adjustment Procedures; Consolidation at Year-end of Bond Acquisition Year—100%-owned Subsidiary**

| | P Company | S Company | Eliminations Dr. | Eliminations Cr. | Consolidated |
|---|---|---|---|---|---|
| **P COMPANY AND SUBSIDIARY (S COMPANY)** Consolidating Statement Worksheet for the Year Ended December 31, 19X4 | | | | | |
| **Income Statement** | | | | | |
| Sales | 680,000 | 280,000 | | | 960,000 |
| Cost of goods sold | (380,000) | (120,000) | | | (500,000) |
| Expenses | (242,200) | (128,500) | | | (370,700) |
| Intercompany Accounts: | | | | | |
| Equity in net income of of subsidiary | 31,000 | | 31,000(1) | | –0– |
| Interest expense | | (2,000) | | 2,000(2) | –0– |
| Interest income | 2,000 | | 2,000(2) | | –0– |
| Gain on extinguishment of debt | 600 | 1,500 | | | 2,100 |
| Net Income | 91,400 | 31,000 | 33,000 | 2,000 | 91,400 |
| **Statement of Retained Earnings** | | | | | |
| Balances, January 1, 19X4 | 163,000 | 65,000 | 65,000(1) | | 163,000 |
| +Net income | 91,400 | 31,000 | 33,000 | 2,000 | 91,400 |
| −Dividends declared | (51,000) | (5,000) | | 5,000(1) | (51,000) |
| Balances, December 31, 19X4 | 203,400 | 91,000 | 98,000 | 7,000 | 203,400 |
| **Balance Sheet** | | | | | |
| Investment in S Company: | | | | | |
| Common stock | 131,000 | | | 131,000(1) | –0– |
| Bonds | 20,000 | | | 20,000(3) | –0– |
| Intercompany interest receivable (payable) | 1,000 | (1,000) | | | –0– |
| Other assets | 600,400 | 311,000 | | | 911,400 |
| Total Assets | 752,400 | 310,000 | | 151,000 | 911,400 |
| Accounts payable and accruals | 249,000 | 127,500 | | | 376,500 |
| Bonds payable | | 30,000 | | | 30,000 |
| Bond premium | | 1,500 | | | 1,500 |
| Intercompany bonds payable | | 20,000 | 20,000(3) | | –0– |
| Common stock | 300,000 | 40,000 | 40,000(1) | | 300,000 |
| Retained earnings | 203,400 | 91,000 | 98,000 | 7,000 | 203,400 |
| Total Liabilities and Equity | 752,400 | 310,000 | 158,000 | 7,000 | 911,400 |
| Proof of debit and credit postings | | | 158,000 | 158,000 | |

Explanation of entries:
(1) The primary elimination entry.
(2) The elimination of intercompany interest income and intercompany interest expense.
(3) The elimination of the bond investment and related intercompany bond payable.

reflect the intercompany premium or discount just as though it had not been eliminated in the general ledger. Although keeping the general ledger for reporting to the parent (rather than to the minority shareholders) slightly complicates the subsidiary's process of reporting to the minority interest, the consolidation process is streamlined—a much greater benefit.

**MODULE 3**   The Partial Equity Method

# MECHANICAL PROCEDURES FOR REPORTING GAIN OR LOSS ON THE EXTINGUISHMENT OF DEBT

**Module Overview.**   Recall from Chapter 7 that under the partial equity method, the parent's net income and retained earnings do not equal consolidated net income and consolidated retained earnings, respectively. In dealing with intercompany bond holdings, this comes about because the gain or loss on extinguishment of debt is reported only in consolidation. The following discussion uses the example given on page 432 in which a $2,100 gain on extinguishment resulted ($1,500 from the subsidiary's premium and $600 from the parent's discount).

**Consolidation at the Bond Acquisition Date.**   If consolidated financial statements are prepared on January 1, 19X4 (the bond acquisition date), the following elimination entry is required in consolidation to (1) reflect this deemed retirement of the bonds and (2) report the gain on extinguishment:

**WORKSHEET ENTRY ONLY**

| | | |
|---|---:|---:|
| Intercompany Bonds Payable | 20,000 | |
| Intercompany Bond Premium | 1,500 | |
|     Investment in S Company Bonds | | 19,400 |
|     Gain on Extinguishment | | 2,100 |

This entry produces the same results as though the subsidiary had acquired and retired the bonds.

## Dealing with Subsequent Amortization of Bond Premium and Discount

In the preceding example, the substance of the deemed bond retirement is to accelerate reporting the $1,500 intercompany bond premium and the $600 bond discount as income. In other words, instead of the $1,500 bond premium being reported as income over the remaining life of the bonds (as a reduction of interest expense through the amortization process), it is reported as income in consolidation at the bond acquisition date. Likewise, instead of the $600 bond discount being reported as income over the remaining life of the bonds (as additional interest income through the amortization process), it is reported as income in consolidation at the bond acquisition date.

Because the $1,500 intercompany bond premium and the $600 discount are reported as income in consolidation at the bond acquisition date, the parent's consolidated retained earnings balance is $2,100 greater than its general ledger Retained Earnings account balance. The parent's general ledger Retained Earnings account balance equals the consolidated retained earnings balance only through the complete amortization of the $1,500 bond premium and $600 discount that takes place in the general ledgers over the remaining life of the bonds. At December 31, 19X6 (the bond maturity date), the entire intercompany bond premium of $1,500 and the discount of $600 have been amortized in the general ledgers. As a result, the parent's general ledger Retained Earnings account balance is $2,100 greater than at January 1, 19X4 (the bond acquisition date).

If nothing is done in consolidation at the end of 19X4, 19X5, and 19X6 concerning this amortization, then the $2,100 has been reported as income twice:

1. First, as a $2,100 gain on extinguishment in 19X4 as a result of the elimination entry made in consolidation to eliminate the bond investment and the related intercompany bond payable and premium accounts.
2. Second, as additional interest income ($600) and lesser interest expense ($1,500) from January 1, 19X4, to December 31, 19X6, as a result of amortizing the $600 discount and the $1,500 intercompany bond premium to income in the general ledgers.

Obviously, the $2,100 can be reported as income only once. Thus, in periods subsequent to the bond acquisition date, elimination entries are needed in consolidation to eliminate this income resulting from the amortization process. This, of course, is consistent with the consolidated viewpoint that the bonds are deemed to be retired at the bond acquisition date. Future-period consolidated income statements cannot report any interest income or expense with respect to these bonds.

## Entries Recorded in Books Subsequent to Bond Acquisition Date

Assume that P Company and S Company use the straight-line method of amortizing bond premium and discount (the results from the straight-line method are not materially different from results under the interest method). The entries that would be recorded in **each company's general ledger** during 19X4, 19X5, and 19X6 relating to the bonds are as follows:

|  | P Company | S Company |
|---|---|---|
| Intercompany Interest Expense...... |  | 2,000 |
| Interest Expense ................... |  | 3,000 |
| Intercompany Interest Payable... |  | 2,000 |
| Interest Payable ................ |  | 3,000 |
| To record interest expense (10% of $50,000, 40% of which is intercompany). |  |  |
|  |  |  |
| Intercompany Interest Receivable.... | 2,000 |  |
| Intercompany Interest Income ... |  | 2,000 |
| To record interest income (10% of $20,000). |  |  |
|  |  |  |
| Intercompany Bond Premium........ |  | 500 |
| Bond Premium .................... |  | 750 |
| Intercompany Interest Expense.. |  | 500 |
| Interest Expense ............... |  | 750 |
| To amortize bond premium. |  |  |
|  |  |  |
| Investment in S Company Bonds..... | 200 |  |
| Intercompany Interest Income ... |  | 200 |
| To amortize bond discount. |  |  |

At the end of each of these years, the balances in the Intercompany Interest Expense and Intercompany Interest Income accounts would be as follows:

| P Company Intercompany Interest Income | | S Company Intercompany Interest Expense | |
|---|---|---|---|
| 2,000 | | 2,000 | |
| 200 | | | 500 |
| 2,200 | | 1,500 | |

The difference between the two accounts is a net credit of $700, which is the result of the amortization of the intercompany bond premium of $500 and the bond discount of $200. Because three such years of amortization occur, the cumulative three-year difference is $2,100 (equal to the gain on extinguishment of debt reportable at January 1, 19X4). As explained in the preceding section, these account balances must be eliminated in consolidation at the end of 19X4, 19X5, and 19X6.

---

**MODULE 3    The Partial Equity Method** (continued)

---

**ILLUSTRATION**    ## Preparing Consolidated Financial Statements

- The Partial Equity Method
- At the End of the Bond Acquisition Year—100%-owned Subsidiary

Assuming P Company is a calendar year-end reporting company, the elimination entries that would be made in consolidation at December 31, 19X4 (one year after the bond acquisition date), are as follows:

1. The elimination of intercompany interest income and intercompany interest expense:

**WORKSHEET ENTRY ONLY**

| | | |
|---|---|---|
| Intercompany Interest Income................. | 2,200 | |
| Intercompany Interest Expense .......... | | 1,500 |
| Gain on Extinguishment of Debt ......... | | 700 |

2. The elimination of the investment in the bonds and the related bond liability and premium accounts:

**WORKSHEET ENTRY ONLY**

| | | |
|---|---|---|
| Intercompany Bonds Payable.................. | 20,000 | |
| Intercompany Bond Premium ($1,500 – $500 | | |
| 19X1 amortization)........................... | 1,000 | |
| Investment in bonds ($19,400 + $200 | | |
| 19X1 amortization) .................. | | 19,600 |
| Gain on Extinguishment of Debt ......... | | 1,400 |

The combination of the two entries results in a $2,100 credit to the Gain on Extinguishment of Debt account, which was the amount of gain determined on January 1, 19X1 (the date the bond investment was made). Because of the actual $700 amortization that was recorded in the general ledgers during 19X1, only $1,400 of premium and discount remain "locked into" the balance sheet at the end of 19X1.

The two preceding entries are posted to the December 31, 19X4, consolidating statement worksheet in Illustration 9-4. The following assumptions were made for simplicity:

1. P Company acquired all of the outstanding common stock of S Company on January 1, 19X1, at an amount equal to the book value of S Company's net assets. Accordingly, no secondary elimination entry is made for cost over or under book value. In 19X4, S Company had net income of $30,000 and declared dividends of $5,000. The primary elimination entry (assuming that P Company uses the equity method of accounting) is as follows:

**MODULE 3    The Partial Equity Method** (continued)

■ **ILLUSTRATION 9-4**

**The Partial Equity Method: Consolidation at the End of the Bond Acquisition Year—100%-owned Subsidiary**

| | P Company | S Company | Eliminations Dr. | Eliminations Cr. | Consolidated |
|---|---|---|---|---|---|
| **P COMPANY AND SUBSIDIARY (S COMPANY)** Consolidating Statement Worksheet for the Year Ended December 31, 19X4 | | | | | |
| **Income Statement** | | | | | |
| Sales | 680,000 | 280,000 | | | 960,000 |
| Cost of goods sold | (380,000) | (120,000) | | | (500,000) |
| Expenses | (242,200) | (128,500) | | | (370,700) |
| Intercompany Accounts: | | | | | |
| Equity in net income of subsidiary | 30,000 | | 30,000(1) | | –0– |
| Interest expense | | (1,500) | | 1,500(2) | –0– |
| Interest income | 2,200 | | 2,200(2) | | –0– |
| Gain on extinguishment of debt | | | | 700(2) 1,400(3) | 2,100 |
| Net Income | 90,000 | 30,000 | 32,200 | 3,600 | 91,400 |
| **Statement of Retained Earnings** | | | | | |
| Balances, January 1, 19X4 | 163,000 | 65,000 | 65,000(1) | | 163,000 |
| + Net income | 90,000 | 30,000 | 32,200 | 3,600 | 91,400 |
| – Dividends declared | (51,000) | (5,000) | | 5,000(1) | (51,000) |
| Balances, December 31, 19X4 | 202,000 | 90,000 | 97,200 | 8,600 | 203,400 |
| **Balance Sheet** | | | | | |
| Investment in S Company: | | | | | |
| Common stock | 130,000 | | | 130,000(1) | –0– |
| Bonds | 19,600 | | | 19,600(3) | –0– |
| Intercompany interest receivable (payable) | 1,000 | (1,000) | | | –0– |
| Other assets | 600,400 | 311,000 | | | 911,400 |
| Total Assets | 751,000 | 310,000 | | 149,600 | 911,400 |
| Accounts payable and accruals | 249,000 | 127,500 | | | 376,500 |
| Bonds payable | | 30,000 | | | 30,000 |
| Bond premium | | 1,500 | | | 1,500 |
| Intercompany bonds payable | | 20,000 | 20,000(3) | | –0– |
| Intercompany bond premium | | 1,000 | 1,000(3) | | –0– |
| Common stock | 300,000 | 40,000 | 40,000(1) | | 300,000 |
| Retained earnings | 202,000 | 90,000 | 97,200 | 8,600 | 203,400 |
| Total Liabilities and Equity | 751,000 | 310,000 | 158,200 | 8,600 | 911,400 |

Proof of debit and credit postings . . . . . . . . . . . . . . . . . . . . . . . . . . . . 158,200    158,200

Explanation of entries:
(1) The primary elimination entry.
(2) The elimination of intercompany interest income and intercompany interest expense.
(3) The elimination of bond investment and related intercompany bond liability and premium accounts.

| MODULE 3 | **The Partial Equity Method** (continued) |

**WORKSHEET ENTRY ONLY**

| Common Stock | 40,000 | |
|---|---|---|
| Retained Earnings (beginning of year) | 65,000 | |
| Equity in Net Income of Subsidiary | 30,000 | |
|     Dividends Declared | | 5,000 |
|     Investment in Subsidiary | | 130,000 |

2. Intercompany interest payable of $1,000 at December 31, 19X4 ($2,500 × 40%), is eliminated against intercompany interest receivable of $1,000 using the rearrangement procedure discussed in Chapter 7. S Company's intercompany payable is shown among its assets in parentheses. Accordingly, no elimination entry is needed for these accounts.

### Review Points for Illustration 9-4.   Note the following:

1. Both consolidated net income and consolidated retained earnings are $1,400 greater than the corresponding account balances in the parent's column. The difference is attributable to P Company's unamortized discount of $400 at December 31, 19X4, and S Company's unamortized intercompany bond premium of $1,000 at December 31, 19X4.
2. The $2,100 gain on extinguishment in the consolidated column is less than 3% of net income. Accordingly, the gain is not reported as an extraordinary item because it is immaterial.

## Bond Elimination Entries for Periods Subsequent to the Bond Acquisition Year

For periods subsequent to the bond acquisition year, the bond-related elimination entries required in consolidation are nearly identical to the two bond elimination entries shown for Illustration 9-4. The differences are as follows:

1. The elimination entry pertaining to the bond investment and related intercompany bond payable and premium accounts contains updated amounts because of the amortization that was recorded in the general ledgers during the year.
2. The Retained Earnings—P Company (beginning of year) account is credited in each of these elimination entries rather than Gain on Extinguishment of Debt. The gain was reported in 19X4 as part of consolidated retained earnings at December 31, 19X4. Thus, the credits to Retained Earnings merely reestablish on the worksheet the portion of the gain on extinguishment that had not yet been recorded in the parent's Retained Earnings account (through the amortization process) at the beginning of the year.

## MODULE 3    The Partial Equity Method *(continued)*

The bond-related elimination entries that would be made in consolidation at December 31, 19X5, and December 31, 19X6, are as follows:

|  |  | December 31, | | | |
|---|---|---|---|---|---|
|  |  | **19X5** | | **19X6** | |
| WORKSHEET ENTRY ONLY | Intercompany Interest Income | 2,200 | | 2,200 | |
|  | Intercompany Interest Expense .............. | | 1,500 | | 1,500 |
|  | Retained Earnings—P Company (beginning of year) ............... | | 700 | | 700 |
| WORKSHEET ENTRY ONLY | Intercompany Bonds Payable | 20,000 | | 20,000 | |
|  | Intercompany Bond Premium | 500 | | | |
|  | Investment in Bonds .... | | 19,800 | | 20,000 |
|  | Retained Earnings—P Company (beginning of year) .............. | | 700 | | |

## Minority Interest Considerations at Bond Acquisition Date

In the preceding discussion, we assumed that S Company was a wholly owned subsidiary. When the subsidiary is partially owned, the entries made in consolidation in connection with intercompany bond transactions require an adjustment to the minority interest if part of the gain or loss on early extinguishment of debt is attributable to the subsidiary's unamortized discount or premium. No adjustment is necessary if the subsidiary issued or acquired bonds at their face amount.

Let us change our example to reflect an 80% ownership in S Company. Of the $2,100 gain on extinguishment of debt, we know that $1,500 is a result of the premium on the subsidiary's books. Only 80%, or $1,200 of this $1,500 accrues to the parent company. The remaining $300 accrues to the minority-interest shareholders. In consolidation, this $300 is reflected as additional minority interest in the subsidiary's net income. Accordingly, if consolidated financial statements are prepared at January 1, 19X4, an additional entry is required to adjust the minority interest. This worksheet entry is as follows:

| WORKSHEET ENTRY ONLY | Minority Interest in Net Income ................ | 300 | |
|---|---|---|---|
|  | Minority Interest in Net Assets........... | | 300 |

## MODULE 3 The Partial Equity Method *(continued)*

As a result of a 20% minority interest in the subsidiary, the consolidated net income is greater by $1,800 ($1,200 + $600 discount) rather than by $2,100.

### Minority Interest Considerations at the End of the Bond Acquisition Year

The minority interest deduction that is derived from the primary elimination entry made at December 31, 19X4 (one year after the purchase of the bonds by the parent), is based on the subsidiary's $30,000 recorded net income for 19X4. This $30,000 includes one year's amortization of the bond premium of $500 (intercompany portion only). However, the amortization of the remaining premium of $1,000 (intercompany portion only) must be accelerated for consolidated reporting purposes. Of this amount, 20%, or $200, accrues to minority shareholders. Consequently, an additional $200 minority interest deduction must be made in consolidation at December 31, 19X4, as follows:

**WORKSHEET ENTRY ONLY**

| | | |
|---|---|---|
| Minority Interest in Net Income .............. | 200 | |
|     Minority Interest in Net Assets........... | | 200 |

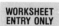

### Preparing Consolidated Financial Statements

- The Partial Equity Method
- At the End of the Bond Acquisition Year—80%-owned Subsidiary

Illustration 9-5 shows Illustration 9-4, revised to reflect 80% ownership of the subsidiary. The preceding minority interest entry is used. The primary elimination is as follows:

**WORKSHEET ENTRY ONLY**

| | | |
|---|---|---|
| Common Stock ............................ | 40,000 | |
| Retained Earnings—S Company (beginning of year) ........................................ | 65,000 | |
| Equity in Net Income of Subsidiary (80% of $30,000) ........................... | 24,000 | |
| Minority Interest in Net Income of S Company (20% of $30,000) ........................... | 6,000 | |
|     Dividends Declared ..................... | | 5,000 |
|     Investment in Subsidiary................ | | 104,000 |
|     Minority Interest in Net Assets of S Company (20% of $130,000).......... | | 26,000 |

**Review Point for Illustration 9-5.** Note that the $6,200 minority interest deduction in the consolidated column can be proven as follows:

| | |
|---|---:|
| Subsidiary's reported net income . . . . . . . . . . . . . . . . . . . . . . . . . | $30,000 |
| Plus—Unamortized intercompany bond premium at December 31, 19X4, recognized in consolidation in 19X4 . . . . . . . . . . . . . . . . . . . . . . . . . | 1,000 |
| | $31,000 |
| Minority interest ownership percentage . . . . . . . . . . . . . . . . . . . . | 20% |
| Reportable minority interest deduction . . . . . . . . . . . . . . . . . . . | $ 6,200 |

## Bond Elimination Entries for Periods Subsequent to the Bond Acquisition Year for Minority Interest Situations

When a minority interest is involved, the following bond-related elimination entries are required in consolidation for periods subsequent to the bond acquisition year:

| | | December 31, | |
|---|---|---|---|
| | | **19X5** | **19X6** |
| WORKSHEET ENTRY ONLY | Intercompany Interest Income | 2,200 | 2,200 |
| | Intercompany Interest Expense . . . . . . . . . . . . . | 1,500 | 1,500 |
| | Minority Interest in Net Income (20% of the $500 intercompany bond premium amortized during the year) . . . . . . . | 100 | 100 |
| | Retained Earnings— P Company (beginning of year) . . . . . . . . . . . . . . | 600 | 600 |

| | | | | | |
|---|---|---|---|---|---|
| WORKSHEET ENTRY ONLY | Intercompany Bonds Payable | 20,000 | | 20,000 | |
| | Intercompany Bond Premium | 500 | | | |
| | Investment in Bonds . . . . | | 19,800 | | 20,000 |
| | Minority Interest in Net Assets . . . . . . . . . . . . | | 100 | | |
| | Retained Earnings— P Company (beginning of year) . . . . . . . . . . . . . . | | 600 | | |

These entries assume that the minority interest deduction in the income statement—based on the subsidiary's reported net income—has already been established from the posting made from the primary elimination entry.

The credits to the parent's Retained Earnings account merely reestablish on the worksheet the portion of the gain on extinguishment that has

## ■ ILLUSTRATION 9-5
### The Partial Equity Method: Consolidation at the End of the Bond Acquisition Year—80%-owned Subsidiary

| P COMPANY AND SUBSIDIARY (S COMPANY) Consolidating Statement Worksheet for the Year Ended December 31, 19X4 | | | | | |
|---|---|---|---|---|---|
| | P Company | S Company | Eliminations Dr. | Eliminations Cr. | Consolidated |
| **Income Statement** | | | | | |
| Sales | 680,000 | 280,000 | | | 960,000 |
| Cost of goods sold | (380,000) | (120,000) | | | (500,000) |
| Expenses | (242,200) | (128,500) | | | (370,700) |
| Intercompany Accounts: | | | | | |
| Equity in net income | 24,000 | | 24,000(1) | | –0– |
| Interest expense | | (1,500) | | 1,500(2) | –0– |
| Interest income | 2,200 | | 2,200(2) | | –0– |
| Gain on extinguishment of debt | | | | 700(2) 1,400(3) | 2,100 |
| Income before Minority Interest | 84,000 | 30,000 | 26,200 200(4) 6,000(1) | 3,600 | 91,400 |
| Minority interest | | | | | (6,200) |
| Net Income | 84,000 | 30,000 | 32,400 | 3,600 | 85,200 |
| **Statement of Retained Earnings** | | | | | |
| Balances, January 1, 19X4 | 154,000 | 65,000 | 65,000(1) | | 154,000 |
| +Net income | 84,000 | 30,000 | 32,400 | 3,600 | 85,200 |
| −Dividends declared | (51,000) | (5,000) | | 5,000(1) | (51,000) |
| Balances, December 31, 19X4 | 187,000 | 90,000 | 97,400 | 8,600 | 188,200 |
| **Balance Sheet** | | | | | |
| Investment in S Company: | | | | | |
| Common stock | 104,000 | | | 104,000(1) | –0– |
| Bonds | 19,600 | | | 19,600(3) | –0– |
| Intercompany interest receivable (payable) | 1,000 | (1,000) | | | –0– |
| Other assets | 611,400 | 311,000 | | | 922,400 |
| Total Assets | 736,000 | 310,000 | | 123,600 | 922,400 |
| Accounts payable and accruals | 249,000 | 127,500 | | | 376,500 |
| Bonds payable | | 30,000 | | | 30,000 |
| Bond premium | | 1,500 | | | 1,500 |
| Intercompany bonds payable | | 20,000 | 20,000(3) | | –0– |
| Intercompany bond premium | | 1,000 | 1,000(3) | | –0– |
| Minority interest in net assets of subsidiary | | | | 200(4) 26,000(1) | 26,200 |
| Common stock | 300,000 | 40,000 | 40,000(1) | | 300,000 |
| Retained earnings | 187,000 | 90,000 | 97,400 | 8,600 | 188,200 |
| Total Liabilities and Equity | 736,000 | 310,000 | 158,400 | 34,800 | 922,400 |
| Proof of debit and credit postings | | | 158,400 | 158,400 | |

Explanation of entries:
  (1) The primary elimination entry.
  (2) The elimination of intercompany interest income and intercompany interest expense.
  (3) The elimination of the bond investment and related intercompany bond liability and premium accounts.
  (4) The adjustment to the minority interest.

not yet been recorded in the parent's retained earnings (through the amortization process) at the beginning of the year. Likewise, the credit to the Minority Interest (balance sheet) account merely reestablishes on the worksheet the portion of the gain on extinguishment that accrues to the minority interest but that has not yet been recorded in the subsidiary's retained earnings (through the amortization process) at this consolidation date; the amount here is 20% of the $500 unamortized intercompany bond premium at December 31, 19X5.

# END-OF-CHAPTER REVIEW

## Summary of Key Points

1. The acquisition of an affiliated company's outstanding bonds is accounted for in consolidation as a retirement of those bonds, even though they are not actually retired.
2. A gain or loss on early extinguishment is reported in the period in which the affiliate's bonds are acquired (only to the extent of the intercompany portion acquired).
3. The gain or loss is the difference between the acquisition cost (excluding amounts paid for interest) and the carrying value of the bonds.

## Glossary of New Terms

**Issuing entity**    The entity that issues bonds.

## Self-Study Questions

*(Answers are at the end of this chapter.)*

1. In intercompany bond holdings in which the issuing company has a premium and the acquiring company has a premium, the following is reported in the consolidated income statement in the year of the bond acquisition:
   a. Always a gain.
   b. Always a loss.
   c. A loss only if the applicable share of the unamortized premium exceeds the acquiring company's premium.
   d. A gain only if the applicable share of the unamortized premium exceeds the acquiring company's premium.
   e. None of the above.
2. A parent company acquired in the open market 30% of its 100%-owned subsidiary's outstanding 10% bonds for $310,000. The outstanding bonds have a

face value of $1,000,000 and a carrying value of $1,020,000 on the acquisition date. The gain or loss to be reported in the consolidated income statement in the bond acquisition year is:

a. A gain of $4,000.
b. A loss of $4,000.
c. A loss of $10,000.
d. A gain of $6,000.
e. None of the above.

*Questions 3 through 7 are based on the following information:*

On April 1, 19X1, Plow Company acquired in the open market 40% of the outstanding 10% bonds of Seed Company (its 80%-owned subsidiary) for $408,000. The bonds have a face value of $1,000,000, a carrying value of $940,000 on the acquisition date, and a maturity date of March 31, 19X3. Corporate policy specifies straight-line amortization of premiums and discounts resulting from bond issuances. Plow reported $100,000 of income for 19X1—excluding any interest income or loss pertaining to its bond investment and excluding any earnings of the subsidiary. Seed Company reported net income of $50,000 for 19X4, which amount is after reported interest expense of $130,000 on the bond issue.

3. The gain or loss on the extinguishment of debt for 19X1 in the consolidated income statement is:
   a. A loss of $32,000.
   b. A loss of $16,000.
   c. A loss of $8,000.
   d. A gain of $16,000.
   e. None of the above.
4. The minority interest share of the subsidiary's 19X1 net income as reported in the 19X1 consolidated income statement is:
   a. $5,200.
   b. $7,000.
   c. $8,200.
   d. $10,000.
   e. None of the above.
5. The consolidated net income for 19X1 is:
   a. $170,000.
   b. $158,000.
   c. $150,000.
   d. $128,000.
   e. None of the above.
6. Plow should report what amount of intercompany interest income in its separate income statement for 19X1?
   a. $40,000.
   b. $30,000.
   c. $27,000.
   d. $22,000.
   e. None of the above.

7. What amount should Plow report in its separate 19X1 income statement for Equity in Net Income of Subsidiary?
   a. $40,000.
   b. $28,000.
   c. $20,800.
   d. $23,000.
   e. None of the above.

# ASSIGNMENT MATERIAL

## Review Questions

1. From a consolidated viewpoint, what is the substance of an intercompany bond purchase?
2. How is the gain or loss on the extinguishment of debt determined?
3. Are gains and losses on extinguishment of debt extraordinary items?
4. Indicate whether a gain or loss results when: (a) each company has a premium; (b) each company has a discount; and (c) one company has a discount and the other a premium.
5. To which entity should the gain or loss on extinguishment of debt be assigned?

## Discussion Cases

**DC 9-1**

### Decision Whether or Not to Use Excess Cash to Purchase a Subsidiary's Bonds

Prose Company owns all of the outstanding common stock of Seth Company. Seth has outstanding $500,000 of 25-year, 10% debenture bonds, which it issued five years ago at a discount of $50,000. Prose has excess cash and is considering purchasing these bonds, which are currently selling at their face value. Its controller has indicated to the treasurer that a loss will be reflected in consolidation when these bonds are purchased. The treasurer replied later that it might be best to avoid this loss by investing the excess cash elsewhere.

**Required:**
Evaluate the validity of these comments.

**DC 9-2**

### Decision Whether or Not to Purchase a Subsidiary's Bonds to Report a Gain on Extinguishment of Debt

Petcon Company owns all of the outstanding common stock of Satrex Company. Satrex has outstanding $1,000,000 of 15-year, 10% debenture bonds, which it issued five years ago at a premium of $75,000. Petcon Company's management anticipates that consolidated earnings for this year will be lower than expected. Accordingly, it is evaluating ways to increase earnings for the remainder of this year. The controller has suggested that Petcon issue $1,000,000 of bonds and use the proceeds to acquire Satrex's outstanding bonds, which are currently selling at 90. Thus, a $150,000 gain can be generated and reported. Petcon's anticipated borrowing rate is approximately 14%.

### Required:

Evaluate the validity and merits of the controller's idea.

---

DC
9-3

### Reissuance of Intercompany Bond Holdings

On July 1, 19X1, Prolight Company acquired for $480,000 bonds of its wholly owned subsidiary, Sender Company. The acquired bonds were initially issued at their face value of $500,000. Prolight needed cash and sold all of the bonds for $505,000 on July 1, 19X3, exactly three years before the maturity date of the bonds. (The above purchase price and proceeds exclude amounts pertaining to interest income.)

### Required:

Using the amounts determinable from the above information, explain the procedures that should be used in consolidation in 19X3 and later years to account for the reissuance of these bonds. Indicate why the procedures you recommend are appropriate.

## Exercises

---

E
9-1

### Calculating Gain or Loss

Parr Company owns 100% of the outstanding common stock of Subb Company. On April 1, 19X4, Parr acquired in the open market 25% of Subb's outstanding 10%, 10-year debentures ($4,000,000 face amount) at a cost of $1,015,000. The bonds were issued at a premium of $320,000. They mature June 30, 19X8, and pay interest semiannually on June 30 and December 31. Assume that the straight-line method is used to amortize the premium.

### Required:

Determine the gain or loss from early extinguishment of debt reported in consolidation for 19X4.

---

E
9-2

### Calculating Gain or Loss and Preparing the Elimination Entry at the Bond Acquisition Date—100%-owned Subsidiary

Pell Company owns 100% of the outstanding common stock of Sull Company. On January 1, 19X2, Pell acquired in the open market 40% of Sull's outstanding 10% bonds at a cost of $430,000. On January 1, 19X2, the carrying value of all of the bonds ($1,000,000 face amount) was $1,040,000, and the maturity date is December 31, 19X5.

**Required:**

1. Determine the gain or loss from early extinguishment of debt reported in consolidation for 19X2.
2. For Modules 1 and 2 only: prepare the general ledger entry or entries required at the bond acquisition date assuming consolidated financial statements are to be prepared at that date.
3. Prepare the bond-elimination entry required in consolidation at January 1, 19X2.

| E 9-3 | **Calculating Gain or Loss and Preparing the Elimination Entry at the Bond Acquisition Date—75%-owned Subsidiary** |

Pelt Company owns 75% of the outstanding common stock of Sable Company. On January 1, 19X4, Pelt acquired in the open market 20% of Sable's outstanding 10% bonds at a cost of $160,000. On that date, the carrying value of all of the bonds ($1,000,000 face amount) was $1,020,000. Their maturity date is December 31, 19X7.

**Required:**

1. Determine the gain or loss from early extinguishment of debt reported in consolidation for 19X4.
2. For Modules 1 and 2 only: prepare the general ledger entry or entries required at the bond acquisition date assuming consolidated financial statements are to be prepared at that date.
3. Prepare the bond-elimination entry required in consolidation at January 1, 19X4.

| E 9-4 | **Calculating Gain or Loss and Preparing the Elimination Entries in the Year of Bond Acquisition—100%-owned Subsidiary** |

Paddle Company owns 100% of the outstanding common stock of Snare Company. On January 1, 19X5, Paddle acquired in the open market 30% of Snare's outstanding 10% bonds at a cost of $340,000. On January 1, 19X5, the carrying value of all of the bonds ($1,000,000 face amount) was $1,035,000, and their maturity date is December 31, 19X9. Assume that each company uses straight-line amortization for bond discount.

**Required:**

1. Determine the gain or loss from early extinguishment of debt reported in consolidation for 19X5.
2. For Modules 1 and 2 only: prepare the general ledger entry or entries required at the bond acquisition date assuming consolidated statements are to be prepared at this date.
3. Prepare the bond-elimination entry required in consolidation at January 1, 19X5.

4. Prepare the bond-related elimination entries required in consolidation at December 31, 19X5. (For Module 1 only: first prepare the parent's required general ledger adjusting entry at this date.)

---

## E 9-5

### Calculating Gain or Loss and Preparing the Elimination Entries in the Year of Bond Acquisition—80%-owned Subsidiary

Pladd Company owns 80% of the outstanding common stock of Shane Company. On January 1, 19X3, Pladd acquired in the open market 60% of Shane's outstanding 10% bonds at a cost of $620,000. On January 1, 19X3, the carrying value of all of the bonds ($1,000,000 face amount) was $1,050,000, and their maturity date is December 31, 19X7. Assume that each company uses straight-line amortization for bond discount.

### Required:

1. Determine the gain or loss from early extinguishment of debt reported in consolidation for 19X3.
2. For Modules 1 and 2 only: prepare the general ledger entry or entries required at the bond acquisition date assuming consolidated statements are to be prepared at this date.
3. Prepare the bond-elimination entry required in consolidation at January 1, 19X3.
4. Prepare the bond-related elimination entries required in consolidation at December 31, 19X3. (For Module 1 only: first prepare the parent's required general ledger adjusting entry at this date.)

## Problems

---

## P 9-1

### Completing Separate Company Income Statements in the Year of Bond Acquisition—100%-owned Subsidiary

The partially completed income statements of Place Company and its wholly owned subsidiary Show Company, for the year ended December 31, 19X6, are as follows:

|  | Place Company | Show Company |
|---|---|---|
| Sales | $7,000,000 | $3,000,000 |
| Cost of goods sold | (4,000,000) | (1,600,000) |
| Expenses | (1,500,000) | (1,000,000) |
| Interest expense | | |
| Intercompany Accounts: | | |
| Equity in net income | | |
| Interest income | | |
| Interest expense | | |
| Gain on extinguishment of debt | | |
| Net Income | $ | $ |

### Additional Information:

1. Assume Place Company's cost for Show Company's common stock equals its share of Show's net assets at book value.
2. On January 1, 19X6, Place acquired 40% of Show's outstanding 10% bonds ($1,000,000 face amount) at 90. Show had initially issued these 10-year bonds on January 1, 19X4, at 105.
3. Assume that neither company had any other investments or indebtedness that would give rise to interest income or interest expense.
4. Assume that corporate policy requires bond premium or discount amortization (if appropriate) to be on the straight-line method.

### Required:

1. Fill in the blanks in the above income statements.
2. Prepare the entries required in consolidation at December 31, 19X6, relating to the intercompany bond holding.

---

### Calculating Gain or Loss and Preparing the Elimination Entries in the Year of Bond Acquisition and Later Years—100%-owned Subsidiary

Point Company owns 100% of the outstanding common stock of Stealth Company. On January 1, 19X3, Stealth issues $10,000,000 of five-year, 10% bonds at 98. Two years later, on January 1, 19X5, Point acquires in the open market 30% of these bonds at 102. (To comply with corporate policy, Stealth uses straight-line amortization for its bond discount.) The maturity date of the bonds is January 1, 19X8.

### Required:

1. Determine the gain or loss from early extinguishment of debt reported in consolidation for 19X5.
2. Prepare the entry or entries required in consolidation at January 1, 19X5, December 31, 19X5, 19X6, and 19X7. (For Modules 1 and 2: first prepare any appropriate general ledger adjusting entries required at these dates.)

---

### Calculating Gain or Loss and Preparing the Elimination Entries in the Year of Bond Acquisition and Later Years—90%-owned Subsidiary

Panda Company owns 90% of the outstanding common stock of Salamander Company. On January 1, 19X1, Salamander issued $10,000,000 of five-year, 10% bonds at 95. On January 1, 19X3 (two years later), Panda acquired in the open market 30% of these bonds at 101. (To comply with corporate policy, Salamander uses straight-line amortization for its bond discount.) The maturity date of the bonds is January 1, 19X6.

### Required:

1. Determine the gain or loss from early extinguishment of debt reported in consolidation for 19X3.

2. Prepare the entry or entries required in consolidation at January 1, 19X3, December 31, 19X3, 19X4, and 19X5. (For Modules 1 and 2: first prepare any appropriate general ledger adjusting entries required at these dates.)

| P 9-4* |
|---|

## Preparing a Consolidation Worksheet in the Year of Bond Acquisition—100%-owned Subsidiary

Pitchco Company acquired 100% of the outstanding common stock of Striker Company on January 1, 19X1. The cost of the investment was $10,000 in excess of the $60,000 book value of the net assets. This excess was assigned to goodwill and is being amortized over 10 years. On March 31, 19X6, Pitchco Company acquired in the open market 25% of Striker Company's outstanding 12%, 10-year bonds for a total cash payment (including interest) of $106,500. Information regarding Striker's bonds as of the bond acquisition date is as follows:

| | |
|---|---|
| Total face amount . . . . . . . . . . . . . . . . . . . . . . . . . . . . . . . . . . | $400,000 |
| Unamortized bond premium . . . . . . . . . . . . . . . . . . . . . . . . | $28,000 |
| Maturity date . . . . . . . . . . . . . . . . . . . . . . . . . . . . . . . . . . . . | December 31, 19X7 |
| Interest payment dates . . . . . . . . . . . . . . . . . . . . . . . . . . . . | July 1 and January 1 |
| Amortization method (to comply with corporate policy) . . . . . . . . . . . . . . . . . . . . . . . . . . . . . . . . . . . . | Straight-line |

The financial statements of each company for the year ended December 31, 19X6, are as follows:

| | Pitchco Company | Striker Company |
|---|---|---|
| **Income Statement (19X6)** | | |
| Sales. . . . . . . . . . . . . . . . . . . . . . . . . . . . . . . . . . . . . . . . | $800,000 | $410,000 |
| Cost of goods sold . . . . . . . . . . . . . . . . . . . . . . . . . . | (430,000) | (210,000) |
| Expenses. . . . . . . . . . . . . . . . . . . . . . . . . . . . . . . . . . | (270,000) | (141,000) |
| Intercompany Accounts: | | |
| Equity in net income of subsidiary. . . . . . . . . . . | 49,000 | |
| Interest income. . . . . . . . . . . . . . . . . . . . . . . . . . | 9,000 | |
| Interest expense. . . . . . . . . . . . . . . . . . . . . . . . . . | | (9,000) |
| Net Income . . . . . . . . . . . . . . . . . . . . . . . . . . . . . | $158,000 | $ 50,000 |
| **Balance Sheet (December 31, 19X6)** | | |
| Investments in Striker Company: | | |
| Common stock . . . . . . . . . . . . . . . . . . . . . . . . . . | $154,000 | |
| Bonds . . . . . . . . . . . . . . . . . . . . . . . . . . . . . . . . . . | 106,500 | |
| Other assets . . . . . . . . . . . . . . . . . . . . . . . . . . . . . . | 539,500 | 600,000 |
| Total Assets. . . . . . . . . . . . . . . . . . . . . . . . . . . . . | $800,000 | $600,000 |
| Accounts payable and accruals. . . . . . . . . . . . . . . | $170,000 | $ 22,000 |

*(continued)*

---

*The financial statement information presented for problems accompanied by asterisks is also provided on Model 9 (filename: Model9) of the software file disk that is available for use with the text, enabling the problem to be worked on the computer.

| | Pitchco Company | Striker Company |
|---|---|---|
| Long-term debt (including premium) . . . . . . . . . . . | 200,000 | 428,000 |
| Common stock . . . . . . . . . . . . . . . . . . . . . . . . . . . | 300,000 | 50,000 |
| Retained earnings . . . . . . . . . . . . . . . . . . . . . . . | 130,000 | 100,000 |
| Total Liabilities and Equity . . . . . . . . . . . . . . | $800,000 | $600,000 |
| Dividends declared and paid in 19X6 . . . . . . . . . | $51,000 | $20,000 |

### Additional information:

1. Neither company has recorded any bond premium or discount amortization since March 31, 19X6.
2. Because of a cash shortage, Striker did not make any bond interest payments to Pitchco during 19X6.
3. In applying the equity method of accounting for 19X6, the accountant recorded 100% of the subsidiary's reported net income of $50,000.

### Required:

1. Prepare an analysis of the appropriate accounts as of the bond acquisition date that shows how the gain or loss on extinguishment of debt is determined.
2. Prepare all general ledger adjusting entries required at December 31, 19X6. Then adjust the financial statements accordingly.
3. Prepare a conceptual analysis of the investment account from January 1, 19X1 through December 31, 19X6.
4. Prepare the entries required in consolidation at December 31, 19X6.
5. Prepare a consolidating statement worksheet at December 31, 19X6.

---

**P 9-5***

### Preparing a Consolidation Worksheet in the Year of Bond Acquisition— 75%-owned Subsidiary

Penn Company acquired 75% of the outstanding common stock of Select Company on January 1, 19X2, for $75,000 cash. The cost of the investment was equal to Penn's share of the $100,000 book value of the net assets. However, Select's Land account was overvalued by $12,000. (This was the only asset or liability having a current value different from its book value.) Goodwill was assigned a 3-year life.

On September 1, 19X4, Penn acquired in the open market 40% of Select's outstanding 10%, 10-year bonds for a total cash payment of $134,000. Information regarding Select's bonds as of the bond acquisition date is as follows:

| | |
|---|---|
| Total face amount . . . . . . . . . . . . . . . . . . . . . . . . . . . . | $300,000 |
| Unamortized bond discount . . . . . . . . . . . . . . . . . . . . | $20,000 |
| Maturity date . . . . . . . . . . . . . . . . . . . . . . . . . . . . . . | December 31, 19X7 |
| Interest payment dates . . . . . . . . . . . . . . . . . . . . . . . . | July 1 and January 1 |
| Amortization method (to comply with corporate policy) . . . . . . . . . . . . . . . . . . . . . . . . . . . . . . . . . . . | Straight-line |

The financial statements of each company for the year ended December 31, 19X4, are as follows:

|  | Penn Company | Select Company |
|---|---|---|
| **Income Statement (19X4)** | | |
| Sales. . . . . . . . . . . . . . . . . . . . . . . . . . . . . . . . . . . | $900,000 | $600,000 |
| Cost of goods sold . . . . . . . . . . . . . . . . . . . . . . . | (500,000) | (350,000) |
| Expenses. . . . . . . . . . . . . . . . . . . . . . . . . . . . . . . | (250,000) | (146,000) |
| Intercompany Accounts: | | |
| Equity in net income of subsidiary. . . . . . . . . . | 72,000 | |
| Interest income. . . . . . . . . . . . . . . . . . . . . . . . | 4,000 | |
| Interest expense. . . . . . . . . . . . . . . . . . . . . . . | | (4,000) |
| Net Income . . . . . . . . . . . . . . . . . . . . . . . . . . . . | $226,000 | $100,000 |
| **Balance Sheet (December 31, 19X4)** | | |
| Investments in Select Company: | | |
| Common stock . . . . . . . . . . . . . . . . . . . . . . . . . | $117,000 | |
| Bonds . . . . . . . . . . . . . . . . . . . . . . . . . . . . . . . | 134,000 | |
| Other assets . . . . . . . . . . . . . . . . . . . . . . . . . . . . | 649,000 | $510,000 |
| Total Assets. . . . . . . . . . . . . . . . . . . . . . . . . | $900,000 | $510,000 |
| Accounts payable and accruals. . . . . . . . . . . . . . | $ 72,000 | $ 62,000 |
| Bonds payable (including discount) . . . . . . . . . . . | | 280,000 |
| Notes payable . . . . . . . . . . . . . . . . . . . . . . . . . . . | 300,000 | |
| Common stock . . . . . . . . . . . . . . . . . . . . . . . . . . . | 200,000 | 60,000 |
| Retained earnings . . . . . . . . . . . . . . . . . . . . . . . . | 328,000 | 108,000 |
| Total Liabilities and Equity. . . . . . . . . . . . . . | $900,000 | $510,000 |
| Dividends declared and paid in 19X4 . . . . . . . . . | $100,000 | $80,000 |

## Additional Information:

1. Neither company has recorded any bond discount or premium amortization since the intercompany bond purchase.
2. The January 1, 19X5, bond interest payment was made on January 2, 19X5.
3. In applying the equity method of accounting for 19X4, the accountant recorded 75% of the subsidiary's reported net income of $100,000.

## Required:

1. Prepare an analysis of the appropriate accounts as of the bond acquisition date that shows how the gain or loss on extinguishment of debt is determined.
2. Prepare all general ledger adjusting entries required at December 31, 19X4. Then adjust the financial statements accordingly.
3. Prepare a conceptual analysis of the investment account from January 1, 19X2 through December 31, 19X4.
4. Prepare the entries required in consolidation at December 31, 19X4.
5. Prepare a consolidating statement worksheet at December 31, 19X4.

**P 9-6\*** **COMPREHENSIVE CHALLENGER (Chapters 3–5, 7, 9)   Preparing a Consolidation Worksheet in the Year of Bond Acquisition—80%-owned Subsidiary; Upstream Inventory Sales**

Pye Company acquired 80% of the outstanding common stock of Slice Company on January 1, 19X1, for $230,000 cash. In addition $14,000 of direct costs were incurred. At the acquisition date, Slice's only assets and liabilities that had current values different from book values were as follows:

| | Book Value | Current Value | Remaining Life |
|---|---|---|---|
| Patent.............................. | $ 70,000 | $160,000 | 6 years |
| 12% Bonds Payable (face value of $500,000)....................... | 532,000 | 492,000 | 8 years |

The difference between the parent's cost and the current value of the net assets was properly allocated to Land inasmuch as the appraisal report indicated that this was the least firm of the appraisal amounts. On January 1, 19X3, Pye paid $50,000 cash to the former owners because Slice's earnings of $90,000 for the two years ended December 31, 19X2, exceeded $80,000. At that date, it was determined that the land was actually undervalued by $30,000. (In retrospect, the conservatism and caution of the appraiser was unjustified.)

On October 1, 19X3, Pye acquired in the open market 50% of Slice's outstanding 12% bonds for a total cash payment of $236,500.

## Additional information:

1. The subsidiary uses straight-line amortization for its bond premium (in accordance with corporate policy). Unlike the subsidiary, the parent has not recorded any amortization of its discount since October 1, 19X3.
2. Goodwill is assigned a 10-year life.
3. The interest payment dates for Slice's bonds are July 1 and January 1. (The January 1, 19X4 payment was made on January 2, 19X4.)
4. Slice did not declare or pay any dividends in 19X1 and 19X2.
5. At December 31, 19X2, Pye held inventory it had acquired from Slice in 19X2 at a cost of $19,000. (Slice's cost was $14,000.)
6. In applying the equity method of accounting for 19X3, the accountant recorded 80% of the subsidiary's reported net income of $75,000. (At no time in 19X2—19X4 did either company make any adjustment to the books for any unrealized intercompany inventory profit or imputed gain or loss relating to the intercompany bond holdings.)

The financial statements of each company for the year ended December 31, 19X3, are as follows:

| | Pye Company | Slice Company |
|---|---|---|
| **Income Statement (19X3)** | | |
| Sales....................................... | $ 800,000 | $500,000 |
| Cost of goods sold.......................... | (400,000) | (250,000) |
| Expenses.................................... | (250,500) | (192,000) |
| Intercompany Accounts: | | |
| Equity in net income....................... | 39,000 | |
| Sales...................................... | | 80,000 |

| | Pye Company | Slice Company |
|---|---|---|
| Cost of goods sold ......................... | | (56,000) |
| Interest income........................... | 7,500* | |
| Interest expense.......................... | | (7,000) |
| Net Income .............................. | $ 196,000 | $ 75,000 |

**Balance Sheet (December 31, 19X3)**

| | Pye Company | Slice Company |
|---|---|---|
| Investment in Slice Company: | | |
| Common stock ........................... | $ 361,000 | |
| Bonds.................................... | 236,500 | |
| Inventory: | | |
| From vendors............................. | 135,000 | $ 80,000 |
| Intercompany ........................... | 25,000 | |
| Other assets ............................. | 842,500 | 820,000 |
| Total Assets............................ | $1,600,000 | $900,000 |
| Accounts payable and accruals............... | $ 150,000 | $ 30,000 |
| Bonds payable (including premium)........... | 700,000 | 520,000 |
| Common stock, $1 par value ................ | 400,000 | 120,000 |
| Retained earnings ........................ | 350,000 | 230,000 |
| Total Liabilities and Equity ............... | $1,600,000 | $900,000 |
| Dividends declared and paid in 19X3.......... | $61,000 | $15,000 |

*Excludes bond premium or discount amortization.

## Required:

1. Prepare an analysis of the appropriate accounts as of the bond acquisition date that shows how the gain or loss on extinguishment of debt is determined.
2. Prepare all general ledger adjusting entries required at December 31, 19X3. Then adjust the financial statements accordingly.
3. Prepare a conceptual analysis of the investment account from January 1, 19X1 through December 31, 19X3.
4. Prepare the entries required in consolidation at December 31, 19X3.
5. Prepare a consolidating statement worksheet at December 31, 19X3.

## ANSWERS TO SELF-STUDY QUESTIONS:

1. d    4. b    6. c (for Modules 1 and 3)
                  b (for Module 2)
2. b    5. c    7. d (for Module 1)
                  b (for Module 2)
3. a           a (for Module 3)

# 10

······

# CHANGES IN PARENT'S OWNERSHIP INTEREST AND SUBSIDIARY WITH PREFERRED STOCK

*TOPIC OUTLINE*

## CHAPTER OVERVIEW

A parent's ownership interest in a subsidiary can change as a result of: (1) the parent or the subsidiary acquiring some or all of the minority interest; (2) the parent disposing of a portion of its common stock holdings (thereby increasing the minority interest); and (3) the subsidiary issuing additional common stock to outside parties (thereby increasing the minority interest). Furthermore, a parent's interest in the subsidiary's net income and net assets is affected by the existence of outstanding preferred stock of a subsidiary.

## THE ACQUISITION OF MINORITY INTEREST

*APB Opinion No. 16* allows only the use of the purchase method to account for the acquisition of minority interests. It states:

> The acquisition . . . of some or all of the stock held by minority stockholders of a subsidiary—whether acquired by the parent, the subsidiary itself, or another affiliate—should be accounted for by the purchase method rather than by the pooling of interests method.[1]

### The Parent Acquires Some or All of the Minority Interest

The parent's acquisition of any or all of the minority interest is merely a block acquisition. The cost of the block of stock acquired must be separated into its components in the same manner that the initial investment cost of a partially owned subsidiary is separated into its components (illustrated in Chapter 5). Thus, the parent's acquisition of any or all of the minority interest presents no new accounting issues. The acquisition of any or all of the minority interest by the subsidiary is also a block acquisition from a consolidated viewpoint; the procedures for this treatment will be explained.

### The Subsidiary Acquires Some or All of the Minority Interest

When the subsidiary acquires any or all of the minority interest and retires the acquired shares (which it does only if directed to do so by the parent), the accounting in consolidation must reflect the purchase method of accounting for the shares acquired. The subsidiary's entries are the same as those made by any corporation acquiring and retiring its outstanding shares—that is, debit the capital accounts and credit Cash (assuming cash is the consideration given). The parent does not adjust

---

[1] *Opinions of the Accounting Principles Board, No. 16,* "Accounting for Business Combinations" (New York: American Institute of Certified Public Accountants, 1970), par. 43.

the total carrying value of its Investment in Subsidiary account regardless of the price paid by the subsidiary to acquire the minority interest. However, if the subsidiary pays more or less than book value per share, the parent's total dollar interest in the subsidiary's net assets at their book value decreases or increases respectively. Accordingly, the expanded analysis of the investment account by components must be adjusted to reflect that the parent's interest in the subsidiary's net assets at book value has changed. To the extent that the parent's total dollar interest decreases (when the subsidiary pays more than book value), the book value element must be decreased and the current value over book value element and/or the goodwill element must be increased by an offsetting amount. The reverse occurs when the subsidiary pays less than book value. Because this adjustment within the expanded analysis does not change the total carrying value of the investment, it is essentially a *reclassification* of amounts from one component to another.

## ILLUSTRATION    The Subsidiary Acquires the Entire Minority Interest at above Book Value

Assume the following information:

|  | Percent | Shares |
|---|---|---|
| Parent's ownership in subsidiary: |  |  |
| Before acquisition of minority interest by subsidiary | 70 | 7,000 |
| After acquisition of minority interest by subsidiary | 100 | 7,000 |
| Purchase price paid by subsidiary to acquire all 3,000 outstanding shares held by minority interest shareholders | $300,000 | |

This information is used in Illustration 10-1 to calculate the decrease in the parent's interest in the subsidiary's net assets. (The procedure is the same when the parent's equity in the subsidiary's net assets increases.)

**Review Points for Illustration 10-1.**   Note the following:

1. The minority shareholders received an additional $60,000 in excess of their ownership interest in the subsidiary's net assets at book value.
2. This excess payment to the minority shareholders dilutes the parent's interest in the subsidiary's net assets at book value by $60,000.
3. The $60,000 excess payment must be treated as cost in excess of book value by the parent. From a consolidated viewpoint, it is irrelevant that the subsidiary acquired the minority interest rather than the parent.

To reflect the $60,000 payment as cost in excess of book value, the parent adjusts its expanded analysis of the investment account by the components of the major conceptual elements. Assuming the parent had

■ **ILLUSTRATION 10-1**

**Calculation of Decrease in Parent's Interest in Subsidiary's Net Assets as a Result of Subsidiary's Acquisition of Entire Minority Interest at Amount in Excess of Book Value**

| | Subsidiary's Equity Accounts | Book Value per Share | Parent's Interest | | Minority Interest | |
|---|---|---|---|---|---|---|
| | | | Percent | Amount | Percent | Amount |
| Before acquisition of minority interest: | | | | | | |
| Common stock....... | $ 80,000 | | 70 | $ 56,000 | 30 | $ 24,000 |
| Retained earnings .... | 720,000 | | 70 | 504,000 | 30 | 216,000 |
| | $ 800,000 | $80 | | $ 560,000 | | $ 240,000 |
| After acquisition of minority interest: | | | | | | |
| Common stock....... | $ 56,000[a] | | 100 | $ 56,000 | | — |
| Retained earnings .... | $ 444,000 | | 100 | $ 444,000 | | — |
| | $ 500,000 | $71.42 | | $ 500,000 | | — |
| Decrease in equity ...... | $(300,000) | | | $ (60,000) | | $(240,000) |

Note: The parent's new ownership percentage is derived by dividing the shares owned by the parent (7,000 shares) by the outstanding shares of the subsidiary (7,000 shares). In other words, the parent's holdings remain constant—only the outstanding shares of the subsidiary (the denominator used in calculating the parent's ownership percentage) decrease.

[a]For simplicity, we assume that the $300,000 payment for the shares acquired and retired was properly charged to the subsidiary's capital accounts as follows:

| | |
|---|---|
| Common stock (30% of $80,000)..................................... | $ 24,000 |
| Retained earnings (residual) ...................................... | 276,000 |
| Total Payment ................................................. | $300,000 |

$200,000 of unamortized cost in excess of its share of the subsidiary's net assets at book value as of the minority interest acquisition date, the required adjustment is determined as follows:

| | Minority Interest | + | Total Cost | = | Book Value Element | | + | Cost in Excess of Book Value[a] |
|---|---|---|---|---|---|---|---|---|
| | | | | | Common Stock | + Retained Earnings | | |
| Balances immediately *before the acquisition* of the minority interest...................... | $ 240,000 | | $760,000 | | $80,000[b] | $720,000[b] | | $200,000 |
| Purchase of minority interest... | (240,000) | | | | (24,000) | (276,000)[c] | | 60,000[d] |
| Balances immediately *after the acquisition* of the minority interest...................... | $ –0– | | $760,000 | | $56,000[b] | $444,000[b] | | $260,000 |

[a]The breakdown of this cost into its individual components is not shown, because it is not necessary with respect to the principle involved.
[b]This amount was obtained from the analysis in Illustration 10-1.
[c]This change of interest in this component element is determined by using the balances *before* and the balances *after* the acquisition of the minority interest.
[d]This is the $60,000 excess payment. It equals the total dilution of the parent's interest in the subsidiary's net assets at book value.

The required adjustment takes place entirely within the expanded analysis of the investment account by the components of the major conceptual elements. The total carrying value of the parent's investment account is unchanged. This adjustment prevents the parent from reporting a loss on the acquisition of the minority interest related to the dilution of the parent's interest in the subsidiary's net assets at book value. The $60,000 cost in excess of book value must be separated into its components in accordance with the purchase method of accounting. After the required adjustment is made within the expanded analysis of the investment account, the analysis is updated in the normal manner. The ending balances as of any future consolidation date are the sources for the primary elimination entry, as illustrated in Chapters 4 and 5.

The following is a "before and after" presentation of the applicable accounts on the consolidating statement worksheet:

### Before the Acquisition of the Minority Interest (thousands of dollars)

|  | P Company | S Company | Eliminations Dr. | Eliminations Cr. | Consolidated |
|---|---|---|---|---|---|
| Cash . . . . . . . . . . . . . . . . . . . . . |  | 300 |  |  | 300 |
| Investment in S Company . . . . . . . . . . . . | 760 |  |  | 760 | –0– |
| Cost in excess of book value . . . . . . . . . . . . . . . . . |  |  | 200 |  | 200 |
| Minority interest in net assets of S Company . . |  |  |  | 240 | 240 |
| Common stock . . . . . . . . . . |  | 80 | 80 |  | –0– |
| Retained earnings . . . . . . . |  | 720 | 720 |  | –0– |

### After the Acquisition of the Minority Interest (thousands of dollars)

|  | P Company | S Company | Eliminations Dr. | Eliminations Cr. | Consolidated |
|---|---|---|---|---|---|
| Cash . . . . . . . . . . . . . . . . . . . . |  | — |  |  | –0– |
| Investment in S Company . . . . . . . . . . . . | 760 |  |  | 760 | –0– |
| Cost in excess of book value . . . . . . . . . . . . . . . . . |  |  | 260 |  | 260 |
| Common stock . . . . . . . . . . |  | 56 | 56 |  | –0– |
| Retained earnings . . . . . . . |  | 444 | 444 |  | –0– |

We can see from this presentation that the effect on the consolidated financial statements is as though the following entry had been made from a consolidated viewpoint.

| | | |
|---|---|---|
| Minority Interest in Net Assets of S Company . . . . . . . . . . . . . . . . . . . . . . . . . . . . . | 240,000 | |
| Cost in Excess of Book Value . . . . . . . . . . . . . . . | 60,000 | |
| Cash . . . . . . . . . . . . . . . . . . . . . . . . . . . . . . . . . | | 300,000 |

**The Subsidiary Acquires Part of the Minority Interest.**  In the preceding example, the subsidiary acquired all of the minority interest. When the subsidiary acquires only a portion of the minority interest at more or less than book value per share, both the parent's **and the remaining minority shareholders'** total dollar interests in the subsidiary's net assets at book value decrease or increase respectively. Only the parent's decrease or increase results in an increase or decrease, respectively, of the current value over book element and/or the goodwill element. For example, if the subsidiary had acquired only 2,000 of the minority interest shares for $200,000 cash (instead of acquiring all of the 3,000 minority interest shares for $300,000 cash), the excess payment would be $40,000 (instead of $60,000). (The $200,000 payment minus $160,000 of book value accruing to these 2,000 shares equals $40,000.) In this case the $40,000 of dilution suffered by the remaining shareholders (7,000 shares being held by the parent and 1,000 shares being held by the remaining minority shareholders) is shared in relation to their respective holdings (a 7:1 ratio). Thus, only $35,000 of the $40,000 dilution is suffered by the parent, which amount is added to its cost in excess of book value. The conceptual analysis of the investment account would be adjusted as follows:

| Minority Interest | + | Total Cost | = | Book Value Element | | Cost in Excess of Book Value |
|---|---|---|---|---|---|---|
| | | | | Common Stock | + Retained Earnings + | |
| $240,000 | | $760,000 | | $80,000 | $720,000 | $200,000 |
| (165,000)[b] | | | | (16,000) | (184,000) | 35,000 |
| $ 75,000[a] | | $760,000 | | $64,000 | $536,000 | $235,000 |

[a]This is $\frac{1}{8}$ of $600,000 (the book value after the acquisition of the 2,000 minority shares).
[b]This is comprised of $160,000 (20% of $800,000) plus $5,000 of dilution suffered by the remaining minority shareholders.

# THE DISPOSAL OF A PORTION OF AN INTEREST IN A SUBSIDIARY

A parent may dispose of a portion or all of its common stock investment in a subsidiary. The former often occurs when the parent wants to raise cash, whereas the latter usually occurs when the parent decides either to (1) dispose of a line of business (the reporting of which is discussed in Chapter 13, "Segment Reporting"), or (2) contract (or reduce) its operations (the reporting of which is governed by APB Opinion No. 30, "Reporting the Results of Operations").

When a parent sells a portion of its common stock holdings in a subsidiary, the accounting problem is that of determining the amount of the reduction to the investment account. This amount is compared with the proceeds from the sale to determine the reportable gain or loss. The two categories of partial disposal are as follows:

1. **Shares acquired in a single acquisition.** When all of the shares owned were acquired at one time, the investment account should be reduced using the average cost of all shares owned.
2. **Shares acquired in block acquisitions.** When the shares owned were acquired at more than one time (in block acquisitions or when the minority interest was subsequently acquired), three methods of reducing the investment account are available:
   a. The average cost method
   b. The specific identification method
   c. The first-in, first-out method

Our preference is the average cost method, because the other two methods introduce an artificial element. For example, the gain or loss reported under the specific identification method could be partially determined by the particular block of stock selected for sale; whereas under the first-in, first-out method, we use an assumed flow concept initially intended for inventory pricing. Furthermore, the manner of acquiring the shares is irrelevant to the accounting for the disposal of shares—the issue is the amount of the total ownership interest that is disposed of. This percentage answer should also apply to the carrying value of the cost of the investment. (Although only the specific identification and the first-in, first-out methods are allowed for federal income tax reporting purposes, this has no bearing on which method should be used for financial reporting purposes.)

Regardless of the method selected to reduce the investment account, it must be applied to each individual component in the expanded analysis of the investment account. Before the investment account is reduced, however, it must be adjusted in accordance with the equity method of accounting up to the date of sale.

 **ILLUSTRATION** ## Partial Disposal Using the Average Cost Method

Assume the following information:

|  | Percent | Shares |
|---|---|---|
| Parent's ownership in subsidiary: |  |  |
|   Before partial disposal | 80 | 800 |
|   After partial disposal | 60 | 600 |
|     Shares sold |  | 200 |
| Subsidiary's net income: |  |  |
|   January 1, 19X8–June 30, 19X8 | $20,000 |  |
|   July 1, 19X8–December 31, 19X8 | 10,000 |  |
|     Total | $30,000 |  |
| Disposal date | July 1, 19X8 |  |
| Proceeds from sale | $40,000 |  |

Subsidiary's dividends:
  On the last day of the first three quarters,
    dividends of $5,000 were declared;
    no dividends were declared in the fourth
    quarter of the year.

The expanded analysis of the investment account in Illustration 10-2 is updated for the year in which a disposal of a portion of shares held in a subsidiary takes place. The following points are important for understanding the illustration:

1. The reportable gain on the disposal of the shares sold is determined as follows:

| | |
|---|---:|
| Proceeds from sale | $40,000 |
| Average cost of shares sold | (25,000) |
| Gain | $15,000 |

2. The following journal entry on the parent's books records this disposal:

| | | |
|---|---:|---:|
| Cash | 40,000 | |
| Investment in S Company | | 25,000 |
| Gain on Sale of Subsidiary's Stock | | 15,000 |

3. The December 31, 19X8, balance in the Equity in Net Income of Subsidiary account in the parent's general ledger is as follows:

| | |
|---|---:|
| Equity in earnings January 1, 19X8–June 30, 19X8 | $16,000 |
| Equity in earnings July 1, 19X8–December 31, 19X8 | 6,000 |
| Total | $22,000 |

4. The minority interest deduction for the year is determined as follows:

| | Jan. 1, 19X8–<br>June 30, 19X8 | July 1, 19X8–<br>Dec. 31, 19X8 | Total |
|---|---:|---:|---:|
| Subsidiary's net income | $20,000 | $10,000 | $30,000 |
| Minority interest ownership percentage | 20% | 40% | |
| Minority interest | $ 4,000 | $ 4,000 | $ 8,000 |

# ■ ILLUSTRATION 10-2
## Updating the Expanded Analysis of the Investment Account for a Partial Disposal Using the Average Cost Method

| | Minority Interest + | Total Cost = | Common Stock + | Book Value Element — Retained Earnings | | | Current Value over Book Value Element — Land (Indef.) + | Goodwill + Element (3 yr.) |
| --- | --- | --- | --- | --- | --- | --- | --- | --- |
| | | | | Prior Year + | Current Year — Earnings | Dividends + | | |
| Remaining life as of January 1, 19X8: | | | | | | | | |
| Balance, January 1, 19X8 ..... | $20,100 | $ 92,400 | $40,000 | $60,500 | | | $9,600 | $2,400 |
| Equity in net income: | | | | | | | | |
| To Parent (80%) ..... | | 16,000 | | | $16,000 | | | |
| To Minority Interest (20%) ..... | 4,000 | | | | 4,000 | | | |
| Dividends—first and second quarters: | | | | | | | | |
| To Parent (80%) ..... | | (8,000) | | | | $ (8,000) | | |
| To Minority Interest (20%) ..... | (2,000) | | | | | (2,000) | | |
| Amortization of cost over book value ..... | | (400) | | | | | | (400) |
| Balance, June 30, 19X8 ..... | $22,100 | $100,000 | $40,000 | $60,500 | $20,000 | $(10,000) | $9,600 | $2,000 |
| Disposal, July 1, 19X8 ..... | 22,100[a] | (25,000)[b] | | | | | (2,400)[b] | (500)[b] |
| Balance, July 1, 19X8 ..... | $44,200 | $ 75,000 | $40,000 | $60,500 | $20,000 | $(10,000) | $7,200 | $1,500 |
| Equity in net income: | | | | | | | | |
| To Parent (60%) ..... | | 6,000 | | | 6,000 | | | |
| To Minority Interest (40%) ..... | 4,000 | | | | 4,000 | | | |
| Dividends—third quarter: | | | | | | | | |
| To Parent (60%) ..... | | (3,000) | | | | (3,000) | | |
| To Minority Interest (40%) ..... | (2,000) | | | | | (2,000) | | |
| Amortization of cost over book value ..... | | (300) | | | | | | (300)[c] |
| Balance, December 31, 19X8 ..... | $46,200 | $ 77,700 | $40,000 | $60,500 | $30,000 | $(15,000) | $7,200 | $1,200 |

[a] This amount is 20% of the book value element at June 30, 19X8 ($40,000 + $60,500 + $20,000 − $10,000) = $110,500: $110,500 × 20% = $22,100).
[b] The June 30, 19X8, balance is reduced by 25%, which is the ratio of the shares sold to total shares held (200 ÷ 800 = 25%).
[c] The $1,500 balance at June 30, 19X8, amortized over 2½ years is $300.

5. The primary elimination entry used to prepare the December 31, 19X8, consolidated financial statements is from the analysis of the investment account as of December 31, 19X8 (in Illustration 10-2). The entry is as follows:

| | | |
|---|---|---|
| Common Stock | 40,000 | |
| Retained Earnings (beginning of year) | 60,500 | |
| Equity in Net Income of Subsidiary | 22,000 | |
| Minority Interest in Net Income of Subsidiary | 8,000 | |
| Land | 7,200 | |
| Goodwill | 1,200 | |
| Dividends Declared | | 15,000 |
| Investment in Subsidiary | | 77,700 |
| Minority Interest in Net Assets of S Company | | 46,200 |

6. By updating the investment account analysis as illustrated, the disposal of a portion of the holdings in a subsidiary's common stock does not affect the basic procedures used to prepare consolidated financial statements.

Illustration 10-3 shows a consolidating statement worksheet for the year ended December 31, 19X8, prepared using the above primary elimination entry. The secondary elimination entry is as follows:

**WORKSHEET ENTRY ONLY**

| | | |
|---|---|---|
| Cost of Goods Sold | 700 | |
| Equity in Net Income of Subsidiary | | 700 |

## THE ISSUANCE OF ADDITIONAL COMMON STOCK BY A SUBSIDIARY

Rather than disposing of a portion of its stock holdings in a subsidiary to raise funds for the consolidated group, a parent may direct the subsidiary to issue additional common stock to the public.

If the shares issued to the public are sold below the current book value per share of the subsidiary's common stock as of the issuance date, the parent's total dollar interest in the subsidiary's net assets at book value is diluted and thus decreases. On the other hand, when the subsidiary issues shares above the existing book value of its common stock as of the issuance date, the parent's total dollar interest in the subsidiary's net assets at book value increases. (This may be understood best by realizing that if the subsidiary were liquidated at no gain or loss in the liquidation process, the parent would receive either more or less than it would have received if the subsidiary had not issued the additional shares.) The issue

■ **ILLUSTRATION 10-3**

**Partial Disposal of Investment in Subsidiary During the Year**

| | | | Eliminations | | |
|---|---|---|---|---|---|
| **P COMPANY AND SUBSIDIARY (S COMPANY)** Consolidating Statement Worksheet for the Year Ended December 31, 19X8 | | | | | |
| | P Company | S Company | Dr. | Cr. | Consolidated |
| **Income Statement** | | | | | |
| Sales............................ | 615,000 | 350,000 | | | 965,000 |
| Cost of goods sold.............. | (309,300) | (180,000) | 700(2) | | (490,000) |
| Expenses....................... | (202,000) | (140,000) | | | (342,000) |
| Gain on sale of subsidiary's stock | 15,000 | | | | 15,000 |
| Intercompany Accounts: | | | | | |
| Equity in net income | | | | | |
| of subsidiary .............. | 21,300ª | | 22,000(1) | 700(2) | –0– |
| Income before Minority Interest.. | 140,000 | 30,000 | 22,700 | 700 | 148,000 |
| Minority interest ............. | | | 8,000(1) | | (8,000) |
| Net Income.................... | 140,000 | 30,000 | 30,700 | 700 | 140,000 |
| **Statement of Retained Earnings** | | | | | |
| Balances, January 1, 19X8...... | 210,000 | 60,500 | 60,500(1) | | 210,000 |
| +Net income................... | 140,000 | 30,000 | 30,700 | 700 | 140,000 |
| −Dividends declared........... | (60,000) | (15,000) | | 15,000(1) | (60,000) |
| Balances, December 31, 19X8 ... | 290,000 | 75,500 | 91,200 | 15,700 | 290,000 |
| **Balance Sheet** | | | | | |
| Investment in subsidiary........ | 77,700 | | | 77,700(1) | –0– |
| Land.......................... | 200,000 | 30,000 | 7,200(1) | | 237,200 |
| Goodwill ...................... | | | 1,200(1) | | 1,200 |
| Other assets................... | 522,300 | 280,000 | | | 802,300 |
| Total Assets ................. | 800,000 | 310,000 | 8,400 | 77,700 | 1,040,700 |
| Liabilities .................... | 210,000 | 194,500 | | | 404,500 |
| Minority interest in net assets | | | | | |
| of subsidiary ................. | | | | 46,200(1) | 46,200 |
| Common stock ................ | 300,000 | 40,000 | 40,000(1) | | 300,000 |
| Retained earnings............. | 290,000 | 75,500 | 91,200 | 15,700 | 290,000 |
| Total Liabilities and Equity.... | 800,000 | 310,000 | 131,200 | 61,900 | 1,040,700 |
| Proof of debit and credit postings........................ | | | 139,600 | 139,600 | |

Explanation of entries:
(1) The primary elimination entry.
(2) The secondary elimination entry.

ªComprised of $22,000 recorded under the equity method minus $700 of amortization of cost over book value.

is how to account for an increase or a decrease in the parent's interest in the subsidiary's net assets at book value as a result of the issuance of the additional shares.

Accountants agree that an increase or a decrease in the parent's interest in the subsidiary's net assets at book value should result in an increase or decrease, respectively, to the carrying value of the investment. Accountants do not agree on the treatment of the offsetting credit or debit. The two alternative accounting treatments are as follows:

1. Record it as an adjustment to the parent's additional paid-in capital. (This treatment carries through to the consolidated balance sheet.)
2. Record it as a gain or loss in the parent's income statement. (The gain or loss **is not eliminated in consolidation.**)

### Rationale for the Additional Paid-in Capital Treatment.
Under the first alternative, the issuance of additional common stock by the subsidiary is a capital-raising transaction for the consolidated group. Because capital-raising transactions do not cause either a gain or a loss on a separate-company basis, they should not cause either a gain or a loss on a consolidated basis. (Recall from intermediate accounting that *APB Opinion No. 9*, "Reporting the Results of Operations" [paragraph 28], requires that gains or losses from transactions in a company's own stock are to be excluded from the income statement.) An increase in the parent's interest in the subsidiary's net assets at book value is deemed in consolidation to be a capital contribution from the minority shareholders to the parent. Similarly, a decrease in the parent's interest in the subsidiary's net assets at book value is treated in consolidation as a capital contribution from the parent to the minority shareholders. This approach fits under the entity theory (see Chapter 5), which maintains that a new reporting entity with two classes of common shareholders results from the consolidation process.

### Rationale for the Income Statement Treatment.
Under the second alternative above, the parent is viewed as either gaining or losing as a result of a subsidiary's issuing additional common stock above or below the book value of its existing outstanding common stock. Gains and losses are reported in the income statement. Accordingly, this type of gain or loss also should be reflected in the income statement. In regard to the requirements of *APB Opinion No. 9*, the argument can be made that this is not a transaction in one's own stock—it is a transaction involving the investment in the subsidiary's stock; thus *APB Opinion No. 9* is not applicable. The advocates of this approach also contend that substantively the sale of a subsidiary's shares by the parent (pursuant to a partial disposal)—whereby a gain or loss is recorded in the income statement—is no different from the issuance of additional common shares by a subsidiary. This approach fits

under the parent company theory (see Chapter 5), which views the parent as the reporting entity in consolidation.

**The Position of the AICPA.**    In 1980, the Accounting Standards Executive Committee of the American Institute for Certified Public Accountants (AICPA) prepared an issues paper, "Accounting in Consolidation for Issuances of a Subsidiary's Stock." This paper's advisory conclusions are that such gains or losses should be reflected in the consolidated income statement. The position taken here seems to be that such transactions are not "transactions in one's own stock." Thus, *APB Opinion No. 9* is not applicable.

**The Position of the Securities and Exchange Commission.**    In 1983, the staff of the Securities and Exchange Commission (SEC) issued *Staff Accounting Bulletin No. 51*, which expresses its views concerning the subsidiary's issuance of additional common stock. According to the SEC staff, companies **may** (an optional reporting treatment) recognize gains or losses resulting from these transactions when the subsidiary's sale of shares is not a part of a corporate reorganization contemplated or planned by the parent company. (The staff had previously required, without benefit of any ruling or publication, that these transactions be accounted for in consolidated financial statements as capital transactions.) This change in position resulted from the SEC's acceptance of the advisory conclusions in the AICPA's 1980 issues paper. The SEC staff considers this paper to be appropriate interim guidance in the matter until the Financial Accounting Standards Board (FASB) addresses this issue as a part of its project "Accounting for the Reporting Entity, including Consolidations, the Equity Method, and Related Matters." Under *SAB No. 51*, companies electing income statement treatment must report the gain or loss as a separate item in the consolidated income statement regardless of size. Furthermore, the gain or loss must be clearly designated as nonoperating. Companies also should include an appropriate description of the transaction in the notes to the financial statements.[2]

In 1989, the staff of the SEC expanded its views on this subject in *Staff Accounting Bulletin No. 84.* In this bulletin, the SEC staff takes the position that no gain should be recognized in consolidation when subsequent capital transactions are contemplated that raise concerns about the likelihood of realization of the gain. Examples of subsequent capital transactions are as follows:

1. A subsequent spin-off of the subsidiary to shareholders is contemplated at the time of issuance.

---

[2]*Staff Accounting Bulletin No. 51,* "Accounting by the Parent in Consolidation for Sale of Stock by Subsidiary," (Washington, D.C.: Securities and Exchange Commission, 1983).

2. A reacquisition of the shares issued by the subsidiary is contemplated at the time of issuance. (A contemplation is deemed to have existed at the issuance date if the shares are repurchased within one year of issuance.)

Furthermore, the bulletin holds that no gain should be recognized if the subsidiary is a newly formed nonoperating entity, a research-and-development start-up or development-stage company, an entity whose ability to continue in existence is in question, or when other similar circumstances exist.

**ILLUSTRATION**

## Issuance of Additional Shares at below Book Value

The journal entry in the following illustration reflects the accounting treatment for additional shares prescribed in the AICPA's 1980 issues paper. Assume the following information:

|  | Percent | Shares |
|---|---|---|
| Parent's ownership in subsidiary: |  |  |
| Before subsidiary issues additional shares to the public | 70 | 7,000 |
| After subsidiary issues additional shares to the public | $58\frac{1}{3}$ | 7,000 |
| Minority ownership in subsidiary: |  |  |
| Before subsidiary issues additional shares to the public | 30 | 3,000 |
| After subsidiary issues additional shares to the public | $41\frac{2}{3}$ | 5,000 |
| Proceeds from issuance of 2,000 additional shares of the subsidiary's no-par common stock at $50 per share | | $100,000 |

This information is used in Illustration 10-4 to calculate the loss to the parent. (The procedure is the same when there is a gain.)

### Review Points for Illustration 10-4.    Note the following:

1. The entry to record the loss on the parent's books is as follows:

| Loss Resulting from Dilution of Interest in | | |
|---|---|---|
| Subsidiary's Net Assets | 35,000 | |
| Investment in Subsidiary | | 35,000 |

This loss is not eliminated in consolidation.

2. The conceptual analysis of the investment account would be adjusted as follows (all amounts are based on Illustration 10-4):

## ■ ILLUSTRATION 10-4
Calculation of Parent's Dilution of Equity in Net Assets of Subsidiary: Subsidiary Sells Additional Common Stock at below Book Value

| | Subsidiary's Equity Accounts | Book Value per Share | Parent's Interest | | Minority Interest | |
|---|---|---|---|---|---|---|
| | | | Percent | Amount | Percent | Amount |
| Before issuance of additional shares: | | | | | | |
| Common stock . . . . . | $ 80,000 | | 70 | $ 56,000 | 30 | $ 24,000 |
| Retained earnings . | 720,000 | | 70 | 504,000 | 30 | 216,000 |
| | $ 800,000 | $80 | | $560,000 | | $ 240,000 |
| After issuance of additional shares: | | | | | | |
| Common stock . . . . . | $ 180,000ᵃ | | $58\frac{1}{3}$ | $105,000 | $41\frac{2}{3}$ | $ 75,000 |
| Retained earnings . | 720,000 | | $58\frac{1}{3}$ | 420,000 | $41\frac{2}{3}$ | 300,000 |
| | $ 900,000 | $75 | | $525,000 | | $ 375,000 |
| Difference . . . . . . . . . . . | $ 100,000 | | | $ (35,000) | | $ 135,000 |
| Proceeds from issuance . . . . . . . . | (100,000) | $50 | | | | (100,000) |
| Parent's dilution/ minority interest accretionᵇ . . . . . . . . | $ –0– | | | $ (35,000) | | $ 35,000 |

ᵃFor simplicity, we assume that the subsidiary's common stock is no-par. Thus, the $100,000 proceeds have been credited to the Common Stock account.
ᵇThe dilution suffered by the parent is offset by the accretion to the minority interest.

| | | | | Book Value Element | |
|---|---|---|---|---|---|
| | Minority Interest | + Total Costᵃ | = Common Stock | + | Retained Earnings |
| Balances before issuance of additional shares . . . . | $240,000 | $560,000 | $ 80,000 | | $720,000 |
| Issuance of additional shares . . . . . . . . . . . . . . . | 100,000 | | 100,000 | | |
| Subtotal. . . . . . . . . . . . . . . . . | $340,000 | $560,000 | $180,000 | | $720,000 |
| Adjustment for parent's dilution/minority interest accretion . . . . | 35,000 | (35,000) | | | |
| Balances after issuance of additional shares . . . . | $375,000 | $525,000 | $180,000 | | $720,000 |

ᵃFor simplicity, we assume that there is no cost in excess of book value.

3. After the adjustment is made for the dilution of the parent's interest in the subsidiary's net assets, the analysis of the investment account is updated in the normal manner. The ending balances as of any future consolidation date are the sources of the primary elimination entry, as illustrated in earlier chapters.

# OTHER CHANGES IN THE SUBSIDIARY'S CAPITAL ACCOUNTS

## Stock Dividends

The treatment of stock dividends is set forth in *ARB No. 51* as follows:

> Occasionally, subsidiary companies capitalize earned surplus [retained earnings] arising since acquisition, by means of a stock dividend or otherwise. This does not require a transfer to capital surplus [additional paid-in capital] on consolidation, inasmuch as the retained earnings in the consolidated financial statements should reflect the accumulated earnings of the consolidated group not distributed to the shareholders of, or capitalized by, the parent company.[3]

In other words, a stock dividend by a subsidiary has no effect on the parent's books or in consolidation. The subsidiary has merely reshuffled amounts within its equity accounts by reducing Retained Earnings and increasing Common Stock and Additional Paid-in Capital in accordance with procedures discussed in intermediate accounting texts. Although no entry is required to adjust the carrying value of the Investment in Subsidiary account, the parent must adjust these accounts as they exist within the expanded analysis of their investment account by components. Assume the following information:

| | Subsidiary's Books | |
| --- | --- | --- |
| | Common Stock | Retained Earnings |
| Balances immediately *before* stock dividend | $ 80,000 | $720,000 |
| Capitalization of retained earnings as a result of stock dividend | 120,000 | (120,000) |
| Balances immediately *after* stock dividend | $200,000 | $600,000 |

The balances in the expanded analysis of the investment account by individual components would be adjusted accordingly.

The reclassification within the parent's expanded analysis of the investment account by components is necessary so that the posting of the

---

[3]*Accounting Research Bulletin No. 51*, "Consolidated Financial Statements" (New York: American Institute of Certified Public Accountants, 1959), par. 18.

primary elimination entry used to prepare consolidated financial statements properly eliminates the subsidiary's equity accounts.

If the capitalization of retained earnings exceeds the total retained earnings as of the acquisition date, an interesting problem results. Under the equity method of accounting, the parent has included amounts in its Retained Earnings account that it cannot obtain from the subsidiary as a result of the capitalization. If this restriction on dividend availability is material, it should be disclosed in the consolidated financial statements.

## Stock Splits

As with stock dividends, when a stock split occurs, no entry is required on the parent's books to adjust the carrying value of its investment in the subsidiary. However, the parent does not make any reclassifications within the expanded analysis of the investment account by individual components, because no changes were made to the subsidiary's capital accounts at the time of the stock split. The parent company makes only a memorandum notation of the stock split.

## Changes from Par Value to No-par and Vice Versa

When a subsidiary changes the par value of its common stock to no-par or vice versa, changes are made on its books in the Common Stock and Additional Paid-In Capital accounts. As a result, the parent makes an adjustment within the expanded analysis of the investment account. The carrying value of the investment itself does not change.

## Appropriation of Retained Earnings

Inasmuch as the amount of the subsidiary's retained earnings existing as of the acquisition date is eliminated in consolidation, any appropriation of retained earnings by the subsidiary that does not exceed the total amount of retained earnings existing as of the acquisition date (including any amount that accrues to minority interests) has no effect on the parent's books or the consolidated financial statements. However, when appropriations of retained earnings exceed this amount, the restriction on dividend availability must be disclosed in the consolidated financial statements if it is material.

## SUBSIDIARY WITH PREFERRED STOCK OUTSTANDING

In consolidated financial statements, a subsidiary's preferred stock not held by the parent company is treated as part of the minority interest. For example, assume a subsidiary has preferred stock recorded on its books at $50,000. At first thought, one would expect to make the following elimination entry in consolidation:

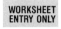

| | | |
|---|---|---|
| Preferred Stock . . . . . . . . . . . . . . . . . . . . . . . . . . . . . . | 50,000 | |
| Minority Interest in Net Assets | | |
| of Subsidiary . . . . . . . . . . . . . . . . . . . . . . . . | | 50,000 |

However, the amount recorded on the subsidiary's books relating to its preferred stock is not necessarily the amount that is added to the minority interest in consolidation. That amount depends on the *features* of the preferred stock—that is, whether it is cumulative or noncumulative, whether it is participating or nonparticipating, and whether it is callable at amounts other than its par value. When cumulative dividends are in arrears, when participating dividends are in arrears, and when call premiums exist, the book value of the preferred stock is greater than its recorded book value. **It is the book value amount that must be added to the minority interest—not the recorded amount of the preferred stock.** The difference between the preferred stock's book value and its recorded value is taken from retained earnings. Thus, a portion of the subsidiary's retained earnings is allocable to the preferred stock interest, with the residual retained earnings being allocable to the common stock interest. These circumstances require special consideration in calculating (1) the parent's cost in excess of (or below) its share of the subsidiary's net assets at book value as of the acquisition date; (2) the amount assigned to the common stock minority shareholder interest at the acquisition date when the subsidiary is partially owned; and (3) the earnings that accrue to each ownership group subsequent to the acquisition date.

## The Determination of Minority Interest as of the Acquisition Date

The procedures for calculating the book value of the preferred stock are the same as discussed in intermediate accounting texts. Briefly, the recorded amount is increased for preferred stock with any of the following features:

- **For cumulative preferred stock:** Add any dividends in arrears through the acquisition date.
- **For participating preferred stock:** Add any unpaid participation amounts through the acquisition date.
- **For callable preferred stock:** Add any premium relating to the call feature.

For example, assume the $5,000 in dividends are in arrears on S Company's 5% **cumulative** preferred stock on January 1, 19X1, the date P Company acquired 80% of the outstanding common stock of S Company for $72,000 cash. The following calculation of the minority interest as of January 1, 19X1, assumes S Company's capital accounts on the acquisition date are as follows:

| | Total | Parent's Interest | Minority Interest |
|---|---|---|---|
| 5% Preferred stock, cumulative..... | $100,000 | | $100,000 |
| Common stock..................... | 40,000 | $32,000 | 8,000 |
| Retained earnings: | | | |
|    Allocable to preferred stock .... | 5,000 | | 5,000 |
|    Allocable to common stock..... | 15,000 | 12,000 | 3,000 |
|     Total Stockholders' Equity ... | $160,000 | $44,000 | $116,000 |

Thus, the parent's interest in the subsidiary's net assets at book value is $44,000 (80% of $55,000)—not $48,000 (80% of $60,000). As a result, the parent's cost in excess of book value at the acquisition date is $28,000 ($72,000 cost − $44,000 share of book value). The interest of the preferred stockholders is easily accounted for by modifying the conceptual analysis of the investment account. Using the above example, the conceptual analysis of the investment account as of the acquisition date would be prepared as follows:

| | | | Book Value Element | | | Cost in |
|---|---|---|---|---|---|---|
| Minority Interest | + Total Cost | = | Preferred Stock | + Common Stock | + Retained Earnings | + Excess of Book Value |
| $116,000 | $72,000 | | $100,000 | $40,000 | $20,000 | $28,000 |

By including the preferred stock in the conceptual analysis, a separate entry eliminating the preferred stock and increasing the minority interest is unnecessary. The preferred stock account balance is eliminated, and the minority interest is established in its entirety from postings made from the primary elimination entry.

In the preceding example, $5,000 of the $20,000 retained earnings balance was allocated to the preferred stockholders' interest. The amount to be allocated to the preferred stockholders is not limited to the balance in retained earnings. If $20,000 of dividends were in arrears and the preferred stock had a $3,000 call premium, then $23,000 would be allocated to the preferred. This would result in a negative $3,000 being allocated to the common stock interest.

## Accounting for Minority Interest Subsequent to the Acquisition Date

In periods subsequent to acquisition, the subsidiary's net income must be allocated between the preferred stockholders' and the common stockholders' interests. Assuming S Company had net income of $15,000 for 19X1 and paid no dividends on its preferred stock, the allocation of the net income for 19X1 is as follows:

| | |
|---|---|
| Total net income ........................................... | $15,000 |
| Less—Preferred stock dividend requirement................. | (5,000) |
| Residual allocable to common stockholders ................ | $10,000 |

The parent company applies the equity method of accounting to the $10,000 and records $8,000 (80% of $10,000) of the subsidiary's earnings. This procedure is in accordance with *APB Opinion No. 18:*

> When an investee has outstanding cumulative preferred stock, an investor should compute its share of earnings (losses) after deducting the investee's preferred dividends, whether or not such dividends are declared.[4]

The conceptual analysis of the investment account would be updated in 19X1 as follows:

| | Minority Interest | + | Total Cost | = | Preferred Stock | + | Common Stock | + | Prior Year | + | Current Year Earnings | + | Cost in Excess of Book Value |
|---|---|---|---|---|---|---|---|---|---|---|---|---|---|
| | | | | | **Book Value Element** | | | | **Retained Earnings** | | | | |
| Balance, Jan.1, 19X1 ........ | $116,000 | | $72,000 | | $100,000 | | $40,000 | | $20,000 | | | | $28,000[a] |
| Equity in net income: | | | | | | | | | | | | | |
| To Preferred | $ 5,000 | | | | | | | | | | $ 5,000 | | |
| To Common —$10,000: | | | | | | | | | | | | | |
| Parent (80%) | | | $ 8,000 | | | | | | | | 8,000 | | |
| Minority Interest (20%).. | 2,000 | | | | | | | | | | 2,000 | | |
| Subtotal ....... | $123,000 | | $80,000 | | $100,000 | | $40,000 | | $20,000 | | $15,000 | | $28,000 |
| Reclassification | | | | | | | | | 15,000 | | (15,000) | | |
| Balance, Dec. 31, 19X1 ........ | $123,000 | | $80,000 | | $100,000 | | $40,000 | | $35,000 | | $ –0– | | $28,000 |

[a]For simplicity, we assume this amount is allocable entirely to Land.

[4]*Opinions of the Accounting Principles Board, No. 18,* "The Equity Method of Accounting for Investments in Common Stock" (New York: American Institute of Certified Public Accountants, 1971), par. 19k.

The primary elimination entry at December 31, 19X1 from this updated analysis is as follows:

| | | |
|---|---:|---:|
| Preferred Stock | 100,000 | |
| Common Stock | 40,000 | |
| Retained Earnings (beginning of year) | 20,000 | |
| Equity in Net Income of Subsidiary | 8,000 | |
| Minority Interest in Net Income of Subsidiary | | |
| ($5,000 + $2,000) | 7,000 | |
| Land | 28,000 | |
|     Investment in S Company | | 80,000 |
|     Minority Interest in Net Assets | | |
|       of Subsidiary | | 123,000 |

When dividends are paid to the preferred stockholders, they are treated in the identical manner as dividends paid to minority common stockholders, that is as a reduction to the minority interest column and the dividends declared column.

### Parent's Acquisition of Subsidiary's Preferred Stock.

Using the data in the preceding example, assume that P Company acquired 40% of the subsidiary's outstanding preferred stock on January 1, 19X2, for $44,000. As with an intercompany bond purchase, for consolidated reporting purposes the preferred stock acquired is treated as retired. The total book value of the preferred stock on that date is $110,000 ($100,000 + $10,000 of dividends in arrears). The parent's share of this book value is $44,000 (40% of $110,000).

The conceptual analysis of the investment account can be modified further to deal with the parent's preferred stock holdings simply by adding a column to the left of the minority interest column and reclassifying the $44,000 interest thereto from the minority interest column. We show this below:

| | Parent's Cost of Preferred Stock | Minority Interest | Total Cost |
|---|---:|---:|---:|
| Balance, January 1, 19X2 | | $123,000 | $80,000 |
|     Reclassification | $44,000 | (44,000) | |
| Subtotal | $44,000 | $ 79,000 | $80,000 |

In consolidation, the $44,000 balance in the parent's preferred stock interest column is posted as a credit to the parent's Investment in Preferred Stock account, thus eliminating the balance in that account.

**Parent's Cost Differs from Book Value.**  In the preceding example, the parent's $44,000 cost equaled its share of the preferred stock's book value. When the parent's cost is above or below its share of the book value, the issue is raised of how the parent should account for the difference. This issue is not specifically addressed in any official accounting pronouncement. Proponents of the entity theory would make an adjustment to Additional Paid-in Capital (using the same reasoning given earlier in situations in which a subsidiary issues additional common stock at more or less than book value). Proponents of the parent company theory would record the difference as a gain or loss to be reported currently in the income statement (using the same reasoning given earlier in situations in which a subsidiary issues additional common stock at more or less than book value).

Assume the parent's cost of the preferred stock was $43,000 (instead of $44,000). The parent would make the following general ledger adjusting entry:

| | | |
|---|---|---|
| Investment in Preferred Stock................. | 1,000 | |
| Additional Paid-in Capital (under the entity theory) *or* Gain on Acquisition of Minority Interest at below Book Value (under the parent company theory)..... | | 1,000 |

Adjusting the parent's carrying value of its preferred stock investment to agree with its share of the book value keeps the consolidation procedures straightforward because the Preferred Stock Investment account can always be eliminated by the posting that comes from the primary elimination entry.

**Accounting for the Parent's Preferred Stock Investment in Subsequent Periods.**
Even though *APB Opinion No. 18* applies only to investments in common stock, it would not be sensible under the equity method to record only some of the subsidiary's earnings that accrue to the parent and not record the remainder. Accordingly, the parent should account for its preferred stock investment using the equity method of accounting. This procedure maintains the carrying value of the investment at the amount shown in the "Parent's Cost of Preferred Stock" column of the conceptual analysis, to which is added the earnings that accrue to these holdings. For example, assume the subsidiary reported $25,000 of net income for 19X2. The appropriate columns of the conceptual analysis of the investment account would be updated as follows (for simplicity all nonaffected columns are not shown):

| | Parent's Cost of Preferred Stock | + | Minority Interest | + | Total Cost | = | Current Year Earnings |
|---|---|---|---|---|---|---|---|
| Balance, January 1, 19X2. | $44,000 | | $79,000 | | $80,000 | | |
| Equity in net income ($25,000 total): | | | | | | | |
| To preferred (5% × $100,000)—Parent (40%). | 2,000 | | | | | | $2,000 |
| Minority interest (60%). | | | 3,000 | | | | 3,000 |
| To common (residual of $20,000)— | | | | | | | |
| Parent (80%). | | | | | 16,000 | | 16,000 |
| Minority interest (20%). | | | 4,000 | | | | 4,000 |
| Subtotal. | $46,000 | | $86,000 | | $96,000 | | $25,000 |

Note in the conceptual analysis above that the minority interest deduction in the income statement would be $7,000. Note also that the parent records $18,000 under the equity method of accounting ($2,000 on the preferred stock and $16,000 on the common stock). We do not illustrate the preparation of a complete set of consolidated financial statements in this preferred stock section because the procedures used to deal with a subsidiary having outstanding preferred stock are but a slight variation from those used when a preferred stock interest does not exist.

# SELECTED REFERENCES

Davis, Michael L., and James A. Largay III, "Reporting Consolidated Gains and Losses on Subsidiary Stock Issuances," *The Accounting Review* (April 1988), pp. 348–63.

Schiff, Jonathan B., "An Unusual Financing Source: Will It Spur New Disclosure Rules?" *Management Accounting* (October 1986). pp. 42–45.

# END-OF-CHAPTER REVIEW

## Summary of Key Points

1. The acquisition of any or all of a subsidiary's common stock minority interest is treated as an acquisition of a block of stock for which purchase accounting must be used. (This holds true whether the parent or the subsidiary acquires the minority shares.)
2. When the subsidiary acquires minority interest shares at above or below book value, the decrease or increase in the parent's interest in the book value of the subsidiary's net assets is treated as an adjustment to cost in excess of book value (with appropriate assignment to the individual components required).

3. For the partial disposal of a parent's interest in a subsidiary, the average cost method is the soundest method of determining the cost to be removed from the Investment account.
4. Any gain or loss on partial disposal is reported in the income statement.
5. The sale of additional common stock to the public by a subsidiary at below book value results in a dilution of the parent's interest in the subsidiary's net assets at book value. (The opposite occurs when sold at above book value.) Under the parent company theory, the loss resulting from this dilution (or the gain when accretion occurs) is reported currently in the income statement. The SEC permits this treatment (in addition to the alternative of debiting or crediting Additional Paid-in Capital, which is entity theory treatment).
6. A subsidiary's preferred stock is treated as additional minority interest in the consolidated financial statements.
7. The special features of preferred stock may require that a portion of the subsidiary's retained earnings be shown as part of the minority interest.
8. When a parent acquires some or all of a subsidiary's outstanding preferred stock, the acquired stock is treated as retired for consolidated reporting.
9. Under parent company theory, a gain or loss on the constructive retirement of a subsidiary's preferred stock is recorded currently in the income statement. (Under entity theory, an adjustment is made to Additional Paid-in Capital.)

## Glossary of New Terms

**Partial disposal**   The disposal by a parent company of a portion of its common stock investment in a subsidiary.

## Self-Study Questions
*(Answers are at the end of this chapter.)*

1. When a parent acquires some or all of the minority interest in a subsidiary, to record the acquisition of the shares, it must use the:
   a. Entity theory.
   b. Parent company theory.
   c. Purchase method.
   d. Cost method.
   e. None of the above.
2. When a subsidiary acquires the minority interest at less than the book value of the minority interest, which of the following takes place or occurs?
   a. A currently reportable gain under the parent company theory.
   b. A change in the carrying value of the Investment in Subsidiary account.
   c. An adjustment to Additional Paid-in Capital under the entity theory.
   d. Dilution of the parent's ownership interest in the net assets of the subsidiary at book value.
   e. None of the above.
3. When a parent sells a portion of its common stock holdings in a subsidiary, which of the following must be applied at the date of the disposal in relieving the investment account?
   a. The cost method.
   b. The parent company theory.

c. The entity theory.

d. *SEC Staff Accounting Bulletin No. 51.*

e. None of the above.

4. On June 1, 19X3, S Company, a 90%-owned subsidiary of P Company, issued 20,000 shares of its $1 par value common stock to the public for $200,000. S Company had 100,000 outstanding shares having a total book value of $1,300,000 just prior to this issuance. The amount the parent would report in its 19X3 income statement under the parent company theory is:

a. –0–.

b. Loss of $45,000.

c. Gain of $45,000.

d. Loss of $50,000.

e. Gain of $50,000.

5. On May 1, 19X1, S Company, a 60%-owned subsidiary of P Company acquired 25,000 shares of its 100,000 outstanding common shares at a cost of $300,000. Prior to this purchase, S Company's net assets had a total book value of $1,500,000. As a result of this purchase, the parent would report in its 19X1 income statement under the parent company theory:

a. –0–.

b. Gain of $60,000.

c. Loss of $60,000.

d. Gain of $75,000.

e. Loss of $75,000.

6. On July 1, 19X6, P Company acquired 60% of the outstanding common stock of S Company. On that date, S Company had the following equity balances:

| | |
|---|---|
| Preferred Stock | $300,000 |
| Common Stock | 200,000 |
| Retained Earnings | 100,000 |

The preferred stock has a call premium of $4,000 and cumulative dividends in arrears of $6,000. The amount to be reported for the minority interest in a consolidated balance sheet on that date is:

a. $116,000.

b. $120,000.

c. $310,000.

d. $426,000.

e. $436,000.

# ASSIGNMENT MATERIAL

## Review Questions

1. When some or all of a minority interest is acquired, is the purchase method or the pooling of interests method of accounting used?

2. Does the accounting method used for the acquisition of some or all of a minority interest depend on whether the parent or the subsidiary acquires the minority interest?

3. When a subsidiary has acquired some or all of its outstanding minority interest at an amount in excess of book value, has the parent's interest in the subsidiary's net assets increased or decreased?

4. When a parent's interest in a subsidiary was acquired in blocks, and a portion of such holdings is sold, what three methods may be used to reduce the investment account?

5. Which of the three methods in Question 5 are acceptable for federal income tax reporting purposes?

6. When a parent disposes of a portion of its common stock holdings in a subsidiary, why must the equity method of accounting be applied up to the date of sale?

7. In which situations does a parent "lose" when a subsidiary issues additional common shares to the public?

8. Does a parent make a general ledger entry when a subsidiary declares a stock dividend?

9. Does a parent make a general ledger entry when a subsidiary effects a stock split?

10. What reasons might explain why a portion of a subsidiary's retained earnings is considered not allocable to common shareholders?

11. Under the equity method of accounting, are preferred stock dividends always deducted from net income?

12. How is the acquisition of an 80%-owned subsidiary's preferred stock similar to the acquisition of 10% of the subsidiary's common shares? How is it different?

13. How is the analysis of a parent company's investment account by the components of the major conceptual elements prepared differently as a result of an acquired subsidiary having preferred stock with dividends in arrears that is callable at above par value?

14. When a partially owned subsidiary has preferred stock that is shown as additional minority interest in the consolidated financial statements, should the acquisition of some or all of the preferred stock above book value be treated as cost in excess of book value in accordance with the purchase method of accounting?

## Discussion Cases

| DC 10-1 | **Acquisition of Minority Interest by Parent: Pooling of Interests versus Purchase Method** |
|---|---|

The controller of Paddle Company indicates to you that the company plans to acquire the entire minority interest of its 92%-owned subsidiary, Steamer Company, by issuing common stock. The terms of the acquisition are identical to those that were used to obtain the 92% interest in Steamer two years ago. The business combination qualified for pooling of interests accounting treatment at that time. The controller asks your advice about how to account for this acquisition.

**Required:**
How would you advise the controller? State your reasons.

| DC 10-2 |
|---|

## Statutory Merger to Eliminate Minority Shareholders: Rights of Minority Shareholders

Several years ago, Paso Company acquired 80% of the outstanding common stock of Sol Company. Paso now decides to merge with Sol. Under state law, the merger requires approval of only two-thirds of Sol's shareholders. Paso votes its 80% of Sol's stock in favor of the merger, which provides that each of Sol's minority stockholders receive one share of Paso's stock in exchange for three shares of Sol's. Your examination of Paso's financial statements after the merger reveals that some of the minority stockholders voted against it. You are concerned that Paso properly disclose in its financial statements the liability, if any, to these stockholders.

### Required:

1. What are the rights of Sol's stockholders who opposed the merger?
2. What steps must minority stockholders ordinarily take to protect their rights in these circumstances?

(AICPA adapted)

| DC 10-3 |
|---|

## Treatment of Gain on Partial Disposal of Interest in a Subsidiary

Phalanx Company sold a portion of its common stock holdings in one of its subsidiaries at a gain of $80,000. The controller is considering the following options:

1. Crediting this gain to the investment account to reduce the remaining $240,000 of unamortized goodwill.
2. Reporting the gain as an extraordinary item, because this is the first such disposal.
3. Reporting the gain as a partial disposal of a segment under the special reporting provisions of *APB Opinion No. 30* for disposals of segments, because neither the parent nor its other subsidiaries are in the same line of business.

### Required:

Evaluate the theoretical merits of these three options.

| DC 10-4 |
|---|

## Treatment of Parent's Dilution after a Sale of Additional Common Stock to the Public by the Subsidiary

Saunders Company is a partially owned subsidiary of Promo Company. In 19X8, Saunders issued additional shares of its common stock to the public at an amount below book value.

Promo is considering the following options in consolidation:

1. Computing the minority interest of these new shareholders based on the amounts they paid for their interest plus their share of earnings minus their share of dividends since the date the additional shares were issued.
2. Computing total minority interest by multiplying the total minority interest ownership percentage by the subsidiary's net assets at book value.

3. Treating the dollar effect of the parent's decrease in interest in the subsidiary's net assets as additional cost in excess of book value.
4. Treating the dollar effect of the parent's decrease in interest in the subsidiary's net assets as a loss in the current period.

**Required:**
Evaluate the theoretical merits of each option.

# Exercises

| E 10-1 |
|---|

## Acquisition of Minority Interest by the Parent

Prost Company owns 80% of the outstanding common stock of Skol Company. The expanded analysis of the parent's investment account by components of the major conceptual elements at January 1, 19X6, is as follows:

| | |
|---|---|
| Book value element: | |
| Common stock . . . . . . . . . . . . . . . . . . . . . . . . . . . . . . . . . . . . . . . . . . . . . . . . . . . | $100,000 |
| Retained earnings . . . . . . . . . . . . . . . . . . . . . . . . . . . . . . . . . . . . . . . . | 90,000 |
| Current value over book value element: | |
| Land . . . . . . . . . . . . . . . . . . . . . . . . . . . . . . . . . . . . . . . . . . . . . . . . . . . . . . . . . | 40,000 |
| Goodwill element . . . . . . . . . . . . . . . . . . . . . . . . . . . . . . . . . . . . . . . . . . . . . . | 28,000 |
| | $258,000 |
| | |
| Total Cost . . . . . . . . . . . . . . . . . . . . . . . . . . . . . . . . . . . . . . . . . . . . . . . . . . . . . . | $220,000 |
| Minority Interest . . . . . . . . . . . . . . . . . . . . . . . . . . . . . . . . . . . . . . . . . . . . . . . | 38,000 |
| | $258,000 |

On January 2, 19X6, Prost acquired 15% of Skol's outstanding common stock from its minority shareholders for $45,000 cash. All of Skol's assets and liabilities have a current value equal to their book value at January 2, 19X6, except land, which is worth $60,000 in excess of its book value.

**Required:**
Update the expanded analysis of the parent's investment account to reflect this acquisition of a portion of the minority holdings.

| E 10-2 |
|---|

## Acquisition of Minority Interest by the Subsidiary: Determining Parent's Increase or Decrease in Net Assets

Penner Company owns 75% of the outstanding common stock of Selff Company. On January 1, 19X6, Selff acquired 15% of that stock from the minority shareholders for $300,000 cash. These shares were immediately retired (the Common Stock account was charged $15,000, the Additional Paid-in Capital account was charged $135,000, and the Retained Earnings account was charged $150,000). The subsidiary's capital accounts immediately before the acquisition are as follows:

| | |
|---|---:|
| Common Stock, $1 par value | $ 100,000 |
| Additional Paid-in Capital | 900,000 |
| Retained Earnings | 600,000 |
| | $1,600,000 |

**Required:**

1. Calculate the total change in the equity in the subsidiary's net assets for the parent and the remaining minority interests as a result of the acquisition of a portion of the minority interest.
2. Determine the changes that must be reflected in the expanded analysis of the investment account.

## E 10-3   Stock Dividend by Subsidiary

On April 1, 19X7, Systems Company, a 75%-owned subsidiary of Pembroke Company, declared a 10% common stock dividend on its 10,000 outstanding shares of $20 par value common stock. Systems recorded the following entry:

| | | |
|---|---:|---:|
| Retained Earnings | 160,000 | |
| Common Stock | | 20,000 |
| Additional Paid-in Capital | | 140,000 |

**Required:**

Determine the appropriate changes that the parent company should make to its expanded analysis of the investment account by individual components as a result of the stock dividend.

## E 10-4   Stock Split by Subsidiary

On January 1, 19X3, Schism Company, a 60%-owned subsidiary of Pergolon Company, split its $10 par value common stock 4 for 1. At the time of the stock split, Schism's capital accounts were as follows:

| | |
|---|---:|
| Common stock | $ 100,000 |
| Additional paid-in capital | 900,000 |
| Retained earnings | 400,000 |
| | $1,400,000 |

**Required:**

Determine the appropriate changes that the parent company should make to its expanded analysis of the investment account by components as a result of the stock split.

## E 10-5   Preferred Stock: Preparing a Conceptual Analysis at Date of Acquisition—75%-owned Subsidiary

On January 1, 19X1, Prater Company acquired 75% of the outstanding common stock of Sergio Company for $220,000 cash. Assume that the total current value of

Sergio's net assets equals the total book value. The equity structure of Sergio Company as of January 1, 19X1, is as follows:

| | |
|---|---:|
| 5% Preferred stock, cumulative, callable at 103 | |
| (dividends of $5,000 in arrears) .............................. | $100,000 |
| Common stock........................................... | 40,000 |
| Additional paid-in capital................................... | 160,000 |
| Retained earnings ....................................... | 80,000 |
| | $380,000 |

### Required:

Prepare an analysis of the investment account by the individual components of the major conceptual elements as of January 1, 19X1.

## Preferred Stock: Preparing a Conceptual Analysis at Date of Acquisition— 80%-owned Subsidiary

On January 1, 19X1, Peg-bit Company acquired 80% of the outstanding common stock of Snap-mate Company for $1,320,000 cash. Assume that the total current value of Snap-mate's net assets equals the total book value. Snap-mate's capital structure as of January 1, 19X1, is as follows:

| | |
|---|---:|
| 5% Convertible bonds........................................ | $ 500,000 |
| 10% Convertible bonds....................................... | 1,000,000 |
| 4% Convertible preferred stock, cumulative, | |
| callable at 103 (dividends of $12,000 in | |
| arrears) ........................................... | 100,000 |
| 8% Preferred stock, cumulative, callable at 102 | |
| (dividends of $16,000 in arrears) ........................... | 200,000 |
| Common stock, $1 par value................................. | 300,000 |
| Additional paid-in capital................................... | 700,000 |
| Retained earnings ....................................... | 400,000 |

Note: Assume that the 5% convertible bonds are common stock equivalents under *APB Opinion No. 15*, "Earnings Per Share."

### Required:

Prepare an expanded analysis of the investment account as of January 1, 19X1.

# Problems

## Acquisition of Minority Interest by the Parent

On January 1, 19X3, Peplite Company acquired all of the minority interest shares of its 90%-owned subsidiary, Spree Company, by issuing 10,000 shares of its $5 par value common stock. Peplite's common stock had a fair market value of $17 per share on January 1, 19X3. The business combination with Spree was recorded as a pooling of interests at the time of the combination. Spree's capital accounts on December 31, 19X2, were as follows:

| | |
|---|---:|
| Common stock . . . . . . . . . . . . . . . . . . . . . . . . . . . . . . . . . . . . . . . . . . . . . . . . . . . | $1,000,000 |
| Retained earnings . . . . . . . . . . . . . . . . . . . . . . . . . . . . . . . . . . . . . . . . . . . . . . . . | 400,000 |
| | $1,400,000 |

All of Spree's assets and liabilities have a current value equal to their book value at January 1, 19X3, except for its building, which is worth $70,000 in excess of book value.

### Required:
Prepare and update the expanded analysis of the parent's investment account to reflect the acquisition of the minority interest.

---

**P 10-2**

## Acquisition of Minority Interest by the Subsidiary

Pebit Company owns 60% of the outstanding common stock of Scredit Company. On January 1, 19X6, Scredit acquired 20% of its outstanding common stock from its minority interest shareholders for $360,000 cash. (These shares were immediately retired by debiting Common Stock for $20,000, Additional Paid-in Capital for $80,000, and Retained Earnings for $260,000.) The expanded analysis of Pebit's investment account by components at December 31, 19X5, is as follows:

| | |
|---|---:|
| **Book value element:** | |
| Common stock . . . . . . . . . . . . . . . . . . . . . . . . . . . . . . . . . . . . . . . . . . . . . . . . | $ 100,000 |
| Additional paid-in capital . . . . . . . . . . . . . . . . . . . . . . . . . . . . . . . . . . . . | 400,000 |
| Retained earnings . . . . . . . . . . . . . . . . . . . . . . . . . . . . . . . . . . . . . . . . . . | 700,000 |
| **Current value over book value element:** | |
| Land . . . . . . . . . . . . . . . . . . . . . . . . . . . . . . . . . . . . . . . . . . . . . . . . . . . . . . . . . | 60,000 |
| Goodwill element . . . . . . . . . . . . . . . . . . . . . . . . . . . . . . . . . . . . . . . . . . . . | 90,000 |
| | $1,350,000 |
| | |
| Total Cost . . . . . . . . . . . . . . . . . . . . . . . . . . . . . . . . . . . . . . . . . . . . . . . . . . . | $ 870,000 |
| Minority Interest . . . . . . . . . . . . . . . . . . . . . . . . . . . . . . . . . . . . . . . . . . . . | 480,000 |
| | $1,350,000 |

All of Scredit's assets and liabilities have a current value equal to their book value on January 1, 19X6, except for land, which has a current value $100,000 over its book value.

### Required:
1. Calculate the amount of the decrease in the parent's interest in the subsidiary's net assets.
2. Update the expanded analysis of the investment account by components to reflect this acquisition of a portion of the minority interest.

---

**P 10-3**

## Acquisition of Minority Interest by the Parent (Problem 10-2 Revised)

Assume the information provided in Problem 10-2, except that the parent acquired 20% of the subsidiary's outstanding common stock from the minority interest shareholders for $360,000 cash.

**Required:**

1. Update the expanded analysis of the investment account by components to reflect this acquisition.
2. Explain why the parent suffered dilution in Problem 10-2 but not in this case.
3. Explain why the parent's cost in excess of book value increased by a greater amount in this case than in Problem 10-2.

---

**P 10-4**

## Partial Disposal: Updating the Analysis of the Investment Account and Preparing Year-end Elimination Entries

On October 1, 19X4, Pyramid Company (a calendar-year reporting company) sold 25% of its common stock holdings in its 80%-owned subsidiary, Schemex Company, for $500,000 cash. All of Schemex's shares were acquired on January 1, 19X1, in a business combination that was accounted for as a purchase. The expanded analysis of the investment account by components as of January 1, 19X4, is as follows:

|  |  | Remaining Life as of January 1, 19X4 |
| --- | --- | --- |
| Book value element: |  |  |
| Common stock | $1,500,000 |  |
| Retained earnings | 500,000 |  |
| Current value over book value element: |  |  |
| Land | 200,000 | Indefinite |
| Patent | 30,000 | 5 years |
| Goodwill element | 24,000 | 12 years |
|  | $2,254,000 |  |
| Total Cost | $1,854,000 |  |
| Minority Interest | 400,000 |  |
|  | $2,254,000 |  |

During 19X4, Schemex had net income of $85,000, $25,000 of which was earned in the fourth quarter, and declared dividends of $10,000 at the end of each quarter.

**Required:**

1. Update the parent company's expanded analysis of the investment account through December 31, 19X4, assuming that Pyramid Company uses the equity method.
2. Prepare the primary elimination entry as of December 31, 19X4.
3. Prepare the entry to record the partial disposal by the parent.

---

**P 10-5**

## Partial Disposal: Updating the Analysis of the Investment Account and Preparing Year-end Elimination Entries

On July 1, 19X7, Pro Company (a calendar-year reporting company) sold 3,000 of the 9,000 Samateur Company common shares it held for $170,000 cash. The

9,000 common shares, a 90% interest, were acquired on January 1, 19X1, in a business combination that was accounted for as a purchase. The expanded analysis of the investment account by components as of January 1, 19X7, is as follows:

|  |  | Remaining Life as of January 1, 19X7 |
|---|---|---|
| Book value element: |  |  |
|   Common stock............................ | $100,000 |  |
|   Retained earnings ........................ | 150,000 |  |
| Current value over book value element: |  |  |
|   Land.................................... | 75,000 | Indefinite |
|   Bonds Payable .......................... | 54,000 | 6 years |
| Goodwill element........................... | 50,000 | 5 years |
|  | $429,000 |  |
|  |  |  |
| Total Cost.................................... | $404,000 |  |
| Minority Interest ........................... | 25,000 |  |
|  | $429,000 |  |

During 19X7, Samateur had the following:

|  | Net Income | Dividends Declared |
|---|---|---|
| January 1, 19X7–June 30, 19X7 .................... | $50,000 | $10,000 |
| July 1, 19X7–December 31, 19X7 ................... | 30,000 | 10,000 |

## Required:

1. Update the parent's expanded analysis of the investment account through December 31, 19X7, assuming that the parent uses the equity method.
2. Prepare the primary elimination entry as of December 31, 19X7.
3. Prepare the entry to record the sale of the 3,000 shares by the parent.

## Issuance of Additional Common Shares by the Subsidiary

On July 1, 19X5, Streeter Company, a 90%-owned subsidiary of Paver Company, issued 20,000 shares of its $10 par value common stock to the public for $1,200,000. The balances in Streeter's equity accounts immediately prior to the issuance are as follows:

| | |
|---|---|
| Common stock....................................................... | $1,000,000 |
| Additional paid-in capital.......................................... | 4,000,000 |
| Retained earnings .................................................. | 2,500,000 |
| | $7,500,000 |

## Required:

1. Determine the "gain" or "loss" that the parent incurs as a result of the issuance.
2. How should the gain or loss be reported?

**P 10-7**

## Issuance of Additional Common Shares by the Subsidiary

On April 1, 19X8, Sweepco Company, an 80%-owned subsidiary of Prush Company, issued 10,000 shares of its $1 par value common stock to the public for $360,000. The balances in Sweepco's equity accounts immediately prior to the issuance are as follows:

| | |
|---|---:|
| Common stock | $ 50,000 |
| Additional paid-in capital | 250,000 |
| Retained earnings | 1,200,000 |
| | $1,500,000 |

### Required:
1. Determine the "gain" or "loss" that the parent incurs as a result of the issuance.
2. How should the gain or loss be reported?

**P 10-8\***

## COMPREHENSIVE (Chapters 3–5, 7, 9, and 10)    Preparing a Consolidation Worksheet: Inventory Transfers, Bond Holdings, and Changes in Parent's Ownership Interest

On January 3, 19X3, Penn Company acquired 80% of the outstanding common stock of Scribe Company by paying $400,000 cash to William Braun, the company's sole stockholder. In addition, Penn acquired a patent from Braun for $40,000 cash. Penn charged the entire $440,000 to the Investment in Scribe Company Common Stock account.

### Additional Information:
1. The book value of Scribe's common stock on the acquisition date was $500,000. The book values of the individual assets and liabilities equaled their current values.
2. The patent had a remaining legal life of four years as of January 3, 19X3. No amortization has been recorded since the acquisition date.
3. During 19X4, Scribe sold merchandise to Penn for $130,000, which included a markup of 50% over Scribe's cost. At December 31, 19X4, $45,000 of this merchandise remained in Penn's inventory. In February 19X5, Penn sold this merchandise at an $8,000 profit.
4. On July 1, 19X5, Penn reduced its investment in Scribe to 75% of Scribe's outstanding common stock by selling shares to an unaffiliated company for $60,000 at a profit of $16,000. Penn recorded the proceeds as a credit to its investment account.
5. In November 19X5, Penn sold merchandise to Scribe for the first time. Penn's cost for this merchandise was $80,000, and it made the sale at 120% of its

*The financial statement information presented for problems accompanied by asterisks is also provided on Model 9 (filename: Model9) of the software file disk that is available for use with the text, enabling the problem to be worked on the computer.

cost. Scribe's December 31, 19X5, inventory contained $24,000 of the merchandise that was purchased from Penn.

6. On December 31, 19X5, a $40,000 payment was in transit from Scribe to Penn. Accounts receivable and accounts payable include intercompany receivables and payables. (Scribe still owes Penn $25,000.)

7. In December 19X5, Scribe declared and paid cash dividends of $100,000 to its stockholders.

8. Scribe had $140,000 of net income for the six months ended June 30, 19X5, and $160,000 of net income for the six months ended December 31, 19X5.

9. On July 1, 19X5, Penn paid $179,000 for 50% of the outstanding bonds issued by Scribe. The bonds mature on December 31, 19X6, and were originally issued at a discount. At December 31, 19X5, the unamortized discount on Scribe's books is $16,000. (Interest at 10% is due on June 30 and December 31 of each year.) The December 31, 19X5, interest payment was made on time. (Both companies use the straight-line method of discount amortization.)

10. At no time in 19X3–19X5 did Penn make any adjustment to its investment account or its financial statements for any unrealized intercompany profit or imputed gain or loss relating to its intercompany bond holdings.

11. The financial statements of each company for the year ended December 31, 19X5, are as follows:

| | Penn Company | Scribe Company |
|---|---|---|
| **Income Statement (19X5)** | | |
| Sales. . . . . . . . . . . . . . . . . . . . . . . . . . . . . . . . . . . . . . . . . . . . . | $4,000,000 | $1,700,000 |
| Cost of goods sold . . . . . . . . . . . . . . . . . . . . . . . . . . . . | (3,000,000) | (1,000,000) |
| Expenses. . . . . . . . . . . . . . . . . . . . . . . . . . . . . . . . . . . . . . . | (399,000) | (400,000) |
| Intercompany Accounts: | | |
| Equity in net income of subsidiary. . . . . . . . . . . | 232,000 | |
| Dividend income. . . . . . . . . . . . . . . . . . . . . . . . . . . . . | 75,000 | |
| Interest income . . . . . . . . . . . . . . . . . . . . . . . . . | 17,000 | |
| Net Income . . . . . . . . . . . . . . . . . . . . . . . . . . . | $ 925,000 | $ 300,000 |
| | | |
| **Balance Sheet (December 31, 19X5)** | | |
| Cash. . . . . . . . . . . . . . . . . . . . . . . . . . . . . . . . . . . . . . . . . . . . | $ 220,000 | $ 80,000 |
| Accounts receivable, net. . . . . . . . . . . . . . . . . . . . . | 370,000 | 255,000 |
| Inventory. . . . . . . . . . . . . . . . . . . . . . . . . . . . . . . . . . . . . . | 479,000 | 355,000 |
| Fixed assets, net. . . . . . . . . . . . . . . . . . . . . . . . . . . . . | 2,230,000 | 710,000 |
| Investments in Scribe Company: | | |
| Common stock . . . . . . . . . . . . . . . . . . . . . . . . . . . . . | 804,000 | |
| Bonds . . . . . . . . . . . . . . . . . . . . . . . . . . . . . . . . . . . . . . . | 186,000 | |
| Total Assets. . . . . . . . . . . . . . . . . . . . . . . . . . . | $4,289,000 | $1,400,000 |
| | | |
| Accounts payable. . . . . . . . . . . . . . . . . . . . . . . . . . . . | $ 384,000 | $ 76,000 |
| Bonds payable. . . . . . . . . . . . . . . . . . . . . . . . . . . . . . . . | | 400,000 |
| Unamortized bond discount. . . . . . . . . . . . . . . . . . | | (16,000) |
| Common stock . . . . . . . . . . . . . . . . . . . . . . . . . . . . . . . | 1,200,000 | 300,000 |
| Retained earnings . . . . . . . . . . . . . . . . . . . . . . . . . . | 2,705,000 | 640,000 |
| Total Liabilities and Equity. . . . . . . . . . . . . . | $4,289,000 | $1,400,000 |
| | | |
| Dividends declared . . . . . . . . . . . . . . . . . . . . . . . . | $170,000 | $100,000 |

### Required:
1. Prepare a conceptual analysis of the investment account from January 3, 19X1 to December 31, 19X5 as it should have been maintained. (Pay particular attention to the requirements of the specific module from Chapters 7 and 9 that you are using in working this problem.)
2. Prepare the appropriate adjusting entries required at December 31, 19X5.
3. Adjust the financial statements for the entries developed in requirement 2. Modify the financial statements to reflect the use of intercompany accounts.
4. Prepare the appropriate elimination entries in consolidation at December 31, 19X5.
5. Prepare a consolidating statement worksheet at December 31, 19X5. (Parent and subsidiary columns should reflect the adjustments made in requirement 3.)

(AICPA adapted)

## Problems: Preferred Stock

### Preferred Stock: Preparing and Updating the Conceptual Analysis— 60%-owned Subsidiary

On January 1, 19X1, Pelt Company acquired 60% of the outstanding common stock of Sable Company for $366,000 cash. All cost in excess of book value is allocable to goodwill, which has a 10-year life. Sable's capital structure as of January 1, 19X1, is as follows:

| | |
|---|---|
| 5% Convertible bonds........................................ | $1,000,000 |
| 6% Convertible preferred stock, callable at 105, cumulative (dividends of $18,000 in arrears)................... | 100,000 |
| Common stock, $10 par value................................. | 500,000 |
| Retained earnings ........................................ | 33,000 |

Sable had net income of $26,000 during 19X1. It declared and paid cash dividends of $12,000 on its preferred stock.

### Required:
1. Prepare an analysis of the investment account as of January 1, 19X1.
2. Update the analysis of the investment account for 19X1 activity under the equity method of accounting.

### Preferred Stock: Preparing and Updating the Conceptual Analysis—Parent Acquires Some of 80%-owned Subsidiary's Preferred Stock

On January 1, 19X1, Plume Company acquired 80% of the outstanding common stock of Samson Comany for $362,000 cash. All cost in excess of the book value of the net assets is allocable to land. Samson's capital structure at January 1, 19X1, is as follows:

| | |
|---|---|
| 5% Preferred stock, cumulative, callable at 102 | |
| (dividends of $18,000 in arrears) . . . . . . . . . . . . . . . . . . . . . . . . . . . | $100,000 |
| Common stock, $10 par value. . . . . . . . . . . . . . . . . . . . . . . . . . . . . . | 350,000 |
| Retained earnings . . . . . . . . . . . . . . . . . . . . . . . . . . . . . . . . . . . . . . | 60,000 |
| | $510,000 |

On December 31, 19X1, Plume acquired 40% of Samson's outstanding pre-ferred stock for $48,000. During 19X1, Samson had net income of $40,000 and declared cash dividends of $5,000 on its preferred stock.

**Required:**
1. Prepare an analysis of the investment account at January 1, 19X1.
2 Update the analysis of the investment account through December 31, 19X1.
3. Determine the entry required in consolidation at December 31, 19X1, relating to the preferred stock.

## Preferred Stock: Preparing a Consolidation Worksheet—Parent Acquires Some of 100%-owned Subsidiary's Preferred Stock

On January 1, 19X1, Perceval Company acquired 100% of the outstanding common stock of Suffolk Company for $450,000 cash. All cost in excess of book value is allocable to land. Suffolk's capital structure on January 1, 19X1, is as follows:

| | |
|---|---|
| 5% Preferred stock, cumulative, callable at 105 | |
| (dividends of $10,000 in arrears). . . . . . . . . . . . . . . . . . . . . . . . . . . | $100,000 |
| Common stock, $100 par value . . . . . . . . . . . . . . . . . . . . . . . . . . . . | 350,000 |
| Retained earnings. . . . . . . . . . . . . . . . . . . . . . . . . . . . . . . . . . . . . . | 50,000 |
| | $500,000 |

On January 3, 19X1, Perceval acquired 60% of Suffolk's outstanding pre-ferred stock for $65,000. In December 19X1, Suffolk declared cash dividends of $10,000 on its preferred stock. The financial statements for each company for the year ended December 31, 19X1, are as follows:

| | Perceval Company | Suffolk Company |
|---|---|---|
| **Income Statement (19X1)** | | |
| Sales. . . . . . . . . . . . . . . . . . . . . . . . . . . . . . . . . . . . . . . . . . . | $750,000 | $350,000 |
| Cost of goods sold. . . . . . . . . . . . . . . . . . . . . . . . . . . . . . | (480,000) | (240,000) |
| Marketing, administrative, and interest expenses. . . . | (150,000) | (50,000) |
| Equity in net income of Suffolk Company . . . . . . . . . . | 55,000 | |
| Dividend income (on Suffolk Company preferred stock) . . . . . . . . . . . . . . . . . . . . . . . . . . . . . | 6,000 | |
| Net Income. . . . . . . . . . . . . . . . . . . . . . . . . . . . . . . . . . . . | $181,000 | $ 60,000 |

|  | Perceval Company | Suffolk Company |
|---|---|---|
| **Balance Sheet (December 31, 19X1)** | | |
| Investments in Suffolk Company: | | |
| Common stock | $505,000 | |
| Preferred stock | 65,000 | |
| Other assets | 380,000 | $585,000 |
| Total Assets | $950,000 | $585,000 |
| Liabilities | $300,000 | $ 35,000 |
| Preferred stock | | 100,000 |
| Common stock | 400,000 | 350,000 |
| Retained earnings | 250,000 | 100,000 |
| Total Liabilities and Equity | $950,000 | $585,000 |
| Dividends declared on common stock | $100,000 | $–0– |

### Required:

1. Prepare all appropriate adjusting entries at year-end: (a) in connection with the preferred stock investment, (use entity theory), and (b) to reflect the equity method of accounting.
2. Prepare an analysis of the investment in common stock of the subsidiary as of January 1, 19X1.
3. Update the analysis of the investment in common stock of the subsidiary through December 31, 19X1, under the equity method of accounting.
4. Prepare the primary elimination entry at December 31, 19X1.
5. Prepare a consolidating statement worksheet for the year ended December 31, 19X1.

## ADVANCED LEVEL ASSIGNMENT MATERIAL

## Advanced Problems

### Structuring a Transaction: Whether to Sell Some of Parent's Holdings or Have Subsidiary Issue Additional Shares

Pewter Company owns 8,000 common shares of Silverado Company's outstanding common stock. Silverado has 10,000 common shares outstanding on June 30, 19X5, the book value of which is $50 per share. On this date, the carrying value of Pewter's investment in Silverado is $400,000. At this time, Pewter's management realizes that its earnings for calendar 19X5 will be below budgeted amounts. To report higher profits for 19X5, management is considering either (1) selling 2,000 shares of its holdings in Silverado at $70 per share, or (2) having the subsidiary sell 2,000 additional shares to the public at $70 per share. Pewter is also experiencing a slight cash flow problem.

**Required:**

1. Calculate the gain that Pewter would report under both alternatives.
2. What are the advantages and disadvantages of each alternative?

<table>
<tr><td>AP<br>10-2</td></tr>
</table>

## Partial Disposals of Investments in Subsidiaries under Unusual Circumstances

Ponzi Equities is a publicly owned company. It has approximately 5,000,000 common shares outstanding, which are traded (thinly) on the over-the-counter market. During the 15 years of its existence, it issued common stock to acquire all of the outstanding common stock of approximately 20 companies, all of which were small family-owned businesses that were relatively debt-free. Immediately after each acquisition, Ponzi would have the subsidiary borrow the maximum amount possible from a financial institution, with its assets pledged as collateral. The cash would then be transferred to the parent either by declaring dividends or making an intercompany loan.

Ponzi Equities' president, Perry King, is the managing partner of King Management Associates (KMA). KMA is the managing general partner in numerous limited partnerships syndicated by KMA. The limited partners are wealthy investors (doctors, professional athletes, and other professionals). Over the years, Ponzi has sold much of its common stock holdings in its subsidiaries to the various limited partnerships (always at a sizeable gain). In other cases, Ponzi has arranged for a subsidiary to sell its land and buildings to the partnerships that are real estate limited partnerships (RELPs). The RELP would then lease the building and land to the subsidiary. Some investors make loans to these partnerships. Ponzi also buys office buildings that it subsequently sells to the RELPs at a gain.

To date, approximately $40,000,000 has been invested by approximately 1,000 investors in these partnerships. Also, Ponzi recently raised $10,000,000 from a convertible debenture offering to the public. KMA and Ponzi proudly boasted that no investor has ever lost a dime investing in either Ponzi or KMA's partnerships. A key element in attracting investors is to be able to satisfy divergent goals. Thus, investors can choose among partnerships, stock interests, and notes of various kinds.

**Required:**

Evaluate these transactions from the perspectives of the investors and the auditors of Ponzi.

# Technical Research Question

1. Certain expenses incurred by a parent on behalf of its subsidiary have not been charged to the subsidiary. The subsidiary files a registration statement with the SEC in connection with a public offering of additional shares.
   a. Should the subsidiary's historical financial statements reflect all of the expenses that the parent incurred on behalf of the subsidiary?

b. How should the amount of expenses incurred on the subsidiary's behalf by its parent be determined, and what disclosure is required in the financial statements?

## ANSWERS TO SELF-STUDY QUESTIONS

1. c    3. e    5. a

2. e    4. b    6. d

# 11

## · · · · · ·

# INDIRECT
# AND RECIPROCAL
# HOLDINGS

## CHAPTER OVERVIEW

The most common intercompany relationship is the parent company's direct investment in a subsidiary's common stock. Other types of relationships are encountered less frequently; they can be categorized as follows:

1. Indirect vertical holdings.
2. Indirect horizontal holdings.
3. Reciprocal (mutual) holdings.

These various relationships are shown in Illustration 11-1. Although this chapter discusses each category independently of the others, the categories are not mutually exclusive; any combination of relationships may occur. Accounting for special corporate relationships involving combinations of indirect vertical holdings, indirect horizontal holdings, and reciprocal holdings can be developed from a careful application of the principles discussed in this chapter.

## INDIRECT VERTICAL HOLDINGS

An **indirect vertical holding** occurs when P Company, for example, owns more than 50% of S Company, and S Company owns more than 50% of T Company. In such relationships, commonly referred to as **chains,** S Company, although a subsidiary of P Company, is a parent with respect to T Company.

The procedures used to consolidate the financial statements of the three companies are as follows:

1. T Company is consolidated into S Company.
2. S Company, which is now consolidated with T Company, is consolidated into P Company.

When minority interests exist at each level, the minority interest deduction in the income statement section and the minority interest in the balance sheet section of the consolidating statement worksheet increase at each higher level of consolidation.

Net income for P Company (the top-level parent) can be determined without consolidation by successive application of the equity method of accounting, starting with the lowest-level parent within the chain. For example, assume the following information for 19X1:

1. P Company owns 80% of S Company, and S Company owns 60% of T Company. The affiliation can be diagrammed as follows:

2. Net income from each company's operations, excluding equity in net income of subsidiary and amortization of cost in excess of book value, is as follows:

P Company . . . . . . . . . . . . . . . . . . . . . . . . . . . . . . . . . . . . . . . . . . . . . . . . $1,000,000
S Company . . . . . . . . . . . . . . . . . . . . . . . . . . . . . . . . . . . . . . . . . . . . . . . . 100,000
T Company . . . . . . . . . . . . . . . . . . . . . . . . . . . . . . . . . . . . . . . . . . . . . . . . 10,000

3. All of P Company's $10,000 cost in excess of book value was allocable to land. All of S Company's $6,000 cost in excess of book value was allocable to goodwill—$1,000 was amortized during 19X1.

The successive application of the equity method of accounting is as follows:

| | |
|---|---:|
| S Company's income from its own operations . . . . . . . . . . . . . . . | $ 100,000 |
| S Company's equity in T Company's net income | |
|   (60% of $10,000) . . . . . . . . . . . . . . . . . . . . . . . . . . . . . . . . . . . . . . | 6,000 |
| Less—Amortization of cost in excess of book value . . . . . . . . . . | (1,000) |
|     Net Income of S Company . . . . . . . . . . . . . . . . . . . . . . . . . . . | $ 105,000 |
| P Company's income from its own operations . . . . . . . . . . . . . . . | $1,000,000 |
| P Company's equity in S Company's net income | |
|   (80% of $105,000) . . . . . . . . . . . . . . . . . . . . . . . . . . . . . . . . . . . . | 84,000 |
|     Net Income of P Company . . . . . . . . . . . . . . . . . . . . . . . . . . . | $1,084,000 |

Note that only 48% of T Company's $10,000 net income is reflected in P Company's net income under the equity method of accounting [80% (60% × $10,000)]. Of the $1,000 amortization of cost in excess of book value expense recorded by S Company, 80%, or $800, accrues to P Company. Thus, the net amount that accrues to P Company is $4,000 ($4,800 − $800). Even though a majority of T Company's net income does not accrue to the consolidated group, successive consolidation is

### ■ ILLUSTRATION 11-1
**Affiliation Diagrams**

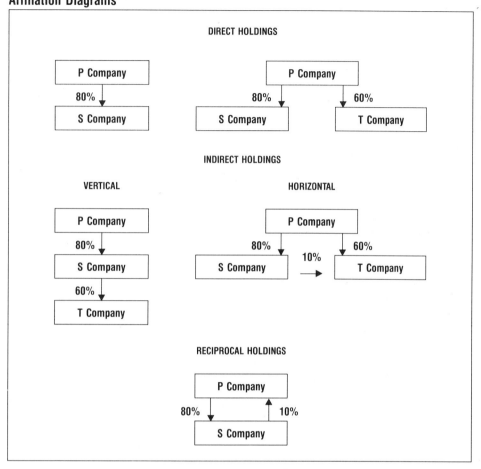

still appropriate, because T Company is controlled indirectly through S Company.

**ILLUSTRATIONS**  ## Preparing Consolidated Financial Statements for Indirect Vertical Holdings

Companies S and T are consolidated as of December 31, 19X1, in Illustration 11-2, and companies P and S are subsequently consolidated as of December 31, 19X1, in Illustration 11-3. The ownership and income information is from the preceding example. (We assume that no intercompany transactions requiring elimination occurred.) The primary and secondary elimination entries for these illustrations are as follows:

# ■ ILLUSTRATION 11-2
## Indirect Vertical Holdings: Consolidation 1

**S COMPANY AND SUBSIDIARY (T COMPANY)**
**Consolidating Statement Worksheet for the Year Ended December 31, 19X1**

| | S Company | T Company | Eliminations Dr. | Eliminations Cr. | S and T Consolidated |
|---|---|---|---|---|---|
| **Income Statement** | | | | | |
| Sales.......................... | 790,000 | 200,000 | | | 990,000 |
| Cost of goods sold.............. | (360,000) | (120,000) | 1,000(2) | | (481,000) |
| Expenses...................... | (330,000) | (70,000) | | | (400,000) |
| Intercompany Accounts: | | | | | |
| Equity in net income......... | 5,000ᵃ | | 6,000(1) | 1,000(2) | –0– |
| Income before Minority Interest.. | 105,000 | 10,000 | 7,000 | 1,000 | 109,000 |
| Minority interest ............. | | | 4,000(1) | | (4,000) |
| Net Income.................... | 105,000 | 10,000 | 11,000 | 1,000 | 105,000 |
| **Statement of Retained Earnings** | | | | | |
| Balances, January 1, 19X1...... | 100,000 | 20,000 | 20,000(1) | | 100,000 |
| +Net income................... | 105,000 | 10,000 | 11,000 | 1,000 | 105,000 |
| −Dividends declared........... | (35,000) | (5,000) | | 5,000(1) | (35,000) |
| Balances, December 31, 19X1... | 170,000 | 25,000 | 31,000 | 6,000 | 170,000 |
| **Balance Sheet** | | | | | |
| Current assets ................. | 338,000 | 115,000 | | | 453,000 |
| Investment in T Company....... | 44,000 | | | 44,000(1) | –0– |
| Fixed assets, net .............. | 350,000 | 155,000 | | | 505,000 |
| Goodwill...................... | | | 5,000(1) | | 5,000 |
| Total Assets.................. | 732,000 | 270,000 | 5,000 | 44,000 | 963,000 |
| Liabilities...................... | 262,000 | 205,000 | | | 467,000 |
| Minority interest in net assets | | | | | |
| of subsidiary................. | | | | 26,000(1) | 26,000 |
| S Company: | | | | | |
| Common stock............... | 300,000 | | | | 300,000 |
| Retained earnings ........... | 170,000 | | | | 170,000 |
| T Company: | | | | | |
| Common stock............... | | 40,000 | 40,000(1) | | –0– |
| Retained earnings ........... | | 25,000 | 31,000 | 6,000 | –0– |
| Total Liabilities and Equity.... | 732,000 | 270,000 | 71,000 | 32,000 | 963,000 |

Proof of debit and credit postings......................... 76,000   76,000

Explanation of entries:
(1) The primary elimination entry.
(2) The secondary elimination entry.

ᵃComprised of $6,000 share of T Company's reported net income, net of $1,000 of amortization of cost in excess of book value.

■ **ILLUSTRATION 11-3**
**Indirect Vertical Holdings: Consolidation 2**

| | P Company | S and T Consolidated[a] | Eliminations Dr. | Eliminations Cr. | P + S + T Consolidated |
|---|---|---|---|---|---|
| **P COMPANY AND SUBSIDIARY (S COMPANY)** Consolidating Statement Worksheet for the Year Ended December 31, 19X1 | | | | | |
| **Income Statement** | | | | | |
| Sales . . . . . . . . . . . . . . . . . . . . . . . . | 7,500,000 | 990,000 | | | 8,490,000 |
| Cost of goods sold. . . . . . . . . . . | (4,000,000) | (481,000) | | | (4,481,000) |
| Expenses. . . . . . . . . . . . . . . . . . | (2,500,000) | (400,000) | | | (2,900,000) |
| Intercompany Accounts: | | | | | |
| Equity in net income . . . . . . . | 84,000 | | 84,000(1) | | —0— |
| Income before Minority Interest | 1,084,000 | 109,000 | 84,000 | | 1,109,000 |
| Minority interest . . . . . . . . . . . | | (4,000) | 21,000(1) | | (25,000) |
| Net Income . . . . . . . . . . . . . . . . . | 1,084,000 | 105,000 | 105,000 | | 1,084,000 |
| **Statement of Retained Earnings** | | | | | |
| Balances, January 1, 19X1 . . . . | 1,700,000 | 100,000 | 100,000(1) | | 1,700,000 |
| + Net income . . . . . . . . . . . . . . . | 1,084,000 | 105,000 | 105,000 | | 1,084,000 |
| − Dividends declared . . . . . . . . . | (700,000) | (35,000) | | 35,000(1) | (700,000) |
| Balances, December 31, 19X1 . . | 2,084,000 | 170,000 | 205,000 | 35,000 | 2,084,000 |
| **Balance Sheet** | | | | | |
| Current assets. . . . . . . . . . . . . . . | 2,068,000 | 453,000 | | | 2,521,000 |
| Investment in S Company. . . . . . | 416,000 | | | 416,000(1) | —0— |
| Fixed assets, net . . . . . . . . . . . . . | 2,600,000 | 505,000 | 40,000(1) | | 3,145,000 |
| Goodwill . . . . . . . . . . . . . . . . . . . | | 5,000 | | | 5,000 |
| Total Assets . . . . . . . . . . . . . . . | 5,084,000 | 963,000 | 40,000 | 416,000 | 5,671,000 |
| Liabilities . . . . . . . . . . . . . . . . . . . | 1,000,000 | 467,000 | | | 1,467,000 |
| Minority interest in T Company and S Company. . . . . . . . . . . | | 26,000 | | 94,000(1) | 120,000 |
| P Company: | | | | | |
| Common stock. . . . . . . . . . . . . | 2,000,000 | | | | 2,000,000 |
| Retained earnings. . . . . . . . . . | 2,084,000 | | | | 2,084,000 |
| S Company: | | | | | |
| Common stock. . . . . . . . . . . . . | | 300,000 | 300,000(1) | | —0— |
| Retained earnings. . . . . . . . . . | | 170,000 | 205,000 | 35,000 | —0— |
| Total Liabilities and Equity. . . | 5,084,000 | 963,000 | 505,000 | 129,000 | 5,671,000 |
| Proof of debit and credit postings. . . . . . . . . . . . . . . . . . . . . . . . | | | 545,000 | 545,000 | |

Explanation of entry:
(1) The primary elimination entry.

[a]From Illustration 11-2.

1. The primary elimination entry:

| | Consolidation of | |
|---|---|---|
| | Companies S and T | Companies P and S |
| Common Stock | 40,000 | 300,000 |
| Retained Earnings (beginning of year) | 20,000 | 100,000 |
| Equity in Net Income of Subsidiary | 6,000 | 84,000 |
| Minority Interest in Net Income of S Company | 4,000 | 21,000 |
| Land | | 40,000 |
| Goodwill | 5,000 | |
|     Dividends Declared | 5,000 | 35,000 |
|     Investment in Subsidiary | 44,000 | 416,000 |
|     Minority Interest in Net Assets of S Company | 26,000 | 94,000 |

2. The secondary elimination entry:

| | | |
|---|---|---|
| Cost of Goods Sold | 1,000 | |
|     Equity in Net Income of Subsidiary | | 1,000 |

**Review Points for Illustration 11-2 and 3.** Note the following:

1. At each higher level of consolidation, the minority interest deduction increases, as does the Minority Interest account in the balance sheet.
2. S Company treats the amortization of cost in excess of book value on its books as a normal expense, thereby reducing its net income, which in turn reduces the minority interest deduction when S Company is consolidated with P Company. In other words, the amortization of cost in excess of book value by S Company is considered a bona fide expense in determining S Company's net income, and the minority interest deduction is based on this net income.
3. The consolidation process starts at the lowest parent–subsidiary level and then works upward.

# INDIRECT HORIZONTAL HOLDINGS

**Indirect horizontal holdings** occur when one subsidiary holds an investment in another subsidiary of a common parent—for example, P Company owns more than 50% of companies S and T, and S Company has an investment in T Company, which obviously must be less than 50%.

Consolidating the financial statements of the three companies is accomplished as follows:

1. S Company (an investor) applies the equity method of accounting with respect to the earnings of T Company (an investee).
2. P Company applies the equity method of accounting to each of its subsidiaries and then consolidates S Company.
3. P Company then consolidates T Company.

When the three companies are consolidated in this sequence, the individual investments in T Company by companies P and S are added together when the latter are consolidated. This combined investment in T Company is then eliminated in a single step when T Company is consolidated with P Company, which is already consolidated with S Company. When eliminating the combined investment in T Company, the individual components of P Company's investment account must be combined with the individual components of S Company's investment account.

Regardless of one subsidiary's ownership percentage in another subsidiary, the equity method of accounting should be used by the investor subsidiary (even if the percentage is less than 20%), because the parent exercises significant influence over the investee subsidiary.

P Company's net income can be determined without consolidation by successive application of the equity method of accounting, starting with the lowest-level investor. Assume the following information for 19X1:

1. P Company owns 80% of S Company and 60% of T Company, and S Company owns 10% of T Company. The affiliations are diagrammed as follows:

2. Income from each company's operations, excluding the equity in net income of any subsidiary or investee, is as follows:

| | |
|---|---:|
| P Company | $1,000,000 |
| S Company | 100,000 |
| T Company | 10,000 |

3. For simplicity, we assume that all cost in excess of book value was allocable to land. Thus, there is no amortization of cost in excess of book value.

The successive application of the equity method of accounting is as follows:

| | |
|---|---|
| S Company's income from its own operations............... | $ 100,000 |
| S Company's equity in T Company's net income (10% of $10,000)......................... | 1,000 |
| Total Net Income of S Company......................... | $ 101,000 |
| P Company's income from its own operations............... | $1,000,000 |
| P Company's equity in S Company's net income (80% of $101,000) ............................... | 80,800 |
| P Company's equity in T Company's net income (60% of $10,000)......................... | 6,000 |
| Total Net Income of P Company...................... | $1,086,800 |

## Preparing Consolidated Financial Statements for Indirect Horizontal Holdings

From the ownership and income information in the preceding example, companies P and S are consolidated as of December 31, 19X1, in Illustration 11-4, and P Company (now consolidated with S Company) is consolidated with T Company as of December 31, 19X1, in Illustration 11-5. (We assume that no intercompany transactions occurred requiring elimination.) The primary elimination entries are given as follows:

| | Consolidation of | | | |
|---|---|---|---|---|
| | **Companies P and S** | | **Companies P and T** (See below for source of these amounts) | |
| Common Stock ............. | 300,000 | | 40,000 | |
| Retained Earnings (beginning of year)......... | 100,000 | | 20,000 | |
| Equity in Net Income of Subsidiary................. | 80,800 | | 7,000 | |
| Minority Interest in Net Income of Subsidiary........ | 20,200 | | 3,000 | |
| Land..................... | 40,000 | | 9,500 | |
| Dividends Declared ..... | | 35,000 | | 5,000 |
| Investment in Subsidiary.............. | | 412,800 | | 55,000 |
| Minority Interest in Net Assets of Subsidiary............. | | 93,200 | | 19,500 |

**WORKSHEET ENTRIES ONLY**

The primary elimination entry to consolidate companies P and T is obtained by combining the individual components of the major conceptual elements of P Company's investment in T Company and S Company's investment in T Company as shown below:

# ■ ILLUSTRATION 11-4
## Indirect Horizontal Holdings: Consolidation 1

| | P COMPANY AND SUBSIDIARY (S COMPANY) Consolidating Statement Worksheet for the Year Ended December 31, 19X1 | | | | |
|---|---|---|---|---|---|
| | P Company | S Company | Eliminations Dr. | Eliminations Cr. | P + S Consolidated |
| **Income Statement** | | | | | |
| Sales | 7,500,000 | 790,000 | | | 8,290,000 |
| Cost of goods sold | (4,000,000) | (360,000) | | | (4,360,000) |
| Expenses | (2,500,000) | (330,000) | | | (2,830,000) |
| Intercompany Accounts: | | | | | |
| Equity of net income—S | 80,800 | | 80,800(1) | | –0– |
| Equity in net income—T | 6,000 | 1,000 | | | 7,000 |
| Income before Minority Interest | 1,086,800 | 101,000 | 80,800 | | 1,107,000 |
| Minority interest | | | 20,200(1) | | (20,200) |
| Net Income | 1,086,800 | 101,000 | 101,000 | | 1,086,800 |
| **Statement of Retained Earnings** | | | | | |
| Balances, January 1, 19X1 | 1,700,000 | 100,000 | 100,000(1) | | 1,700,000 |
| + Net income | 1,086,800 | 101,000 | 101,000 | | 1,086,800 |
| – Dividends declared | (700,000) | (35,000) | | 35,000(1) | (700,000) |
| Balances, December 31, 19X1 | 2,086,800 | 166,000 | 201,000 | 35,000 | 2,086,800 |
| **Balance Sheet** | | | | | |
| Current assets | 2,029,000 | 368,000 | | | 2,397,000 |
| Investment in Subsidiaries: | | | | | |
| S Company | 412,800 | | | 412,800(1) | –0– |
| T Company | 45,000 | 10,000 | | | 55,000 |
| Fixed assets, net | 2,600,000 | 350,000 | 40,000(1) | | 2,990,000 |
| Total Assets | 5,086,800 | 728,000 | 40,000 | 412,800 | 5,442,000 |
| Liabilities | 1,000,000 | 262,000 | | | 1,262,000 |
| Minority interest in net assets of subsidiary | | | | 93,200(1) | 93,200 |
| P Company: | | | | | |
| Common stock | 2,000,000 | | | | 2,000,000 |
| Retained earnings | 2,086,800 | | | | 2,086,800 |
| S Company: | | | | | |
| Common stock | | 300,000 | 300,000(1) | | –0– |
| Retained earnings | | 166,000 | 201,000 | 35,000 | –0– |
| Total Liabilities and Equity | 5,086,800 | 728,000 | 501,000 | 128,200 | 5,442,000 |
| Proof of debit and credit postings | | | 541,000 | 541,000 | |

Explanation of entry:
(1) The primary elimination entry.

■ **ILLUSTRATION 11-5**

**Indirect Horizontal Holdings: Consolidation 2**

| | P and S Consolidated[a] | T Company | Eliminations Dr. | Eliminations Cr. | P+S+T Consolidated |
|---|---|---|---|---|---|
| **P AND S COMPANIES (Consolidated) AND SUBSIDIARY (T COMPANY)** Consolidating Statement Worksheet for the Year Ended December 31, 19X1 | | | | | |
| **Income Statement** | | | | | |
| Sales | 8,290,000 | 200,000 | | | 8,490,000 |
| Cost of goods sold | 4,360,000 | (120,000) | | | (4,480,000) |
| Expenses | (2,830,000) | (70,000) | | | (2,900,000) |
| Intercompany Accounts: | | | | | |
| Equity in net income— | | | | | |
| T Company | 7,000 | | 7,000(1) | | –0– |
| Income before Minority Interest | 1,107,000 | 10,000 | 7,000 | | 1,110,000 |
| Minority interest | (20,200) | | 3,000(1) | | (23,200) |
| Net Income | 1,086,800 | 10,000 | 10,000 | | 1,086,800 |
| **Statement of Retained Earnings** | | | | | |
| Balances, January 1, 19X1 | 1,700,000 | 20,000 | 20,000(1) | | 1,700,000 |
| +Net income | 1,086,800 | 10,000 | 10,000 | | 1,086,800 |
| −Dividends declared | (700,000) | (5,000) | | 5,000(1) | (700,000) |
| Balances, December 31, 19X1 | 2,086,800 | 25,000 | 30,000 | 5,000 | 2,086,800 |
| **Balance Sheet** | | | | | |
| Current assets | 2,397,000 | 115,000 | | | 2,512,000 |
| Investment in T Company | 55,000 | | | 55,000(1) | –0– |
| Fixed assets, net | 2,990,000 | 155,000 | 9,500(1) | | 3,154,500 |
| Total Assets | 5,442,000 | 270,000 | 9,500 | 55,000 | 5,666,500 |
| Liabilities | 1,262,000 | 205,000 | | | 1,467,000 |
| Minority interest in net assets of subsidiaries | 93,200 | | | 19,500(1) | 112,700 |
| P Company: | | | | | |
| Common stock | 2,000,000 | | | | 2,000,000 |
| Retained earnings | 2,086,800 | | | | 2,086,800 |
| T Company: | | | | | |
| Common stock | | 40,000 | 40,000(1) | | –0– |
| Retained earnings | | 25,000 | 30,000 | 5,000 | –0– |
| Total Liabilities and Equity | 5,442,000 | 270,000 | 70,000 | 24,500 | 5,666,500 |
| Proof of debit and credit postings | | | 79,500 | 79,500 | |

Explanation of entry:
(1) The primary elimination entry.

[a]From Illustration 11-4.

| | P Company's Investment in T Company | S Company's Investment in T Company | Total |
|---|---|---|---|
| Common Stock . . . . . . . . . . . . . . . . . . . | $36,000[a] | $ 4,000 | $40,000 |
| Retained Earnings (beginning of year) . . . . . . . . . . . . . . . . . . . . . . . . | 18,000[a] | 2,000 | 20,000 |
| Equity in Net Income of T Company . | 6,000 | 1,000 | 7,000 |
| Minority Interest in Net Income of T Company . . . . . . . . . . . . . . . . . . | 3,000 | | 3,000 |
| Dividends . . . . . . . . . . . . . . . . . . . . . . . | (4,500) | (500) | (5,000) |
| Land . . . . . . . . . . . . . . . . . . . . . . . . . . . | 6,000 | 3,500 | 9,500 |
| | $64,500 | $10,000 | $74,500 |
| Total Cost . . . . . . . . . . . . . . . . . . . . . . . | $45,000 | $10,000 | $55,000 |
| Minority Interest . . . . . . . . . . . . . . . . . | 19,500 | | 19,500 |
| | $64,500 | $10,000 | $74,500 |

[a]Because of the 10% horizontal investment, this amount is only 90% of the book value rather than 100%.

### Review Points for Illustrations 11-4 and 11-5.  Note the following:

1. For the percentage investment held in T Company, S Company's cost in excess of book value was greater than that of P Company. We assumed that (a) S Company made its investment in T Company after P Company made its investment in T Company, and (b) the land appreciated in value during that interval.
2. The consolidation can also be performed using one consolidation worksheet in which companies S and T are simultaneously consolidated with P Company. This is the common procedure in practice; separate consolidations of each company are used here for instructional purposes.

## RECIPROCAL HOLDINGS

**Reciprocal holdings** occur when a subsidiary invests in its parent company's common stock. Two accounting questions are raised by such holdings:

1. How should the subsidiary account for the investment in the parent company?
2. How should the investment in the parent company be accounted for in consolidation?

### Accounting by the Subsidiary

An investment by a subsidiary in its parent's common stock must be considered a long-term investment. Because such investments rarely, if ever, reach the 20% level, ownership in the parent's common stock is usually less than 20%. In this situation, the subsidiary must account for the investment under the lower of cost or market method, as prescribed by *FASB Statement No. 12*, "Investments in Certain Marketable Securities."

Remember that a subsidiary, as a separate legal entity, must follow generally accepted accounting principles without regard to the fact that it is a subsidiary. Many subsidiaries must issue separate financial statements pursuant to loan indenture agreements. When contingent consideration based on the subsidiary's postcombination sales or earnings amounts is a provision of the business combination agreement, separate audited financial statements are often required.

## Accounting in Consolidation

The subsidiary's method of accounting for its investment in the parent when preparing consolidated financial statements is prescribed by *ARB No. 51* as follows:

> Shares of the parent held by a subsidiary should not be treated as outstanding stock in the consolidated balance sheet.[1]

If the parent had acquired its own shares, then the cost would be treated as a cost of treasury shares. But the parent directed the subsidiary to acquire the shares, which is usually the way such investments are made. If the subsidiary is wholly owned, this treatment makes sense. However, if the subsidiary is partially owned, the requirement to treat all of the shares it owns as not outstanding ignores the reality that the subsidiary's minority shareholders are indirectly shareholders of the parent. The requirement can cause a misleading earnings per share amount to be reported, as demonstrated later in the chapter.

This requirement of *ARB No. 51*, therefore, means that **in consolidation the cost of the investment in the parent's common stock is treated as a cost of treasury shares.** Accordingly, a reclassification must be made in the balance sheet section of the consolidating statement worksheet as follows:

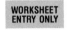

| | | |
|---|---|---|
| Cost of Treasury Stock...................... | xxx | |
|     Investment in Parent Company's | | |
|         Common Stock ...................... | | xxx |

When a subsidiary has lowered the carrying value of its investment in its parent through a valuation allowance, the offsetting charge to its

---

[1]*Accounting Research Bulletin No. 51*, "Consolidated Financial Statements" (New York: American Institute of Certified Public Accountants, 1959), par. 13.

stockholders' equity section (required under *FASB Statement No. 12*) must be reclassified in consolidation as part of the total cost of the treasury shares. Until the subsidiary disposes of some or all of its investment in its parent, the balance of the cost of the treasury shares, as reported in the consolidated financial statements, remains unchanged.

When a subsidiary is wholly owned, consolidated net income is the sum of (1) the parent's earnings from its own operations, exclusive of earnings on its investment in the subsidiary and (2) the subsidiary's earnings from its own operations, exclusive of earnings on its investment in the parent. These situations present no accounting issues in preparing consolidated financial statements.

When a subsidiary is partially owned, the accounting issue is how to report the combined earnings for financial reporting purposes **in view of the fact that the subsidiary's minority shareholders are indirectly shareholders of the parent.** *ARB No. 51* does not specify the procedures for these situations. Two schools of thought explain how the combined earnings should be reported—one advocating the **treasury stock method** and the other advocating the **traditional allocation method.** Each of these methods is best discussed using an example. Assume the following information:

| | P Company | S Company |
|---|---|---|
| Number of common shares outstanding ..... | 100,000 | 20,000 |
| Ownership interest in the other: | | |
|     Percentage ............................... | 70% | 10% |
|     Number of shares ....................... | 14,000 | 10,000 |
| Net income for the year (from own separate operations, exclusive of earnings on investments in the other)................ | $1,000,000 | $500,000 |

The affiliation diagram is as follows:

## The Treasury Stock Method

The **treasury stock method** essentially comes under the parent company theory, which is discussed in Chapter 5. Recall that under the parent company theory the parent is the reporting entity. The consolidation process is merely the substitution of the subsidiary's assets and liabilities for the parent's Investment in Subsidiary account. From this perspective, consolidated net income should be the sum of (1) the parent's earnings from its own separate operations, and (2) the parent's share of the subsidiary's earnings from its own separate operations.

From the above information, **consolidated net income under this method is $1,350,000** [$1,000,000 + (70% × $500,000)]. Thus, the minority interest deduction is based solely on the percentage of minority interest ownership in the subsidiary's earnings from its own separate operations, exclusive of earnings on its investment in the parent. Thus, the minority interest deduction would be $150,000 (30% of $500,000).

The consolidated net income, therefore, is the amount by which the parent's retained earnings would increase if the subsidiary distributed as dividends all of its earnings from its own separate operations, exclusive of its earnings on its investment in the parent. Dividend distributions to the parent's stockholders are ignored in calculating the amount of this increase. Whether the parent uses the equity method or the cost method to account for its investment in the subsidiary is irrelevant.

When the parent accounts for its investment in the subsidiary under the equity method of accounting, it merely applies its ownership percentage in the subsidiary to the subsidiary's earnings from its own separate operations, not including the subsidiary's earnings on its investment in the parent. In the example, this would be $350,000 (70% of $500,000). As a result, the parent's $1,350,000 recorded net income equals the $1,350,000 consolidated net income.

**Earnings per Share: Is It Meaningful?**   The amount of earnings per share on a consolidated basis (assuming no other dilutive securities) is computed by dividing the consolidated net income of $1,350,000 by the 90,000 shares deemed outstanding (100,000 shares issued − 10,000 shares held by the subsidiary treated as not outstanding). This computation gives $15 per share. However, treating all 10,000 shares of the parent's stock held by the subsidiary as not outstanding results in a meaningless earnings per share amount. If the parent distributed as dividends all of its $1,350,000 consolidated net income, this amount would not be distributed solely to the holders of the 90,000 shares. Because 10,000 shares of the parent's stock are held by the subsidiary and because the subsidiary is only 70% owned by the parent, the subsidiary's minority shareholders are effectively indirect shareholders of the parent to the extent of 3,000 shares (30% of 10,000). Assume that the subsidiary was liquidated immediately after it distributed as dividends its net income from its own separate operations. The 10,000 shares held as an investment in the parent would be distributed to the subsidiary's shareholders—7,000 to the parent and 3,000 to the minority shareholders. Thus, the parent's consolidated net income of $1,350,000 would be distributed to holders of 93,000 shares, not 90,000 shares. Dividing $1,350,000 by 93,000 gives $14.52 per share. In terms of dollars, the holders of the 90,000 shares would receive $1,306,452 (90,000 ÷ 93,000) of the consolidated net income of $1,350,000. The minority interest shareholders would receive $43,548 (3,000 ÷ 93,000) of the $1,350,000 consolidated net income. The $14.52 earnings per share amount is therefore more meaningful.

## The Traditional Allocation Method

The **traditional allocation method** essentially comes under the entity theory, which is discussed in Chapter 5. Recall that under the entity theory a "new reporting entity" is deemed to exist as a result of consolidation. This new reporting entity has two classes of shareholders:

1. The controlling interests (in the example, holders of 90,000 shares of the parent's outstanding common stock).
2. The subsidiary's minority shareholders (who indirectly own 3,000 shares of the parent's outstanding common stock in the example).

From this perspective, the combined earnings of the parent and the subsidiary should appear in the consolidated income statement so that the amount that accrues to each class of shareholders is shown. As demonstrated in the discussion of the treasury stock method, the holders of the 90,000 shares are entitled to $1,306,452 of the combined earnings of $1,500,000 ($1,000,000 + $500,000), and the minority shareholders are entitled to $193,548. The amount that accrues to the minority shareholders can be thought of as comprising two amounts, as follows:

1. The minority shareholders' interest in the subsidiary's earnings from its own separate operations, exclusive of earnings from its investment in the parent (30% of $500,000). . . . . . . . . . .  $150,000
2. The minority shareholders' interest in:
   a. The parent's earnings from its separate operations. . . . . . . . . . . . . . . . . . . . .  $1,000,000
   b. The parent's share of the subsidiary's earnings of $500,000 from its own separate operations (70% of $500,000). . . . . . . . . . . . . . . . . . . . . . . . . .  350,000
   
   $1,350,000

As shown in the discussion of the treasury stock method, the minority interest in these amounts is in the ratio of 3,000 shares to 93,000 shares (3,000 ÷ 93,000) × $1,350,000 = . . . . . . . . . . . . . . . . . .  43,548

Portion of combined earnings that accrues to the minority shareholders . . . . . . . . . . . . . . . . . . . . . . . .  $193,548

Recall from Chapter 5 that under the entity theory, the combined earnings of the parent and the subsidiary are presented in the consolidated income statement as follows:

Earnings accruing to controlling interests................. $1,306,452
Earnings accruing to minority interests .................... 193,548
    Consolidated Net Income ............................... $1,500,000

Some accountants advocate an alternative presentation that deducts the amount accruing to the minority interests from the combined earnings of $1,500,000 to arrive at a consolidated net income of $1,306,452. This presentation is inconsistent with the underlying premise of the traditional allocation method, in which the parent is not viewed as the reporting entity.

Reporting the combined earnings using either of these manners of presentation is obviously inconsistent with the equity method of accounting and the amount reported as consolidated net income. In a strict application of the equity method, the parent would record $350,000 as its share of the subsidiary's earnings (70% of $500,000). Thus, the parent's net income under the equity method would be $1,350,000, which is not reported using either of the above methods of presenting the combined earnings.

**Earnings per Share—On the Mark.** The amount of earnings per share on a consolidated basis (assuming no other dilutive securities) is computed by dividing the $1,306,452 earnings that accrue to the controlling interests by 90,000 shares deemed outstanding (100,000 shares issued − 10,000 shares held by the subsidiary treated as not outstanding). This computation gives $14.52 per share, which is a meaningful amount to the holders of the 90,000 shares. (The same earnings per share amount was calculated under the treasury stock approach using 93,000 as the denominator.)

**Using Simultaneous Equations.** Mathematically, the amount of the combined earnings that accrues to each class of shareholders is usually determined under this approach using simultaneous equations. In Illustration 11-6, the data from the example in this section are used with simultaneous equations to arrive at these amounts.

## Which Method Is Correct?

Whether to use the treasury stock method or the traditional allocation method depends on whether the parent company theory or the entity theory produces the more meaningful form of reported combined earnings.

■ **ILLUSTRATION 11-6**
**Application of Simultaneous Equations to Traditional Allocation Method**

Let $P$ equal P Company's net income from its own separate operations plus its share of S Company's net income that would accrue to it on S Company's liquidation. Let $S$ equal S Company's net income from its own separate operations plus its share of P Company's net income that would accrue to it on P Company's liquidation. Thus:

$$P = \$1,000,000 + (.70 \times S)$$
$$S = \$500,000 + (.10 \times P)$$

Substituting for $P$:

$$S = \$500,000 + .10(\$1,000,000 + .70 \times S)$$
$$S = \$500,000 + \$100,000 + .07S$$
$$.093S = \$600,000$$
$$S = \$645,161$$

S Company's minority shareholders would be entitled to $193,548 (30% of $645,161). Subtracting $193,548 from the combined earnings of $1,500,000 gives earnings of $1,306,452, which accrue to the controlling interests.

Alternatively, the earnings that accrue to the controlling interests can be computed by solving the equation for $P$ by substituting for $S$ as follows:

$$P = \$1,000,000 + .70(\$500,000 + .10 \times P)$$
$$P = \$1,000,000 + \$350,000 + .07P$$
$$.093P = \$1,350,000$$
$$P = \$1,451,613$$

Because P Company's existing shareholders (other than S Company) own 90% of its outstanding common stock, they would be entitled to $1,306,452 (90% of $1,451,613) in the event of a double liquidation.

This purely subjective evaluation is based on whether or not the reporting entity is transformed into a new reporting entity by the consolidation process. The treasury stock method is widely practiced, whereas the traditional allocation method is not, partly because of the simplicity of the treasury stock method and management's reluctance to treat part of the parent's earnings as accruing to the minority shareholders.

# INTERCOMPANY PROFIT ON ASSET TRANSFERS

Regardless of the degree of complexity of the relationship among the entities within the consolidated group, any unrealized profit on intercompany asset transfers cannot be reported in the consolidated financial statements. When the complete equity method (explained in Chapters 7 and 8) is used, any unrealized intercompany profit is deferred in the general ledger or ledgers. Consequently, no special procedures are needed in consolidation merely because of the added complexity of the relationship among the entities within the consolidated group. However, when the partial equity method is used (also explained in Chapters 7 and 8), a careful analysis must be made to determine how much of the total unrealized intercompany profit (being deferred *in the consolidation process*) is allocable to the minority interest.

# END-OF-CHAPTER REVIEW

## Summary of Key Points

1. For **indirect vertical holdings:** In applying the equity method of accounting, the lowest-level parent must apply the equity method before it is applied at the next higher level in the chain. The consolidation process starts at the lowest parent-subsidiary level and then works upward.
2. For **indirect horizontal holdings:** In applying the equity method of accounting, the investor-subsidiary must apply the equity method of accounting to its investee's earnings before the parent applies the equity method to the investor-subsidiary's earnings (even if the horizontal holding is less than 20%).
3. For **reciprocal holdings:** Under the treasury stock method, the minority interest deduction is based solely on the subsidiary's earnings from its own separate operations, excluding earnings on its investment in the parent. Under the traditional allocation method, the portion of the combined earnings that accrues to the minority shareholders includes a portion of the parent's earnings from its own separate operations.

## Glossary of New Terms

**Indirect horizontal holdings**  An intercorporate relationship in which a subsidiary has a common stock investment in another subsidiary of their common parent.

**Indirect vertical holdings**  An intercorporate relationship in which a subsidiary has a controlling common stock interest in another company.

**Reciprocal holdings**  An intercorporate relationship in which two entities of an affiliated group of companies have common stock investments in each other.

**Treasury stock method**  A procedure whereby the combined earnings of companies having reciprocal holdings (the controlled company being partially owned) are presented in a manner that portrays the parent as the reporting entity in consolidation. Under this method, the fact that the subsidiary's minority shareholders are indirectly shareholders of the parent is considered irrelevant.

**Traditional allocation method** A procedure whereby the combined earnings of companies having reciprocal holdings (the controlled company being partially owned) are presented in a manner that implies the existence of a new reporting entity from the consolidation process. Under this method, the combined earnings are divided between amounts that accrue to the controlling interests and amounts that accrue to the minority interests, based on their respective interests in the new reporting entity.

## Self-Study Questions

*(Answers are at the end of this chapter.)*

1. In indirect vertical holdings:
   a. A third-tier subsidiary cannot be consolidated unless more than 50% of its earnings accrue to the top-level parent.
   b. A subsidiary has an investment in the parent.
   c. The sequence of consolidation starts at the highest parent-subsidiary level and then works downwards.
   d. Either the treasury stock method or the traditional allocation method can be used.
   e. None of the above.

2. In indirect horizontal holdings:
   a. Investments of less than 20% can be accounted for under the equity method.
   b. The parent must consolidate the subsidiary having the investment in the other subsidiary before it consolidates the other subsidiary.
   c. A subsidiary is also a parent.
   d. A portion of the parent's own separate earnings are excluded from consolidated net income.
   e. None of the above.

3. In reciprocal holdings:
   a. The traditional allocation method fits under the parent company theory.
   b. The minority interest is shown as a deduction in arriving at the consolidated net income under the traditional allocation method.
   c. The cost of the investment in the parent's common stock is treated as a cost of treasury shares in consolidation under both the treasury stock method and the traditional allocation method.
   d. The equity method can be used under the traditional allocation method.
   e. None of the above.

4. P Company owns 60% of the stock of S Company. S Company owns 70% of the stock of T Company. For 19X1, each company had $100,000 of earnings from its own separate operations, exclusive of earnings on its investment in affiliates and amortization of cost in excess of book value. For 19X1, P Company and S Company had amortization of cost in excess of book value of $20,000 and $10,000, respectively. The consolidated net income for 19X1 is:
   a. $172,000.
   b. $176,000.
   c. $182,000.
   d. $185,800.
   e. None of the above.

5. P Company owns 80% of the common stock of S Company and 80% of the common stock of T Company. S Company owns 10% of the common stock of T Company. For 19X1, each company had $500,000 of earnings from its own separate operations, exclusive of earnings on investments in affiliates and amortization of cost in excess of book value. For 19X1, P Company had amortization of cost in excess of book value of $40,000 relating to S Company and $50,000 relating to T Company. The consolidated net income for 19X1 is:
   a. $1,210,000.
   b. $1,250,000.
   c. $1,260,000.
   d. $1,350,000.
   e. None of the above.

6. P Company owns 80% of the common stock of S Company. S Company owns 20% of the common stock of P Company. For 19X1, each company had net income of $500,000 from its own separate operations, exclusive of earnings on its investment in the other. Under a proper presentation of the traditional allocation method, consolidated net income for 19X1 is:
   a. $857,143.
   b. $900,000.
   c. $940,000.
   d. $1,000,000.
   e. None of the above.

## ASSIGNMENT MATERIAL

## Review Questions

1. What is the difference between an indirect vertical holding and an indirect horizontal holding?
2. What are the two methods of accounting for reciprocal holdings?
3. Can a group of affiliated companies simultaneously have indirect vertical holdings, indirect horizontal holdings, and reciprocal holdings?
4. What is the sequence of the consolidation process when indirect vertical holdings exist?
5. What is the sequence of the consolidation process when indirect horizontal holdings exist?
6. How should a subsidiary account for an investment in its parent company?
7. From a consolidated viewpoint, are shares of a parent company that are held by a subsidiary considered issued stock or outstanding stock?
8. How is the cost of a subsidiary's investment in its parent's stock treated in consolidated financial statements?
9. Under the traditional allocation method, is the parent viewed as the reporting entity in consolidation? Why or why not?
10. Under the treasury stock method, why is it misleading to treat all of the parent's common shares held by a partially owned subsidiary as not outstanding when computing consolidated earnings per share?

## Discussion Cases

| DC 11-1 | **Reciprocal Holdings: Selection of Accounting Method** |

During 19X1, Piper Company acquired 80% of Sonoma Company's outstanding common stock, and Sonoma acquired 10% of Piper's outstanding common stock. Piper's top management has indicated to its controller that Sonoma's minority interest shareholders will probably not share in Piper's earnings for many years to come because Piper does not expect to pay any dividends on its common stock inasmuch as it intends to retain earnings for growth.

**Required:**

Decide whether to use the treasury stock method or the traditional allocation method. How does this dividend policy influence your decision?

| DC 11-2 | **Reciprocal Holdings: Determining Dividends to Be Reported in the Consolidated Statement of Retained Earnings—Treasury Stock Method** |

Perk Company has an 80%-owned subsidiary that in turn owns 10% of the parent company's outstanding common stock. Perk uses the treasury stock method to determine consolidated net income. It declared and paid cash dividends of $100,000 on its outstanding common stock during 19X1, $10,000 of which went to its subsidiary. Perk's controller is uncertain whether the consolidated statement of retained earnings for 19X1 should show dividends declared of $100,000, $90,000, or $92,000.

**Required:**

How would you advise the controller?

| DC 11-3 | **Reciprocal Holdings: Theory** |

Pey Company has a partially owned subsidiary that recently acquired some of Pey's outstanding common stock. You are the staff accountant in charge of preparing the consolidated financial statements for the first year after the reciprocal investment was established. Pey's controller has indicated that you should calculate the minority interest deduction by using the traditional allocation method.

**Required:**

How would you respond to this instruction?

| DC 11-4 | **Reciprocal Holdings: Ramifications of Dual Intercorporate Control** |

Proofer Company owns 100% of Storm Company's outstanding common stock. Storm owns 100% of Proofer's outstanding common stock.

**Required:**

What are the ramifications of such intercorporate holdings?

# Exercises

### Indirect Vertical Holdings: Cost Equals Book Value of Net Assets

Pargo Company owns 90% of Solomon Company's outstanding common stock, and Solomon Company owns 80% of the outstanding common stock of Tsar Company. Each company earned $100,000 during 19X1 from its own operations, exclusive of earnings on its investment in its subsidiary. (Assume there was no cost in excess of or below book value to amortize.)

**Required:**

1. Determine Pargo's consolidated net income for 19X1 through successive application of the equity method of accounting.
2. Determine the minority interest deduction in Pargo's consolidated income statement for 19X1.
3. Indicate the sequence of the consolidation process.

### Indirect Vertical Holdings: Cost Equals Book Value of Net Assets

On January 1, 19X1, Delta Company acquired 80% of the outstanding common stock of Echo Company. On January 1, 19X2, Echo Company acquired 80% of the outstanding common stock of Fox Company. On January 1, 19X3, Pratt Company acquired 75% of the outstanding common stock of Delta Company. Each company's earnings for 19X3 (exclusive of earnings on investments in affiliates) are as follows:

| | |
|---|---:|
| Pratt Company | $400,000 |
| Delta Company | 300,000 |
| Echo Company | 200,000 |
| Fox Company | 100,000 |

Each company declared cash dividends on its common stock of $10,000 during 19X1, 19X2, and 19X3. (Assume there was no cost in excess of or below book value to amortize.)

**Required:**

1. Determine the net income of Pratt Company and its subsidiaries for 19X3 through successive application of the equity method of accounting.
2. Determine the total minority interest deduction shown in Pratt's consolidated income statement for 19X3.
3. Indicate the sequence of the consolidation process.

## Indirect Horizontal Holdings: Cost Equals Book Value of Net Assets

On January 1, 19X1, Pulse Company acquired 80% of Sound Company's outstanding common stock and 70% of Tape Company's outstanding common stock. On July 1, 19X1, Sound acquired 10% of Tape's outstanding common stock. (Assume all investments were made at a cost equal to the applicable share of net assets at book value.) For 19X2, the following amounts were reported:

| | Income from Own Operations (exclusive of earnings on investments in affiliates) | Dividends Declared |
|---|---|---|
| Pulse Company . . . . . . . . . . . . . . | $300,000 | $50,000 |
| Sound Company. . . . . . . . . . . . . . | 100,000 | 20,000 |
| Tape Company . . . . . . . . . . . . . . | 50,000 | 10,000 |

### Required:
1. Determine the consolidated net income of Pulse Company and its subsidiaries for 19X2 through successive application of the equity method of accounting.
2. Determine the total minority interest deduction shown in Pulse's consolidated income statement for 19X2.
3. Indicate the sequence of the consolidation process.

## Several Indirect Horizontal Holdings: Cost Equals Book Value of Net Assets

Potter Company, a nonoperating holding company, is a parent of the following subsidiaries with the indicated ownership percentages:

| Subsidiary Company | Ownership Percentage |
|---|---|
| B | 90 |
| C | 80 |
| D | 70 |
| E | 60 |

In addition, B Company owns 10% of the outstanding common stock of C Company, D Company, and E Company; D Company owns 20% of the outstanding common stock of E Company. (Assume all investments were made at a cost equal to the applicable share of net assets at book value.)

Each company's net income from its own operations (exclusive of earnings on investments in affiliates) is as follows for 19X1:

| | |
|---|---|
| Potter Company. . . . . . . . . . . . . . . . . . . . . . . . . . . . . . . . . . . . . . . . . . . . . . . . . . | $   –0– |
| B Company . . . . . . . . . . . . . . . . . . . . . . . . . . . . . . . . . . . . . . . . . . . . . . . . . . . . . . . . | 10,000,000 |
| C Company . . . . . . . . . . . . . . . . . . . . . . . . . . . . . . . . . . . . . . . . . . . . . . . . . . . . . . . . | 1,000,000 |
| D Company . . . . . . . . . . . . . . . . . . . . . . . . . . . . . . . . . . . . . . . . . . . . . . . . . . . . . . . . | 100,000 |
| E Company . . . . . . . . . . . . . . . . . . . . . . . . . . . . . . . . . . . . . . . . . . . . . . . . . . . . . . . . | 10,000 |

E 11-3

E 11-4

**Required:**

1. Determine Potter Company's 19X1 net income through successive application of the equity method of accounting.
2. Determine the total minority interest deduction shown in Potter's consolidated income statement for 19X1.
3. Indicate the sequence of the consolidated process.

---

## Reciprocal Holdings: Parent's Cost Equals Book Value of Net Assets

Premier Company owns 80% of the outstanding common stock of Smidgeon Company, which in turn owns 10% of the outstanding common stock of Premier. During 19X1, Premier earned $500,000 from its own operations, exclusive of earnings on its investment in Smidgeon. (Assume the cost of the parent company's investment equals its share of the net assets at book value.) Smidgeon earned $100,000 from its own separate operations in 19X1. Neither company declared dividends during 19X1.

**Required:**

1. Compute the consolidated net income and the minority interest deduction for 19X1 under the treasury stock method.
2. Compute the amount of the combined earnings that accrues to the controlling interests and the minority interests for 19X1 under the traditional allocation method.

## Problems

## Indirect Vertical Holdings: Cost Exceeds Book Value of Net Assets

On January 1, 19X1, Posit Company acquired 80% of Syncron Company's outstanding common stock at a cost of $40,000 in excess of its share of net assets at book value. Assume that this excess is allocable to goodwill, which has a 10-year life.

On January 1, 19X2, Syncron Company acquired 60% of Techna Company's outstanding common stock at a cost of $20,000 in excess of its share of net assets at book value. Assume that this excess is allocable to goodwill, which has a 10-year life.

For 19X2, the companies reported the following:

| | Income from Own Operations (exclusive of earnings and amortization on investments in affiliates) | Dividends Declared |
|---|---|---|
| Posit Company | $500,000 | $100,000 |
| Syncron Company | 100,000 | 50,000 |
| Techna Company | 20,000 | 10,000 |

**Required:**
1. Determine the consolidated net income of Posit Company and its subsidiaries for 19X2 through successive application of the equity method of accounting.
2. Determine the total minority interest deduction shown in Posit's consolidated income statement for 19X2.
3. Indicate the sequence of the consolidation process.

## Indirect Horizontal Holdings: Cost Exceeds Book Value of Net Assets

**P 11-2**

On January 1, 19X1, Packager Company acquired 80% of Shipper Company's outstanding common stock at a cost of $100,000 in excess of its share of net assets at book value. Assume that this excess is allocable to goodwill, which has an estimated 20-year life.

On January 1, 19X2, Packager acquired 65% of Tender Company's outstanding common stock at a cost of $20,000 in excess of its share of net assets at book value. Assume that this excess is allocable to goodwill, which has an estimated 10-year life.

On January 1, 19X3, Shipper acquired 20% of Tender's outstanding common stock at a cost of $5,000 in excess of its share of net assets at book value. Assume that this excess is allocable to goodwill, which has an estimated 10-year life.

Each company reported the following amounts during 19X3:

|  | Income from Own Operations (excluding income and amortization on investments in affiliates) | Dividends Declared |
|---|---|---|
| Packager Company . . . . . . . . . . . | $1,000,000 | $500,000 |
| Shipper Company . . . . . . . . . . . . | 100,000 | 50,000 |
| Tender Company . . . . . . . . . . . . | 10,000 | 5,000 |

**Required:**
1. Determine the amount of consolidated net income for Packager Company and its subsidiaries for 19X3 through successive application of the equity method of accounting.
2. Determine the total minority interest deduction shown in Packager's consolidated income statement for 19X3.
3. Indicate the sequence of the consolidation process.

## Indirect Horizontal Holdings: Cost Exceeds Book Value of Net Assets

**P 11-3**

On January 1, 19X1, Polar Bank acquired 80% of the outstanding common stock of Solar Savings and 70% of the outstanding common stock of Tanner Trust. On January 2, 19X1, Solar acquired 20% of Tanner's outstanding common stock. The analysis of the investment accounts by the components of the major conceptual elements for each acquisition at the acquisition date is as follows:

| | Polar's Investment[a] | | Solar's Investment |
|---|---|---|---|
| | Solar | Tanner | Tanner |
| Book value element: | | | |
| Common stock . . . . . . . . . . . . . . . . . . . . . . . | $ 16,000 | $ 7,000 | $ 2,000 |
| Additional paid-in capital . . . . . . . . . . . . . . | 144,000 | 63,000 | 18,000 |
| Retained earnings . . . . . . . . . . . . . . . . . . . | 40,000 | 21,000 | 6,000 |
| Current value over book value element: | | | |
| Land . . . . . . . . . . . . . . . . . . . . . . . . . . . . . . | 20,000 | 7,000 | 4,000 |
| Goodwill element . . . . . . . . . . . . . . . . . . . . . . | 40,000 | 10,000 | 5,000 |
| Total Cost . . . . . . . . . . . . . . . . . . . . . . . | $260,000 | $108,000 | $35,000 |

[a]Note that the conceptual analysis has *not* been modified to include the minority interest.

Assume goodwill has a five-year life from the purchase date. Data for 19X1 for each company are as follows:

| | Income from Own Operations (exclusive of earnings and amortization on investments in affiliates) | Quarterly Dividends Declared |
|---|---|---|
| Polar . . . . . . . . . . . . . . . . . . . . . . | $600,000 | $100,000 |
| Solar . . . . . . . . . . . . . . . . . . . . . . | 80,000 | 30,000 |
| Tanner . . . . . . . . . . . . . . . . . . . . . | 40,000 | 10,000 |

Assume earnings for each company occurred evenly during the year.

### Required:

1. Calculate the amount of Polar's consolidated net income for 19X1 through successive application of the equity method of accounting.
2. Determine the minority interest deduction shown in Polar's consolidated income statement for 19X1.
3. Indicate the sequence of the consolidation process.

## Reciprocal Holdings: Parent's Cost Exceeds Book Value of Net Assets

Picolo Company owns 90% of Sayers Company's outstanding common stock. In turn, Sayers owns 10% of Picolo's outstanding common stock. Data for each company for 19X1 are as follows:

| | Income from Own Operations (exclusive of earnings on investments in affiliates) | Dividends Declared |
|---|---|---|
| Picolo Company . . . . . . . . . . . . . . | $800,000 | $200,000 |
| Sayers Company . . . . . . . . . . . . . | 100,000 | 30,000 |

In addition, Picolo had $12,000 amortization of cost in excess of book value during 19X1, which is not reflected in its separate earnings of $800,000.

**Required:**

1. Calculate the consolidated net income and the minority interest deduction for 19X1 using the treasury stock method.
2. Calculate the amount of combined earnings that accrues to the controlling interests and the minority interests under the traditional allocation method.

### CHALLENGER Reciprocal Holdings: Parent's Cost Exceeds Book Value; Preparing Consolidated Statement of Retained Earnings in Year Subsequent to Acquisition

Perigee Company acquired 60% of Syzygy Company's outstanding common stock on January 1, 19X1. On January 2, 19X1, Syzygy acquired 10% of Perigee's outstanding common stock. Data for each company for 19X1 are as follows:

|  | Perigee Company | Syzygy Company |
|---|---|---|
| Retained earnings, January 1, 19X1 . . . . . . . . . . . . . | $900,000 | $300,000 |
| Income from own operations for 19X1, exclusive of earnings on investments in affiliates and amortization of cost in excess of book value . . . . | 400,000 | 100,000 |
| Amortization of cost in excess of book value. . . . . . | 10,000 | |
| Dividends declared in 19X1. . . . . . . . . . . . . . . . . . . . | 150,000 | 30,000 |
| Common shares outstanding . . . . . . . . . . . . . . . . . | 100,000 | 20,000 |

**Required:**

1. Calculate the consolidated net income and the minority interest deduction for 19X1 under the treasury stock method.
2. Prepare a consolidated statement of retained earnings for 19X1 assuming that the parent uses the treasury stock method.
3. Calculate the amount of combined earnings that accrues to the controlling interests and the minority interests for 19X1 under the traditional allocation method.
4. Prepare a consolidated statement of retained earnings for 19X1 assuming the parent uses the traditional allocation method.

### Indirect Vertical Holdings: Intercompany Inventory Profit in Ending Inventory from Upstream Sale

Peter Company acquired 75% of Steven Company's outstanding common stock on January 1, 19X1, and Steven acquired 80% of Theo Company's outstanding common stock on January 1, 19X2. The cost of these acquisitions was at the applicable percentage of net assets at book value.

During 19X2, each company reported $100,000 of income (after income taxes) from its own operations, exclusive of earnings on investments in affiliates. At December 31, 19X2, Steven's ending inventory included merchandise it had acquired from Theo at a cost of $50,000. Theo's cost was $30,000.

**Required:**

1. Determine the consolidated net income that Steven Company reports to its parent company for 19X2 through successive application of the equity method of accounting.
2. Determine the consolidated net income that Peter reports to its stockholders for 19X2 through successive application of the equity method of accounting.
3. Determine the total minority interest deduction for 19X2.

### SOLUTIONS TO SELF-STUDY QUESTIONS

1. e    4. b
2. a    5. b
3. c    6. d

# 12

# INCOME TAXES, EARNINGS PER SHARE, AND CONSOLIDATED STATEMENT OF CASH FLOWS

## *TOPIC OUTLINE*

**INCOME TAXES**

An Overview

Recognizing Deferred Taxes at the Combination Date

Recording Income Taxes on Earnings of Subsidiaries

Tax Treatment of Parent's Amortization of Cost above or below Its Interest in Subsidiary's Net Assets at Book Value

Calculating Consolidated Income Tax Expense

**EARNINGS PER SHARE**

An Overview

Requirements of *APB Opinion No. 15*

The Basic Approach

Comprehensive Illustration

**CONSOLIDATED STATEMENT OF CASH FLOWS**

The Two Approaches

Areas Requiring Special Consideration

# INCOME TAXES

## AN OVERVIEW

### Purchase Business Combination

For purchase business combinations (as distinct from pooling of interests business combinations), the issue is whether or not deferred taxes should be recorded at the combination date for differences between the assigned values of assets and liabilities of the acquired business and the tax basis of those assets and liabilities. *FASB Statement No. 96* amended paragraphs 87 to 89 of *Accounting Principles Board Opinion No. 16,* such that deferred income taxes must be recorded for these differences.

### Earnings of Subsidiaries

For income tax reporting purposes, investor companies must pay income taxes on dividends *received* from investee companies. (Some exceptions to this requirement are discussed later in the chapter.) In this respect, the income tax rules are on the cash basis. The financial reporting issue is determining whether investor companies should record such income taxes in their books on the cash basis (consistent with income tax reporting) or on the accrual basis, whereby income taxes on an investor's share of an investee's net income are recorded in the year the investee reports its earnings. *APB Opinion No. 23,* "Accounting for Income Taxes—Special Areas," is the governing pronouncement in this area, and it requires income taxes to be recorded on the accrual basis. (*FASB Statement No. 96* did not supersede this pronouncement as it did *APB Opinion No. 11.*)

## RECOGNIZING DEFERRED TAXES AT THE COMBINATION DATE

To properly account for income taxes on the accrual basis, *FASB Statement No. 96* takes the position that the tax consequences of an event must be recognized in the same period in which the event is recognized in the financial statements. For purchase business combinations, differences between the assigned values of assets and liabilities and the tax bases of those assets and liabilities will result in taxable or tax deductible amounts when the asset or liability in the financial statements is later recovered or settled at its reported amount. Under *FASB Statement No. 96,* a deferred tax liability or asset is to be recognized for such differences. (Goodwill and unextinguished bargain purchase elements are excluded from this requirement.)

## Taxable versus Nontaxable Purchase Business Combinations

Recall from Chapter 2 that most purchase business combinations are taxable combinations for tax reporting purposes; only a minor percentage are nontaxable (tax-deferred). Differences between the assigned values of assets and liabilities and the tax bases of those assets and liabilities nearly always exist in nontaxable purchase business combinations. For taxable purchase business combinations, however, such differences are the exception rather than the rule. This is because the acquiring entity assigns its purchase price to the assets and liabilities of the target company for both financial reporting and tax reporting purposes. (For this assignment to be done for tax purposes when common stock is acquired, the parent would have to make an election under Section 338 of the Internal Revenue Code, as explained on page 545, to step up the bases of the subsidiary's assets based on the purchase price.) The following section shows how deferred taxes are recognized in nontaxable purchase business combinations.

## Nontaxable Purchase Business Combinations: The Acquired Business Has No Deferred Tax Accounts at the Combination Date

Assume that P Company and S Company's stockholders entered into a nontaxable purchase business combination on January 1, 19X1. Other assumptions follow:

1. P Company issued 1,000 shares of its $1 par value common stock, which has a market value of $90,000.
2. The book value of S Company's assets is $250,000, and the book value of its liabilities is $190,000. Thus the book value of the net assets is $60,000.
3. The book values of S Company's assets and liabilities are equal to their tax bases. Thus no deferred tax liability or asset accounts exist on S Company's books at the combination date.
4. S Company's assets have a current value of $20,000 in excess of their book values.
5. The enacted income tax rate for future years is 40%. (Here and in some other aspects of dealing with income taxes, we use an assumed tax rate of 40% for simplicity, instead of the statutory rate of 34%.)

Because of the temporary difference of $20,000 between the assigned values of the assets and their tax bases, a deferred tax liability of $8,000 ($20,000 × 40%) must be recognized in recording the business combination. Illustration 12-1 presents the entries that would be made assuming that the assets are acquired (part 1) and the common stock is acquired (part 2). The analysis of the investment by its major conceptual elements is also shown for the latter situation.

## ■ ILLUSTRATION 12-1
### Nontaxable Purchase Business Combination: The Acquired Business Has No Deferred Tax Accounts at the Combination Date

**1. Acquisition of Assets**

| | | |
|---|---:|---:|
| Assets ($250,000 + $20,000) . . . . . . . . . . . . . . . . . . . . . . | 270,000 | |
|     Liabilities. . . . . . . . . . . . . . . . . . . . . . . . . . . . . . . | | 190,000 |
|     Deferred Tax Liability . . . . . . . . . . . . . . . . . . . . . . | | 8,000 |
|     Common Stock (1,000 shares × $1). . . . . . . . . . . | | 1,000 |
|     Additional Paid-in Capital. . . . . . . . . . . . . . . . . . | | 89,000 |
| Goodwill (residual amount) . . . . . . . . . . . . . . . . . . . . . | 18,000 | |

**2. Acquisition of Common Stock**

| | | |
|---|---:|---:|
| Investment in Subsidiary . . . . . . . . . . . . . . . . . . . . . . . | 90,000 | |
|     Common Stock (1,000 shares × $1). . . . . . . . . . . | | 1,000 |
|     Additional Paid-in Capital. . . . . . . . . . . . . . . . . . | | 89,000 |

Conceptual Analysis of Investment Account by Major Conceptual Elements:

| Total Cost | = | Book Value Element | + | Various Assets | + | Deferred Tax Liability | + | Goodwill Element |
|---|---|---|---|---|---|---|---|---|
| | | | | Current Value over (under) Book Value Element | | | | |
| $90,000 | | $60,000 | | $20,000 | | $(8,000) | | $18,000 |

## Nontaxable Purchase Business Combinations: The Acquired Business Has a Deferred Tax Liability at the Combination Date

Based on the facts in the preceding illustration, let us assume that: (1) the acquired business has used accelerated depreciation for income tax reporting purposes; and (2) the acquired business has a $4,000 deferred tax liability on its books at the combination date as a result of having deducted $10,000 more depreciation expense for tax purposes than for financial reporting purposes. Accordingly, there is a $30,000 difference between the assigned values and the tax bases of the assets. Thus, a $12,000 deferred tax liability needs to be recognized at the combination date ($30,000 × 40%). However, because of the deferred tax situation, the target company would have $4,000 of additional assets in addition to the deferred tax liability of $4,000. (S Company retained $4,000 cash that otherwise would have been remitted to the government.) If assets are acquired, the entry by P Company is:

| | | |
|---|---:|---:|
| Assets ($254,000 + $20,000) . . . . . . . . . . . . . . . . . | 274,000 | |
|     Liabilities . . . . . . . . . . . . . . . . . . . . . . . . . . . . . | | 190,000 |
|     Deferred Tax Liability . . . . . . . . . . . . . . . . . . | | 12,000 |

| | | |
|---|---|---|
| Common Stock (1,000 shares × $1)...... | | 1,000 |
| Additional Paid-in Capital............... | | 89,000 |
| Goodwill (residual amount)................. | 18,000 | |

If common stock is acquired, the entry is the same as shown in Illustration 12-1, inasmuch as S Company has a $4,000 deferred tax liability recorded on its books.

# RECORDING INCOME TAXES ON EARNINGS OF SUBSIDIARIES

## Consolidated Income Tax Return Situations

A parent company and its **domestic** subsidiaries may file a consolidated federal income tax return if the parent owns directly or indirectly at least 80% of both the voting power of all classes of stock of each subsidiary and the value of all classes of stock of each subsidiary included in the consolidated return. (At least one subsidiary must be at least 80% directly owned by the parent.)[1] Filing a consolidated income tax return relieves each subsidiary of the responsibility of filing a separate federal income tax return.

**Advantages of Consolidated Returns.**  Preparing a consolidated federal tax return is similar to preparing a consolidated income statement for financial reporting purposes. Often only an appropriate adjustment is needed to the consolidated income statement that was prepared for financial reporting purposes to arrive at consolidated taxable income. The major advantages are as follows:

1. **Offsetting losses against profits.** Losses of companies within the consolidated group that do not generate profits can offset profits of the other members of the consolidated group. (The same holds true for capital losses and capital gains.)
2. **Deferral of income on intercompany transactions.** Intercompany profits recorded on the sale of assets between entities are deferred until such assets are either sold (for inventory transfers) or depreciation occurs (for depreciable asset transfers).
3. **Elimination of tax on intercompany dividends.** Intercompany dividends are not taxable to the parent at all.
4. **Use of excess foreign tax credits.** The group may be able to use a member's excess foreign tax credit. (Foreign tax credits are discussed later.)

**Disadvantages of Consolidated Returns.**  Some of the disadvantages of consolidated returns are:

[1]The detailed requirements are set forth in the U.S. Internal Revenue Code of 1954, Sec. 1504(a).

1. Deferral of losses on intercompany transactions.
2. The greater risk of the alternative minimum tax.

**Implications of Consolidated Tax Returns for Financial Reporting.** The obvious implication for financial reporting purposes of a consolidated income tax return is that no income taxes need to be recorded by a parent with respect to the subsidiary's **net income.** This holds true whether or not the subsidiary actually makes dividend payments to the parent. Thus, from a consolidated viewpoint, these situations involve no accounting issues. From a separate-company viewpoint, the total consolidated income tax expense must be allocated among the companies included in the consolidated income tax return. For subsidiaries included in consolidated tax returns that issue separate financial statements, *FASB Statement No. 96* requires the following disclosures:

a. The amount of current and deferred tax expense for each statement of earnings presented and the amount of any tax-related balances due to or from affiliates as of the date of each statement of financial position presented.

b. The principal provisions of the method by which the consolidated amount of current and deferred tax expenses is allocated to members of the group and the nature and effect of any changes in that method (and in determining related balances to or from affiliates) during the years for which the disclosures in (a) above are presented.[2]

The following section focuses on situations in which subsidiaries file separate federal income tax returns. These situations involve accounting issues from a consolidated viewpoint.

## Separate Income Tax Returns

**The Accounting Issue.** Subsidiaries that file separate federal income tax returns record the income taxes they will pay individually. Parent companies include in their tax return only **dividends received** from their subsidiaries, not their full share of subsidiary earnings. Such dividends are taxable to the parent. However, an **80% dividends received deduction** is allowed; thus, only 20% of the dividends received is taxed. The accounting issue is determining if and when income taxes should be recorded by the parent on the subsidiary's **net income** for financial reporting purposes. There are two obvious possibilities:

1. Under the **cash basis,** income taxes are recorded in **the year in which the parent receives the dividends.** Thus, for a wholly owned domestic

---

[2]*FASB Statement No. 96*, par. 30.

subsidiary with net income of $300,000 and paying dividends of $100,000 in a given year, the parent would record income taxes of $8,000, assuming a 40% income tax rate and the application of the 80% dividends received deduction [.40(1 − .80) × $100,000]. No income taxes would be recorded on the undistributed earnings of $200,000. (Of course, under the equity method of accounting, the parent would record $300,000 earnings.)

2. Under the **accrual basis,** income taxes are recorded in **the year in which the subsidiary reports income,** rather than the year in which it pays dividends. Timing differences result between financial reporting and tax reporting when current earnings are not distributed. Compared with the preceding example using the cash basis, the parent would record income taxes of $24,000 under the accrual approach [.40(1 − .80) × $300,000]. (Although the 80% dividends received deduction is an income tax provision applicable only to dividends actually received, we apply the concept to the full $300,000 of earnings in computing income tax expense for financial reporting purposes, not just to the $100,000 of dividends actually received. Hereafter, for financial reporting purposes, we refer to the 80% dividends received deduction as the 80% **dividend exclusion** to signify that the 80% is not applied solely to dividends received.)

To be consistent with the accrual basis of accounting, the apparent solution would have the parent record any required federal income taxes in the period in which the subsidiary reports the income. This is the general requirement of *APB Opinion No. 23*, "Accounting for Income Taxes— Special Areas." However, *APB Opinion No. 23* allows exceptions to this requirement, whereby the parent does not have to provide income taxes on earnings of its subsidiaries when certain conditions are met.

**The Tax-free Liquidation Condition.** Section 332 of the Internal Revenue Code allows a subsidiary to remit its undistributed earnings to its parent in a tax-free liquidation, providing certain conditions are met. Under *APB Opinion No. 23*, a parent need not provide income taxes on such earnings if the earnings could be remitted tax-free.

**The Invested Indefinitely Condition.** If evidence shows that **some** or **all** of the undistributed subsidiary earnings have been or will be invested indefinitely, parent companies do not have to provide income taxes on their share of their subsidiaries' **undistributed earnings.** Appropriate income taxes must always be recorded on subsidiary earnings that are distributed or are expected to be distributed. (Calculations are shown later in the chapter.) Note that *indefinitely* does not mean permanently. In other words, parent companies are not required to invest the undistributed earnings of their subsidiaries forever—only for the foreseeable future. Two examples of evidence required to satisfy this condition are **experience** and **future programs of operations.**

In effect, the parent records income taxes only to the extent that their payment is reasonably expected. Thus, in addition to the extreme cases of either 100% reinvestment on an indefinite basis, or no intention to reinvest any earnings on an indefinite basis, possible hybrid situations exist in which a percentage of current earnings has been or is expected to be distributed as dividends and the remainder is reinvested indefinitely. With respect to changing circumstances, the pronouncement states:

[1] If circumstances change and it becomes apparent that some or all of the undistributed earnings of a subsidiary will be remitted in the foreseeable future but income taxes have not been recognized by the parent company, it should accrue as an expense of the current-period income taxes attributable to that remittance; income tax expense for such remittance should not be accounted for as an extraordinary item.

[2] If it becomes apparent that some or all of the undistributed earnings of a subsidiary on which income taxes have been accrued will not be remitted in the foreseeable future, the parent company should adjust income tax expense of the current period; such adjustment of income tax expense should not be accounted for as an extraordinary item.[3]

Situation 1 typically occurs when a parent company anticipates either: (a) a significant decrease in the direct exchange rate of the currency of the country in which its subsidiary is located (whether from an expected weakening of the foreign currency or a strengthening of the dollar); or (b) the foreign government's imposition of currency transfer restrictions. Situation 2 typically occurs during a continuing increase in the direct exchange rate of the currency of the country in which the subsidiary is located or when the foreign government encourages the expansion of existing operations by granting inducements.

**Rationale of *APB Opinion No. 23*.** The rationale of *APB Opinion No. 23* is that a subsidiary may not distribute all of its earnings because funds are needed to finance internal growth. This situation is most common for newly established foreign subsidiaries, when parent companies desire to limit the amount of equity capital the subsidiary obtains directly from the parent. Thus, the parent views all or a large portion of the subsidiary's retained earnings as *permanent capital.* From this viewpoint, no U.S.

---

3*APB Opinion No. 23*, par. 12.

income taxes would ever be paid on the amount deemed permanent capital, because it would never be distributed as dividends. Consequently, the parent would not record any income taxes on that portion of a subsidiary's earnings that is invested in the subsidiary indefinitely.

### Domestic versus Foreign Subsidiaries.
When income taxes are to be recorded on earnings of subsidiaries, the calculation of income taxes is different for a domestic subsidiary than for a foreign subsidiary. The following sections illustrate these separate calculations.

### Domestic Subsidiaries: Computing and Recording Income Taxes.
Income taxes recorded on the parent's equity in a domestic subsidiary's net income are calculated using the 80% dividend exclusion. For a 90%-owned subsidiary with net income of $100,000, the calculation is as follows:

| | |
|---|---:|
| Net income of subsidiary | $100,000 |
| Parent's ownership percentage | 90% |
| Parent's equity in earnings of subsidiary | $ 90,000 |
| Less—Dividend exclusion @ 80% | 72,000 |
| Net income subject to taxation | $ 18,000 |
| Assumed income tax rate | 40% |
| Income taxes | $ 7,200 |

To the extent that all of the current earnings are not distributed in the current year, timing differences result, and the Deferred Tax Liability account must be credited for the income taxes relating to the undistributed current earnings. Assuming the subsidiary paid total dividends of $25,000 (25% of its net income) during the year, the parent company's entries with respect to the subsidiary's operations for the year are as follows:

1. To record equity in earnings of subsidiary:

| | | |
|---|---:|---:|
| Investment in Subsidiary | 90,000 | |
| Equity in Net Income of Subsidiary | | 90,000 |
| (90% of $100,000) | | |

2. To record dividend received from subsidiary:

| | | |
|---|---:|---:|
| Cash | 22,500 | |
| Investment in Subsidiary | | 22,500 |
| (90% of $25,000) | | |

3. To record income tax expense on equity in earnings of subsidiary:

| Income Tax Expense | 7,200 | |
|---|---|---|
| Income Taxes Currently Payable | | |
| [($22,500 ÷ $90,000) × $7,200] | | 1,800 |
| Deferred Tax Liability | | |
| [($67,500 ÷ $90,000) × $7,200] | | 5,400 |

**An Overview of Tax Rules for Foreign Subsidiaries.** A foreign subsidiary files an income tax return in the country in which it is domiciled (that is, where incorporated). Dividends paid to a U.S. parent are not eligible for the 80% dividends received deduction. However, the parent pays U.S. federal income taxes on these dividends only if the subsidiary's foreign income tax credits cannot offset amounts otherwise payable to the U.S. government. For foreign subsidiaries, the income taxes recorded on the parent's equity in the subsidiary's net income are calculated as follows:

1. The subsidiary's net income is irrelevant; instead, the subsidiary's pretax income is treated as though it had been earned in the United States.
2. U.S. income taxes are calculated on this foreign pretax income using regular income tax rates.
3. Foreign tax credits are subtracted from the taxes calculated in step 2. If a positive balance exists, then that amount of U.S. income tax is payable. If a zero or negative balance exists, then no U.S. income tax is payable. There are two kinds of foreign tax credits:
   a. Foreign income taxes.
   b. Dividend withholding taxes. These taxes are withheld by the foreign government when a dividend is remitted. (One of the avowed purposes of this tax is to collect taxes that otherwise would have been collected at the individual taxpayer level had the corporation been owned by local citizens.)

A table of statutory income tax rates for several countries appears in Illustration 12-2.

In addition to any U.S. income taxes, the parent must record on its books the dividend withholding tax payable. **The dividend withholding tax is a tax to the recipient; accordingly, it is never recorded as an expense on the foreign subsidiary's books.**

**Foreign Subsidiaries: Computing and Recording Income Taxes.** The following examples show how to calculate and record income taxes on earnings of foreign subsidiaries:

| | Country A | Country B |
|---|---|---|
| Assumed foreign income tax rate | 20% | 50% |
| Assumed foreign dividend withholding rate | 10% | 15% |

|  | Country A | Country B |
|---|---|---|
| Foreign subsidiary's pretax income . . . . . . . | $200,000 | $200,000 |
| Foreign income tax expense . . . . . . . . . . . . . | (40,000) | (100,000) |
| Foreign subsidiary's net income. . . . . . . . . . . | $160,000 | $100,000 |
| U.S. income taxes at assumed rate of 34% on pretax income . . . . . . . . . . . . . . . . . . . . . . | $ 68,000 | $ 68,000 |
| Less foreign tax credits: |  |  |
| Foreign income taxes (as above) . . . . . . . . . | (40,000) | (100,000) |
| Dividend withholding taxes (10% and 15%, respectively, of subsidiary's net income) | (16,000) | (15,000) |
| U.S. income taxes recorded by the parent company (assuming 100% ownership). . | $ 12,000 | $ –0– |

Timing differences result when all current earnings are not distributed in the current year, and the Deferred Tax Liability account must be credited for taxes on the undistributed current earnings. Assuming each subsidiary paid $20,000 total dividends during the year (one-eighth

■ **ILLUSTRATION 12-2**
**Examples of Foreign Income Tax Rates**

|  | Statutory Income Tax Rate[a] (percent) | Dividend Withholding Tax Rate[b] (percent) |
|---|---|---|
| Brazil | 25–40 | 25 |
| Canada |  |  |
| Manufacturing | 41 | 10–15 |
| Other | 47 | 10–15 |
| France | 42 | 5 |
| Ireland (Republic of) |  |  |
| Manufacturing | 10 | None |
| Other | 50 | None |
| Italy | 36 | 5 |
| Japan | 46–56 | 10–15 |
| Mexico | 35 | 50 |
| Switzerland | 23–36 | 5–15 |
| United Kingdom | 27–35 | 5 |
| United States | 15–34 | 15–30 |
| Venezuela | 50 | 15 |
| West Germany | 36–56 | 15 |

[a]For countries that have a range of income tax rates indicated, the exact rate is a function of one or more of the following factors: amount of income, amount of capitalization, whether earnings are distributed or retained, type of business, and whether the corporation is a resident or nonresident company.
[b]For foreign countries, the withholding tax rate indicated is that existing under tax treaties with the United States.
Source: Latest available published statutory rates.

and one-fifth of their respective net incomes), the parent's entries with respect to each subsidiary's operations for the year are as follows:

1. To record equity in earnings of subsidiary:

|  | Country A | | Country B | |
|---|---|---|---|---|
| Investment in Subsidiary... | 160,000 | | 100,000 | |
| Equity in Net Income of Subsidiary......... | | 160,000 | | 100,000 |
| (100% of $160,000 and $100,000, respectively.) | | | | |

2. To record the dividend withholding tax:

|  | Country A | | Country B | |
|---|---|---|---|---|
| Income Tax Expense........ | 16,000 | | 15,000 | |
| Income Taxes Payable— Foreign ($\frac{1}{8}$ and $\frac{1}{5}$, respectively)........... | | 2,000 | | 3,000 |
| Deferred Tax Liability— Foreign ($\frac{7}{8}$ and $\frac{4}{5}$, respectively)........... | | 14,000 | | 12,000 |
| (100% of $16,000 and $15,000, respectively.) | | | | |

3. To record dividend received from subsidiary:

|  | Country A | | Country B | |
|---|---|---|---|---|
| Cash...................... | 18,000 | | 17,000 | |
| Income Taxes Payable— Foreign .................... | 2,000 | | 3,000 | |
| Investment in Subsidiary............ | | 20,000 | | 20,000 |

Note: The debit to Income Taxes Payable—Foreign equals the taxes withheld at the time of remittance.

4. To record U.S. income taxes on equity in earnings of subsidiary:

|  | Country A | |
|---|---|---|
| Income Tax Expense........ | 12,000 | |
| Income Taxes Payable— U.S. .................... | | 1,500 |
| Deferred Tax Liability— U.S. .................... | | 10,500 |
| ($\frac{1}{8}$ and $\frac{7}{8}$, respectively.) | | |

The greater the foreign income tax and dividend withholding tax rates, the greater are the credits against the U.S. income taxes otherwise payable. The preceding examples assume no limitations on the credit amount allowable against these taxes. However, on a per-country and an overall basis, the Internal Revenue Code does limit the credit amount allowable against U.S. income taxes otherwise payable. The specific limitations are beyond the scope of this text, but students should be aware that they exist.

## TAX TREATMENT OF PARENT'S AMORTIZATION OF COST ABOVE OR BELOW ITS INTEREST IN SUBSIDIARY'S NET ASSETS AT BOOK VALUE

Chapters 4 and 5 illustrated the amortization procedures appropriate for that portion of a parent's cost that is in excess of or below its interest in the subsidiary's net assets at book value. (Recall that this occurs only under the non-push-down basis of accounting.) For income tax reporting purposes, the amortization of cost in excess of book value (which is recorded in the parent's general ledger) is not tax deductible. This holds true even though some amortization relates to depreciable, tangible assets. Likewise, when a parent's cost is below book value, the amortization (which is a credit to income in these situations) is not taxable.

However, under Section 338 of the Internal Revenue Code, an acquiring company in a taxable transaction may treat the acquisition of a target company's common stock as an asset purchase. If it does, the tax basis of the target company's assets is "stepped up" based on the purchase cost of the common stock of the target company, just as though the assets had been acquired instead of common stock. (In substance, this is nothing more than applying push-down accounting for tax reporting purposes.) From a consolidated viewpoint, the end result is as though the parent's cost in excess of book value were tax deductible. (Note that it is the *subsidiary* that receives greater depreciation and amortization deductions— not the parent. The parent's cost of the investment in the subsidiary becomes the tax basis of its common stock investment in the subsidiary.)

Section 338 also includes the following requirements:

- The subsidiary must be 80% owned. (The 80% ownership level must have been obtained within a 12-month period.)
- The election must be made within 75 days after obtaining 80% ownership of the target company's common stock.
- Amounts assigned to goodwill are not tax deductible.

It would be simpler for the parent to acquire the assets rather than the common stock. Recall from Chapter 2, however, that there may be certain nontax reasons for not doing so.

In practice, the Section 338 election is usually quite unattractive because the subsidiary must pay taxes currently on the amount of the step-up in basis. (Few companies, if any, would pay taxes now to obtain greater tax deductions at later dates.) However, the Section 338 is worth considering in certain limited situations, all of which are beyond the scope of this chapter.

## CALCULATING CONSOLIDATED INCOME TAX EXPENSE

Income tax expense was not shown as a separate line item in the consolidating statement worksheet illustrations in Chapters 4 to 11. For the sake of simplicity, the tax expense was assumed to be included in the Expenses account in the worksheets. However, this is not the customary practice. Illustration 12-3 shows a consolidating statement worksheet with the income tax expense included as a separate line item. At year-end there is $20,000 of unrealized intercompany profit, which the parent has deferred in its general ledger under the complete equity method. We arbitrarily showed the deferral of the $20,000 unrealized intercompany profit by using a Deferral of Profit account (the Noninvestment Account Adjustment Procedure in Module 2 in Chapter 7). If the Investment Account Adjustment Procedure in Module 1 in Chapter 7 were used instead, then the Equity in Net Income of S Company amount of $40,000 would be $20,000. Thus, regardless of which of the two complete equity method modules is used, the parent's income before taxes amount of $316,000 is the same. Illustration 12-4 shows the calculation of the income tax expense amounts in Illustration 12-3 for the parent and the subsidiary, the total of which is consolidated income tax expense.

**The Entry under the Partial Equity Method.** If the partial equity method had been used by the parent, its general ledger net income would have been $20,000 more. As a result, it would record an additional $8,000 of income tax expense (40% of $20,000) and $8,000 less prepaid income taxes. The parent's general ledger entry follows:

| | | |
|---|---|---|
| Income Tax Expense............................ | 122,000 | |
| Prepaid Income Taxes ($5,000 × 40%)......... | 2,000 | |
|     Income Taxes Currently Payable......... | | 118,400 |
|     Deferred Tax Liability (40% of $14,000). | | 5,600 |

In consolidation, the $20,000 of unrealized intercompany profit would be deferred. In addition, the related income tax effect of $8,000 (40% of $20,000) would also be deferred on the worksheet, as follows:

| | | |
|---|---|---|
| Prepaid Income Taxes ........................ | $8,000 | |
| Income Tax Expense..................... | | 8,000 |

# EARNINGS PER SHARE

## AN OVERVIEW

Fundamentally, consolidated earnings per share is simply consolidated net income (income accruing to the benefit of the parent's shareholders) divided by the average number of the parent company's common shares outstanding (adjusted for the parent's common equivalent shares and its other potentially dilutive securities, if any).

### ■ ILLUSTRATION 12-3
Consolidating Income Statement Showing Income Tax Expense (Wholly Owned Subsidiary); Unrealized Intercompany Profit Deferred in Parent's General Ledger under the Complete Equity Method

| **P COMPANY AND SUBSIDIARY (S COMPANY)** | | | | | |
|---|---|---|---|---|---|
| **Consolidating Income Statement for the Year Ended December 31, 19X5** | | | | | |
| | P Company | S Company | Eliminations Dr. | Eliminations Cr. | Consolidated |
| **Income Statement** | | | | | |
| Sales.................... | 900,000 | 600,000 | | | 1,500,000 |
| Cost of goods sold....... | (500,000) | (300,000) | 30,000(2) | 80,000(4) | (750,000) |
| Expenses............... | (204,000) | (200,000) | | | (404,000) |
| Intercompany Accounts: | | | | | |
| Equity in net income of | | | | | |
| S Company ......... | 40,000[a] | | 70,000(1) | 30,000(2) | –0– |
| Sales................. | 200,000 | | 200,000(4) | | –0– |
| Cost of goods sold..... | (100,000) | | | 100,000(4) | –0– |
| Deferral of profit ...... | (20,000) | | | 20,000(3) | –0– |
| Income before taxes ..... | 316,000 | 100,000 | 300,000 | 230,000 | 346,000 |
| Income tax expense ... | (114,000)[b] | (30,000)[b] | | | (144,000) |
| Net Income............. | 202,000 | 70,000 | 300,000 | 230,000 | 202,000 |

Explanation of entries:
(1) The primary elimination entry.
(2) The secondary elimination entry.
(3) The reversal of the parent's year-end general ledger unrealized intercompany profit entry (made under the complete equity method—Noninvestment Account Adjustment Procedure shown in Module 2 in Chapter 7).
(4) The intercompany sales elimination entry.

[a]Comprised of $70,000 of subsidiary's reported net income less $30,000 of amortization of cost in excess of book value. (In Illustration 12-4, we assume that $5,000 of this amortization pertains to goodwill.)
[b]See Illustration 12-4 for the calculation of this amount.

### ■ ILLUSTRATION 12-4
### Calculation of Consolidated Income Taxes

Assumptions:

1. S Company is a wholly owned domestic subsidiary of P Company. (Thus, the 80% dividend exclusion applies.)
2. Parent and subsidiary file separate income tax returns. (Thus, unrealized intercompany profit at year-end must still be reported for tax reporting purposes—this will result in a deferred tax asset.)
3. The parent makes a Section 338 election under the Internal Revenue Code, whereby the subsidiary steps up the bases of its assets based on the parent's purchase price. (Thus, the subsidiary has additional depreciation and amortization of $25,000; the other $5,000 of amortization of cost in excess of book value is goodwill, which is not deductible for tax reporting purposes resulting in a deferred tax asset.)
4. S Company declared no dividends during 19X5. However, the earnings are **not being reinvested indefinitely.** (Thus, income taxes will be recorded by the parent on the earnings of the subsidiary; however, these taxes are not payable currently because no dividends were declared and paid—resulting in a deferred tax liability.)
5. The enacted income tax rate for the current and future years is 40%.

|  | P Company | | S Company |
|---|---|---|---|
|  | Tax Reporting | Financial Reporting | Tax and Financial Reporting |
| Income before income taxes (from Illustration 12-3) . . . . . . . . | $316,000 | $316,000 | $100,000 |
| Dividend exclusion: |  |  |  |
| ($70,000 × 80%) . . . . . . . . . . . . |  | (56,000) |  |
| ($70,000 × 100%) . . . . . . . . . . | (70,000) |  |  |
| Amortization of cost in excess of book value: |  |  |  |
| Inventory and equipment . . | 25,000 | 25,000 | (25,000) |
| Goodwill . . . . . . . . . . . . . . . . | 5,000 |  |  |
| Unrealized intercompany profit at year-end . . . . . . . . . . . . | 20,000 |  |  |
| Taxable income . . . . . . . . . . . . . . . . . | $296,000 | $285,000 | $ 75,000 |
| Income tax rate assumed . . . . . . . | 40% | 40% | 40% |
| Income Tax Expense . . . . . . . . . . . . | $118,400 | $114,000 | $ 30,000 |

General ledger entries to record income taxes:

|  | P Company | | S Company |
|---|---|---|---|
| Income Tax Expense . . . . . . . . . . . . . . . . . . | 114,000 |  | 30,000 |
| Prepaid Income Taxes [40% of $25,000 ($5,000 for goodwill amortization and $20,000 for unrealized profit)] . . . . . . . . | 10,000 |  |  |
| Income Taxes Currently Payable . . . . . |  | 118,400 | 30,000 |
| Deferred Tax Liability [40% of $14,000 ($70,000 − $56,000)] . . . . . . |  | 5,600[a] |  |

[a]In the published balance sheet, the prepaid income taxes and the deferred tax liability would be netted and shown as one amount.

Most subsidiaries are wholly owned and do not have outstanding any potentially dilutive securities such as stock options, warrants, convertible bonds, and convertible preferred stocks. The parent's calculation of earnings per share on a consolidated basis presents no special problems in these cases. To make the calculations, the parent company merely uses the income it has recorded under the equity method of accounting with respect to the subsidiary's earnings, along with the net income from its own operations.

When a subsidiary is partially owned and has no potentially dilutive securities outstanding, the procedures are identical to those in situations in which a subsidiary is wholly owned and has no potentially dilutive securities outstanding. The subsidiary's earnings that accrue to the minority shareholders and the minority interest shares outstanding are excluded in the calculation of consolidated earnings per share.

When a subsidiary has potentially dilutive securities outstanding (whether the subsidiary is wholly owned or partially owned), the above procedures are not proper. A parent company must follow different procedures to determine the amount of a subsidiary's earnings that may be included with a parent company's net income for purposes of computing earnings per share on a consolidated basis.

At this point, students should have a solid understanding of the procedures used to compute earnings per share as discussed in *APB Opinion No. 15*, "Earnings per Share." This pronouncement is discussed in detail in intermediate accounting texts.

## REQUIREMENTS OF *APB OPINION NO. 15*

*APB Opinion No. 15* specifies the accounting procedures used to compute earnings per share on a consolidated basis:

> If a subsidiary has dilutive warrants or options outstanding or dilutive convertible securities which are common stock equivalents from the standpoint of the subsidiary, consolidated . . . primary earnings per share should include the portion of the subsidiary's income that would be applicable to the consolidated group based on its holdings and the subsidiary's primary earnings per share.
>
> If a subsidiary's convertible securities are not common stock equivalents from the standpoint of the subsidiary, only the portion of the subsidiary's income that would be applicable to the consolidated group based on its holdings and the fully diluted earnings per share of the subsidiary should be included in consolidated . . . fully diluted earnings per share.[4]

---

[4]*Opinions of the Accounting Principles Board, No. 15*, "Earnings per Share" (New York: American Institute of Certified Public Accountants, 1969), pars. 66–67.

The procedures for determining "the portion of the subsidiary's income that would be applicable to the consolidated group based on its holdings" and the subsidiary's primary and fully diluted earnings per share are explained in the next section.

## THE BASIC APPROACH

When a subsidiary has potentially dilutive securities outstanding, the effect of their potential dilution must be considered when computing earnings per share on a consolidated basis. This is done by substituting an earnings amount (the calculation of which is explained and illustrated later in this chapter) for the subsidiary's earnings that the parent has recorded under the equity method of accounting. The latter amount is usable for calculating consolidated earnings per share only when the subsidiary has no potentially dilutive securities outstanding.

This substitution effectively adjusts the numerator that the parent uses to calculate the primary and fully diluted earnings per share on a consolidated basis. Because this adjustment to the numerator is made only to compute earnings per share, it is accomplished on a worksheet outside the general ledger: the Equity in Earnings of Subsidiary account recorded on the parent company's books is not adjusted.

The denominator that the parent uses to calculate the primary and fully diluted earnings per share on a consolidated basis is determined using only the parent's outstanding common stock and potentially dilutive securities.

To determine how a subsidiary's potentially dilutive securities affect earnings per share on a consolidated basis, the subsidiary must make available to the parent (1) the numerator and denominator used in calculating its own primary earnings per share, and (2) the numerator and denominator used in calculating its fully diluted earnings per share. (The actual earnings per share amounts for the subsidiary are not used for our purposes—only the numerator and denominator used in each calculation are needed.) The numerator represents the earnings for purposes of earnings per share. The objective is to determine how much of this numerator accrues to the parent company so that earnings per share on a consolidated basis can be calculated.

This is done by developing a percentage from the denominator used to compute the subsidiary's earnings per share; this percentage is then applied to the numerator. The percentage is developed from the following ratio:

$$\frac{\text{Number of shares in denominator that are owned by or accrue to the parent}}{\text{Total number of shares in denominator}} = \text{Percentage}$$

This is the percentage of the numerator in the subsidiary's calculations of primary earnings per share and fully diluted earnings per share that accrues to the parent company.

This approach produces the same results as those illustrated in an unofficial accounting interpretation of *APB Opinion No. 15* issued by the American Institute of Certified Public Accountants.[5] However, the illustration in that interpretation uses a different and more.involved mechanical procedure than the one illustrated here.

## COMPREHENSIVE ILLUSTRATION

### Computing Earnings per Share on a Consolidated Basis When Subsidiary Has Potentially Dilutive Securities Outstanding

Assume the following information with respect to P Company and its 90%-owned subsidiary, S Company, for 19X1:

1. For P Company:

Income data:

| | |
|---|---:|
| Income from its own separate operations . . . . . . . . . . . . . . . . | $150,000 |
| Equity in net income of subsidiary (90% of $80,000) . . . . . . | 72,000 |
| Amortization of cost in excess of book value. . . . . . . . . . . . . | (12,000) |
| Consolidated net income . . . . . . . . . . . . . . . . . . . . . . . . | $210,000 |

Securities data:

| | |
|---|---:|
| Average number of common stock shares outstanding during the year. . . . . . . . . . . . . . . . . . . . . . . . . . . . . . . . . | 250,000 |
| Common equivalent shares deemed outstanding, net of shares assumed repurchased under the treasury stock method . . . . . . . . . . . . . . . . . . . . . . . . . . . . . . . . | 50,000 |
| Denominator for purposes of computing consolidated primary earnings per share . . . . . . . . . . . . . | 300,000 |
| Other potentially dilutive securities . . . . . . . . . . . . . . . . . . . . | None |

(On the basis of the structure of P Company's securities, fully diluted earnings per share on a consolidated basis is not necessary because P Company has no other potentially dilutive securities outstanding.)

2. For S Company:

Income data:

| | |
|---|---:|
| Net income . . . . . . . . . . . . . . . . . . . . . . . . . . . . . . . . . . . . . . . | $100,000 |

*(continued)*

---

[5]*Unofficial Accounting Interpretations of APB Opinion No. 15*, "Computing Earnings per Share" (New York: American Institute of Certified Public Accountants AICPA, 1970), *Definitional Interpretation No. 93.*

| | |
|---|---:|
| Less—Preferred stock dividend requirement.............. | (20,000) |
| Net income allocable to common stock ................. | $ 80,000 |

Securities data:

| | |
|---|---:|
| Average number of common stock shares outstanding during the year......................... | 60,000 |
| Common equivalent shares deemed outstanding (stock options and warrants), net of shares assumed repurchased under the treasury stock method (P Company owns 40% of these outstanding securities) ........................................ | 20,000 |
| Denominator for purposes of computing primary earnings per share .................................... | 80,000 |

Other potentially dilutive securities:

| | |
|---|---:|
| Preferred stock, convertible into 40,000 shares of common stock, annual cumulative dividend requirement is $20,000 (P Company owns none of these preferred shares)................................. | 40,000 |
| Denominator for purposes of computing fully diluted earnings per share ..................................... | 120,000 |

S Company's primary and fully diluted earnings per share are calculated as follows:

Calculation of primary earnings per share—S Company:

| | |
|---|---:|
| Net income......................................... | $100,000 |
| Less—Preferred stock dividend requirements ............ | (20,000) |
| Numerator......................................... | $ 80,000 |
| Denominator ....................................... | 80,000 shares |
| Primary earnings per share ............................ | $1.00 |

Calculation of fully diluted earnings per share—S Company:

| | |
|---|---:|
| Net income (numerator)................................. | $100,000 |
| Denominator ....................................... | 120,000 shares |
| Fully diluted earnings per share ....................... | $.83 |

The preceding calculation of the amounts for earnings per share is unnecessary. The numerator and denominator used in each calculation, however, are needed to determine the amount of the subsidiary's earnings that may be included with the parent's own separate earnings when computing consolidated earnings per share. This amount is calculated as follows:

|  | Shares Owned by or That Accrue to P Company | Total |
|---|---|---|
| Average number of common stock shares outstanding during the year . . . . . . . . . . . . . . | 54,000 (90%) | 60,000 |
| Common stock equivalents deemed outstanding, net of shares assumed repurchased under the treasury stock method. . . . . . . . . . . . . . . . . . . . . . . . . . . . . . . . | 8,000 (40%) | 20,000 |
|  | 62,000 | 80,000 |

The ratio (62,000 ÷ 80,000) is equivalent to 77.5%, which is multiplied by the numerator used by S Company to compute its primary earnings per share as follows:

| | |
|---|---|
| Numerator used by S Company to compute its primary earnings per share . . . . . . . . . . . . . . . . . . . . . . . . . . . . . . . | $80,000 |
| Percentage calculated above. . . . . . . . . . . . . . . . . . . . . . . | 77.5% |
| Amount of S Company earnings that P Company must use to compute consolidated primary earnings per share . . . . . | $62,000 |

The consolidated primary earnings per share is calculated as follows:

**Calculation of consolidated primary earnings per share:**

| | |
|---|---|
| Amount of S Company's earnings that P Company can include in computing consolidated primary earnings per share (per preceding calculation) . . . . . . . . . . . . . . . . . | $ 62,000 |
| P Company's earnings from its own separate operations. . . . . . . . . . . . . . . . . . . . . . . . . . . . . . . . . . . . . | 150,000 |
| Less—Amortization of cost in excess of book value. . . . . . . | (12,000) |
| Numerator for computing consolidated primary earnings per share. . . . . . . . . . . . . . . . . . . . . . . . . . . . . . . . . . . . | $200,000 |
| Denominator . . . . . . . . . . . . . . . . . . . . . . . . . . . . . . . . . . . . | 300,000 shares |
| Primary earnings per share (consolidated). . . . . . . . . . . . . . | $.67 |

The amount of the subsidiary's earnings that P Company can include in its numerator for purposes of computing consolidated fully diluted earnings per share is computed as follows:

|  | Shares Owned by or That Accrue to P Company | Total |
|---|---|---|
| Average number of common stock shares outstanding during the year . . . . . . . . . . . . . . | 54,000 (90%) | 60,000 |

*(continued)*

| | Shares Owned by or That Accrue to P Company | Total |
|---|---|---|
| Common stock equivalents deemed outstanding, net of shares assumed repurchased under the treasury stock method .......................... | 8,000 (40%) | 20,000 |
| Other potentially dilutive securities (preferred stock) ........................ | | 40,000 |
| | 62,000 | 120,000 |

The ratio (62,000 ÷ 120,000) is equivalent to 51.67%, which is multiplied by the numerator used by S Company to compute its fully diluted earnings per share as follows:

| | |
|---|---|
| Numerator used by S Company to compute its fully diluted earnings per share ...................... | $100,000 |
| Percentage calculated above........................... | 51.67% |
| Amount of S Company's earnings that P Company must use to compute consolidated fully diluted earnings per share......................................... | $ 51,667 |

The consolidated fully diluted earnings per share is calculated as follows:

Calculation of consolidated fully diluted earnings per share:

| | |
|---|---|
| Amount of S Company's earnings per share that the parent can include to compute consolidated fully diluted earnings per share (from preceding calculation) ........ | $ 51,667 |
| P Company's earnings from its own separate operations ... | 150,000 |
| Less—Amortization of cost in excess of book value........ | (12,000) |
| Numerator for purposes of computing consolidated fully diluted earnings per share............................. | $189,667 |
| Denominator (same as in primary earnings per share because P Company has no other potentially dilutive securities outstanding)................................. | 300,000 shares |
| Consolidated fully diluted earnings per share.............. | $.63 |

**Review Points for Comprehensive Illustration.**   Note the following:

1. The equity in the subsidiary's earnings recorded by P Company was calculated after the preferred stock dividend requirement was subtracted from S Company's net income, as required by paragraph 19k of *APB Opinion No. 18*.
2. The $72,000 equity in the subsidiary's earnings, recorded by P Company under the equity method of accounting, was greater than both

the $62,000 used in computing consolidated primary earnings per share and the $51,667 used in computing consolidated fully diluted earnings per share.

3. Initially, P Company did not have to calculate a fully diluted earnings per share amount, inasmuch as it does not have any "other potentially dilutive securities" outstanding. The subsidiary, however, does have such securities outstanding, which significantly reduce the parent's interest in the subsidiary's net income. Accordingly, a fully diluted earnings-per-share amount must be calculated on a consolidated basis.

4. We assumed that no unrealized profit existed pertaining to intercompany transactions that required eliminations in arriving at consolidated net income. Any unrealized profit deferred in consolidation would have to be subtracted from the numerators used above to compute consolidated primary and fully diluted earnings per share.

## CONSOLIDATED STATEMENT OF CASH FLOWS

When a consolidated balance sheet and income statement are presented, a consolidated statement of cash flows is also necessary. A few additional areas require special consideration when the statement of cash flows is prepared on a consolidated basis rather than on a separate-company-only basis. These areas of special consideration are discussed later in this chapter.

## THE TWO APPROACHES

Two approaches can be used to prepare the consolidated statement of cash flows: (1) combining the separate statements and (2) analyzing the changes in the consolidated balance sheets. Regardless of which approach is taken, a parent company usually requires each subsidiary to submit a statement of cash flows to facilitate its preparation of the consolidated statement. Thus, information is provided for each company within the consolidated group as to property additions, retirements, depreciation expense, borrowings, and repayments—items commonly set out separately in a statement of cash flows.

**Combining the Separate Statements Approach.**   A multicolumn worksheet can be used to consolidate the separate company statements of cash flows. The columnar headings for the worksheet would be as follows:

| P Company | S Company | Eliminations Dr. | Cr. | Consoli- dated |
|-----------|-----------|------|-----|---------|

This approach is practical when no intercompany inventory, fixed asset, or bond transactions have occurred. Elimination entries are needed only to: (1) eliminate the parent's interest in the subsidiary's net income (to prevent double-counting); (2) eliminate intercompany dividends; and (3) eliminate the minority interest in the subsidiary's net income and reflect the minority interest deduction as a charge that did not require the use of funds. (We explain the last point more fully later.)

**Analyzing the Changes in the Consolidated Balance Sheet Approach.** A company can use its consolidated balance sheets for the beginning and end of a year to prepare a statement of cash flows. The change in each individual account balance for the year is analyzed in terms of sources and uses of cash. (This approach was covered in intermediate accounting.) When transactions for intercompany inventory, fixed assets, or bonds have occurred, this method is much quicker because these intercompany transactions have been eliminated in preparing the consolidated balance sheet and income statement. Thus, these intercompany transactions are not dealt with again in preparing the consolidated statement of cash flows, as they must be under the combining the separate statements approach.

# AREAS REQUIRING SPECIAL CONSIDERATION

The following areas require special consideration in preparing the consolidated statement of cash flows:

1. Amortization of cost in excess of book value.
2. Minority interest.
3. Subsidiary with preferred stock.
4. Changes in the parent's ownership interest.

**Amortization of Cost in Excess of Book Value.** Recall that when the non-push-down basis of accounting is used in purchase accounting situations, the parent will have amortization of cost in excess of (or below) book value. This amortization is added back to consolidated net income (along with depreciation expense and any other charges that do not require the use of cash) to arrive at the amount of cash provided from operations. (Amortization of cost below book value would be shown as a reduction from consolidated net income because it is a credit that does not result in an inflow of cash.)

**Minority Interest.** Recall that the minority interest in a subsidiary's net income is shown in the consolidated income statement as a deduction in arriving at consolidated net income. This minority interest deduction, however, does not require the use of cash. Accordingly, it is added back to consolidated net income to arrive at cash provided from operations. Dividends paid to minority shareholders constitute a use of cash and are shown as such in the consolidated statement of cash flows, along with dividends paid to the parent's stockholders.

**Subsidiary with Preferred Stock.**    When a subsidiary issues preferred stock, the proceeds are reported as a source of cash in the consolidated statement of cash flows. (We discussed earlier that such preferred stock is classified as part of the minority interest in the consolidated balance sheet.) The purchase of the preferred stock by the parent, or its retirement by the subsidiary, is treated as a use of cash. Any dividends paid on the preferred stock owned by outsiders are shown as a use of cash in the consolidated statement of cash flows.

**Changes in Parent's Ownership Interest.**    Similarly, when the parent (or the subsidiary) acquires some or all of a minority interest, the amount paid is reported as a use of cash in the consolidated statement of cash flows. When a subsidiary issues additional common stock, the proceeds are reported as a source of cash in the consolidated statement of cash flows.

ILLUSTRATION    ## Consolidating Statement of Cash Flows

Illustration 12-5 shows a consolidating statement of cash flows worksheet using the combining the separate statements approach.

# END-OF-CHAPTER REVIEW

## Summary of Key Points (for Income Taxes)

1. For purchase business combinations, a deferred tax liability or asset must be recognized at the combination date for differences between the assigned values of assets and liabilities and their tax bases.
2. Consolidated tax returns have several advantages over separate-company tax returns, such as the ability to offset losses of one entity against the profits of another entity and the nontaxability of intercompany dividends.
3. If separate returns are filed, the parent must record income taxes on the earnings of subsidiaries (although an 80% dividend exclusion is available for domestic subsidiaries and certain tax credits are available for foreign subsidiaries) unless certain conditions of tax-free liquidation or indefinite investment are met.
4. Two examples of evidence required to satisfy the indefinite investment condition are experience and future programs of operations.

## ■ ILLUSTRATION 12-5
### Consolidating Statement of Cash Flows

| | | | Eliminations | | |
|---|---|---|---|---|---|
| **P COMPANY AND SUBSIDIARY (S COMPANY)** Consolidating Statement of Cash Flows for the Year Ended December 31, 19X1 | | | | | |
| | P Company | S Company | Dr. | Cr. | Consolidated |
| **Cash flows from operating activities:** | | | | | |
| Net income...................... | 58,800 | 15,000 | 12,000(1) 3,000(3) | | 58,800 |
| Charges (credits) not affecting cash: | | | | | |
| Depreciation expense.......... | 40,000 | 13,000 | | | 53,000 |
| Amortization of cost in excess of book value............... | 3,200 | | | | 3,200 |
| Equity in reported net income of subsidiary............... | (12,000) | | | 12,000(1) | –0– |
| Net change in receivables, inventory, and payables ..... | (43,000) | (47,000) | | | (90,000) |
| Minority interest in net income of S Company.............. | | | | 3,000(3) | 3,000 |
| Net cash flow from operating activities............ | 47,000 | (19,000) | 15,000 | 15,000 | 28,000 |
| **Cash flows from investing activities:** | | | | | |
| Payment for purchase of S Company ................. | (72,000) | | | | (72,000) |
| Cash of S Company at acquisition date.............. | | | | | 15,000 |
| Dividends received from S Company ................. | 4,000 | | 4,000(2) | | –0– |
| Net cash flow from investing activities.................... | (68,000) | | 4,000 | | (57,000) |
| **Cash flows from financing activities:** | | | | | |
| Increase in long-term debt....... | –0– | 20,000 | | | 20,000 |
| Dividends paid................ | (45,000) | (5,000) | | 4,000(2) | (46,000) |
| Net cash flow from financing activities.................... | (45,000) | 15,000 | | 4,000 | (26,000) |
| Net increase (decrease) in cash .. | (66,000) | (4,000) | 19,000 | 19,000 | (55,000) |

Explanation of entries:
  (1) To eliminate parent's equity in net income.
  (2) To eliminate intercompany dividends.
  (3) To eliminate minority interest share of S Company's net income and show the minority interest
      deduction (that is present in the consolidated income statement) as a charge that did not require
      the use of cash.

Note: The amounts shown in this illustration were obtained using: (1) the balance sheets at January 1, 19X1, as shown in
Illustration 5-3; (2) the financial statements as of December 31, 19X1, (or for the year then ended), as shown in Illustration 5-5;
and (3) the assumed activity for 19X1 as shown in Illustration 5-4. P Company's cash balance at December 31, 19X0, was
$108,000 ($36,000 on January 1, 19X1, as shown in Illustration 5-3 plus $72,000 cash paid out on January 1, 19X1, to acquire
80% of S Company's outstanding common stock). Because liabilities were given in total in Illustration 5-5 (and at January 1,
19X1, in Illustration 5-3), we assumed that: (1) the parent had long-term debt of $200,000 at the beginning and end of the year;
and (2) the subsidiary had $140,000 of long-term debt at the beginning of the year and $160,000 at the end of the year.

## Summary of Key Points (for Earnings per Share)

1. When a subsidiary has common stock equivalents or other potentially dilutive securities, the parent company cannot use the earnings it has recorded in its general ledger under the equity method of accounting to compute consolidated primary and fully diluted earnings per share.

2. Instead, another amount that reflects the parent's interest in the subsidiary's earnings must be used, assuming the subsidiary's common stock equivalents and other potentially dilutive securities had been exercised or converted into common stock. To determine this other amount involves analyzing the number of shares that the subsidiary uses as its denominators to compute the amounts for its individual primary and fully diluted earnings per share. This analysis produces a ratio, which when applied to the numerators used by the subsidiary to compute its individual primary and fully diluted earnings per share amounts, produces the proper amount the parent must use to compute consolidated primary and fully diluted earnings per share amounts.

## Glossary of New Terms

**Dividends received deduction**   The 80% deduction allowed to parent companies by the IRS when reporting as income the dividends received from their subsidiaries.

## Self-Study Questions
*(Answers are at the end of this chapter.)*

1. Deferred income taxes must be recognized at the business combination date in purchase combinations:
   a. Only if assets are acquired.
   b. Only if common stock is acquired.
   c. If the transaction is a taxable combination.
   d. If the transaction is a nontaxable combination.
   e. Only if the target company has no deferred tax accounts at the combination date.

2. Which of the following is *not* an advantage of filing a consolidated tax return?
   a. The nontaxability of intercompany dividends.
   b. The deferral of intercompany profits and losses on the intercompany transactions.
   c. The offsetting of loss operations against profitable operations.
   d. The use of excess foreign tax credits.
   e. None of the above.

3. For financial reporting purposes, parent companies must provide income taxes on their share of their subsidiaries' earnings:
   a. If a tax-free liquidation is planned.
   b. If earnings have been or will be invested indefinitely.
   c. If a consolidated income tax return cannot be filed.
   d. If the dividend exclusion is not applicable.
   e. None of the above.

4. S Company is a wholly owned domestic subsidiary of P Company. For 19X1, S Company had $200,000 of pretax income and $120,000 of net income. A tax

rate of 40% is assumed. At the end of 19X1, P Company had S Company declare and pay a dividend of $70,000. The remaining $50,000 of net income is expected to be invested indefinitely. For 19X1, P Company should provide income taxes relating to S Company of:

a. $–0–.
b. $5,600.
c. $9,600.
d. $28,000.
e. None of the above.

5. P Company owns all the common stock of S Company, a foreign subsidiary located in a country that has a 20% income tax rate and a 10% dividend withholding tax. Assume the income tax rate in the United States is 34%. S Company reported net income of $400,000 for 19X1 and remitted $250,000 of these earnings as dividends to the parent in 19X1. The remaining earnings are expected to be remitted in 19X2. What is the total amount of income taxes relating to the foreign subsidiary that should be provided on the parent's books for 19X1?

a. $–0–.
b. $25,000.
c. $30,000.
d. $40,000.
e. $70,000.

6. In calculating consolidated earnings per share when a subsidiary has potentially dilutive securities, the parent must:

a. Use the income recorded under the equity method of accounting.
b. Add the numerator used by the subsidiary in computing its earnings per share to the numerator used by the parent in computing its parent company earnings per share.
c. Add the denominator used by the subsidiary in computing its earnings per share to the denominator used by the parent in computing its parent company earnings per share.
d. Adjust its denominator used in calculating earnings per share for the potential dilution of the subsidiary's common stock.
e. None of the above.

7. In the consolidated statement of cash flows, which of the following amounts is not shown as a separate line item (in the indirect method):

a. Minority interest in net income of subsidiary.
b. Dividends received by the parent from the subsidiary.
c. Amortization of cost in excess of book value.
d. Proceeds from issuance of preferred stock by subsidiary.
e. None of the above.

# ASSIGNMENT MATERIAL

## Review Questions

1. Under what conditions must a deferred tax liability or asset be recognized at the business combination date?

2. What bearing does the taxability or nontaxability of a combination have on recognizing a deferred tax liability or asset at the business combination date?
3. What are the main advantages of a consolidated tax return?
4. What disclosures are required for a subsidiary that is included in a consolidated tax return and issues separate financial statements?
5. Explain how earnings of domestic subsidiaries are taxed at the parent company level.
6. In general, how are the earnings of foreign subsidiaries taxed in the United States?
7. On whose books is the dividend withholding tax recorded? Why?
8. When a parent company's cost is in excess of its share of its subsidiary's net assets at book value, and such excess is assigned to depreciable assets, is that excess deductible for income tax reporting purposes?
9. What steps are necessary to make cost in excess of book value deductible for income tax reporting purposes?
10. Summarize the basic approach to calculating consolidated earnings per share when a subsidiary has potentially dilutive securities outstanding.
11. When a subsidiary has potentially dilutive securities outstanding, is the denominator used by a parent company adjusted to compute consolidated earnings per share? Why or why not?

## Discussion Cases

| DC 12-1 | **Income Tax Planning** |

On January 1, 19X1, Paul Company acquired all of Saul Company's outstanding common stock in such a manner that the business combination did not qualify either as a pooling of interests for financial reporting purposes or as a tax-free reorganization for income tax reporting purposes. The value of the consideration given by Paul greatly exceeded the book value of Saul's net assets. The cost in excess of book value was assignable to land, depreciable fixed assets, and goodwill.

**Required:**
What important income tax consideration should be addressed?

| DC 12-2 | **Determining If and When to Record Income Taxes** |

Expando Company is establishing a foreign subsidiary. The plans call for investing $500,000 to establish initial operations. The subsidiary will retain all earnings for the first five years to finance internal growth. At the end of the five-year period, future internal growth is expected to be more moderate, and all of the future earnings will not be needed to finance additional internal growth.

**Required:**
Evaluate if and when Expando Company should record income taxes on the foreign subsidiary's earnings, assuming foreign income tax credits will not offset income taxes that would otherwise be payable.

# Exercises

<table>
<tr><td>

**E
12-1**

</td><td>

### Recognizing Deferred Taxes at the Business Combination Date

Pirouette Company acquired the business of Swirl Company in a nontaxable purchase business combination on July 1, 19X5. Other information follows:

</td></tr>
</table>

1. Pirouette issued 5,000 shares of its $1 par value common stock, which had a fair market value of $40 per share.
2. The book value of Swirl's net assets is $160,000.
3. The book value of Swirl's assets and liabilities equals their tax bases just prior to the combination.
4. Swirl's fixed assets have a current value of $330,000 and a book value of $355,000.
5. Swirl's liabilities of $500,000 equal their current value.
6. The enacted income tax rate for current and future years is 40%.

#### Required:

1. Prepare the entry made to record the acquisition assuming the assets are acquired.
2. Prepare the entry made to record the acquisition, assuming all the common stock is acquired. Also prepare a conceptual analysis of the investment account.

<table>
<tr><td>

**E
12-2**

</td><td>

### Recording Income Taxes on Earnings of a Subsidiary

Pann Company owns 100% of the outstanding common stock of Sluce Company, a domestic company that had net income of $150,000 in 19X1. Sluce's earnings are not intended to be retained in the business indefinitely. In 19X1, Sluce paid cash dividends of $80,000 on its common stock. Assume a 40% income tax rate.

</td></tr>
</table>

#### Required:

Prepare Pann Company's 19X1 entries with respect to its investment in Sluce Company.

<table>
<tr><td>

**E
12-3**

</td><td>

### Recording Income Taxes on Earnings of a Subsidiary

Assume the information in Exercise 12-2, except that all of Sluce Company's earnings are intended to be retained in the business for internal expansion and that Sluce has not paid any dividends on its common stock since its inception.

</td></tr>
</table>

#### Required:

The requirement is the same as for Exercise 12-2.

<table>
<tr><td>

**E
12-4**

</td><td>

### Recording Income Taxes on Earnings of a Subsidiary

Pike Company owns 100% of the outstanding common stock of Shantal Company, a foreign subsidiary that had net income of $140,000 in 19X1. Shantal consis-

</td></tr>
</table>

tently declares no dividends on its common stock, because the earnings are used each year for internal expansion, which is expected to continue into the foreseeable future. Assume a 40% domestic income tax rate, a 30% foreign income tax rate, and a 10% withholding tax rate.

### Required:
Prepare Pike Company's 19X1 entries with respect to its investment in Shantal Company.

### EPS: Partially Owned Subsidiary with Warrants; Parent with Simple Capital Structure

Powell Company owns 75% of Somas Company's outstanding common stock. Income and securities data for each company for 19X1 are as follows:

|  | Powell Company | Somas Company |
|---|---|---|
| Income from own operations. . . . . . . . . . . . . . . . . . . . . . | $500,000 | $100,000 |
| Average number of common stock shares outstanding during 19X1 . . . . . . . . . . . . . . . . . . . . . . . . . . . . . . . . | 200,000 | 20,000 |
| Common equivalent shares: |  |  |
| Warrants— |  |  |
| Average number of warrants outstanding during 19X1 . . . . . . . . . . . . . . . . . . . . . . . . . . . . . . . . . . . |  | 15,000 |
| Shares assumed repurchased under the treasury stock method. . . . . . . . . . . . . . . . . . . . . . . . . . . . . . . . . |  | 10,000 |

### Required:
1. Calculate primary earnings per share on a consolidated basis assuming:
   a. The parent company owns none of the subsidiary's warrants.
   b. The parent company owns 20% of the subsidiary's warrants.
2. Determine consolidated net income.

### EPS: Wholly Owned Subsidiary with Convertible Preferred Stock; Parent with Simple Capital Structure

Press Company owns 100% of Stamp Company's outstanding common stock. Income and securities data for each company for 19X1 are as follows:

|  | Press Company | Stamp Company |
|---|---|---|
| Income from own operations. . . . . . . . . . . . . . . . . . . . . . | $1,000,000 | $500,000 |
| Average number of common stock shares outstanding during 19X1 . . . . . . . . . . . . . . . . . . . . . . . . . . . . . . . . | 100,000 | 75,000 |
| Common equivalent shares: |  |  |
| Convertible preferred stock— |  |  |
| Shares outstanding during 19X1. . . . . . . . . . . . . . . . |  | 5,000 |

*(continued)*

| | Press Company | Stamp Company |
|---|---|---|
| Dividends per share (cumulative) . . . . . . . . . . . . . . | | $10 |
| Number of common shares obtainable on conversion . . . . . . . . . . . . . . . . . . . . . . . . . . . . . . . . | | 25,000 |

### Required:

1. Calculate primary earnings per share on a consolidated basis assuming:
   a. The parent company owns none of the subsidiary's convertible preferred stock.
   b. The parent company owns 40% of the subsidiary's convertible preferred stock.
2. Determine consolidated net income.

---

| E 12-7 |
|---|

## EPS: Wholly Owned Subsidiary with Convertible Bonds; Parent with Simple Capital Structure

Pandora Company owns all of Scylla Company's outstanding common stock. Income and securities data for each company for 19X1 are as follows:

| | Pandora Company | Scylla Company |
|---|---|---|
| Income from own operations . . . . . . . . . . . . . . . . . . . . . . | $600,000 | $200,000 |
| Average number of common stock shares outstanding during 19X1 . . . . . . . . . . . . . . . . . . . . . . . . . . . . . . . . | 300,000 | 100,000 |
| Preferred stock (nonconvertible)— | | |
| Average number of shares outstanding during 19X1 | 25,000 | |
| Dividends per share (cumulative) . . . . . . . . . . . . . . . | $4 | |
| Common equivalent shares: | | |
| Convertible bonds— | | |
| Face amount outstanding during 19X1 . . . . . . . . . . | | $1,000,000 |
| Interest rate . . . . . . . . . . . . . . . . . . . . . . . . . . . . . . . | | 10% |
| Assumed income tax rate . . . . . . . . . . . . . . . . . . . . . | | 40% |
| Number of common shares obtainable on conversion . . . . . . . . . . . . . . . . . . . . . . . . . . . . . . . . | | 50,000 |

### Required:

1. Calculate primary earnings per share on a consolidated basis assuming:
   a. The parent company owns none of the subsidiary's convertible bonds.
   b. The parent company owns 60% of the subsidiary's convertible bonds.
2. Determine consolidated net income and consolidated net income accruing to common stockholders.

## Problems

| P 12-1 |
|---|

## Recognizing Deferred Taxes at the Business Combination Date

Parrish Company entered into an agreement with the stockholders of Sermonetti Company providing for a nontaxable purchase business combination. Other information as of the combination date follows:

1. Parrish issued 10,000 shares of its $5 par value common stock, which had a fair market value of $70 per share on the combination date.
2. Sermonetti's net assets have a book value of $600,000.
3. Sermonetti has a deferred tax liability of $24,000 as a result of using accelerated depreciation for tax reporting purposes.
4. Sermonetti's fixed assets have a current value of $490,000 and a book value of $410,000.
5. Sermonetti's long-term debt has a current value of $500,000 and a book value of $450,000.
6. The enacted income tax rate for current and future years is 40%.

### Required:

1. Prepare the entry made to record the acquisition assuming the assets are acquired.
2. Prepare the entry made to record the acquisition assuming all the common stock is acquired. Also prepare a conceptual analysis of the investment account.

---

| P |
| 12-2 |

## Recording Income Taxes on Earnings of a Foreign Subsidiary

On January 1, 19X1, Problemex Company formed a wholly owned foreign subsidiary, Solvco. Solvco is domiciled in a foreign country that has a 27% corporate income tax rate and a 10% dividend withholding rate. Assume a 40% U.S. income tax rate. Problemex expects Solvco to be operational for five to ten years, after which its total accumulated earnings will be remitted to Problemex in a tax-free liquidation. The subsidiary had a net income of $200,000 in 19X1.

### Required:

Prepare Problemex Company's 19X1 entries related to its investment in Solvco.

---

| P |
| 12-3 |

## Recording Income Taxes on Earnings of a Foreign Subsidiary

Pavlov Company owns 100% of the outstanding common stock of Skinner Company, a foreign subsidiary domiciled in a foreign country that imposes a 20% corporate income tax and a 10% dividend withholding tax. Assume a 40% U.S income tax rate. Skinner had net income of $200,000 in 19X1. Skinner's earnings are not being reinvested indefinitely; it declared and paid cash dividends of $120,000 on its common stock in 19X1.

### Required:

1. Prepare Pavlov Company's 19X1 entries related to its investment in Skinner Company.
2. What amounts for the earnings of the subsidiary will be reported on the parent's U.S. Federal Form 1120 corporate income tax return for 19X1?

---

| P |
| 12-4 |

## Recording Income Taxes on Earnings of a Foreign Subsidiary

Parias Company owns 100% of the outstanding common stock of Sonata Company, a foreign subsidiary that had net income of $600,000 in 19X1. The foreign country in which Sonata is domiciled has a 25% corporate income tax rate and a 15% dividend withholding tax. Assume a 40% U.S. income tax rate. Sonata consistently pays cash dividends on its common stock. Parias instructs this foreign subsidiary to remit dividends to the maximum extent possible, considering cash requirements for normal operations that are not expected to expand. In 19X1, it declared $500,000 of dividends but paid only $400,000.

### Required:

1. Prepare Parias Company's 19X1 entries related to its investment in Sonata Company.
2. What amounts for the earnings of the subsidiary will appear on the parent's U.S. Federal Form 1120 corporate income tax return for 19X1?

## Calculating Consolidated Income Taxes: Wholly Owned Domestic Subsidiary

The partially completed income statements of Plowe Company and Snowe Company (a wholly owned domestic subsidiary) for 19X7 follow:

| | Plowe Company | Snowe Company |
|---|---|---|
| **Income Statement** | | |
| Sales. | $2,000,000 | $1,000,000 |
| Cost of goods sold | (1,100,000) | (500,000) |
| Expenses | (400,000) | (310,000) |
| Intercompany Accounts: | | |
| Equity in net income of S Company | (50,000)[a] | |
| Sales | 400,000 | |
| Cost of goods sold | (200,000) | |
| Income before Taxes | | 190,000 |
| Income tax expense | | |
| Net Income | | |

[a]This $(50,000) is the parent's amortization of cost in excess of book value.

### Additional Information:

1. Separate income tax returns are filed.
2. Snowe Company declared and paid dividends of $100,000 during 19X7. (The remainder of the net income will be remitted to the parent in 19X8.)
3. The acquisition of Snowe in 19X5 was a taxable combination. The parent made a Section 338 election under the Internal Revenue Code to step up the bases of the subsidiary's assets for tax reporting purposes. Of the $50,000 amortization of cost in excess of book value recorded by the parent, $40,000 pertains to depreciable assets, the remaining $10,000 is goodwill.
4. The enacted income tax rate for current and future years is 40%.
5. At the end of 19X7, $20,000 of intercompany profit is unrealized. The parent has not made any adjustment in its general ledger for this unrealized profit. (No unrealized intercompany profit existed at the beginning of the year.)

**Required:**

1. Calculate the income tax expense for each company for 19X7.
2. Prepare the general ledger entries to record income taxes.
3. Prepare a consolidating income statement.

## P 12-6  Calculating Consolidated Income Taxes: Wholly Owned Foreign Subsidiary

The partially completed income statements of Powersburg Company and its wholly owned foreign subsidiary, Strongsville Company, for 19X8 follow:

| | Powersburg Company | Strongsville Company |
|---|---|---|
| **Income Statement** | | |
| Sales. . . . . . . . . . . . . . . . . . . . . . . . . . . . . . . . . . . . . | $4,000,000 | $2,400,000 |
| Cost of goods sold . . . . . . . . . . . . . . . . . . . . . . . . . | (2,100,000) | (1,100,000) |
| Expenses. . . . . . . . . . . . . . . . . . . . . . . . . . . . . . . . . | (900,000) | (800,000) |
| Intercompany Accounts: | | |
| Equity in net income of subsidiary. . . . . . . . . . | (100,000)[a] | |
| Sales. . . . . . . . . . . . . . . . . . . . . . . . . . . . . . . . . . | 600,000 | |
| Cost of goods sold . . . . . . . . . . . . . . . . . . . . . . | (300,000) | |
| Income before Taxes . . . . . . . . . . . . . . . . . . . . . . . | | |
| Income tax expense . . . . . . . . . . . . . . . . . . . . . . . . | | |
| Net Income . . . . . . . . . . . . . . . . . . . . . . . . . . . . . . | | |

[a]This $(100,000) is the parent's amortization of cost in excess of book value.

### Additional Information:

1. The subsidiary is located in a country that imposes a 20% income tax and a 10% dividend withholding tax.
2. Dividends of $300,000 were declared during 19X8, of which $240,000 was paid in 19X8. The remaining $60,000 was paid on January 10, 19X9. The remainder of the subsidiary's net income will be remitted to the parent in March 19X9.
3. Of the parent's 19X8 amortization of cost in excess of book value, $80,000 pertains to depreciable assets; the remaining $20,000 is goodwill.
4. At December 31, 19X8, the subsidiary reported $210,000 of intercompany acquired inventory in its balance sheet. The parent has not made any adjustment in its general ledger for unrealized intercompany profit at the end of 19X8. (No unrealized intercompany profit existed at the beginning of the year.)
5. The acquisition of the subsidiary was a nontaxable transaction to the selling stockholders.
6. The enacted U.S. income tax rate for current and future years is 40%.

### Required:

1. Calculate the income tax expense for each company for 19X8.
2. Prepare the general ledger entries to record income taxes.
3. Prepare a consolidating income statement.

## EPS: Partially Owned Subsidiary with Warrants; Parent with Warrants

**P 12-7**

Powers Company owns 80% of Sanders Company's outstanding common stock. Income and securities data for each company for 19X1 are as follows:

|  | Powers Company | Sanders Company |
|---|---|---|
| Income from own operations | $2,000,000 | $600,000 |
| Average number of common stock shares outstanding during 19X1 | 1,450,000 | 200,000 |
| Common equivalent shares: | | |
| Warrants— | | |
| Average number of warrants outstanding during 19X1 | 200,000 | 45,000 |
| Shares assumed repurchased under the treasury stock method | 150,000 | 25,000 |

**Required:**

1. Calculate primary earnings per share on a consolidated basis assuming:
   a. The parent company owns none of the subsidiary's warrants.
   b. The parent company owns 75% of the subsidiary's warrants.
2. Determine consolidated net income and consolidated net income accruing to common stockholders.

## EPS: Partially Owned Subsidiary with Convertible Preferred Stock; Parent with Convertible Preferred Stock

**P 12-8**

Presco Company owns 60% of Slicex Company's outstanding common stock. Income and securities data for each company for 19X1 are as follows:

|  | Presco Company | Slicex Company |
|---|---|---|
| Income from own operations | $700,000 | $250,000 |
| Average number of common stock shares outstanding during 19X1 | 800,000 | 200,000 |
| Common equivalent shares: | | |
| Convertible preferred stock— | | |
| Shares outstanding during 19X1 | 20,000 | 50,000 |
| Dividends per share (cumulative) | $5 | $1 |
| Number of common shares obtainable on conversion | 200,000 | 80,000 |

**Required:**

1. Calculate primary earnings per share on a consolidated basis assuming:
   a. The parent company owns none of the subsidiary's convertible preferred stock.
   b. The parent company owns 25% of the subsidiary's convertible preferred stock.

2. Determine consolidated net income and consolidated net income accruing to common stockholders.

| P 12-9 |
|---|

### EPS: Partially Owned Subsidiary with Warrants and Convertible Bonds; Parent with Warrants and Convertible Preferred Stock

Parker Company owns 80% of Sheldon Company's outstanding common stock. Income and securities data for each company for 19X1 are as follows:

|  | Parker Company | Sheldon Company |
|---|---|---|
| Income from own operations. . . . . . . . . . . . . . . . . . . . . . | $1,500,000 | $470,000 |
| Average number of common stock shares outstanding during 19X1 . . . . . . . . . . . . . . . . . . . . . . . . . . . . . . | 900,000 | 200,000 |
| Common equivalent shares: | | |
| Warrants— | | |
| Average number of warrants outstanding during 19X1 . . . . . . . . . . . . . . . . . . . . . . . . . . . . . . . . . . . | 250,000 | 80,000 |
| Shares assumed repurchased under the treasury stock method. . . . . . . . . . . . . . . . . . . . . . . . . . . . | 150,000 | 50,000 |
| Convertible bonds— | | |
| Face amount outstanding during 19X1. . . . . . . . . . . | | $500,000 |
| Interest rate. . . . . . . . . . . . . . . . . . . . . . . . . . . . . . . . | | 10% |
| Assumed income tax rate . . . . . . . . . . . . . . . . . . . . . | | 40% |
| Number of common shares obtainable on conversion . . . . . . . . . . . . . . . . . . . . . . . . . . . . . . . . | | 20,000 |
| Other potentially dilutive securities: | | |
| Convertible preferred stock— | | |
| Shares outstanding during 19X1. . . . . . . . . . . . . . . | 80,000 | |
| Dividends per share. . . . . . . . . . . . . . . . . . . . . . . . . | $2.50 | |
| Number of common shares obtainable on conversion . . . . . . . . . . . . . . . . . . . . . . . . . . . . . . . . | 300,000 | |

### Required:
1. Calculate primary and fully diluted earnings per share on a consolidated basis assuming:
   a. The parent company owns none of the subsidiary's warrants or convertible bonds.
   b. The parent company owns 75% of the subsidiary's warrants and none of the convertible bonds.
2. Determine consolidated net income and consolidated net income accruing to common stockholders.

| P 12-10 |
|---|

### Consolidated Statement of Cash Flows

The 19X1 separate-company statements of cash flows for Pacific Company and its 90%-owned subsidiary, South Company, follow:

| | Pacific Company | South Company |
|---|---|---|
| **Statement of Cash Flows (19X1)** | | |
| Cash flows from operating activities: | | |
| Net income. . . . . . . . . . . . . . . . . . . . . . . . . . . . . . . . . . . . | $127,000 | $ 30,000 |
| Charges (credits) not affecting cash: | | |
| Depreciation expense. . . . . . . . . . . . . . . . . . . . . . . . | 14,000 | 6,000 |
| Goodwill amortization . . . . . . . . . . . . . . . . . . . . . . . | 4,000 | |
| Equity in reported net income of subsidiary | (27,000) | |
| Net increase in receivables, inventory, | | |
| and payables . . . . . . . . . . . . . . . . . . . . . . . . . . . | (11,000) | (5,000) |
| Net cash flow from operating activities . . . . . . | $107,000 | $ 31,000 |
| Cash flows from investing activities: | | |
| Purchase of equipment . . . . . . . . . . . . . . . . . . . . . . . | $ (71,000) | $(19,000) |
| Dividends received from South Company . . . . . . . . . | 9,000 | |
| Net cash flow from investing activities . . . . . . | $ (62,000) | $(19,000) |
| Cash flows from financing activities: | | |
| Sale of common stock . . . . . . . . . . . . . . . . . . . . . . . . | $ 50,000 | |
| Sale of preferred stock . . . . . . . . . . . . . . . . . . . . . . . | 40,000 | |
| Sale of bonds at par . . . . . . . . . . . . . . . . . . . . . . . . . | | $ 20,000 |
| Retirement of debt . . . . . . . . . . . . . . . . . . . . . . . . . . | (30,000) | (15,000) |
| Dividends on common stock . . . . . . . . . . . . . . . . . . | (60,000) | (10,000) |
| Dividends on preferred stock. . . . . . . . . . . . . . . . . . | (2,000) | |
| Net cash flow from investing activities . . . . . . | $ (2,000) | $ (5,000) |
| Net Increase (Decrease) in Cash . . . . . . . . . . . . . . . . | $ 43,000 | $ 7,000 |

## Additional Information:

1. The only intercompany transaction during 19X1 was the payment of dividends to the parent.
2. The parent acquired the 90% interest in the subsidiary two years ago.

## Required:

Prepare a consolidated statement of cash flows using the combining the separate statements approach.

## Consolidated Statement of Cash Flows

The following consolidated income statement and comparative balance sheets are for Pumper Company and its 80%-owned subsidiary, Stress-lok Company:

| Income Statement (19X1) | |
|---|---|
| Sales. . . . . . . . . . . . . . . . . . . . . . . . . . . . . . . . . . . . . . . . . . . . . . . . . . . . . . . . . | $600,000 |
| Cost of goods sold . . . . . . . . . . . . . . . . . . . . . . . . . . . . . . . . . . . . . . . . . . . . | (350,000) |
| Marketing and administrative expenses . . . . . . . . . . . . . . . . . . . . . . . . | (141,000) |
| Interest expense. . . . . . . . . . . . . . . . . . . . . . . . . . . . . . . . . . . . . . . . . . . . . . | (22,000) |
| Gain on sale of equipment . . . . . . . . . . . . . . . . . . . . . . . . . . . . . . . . . . . . | 3,000 |
| Minority interest . . . . . . . . . . . . . . . . . . . . . . . . . . . . . . . . . . . . . . . . . . . . | (6,000) |
| Net Income. . . . . . . . . . . . . . . . . . . . . . . . . . . . . . . . . . . . . . . . . . . . . . . . | $ 84,000 |

| | December 31, | |
|---|---|---|
| **Balance Sheets** | **19X1** | **19X0** |
| Cash . . . . . . . . . . . . . . . . . . . . . . . . . . . . . . . . . . . . . . . . . . . . . . | $ 75,000 | $ 60,000 |
| Receivables, net . . . . . . . . . . . . . . . . . . . . . . . . . . . . . . . . . . | 90,000 | 70,000 |
| Inventory . . . . . . . . . . . . . . . . . . . . . . . . . . . . . . . . . . . . . . . . . | 200,000 | 170,000 |
| Fixed assets—Cost . . . . . . . . . . . . . . . . . . . . . . . . . . . . . . . . . | 506,000 | 465,000 |
| —Accumulated depreciation . . . . . . . . . . . | (103,000) | (100,000) |
| Goodwill . . . . . . . . . . . . . . . . . . . . . . . . . . . . . . . . . . . . . . . . . . | 32,000 | 35,000 |
| Total Assets . . . . . . . . . . . . . . . . . . . . . . . . . . . . . . . . . | $800,000 | $700,000 |
| Accounts payable . . . . . . . . . . . . . . . . . . . . . . . . . . . . . . . . . . | $180,000 | $164,000 |
| Bonds payable—Current . . . . . . . . . . . . . . . . . . . . . . . . . . . | 20,000 | 20,000 |
| —Long-term . . . . . . . . . . . . . . . . . . . . . . . | 160,000 | 180,000 |
| Minority interest . . . . . . . . . . . . . . . . . . . . . . . . . . . . . . . . . . | 66,000 | 36,000 |
| Common stock . . . . . . . . . . . . . . . . . . . . . . . . . . . . . . . . . . . . | 250,000 | 200,000 |
| Retained earnings . . . . . . . . . . . . . . . . . . . . . . . . . . . . . . . . | 124,000 | 100,000 |
| Total Liabilities and Equity . . . . . . . . . . . . . . . . . . | $800,000 | $700,000 |

## Additional Information:

1. On January 1, 19X1, Pumper increased its ownership in Stress-lok from 70% to 80% by paying $17,000 cash to certain minority shareholders. (The cost in excess of book value was designated as goodwill.)
2. On December 31, 19X1, Stress-lok issued preferred stock at par totaling $40,000 (shown as part of the minority interest in the December 31, 19X1, consolidated balance sheet). Stress-lok had no preferred stock outstanding prior to this issuance.
3. As of January 1, 19X1, goodwill has a five-year remaining life (including the goodwill paid for on January 1, 19X1).
4. On July 1, 19X1, Pumper issued 5,000 shares of common stock for $10 per share.
5. During 19X1, dividends on common stock were declared and paid as follows:

| | |
|---|---|
| Pumper Company . . . . . . . . . . . . . . . . . . . . . . . . . . . . . . . . . . . . . . . . | $60,000 |
| Stress-lok Company . . . . . . . . . . . . . . . . . . . . . . . . . . . . . . . . . . . . | 20,000 |

6. On January 2, 19X1, Pumper sold equipment to Stress-lok for $21,000. The equipment had cost Pumper $30,000 and was 60% depreciated at the time of the intercompany transfer. Stress-lok assigned a three-year life to the equipment. In consolidation at December 31, 19X1, the following elimination entry was made as a result of this transfer:

| | | |
|---|---|---|
| Gain on Sale of Equipment . . . . . . . . . . . . . . . . . . . . . . . . . | 9,000 | |
| Equipment . . . . . . . . . . . . . . . . . . . . . . . . . . . . . . . . . . . . . . . | 9,000 | |
| Depreciation Expense . . . . . . . . . . . . . . . . . . . . . . . | | 3,000 |
| Accumulated Depreciation . . . . . . . . . . . . . . . . . . . | | 15,000 |

7. The only fixed-asset retirement during 19X1 was a machine that had cost $33,000, had accumulated depreciation of $22,000, and was sold for $14,000.

**Required:**

Prepare a consolidated statement of changes in cash flow for 19X1.

## ANSWERS TO SELF-STUDY QUESTIONS

1. d    5. e
2. e    6. e
3. e    7. b
4. b

# 13
..... 

# SEGMENT REPORTING AND DISPOSALS OF SEGMENTS

### *TOPIC OUTLINE*

## CHAPTER OVERVIEW

The foregoing chapters focus on the preparation of combined and consolidated financial statements, which are important to investors and lenders in evaluating the overall performance and condition of an enterprise. Historically, financial statements have also been used by investors and lenders to prepare trends and ratios that are useful in assessing the future prospects of an enterprise. For companies that have expanded into different industries or geographic areas, this task is usually more complicated because of different opportunities for growth, degrees and types of risk, and return on investments among the various segments. As is discussed in Chapter 15, significant additional risks arise in conducting operations in foreign countries. Even when a company has only domestic operations, substantial differences in future prospects may exist among the industry segments.

Because of two major events, accountants feel that lenders and investors would be better served if combined or consolidated financial statements were supplemented with information concerning the industries and geographic areas in which an enterprise operates. The first event was the substantial foreign investment that occurred after World War II. The second event was the extensive diversification of products carried out by scores of companies beginning in the 1960s. In 1976, the Financial Accounting Standards Board (FASB) issued *Statement No. 14*, "Financial Reporting for Segments of a Business Enterprise," in response to these events. This pronouncement requires the disclosure of information in addition to the basic financial statements. This information fits into three broad categories:

1. Operations in different industries.
2. Foreign operations and export sales.
3. Major customers.

If a complete set of the basic financial statements is presented for more than one year (for comparative purposes), then the information to be disclosed under *FASB Statement No. 14* must be presented for each such year.

The reporting requirements of this pronouncement are substantial for companies obliged to comply (certain companies are exempted from this pronouncement's reporting requirements). Before *FASB Statement No. 14* was issued, the Securities and Exchange Commission (SEC) had imposed line of business reporting requirements on publicly owned companies. The current SEC reporting requirements in Regulation S-K, an integrated disclosure regulation adopted in 1977, are closely patterned after *FASB Statement No. 14*. (Regulation S-K is discussed in detail in Chapter 18).

## The Principles Used to Present Segment Information

Recall that a basic principle in the preparation of consolidated financial statements is that all intercompany transactions (and intracompany transactions when divisions are used) are completely eliminated just as though the transactions had never occurred. This principle is also used in the preparation of segment information, with the modification that any **intersegment** sales should be separately **disclosed** but then also **eliminated** in reconciling to the consolidated revenues—and this disclosure and elimination must be shown together. Any **intrasegment** sales, (such as those within a vertically integrated operation), need not be disclosed.

With respect to reporting information by geographic areas, the modified basic principle requires separate disclosure of transfers between geographic areas with the elimination of these transfers in reconciling to consolidated revenues; this disclosure and elimination also are shown together. "Transfer" means shipments of inventory, whether or not accounted for as a sale by the shipping organization. (The statement ignores the organizational structure of companies—that is, whether divided into branches, divisions, or subsidiaries.)

A comprehensive illustration of the type of disclosure required by *FASB Statement No. 14* is provided at the end of the chapter. Before proceeding, lightly review this illustration to obtain a general understanding of the disclosure required under this pronouncement. Specific sections of the illustration are referred to later in the chapter as the material is discussed.

## APPLICABILITY OF *FASB STATEMENT NO. 14*

**Public Enterprises Only.**    When it was issued, *FASB Statement No. 14* applied to all enterprises. Later, however, it was evident that (1) the reporting requirements of this pronouncement burdened small, closely held enterprises; and (2) its benefit to nonmanagement investors and creditors was too limited. Consequently, *FASB Statement No. 21*, "Suspension of the Reporting of Earnings per Share and Segment Information by Nonpublic Enterprises," was issued, suspending the requirements of *FASB Statement No. 14* for nonpublic enterprises. *FASB Statement No. 21* defines a nonpublic enterprise as follows:

> For purposes of this Statement, a nonpublic enterprise is an enterprise other than one (a) whose debt or equity securities trade in a public market on a foreign or domestic stock exchange or in the over-the-counter market (including securities quoted only locally or regionally) or (b) that

is required to file financial statements with the Securities and Exchange Commission. An enterprise is no longer considered a nonpublic enterprise when its financial statements are issued in preparation for the sale of any class of securities in a public market.[1]

**Interim Financial Statements.** *FASB Statement No. 14* required that segment information be included in interim financial reports that constituted a complete set of financial statements in conformity with generally accepted accounting principles. However, *FASB Statement No. 18*, "Financial Reporting for Segments of a Business Enterprise—Interim Financial Statements," later rescinded this requirement.

**Financial Statements Presented in Another Enterprise's Financial Report.** Many situations arise in which a complete set of an entity's financial statements is presented in another enterprise's financial report. The three most common such situations are the following:

1. "Parent company only" statements are presented in addition to the consolidated financial statements.
2. The financial statements of an unconsolidated subsidiary are presented in footnotes to the parent's financial statements (which may be consolidated with the financial statements of other subsidiaries).
3. The financial statements of a 50%-or-less-owned investee are presented in the footnotes to the investor's financial statements.

In a literal interpretation of paragraph 7 of *FASB Statement No. 14*, the separate "additional" set of financial statements described in the above three situations must include the information required by *FASB Statement No. 14*. *FASB Statement No. 24*, "Reporting Segment Information in Financial Statements That Are Presented in Another Enterprise's Financial Report," later amended this paragraph to delete this reporting requirement in certain situations. For the three situations listed above, the *FASB Statement No. 24* provisions are as follows:

1. The disclosure requirements of *FASB Statement No. 14* do not apply to "parent company" financial statements (because such statements are included in the consolidated statements).
2. The disclosure requirements of *FASB Statement No. 14* apply to the financial statements of unconsolidated subsidiaries "if that information is significant in relation to the financial statements of the primary reporting entity in that financial report.

---

[1]*Statement of Financial Accounting Standards, No. 21*, "Suspension of the Reporting of Earnings per Share and Segment Information by Nonpublic Enterprises" (Stamford: Financial Accounting Standards Board, 1978), par. 13.

3. The disclosure requirements of *FASB Statement No. 14* in these situations depend on whether the 50%-or-less-owned investee is a domestic or foreign entity.

    a. **Domestic entity:** The requirements of *FASB Statement No. 14* apply to a domestic entity's financial statements "if that information is significant in relation to the financial statements of the primary reporting entity in that financial report.

    b. **Foreign entity:** The requirements of *FASB Statement No. 14* do not apply to a foreign entity's financial statements "unless that foreign entity's *separately issued* financial statements disclose the information required by *FASB Statement No. 14.*

In summary, the disclosure requirements of *FASB Statement No. 14* currently pertain to **annual** financial statements of **publicly held** companies. When the financial reports of these companies also include a complete set of financial statements of an unconsolidated subsidiary or a 50%-or-less-owned entity, then the requirements of *FASB Statement No. 14* may also apply to the investee's financial statements (as included in the financial report of the investor), depending on the individual circumstances.

## INFORMATION ABOUT DIFFERENT INDUSTRIES

*FASB Statement No. 14* specifies detailed mathematical tests for determining the components of a business that must disclose certain information regarding their operations. Components that meet these tests are "reportable industry segments." Before discussing these mathematical tests, we present the information that must be disclosed for each reportable industry segment and the manner of reporting this information.

### Information Presented for Reportable Industry Segments

The following information must be presented for each reportable industry segment and in total for all nonreportable industry segments:

    1. *Revenue.* Sales to unaffiliated customers and sales or transfers to other industry segments. . . .

    2. *Profitability.* Operating profit or loss . . . [along with an explanation of] the nature and amount of any unusual or infrequently occurring items . . . that have been added or deducted in computing the operating profit or loss. . . .

    3. *Identifiable assets.* The aggregate carrying amount of identifiable assets. . . .

4. *Other related disclosures:*

a. The aggregate amount of depreciation, depletion, and amortization expense. . . .

b. The amount of . . . capital expenditures, i.e., additions to its property, plant, and equipment. . . .

c. The . . . equity in the net income from and investment in the net assets of unconsolidated subsidiaries and other equity method investees whose operations are vertically integrated with the operations of that segment. . . .

d. The effect . . . on the operating profit [of a change in accounting principle].[2]

The pronouncement defines items 1, 2, and 3 as follows:

**Revenue.** The revenue of an industry segment includes revenue both from sales to unaffiliated customers (i.e., revenue from customers outside the enterprise as reported in the enterprise's income statement) and from intersegment sales or transfers, if any, of products and services similar to those sold to unaffiliated customers. . . .

**Operating Profit or Loss.** The operating profit or loss of an industry segment is its revenue as defined . . . minus all operating expenses. As used herein, operating expenses include expenses that relate to both revenue from sales to unaffiliated customers and revenue from intersegment sales or transfers. . . .

**Identifiable Assets.** The identifiable assets of an industry segment are those tangible and intangible enterprise assets that are used by the industry segment, including (1) assets that are used exclusively by that industry segment and (2) an allocated portion of assets used jointly by two or more industry segments. . . .[3]

The identifiable assets of segments that were acquired in a business combination accounted for as a purchase include the amount of the parent's cost of an investment in excess of its interest in a subsidiary's net assets. This is necessary so that the amount of a segment's identifiable net assets is the same whether assets or common stock was acquired.

## Methods of Presenting Information on Reportable Segments

The required information pertaining to reportable segments must be included in the financial statements in one of the following ways:

[2]*Statement of Financial Accounting Standards, No. 14,* "Financial Reporting for Segments of a Business Enterprise" (Stamford: Financial Accounting Standards Board, 1976), pars. 22–27.

[3]*FASB Statement No. 14,* par. 10.

1. Within the body of the financial statements, with appropriate explanatory disclosures in the footnotes to the financial statements.
2. Entirely in the footnotes to the financial statements.
3. In a separate schedule that is included as an integral part of the financial statements.[4]

The information that must be presented for individual reportable industry segments and in the aggregate for industry segments not deemed reportable must be reconciled to the consolidated financial statements as follows:

1. Revenue shall be reconciled to revenue reported in the consolidated income statement. . . .
2. Operating profit or loss shall be reconciled to pretax income from continuing operations (before gain or loss on discontinued operations, extraordinary items, and cumulative effect of a change in accounting principle) in the consolidated income statement. . . .
3. Identifiable assets shall be reconciled to consolidated total assets, with assets maintained for general corporate purposes separately identified in the reconciliation.[5]

Reconciling items 2 and 3 to consolidated amounts requires the use of procedures discussed and illustrated in Chapters 7 and 8 for the recognition and deferral of gross profit or gain on intercompany asset transfers.

## Transfer Pricing

The definition of revenue includes revenues from intersegment sales and transfers, if any, of products and services similar to those sold to unaffiliated customers. Accordingly, the reported profitability of each segment is directly affected by the sales or transfer prices used. Because such sales or transfers are not determined on an "arm's length" basis from a consolidated viewpoint, substantial latitude exists for top management to shift profits between the selling and buying segments.

It would be impractical for the FASB to try to establish a basis to set prices for sales or transfers between segments. Instead, the board requires companies to use the same transfer prices (for reporting purposes under the pronouncement) as those used internally to price the intersegment sales or transfers. Because transfer pricing has been associated in the past with vertically integrated operations (which need not be disaggregated), the potential for shifting profits is of less apparent concern.

---

[4]*FASB Statement No. 14*, par. 28.
[5]*FASB Statement No. 14*, par. 30.

Furthermore, when sales or transfers take place between segments, most often the organizational structures of the segments are similar to profit centers. This organizational structure is a substantial motivating factor for each segment to sell or transfer at no more or no less than independent market prices, as the case may be. The basis of accounting for sales or transfers between industry segments and between geographic areas must be disclosed. If the basis is changed, the nature and effect of the change must be disclosed in the period of change.

## Allocation of Common Costs

When determining an industry segment's operating profit or loss, the operating expenses subtracted from revenue (as defined in the pronouncement) include expenses related to both revenue from sales to unaffiliated customers and revenue from intersegment sales or transfers. Operating expenses not directly traceable to an industry segment are allocated on a reasonable basis among those industry segments for whose benefit the expenses were incurred.

The methods used to allocate operating expenses among industry segments must be consistently applied from period to period. If the methods are changed, however, the nature of the change and the effect on the operating profit or loss of reportable segments must be disclosed in the period of change.

Because many items would have to be allocated on an arbitrary basis, *FASB Statement No. 14* specifies that the following items are neither added nor deducted, as the case may be, in computing an industry segment's operating profit or loss:

1. Revenue earned at the corporate level and not derived from the operations of any industry segment.
2. General corporate expenses.
3. Interest expense.
4. Domestic and foreign income taxes.
5. Equity in income or loss from unconsolidated subsidiaries and other unconsolidated investees.
6. Gain or loss on discontinued operations.
7. Extraordinary items.
8. Minority interest.
9. The cumulative effect of a change in accounting principle.

Note that items 3 to 9 appear below the operating income or loss line as that term is customarily used in income statements. Thus, the meaning of operating profit or loss for a segment is consistent with the customary definition of those terms.

In the Comprehensive Illustration at the end of this chapter, exhibits A and B and the note to exhibit B contain the industry segment information discussed to this point.

## Determination of Industry Segments

An industry segment is defined as follows:

> A component of an enterprise engaged in providing a product or service or a group of related products and services primarily to unaffiliated customers (i.e., customers outside the enterprise) for a profit. By defining an industry segment in terms of products and services that are sold primarily to unaffiliated customers, the Statement does not require the disaggregation of the vertically integrated operations of an enterprise.[6]

The products and services that are sold to outside customers must be grouped by industry lines to arrive at industry segments. Because the available classification systems are not entirely suitable, the grouping of products and services into appropriate industry segments is left to management's judgment, with the following considerations:

1. The nature of the product.
2. The nature of the production process.
3. Markets and marketing methods.

> Broad categories such as *manufacturing, wholesaling, retailing,* and *consumer products* are not per se indicative of the industries in which an enterprise operates, and those terms should not be used without identification of a product or service to describe an enterprise's industry segments.[7]

The underlying philosophy is to disaggregate the total business into segments with distinct markets and thus different profitability, growth potential, and/or risk patterns. The enterprise's internal data by organizational, divisional, or parent–subsidiary lines *may* be used, but only if consistent with this philosophy.

## Determination of Reportable Industry Segments

A reportable industry segment is

> an industry segment (or, in certain cases, a group of two or more closely related industry segments . . . ) for which information is required to be reported by this Statement.[8]

An industry segment is "reportable" simply if it is big enough. Any industry segment that satisfies **any one** of the following criteria is considered a reportable segment for which specific information should be disclosed:

[6]*FASB Statement No. 14*, par. 10.
[7]*FASB Statement No. 14*, par. 101.
[8]*FASB Statement No. 14*, par. 10.

1. Its revenue (including both sales to unaffiliated customers and inter-segment sales or transfers) is 10% or more of the combined revenue (sales to unaffiliated customers and intersegment sales or transfers) of all of the enterprise's industry segments.
2. The absolute amount of its operating profit or operating loss is 10% or more of the greater, in absolute amount, of:
   a. The combined operating profit of all industry segments that did not incur an operating loss, or
   b. The combined operating loss of all industry segments that did incur an operating loss.
3. Its identifiable assets are 10% or more of the combined identifiable assets of all industry segments.[9]

**An Illustration of the Operating Profit or Operating Loss Test.**    To illustrate the application of the second test, assume that a company has eight industry segments, which are grouped as follows:

| Industry Segment | Operating Profit | Operating Loss |
|---|---|---|
| A | $    80,000 | |
| B | 300,000 | |
| C | 400,000 | |
| D | 220,000 | |
| E | 500,000 | |
| F | | $160,000 |
| G | | 90,000 |
| H | | 250,000 |
| | $1,500,000 | $500,000 |

The total of the operating profits is greater than the total of the operating losses. Applying the 10% test to the total of the operating profits gives $150,000. Any segment that has an operating profit or loss equal to or above $150,000 satisfies the test and is a reportable segment. In this situation, only segments A and G do not pass the test. Segments that do not satisfy the tests of a reportable segment are shown as a combined group of segments, appropriately described.

**The Judgment Factor.**    After applying the three 10% tests, an enterprise must exercise judgment in evaluating the results of the tests. In this respect, it may be appropriate to:

1. Exclude a segment that satisfies one of the tests if the result is a freak occurrence, such as an abnormally high revenue or operating profit or loss for the segment.

[9]FASB Statement No. 14, par. 15.

2. Include a segment that does not meet one of the tests if the result is a freak occurrence, such as an abnormally low revenue or operating profit or loss.

This latitude was granted so that interperiod comparability could be maintained. When a "reportable" segment is excluded or a "non-reportable" segment is included, appropriate disclosure of such circumstances is required.

**The 75% Test.** Enough individual segments must be shown so that at least 75% of the combined revenues (from sales to unaffiliated customers of all industry segments) is shown by reportable segments. To illustrate how the 75% test is applied, assume a company with eight industry segments has the following revenues:

| Industry Segment | Sales to Unaffiliated Customers | Intersegment Sales | Total |
|---|---|---|---|
| A | $ 100,000 | | $ 100,000 |
| B | 200,000 | | 200,000 |
| C | 310,000 | $ 40,000 | 350,000 |
| D | 340,000 | | 340,000 |
| E | 550,000 | | 550,000 |
| F | 600,000 | 60,000 | 660,000 |
| G | 700,000 | | 700,000 |
| H | 800,000 | 300,000 | 1,100,000 |
| | $3,600,000[a] | $400,000 | $4,000,000 |
| | 75% | | |
| | $2,700,000 | | |

[a]Note that this amount is consolidated sales.

Assume that the operating profit or loss test and the identifiable assets test do not result in any reportable segments other than those determined below in the 10% of total revenues test.

| Industry Segment | Sales to Unaffiliated Customers |
|---|---|
| E | $ 550,000 |
| F | 600,000 |
| G | 700,000 |
| H | 800,000 |
| | $2,650,000 |

An additional segment must be selected so that at least $2,700,000 of sales to unaffiliated customers is shown by individual segments. This 75%

requirement is determined after the three tests pertaining to revenues, operating profit or loss, and identifiable assets have been performed.

There may be situations in which a substantial number of segments must be presented to comply with the 75% test. No specific limit is imposed on the number of segments for which information is reported. However, for practical reasons, the FASB has indicated that if more than ten industry segments are reportable segments, a company may combine "the most closely related industry segments into broader reportable segments.[10]

## INFORMATION ABOUT FOREIGN OPERATIONS AND EXPORT SALES

### Foreign Operations Defined

Foreign operations are revenue-producing operations (except for unconsolidated subsidiaries and other unconsolidated investees) that

> (a) are located outside of the enterprise's home country (the United States for U.S. enterprises) and (b) are generating revenue either from sales to unaffiliated customers or from intraenterprise sales or transfers between geographic areas.[11]

### Determination of Reportable Foreign Operations

Information about foreign operations must be presented if either of the following criteria is met:

1. Revenue generated by the enterprise's foreign operations from sales to unaffiliated customers is 10% or more of consolidated revenue as reported in the enterprise's income statement.
2. Identifiable assets of the enterprise's foreign operations are 10% or more of consolidated total assets as reported in the enterprise's balance sheet.[12]

**These two tests are based on the consolidated amounts, whereas the revenue and identifiable assets tests used to determine reportable industry segments are based on total industry segment amounts.** Note that the 10% operating profit or loss test used for industry segments is not used for geographic segments. This test was apparently excluded because potential misinterpretations could occur as a result of significant differences in tax structures among geographic areas.

[10]*FASB Statement No. 14*, par. 19.
[11]*FASB Statement No. 14*, par. 31.
[12]*FASB Statement No. 14*, par. 32.

## Determination of Geographic Areas

Disclosures required for foreign operations are presented in total or by geographic area. The grouping of foreign countries into geographic areas is left to the judgment of management, which should consider the following factors: "proximity, economic affinity, similarities in business environment, and the nature, scale, and degree of interrelationship of the various countries."[13] These factors could create differing patterns of risk, profitability and growth.

## Determination of Reportable Geographic Areas

When foreign operations are conducted in more than one geographic area, information must be presented for any geographic area meeting one of the following conditions:

1. Its revenues from sales to unaffiliated customers are 10% or more of consolidated revenues.
2. Its identifiable assets are 10% or more of consolidated total assets.

## Information Presented about Foreign Operations

The following information must be presented in total (when only one foreign geographic area exists) or for each reportable geographic area, and in the aggregate for all other foreign geographic areas that individually are not reportable as geographic areas:

1. Revenue . . . with sales to unaffiliated customers and sales or transfers between geographic areas shown separately. . . .
2. Operating profit or loss . . . or net income, or some other measure of profitability between operating profit or loss and net income. . . .
3. Identifiable assets . . .[14]

With respect to item 2, a wide range of profitability can be used in lieu of operating profit and loss (as required for industry segment reporting). The apparent reason for allowing this flexibility is that when there are significant differences among the tax structures of foreign countries and the United States, misleading conclusions could result if the operating income or loss level alone were imposed.

A multinational company that has diversified operations may have to disclose both industry segment information *and* information about its foreign operations.

[13]*FASB Statement No. 14*, par. 34.
[14]*FASB Statement No. 14*, par. 35.

## Information Presented about Export Sales

When sales to unaffiliated foreign customers by a domestic company (export sales) are 10% or more of total revenue from sales to unaffiliated customers as reported in the consolidated income statement, the total export sales must be separately reported, in total and by geographic area.

## Methods of Presenting Foreign Operations and Export Sales Information

Foreign operations and export sales information may be presented in any of the ways shown previously for presenting industry segment information. The information presented for foreign operations, however, must be presented with the same information for domestic operations. The information for domestic operations and for foreign operations must then be reconciled to the related amounts in the consolidated financial statements in a manner similar to that described for industry segment information.

Information regarding export sales may have to be presented even though segment data need not be disclosed. In these cases, the information would normally be presented in a simple narrative footnote rather than as part of a more complex schedule dealing with segment data.

At the end of this chapter, exhibit C and the note to exhibit C illustrate the type of disclosure required with respect to foreign operations and export sales.

## INFORMATION ABOUT MAJOR CUSTOMERS

Some enterprises rely heavily on major customers. *FASB Statement No. 14*, as amended by *FASB Statement No. 30*, "Disclosure of Information about Major Customers," requires enterprises having revenues from any single customer in excess of 10% of total revenues to disclose the following information:

1. The fact that the enterprise has revenues from one or more single customers in excess of 10% of total revenues.
2. The amount of revenues from each such customer but not the identity of each such customer.
3. The industry segment making the sales to each such customer.

The federal government (including its agencies), a state government, a local government unit (such as a county or a municipality), a foreign government, and a group of entities under common control are each considered a single customer. As in the case of export sales, information about major customers may have to be presented even though segment data need not be disclosed. A simple narrative footnote usually suffices in these cases.

# REPORTING THE DISPOSAL OF A SEGMENT OF A BUSINESS

## A Short History

**The Professional Management Approach.**  In the 1960s and 1970s, a professional management approach became exceedingly popular. Under this approach, it was thought that acquired businesses could be managed by professional managers, whose skills could be applied successfully to almost any acquired business. Managing a diverse group of acquired businesses was likened to managing a portfolio of investments. This thinking contributed to the rapid rise in the number of conglomerates during this period (discussed in Chapter 2).

**The Reversal of the Professional Management Approach and the Deconglomeration Trend.**  By the early 1980s, it was evident that this approach had not been that successful. After an acquisitions binge, many companies found that they had bitten off more than they could chew. Many companies had bought into the wrong industry, or they simply did not have the managerial talent to manage a diverse group of industries effectively. In fact, of the fourteen companies identified as having supremely excellent management by Peters and Waterman in their 1982 best-selling book *In Search of Excellence: Lessons from America's Best-Run Companies*, not one was a conglomerate.

In recent years, scores of top managements have undone much of the external expansion of their predecessors because the acquired businesses had lower than expected rates of return or continuous operating losses. Such undoings are referred to as "divestiture programs" rather than "selling your losers." In the 1980s, the number of disposals of unwanted businesses per year has increased dramatically (approaching a thousand for several of the recent years). Clearly, there is a trend away from "making deals" and toward operating businesses that managements know best. Recent notable divestiture programs include the following:

1. From 1979 until 1985, International Telephone and Telegraph (ITT), in a move to reverse an earnings decline in almost all of its lines of businesses, sold approximately 80 business units having estimated sales of $2 billion. (ITT has been called the "ultimate conglomerate"; from 1959 to 1977 it acquired approximately 350 businesses in nearly 20 countries; the products and services it made and offered included Hostess Twinkies, radar surveillance systems, and the Sheraton hotel chain.)
2. From 1983 to 1988, Gulf and Western Industries, Inc., a conglomerate, sold more than 60 of its business units to streamline and reshape the direction of the company.

3. From 1980 to 1988, General Electric Co. sold nearly 200 subsidiaries in a relentless divestiture of low-profit business units.

**Results of Divestitures.** Divesting companies are leaner and healthier after divesting unwanted units. New management may run the divested units more effectively. If existing management buys the business, it may be entrepreneurially oriented and able to make decisions faster than allowed in a major corporation's rigid and stifling reporting structure.

**Manner of Divesting.** Companies commonly employ investment advisers (at substantial fees) to assist them in their divestitures. Divestitures can take the following forms: (a) selling segments to other companies (a business combination for the acquiring company); (b) selling segments to managers, employees, or investors in a **leveraged buyout** (increasingly common in recent years); (c) spinning off segments as separate companies (distributing the common stock of the subsidiary to the parent company's shareholders); and, when all else fails, (d) liquidating the business.

## Accounting Issues

The following accounting issues are associated with the disposal of a segment of a business:

1. How should a gain or loss on the disposal of a segment be measured and classified in the income statement?
2. How should the results of operations of the discontinued operation be reported in the income statement?

The reporting and accounting for the disposal of a segment of a business are governed by *APB Opinion No. 30*, "Reporting the Results of Operations." This pronouncement introduced the idea that the results of operations of a discontinued segment and any gain or loss on the disposal should be reported separately from continuing operations. Before *APB Opinion No. 30* was issued, losses on the disposals of segments were commonly reported as extraordinary items, whereas gains were not commonly shown as extraordinary items; the results of operations of the discontinued segments were not separated from the continuing operations.

## Manner of Reporting a Disposal of a Segment

*APB Opinion No. 30* specifies the manner of reporting the disposal of a segment as follows:

> For purposes of this Opinion, the term "discontinued operations" refers to the operations of a segment of a business . . . that has been sold, abandoned, spun off, or otherwise disposed of or, although still operating, is the subject of a formal plan for disposal. . . .

The Board concludes that the results of continuing operations should be reported separately from discontinued operations and that any gain or loss from disposal of a segment of a business . . . should be reported in conjunction with the related results of discontinued operations and not as an extraordinary item. Accordingly, operations of a segment that has been or will be discontinued should be reported separately as a component of income before extraordinary items and the cumulative effect of accounting changes (if applicable) in the following manner:

| | | |
|---|---:|---:|
| Income from continuing operations before income taxes | $xxxx | |
| Provision for income taxes | xxx | |
| Income from continuing operations | | $xxxx |
| Discontinued operations (Note ____ ): | | |
| Income (loss) from operations of discontinued Division X (less applicable income taxes of $ ____ ) | $xxxx | |
| Loss on disposal of Division X, including provision of $ ____ for operating losses during phase-out period (less applicable income taxes of $ ____ ) | xxxx | xxxx |
| Net Income | | $xxxx |

Amounts of income taxes applicable to the results of discontinued operations and the gain or loss from disposal of the segment should be disclosed on the face of the income statement or in related notes. Revenues applicable to the discontinued operations should be separately disclosed in the related notes.[15]

If prior-period income statements are presented for comparative purposes, such statements are **restated** to report the results of operations of the segment being disposed of as a separate component of income before extraordinary items, net of taxes.

## Definition of a Segment of a Business

The precise definition of a segment of a business in *APB Opinion No. 30,* which is different from the definition in *FASB Statement No. 14,* is as follows:

For purposes of this Opinion, the term "segment of a business" refers to a component of an entity whose activities represent a separate major line of

---

[15]*Opinions of the Accounting Principles Board, No. 30,* "Reporting the Results of Operations" (New York: American Institute of Certified Public Accountants, 1973), par. 8. Copyright © 1973 by the American Institute of Certified Public Accountants, Inc.

business or class of customer. A segment may be in the form of a subsidiary, a division, or a department, and in some cases a joint venture or other nonsubsidiary investee, provided that its assets, results of operations, and activities can be clearly distinguished, physically and operationally and for financial reporting purposes, from the other assets, results of operations, and activities of the entity. . . . The fact that the results of operations of the segment being sold or abandoned cannot be separately identified strongly suggests that the transaction should not be classified as the disposal of a segment of the business. The disposal of a segment of a business should be distinguished from other disposals of assets incident to the evolution of the entity's business, such as the disposal of part of a line of business, the shifting of production or marketing activities for a particular line of business from one location to another, the phasing out of a product line or class of service, and other changes occasioned by technological improvements.[16]

This definition is apparently narrower than the definition used in *FASB Statement No. 14* in that the disposal of a discrete operation within a vertically integrated operation would be considered a disposal of a segment. (Actually, this would be a disposal of a portion of a segment as that term is used in *FASB Statement No. 14.*) This interpretation is consistent with the intent of *FASB Statement No. 14*, because an appendix to the statement illustrates the disposal of a portion of a segment (as that term is defined in *FASB Statement No. 14*), which is reported in accordance with the procedures set forth in *APB Opinion No. 30*.

## Definition of Measurement and Disposal Dates

*APB Opinion No. 30* distinguishes between the operations of a segment that occur before a decision to dispose of that segment and operations that occur after that time. The particular point in time, referred to as the **measurement date,** is defined as follows:

The "measurement date" of a disposal is the date on which management, having authority to approve the action, commits itself to a formal plan to dispose of a segment of the business, whether by sale or abandonment. The disposal should include, as a minimum, identification of the major assets to be disposed of, the expected method of disposal, the period expected to be required for completion of the disposal, an active program to find a buyer if disposal is by sale, the estimated results of operations of the segment from the measurement date to the disposal date, and the estimated proceeds or salvage to be realized by disposal.[17]

[16]*APB Opinion No. 30*, par. 13.
[17]*APB Opinion No. 30*, par. 14.

The **disposal date** as used in the preceding definition is defined as follows:

> The "disposal date" is the date of closing the sale if the disposal is by sale or the date that operations cease if the disposal is by abandonment.[18]

The format for reporting the discontinued operations of a business includes two categories. The first category, the income or loss from operations of a discontinued segment of a business, includes all operations up to the measurement date. The second category, the gain or loss on disposal of a segment of a business, includes the following:

1. The income or loss from operations **during the phase-out period** (from the measurement date to the disposal date).
2. The gain or loss on the sale or abandonment of the segment.

The amount reported in the second category **as of the measurement date** depends on the relative amounts determined for items 1 and 2, above, and whether the amounts are positive or negative. The pronouncement requires companies to recognize losses currently and to recognize income and gains only when realized, but some offsetting is also required. Thus, an anticipated loss on the sale or abandonment of the segment is recognized as of the measurement date, whereas an anticipated gain is recognized when realized. However, estimated losses from operations during the phase-out period are included in this calculation. Estimated income from operations during the phase-out period is included only to the extent of the estimated loss on the sale or abandonment of the segment (with any remaining amount to be recognized when realized).

To illustrate, assume that on October 1, 19X1, a company with a calendar year-end decides to dispose of a segment of its business. The expected sales date is March 31, 19X2. Illustration 13-1 shows the amounts reported for 19X1 and 19X2 under various assumptions.

## Guidelines for Determining Gain or Loss on Disposal

*APB Opinion No. 30* specifies the following guidelines to determine the amount of gain or loss on disposal:

> Estimated amounts of income or loss from operations of a segment between measurement date and disposal date included in the determination of loss on disposal should be limited to those amounts that can be projected with reasonable accuracy. In the usual circumstance, it would

---

[18]*APB Opinion No. 30*, par. 14.

■ **ILLUSTRATION 13-1**

**Determining the Amount Reported for Category 2: Loss or Gain on Disposal (thousands of dollars)**

| | Estimated Income (Loss) from Operations during the Phase-out Period (October 1, 19X1 to March 31, 19X2) | | | Estimated Gain (Loss) on Sale of Segment | Category 2 Gain (Loss) to Be Reported | |
|---|---|---|---|---|---|---|
| | **19X1** | **19X2** | **Total** | **March 31, 19X2** | **19X1** | **19X2** |
| A. | $(30) | $(70) | $(100) | $(140) | $(240)[a] | |
| B. | (30) | (70) | (100) | 80 | (20)[a] | |
| C. | (30) | (70) | (100) | 130 | | $ 30[b] |
| D. | 30 | 70 | 100 | (140) | (40)[a] | |
| E. | 30 | 70 | 100 | (90) | | 10[b] |
| F. | 30 | 70 | 100 | 160 | 30[b] | 230[b] |

Note: For simplicity, income tax effects were not considered.

[a]Reported as of the measurement date (October 1, 19X1).
[b]Reported when realized.

be expected that the plan of disposal would be carried out within a period of one year from the measurement date and that such projections of operating income or loss would not cover a period exceeding approximately one year.

Gain or loss from the disposal of a segment of a business should not include adjustments, costs, and expenses associated with normal business activities that should have been recognized on a going-concern basis up to the measurement date, such as adjustments of accruals on long-term contracts or write-down or write-off of receivables, inventories, property, plant, and equipment used in the business, equipment leased to others . . . or other intangible assets. However, such adjustments, costs, and expenses which (a) are clearly a "direct" result of the decision to dispose of the segment and (b) are clearly not the adjustments of carrying amounts or costs, or expenses that should not have been recognized on a going-concern basis prior to the measurement date should be included in determining the gain or loss on disposal. Results of operations before the measurement date should not be included in the gain or loss on disposal.

Costs and expenses "directly" associated with the decision to dispose include items such as severance pay, additional pension costs, employee relocation expenses, and future rentals on long-term leases to the extent they are not offset by sublease rentals.[19]

---

[19]*APB Opinion No. 30*, pars. 15–17. Copyright © 1973 by the American Institute of Certified Public Accountants, Inc.

## Disclosure

In addition to the manner of reporting in the income statement gains or losses on the disposal of a segment, the notes to the financial statements for the period encompassing the measurement date should disclose the following:

1. The identity of the business segment that has or will be discontinued.
2. The expected disposal date, if known.
3. The expected manner of disposal.
4. A description of the remaining assets and liabilities of the segment at the balance sheet date, and
5. The income or loss from operations and any proceeds from disposal of the segment during the period from the measurement date to the date of the balance sheet.[20]

## COMPREHENSIVE ILLUSTRATION

This comprehensive illustration contains illustrations of the type of information required by *FASB Statement No. 14*, as follows:

Exhibit A    Consolidated income statement of a hypothetical company for the year ended December 31, 19X1.

Exhibit B    Information about operations in different industries and sales to major customers.

Exhibit C    Information about operations in different geographic areas and export sales.

The consolidated income statement in Exhibit A is not required pursuant to *FASB Statement No. 14;* it is included so that amounts in Exhibits B and C can be identified in the consolidated income statement.

Exhibits A, B, and C, and the notes to B and C in the text, were adapted from *FASB Statement No. 14,* "Financial Reporting for Segments of a Business Enterprise" (Stamford: Financial Accounting Standards Board, 1976), Appendix F. Amounts in the notes are in thousands.

## Note to Exhibit B

X Company operates principally in three industries—computers, food processing, and can manufacturing. Operations in the computer industry include the design, development, manufacture, and marketing of large

---

[20]*APB Opinion No. 30,* par. 18.

**Exhibit A**

---

### X Company
### Consolidated Income Statement
### For the Year Ended December 31, 19X1
### (thousands of dollars)

| | | |
|---|---:|---:|
| Sales . . . . . . . . . . . . . . . . . . . . . . . . . . . . . . . . . . . . . . . . . . . . | | $4,700 |
| Cost of sales . . . . . . . . . . . . . . . . . . . . . . . . . . . . . . . . . . . | $3,000 | |
| Selling, general, and administrative expense . . . . . . . . . | 700 | |
| Interest expense. . . . . . . . . . . . . . . . . . . . . . . . . . . . . . . . . | 200 | (3,900) |
| | | $  800 |
| Equity in net income of Z Company (25% owned) . . . . . | | 100 |
| Income from continuing operations before income | | |
|   taxes. . . . . . . . . . . . . . . . . . . . . . . . . . . . . . . . . . . . . . . . . | | $  900 |
| Income taxes. . . . . . . . . . . . . . . . . . . . . . . . . . . . . . . . . . . | | (400) |
| Income from continuing operations . . . . . . . . . . . . . . . . . | | $  500 |
| Discontinued operations: | | |
|   Loss from operations of discontinued farm | | |
|     machinery manufacturing business (net of $50 | | |
|     income tax effect) . . . . . . . . . . . . . . . . . . . . . . . . . . . . . | $    70 | |
|   Loss on disposal of farm machinery manufacturing | | |
|     business (net of $100 income tax effect). . . . . . . . . . . | 130 | (200) |
| Income before extraordinary gain and before | | |
|   cumulative effect of change in accounting principle . | | $  300 |
| Extraordinary gain (net of $80 income tax effect) . . . . . | | 90 |
| Cumulative effect on prior years of change from | | |
|   straight-line to accelerated depreciation (net of $60 | | |
|   income tax effect) . . . . . . . . . . . . . . . . . . . . . . . . . . . . . . | | (60) |
| Net Income. . . . . . . . . . . . . . . . . . . . . . . . . . . . . . . . . . . . . | | $  330 |

---

computers. Operations in the food-processing industry include the cleaning, cooking, canning, and marketing of vegetables. Operations in the can-manufacturing industry include the production and sale of aluminum and steel cans for the canning industry. Total revenue by industry includes both sales to unaffiliated customers, as reported in the company's consolidated income statement, and intersegment sales, which are accounted for at negotiated prices between the segments. The company feels these negotiated prices approximate outside market prices.

Operating profit is total revenue less operating expenses. In computing operating profit, none of the following items has been added or deducted: general corporate expenses, interest expense, income taxes, equity in income from unconsolidated investee, loss from discontinued operations of the farm machinery manufacturing business (which was a separate industry), extraordinary gain (which relates to the company's operations in the computer industry, and the cumulative effect of the change from straight-line to accelerated depreciation, of which $30 relates to the company's operations in the computer industry, $10 to the food-processing industry, and $20 to the can-manufacturing industry). Depreciation for these three industries was $80, $100, and $150, respectively. Capital expenditures for the three industries were $100, $200, and $400, respectively.

Changing from straight-line to accelerated depreciation reduced the 19X1 operating profit of the computer industry, the food-processing industry, and the can-manufacturing industry by $40, $30, and $20, respectively.

Identifiable assets by industry are assets that are used in the company's operations in each industry. Corporate assets are principally cash and marketable securities.

**Exhibit B**

| | | | | | | |
|---|---|---|---|---|---|---|
| X COMPANY<br>Information about the Company's Operations<br>in Different Industries<br>(thousands of dollars) | | | | | | |
| | Com-<br>puters | Food<br>Pro-<br>cessing | Can<br>Manufac-<br>turing | Other<br>Indus-<br>tries | Adjust-<br>ments<br>and<br>Elimi-<br>nations | Consoli-<br>dated |
| Sales to unaffiliated customers...... | $1,200 | $2,000 | $1,300 | $  200 | | $  4,700 |
| Intersegment sales ................. | | | 700 | | $(700) | |
| Total Revenue.................... | $1,200 | $2,000 | $2,000 | $  200 | $(700) | $  4,700 |
| Operating profit................... | $  200 | $  290 | $  600 | $   50 | $  (40)[a] | $  1,100 |
| Equity in net income of Z Company | | | | | | 100 |
| General corporate expenses......... | | | | | | (100) |
| Interest expense................... | | | | | | (200) |
| Income from continuing<br>operations before income taxes | | | | | | $    900 |
| Identifiable assets at December 31,<br>19X1........................... | $2,000 | $4,050 | $6,000 | $1,000 | $  (50)[b] | $13,000 |
| Investment in net assets of<br>Z Company ..................... | | | | | | 400 |
| Corporate assets ................. | | | | | | 1,600 |
| Total Assets at December 31, 19X1 | | | | | | $15,000 |

See accompanying note in text.

[a]$10,000 of intersegment operating profit in beginning inventory, net of $50,000 of intersegment operating profit in ending inventory.
[b]$50,000 of intersegment operating profit in ending inventory.

The company has a 25% interest in Z Company whose operations are in the United States and are vertically integrated with the company's operations in the computer industry. The equity in Z Company's net income was $100; the investment in Z Company's net assets was $400.

To reconcile industry information with consolidated amounts, the following eliminations have been made: $700 of intersegment sales; $40 from the net change in intersegment operating profit in beginning and ending inventories; and $50 intersegment operating profit in inventory at December 31, 19X1.

Contracts with a U.S. government agency account for $1,000 of the sales to unaffiliated customers of the food-processing industry.

### Note to Exhibit C

Transfers between geographic areas are accounted for at prices negotiated between the buying and selling units. The company feels such prices approximate outside market prices. Operating profit is total revenue less

### Exhibit C

**X COMPANY**
**Information about the Company's Operations**
**in Different Geographic Areas**
**For the Year Ended December 31, 19X1**
**(thousands of dollars)**

|  | United States | Western Europe | South America | Adjustments and Eliminations | Consolidated |
|---|---|---|---|---|---|
| Sales to unaffiliated customers............. | $3,000 | $1,000 | $ 700 | | $ 4,700 |
| Transfers between geographic areas......... | 1,000 | | | $(1,000) | |
| Total Revenue.......................... | $4,000 | $1,000 | $ 700 | $(1,000) | $ 4,700 |
| Operating profit........................... | $ 800 | $ 400 | $ 100 | $ (200) | $ 1,100 |
| Equity in net income of Z Company......... | | | | | 100 |
| General corporate expenses................. | | | | | (100) |
| Interest expense........................... | | | | | (200) |
| Income from continuing operations before income taxes........................... | | | | | $ 900 |
| Identifiable assets at December 31, 19X1.... | $7,300 | $3,400 | $2,450 | $ (150) | $13,000 |
| Investment in net assets of Z Company...... | | | | | 400 |
| Corporate assets ........................... | | | | | 1,600 |
| Total Assets at December 31, 19X1........ | | | | | $15,000 |

See accompanying note in text.

operating expenses. In computing operating profit, none of the following items has been added or deducted: general corporate expenses, interest expense, income taxes, equity in income from unconsolidated investee, loss from discontinued operations of the farm machinery manufacturing business (which was part of the company's domestic operations), extraordinary gain (which relates to the company's operations in Western Europe), and the cumulative effect of the change from straight-line to accelerated depreciation (which relates entirely to the company's operations in the United States).

The company's identifiable assets are identified with the operations in each geographic area. Corporate assets are principally cash and marketable securities.

Of the $3,000 U.S. sales to unaffiliated customers, $1,200 were export sales, principally to South America.

# END-OF-CHAPTER REVIEW

## Summary of Key Points

1. Because of the limitations of consolidated financial statements, supplemental data on industry segments and foreign operations are considered necessary to assist users of financial statements to assess future prospects.
2. The process of supplying information by industry involves: (1) identifying the various industry segments in which the enterprise operates; (2) applying three tests to each industry segment to determine if it is considered a reportable industry segment; and (3) presenting financial information for each reportable industry segment and all other industry segments combined in such a manner that the amounts shown tie into the consolidated financial statements.
3. The basic criterion for determining whether a component of a business is an industry segment is whether or not that component sells products or provides services primarily to unaffiliated customers for a profit.
4. The three major disclosures for a reportable industry segment pertain to revenues, operating profit or loss, and identifiable assets used by the segment. In addition, a fourth category of miscellaneous disclosures relates primarily to capital investments, depreciation, and effects of changes in accounting principles.
5. The process of disclosing information about foreign operations involves (1) grouping the various foreign countries in which the enterprise operates into meaningful, related geographic areas; (2) applying two tests to each geographic area to determine if it is reportable; and (3) presenting financial information and data for each reportable geographic area and all other geographic areas combined in such a manner that the amounts shown tie into the consolidated financial statements.
6. The three major disclosures for geographic areas pertain to revenues, operating profit or loss, and identifiable assets used by each segment.

7. Disposals of segments (or part of a segment) are reported in the income statement separately from all other operations, which are referred to as continuing operations.
8. Losses projected to occur after the current year-end may have to be recorded in the current year.

## Glossary of New Terms

**Disposal date**   "The disposal date is the date of closing the sale if the disposal is by sale or the date that operations cease if the disposal is by abandonment."*

**Identifiable assets**   "The identifiable assets of an industry segment are those tangible and intangible enterprise assets that are used by the industry segment, including (1) assets that are used exclusively by that industry segment and (2) an allocated portion of assets used jointly by two or more industry segments."†

**Industry segments**   "A component of an enterprise engaged in providing a product or service or a group of related products and services primarily to unaffiliated customers (i.e., customers outside the enterprise) for a profit. By defining an industry segment in terms of products and services that are sold primarily to unaffiliated customers, the Statement does not require the disaggregation of the vertically integrated operations of an enterprise."†

**Measurement date**   "The measurement date of a disposal is the date on which management, having authority to approve the action, commits itself to a formal plan to dispose of a segment of the business, whether by sale or abandonment."*

**Operating profit or loss**   "The operating profit or loss of an industry segment is its revenue as defined . . . minus all operating expenses. Operating expenses include expenses that relate to both revenue from sale to unaffiliated customers and revenue from intersegment sales or transfers."†

**Reportable segments**   "An industry segment (or, in certain cases, a group of two or more closely related industry segments . . .) for which information is required to be reported by the Statement."†

**Revenue**   "The revenue of an industry segment includes revenue both from sales to unaffiliated customers (i.e., revenue from customers outside the enterprise as reported in the enterprise's income statement) and from intersegment sales or transfers, if any, of products and services similar to those sold to unaffiliated customers."†

## Self-Study Questions

*(Answers are at the end of this chapter.)*

1. Select the items that are part of the additional information disclosure requirements of *FASB Statement No. 14.*
   a. Major customers
   b. Different industries
   c. Imports
   d. Major suppliers
   e. Export sales
   f. Foreign operations
2. Select the items that are used in one of the three 10% tests for determining reportable industry segments.
   a. Total revenues
   b. Operating profit or loss
   c. Segment net income
   d. Revenues to unaffiliated customers
   e. Identifiable assets
   f. Nonidentifiable assets

---

*Definitions quoted from *APB Opinion No. 30,* par. 14.
†Definitions quoted from *FASB Statement No. 14,* par. 10.

3. Select the items that are to be disclosed for reportable industry segments.
   a. Identifiable assets
   b. Capital expenditures
   c. Pretax accounting income
   d. Depreciation expense
   e. Operating profit or loss
   f. Total revenues
   g. Revenues from sales to unaffiliated customers and sales or transfers to other industry segments

4. Select the items reportable by industry segment that must be reconciled to consolidated amounts.
   a. Net income
   b. Identifiable assets
   c. Cost of goods sold
   d. Operating profit or loss
   e. Intersegment sales
   f. Revenues

5. Select the items that cannot be added or deducted, as the case may be, in computing the operating profit or loss of an industry segment.
   a. Income taxes
   b. General corporate expenses
   c. Interest expense
   d. Property taxes
   e. Research and development expenses
   f. Gain on early extinguishment of debt
   g. Extraordinary items

6. Indicate whether the following statements are true or false:
   a. The definition of *revenue* under *FASB Statement No. 14* includes revenues from intersegment sales or transfers.
   b. The FASB has established a basis that should be used to set prices for intersegment sales.
   c. The FASB has allowed management to determine the procedures for allocating general corporate expenses to individual segments.
   d. *FASB Statement No. 14* applies to companies having consolidated sales under $100,000,000.
   e. The emphasis of *FASB Statement No. 14* is on organizational structure—that is, branches, divisions, and subsidiaries.
   f. An industry segment is the component of a business that sells only to unaffiliated customers.
   g. Revenue (as defined) minus all operating expenses equals the operating profit or loss of an industry segment.
   h. The definition of operating expenses does not include expenses related to both revenues from sales to unaffiliated customers and revenues from intersegment sales or transfers.
   i. Identifiable assets of an industry segment may include an allocated portion of assets used jointly by two or more segments.
   j. Management determines the grouping of products and services into appropriate industry segments.

7. Fill in the blanks with the appropriate word or phrase.
   a. If more than _____ reportable industry segments exist, a company may appropriately combine the most closely related segments into broader segments.
   b. Enough individual segments must be presented so that at least _____ % of the combined revenues (from sales to _____ _____ of all industry segments) is shown by reportable segments.
   c. An industry segment is a component of an enterprise engaged in providing a _____ or _____ or a group of related _____ and _____ primarily to _____ customers for a _____ .

d. Segment reporting is not required for _____ companies.

e. The percentage used in the three tests for determining if an industry segment is reportable is _____ .

f. The revenues test used to determine if an industry segment is reportable is based on _____ _____, which includes sales to _____ customers and _____ sales.

g. The revenues test and the identifiable assets test used to determine if a geographic area is separately reportable are based on _____ amounts.

h. The three basic types of information provided for a reportable geographic area are _____ , _____ , and _____ _____ .

# ASSIGNMENT MATERIAL

## Review Questions

1. Why are consolidated financial statements alone considered insufficient and inadequate financial reports?
2. What three basic disclosures relate to industry segment reporting?
3. Define *industry segment* according to *FASB Statement No. 14.*
4. Distinguish between an industry segment and a reportable segment.
5. What tests determine whether an industry segment is a reportable segment?
6. What amounts for industry segments must be reconciled to consolidated amounts?
7. Under *FASB Statement No. 14,* how should prices be determined for transfers between segments?
8. Name five items that cannot be allocated to industry segments in computing a segment's operating profit or loss.
9. What two tests determine whether foreign operations are reportable?
10. How are foreign countries grouped into geographic areas under *FASB Statement No. 14?*
11. What three types of information must be disclosed for a reportable geographic area?
12. Explain the difference between the definition of an industry segment under *FASB Statement No. 14* and the definition under *APB Opinion No. 30.*
13. Distinguish between the measurement date and the disposal date as those terms are used in *APB Opinion No. 30.*
14. How are revenues, cost of goods sold, and operating expenses from the beginning of the year to the measurement date reported for a segment being disposed of?

## Discussion Cases

| DC 13-1 |
|---------|

### Procedures Used to Determine Industry Segments

Knotter Company has the following operations: (1) planting and growing trees, (2) harvesting trees, (3) processing cut trees into building materials (lumber and plywood), (4) manufacturing paper and paper products, and (5) manufacturing container and packaging products.

The controller has asked your advice on determining industry segments.

**Required:**

1. How would you determine which operations constitute industry segments?
2. Make several possible assumptions as to the key determinant, and proceed accordingly.

### DC 13-2

### Treatment of Central Research and Development Costs

Foursome Company operates in four industries, each of which is conducted through subsidiaries. The operations of these subsidiaries are located some distance from the parent's headquarters location. Each subsidiary conducts research and development at its separate location. In addition, the parent maintains a central research department at its own headquarters location, which benefits all of the segments in the same manner that top management at the headquarters location benefits all segments.

**Required:**

Evaluate the treatment used to record the facilities and expenses of the central research department in preparing segment information disclosures.

### DC 13-3

### Manner of Reconciling Segment Information to Consolidated Amounts

Tres Company operates in three industry segments—A, B, and C. Industry segment A comprises three companies (X, Y, and Z), which constitute a vertically integrated operation. Company X sells solely to Company Y, which sells solely to Company Z, which sells solely to unaffiliated customers. In addition, Segment B sells about 10% of its production output to Segment C. Segments B and C are not vertically integrated operations. All of these intercompany sales are at prices approximating outside market prices. Assume Company Y, Company Z, and Segment C have intercompany inventory purchases on hand at the beginning and end of the current reporting year.

**Required:**

How are intercompany sales and intercompany profits on such intercompany inventory sales presented in disclosing industry segment information? Be specific as to the effect on presenting revenues, operating profit or loss, and identifiable assets.

## Exercises

### E 13-1

### Segment Reporting: Treatment of Common Costs

Sulovsky Company operates in three different industries, each of which is appropriately regarded as a reportable segment. Segment 1 contributed 60% of Sulovsky's total sales. Sales for Segment 1 were $900,000 and traceable costs were $400,000. Total common costs for Sulovsky were $300,000. Sulovsky allocates common costs based on the ratio of a segment's sales to total sales, an appropriate method of allocation. Assume a 40% income tax rate.

**Required:**

Determine the operating profit presented for Segment 1.

(AICPA adapted)

| E 13-2 |
|:---:|

## Segment Reporting: Determining Reportable Segments—Revenues Test

Ming Company has the following revenues (stated in thousands of dollars) for its industry segments:

| Segment | Sales to Unaffiliated Customers | Intersegment Sales | Total Sales |
|---|---|---|---|
| A | $ 170 | | $ 170 |
| B | 150 | | 150 |
| C | 75 | | 75 |
| D | 300 | $125 | 425 |
| E | 80 | | 80 |
| F | 125 | | 125 |
| G | 200 | 175 | 375 |
| | $1,100 | $300 | $1,400 |

**Required:**

1. Determine the reportable segments based on the revenues test.
2. Assuming the other two 10% tests based on operating profit or loss and identifiable assets do not result in any additional reportable segments, perform the 75% test.

| E 13-3 |
|:---:|

## Segment Reporting: Determining Reportable Geographic Areas—Revenues Test

Clover Company earns revenues (in thousands of dollars) in the following geographic areas:

| Geographic Area | Sales to Unaffiliated Customers | Transfers between Geographic Areas | Total |
|---|---|---|---|
| Western Europe | $ 100 | $100 | $ 200 |
| Africa | 200 | 150 | 350 |
| South America | 300 | | 300 |
| Australia | 400 | 100 | 500 |
| Middle East | 500 | | 500 |
| United States | 1,000 | 150 | 1,150 |
| | $2,500 | $500 | $3,000 |

**Required:**

Determine which foreign geographic areas are reportable areas based on the revenues test.

| | | |
|---|---|---|
| **E** | | |
| **13-4** | | |

## Disposal of a Segment: Determining Amounts to Be Reported

The following condensed income statement for Divesto Corporation, a diversified company, is presented for the two years ended December 31, 19X7 and 19X6:

| | 19X7 | 19X6 |
|---|---|---|
| Net sales | $5,000,000 | $4,800,000 |
| Cost of goods sold | (3,100,000) | (3,000,000) |
| Gross profit | $1,900,000 | $1,800,000 |
| Operating expenses | (1,100,000) | (1,200,000) |
| Operating income | $ 800,000 | $ 600,000 |
| Gain on sale of division | 450,000 | |
| Income before Income Taxes | $1,250,000 | $ 600,000 |
| Provision for income taxes | (500,000) | (240,000) |
| Net Income | $ 750,000 | $ 360,000 |

On January 1, 19X7, Divesto entered into an agreement to sell for $1,600,000 the assets and product line of its separate Data PC division. The sale was consummated on December 31, 19X7, and resulted in a pretax gain on disposition of $450,000. This division's contribution to Divesto's reported pretax operating income for each year was as follows: 19X6, $(250,000) loss; 19X7, $(320,000) loss. Assume an income tax rate of 40%.

**Required:**

Determine the following amounts that Divesto should report in its comparative income statement for 19X7 and 19X6:

a. Income from continuing operations (after income taxes).
b. Discontinued operations.
c. Net income.

(AICPA adapted)

| | | |
|---|---|---|
| **E** | | |
| **13-5** | | |

## Disposal of a Segment: Determination of Loss Related to Discontinued Operations

The Rodney Company is disposing of a segment of its business. With respect to this disposal, the following information is given:

| | |
|---|---|
| Estimated operating loss from the measurement date to the end of the current year | $200,000 |
| Severance pay | 100,000 |
| Relocation costs (for employees) | 50,000 |

*(continued)*

Actual operating loss from the beginning of the year to the
measurement date . . . . . . . . . . . . . . . . . . . . . . . . . . . . . . . . . . . . . . . . .    300,000
Estimated operating loss from the end of the current year to the
estimated disposal date . . . . . . . . . . . . . . . . . . . . . . . . . . . . . . . . . . . .    400,000
Estimated loss on the sale of the segment's assets in the
following year . . . . . . . . . . . . . . . . . . . . . . . . . . . . . . . . . . . . . . . . . . . .    500,000

The severance pay and the employee relocation costs are directly associated with
the decision to dispose of this segment. Assume a 40% income tax rate.

**Required:**
Prepare the discontinued operations section of the income statement for the current year.

# Problems

## Segment Reporting: Determining Reportable Segments—Revenues Test, Operating Profit or Loss Test, and Identifiable Assets Test

Information (in thousands of dollars) with respect to Mogambu Company's industry segments for 19X1 follows:

| Segment | Total Revenue | Operating Profit (Loss) | Identifiable Assets |
|---|---|---|---|
| A | $    30 | $  (10) | $    75 |
| B | 210 | 100 | 400 |
| C | 80 | (40) | 125 |
| D | 190 | 20 | 100 |
| E | 170 | (60) | 250 |
| F | 70 | 10 | 100 |
| G | 250 | 110 | 450 |
| | $1,000 | $130 | $1,500 |

The only intersegment revenues were $60,000 from segment E to segment D.

**Required:**
1. Determine which industry segments are reportable segments.
2. Perform the 75% test.

## Segment Reporting: Presenting Industry Segment Information— Intersegment Inventory Sales (Intercompany Profit in Ending Inventory)

Kasagi Company operates in five major industry segments, all of which are reportable segments. Financial information for each segment for 19X8 follows:

| | Segment | | | | |
|---|---|---|---|---|---|
| | **A** | **B** | **C** | **D** | **E** |
| Total revenues . . . . . | $70,000 | $60,000 | $50,000 | $40,000 | $30,000 |
| Operating profit . . . . | 30,000 | 25,000 | 20,000 | 15,000 | 10,000 |
| Identifiable assets . . | 40,000 | 35,000 | 30,000 | 25,000 | 20,000 |

Intersegment sales (included in the above total revenues) were as follows:

1. Segment C sold inventory costing $5,000 to segment D for $8,000. At December 31, 19X8, all of this inventory had been sold by segment D.
2. Segment A sold inventory costing $6,000 to segment B for $10,000. At December 31, 19X8, 20% of this inventory had not been sold by segment B.

Assume no intercompany inventory was on hand at December 31, 19X7, and assume a consolidated income tax return is filed. Data related to the corporate offices are as follows:

| | |
|---|---|
| Corporate expenses . . . . . . . . . . . . . . . . . . . . . . . . . . . . . . . . . . . . . . . . . . . . . . | $12,000 |
| Interest expense . . . . . . . . . . . . . . . . . . . . . . . . . . . . . . . . . . . . . . . . . . . . . . . . | 18,000 |
| Interest income . . . . . . . . . . . . . . . . . . . . . . . . . . . . . . . . . . . . . . . . . . . . . . . . | 5,000 |
| Corporate assets . . . . . . . . . . . . . . . . . . . . . . . . . . . . . . . . . . . . . . . . . . . . . . . . | 15,000 |
| Overall corporate income tax rate . . . . . . . . . . . . . . . . . . . . . . . . . . . . . . | 40% |

### Required:

Prepare a report presenting industry segment information, reconciling, when required, to amounts that would appear in the consolidated financial statements. (Use the Comprehensive Illustration on pages 593–97, as a guide.)

### P 13-3 Segment Reporting: Presenting Industry Segment Information—Intrasegment and Intersegment Sales (Intracompany Profit in Beginning and Ending Inventories)

Dubbler Company operates in two industries, both of which qualify as reportable industry segments. Applicable data follow (amounts are in thousands):

| | **19X2** |
|---|---|
| **Segment A** | |
| Sales to unaffiliated customers . . . . . . . . . . . . . . . . . . . . . . . . . . . . . . . | $500 |
| *Inter*segment sales . . . . . . . . . . . . . . . . . . . . . . . . . . . . . . . . . . . . . . . . | 400 |
| *Intra*segment sales . . . . . . . . . . . . . . . . . . . . . . . . . . . . . . . . . . . . . . | 200 |
| Operating profit . . . . . . . . . . . . . . . . . . . . . . . . . . . . . . . . . . . . . . . . | 300 |
| *Inter*segment gross profit that could not be reported at the end of: | |
| 19X2 . . . . . . . . . . . . . . . . . . . . . . . . . . . . . . . . . . . . . . . . . . . . . . . | 60 |
| 19X1 . . . . . . . . . . . . . . . . . . . . . . . . . . . . . . . . . . . . . . . . . . . . . . . | 20 |
| *Intra*segment gross profit that could not be reported at the end of: | |
| 19X2 . . . . . . . . . . . . . . . . . . . . . . . . . . . . . . . . . . . . . . . . . . . . . . . | 10 |
| 19X1 . . . . . . . . . . . . . . . . . . . . . . . . . . . . . . . . . . . . . . . . . . . . . . . | —0— |

*(continued)*

|  | 19X2 |
|---|---|

**Segment B**

| | |
|---|---|
| Sales to unaffiliated customers. . . . . . . . . . . . . . . . . . . . . . . . . . . . . . . . . . | 800 |
| Operating profit . . . . . . . . . . . . . . . . . . . . . . . . . . . . . . . . . . . . . . . . . . . . | 100 |

**Required:**

Determine the proper amounts for revenues and operating profit to be presented in the industry segment information disclosure schedule for 19X2 shown below:

| | Segment A | Segment B | Adjustments and Eliminations | Consolidated |
|---|---|---|---|---|
| Revenues | | | | |
| Operating profit | | | | |

## Segment Reporting: Presenting Industry Segment Information—Intrasegment and Intersegment Sales (Intercompany Profit in Beginning and Ending Inventories)

Maui Company has three industry segments—A, B, and C, each of which is a reportable industry segment. Data (in thousands of dollars) for these segments for 19X2 are as follows:

| | Revenues | | Operating Profit | Identifiable Assets |
|---|---|---|---|---|
| | Inter-company | Unaffiliated Customers | | |
| **Segment A:** | | | | |
| Company X . . . . . . . . . . . . . . . | $100 | | $ 30 | $240 |
| Company Y . . . . . . . . . . . . . . . | | $700 | 170 | 660 |
| **Segment B:** | | | | |
| Company M . . . . . . . . . . . . . . . | | 300 | 80 | 310 |
| Company N . . . . . . . . . . . . . . . | 50 | 560 | 120 | 490 |
| **Segment C:** | | | | |
| Company T . . . . . . . . . . . . . . . | | 300 | 50 | 200 |

**Additional Information:**

1. Segment A is a vertically integrated operation. Company X sells all of its output to Company Y.
2. Segments B and C are not vertically integrated operations. Company N's intercompany sales are to Company T.
3. All intercompany sales are at prices that approximate outside market prices. Assume a 40% gross profit margin on all intercompany sales.
4. At the end of the current reporting year, each company has 10% of its current-year intercompany inventory purchases on hand.
5. Data relating to the corporate offices are as follows:

| Corporate expenses. | $35,000 |
| Interest expense. | 29,000 |
| Corporate assets | 40,000 |

6. Assume a consolidated federal income tax return is filed and a 40% income tax rate.

### Required:

1. Present the above data in a schedule that satisfies the disclosure requirements of *FASB Statement No. 14*, assuming no intercompany inventory purchases were on hand at the beginning of the year. The following steps will help:
   a. Prepare the intercompany transaction elimination entry in consolidating Company X and Company Y.
   b. Post the entry in (a) to a mini-worksheet containing the sales and profit data provided in the problem.
2. Present the above data in a schedule that satisfies the disclosure requirements of *FASB Statement No. 14*, assuming that (a) Company Y had $25,000 of intercompany inventory on hand at the beginning of the year, and (b) Company T had $4,000 of intercompany inventory on hand at the beginning of the year. (Assume a 40% gross profit rate for the prior year.)

---

**P 13-5**

## Segment Reporting: Presenting Geographic Area Information—Intrageographic and Intergeographic Transfers (Intercompany Profit in Ending Inventory)

Klaus Company has operations in the United States, Mexico, and England, each of which qualifies as a reportable geographic area. Data (in thousands of dollars) with respect to these areas for 19X3 are as follows:

| | Revenues | | Operating Profit | Identifiable Assets |
| --- | --- | --- | --- | --- |
| | Inter-company | Unaffiliated Customers | | |
| **United States** | | | | |
| Company A | | $800 | $200 | $300 |
| Company B | $150 | 450 | 150 | 200 |
| Company C | 60 | 600 | 240 | 350 |
| **Mexico** | | | | |
| Company X | 100 | | 30 | 180 |
| **England** | | | | |
| Company S | | 280 | 110 | 90 |

### Additional Information:

1. Company X is part of a vertically integrated industry and sells all of its output to Company B.
2. Company B is part of a vertically integrated industry and sells part of its output to Company S.

3. Company C's intercompany sales are to Company A.
4. All intercompany sales are at prices that approximate outside market prices. Assume a 40% gross profit margin on all intercompany sales.
5. At the end of the current reporting year, each company has 10% of its current-year intercompany inventory purchases on hand.
6. Data as to the corporate offices are as follows:

| | |
|---|---|
| General corporate expenses . . . . . . . . . . . . . . . . . . . . . . . . . . . . . . . . . . | $37,000 |
| Interest expense. . . . . . . . . . . . . . . . . . . . . . . . . . . . . . . . . . . . . . . . . | 28,000 |
| Corporate assets . . . . . . . . . . . . . . . . . . . . . . . . . . . . . . . . . . . . . . . . | 65,000 |

7. Assume a 40% income tax rate.

### Required:

Present the above data in a schedule that satisfies the disclosure requirements of *FASB Statement No. 14*, assuming no intercompany inventory purchases were on hand at the beginning of the year.

## P 13-6   Disposal of a Segment: Determining Amounts to Report

On June 30, 19X1, Zapata Enterprises (a calendar year-end reporting company) announced plans to dispose of several of its segments. Data (in thousands of dollars) gathered at that time for these segments follow:

| Segment | Year-to-Date Income (Loss) from Operations | Estimated Future Income (Loss) from Operations through the Disposal Date 19X1 | 19X2 | Estimated Gain (Loss) on Disposal | Estimated Disposal Date |
|---|---|---|---|---|---|
| A | $(400) | $(300) | $(200) | $(100) | 2/1/X2 |
| B | (100) | (400) | (300) | 800 | 2/1/X2 |
| C | 200 | (500) | 100 | 300 | 2/1/X2 |
| D | (300) | (400) | | 200 | 10/1/X1 |
| E | (300) | (200) | | 400 | 10/1/X1 |
| F | 300 | 200 | | (400) | 10/1/X1 |
| G | 200 | 200 | 200 | 300 | 3/1/X2 |
| H | 200 | 400 | 200 | (300) | 3/1/X2 |
| I | 600 | 300 | (100) | (300) | 3/1/X2 |

These amounts do not reflect income taxes.

### Required:

Determine the amounts to be reported in the two categories of the discontinued operations section of the income statement for each of the above segments. Use the following reporting periods:

| First and Second Quarters—19X1 | Third and Fourth Quarters—19X1 | First Quarter— 19X2 |
|---|---|---|

For simplicity, assume future operations and sales of the segments proceed according to plan. Ignore income tax effects.

## P 13-7 — Disposal of a Segment: Preparing Income Statement and Statement of Retained Earnings—Variety of Events and Transactions

Variety Company had the following events and transactions in 19X5:

| | |
|---|---|
| Sales . . . . . . . . . . . . . . . . . . . . . . . . . . . . . . . . . . . . . . . . . . . . . . . . . . . . . . | $10,000,000[a] |
| Cost of goods sold (corrected for inventory pricing error at December 31, 19X4) . . . . . . . . . . . . . . . . . . . . . . . . . . . . . . . . . . . . . . . | 5,700,000[a] |
| Understatement of December 31, 19X4 inventory (pricing error). . . . | 250,000 |
| Marketing and administrative expenses . . . . . . . . . . . . . . . . . . . . . . . . | 2,000,000[a] |
| Operating loss for 19X5 related to Gismo Division, $150,000 of which occurred after the decision to dispose of the division . . . . . | 500,000 |
| Estimated 19X6 operating loss for Gismo Division. . . . . . . . . . . . . . . | 300,000 |
| Estimated loss on sale of Gismo Division's net assets (a separate industry segment), disposal to be completed in 19X6 . . . . . . . . . . . . . . . . . . . . . . . . . . . . . . . . . . . . . . . . . . . . . | 550,000 |
| Gain on early extinguishment of debt . . . . . . . . . . . . . . . . . . . . . . . . . | 600,000 |
| Flood loss, uninsured. . . . . . . . . . . . . . . . . . . . . . . . . . . . . . . . . . . . . . | 700,000[b] |
| Settlement of lawsuit related to 19X3 activity (not accrued in prior years) . . . . . . . . . . . . . . . . . . . . . . . . . . . . . . . . . . . . . . . . . | 400,000[c] |

[a]Excludes Gismo Division.
[b]The last major flood in the area was 60 years ago.
[c]From the time the lawsuit was filed in 19X3, legal counsel felt that the company would not win the lawsuit. Legal counsel could not estimate either the ultimate settlement amount or a likely range within which the settlement amount would fall. Future such lawsuits are possible.

Assume a combined federal and state income tax rate of 40%. Assume that no timing or permanent differences exist between pretax accounting income and taxable income. Retained earnings were $2,000,000 on January 1, 19X5, and cash dividends of $100,000 were declared during 19X5.

### Required:
Prepare an income statement and a statement of retained earnings for 19X5.

# ADVANCED LEVEL ASSIGNMENT MATERIAL

## Advanced Problem

## AP 13-1 — Sale of a Subsidiary in a Leveraged Buyout

On June 30, 19X1, Pylox Company sold its 100% interest in its subsidiary, Shylock Company, to Newco Company. Shylock Company has been reported as a separate reportable industry segment prior to the sale. Newco was recently formed by the top management of Shylock and a group of wealthy outside investors. The transaction is a leveraged buyout (LBO). The carrying value of Pylox's investment in Shylock at the sale date was $7,000,000. Newco paid Shylock $10,000,000 cash (virtually all borrowed from a financial institution). The sales agreement provided that Pylox guarantee payment of $2,000,000 of the Newco debt. Furthermore, if Newco's cash flow falls below certain levels, Pylox is obligated to purchase $500,000 of preferred stock of Newco.

### Required:
Determine how Pylox should report its $3,000,000 gain.

### ANSWERS TO SELF-STUDY QUESTIONS
1. a, b, e, and f
2. a, b, and e
3. a, b, d, e, and g.
4. b, d, and f
5. a, b, c, f, (an extraordinary item, if material), and g
6. Only questions a, d, g, i, and j are true.
7. a. ten
   b. 75; unaffiliated customers
   c. product; service; products; services; unaffiliated; profit
   d. nonpublic
   e. 10%
   f. total revenues; unaffiliated; intersegment
   g. consolidated
   h. revenues; operating profit or loss; identifiable assets

# OMNIBUS AREA

■ ■ ■ ■ ■

# 14
## .....

# TRANSLATION OF FOREIGN CURRENCY TRANSACTIONS

*TOPIC OUTLINE*

## CHAPTER OVERVIEW

The expansion of international business in the last 40 years has been phenomenal. Total U.S. exports are nearly $400 billion annually (approximately $110 billion less than imports). Currently, investments overseas by U.S. companies exceed $225 billion (up from approximately $12 billion in 1950), producing over $45 billion in earnings per year. As a result, international business now constitutes a significant part of the overall activities of a large number of domestic corporations.

In this chapter, we first lay the theoretical groundwork for dealing with currency exchange rates, and then discuss and illustrate how to translate foreign currency transactions into U.S. dollars. **Foreign currency transactions** are transactions that require settlement (payment or receipt) in a foreign currency. The foreign currency transactions we examine in this chapter are (1) importing and exporting transactions, (2) hedging transactions entered into to protect against potential adverse changes in the exchange rate on unsettled importing and exporting transactions, and (3) speculation in foreign currencies.

Chapters 15 and 16 discuss and illustrate how to translate the financial statements of foreign subsidiaries (formally called *foreign currency financial statements*) into U.S. dollars. Chapter 16 also covers (1) intercompany transactions between a domestic company and its foreign subsidiary, and (2) hedging transactions a domestic company may enter into to protect its investment in a foreign subsidiary against adverse exchange rate changes.

### The Governing Pronouncement

*FASB Statement No. 52*, "Foreign Currency Translation," sets forth the accounting principles and procedures for the translation of foreign currency transactions and deals with translating foreign currency financial statements. The issues involved in the translation of foreign currency transactions are not controversial, whereas the issues pertaining to the translation of foreign currency financial statements are highly controversial and will be discussed in Chapter 15.

## CURRENCY EXCHANGE RATES

### Conversion versus Translation

Actually changing one currency into another currency is called **conversion.** Foreign currencies are usually purchased through commercial banks. Likewise, when payment is received in a foreign currency, that currency may be converted into dollars at such institutions. Conversion must be differentiated from **translation,** which is the process of expressing amounts stated in one currency in terms of another currency by using the appropriate **currency exchange rates.**

## Methods of Expressing Exchange Rates

The ratio of the number of units of one currency needed to acquire one unit of another currency constitutes the exchange rate between the two currencies. The exchange rate may be expressed in two ways, indirect quotation and direct quotation:

1. **Indirect quotation.** The number of units of the foreign currency needed to acquire one unit of the domestic currency is the **indirect** quotation of the exchange rate (for example, 1 dollar = .625 pounds). To determine the dollar equivalent of an amount stated in a foreign currency, the foreign currency is **divided** by the exchange rate. (Professional traders in foreign currencies use the indirect quotation rate.)
2. **Direct quotation.** The number of units of the domestic currency needed to acquire one unit of the foreign currency is a **direct** quotation of the exchange rate (for example, 1 pound = $1.60). To determine the dollar equivalent of an amount stated in a foreign currency, the foreign currency amount is **multiplied** by the exchange rate. (Travelers prefer the direct quotation rate.)

Banks and daily newspapers in the United States quote exchange rates both indirectly and directly. Translation of amounts stated in foreign currencies is usually performed using direct quotations. In all examples and illustrations in this chapter, we use the direct quotation of the exchange rate. Direct quotations of the exchange rates between the dollar and several major foreign currencies are as follows:

| Country (currency) | Dollar Equivalent of One Unit of Foreign Currency | | | Percent Change | |
| --- | --- | --- | --- | --- | --- |
| | 12/31/81 | 12/31/88 | 12/31/89 | 8 year | 1 year |
| Brazil (cruzeiro) | $8,010.0000 | 1.3110 | .1130 | − 99 | − 92 |
| Britain (pound) | 1.9170 | 1.7982 | 1.6140 | − 16 | − 10 |
| Canada (dollar) | .8435 | .8395 | .8635 | + 2 | + 2 |
| France (franc) | .1757 | .1644 | .1731 | − 1 | + 5 |
| Italy (lira) | .0008 | .0008 | .0008 | nil | nil |
| Japan (yen) | .0045 | .0079 | .0069 | + 53 | − 13 |
| Mexico (peso) | .0381 | .0004 | .0004 | − 99 | nil |
| Switzerland (franc) | .5602 | .6624 | .6485 | + 16 | − 2 |
| West Germany (mark) | .4460 | .5613 | .5918 | + 33 | + 5 |

**Spot and Forward Exchange Rates.** Exchange rates at which currencies could be converted immediately (for settlement in two days) are termed **spot rates.** Exchange rates also exist for transactions whereby conversion could be made at some stipulated date (normally up to 12 months) in the future. Such rates are called **future** or **forward rates** (discussed on pages 627–28).

## The Exchange Rate System: Floating versus Fixed Exchange Rates

Currency exchange rates are a function of market conditions, which in turn are a function of changing economic and political conditions such as the internal inflation rate, the balance of payments surplus or deficit, the internal spending surplus or deficit, and the imminence of various civil disorders. Exchange rates determined by market conditions are commonly referred to as either **floating** or **free** rates.

Before 1974, the dollar was tied to gold, and most currencies were tied to the dollar. As a result, **fixed** or **official** exchange rates existed. When fixed rates no longer reflected economic conditions, governments were forced to devalue or revalue their currencies (as the U.S. government did in 1973 when it announced a 10% devaluation). Although devaluations of certain currencies were often expected, it was impossible to determine exactly when they would occur or the amount of the devaluation. This major drawback and the fact that the system could not deal with rapid inflation made the system unsustainable. In 1974, the dollar was taken off the gold standard (that is, the dollar was no longer backed by gold reserves), and most currencies that had not already been allowed to float were allowed to do so. As a result, changing international economic conditions are reflected in the currency exchange rates on a daily basis.

Even under the floating exchange rate system, governments may intervene in the exchange markets by buying and selling currencies (as the U.S. government did in the late 1970s to bolster the dollar). An extreme example of intervention is the Mexican peso. After nearly 25 years of stability, the Mexican government allowed the peso to float in 1976; it promptly declined 50% in value against the dollar. In theory, the peso became a floating currency in the international money markets at that time. However, by buying and selling dollars, the central bank of Mexico tried to control the value of the peso at a fairly fixed level against the dollar. In early 1982, the central bank's reserves of U.S. dollars were nearly exhausted, and the government announced that it would withdraw temporarily from the foreign exchange markets. The peso promptly declined nearly 40% in value against the dollar. Two subsequent interventions and temporary withdrawals occurred in 1982; the peso declined approximately 85% in value against the dollar in 1982.

A change in a floating exchange rate is appropriately referred to as a **strengthening** or **weakening** of one currency in relation to another.

**Strengthening Currencies.** A foreign currency that is *strengthening* in value in relation to the dollar requires more dollars to obtain a unit of the foreign currency; accordingly, the direct exchange rate increases. A weakening of the dollar has the same effect on the direct exchange rate as does the strengthening of the foreign currency.

**Weakening Currencies.** A foreign currency that is *weakening* in value in relation to the dollar requires fewer dollars to obtain a unit of the foreign currency; accordingly, the direct exchange rate decreases. A strengthening of the dollar has the same effect on the direct exchange rate as does the weakening of the foreign currency.

## WHAT CAUSES CURRENCY EXCHANGE RATES TO CHANGE

Earlier we stated that exchange rates are determined by market conditions. Thus, the price of a foreign currency (the exchange rate) is governed by the laws of supply and demand, as is the case for commodities such as corn, cotton, and gold. *Supply* is the quantity of a currency that companies and individuals are trying to sell; *demand* is the quantity of a currency that companies and individuals are trying to buy.

Many factors affect supply and demand, such as the money supply, the rate of inflation, interest rates (which are determined to a certain extent by inflation), the level of a country's imports versus its exports, the level of investment made domestically by foreign investors versus the level of investment made in foreign countries by domestic investors, government-imposed restrictions on currency transfers, civil disorders, and wars. Some of these factors have only a short-term effect, while the effect of others is long-term. It is beyond the scope of this book to examine and discuss each of these factors, inasmuch as an entire chapter could be devoted to the topic (as is done in textbooks on international finance). However, we look at some of these factors in order to give you a fuller understanding of the more important ones.

### The Foreign Trade Deficit

For many years, the continuous and substantial foreign trade deficit of the U.S., in which imports far exceed exports, has been of considerable concern. Because much of this trade deficit is with Japan (currently $50 billion a year), let us assume for simplicity that: (1) the only trading partner of the U.S. is Japan; (2) trade between the two countries began in 19X1; and (3) exporters in each country demand payment in their own currency.

When a U.S. company imports goods from Japan to sell domestically, it must purchase yen from a foreign currency dealer to pay the Japanese exporter, which creates demand for yen. When a U.S. company exports U.S. goods to sell in Japan, the Japanese importer must purchase dollars from a foreign currency dealer to pay the U.S. exporter, which creates demand for dollars. Therefore, when the U.S. imports more than it exports, more demand is created for yen than is created for dollars. Disregarding all other factors, one would expect the yen to strengthen and the dollar to weaken when this occurs, resulting in an increase in the direct exchange rate.

Given these circumstances due to foreign trade, at the end of 19X1 the Japanese foreign currency dealers would hold many more dollars than U.S. foreign currency dealers would hold yen. If a trade deficit with Japan continues year after year, then the Japanese foreign currency dealers will continue to accumulate substantial sums in dollars. Assuming the dollars can be spent only in the U.S., the question arises: Why are the Japanese foreign currency dealers willing to accumulate all those dollars? The answer is that they are convinced they can sell the dollars to Japanese investors who desire to invest in the U.S. This leads to foreign investment as a factor of currency supply and demand.

## Foreign Investment

When U.S. companies desire to invest in Japan, they must purchase yen from a foreign currency dealer because they need yen in order to consummate these investment transactions, which creates demand for yen. When Japanese companies invest in the U.S., they must purchase dollars to consummate their investment transactions in the U.S., which creates demand for dollars. Therefore, when Japanese investors invest in the U.S. more than U.S. investors invest in Japan, more demand is created for dollars than for yen. Disregarding all other factors, we would expect the dollar to strengthen and the yen to weaken when this occurs, thus resulting in a decrease in the direct exchange rate.

Given such circumstances due to foreign investment, at the end of 19X1 the U.S. foreign currency dealers would hold many more yen than Japanese foreign currency dealers would hold dollars. If the investment deficit continues year after year, the U.S. foreign currency dealers will continue to accumulate substantial sums in yen. Assuming the yen can be spent only in Japan, the question is raised: Why are the U.S. foreign currency dealers willing to accumulate all those yen? The answer is that they are convinced that they can sell the yen to U.S. companies that desire to import products from Japan. This leads to the interrelationship between trading and investing as a factor of currency supply and demand.

## The Interrelationship between Foreign Trade and Foreign Investment

To make the basic relationship clearer, let us assume that there are no foreign currency dealers (who merely act as intermediaries in matching up buyers and sellers of currencies). Under such a scenario, a U.S. trade deficit with Japan would result in many Japanese companies holding dollars at the end of 19X1. This is because the Japanese exporters must accept dollars in payment (otherwise, we would revert to a barter system). Thus, the Japanese companies would accumulate substantial sums in dollars each year that the U.S. trade deficit continues. These Japanese exporters, however, are willing to take dollars only if they are convinced that they can: (1) use the dollars to import products from the U.S. that they may desire; (2) use the dollars to purchase items such as real estate or securities in the U.S. (thereby making the Japanese companies investors in the U.S.); or (3) sell the dollars to other Japanese citizens or Japanese companies who want to import products from the U.S. or invest in the U.S. The key point is that **no foreign company will accept U.S. dollars unless it is convinced that the dollars can be exchanged for something of value from or in the U.S.** Otherwise, countries would be able to import whatever they desired merely by printing money.

This means that when the U.S. imports from Japan more goods than it exports to Japan, there is an equal and offsetting effect by Japanese investors. Stated differently, a $50 billion trade deficit with Japan is exactly offset by Japanese investors investing $50 billion more in the U.S. than invested in Japan by U.S. investors. Thus, there is offsetting demand, which means that there should be no long-term effect on exchange rates. In the short run, however, there usually is some effect because at any given time or during any short period of time, a perfect balance between trade and investment does not exist. **Note that the U.S. trade deficit can last as long as (1) foreign investors are willing to invest in the U.S., and (2) U.S. companies and citizens are willing to sell their real estate and securities (if they have any left to sell) to foreign investors.**

## Inflation

Under the theory of **purchasing power parity** (sometimes referred to as the "law of one price"), **the differential rate of inflation between two countries can be expected to result over the long run in an equal but opposite change in the exchange rate between the two currencies.** For example, assume that on January 1, 19X1, the direct exchange rate between the U.S. dollar and the British pound is 1 pound equals $1. Also assume that on this date a bushel of wheat can be purchased in the United States for $1 and in Great Britain for 1 pound. Thus, a U.S. citizen will pay the same (one) price ($1) for a bushel of wheat—regardless whether the wheat is purchased domestically or in Great Britain. (The same can be said for British citizens using the pound from their perspective.) For 19X1, assume that the inflation rate is zero in the United States and 100% in Great Britain. Accordingly, at December 31, 19X1, a bushel of wheat in Great Britain costs 2 pounds. If the exchange rate did not change in 19X1, then a British citizen would be able to purchase wheat at two prices: 2 pounds if purchased in Great Britain and 1 pound if purchased in the United States. British citizens would most likely purchase the wheat in the United States, thereby saving 1 pound per bushel. However, this would create more demand for U.S. dollars and would cause the value of the dollar to rise against the pound. Under the theory, the exchange rate at December 31, 19X1, should adjust so that there is only one price to British citizens: 1 pound would become equal to $.50.

Studies have shown that in the short run other factors influence exchange rates much more than differential rates of inflation. In the long run, however, studies have shown that the effects of all the other factors tend to reverse or cancel out, and eventually exchange rates closely approximate the results expected under the purchasing power parity theory. A more extensive discussion of this theory may be found in textbooks on international business finance.

We should note that in many South American countries that have highly inflationary economies, in the short run inflation is the primary cause of the continual weakening of these foreign currencies.

## IMPORTING AND EXPORTING TRANSACTIONS

### Measured versus Denominated

The currency in which a transaction is to be settled must be stipulated. When the transaction is to be settled by the receipt or payment of a fixed amount of a specified currency, the receivable or payable, respectively, is said to be **denominated** in that currency. When the transaction is to be settled by the receipt or payment of a fixed amount of a currency other than the U.S. dollar, from the perspective of a U.S. reporting entity, the receivable or payable is denominated in a foreign currency. A party to a transaction **measures** and records the transaction in the currency of the country in which that party is located. A transaction may be measured and denominated in one currency, or a transaction may be measured in one currency and denominated in another currency. The following examples illustrate this process:

1. A U.S. importer purchases goods on credit from a Swiss exporter, with payment to be made in a specified number of Swiss francs. The domestic importer measures and records the transaction in dollars, and the Swiss exporter measures and records the transaction in Swiss francs. The domestic importer's liability is denominated in a foreign currency, the Swiss franc. The Swiss exporter's receivable is denominated in Swiss francs. (If the terms of the transaction called for payment to be made in dollars, the transaction would be measured and denominated in dollars, from the perspective of the importer.)

2. A Swiss subsidiary of a U.S. company purchases goods on credit from another Swiss company, with payment to be made in a specified number of Swiss francs. The Swiss subsidiary measures the asset acquired and the liability incurred in Swiss francs. The Swiss subsidiary's liability is not denominated in a foreign currency, because the liability is denominated in Swiss francs. From the perspective of the U.S. parent, however, the Swiss subsidiary's liability is denominated in a foreign currency, because the liability is not payable in dollars.

3. A Swiss subsidiary of a U.S. company purchases goods on credit from an Italian company, with payment to be made in Italian lira. The Swiss subsidiary measures the asset acquired and liability incurred in Swiss francs. The Swiss subsidiary's liability is denominated in a foreign currency. From the perspective of the U.S. parent, the Swiss subsidiary's liability is denominated in a foreign currency, because the liability is not payable in dollars.

## Foreign Currency Transactions versus Foreign Transactions

For each international transaction, only one party has a foreign currency transaction, because payment is usually specified in only one currency. The party that must make or receive payment in other than its own local currency has the **foreign currency transaction.** For example, a domestic importer who pays for goods in the supplier's currency has a foreign currency transaction, whereas the supplier has only a **foreign transaction.** Likewise, a domestic exporter who receives payment in the customer's currency has a foreign currency transaction, whereas the customer has only a foreign transaction.

When the domestic company makes or receives payment in dollars, no special accounting procedures are necessary because no accounting issues exist. When the domestic company pays or receives in the foreign currency, however, several accounting issues arise. Before discussing these issues, we must define the following three dates that may be involved in a foreign currency transaction:

1. The **transaction date** is the date on which the transaction is initially recordable under generally accepted accounting principles.
2. **Intervening balance sheet dates** occur between the transaction date and the settlement date. A transaction recorded on August 20, 19X5, and settled on January 10, 19X6, would have five intervening balance sheet dates, assuming that monthly financial statements are prepared. Intervening balance sheet dates exist only for transactions in which credit terms are granted and used.
3. Payment is made on the **settlement date.** On this date, one currency is **converted** into the other currency. (When credit terms are not granted, the transaction date and the settlement date coincide.)

## Conceptual Issues

In foreign currency transactions, the first accounting issue pertains to how the transaction should be recorded in dollars at the transaction date. Accountants generally agree that the transaction should be recorded at the transaction date using the exchange rate in effect at that date. For an import transaction, therefore, the acquired asset is initially recorded at the dollar amount needed to purchase the amount of foreign currency that would settle the transaction at the transaction date. For an export transaction, the export sale is recorded at the dollar amount that would be received from converting the foreign currency into dollars if full payment were made at the transaction date.

If credit terms are not granted, no other accounting issues exist. If credit terms are granted and used, the following additional accounting issues arise:

1. If the exchange rate used to record the transaction at the transaction date has changed between the transaction date and an intervening balance sheet date, should the receivable or payable pertaining to the unsettled portion of the transaction be adjusted to reflect the current rate at such intervening balance sheet date?
2. If the transaction is settled at an amount different from that at which it was initially recorded, how should the difference be recorded?

With respect to the first issue, most accountants agree that any unsettled portion of the transaction represented by a payable or receivable should be adjusted at intervening balance sheet dates to reflect the exchange rate in effect at those dates. It makes sense to carry the receivable or payable at the amount of dollars that would be received or paid, respectively, if the transaction were settled on that date. **(This is essentially current-value accounting.)** There are two viewpoints concerning the second issue:

1. Under the **one-transaction perspective,** all aspects of the transaction are viewed as part of a single transaction. A company's commitment to pay or receive foreign currency is considered a necessary and inseparable part of the transaction to purchase or sell goods, respectively. The amount initially recorded at the transaction date is considered an estimate until the final settlement. As a result, the initially recorded cost of goods acquired or revenue is subsequently adjusted for any difference between the amount recorded at the transaction date and the amount at which the transaction is ultimately settled.

2. Under the **two-transaction perspective,** the commitment to pay or receive foreign currency is considered a separate transaction from the purchase or sale of goods. The decision to grant or use credit is considered a separate decision from that of purchasing or selling goods. As a result, any difference between the amount initially recorded at the transaction date and the amount at which the transaction is ultimately settled is considered a foreign currency transaction gain or loss—no adjustment is made to the initially recorded cost of goods acquired or revenues recorded pertaining to goods sold, as the case may be.

From either perspective, the risk in a foreign currency transaction from potential adverse exchange rate changes can be eliminated by not granting or using credit or by using a *forward exchange contract* (discussed later in the chapter).

**FASB Adopts the Two-Transaction Perspective.** The Financial Accounting Standards Board rejected the one-transaction approach in *FASB Statement No. 52* (as it did in *FASB Statement No. 8*) on the grounds that the consequences of the risks associated with foreign currency transactions should be accounted for separately from the purchase or sale of goods. Thus, the requirements of *FASB Statement No. 52* reflect the two-transaction perspective, and a domestic importer or exporter would account for such transactions as follows:

1. At the **transaction date,** measure and record in dollars each asset, liability, revenue, expense, gain or loss arising from the transaction

using the **current exchange rate** (the rate that could be used to settle the transaction at that date).

2. At each **intervening balance sheet date,** adjust the recorded balances of any foreign currency receivable or payable to reflect the current exchange rate (the rate at which the receivable or payable could be settled at that date).
3. Report in the income statement a **foreign currency transaction gain or loss** resulting from (a) adjustments made at any intervening balance sheet dates, and (b) any adjustments from settling the transaction at an amount different from that recorded at the latest intervening balance sheet date (or the transaction date when there are no intervening balance sheet dates).

In summary, the cost or the revenue arising from a transaction should be determined only once: when the transaction is initially recorded. The fact that credit terms are granted should not result in a later adjustment to the asset or service acquired, or to the revenue initially recorded, if the exchange rate changes between the transaction date and the settlement date. Any additional or lesser amount than that initially recorded represents a gain or loss that could have been avoided had the transaction been fully paid for when it occurred. Thus, any additional or lesser amount payable involves a decision to grant or exercise credit, which should be charged or credited to income in the period in which the exchange rate changes.

**ILLUSTRATION**    ## Import and Export Transactions

Assume a domestic company has the following import and export transactions with suppliers and customers in Britain:

1. On December 11, 19X1, inventory is acquired from Vendor A for 100,000 pounds. Payment is due in pounds on January 10, 19X2.
2. Inventory is sold to Customer X for 200,000 pounds on December 21, 19X1. Payment is due in pounds on January 20, 19X2.

Illustration 14-1 shows these transactions as initially recorded and as adjusted at the intervening balance sheet date (December 31, 19X1). Payments are made as required. The direct exchange rates (spot rates) for the applicable dates in December 19X1 and January 19X2 (when the pound was strengthening) are as follows:

| | |
|---|---|
| December 11, 19X1 | $1.50 |
| December 21, 19X1 | 1.52 |
| December 31, 19X1 | 1.55 |
| January 10, 19X2 | 1.57 |
| January 20, 19X2 | 1.60 |

### ■ ILLUSTRATION 14-1
### Recording Foreign Currency Transactions

| | | |
|---|---:|---:|
| **Entries Related to Vendor A** | | |
| **December 11, 19X1:** | | |
| Inventory (or Purchases) .......................... | 150,000 | |
|    Foreign Currency Payable .................... | | 150,000 |
|   To record purchase of inventory. | | |
|   (100,000 pounds × $1.50 = $150,000) | | |
| **December 31, 19X1:** | | |
| Foreign Currency Transaction Loss ................. | 5,000 | |
|    Foreign Currency Payable .................... | | 5,000 |
|   To adjust foreign currency payable to the current | | |
|    spot rate. | | |
|   ($1.55 − $1.50 = $.05) | | |
|   ($.05 × 100,000 pounds = $5,000) | | |
| **January 10, 19X2:** | | |
| Foreign Currency Transaction Loss ................. | 2,000 | |
|    Foreign Currency Payable .................... | | 2,000 |
|   To adjust foreign currency payable to the current | | |
|    spot rate. | | |
|   ($1.57 − $1.55 = $.02) | | |
|   ($.02 × 100,000 pounds = $2,000) | | |
| Foreign Currency................................. | 157,000 | |
|    Cash ....................................... | | 157,000 |
|   To record purchase of foreign currency. | | |
| Foreign Currency Payable.......................... | 157,000 | |
|    Foreign Currency ........................... | | 157,000 |
|   To record payment to vendor. | | |

In an alternative (shortcut) approach at January 10, 19X2, the Foreign Currency Payable account is not adjusted, but the following entry is made (rather than the first and third entries shown above for January 10, 19X2):

| | | |
|---|---:|---:|
| Foreign Currency Payable.......................... | 155,000 | |
| Foreign Currency Transaction Loss ................. | 2,000 | |
|    Foreign Currency ........................... | | 157,000 |

**Review Points for Illustration 14-1.** Note the following:

1. When its payments are due in pounds, the domestic company has a foreign currency transaction, not a foreign transaction.
2. Adjustments for the foreign currency transactions were necessary at December 31, 19X1, because the exchange rates had changed since the dates the transactions were initially recorded. Such adjustments would have been avoided if full payment had been made when the transactions were initially recorded.
3. The 19X1 net foreign currency transaction gain is $1,000 ($6,000 gain on receivable − $5,000 loss on payable). The net foreign currency transaction gain is credited to income in 19X1.
4. Foreign currency transaction gains are almost always taxable; thus, income taxes must be provided on the net foreign currency transac-

**■ ILLUSTRATION 14-1 (continued)**

**Entries Related to Customer X**
**December 21, 19X1:**

| | | |
|---|---:|---:|
| Foreign Currency Receivable . . . . . . . . . . . . . . . . . . . . . . | 304,000 | |
|    Sales . . . . . . . . . . . . . . . . . . . . . . . . . . . . . . . . | | 304,000 |

  To record sale.
  (200,000 pounds × \$1.52 = \$304,000)

**December 31, 19X1:**

| | | |
|---|---:|---:|
| Foreign Currency Receivable . . . . . . . . . . . . . . . . . . . . . . | 6,000 | |
|    Foreign Currency Transaction Gain . . . . . . . . . . . . . | | 6,000 |

  To adjust foreign currency receivable to the current
    spot rate.
  (\$1.55 − \$1.52 = \$.03)
  (\$.03 × 200,000 pounds = \$6,000)

**January 20, 19X2:**

| | | |
|---|---:|---:|
| Foreign Currency Receivable . . . . . . . . . . . . . . . . . . . . . . | 10,000 | |
|    Foreign Currency Transaction Gain . . . . . . . . . . . . . | | 10,000 |

  To adjust foreign currency receivable to the current
    spot rate.
  (\$1.60 − \$1.55 = \$.05)
  (\$.05 × 200,000 pounds = \$10,000)

| | | |
|---|---:|---:|
| Foreign Currency . . . . . . . . . . . . . . . . . . . . . . . . . . . . . | 320,000 | |
|    Foreign Currency Receivable . . . . . . . . . . . . . . . . . . | | 320,000 |

  To record collection from customer.
  (200,000 pounds × \$1.60 = \$320,000)

| | | |
|---|---:|---:|
| Cash . . . . . . . . . . . . . . . . . . . . . . . . . . . . . . . . . . . . . . | 320,000 | |
|    Foreign Currency . . . . . . . . . . . . . . . . . . . . . . . . . . | | 320,000 |

  To convert foreign currency into U.S. dollars.

In the alternative (shortcut) approach at January 20, 19X2, the Foreign Currency Receivable account is not adjusted, but the following entry is made (rather than the first two entries shown above for January 20, 19X2):

| | | |
|---|---:|---:|
| Foreign Currency . . . . . . . . . . . . . . . . . . . . . . . . . . . . . | 320,000 | |
|    Foreign Currency Receivable . . . . . . . . . . . . . . . . . . | | 310,000 |
|    Foreign Currency Transaction Gain . . . . . . . . . . . . . | | 10,000 |

tion gain. (Likewise, net foreign currency transaction losses are almost always tax deductible.)

5. When one of the parties to a foreign transaction incurs a foreign currency transaction gain or loss, the other party does not incur an opposite, offsetting foreign currency transaction gain or loss. Foreign currency transaction gains and losses, therefore, are one-sided.

## THE BASICS OF HEDGING

In addition to the basic importing and exporting transactions settled in a foreign currency, companies often enter into foreign currency transactions with dealers in foreign currency to hedge an existing foreign currency transaction (exposure), and to speculate. By *hedging*, a company can avoid a loss that may arise from an existing foreign currency transaction; the idea is to have a counterbalancing gain on the hedging transaction if a loss occurs on the existing foreign currency transaction. Three types of hedging transactions exist:

1. A hedge of a **recorded but unsettled** foreign currency transaction (such as from importing or exporting inventory).
2. A hedge of an **identifiable foreign currency commitment** (such as an order for inventory or equipment from a foreign company); in other words, a transaction that is **not yet recordable.**
3. A hedge of a **net investment** in a foreign operation or a hedge of a **net monetary position.** (Both are discussed in Chapter 16.)

The most common hedging or speculating transactions involve a forward exchange contract. (Less frequently used methods are discussed next along with forward exchange contracts.)

## Forward Exchange Contracts

A **forward exchange contract** is an agreement to buy or sell a foreign currency at a specified future date (usually within twelve months) at a specified exchange rate, commonly called the **forward rate.** Invariably, the forward rate is slightly above or slightly below the spot rate. The difference is primarily attributable to the difference in interest rates obtainable on the two currencies in the international money market for the duration of the contract.

When the interest rate obtainable on the dollar is higher than the interest rate obtainable on the foreign currency, the forward exchange rate is higher than the spot rate, and the foreign currency is said to be selling at a **premium** on the forward market. On the other hand, when the interest rate obtainable on the dollar is lower than the interest rate obtainable on the foreign currency, the forward exchange rate is lower than the spot rate, and the foreign currency is said to be selling at a **discount** on the forward market. The premium or discount rate multiplied by the units of foreign currency to be received or delivered under the contract equals the total amount of premium or discount on the forward exchange contract. This interest parity system, in effect, prevents the transfer of money between international money markets merely to obtain a higher interest rate relatively risk-free through the use of a forward exchange contract.

The following table summarizes when premiums and discounts occur and whether a debit or credit balance for the premium or discount results in recording the forward exchange contract:

| Buying or Selling Foreign Currency | Direct Rate | | Result[a] | |
|---|---|---|---|---|
| | Spot Rate | Forward Rate | Premium | Discount |
| Buying | $1.00 | $1.01 | x (Debit) | |
| Buying | $1.00 | $ .99 | | x (Credit) |
| Selling | $1.00 | $1.01 | x (Credit) | |
| Selling | $1.00 | $ .99 | | x (Debit) |

[a]Debits eventually reduce stockholders' equity, whereas credits eventually increase stockholders' equity.

When a currency is strengthening or weakening to a limited extent, the difference between the spot rate and the forward rate may also be attributable somewhat to expectations of what the spot rate will be at the specified future date. When a currency is strengthening or weakening to a greater extent and substantial economic or political uncertainties exist, the risks may be significant enough to cause the futures market to cease temporarily until stability is achieved.

Accounting for forward exchange contracts is different for the three types of hedging transactions and for speculative transactions. We discuss each of these areas separately.

# HEDGING A RECORDED BUT UNSETTLED FOREIGN CURRENCY TRANSACTION

A company that has a liability in a foreign currency is said to be in an **exposed liability position.** A company that has a receivable in a foreign currency is said to be in an **exposed asset position.** Because accounting for these situations is symmetrical, we illustrate only the first situation.

## Exposed Liability Position

The domestic company in Illustration 14-1 agreed to pay Vendor A 100,000 pounds for inventory on January 10, 19X2; the domestic company is in an exposed liability position. To avoid the risk of an exchange rate increase during the period from the transaction date (December 11, 19X1) to the settlement date (January 10, 19X2), the domestic company could enter into a 30-day forward exchange contract on December 11, 19X1, whereby it agreed to purchase 100,000 pounds on January 10, 19X2, at the currently existing forward exchange rate. Thus, the domestic company can determine now, rather than on January 10, 19X2, how many dollars are needed to obtain 100,000 pounds.

Entering into a forward exchange contract is an immediately recordable transaction. The domestic company has (1) a fixed dollar liability to the foreign currency dealer that is determined by multiplying the forward rate by the number of units of foreign currency to be acquired, and (2) a foreign currency receivable that is initially valued at the spot rate multiplied by the number of units of foreign currency to be acquired. At subsequent balance sheet dates before the forward contract expiration date, the foreign currency receivable is adjusted to reflect **the spot rate on that date.** The difference, if any, between the amounts initially recorded at 1 and 2 above represent either a premium or a discount that must be amortized over the life of the contract.

At the end of the contract, the fixed liability to the foreign currency dealer is extinguished by the payment of cash (dollars) to the dealer, and the foreign currency receivable is extinguished by receipt of the foreign currency from the foreign currency dealer. The latter part of the exchange requires a debit to a Foreign Currency account. When the foreign currency is delivered to Vendor A, the Foreign Currency account is credited and the Foreign Currency Payable account is debited.

By valuing the foreign currency receivable at the current spot rate (both initially and subsequently), the foreign currency receivable always equals the amount payable to Vendor A, because that amount is always adjusted to the current spot rate, as shown in Illustration 14-1. Accordingly, any exchange loss on the payable to Vendor A is exactly offset by an exchange gain on the foreign currency receivable—such is the purpose of the forward exchange contract. The shifting of risk to the foreign currency dealer also involves paying a commission charge that would be amortized over the life of the contract.

**ILLUSTRATION**

## Hedging a Recorded but Unsettled Foreign Currency Transaction

Illustration 14-2 shows the entries that would be made under a forward exchange contract entered into to protect the exposed liability position of the 100,000-pound purchase transaction with Vendor A. (For simplicity, we ignore commission charges.) The direct exchange rates for the applicable dates in December 19X1 and January 19X2 (when the pound was strengthening) were the following:

|  | Spot Rate | Forward Rate |
|---|---|---|
| December 11, 19X1 (the date the forward exchange contract was entered into) | $1.50 | $1.54 |
| December 31, 19X1 (the intervening balance sheet date) | 1.55 | n/a |
| January 10, 19X2 (the expiration date of the forward exchange contract) | 1.57 | n/a |

■ **ILLUSTRATION 14-2**

*Spot Rate*

*Forward Rate*

## Hedging a Recorded but Unsettled Transaction

| | | |
|---|---:|---:|
| **December 11, 19X1:** | | |
| Foreign Currency Receivable ($1.50 × 100,000 pounds) . | 150,000 | |
| Deferred Premium on Forward Exchange Contract . . . . . | 4,000 | |
|     Liability to Foreign Currency Dealer | | |
|       ($1.54 × 100,000 pounds) . . . . . . . . . . . . . . . . . . . . | | 154,000 |
|     To record initially the forward exchange contract. | | |
| **December 31, 19X1:** | | |
| Foreign Currency Receivable . . . . . . . . . . . . . . . . . . . . . . . | 5,000 | |
|     Foreign Currency Transaction Gain . . . . . . . . . . . . | | 5,000[a] |
|     To adjust the foreign currency receivable to the | | |
|       current spot rate. | | |
|     ($1.55 − $1.50 = $.05) | | |
|     ($.05 × 100,000 pounds = $5,000) | | |
| Premium Amortization Expense . . . . . . . . . . . . . . . . . . . . | 2,667 | |
|     Deferred Premium on Forward Exchange Contract | | 2,667 |
|     To amortize the premium on the contract. | | |
|     [(20 ÷ 30) × $4,000 = $2,667] | | |
| **January 10, 19X2:** | | |
| Foreign Currency Receivable . . . . . . . . . . . . . . . . . . . . . . | 2,000 | |
|     Foreign Currency Transaction Gain . . . . . . . . . . . . | | 2,000[b] |
|     To adjust the foreign currency receivable to the | | |
|       current spot rate. | | |
|     ($1.57 − $1.55 = $.02) | | |
|     ($.02 × 100,000 pounds = $2,000) | | |
| Premium Amortization Expense . . . . . . . . . . . . . . . . . . . . | 1,333 | |
|     Deferred Premium on Forward Exchange Contract | | 1,333 |
|     To amortize the premium on the contract. | | |
|     (10 ÷ 30 × $4,000 = $1,333) | | |
| Liability to Foreign Currency Dealer . . . . . . . . . . . . . . . . | 154,000 | |
|     Cash . . . . . . . . . . . . . . . . . . . . . . . . . . . . . . . . . . . . . . . . | | 154,000 |
| Foreign Currency . . . . . . . . . . . . . . . . . . . . . . . . . . . . . . . . | 157,000 | |
|     Foreign Currency Receivable . . . . . . . . . . . . . . . . . . . | | 157,000 |
|     To pay the foreign currency dealer in exchange for the | | |
|       receipt of 100,000 pounds. | | |

Note: In addition to the preceding entries (which relate only to the forward exchange contract), the following entry is necessary to discharge the liability to Vendor A:

| | | |
|---|---:|---:|
| Foreign Currency Payable . . . . . . . . . . . . . . . . . . . . . . . . . | 157,000 | |
|     Foreign Currency . . . . . . . . . . . . . . . . . . . . . . . . . . . . . | | 157,000 |

T-account Comparison: Note below how the receivable on the hedging contract is symmetrical to the payable on the inventory purchase transaction:

| | Hedging Contract | | | Inventory Purchase in Illustration 14-1 | |
|---|---|---|---|---|---|
| | **Foreign Currency Receivable** | | | **Foreign Currency Payable** | |
| Dec. 11 | 150,000 | | | 150,000 | Dec. 11 |
| Dec. 31 | 5,000 | | | 5,000 | Dec. 31 |
| | 155,000 | | | 155,000 | |
| Jan. 10 | 2,000 | | | 2,000 | Jan. 10 |
| | 157,000 | | | 157,000 | |
| | | 157,000 | Jan. 10    157,000 | | |
| | –0– | | | –0– | |

[a]This gain offsets the $5,000 foreign currency transaction loss on the importing transaction; see the journal entry on page 624.

[b]This gain offsets the $2,000 foreign currency transaction loss on the importing transaction; see the journal entry on page 624.

**Review Points for Illustration 14-2.**    Note the following:

1. During the 30-day period of the forward exchange contract, the pound strengthened from $1.50 to $1.57. Without the forward exchange contract, the $7,000 additional amount payable to Vendor A would not have been offset by the $7,000 foreign currency transaction gain.
2. Inasmuch as the foreign currency transaction loss on the amount payable to Vendor A is offset by the foreign currency transaction gain on the forward exchange contract, the net cost of the forward exchange contract is the $4,000 premium.
3. The forward exchange contract is an independent transaction in relation to the transaction with Vendor A. Accounting for one is independent of accounting for the other.

## Exposed Asset Position

An exposed asset position most often results from an exporting transaction in which payment is to be received in the foreign currency. In these situations, the domestic exporter agrees to **sell a specified number of foreign currency units at a specified future date.** Because the domestic company is selling foreign currency under the forward exchange contract, it also has a fixed receivable amount from the foreign currency dealer and a foreign currency amount payable (which is valued at the spot rate) to the foreign currency dealer. Any premium or discount is amortized to income over the life of the contract, along with the commission.

# HEDGING AN IDENTIFIABLE FOREIGN CURRENCY COMMITMENT

## Commitment to Purchase

A domestic company often enters into an agreement with a foreign company whereby the domestic company purchases goods to be delivered and paid for in the future in the foreign currency. In such situations, the future transaction date may be known or reasonably determinable, but the exchange rate cannot be known. Accordingly, the domestic company may desire to protect itself from the risks of exchange-rate fluctuations by entering into a forward exchange contract under which the domestic importer agrees to **purchase a specified number of foreign currency units at a specified future date.** In these situations, any gain or loss that arises from the forward exchange contract must be deferred until the transaction is recorded. The gain or loss is then subtracted from or added to the cost of the goods acquired. In addition, the premium or discount on the forward exchange contract may be either amortized over the life of the contract (as is required in exposed asset or exposed liability situations) or treated the same as a gain or loss arising from the forward exchange contract—that is, it may be deferred and added to or subtracted from, respectively, the cost of the goods acquired.

The rationale for deferring the foreign currency transaction gain or loss is that of the one-transaction perspective, introduced earlier. The one-transaction perspective makes sense in this situation because we are dealing with a commitment rather than a recorded purchase or sales transaction in which the cost or revenue has already been determined. This rationale also allows the premium or discount to be treated the same as a foreign currency transaction gain or loss. (Although *FASB Statement No. 52* does not specifically address them because of their immateriality, commission costs could also be treated in this manner under the one-transaction perspective.)

## ILLUSTRATION

### Hedging an Identifiable Foreign Currency Commitment (Purchase Commitment)

Assume a domestic company with a calendar year-end entered into the following transactions on October 10, 19X1:

1. It ordered equipment built to its specifications from a French manufacturer. The purchase price is 1,000,000 francs. Delivery is to be in 90 days (January 8, 19X2), and the payment is due then.
2. It contracted with a foreign currency dealer to purchase 1,000,000 francs on January 8, 19X2, at the forward exchange rate of $.098 plus a commission of $750.

Illustration 14-3 shows these transactions as initially recorded and as adjusted at the intervening balance sheet date (December 31, 19X1). Delivery and payments are made as required. The direct exchange rates for the applicable dates were the following:

|  | Exchange Rate | |
|  | Spot | Forward |
|---|---|---|
| October 10, 19X1 | $.100 | $.098 |
| December 31, 19X1 | .105 | n/a |
| January 8, 19X2 | .104 | n/a |

**Review Points for Illustration 14-3.** Note the following:

1. The capitalized cost of the equipment ($98,750) is determined as follows:

| | |
|---|---|
| Dollar equivalent of foreign currency paid to supplier (1,000,000 francs × $.104) | $104,000 |
| Less—Deferred transaction gain on forward exchange contract | (4,000) |
| Deferred discount on forward exchange contract | (2,000) |
| Plus—Deferred commission costs | 750 |
| | $ 98,750 |

## ■ ILLUSTRATION 14-3
### Hedging an Identifiable Foreign Currency Commitment

| October 10, 19X1: | | |
|---|---:|---:|
| Foreign Currency Receivable | | |
| (1,000,000 francs × $.10) . . . . . . . . . . . . . . . . . . . . . . . | 100,000 | |
| Deferred Commission Costs . . . . . . . . . . . . . . . . . . . . . . | 750 | |
| Liability to Foreign Currency Dealer | | |
| (1,000,000 francs × $.098 + $750 | | |
| commission) . . . . . . . . . . . . . . . . . . . . . . . . . . . . . | | 98,750 |
| Deferred Discount on Forward Exchange | | |
| Contract (1,000,000 francs × $.002) . . . . . . . . . | | 2,000 |
| To record initially the forward exchange contract. | | |

| December 31, 19X1: | | |
|---|---:|---:|
| Foreign Currency Receivable . . . . . . . . . . . . . . . . . . . . . . | 5,000 | |
| Deferred Foreign Currency Transaction Gain. . . . . | | 5,000 |
| To adjust the foreign currency receivable to the | | |
| current spot rate. | | |
| ($.105 − $.100 = $.005) | | |
| ($.005 × 1,000,000 francs = $5,000) | | |

The deferred discount and deferred commission costs need not be amortized, as it is assumed that they will be treated as adjustments to the purchase price of the equipment at the time of delivery.

| January 8, 19X2: | | |
|---|---:|---:|
| Deferred Foreign Currency Transaction Gain . . . . . . . . . . | 1,000 | |
| Foreign Currency Receivable. . . . . . . . . . . . . . . . . | | 1,000 |
| To adjust the foreign currency receivable to the | | |
| current spot rate. | | |
| ($.105 − $.104 = $.001) | | |
| (.001 × 1,000,000 francs = $1,000) | | |
| Liability to Foreign Currency Dealer. . . . . . . . . . . . . . . . | 98,750 | |
| Cash . . . . . . . . . . . . . . . . . . . . . . . . . . . . . . . . . | | 98,750 |
| Foreign Currency . . . . . . . . . . . . . . . . . . . . . . . . . . . . . | 104,000 | |
| Foreign Currency Receivable. . . . . . . . . . . . . . . . . | | 104,000 |
| To pay the foreign currency dealer in exchange | | |
| for the receipt of 1,000,000 francs. | | |

Note: In addition to the preceding entries (which relate only to the forward exchange contract), the following entry would be made to record the purchase of the equipment on January 8, 19X2 (when delivery and payment were made):

| | | |
|---|---:|---:|
| Deferred Discount on Forward Exchange Contract. . . . . . . . . . . . | 2,000 | |
| Deferred Foreign Currency Transaction Gain. . . . . . . . . . . . . . | 4,000 | |
| Equipment . . . . . . . . . . . . . . . . . . . . . . . . . . . . . . . . | 98,750 | |
| Deferred Commission Costs . . . . . . . . . . . . . . . . . . . . . | | 750 |
| Foreign Currency. . . . . . . . . . . . . . . . . . . . . . . . . . . . | | 104,000 |

2. If the forward exchange contract had not been entered into, the capitalized cost would have been $104,000.

3. The $4,000 foreign currency transaction gain can be treated as an adjustment to the $104,000 purchase price because the company's expected purchase price was $100,000 (based on the exchange rate existing when the equipment was ordered). The forward exchange contract merely locks in this price.

4. The discount and commission cost can be treated as adjustments to the locked-in purchase price of $100,000 because these items are necessary and incidental costs to protect or lock in the $100,000 purchase price.

## Commitment to Sell

Parallel accounting procedures are used when (1) the domestic company has entered into an agreement to sell goods to a foreign company in the future, with payment to be received in the foreign currency, and (2) the domestic company wishes to protect itself from the risk of exchange rate fluctuations by entering into a forward exchange contract to **sell a specified number of foreign currency units at a specified future date.**

## Qualifying Conditions

The following two conditions must be met for a forward exchange contract (or other foreign currency transaction) to qualify as a hedge of an identifiable foreign currency commitment:

a. The foreign currency transaction is designated as, and is effective as, a hedge of a foreign currency commitment.
b. The foreign currency commitment is firm.[1]

The "designation" part of the first condition merely means that **the company must identify the intent of the hedge with the foreign currency commitment.** Whether or not a hedge transaction is effective is an after-the-fact determination. Clearly, the hedge is effective if (1) the forward exchange contract is in the same currency as the transaction being hedged, and (2) the gain or loss on the hedging transaction is in the **opposite direction** to the loss or gain on the transaction being hedged.

The second condition is not defined in *FASB Statement No. 52.* However, it implies that the foreign currency commitment is either noncancelable or that the probability of cancellation is remote because of a severe monetary penalty.

**Transactions Other Than Forward Exchange Contracts.** The preceding two conditions are sufficiently broad that foreign currency transactions other than forward exchange contracts may qualify as hedges of foreign currency commitments. For example:

1. A U.S. company committed to constructing a building in France and receiving payment in francs could borrow francs to finance the

---

[1]*Statement of Financial Accounting Standards, No. 52,* "Foreign Currency Translation" (Stamford: Financial Accounting Standards Board, 1981), par. 21.

construction and designate the borrowing as a hedge of the commitment.

2. A U.S. company committed to purchasing inventory or equipment from a Japanese company could convert dollars into yen, hold or invest the yen, and designate them as a hedge of the commitment.

3. A U.S. company, or its Spanish subsidiary, could designate a foreign currency receivable in Italian lira as a hedge against a foreign currency purchase commitment in Italian lira.

**Other Technical Points.** The hedging transaction need not be entered into at the same time as the foreign currency commitment; nor must it extend from the foreign currency commitment date to the anticipated transaction date. Other technical points include the following:

1. If the hedging transaction extends **beyond the foreign currency commitment transaction date,** any gain or loss on the hedging transaction that occurs after that date cannot be deferred; it must be reported in the income statement as it arises.

2. If the hedging is terminated **before the foreign currency transaction commitment date,** any deferred gain or loss on the hedging transaction up to that point is still deferred and treated as part of the cost of the asset acquired or as an adjustment to the sales price of the asset sold.

3. If the hedging transaction amount **exceeds the foreign currency transaction commitment amount,** only the gain or loss on the hedging transaction up to the foreign currency transaction commitment amount may be deferred and included as an adjustment to the cost of the asset acquired or as an adjustment to the sales price of the asset sold.

4. Losses on hedging transactions related to a foreign currency transaction commitment cannot be deferred (but must be reported currently in the income statement) if such deferral would lead to recognizing losses in a later period.

## SPECULATING IN FOREIGN CURRENCY

When a company enters into a forward exchange contract that does not relate to a foreign currency exposure, the forward exchange contract is intended to produce an investment gain. Any gains or losses on such contracts are recognized currently in the income statement as they arise (no special deferral provisions exist for this type of hedging). In calculating gains and losses, the foreign currency receivable or payable must be **carried in the balance sheet at the current forward exchange rate for the**

**remaining life of the forward exchange contract** (rather than at the current exchange rate existing at each intervening balance sheet date). The current forward exchange rate is presumably a better indicator of the ultimate amount that will be received or paid when the contract expires. Because the foreign currency receivable or payable is initially recorded at the fixed liability to or receivable from the foreign currency dealer no accounting recognition is given to premiums and discounts.

ILLUSTRATION

## Speculating in Foreign Currency

Assume a domestic company with a calendar year-end concludes that the Swiss franc will strengthen within 90 days. Accordingly, it contracts with a foreign currency dealer on November 11, 19X1, to purchase 100,000 Swiss francs at the 90-day forward rate of $.49. (For simplicity, we ignore the commission charge, which would be amortized over the life of the contract.) Illustration 14-4 shows the entries that would be made for this contract using the following assumed direct exchange rates:

### ■ ILLUSTRATION 14-4
### Speculating in Foreign Currency

| November 11, 19X1: | | |
|---|---|---|
| Foreign Currency Receivable . . . . . . . . . . . . . . . . . . . . . . . . . | 49,000 | |
|     Liability to Foreign Currency Dealer . . . . . . . . . . . | | 49,000 |
|     To record initially the forward exchange contract. | | |
|     (100,000 francs × $.49 = $49,000) | | |
| **December 31, 19X1:** | | |
| Foreign Currency Receivable . . . . . . . . . . . . . . . . . . . . . . . . | 3,000 | |
|     Foreign Currency Transaction Gain. . . . . . . . . . . . . . | | 3,000 |
|     To adjust the foreign currency receivable to the forward | | |
|       rate available at the expiration of the contract. | | |
|     ($.52 − $.49 = $.03) | | |
|     (100,000 francs × $.03 = $3,000) | | |
| **February 9, 19X2:** | | |
| Foreign Currency Receivable . . . . . . . . . . . . . . . . . . . . . . . . | 5,000 | |
|     Foreign Currency Transaction Gain. . . . . . . . . . . . . . | | 5,000 |
|     To adjust the foreign currency receivable to the spot | | |
|       rate at the expiration of the contract. | | |
|     ($.57 − $.52 = $.05) | | |
|     (100,000 francs × $.05 = $5,000) | | |
| Liability to Foreign Currency Dealer. . . . . . . . . . . . . . . . | 49,000 | |
|     Cash . . . . . . . . . . . . . . . . . . . . . . . . . . . . . . . . . . . . . . . . . | | 49,000 |
| Foreign Currency. . . . . . . . . . . . . . . . . . . . . . . . . . . . . . . . . | 57,000 | |
|     Foreign Currency Receivable. . . . . . . . . . . . . . . . . . . | | 57,000 |
|     To pay the foreign currency dealer in exchange for the | | |
|       100,000 francs. | | |

Note: At February 9, 19X2, the company could convert the foreign currency of 100,000 francs into $57,000.

| | Spot Rate | Forward Rate for February 9, 19X2 |
|---|---|---|
| November 11, 19X1 (the date the forward exchange contract was entered into).. | n/a | $.49 |
| December 31, 19X1 (the intervening balance sheet date)................ | n/a | .52 |
| February 9, 19X2 (the expiration date of the forward exchange contract)....... | $.57 | n/a |

**Review Points for Illustration 14-4.**   Note the following:

1. The ultimate gain on the contract depends on the spot rate existing when the contract expires.
2. If the spot rate were used to value the foreign currency receivable at December 31, 19X1, (rather than the forward rate available for February 9, 19X2), the $8,000 total gain would have been reported differently than as shown in the illustration.

# END-OF-CHAPTER REVIEW

## Summary of Key Points

1. A foreign currency transaction involves a commitment to receive or purchase foreign currency in settlement of the transaction. When the transaction involves credit, the party engaging in the foreign currency transaction assumes the risk that the currency exchange rate may change between the transaction date and the settlement date.
2. The effect of exchange rate changes that occur between these two dates is called a foreign currency transaction gain or loss. Such gains or losses are accounted for separately from the purchase or sale of goods, as recorded on the transaction date. Transaction gains or losses are reported in the income statement in the period in which they occur.
3. A company usually enters into special foreign currency transactions to protect its exposure to exchange rate changes. (Illustration 14-5 summarizes how to account for gains and losses on such transactions.)

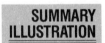

## Summary of Accounting for Special Foreign Currency Transactions

Illustration 14-5 summarizes the accounting treatment of the special foreign currency transactions.

## Glossary of New Terms

**Conversion**   The exchange of one currency for another.

**Discount or premium on forward exchange contract**   "The foreign currency amount of the contract multiplied by the difference between the contracted forward rate and the spot rate at the date of inception of the contract."*

**Foreign currency transactions**   "Transactions whose terms are denominated in a currency other than the entity's functional currency."* (As explained in Chapter

*FASB Statement No. 52, Appendix E, pp. 75–78.

# ■ ILLUSTRATION 14-5
## Summary of Accounting for Special Foreign Currency Transactions

| Type of Transaction | Accounting Treatment Accorded Gains and Losses | |
| --- | --- | --- |
| | Recognize Currently in the Income Statement | Special Treatment |
| A. Hedge of a recorded but unsettled foreign currency transaction | X | |
| B. Hedge of an identifiable foreign currency commitment | | Defer and treat as an adjustment to cost of item acquired or sales price of item sold. |
| C. Speculation in foreign currency | X | |

Other considerations pertaining to foreign currency transactions involving forward exchange contracts include the following:

1. In determining the gain or loss on the contract, the foreign currency receivable or payable is carried at the current (spot) rate (except in speculation situations, for which the available forward rate is used).

2. Premiums and discounts on forward exchange contracts are recognized currently in the income statement if the gain or loss on the contract is treated in that manner. If the gain or loss is given special treatment (as shown above), the premium or discount *may be given the same special treatment* or be recognized currently in the income statement. (Premiums and discounts are not recognized in speculation situations.)

15, a company's "functional" currency is that currency in which it primarily conducts its operations.)

**Forward exchange contract**   "An agreement to exchange at a specified future date currencies of different countries at a specified rate (forward rate)."*

**Forward rate**   *See* Forward exchange contract.

**Settlement date**   The date at which a receivable is collected or payable is paid.

**Spot rate**   "The exchange rate for immediate delivery of currencies exchanged."*

**Transaction date**   "The date at which a transaction (for example, a sale or purchase of merchandise or services) is recorded in accounting records in conformity with generally accepted accounting principles."*

**Transaction gain or loss**   "Transaction gains or losses result from a change in exchange rates between the functional currency and the currency in which a foreign currency transaction is denominated. They represent an increase or decrease in (a) the functional currency cash flows realized upon settlement of foreign currency transactions and (b) the expected functional currency cash flows on unsettled foreign currency transactions."*

# Self-Study Questions
*(Answers are at the end of this chapter.)*

1. A domestic exporter sold inventory to a foreign company on credit, with the transaction denominated in the foreign currency. Between the transaction date and the settlement date, the U.S. dollar strengthened. There was no intervening balance sheet date. The exporter should account for the change in the exchange rate as:

    a. A decrease to the initially recorded sales amount.

    b. An increase to the initially recorded sales amount.

    c. A gain or loss recognized currently in the income statement.

    d. A gain or loss to be deferred.

    e. None of the above.

2. On December 10, 19X1, a domestic importer purchased inventory on credit from a foreign vendor, with payment to be made in the foreign currency. The direct exchange rate was $.80 on December 10, 19X1, and $.83 on December 31, 19X1 (the importer's year-end). On January 5, 19X2 (the settlement date), the direct exchange rate was $.79. At December 31, 19X1, the importer should report:

    a. An increase to the amount initially recorded for inventory.

    b. A decrease to the amount initially recorded for inventory.

    c. A gain or loss to be deferred.

    d. A gain currently in the income statement.

    e. A loss currently in the income statement.

3. A domestic company that enters into a forward exchange contract to sell foreign currency when the spot rate is $.55 and the forward exchange rate is $.53 has:

    a. A premium that is recorded as a debit.

    b. A premium that is recorded as a credit.

    c. A discount that is recorded as a debit.

    d. A discount that is recorded as a credit.

4. A domestic exporter that enters into a forward exchange contract to hedge a recorded but unsettled exporting transaction must do the following:

    a. Any foreign currency transaction gain or loss on the hedging transaction is to be deferred until the settlement date.

    b. The receivable from the foreign currency dealer is to be initially recorded at the spot rate.

    c. The liability to the foreign currency dealer is to be initially recorded at the contractually fixed amount to be paid.

    d. The foreign currency receivable is to be continuously carried at the forward exchange rate.

    e. None of the above.

5. A domestic buyer enters into a forward exchange contract to hedge an identifiable foreign currency commitment. Which of the following is correct?

    a. Any foreign currency transaction gain or loss on the forward exchange contract (up to the transaction date for the item being bought) may be deferred and treated as an adjustment to the cost of the item being bought.

    b. The receivable from the foreign currency dealer is to be initially recorded at the fixed contractual amount.

    c. The receivable from the foreign currency dealer is to be continually carried at the forward exchange rate.

    d. The gain or loss on the forward exchange contract will exactly offset the loss or gain on the purchase contract.

    e. None of the above.

6. On December 10, 19X1, Hedgley Company entered into a 90-day forward exchange contract involving 1,000,000 French francs in anticipation that the French franc would weaken. The following direct exchange rates are assumed:

|  | Spot Rate | Forward Rate (for March 10, 19X2) |
|---|---|---|
| December 10, 19X1 . . . . . . . . . . . . . . . . . . . . . . . . | $.90 | $.86 |
| December 31, 19X1 | | |
| (Hedgley's year-end) . . . . . . . . . . . . . . . . . . . . . | .88 | .87 |
| March 10, 19X2 . . . . . . . . . . . . . . . . . . . . . . . . . | .91 | n/a |

The amount of the foreign currency transaction gain or loss that would be reported in the income statement for 19X1 on the forward exchange contract, assuming the contract is a hedge of a recorded but unsettled inventory sale transaction, is:

a. $10,000 gain.   f. $30,000 loss.
b. $10,000 loss.   g. $40,000 gain.
c. $20,000 gain.   h. $40,000 loss.
d. $20,000 loss.   i. $–0–.
e. $30,000 gain.   j. None of the above.

7. Use the information in question 6, but assume that the forward exchange contract pertains to a hedge of an identifiable foreign currency involving the sale of special equipment.

8. Use the information in question 6, but assume that the forward exchange contract pertains to speculation in foreign currency.

# ASSIGNMENT MATERIAL

## Review Questions

1. Differentiate between conversion and translation.
2. What is the direct quotation rate? the indirect quotation rate?
3. What is meant when a currency is said to be strengthening? weakening?
4. What does *denominated* mean?
5. What is the difference between a foreign transaction and a foreign currency transaction?
6. Summarize the two-transaction perspective.
7. Summarize the one-transaction perspective.
8. Why would a company enter into a forward exchange contract?
9. How does a company treat gains and losses on forward exchange contracts related to hedges of identifiable foreign currency commitments?
10. What two conditions must be met to qualify a forward exchange contract as a hedge of an identifiable foreign currency commitment?

## Exercises

| E |
|---|
| 14-1 |

### Exchange Rates

On January 1, 19X1, 100,000 pesos could be converted into $400. On December 31, 19X1, 100,000 pesos could be converted into $500.

**Required:**
1. Express the relationship between the two currencies at each date directly and indirectly.
2. Did the peso strengthen or weaken during 19X1? Did the dollar strengthen or weaken during 19X1?

## Basic Understanding of Foreign Currency Exposure

**E 14-2**

The Docker Company has many importing and exporting transactions that require settlement in foreign currency (LCU). Credit terms are granted and used.

**Required:**
1. Docker should be concerned about whether the direct exchange rate:
   a. Goes up.
   b. Goes down.
2. Indicate in the following table what the foreign currency exposure concern should be:

| Transaction | Billing Currency | Whether the Dollar Will Strengthen | Weaken | Whether the LCU Will Strengthen | Weaken |
|---|---|---|---|---|---|
| Importing | Dollar | _____ | _____ | _____ | _____ |
| Importing | LCU | _____ | _____ | _____ | _____ |
| Exporting | Dollar | _____ | _____ | _____ | _____ |
| Exporting | LCU | _____ | _____ | _____ | _____ |

## Basic Understanding of Forward Exchange Contracts

**E 14-3**

The Hedgley Company has foreign operations and importing and exporting transactions that require settlement in a foreign currency. The company often enters into forward exchange contracts to hedge its foreign currency exposure and occasionally to speculate. Hedgley must determine whether it should contract to buy or sell a foreign currency in each of the following situations:

| Area of Foreign Currency Exposure | Direct Rate or Currency | Direction | Buy | Sell |
|---|---|---|---|---|
| 1. Exporting | Direct rate | Up | — | — |
|  | Direct rate | Down | — | X |
|  | U.S. dollar | Strengthen | — | X |
|  | U.S. dollar | Weaken | — | — |
|  | Foreign | Strengthen | — | — |
|  | Foreign | Weaken | — | X |
| 2. Importing | Direct rate | Up | X | — |
|  | Direct rate | Down | — | — |
|  | U.S. dollar | Strengthen | — | — |

| Area of Foreign Currency Exposure | Future Expectation | | | |
|---|---|---|---|---|
| | Direct Rate or Currency | Direction | Buy | Sell |
| | U.S. dollar | Weaken | X | — |
| | Foreign | Strengthen | X | — |
| | Foreign | Weaken | — | — |
| 3. n/a—Speculation | Foreign | Strengthen | X | — |
| | Foreign | Weaken | — | X |

### Required:

Put an X in the appropriate buy or sell column in the table.

---

> **E 14-4**

## Accounting for a Travel Advance

On December 26, 19X1, the vice-president of marketing of Plano Company was given a $6,000 travel advance for a 10-day trip to the United Kingdom. On that date, the vice-president converted the $6,000 into 12,000 pounds. During this 10-day trip, the pound steadily weakened against the dollar. The exchange rate at December 31, 19X1, was 1 pound equals $.48. On January 5, 19X2, the vice-president returned and submitted to the company cashier 1,100 pounds and receipts for 10,900 pounds that had been spent. On this date, the exchange rate was 1 pound equals $.42. Of the 10,900 pounds spent during the trip, 5,700 had been spent by December 31, 19X1.

### Required:

Prepare all entries required at December 31, 19X1, and January 5, 19X2, in connection with this travel advance.

## Problems

> **P 14-1**

## Importing and Exporting Transactions: No Intervening Balance Sheet Date

During July 19X5, the Billings Company had the following transactions with foreign businesses:

| Date | Nature of Transaction | Billing Currency | Exchange Rate (Direct) |
|---|---|---|---|
| **Vendor A** | | | |
| July 1, 19X1 | Imported merchandise costing 1,000,000 pesos from Mexico City wholesaler.................... | Pesos | $.0070 |
| July 10, 19X1 | Paid 50% of amount owed........... | | .0071 |
| July 31, 19X1 | Paid remaining amount owed........ | | .0066 |
| **Customer A** | | | |
| July 15, 19X1 | Sold merchandise for 50,000 francs to French wholesaler ............. | Francs | $.130 |
| July 20, 19X1 | Received 50% payment ............. | | .120 |
| July 30, 19X1 | Received entire payment............ | | .125 |

**Required:**

Prepare journal entries for these transactions.

## Importing and Exporting Transactions: Intervening Balance Sheet Date

P 14-2

During June and July of 19X1, the Quartex Company (which reports on a calendar-year basis and issues quarterly financial statements) had the following transactions with foreign businesses:

| Date | Nature of Transaction | Billing Currency | Exchange Rate (Direct) |
|------|----------------------|------------------|------------------------|
| **Vendor A** | | | |
| June 15, 19X1 | Imported merchandise costing 100,000 Canadian dollars from Canadian manufacturer . | Canadian dollars | $ .80 |
| July 15, 19X1 | Paid entire amount owed . . . . . . . | | .77 |
| **Customer A** | | | |
| June 20, 19X1 | Sold merchandise for 10,000 pounds to London retailer . . . . | Pounds | $1.55 |
| June 30, 19X1 | Received 50% payment. . . . . . . . | | 1.52 |
| July 10, 19X1 | Received remaining amount owed . . . . . . . . . . . . . . . . . . . . | | 1.54 |

The exchange rate on June 30, 19X1, for Canadian dollars was $.79.

**Required:**

Prepare journal entries for the above transactions. (Be sure to prepare journal entries at June 30, 19X1, when necessary.)

## Hedging an Exposed Liability Position: Intervening Balance Sheet Date

P 14-3

On October 17, 19X1, Bavaro Company purchased merchandise costing 40,000,000 lira from the Vinnie Company of Italy. The spot rate (direct) on that date was $.00062. Payment is due in lira in 90 days.

Concurrently, Bavaro entered into a foreign exchange contract, whereby it agreed to purchase 40,000,000 lira for delivery in 90 days at $.00065 (the forward rate). On December 31, 19X1, the spot rate was $.00068, and on January 15, 19X2 (the date Vinnie was paid in full), the spot rate was $.00066. Bavaro has a June 30 fiscal year-end and issues quarterly financial reports.

**Required:**

Prepare the journal entries to record the above transactions. (Be sure to prepare journal entries at December 31, 19X1, when necessary.)

P 14-4

## Hedging an Exposed Asset Position: Intervening Balance Sheet Date

On April 1, 19X3, Niagara Company, a calendar-year reporting company that issues quarterly financial reports, sold merchandise to a Canadian company for 100,000 Canadian dollars. The spot rate (direct) on April 1, 19X3, was $.81. Payment is due in 120 days.

Concurrently, Niagara entered into a forward exchange contract to sell 100,000 Canadian dollars at $.80 (the forward rate). The spot rate on July 30, 19X3, was $.82. Assume that payment was made on July 30, 19X3. (The spot rate on June 30, 19X3, was $.825.)

### Required:

Prepare the entries related to the above transactions, including appropriate June 30, 19X3, adjustments.

P 14-5

## Hedging an Identifiable Foreign Currency Commitment: Intervening Balance Sheet Date

On October 1, 19X1, Vail Company, a calendar-year reporting company, entered into a noncancelable contract with a Swiss company, whereby the Swiss company would manufacture a custom-built aerial tram for 1,000,000 francs, with delivery to be in 180 days and payment to be in Swiss francs. On October 1, 19X1, the exchange rate (direct) was $.47.

Concurrently, Vail entered into a forward exchange contract (at a commission cost of $1,000) to acquire 1,000,000 Swiss francs in 180 days at $.48. At December 31, 19X1 (the only intervening balance sheet date for purposes of this problem), the current exchange rate was $.463. Assume that delivery and payment were made in 180 days and that Vail desires to maximize earnings in 19X1. Assume that the spot rate on March 30, 19X2, was $.45.

### Required:

Prepare the entries related to the above transactions, including appropriate adjustments at the intervening month-end.

### SOLUTIONS TO SELF-STUDY QUESTIONS

| | |
|---|---|
| 1. c | 5. a |
| 2. e | 6. c |
| 3. c | 7. i |
| 4. e | 8. b |

# 15
# •••••

# TRANSLATION OF FOREIGN CURRENCY FINANCIAL STATEMENTS: CONCEPTS

## *TOPIC OUTLINE*

# CHAPTER OVERVIEW

I n the first section of this chapter, we cover some basics of international business and explain why so many U.S. companies have overseas manufacturing subsidiaries. We then examine the diversity of accounting practices around the world. Finally, we discuss the conceptual issues pertaining to the translation of foreign currency financial statements into U.S. dollars. The detailed specific requirements of *FASB Statement No. 52*, insofar as it pertains to the translation of foreign currency financial statements, are discussed in Chapter 16.

## The Accounting Issues

**Foreign Operations.** Through internal or external expansion, some companies build or acquire overseas manufacturing or marketing organizations, which may conduct import or export activities with the domestic operation. Such foreign operations may be conducted through either branches or subsidiaries, but the most common form of organization is the subsidiary, because it best insulates legally the foreign operation from the domestic operation. There are three accounting issues for foreign operations of a domestic parent:

1. How should the earnings and losses of the foreign units be determined in U.S. dollars?
2. What additional risks must be considered in reporting earnings from foreign operations? Is consolidation appropriate?
3. Should supplemental information disclose the extent of a company's foreign operations?

## The Governing Pronouncements

**Translation.** The translation of foreign currency financial statements into U.S. dollars is widely recognized as one of the most complex and controversial of all accounting issues. *FASB Statement No. 52*, "Foreign Currency Translation," was issued in 1981 after three years of intensive research and extensive participation by professionals in industry, public accounting, higher education, and finance. *FASB Statement No. 52* replaced *FASB Statement No. 8*, "Accounting for the Translation of Foreign Currency Transactions and Foreign Currency Financial Statements," which was issued in 1975. *FASB Statement No. 8* outlined uniform translation procedures for the translation of foreign currency financial statements (an area previously characterized by numerous practices that often produced widely different results). However, the results under the uniform treatment prescribed by *FASB Statement No. 8* were widely criticized as not reflective of economic changes, and the business community's strong opposition to and continued criticism of the pronouncement resulted in FASB's decision in 1979 to reconsider the entire translation issue.

**Additional Risks and the Appropriateness of Consolidation.**   The additional risks associated with foreign operations are discussed later in this chapter. The appropriateness of consolidating foreign subsidiaries was addressed in Chapter 3. Recall that consolidation of a subsidiary is mandatory, unless control is lacking, in which case consolidation is not allowed.

**Supplemental Disclosures.**   The issue of presenting in financial statements supplemental information pertaining to the extent of a company's foreign operations is addressed in *FASB Statement No. 14*, "Financial Reporting for Segments of a Business Enterprise." This pronouncement was discussed in detail in Chapter 13, which covers segment reporting.

## GOING INTERNATIONAL

American companies conduct business abroad in two general ways: They either export goods and services from the United States, or they produce goods and services in foreign countries. Any domestic company considering international business must also understand the variations within these two general categories so as to select the alternative that best meets its goals. This discussion follows Chapter 14 because it is first necessary to have a basic familiarity with exchange rates and exposure to foreign currency transactions and their attendant risks (as discussed in Chapter 14). These various alternatives are as follows:

I. **Exporting:**
   1. Export to an independent distributor.
   2. Export through a foreign commission agent.
   3. Export by establishing a foreign marketing branch.
   4. Export by establishing a foreign marketing subsidiary.
   5. Export using an export trade vehicle, such as a Foreign Sales Corporation (FSC) or an Interest Charge-Domestic International Sales Corporation (IC-DISC).
II. **Manufacturing Overseas:**
   1. Establish a foreign manufacturing branch.
   2. Establish a foreign manufacturing subsidiary.
   3. Establish a domestic subsidiary that establishes a foreign manufacturing branch.

It is beyond the scope of this book to discuss each of these alternatives more than briefly, as that is more appropriate in an international business or tax course. Because tax considerations are usually of great importance, we also briefly examine federal income tax considerations pertaining to each alternative. Finally, we discuss in general some of the major reasons why U.S. companies prefer manufacturing overseas to exporting goods to foreign countries.

---

### Fortune 500 Company Profile

**Raychem Corporation**

- Founded in 1957
- 1989 sales of $1.1 billion
- Number of foreign sales offices: 45 (in 45 countries)
- Number of foreign manufacturing plants: 20
- Percentage of foreign sales to total sales: 62%

---

## EXPORTING

### Exporting to an Independent Distributor

To demonstrate this first alternative, we will take the example of a domestic manufacturer that sells its product to an unrelated, independent distributor in Switzerland. The Swiss distributor takes physical possession and legal title to the inventory, which it sells to the ultimate Swiss consumer using its own marketing efforts. The U.S. company is subject to U.S. federal, state, and local income taxes on its profit (the sales price minus the cost of goods sold and other related expenses). Because the U.S. company has no physical presence in Switzerland, it is not subject to the Swiss tax system. Of course, the Swiss distributor is subject to Swiss income taxes on its profit (but the Swiss company is not subject to U.S. taxes, because it has no business activity in the U.S.).

### Exporting through a Foreign Commission Agent

To illustrate this alternative, assume a U.S. manufacturer uses a British broker as its commission agent. The broker solicits British customers for the U.S. company and receives a commission on each sale obtained. The commission is tax deductible by the U.S. manufacturer. Generally, the U.S. company is not subject to British income taxes under this arrangement. However, if the U.S. company establishes a physical presence in Great Britain, such as by renting a warehouse or hiring employees, then the chances of being subject to British income taxes increase. To determine if the U.S. company is subject to British income taxes, it is necessary to examine British tax statutes and the U.S.–Great Britain income tax treaty.

## Exporting by Establishing a Foreign Marketing Branch

A **branch** can be an office, a warehouse, or U.S. employees conducting activities in a foreign country on behalf of the U.S. home office. These activities are deemed to represent the physical presence of the U.S. company in the foreign country and make the branch subject to the foreign country's income taxes. For U.S. tax purposes, the branch's profits are also taxable in the U.S. (Likewise, branch losses are tax deductible in the U.S.) To avoid double taxation on branch profits, U.S. tax laws allow foreign income taxes to be treated as credits against any U.S. income taxes.

For example, assume a domestic company establishes a branch in France, which has a statutory income tax rate of 42%, compared to the U.S. income tax rate of 34%. If the branch has $100,000 of profit, then it will pay $42,000 in taxes to the French government. No additional tax will be paid to the U.S. government because $42,000 of tax credits more than offset the $34,000 of taxes otherwise payable. Thus, the domestic company has what is commonly called "excess foreign tax credits." This means that the domestic company is paying taxes on its worldwide income at more than the U.S. statutory rate of 34%. With most foreign countries having income tax rates higher than 34%, many companies operating with foreign marketing branches have this problem.

A highly specialized area of income tax law has developed around "managing excess foreign tax credits" for the purpose of developing strategies designed to minimize and use excess foreign tax credits so that the income taxes on worldwide income are as close as is legally possible to 34%. (At many universities that offer graduate degrees in taxation, one course in the program deals almost exclusively with this topic.)

**Fair Transfer Pricing Rules.** A domestic company that transfers inventory to its foreign marketing branch must take into consideration the U.S. and foreign country's arm's length transfer pricing rules, so that gross profit is not artificially shifted from the high income tax rate country to the low income tax rate country (thereby depriving one country of its fair share of taxes). To prevent the possibility of later adjustments by taxing authorities, the fairness of the transfer prices must be supportable.

## Exporting by Establishing a Foreign Marketing Subsidiary

To insulate the foreign marketing operation legally from the domestic operation, a foreign subsidiary would be used instead of the branch form of organization. Setting up a foreign subsidiary is a more critical consideration for a U.S. company's overseas manufacturing operations, however,

## PERSPECTIVE

## Fair Transfer Pricing Becomes a Hot Issue

As this book goes to print, the Internal Revenue Service is investigating hundreds of U.S. subsidiaries owned by foreign corporations on the suspicion that they have underpaid U.S. corporate income taxes by billions in the 1980s. For 1986, the latest year for which figures are available, the nearly 37,000 foreign-owned companies that filed tax returns in the U.S. reported revenues of $543 billion and costs and expenses of $544 billion. More than half of these companies reported losses. Many of these foreign-owned subsidiaries are distributors of manufactured goods in the automobile and electronics industry, a high percentage of which are owned by Japanese companies.

At issue is the fairness of the intercompany transfer price. An artificially high transfer price on sales to a U.S. subsidiary would result in little or no income taxes being paid to the U.S. government. As a result, virtually all of the profit would be reported in the foreign countries, with virtually all of the income taxes being paid to the foreign governments. At first glance, it would appear that the foreign manufacturing parent companies would set the transfer prices artificially low rather than artificially high, inasmuch as the U.S. corporate income tax rate of 34% is significantly lower than the corporate income tax rate of almost all major trading nations. This would result in a lower overall corporate income tax rate on worldwide income. The motivation for the alleged high transfer prices, however, may be the "nationalism" factor—that is, foreign companies may rather pay income taxes to their own governments (many of which subsidize certain industries) than to a foreign government (the U.S.) even though they will pay more taxes than they otherwise would have to pay.

For many years, the IRS has been frustrated by (1) the lack of cooperation by the foreign parent companies of U.S. subsidiaries, and (2) the difficulty in auditing the transfer prices (since records are kept in foreign countries, in foreign languages, and in much less detail than would be required in the United States). In 1989, Congress passed a law that increases the IRS's broad authority to levy fines up to $10,000 a month (from $1,000) if a foreign government does not promptly comply with demands for records or testimony. (The former $24,000 cap on such fines was removed as well.) Possibly of greater importance, the IRS was empowered to determine what it thinks a fair transfer price should be if a foreign company does not produce records. In determining fair transfer prices, the IRS is employing economists to assist them in addressing questions such as: Why keep a marginally profitable or loss-incurring U.S. subsidiary operating year after year? Some former top executives of electronic subsidiaries have admitted the transfer prices set by the Japanese parent companies were purposely set artificially high so that the U.S. subsidiary would not report a profit and, thus, not have to pay any U.S. income taxes.

Source: Certain information in this perspective was drawn from the following articles: "IRS Suspects Foreign Firms Owe It Billions," *The Wall Street Journal*, February 20, 1990, p. 3.; "Many Japanese Companies' U.S. Subsidiaries under Investigation by IRS for Tax Fraud," *San Jose Mercury News*, February 18, 1990, p. 12A (a reprint from the New York Times); and "The Independence Issue," *San Jose Mercury News*, March 20, 1988, p. 6A. Also, certain information was obtained from an interview with an IRS official handling audits involving transfer pricing issues.

and we discuss these implications later in the section covering foreign manufacturing subsidiaries. The transfer pricing problem discussed earlier also applies here.

Unlike a foreign marketing branch (whose profits are taxed currently in the U.S.), the profits of a foreign subsidiary are not taxed in the United States until paid out in dividends. Most foreign countries withhold a portion of the dividends being repatriated to the U.S. (formally called dividend withholding taxes, which range generally from 5% to 15%). The system of allowable credits previously explained for branches (to prevent double taxation) is equally applicable to subsidiaries. When dividends are paid, the taxes withheld on dividends by the foreign government are also allowed as credits against U.S. income taxes otherwise payable on the foreign subsidiary's earnings.

**"Controlled Foreign Corporation" Rules.**    If a foreign subsidiary is controlled by one or several domestic companies and has certain types of income activity, some or all of the foreign corporation's earnings must be reported currently for U.S. tax purposes by the U.S. parent—even though such earnings remain undistributed. These rules are commonly known as the **"controlled foreign corporation"** (CFCs) or **"Subpart F"** provisions. For example, certain passive income (interest, dividends, and rents) or income from certain foreign sales, services, or shipping subsidiaries will be taxed to the controlling U.S. parent corporation just as if the equity method of accounting were used for tax purposes.

## Using an Export Trade Vehicle

The Revenue Act of 1971 established a new type of domestic corporation, referred to as a **Domestic International Sales Corporation (DISC).** The purpose of this act was to give tax incentives to U.S. companies to increase their exports. Because the European Community objected to DISCs on the grounds that they resulted in an illegal export subsidy on export income earned in the U.S. (in violation of tariff and trade agreements), the DISC system was replaced (for the most part) in 1984 with the newly created system of **Foreign Sales Corporations (FSC).** A discussion of these vehicles follows:

1. **Foreign Sales Corporation.** A domestic company that establishes a foreign corporation (one not chartered in the U.S.) may elect to have that corporation treated as a Foreign Sales Corporation. Under the FSC system, a portion (15%) of the foreign trade income of an FSC is exempt from U.S. federal income taxes. Although potential tax savings vary with the particular circumstances, the 34% U.S. income tax rate can be reduced by as much as 5.1% (34% × 15%). Numerous requirements must be met for qualification as an FSC. (A "small FSC"

having fewer compliance requirements is available for smaller businesses.) The foreign trade income of the FSC must result from the foreign presence and activity of the FSC. Thus, a domestic company cannot set up a shell corporation overseas merely to obtain tax benefits. (The system of tax credits discussed earlier for foreign branches is equally applicable to FSCs.)

2. **Interest Charge–Domestic International Sales Corporation (IC–DISC).** Domestic International Sales Corporations that were not eliminated by the Tax Reform Act of 1984 are treated as interest charge–DISCs, the benefits of which are designed for small businesses. An IC–DISC is a U.S. corporation that earns profit on export sales. Approximately 50% of the profit is deferred from current U.S. taxation. However, a favorably low rate of interest must be paid to the U.S. government on the deferred tax liability. Consequently, this vehicle can be viewed as merely a means of obtaining a low interest loan from the U.S. government.

## MANUFACTURING OVERSEAS

### Establishing a Foreign Manufacturing Branch

Earlier we described the use of a foreign marketing branch as a means of generating export sales. A foreign branch can be used to manufacture products (as well as to market products). All of the tax rules discussed earlier for foreign marketing branches apply equally as well here. However, many foreign countries prohibit the establishment of manufacturing branches because they insist on a percentage of the operation being owned locally. This forces a company into forming a foreign subsidiary if it intends to manufacture in that particular country. **A domestic company that sells inventory to its foreign manufacturing branch must take into consideration the U.S. and foreign country's arm's length transfer pricing rules, which were discussed earlier in connection with foreign marketing branches.**

### Establishing a Foreign Manufacturing Subsidiary

By forming a foreign subsidiary, the parent, in theory, has legally insulated the foreign subsidiary's operations from those of the parent. For instance, if a major disaster happens at the foreign manufacturing plant, the parent's monetary exposure is limited to the amount it has invested in the subsidiary. Sometimes, however, a parent company (possibly for public relation purposes) will assume responsibility for liabilities beyond those that can be paid by the foreign subsidiary (as did Union Carbide Corporation by paying $470 million after the tragic disaster in 1984 at its manufacturing subsidiary in Bhopal, India, where more than 3,300 people were killed in an explosion).

**The transfer pricing issue and the manner of taxation (including the controlled foreign corporation rules) discussed earlier, apply here.** Manufacturing subsidiaries established in certain U.S. possessions (such as Puerto Rico) may be exempt from both U.S. federal income taxes and Puerto Rican taxes.

## Establishing a Domestic Subsidiary That Establishes a Foreign Manufacturing Branch

Sometimes a domestic company desires to manufacture in a foreign country using the branch form of organization but while insulating the foreign operations from the domestic. By forming a domestic subsidiary, the subsidiary can then establish a foreign manufacturing branch. A reason for using the branch form of organization overseas is to have any technology and patents that are used by the foreign operation remain subject to U.S. patent laws. Some foreign countries (such as the Philippines) have virtually no patent laws. If such technology and patents were transferred to a foreign subsidiary, then U.S. patent protection could be lost inasmuch as the foreign subsidiary would be subject to the laws of the foreign country.

## EXPORTING VERSUS MANUFACTURING OVERSEAS—PRIMARY REASONS FOR MANUFACTURING OVERSEAS

Historically, a primary reason for a U.S. company deciding to manufacture domestically and export to foreign countries was to keep the technology at home, as well as the jobs. In the last 30 years, however, the lure of cheaper foreign labor abroad has enticed many companies to manufacture abroad. Many foreign countries also grant "tax holidays" as an incentive for U.S. corporations to build manufacturing plants in their countries. This makes manufacturing overseas extremely attractive, inasmuch as companies will pay very low or no income taxes until the earnings are repatriated to the U.S. For example, in the 1980s, Ireland granted total income tax relief until 1990 and then a 10% income tax rate until the year 2000. Some companies have also found from internal studies over many decades that the most successful way to generate sales abroad is to have a manufacturing presence in foreign countries.

## The Fluctuating Exchange Rate Problem—Another Major Incentive to Manufacture Overseas

During the last 15 years under the floating exchange rate system, exchange rates have fluctuated tremendously. A major problem for domestic exporters under the floating exchange rate system is that whenever the U.S. dollar strengthens considerably, foreign customers must pay higher prices for U.S. exports because they need to come up with more units of their currency than if the dollar had not strengthened. A strong dollar makes it difficult for U.S. companies to sell abroad (unless they are willing to lower their prices and thereby reduce their operating margins). Of course, the ability to sell U.S. products overseas is made easier when the dollar weakens.

Rather than continually dealing with this roller-coaster exchange rate environment, scores of companies have decided to produce products overseas in the country in which the product will be sold, thus neutralizing the impact of exchange rate changes. This is just one more reason for U.S. companies to manufacture overseas rather than to export domestically.

## The Risks of Investing Abroad

Against all of the considerable advantages to manufacturing overseas versus exporting must be weighed the risks of having U.S. funds invested overseas. An asset held in a foreign country is not the same as an asset held domestically. Assets held in foreign countries entail the following additional risks:

1. **Expropriation,** or the seizure of assets.
2. **Devaluation,** or the diminution of value of the cash flows from future operations because of adverse changes in the exchange rate.
3. **Currency transfer restrictions,** or the limitation on repatriation of foreign profits and invested capital. (Many companies must go to extreme lengths to get earnings sent back to the U.S.)
4. **Wars and civil disorders.**

The remainder of this chapter deals with translating the financial statements of foreign subsidiaries into U.S. dollars.

## GETTING IN STEP WITH U.S. GENERALLY ACCEPTED ACCOUNTING PRINCIPLES

Companies establish foreign operations with the expectation that these units will generate profits on the investments made. Domestic companies, therefore, want to isolate for analysis the profit or loss generated by their foreign units. Each foreign unit keeps its books and records in its own local currency. However, the profit or loss of a foreign unit as stated in the foreign currency is not meaningful to the domestic parent or home office; domestic companies must be able to determine the profit or loss of each of their foreign units in dollars. This is done by translating the foreign currency financial statements into dollars, using appropriate currency exchange rates. However, translating profit or loss amounts of foreign units into dollars is complicated by the fact that foreign units use the accounting principles of the countries in which they are located—not U.S. generally accepted accounting principles.

## The Diversity of Worldwide Accounting Principles

Accounting principles are not uniform worldwide. Different national laws, different tax laws, and varying degrees of formalization of accounting and reporting practices by standard-setting bodies in the private sector are the main reasons for these differences. Some of the major differences are as follows:

1. **LIFO inventory costing.** Although widely used in the United States, this method has virtually no acceptance in other countries.
2. **Interperiod income tax allocation.** Although mandatory in the United States, only a handful of other countries require it.
3. **Pooling of interests.** Although required in the United States when the specified criteria are met, it is allowed in only a few other countries and then only under rigid constraints. Pooling of interests is unheard of in many countries.
4. **Goodwill amortization.** Amortization is mandatory in the United States, but most foreign countries do not require it, allowing goodwill to appear on the balance sheet practically forever.

The following examples demonstrate the range and diversity of accounting practices in foreign countries.

### Australia

- Land and buildings are reported at either cost or appraised values (or a mixture of both), less depreciation.
- Certain nonmanufacturing assets may not be depreciated.
- All cost in excess of an acquired business's net assets at book value is usually deemed to be goodwill. Goodwill may be shown as a deduction from capital or charged to capital.

### Brazil

- All fixed assets are written up once a year, using indexes published by the federal government that are based on the percentage of inflation that occurred during the year. Depreciation for financial and tax reporting purposes is based on the revalued amounts.
- A provision for "maintenance of working capital" may be recorded to remove from profit the effect of inflation on current and long-term assets (excluding fixed assets) and liabilities. This provision is also deductible for tax-reporting purposes.

### France

- Pension costs are provided only to the extent that such provisions are deductible for income tax purposes.

### Italy

- The national legislative body periodically authorizes companies to revalue their fixed assets to reflect inflation.

### Japan

- Goodwill may be expensed as incurred or amortized over a maximum of five years.
- Research and development costs may be deferred over a maximum of five years.
- Losses generally are not provided on inventory that is obsolete or slow-moving.

### Mexico

- Most industrial and retail firms revalue their fixed assets annually to current appraised value.
- Some companies report income tax expense on the cash basis.
- All cost in excess of an acquired business's net assets at book value is deemed to be goodwill.

### Switzerland

- The equity method is not used to account for long-term investments.
- Machinery and equipment may be expensed at the time of purchase.

### United Kingdom

- Goodwill may be written off immediately to stockholders' equity or amortized to income. No maximum amortization period exists.

### West Germany

- Intangible assets cannot be amortized over more than five years (compared to 40 years in the U.S.).
- Certain inventory valuation methods may result in a valuation lower than that produced by applying the lower of cost or market rule.

Just as it does not make sense to add together financial statement amounts in dollars and foreign currencies, it would not be meaningful financial reporting to report worldwide operations using one set of accounting principles for domestic operations and a variety of accounting principles for foreign operations. Accordingly, when foreign currency financial statements are prepared using accounting principles and practices that are materially different from U.S. generally accepted accounting principles, such statements must be **restated** to reflect U.S. generally accepted accounting principles **before they are translated into dollars.**

The lack of worldwide uniform accounting principles and practices is unfortunate, as the article on page 657 reflects. Some international accounting organizations (most notably the International Accounting Standards Committee, which has issued nearly 30 international accounting standards) are seeking to promote worldwide uniform accounting principles and practices. The problem is not only one of reaching agreement on what the worldwide accounting principles should be but also of persuading countries to adopt uniform accounting principles. Both aspects of the problem are monumental, and efforts to date have produced only limited results. However, the increasing propensity of companies to try to raise capital in world markets (outside their home countries) is becoming a factor in internationalizing accounting principles.

National preferences aside, adjusting a foreign subsidiary's financial statements to the U.S.'s generally accepted accounting principles is nothing more complicated than making correcting entries, a subject that is covered in intermediate accounting. However, the difficulty lies in the fact that there are usually many such restatement entries for each foreign subsidiary.

## CONCEPTUAL ISSUES

The process of translating foreign currency financial statements into dollars is merely a mechanical process, once the exchange rate for each account has been determined. However, for many years a raging controversy has existed over the following two conceptual issues:

1. Which exchange rates should be used to translate the foreign currency financial statements into dollars?
2. How should the effect of a change in the exchange rate be reported?

In this section we devote considerable attention to the substance of this controversy and the solutions that have been tried and rejected. This background is a solid base for understanding the rationale for and the requirements of *FASB Statement No. 52*. More importantly, this section emphasizes thinking rather than memorization of detailed rules and requirements, thereby enabling you to better evaluate the requirements of *FASB Statement No. 52* independently.

### CONCEPTUAL ISSUE 1: WHICH EXCHANGE RATES TO USE?
### Criteria Used as a Frame of Reference

The first conceptual issue is determining the appropriate exchange rates for translating the individual assets and liabilities in the balance sheet.

## PERSPECTIVE

### Where Boards and Governments Have Failed, the Market Could Internationalize Accounting

A French manufacturing company listed recently on the Paris Bourse looks like a promising investment. Its financial statement shows booming international sales and a healthy profit. The company's earnings outshine the disappointing results of a comparable U.S. concern in the same business.

There's only one problem. The two companies used different foreign-currency translation methods during a year of wild exchange-rate fluctuations. Because the concerns took different paths to the bottom line, the figures there could differ by millions of dollars.

Accounting experts warn that this lack of uniformity in financial statements—the absence of a world-wide accounting language—threatens the growing internationalization of trade, investment, and securities markets. If investors and managers of multinational enterprises can't get understandable financial information about foreign companies and subsidiaries, they are less likely to venture abroad.

Consequently, all kinds of international bodies are trying to harmonize accounting standards. But their success has been limited, and the real changes may come from the companies themselves. As more large European firms seek to raise funds on world markets, especially in the U.S., they have had to upgrade their accounting practices and, in many cases, adopt U.S. accounting standards to attract investors and meet government filing requirements.

Such de facto harmonization could force national governments and accounting bodies to harmonize their standards. "Economics may force something that has been lagging for the last 30 years," says Edmund Coulson, deputy chief accountant of the U.S. Securities and Exchange Commission.

Many groups are working on the problem. The Organization for Economic Cooperation and Development, which monitors developed economies, gathered international business and accounting leaders here recently to discuss the barriers to standardization. The International Accounting Standards Committee, representing accountants in 65 nations, has issued more than 20 nonbinding international accounting standards. The United Nations has a group working on the problem, and the European Common Market has issued several directives requiring European companies to standardize their financial statements.

But widely varying national laws, as well as national pride, still are roadblocks. "Given the complexity of the subject and the weight of the past, the goal of harmonization still seems to be a rather long way off," says Jean-Claude Paye, the OECD's secretary-general. Donald J. Kirk, chairman of the Financial Accounting Standards Board, the professional body that hammers out accounting standards for U.S. companies, says: "Harmonization even within the U.S. is difficult, so I have to be a pessimist about international prospects."

But the growing influence of standards issued by Mr. Kirk's group may spur that harmonization. U.S. accounting rules—the so-called generally accepted accounting principles—are observed in most audits by large U.S. accounting firms. In addition, the SEC requires all companies seeking a public listing in the U.S. to comply with these principles. Some European companies, anxious to tap the deep pool of funds available in U.S. markets, have adopted the guidelines.

The number of foreign companies seeking listings in the U.S. is growing rapidly. Transactions in the U.S. in stock of foreign companies rose from $2.03 billion in 1970 to nearly $30 billion in 1983. Eighteen companies located outside the U.S. and Canada raised about $1 billion in the U.S. in 1983.

Aside from capital, a U.S. listing "gives the impression that the company is on the move

---

**Where Boards and Governments Have Failed, the Market Could Internationalize Accounting** (continued)

and a major player," says Alfredo Scotti, who helped direct Saipem S.p.A's adoption of U.S. accounting standards in anticipation of a New York Stock Exchange offering.

Mr. Scotti says Saipem, the engineering and oil services unit of Ente Nazionale Idrocarburi, Italy's state energy holding company, came out of the process a changed entity. For one thing, earnings increased because of different rules governing the depreciation of fixed assets. (Continental European accounting practices tend to minimize profits, with the aim of minimizing taxes, while U.S. practices tend to maximize profits, with the aim of impressing potential investors.)

Some of the differences in accounting practices have a national rationale that causes European accountants to resist the wholesale, "imperialistic" imposition of U.S. standards. While countries should seek to promote international harmonization of accounting standards, "each should be free to use the methods best suited to it and its traditions," says French Finance Minister Pierre Beregovoy.

"There's a danger in trying to apply in France standards hammered out for a different country—that is, America," says Bertrand d'Illiers, chief accountant at the Paris Bourse.

Even advocates of U.S. standards express concern that they may have become too detailed and rigid. The FASB, in its 12 years of existence, has issued 80 statements refining general accounting principles, a trend Mr. Kirk worries may lead to "standards overload."

In fact, the SEC has modified some of its requirements for offerings by foreign companies. For example, companies don't need to report the salaries of individual officers, but only aggregate executive compensation. And differences in national accounting practices are permitted if the required information is provided and a means exists to reconcile it with U.S. standards.

Source: Paul Hemp, "Where Boards and Governments Have Failed, the Market Could Internationalize Accounting," *The Wall Street Journal*, May 8, 1985, p. 38. Reprinted by permission of *The Wall Street Journal*, © Dow Jones & Company, Inc. 1985. All rights reserved worldwide.

---

The translation of the stockholders' equity accounts is not part of the issue, because the total translated stockholders' equity is a forced residual amount that is the difference between the total translated assets and the total translated liabilities. Once the appropriate exchange rates have been determined for the assets and liabilities, consistency and logic dictate the appropriate exchange rates for translating the income statement accounts.

Balance sheet accounts may be conveniently grouped into **monetary** and **nonmonetary** classifications (the same classification scheme used in constant-dollar accounting). Monetary items include cash and accounts that are contractually obligated to be settled in cash—namely receivables and payables. All other accounts—Inventory, Fixed Assets, and the equity accounts, for example—are nonmonetary. This first conceptual issue is discussed shortly for each of these categories.

Accountants have used the following criteria as a frame of reference for determining the appropriate exchange rates:

1. Does the exchange rate selected for a specific account result in a meaningful dollar amount?

2. Does the exchange rate selected for a specific account change the basis of accounting in translation? (For example, is the historical cost basis for fixed assets in the foreign currency retained when translation is made into dollars?)
3. When a change has occurred in the exchange rate, do the translated results reflect the economic impact of the change?

The first two criteria require no explanation. For the last criterion, understand that when a U.S. company has invested money in a foreign country, an increase in the direct exchange rate is a favorable economic event that should result in a positive report. Likewise, a decrease in the direct exchange rate is an unfavorable economic event that should result in an adverse report. For example, assume someone invested $1,000 in a savings account in a Mexican bank when the direct exchange rate was $.08 (as many U.S. citizens did in 1975–1976 because of the high interest rates). The bank would credit the account for 12,500 pesos ($1,000 ÷ $.08). Assume that the direct exchange rate then dropped to $.04 (as it did in 1976). If he or she then withdrew the 12,500 pesos and converted them into dollars, he or she would have only $500 (12,500 × $.04). This decrease in the direct exchange rate was indeed an adverse economic event that caused the net worth to decrease by $500.

In the discussion to follow of the first conceptual issue, we refer to the effect of a change in the exchange rate as a **translation adjustment.** How to report a change in the exchange rate is a controversial issue that we address in our discussion of the second conceptual issue.

## Translating Monetary Accounts

Most accountants agree that the only sensible way to translate monetary items is to use the exchange rate in effect at the balance sheet date (a current exchange rate). This procedure effectively values these items on a current-value basis, which is considered the most useful reporting basis. For example, assume the following information:

1. A domestic company formed a West German subsidiary on January 1, 19X1.
2. The domestic company acquired the subsidiary's common stock for $400,000 on that date when the direct exchange rate was $.40. (The subsidiary immediately converted the $400,000 into 1,000,000 marks.)
3. The subsidiary had no other transactions from its inception to December 31, 19X1 (the parent's and its year-end).
4. The direct exchange rate at December 31, 19X1, was $.50. (Thus, either the mark strengthened or the dollar weakened during this period—from the companies' viewpoint it does not matter which occurred.)

What is the appropriate exchange rate to translate the 1,000,000 marks at December 31, 19X1, into dollars? The only meaningful dollar amount is the dollar equivalent of marks—that is, the number of dollars into which the 1,000,000 marks could be converted. Obviously, only the $.50 direct exchange rate at December 31, 19X1, gives a meaningful answer ($500,000). Using the $.40 exchange rate that existed at January 1, 19X1, would give $400,000, an amount that has absolutely no meaning or usefulness at this time. Accordingly, the translation process for the Cash and the Common Stock accounts as of January 1, 19X1, and December 31, 19X1, would be as follows:

| | Amount (marks) | January 1, 19X1 Rate | January 1, 19X1 Amount | December 31, 19X1 Rate | December 31, 19X1 Amount |
|---|---|---|---|---|---|
| Cash . . . . . . . . . . | 1,000,000 | $.40 | $400,000 | $.50 | $500,000 |
| Common stock . | 1,000,000 | .40 | 400,000 | .40[a] | 400,000 |
| Translation adjustment (the effect of the change in the exchange rate). . . . . . . . . . . . . . . . . . . . . . . . . . . . . . . . . . . . . . | | | | | 100,000 |

[a]The historical exchange rate of $.40 must be used here to isolate the effect of the change in the exchange rate.

If the parent liquidated the foreign subsidiary on December 31, 19X1, it would receive $500,000, not the $400,000 it initially invested. The parent's investment actually increased in value during 19X1 by $100,000. The use of the $.50 exchange rate existing at the balance sheet date reflects the economics of what has transpired. (Recall that the increase in the direct exchange rate is a favorable economic event.) In summary, all three criteria listed on pages 658–59 are satisfied.

**Monetary Items Other Than Cash.** To translate the remaining monetary items (receivables and payables), we use the logic that was applied to the Cash account. Because receivables are one step away from cash, the only meaningful dollar amount is the dollar equivalent of the receivables. Likewise, payables require the use of cash, so the only meaningful dollar amount is the dollar equivalent that would be needed to settle the payables. The direct exchange rate existing at the balance sheet date is the only exchange rate that produces meaningful dollar amounts. Furthermore, the use of the exchange rate existing at the balance sheet date does not change the valuation basis of these accounts in translation. (For example, the valuation basis of receivables in a foreign currency is *net realizable value*, and the use of the exchange rate existing at the balance sheet date produces the dollar equivalent of the net amount expected to be realized.) Finally, as with Cash, the use of the exchange rate existing at the balance sheet date reflects the economic impact of any change in the exchange rate. Thus, all three criteria listed on pages 658–59 are satisfied.

## Translating Nonmonetary Accounts: An Introduction to the Controversy

Accountants do not agree on the appropriate exchange rates to translate nonmonetary accounts at the balance sheet date. Two schools of thought have evolved concerning the appropriate exchange rate to use at the balance sheet date to translate nonmonetary accounts into dollars: the **U.S. dollar perspective** and the **foreign currency perspective,** discussed shortly.

### Is the Monetary–Nonmonetary Distinction Relevant?
Under the U.S. dollar perspective, the distinction between monetary and nonmonetary items is crucial, and, therefore, the use of the exchange rate existing at the balance sheet date (a current exchange rate) is deemed inappropriate for nonmonetary accounts. Under the foreign currency perspective, the distinction between monetary and nonmonetary items is irrelevant, and the exchange rate existing at the balance sheet date may be used for nonmonetary accounts.

In deciding whether a distinction between monetary and nonmonetary is relevant, it is important to realize that a foreign unit's buildings and equipment, although classified as nonmonetary items, are actually transformed from nonmonetary into monetary assets. Nonmonetary assets generate a cash flow, part of which constitutes a recovery of the cost of these assets. Of course, the process takes as long as the depreciation lives selected, and the transformation is not as evident as when nonmonetary assets are sold (disposed of) outright for cash. Because of this transformation process, when the exchange rate changes, the cash flow generated by these nonmonetary assets is worth either a greater number of dollars (when the direct exchange rate increases) or a lesser number of dollars (when the direct exchange rate decreases). Thus, in determining the appropriate exchange rate to translate nonmonetary items into dollars, we may view nonmonetary assets as being on the way to becoming monetary assets.

## The U.S. Dollar Perspective

To illustrate the U.S. dollar perspective, let us change slightly the facts from the example used in the discussion of monetary accounts by assuming the foreign subsidiary used the 1,000,000 marks from the issuance of the common stock to purchase a parcel of land on January 1, 19X1. Thus, at December 31, 19X1, it has Land reported at 1,000,000 marks in its balance sheet instead of Cash of 1,000,000 marks.

**The Rationale.** From the **U.S. dollar perspective,** foreign operations are viewed as extensions of the parent company. Therefore, **all transactions must be translated in a manner that produces the dollar equivalent of the transaction at the time the transaction occurred.** From this perspective, the historical cost of the land in dollars is the amount of dollars that were needed to acquire it on January 1, 19X1. Because we know this amount is $400,000, the only exchange rate that translates the 1,000,000 marks into this amount is the historical exchange rate of $.40 (the rate in effect on January 1, 19X1). Using the historical exchange rate not only expresses the cost of the land in dollars, but it also **changes the unit of measure from the foreign currency to the dollar.** Thus, the cost of the land has been **"remeasured" and expressed in U.S. dollars.** (This concept is difficult to grasp now; at this point, you should understand it fully after you have studied the foreign currency perspective, discussed later, under which the foreign currency is retained as the unit of measure in the translation process.) The historical exchange rate retains or preserves the historical cost measurement basis in dollars. Fixed assets of the domestic parent and its foreign units are therefore reported in consolidation on the same historical cost basis in terms of the reporting currency (U.S. dollars). Proponents of this approach claim that the results are clearly meaningful dollar amounts.

**Its Shortcoming.**   The shortcoming of the U.S. dollar perspective is that **it completely disregards how changes in the exchange rate affect the nonmonetary accounts.** Changes in the exchange rate are economic events that have considerable impact on the U.S. parent company, which has invested money in the foreign unit. This fact holds true regardless of whether the foreign unit holds all monetary assets, all nonmonetary assets, or any combination of the two. When the effects of a change in the exchange rate are not reflected in the reporting results, the parent is effectively pretending that the exchange rate did not change.

To illustrate this shortcoming, we first deal with a situation in which the exchange rate changes and nonmonetary assets are financed entirely by a capital (common stock) investment by the parent. In a second situation, the nonmonetary assets are financed entirely by a local loan in the foreign country, and the parent has a nil investment in the subsidiary.

### Situation 1: Parent Company Financing of Nonmonetary Assets

Let us continue with the example in the preceding discussion to see how a favorable economic event (an increase in the direct exchange rate) is not reported because the historical exchange rate is used to translate the nonmonetary accounts into dollars. Using the information presented so far, we know the translation process for the Land and Common Stock accounts as of January 1, 19X1, and December 31, 19X1, would be as follows:

| | Amount (marks) | January 1, 19X1 Rate | January 1, 19X1 Amount | December 31, 19X1 Rate | December 31, 19X1 Amount |
|---|---|---|---|---|---|
| Land . . . . . . . . . . | 1,000,000 | $.40 | $400,000 | $.40 | $400,000 |
| Common stock . | 1,000,000 | .40 | 400,000 | .40 | 400,000 |

This presentation clearly shows that the economic impact of the change in the exchange rate is not reported under this approach. However, from an economic viewpoint, the parent's $400,000 initial investment has increased in value to $500,000, because the direct exchange rate has increased from $.40 at January 1, 19X1, to $.50 at December 31, 19X1. (The $100,000 increase would be considered an unrealized increase in value.)

This concept is more understandable if we assume that the land was sold on December 31, 19X1, for cash of 1,000,000 marks, its book value on that date. On the date of sale, cash of 1,000,000 marks would be translated at $.50, resulting in $500,000. This translated amount is $100,000 more than the Land account would show if the land were still owned. (Note that we do not assume that the land has appreciated in value in marks—the value in marks holds constant at 1,000,000.) However, because historical exchange rates are used to translate nonmonetary accounts, this favorable economic event (the increase in the direct exchange rate) is never reported. What is equally misleading is that if the land is sold on January 1, 19X2 (instead of December 31, 19X1), for cash of 1,000,000 marks (its book value), a $100,000 favorable result would be reportable at that time (assuming the exchange rate did not change from December 31, 19X1), even though nothing happened economically on January 1, 19X2. (Likewise, a decrease in the exchange rate in 19X1 from $.40 to $.32—an unfavorable economic event—would be ignored in the reporting process, even though from an economic viewpoint the parent's $400,000 initial investment has decreased in value by $80,000 to $320,000.)

### Situation 2: Foreign Financing of Nonmonetary Assets

To minimize the risk of investing in foreign companies (including the risk that the exchange rate could change adversely), U.S. companies commonly finance foreign operations through foreign borrowings to the extent possible, thereby keeping their investments in the foreign units as small as possible. To illustrate this situation, let us change the example in the preceding discussion as follows:

1. The foreign subsidiary was so thinly capitalized by the parent on January 1, 19X1, that we can ignore the translation of the Common Stock account.
2. The foreign subsidiary borrowed 1,000,000 marks from a local bank on January 1, 19X1, and used the proceeds to purchase the parcel of land. (The loan is payable in marks.)
3. For simplicity, interest expense on the loan is ignored.
4. No principal payments were made on the loan in 19X1.

From this we determine the translation process for the Land and Notes Payable accounts (the loan is a monetary item) as of January 1, 19X1, and December 31, 19X1, as follows:

| | Amount | January 1, 19X1 | | December 31, 19X1 | |
|---|---|---|---|---|---|
| | (marks) | Rate | Amount | Rate | Amount |
| Land . . . . . . . . . . | 1,000,000 | $.40 | $400,000 | $.40 | $400,000 |
| Notes payable . . | 1,000,000 | .40 | 400,000 | .50 | 500,000 |
| Translation adjustment (the effect of the change in the exchange rate). . . . . . . . . . . . . . . . . . . . . . . . . . . . . . . . . . . . . . . . . . . . . . . . . | | | | | (100,000) |

An adverse result of $100,000 would be reported under this translation approach. We might conclude from this result that it would take $100,000 more to pay off the loan at December 31, 19X1, than were needed at December 1, 19X1. However, the adverse result exactly offsets the $100,000 increase in value of the land, which is completely ignored because of the use of the historical exchange rate of $.40 for the land at December 31, 19X1.

We may more easily understand why nothing adverse has actually occurred from an economic viewpoint by assuming that the land was sold on December 31, 19X1, for cash of 1,000,000 marks, its book value on that date. On the date of sale, cash of 1,000,000 marks would be translated at $.50 into $500,000 rather than at $.40 into $400,000. The translated cash amount of $500,000 equals the translated note payable amount of $500,000, and no translation adjustment is needed. Interestingly, if the land is sold on January 1, 19X2 (rather than on December 31, 19X1), for cash of 1,000,000 marks (its book value), a favorable result of $100,000 would be reportable at that time (assuming the exchange rate does not change from December 31, 19X1), even though nothing happened economically on January 1, 19X2. Note also that this $100,000 favorable result for 19X2 completely offsets the $100,000 unfavorable result reportable for 19X1.

The most convincing proof that nothing adverse has happened during 19X1, as far as the parent's investment in the subsidiary is concerned, is the fact that the parent's investment is negligible. It had nothing invested and therefore nothing at risk. To report a $100,000 adverse result for 19X1 under these conditions makes no sense. (The same logic would be applied if the exchange rate decreased during 19X1 from $.40 to $.32 but the reporting results would be reversed.) Accordingly, when the parent can finance the foreign unit's nonmonetary assets with foreign borrowings that are repayable in the foreign currency, a change in the exchange rate has no economic impact on the parent. In this situation, the reporting of favorable and unfavorable results is viewed as mere paper gains and losses that are reversed in later periods—in other words, timing differences. From this viewpoint, it is not sensible to report adverse results in one period that are offset by favorable results in later periods and vice versa.

### The Two Translation Methods That Fit under the U.S. Dollar Perspective.

Two translation methods fit under the U.S. dollar perspective—the temporal method and the monetary–nonmonetary method. Under the **temporal method,** which can accommodate any measurement basis (historical cost, current replacement price, or current market price), a foreign currency measurement is changed into a dollar measurement without changing the measurement basis. Thus, **the accounting principles are not changed** (even though the unit of measure has been changed to the dollar). The measurement basis of an asset or liability determines the exchange rate used in translating that asset or liability. Accordingly, different exchange rates are used for different measurement bases (for example, historical exchange rates, for fixed assets and a current exchange rate for receivables). The **monetary–nonmonetary** method is merely a classification scheme whereby all monetary assets and liabilities are translated at the exchange rate existing at the balance sheet date, and all nonmonetary assets and liabilities are translated at historical exchange rates. Under current generally accepted accounting principles, the results of the temporal method coincide with those of the monetary–nonmonetary method. However, if accounting principles change so that nonmonetary assets (such as marketable equity securities) are measured at current prices instead of at historical prices or at the lower of cost or market, the results would be different. The temporal method could accommodate such accounting principles, whereas the monetary–nonmonetary method could not, because the measurement basis would not be maintained in the translation process.

### The Focus for Both Methods: Net Monetary Position.

Under both the temporal and the monetary–nonmonetary translation methods, the monetary or nonmonetary composition of the individual assets and liabilities is critical in determining whether a favorable or unfavorable result is reported as a consequence of a change in the exchange rate. In this respect, the focus is on the *net monetary position.* An excess of monetary assets over monetary liabilities is referred to as a **net monetary asset position;** an excess of monetary liabilities over monetary assets is referred to as a **net monetary liability position.** If the direct exchange rate has increased since the beginning of the period (a favorable economic event), a company in a net monetary asset position reports a favorable result; if it is in a net monetary liability position, the company reports an unfavorable result. On the other hand, if the direct exchange rate has decreased since the beginning of the period (an unfavorable economic event), a company in a net monetary asset position reports an unfavorable result, but if a company is in a net monetary liability position, it reports a favorable result.

### The FASB's First Attempt in Addressing the Translation Issue.

In 1975, the Financial Accounting Standards Board (FASB) adopted the U.S. dollar perspective by requiring the temporal method of translation in all cases.

The unusual results that occur under the U.S. dollar perspective led to a reconsideration of the entire translation issue in 1979. *FASB Statement No. 52* superseded *FASB Statement No. 8* in 1981, and the U.S. dollar perspective is now called for only in certain situations discussed in Chapter 16.

## The Foreign Currency Perspective

**The Rationale.**   From the foreign currency perspective, a foreign operation is a separate business unit whose only factual financial statements are those prepared in its foreign currency. From this premise, we reason that **the relationships of items must be maintained in the translation process.** The only way to maintain the relationships of items in translation is to use a single exchange rate for all assets and liabilities. For example, assume a British subsidiary has total assets of 500,000 pounds. If Land is reported at 150,000 pounds, then Land is 30% of the total assets. In translating into U.S. dollars, the only way to maintain the Land at 30% of the total assets in dollars is to use the same exchange rate for all assets. The use of the current rate for monetary assets and historical rates for nonmonetary assets would result in Land being more or less than 30% of total assets in dollars.

The exchange rate existing at the balance sheet date (a current exchange rate) is presumably the single most meaningful exchange rate. For translation using a single exchange rate, **the foreign currency is the "unit of measure"** in the dollar financial statements. **Thus, the nonmonetary accounts are not translated to their dollar equivalent when the transactions were recorded.** Consequently, **the nonmonetary accounts are not remeasured in dollars—they are only expressed in dollars.** The use of the exchange rate existing at the balance sheet date clearly overcomes the objections raised for the U.S. dollar perspective—namely, that the economic impact of the change in the exchange rate is completely ignored in the translation of the nonmonetary accounts. As a result, the proponents of the foreign currency perspective assert that the translated amounts are obviously meaningful dollar amounts.

**Is the Translated Amount Historical Cost?**   The most difficult result to understand under the foreign currency perspective is whether the amount expressed in dollars should be considered historical cost or some form of current value. Let us continue with the example of translating the value of land that we used in discussing the U.S. dollar perspective. Under the foreign currency perspective, the foreign subsidiary's Land and Common Stock accounts would be translated into dollars at January 1, 19X1, and December 31, 19X1, as follows:

|  | Amount (marks) | January 1, 19X1 | | December 31, 19X1 | |
|---|---|---|---|---|---|
|  |  | Rate | Amount | Rate | Amount |
| Land . . . . . . . . . . | 1,000,000 | $.40 | $400,000 | $.50 | $500,000 |
| Common stock . | 1,000,000 | .40 | 400,000 | .40[a] | 400,000 |
| Translation adjustment (the effect of the change in the exchange rate) . . . . . . . . . . . . . . . . . . . . . . . . . . . . . . . . . . . . . . . . . |  |  |  |  | 100,000 |

[a]The historical exchange rate of $.40 must be used here to isolate the effect of the change in the exchange rate.

The $500,000 translated amount for the land at December 31, 19X1, is not historical cost in terms of the equivalent number of dollars that were needed to acquire the land on January 1, 19X1 (that is, $400,000). Advocates of the foreign currency perspective claim that **the $500,000 is the historical cost of the land using the foreign currency as the unit of measure rather than the dollar.** If the direct exchange rate were $.60 at December 31, 19X2 (one year later), then the historical cost using the foreign currency as the unit of measure would be $600,000 (1,000,000 marks × $.60). Thus, the land would be reported in the consolidated financial statements at a different amount every year as the exchange rate changed each year. Critics of the foreign currency perspective contend that, in substance, this is merely an abandonment of historical cost and a change to a form of current-value accounting.

## Is the Translated Amount Current Value?

Let us continue with the preceding example dealing with Land but assume that the land appreciated in value by 100,000 marks during 19X1. Its current value in marks at December 31, 19X1, is 1,100,000 marks. To obtain the land's current value in dollars at that date, this amount would have to be multiplied by the $.50 exchange rate existing at December 31, 19X1, which is $550,000. However, nonmonetary accounts are not adjusted for inflation prior to translation. Accordingly, the use of the exchange rate existing at the balance sheet date would result in current value only if the nonmonetary account were restated for the effects of inflation. Furthermore, when dealing with depreciable assets, the amounts expressed in dollars would approximate current value only if the depreciation lives and methods used gave results that closely corresponded to the decline in the assets' values.

## The Disappearing Plant Problem.

About fifteen countries (primarily in South America) currently have highly inflationary economies (approximately 100% or more over a three-year period). The use of the foreign currency perspective can result in meaningless figures in these situations. To illustrate, consider the following example of a manufacturing plant in Argentina that cost 10,000,000 australs when it was purchased on December 31, 1974:

| | Amount (australs) | December 31, 1974 | | December 31, 1989 | |
|---|---|---|---|---|---|
| | | Rate | Amount | Rate | Amount |
| Plant..... | 10,000,000 | $.20 | $2,000,000 | $.00000002 | $.20 |

The application of the December 31, 1989, current exchange rate to the historical cost in australs produces an amount that bears no relationship to current value or a reasonable historial cost amount. The use of the current exchange rate would produce a meaningful amount only if it were applied to the inflation-adjusted historical cost in australs. However, this procedure would depart from historical cost in the foreign currency. Accordingly, operations in highly inflationary economies require special consideration. Chapter 16 shows how *FASB Statement No. 52* deals with these situations.

**The Current-rate Method of Translation.** Only one translation method fits under the foreign currency perspective—the current-rate method. Under the **current-rate method,** an increase in the direct exchange rate results in a favorable translation adjustment, and a decrease in the direct exchange rate results in an unfavorable translation adjustment.

**The Focus: The Net Investment.** The current-rate method focuses on the parent's net investment (total assets – total liabilities), not on the composition of the individual assets and liabilities. In other words, the monetary or nonmonetary classification of the individual assets and liabilities is irrelevant. This approach emphasizes that the foreign operation's net assets are at risk (described as a **net investment** view as opposed to the individual asset and liability view under the temporal method).

**SUMMARY ILLUSTRATION**

### The Effect of Changes in the Exchange Rate

Illustration 15-1 summarizes the effect of exchange rate changes under both the U.S. dollar perspective and the foreign currency perspective.

**The FASB's Second Attempt: The "Functional Currency" Concept.** *FASB Statement No. 52* adopted the foreign currency perspective in addition to the U.S. dollar perspective. However, the foreign currency perspective is dominant because its use is required far more often than the U.S. dollar perspective. *FASB Statement No. 52* introduced the "functional currency" concept as a basis for determining whether the foreign currency or the U.S. dollar perspective should be used for each foreign operation. In a nutshell, a foreign unit's functional currency is that currency in which it primarily conducts its operations. If a foreign unit's functional currency is its local currency, then the foreign currency perspective must be used. If a foreign unit's functional currency is the U.S. dollar, the U.S. dollar per-

## ■ ILLUSTRATION 15-1
### The Effect of Changes in the Exchange Rate

| Perspective | Possible Financial Positions | Economic Result of Direct Rate | |
|---|---|---|---|
| | | Increase[a] (Foreign Currency Has Strengthened or Dollar Has Weakened) | Decrease[b] (Foreign Currency Has Weakened or Dollar Has Strengthened) |
| Foreign currency | Net asset | Favorable | Unfavorable |
| Foreign currency | Net liability | Unfavorable | Favorable |
| U.S. dollar | Net monetary asset | Favorable | Unfavorable |
| U.S. dollar | Net monetary liability | Unfavorable | Favorable |

[a]In all situations, the effect is favorable on the assets and unfavorable on the liabilities.
[b]In all situations, the effect is unfavorable on the assets and favorable on the liabilities.

spective must be used. Chapter 16 discusses the factors to consider in determining a foreign unit's functional currency.

## CONCEPTUAL ISSUE 2: HOW TO REPORT THE EFFECT OF A CHANGE IN THE EXCHANGE RATE

The issue of how to report the effect of a change in the exchange rate centers on whether or not the translation adjustment should be reported in the income statement in the period in which the rate changes. There are arguments for both sides, and the FASB takes a dual approach to the issue in its *Statement No. 52*.

## Arguments for Reporting It Immediately in the Income Statement

The following list contains the principal arguments for including the translation adjustment immediately in the income statement:

1. The possibility of changes in the exchange rate is a risk of investing in a foreign country. The effects of this possibility can be economically favorable or unfavorable. Favorable effects are gains; unfavorable effects are losses. Gains and losses should be recognized in the period in which they occur.
2. Recognizing in the income statement the effects of changes in the exchange rate is consistent with the all-inclusive income statement approach that has prevailed in accounting in recent years.
3. Past exchange rate changes are historical facts, and each accounting period should reflect the economic events that occurred during that time frame.

4. Exchange rates fluctuate. Not including the effects of such fluctuations in net income when they occur gives the impression that exchange rates are stable.

## Arguments for Not Reporting It Immediately in the Income Statement

The following list contains the principal arguments for excluding the translation adjustment from the income statement:

1. If exchange rates are likely to reverse, the effect should be deferred. (This argument presumes that managements are reasonably adept at predicting future exchange rates; in reality, a high degree of uncertainty exists with future exchange rates.)
2. Exchange rate changes often reverse, causing unnecessary fluctuations in net income. (This argument implies that a function of accounting is to minimize the reporting of fluctuations.)
3. When the U.S. dollar perspective is used and when monetary liabilities exceed monetary assets (nonmonetary assets thus financed to some degree by borrowings), the translation adjustment should be deferred to offset (a) the unrecognized decrease in value on these assets (when the direct exchange rate decreases), and (b) the unrecognized increase in value of these assets (when the direct exchange rate increases). This approach would eliminate some of the unusual reporting results that occur under the U.S. dollar perspective; however, it is merely a disguised manner of revaluing the nonmonetary assets upward or downward. As a result, these items are translated at exchange rates that are between the historical exchange rate and the exchange rate existing at the balance sheet date, depending on the amount of borrowings to finance these nonmonetary assets.
4. For many foreign operations, translation adjustments do not affect the operations or cash flows of the foreign unit. They arise only in translation and thus do not affect directly the cash flows of the reporting currency (dollars).
5. The effect of changes in the exchange rate **lack the characteristics of items generally reported in the income statement.** This is because **the effect is unrealized,** therefore, possessing a high degree of uncertainty prior to the sale or liquidation of the investment. (Comments in the following two paragraphs relate to this and the preceding argument.)

**The Dual Approach of *FASB Statement No. 52.***   In *FASB Statement No. 52,* how to report the effect of a change in the exchange rate is a function of the perspective used for each foreign operation. When the foreign currency perspective is used (requiring the use of the current-rate method of translation), the effect of a change in the exchange rate is called a **transla-**

**tion adjustment** (in *FASB Statement No. 52*), and it is **reported as a separate component of stockholders' equity,** bypassing the income statement until disposal or liquidation of the investment. (Argument 4 above, which was first presented in *FASB Statement No. 52*, is the basis for this position.) When the U.S. dollar perspective is used (requiring the use of procedures that are nearly identical to the temporal method of translation), the effect of a change in the exchange rate is called a **foreign currency transaction gain or loss** (in *FASB Statement No. 52*), and it is **reported currently in the income statement.**

**Why the Separate Component of Stockholders' Equity?**   Recall that the foreign currency perspective is now required more often than the parent company perspective. Thus, one might think that the criticisms of *FASB Statement No. 8* (which required the U.S. dollar perspective in all cases) have been addressed. A major part of the business community's dissatisfaction with *FASB Statement No. 8* was not only the results produced under the U.S. dollar perspective but the requirement to report the effects of the change in the exchange rate currently in the income statement when subsequent reversals were expected (the paper gain and loss conclusion discussed earlier). Wild gyrations in adjustments often resulted on a quarter-to-quarter basis. Even under the foreign currency perspective (which requires the use of the current-rate method of translation), significant fluctuations in translation adjustments occur as long as exchange rates continue to change back and forth significantly; this is possible under the current floating exchange rate system. In fact, the fluctuations may be even greater under the foreign currency perspective—the only requirement is that a foreign operation's net asset position must be greater than its net monetary asset or liability position. Thus, although the business community has available a method that it believes produces results that better reflect economic reality (that is, the current rate method), it opposes reporting translation adjustments currently in the income statement because of the significant fluctuations. The FASB's decision to require companies to report translation adjustments resulting from the use of the current-rate method as a separate component of stockholders' equity may have been partly attributable to the practical aspects of the environment in which the FASB operates.

## USING THE PURCHASING POWER PARITY THEORY IN EVALUATING TRANSLATION RESULTS

Recall from Chapter 14 that under the purchasing power parity theory, the change in the exchange rate—in the long run—is a function of the differential rate of inflation between two countries. (This assumes the absence of civil disorders, wars, and currency exchange restrictions.) Assuming that the purchasing power parity theory holds true, we now examine four different assumed inflation scenarios to see how the U.S. dollar perspective and the foreign currency perspective reflect economic reality. We use the example in the chapter in which a foreign subsidiary is formed on January 1, 19X1, in West Germany and purchases land on this date for 1,000,000 marks. **Economic reality is defined as the number of U.S. dollars the parent is ahead (or behind) at December 31, 19X1, (assuming a complete liquidation of the subsidiary at December 31, 19X1) in comparison to the amount the parent invested at January 1, 19X1, when the subsidiary was formed.** Both debt and equity financing alternatives are shown.

**Situation 1: Zero Inflation in West Germany in 19X1; 25% Inflation in the United States**
The translation illustrations in the chapter used a direct exchange rate of $.40 at January 1, 19X1, and a direct exchange rate of $.50 at December 31, 19X1. Under purchasing power parity theory, this increase in the direct exchange rate is a function of greater inflation in the United States than in West Germany. For simplicity, we assume for 19X1 that the U.S. had 25% inflation and West Germany had zero inflation. Such a scenario would account for the entire change in the exchange rate in 19X1.

The following table compares the reporting results under the U.S. dollar perspective and the foreign currency perspective to economic reality:

| | Economic Reality (Dollars Ahead upon Liquidation at Dec. 31, 19X1)[a] | Favorable (or Unfavorable) Reporting Result under | |
| | | U.S. Dollar Perspective | Foreign Currency Perspective |
| Land Financed by | | | |
|---|---|---|---|
| Debt. . . . . . . . . . . . . . . . . | $ –0– | $(100,000) | $ –0– |
| Equity. . . . . . . . . . . . . . . | $100,000 | $ –0– | $100,000 |

[a]At December 31, 19X1, the land would be sold at its current value of 1,000,000 marks (historical cost of 1,000,000 marks plus zero inflation in West Germany during 19X1). All cash would then be returned to the parent (after repayment of the debt when debt is used).

**Note that when inflation occurs only in the United States, only the reporting results of the foreign currency perspective coincide with economic reality.** This is because the reporting results of the foreign currency perspective always coincide with the results under current value accounting in this situation. In this example, the land is reported at year-end at its current realizable value in dollars of $500,000 (1,000,000 marks × $.50). Under the U.S. dollar perspective, the land is reported at $400,000 at year-end (1,000,000 marks × $.40) under both financing alternatives, thereby suppressing $100,000 of valuation. Thus, the impact of inflation in the United States on the exchange rate is ignored under the U.S. dollar perspective.

### Situation 2: 25% Inflation in West Germany in 19X1; Zero Inflation in the United States

Let us assume the direct exchange rate for 19X1 went from $.40 to $.32. Under purchasing power parity theory, this decrease is a function of greater inflation in West Germany than in the United States. For simplicity, we assume for 19X1 that the United States had zero inflation and West Germany had 25% inflation. Such a scenario would account for the entire decrease in the exchange rate in 19X1.

The following table compares the reporting results under the U.S. dollar perspective and the foreign currency perspective to economic reality:

| Land Financed by | Economic Reality (Dollars Ahead upon Liquidation at Dec. 31, 19X1)[a] | Favorable (or Unfavorable) Reporting Result under | |
|---|---|---|---|
| | | U.S. Dollar Perspective | Foreign Currency Perspective |
| Debt.................. | $80,000 | $80,000 | $   –0– |
| Equity................ | $  –0– | $  –0– | $(80,000) |

[a]At December 31, 19X1, the land would be sold at its current value of 1,250,000 marks (historical cost of 1,000,000 marks plus 250,000 marks of appreciation during 19X1). All cash would then be returned to the parent (after repayment of the debt when debt is used).

**Note that when inflation occurs only in the foreign country, only the reporting results of the U.S. dollar perspective coincide with economic reality.** This is because the reporting results of the U.S. dollar perspective always coincide with the results under current value accounting in this situation. In this example, the land is reported at year-end at its current realizable value in dollars of $400,000 (current value of 1,250,000 marks × the current exchange rate of $.32). This current value coincides with the amount obtained in translating under the U.S. dollar perspective whereby historical cost of 1,000,000 marks is multiplied by the historical exchange rate of $.40. The flaw in the foreign currency perspective in this situation is that while the current rate at year-end is used, that rate (which bears the effect of inflation during the year) is not applied to an inflation adjusted number (the 1,250,000 marks), thus suppressing $80,000 of valuation (250,000 marks × $.32) for each financing alternative.

### Situation 3: 25% Inflation in West Germany; 25% Inflation in the United States

Let us assume inflation rates in 19X1 of 25% for West Germany and 25% for the United States. Under these assumptions, the direct exchange rate at January 1, 19X1, of $.40 would remain unchanged during 19X1 under the purchasing power parity theory.

The following table compares the reporting results under the U.S. dollar perspective and the foreign currency perspective to economic reality:

| Land Financed by | Economic Reality (Dollars Ahead upon Liquidation at Dec. 31, 19X1)[a] | Favorable (or Unfavorable) Reporting Result under | |
| | | U.S. Dollar Perspective | Foreign Currency Perspective |
| --- | --- | --- | --- |
| Debt.................. | $100,000 | $  –0– | $  –0– |
| Equity............... | $100,000 | $  –0– | $  –0– |

[a]At December 31, 19X1, the land would be sold at its current value of 1,250,000 marks (historical cost of 1,000,000 marks plus 250,000 marks of appreciation during 19X1). All cash would then be returned to the parent (after repayment of the debt when debt is used).

**Note that when the inflation rate is the same for both countries, neither the U.S. dollar perspective nor the foreign currency perspective coincide with economic reality.** This is because neither method reflects current value accounting. Under current value accounting, the realizable value of the land at year-end in dollars is $500,000 (1,250,000 marks × $.40).

Under the U.S. dollar perspective, the land is reported at $400,000 (1,000,000 marks × $.40), thereby suppressing $100,000 of valuation. As in Situation 1, which had inflation only in the United States, the U.S. dollar perspective ignores the impact of inflation in the United States on the exchange rate. (Although the translation process here is 1,000,000 marks × $.40, it effectively is 1,250,000 marks × $.32—the $.32 is not adjusted upward to $.40 as a result of inflation in the United States.)

Under the foreign currency perspective, the land is reported at $400,000 (1,000,000 × $.40), thereby suppressing $100,000 of valuation. As in Situation 2, which had inflation only in the foreign country, the foreign currency perspective multiplies an inflation impacted exchange rate to an amount that has not been adjusted for inflation (the 1,000,000 marks).

### Situation 4: 50% Inflation in West Germany; 25% Inflation in United States

Let us assume inflation rates in 19X1 of 50% for West Germany and 25% for the United States. Under these assumptions the direct exchange rate at January 1, 19X1, of $.40 would decline to $.333 at December 31, 19X1, under the purchasing power parity theory ($.40 × 125% equals $.50; $.50 ÷ 150% equals $.333).

The following table compares the reporting results under the U.S. dollar perspective and the foreign currency perspective to economic reality:

| Land Financed by | Economic Reality (Dollars Ahead upon Liquidation at Dec. 31, 19X1)[a] | Favorable (or Unfavorable) Reporting Result under | |
|---|---|---|---|
| | | U.S. Dollar Perspective | Foreign Currency Perspective |
| Debt.................. | $166,667 | $66,667 | $ –0– |
| Equity................ | $100,000 | $ –0– | $(66,667) |

[a]At December 31, 19X1, the land would be sold at its current value of 1,500,000 marks (historical cost of 1,000,000 marks plus 500,000 marks of appreciation during 19X1). All cash would then be returned to the parent (after repayment of the debt when debt is used).

Note that neither the U.S. dollar perspective nor the foreign currency perspective portrays economic reality when both countries experience inflation (the most common situation). The explanation is the same as that provided in Situation 3.

## Concluding Comments

**When nonmonetary assets are financed by the parent's equity investment,** the reporting results under each of the perspectives do not always reflect the number of U.S. dollars the parent would be ahead if the subsidiary were liquidated at year-end. However, a closer examination reveals that the reporting results under the U.S. dollar perspective—in each inflation scenario—reflect how much better off the parent is at year-end in relation to the parent's purchasing power at the beginning of the year (which was $400,000 in the examples). **Thus, the U.S. dollar perspective achieves results under price-level accounting when equity financing is used.**

**When nonmonetary assets are financed by borrowings in the foreign country,** the reporting results under each of the perspectives do not—in most inflation scenarios—reflect the number of dollars the parent would be ahead if the subsidiary were liquidated at year-end. Because of the use of debt financing, the number of dollars the parent would be ahead upon liquidation at year-end—in all inflation scenarios—is equal to how much better off the parent is at year-end than it was at the beginning of the year. Accordingly, the reporting results under each of the perspectives do not—in most inflation scenarios—portray how much better off the parent is at year-end in relation to the parent's purchasing power at the beginning of the year.

Purchasing power parity theory is implicitly recognized by the financial heads of most multinational corporations. Moreover, it is recognized by many economists (as well as the editorial board of *The Wall Street Journal*) as the best explanation of changes in exchange rates over long periods of time. The results produced under both the U.S. dollar perspective and the foreign currency perspective, when both countries have inflation in light of this theory, raise serious questions about whether the translation issue should be reexamined.

## END-OF-CHAPTER REVIEW

### Summary of Key Points

1. A domestic company seeking to sell abroad must have a full understanding of the various alternatives, including the related accompanying factors (such as legal, tax, and foreign currency exposure considerations).
2. Rather than continually deal with swings in the exchange rates, many domestic exporters have minimized this problem by manufacturing overseas.
3. The diversity of worldwide accounting principles is enormous. Before translating foreign currency financial statements into U.S. dollars, the foreign currency financial statements must be restated to U.S. GAAP.
4. All translation methods fit under either the U.S. dollar perspective (the temporal method and the monetary–nonmonetary method) or the foreign currency perspective (the current rate method). The difference between the two perspectives results in different rates used in translating nonmonetary accounts.
5. Under the U.S. dollar perspective, the focus is on the net monetary position. Under the foreign currency perspective, the focus is on the net investment position.
6. To the extent that changes in exchange rates are caused by inflation, the amounts expressed in dollars must be carefully evaluated inasmuch as the use of the translation methods that fit under both the U.S. dollar perspective and the foreign currency perspective can produce results that are not reflective of economic reality.

### Glossary of New Terms

**Foreign operation**   "An operation (for example, subsidiary, division, branch, joint venture, and so on) whose financial statements (a) are prepared in a currency other than the reporting currency of the reporting enterprise and (b) are combined or consolidated with or accounted for on the equity basis in the financial statements of the reporting enterprise."*

**Monetary accounts**   Cash and receivables and payables to be settled in currency.

**Net asset position**   Having assets in excess of liabilities.

**Net liability position**   Having liabilities in excess of assets.

**Net monetary asset position**   Having monetary assets in excess of monetary liabilities.

**Net monetary liability position**   Having monetary liabilities in excess of monetary assets.

**Nonmonetary accounts**   All balance sheet accounts that are not monetary accounts.

*\*FASB Statement No. 52*, Appendix E, pp. 75–78.

## Self-Study Questions

*(Answers are at the end of this chapter.)*

1. A translation method that fits under the foreign currency perspective is the:
   a. Current rate method.
   b. Monetary–nonmonetary method.
   c. Current–noncurrent method.
   d. Temporal method.

2. Under the U.S. dollar perspective, the focus is on the:
   a. Net monetary asset position.
   b. Net monetary liability position.
   c. Net exposed asset position.
   d. Net exposed liability position.
   e. None of the above.

3. Under the foreign currency perspective, the focus is on the:
   a. Net liability position.
   b. Net asset position.
   c. Net monetary position.
   d. Net monetary asset or liability position.
   e. None of the above.

4. When the direct exchange rate decreases during the year and a favorable effect for this change in the exchange rate is reported currently in the income statement, the foreign unit had to be in a:
   a. Net asset position.
   b. Net liability position.
   c. Net monetary position.
   d. Net monetary asset position.
   e. Net monetary liability position.

5. The effect of a change in the exchange rate should be reported as a charge or credit to:

|  | Under the U.S. Dollar Perspective | Under the Foreign Currency Perspective |
|---|---|---|
| a. | The income statement | The income statement |
| b. | Stockholders' equity | The income statement |
| c. | The income statement | Stockholders' equity |
| d. | Stockholders' equity | Stockholders' equity |

6. On January 1, 19X1, the direct exchange rate is $.24. Management forecasts that the U.S. will have 5% inflation during 19X1 and that the foreign country will have 20% inflation during 19X1. Under purchasing power parity theory, what is the expected exchange rate at December 31, 19X1?
   a. $.20.
   b. $.21.
   c. $.274.
   d. $.208.

# ASSIGNMENT MATERIAL

## Review Questions

1. What are some of the major reasons for domestic exporters establishing overseas manufacturing operations?
2. How do fluctuations in the exchange rates impact domestic exporters?
3. In general, what results in a domestic company becoming subject to the income tax laws of a foreign country?
4. What is the significance of establishing arbitrary transfer prices between a domestic company and its overseas units?
5. How does the U.S. government taxing authorities treat foreign earnings of a domestic company?
6. Restate and then translate or translate and then restate—which is correct? Why?
7. What is meant by the current exchange rate? historical exchange rate?
8. What is meant by the term *monetary accounts?*
9. Summarize the U.S. dollar perspective.
10. What is the focus under the U.S. dollar perspective?
11. Which translation methods fit under the U.S. dollar perspective?
12. Summarize the foreign currency perspective.
13. What is meant by the term *functional currency?*
14. What is the focus under the foreign currency perspective?
15. Explain the purchasing power parity concept.

## Discussion Cases

| DC 15-1 |
|---|

### Evaluation of the Impact of a Weakening Foreign Currency

Assume you are the controller of a domestic company that established operations in Mexico two years ago. These foreign operations are conducted through a Mexican subsidiary. The subsidiary has three operational manufacturing plants, all of which cost approximately the same amount and were financed as follows:

1. The first plant was financed entirely from a capital stock investment made by the parent in the subsidiary.
2. The second plant was financed entirely from a long-term loan from a local Mexican bank, none of which has been repaid.
3. The third plant was financed entirely from an interest-bearing, long-term loan from the parent, none of which has been repaid. (The loan is payable in dollars.)

During the month preceding the annual shareholders' meeting, the Mexican peso declined approximately 30% in value. You are sure a question will arise at the shareholders' meeting concerning the financial consequences of this decline.

**Required:**

1. Without regard to whether the functional currency is the dollar or the peso, prepare a brief summary of the impact of the decline in the value of the peso on the company's foreign operations.
2. Indicate the effect of the change in the exchange rate that will be reported for the current year of each of the plants assuming that the functional currency is the:
    a. Peso.
    b. Dollar.

---

DC
15-2

## Evaluation of the Impact of a Weakening Dollar

Rosebud Corporation is a domestic company that established a manufacturing subsidiary in West Germany four years ago. In establishing this foreign operation, Rosebud minimized the number of dollars taken out of the United States by financing the subsidiary's manufacturing plant through a loan obtained from a West German financial institution. This loan is being repaid over 25 years. As a result, the subsidiary is thinly capitalized.

During the current year, the dollar weakened approximately 20% against the mark, as concerns arose over the sizable U.S. foreign trade deficit, the federal spending deficit, and the inability to control inflation. (The mark held steady against the other major currencies of the world.) In marks, the subsidiary had a profit for the current year comparable to the prior year. In dollars, the subsidiary had a loss for the current year, compared with a profit for the prior year.

**Required:**

Rosebud's president, Orson Wellsby, has asked you, the controller, to respond to the following questions:

1. How is it possible to report a loss on the foreign operation for the current year, considering the following:
    a. The parent minimized its dollars at risk by financing the foreign plant with local borrowings.
    b. The operation was run as efficiently this year as in the prior year.
2. Is this an economic loss or a paper loss? Explain your answer.
3. Is there any way the loss could have been avoided?

# Exercises

---

E
15-1

## Getting in Step with U.S. Generally Accepted Accounting Practices

A foreign subsidiary must adjust its fixed assets annually for inflation. Amounts of these adjustments are maintained in separate general ledger accounts. The balances in these accounts at year-end are as follows:

|  | Debit | Credit |
|---|---|---|
| Land—revaluation . . . . . . . . . . . . . . . . . . . . . . . . . . . . . . . . . | 500,000 |  |
| Building—revaluation . . . . . . . . . . . . . . . . . . . . . . . . . . . . . | 800,000 |  |
| Accumulated depreciation—revaluation . . . . . . . . |  | 200,000 |
| Depreciation Expense—revaluation (19X1) . . . . . . . . . . | 40,000 |  |

When the fixed assets were revalued for inflation, the appropriate account was credited. The depreciation expense increment is deductible for foreign federal tax purposes. Assume the foreign tax rate is 40%.

**Required:**

Prepare the adjusting entry necessary to convert to U.S. generally accepted accounting principles at the end of 19X1.

## E 15-2 Comparing Reporting Results

On December 31, 19X1, Pella Company formed a wholly owned real estate development subsidiary, Sella Company, in France. Pella paid $2,500,000 cash for common stock of Sella on this date. Also on this date, Sella converted the $2,500,000 into 5,000,000 francs on the formation date. It immediately acquired land for 4,000,000 francs and left the remaining 1,000,000 francs in a checking account for all of 19X2 (earning no interest). Sella had no expenses in 19X2. The exchange rate at December 31, 19X2, is 1 franc equals $.40. France had 25% inflation during 19X2.

**Required:**

1. Translate Sella's balance sheet at December 31, 19X2, under the U.S. dollar perspective.
2. Translate Sella's balance sheet at December 31, 19X2, under the foreign currency perspective.
3. Calculate the parent's increase or decrease in cash for 19X2 if the subsidiary were liquidated at December 31, 19X2 (with the land being sold at its current value of 5,000,000 francs). Compare this reporting result to the results in requirements 1 and 2. Comment accordingly.

## E 15-3 Calculating the Effect of a Change in the Exchange Rate

The Berkshire Corporation has a foreign subsidiary in a country in which the direct exchange rate has decreased from $.25 at January 1, 19X1, to $.20 at December 31, 19X1. The average balances of the individual assets and liabilities during the year were as follows:

|  | Units of Foreign Currency |
|---|---|
| Cash . . . . . . . . . . . . . . . . . . . . . . . . . . . . . . . . . . . . . . . . . . . . . . . . . . . . . . . | 80,000 |
| Accounts Receivable . . . . . . . . . . . . . . . . . . . . . . . . . . . . . . . . . . . . . . . . . . | 220,000 |
| Inventory . . . . . . . . . . . . . . . . . . . . . . . . . . . . . . . . . . . . . . . . . . . . . . . . . . . | 275,000 |

|  | Units of Foreign Currency |
|---|---|
| Fixed Assets, net . . . . . . . . . . . . . . . . . . . . . . . . . . . . . . . . . . . . . . . . . . . . | 425,000 |
|  | 1,000,000 |
| Accounts Payable and Accruals . . . . . . . . . . . . . . . . . . . . . . . . . . . | 325,000 |
| Current portion of Long-term Debt . . . . . . . . . . . . . . . . . . . . . . . | 25,000 |
| Intercompany Payable. . . . . . . . . . . . . . . . . . . . . . . . . . . . . . . . . . . | 100,000 |
| Long-term debt. . . . . . . . . . . . . . . . . . . . . . . . . . . . . . . . . . . . . . . . | 300,000 |
| Deferred Income Taxes Payable. . . . . . . . . . . . . . . . . . . . . . . . . . | 50,000 |
|  | 800,000 |

**Required:**
Determine the effect of the change in the exchange rate for 19X1 assuming the foreign operation's functional currency is the:
a. Foreign currency.
b. Dollar.

## Determining the Financial Position of Foreign Operations from Effect and Direction of Exchange Rate Changes

Information for Extent Corporation's overseas subsidiaries for 19X1 is presented below:

| Country | Functional Currency | Direction of Direct Exchange Rate in 19X1 | Effect of Change in Exchange Rate |
|---|---|---|---|
| Brazil | Dollar | Decreased | Favorable |
| Mexico | Dollar | Decreased | Unfavorable |
| Sweden | Krona | Increased | Favorable |
| Belgium | Franc | Increased | Unfavorable |
| Ireland | Punt | Decreased | Unfavorable |
| Spain | Peseta | Decreased | Favorable |
| Saudi Arabia | Dollar | Increased | Favorable |
| Japan | Dollar | Increased | Unfavorable |

**Required:**
Determine the appropriate financial position that each of the above foreign operations was in during the year for the above listed effect to have resulted.

## Calculating the Projected Exchange Rate

**E 15-5**

On January 1, 19X1, the exchange rate between the United States and the foreign country in which a domestic parent has a subsidiary was 1 LCU equals $.50. (LCU stands for local currency unit). For 19X1, management expects 10% inflation for the United States and 25% inflation for the foreign country.

**Required:**

Calculate the expected exchange rate at December 31, 19X1, under purchasing power parity theory.

## ANSWERS TO SELF-STUDY QUESTIONS

1. a    4. e
2. e    5. c
3. b    6. b

# 16
......

# TRANSLATION OF FOREIGN CURRENCY FINANCIAL STATEMENTS: PRACTICE

*TOPIC OUTLINE*

The Functional Currency Concept
The Translation Process
The Remeasurement Process
Intercompany Transactions with Foreign Units
The Manner of Reporting Foreign Operations
Concluding Comments
APPENDIX: Hedging the Foreign Operation's Exposed Position

This chapter focuses on the requirements of *FASB Statement No. 52*, "Foreign Currency Translation."

# THE FUNCTIONAL CURRENCY CONCEPT

## The Objectives of Translation

*F*ASB Statement No. 52 states the following objectives for translation of foreign currency financial statements:

a. Provide information that is generally compatible with the expected economic effects of a rate change on an enterprise's cash flows and equity.

b. Reflect in consolidated statements the financial results and relationships of the individual consolidated entities as measured in their *functional currencies* in conformity with U.S. generally accepted accounting principles.[1]

The first objective merely states that the selected exchange rate and the reporting of the effect of a change in the exchange rate should reflect the economics of what has transpired. The second objective allows for the use of both the U.S. dollar perspective (when the dollar is the foreign unit's functional currency) and the more prevalent foreign currency perspective (when the foreign currency is the foreign unit's functional currency). To achieve these two objectives, the **functional currency concept** was developed.

## The Basis for the Functional Currency Concept

*FASB Statement No. 52* presumes that an enterprise's foreign operations may be conducted in one or more economic and currency environments. The primary economic environment must be determined for each separate foreign operation. However, the pronouncement does not specifically define the economic environment concept. Each foreign country has its own economic environment composed of taxation policies, currency controls, government policies toward intervention in the international currency markets, economic instability, and inflation. The primary economic environment concept, however, pertains to the manner in which the foreign operation conducts its operations—**the currency it primarily uses to generate and expend cash.** (This concept presumes that each foreign operation has a primary currency.)

---

[1]*Statement of Financial Accounting Standards, No. 52*, "Foreign Currency Translation" (Stamford: Financial Accounting Standards Board, 1981), par. 4.

The currency of the primary economic environment is then designated as that foreign operation's functional currency. The FASB has developed some economic factors that are to be considered individually and collectively in determining the functional currency for each foreign operation of an enterprise. (A list of these economic factors appears in Illustration 16-1.) The functional currency determined for each foreign operation is the basis for the method of translation into dollars. When the foreign currency is designated the functional currency (which occurs most of the time), the foreign currency perspective must be used; thus, the current-rate method is used to translate the foreign currency financial statements into dollars. When the dollar is designated the functional currency, the U.S. dollar perspective must be used; thus, translating foreign currency financial statements into dollars is accomplished using procedures that are nearly identical to the temporal method (which *FASB Statement No. 8* required for all situations).

**Two Categories of Foreign Operations.** In reviewing Illustration 16-1, realize that most foreign operations conveniently fit into one of two categories. The **first category** includes **foreign operations that are relatively self-contained and independent of the parent's operations.** These operations primarily generate and expend the foreign currency of the country in which they are located. Earnings may be reinvested or distributed to the parent. In these cases, the foreign currency is obviously the functional currency. (An example would be a foreign subsidiary that manufactures automobiles for sale in the foreign country, purchasing no parts from the parent's operations.) The **second category** includes **foreign operations that are not relatively self-contained and independent of the parent's operations.** These operations may be viewed as direct extensions or integral components of the parent's operations. The day-to-day operations of these units directly affect the parent company's dollar cash flows. In these cases, the dollar is the functional currency. (An example would be a foreign subsidiary that manufactures automobile transmissions that are shipped to the parent for inclusion in cars produced domestically.)

**No Arbitrary Selection Allowed.** The determination of the functional currency should be based on the economic facts—it cannot be an arbitrary selection. Because significant differences in reported net income can occur as a result of choosing the foreign currency or the dollar as the functional currency, managements must be prevented from arbitrarily choosing their accounting principles. When the economic factors listed in Illustration 16-1 do not clearly point to which functional currency a foreign operation should use, management can weigh the individual economic factors and use its judgment, considering the stated objectives of translation.

## ■ ILLUSTRATION 16-1
**Economic Factors to Be Considered in Determining the Functional Currency**

| Type of Factor | Factors Pointing to a Foreign Functional Currency | Factors Pointing to a Dollar Functional Currency |
|---|---|---|
| Cash flows | Cash flows related to the foreign entity's individual assets and liabilities are primarily in the foreign currency and do not directly impact the parent company's cash flows. | Cash flows related to the foreign entity's individual assets and liabilities directly impact the parent's cash flows on a current basis and are readily available for remittance to the parent company. |
| Sales prices | Sales prices for the foreign entity's products are not primarily responsive on a short-term basis to changes in exchange rates but are determined more by local competition or local government regulation. | Sales prices for the foreign entity's products are primarily responsive on a short-term basis to changes in exchange rates; for example, sales prices are determined more by worldwide competition or by international prices. |
| Sales market | An active local sales market exists for the foreign entity's products, although significant amounts of exports might also be available. | The sales market is mostly in the parent's country, or sales contracts are denominated in the parent's currency. |
| Cost and expenses | Labor, materials, and other costs for the foreign entity's products or services are primarily local costs, even though imports from other countries might also be available. | Labor, materials, and other costs for the foreign entity's products or services, on a continuing basis, are primarily costs for components obtained from the country in which the parent company is located. |
| Financing | Financing is primarily denominated in foreign currency, and funds generated by the foreign entity's operations are sufficient to service existing and normally expected debt obligations. | Financing is primarily from the parent or other dollar-denominated obligations, or funds generated by the foreign entity's operations are not sufficient to service existing and normally expected debt obligations without the infusion of additional funds from the parent company. Infusion of additional funds from the parent company for expansion is not a factor, provided funds generated by the foreign entity's expanded operations are expected to be sufficient to service that additional financing. |
| Intercompany transactions and arrangements | There is a low volume of intercompany transactions, and an extensive interrelationship does not exist between the operations of the foreign entity and the parent company. However, the foreign entity's operations may rely on the parent's or affiliates' competitive advantages such as patents and trademarks. | There is a high volume of intercompany transactions, and an extensive interrelationship exists between the operations of the foreign entity and the parent company. Additionally, the parent's currency generally would be the functional currency if the foreign entity is a device or shell corporation for holding investments, obligations, intangible assets, and so on, that could readily be carried on the parent's or an affiliate's books. |

Source: Adapted from *Statement of Financial Accounting Standards, No. 52,* "Foreign Currency Translation" (Stamford: Financial Accounting Standards Board, 1981), Appendix A, par. 42.

**Highly Inflationary Economies.**   An exception to the approach of determining the functional currency from economic facts is made for operations in highly inflationary economies. *FASB Statement No. 52* defines an inflationary economy as "one that has cumulative inflation of approximately 100 percent or more over a three-year period.[2] In these cases, the dollar is used as the functional currency. The purpose of the exception is to deal with the "disappearing plant" problem discussed in Chapter 15. Recall that applying the current exchange rate to historical cost amounts in foreign currency financial statements can produce meaningless dollar amounts for fixed assets in such economies. The problem is the foreign currency's lack of stability, which makes it completely unsuitable for use as a functional currency. In the exposure draft that preceded the issuance of *FASB Statement No. 52*, the FASB proposed restating the historical cost amounts for inflation prior to translation (and then allowing the use of the current-rate method). However, the proposal was dropped because of conceptual objections to mixing historical cost with inflation-adjusted amounts and the inadequacy of published indices for several countries. As a practical alternative, which is an acknowledged conceptual compromise, the FASB designated the dollar as the functional currency in highly inflationary economies (whereby the historical cost amounts are translated at historical exchange rates). The results are more reasonable dollar amounts for the fixed assets of these foreign operations. Numerous countries, primarily in South America, have cumulative inflation rates near or exceeding 100% over three-year periods. Although 100% may seem high, an annual inflation rate of only 26% results in 100% inflation cumulatively over a three-year period.

**The Judgment Factor in Highly Inflationary Economies.**   The use of 100% is arbitrary, but the use of the modifier "approximately" in the pronouncement allows management some latitude in judgment. Thus, a cumulative inflation rate of 90%, for example, could be sufficient grounds for using the dollar as the functional currency, whereas a foreign unit operating with a cumulative inflation rate of 110% could still use the foreign currency as the functional currency. We must also consider management's latitude when the economic facts do not clearly indicate the functional currency. In such a case and when the cumulative inflation rate is high but below 100%, management may lean toward using the dollar as the functional currency.

## Distinguishing "Translation" from "Remeasurement"

For simplicity, we have referred to the process of applying exchange rates to a foreign operation's financial statements to arrive at dollar amounts as

2*FASB Statement No. 52*, par. 11.

*translation.* Historically, this has been the definition of the term. The use of the functional currency concept, however, has resulted in a narrower definition of this term in *FASB Statement No. 52.*

### Translation (from the Functional Currency to the Reporting Currency).

In *FASB Statement No. 52*, **translation** refers to the process of **expressing functional currency amounts in the reporting currency.** Accordingly, the term is restricted to situations in which the foreign currency is the functional currency. Recall that when the foreign currency is the functional currency, the current-rate method is required, and it merely *expresses* the foreign currency financial statements in dollars. (It does not "remeasure" the nonmonetary accounts to obtain their dollar equivalents at the time the transactions were recorded.) The effect of a change in the exchange rate in these "translation" situations is called a **translation adjustment.** Translation adjustments are reported separately in stockholders' equity (a less closely monitored section of the financial statements, unfortunately) pending sale or liquidation of the investment.

### Remeasurement (from a Nonfunctional Currency to the Functional Currency).

In *FASB Statement No. 52*, **remeasurement** is the process of applying exchange rates to a foreign operation's financial statements when they are not stated in the functional currency. **Thus, amounts in a different currency are expressed in the functional currency.** The most common example occurs when the functional currency of the foreign operation is the dollar. Foreign operations normally maintain their books and prepare their financial statements in the currency of the country in which they are located, regardless of whether the dollar is their functional currency. Recall that when the dollar is the functional currency, a combination of current and historical exchange rates is used whereby the nonmonetary accounts are remeasured in dollars to obtain the dollar equivalent of the transactions at the time they were recorded. Thus, the remeasurement process in *FASB Statement No. 52* refers to the remeasuring in the functional currency. Note that when the dollar is the functional currency, translation (as narrowly defined in the preceding paragraph) is not necessary because the functional currency is also the reporting currency. The effect of a change in the exchange rate from the remeasurement process is called a **foreign currency transaction gain or loss,** which must be reported currently in the income statement.

### Remeasurement and Translation Situations.

Infrequently, a foreign operation's functional currency is a foreign currency that is different from the currency it uses to maintain its books and prepare its financial statements. An example would be a Swiss operation that keeps its books in Swiss francs (most likely because of tax laws) but uses the French franc as its functional currency. In such a case, the Swiss financial statements must be "remeasured" and expressed in French francs. Then, the French franc financial statements must be "translated" into dollars. Thus, a two-step process is required to obtain amounts in dollars. However, most foreign operations require only a one-step process—either the translation process or the remeasurement process.

**Comparison Comment.**   The translation process is relatively simple because of the use of the current-rate method. In comparison, the remeasurement process is slightly more involved because of the use of current and historical exchange rates. When the remeasurement process is illustrated later in the chapter, we list the accounts to be remeasured using historical exchange rates. (For now, understand only that these are nonmonetary accounts and their amortizations.)

# THE TRANSLATION PROCESS

In this section, we deal with the actual translation of foreign currency financial statements into dollars. Recall that in the translation process the foreign currency is the functional currency.

## Basic Procedures before Translation

Certain fundamental procedures must be performed before the financial statements of foreign subsidiaries or branches may be translated into dollars.

### Adjustments to Conform to U.S. Generally Accepted Accounting Principles.   Operations conducted in a foreign country must be accounted for using that country's accounting principles. When foreign currency financial statements use accounting principles that are different from U.S. generally accepted accounting principles, appropriate adjustments must be made to those statements before translation so that they conform to U.S. generally accepted accounting principles. These adjustments, which are **made on a worksheet,** are never posted to the general ledger of the foreign accounting entity. The adjustments are necessary regardless of (1) the organizational form through which foreign operations are conducted, and (2) whether or not the foreign operation's statements are consolidated (if a subsidiary) or combined (if a division or a branch) with the financial statements of the domestic accounting entity.

Similarly, when a domestic company has a 20% to 50% interest in a foreign operation, which must be accounted for under the equity method of accounting, the investee's foreign statements must be adjusted to conform to U.S. generally accepted accounting principles before translation into dollars. The equity method is then applied after the translation process in accordance with *FASB Statement No. 52*.

**Adjustments to Receivables and Payables.**   A foreign operation's receivables or payables in other than its local currency must be adjusted to reflect the current rate between the local currency (of the foreign country) and the currency in which the receivable or payable is stated. Recall that how to make and account for such adjustments was discussed in Chapter 14. (In the illustration of the translation process in this section, we assume that any such adjustments have already been made.)

**Reconciliation of Inter- or Intracompany Receivable and Payable Accounts.**   Inventory and cash are commonly transferred between domestic and foreign operations. Such transactions are usually recorded in separate inter- or intracompany receivable and payable accounts by each accounting entity. Such accounts must be reconciled to each other before translation to ensure that no clerical errors or unrecorded in-transit items exist. Only by performing this reconciliation will these accounts completely offset each other after translation.

Furthermore, when the inter- or intracompany account is to be settled in dollars (rather than in the foreign unit's local currency), the foreign unit's accounts must be adjusted as described in the preceding section. If settlement is to be made in the foreign unit's local currency, the domestic operation must adjust its books. (Such adjustments are illustrated later in the chapter where the fine points of intercompany transactions with foreign subsidiaries are discussed.)

## Exchange Rates Used in Translation

**Current Exchange Rate.**   *FASB Statement No. 52* has a dual definition of the current exchange rate. For the balance sheet, this is the exchange rate existing at the balance sheet date. For the income statement, this is the exchange rate in effect when an item is recognized in the income statement. Thus, there can exist up to 365 different exchange rates in translating the income statement.

**Average Exchange Rates.**   Because it is impractical to translate the various income statement items at the numerous exchange rates that could apply throughout a period, *FASB Statement No. 52* allows firms to use appropriately weighted average exchange rates for the period.

**Multiple Exchange Rates.**   In addition to the floating rates, many countries declare one or more official rates for certain types of currency conversions. For example, to discourage the repatriation of dividends to a foreign parent company, a country would use a rate whereby the parent company would receive a lesser amount of its own currency than it otherwise would receive had the free rate been used. When such multiple rates exist, the current exchange rate is the rate **that could be used for dividend remittances.**

## Specific Translation Procedures

**Balance Sheet Accounts.** The following procedures translate the individual balance sheet accounts:

1. All assets and liabilities are translated at the exchange rate existing at the balance sheet date.
2. Common stock and additional paid-in capital are translated at historical exchange rates (to isolate the effect of the change in the exchange rate for the current period).
3. Beginning retained earnings is the dollar balance in the Retained Earnings account at the end of the prior period.
4. Dividend payments, if any, are translated using the exchange rate in effect at the time of the declaration.

**Revenue, Cost of Goods Sold, and Expense Accounts.** All revenues, costs of sales, and expenses (as well as gains and losses) are translated using exchange rates that were in effect when these items were **recognized** in the income statement. Thus, exchange rates **in effect during the current period** are used. The following two paragraphs explain how this process can be simplified.

**The Use of Average Exchange Rates.** When translating income statement accounts, average exchange rates may be used, provided that approximately the same results can be obtained from translating each individual transaction into dollars using the exchange rate that was in effect when the transaction occurred. If the item being translated occurred evenly throughout the period (month, quarter, or year), a simple average is sufficient. Otherwise, a weighted average is necessary. (Most publicly owned companies achieve a weighted average result by multiplying each individual month's amount by each month's average exchange rate.) Average exchange rates must be calculated using the direct exchange rates that existed during the period; indirect exchange rates would not give the proper translated amounts.

**The Substitution Technique.** A simplifying technique commonly used to translate income statement accounts that arise from activity with the parent or home office is to **substitute the amount in the domestic company's**

**account for the subsidiary's or branch's account.** For example, the Intercompany Interest Expense account on the foreign subsidiary's books would be translated at the amount recorded in the Intercompany Interest Income account on the parent company's books. Likewise, the Intercompany Sales account on the foreign subsidiary's books would be translated at the amount recorded in the Intercompany Purchases account on the parent's books. This procedure automatically translates these items at the rates in effect on each transaction date, thus negating the need to use average rates. (This technique cannot be used in the translation process for downstream sales because it would result in a cost of goods sold amount based on exchange prices in existence when the inventory was acquired by the foreign unit rather than when the foreign unit sold the inventory. The latter is required under the translation process.)

In most cases, inter- or intracompany revenue and expense accounts need not be reconciled before doing the substitution. By reconciling the inter- or intracompany receivable and payable accounts before this substitution is made (as discussed on page 690), any clerical errors or unrecorded in-transit items affecting these income statement accounts would have been detected.

---

**ILLUSTRATION**

## Translation of Foreign Currency Financial Statements

Assume the following information for a wholly owned subsidiary located in West Germany.

1. **Conformity with U.S. generally accepted accounting principles:** The financial statements in marks have been adjusted to conform with U.S. generally accepted accounting principles. No adjustments are necessary on the worksheet before translation.
2. **Intercompany Receivable and Payable accounts:** The parent company and the subsidiary have no intercompany transactions (other than dividends declared by the subsidiary). Accordingly, no intercompany receivable and payable accounts exist, and no adjustments must be made at the balance sheet date prior to the translation process relating to changes in the exchange rate.
3. **Exchange rates:** The direct exchange rate at the beginning of the year was $.45. The mark weakened or the dollar strengthened during the year such that the direct exchange rate at year-end was $.40. The average rate for the year was $.42.
4. **Common stock:** The subsidiary was formed several years ago when the direct exchange rate was $.50. No additional capital stock changes have occurred since then.
5. **Retained earnings—beginning of year:** The translated amount of retained earnings at the end of the prior year was $42,300.

6. **Dividends declared:** The subsidiary declared dividends of 25,000 marks in 19X1 when the direct exchange rate was $.44.
7. **Sales, costs, and expenses:** All sales, costs, and expenses occurred evenly throughout the year.
8. **Cumulative translation adjustment—beginning of year:** The amount of the cumulative translation adjustment at the end of the prior year was a debit balance of $6,800.
9. **Current year translation adjustment:** The current year translation adjustment is a debit of $9,700. The manner of calculating this amount is shown in a supporting schedule to this illustration.

Illustration 16-2 uses the information above to translate the foreign subsidiary's financial statements into dollars. The calculation of the current year translation adjustment is shown in Illustration 16-3.

## Parent's Procedures after Translation

Under the equity method of accounting, the parent company would make the following entries:

| | | |
|---|---|---|
| Investment in Subsidiary . . . . . . . . . . . . . . . . . . . . . | 25,200 | |
| Equity in Net Income of Subsidiary . . . . . . . | | 25,200 |
| To record equity in net income. | | |

| | | |
|---|---|---|
| Cumulative Translation Adjustment . . . . . . . . . . . | 9,700 | |
| Investment in Subsidiary . . . . . . . . . . . . . . . | | 9,700 |
| To record effect of change in exchange rate. | | |

Note: These entries always maintain the book value element of the investment account balance at the difference between the subsidiary's assets and liabilities.

The conceptual analysis of the parent's investment account would be updated in 19X1 as follows:

| | | | | Book Value Element | | | |
|---|---|---|---|---|---|---|---|
| | | | | Retained Earnings | | | |
| | | | | | Current Year | | Cumulative |
| | Total | | Common | Prior | | Divi- | Translation |
| | Cost | = | Stock | + Years | + Earnings | − dends | + Adjustment |
| Balance, Jan. 1, 19X1 . . . . . . | $85,500[a] | | $50,000 | $42,300 | | | $ (6,800) |
| Equity in net income . . . . . | 25,200 | | | | $25,200 | | |
| Dividends declared . . . . . . | (11,000) | | | | | $(11,000) | |
| Translation adjustment . . | (9,700) | | | | | | (9,700) |
| Subtotal . . . . . . . . . . . . . . . . . | $90,000 | | $50,000 | $42,300 | $25,200 | $(11,000) | $(16,500) |
| Reclassification . . . . . . . . . | | | | 14,200 | (25,200) | 11,000 | |
| Balance, Dec. 31, 19X1 . . . . . | $90,000 | | $50,000 | $56,500 | $ –0– | $ –0– | $(16,500) |

[a]There is no cost in excess of book value because the subsidiary was formed by the parent company.

# ■ ILLUSTRATION 16-2

**Translation of Foreign Subsidiary's Financial Statements for the Year Ended December 31, 19X1**

| | Marks | Exchange Rates Code | Exchange Rates Rate | Dollars |
|---|---|---|---|---|
| **Income Statement** | | | | |
| Sales. . . . . . . . . . . . . . . . . . . . . . . . . . . . . | 800,000 | A | $.42 | $336,000 |
| Cost of goods sold. . . . . . . . . . . . . . . . . . | (500,000) | A | .42 | (210,000) |
| Depreciation expense. . . . . . . . . . . . . . . . | (20,000) | A | .42 | (8,400) |
| Operating expenses . . . . . . . . . . . . . . . . . | (180,000) | A | .42 | (75,600) |
| Income before Income Taxes . . . . . . . . . | 100,000 | | | $ 42,000 |
| Income tax expense @ 40% . . . . . . . . . . . | (40,000) | A | .42 | (16,800) |
| Net Income . . . . . . . . . . . . . . . . . . . . . . | 60,000 | | | $ 25,200 |
| **Statement of Retained Earnings** | | | | |
| Balance, January 1, 19X1. . . . . . . . . . . . . | 90,000 | | | $ 42,300 |
| + Net income. . . . . . . . . . . . . . . . . . . . . . | 60,000 | (Per net income above*) | | 25,200 |
| − Dividends declared . . . . . . . . . . . . . . . . | (25,000) | (1) | $.44 | (11,000) |
| Balance, December 31, 19X1 . . . . . . . . . . | 125,000 | | | $ 56,500 |
| **Balance Sheet** | | | | |
| Cash . . . . . . . . . . . . . . . . . . . . . . . . . . . . . | 50,000 | C | $.40 | $ 20,000 |
| Accounts receivable, net. . . . . . . . . . . . . . | 150,000 | C | .40 | 60,000 |
| Inventory . . . . . . . . . . . . . . . . . . . . . . . . . . | 200,000 | C | .40 | 80,000 |
| Fixed assets . . . . . . . . . . . . . . . . . . . . . . . | 400,000 | C | .40 | 160,000 |
| Accumulated depreciation . . . . . . . . . . . . | (50,000) | C | .40 | (20,000) |
| Total Assets . . . . . . . . . . . . . . . . . . . . . | 750,000 | | | $300,000 |
| Accounts payable . . . . . . . . . . . . . . . . . . | 235,000 | C | .40 | $ 94,000 |
| Income taxes payable. . . . . . . . . . . . . . . . | 40,000 | C | .40 | 16,000 |
| Long-term debt . . . . . . . . . . . . . . . . . . . . . | 250,000 | C | .40 | 100,000 |
| Total Liabilities . . . . . . . . . . . . . . . . . . . | 525,000 | | | $210,000 |
| Common stock. . . . . . . . . . . . . . . . . . . . . | 100,000 | H | .50 | $ 50,000 |
| Retained earnings . . . . . . . . . . . . . . . . . . | 125,000 | (Per above) | | 56,500 |
| Cumulative translation adjustment, net: | | | | |
| Prior years . . . . . . . . . . . . . . . . . . . . . . . | | | | (6,800) |
| Current year. . . . . . . . . . . . . . . . . . . . . . | | (Per Illus. 16-3) | | (9,700) |
| Total Equity . . . . . . . . . . . . . . . . . . . . . . | 225,000 | | | $ 90,000 |
| Total Liabilities and Equity. . . . . . . . . | 750,000 | | | $300,000 |

Code:
 C  =  Current rate existing at the balance sheet date.
 A  =  Average rate, as given in the introduction to this illustration.
 H  =  Historical rate.
 (1)  =  The $.44 spot rate at the declaration date.

*The amount in dollars is given in the introduction to this illustration.

## ■ ILLUSTRATION 16-3
### Calculation of Current Year Translation Adjustment: Supporting Schedule to Illustration 16-2

#### METHOD I: THE NET ASSET ANALYSIS APPROACH

| | Marks | Direct Exchange Rate | Dollars |
|---|---|---|---|
| Net assets, January 1, 19X1 | 190,000 | $.45 | $85,500 |
| + Net income | 60,000 | .42 | 25,200 |
| − Dividends declared | (25,000) | .44 | (11,000) |
| Net assets, December 31, 19X1 | 225,000 | | $99,700 |
| Net assets, December 31, 19X1 | 225,000 | .40 | 90,000 |
| Current Year Translation Adjustment | | | $ 9,700 |

An alternate way of analyzing the effect on the net assets is as follows:

| | Marks | Decrease in Direct Exchange Rate | Dollars |
|---|---|---|---|
| Net assets at January 1, 19X1, that lost $.05 of valuation | 165,000 | $.05 | $8,250 |
| Net assets at January 1, 19X1, that lost $.01 of valuation | 25,000 | .01 | 250 |
| Net assets that lost $.02 of valuation (19X1 net income) | 60,000 | .02 | 1,200 |
| Current Year Translation Adjustment | | | $9,700 |

#### METHOD II: THE FORCING OUT APPROACH

| | | |
|---|---|---|
| 1. | Translated assets | $300,000 |
| 2. Less | Translated liabilities | 210,000 |
| 3. Equals | Total stockholders' equity | $ 90,000 |
| 4. Less | Translated common stock and additional paid-in capital accounts | 50,000 |
| 5. Equals | Total retained earnings and the cumulative translation adjustment | $ 40,000 |
| 6. Less | Ending retained earnings | 56,500 |
| 7. Equals | The cumulative translation adjustment | $ (16,500) |
| 8. Less | The cumulative translation adjustment as of the beginning of the period | (6,800) |
| 9. Equals | The current-period translation adjustment | $ (9,700) |

Comparison Note: In practice, most companies perform their translations using templates on electronic spreadsheet software. The templates are designed so that the current period translation adjustment is forced out.

The primary elimination entry to consolidate the subsidiary at December 31, 19X1, is developed from the preceding analysis and is as follows:

| | Dr. | Cr. |
|---|---|---|
| **WORKSHEET ENTRY ONLY** | | |
| Common Stock | 50,000 | |
| Retained Earnings (beginning-of-year balance) | 42,300 | |
| Equity in Net Income of Subsidiary | 25,200 | |

*(continued)*

| | Dr. | Cr. |
|---|---|---|
| Dividends declared............................ | | 11,000 |
| Cumulative Translation Adjustment ...... | | 16,500 |
| Investment in Subsidiary................ | | 90,000 |

The equity accounts on the consolidation worksheet would appear as follows:

| | P Company | S Company | Eliminations Dr. | Eliminations Cr. | Consolidated |
|---|---|---|---|---|---|
| **P Company** | | | | | |
| Common stock .................. | 300,000[a] | | | | 300,000 |
| Retained earnings ............... | 125,200[a] | | | | 125,200 |
| Cumulative translation adjustment | (16,500) | | | | (16,500) |
| **S Company** | | | | | |
| Common stock .................. | | 50,000 | 50,000(1) | | –0– |
| Retained earnings ............... | | 56,500 | 67,500[b] | 11,000[b] | –0– |
| Cumulative translation adjustment | | (16,500) | | 16,500(1) | –0– |

(1) This posting comes from the primary elimination entry.
[a]Assumed amount.
[b]Carried forward from statement of retained earnings.

## Income Tax Consequences of Exchange Rate Changes

Translation adjustments are temporary differences under *FASB Statement No. 96*, "Accounting for Income Taxes." If the translation adjustment is positive, then a deferred tax liability is to be recorded—the offsetting debit is made to the cumulative translation adjustment account. This requirement becomes inoperable if the parent is using the loophole available in *APB Opinion No. 23*, "Accounting for Income Taxes—Special Areas," that allows no income taxes to be provided on foreign earnings (discussed in Chapter 12). If the translation adjustment is negative, then the parent will have to make the appropriate calculations under *FASB Statement No. 96* to determine whether a deferred tax asset can be recorded—the offsetting credit is made to the cumulative translation adjustment account.

## Disposition of Translation Adjustments

The translation adjustments reported as a separate component of stockholders' equity are removed from that component (along with any related income taxes) and reported in the income statement on (a) complete or substantially complete liquidation or (b) sale of the investment. (*FASB Interpretation No. 37* requires such treatment on a pro rata basis when only part of the ownership in a foreign operation is sold.) Further interpretations are needed in this area to address the following questions:

1. Does the conversion of all operating assets into cash constitute a liquidation?
2. Does the conversion of all operating assets into passive investments constitute a liquidation?
3. What percentage of the operating assets would have to be sold to constitute a substantially complete liquidation?

A company that has foreign operations in more than one foreign country must, of course, maintain the separate translation component of equity for each such foreign operation that has translation adjustments.

# THE REMEASUREMENT PROCESS

This section deals with the actual remeasurement of a foreign operation's financial statements into dollars, which in this case is the foreign unit's functional currency.

Recall that the intent of the remeasurement process is to produce the same results as though the foreign unit's transactions had been recorded in the functional currency (dollars, in this case) using the exchange rates in effect when the transactions occurred. Accordingly, historical exchange rates are used for nonmonetary accounts.

## Specific Remeasurement Procedures

The basic procedures required before translation that were discussed in the preceding section on the translation process also apply to the remeasurement process—that is, making adjustments to conform to U.S. generally accepted accounting procedures, adjusting foreign currency receivable and payable accounts, and reconciling inter- or intracompany accounts.

**Historical Exchange Rate.**   *FASB Statement No. 52* requires the use of both the current exchange rate and the historical exchange rate (depending on the individual item) when the current rate method of translation is not appropriate. For example, the exchange rate in effect last year when a building was acquired (the current rate at that time) is now the historical exchange rate, which is used rather than the current exchange rate existing at the balance sheet date. Likewise, the historical exchange rate would be used for depreciation expense related to the building rather than the rate in effect when the depreciation was recognized in the income statement. The accounts for which historical exchange rates are to be used are listed in Illustration 16-4.

■ **ILLUSTRATION 16-4**
**Accounts Remeasured Using Historical Exchange Rates**

**Assets**

Marketable securities carried at cost:
   Equity securities
   Debt securities not intended to be held until maturity
Inventories carried at cost
Prepaid expenses, such as insurance, advertising, and rent
Property, plant, and equipment
Accumulated depreciation on property, plant, and equipment
Patents, trademarks, licenses, and formulas
Goodwill
Other tangible assets

**Liabilities**

Deferred income

**Equity**

Common stock
Preferred stock carried at issuance price

**Revenues, Costs, and Expenses (examples of accounts related to nonmonetary items)**

Cost of goods sold
Depreciation of property, plant, and equipment
Amortization of intangible items, such as goodwill, patents, licenses,
   and so on
Amortization of deferred charges or credits, except deferred income taxes
   and policy acquisition costs for life insurance companies

Comments:
1. **Additional Paid-in Capital:** Although not listed above, this account would be re-measured at historical exchange rates. (The Common Stock account listed was obviously intended to include this account.)
2. **Retained Earnings:** This account is not listed above, not because the current rate is used, but because it is a "forced out" amount.

Note: The above list excludes deferred income taxes; they would be remeasured using the current rate.

Source: Based on *FASB Statement No. 52*, par. 48.

---

ILLUSTRATION

## Remeasurement of a Foreign Operation's Financial Statements into Dollars

To compare the results of the remeasurement process with the results of the translation process illustrated in the previous section, we use the financial statements for the same West German foreign subsidiary in the following illustration. In addition, we reflect an Intercompany Payable account of 50,000 marks (long-term debt was reduced by 50,000 marks). The assumptions for this illustration, some of which are identical to those used in the translation process, are as follows:

1. **Conformity with U.S. generally accepted accounting principles:** The financial statements in marks have been adjusted to conform with U.S. generally accepted accounting principles. No adjustments are necessary on the worksheet before remeasurement.

2. **Intercompany Receivable and Payable accounts:** The parent company and the subsidiary have considerable intercompany transactions (involving mainly inventory transfers). The subsidiary's intercompany payable account is payable in marks. Accordingly, the parent company has a foreign currency transaction and is the entity that must adjust its intercompany receivable account at year-end to reflect the exchange rate existing at the balance sheet date. (We discuss these intercompany accounts more fully later in the chapter within the section dealing with some of the fine points of intercompany transactions.)

3. **Exchange rates:** The direct exchange rate at the beginning of the year was $.45. The mark weakened or the dollar strengthened during the year such that the direct exchange rate at year-end was $.40. The average rate for the year was $.42.

4. **Inventory:** The beginning inventory was remeasured at $46,000 in last year's financial statements. Ending inventory cost was below market in marks, resulting in no adjustment in marks for valuation purposes. The subsidiary determines that its ending inventory was acquired when the exchange rates were as follows:

| Marks | Rate | Dollars |
|---|---|---|
| 20,000 | $.42 | $ 8,400 |
| 60,000 | .41 | 24,600 |
| 120,000 | .40 | 48,000 |
| 200,000 | | $81,000 |

5. **Fixed assets:** All fixed assets were acquired in prior years when the exchange rate was $.50. No fixed assets were retired during the year.

6. **Common stock:** The subsidiary was formed several years ago when the exchange rate was $.50. No additional capital stock changes have occurred since then.

7. **Retained earnings—beginning of year:** The translated retained earnings amount at the end of the prior year was $55,000.

8. **Dividends declared:** The subsidiary declared dividends of 25,000 marks in 19X1 when the direct exchange rate was $.44.

9. **Sales, purchases, and expenses:** All sales, purchases, and expenses occurred evenly throughout the year.

10. **Certain monetary information:** At January 1, 19X1, the subsidiary had monetary assets of 240,000 marks and monetary liabilities of 520,000 marks. During 19X1, cash disbursements in payment of liabilities totaled 815,000 marks.

Illustration 16-5 uses the above information to remeasure the foreign subsidiary's financial statements into dollars. The calculation of the transaction gain from remeasurement is shown in Illustration 16-6.

### Review Points for Illustration 16-5.   Note the following:

1. **Applying the equity method.** The equity method of accounting would be applied to the subsidiary's net income of $32,000 as follows:

| | | |
|---|---|---|
| Investment in Subsidiary.................... | 32,000 | |
| Equity in Net Income of Subsidiary ..... | | 32,000 |

Note: Recall that the $15,400 transaction gain from remeasurement is included in determining net income.

2. **Comparison to Illustration 16-2.** Total assets and total equity are both higher by $36,000 in Illustration 16-5 than in Illustration 16-2, in which the translation process was shown. This difference is the result of using historical exchange rates in Illustration 16-5 for inventory (a $1,000 difference) and fixed assets (a $35,000 difference) rather than the rate existing at the balance sheet date (a current rate).

3. **Managing the monetary position.** The $15,400 transaction gain from remeasurement would not have resulted if the company had kept monetary assets and monetary liabilities at approximately the same level throughout the year. Doing this merely to minimize transaction gains and losses from remeasurement, however, counteracts the long-standing principle of minimizing the risks associated with foreign operations by financing them with foreign borrowings (payable in the foreign currency of the foreign operation) to the maximum extent possible. Obviously, companies must carefully weigh these conflicting objectives. (In the appendix, we discuss other means of minimizing gains and losses resulting from remeasurement.)

4. **Income tax consequences of exchange rate changes.** As was the case for "translation adjustments" discussed earlier, the gain or loss on remeasurement is a temporary difference under *FASB Statement No. 96* for which the parent may have to provide deferred income taxes.

5. **Possibility that the gain from remeasurement is imaginary.** The decrease in the direct exchange rate was an adverse economic event; however, a $15,400 favorable result was reported for the effect of the change in the exchange rate. (This unusual result situation was discussed in detail in the conceptual issues section of Chapter 15.) In such a situation, the gain from remeasurement may be imaginary. If the nonmonetary assets can be sold for no more than their book values, then their realizable value in dollars is only $220,000 (inventory and fixed assets at book value of 550,000 marks × $.40). This

## ■ ILLUSTRATION 16-5
### Remeasurement of Foreign Subsidiary's Financial Statements into Dollars for the Year Ended December 31, 19X1

| | Marks | Exchange Rates Code | Exchange Rates Rate | Dollars |
|---|---|---|---|---|
| **Income Statement** | | | | |
| Sales......................... | 800,000 | A | $.42 | $336,000 |
| Cost of goods sold: | | | | |
| Beginning inventory.......... | 100,000 | | * | $ 46,000 |
| Purchases................... | 600,000 | A | .42 | 252,000 |
| Goods available for sale ..... | 700,000 | | | $298,000 |
| Less: Ending inventory........ | (200,000) (500,000) | (Per balance sheet) | | (81,000) (217,000) |
| Depreciation expense .......... | (20,000) | H | .50 | (10,000) |
| Operating expenses............ | (180,000) | A | .42 | (75,600) |
| Income before Income Taxes ... | 100,000 | | | $ 33,400 |
| Income tax expense @ 40%...... | (40,000) | A | .42 | (16,800) |
| Income before Transaction Gain from Remeasurement ... | 60,000 | | | $ 16,600 |
| Transaction gain from remeasurement ............. | | (Per Illus. 16-6) | | 15,400 |
| Net Income................ | 60,000 | | | $ 32,000 ─┐ |
| **Statement of Retained Earnings** | | | | |
| Balance, January 1, 19X1....... | 90,000 | | * | $55,000 |
| + Net income ................ | 60,000 | | | 32,000 ◄┘ |
| − Dividends declared.......... | (25,000) | (1) | $.44 | (11,000) |
| Balance, December 31, 19X1 .... | 125,000 | | | $ 76,000 ─┐ |
| **Balance Sheet** | | | | |
| Cash........................ | 50,000 | C | $.40 | $ 20,000 |
| Accounts receivable, net......... | 150,000 | C | .40 | 60,000 |
| Inventory .................... | 200,000 | | * | 81,000 |
| Fixed assets.................. | 400,000 | H | .50 | 200,000 |
| Accumulated depreciation ....... | (50,000) | H | .50 | (25,000) |
| Total Assets ................ | 750,000 | | | $336,000 |
| Accounts payable.............. | 235,000 | C | .40 | $ 94,000 |
| Income taxes payable .......... | 40,000 | C | .40 | 16,000 |
| Intercompany payable.......... | 50,000 | C | .40 | 20,000 |
| Long-term debt .............. | 200,000 | C | .40 | 80,000 |
| Total Liabilities ............. | 525,000 | | | $210,000 |
| Common stock .............. | 100,000 | H | .50 | $ 50,000 |
| Retained earnings ............ | 125,000 | | | 76,000 ◄┘ |
| Total Equity................. | 225,000 | | | $126,000 |
| Total Liabilities and Equity .... | 750,000 | | | $336,000 |

Code:
C  =  Current rate existing at the balance sheet date.
H  =  Historical rate.
A  =  Average rate, as given in the introduction to this illustration.
(1)  =  The $.44 spot rate at the declaration date.
*The amount in dollars is given in the introduction to this illustration.

# ■ ILLUSTRATION 16-6
## Calculation of the Transaction Gain from Remeasurement: Supporting Schedule to Illustration 16-5

### METHOD 1: ANALYZING THE MONETARY ACCOUNTS

**Analysis of Monetary Assets and Monetary Liabilities for 19X1 (in marks):**

|  | Monetary Assets | Monetary Liabilities | Net Monetary Liability Position |
|---|---|---|---|
| Monetary items, January 1, 19X1 . . . . . . . . . . . . . . . . . . . . . . . . . . . . . . . . | 240,000 | 520,000 | 280,000 |
| Sales . . . . . . . . . . . . . . . . . . . . . . . . . . . . . . . . . . . . . . . . . . . . . . . | 800,000 |  | (800,000) |
| Purchases . . . . . . . . . . . . . . . . . . . . . . . . . . . . . . . . . . . . . . . . . . . . |  | 600,000 | 600,000 |
| Operating expenses (excluding depreciation expense) . . . . . . . . . . . . . |  | 180,000 | 180,000 |
| Income tax expense . . . . . . . . . . . . . . . . . . . . . . . . . . . . . . . . . . . . . . |  | 40,000 | 40,000 |
| Payment of liabilities . . . . . . . . . . . . . . . . . . . . . . . . . . . . . . . . . . . . | (815,000) | (815,000) |  |
| Dividend payment . . . . . . . . . . . . . . . . . . . . . . . . . . . . . . . . . . . . . . . | (25,000) |  | 25,000 |
| Monetary items, December 31, 19X1 . . . . . . . . . . . . . . . . . . . . . . . . . . . | 200,000 | 525,000 | 325,000 |

**Calculating the Transaction Gain from Remeasurement Using the Above Analysis of the Monetary Accounts:**

|  | Loss on Monetary Assets | Gain on Monetary Liabilities | Transaction Gain (Loss) from Remeasurement |
|---|---|---|---|
| Monetary assets at January 1, 19X1 that lost $.05 of valuation (240,000 marks − 25,000 marks for the dividend) . . . . . . . . . . . . . . . . . . . . . . . . . . . . . . . . . . . . | $(10,750) |  | $(10,750) |
| Monetary assets at January 1, 19X1 that lost $.01 of valuation (25,000 marks for the dividend) . . . . . . . . . . . . . . . . . . . . . | (250) |  | (250) |
| Monetary liabilities at January 1, 19X1 that lost $.05 of valuation (the entire 520,000 marks) . . . . . . . . . . . . . . . . . . . . . . . |  | $26,000 | 26,000 |
| Sales (a loss of $.02 of valuation) . . . . . . . . . . . . . . . . . . . . . . . . . . . . | (16,000) |  | (16,000) |
| Purchases (a loss of $.02 of valuation) . . . . . . . . . . . . . . . . . . . . . . . . |  | 12,000 | 12,000 |
| Operating expenses (a loss of $.02 of valuation) . . . . . . . . . . . . . . . . |  | 3,600 | 3,600 |
| Income tax expense (a loss of $.02 of valuation) . . . . . . . . . . . . . . . . |  | 800 | 800 |
|  | $(27,000) | $42,400 | $15,400 |

### METHOD II—THE FORCING OUT APPROACH

| | | | |
|---|---|---|---|
| 1. | | Remeasured assets . . . . . . . . . . . . . . . . . . . . . . . . . . . . . . . . . . . . . . . . . | $336,000 |
| 2. | Less | Remeasured liabilities . . . . . . . . . . . . . . . . . . . . . . . . . . . . . . . . . . . . . . . | 210,000 |
| 3. | Equals | Total stockholders' equity . . . . . . . . . . . . . . . . . . . . . . . . . . . . . . . . . . . . | $126,000 |
| 4. | Less | Remeasured common stock and additional paid-in capital . . . . . . . . . . . . . . . . . . . . . . . . . . . . . . . . . . . . . . . | 50,000 |
| 5. | Equals | Total retained earnings . . . . . . . . . . . . . . . . . . . . . . . . . . . . . . . . . . . . | $ 76,000 |
| 6. | Less | Beginning retained earnings in dollars as reported in the prior period's remeasured financial statements reduced for any dividends declared ($55,000 − $11,000) . . . . . . | 44,000 |
| 7. | Equals | Current-period net income . . . . . . . . . . . . . . . . . . . . . . . . . . . . . . . . . . | $ 32,000 |
| 8. | Less | Remeasured revenues and expenses (as shown in Illustration 16-5) . . . . . . . . . . . . . . . . | 16,600 |
| 9. | Equals | The current-period foreign currency transaction gain from remeasurement . . . . . . . . . . | $ 15,400 |

$220,000 is $36,000 below the $256,000 amount shown in dollars. Accordingly, a write-down of $36,000 would be necessary (more than offsetting the 15,400 gain from remeasurement). The procedures for assessing realization in dollars are discussed after the following review point.

6. **What if the exchange rate had increased?** If the direct exchange rate had increased rather than decreased in Illustration 16-5, a transaction loss from remeasurement would have resulted; however, the loss would be imaginary if the nonmonetary assets can be sold for at least their book values. If so, their realizable value in dollars would be much greater than the amounts reported in dollars from the remeasurement process. However, no provisions exist for revaluing inventory and fixed assets upward in dollars to obtain an offsetting effect (as is possible when the direct exchange rate decreases). Accordingly, the reporting of a current-period transaction loss from remeasurement is offset in later periods as the nonmonetary assets are realized (transformed into monetary assets).

## Realization Review Procedures for Nonmonetary Assets

Because of the use of historical exchange rates for most nonmonetary assets, the results of the remeasurement process create a special problem that does not arise with the translation process. Nonmonetary assets remeasured at historical exchange rates are not necessarily realizable in dollars (even though no realizability problem exists in the foreign currency). (This problem usually arises only when the direct exchange rate has decreased; however, the problem also could exist when the direct exchange rate has not changed or has increased. Accordingly, it must be addressed in each individual remeasurement process.) Thus, the foreign operation's remeasured nonmonetary assets must be reviewed and evaluated for their realizability in dollars. Prior to consolidation, the dollar amounts of such assets on the worksheet must be adjusted to the extent that they are not realizable in dollars. *FASB Statement No. 52* discusses the realization of inventory in dollars in great detail; however, it only briefly touches on the realization of fixed assets, which may be an even greater problem.

**Inventory.**   The lower of cost or market test must also be performed in dollars, to ensure that the realizable value in dollars is not less than remeasured historical cost. Such situations usually arise when ending inventory is acquired before the direct exchange rate decreases significantly, and the inventory is thus priced at historical cost and remeasured at the historical rate. In applying the lower of cost or market test in dollars, we determine current replacement cost, net realizable value, and net realizable value reduced for a normal profit margin (a percentage concept) in the foreign currency and then express each one in dollars using the exchange rate existing at the balance sheet date. (These are current-value concepts; thus, the exchange rate existing at the balance sheet date is the only sensible rate.)

To illustrate this procedure, we must use a more drastic decrease in the exchange rate than the one assumed in Illustration 16-5. Let us use the 85% decline in the value of the Mexican peso that occurred in 1982. We assume that ending inventory was acquired for 1,000,000 pesos before the decrease in the direct exchange rate. The exchange rate before the decrease was $.04, and the exchange rate after the decrease was $.006. The lower of cost or market calculation in dollars is as follows:

|  | Pesos | Rate | Dollars |
|---|---|---|---|
| Historical cost................. | 1,000,000 | $.04 | $40,000 |
| Replacement cost.............. | 1,000,000 | .006 | 6,000 |
| Net realizable value............ | 1,200,000 | .006 | $ 7,200 (ceiling) |
| Net realizable value reduced for a normal profit margin .... | 1,000,000 | .006 | $ 6,000 (floor) |

Accordingly, the inventory must be valued at $6,000, a write-down of $34,000. This write-down is made to the dollar column; it would never be posted to the peso general ledger. This process is necessary regardless of whether a write-down was needed in applying the lower of cost or market test in pesos. In an alternative view of the rationale for performing the lower of cost or market test in dollars, we assume that the inventory was sold on the last day of the year for 1,200,000 pesos. The 1,200,000 pesos (cash or receivables) would be remeasured to $7,200, which is below the remeasured historical cost of $40,000.

This example assumes that selling prices and purchase prices did not advance after the weakening of the peso. When selling prices neither advance nor decline, replacement cost always equals the floor. If selling prices had advanced in pesos after the weakening of the peso, the ceiling and floor would have been higher, thus necessitating a lower write-down. The process of performing a lower of cost or market test for inventory in dollars is discussed at length in paragraphs 49 through 53 of *FASB Statement No. 52.*

**Assets Other than Inventory.** Fixed assets may be realizable in the foreign currency, but the future cash flow that such assets generate (including that portion of the future cash flow that presumably represents a recovery of the investment in fixed assets) is worth significantly less (in dollars) as a result of a weakening of the foreign currency. Surprisingly, the use of historical rates in remeasuring assets other than inventory and the potential realization problems that may arise are given only footnote attention in *FASB Statement No. 52.* Footnote 5 to paragraph 49 states:

> An asset other than inventory may sometimes be written down from historical cost. Although that write-down is not under the rule of cost or market, whichever is lower, the approach described in this paragraph might be appropriate. . . .[3]

If a substantial decline in the direct exchange rate occurs (such as the 85% devaluation of the Mexican peso in 1982), the realization of fixed assets in dollars represents a major problem that could be a much greater one than the realization of inventory in dollars.

**The Role of Inflation.**  Recall from Chapter 14 that under purchasing power parity theory, the differential rate of inflation between two countries causes an opposite effect on the exchange rate between those two countries (in the long run). Thus, if the inflation rate for 19X1 was zero in the U.S. and 25% in West Germany, a direct exchange rate of $.40 on January 1, 19X1, would decrease to $.32 ($.40 ÷ 125%) by December 31, 19X1. Under such a scenario, a realization problem in dollars would not occur. Furthermore, any gain from remeasurement would not be imaginary inasmuch as it substantively would be an inflationary holding gain (holding nonmonetary assets that appreciate in value but are financed by debt, the value of which is fixed in the foreign currency).

# INTERCOMPANY TRANSACTIONS WITH FOREIGN UNITS

We now discuss the specific reporting requirements pertaining to intercompany transactions between a parent company and a foreign subsidiary.

## Adjusting Intercompany Receivables and Payables

When intercompany receivables and payables exist, the entity that makes or receives payment in the foreign currency (that is, in other than its own currency) must adjust its intercompany receivable or payable to reflect the new exchange rate. In Illustration 16-5 (page 701), which dealt with the remeasurement process, the foreign subsidiary had an intercompany payable to the parent company. The payable was denominated in marks; thus, the parent company had the foreign currency transaction and was

---

[3]*FASB Statement No. 52,* par. 49, footnote 5.

the entity that made the adjustment to reflect the current rate. Let us assume that the payable of 50,000 marks arose when the direct exchange rate was $.45 (the parent's receivable was therefore $22,500). The direct exchange rate at December 31, 19X1, was $.40, making the receivable worth only $20,000 (50,000 marks × $.40). Accordingly, the parent would make the following adjustment:

| | | |
|---|---|---|
| Foreign Currency Transaction Loss ........... | 2,500 | |
|     Intercompany Receivable ................. | | 2,500 |
|   To adjust intercompany receivable to reflect | | |
|   the new exchange rate of $.40. | | |
|   ($22,500 − $20,000 = $2,500) | | |

If the intercompany payable had been repayable in dollars instead of marks, the foreign subsidiary would have made the adjustment at December 31, 19X1 ($22,500 ÷ $.40 = 56,250 marks):

| | | |
|---|---|---|
| Foreign Currency Transaction Loss | 6,250 (marks) | |
|     Intercompany Payable ........ | | 6,250 (marks) |
|   To adjust the intercompany | | |
|   payable to reflect the new | | |
|   exchange rate of $.40. (56,250 | | |
|   marks − 50,000 marks = | | |
|   6,250 marks) | | |

When expressing the foreign subsidiary's financial statements in dollars, the parent company must use the direct exchange rate to which the intercompany payable was adjusted ($.40) in dealing with the foreign currency transaction loss of 6,250 marks. This calculation gives $2,500 (6,250 marks × $.40), which equals the amount of loss the parent company would have recorded if the payable had been repayable in marks instead of dollars. (Alternatively, we could obtain this answer by multiplying the 50,000 marks by the $.05 change in the direct exchange rate.)

Of course, if the appropriate adjusting entries are not made at the balance sheet date, the intercompany receivable and payable accounts would not agree and would not eliminate in consolidation.

**The Wash Effect.** The preceding entries indicate that a $2,500 transaction loss would be reported as a result of adjustments to the intercompany receivable or payable accounts. **However, the parent company's equity is never affected by adjustments to the intercompany accounts.** This fact holds true whether the amounts are denominated in the dollar or in the foreign operation's local currency. The zero net answer results from the translation process or the remeasurement process, as the case may be.

When the dollar is the foreign operation's functional currency, a $2,500 transaction gain from remeasurement arises on the 50,000 mark intercompany payable (50,000 marks × $.05 decrease in direct exchange rate). This amount offsets the $2,500 transaction loss in the income statement. When the foreign currency is the functional currency, a $2,500 translation adjustment arises on the 50,000 mark intercompany payable. This $2,500 translation adjustment, however, is reported in the translation adjustment component of stockholders' equity. Thus, the income statement contains no offsetting entry, but Stockholders' Equity does.

**Long-term Intercompany Receivables and Payables.** A long-term intercompany receivable on the parent company's books is, in substance, an addition to its investment. Likewise, a long-term intercompany payable on the parent company's books is, in substance, a reduction of its investment. When such receivables and payables exist **and settlement is not planned or anticipated in the foreseeable future,** *FASB Statement No. 52* requires that transaction gains and losses resulting from adjusting these accounts (as a result of exchange rate changes) should be treated as translation adjustments. They are **accumulated in the separate component of stockholders' equity** rather than reported currently in the income statement. This provision ensures that the entire effect of a rate change on the true net investment in a foreign unit is shown as part of the separate component of stockholders' equity. This requirement applies **only when the "translation" process is involved, that is, when the foreign currency is the functional currency.**

## Intercompany Profits

All intercompany profit from intercompany transactions must, of course, be eliminated. Under *FASB Statement No. 52*, no special problems are involved when the foreign unit has the dollar as its functional currency, because all foreign-unit account balances are remeasured into the equivalent dollar amounts. However, when the foreign unit has a foreign currency as its functional currency, the translated cost of any remaining intercompany-acquired inventory or fixed assets does not equal the parent's selling price if the exchange rate has changed since the transfer date. The difference between the translated cost at the transfer date and the translated cost at the balance sheet date is treated as part of the effect of the change in the exchange rate—that is, as part of the translation adjustment accumulated in the special component of stockholders' equity. *FASB Statement No. 52* requires that **any intercompany profit be eliminated using the exchange rate existing at the time of the transfer. The gross profit determined at the time of the transfer is used for subsequent eliminations, regardless of any subsequent exchange rate changes.**

**Illustration.** Assume S Company has at year-end 25,000 marks of inventory that was acquired from the parent when the direct exchange rate was $.40. Thus, the parent's selling price was $10,000 (25,000 marks × $.40). Assume the parent's cost was $6,000, which means the intercompany mark-up is 40% of the transfer price. If the exchange rate has not changed since the transfer date, then the inventory will be translated into $10,000. Clearly, $4,000 of intercompany profit must be deferred at year-end. However, if the direct exchange rate at year-end is $.10, the inventory would be translated into $2,500, which amount is less than the $4,000 of intercompany profit associated with this inventory. It would be improper to defer only $1,000 of intercompany profit (40% of $2,500). Regardless of the inventory's translated amount in dollars, $4,000 of intercompany profit must be deferred at year-end.

## Intercompany Dividends

The parent company uses **the exchange rate existing when dividends are declared** to record a dividend receivable. Any changes in the exchange rate between the declaration date and the remittance date result in a foreign currency transaction gain or loss recorded by one of the entities. Such gains and losses can be avoided if dividends are remitted at their declaration date.

# THE MANNER OF REPORTING FOREIGN OPERATIONS

## Disclosures Concerning Translation and Remeasurement

**Translation.** For the separate component of stockholders' equity containing the cumulative translation adjustments, the FASB requires an analysis of the following changes during the period:

a. Beginning and ending amount of cumulative translation adjustments.
b. The aggregate adjustment for the period resulting from translation adjustments and gains and losses from certain hedges and intercompany balances [the latter items are discussed in the appendix.]
c. The amount of income taxes for the period allocated to translation adjustments.
d. The amounts transferred from cumulative translation adjustments [including all items above] and included in determining net income for the period as a result of the sale or complete or substantially complete liquidation of an investment in a foreign subsidiary.[4]

[4]*FASB Statement No. 52*, par. 31.

This analysis may be shown (1) in a separate financial statement, (2) in notes of the financial statements, or (3) as part of a statement of changes in stockholders' equity.

**Remeasurement.** The total of all transaction gains and losses from remeasurement (along with other foreign currency transaction gains and losses that are reported in the income statement—such as those resulting from importing and exporting transactions) is disclosed as a net amount either in the income statement or in notes to the financial statements. Transaction gains and losses are not considered extraordinary items, no matter how material they might be.

## Consolidation of Foreign Subsidiaries

Recall from Chapter 3 that *FASB Statement No. 94*, "Consolidation of All Majority-owned Subsidiaries" requires all subsidiaries to be consolidated unless control is lacking or is likely to be temporary. When a foreign government imposes currency exchange restrictions or other severe governmental controls, the parent no longer has complete control over the subsidiary. In such situations, consolidation is inappropriate.

**Nonconsolidation of a Foreign Operation.** If a foreign subsidiary is not consolidated, then the parent must evaluate whether or not it can realize its investment in the subsidiary. If a realization problem exists, the investment must be written down.

**Disclosures Concerning Foreign Assets, Revenues, and Profitability.** *FASB Statement No. 14*, "Financial Reporting for Segments of a Business Enterprise," requires disclosures of foreign assets, revenues, and profitability of consolidated foreign operations if specific tests are met. We discussed these tests and the disclosure requirements in Chapter 13, which deals with segment reporting.

## CONCLUDING COMMENTS

Knowledgeable people, many with substantial experience in assessing and dealing with foreign operations, draw completely different conclusions concerning how to account for the effects of changes in the exchange rate in reporting foreign operations. For example, *FASB Statement No. 52* was passed by a mere 4 to 3 vote. We summarize the views of the dissenting members of the FASB on the following page.

## Views of the Dissenting FASB Members

The substantial objections and views of the three dissenting FASB members are presented in pages 15 to 23 of *FASB Statement No. 52*. They basically objected to allowing the use of a foreign currency as the unit of measure (when the dollar is not the functional currency). (This objection essentially rejects the functional-currency concept as a relevant factor in determining how foreign operations should be expressed in dollars.) In their view, the dollar should be used as the unit of measure in all cases. Furthermore, dissenting members felt that the translation adjustments should not be reported directly in stockholders' equity. In their view, translation adjustments are gains and losses from a dollar perspective that should be currently reported in the income statement. In summary, these members felt that *FASB Statement No. 8* was conceptually sound and that the temporal method of translation should be used in all cases. (They would have allowed a practical modification for inventory; locally acquired inventory could be translated at the current exchange rate.)

## Has the Controversy Ended?

Whether *FASB Statement No. 52* is the last chapter concerning the foreign currency translation issue or merely the latest chapter remains to be seen. An adequate assessment of the reporting results from using the functional currency concept and not reporting translation adjustments currently in the income statement will probably require a fairly long period of time. Considering the extensive monumental effort that the FASB and its staff devoted to *FASB Statement No. 52*, it is likely that they will not want to readdress this issue for quite a while.

## END-OF-CHAPTER REVIEW

## Summary of Key Points

1. The cornerstone of *FASB Statement No. 52* is the functional currency concept. The functional currency for each foreign operation must be determined.
2. The currency in which the foreign operation primarily generates and expends cash is its functional currency, and this currency is not necessarily the one in which it maintains its books and prepares its financial statements.
3. Illustration 16-7 contains a summary of accounting for the translation of foreign currency financial statements once the functional currency has been determined.
4. Gains or losses from adjusting intercompany receivable and payable balances for exchange rate changes are reported currently in the income statement unless (1) the adjustment pertains to long-term receivables and payables, and (2) the foreign unit's functional currency is *not* the dollar.

5. When intercompany asset transfers occur, the gross profit eliminated is based on the gross profit determined at the time of the transfer. Subsequent changes in the exchange rate have no bearing in this respect.

## Glossary of New Terms

**Current exchange rate**   "The current exchange rate is the rate at which one unit of a currency can be exchanged for (converted into) another currency. For purposes of translation . . . , the current exchange rate is the rate as of the end of the period covered by the financial statements or as of the dates of recognition in those statements in the case of revenues, expenses, gains, and losses."*

**Foreign currency translation**   "The process of expressing in the reporting currency of the enterprise those amounts that are denominated or measured in a different currency."*

**Remeasurement**   The process of measuring in the functional currency amounts denominated or stated in another currency.

**Translation (distinguished from remeasurement)**   The process of expressing functional currency measurements in the reporting currency.

### ■ ILLUSTRATION 16-7
### Summary of Accounting for the Translation of Foreign Currency Financial Statements

|  | Functional Currency | |
|---|---|---|
|  | **Foreign Currency** | **U.S. Dollar** |
| Perspective taken | Foreign currency | U.S. dollar |
| Name given to process | Translation | Remeasurement |
| Exchange rates to be used for: | | |
|   Assets and liabilities | Current rate[a] | Combination of current[a] and historical rates |
|   Income statement accounts | Current rate[b] | Combination of current[b] and historical rates |
| Term used to describe the effect of a change in the exchange rate | Translation adjustment | Foreign currency transaction gain or loss |
| Treatment to be accorded the effect of a change in the exchange rate | Accumulate in separate component of stockholders' equity (pending liquidation or disposal of the investment) | Report currently in the income statement |

Note: For operations located in countries that have highly inflationary economies, the dollar is deemed to be the functional currency.

[a]Current rate here means the exchange rate existing at the balance sheet date.
[b]Current rate here means the exchange rate existing when the items were recognized in the income statement.

**Translation adjustments** Adjustments that result from translating financial statements from the entity's functional currency into the reporting currency.

**Unit of measure** The currency in which assets, liabilities, revenues, expenses, gains, and losses are measured.*

## Self-Study Questions

*(Answers are at the end of this chapter, preceding the appendix.)*

1. A subsidiary located in a foreign country having a highly inflationary economy should use which of the following methods in expressing the financial statements in dollars?
   a. The current rate method.
   b. The temporal method.
   c. The monetary–nonmonetary method.
   d. A combination of current and historical rates as specified in *FASB Statement No. 52*.
   e. None of the above.

2. Which of the following methods should be used for expressing in dollars the financial statements of a foreign operation that is relatively self-contained and independent of the parent's operations?
   a. The current rate method.
   b. The monetary–nonmonetary method.
   c. The temporal method.
   d. A combination of current and historical rates as specified in *FASB Statement No. 52*.
   e. None of the above.

3. A subsidiary's functional currency is the local currency, which has not experienced significant inflation. Which exchange rate should be used in expressing the following accounts in dollars?

   | | Depreciation Expense | Plant and Equipment |
   |---|---|---|
   | a. | Current | Current |
   | b. | Historical | Historical |
   | c. | Current | Historical |
   | d. | Historical | Current |
   | e. | None of the above. | |

4. Assume the same information in Question 3, except that the functional currency is the dollar.

5. Which exchange rates should be used in expressing cost of goods sold in dollars for a foreign subsidiary under each of the following processes?

   | | Translation | Remeasurement |
   |---|---|---|
   | a. | Current | Current |
   | b. | Historical | Historical |
   | c. | Current | Historical |
   | d. | Historical | Current |
   | e. | None of the above. | |

*FASB Statement No. 52, Appendix E, pp. 75–78.

6. A parent company has a long-term receivable from its foreign subsidiary. The receivable is not expected to be settled in the foreseeable future. The functional currency of the subsidiary is its local currency. The receivable is denominated in the foreign subsidiary's functional currency. During 19X1, the direct exchange rate increased steadily throughout the year. At year-end, the parent should:
   a. Adjust the receivable and credit an income statement account.
   b. Adjust the receivable and debit an income statement account.
   c. Adjust the receivable and credit the cumulative translation adjustment account.
   d. Adjust the receivable and debit the cumulative translation adjustment account.
   e. None of the above.
7. A domestic parent company sold inventory costing $70,000 to its British subsidiary for $100,000. At year-end, the subsidiary reported in its balance sheet 40,000 pounds of this inventory. At the time of the sale, the direct exchange rate was $.50. At year-end, the direct exchange rate was $.40. How much intercompany profit must be deferred at year-end under each of the following processes?

| Translation | Remeasurement |
|---|---|
| a. $6,000 | $6,000 |
| b. $4,800 | $4,800 |
| c. $6,000 | $4,800 |
| d. $4,800 | $6,000 |
| e. None of the above. | |

# ASSIGNMENT MATERIAL

## Review Questions

1. How does *FASB Statement No. 52* define a highly inflationary economy?
2. How are highly inflationary economies dealt with in *FASB Statement No. 52*?
3. Differentiate between translation and remeasurement.
4. How are the effects of changes in the exchange rate treated in translation situations? In remeasurement situations?
5. List the basic procedures required before the translation or remeasurement process begins.
6. Name six balance sheet accounts for which historical exchange rates are used in remeasurement.

## Discussion Case

| DC 16-1 |
|---|

### Determination of the Functional Currency

The Handy Company manufactures soap domestically and in a foreign country, which has low labor costs. The foreign operation (conducted through a wholly owned subsidiary) purchases all of its raw materials from the parent company, which can obtain volume discounts because of its size. (Were it not for the volume discount, the foreign subsidiary would purchase the raw materials directly from suppliers.) The foreign subsidiary's purchases from the parent company are denominated in dollars.

All of the subsidiary's sales are in its local currency, the mun, and all employees are paid in muns. The parent company has established that the subsidiary's dividend policy is to convert its available funds into dollars as quickly as possible each month for current or near-term distribution to the parent.

**Required:**
Determine whether the functional currency is the dollar or the mun.

# Exercises

## Selection of the Proper Exchange Rate: Balance Sheet Accounts

The following accounts exist in a foreign subsidiary's books:

1. Allowance for Doubtful Accounts
2. Inventory (carried at cost)
3. Inventory (carried at market, which is below cost)
4. Marketable Equity Securities (carried at cost)
5. Marketable Equity Securities (carried at market, which exceeds historical cost)
6. Marketable Bonds
7. Patents
8. Equipment
9. Accumulated Depreciation
10. Intercompany Payable
11. Long-term Debt
12. Income Taxes Payable
13. Deferred Income Taxes Payable
14. Common Stock
15. Additional Paid-in Capital
16. Retained Earnings

**Required:**
1. Assuming that the subsidiary's local currency is its functional currency, determine whether the historical exchange rate, the current exchange rate, an average exchange rate, or some other procedure should be used to translate the above accounts.
2. Assuming that the dollar is the subsidiary's functional currency, determine whether the historical exchange rate, the current exchange rate, an average exchange rate, or some other procedure should be used to remeasure the above accounts in dollars.

| E |
|---|
| 16-2 |

## Selection of the Proper Exchange Rate: Income Statement Accounts

The following accounts exist in a foreign subsidiary's books:

1. Revenues
2. Intercompany Sales to Parent Company
3. Purchases
4. Intercompany Purchases from Parent Company
5. Cost of Goods Sold
6. Selling Expenses
7. Depreciation Expense
8. Income Tax Expense
9. Goodwill Amortization
10. Gain on Sale of Equipment
11. Intercompany Interest Expense
12. Depreciation Expenses (incremental amount resulting from adjusting assets for inflation)

### Required:
The requirements are the same as those in Exercise 16-1.

| E |
|---|
| 16-3 |

## Translation of Depreciation Expense

The Willinger Company owns a foreign subsidiary with 3,600,000 local currency units (LCU) of property, plant, and equipment before accumulated depreciation at December 31, 19X5. Of this amount, 2,400,000 LCU were acquired in 19X3 when the exchange rate was 5 LCU to $1; 1,200,000 LCU were acquired in 19X4 when the exchange rate was 8 LCU to $1.

The exchange rate in effect at December 31, 19X5, was 10 LCU to $1. The average of exchange rates that were in effect during 19X5 was 12 LCU to $1. Assume that the property, plant, and equipment are depreciated using the straight-line method over a 10-year period with no salvage value.

### Required:
1. Are the exchange rates given above the direct rates or the indirect rates?
2. Determine the dollar amount of depreciation expense for 19X5 assuming that the foreign operation's functional currency is the
   a. LCU.
   b. Dollar.

(AICPA adapted)

| E |
|---|
| 16-4 |

## Translating/Remeasuring a Gain in Dollars for Fixed Assets

A Mexican subsidiary sold equipment acquired in prior years costing 6,000,000 pesos on April 1, 19X1, for 2,500,000 pesos when the exchange rate was $.008. (The exchange rate existing when the equipment was purchased several years ago was $.04.) A 1,000,000-peso gain relating to this disposal is recorded in the general ledger.

The exchange rate at December 31, 19X1, is 200 pesos to $1; however, the average relationship for 19X1 was 150 pesos to $1.

**Required:**
Determine the amount of the gain in dollars assuming that:
a. The peso is the functional currency.
b. The dollar is the functional currency.

## E 16-5 — Translating/Remeasuring and Performing a Lower of Cost or Market Test in Dollars for Inventory

The following selected information is provided in connection with the translation of a Mexican subsidiary's December 31, 19X1, financial statements:
The December 31, 19X1, inventory was acquired when the following exchange rates existed:

| Pesos | Direct Rate |
|---|---|
| 1,000,000 | $.009 |
| 3,000,000 | .008 |
| 7,000,000 | .007 |
| 10,000,000 | .006 |
| 15,000,000 | .005 |
| 36,000,000 | |

The replacement cost of the inventory is 38,000,000 pesos; the net realizable value is 60,000,000 pesos; and the net realizable value less a normal profit margin is 40,000,000 pesos.

The exchange rate at December 31, 19X1, is 200 pesos to $1; however, the average relationship for 19X1 was 150 pesos to $1.

**Required:**
Perform a lower of cost or market test in dollars assuming that:
a. The peso is the functional currency.
b. The dollar is the functional currency.

## E 16-6 — Adjusting Intercompany Accounts

The Sunset Company formed a foreign subsidiary on December 30, 19X1. The parent company lent the subsidiary $90,000 at that time when the direct exchange rate between the dollar and the widgetta (the foreign country's currency) was $.10. The subsidiary immediately converted the $90,000 into widgettas and used the entire amount to purchase land on December 30, 19X1. At December 31, 19X1, the year-end of the parent company and the subsidiary, the direct exchange rate was $.09.

**Required:**
1. Make the appropriate adjustments at December 31, 19X1, assuming the loan is denominated in widgettas.

2. Make the appropriate adjustments at December 31, 19X1, assuming the loan is denominated in dollars.
3. Express in dollars the effect of the adjustments made in requirement 2. (Show the calculations for the two ways of determining this amount.)

## Accounting for a Dividend from the Foreign Subsidiary

**E 16-7**

For the year ended December 31, 19X5, Moonglow Corporation's foreign subsidiary had net income of 60,000,000 local currency units (LCU), which was appropriately translated into $2,900,000. On July 25, 19X5, when the exchange rate was 20 LCU to $1, the foreign subsidiary declared a dividend to Moonglow of 30,000,000 LCU. The dividend represented the foreign subsidiary's net income for the six months ended June 30, 19X5, during which time the weighted average of the exchange rate was 21 LCU to $1. The dividend was paid on August 3, 19X5, when the exchange rate was 19 LCU to $1. The exchange rate existing at December 31, 19X5, was 18.5 LCU to $1. Moonglow uses the equity method of accounting for the foreign subsidiary.

### Required:
1. Prepare the parent company's entry to record the dividend receivable.
2. Prepare the entry related to the receipt of the dividend on August 3, 19X5.

# Problems

## MINI-COMPREHENSIVE    Translation and Remeasurement

**P 16-1**

Following are certain items (accounts or account totals) that have been translated or remeasured into dollars at or for the year ended December 31, 19X2:

| | |
|---|---:|
| Total Assets | $200,000 |
| Total Liabilities | 110,000 |
| Common Stock | 20,000 |
| Revenues | 80,000 |
| Expenses | 50,000 |

| | Functional Currency | |
|---|---|---|
| | Pound | Dollar |
| Amounts Reported at the End of the Prior Year (December 31, 19X1): | | |
| Retained Earnings | $12,000 | $30,000 |
| Cumulative translation adjustment | 15,000 | |

The subsidiary did not declare any dividends in 19X2.

### Required:
1. Assuming that the pound is the functional currency, use the "forcing out" process to determine the following items:
   a. Ending balance for Retained Earnings at December 31, 19X2.
   b. Current-period effect of the change in the exchange rate.

2. Assuming that the dollar is the functional currency, use the "forcing out" process to determine the following items:
   a. Ending balance of Retained Earnings at December 31, 19X2.
   b. Current-period effect of the change in the exchange rate.

<table>
<tr><td>P<br>16-2*</td></tr>
</table>

## Translation (Foreign Currency Is the Functional Currency)

The financial statements of the Maginot Company, a foreign subsidiary domiciled in France, for the year ended December 31, 19X2, are as follows:

|  |  | **Francs** |
|---|---:|---:|
| **Income Statement (19X2)** | | |
| Sales | | 10,000,000 |
| Cost of goods sold: | | |
|     Beginning inventory | 1,500,000 | |
|     Purchases | 6,000,000 | |
| | 7,500,000 | |
|     Less—Ending inventory | (2,000,000) | (5,500,000) |
| Depreciation expense (total) | | (200,000) |
| Operating expenses | | (3,300,000) |
|   Income before Income Taxes | | 1,000,000 |
| Income tax expense | | (400,000) |
|   Net Income | | 600,000 |
| **Balance Sheet (December 31, 19X2)** | | |
| Cash | | 300,000 |
| Accounts receivable, net | | 1,000,000 |
| Inventory | | 2,000,000 |
| Land | | 1,000,000 |
| Buildings and equipment | | 5,200,000 |
| Accumulated depreciation | | (500,000) |
|   Total Assets | | 9,000,000 |
| Accounts payable | | 2,500,000 |
| Income taxes payable | | 200,000 |
| Long-term debt | | 2,800,000 |
|   Total Liabilities | | 5,500,000 |
| Common stock | | 1,500,000 |
| Retained earnings | | 2,000,000 |
|   Total Equity | | 3,500,000 |
|   Total Liabilities and Equity | | 9,000,000 |

### Additional Information:

1. **Conformity with U.S. generally accepted accounting principles:** Assume the financial statements in francs have been adjusted to conform with U.S. generally accepted accounting principles.

---

*The financial statement information presented for problems accompanied by asterisks is also provided on Model 16T (for translation problems) and Model 16R (for remeasurement problems) of the software file disk (filenames: Model16T or Model16R) that is available for use with the text, enabling the problem to be worked on the computer.

2. **Exchange rates:**

|  | Direct Rate |
|---|---|
| Current rate at December 31, 19X1 .......................... | $.15 |
| Average rate for 19X2 ....................................... | .12 |
| Current rate at December 31, 19X2 .......................... | .10 |

3. **Inventory:** The ending inventory is valued at the lower of cost or market in francs; however, no write-down to market was necessary on the subsidiary's books. Assume that the inventory at December 31, 19X2, was acquired when the exchange rate was $.11. Inventory at December 31, 19X1, was acquired when the exchange rate was $.16.

4. **Property, plant and equipment:** All were acquired in prior years when the exchange rate was $.16, except equipment costing 200,000 francs, which was acquired in late December 19X2 when the exchange rate was $.11. (No depreciation was recorded on this equipment for 19X2.)

5. **Sales, purchases, and operating expenses:** All occurred evenly throughout the year.

6. **Common stock:** The subsidiary was formed two years ago when the direct exchange rate was $.16. No additional capital transactions have occurred since that time.

7. **Dividends:** The subsidiary did not declare any dividends during the year.

## Required:

1. Calculate the translation adjustment for 19X2 using the net asset analysis approach.
2. Translate the financial statements into dollars assuming that
   a. The franc is the functional currency.
   b. Retained earnings at December 31, 19X1 (per the translated financial statements) were $217,000.
   c. The cumulative translation adjustment at December 31, 19X1, was $(22,000).
3. Prepare the parent company's entry or entries at December 31, 19X2, relating to the equity method of accounting.

## Remeasurement (Dollar Is the Functional Currency)

Assume the information provided in Problem 16-2.

## Required:

1. Calculate the gain or loss from remeasurement for 19X2 by analyzing the monetary items. (Assume that at the beginning of 19X2 the subsidiary had monetary assets of 1,400,000 pounds and monetary liabilities of 5,700,000 pounds. Also assume that cash disbursed in payment of liabilities during 19X2 was 9,900,000 pounds.)
2. Remeasure the financial statements into dollars assuming that
   a. The dollar is the functional currency.
   b. From the dollar financial statements, retained earnings at December 31, 19X1, were $267,000.

3. Prepare the parent company's entry or entries at December 31, 19X2, relating to the equity method of accounting.
4. After you have completed the remeasurement process, evaluate whether any other important areas should be addressed.

## Translation (Foreign Currency Is the Functional Currency)

The financial statements of Tipperary Company, a foreign subsidiary domiciled in Ireland, for the year ended December 31, 19X4, are as follows:

|  |  | Punts |
|---|---:|---:|
| **Income Statement (19X4)** | | |
| Sales | | 4,000,000 |
| Cost of goods sold: | | |
| Beginning inventory | 800,000 | |
| Purchases | 3,200,000 | |
| | 4,000,000 | |
| Less—Ending inventory | (900,000) | (3,100,000) |
| Depreciation expense (in total) | | (50,000) |
| Operating and interest expenses | | (450,000) |
| Income before Income Taxes | | 400,000 |
| Income tax expense @ 25% | | (100,000) |
| Net Income | | 300,000 |
| **Balance Sheet (December 31, 19X4)** | | |
| Cash | | 200,000 |
| Accounts receivable | | 500,000 |
| Allowance for doubtful accounts | | (50,000) |
| Inventory (Fifo) | | 900,000 |
| Land | | 300,000 |
| Buildings and equipment | | 1,100,000 |
| Accumulated depreciation | | (250,000) |
| Total Assets | | 2,700,000 |
| Accounts payable and accrued liabilities | | 700,000 |
| Accrued income taxes payable | | 100,000 |
| Intercompany payable (to parent) | | 500,000 |
| Long-term debt | | 600,000 |
| Total Liabilities | | 1,900,000 |
| Common stock | | 100,000 |
| Retained earnings | | 700,000 |
| Total Equity | | 800,000 |
| Total Liabilities and Equity | | 2,700,000 |

### Additional Information:

1. **Conformity with U.S. generally accepted accounting principles:** Assume the financial statements in punts are in accordance with U.S. generally accepted accounting principles; thus no adjustments are required.

2. **Exchange rates:**

|  | Direct Rate |
|---|---|
| Current rate at December 31, 19X3 ............................... | $1.25 |
| Average rate for 19X4 ......................................... | 1.40 |
| Current rate at December 31, 19X4 ............................... | 1.50 |

3. **Inventory:** The ending inventory is valued at the lower of cost or market in punts; however, no write-down to market was necessary on the subsidiary's books. Assume that the inventory at December 31, 19X4, was acquired evenly during the last quarter of 19X4 (which had an average exchange rate of $1.45).

   The beginning inventory was all acquired when the exchange rate was $1.20, and no market adjustment in punts was necessary.

4. **Fixed assets:** The land, buildings, and equipment were acquired in 19X2 when the exchange rate was $1.60, except for some office equipment costing 100,000 punts that was acquired in late December 19X4 when the exchange rate was $1.49. (No depreciation was recorded on this equipment for 19X4.)

5. **Sales and operating expenses:** Assume sales and expenses occurred evenly throughout the year.

6. **Purchases:** Assume purchases occurred evenly throughout the year.

7. **Intercompany payable:** The intercompany payable is denominated in punts.

8. **Common stock:** The subsidiary was formed in 19X2, when the exchange rate was $1.60. No additional capital transactions have occurred since then.

9. **Dividends.** Dividends of 200,000 punts were declared and paid in 19X4 when the direct exchange rate was $1.45.

### Required:

1. Calculate the translation adjustment for 19X4 using the net asset analysis approach.
2. Translate the financial statements into dollars assuming that:
   a. The punt is the functional currency.
   b. From the dollar financial statements, retained earnings at December 31, 19X3, were $840,000.
   c. The cumulative translation adjustment at December 31, 19X3, was $(125,000).
3. Prepare the parent company's entry or entries at December 31, 19X4, under the equity method of accounting.

## Remeasurement (Dollar Is the Functional Currency)

Assume the information provided in Problem 16-4.

### Required:

1. Calculate the gain or loss from remeasurement for 19X4 by analyzing the monetary items. (Assume that at the beginning of 19X4 the subsidiary had monetary assets of 800,000 punts and monetary liabilities of 2,000,000 punts. Also assume that cash disbursed in payment of liabilities during 19X4 was 3,850,000 punts.)

2. Remeasure the financial statements into dollars assuming that:
   a. The dollar is the functional currency.
   b. From the dollar financial statements, retained earnings at December 31, 19X3, were $1,060,000.
3. Prepare the parent company's entry or entries at December 31, 19X4, under the equity method of accounting.

---

| P 16-6 | **Intercompany Inventory Transactions: Adjusting Intercompany Accounts and Calculating Unrealized Intercompany Profit** |
|---|---|

Below are certain accounts of PBX Company and its 100%-owned foreign subsidiary SDX Company for the year ended December 31, 19X5.

|  | PBX (in dollars) | SDX (in pounds) |
|---|---|---|
| Intercompany Sales. . . . . . . . . . . . . . . . . . . . . . . | $400,000 | |
| Intercompany Cost of Sales. . . . . . . . . . . . . . . . | (300,000) | |
| Intercompany Receivable . . . . . . . . . . . . . . . . . . | 400,000 | |
| Intercompany Payable. . . . . . . . . . . . . . . . . . . . . | | 200,000 pounds |
| **Inventory** | | |
| Vendor acquired . . . . . . . . . . . . . . . . . . . . . . . . | | 500,000 pounds |
| Intercompany acquired . . . . . . . . . . . . . . . . . | | 50,000 pounds |
| **Direct Exchange Rates for 19X5** | | |
| December 31, 19X4 . . . . . . . . . . . . . . . . . . . . . | $2.40 | |
| December 31, 19X5 . . . . . . . . . . . . . . . . . . . . . | 1.20 | |
| Average rate for 19X5 . . . . . . . . . . . . . . . . . . . | 1.80 | |
| Exchange rate at time of intercompany sale . | 2.00 | |

### Additional Information:

1. The subsidiary's intercompany payable is denominated in pounds.
2. At year-end, the subsidiary still owes the parent the entire amount relating to this inventory purchase.
3. No adjustment has been made at year-end because of the change in the exchange rate.

### Required:

1. Make the necessary adjustment at December 31, 19X5, to the appropriate intercompany receivable or intercompany payable account balance.
2. What adjusting entry would be made if the intercompany payable were denominated in dollars?
3. Complete the following analysis:

| | Total | Sold | On Hand |
|---|---|---|---|
| | $400,000 | | |
| | (300,000) | _____ | _____ |
| | $100,000 | ════════ | ════════ |

4. Prepare the universal intercompany elimination entry or entries (discussed in Chapter 7) required in consolidation at December 31, 19X5, relating to the above intercompany transaction.
5. Repeat requirement 3 assuming the $1.20 direct exchange rate at year-end is to be used in determining the inventory on hand at year-end in dollars.
6. Repeat requirement 3 assuming:
   a. The December 31, 19X5, direct exchange rate is $.08.
   b. This exchange rate is to be used in determining the inventory on hand at year-end in dollars.
7. Note that the amount of gross profit deferred at year-end using a year-end exchange rate (as in requirements 5 and 6) can differ significantly from the amount deferred using the exchange rate prescribed by *FASB Statement No. 52*. Which exchange rate makes the most sense to use? Why?

| | |
|---|---|
| **P 16-7** | **Determining the Net Effect of Adjustments to Intercompany Account** |

A domestic company formed a foreign subsidiary on December 1, 19X1. On that date, the parent company lent the foreign subsidiary $180,000; the subsidiary converted the $180,000 into laffers (its local currency) and used all of them to purchase land. The direct exchange rate was $.40 at December 1, 19X1, and $.45 at December 31, 19X1. For simplicity, assume that the subsidiary was so thinly capitalized that we can ignore the Common Stock account.

### Required:

1. Make the appropriate December 31, 19X1, adjusting entry, assuming that the loan is denominated in dollars.
2. Translate the subsidiary's December 31, 19X1, financial statement into dollars, assuming that the laffer is the foreign subsidiary's functional currency.
3. Remeasure the subsidiary's December 31, 19X1, financial statements in dollars, assuming that the dollar is the foreign subsidiary's functional currency.
4. Considering the effect of the adjustment made for requirement 1, determine the net effect of the change in the exchange rate in the 19X1 consolidated statements assuming that:
   a. The laffer is the functional currency.
   b. The dollar is the functional currency.

| | |
|---|---|
| **P 16-8** | **Determining the Net Effect of Adjustments to Intercompany Account** |

Assume the information in Problem 16-7, except that the subsidiary used the money from the loan to open a checking account rather than buying land.

### Required:

The requirements are the same as in Problem 16-7.

| | |
|---|---|
| **P 16-9\*** | **COMPREHENSIVE (Chapters 4, 7, 14–16)   Translation, Consolidation, and Intercompany Transactions (Foreign Currency Is Functional Currency)** |

The financial statements of Piper Company and its wholly owned subsidiary, Swan Company (located in Great Britain), for the year ended December 31, 19X5, are as follows:

|  | Piper Company (dollars) | Swan Company (pounds) |
|---|---|---|
| **Income Statement (19X5)** | | |
| Sales | $7,000,000 | £1,500,000 |
| Cost of goods sold | (4,000,000) | (800,000) |
| Depreciation expense | (86,000) | (30,000) |
| Expenses | (1,900,000) | (470,000) |
| Intercompany Accounts: | | |
| Sales | 465,000 | |
| Cost of goods sold | (279,000) | |
| Net Income | $1,200,000 | £ 200,000 |
| **Balance Sheet (December 31, 19X5)** | | |
| Cash | $ 569,000 | £ 50,000 |
| Accounts receivable | 800,000 | 300,000 |
| Intercompany receivable | 472,000 | |
| Inventory: | | |
| Vendor acquired | 700,000 | 400,000 |
| Intercompany acquired | | 100,000 |
| Investment in Swan Company | 359,000 | |
| Land | 200,000 | 150,000 |
| Buildings and equipment | 1,000,000 | 500,000 |
| Accumulated depreciation | (300,000) | (100,000) |
| Total Assets | $3,800,000 | £1,400,000 |
| Accounts payable | $ 700,000 | £ 160,000 |
| Accrued liabilities | 500,000 | 40,000 |
| Intercompany payable | | 300,000 |
| Long-term debt | 1,500,000 | 500,000 |
| Total Liabilities | $2,700,000 | £1,000,000 |
| Common stock | $ 500,000 | £ 100,000 |
| Retained earnings | 610,000 | 300,000 |
| Cumulative translation adjustment | (10,000) | |
| Total Equity | $1,100,000 | £ 400,000 |
| Total Liabilities and Equity | $3,800,000 | £1,400,000 |
| Dividends declared | $900,000 | £100,000 |

## Additional Information:

1. **Conformity with U.S. generally accepted accounting principles:** Assume the financial statements of the subsidiary are in accordance with U.S. generally accepted accounting principles.
2. **Exchange rates:**

|  | Direct Rate |
|---|---|
| Current rate at December 31, 19X4 | $1.70 |
| Average rate for 19X5 | 1.60 |
| Current rate at December 31, 19X5 | 1.50 |

The pound is the functional currency.

3. **Inventory:** The ending inventory was acquired during the last quarter of 19X5 when the average exchange rate was $1.55. (No intercompany acquired inventory was on hand at the beginning of 19X5.)
4. **Fixed assets:** The fixed assets were acquired when the subsidiary was formed in 19X2, at which time the exchange rate was $1.75.
5. **Sales and operating expenses:** These occurred evenly throughout the year.
6. **Intercompany accounts:** All intercompany transactions are denominated in pounds. No adjustment has been made at year-end because of changes in the exchange rate during the year. The activity in the intercompany accounts for 19X5 follows:

| Parent's Intercompany Receivable (in dollars) | | | | Subsidiary's Intercompany Payable (in pounds) | | |
|---|---|---|---|---|---|---|
| Bal., 1/1/X5 | $102,000 | | | | 60,000 | Bal., 1/1/X5 |
| | | $ 96,000[a] | 7/1/X5 | 6/30/X5 | 60,000[a] | |
| 11/15/X5 | 465,000[b] | | | | 300,000[b] | 11/20/X5 |
| 12/20/X5 | 151,000[c] | | | | 100,000[c] | 12/20/X5 |
| | | 150,000[d] | 12/30/X5 | 12/30/X5 | 100,000[d] | |
| Bal., 12/31/X5 | $472,000 | | | | 300,000 | Bal., 12/31/X5 |

[a]Cash payment to parent when direct rate was $1.60
[b]Inventory transfer
[c]Dividend declaration
[d]Dividend payment

7. **Common stock:** No common stock transactions have occurred since the formation of the subsidiary by the parent in 19X2.
8. **Retained earnings:** From the dollar financial statements the subsidiary's retained earnings account at December 31, 19X4, was $345,000.
9. **Cumulative translation adjustment:** The cumulative translation adjustment at December 31, 19X4, was $(10,000).
10. **Dividends:** The subsidiary declared its 19X5 dividends on December 20, 19X5 (when the exchange rate was $1.51), and paid the dividend on December 30, 19X5 (when the exchange rate was $1.50). (Intercompany dividends are recorded in the intercompany payable and intercompany receivable accounts and were properly recorded by both entities.)
11. **Income taxes:** For simplicity, ignore income tax considerations.
12. **Equity method of accounting:** The parent uses the equity method of accounting, but has yet to record the earnings of the subsidiary for 19X5. No adjustment has been made to the parent's books for unrealized intercompany profit.

### Required:

1. Calculate the translation adjustment for 19X5 using the net asset analysis approach.
2. Translate the subsidiary's financial statements into dollars.
3. Prepare the appropriate adjusting entry to bring the Intercompany Receivable and Intercompany Payable accounts into agreement.

4. Prepare an analysis showing the amount of intercompany profit that is unrealized at year-end.
5. Prepare the entries the parent would record under the equity method of accounting. If you are using the procedures shown in Module 2 in Chapter 7 (the complete equity method using noninvestment account adjustment procedures), also prepare the general ledger adjusting entry at year-end to defer the unrealized intercompany profit.
6. Prepare a conceptual analysis of the investment account as of December 31, 19X4, and update it through December 31, 19X5. (Hint: The components at December 31, 19X4, total $510,000.)
7. Prepare all elimination entries needed at December 31, 19X5, in order to consolidate the subsidiary's financial statements properly.
8. Prepare a consolidating statement worksheet.

# ADVANCED LEVEL ASSIGNMENT MATERIAL

## Advanced Problems

AP
16-1

### Calculating Parent's Return on Investment—Subsidiary Disposed of after Three Years

PDX Company formed a wholly owned foreign subsidiary on January 1, 19X1, with a capital investment of $400,000 when the direct exchange rate was $0.50. The subsidiary's functional currency is its local currency (LCU). Selected data for the subsidiary follows:

| | Net Income | | Dividends Declared | | Current Year Translation Adjustment | Direct Exchange Rate at Year-end |
|---|---|---|---|---|---|---|
| Year | LCU | Dollars | LCU | Dollars | | |
| 19X1 | 200,000 | $100,000 | –0– | $ –0– | $ –0– | $.50 |
| 19X2 | 200,000 | 90,000 | 200,000 | 80,000 | (110,000) | .40 |
| 19X3 | 200,000 | 70,000 | 200,000 | 80,000 | (90,000) | .30 |

### Additional Information:

1. The subsidiary declared and paid its 19X2 dividend at the *end* of 19X2 and its 19X3 dividend at the *beginning* of 19X3.
2. At December 31, 19X3, the parent sold its entire interest in the subsidiary to a group of local investors for cash of 1,120,000 LCU.
3. The subsidiary's reported net income each year was earned evenly throughout the year.

### Required:

1. Prepare a "T" account analysis of the parent's Investment in Subsidiary account for 19X1 through 19X3.
2. Calculate the parent's return on investment for 19X1 through 19X3.

3. Explain whether it is correct to use the beginning of year investment balance or the average investment balance for the year in the denominator in requirement 2.

4. Determine if and how the current period translation adjustment should be considered in requirement 2. Hint: Be consistent, and make sure your percentages from an overall perspective make sense in relation to the percent obtained in requirement 5.

5. Calculate the internal rate of return (IRR) over the life of the investment.*

6. Explain why the internal rate of return (IRR) in requirement 5 differs from the return on investment calculations in requirement 2. Which should be used in evaluating the profitability of the subsidiary?

## Accounting for a Loan from a Foreign Government

As an inducement to build a manufacturing plant in Spain, the Spanish government on December 31, 19X0, made a $1,000,000 noninterest bearing loan to Parallel Company (a U.S. company). The loan is repayable *in dollars* on December 31, 19X2 (a two-year loan). (Parallel Company received exactly $1,000,000 (U.S. currency) on December 31, 19X0.)

### Additional Information:

1. The present value of the note payable (discounted at 10%) is $826,000.

2. Parallel Company (a conservatively run company) invested the $1,000,000 cash in a two-year U.S. Treasury Note that pays 10% interest annually. (Ignore reinvestment of interest received at the end of 19X1.)

3. No other right or privilege is exchanged.

### Required:

1. Assuming the note payable is initially recorded on the books of the company at December 31, 19X0, at its face amount of $1,000,000, show the effect on the income statement for 19X0, 19X1, and 19X2 of the above transactions (both the loan transaction *and* the investment transaction). Explain the rationale for this accounting treatment.

2. Repeat requirement 1, but assume the note payable is initially recorded at its present value of $826,000.

3. Make cash flow projections and present value calculations from the perspective of financial analysts and potential common stock investors. (Be sure to evaluate the impact of these transactions on the market price of the stock.)

4. Compare the results in requirement 2 to the results in requirement 3. Which treatment do you feel better reflects the economics of the transactions? Why?

### ANSWERS TO SELF-STUDY QUESTIONS:

| | | | |
|---|---|---|---|
| 1. d | 3. a | 5. c | 7. a |
| 2. a | 4. b | 6. c | |

*You may readily obtain this answer using the IRR function available in Lotus 1-2-3®. (You merely need to set up a cash flow table and *then* program the IRR function with the cell cursor located in the cell in which you want your answer to appear.)

## Appendix   HEDGING THE FOREIGN OPERATION'S EXPOSED POSITION

### Hedging a Net Investment Position

Companies with foreign operations normally have a person or department responsible for monitoring foreign currency changes and handling foreign currency operations. Because of the potentially substantial economic losses from adverse exchange-rate changes, the person in charge is often a vice president.

Forward exchange contracts and other foreign transactions (such as borrowings in a foreign currency) are also commonly used to hedge a net investment in a foreign operation. For example, in 1982 before the Mexican peso declined sharply in value, some domestic companies with operations in Mexico correctly concluded that a decline was imminent. Accordingly, the parent company or the Mexican subsidiary borrowed pesos to hedge some or all of the company's net asset position. (The borrowings were immediately converted into dollars.) When the direct exchange rate then declined, the adverse effect on the net asset position was partially or fully offset by the fewer number of dollars required to buy pesos to repay the loan. Accounting for the gain or loss on such transactions depends on whether the foreign currency or the dollar is the foreign operation's functional currency.

**When the Foreign Currency is the Functional Currency.**   When the foreign currency is the functional currency, the gain or loss on the hedging transaction (net of the related tax effect) must be **accumulated in the separate component of stockholders' equity.** This requirement allows a foreign currency translation adjustment to be offset partially or fully by the effect of a rate change on the hedging transaction. For the gain or loss to be deferred in this manner, however, **the transaction must be designated as a hedge of the net investment** and **it must be effective** (go in the opposite direction to the translation adjustment).

**ILLUSTRATION**

### Hedging a Net Investment Position: The Foreign Currency Is the Functional Currency

Assume a domestic company with a calendar year-end and a $500,000 investment in a wholly owned Japanese subsidiary expects the Japanese yen to weaken considerably within six months. Accordingly, it contracts with a foreign currency dealer on July 10, 19X1, to sell 100,000,000 yen in 180 days at the forward rate of $.0049. Illustration 16-8 shows the accounting treatment for this contract. (For simplicity, we ignore commission costs and assume that the only intervening balance sheet date is December 31, 19X1.) The following direct exchange rates are assumed:

|  | Spot Rate | Forward Rate for January 6, 19X2 |
|---|---|---|
| July 10, 19X1 (the date the forward exchange contract was entered into) . . . . . . . . | $.0050 | $.0049 |
| December 31, 19X1 (the intervening balance sheet date) . . . . . . . . . . . . . . . . . . . . . | .0043 | n/a |
| January 6, 19X2 (the expiration of the forward exchange contract) . . . . . . . . . . . . . . . | .0042 | n/a |

### Review Points for Illustration 16-8. Note the following:

1. The following amount may be deferred and accumulated in the separate component of stockholder's equity at December 31, 19X1:

| | |
|---|---|
| Foreign currency transaction gain . . . . . . . . . . . . . . . . . . . . . . . . . . . . . | $70,000 |
| Less—Discount amortization expense . . . . . . . . . . . . . . . . . . . . . . . . | (9,667) |
| Net deferrable amount . . . . . . . . . . . . . . . . . . . . . . . . . . . . . . . . . . . | $60,333 |

2. Assuming a $68,000 unfavorable translation adjustment for 19X1, the net charge to the separate component of stockholders' equity for 19X1 (ignoring income tax effects) would be $7,667 ($68,000 − $60,333). Obviously, the hedge was effective.

### When the Dollar Is the Functional Currency.

When the dollar is the functional currency, the gain or loss on the hedging transaction is **reported in the income statement.** Recall that when the dollar is the functional currency the remeasurement process is required (instead of the "translation" process), and any gains or losses from remeasurement are reported currently in the income statement. Hedging a net asset position when the dollar is the functional currency may or may not cause an offsetting effect, which occurs when the foreign currency is the functional currency. The gain or loss resulting from the remeasurement process is **not based on the net asset position but on the net monetary position.** Being in a net monetary asset position causes an offsetting effect in the income statement. However, being in a net monetary liability position does not cause an offsetting effect in the income statement. Instead, two gains or two losses are reported—such as a gain on the hedging transaction and a gain resulting from the remeasurement process (or a loss on each). Some companies with foreign operations that use the dollar as the functional currency hedge the net asset position, wisely realizing that the gain or loss from remeasurement (in net monetary liability situations) is merely a paper gain or loss that will reverse itself in the future as the nonmonetary assets are financially transformed into monetary assets. (The amount of the gain or loss on the hedging transaction could be more, less, or equal to the gain or loss from remeasurement, depending on the amount of the net investment hedged and the amount of the net monetary position.)

■ **ILLUSTRATION 16-8**
**Hedging a Net Investment Position**

| | | |
|---|---:|---:|
| **July 10, 19X1:** | | |
| Receivable from Foreign Currency Dealer | | |
| (100,000,000 yen × $.0049) . . . . . . . . . . . . . . . . . . . . | 490,000 | |
| Deferred Discount on Forward Exchange Contract . . . . . . | 10,000 | |
| Foreign Currency Payable | | |
| (100,000,000 yen × $.005) . . . . . . . . . . . . . . . . . . | | 500,000 |
| To record initially the forward exchange contract. | | |
| **December 31, 19X1:** | | |
| Foreign Currency Payable . . . . . . . . . . . . . . . . . . . . . . . . | 70,000 | |
| Foreign Currency Transaction Gain . . . . . . . . . . . . | | 70,000 |
| To adjust the foreign currency payable to the current | | |
| spot rate. | | |
| ($.0050 − $.0043 = $.0007) | | |
| (100,000,000 yen × $.0007 = $70,000) | | |
| Discount Amortization Expense . . . . . . . . . . . . . . . . . . . . | 9,667 | |
| Deferred Discount on Forward Exchange Contract | | 9,667 |
| To amortize the discount on the contract. | | |
| (174 ÷ 180 × $10,000 = $9,667) | | |
| **January 6, 19X2:** | | |
| Foreign Currency Payable . . . . . . . . . . . . . . . . . . . . . . . . | 10,000 | |
| Foreign Currency Transaction Gain . . . . . . . . . . . . | | 10,000 |
| To adjust the foreign currency payable to the current | | |
| spot rate. | | |
| ($.0043 − $.0042 = $.0001) | | |
| (100,000,000 yen × $.0001 = $10,000) | | |
| Discount Amortization Expense . . . . . . . . . . . . . . . . . . . . | 333 | |
| Deferred Discount on Forward Exchange Contract | | 333 |
| To amortize the discount on the contract. | | |
| (6 ÷ 180 × $10,000 = $333) | | |
| Foreign Currency . . . . . . . . . . . . . . . . . . . . . . . . . . . . . . | 420,000 | |
| Cash . . . . . . . . . . . . . . . . . . . . . . . . . . . . . . . . . . . . | | 420,000 |
| To record purchase of 100,000,000 yen. | | |
| (100,000,000 × $.0042 = $420,000) | | |
| Foreign Currency Payable . . . . . . . . . . . . . . . . . . . . . . . . | 420,000 | |
| Foreign Currency . . . . . . . . . . . . . . . . . . . . . . . . . . . | | 420,000 |
| Cash . . . . . . . . . . . . . . . . . . . . . . . . . . . . . . . . . . . . . . . . | 490,000 | |
| Receivable from Foreign Currency Dealer . . . . . . . . | | 490,000 |
| To collect the amount due from the foreign currency | | |
| dealer in exchange for the 100,000,000 yen. | | |

## Hedging a Net Monetary Position

When the dollar is the foreign unit's functional currency, a company may decide to hedge the net monetary position instead of the net asset position to ensure an offsetting effect in the income statement. An interesting dilemma occurs when the foreign operation is in a net monetary liability position and the foreign currency is expected to strengthen or the dollar is expected to weaken. To prevent the reporting of a transaction loss from remeasurement if the direct exchange rate increases, the company may decide to enter into a forward exchange contract (or other type of hedging transaction) to purchase foreign currency to the extent of the net monetary liability position. If the direct exchange rate increases as expected, the transaction loss from remeasurement offsets the gain on the forward exchange contract. However if the direct exchange rate decreases, a loss on the forward exchange contract and a transaction gain from the remeasurement process occur. As explained previously, the transaction gain from remeasurement (in net monetary liability position situations) may be viewed as a paper gain that will reverse itself in later periods. The loss on the forward exchange contract, however, is an actual loss that will not reverse in later periods.

One of the criticisms leveled at the temporal method of translation required under *FASB Statement No. 8* was that companies focused their attention on hedging net monetary positions to minimize the impact of currency exchange rate changes on consolidated income. Because the remeasurement process procedures are nearly identical to the temporal method, this problem continues to exist when the dollar is the functional currency.

## Whether to Hedge the Net Asset Position, the Net Monetary Position, or Projected Cash Flows

Some companies are driven by *FASB Statement No. 52* in that the functional currency for a given foreign operation is used as a basis for deciding whether to hedge the net asset position or the net monetary position, so as to achieve an offsetting effect to the result reported for the translation process or the remeasurement process. Some companies ignore *FASB Statement No. 52* and focus their hedging on what they deem to be their economic exposure. For companies that accept purchasing power parity theory (inflation causes exchange rates to change), they consider the foreign unit to have exposure only when it is in a net monetary asset position. Other companies disregard financial positions and hedge only projected cash flows to the parent.

## Review Questions for Appendix

1. Distinguish between hedging a net investment and hedging a net monetary position.
2. How are gains and losses on hedging a net investment treated?

## Problems for Appendix

### Hedging a Net Investment Position

The functional currency for Kimberly Company's foreign subsidiary is its local currency, the debita. For 19X1, the subsidiary's net income was 100,000 debitas, which translated into $35,000. (Earnings occurred evenly throughout the year and were remitted to the parent monthly.) An unfavorable translation adjustment of $75,000 resulted for 19X1.

On January 5, 19X1, in expectation that the debita would weaken throughout 19X1, management entered into a 360-day forward exchange contract with a foreign currency dealer to sell 600,000 debitas (which approximates its net investment in the subsidiary) on December 31, 19X1, at the forward rate of $.41 plus a commission of $850. The following exchange rates are for 19X1:

| | Spot | Forward (for 12/31/X1) |
|---|---|---|
| | **Exchange Rates** | |
| January 1, 19X1 . . . . . . . . . . . . . . . . . . . . . . . . . . . . . | $.401 | n/a |
| January 5, 19X1 . . . . . . . . . . . . . . . . . . . . . . . . . . . . | .400 | $.410 |
| June 30, 19X1 (assumed to be the only intervening balance sheet date) . . . . . . . . . . . . . . . . | .360 | .340 |
| December 31, 19X1. . . . . . . . . . . . . . . . . . . . . . . . . . . | .300 | n/a |
| Average rate for 19X1 . . . . . . . . . . . . . . . . . . . . . . . . | .350 | n/a |

**Required:**

1. Prepare the journal entries pertaining to the forward exchange contract.
2. Determine the amount to be charged or credited to the special component of stockholders' equity for 19X1.

## Hedging Net Investments and Net Monetary Positions

McLaughlin Company's foreign subsidiary had the following average account balances for 19X1 (expressed in its local currency, the krebit):

| Monetary Assets . . . . . | 400,000 | Monetary Liabilities . . . . | 300,000 |
|---|---|---|---|
| Nonmonetary Assets . | 400,000 | Stockholders' Equity . . . | 500,000 |

Net income for 19X1 was 100,000 krebits, earned evenly throughout the year and remitted to the parent monthly. During 19X1, the krebit weakened 25%, the direct (spot) rate going from $.40 to $.30. Various assumptions for different situations follow:

| Situation | Functional Currency | Item Hedged |
|---|---|---|
| A | Krebit | Net investment |
| B | Krebit | Net monetary asset position |
| C | U.S. dollar | Net investment |
| D | U.S. dollar | Net monetary asset position |
| E | U.S. dollar | Net monetary liability position |
| | | (For situation E, assume average monetary liabilities were 500,000 krebits and average stockholders' equity was 300,000 krebits.) |

For situations A, B, C, and D, assume that management expected the krebit to weaken during 19X1 and it hedged the item indicated using forward exchange contracts entered into on January 1, 19X1, and terminated December 31, 19X1. For situation E, assume that management expected the krebit to strengthen during 19X1 and it hedged accordingly. (For simplicity, assume that the forward rate on January 1, 19X1, for a one-year forward exchange contract was $.40.)

### Required:

For each situation, determine the following and indicate how the amounts should be reported for 19X1:

1. The hedging gain or loss.
2. The translation adjustment or the gain or loss from the remeasurement process, as appropriate.

# 17
. . . . .

# INTERIM REPORTING

## TOPIC OUTLINE

# CHAPTER OVERVIEW

## Applicability

Users of financial data need continuous, timely information about the performance of an enterprise to make investment or credit-related decisions. Although it has the benefit of an independent audit, an annual report is inadequate by itself in meeting these needs. Accordingly, the reporting of quarterly financial data has become a basic part of the corporate reporting process. Quarterly periods are sufficiently short to reveal business turning points, which may be obscured in annual reports. For companies that have significant seasonal variations in their operations, quarterly financial reports may give investors a better understanding of the nature of the business.

Quarterly financial reporting is not required by any official accounting pronouncement of the Financial Accounting Standards Board (FASB) or any of its predecessor organizations. However, the New York Stock Exchange and the American Stock Exchange require their listed companies to furnish interim quarterly operating results to their stockholders. Companies not subject to these stock exchange listing requirements usually furnish such reports voluntarily. In fact, many privately owned companies furnish financial information to their stockholders as often as monthly.

**Requirements of the Securities and Exchange Commission.** Publicly owned companies that are subject to the continuous reporting requirements of the Securities and Exchange Commission (SEC) must file interim financial statements with the SEC on Form 10-Q. This form must be filed for each of the first three quarters of each fiscal year within 45 days after the end of each such quarter.[1] Furthermore, the SEC requires specified quarterly financial data pertaining to operations for the latest two years to be presented in the annual report sent to stockholders and in the annual financial statements that must be filed with the SEC on Form 10-K.[2] (Forms 10-Q and 10-K are discussed in detail in Chapter 18.) Such disclosures inform investors of the pattern of corporate activities throughout the year.

## Official Accounting Pronouncements

The first and still current pronouncement specifically dealing with interim reports is *APB Opinion No. 28*, "Interim Financial Reporting," which was

---

[1]Companies whose securities are listed on a stock exchange and companies meeting certain size tests whose securities are traded in the over-the-counter market are subject to the continuous reporting requirements of the SEC.

[2]Proxy and Information Statement Rule 14a-3(b)(3); Form 10-K, Item 8; and Regulation S-K, Item 302 (a) (Washington, D.C.: Securities and Exchange Commission).

issued in 1973. This pronouncement has been amended by *FASB Statement No. 3*, "Reporting Accounting Changes in Interim Financial Statements," and interpreted by *FASB Interpretation No. 18*, "Accounting for Income Taxes in Interim Periods." Also, slight amendments were made to the pronouncement by *FASB Statement No. 96*, "Accounting for Income Taxes." *APB Opinion No. 28* is divided into the following two major parts:

1. Part I does not require interim financial reports to be issued but sets forth accounting standards to be used in preparing them.
2. Part II sets forth minimum disclosures to be included in interim financial reports issued by publicly owned companies.

Interim financial statements filed with the SEC on Form 10-Q must be prepared in accordance with the provisions of *APB Opinion No. 28* and any amendments. Before discussing the detailed requirements of this pronouncement and the related amendment and interpretation, we discuss the conceptual issues associated with interim reporting.

## CONCEPTUAL ISSUES

The fundamental conceptual issue concerning interim financial statements (whether complete or condensed) is whether or not they should be prepared in accordance with the same accounting principles and practices used to prepare annual financial statements. This issue pertains almost solely to the recognition of costs and expenses, because accountants generally agree that for interim reporting purposes no sensible alternatives exist to the long-established practice of recognizing revenue when it is earned. The following examples of costs and expenses illustrate the problems associated with their treatment for interim reporting purposes:

1. **Major advertising expenditures.** Suppose that a major advertising campaign is launched early in the year. For interim reporting purposes, should the cost be deferred as an asset and amortized throughout the year, even though no portion of advertising costs can be deferred and reported as an asset at the end of the annual reporting period?
2. **Seasonal repairs.** Suppose a company historically makes major annual repairs late in the year. Accruing liabilities for future repair costs (other than warranty-related costs) is not proper at the end of an annual reporting period. Is it proper, therefore, to spread total estimated repairs throughout the year by accruing such costs in interim periods prior to their incurrence?
3. **Depreciation and rent.** In most cases, depreciation and rent expenses are computed for annual reporting purposes based on the passage of

time. Should a year's depreciation and rent expense be assigned to interim periods for interim reporting purposes on this same basis, or should some other basis (such as sales) be used?

4. **Social security taxes.** Social security taxes are paid by the employer only during a portion of the year for employees who have incomes greater than the maximum amount on which employer social security taxes must be paid. Should the employer's social security taxes for these employees be charged to expense over the entire year, using deferrals?

5. **Year-end bonuses.** Should year-end bonuses be anticipated and accrued for interim reporting purposes?

There are three schools of thought concerning the approach used in interim reporting: the discrete view, the integral view, and the combination discrete–integral view.

## The Discrete View

Under the **discrete view,** an interim period is a discrete, self-contained segment of history, just as an annual period is; therefore, an interim period must stand on its own. From this perspective, the results of operations for each interim period are determined using the same accounting principles and practices used to prepare annual reports. No special deferral or accrual practices are used for interim reporting purposes that cannot be used for annual reporting purposes. As a result, the components of Assets, Liabilities, Revenues, Expenses, and Earnings are defined for interim reporting purposes the same way as they are for annual reporting purposes. Under the discrete view, the function of accounting is to record transactions and events as they occur. Thus, the period of time for which results of operations are determined should not influence how such transactions and events are reported.

This approach is unacceptable to most accountants because it does not allow accruals, deferrals, and estimations at interim dates for annual items.

## The Integral View

Under the **integral view,** an interim period is an integral part of an annual period. From this perspective, the expected relationship between revenues and expenses for the annual period should be reflected in the interim periods so that reasonably constant operating profit margins can be reported throughout the year. Under this "pure form" of the integral view, annual expenses are estimated and assigned to interim periods in proportion to revenues recognized. Special deferral and accrual practices are used for interim reporting purposes that may not be used for annual reporting purposes. As a result, the components of Assets, Liabilities, Revenues, Expenses, and Earnings are defined differently for interim reporting purposes than for annual reporting purposes. The costs of unforeseen events and certain other nonoperating items—such as settlement of litigation, discontinued operations, and asset disposals—are recorded in the interim period in which they occur.

This approach is also unacceptable to most accountants because of the artificial assumption that each dollar of revenue attracts the same rate of operating profit margin. Such an assumption is no more appropriate for periods within a year than it is over a company's entire life cycle.

## The Combination Discrete–Integral View

Between the extremes of the discrete view and the pure form of the integral view are various combination **discrete–integral approaches.** Under these approaches, the integral view is used for some costs and the discrete view is used for the remaining costs. All methods of deciding which costs are treated with integral techniques and which are treated under the discrete view are arbitrary. The remainder of this chapter discusses *APB Opinion No. 28,* which prescribes a combination discrete–integral approach.

# THE REQUIREMENTS OF *APB OPINION NO. 28*

## Revenues

> Revenue from products sold or services rendered should be recognized as earned during an interim period on the same basis as followed for the full year.[3]

This provision, which requires that each interim period be viewed as an annual period, produces the following results:

1. Companies that have seasonal revenues must report such revenues in the interim period in which they are earned as opposed to allocating them over the full year.
2. When receipts at an interim date precede the earnings process, the revenues are deferred until the interim period in which the product is delivered or the service is rendered.
3. Companies using the percentage-of-completion method for long-term construction-type contracts must recognize revenues in interim periods using the same procedures that are used at the end of the annual period.

[3]*Opinions of the Accounting Principles Board, No. 28,* "Interim Financial Reporting" (New York: American Institute of Certified Public Accountants, 1973), par. 11.

## Costs Associated with Revenues (Product Costs)

> Those costs and expenses that are associated directly with or allocated to the products sold or to the services rendered for annual reporting purposes (including for example, material costs, wages and salaries and related fringe benefits, manufacturing overhead, and warranties) should be similarly treated for interim reporting purposes. . . . Companies should generally use the same inventory pricing methods and make provisions for write-downs to market at interim dates on the same basis as used at annual inventory dates. . . .[4]

Although this provision appears to treat each interim period as though it were an annual period, the following four specified exceptions allow each interim period to be viewed as part of an annual period:

1. Estimated gross profit rates may be used to determine the cost of goods sold during interim periods. This procedure is merely a practical modification, as complete physical inventories are usually not taken at interim dates.
2. Liquidation at an interim date of LIFO base-period inventories that the company expects to replace by the end of the annual period does not affect interim results; that is, cost of goods sold for the interim reporting period should include the expected cost of replacing the liquidated LIFO base.
3. Declines in market price at interim dates that will probably be recovered by the end of the annual period (temporary declines) "need not" be recognized at the interim date. If inventory losses from market declines are recognized at an interim date, any subsequent recoveries should be recognized as gains in those periods, but only to the extent of previously recognized losses.
4. For companies using standard cost accounting systems, purchase price variances or volume or capacity variances of costs that are inventoriable "should ordinarily" be deferred at interim reporting dates, providing such variances are planned and expected to be absorbed by the end of the annual period.

With respect to exception 3 above, assume that a company has on hand at the beginning of the year 15,000 units of a particular inventory item, which are valued at their historical FIFO cost of $20 per unit. For simplicity, we assume that no additional purchases of this item are made during the year. Assumed sales for each quarter and replacement costs (assumed to be market) at the end of each quarter are as follows:

---

[4]*APB Opinion No. 28*, pars. 13–14.

| Quarter | Units Sold during Quarter | Replacement Cost at End of Quarter |
|---------|----------------------------|-------------------------------------|
| 1 | 1,000 | $16 (Not considered a temporary decline) |
| 2 | 2,000 | 14 (Considered a temporary decline) |
| 3 | 3,000 | 17 |
| 4 | 4,000 | 21 |

Illustration 17-1 shows the adjustments that would be made to the Inventory account for this item during the year for market changes.

In reviewing Illustration 17-1, note that no market adjustment was made at the end of the second quarter. The market decline during that quarter was considered a temporary decline that was reasonably expected to disappear by the end of the annual period.

Note also that the use of the language "need not" in the pronouncement (rather than the mandatory term "should") permits companies to recognize temporary market declines in the interim period in which they occur if they choose to do so. Thus, alternative treatments for temporary market declines are sanctioned.

With respect to exception 4 that deals with companies using standard cost accounting systems, the use of the language "should ordinarily" in the pronouncement (rather than an unqualified "should") permits alternative treatments for purchase price and volume variances that are planned and

■ **ILLUSTRATION 17-1**
**Analysis of the Inventory Account for the Year**

| | Units | | | Amount |
|---|---|---|---|---|
| Balance, January 1 | 15,000 | × | $20 | = $300,000 |
| First-quarter sales | (1,000) | × | 20 | = (20,000) |
| | | | | $280,000 |
| First-quarter market adjustment | 14,000 | × | (4) [$20 − $16] | = (56,000) |
| Balance, March 31 | 14,000 | × | 16 | = $224,000 |
| Second-quarter sales | (2,000) | × | 16 | = (32,000) |
| Balance, June 30 | 12,000 | × | 16 | = $192,000 |
| Third-quarter sales | (3,000) | × | 16 | = (48,000) |
| | | | | $144,000 |
| Third-quarter market adjustment | 9,000 | × | 1[$17 − $16] | = 9,000 |
| Balance, September 30 | 9,000 | × | 17 | = $153,000 |
| Fourth-quarter sales | (4,000) | × | 17 | = (68,000) |
| | | | | $ 85,000 |
| Fourth-quarter market adjustment | 5,000 | × | 3 [$20 − $17] | = 15,000 |
| Balance, December 31 | 5,000 | × | 20 | = $100,000 |

expected to be absorbed by year-end. In summary, *APB Opinion No. 28* allows substantial leeway for dealing with certain aspects of inventorycosting and manufacturing cost variances in interim reports.

## All Other Costs and Expenses

The Accounting Principles Board (APB) developed the following standards for all costs and expenses other than product costs:

a. Costs and expenses other than product costs should be charged to interim periods as incurred, or be allocated among interim periods based on an estimate of time expired, benefit received or activity associated with the periods. Procedures adopted for assigning specific cost and expense items to an interim period should be consistent with the bases followed by the company in reporting results of operations at annual reporting dates. However when a specific cost or expense item charged to expense for annual reporting purposes benefits more than one interim period, the cost or expense item may be allocated to those interim periods.

b. Some costs and expenses incurred in an interim period, however, cannot be readily identified with the activities or benefits of other interim periods and should be charged to the interim period in which incurred. Disclosure should be made as to the nature and amount of such costs unless items of a comparable nature are included in both the current interim period and in the corresponding interim period of the preceding year.

c. Arbitrary assignment of the amount of such costs to an interim period should not be made.

d. Gains and losses that arise in any interim period similar to those that would not be deferred at year end should not be deferred to later interim periods within the same fiscal year.[5]

These standards do the following:

1. They prohibit the "normalizing" or "spreading" of expenditures over a fiscal year on a revenue basis as under a pure integral approach.
2. They require that most expenditures be treated as though each interim period were an annual reporting period.
3. They permit certain expenditures that clearly benefit more than one interim period to be allocated among the interim periods benefited. Note that this treatment is **permissive, not mandatory.** Some examples of expenditures that may qualify for allocation among interim periods are major annual repairs, costs of periodic advertising campaigns, social security taxes, and charitable contributions.

[5]*APB Opinion No. 28*, par. 15.

In addition to the preceding standards, the pronouncement requires that estimation procedures be used at interim dates for items that historically have resulted in year-end adjustments (usually charges to income) or that can be reasonably approximated at interim dates. Examples are allowances for uncollectible accounts, inventory shrinkage, quantity discounts, and accruals for discretionary year-end bonuses. This requirement clearly attempts to prevent the reporting of material fourth-quarter adjustments that cast a shadow on the reliability of prior interim reports and undermine the integrity of the interim reporting process.

## Seasonal Revenues, Costs, and Expenses

Many businesses—such as amusement parks, professional sports teams, farming corporations, department stores, and toy manufacturers—receive all or a major portion of their revenues in one or two interim periods. As a result, these companies report wide fluctuations in revenues and profitability in their interim reports. Such companies must disclose the seasonal nature of their activities to avoid misleading inferences about revenues and profitability for the entire year. Furthermore, these companies should consider providing supplemental financial information for the 12-month periods ended at the interim date for the current and prior years.

## Income Tax Provisions

The basic provision for the computation of income taxes for interim periods is as follows:

> At the end of each interim period the company should make its best estimate of the effective tax rate expected to be applicable for the full fiscal year. The rate so determined should be used in providing for income taxes on a current year-to-date basis. The effective tax rate should reflect anticipated investment tax credits, foreign tax rates, percentage depletion, capital gains rates, and other available tax planning alternatives.[6]

The following points concerning this provision should be understood:

1. Each interim period is *not* a separate taxable period.
2. If the estimated tax rate for the year changes as the year proceeds, the effect of the change is included in the appropriate interim period as a change in estimate. No retroactive restatement of prior interim periods is made. The provision for income taxes for the third quarter of a company's fiscal year, for example, is the result of applying the expected tax rate to year-to-date earnings and subtracting the provisions reported for the first and second quarters.

[6]*APB Opinion No. 28*, par. 19.

The basic provision as stated above is supplemented for the tax effects of unusual or extraordinary items as follows:

> However, in arriving at this effective tax rate no effect should be included for the tax related to significant unusual or extraordinary items that will be separately reported or reported net of their related tax effect in reports for the interim period or for the fiscal year.[7]

Illustration 17-2 shows how to calculate the estimated effective annual income tax rate at interim periods and how to determine the income tax provision for the first interim quarter and subsequent interim quarters. For simplicity, the assumed facts do not involve any unusual or extraordinary items. Computing interim-period income taxes is more involved when one or more of the following items is present:

1. Unusual items reported separately.
2. Extraordinary items reported net of related tax effects.
3. Losses in one or more interim periods.
4. Prior year operating loss carryforwards available.
5. Discontinued operations.
6. Changes in accounting principles.
7. Effects of new tax legislation.

A discussion and illustration of each of these items is beyond the scope of this chapter. However, item 3 deserves some attention here as it relates to seasonal businesses that may have losses during early interim periods but that are expected to be profitable for the entire year. In these cases, the tax effects of losses arising in the early portion of a fiscal year are recognized only if (1) the carryback of such losses to prior years is possible, or (2) realization is assured beyond reasonable doubt as a result of profitable operations expected for the entire year. A historical pattern of losses in early interim periods that have been offset by profits in later interim periods normally constitutes sufficient evidence that realization is assured beyond a reasonable doubt, unless other facts indicate that the historical pattern will not repeat.

Illustration 17-3 shows the income tax expense or benefit reported in each interim reporting period for an enterprise engaged in a seasonal business that shows a loss for the first interim reporting period. We assume that the enterprise anticipates being profitable for the entire year and that this expectation proves to be correct. Established seasonal patterns ensure realization of the tax benefit related to the loss in the first interim reporting period. For simplicity, we also assume that (1) the estimated annual effective tax rate is 40%, (2) this rate does not change during the year, and (3) no unusual or extraordinary items are present.

---

[7]*APB Opinion No. 28*, par. 19.

■ **ILLUSTRATION 17-2**

**Calculation of Estimated Effective Annual Income Tax Rate and Interim Tax Provisions**

**1. Assumptions**

Income before income taxes for 19X1:

| | |
|---|---:|
| First quarter (actual) | $100,000 |
| Remainder of the year (estimated) | $500,000 |
| Federal income tax rate | 34% |
| State income tax rate | 5% |
| Estimated federal research and development tax credits for 19X1 | $ 11,500 |
| Estimated officers' life insurance premiums not deductible for state or federal income tax | $ 10,000 |

**2. Calculation of Estimated Effective Annual Income Tax Rate and First-quarter Income Tax Provision**

Calculation of estimated state income taxes for 19X1:

| | |
|---|---:|
| Estimated annual income before income taxes ($100,000 + $500,000) | $600,000 |
| Add—Officers' life insurance premiums | 10,000 |
| Estimated state taxable income for 19X1 | $610,000 |
| State income tax rate | 5% |
| Estimated state income taxes for 19X1 | $ 30,500 |

Calculation of estimated federal income taxes for 19X1:

| | |
|---|---:|
| Estimated annual income before income taxes ($100,000 + $500,000) | $600,000 |
| Add—Officers' life insurance premiums | 10,000 |
| Less—State income taxes | (30,500) |
| Estimated federal taxable income for 19X1 | $579,500 |
| Federal income tax rate | 34% |
| | $197,030 |
| Less—Research and development tax credits | (11,500) |
| Estimated federal income taxes for 19X1 | $185,530 |

Calculation of estimated effective annual income tax rate for 19X1:

| | |
|---|---:|
| Combined estimated federal and state income taxes for 19X1 ($185,530 + $30,500) | $216,030 |
| Estimated income before income taxes for 19X1 | $600,000 |
| Estimated effective annual income tax rate ($216,030 ÷ $600,000) | 36% |

Calculation of income tax provision for the first quarter:

| | |
|---|---:|
| Income before income taxes for first quarter | $100,000 |
| Estimated effective annual income tax rate | 36% |
| Income tax provision | $ 36,000 |

■ **ILLUSTRATION 17-2 (continued)**

**3. Calculation of Second-quarter Income Tax Provision**

At the end of the second quarter, another calculation would be made of the estimated effective annual income tax rate for 19X1 using the same procedures used at the end of the first quarter. Assume that the calculation at the end of the second quarter produces an estimated effective annual income tax rate of 35%. The calculation of the income tax provision to be reported for the second quarter, assuming second quarter income before income taxes of $180,000, is as follows:

| | |
|---|---:|
| Income before income taxes for the first six months ($100,000 + $180,000)................................. | $280,000 |
| Estimated effective annual income tax rate (calculated at the end of the second quarter)............................... | 35% |
| Cumulative income tax provision............................. | $ 98,000 |
| Less—Income tax provision reported for the first quarter........ | (36,000) |
| Income tax provision for second quarter..................... | $ 62,000 |

Note that 35% of $180,000 is $63,000. The difference between this amount and the $62,000 amount calculated above is the 1% change in the estimated annual tax rate multiplied by the first quarter income before income taxes of $100,000.

*FASB Interpretation No. 18*, "Accounting for Income Taxes in Interim Periods," clarifies the application of *APB Opinion No. 28* with respect to accounting for income taxes. This interpretation, containing more than 20 detailed examples spread over more than 40 pages, shows how to compute interim period income taxes involving the more complex areas listed on page 743. Refer to that pronouncement for a complete discussion and related examples.

## Disposal of a Segment of a Business and Extraordinary, Unusual, Infrequently Occurring, and Contingent Items

The effects of the disposal of a segment of a business and extraordinary, unusual, and infrequently occurring items are reported in the period in

■ **ILLUSTRATION 17-3**
**Income Tax Expense or Benefit to Be Reported for a Seasonal Business**
**(in thousands of dollars)**

| | Reporting Quarter | | | | Fiscal Year |
|---|---:|---:|---:|---:|---:|
| | 1 | 2 | 3 | 4 | |
| Income (loss) before income taxes.. | $(200) | $100 | $150 | $950 | $1,000 |
| Income tax benefit (expense) @ 40% | 80 | (40) | (60) | (380) | (400) |
| Net income (loss)................. | $(120) | $ 60 | $ 90 | $570 | $ 600 |

which they occur. If the effects are material in relation to the operating results of the interim period, they are reported separately.

The basic thrust of *APB Opinion No. 28* concerning contingencies is a discrete approach; that is, disclosures are made in interim reports in the same manner as they are made in annual reports, except that the significance of a contingency should be judged in relation to annual financial statements. *FASB Statement No. 5*, "Accounting for Contingencies," was issued after *APB Opinion No. 28*. The application of *FASB Statement No. 5* provisions to interim periods as though each interim period were an annual period is consistent with the basic thrust of *APB Opinion No. 28* in this area. Thus, the **probable** and **reasonably estimatable** criteria of *FASB Statement No. 5* would be used to determine in which interim period a loss contingency should be accrued.

## Accounting Changes

Interim financial reports must disclose any changes in accounting principles or practices. The basic provisions of *APB Opinion No. 20*, "Accounting Changes," apply to interim reporting. Changes in accounting principles that require **retroactive restatement** of previously issued annual financial statements result in the similar restatement of previously issued interim financial statements when such accounting changes are made in other than the first interim reporting period. (*APB Opinion No. 20* specifically sets forth the few changes that can be accorded retroactive restatement, such as a change in the method of accounting for long-term construction contracts.)

The **cumulative effect** of a change in accounting principles is reported as an adjustment in the current-year income statement as prescribed by *FASB Statement No. 3*, an amendment to *APB Opinion No. 28*. If such a change is made during the *first* interim reporting period, the cumulative effect as of the beginning of that year is included in the net income of that first interim reporting period. If such a change is made in *other than the first* interim reporting period, however, the prior interim reporting periods of the current year are restated by applying the new accounting principles, and the cumulative effect as of the beginning of that year is included in the restated net income of the first interim reporting period of the current year. The end result, therefore, is as though all such changes had been made in the first interim reporting period.

Changes in accounting estimates must be accounted for in the interim period in which the change is made on a prospective basis, regardless of the interim period of the change. Thus, restatement of previously reported interim information is prohibited for such changes.

Previously issued interim reports may be restated for corrections of an error just as previously issued annual financial statements may be restated for such items.

## Disclosures of Summarized Interim Financial Data by Publicly Owned Companies

The following minimum disclosures must be furnished to stockholders in interim reports (including fourth-quarter reports):

    a. Sales or gross revenues, provision for income taxes, extraordinary items (including related income tax effects), cumulative effect of a change in accounting principles or practices, and net income.

    b. Primary and fully diluted earnings per share data for each period presented . . .

    c. Seasonal revenue, costs or expenses.

    d. Significant changes in estimates or provisions for income taxes.

    e. Disposal of a segment of a business and extraordinary unusual or infrequently occurring items.

    f. Contingent items.

    g. Changes in accounting principles or estimates.

    h. Significant changes in financial position.[8]

Most publicly owned companies exceed these requirements by furnishing either a condensed or a complete income statement. These income statements (condensed or complete) are usually presented in comparative form. For reports other than the first quarter, quarterly data and **year-to-date** amounts are usually presented. Many companies also furnish complete or condensed balance sheets (usually in comparative form) in their interim reports. In addition to financial data, these interim reports usually contain a narrative discussion of interim period highlights.

Many publicly traded companies do not issue a separate report covering fourth-quarter interim results. Such companies often disclose fourth-quarter results (as outlined in paragraph 30 of *APB Opinion No. 28*) in the annual report. If the results of the fourth quarter are not furnished in a separate report or in the annual report, a company must disclose the following items recognized in the fourth quarter in a note to the annual financial statements:

    1. Disposals of segments.

    2. Extraordinary items.

    3. Unusual or infrequently occurring items.

    4. The aggregate effect of year-end adjustments that are material to the results of the fourth quarter.[9]

In addition, the effects of accounting changes made during the fourth quarter are disclosed in a note to the annual financial statements in the

[8]*APB Opinion No. 28*, par. 30.
[9]*APB Opinion No. 28*, par. 31.

absence of a separate fourth-quarter report or disclosure in the annual report.

## The Requirements of *APB Opinion No. 28* and of SEC Form 10-Q Compared

The disclosure requirements of SEC Form 10-Q are more extensive than those of *APB Opinion No. 28*. Form 10-Q requires that the following condensed financial statements be included in interim reports filed with the SEC:

1. **Balance sheets.** Balance sheets are presented for the end of the most recent fiscal quarter and for the end of the preceding fiscal year.
2. **Income statements.** Income statements are presented for the most recent fiscal quarter, for the period between the end of the last fiscal year and the end of the most recent fiscal quarter (year-to-date amounts in second- and third-quarter reports), and for corresponding periods of the preceding fiscal year.
3. **Statements of cash flows.** Statements of cash flows are presented for the period between the end of the last fiscal year and the end of the most recent fiscal quarter, and for the corresponding period of the preceding fiscal year.

As stated earlier, financial statements included in Form 10-Q reports are prepared in accordance with *APB Opinion No. 28* provisions and any amendments to the opinion that may be adopted by the FASB. Disclosures must be complete enough so that none of the information presented is misleading. Furthermore, management must provide an analysis of the quarterly results of operations. Information required in Form 10-Q may be omitted from that form if such information is contained in a quarterly report to the stockholders and a copy of that quarterly report is filed with Form 10-Q.

## INVOLVEMENT OF CERTIFIED PUBLIC ACCOUNTANTS IN INTERIM REPORTING

Audited interim financial reports are virtually nonexistent. For many years prior to 1975, common deficiencies in unaudited reports included a preponderance of unusual charges and, less often, credits to income late in the year and corrections to previously issued interim financial data. In recognition of such significant, continuing deficiencies and abuses in the interim reporting process, the SEC took steps in 1975 to improve the quality of interim financial reports by effectively forcing the accounting profession to accept auditor involvement in the interim reporting process. At that time, most members of the profession did not want to be associated with interim financial reports on anything less than a complete audit basis, fearing potential lawsuits in the event interim financial report data proved to be false or misleading. The SEC obtained auditor involvement in quite an interesting way. First, it passed a rule requiring that quarterly financial data appear in a note to the annual financial statements included in the annual 10-K report filed with the SEC. This requirement caused auditors to be "associated" with these data by virtue of reporting on the financial statements in which the note was included. This occurred even though the SEC allowed the note to be labeled "unaudited" and the auditors had not audited the data in the note.

Second, the SEC passed a rule informing auditors that the SEC presumed that auditors applied "appropriate professional standards and procedures with respect to the data in the note." Thus, auditors had to perform some form of "review" of the data included in this note. Furthermore, the SEC indicated that unless the American Institute of Certified Public Accountants (AICPA) developed professional standards and procedures in connection with reviewing the data in this note, the SEC would do so. The AICPA chose to do so, and these standards and procedures are contained in *Statement on Auditing Standards No. 36,* "Review of Interim Financial Information."[10] Because this pronouncement is the subject of an auditing course, it is not discussed in detail here. Briefly, auditors must perform certain procedures that are **substantially less than an audit.**

Auditors are not specifically required as part of the interim reporting process to perform these review procedures during the year. Thus, the review can be made at year-end. The SEC took these steps, however, in the belief that companies would have the reviews made as part of the interim reporting process for the following reasons:

1. The likelihood of having to revise quarterly data when the annual statements are published should be less.
2. The likelihood of discovering needed adjustments on a timely basis should be greater, so that unusual charges and credits are less frequent in the last month of the year.
3. The added expertise of professional accountants increases the quality of the interim reporting process.[11]

To encourage auditors to be more involved in the interim reporting process, the SEC adopted a rule in 1979 that exempts interim financial reports from a federal securities law provision automatically making certified public accountants liable for a client's false and misleading financial statements unless such accountants can prove they were diligent.

---

[10]*Statement on Auditing Standards No. 36,* "Review of Interim Financial Information" (New York: American Institute of Certified Public Accountants, 1981). This pronouncement supersedes *Statement on Auditing Standards No. 24,* which was issued in 1979.

[11]*Accounting Series Release No. 177* (Washington, D.C.: Securities and Exchange Commission, 1975).

(Certified public accountants are not exempted, however, from the section of the federal securities law that deals with fraud.) Even before the adoption of this rule, the opposition of auditors to involvement in the interim reporting process had, for the most part, dissipated. Most auditors of publicly held companies now encourage their clients to have the review performed as part of the interim reporting process rather than at year-end. (As this book goes to print, the SEC has released a proposal requiring all quarterly reports to be reviewed on a timely basis by outside auditors.)

In 1980, the SEC revised its reporting requirements, so that (1) quarterly financial data may be presented outside of the notes to the annual financial statements, and (2) auditors must follow the AICPA's review standards and procedures regardless of the placement of the quarterly financial data.[12]

# END-OF-CHAPTER REVIEW

## Summary of Key Points

1. Interim reporting raises the fundamental issue of whether or not interim financial statements should be prepared using the same accounting principles and practices used in preparing annual financial statements.
2. Under the discrete view, each interim period must stand on its own without regard to the fact that it is part of an annual reporting period.
3. Under the integral view, the fact that an interim period is part of an annual reporting period is a basis for assigning the total estimated annual costs and expenses to interim periods based on revenues to report reasonably constant operating margins.
4. *APB Opinion No. 28* adopted a combination discrete–integral approach, whereby revenues, extraordinary items, gains or losses from the disposal of a segment, unusual items, and infrequently occurring items are treated under the discrete view.
5. For costs associated with revenue (product costs), the discrete view is used. (Four specified exceptions to this rule produce integral results.)
6. The discrete view must be used for all other costs and expenses, unless an item meets specified standards for integral treatment. If the standards are met, the company may use integral techniques.
7. For income taxes, the integral view is prescribed.

## Glossary of New Terms

**Discrete view**   A manner of measuring interim period earnings by viewing each interim period as an independent period that must stand on its own.

---

[12]Regulation S-K, Item 302(a)(1) and (4) (Washington, D.C.: Securities and Exchange Commission, 1980).

**Integral view** A manner of measuring interim period earnings by viewing t. interim period as an integral part of an annual reporting period. Under thi. view, each interim period should bear part of the annual expenses that are incurred in generating revenues for the entire year.

**Combination discrete–integral view** A manner of measuring interim period earnings by accepting the integral view for certain costs and expenses and using the discrete view for all other costs and expenses.

## Self-Study Questions

*(Answers are at the end of this chapter.)*

1. Under the discrete view,
   a. An interim period cannot stand on its own.
   b. The period of time for which results of operations are being determined influences how such transactions and events are reported.
   c. Accounting procedures are used that result in reasonably constant operating profit margins throughout the year.
   d. Events and transactions are recorded as they occur.
   e. None of the above.

2. Under *APB Opinion No. 28,*
   a. Revenues may be artificially smoothed over the four quarters providing full disclosure is made of the procedures used.
   b. Unplanned capacity variances arising at an interim date should *not* be deferred at interim reporting dates.
   c. Certain expenditures (other than product costs) that clearly benefit more than one interim period are required to be allocated among interim periods benefited.
   d. Extraordinary items must be prorated over the current and remaining interim periods.
   e. None of the above.

3. Under *APB Opinion No. 28,*
   a. Temporary declines in inventory market prices are to be recognized at interim reporting dates.
   b. Inventory price declines at interim dates that are considered to be not temporary need not be recognized at the interim date.
   c. Physical inventories must be taken at the end of each interim quarter.
   d. Temporary and nontemporary declines in inventory market prices are to be recognized at interim reporting dates.
   e. None of the above.

4. Under *APB Opinion No. 28,* if annual major repairs made in the first quarter and paid for in the second quarter clearly benefit the entire year, they
   a. Must be expensed in the first quarter.
   b. Must be expensed in the second quarter.
   c. Must be expensed in each of the four quarters using allocation procedures.
   d. May be expensed in the first quarter or allocated over the four quarters.
   e. None of the above.

## ASSIGNMENT MATERIAL

### Review Questions

1. Do the principles and practices that apply to interim reporting apply only to publicly owned companies?
2. What is the fundamental issue pertaining to interim reporting?
3. Are the issues associated with interim reporting primarily related to revenues or to costs and expenses?
4. Name the three schools of thought that exist concerning the approach to interim reporting.
5. Under which approach must each interim period stand on its own?
6. Does *APB Opinion No. 28* impose integral techniques for costs and expenses not associated with revenue? Explain.
7. What factors could cause the estimated annual income tax rate to change from quarter to quarter?
8. If fourth-quarter results are not furnished in a separate report or in the annual report, which items recognized in the fourth quarter must be disclosed in a note to the annual financial statements?

## Discussion Cases

**DC 17-1**

### Treatment of Annual Furnace Relining Costs

Harth Company was formed in 19X1 to produce steel. Production commenced in October 19X2, and sales began in November 19X2. The company expects to close down its furnaces each September to reline them, which takes about a month. Members of the controller's staff disagree on how the costs of relining the furnaces should be reported. The following approaches are advocated:

1. Expense the costs in the period in which they are incurred.
2. Expense the costs over the company's calendar reporting year.
3. Expense the costs over a period from September to August of the following year.

#### Required:

Evaluate the theoretical soundness of these proposed treatments and comment on their conformity with the provisions of *APB Opinion No. 28*.

**DC 17-2**

### Treatment of Accounting and Legal Fees Related to Reporting to Stockholders

Callex Company reports on a calendar year-end basis. The accounting firm that performs the annual year-end audit renders approximately one-third of its audit-related services in the fourth quarter of each calendar year and approximately two-thirds of its audit-related services in the first quarter of each calendar year. (The accounting firm renders an interim billing in the fourth quarter for services performed during that quarter.)

The legal firm that assists the company in preparing its annual 10-K report, which must be filed with the SEC within 90 days after year-end, renders all of its 10-K related services in the first calendar quarter of each year. (The legal firm renders its billing sometime in the second quarter.)

### Required:

Determine how these accounting and legal fees should be reported in the quarterly financial statements.

## DC 17-3 Material Year-end Physical Inventory Adjustment

Pilferex Company uses a periodic inventory system and takes an annual physical inventory at year-end. Historically, the company's adjustments from book value to physical inventory have been insignificant. Current-year sales and production increased substantially over the prior year, and a material book to physical inventory adjustment (a shortage) occurred. Management has not determined the cause of the physical inventory adjustment.

The market price of the company's common stock rose during the year due to the favorable sales and earnings pattern reported for the first three quarters. The market price declined sharply when the company announced that the annual earnings would be below estimated amounts as a result of the large physical inventory adjustment.

### Required:

1. How should the physical inventory adjustment be reported?
2. What are the possible consequences of large fourth-quarter adjustments?

## DC 17-4 Revising Previously Issued Quarterly Results

In November 1982, Tandem Computers, Inc., announced results for its fourth quarter (ended September 30, 1982) prior to the completion of its annual audit. (The company assumed that its outside auditors would not have any proposed adjustments.) In December 1982, after the auditors had completed their work, the company announced a restatement of third- and fourth-quarter results because (a) recorded sales included shipments that had occurred after the end of these quarters, and (b) previously recorded sales did not have sufficient documentation. Reported results (in millions of dollars) follow:

|  | Initially Reported | Restated | Decrease Amount | Decrease Percent |
|---|---|---|---|---|
| Sales | $336.9 | $312.1 | $(23.8) | (7) |
| Net income | 37.3 | 29.9 | (7.4) | (20) |

After this announcement, the price of the company's common stock immediately fell 6 points, a 20% decline.

**Required:**

1. What are the ramifications of restating results for these quarters?
2. If the auditors reviewed quarterly information at the end of each quarter, why did they not discover this problem at the end of the third quarter?

---

**DC 17-5**

## Treatment of Unresolved Item

During its second quarter, Newby Company entered into a new type of transaction, which will result in the immediate reporting of substantial income. The company feels that its proposed accounting treatment is in accordance with generally accepted accounting principles. However, its outside auditors have been noncommittal as to whether the company's interpretation of the applicable FASB accounting standard is proper. At the end of the second quarter, the auditors indicate that they need more time to study the issue and do research. (Assume the auditors review quarterly results at year-end.)

**Required:**

1. Should the company record the transaction and report the income in the second quarter? State your reasons for your position.
2. What steps might the outside auditors take in doing research?
3. What other steps should the auditors consider?

# Exercises

**E 17-1**

## Inventory Loss from Market Decline

An inventory loss of $420,000 from marked declines occurred in April 19X6. At that time, the market decline was not considered temporary. Of this loss, $100,000 was recovered in the fourth quarter ended December 31, 19X6.

**Required:**

How should this loss be reflected in the quarterly income statements for 19X6?

(AICPA adapted)

**E 17-2**

## Annual Major Repairs and Property Taxes

On January 1, 19X6, Luca Company paid property taxes of $40,000 on its plant for calendar year 19X6. In March 19X6, Luca made its annual type major repairs to its machinery amounting to $120,000. These repairs benefit the entire calendar year's operations.

**Required:**

How should these expenditures be reflected in the quarterly income statements for 19X6?

(AICPA adapted)

## E 17-3

### Year-end Bonuses

In January 19X7, Gelt Company estimated that its 19X7 year-end bonuses to executives would be $240,000. The actual amount paid for 19X6 year-end bonuses was $224,000. The 19X7 estimate is subject to year-end adjustment.

#### Required:

What amount, if any, of expense should be reflected in the quarterly income statement for the three months ended March 31, 19X7?

(AICPA adapted)

## E 17-4

### Percentage-of-completion Method on Long-term Contracts

For annual reporting purposes, Candu Company appropriately accounts for revenues from long-term construction contracts under the percentage-of-completion method. In December 19X5, for budgeting purposes, Candu estimated that these revenues would be $1,600,000 for 19X6. As a result of favorable business conditions in October 19X6, Candu recognized revenues of $2,000,000 for the year ended December 31, 19X6. If the percentage-of-completion method had been used for the quarterly income statements on the same basis as followed for the year-end income statement, revenues would have been as follows:

| | |
|---|---:|
| Three months ended March 31, 19X6 | $ 300,000 |
| Three months ended June 30, 19X6 | 400,000 |
| Three months ended September 30, 19X6 | 200,000 |
| Three months ended December 31, 19X6 | 1,100,000 |
| Total | $2,000,000 |

#### Required:

What amount of revenues from long-term construction contracts should be reflected in the quarterly income statement for the three months ended December 31, 19X6?

(AICPA adapted)

## E 17-5

### Severance Pay

During the second quarter of its current reporting year, Shears Company announced that it would trim its work force by 7% as a result of below-normal demand for its products. Employees being laid-off are given 3 to 6 weeks severance pay, depending on their length of employment.

#### Required:

Assuming the severance pay was paid in the second quarter, how should it be accounted for in the quarterly reports for the current year?

# Problems

P
17-1

## Income Tax Provision: Change in Estimated Rate

Reviso Company had the following pretax income for the first two reporting quarters of 19X2:

| | |
|---|---|
| First quarter | $500,000 |
| Second quarter | 700,000 |

Reviso's actual annual effective income tax rate for 19X1 was 40%. For budgeting purposes, Reviso estimated that the effective annual income tax rate for 19X2 would also be 40%. Near the end of the second quarter, Reviso changed its estimated effective annual income tax rate for 19X2 to 35%. Reviso issues its quarterly reports within 45 days of the end of the quarter.

**Required:**

Determine the amount of income tax expense reported for the first and second quarters of 19X2.

P
17-2

## Incentive Compensation Plan for Sales Personnel

Pavlov Company uses an incentive system for its sales personnel whereby each salesperson receives:

1. A base salary of $1,000 per month.
2. A commission of 2% of the individual salesperson's sales.
3. A bonus of 10% on the individual salesperson's annual sales in excess of $1,200,000. (This bonus is paid in the first quarter of the year following the year on which the bonus is based.)

The company's sales do not occur in a seasonal pattern. Sales generated by certain sales personnel for the first and second quarters of 19X3 are as follows:

| | First Quarter | Second Quarter | Cumulative |
|---|---|---|---|
| Buffet | $ 400,000 | $ 350,000 | $ 750,000 |
| Cook | 340,000 | 220,000 | 560,000 |
| Dillon | 260,000 | 380,000 | 640,000 |
| Holly | 280,000 | 290,000 | 570,000 |
| Total | $1,280,000 | $1,240,000 | $2,520,000 |

Payments made during the first quarter of 19X3 for bonuses based on total 19X2 sales are as follows:

| | |
|---|---|
| Buffet | $24,000 |
| Holly | 3,000 |

**Required:**

Determine the amount of compensation reported as expense for the first and second quarters of 19X3 using two different approaches for the bonuses.

| | |
|---|---|
| **P**<br>**17-3** | ## Calculation of Estimated Effective Annual Income Tax Rate and Interim Tax Provisions |

Domino Company has developed the following data for 19X2 at the end of its first reporting quarter:

Income before income taxes:

| | |
|---|---:|
| First quarter (actual). | $200,000 |
| Remainder of year (estimated). | $800,000 |
| Federal income tax rate. | 40% |
| State income tax rate | 10% |
| Estimated research and development tax credits | $ 44,600 |
| Officers' life insurance premiums not deductible for state or federal purposes | $ 10,000 |
| Excess of accelerated depreciation over straight-line depreciation for state and federal purposes. | $ 50,000 |

*irrelevant to solution*

### Required:

1. Calculate the estimated effective annual income tax rate at the end of the first quarter.
2. Calculate the income tax provision for the first quarter.
3. Calculate the estimated effective annual income tax rate at the end of the second quarter assuming:
   a. Income before income taxes for the second quarter was $400,000.
   b. The estimated income before income taxes for the third and fourth quarters is $500,000 in total.
4. Calculate the income tax provision for the second quarter.

| | |
|---|---|
| **P**<br>**17-4** | ## COMPREHENSIVE   Identifying Weaknesses in an Interim Report and Evaluating Treatment of Selected Items |

Budd Company, which is listed on the American Stock Exchange, budgeted activities for 19X5 as follows:

| | Amount | Units |
|---|---:|---:|
| Sales, net. | $6,000,000 | 1,000,000 |
| Cost of goods sold. | (3,600,000) | 1,000,000 |
| Gross margin | $2,400,000 | |
| Selling, general, and administrative expenses | (1,400,000) | |
| Operating income. | $1,000,000 | |
| Nonoperating revenue and expenses | –0– | |
| Income before Income Taxes | $1,000,000 | |
| Estimated income taxes (current and deferred). | (400,000) | |
| Net Income | $ 600,000 | |
| Earnings per share of common stock | $6.00 | |

*not disclosing seasonal business*

The company has operated profitably for many years and has experienced a seasonal pattern of sales volume and production similar to the ones forecasted for

19X5. Sales volume is expected to follow a quarterly pattern of 10%, 20%, 35%, and 35%, respectively, because of the seasonality of the industry. Because of production and storage capacity limitations, production is expected to follow a pattern of 20%, 25%, 30%, and 25% per quarter, respectively.

At the conclusion of the first quarter of 19X5, the controller prepared and issued the following interim report for public release:

|  | Amount | Units |
|---|---|---|
| Sales, net. . . . . . . . . . . . . . . . . . . . . . . . . . . . . . . . . . . . . . . | $ 600,000 | 100,000 |
| Cost of goods sold. . . . . . . . . . . . . . . . . . . . . . . . . . | (360,000) | 100,000 |
| Gross margin . . . . . . . . . . . . . . . . . . . . . . . . . . . . . . . | $ 240,000 | |
| Selling, general, and administrative expenses. . . . . | (260,000) | |
| Operating loss . . . . . . . . . . . . . . . . . . . . . . . . . . . . | $ (20,000) | |
| Loss from warehouse fire. . . . . . . . . . . . . . . . . . . . . | (140,000) | |
| Loss before Income Taxes . . . . . . . . . . . . . . . . . . . | $ (160,000) | |
| Estimated income taxes . . . . . . . . . . . . . . . . . . . . . . | –0– | |
| Net Loss. . . . . . . . . . . . . . . . . . . . . . . . . . . . . . . . . . . . | $ (160,000) | |
| Loss per share of common stock . . . . . . . . . . . . . . | $(1.60) | |

The following additional information is available for the first quarter just completed but was not included in the information released to the public:

a. The company uses a standard costing system, in which standards are set annually at currently attainable levels. At the end of the first quarter, an underapplied fixed factory overhead (volume variance) of $50,000 was treated as an asset at the end of the quarter. Production during the quarter was 200,000 units, of which 100,000 units were sold.

b. The selling, general, and administrative expenses were budgeted on a basis of $800,000 fixed expenses for the year plus $.50 variable expenses per unit of sales. (An unfavorable variance of $10,000 was incurred in the first quarter.)

c. Assume that the warehouse fire loss met the conditions of an extraordinary loss. The warehouse had an undepreciated cost of $320,000; $180,000 was recovered from insurance on the warehouse. No other gains or losses are anticipated this year from similar events or transactions, nor has the company had any similar losses in preceding years; thus, the full loss is deductible as an ordinary loss for income tax purposes.

d. The effective income tax rate, for federal and state taxes combined, is expected to average 40% of earnings before income taxes during 19X5. No permanent differences exist between pretax accounting earnings and taxable income.

e. Earnings per share were computed on the basis of 100,000 shares of capital stock outstanding. Budd has only one class of stock issued, no long-term debt outstanding, and no stock option plan.

## Required:

1. Without reference to the specific situation described above, what standards of disclosure exist for interim financial data (published interim financial reports) for publicly traded companies? Explain.

2. Identify the form and content weaknesses of the interim report without reference to the additional information.
3. Indicate for interim reporting purposes the preferable treatment for each of the five items of additional information and explain why that treatment is preferable.

(AICPA adapted)

**ANSWERS TO SELF-STUDY QUESTIONS**
1. d
2. b
3. e
4. d

# 18

**. . . . .**

# SECURITIES
# AND EXCHANGE
# COMMISSION
# REPORTING

# AN OVERVIEW OF SEC REPORTING

## Historical Background

The nature of securities is such that their purchase and sale can create substantial opportunities for misrepresentation, manipulation, and other fraudulent acts. In reaction to a rapidly increasing number of flagrant abuses in this area, all but one state enacted some form of legislation between 1911 and 1933 to regulate the purchase and sale of corporate securities. Commonly referred to as the **blue sky laws,** these laws vary widely among the states. In addition, because these laws apply only to intrastate transactions, from an overall standpoint in protecting the public, they have proved to be ineffective. The stock market crash of 1929, testimonial to the inadequacy of this type of regulation, was preceded by (1) the issuance of billions of dollars of securities during the preceding decade that proved to be worthless; (2) the excessive use of credit to purchase stocks on margin; (3) the extensive manipulation of stock prices by various means; (4) the extensive use of inside information by officers and directors for purposes of self-enrichment; and (5) lax standards governing the solicitation of votes from shareholders whereby managements were often able to perpetuate themselves in power. The magnitude of the inadequate financial reporting and questionable ethical standards that led to this financial collapse substantially undermined the integrity of the capital markets and thus raised serious questions concerning the survival of our system of free capital markets.

To restore investor confidence and reestablish integrity in the capital markets, Congress passed the Securities Act of 1933 ("the 1933 Act") and the Securities Exchange Act of 1934 ("the 1934 Act"). These two acts do not replace the intrastate regulation provided by the blue sky laws but merely supplement them. The 1933 Act applies to the initial distribution of securities to the public. The purpose of this act, as expressed in its preamble, is

> to provide full and fair disclosure of the character of securities sold in interstate and foreign commerce and through the mails, and to prevent frauds in the sale thereof . . .

This required disclosure is accomplished by "registering" securities with the Securities and Exchange Commission (SEC) before they may be offered to the public. The registration procedure involves filing specified financial and nonfinancial information with the SEC for examination.

The 1934 Act applies to the subsequent trading in outstanding securities that are listed on organized stock exchanges and in the over-the-counter markets. The purpose of this act, as expressed in its preamble, is to provide for the regulation of securities exchanges and of over-the-counter markets operating in interstate and foreign commerce and through the mails to prevent inequitable and unfair practices on such exchanges and markets . . .

Companies that come under the provisions of the 1934 Act must file periodic reports with the SEC of specified financial and nonfinancial information. In addition, certain practices are prohibited. '

Because each act constitutes a major piece of legislation, we cannot discuss them in great detail in one chapter. Accordingly, this chapter provides a general familiarity with selected portions of each act and the means of complying with the financial reporting requirements established by the SEC.

## The Functions of the SEC

Before discussing the two acts, we must examine the functions and organizational structure of the Securities and Exchange Commission. The SEC is a quasi-judicial agency of the U.S. government that was created in 1934 to administer the 1933 Act and the 1934 Act (the 1933 Act was administered for one year by the Federal Trade Commission). Since that time, the SEC's responsibilities have broadened so that it now administers and enforces the following additional acts:

1. **The Public Utility Holding Company Act of 1935** requires geographic integration of operations and simplification of unduly cumbersome and complex capital structures of public utility holding companies. Because these objectives were accomplished many years ago through the registration process, current efforts are directed toward maintaining the status quo.
2. **The Trust Indenture Act of 1939** requires the use of a trust indenture that meets certain requirements for debt securities offered to the public to protect the rights of investors in such securities. Although a separate act, it is substantively an amendment to the 1933 Act.
3. **The Investment Company Act of 1940** regulates investment companies, that is, companies engaged primarily in the business of investing, reinvesting, owning, holding, or trading in securities. Mutual funds are the most visible investment companies. Regulation is effected through the registration process.
4. **The Investment Advisers Act of 1940** regulates the conduct of investment advisers similarly to the manner in which the conduct of brokers and dealers is regulated under the 1934 Act. Regulation is effected through the registration process.

# The Organizational Structure of the SEC

The Securities and Exchange Commission is composed of five members appointed by the president, with the advice and consent of the Senate, for a five-year term, with one term expiring each year. No more than three members may be of the same political party. An extensive professional staff—comprising primarily lawyers, accountants, and financial analysts—has been organized into the following separate offices and divisions:

| Offices | Operating Divisions |
|---|---|
| Administrative Law Judges | Corporation Finance |
| Opinions and Review | Enforcement |
| Secretary | Investment Management |
| Chief Accountant | Market Regulation |
| Chief Economic Adviser | Corporate Regulation |
| General Counsel | |
| Executive Director | |

The following additional offices report to the Executive Director:

Consumer Affairs
Public Affairs
Reports and Information Services
Comptroller
Data Processing
Administrative Services
Personnel

These offices and divisions are responsible to the commission and carry out its orders and legal responsibilities. In addition to this bureaucracy located in Washington, D.C., nine regional offices and eight branch offices are located in major cities throughout the country. The roles of the office of the Chief Accountant and the division of Corporation Finance are pertinent to this chapter.

**The Division of Corporation Finance.** The division of Corporation Finance reviews the registration statements and reports that registrants file with the SEC. The review determines (1) that all required financial statements and supporting schedules have been included, and (2) that such financial statements apparently have been prepared in accordance with generally accepted accounting principles, as well as the rules, regulations, and policies issued by the SEC. Because the SEC does not perform audits of registrants' financial statements, it cannot absolutely determine whether they have been prepared in accordance with generally accepted accounting principles. For this it relies on the reports of registrants' outside certified public accountants (discussed later in the chapter).

**The Chief Accountant.** The Chief Accountant is the commission's chief accounting officer for all accounting and auditing matters in connection with the administration of the various acts. The Chief Accountant advises the commission of accounting problems and recommends courses of action. For example, in 1986 the Chief Accountant proposed that the full cost method used by oil- and gas-producing companies be abolished. Following an outcry by two cabinet members and ten senators from oil- and gas-producing states, the SEC's commissioners voted to abandon the proposal. Accordingly, the power to establish accounting principles (discussed in detail in the following section) resides with the SEC's commissioners—not with the Chief Accountant. Administratively, the Chief Accountant drafts rules and regulations governing the form and content of the financial statements that must be filed with the commission under the various acts.

## THE ROLE OF THE SEC IN RELATION TO THE FASB

### The Statutory Authority of the SEC

Under the 1933 Act and the 1934 Act, the SEC has the power to do the following:

1. Adopt, amend, and rescind rules and regulations as necessary to carry out the provisions of these Acts.
2. Prescribe the form or forms on which required information is filed with the SEC.
3. Prescribe the accounting methods to be followed in the financial statements filed with the SEC.
4. Prescribe the items or details to be shown in the financial statements filed with the SEC.

In item 3, the SEC has the statutory authority to prescribe accounting principles for companies falling under its jurisdiction. Recognizing the expertise and substantial resources of the public accounting profession, however, the SEC has usually looked to the accounting profession's standard-setting bodies to establish and improve accounting and reporting standards. When the Financial Accounting Standards Board (FASB) was established in 1973, for example, the SEC specifically announced that

principles, standards and practices promulgated by the FASB in its Statements and Interpretations will be considered by the Commission as having substantial authoritative support and those contrary to such FASB promulgations will be considered to have no such support.[1]

This policy of looking to the private sector in establishing and improving standards is by no means an abdication of its responsibilities or authority. When the SEC has concluded that such bodies were moving too slowly or in the wrong direction, it has not hesitated to take one of the following courses of action:

1. Establish its own additional financial reporting requirements (calling for additional disclosures).
2. Impose a moratorium on accounting practices.
3. Overrule a pronouncement of the FASB.

Concerning items 1 and 2, in most instances the SEC has later rescinded its own action as a result of the passage of new or revised accounting principles or disclosure requirements by the profession's standard-setting bodies. The following two paragraphs contain examples of the most recent major actions of the SEC along these lines.

**Examples of Additional Disclosures Required.**    The SEC imposed line-of-business disclosure requirements long before the 1976 issuance of *FASB Statement No. 14,* "Financial Reporting for Segments of a Business Enterprise." Shortly after this statement was issued, the SEC modified its previous line-of-business disclosure requirements to conform in most respects with the requirements of *FASB Statement No. 14.* In 1976, the SEC required certain large companies to disclose replacement cost data (*Accounting Series Release No. 190*). After *FASB Statement No. 33,* "Financial Reporting and Changing Prices," was issued in 1979, the SEC rescinded its requirements in this area. (In 1986, *FASB Statement No. 89,* "Financial Reporting and Changing Prices," superseded *FASB Statement No. 33* and made voluntary the supplementary disclosure of current cost/constant purchasing power information.)

**Examples of Prohibiting Accounting Practices.**    In 1974, the SEC imposed a moratorium on the capitalization of interest (*Accounting Series Release No. 163*). It had noted with concern an increase in the number of companies changing their accounting methods to a policy of capitalizing interest cost. Because no authoritative statement on this subject existed at that time (except for two specific industries), this action stopped a developing trend until the FASB could deal with the issue. In 1979, after the FASB

---

[1]*Accounting Series Release No. 150,* "Statement of Policy on the Establishment and Improvement of Accounting Principles and Standards" (Washington, D.C.: Securities and Exchange Commission), 1973. In April 1982, *Accounting Series Release No. 150* was codified in *SEC Financial Reporting Release No. 1,* Section 101.

issued *FASB Statement No. 34*, "Capitalization of Interest Cost," the SEC rescinded its moratorium. In another action, in 1983 the SEC moved to halt the spread of a controversial accounting method that more than a dozen computer software companies were using to increase their earnings. The SEC had noticed a trend in the industry toward capitalization without adequate criteria—the accounting standards and related interpretation that existed then were somewhat fuzzy. Therefore, the SEC imposed a moratorium on the capitalization of software development costs for companies that had not publicly disclosed the practice of capitalizing those costs prior to April 14, 1983 (Financial Reporting Release No. 12). In 1985, after the FASB issued *FASB Statement No. 86*, "Accounting for the Costs of Computer Software to be Sold, Leased, or Otherwise Marketed," the SEC rescinded its moratorium.

**Overruling the FASB.**   Only once has the SEC overruled a pronouncement of the FASB. This ruling occurred in 1978 when the SEC rejected the standards set forth in *FASB Statement No. 19*, "Financial Accounting and Reporting for Oil and Gas Producing Companies." The SEC favored developing a new system of "reserve recognition accounting" (RRA). The conflict between the requirements of *FASB Statement No. 19* and those of the SEC (as set forth in *Accounting Series Release No. 253*) resulted in an untenable situation. (Privately owned companies were subject to *FASB Statement No. 19* and publicly owned companies were subject to *ASR No. 253*. Lack of comparability resulted.) Accordingly, the FASB voluntarily (and to be practical) issued *FASB Statement No. 25*, which suspended the effective dates of most requirements in *FASB Statement No. 19*. In 1981, the SEC abandoned its effort to develop RRA and announced it would support FASB's efforts to develop disclosure requirements for oil and gas producers. In 1982, the FASB issued *FASB Statement No. 69*, "Disclosures about Oil and Gas Producing Activities," which amended *FASB Statements No. 19* and *No. 25*. Shortly thereafter, the SEC amended its disclosure requirements for oil and gas producers to require compliance with the provisions of *FASB Statement No. 69*.

**Current Working Relationship.**   The Securities and Exchange Commission and the FASB now try to maintain a close working relationship to prevent any future conflicts. FASB members meet with the SEC's commissioners on a regular basis to exchange information on the status of projects and plans, and to discuss other matters of mutual interest. Members of the Chief Accountant's staff are responsible for keeping track of the development of specific FASB technical projects. SEC staff members participate in advisory task force meetings on those projects and frequently observe FASB meetings. When the SEC proposes changes to its rules and regulations, the FASB has occasionally expressed its views on such proposals.

In summary, both organizations strive for a climate of mutual cooperation and no surprises.

**SEC Involvement in the FASB's Emerging Issues Task Force.**  In 1984, the FASB responded to criticism that its lengthy due-process procedures were not dealing with emerging issues on a timely basis by forming the "emerging issues task force." The task force is comprised of representatives of eleven certified public accounting firms, (including senior technical partners from each of the six largest accounting firms), four major companies, the Chief Accountant, and the FASB. The task force meets every six weeks in an open meeting. Since its inception, it has debated more than 200 accounting issues. Designed to deal promptly with areas in which no standards exist, its consensus views have become generally accepted accounting principles for publicly owned companies even though the task force has no formal authority. This is primarily because the Chief Accountant has taken the position that the conclusions of the task force represent the best thinking on areas for which there are no specific standards. As a result, the SEC challenges any registrant's accounting practices that differ from the consensus views of the task force.

**The Open Door Policy.**  The SEC encourages registrants to bring novel accounting treatments and new types of accounting transactions to its attention for immediate resolution before reporting the accounting effects to stockholders. Unfortunately, many registrants do not avail themselves of this opportunity (possibly fearing that the answer will be no). Instead, they try to slip liberal accounting practices and interpretations past the SEC—hoping that it will not notice these practices when making its reviews—and placing themselves in the position of having enforcement actions brought against them.

# ENFORCEMENT ROLE

## Actions against Registrants

The Securities and Exchange Commission does not hesitate to question the accounting and reporting practices of the financial statements filed with it, regardless of whether a registrant's outside auditors concur with the registrant's accounting treatment. Unlike the FASB, the SEC can order companies to revise their financial statements if it concludes that a particular accounting treatment is not proper. In this respect, the SEC pays great attention to ensuring that substance prevails over form. Countless instances have occurred in which the SEC has cast aside a registrant's literal interpretation of generally accepted accounting principles that the

SEC deemed superficial and unreflective of the economics. Some of the more notable and recent such actions are as follows:

1. Financial Corp. of America had to restate its net income for the first half of 1984 to a loss of $79.9 million from the previously reported profit of $73.3 million. The SEC required the company to change its method of accounting for its reverse repurchase agreement transactions.

2. BankAmerica Corp. had to reclassify as an extraordinary item a $30.8 million gain from a debt-equity exchange that it previously reported as part of operating income.

3. Aetna Life & Casualty Co. was prohibited from giving tax effects to items through the use of the operating loss carryforward provisions of *APB Opinion No. 11*.

4. Alexander and Alexander Services, Inc., had to report as an extraordinary loss an unanticipated $40 million it proposed to add to goodwill and amortize over 40 years. The registrant had purchased a target company and shortly after the consummation discovered that the acquired company's liabilities had been understated by $40 million.

5. Several financial institutions were ordered to reduce their goodwill amortization lives from 40 years to 25 years or less because of SEC's perception that artificial income was being reported in the use of 40 years for goodwill and a much shorter life for loan discounts (the amortization of which increased income). (The FASB subsequently addressed the issue in *FASB Statement No. 72*, "Accounting for Certain Acquisitions of Banks or Thrift Institutions," with similar conclusions.)

6. Numerous companies having contractual arrangements with their research and development limited partnerships were required to recognize a liability for the eventual acquisition of the R&D product and charge a like amount to income as R&D expense. (The FASB later addressed the issue in *FASB Statement No. 68*, "Research and Development Arrangements" with similar conclusions concerning if and when a liability should be recognized.)

7. Several companies that formed "nonsubsidiary subsidiaries" (discussed in Chapter 3) to avoid recognition of expenses or losses in their statements during the early years of the affiliates' operations were ordered to consolidate such companies.

During economically troubled times, the SEC usually scrutinizes financial reports closely, because fraudulent and deceptive practices are much more likely when companies attempt to conceal their financial difficulties. Overall, the SEC is given high marks and has won the reputation as a tough police officer of corporate conduct.

## Disciplinary Actions against Auditors

If the SEC finds that a registrant's certified public accountants are not qualified, lack integrity, have engaged in unethical or improper professional conduct, or have willfully violated or aided and abetted the violation of any provision of the federal securities laws or rules thereunder, the SEC is empowered to take the following steps:

1. Bar the auditor(s) from practicing before the SEC either permanently or for a specified period of time.
2. Bar the auditor(s) from accepting new publicly owned companies as clients for a stipulated period of time.
3. Censure the auditor(s).
4. Require the auditor(s) to submit to a peer review.
5. Recommend criminal proceedings against the auditor(s) (as the SEC did in the well-publicized Continental Vending case and the National Student Marketing case of the early 1970s in which partners of two large accounting firms were convicted and sent to prison).

# SEC PROMULGATIONS

To carry out its responsibilities, the SEC issues various rules, regulations (a group of rules), releases, and staff accounting bulletins, and prescribes certain forms that companies must use in filing registration statements and reports. The 1933 Act and the 1934 Act have their own regulations, rules, releases, and forms. In addition, certain regulations and releases apply to both the 1933 Act and the 1934 Act. The Staff Accounting Bulletins also apply to both acts. An understanding of all of these items is essential to comply with the registration and reporting requirements of these acts.

## The General Rules and Regulations, Forms, and Releases

**General Rules and Regulations.**   The Securities Act of 1933 is divided into 26 sections, and the Securities Exchange Act of 1934 is divided into 35 sections. The SEC has adopted rules pertaining to the 1933 Act, which are assigned three-digit numbers starting with 100. The rules are grouped into various categories, most of which are designated *regulations*. For example, Rules 400–494 make up Regulation C, which deals with the mechanics of registering securities with the SEC.

Rules and regulations pertaining to the 1934 Act are assigned numbers that correspond to the section of the act to which they relate. The major sections are referred to as *regulations*, and the detailed rules within each regulation are *rules*. For example, Section 10(b) of the act is called Regulation 10B, and the individual rules within that section are referred to as Rule 10b-1 through Rule 10b-17.

**Forms.** The *forms* are enumerations of the form and content of the information included in registration statements and reports. (They are not blank forms to be filled out, as the term is used by the Internal Revenue Service and other taxing authorities.) Each act has its own forms.

**Releases.** *Releases* are announcements pertaining to the various rules, regulations, and forms. Releases are numbered sequentially as issued. To date, approximately 6,900 releases have been issued under the 1933 Act and approximately 27,000 under the 1934 Act. A release is formally designated as follows: Securities Act of 1933, Release No. 5307. A release is informally referred to simply as Release 33-5307, for example, under the 1933 Act, and Release 34-9310, for example, under the 1934 Act. Some SEC releases under the 1934 Act also apply under the 1933 Act. In these cases, a release is assigned a number under the 1933 Act and a different number under the 1934 Act. Except for Interpretative Releases, they are subject to the Administrative Procedures Act and must be exposed for public comment before becoming effective. The primary matters to which these releases pertain are as follows:

1. **Proposals to amend or adopt new rules and forms.** Changes are often necessary to keep up with the times. In some instances, better ways of disclosure are found. For example, to improve the readability of information provided to investors, the SEC issued Release 33-5164, which proposed certain amendments to Rules 425A and 426 of the Securities Act of 1933.

   Interested companies and certified public accountants usually make comments and suggestions to the SEC. The final adopted amendment or new rule or form probably reflects many of these comments and suggestions. Sometimes a proposed item is not adopted for various reasons.
2. **Adoption of amendments or new rules and forms.** To continue with the preceding example, the proposals contained in Release 33-5164 were revised to reflect the comments and suggestions that the SEC considered significant and were subsequently adopted in Release 33-5278.

## Regulation S-K and Regulation S-X

All nonfinancial disclosure requirements are contained in Regulation S-K. All financial disclosure requirements are contained in Regulation S-X.

Each form under the 1933 Act and the 1934 Act specifies the disclosures contained in Regulations S-K and S-X that are to be made for that form.

**Regulation S-K (Nonfinancial Statement Disclosure Requirements).** The major disclosure requirements contained in Regulation S-K deal with (1) a description of the company's business; (2) a description of the company's properties; (3) a description of the company's legal proceedings; (4) selected financial data for the last five years (including sales, income from continuing operations, cash dividends per common share, total assets, and long-term obligations); (5) supplementary financial information (quarterly financial data and information on the effects of changing prices); (6) information about the company's directors and management (including management remuneration); and (7) management's discussion and analysis (commonly referred to as the "MDA") of financial condition and results of operations.

**Regulation S-X (Financial Statement Disclosure Requirements).** Regulation S-X, which accountants deal with most often, not only lists the **specific financial statements** that must be filed under all Acts administered by the SEC but also details the **form and content of such financial statements.** The term **"financial statements"** as used in this regulation includes all notes to the financial statements and all related financial statement supporting schedules. The financial statements filed under Regulation S-X are (1) audited balance sheets as of the end of the two most recent fiscal years, and (2) audited statements of income and cash flows for the three fiscal years preceding the date of the most recent audited balance sheet being filed. (Variations from these requirements are permitted for certain specified filings.) In addition, the regulation contains requirements for filing interim financial statements. (Regulation S-X is discussed in more detail later in the chapter.)

## Financial Reporting Releases

The Financial Reporting Releases (FRRs), numbered sequentially, pertain solely to accounting matters. Approximately, 30 Financial Reporting Releases have been issued. Prior to 1982, such accounting matters (as well as enforcement matters) were dealt with in the now discontinued Accounting Series Releases (of which 307 had been issued). *Financial Reporting Release No. 1* is the codification of the earlier releases that had continuing relevance to financial reporting. This codification (with its topical index) makes thousands of pages of material available in a concise and much more accessible format. These releases pertain to the following major areas of accounting:

1. **Adoption of amendment or revision of Regulation S-X.** Many FRRs include financial reporting requirements that go beyond the pronouncements of the FASB and its predecessor organizations. In addition to setting forth an amendment or revision to Regulation S-X, such FRRs also discuss the purpose of the new reporting requirements and comments received in response to the SEC's proposed revisions to Regulation S-X (including the SEC's reaction to those comments). In some cases, an FRR contains exhibits and examples to assist companies in understanding and complying with the new reporting requirements of Regulation S-X.

   Many FRRs have been rescinded as a result of the issuance of subsequent accounting pronouncements. However, the SEC rescinds such requirements only when it concurs with an accounting pronouncement.

2. **Policy/interpretive statements regarding particular accounting areas.** *Accounting Series Release Nos. 130, 135, 146,* and *146A* (now part of *FRR No. 1*), for example, deal with how the SEC interprets certain provisions of *APB Opinion No. 16,* "Accounting for Business Combinations." Accountants must be familiar with such releases in addition to the provisions of the professional pronouncements. (Recall that *Accounting Series Release Nos. 146* and *146A* were discussed in Chapter 6 in connection with pooling of interests accounting.)

## Accounting and Auditing Enforcement Releases

Accounting and Auditing Enforcement Releases (AAERs) announce accounting and auditing matters related to the SEC's enforcement activities. Because of their nature, AAERs are not codified.

## Staff Accounting Bulletins

The Staff Accounting Bulletins (SABs) represent interpretations and practices followed by certain departments of the SEC that are responsible for reviewing the disclosure requirements of the federal securities laws. These bulletins do not constitute official rules or regulations, nor do they have the official approval of the SEC. The bulletins essentially accomplish on an informal basis what otherwise would be dealt with formally through releases. Much of the subject matter of the bulletins arises from specific questions raised by registrants. The dissemination of answers to these questions in this manner rather than solely to the company making an inquiry avoids needless repetition of inquiries pertaining to the same subject. More than 80 SABs have been issued to date. In 1981, the staff codified by topic all bulletins issued to date in *Staff Accounting Bulletin No. 40,* making the SABs substantially more easy to use. (Recall from

Chapter 3 that push-down accounting was implemented as a result of the issuance of *Staff Accounting Bulletin No. 54.*)

# THE SECURITIES ACT OF 1933

## Registration

The Securities Act of 1933 prohibits sales of, or offers to sell, securities to the public (in interstate commerce or through the use of the mails) by an **issuer** or an underwriter unless the securities have been registered with the SEC. Certain exemptions to this prohibition are discussed later in the chapter. A **security** is defined broadly as:

> any note, stock, treasury stock, bond, debenture, evidence of indebtedness, certificate of interest or participation in any profit-sharing agreement, . . . transferable share, investment contract, voting trust certificate . . . or in general any interest or instrument commonly known as a security. . . .

To avoid having a technical loophole in the law, the prohibition also applies to underwriters. An **underwriter** is defined as:

> any person who has purchased from an issuer with a view to, or offers or sells for an issuer in connection with, the distribution of any security, or participates [directly or indirectly] . . . in any such undertaking. . . .

It is important at this point to understand that registration under the 1933 Act refers only to the **actual quantity of securities being registered** and not the registration of an **entire class of securities.** This is just the opposite of the 1934 Act, which is discussed in detail later in the chapter.

**The Essence of Registration.** **Registration** of a security offering under the 1933 Act begins with the filing of specified financial and nonfinancial information with the SEC using the appropriate form. The appropriate SEC form in a particular case is a legal determination. All specified financial and nonfinancial information submitted as set forth in the appropriate form is called a **registration statement.** The SEC examines the registration statement and almost always issues a **letter of comments** (commonly referred to as a **deficiency letter**). The registrant must respond to this letter of comments to the SEC's satisfaction before it may sell the securities to the public. Responding to a letter of comments usually involves a combination of direct written responses to the SEC in a letter, revision of certain information in the registration statement, and addition of information to the statement. The revised registration statement, called an **amended registration statement,** is filed with the SEC for reexamination. When the SEC is satisfied that the items in its letter of comments have been appropriately addressed, it permits the amended registration statement to become "effective," and the securities being offered are deemed registered under the 1933 Act and may be sold to the public.

**Prospectuses.**    Prospective investors in a security being registered with the SEC under the 1933 Act must be furnished a **prospectus.** The registration statement is divided into two basic parts:

- Part I   Information required to be included in the prospectus.
- Part II   Information not required to be included in the prospectus.

Part I is the major part of the registration statement. It includes all required financial statements and related notes (according to the provisions of Regulation S-X), as well as reports by the registrant's auditors on financial statements that must have been audited. Part I also includes, among other things, such nonfinancial information as an extensive description of the registrant's business (including risk factors associated with the purchase of the securities offered) and properties, an explanation of how the proceeds are to be used, a description of any current legal proceedings, the names of the registrant's directors and officers (including their backgrounds), and the amount of their remuneration. The financial and nonfinancial disclosures included in the prospectus should provide potential investors with an adequate basis for deciding whether to invest in the securities offered. Preliminary prospectuses, which may be distributed to potential investors before the effective date, are commonly referred to as "red herrings" because certain information on the cover is printed in red ink.

Part II of the registration statement lists all exhibits filed with the registration statement and includes specified financial statement supporting schedules and other miscellaneous information not deemed necessary for distribution to potential investors.

**Regulation C.**    Regulation C deals with the mechanics of registering securities under the 1933 Act. A company's legal counsel usually assumes responsibility for ensuring that the registration statement complies with Regulation C.

**Unlawful Representations Relating to Registration Statements.**    The 1933 Act expressly states the responsibility of the SEC with respect to its examination of registration statements:

> Neither the fact that the registration statement for a security has been filed or is in effect . . . shall be deemed a finding by the Commission that

the registration statement is true and accurate on its face or that it does not contain an untrue statement of fact or omit a material fact, or be held to mean that the Commission has in any way passed upon the merits of, or given approval to, such security. It shall be unlawful to make, or cause to be made, to any prospective purchaser any representation contrary to the foregoing provisions of this section [Section 23].

A statement to this effect must be made on the cover page of each prospectus. The SEC cannot evaluate the investment quality of the securities offered. This contrasts sharply with the blue sky laws of many states, which allow state regulatory commissions to prohibit the sale of securities considered potentially fraudulent, dangerously speculative, or lacking sufficient investment quality.

## Exemptions from Registration

Certain types of securities and securities transactions, which have no practical need for registration or for which the benefits of registration are too remote, are exempt from the registration requirements. The major categories of exemptions are discussed below.

**Regulation A Offerings.**  Regulation A (Rules 251–263 of the 1933 Act) pertains to offerings whose total amount, together with other exempt offerings within a one-year period, does not exceed $1,500,000. If the total offering price is more than $100,000, however, a Regulation A Offering Statement (containing specified financial and nonfinancial information) must be filed with a regional or branch office of the SEC for examination. Furthermore, an offering circular (Part II of the Offering Statement) must be furnished to prospective purchasers.

**Regulation D Offerings.**  Regulation D (Rules 501–506 of the 1933 Act) was adopted in 1982 to facilitate the capital-raising process for small companies. The amount of offerings exempted within a twelve-month period is $500,000 or $5,000,000, depending on the type of company and whether it is subject to the continuous reporting requirements of the SEC. Under Regulation D, only a notice of the sale must be filed with the SEC (on Form D).

**Private Offerings.**  The 1933 Act exempts "transactions by an issuer not involving a public offering [Section 4(2)]." Such transactions are also commonly referred to as **private placements**. This exemption is available for offerings to persons (individuals, partnerships, and corporations) having access to substantially the same information concerning the issuer that registration would provide and who can fend for themselves.[2] The fundamental consideration in determining whether this exemption applies is the potential investor's level of sophistication and such investor's access to information about the issuer. Generally, sophisticated investors have either sufficient economic power or a family or employment relationship that enables them to obtain adequate information from the issuer for purposes of evaluating the merits and risks of the investment. Private offerings are commonly made to venture capital firms and insurance companies. Because the security is not sold through a public offering, it is referred to as a **restricted security**. The restrictions are discussed in the following exemption category.

**Transactions by Individual Investors.**  The 1933 Act exempts "transactions by any person other than an issuer, underwriter or dealer [Section 4(1)]." This section was intended to exempt only transactions between individual investors with respect to securities already issued and not distributions by issuers or acts of other individuals who engage in steps necessary to such distributions.[3] Investors who acquire an issuer's securities by means that do not involve a public offering (such as a private offering) may resell the securities to the public other than through registration only if certain conditions are met. Otherwise, the sale is considered a distribution of securities to the public because the investor is acting as a conduit for sale to the public on behalf of the issuer—that is, as an underwriter. In such cases, the resale of the security to the public must be registered. Rule 144 sets forth conditions that must be satisfied in order to resell restricted securities to the public other than through registration. This rule emphasizes that (1) the investor must have paid for and held the security for a reasonable period of time (a minimum of two to four years, depending on the category of the issuer), and (2) adequate current public information with respect to the issuer of the securities must be available.

**Strictly Intrastate Issues.**  For intrastate issues, the security must be offered and sold only to the residents of the state in which the corporate issuer is incorporated and doing business [Section 3(11)].

**Commercial Paper.**  This category, commercial paper, pertains to a borrowing "which arises out of a current transaction or the proceeds of which have been or are able to be used for current transactions, and which has a

[2]*SEC v. Ralston Purina Co.*, 346 U.S. 119 (1953).
[3]*SEC v. Chinese Consol. Benev. Ass'n.*, 120 F. 2d 738 (2nd. Cir., 1941). *Certiorari* denied, 314 U.S. 618.

maturity at the time of issuance of not exceeding nine months . . . [Section 3(3)]." This category is a practical necessity; an example is a bank borrowing under a 90-day note.

**Securities of Governments and Banks.** According to Section 3(2), the governmental category of securities includes federal, state, and local governmental units (including municipalities) and agencies thereof.

Whether or not a security offering or transaction is exempt from registration under the 1933 Act is strictly a legal and factual determination and outside the expertise of accountants.

## Forms Used in Registration

The Securities and Exchange Commission has devised numerous forms to deal with the diverse companies (and their maturity) seeking to offer securities to the public. Although the general contents of a registration statement have already been descibed, each form has it own detailed table of contents and related instructions. (Recall that the financial statement requirements for these forms are set forth in Regulation S-X.) Two categories of forms are used under the 1933 Act: general forms and special forms.

**General Forms.** The SEC has three **general forms:** S-1, S-2, and S-3. These three forms are set up on a tier system based on the issuer's following in the stock market. Although all three forms basically require the same information to be furnished to potential investors, the method of furnishing that information varies. Form S-1, the most widely used of the forms, is required when one of the special forms is not authorized or prescribed, or when a company eligible to use Form S-2 or S-3 chooses to use Form S-1 instead. Basically, Form S-1 is used by new registrants and by companies that are already registered under the 1934 Act but have been filing reports with the SEC for less than 36 months. All financial and nonfinancial disclosures must be included in the prospectus. The detailed table of contents to Form S-1 appears in Exhibit 18-1.

To be eligible to use Forms S-2 and S-3, a company must have been subject to the reporting requirements of the 1934 Act for at least 36 months and satisfy other conditions. Form S-3 is used by large companies having a wide following in the stock market; accordingly, such firms must meet an additional requirement based on annual trading volume and outstanding voting stock. The advantage to these forms is time and effort; that is, financial and nonfinancial information need not be included in the prospectus—it may simply be incorporated by reference to reports already filed with the SEC under the 1934 Act. Thus, these forms are effectively a simplified Form S-1.

## ■ EXHIBIT 18-1
### Table of Contents of Form S-1

The following is the table of contents from Form S-1, the most widely used of the SEC's forms. It is reprinted here in order to provide a more complete look at what is called for in a registration statement.

**General Instructions**

    I. Eligibility requirements for use of Form S-1
    II. Application of general rules and regulations
    III. Exchange offers

**Facing Sheet**

**I. Information Required in Prospectus**

**Item**

    1. Forepart of the registration statement and outside front cover page of prospectus
    2. Inside front and outside back cover page of prospectus
    3. Summary information, risk factors, and ratio of earnings to fixed charges
    4. Use of proceeds
    5. Determination of offering price
    6. Dilution
    7. Selling security holders
    8. Plan of distribution
    9. Description of securities being registered
  10. Interest of named experts and counsel
  11. Information with respect to the registrant[4]
  12. Disclosure of commission position on indemnification for securities act liabilities

**II. Information Not Required in Prospectus**

  13. Other expenses of issuance and distribution
  14. Indemnification of directors and officers
  15. Recent sales of unregistered securities
  16. Exhibits and financial statement schedules
  17. Undertakings

**Signatures**

**Instructions as to Summary Prospectuses**

[4]This item specifies (a) the nonfinancial disclosure requirements in Regulation S-K and (b) the financial statement requirements of Regulation S-X that are to be included.

**Special Forms.** The SEC has twelve **special forms,** five of which are commonly used:

    1. **Form S-4,** for registration of securities issued in connection with most business combinations and reofferings. (Substantial information may be incorporated by reference.)
    2. **Form S-8,** for securities offered to employees pursuant to employee benefit plans, such as stock option plans.

3. **Form S-11,** applicable to real estate investment trusts and real estate companies.
4. **Form S-15,** for securities issued in certain business combinations (involving a large company and a much smaller company). This streamlined form requires only an abbreviated prospectus.
5. **Form S-18,** for offerings up to $7.5 million. This form gives small initial registrants (including limited partnerships) a fast and simple method of raising capital in public markets because (1) the disclosure requirements are less extensive than in Form S-1, and (2) the filing may be made at an SEC regional office rather than in Washington, D.C.

## Legal Liability for Filing a False Registration Statement

Section 6 of the Securities Act of 1933 requires that the registration statement be signed by the following persons:

1. The principal executive officer or officers.
2. The principal financial officer.
3. The controller or principal accounting officer.
4. The majority of the board of directors or persons performing similar functions.

The 1933 Act sets forth the following civil liabilities for a false registration:

> In case any part of the registration statement, when such part became effective, contained an untrue statement of a material fact or omitted to state a material fact required to be stated therein or necessary to make the statements therein not misleading, any person acquiring such security (unless it is proved that at the time of such acquisition he knew of such untruth or omission) may . . . sue [for recovery of losses suffered]—
>
> 1. every person who signed the registration statement;
> 2. every person who was a director of . . . the issuer . . . ;
> 3. every person who, with his consent, is named in the registration statement as being or about to become a director . . . ;
> 4. every accountant, engineer, appraiser, or any person whose profession gives authority to a statement made by him, who has with his consent been named as having prepared or certified part of the registration statement, . . . with respect to the statement in such registration statement, report, or valuation, which purports to have been prepared or certified by him;
> 5. every underwriter with respect to such security [Section 11].

In addition to these civil proceedings whereby a purchaser may recover damages suffered, Section 24 of the 1933 Act provides for criminal penalties (monetary fines and imprisonment) if the untrue statement of a material fact or omission thereof was "willful."

### Shareholders Often Sue If Stock Prices Fall.

Countless instances have occurred in which stock prices have substantially declined from the offering price within six to twelve months of the offering. In such cases, it is common for disgruntled stockholders to file class-action lawsuits alleging that unfavorable information was purposely omitted from the prospectus. (Such information could include known problems in developing anticipated new products, or shipping and order delays.) In fact, many attorneys actively search out investors who have sustained losses on public offerings, hoping to represent them in such lawsuits, which have a high settlement potential.

### Ramifications to Outside Auditors.

This section of the 1933 Act has special significance to certified public accountants of companies registering securities. When securities are not registered, **gross negligence** must be proved for a company's certified public accountants to be held liable for civil damages. When a company registers securities under the 1933 Act, however, the focal point is not whether the outside auditors were grossly negligent in the performance of their duties. Instead, the issue is merely whether or not the financial statements and related notes in the registration statement **contained an untrue statement of a material fact or omitted a material fact.** Thus, the 1933 Act imposes an additional potential liability on the certified public accountants of companies registering securities. However, certain defenses are available to the outside auditors under Section 11 of the 1933 Act that relate to their having made a "reasonable investigation" and having "reasonable grounds for belief."

## THE SECURITIES EXCHANGE ACT OF 1934

The Securities Exchange Act of 1934, which deals with the trading in (exchange of) securities, has two broad purposes:

1. To require publicly held companies to disclose on a continual basis current information to holders and prospective purchasers of their securities comparable to the information that must be disclosed in a registration statement under the 1933 Act. In this respect, the 1934 Act supplements the 1933 Act, which applies only to public offerings of securities and not to subsequent trading in such securities.
2. To regulate the public trading markets (organized exchanges and over-the-counter markets) and the broker-dealers who operate in such markets.

## Major Provisions of the 1934 Act

Unlike the 1933 Act, which is a unified piece of legislation, the 1934 Act covers a wide range of areas. Its major provisions are discussed in the following paragraphs.

**Registration of Securities Exchanges.**    Securities exchanges (such as the New York Stock Exchange) must be registered with the SEC, which has supervisory control over them.

**Registration of Securities on Securities Exchanges.**    Securities exchanges cannot effect transactions in any security unless that security is registered on the exchange. The registration process involves filing a registration statement on Form 10 (or another appropriate form) with the securities exchange and with the SEC. Form 10 requires information comparable to that required in Form S-1 under the 1933 Act. A security that is traded on a securities exchange is referred to as a "listed" security. Companies having securities registered on a securities exchange are referred to as Section 12(b) companies.

**Registration of Over-the-counter Securities.**    The *over-the-counter* market encompasses all securities transactions that do not take place on organized securities exchanges. The 1934 Act was amended in 1964 to require registration of securities traded in the over-the-counter market that meet certain size tests. Companies that have total assets exceeding $5 million *and* a class of equity security with 500 or more stockholders must register such security with the SEC by filing a registration statement (usually Form 10). Securities traded in the over-the-counter market are referred to as "unlisted" securities. Companies meeting these tests are referred to as Section 12(g) companies. Once a company meets these size tests, it is subject to all the requirements of the 1934 Act that are imposed on listed companies.

A Section 12(g) company may deregister when it has (1) less than 500 shareholders for the class of equity security and total assets of less than $5 million at the end of each of its last three fiscal years; or (2) fewer than 300 shareholders.

**Filing of Periodic and Other Reports.**    Issuers of securities that must be registered under the 1934 Act must file annual and quarterly reports with the SEC containing specified financial and nonfinancial information. In addition, reports describing specified important events must be filed promptly after they occur. These periodic reports are discussed in detail on page 783.

**Proxy Regulations.** For companies subject to the registration requirements of the 1934 Act, the SEC is authorized to prescribe regulations and rules governing the solicitation of proxies by management from shareholders regarding matters to be voted on by shareholders. A **proxy** is merely a document empowering one person to vote for another. Because all shareholders do not normally attend annual or special shareholders' meetings, companies typically request each shareholder to sign a proxy empowering management to vote either as the shareholder indicates or in accordance with the recommendations of management. When soliciting proxies, a **proxy statement** containing information specified by the SEC must be furnished to the stockholders. Furthermore, preliminary proxy material must be filed with the SEC for review at least ten days before the proposed mailing date.

**Antifraud and Insider Trading Provisions.** Section 10 of the 1934 Act makes it unlawful for any person directly or indirectly to use deceptive or fraudulent practices or to misstate or omit any material fact in connection with the purchase or sale of a security. Criminal fines up to $100,000 can be imposed. Persons suffering losses as a result of fraud are entitled to sue for recovery of actual losses.

Corporate "insiders" are prohibited from trading in a corporation's securities using material information that has not been disseminated to the public. Inside traders can be forced to give up their profits and be fined up to three times their profits. Also, criminal fines of $100,000 can be imposed. An **insider** is any person who has material nonpublic information, including any officer or director or any person who obtains such information from others. In addition, under the "short-swing profit" rule in Section 16(b), any profit realized from any purchase and sale (or from any sale and purchase) of any such issuer's equity security within any period of less than six months by certain persons accrues to the issuer and is recoverable by the issuer, with certain exceptions. These certain persons are officers, directors, or any person who is the beneficial owner of more than 10% of any security that is registered under the 1934 Act. Under Section 16(a), officers, directors, and such 10% security holders must report to the SEC any changes in their beneficial ownership of registered securities. Changes in ownership are reported using either Form 3 (Initial Statement of Ownership) or Form 4 (Changes in Ownership). The form must be filed within 10 days after the end of the month in which the transaction occurs.

**Brokers and Dealers.** The 1934 Act requires brokers and dealers to register with the SEC and to comply with regulations imposed on them. Certain trading practices are prohibited. Specific sections of the 1934 Act deal with unlawful representations, liability for misleading statements, and criminal penalties.

## Forms Used in Reporting

The SEC has devised approximately 20 forms to be used by companies whose securities are registered under the 1934 Act. Because most of these forms are of a specialized nature, a complete list is not presented. By far the most commonly used forms are the following:

- Form 8-K, current reports
- Form 10-K, annual report
- Form 10-Q, quarterly report

Regulation 12B of the 1934 Act sets forth the mechanics of reporting in the same manner that Regulation C does under the 1933 Act.

## Form 8-K, Current Reports

Form 8-K provides certain information to investors on a reasonably current basis. A report on this form must be filed when one of the following events occurs:

1. Changes in control of the registrant.
2. Significant acquisitions or dispositions of assets (including business combinations).
3. Bankruptcy or receivership.
4. Changes in the registrant's certifying accountant. (The disclosures here are designed to discourage "opinion shopping." We discuss this event more fully in the following section.)
5. Other events (that the registrant deems important to its security holders).
6. The resignation of a director.

Form 8-K reports must be filed within fifteen days after the occurrence of the earliest event (five days for item 4).

**Changes in Auditors.**   Companies must report to the SEC when their auditors are fired, resign, or inform the company that they do not intend to seek reappointment for the following year. The report must state whether the company and its auditor disagreed about accounting principles or practices, financial statement disclosures, or auditing scope or procedures. (Form 8-K elaborates on what circumstances are deemed to be disagreements.) Within 10 days after the 8-K report is filed, the former auditor must submit a letter to the SEC stating whether they agree or disagree with the company's statement. Furthermore, if the company has held discussions with its new auditors concerning accounting and financial reporting matters within the two years prior to their appointment, the issues discussed must be reported.

## Form 10-K, Annual Report

Within 90 days after the end of the fiscal year, a company must file an annual report with the SEC, using Form 10-K if no other form is prescribed. Although it must be furnished to stockholders on request, this report is in addition to the company's annual report to its stockholders. Form 10-K must include substantially all nonfinancial statement disclosure requirements set forth in Regulation S-K (the major items were indicated on page 771) and the financial statement information specified in Regulation S-X (described on page 771).

**Form 10-K Compared with the Annual Report to Stockholders.** As part of the SEC's three-year effort from 1980 to 1982 to streamline its reporting requirements, substantially all the information called for in the 10-K annual report also must be included in the annual report sent to the stockholders. Companies may omit information from the 10-K annual report if it is included in the annual report sent to the stockholders. A copy of the annual report sent to the stockholders must be filed with the 10-K annual report, and the 10-K annual report must indicate that the omitted information is included in the annual report sent to the stockholders. (This is known as **incorporation by reference.**)

## Form 10-Q, Quarterly Report

Within 45 days of the end of each of the first three fiscal quarters of each fiscal year, a company must file a quarterly report with the SEC on Form 10-Q. No report is necessary for the fourth quarter. Form 10-Q calls for the interim financial statements specified in Regulation S-X. These financial statements, which may be condensed, are as follows:

1. An interim **balance sheet** as of the end of the most recent fiscal quarter, and a balance sheet at the end of the preceding fiscal year.
2. Interim **income statements** for the most recent fiscal quarter; for the period between the end of the last fiscal year and the end of the most recent fiscal quarter (year-to-date amounts in second- and third-quarter reports); and corresponding periods of the preceding fiscal year.
3. Statements of **cash flows** for the period between the end of the last fiscal year and the end of the most recent fiscal quarter and for the corresponding period of the preceding fiscal year.

Detailed footnotes are not required; however, disclosures must be complete enough so that the information presented is not misleading. In this respect, companies may presume that users of the interim financial information have read or have access to the audited financial statements for the preceding fiscal year. Thus, disclosures deal primarily with events after the end of the most recent fiscal year. The interim financial information need not be audited or reviewed by an independent public accountant.

Form 10-Q also calls for a *management discussion and analysis* (MDA) of the financial condition and results of operations pursuant to the nonfinancial statement disclosure requirements of Regulation S-K.

**Form 10-Q Compared with the Quarterly Report to Stockholders.** As with the rules concerning the 10-K annual report, information called for on Form 10-Q may be omitted if such information is contained in a quarterly report to the stockholders and a copy of that report is filed with Form 10-Q.

## REGULATION S-X: A CLOSER LOOK

Recall from the introduction to Regulation S-X on page 771 that this regulation sets forth not only the financial statements filed with the SEC under the various acts but also the form and content of those financial statements. As a result of recent revisions to modernize Regulation S-X and integrate the various reporting requirements of companies, the regulation also applies to annual reports to stockholders. Accordingly, the financial statements included in Form 10-K annual report are now identical to the financial statements in annual reports to stockholders.

Because this regulation is approximately 100 pages long, a detailed discussion is beyond the scope of this book. The objective here is to provide a general familiarity with the contents of Regulation S-X.

Regulation S-X is composed of the following articles, each of which has its own rules:

| Article | Description |
|---------|-------------|
| 1 | Application of Regulation S-X |
| 2 | Qualifications and reports of accountants |
| 3 | General instructions for financial statements |
| 3A | Consolidated and combined financial statements |
| 4 | Rules of general application |
| 5 | Commercial and industrial companies |
| 5A | Companies in the development stage |
| 6 | Registered investment companies |
| 6A | Employee stock purchase, savings, and similar plans |
| 7 | Insurance companies |
| 9 | Bank holding companies |
| 10 | Interim financial statements |
| 11 | Pro forma financial information |
| 12 | Form and content of schedules |

Because Articles 5A, 6, 6A, 7, and 9 have at most only limited application to most companies, they are not discussed in this chapter. The remaining articles are discussed briefly.

## Article 1: Application of Regulation S-X

Article 1 specifies the nature of Regulation S-X, states the Acts to which it applies, and defines the terms used in the regulation.

## Article 2: Qualifications and Reports of Accountants

Article 2 discusses (1) the qualification of certified public accountants (primarily, conditions necessary for their independence), and (2) specific requirements concerning the content of a certified public accountant's report on audited financial statements included in one of the designated forms filed with the SEC.

## Article 3: General Instructions for Financial Statements

Article 3 specifies the balance sheets, income statements, and statements of changes in financial position to be included in registration statements and reports filed with the SEC.

## Article 3A: Consolidated and Combined Financial Statements

Article 3A deals with the presentation of consolidated and combined financial statements. It specifies which subsidiaries should not be consolidated and requires, in general, that all intercompany items and transactions be eliminated.

## Article 4: Rules of General Application

Article 4, the rules of general application, pertains to a variety of items regarding form, classification, and the content of notes to the financial statements. Rule 4-08, "General Notes to Financial Statements," comprises most of this article. Rule 4-08 is an extensive rule specifying certain information to be set forth in notes to the financial statements. This rule is not a duplication of FASB disclosure requirements. Instead, the requirements pertain to items not specifically addressed in pronouncements of the FASB and its predecessor organizations. Generally, preparing the additional disclosures called for by this Article is not a major task.

## Article 5: Commercial and Industrial Companies

Article 5 applies to all companies that are not required to follow Articles 5A, 6, 6A, 7, and 9. Rules 5-02 and 5-03 set forth the various line items and certain additional disclosures that should appear in the balance sheet, income statement, or related notes.

Rule 5-04 is a list and description of 13 financial statement supporting schedules (commonly referred to as **schedules**) that are filed in support of the basic financial statements. These schedules pertain to such things as analyses of property, plant, and equipment and analyses of valuation accounts for specified periods of time. In most cases, only four or five schedules apply. The exact form and content of the schedules are specified by Article 12.

## Article 10: Interim Financial Statements

Article 10 deals with the form and content of presentation of interim financial statements (quarterly reports under the 1934 Act and interim financial statements in registration statements filed under the 1933 Act).

## Article 11: Pro Forma Financial Information

Article 11 specifies when pro forma financial statements must be presented. Such financial statements are required when business combinations have occurred or are probable.

## Article 12: Form and Content of Schedules

Article 12 prescribes the form and content of the financial statement supporting schedules required by Rule 5-04 under Article 5 and certain rules in other articles. The exact columnar headings used for each schedule are specified, along with detailed instructions on how to prepare each schedule.

# END-OF-CHAPTER REVIEW

## Summary of Key Points

1. The Securities Act of 1933 and the Securities Exchange Act of 1934 protect investors from fraudulent actions and unethical practices by the promoters of securities and the managements of companies issuing securities.
2. The Securities and Exchange Commission administers the 1933 Act and the 1934 Act, as well as several other acts.
3. The SEC has the statutory authority (granted by Congress) to establish GAAP. To date, the SEC has allowed the private sector to establish GAAP. The SEC works closely with the FASB and the Emerging Issues Task Force in establishing GAAP.
4. Unlike the FASB, the SEC has enforcement powers that it uses as necessary to order a company to change their interpretation of GAAP. Also, the SEC is empowered to take disciplinary actions against auditors.
5. Companies subject to the registration and reporting requirements of these statutes must be familiar with a labyrinth of regulations, rules, releases, forms, and bulletins to comply with these statutes. For the disclosure of non-financial information, companies usually rely heavily on their legal counsel for assistance and guidance. For the disclosure of financial information,

company accountants must be intimately familiar with the detailed requirements of Regulation S-X.

6. In some areas, Regulation S-X imposes significant additional reporting requirements beyond those required under generally accepted accounting principles.

## Glossary of New Terms

**Blue sky laws**    State laws dealing with the purchase and sale of securities.

**Exempt offering**    An offering of securities that need not be registered with the SEC because of an available statutory exemption.

**Forms**    Specific enumerations of the form and content of information included in registration statements and reports filed with the SEC.

**Private offering**    "Transactions by an issuer not involving a public offering."*

**Prospectus**    The portion of a registration statement that must be furnished to prospective investors in connection with an offering of securities being registered with the SEC.

**Proxy**    A document empowering a person to vote for another person.

**Proxy statement**    A statement containing specified information furnished to stockholders in connection with the solicitation of proxies for use at an annual meeting (or special meetings) of shareholders.

**Registration statement**    All of the specified financial and nonfinancial information filed with the SEC (set forth according to an appropriate form) for purposes of registering an offering of securities to the public.

**Restricted security**    Securities acquired by means that did not involve a public offering.

**Security**    "Any note, stock, treasury stock, bond, debenture, evidence of indebtedness, certificate of interest or participation in any profit-sharing agreement, . . . transferable share, investment contract, voting trust certificate, . . . or in general any interest or instrument commonly known as a security . . ."*

**Underwriter**    "Any person who has purchased from an issuer with a view to, or offers or sells for an issuer in connection with, the distribution of any security, or participates [directly or indirectly] . . . in any such undertaking . . ."*

## Self-Study Questions

*(Answers are at the end of this chapter.)*

1. The SEC is empowered to do all of the following except
   a. Require additional disclosures.
   b. Prohibit accounting practices.
   c. Overrule the FASB.
   d. Establish GAAP.
   e. None of the above.
2. The statutory authority to establish GAAP resides with
   a. The SEC Commissioners.
   b. The Chief Accountant of the SEC.

---

*Securities Act of 1933.

   c. The Division of Corporate Finance.

   d. The FASB.

   e. None of the above.

3. The SEC can take the following disciplinary actions against auditors except

   a. Censure the auditors.

   b. Require the auditor to submit to a peer review.

   c. Institute criminal proceedings.

   d. Bar the auditor(s) from practicing before the SEC either temporarily or permanently.

   e. None of the above.

4. Interpretations and practices followed by certain departments of the SEC that are responsible for reviewing the disclosure requirements of the federal securities law would be found in

   a. Regulation S-K.

   b. Regulation S-X.

   c. Financial Reporting Releases.

   d. Staff Accounting Bulletins.

   e. Accounting and Auditing Enforcement Releases.

   f. None of the above.

5. A company desiring to issue common stock to the public must file with the SEC a(n)

   a. Prospectus.

   b. Registration statement.

   c. Proxy statement.

   d. Offering circular.

   e. None of the above.

6. The Securities Act of 1933, in general, exempts certain stock offerings from full registration. Which of the following is *not* exempt from full registration?

   a. Private offerings.

   b. Regulation A offerings.

   c. Strictly intrastate issues.

   d. Securities of governmental units.

   e. None of the above.

7. In filings with the SEC, the financial statements to be included in the material being filed are found in

   a. The appropriate form being used.

   b. Regulation S-X.

   c. Regulation S-K.

   d. Staff Accounting Bulletins.

   e. None of the above.

8. Which form is used to report a change in auditors?

   a. Form S-1.

   b. Form 10-K.

   c. Form 8-K.

   d. Form F-4.

   e. Form S-X.

   f. None of the above.

## ASSIGNMENT MATERIAL

### Review Questions

1. How does the Securities Exchange Act of 1934 differ from the Securities Act of 1933?
2. What purpose is served by the SEC's Staff Accounting Bulletins?
3. What purpose do SEC releases serve?
4. Describe the SEC's role in the formation and improvement of generally accepted accounting principles.
5. Distinguish between a registration statement and a prospectus.
6. What is the distinction between Form S-1 and Form 10-K?
7. What do Regulations A and D have in common?
8. What do Forms 8-K, 10-K, and 10-Q have in common?
9. How is Regulation C under the 1933 Act similar to Regulation 12B under the 1934 Act?
10. What is the distinction between Regulation S-X and Regulation S-K?
11. Distinguish between a proxy and a proxy statement.
12. How are financial statements that are prepared in accordance with Regulation S-X requirements different from financial statements prepared in accordance with generally accepted accounting principles?

### Exercises

| E |
| 18-1 |

#### The Role of the SEC in Relation to the FASB

Indicate whether the following statements are true or false. Discuss your reasons for your answers.

1. The pronouncements of the Financial Accounting Standards Board must be approved by the SEC before they can be issued.
2. The accounting related pronouncements of the SEC must be approved by the FASB before they are issued.
3. The SEC has given the FASB the statutory authority to prescribe accounting principles.
4. Publicly owned companies are subject to the financial reporting requirements of the SEC and FASB.
5. Privately owned companies are not subject to the financial reporting requirements of the SEC.
6. The SEC automatically rescinds a pronouncement when the FASB issues a Statement of Financial Accounting Standards involving a particular accounting issue.
7. When the SEC notices an emerging accounting practice that has not been addressed by the FASB, it most likely will establish accounting principles in that area until the FASB can address the issue.
8. Unlike the FASB, the SEC can order a company subject to its reporting requirements to alter its financial statements.

| E |
|---|
| **18-2** |

## SEC Promulgations

Complete the following statements:

1. The form and content of financial statements included with filings with the SEC are set forth in _____.
2. The pronouncements that announce the SEC's proposed revisions to its rules and regulations are called _____.
3. Nonfinancial statement disclosure requirements are set forth in _____.
4. An SEC regulation is merely a collection of _____.
5. The SEC rules and regulations that pertain to the various sections of the 1933 Act and the 1934 Act are referred to as the _____ rules and regulations.
6. The regulation that specifies the financial statements included in SEC filings is _____.
7. The interpretations and practices followed by certain departments of the SEC are called _____.
8. Accounting related releases used to be announced in _____, but now they are set forth in _____.
9. The promulgation of the SEC that accountants deal with more than any other is _____.
10. A list of instructions concerning what is included in a particular SEC filing is called a _____.

| E |
|---|
| **18-3** |

## The 1933 and 1934 Acts: Terminology

Complete the following statements:

1. Under the 1933 Act, issuers of securities must furnish potential investors with a _____.
2. A registration statement is divided into the following two basic parts:
   a. Information _____.
   b. Information _____.
3. A "red herring" is a _____.
4. Stocks and bonds are _____.
5. A person who purchases an issuer's stock with a view to distributing that stock to the public is a(n) _____.
6. Security offerings that need not be registered with the SEC are considered _____ offerings.
7. All the information filed with the SEC using an appropriate form under the 1933 Act is called a _____.
8. The Securities Act of 1933 pertains to the _____ of securities.
9. The Securities Exchange Act of 1934 pertains to _____ of issued securities.
10. Securities acquired by means that did not involve a public offering are called _____.
11. A document authorizing one person to vote for another person is a _____.
12. A statement furnished to stockholders in connection with soliciting their votes is called a _____.

| E 18-4 |

## The 1933 and 1934 Acts: Forms Used in Registrations and Filings

Indicate the SEC form applicable to each of the following items:

1. The most commonly used annual reporting form under the 1934 Act.
2. The most commonly used registration form under the 1933 Act.
3. The quarterly reporting form under the 1934 Act.
4. The form used under the 1934 Act to report certain transactions or events that arise during the year.
5. The form that may be used to register stock option plans, providing certain other conditions are met.
6. The most commonly used registration form under the 1934 Act.
7. The three general forms used under the 1933 Act.
8. The item filed with the SEC when a Regulation A offering is involved.

| E 18-5 |

## The Securities Act of 1933: The Role of the SEC and Responsibility of Outside Auditors

Select the best answer for each of the following items:

1. One of the SEC's functions is to
    a. Judge the merits of the securities being offered to the public.
    b. Ascertain the wisdom of investing in securities being offered to the public.
    c. Warrant that registration statements contain all necessary financial and nonfinancial statement information required by the investing public to evaluate the merit of the securities being offered.
    d. Warrant that the information contained in registration statements examined and approved by the SEC is true and accurate.
    e. None of the above.
2. A company registers securities with the SEC under the 1933 Act. As this event concerns its outside auditors, which of the following is correct?
    a. The SEC will defend any action brought against certified public accountants who have reported on financial statements included in a registration statement examined and approved by the SEC.
    b. Any action brought against the auditors would have to be decided on the basis of ordinary negligence versus gross negligence.
    c. The auditors could be held liable in the event of ordinary negligence as well as gross negligence.
    d. The auditors could be held liable for misleading statements in the notes to the financial statements even if negligence is not involved.
    e. None of the above.
3. One of the major purposes of the federal security statutes is to
    a. Establish the qualifications for accountants who are members of the profession.
    b. Eliminate incompetent attorneys and accountants who participate in the registration of securities offered to the public.
    c. Provide a set of uniform standards and tests for accountants, attorneys, and others who practice before the Securities and Exchange Commission.

    d. Provide sufficient information to the investing public who purchase securities in the marketplace.

    e. None of the above.

4. Under the Securities Act of 1933, subject to some exceptions and limitations, it is unlawful to use the mails or instruments of interstate commerce to sell or offer to sell a security to the public unless

    a. A surety bond sufficient to cover potential liability to investors is obtained and filed with the SEC.

    b. The offer is made through underwriters qualified to offer the securities on a nationwide basis.

    c. A registration statement that has been properly filed with the SEC has been found to be acceptable and is in effect.

    d. The SEC approves of the financial merit of the offering.

    e. None of the above.

5. A company registers securities with the SEC under the 1933 Act. As this event concerns its outside auditors, which of the following is correct?

    a. The outside auditors may disclaim any liability under the federal securities acts by an unambiguous, boldfaced disclaimer of liability on its audit report.

    b. The outside auditors must determine which SEC form the company should use in the filing.

    c. As long as the outside auditors engage exclusively in intrastate business, the federal securities laws do not apply to them.

    d. The outside auditors have primary responsibility for the nonfinancial statement portions of the registration statement as well as responsibility for the financial statement portions of the registration statement.

    e. None of the above.

## The 1933 and 1934 Acts: Technical Understanding

**E
18-6**

Select the best answer for each of the following items:

1. Regulation A and Regulation D deal with

    a. The mechanics of registering securities under the 1933 Act.

    b. The responsibilities of outside auditors under the 1933 Act.

    c. The forms used under the 1933 Act.

    d. Allowable exemptions from registration under the 1933 Act.

    e. None of the above.

2. Concerning the relationship between the 1933 Act and the 1934 Act, which of the following is correct?

    a. Having once become subject to the reporting requirements of the 1934 Act, a company may offer securities to the public in the future without having to register such securities with the SEC under the 1933 Act.

    b. If a privately owned company having 200,000 common shares outstanding registers the sale of 50,000 new shares under the 1933 Act, then all 250,000 common shares are deemed to be registered under the 1933 Act.

    c. A company that registers securities under the 1933 Act becomes subject to the reporting requirements of the 1934 Act.

d. If a privately owned company having 500,000 common shares outstanding registers the sale of 100,000 new shares under the 1933 Act, then only the 100,000 new shares may be registered under the 1934 Act.

e. None of the above.

3. Under the 1933 Act, which of the following is the most important criterion of whether a private placement to a limited number of persons or a public offering has been made?

a. The size of the issuing corporation.

b. The type of security offered.

c. The prompt resale of the securities by the purchasers.

d. Whether the company engages exclusively in intrastate business.

e. None of the above.

4. Which of the following is not exempt from registration under the 1933 Act?

a. Securities offered through underwriters.

b. Securities offered to a limited number of persons in a private placement.

c. Securities offered only to residents of the state in which the company is located.

d. Securities offered by a government unit.

e. None of the above.

5. Concerning the 1934 Act, which of the following is correct?

a. A company may be subject to the reporting requirements of the 1934 Act even though it never has registered securities under the 1933 Act.

b. A company that has been subject to the reporting requirements of the 1934 Act is always subject to such requirements unless the company becomes privately held again.

c. A company is no longer subject to the reporting requirements of the 1934 Act if its total assets are below $5 million at the end of its last three fiscal years.

d. A company that is no longer subject to the reporting requirements of the 1934 Act is also no longer subject to the requirements of the 1933 Act.

e. None of the above.

## Regulation S-X: True or False

**E
18-7**

Indicate whether the following statements are true or false.

1. Regulation S-X specifies the financial statements included in registration statements and reports filed with the SEC.

2. Some Financial Reporting Releases explain and illustrate certain rules in Regulation S-X.

3. Regulation S-X applies to the 1933 Act but not the 1934 Act.

4. Some Regulation S-X rules permit the deletion of certain notes to financial statements otherwise required by generally accepted accounting principles.

5. The form and content of financial statements included in registration statements and reports filed with the SEC are set forth in Regulation S-X.

6. The SEC automatically amends Regulation S-X to comply with any new FASB pronouncements.

7. Annual reports to shareholders need not present financial statements in compliance with Regulation S-X.
8. In general, it is a major task to convert financial statements and the related footnotes (prepared in accordance with generally accepted accounting principles) to meet the requirements of Regulation S-X.
9. Regulation S-X is a guide for preparing financial statements included in the registration statements and reports filed with the SEC—it need not be strictly followed.
10. Regulation S-X does not specify which SEC form is used in preparing reports filed under the 1934 Act.
11. Certain rules in Regulation S-X require additional financial disclosures above and beyond disclosures normally made pursuant to generally accepted accounting principles.
12. Changes in Regulation S-X can be announced through the issuance of a Financial Reporting Release.

## Problems

| P |
| 18-1 |

### The Securities Exchange Act of 1934: Stock Transactions by Employees

Discovery Corporation is a manufacturing company whose securities are registered on a national securities exchange. On February 6, 19X5, one of the company's engineers disclosed to management that he had discovered a new product that he believed would be quite profitable to the corporation. Messrs. Prescott and Trout, the corporation's president and treasurer and members of its board of directors, were quite impressed with the prospects of the new product's profitability.

Trout had such confidence in the corporation's prospects that on February 12, 19X5, he purchased on the open market 1,000 shares of the corporation's common stock at $10 per share. This purchase occurred before news of the new product reached the public in late February and caused a rise in the market price to $30 per share. Prescott did not purchase any shares in February because he had already purchased 600 shares of the corporation's common stock on January 15, 19X5, for $10 per share.

On April 16, 19X5, because of unexpected expenses arising from a fire in his home, Prescott sold on the open market the 600 shares of stock he purchased in January for $35 per share. Trout continues to hold his 1,000 shares.

#### Required:
1. What questions arising out of the federal securities laws are suggested by these facts? Discuss.
2. What would be a reasonable corporate policy designed to have employees buy and sell stock on the same basis as nonemployees?

| P |
| 18-2 |

### The Securities Exchange Act of 1934: Public Disclosures

B&S Corporation's sole issue of stock is traded on a national exchange. In conducting the year-end examination of its financial statements, the auditor learned that

B&S's research department had perfected a manufacturing process that would have a positive material effect on future earnings. B&S did not announce the development.

When a rumor about the new process started in late January, B&S's president promptly telephoned financial papers in several states and announced that there was no substance to the rumor. A number of papers reported the president's denial of the rumor. Thereafter, B&S's stock traded in its normal narrow range. In February, relying on the information reported in the financial press, Sellinger (an outside shareholder) sold a large block of his B&S stock at the current market price.

B&S's president made a public announcement about the perfection of the new process the following June. The announcement precipitated a dramatic increase in both the price and volume of trading of B&S's stock. Neither B&S nor any person with knowledge of the process engaged in trading B&S's stock before the public announcement of the discovery.

### Required:

What questions arising out of federal securities laws are suggested by these facts? Discuss.

(AICPA adapted)

### ANSWERS TO SELF-STUDY QUESTIONS

1. e    5. b
2. a    6. e
3. c    7. b
4. d    8. c

# 19

......

# TROUBLED DEBT
# RESTRUCTURINGS,
# BANKRUPTCY
# REORGANIZATIONS,
# AND LIQUIDATIONS

*TOPIC OUTLINE*

# CHAPTER OVERVIEW

## Options for Financially Distressed Companies

**A**ny type of economic entity (including corporations, partnerships, sole proprietorships, and municipalities) can encounter financial difficulties. Business entities in financial difficulty first usually retrench and undertake cost-cutting steps to conserve cash and reduce operating losses. Such steps may include revamping the organizational structure to eliminate or consolidate functions (often resulting in the termination of a substantial number of personnel), seeking wage and fringe-benefit concessions from employees, seeking relaxation of restrictive union work rules, and disposing of unprofitable segments. In addition, the entity may eventually need to (1) raise additional capital, (2) dispose of profitable segments, (3) combine with another business, (4) restructure its debt outside of the bankruptcy courts, (5) reorganize through the bankruptcy courts, or (6) liquidate.

This chapter deals with corporations that select the last three options. Option 4, restructuring debt outside of the bankruptcy courts, usually consists of extending due dates, forgiving some portion of debt, and reducing the interest rate on the debt. This option gives the business a reasonable chance to continue as a viable entity and recover from the financial difficulties, thereby avoiding liquidation, at least for the time being. Although option 5, reorganization through the bankruptcy courts, is identical in its objective to that of option 4, it is considered less desirable even though it usually results in a substantial forgiveness of debt. Option 6, liquidation, consists of converting all noncash assets into cash, paying creditors to the extent possible, and ending the legal existence of the corporation. In discussing the options of restructuring debt and reorganizing through the bankruptcy courts, we exclude railroads and municipalities because of their special nature. We also exclude these special entities from the discussion of liquidation, because public policy dictates that these entities not be liquidated.

# BANKRUPTCY STATUTES

## Their Purpose

Debt capital markets would be inhibited without some provisions for ensuring fair and equitable means of resolving rights and protecting public interests. This is the purpose of the bankruptcy laws. Distressed companies and their creditors must decide whether it is necessary to resort to the bankruptcy process. Accordingly, we now discuss the federal bankruptcy statutes.

## Their Substance

Under the bankruptcy statutes, a company or an individual is placed under the protection of the court, whereby creditors (including creditors possessing security interests, unsecured creditors, tax collectors, and public utilities) are prevented from taking other legal action (such as fore-closing on loans, filing lawsuits, repossessing or seizing assets, and placing padlocks on the doors of the company's real property). When a company's rehabilitation and future viable operations are feasible, its debt is restructured under the supervision and control of the court in such a manner that the debtor may be legally freed from the payment of certain past debts. When rehabilitation and recovery are not feasible, an orderly liquidation takes place under the supervision and control of the bankruptcy court.

## Federal Bankruptcy Statutes

Article I, Section 8 of the U.S. Constitution grants to the Congress the power to establish uniform laws throughout the United States pertaining to the subject of bankruptcies. Federal statutes pertaining to bankruptcy prevail over state laws that conflict with federal laws.

In 1978, the U.S. Congress rewrote the federal bankruptcy statutes under the Bankruptcy Reform Act of 1978. Taking effect on October 1, 1979, the new law replaced the National Bankruptcy Act of 1898. The new law established separate bankruptcy courts (adjuncts to the district courts) with special judges (commonly referred to as "bankruptcy judges") who supervise and review all bankruptcy petitions and proceedings. (If a case involves broad bankruptcy issues, however, such issues are to be decided by district judges, not the bankruptcy judges.)

The Bankruptcy Reform Act of 1978 (as amended in 1984) consists of the following eight chapters (even-numbered chapters do not exist):

| | |
|---|---|
| Chapter 1 | General provisions |
| Chapter 3 | Case administration |
| Chapter 5 | Creditors, the debtor, and the estate |
| Chapter 7 | Liquidation |
| Chapter 9 | Adjustment of debts of a municipality |
| Chapter 11 | Reorganization |
| Chapter 13 | Adjustment of debts of an individual with regular income |
| Chapter 15 | United States trustees |

The general provisions of Chapters 1, 3, and 5 pertain to Chapters 7, 9, 11, and 13, unless otherwise indicated. In this section, we discuss certain basic aspects of Chapters 1, 3, and 5. Chapters 9 and 13 do not pertain to corporations organized to make a profit; accordingly, they are not discussed in this chapter. (Chapter 9 applies only to municipalities that seek relief voluntarily—a municipality cannot be forced into bankruptcy proceedings against its will by its creditors.) Chapter 7 is discussed later in this chapter in the section dealing with liquidations. Chapter 11 is also discussed later in this chapter in the section dealing with bankruptcy reorganizations.

In the 1978 Act, the subject of the bankruptcy proceedings is referred to as a **debtor.** The commencement of a bankruptcy case creates an **estate.** The estate includes all of the debtor's property no matter where located (Section 541).[1]

## Applicability of the Bankruptcy Statutes

The bankruptcy statutes apply to individuals, partnerships, corporations (all of which are collectively referred to as "persons"), and municipalities. Insurance companies and certain financial institutions (such as banks, savings and loan associations, building and loan associations, and credit unions) are excluded because they are subject to alternative regulations. Railroads may not use the liquidation provisions of Chapter 7, only the reorganization provisions of Chapter 11. Stockbrokers and commodity brokers are not eligible for the reorganization provisions of Chapter 11, only the liquidation provisions of Chapter 7 (Section 109[b]).

## Voluntary Petitions

An eligible corporation (that is, a corporation other than an insurance company or certain financial institutions) may file a voluntary petition with the bankruptcy courts under Chapter 7 or 11 and thereby obtain the benefits available under the statutes (Section 109). Filing a voluntary petition constitutes an **order for relief,** which has the full force and effect as if the bankruptcy court had issued an order that the debtor be granted relief under the statutes (Section 301). However, the court can dismiss a voluntary filing if it is in the best interests of creditors (Section 707 and 1112[b]).

The petition initiates bankruptcy proceedings and is an official form that must be accompanied by a summary of the debtor's property (at market or current values) and debts, including supporting schedules, all on official forms. The supporting schedules for property consist of separate schedules for real property, personal property and property not otherwise scheduled. The supporting schedules for debts consist of separate schedules for *creditors with priority* (a special class of creditors explained later in the book), creditors holding security, and creditors having unsecured

---

[1]This reference is to the Bankruptcy Reform Act of 1978. Hereafter, only the section number of the act is provided.

claims without priority. Information also must include each creditor's address (if known), when the debt was incurred, and whether the debt is contingent, disputed, or subject to setoff. In addition, the petitioner must respond to a questionnaire regarding all aspects of its financial condition and operations. Although this questionnaire is called the *statement of affairs,* it should not be confused with the statement of affairs that accountants prepare regarding asset values and debts owed, which is explained later in the chapter.

## Involuntary Petitions

Under Chapter 7 or 11, an eligible corporation may be forced into bankruptcy proceedings against its will by its creditors. One or more creditors may file an involuntary petition with the bankruptcy court. If a debtor has twelve or more creditors, at least three of them who have claims totaling a minimum of $5,000 more than the value of any lien on the property of the debtor securing such claims must sign the petition (Section 303[b][1]). If a company has fewer than twelve creditors, one or more creditors having such claims of at least $5,000 must sign the petition (Section 303[b][2]). These dollar amounts apply to both liquidation and reorganization cases.

For an involuntary petition filed under Chapter 7 or 11, the bankruptcy court enters an order for relief against the debtor only if either of the following conditions pertain:

1. The debtor is generally not paying its debts as they become due.
2. A custodian was appointed or took possession of the debtor's property within 120 days before the date of the filing of the petition. (This does not apply to a trustee, receiver, or agent appointed or authorized to take charge of less than the majority of the debtor's property for the purpose of enforcing a lien against such property.) (Section 303[h]).

The first test above is an equity insolvency test; that is, the debtor's assets equitably belong to the creditors to the extent of their claims. In the second test, the appointment of a custodian presumes that the debtor cannot pay its debts as they mature.

In practice, voluntary bankruptcies occur much more frequently than involuntary bankruptcies. Regardless of whether a company enters bankruptcy proceedings voluntarily or involuntarily, it should immediately obtain the assistance of an attorney who specializes in bankruptcy proceedings.

## Creditors with Priority

A company entering bankruptcy proceedings can have two general classes of creditors—secured creditors and unsecured creditors. **Secured** creditors have been pledged certain of the company's assets as security on their claims. Creditors that have no right to any of the company's specific assets are **unsecured** creditors. In addition to these two general classes of creditors, the bankruptcy statutes create a special class of creditors termed **creditors with priority.** Debts with priority are listed in the order of their priority, as follows:

1. **Administrative expenses, fees, and charges assessed against the estate.** Administrative expenses are the actual and necessary costs and expenses of preserving the estate after the petition has been filed. This includes trustee's fees, legal, accounting, and appraisal fees incurred in connection with the bankruptcy proceedings, filing fees paid by creditors in an involuntary bankruptcy petition, and expenses incurred in recovering assets that were concealed or fraudulently transferred.

2. **Certain postfiling "gap" claims.** This category, which exists only for involuntary filings, includes unsecured claims arising in the ordinary course of the debtor's business after the involuntary filing but before the appointment of a trustee or an order of relief is entered, whichever occurs first.

3. **Wages, salaries, and commissions.** Wages, salaries, and commissions are limited to unsecured amounts earned by an individual within 90 days before the filing date or the date of the cessation of the debtor's business, whichever occurs first, but only up to $2,000 for each individual. This category includes vacation, severance, and sick leave pay.

4. **Employee benefit plans.** This category pertains to unsecured claims for contributions to employee benefit plans arising from services rendered by the employees within 180 days before the date of the filing of the petition or the date of the cessation of the debtor's business, whichever occurs first. The claims are limited to the number of employees covered by each such plan multiplied by $2,000, minus (a) the total amount paid to such employees as items in priority 3 above, and (b) the total amount paid by the estate on behalf of such employees to any other employee benefit plan.

5. **Deposits by individuals.** This category includes unsecured claims of up to $900 for each such individual, arising from the deposit of money before the commencement of the case in connection with the purchase, lease, or rental of property, or the purchase of services for the personal, family, or household use of such individuals, that were not delivered or provided.

6. **Taxes.** This category includes income taxes, property taxes, withholding taxes, employer payroll taxes, excise taxes, and customs duties. Most of these taxes are limited to amounts relating to a specified period of time preceding the date of the filing, usually one or three years, depending on the item.

Creditors with priority are given a statutory priority over the claims of other unsecured creditors with regard to payment. Later in the chapter, we illustrate this priority in a liquidation through the bankruptcy courts.

# TROUBLED DEBT RESTRUCTURINGS

In troubled debt restructurings, steps are taken outside of the bankruptcy courts to give the distressed company a reasonable chance of surviving. This option is considered much more desirable than a Chapter 11 reorganization.

## The Advantages of Restructuring versus Reorganizing

One advantage of restructuring outside of the bankruptcy courts is that the restructuring can be completed in far less time than a Chapter 11 reorganization, which takes a minimum of approximately 18 months. However, of greater importance is the desire to avoid the stigma associated with being or having been subject to bankruptcy proceedings. More uncertainty is associated with Chapter 11 reorganizations concerning the distressed company's chances of survival—many companies that file for Chapter 11 reorganizations are unable to work out a successful plan of reorganization and are liquidated instead. Thus, filing for reorganization under Chapter 11 is considered the last resort, short of liquidation.

Needless to say, filing for a Chapter 11 reorganization has far greater consequences to the distressed company in terms of its impact on suppliers, competitors, customers, and employees than does a restructuring outside of the bankruptcy courts. For example, a distressed company that is restructuring may be able to obtain some credit from suppliers; when a company reorganizes under Chapter 11, suppliers usually require payment on delivery. During restructuring, competitors tend to get sales leverage from a distressed company's problems; during a Chapter 11 reorganization, competitors have that much more ammunition. (Competitors often show customers press clippings of the distressed company's financial problems.)

When a company has filed for reorganization under Chapter 11, customers have that much less assurance of the company's survival—this can be critical for a distressed company that sells products requiring the company's continued existence for purposes of providing service and stocking spare parts. Employees are more likely to look for greener pastures once a company files for reorganization under Chapter 11 because of the uncertainty associated with bankruptcy proceedings. (Personnel placement firms tend to zero in on distressed companies to hire away their employees; their chances of success increase when a company files for a Chapter 11 reorganization.)

Working out a troubled debt restructuring agreement is usually a substantial and difficult undertaking, especially when major differences exist among various groups of creditors as to the sacrifices each is willing to make. A distressed company often resorts to a Chapter 11 reorganization when it is impossible to work out a troubled debt restructuring agreement with its creditors, when its lenders refuse to lend any more money, or when suppliers begin requiring payment on delivery. Although the advantages of restructuring debt outside of the bankruptcy courts are considerable, there are certain advantages in filing for reorganization under Chapter 11. These advantages are discussed later in the chapter when reorganization under Chapter 11 is discussed in detail.

## The Nature of Troubled Debt Restructurings

The accounting procedures for most debt restructurings are prescribed by *FASB Statement No. 15*, "Accounting by Debtors and Creditors for Troubled Debt Restructurings." Before discussing the accounting issues and procedures in detail, we (1) define a troubled debt restructuring, (2) show transactions that may be considered troubled debt restructurings, and (3) show some ways in which a distressed company can restructure its debt.

**Definition.**   *FASB Statement No. 15* defines a troubled debt restructuring as follows:

> A restructuring of a debt constitutes a **troubled debt restructuring** for purposes of this Statement if the creditor for economic or legal reasons related to the debtor's financial difficulties grants a concession to the debtor that it would not otherwise consider.[2]

The statement expounds on this definition as follows:

> Whatever the form of concession granted by the creditor to the debtor in a troubled debt restructuring, the creditor's objective is to make the best of a difficult situation. That is, the creditor expects to obtain more cash or other value from the debtor, or to increase the probability of receipt, by granting the concession than by not granting it.[3]

**Categories of Transactions.**   The statement lists the following types of transactions that may constitute troubled debt restructurings:

[2]*Statement of Financial Accounting Standards, No. 15,* "Accounting by Debtors and Creditors for Troubled Debt Restructurings" (Stamford: Financial Accounting Standards Board, 1977), par. 2.
[3]*FASB Statement No. 15,* par. 3.

a. Transfer from the debtor to the creditor of receivables from third parties, real estate, or other assets to satisfy fully or partially a debt (including a transfer resulting from foreclosure or repossession).

b. Issuance or other granting of an equity interest to the creditor by the debtor to satisfy fully or partially a debt unless the equity interest is granted pursuant to existing terms for converting the debt into an equity interest.

c. Modification of terms of a debt, such as one or a combination of:

1. Reduction (absolute or contingent) of the stated interest rate for the remaining original life of the debt.

2. Extension of the maturity date or dates at a stated interest rate lower than the current market rate for a new debt with similar risk.

3. Reduction (absolute or contingent) of the face amount or maturity amount of the debt as stated in the instrument or other agreement.

4. Reduction (absolute or contingent) of accrued interest.[4]

**Individual Creditor Agreements.** The most frequently used manner of restructuring debt is the **individual creditor agreement** between a debtor and a creditor whereby the payment terms are restructured pursuant to negotiated terms. Within the last ten years, dozens of large companies have restructured their debt in this manner or have at least attempted to do so. Typically, the creditors involved are banks. The most major, widely publicized completed restructurings in the 1980s were those of Chrysler Corp., which owed $4.4 billion to more than 400 banks, and International Harvester Corp., which owed $3.4 billion to more than 200 banks.

**Composition Agreements.** A **composition agreement** is a formal agreement between a debtor and its creditors (and among the creditors) whereby the creditors collectively agree to accept a percentage of their claims—such as 60 cents on the dollar—in full settlement of their claims. For example, a composition agreement may include only the debtor's major creditors, with all other creditors still entitled to full payment. The payment terms of the composition agreement may require immediate, partial, or full payment of the reduced amount. To the extent that payment of the reduced amount is deferred, a debtor may execute notes payable bearing interest on the deferred amount.

Composition agreements are usually negotiated when a company's filing for a Chapter 11 reorganization is imminent. As a result of the agreement, the company does not suffer the taint of having gone through a bankruptcy proceeding, a potentially lengthy and involved bankruptcy process is avoided, and the creditors expect to recover more than they would in a Chapter 11 reorganization.

---

[4]*FASB Statement No. 15*, par. 5.

## Conceptual Issues

Troubled debt restructurings usually result in the creditors' substantial reduction of the debtor's financial obligations (required payments for principal and interest). This procedure requires a comparison of (1) the total amount owed (including unpaid interest) immediately before the restructuring, which is commonly referred to as the **carrying amount of the debt,** with (2) the **total future payments** (including amounts designated as interest) to be made pursuant to the restructuring agreement. If the carrying amount of the debt exceeds the total future payments, the debtor's liabilities must be reduced. This reduction constitutes a **forgiveness of debt.** If the debtor's total future payments exceed the carrying amount of the debt, the excess is reported as interest expense in future periods. This situation presents no accounting issue. The accounting issues pertain solely to the forgiveness of debt and are as follows:

1. *How should any forgiveness of debt be measured?* The focus of this issue is primarily whether the new (post-restructuring) liability amount should be measured and reported as (a) the undiscounted total future payments to be made, or (b) the present value of total future payments. The difference between (a) or (b) and the carrying amount of the debt is the amount of the forgiveness. Obviously, the choice between (a) and (b) affects the amount of forgiveness.
2. *How should a forgiveness of debt be classified and reported?* This issue is concerned with whether a forgiveness of debt should be considered (a) a **gain** and, therefore, reported in the **income statement,** or (b) a **capital contribution** by the creditor or creditors and, therefore, credited directly to an **equity account.**

The resolution of these issues should be based on the **substance** of the restructuring, rather than its **form.** However, varying perceptions exist as to what constitutes the substance.

### Conceptual Issue 1: Calculation of Forgiveness of Debt

In some situations, the calculation of forgiveness of debt is quite simple. For example, assume a creditor that is owed $100,000 agrees to cancel $40,000 of the debt in return for the immediate payment of the remaining $60,000. Obviously, the amount of debt forgiven is $40,000. Most situations, however, are more complex. For example, assume that (1) a creditor is owed $100,000 of principal related to a delinquent loan bearing interest at 10% (for simplicity, we assume no interest is owed); and (2) the creditor agrees to be paid in full in two years with no interest to be charged. Two approaches have been advocated for such situations—one that **imputes interest** and one that **does not impute interest.** When interest is not imputed, the calculation to determine any forgiveness of debt is as follows:

| | |
|---|---|
| Carrying amount of debt............................... | $100,000 |
| Total future payments ............................. | 100,000 |
| Amount of forgiveness.................................. | $ –0– |

Under this approach, the liability reported in the balance sheet immediately after the restructuring is $100,000, and it bears a zero interest rate. No interest expense would be reported in either year.

When interest is imputed (using present value techniques), the amount of forgiveness, if any, depends on the imputed interest rate used. Assuming that the 10% pre-restructuring interest rate is appropriate, the calculation to determine any forgiveness of debt is as follows:

| | | |
|---|---|---|
| Carrying amount of debt..................... | | $100,000 |
| Total future payments ..................... | $100,000 | |
| Present value factor (10%, 2 years)......... | .82645 | |
| Present value of total future payments....... | | 82,645 |
| Amount of forgiveness.................... | | $ 17,355 |

Under this approach, the liability reported in the balance sheet immediately after the restructuring is $82,645, and it bears interest at 10%. Interest expense of $8,264 (10% of $82,645) would be reported in year one, and $9,091 [10% of ($82,645 + $8,264)] would be reported in year two.

**Rationale for Not Imputing Interest.** Arguments for not imputing interest are as follows:

1. Troubled debt restructurings *are not* "exchanges of debt" and, therefore, *do not* require the use of present value techniques as set forth in *APB Opinion No. 21*, "Interest on Receivables and Payables," which deals with "exchanges."
2. A creditor does not grant any forgiveness under the restructuring so long as the total future payments to be received equal or exceed the recorded investment in the receivable; that is, the **recoverability** of the recorded investment in the receivable is not affected.
3. A reduction of the debtor's financial obligations (before the restructuring) to the amount of the recorded investment in the receivable merely changes the creditor's **future profitability** on the loan. Thus, a creditor's effective interest rate after the restructuring could vary from the pre-restructuring interest rate of 10%, for example, down to zero.

Recall from the nonimputing example that no forgiveness of debt existed because the total future payments of $100,000 were not below the $100,000 carrying amount of the debt. Thus, from the creditor's perspective, the future profitability on the loan had been reduced to zero, but the recoverability of the recorded amount of the receivable had not been affected.

**Rationale for Imputing Interest.** Arguments for imputing interest are as follows:

1. The debtor's liability after restructuring ($82,645 in the imputing example) is reported on the same basis as the borrowings of all debtors—that is, the present value of the future cash outflows for principal and interest.
2. The debtor's future income statements will reflect a reasonable amount of interest expense, which should enhance comparability of those statements with the debtor's past income statements and with future income statements of other companies.

An implementation issue under this approach is whether the **pre-restructuring** interest rate or a current market interest rate should be used. Most accountants feel that the debtor's obligation after the restructuring results from a modification of an existing loan. Therefore, the pre-restructuring rate should be used. Other accountants who view the debtor's obligation after restructuring as arising from the execution of a new lending agreement conclude that a current market interest rate should be used. An advantage of the pre-restructuring approach is that the interest rate is known. However, the current market rate approach involves determining the interest rate at which a debtor in a precarious financial position might be able to borrow when, in fact, no lenders may be available.

## Conceptual Issue 2: Reporting Forgiveness of Debt

A forgiveness of debt may be reported in the income statement. In this approach, **a forgiveness of debt is a gain on restructuring,** which is **similar to a gain on extinguishment of debt.** Under *APB Opinion No. 26*, "Early Extinguishment of Debt," gain on extinguishment of debt must be reported in the income statement. Most advocates of this position agree that such a gain should be reported as an extraordinary item because the criteria of unusual and infrequent would be met.

In a second alternative, **a forgiveness of debt may be reported as a direct addition to paid-in capital.** The arguments for this approach are as follows:

1. Because the transaction infuses capital to the debtor, in substance, the debtor has received a capital contribution from the creditor.
2. It should make no difference whether the additional capital needed to keep the debtor in business comes from stockholders or creditors.
3. A company in serious financial difficulty, which has probably reported substantial operating losses, should not report income on a transaction intended to assist it in eventually returning to profitable operations.

## Requirements of *FASB Statement No. 15*

After considering the various viewpoints on imputing or not imputing interest, the Financial Accounting Standards Board (FASB) concluded that (1) **interest should not be imputed** in the calculation to determine if any forgiveness of debt exists; (2) the amount of debt forgiven should be **reported as a gain on restructuring**; and (3) such gain, if material, should be **reported as an extraordinary item,** net of its related income tax effect. Accordingly, in calculating the amount of debt forgiven, the carrying amount of the debt is compared with any one (or more) of the following that was included in the restructuring plan:

1. The total future cash payments specified in the new terms, **not discounted** back to their present value.
2. The fair value of the noncash assets transferred.
3. The fair value of the equity interest granted.

To the extent that the carrying amount of the debt exceeds the relevant factor or factors listed above, a gain on restructuring is reportable.

We now define in detail certain terms used in *FASB Statement No. 15.*

1. **The carrying amount of the debt** is the face, or principal, amount, plus any accrued interest payable, less any unamortized discount (or plus any premium), finance charges, or debt issuance costs.
2. **Total future cash payments** include amounts that are designated principal and interest. Thus, the labels traditionally assigned to amounts to be paid to creditors lose their significance for purposes of determining if a gain on restructuring of debt exists.
3. **Fair value** is defined as "the amount that the debtor could reasonably expect to receive . . . in a current sale between a willing buyer and a willing seller, that is, other than in a forced or liquidation sale."[5]

In most respects, this approach for calculating the amount of debt forgiven is relatively simple to apply. However, subsequent income statements reflect either no interest expense (when a forgiveness of debt is reportable) or unrealistically low interest expense (when no forgiveness of debt is reportable) until the maturity date of the restructured debt. Consequently, reported earnings are higher than the earnings reported if the company paid interest (or at least measured interest expense) at the current rate. Because of the potentially misleading inferences that can be made from subsequent income statements immediately after a complex restructuring, it is important to disclose in the notes to the financial statements of the appropriate subsequent periods the fact that reported interest expense is artificially low because the restructuring was accounted for in this manner.

---

[5]*FASB Statement No. 15*, par. 13.

**Other Important Technical and Procedural Points.** Other important technical and procedural points of *FASB Statement No. 15* are the following:

1. The *date of consummation* is the point in time at which the restructuring occurs.
2. The restructuring of each payable is accounted for individually, even if the restructuring was negotiated and restructured jointly.
3. When a noncash asset is transferred to a creditor in full settlement of a debt, the difference between the carrying amount of the noncash asset and its fair value is recognized as a gain or loss in the transfer of the asset. (Such gain or loss is reported in the income statement in the period of transfer as provided in *APB Opinion No. 30*, "Reporting the Results of Operations.")
4. To the extent that the total future cash payments specified in the new terms exceed the carrying amount of the debt, the difference is reported as interest expense between the restructuring date and the maturity date.
5. The "interest" method prescribed by *APB Opinion No. 21* is used to calculate the amount of the interest expense for each year between the restructuring date and the maturity date. This method causes a constant effective interest rate to be applied to the carrying amount of the debt at the beginning of each period between the restructuring date and the maturity date.
6. When a gain on restructuring has been recognized, all future cash payments are charged to the carrying amount of the payable. In other words, if a gain on restructuring is reported, then there cannot be any future interest expense with respect to that debt.
7. For determining if a gain on restructuring exists, the total future cash payments include amounts that may be contingently payable.
8. When the debtor grants an equity interest to a creditor to settle fully a payable, the equity interest is recorded in the debtor's capital accounts at its fair value, and any remaining liability in excess of this fair value is recognized as a gain on restructuring of payables.
9. When either noncash assets or an equity interest is given to a creditor in partial settlement of a payable and the payment terms of the remaining payable are modified, the fair value of the assets transferred or the equity interest granted is first subtracted from the carrying amount of the payable. The residual amount of the payable is then compared with the total future cash payments specified in the new terms to determine if a gain on restructuring exists.

**ILLUSTRATION**  ## Application of *FASB Statement No. 15*

Assume that the financially distressed Never-Quit Company has consummated a troubled debt restructuring with substantially all of its unsecured

### ■ ILLUSTRATION 19-1
**Balance Sheet before Restructuring of Debt**

| NEVER-QUIT COMPANY<br>Balance Sheet<br>August 31, 19X1<br>(immediately before restructuring) | | |
|---|---:|---:|
| **Assets** | | |
| **Current Assets** | | |
| Cash | | $    450,000 |
| Accounts receivable | $   650,000 | |
| Less—Allowance for uncollectibles | (240,000) | 410,000 |
| Inventories | | 800,000 |
| Total Current Assets | | $ 1,660,000 |
| **Noncurrent Assets** | | |
| Property, plant, and equipment | $2,700,000 | |
| Less—Accumulated depreciation | (1,500,000) | 1,200,000 |
| Other assets | | 140,000 |
| Total Assets | | $ 3,000,000 |
| **Liabilities and Stockholders' Deficiency** | | |
| **Current Liabilities** | | |
| Note payable, secured by land and buildings | | $ 1,000,000 |
| Notes payable, unsecured | | 2,050,000 |
| Accrued interest (all on unsecured notes) | | 540,000 |
| Accounts payable | | 925,000 |
| Other accrued liabilities | | 75,000 |
| Total Liabilities | | $ 4,590,000 |
| **Stockholders' Deficiency** | | |
| Common stock, $1 par value, 200,000 shares issued and outstanding | | $    200,000 |
| Additional paid-in capital | | 1,850,000 |
| Accumulated deficit | | (3,640,000) |
| Total Stockholders' Deficiency | | $(1,590,000) |
| Total Liabilities in Excess of Stockholders' Deficiency | | $ 3,000,000 |

creditors on August 31, 19X1. Never-Quit's August 31, 19X1, balance sheet before the restructuring is shown in Illustration 19-1. We assume that all notes payable (secured and unsecured) are currently due and payable as a result of defaults under related loan agreements.

The following items are part of the restructuring. For each of these items (except the last item), the application of *FASB Statement No. 15* is explained and the journal entry to reflect the restructuring is given. (All solutions ignore income tax effects.)

1. **Payment of cash in full settlement.** Never-Quit owes $600,000 to 80 vendors. These vendors have collectively agreed to settle their claims fully for 40 cents on the dollar. Payment of $240,000 was made on August 31, 19X1. Because the carrying amount of the $600,000 debt exceeds the total future cash payments of $240,000, a $360,000 gain on restructuring of debt is reportable in the 19X1 income statement, recorded as follows:

| | | |
|---|---|---|
| Accounts Payable | 600,000 | |
| Cash | | 240,000 |
| Gain on Restructuring of Debt | | 360,000 |
| To record payment to vendors and gain on restructuring of debt. | | |

2. **Transfer of receivables in full settlement.** The company owes $325,000 to a vendor who has agreed to accept certain of the company's accounts receivable totaling $280,000. The company has an allowance of $100,000 recorded on the books against these receivables. The receivables were assigned to the creditor on August 31, 19X1. The company has not guaranteed the collectibility of these receivables.

Because the $325,000 carrying amount of the debt exceeds the $180,000 fair value of the assets (the net amount expected to be collectible by the debtor), a gain on restructuring of $145,000 is reportable in the 19X1 income statement, recorded as follows:

| | | |
|---|---|---|
| Accounts Payable | 325,000 | |
| Allowance for Uncollectibles | 100,000 | |
| Accounts Receivable | | 280,000 |
| Gain on Restructuring of Debt | | 145,000 |
| To record transfer of assets to vendor and gain on restructuring of debt. | | |

3. **Grant of an equity interest in full settlement.** The company owes $500,000 ($430,000 principal and $70,000 interest) to a financial institution that has agreed to cancel the entire amount owed in exchange for 100,000 shares of the debtor's common stock. The market value of the common stock on August 31, 19X1, is $3.50 per share. The company issued the 100,000 shares of common stock to the creditor on this date.

Because the $500,000 carrying amount of the debt exceeds the $350,000 fair value of the equity interest granted (100,000 shares × $3.50 per share), a gain on restructuring of debt of $150,000 is reportable in the 19X1 income statement, recorded as follows:

| | | |
|---|---|---|
| Notes Payable. . . . . . . . . . . . . . . . . . . . . . . . . . . . . . . . . . | 430,000 | |
| Accrued Interest Payable . . . . . . . . . . . . . . . . . . . . | 70,000 | |
| Common Stock . . . . . . . . . . . . . . . . . . . . . . . | | 100,000 |
| Additional Paid-in Capital. . . . . . . . . . . . . . | | 250,000 |
| Gain on Restructuring of Debt . . . . . . . . . | | 150,000 |
| To record grant of equity interest and gain on restructuring of debt. | | |

4. **Modification of debt terms (no contingent interest).** The company owes $260,000 ($220,000 principal and $40,000 interest) to a financial institution that has agreed to cancel $20,000 of principal and the $40,000 of accrued interest and reduce the interest rate on the remaining principal to 5% for five years, at the end of which time the note is to be paid in full.

   Because the $260,000 carrying amount of the debt exceeds the $250,000 total future cash payments as specified in the terms of the agreement ($200,000 designated as a principal payment and $50,000 designated as interest payments), a gain on restructuring of debt of $10,000 is reportable in the 19X1 income statement, recorded as follows:

| | | |
|---|---|---|
| Notes Payable. . . . . . . . . . . . . . . . . . . . . . . . . . . . . . . . . . | 220,000 | |
| Accrued Interest Payable . . . . . . . . . . . . . . . . . . . . | 40,000 | |
| Restructured Debt. . . . . . . . . . . . . . . . . . . . . . | | 250,000 |
| Gain on Restructuring of Debt . . . . . . . . . | | 10,000 |
| To record the restructuring of the debt and the resultant gain. | | |

Because a gain on restructuring of debt exists, no interest expense is reported for the next five years on this debt.

5. **Modification of debt terms (contingent interest).** The company owes a total of $750,000 ($500,000 principal and $250,000 interest) to a financial institution that has agreed to the following:
   a. The $250,000 accrued interest is canceled.
   b. The due date of the $500,000 principal is extended six years from August 31, 19X1.
   c. The interest rate for the first three years is 5% (a reduction of 5% from the old rate).
   d. The interest rate for the following three years is 10%.
   e. If the debtor's cumulative earnings for the next six years exceed $1,000,000, then interest for the first three years must be paid at 10% rather than 5%. (The cumulative earnings will probably not exceed $1,000,000 for the next six years.)

The total minimum and maximum future payments are determined as follows:

| | |
|---|---:|
| Principal . . . . . . . . . . . . . . . . . . . . . . . . . . . . . . . . . . . . . . . . . . . . . . . . . . . . . | $500,000 |
| Interest—years 1, 2, and 3 @ 5% . . . . . . . . . . . . . . . . . . . . . . . . . . | 75,000 |
| Interest—years 4, 5, and 6 @ 10% . . . . . . . . . . . . . . . . . . . . . . . . | 150,000 |
| Minimum Total Future Payments . . . . . . . . . . . . . . . . . . . . . . . . . | $725,000 |
| Contingent interest—years 1, 2, and 3 . . . . . . . . . . . . . . . . . . . . . | 75,000 |
| Maximum Total Future Payments . . . . . . . . . . . . . . . . . . . . . . . . . | $800,000 |

The $750,000 carrying value of the debt does not exceed the $800,000 total maximum future payments that may be made under the new terms. Thus, no gain on restructuring of debt is reportable in 19X1:

| | | |
|---|---:|---:|
| Notes Payable . . . . . . . . . . . . . . . . . . . . . . . . . . . . . . . . | 500,000 | |
| Accrued Interest Payable . . . . . . . . . . . . . . . . . . . . . . . | 250,000 | |
| Restructured Debt. . . . . . . . . . . . . . . . . . . . . . . . | | 750,000 |
| To record the restructuring of the debt. | | |

If the end of the sixth year the cumulative earnings have not exceeded $1,000,000, then a $25,000 gain on restructuring is reported at that time. If it becomes probable during the six years that the cumulative earnings will exceed $1,000,000, then additional interest expense of $50,000 ($800,000 − $750,000 carrying amount of the debt) must be provided over the remaining life of the loan.

6. **Combination grant of equity interest and modification of debt terms.** Never-Quit owes $1,080,000 ($900,000 principal and $180,000 interest) to some of its major stockholders, who have agreed to the following:
   a. Accrued interest of $80,000 is canceled.
   b. Principal of $400,000 is canceled in exchange for the issuance of 4,000 shares of 6%, $100 par value, convertible preferred stock with cumulative dividends. (We assume that the articles of incorporation were amended to approve the authorization for this new class of stock, which was issued on August 31, 19X1.)
   c. The remaining principal of $500,000 and the uncanceled interest of $100,000 bear interest at 5%, with $300,000 to be paid in six months and the remaining $300,000 to be paid in 18 months.

Because no established market price is available for the preferred stock, we assume that the fair value of the preferred stock equals the $400,000 amount of the principal canceled. This assumed fair value of the preferred stock is subtracted from the $1,080,000 carrying value of the debt to arrive at an **adjusted carrying value** of $680,000. The adjusted carrying value of $680,000 is then compared with the total future payments to determine if a gain on restructuring exists. The total future payments are $630,000 ($600,000 designated as principal and

$30,000 designated as interest). Accordingly, a gain on restructuring of debt of $50,000 ($680,000 − $630,000) is reportable in the 19X1 income statement, recorded as follows:

| | | |
|---|---|---|
| Notes Payable | 900,000 | |
| Accrued Interest Payable | 180,000 | |
|     Preferred Stock | | 400,000 |
|     Restructured Debt | | 630,000 |
|     Gain on Restructuring of Debt | | 50,000 |
|   To record the restructuring of the debt. | | |

7. **Reclassification by secured creditor.** None of the preceding items pertains to the company's secured creditor (who is owed $1,000,000), because a secured creditor is under no economic compulsion to make concessions. Because of the preceding restructurings, however, this creditor agrees to allow Never-Quit to repay $960,000 of the $1,000,000 owed after August 31, 19X2, leaving only $40,000 as a current liability as of August 31, 19X1. (The interest rate was not changed.)

Never-Quit's August 31, 19X1, balance sheet, which reflects the financial terms of the restructurings, is shown in Illustration 19-2. In comparing Illustration 19-2 with Illustration 19-1, note that the stockholders' deficiency has been almost eliminated as a result of the restructuring. Although a substantial portion of the stockholders' deficiency is usually eliminated in a troubled debt restructuring, the entire deficiency need not be eliminated for the rehabilitation efforts to be successful.

Never-Quit's 19X1 income statement reflects the gain on restructuring as an extraordinary item, part of the period's income but separate from income (loss) from operations. The illustration has omitted tax effects, which we address in a later section.

## Nonapplicability of *FASB Statement No. 15* to Quasi-Reorganizations

Although a debt restructuring may eliminate most or all of the stockholders' deficiency, some companies try to eliminate the accumulated deficit by using the "quasi-reorganization" procedures provided by many state laws.

Recall from intermediate accounting that adjustments made to restate (usually write down) assets in a quasi-reorganization are charged directly to equity.[6] Adjustments to restate (reduce) liabilities in a quasi-reorganization are similarly credited directly to equity. Treating such adjustments to assets and liabilities as capital transactions is desirable,

[6]This procedure is required pursuant to the provision of *Accounting Research Bulletin No. 43*, Chapter 7, Section A, "Capital Accounts," par. 6. This position was reaffirmed in *Opinions of the Accounting Principles Board, No. 9*, "Reporting the Results of Operations," par. 28.

■ **ILLUSTRATION 19-2**
**Balance Sheet after Restructuring of Debt**

| NEVER-QUIT COMPANY<br>Balance Sheet<br>August 31, 19X1<br>(after the restructuring) | | |
|---|---:|---:|
| **Assets** | | |
| **Current Assets** | | |
| Cash.................................................. | | $ 210,000 |
| Accounts receivable............................ | $ 370,000 | |
| Less—Allowance for uncollectibles............ | (140,000) | 230,000 |
| Inventories........................................ | | 800,000 |
| Total Current Assets...................... | | $1,240,000 |
| **Noncurrent Assets** | | |
| Property, plant, and equipment............... | $2,700,000 | |
| Less—Accumulated depreciation.............. | (1,500,000) | 1,200,000 |
| Other assets...................................... | | 140,000 |
| Total Assets................................ | | $2,580,000 |
| **Liabilities and Stockholders' Deficiency** | | |
| **Current Liabilities** | | |
| Other accrued liabilities...................... | | $ 75,000 |
| Current portion of secured note payable...... | | 40,000 |
| Current portion of restructured debt, unsecured......... | | 300,000 |
| Total Current Liabilities.................. | | $ 415,000 |
| **Long-Term Debt** | | |
| Secured note payable........................... | | $ 960,000 |
| Restructured debt, unsecured.................. | | 1,330,000 |
| Total Long-Term Debt...................... | | $2,290,000 |
| **Stockholders' Deficiency** | | |
| Preferred stock, 6%, $100 par value, cumulative,<br>40,000 shares issued and outstanding................. | | $ 400,000 |
| Common stock, $1 par value, 300,000 shares<br>issued and outstanding............................ | | 300,000 |
| Additional paid-in capital...................... | | 2,100,000 |
| Accumulated deficit............................. | | (2,925,000) |
| Total Stockholders' Deficiency........... | | $ (125,000) |
| Total Liabilities in Excess of Stockholders' Deficiency ... | | $2,580,000 |

because otherwise asset write-downs would be reported as capital transactions and liability reductions would be reported (per the general rule of
*FASB Statement No 15*) as noncapital (income statement) transactions.

*FASB Statement No. 15* does not apply to a troubled debt restructuring
that coincides with quasi-reorganization procedures if the debtor "re-

states its liabilities generally" in that quasi-reorganization. The phrase **"restates its liabilities generally"** is a new term introduced into the accounting literature by *FASB Statement No. 15*. Although the pronouncement does not define the term, it means a restructuring that encompasses most of a company's liabilities, as would usually occur when restructuring is part of the quasi-reorganization plan. Although *FASB Statement No. 15* does not explain why it does not apply to these situations, we may assume that the FASB wants to allow consistent treatment for both asset and liability adjustments in quasi-reorganizations.

This explanation does not help in the more common situation in which the stockholders' deficiency resulted from several years of large operating losses—that is, not from a restatement of the assets. Regardless of what caused the accumulated deficit (whether from restating assets or from operating losses), the following question is raised: Why should the decision to eliminate the accumulated deficit using quasi-reorganization procedures (a mere formality under state law) change the perception of forgiveness of debt from an income statement gain (in *FASB Statement No. 15*) to a capital transaction? The answer evidently lies in the "fresh start" objective of a quasi-reorganization. A restructuring not involving a quasi-reorganization maintains the company's basic continuity. A quasi-reorganization results in the assumed death of the old company and the assumed creation of a new one. A "break" exists that usually destroys any pre- versus post-income statement comparability. Because of this fresh-start objective, treating the forgiveness as a capital transaction makes more sense.

## Tax Consequences of Gains on Restructurings

The Internal Revenue Code treats gains on troubled debt restructurings as taxable only to the extent that such restructurings result in a positive balance in total stockholders' equity (not retained earnings). Any income taxes provided would be netted against the gain on the restructuring, because in financial reporting, the gain must be reported as an extraordinary item net of income tax effects.

## Accounting by Creditors

Although this chapter is concerned with accounting by a debtor, *FASB Statement No. 15* applies to creditors as well. In most respects, accounting by a creditor is symmetrical to the accounting by a debtor. Thus, if the debtor reports a gain on restructuring, the creditor simultaneously reports an offsetting loss on restructuring of its receivables, except to the extent that such loss has already been provided for in allowances for uncollectibles or write-offs, or both.

Interestingly, the banking industry uniformly and vehemently opposed the imputed interest (discounted present value) approach of calculating the amount of debt forgiven as presented in the FASB discussion memorandum that preceded *FASB Statement No. 15.* This approach would have had creditors reporting much greater losses than under the "no-discount" alternative adopted by the FASB. How the banking industry's strong vocal position influenced the FASB in its deliberations is conjecture. It is interesting to note, however, that the FASB's first exposure draft on troubled debt restructurings (dated November 7, 1975, and encompassing only accounting by debtors) called for the imputed interest approach. Because of the obvious implications to creditors—that is, if a debtor reports a gain, the creditor should simultaneously report a loss—the project was expanded to include accounting by creditors as well.

## Subsequent-Period Interest Expense in "No Reportable Gain" Restructurings

Procedural points 4 and 5 of *FASB Statement No. 15* (shown on page 810) indicate that when the total future payments exceed the carrying amount of the debt, the excess is reported as interest expense between the restructuring date and the maturity date using the interest method prescribed by *APB Opinion No. 21.* In such cases, the effective interest rate must be calculated. Assume the following information:

1. Carrying amount of the debt at January 1, 19X1:

| | |
|---|---:|
| Principal owed . . . . . . . . . . . . . . . . . . . . . . . . . . . . . . . . . . . . . . | $1,100,000 |
| Interest owed . . . . . . . . . . . . . . . . . . . . . . . . . . . . . . . . . . . . . . | 33,947 |
| | $1,133,947 |

2. Cancellation of debt per restructuring agreement consummated January 1, 19X1:

| | |
|---|---:|
| Principal . . . . . . . . . . . . . . . . . . . . . . . . . . . . . . . . . . . . . . | $  100,000 |
| Interest . . . . . . . . . . . . . . . . . . . . . . . . . . . . . . . . . . . . . . | 33,947 |
| | $  133,947 |

3. Total future payments to be made:

| | |
|---|---:|
| Amount designated as principal (due December 31, 19X2) . . . . . . . . . . . . . . . . . . . . . . | $1,000,000 |
| Amounts designated as interest (10% of $1,000,000 payable annually at year-end for two years) . . . . . . . . . . . . . . . . . . . . . . . . . . . . | 200,000 |
| | $1,200,000 |

Because the $1,200,000 total future payments exceed the $1,133,947 carrying amount of the debt, $66,053 interest expense ($1,200,000 − $1,133,947) is reported in the income statements during the two years following the restructuring. What interest rate is needed for the total future payments of $1,200,000 to equal the present value of the carrying amount of the debt of $1,133,947? A trial-and-error approach to the present value tables reveals that the effective interest rate is 3%. The present value calculations are shown below:

| Designation | Total Future Payments | Present Value Factor at 3% | Present Value |
|---|---|---|---|
| Principal | $1,000,000 | .94260 | $ 942,600 |
| Interest | 200,000 | 1.91347 | 191,347 |
| | $1,200,000 | | $1,133,947 |

ªObtained from an annuity present value table (applied to the $100,000 annual amount).

This example was designed so that the effective interest rate would be an even number to avoid the additional complexity of interpolating. In practice, of course, interpolating is usually necessary.

The following entries would be made for the restructuring, the recording of interest using the effective interest rate, and the payments made under the restructuring agreement:

1. January 1, 19X1:

| | | |
|---|---|---|
| Notes Payable | 1,100,000 | |
| Interest Payable | 33,947 | |
| Restructured Debt | | 1,133,947 |

To record the effect of the restructuring.

2. December 31, 19X1:

| | | |
|---|---|---|
| Interest Expense | 34,018 | |
| Restructured Debt | 65,982 | |
| Cash | | 100,000 |

To record interest expense at 3% of $1,133,947 and the first payment of $100,000.

3. December 31, 19X2:

| | | |
|---|---|---|
| Interest Expense | 32,035 | |
| Restructured Debt | 67,965 | |
| Cash | | 100,000 |

To record interest expense at 3% of $1,067,965 ($1,133,947 − $65,982) and the second payment of $100,000.

| | | |
|---|---|---|
| Restructured Debt | 1,000,000 | |
| Cash | | 1,000,000 |

To record the $1,000,000 payment at its maturity date.

The entries affecting the Restructured Debt account are recorded in the following T-account to illustrate how the use of the exact effective interest rate results in a zero balance after the last required payment.

| | Restructured Debt | | |
|---|---|---|---|
| | | 1,133,947 | Jan. 1, 19X1 |
| Dec. 31, 19X1 | 65,982 | | |
| | | 1,067,965 | |
| Dec. 31, 19X2 | 67,965 | | |
| | | 1,000,000 | |
| Dec. 31, 19X2 | 1,000,000 | | |
| | | –0– | |

# BANKRUPTCY REORGANIZATIONS

Although Chapter 11 of the bankruptcy statutes is the reorganization chapter, the statutes do not define the term *reorganization*. However, we may assume from the Chapter 11 purpose and the procedures that the chapter allows that the term is intended to have a broad meaning. Basically, a **reorganization** encompasses the development of a plan—called a *plan of reorganization*—to alter the company's liability and/or equity structure so that the company has a reasonable chance of surviving bankruptcy proceedings and prospering on its own.

Most reorganization plans involve a negotiated settlement between the company and its unsecured creditors to repay debts, usually at so many cents on the dollar. Thus, the company is provided with a "fresh start" a unique opportunity in business. Approximately 10 to 20% of all business bankruptcy filings are Chapter 11 filings (the remainder being Chapter 7 filings).

## Advantages and Disadvantages of Reorganizing under Chapter 11 versus Restructuring Outside of the Bankruptcy Courts

The primary advantage to a distressed company of a Chapter 11 reorganization is that it usually results in a massive reduction of the debtor's liabilities (forgiveness of debt) compared with the amount of debt forgiven in a restructuring outside of the bankruptcy courts. In addition, a considerable amount of cash is saved because interest on unsecured debt does not accrue during the period of the bankruptcy proceeding—the amount of unsecured creditors' claims is fixed at the bankruptcy filing. For example, Wickes Cos., a giant retailing conglomerate, saved more than $350 million of interest related to its unsecured debt during the 33 months that it was in Chapter 11 reorganization (concluded in 1985). Furthermore, filing for reorganization under Chapter 11 places a company in sanctuary from its creditors because they cannot sue for overdue payments. As a result, the distressed company has some "breathing room" to develop a plan of reorganization. When recessions and high interest rates occur, as they did in the early 1980s, increasing numbers of companies flee to the bankruptcy courts for protection from creditors and for the opportunity to salvage the potentially productive (profitable) portions of the existing organization. Also of major importance is that, with court approval, companies in Chapter 11 can make substantial wage reductions by rejecting or altering union contracts.

**What Percentage Survive Chapter 11?**   To file for reorganization under Chapter 11 is to flirt with extinction. Of all Chapter 11 filings, about only 15% emerge as viable companies—and then usually with new top management; the remainder are transferred to Chapter 7 and liquidated.

## The Sequence of Events in a Chapter 11 Filing

The typical sequence of events in a Chapter 11 filing is as follows:

1. **Filing the petition.** Either a voluntary or an involuntary petition can initiate bankruptcy proceedings. The company in question may prepare a statement showing asset values and amounts that would be paid to each class of creditor in the event of liquidation. As noted earlier, accountants called this a *statement of affairs.* We illustrate the preparation of this statement later in the chapter in connection with liquidations.
2. **Management of the company.** The debtor company's management usually continues to control and operate the debtor's day-to-day activities. Under certain conditions and for just cause (such as fraud, incompetence, or gross mismanagement of the company), and if in the best interests of creditors, the court may appoint a trustee to manage the debtor's business (Section 1104[a]). **The appointment of a trustee in a Chapter 11 filing is infrequent.** We discuss the duties of trustees later in the chapter in connection with liquidations, for which trustees are always appointed.
3. **Creditors' and equity security holders' committees.** After an order for relief has been entered, the court appoints a committee of unsecured creditors. (The court may also appoint additional committees of creditors, or of equity security holders if necessary, to ensure adequate representation of these groups. Such a court-appointed committee may

   a. select and authorize [with the court's approval] the employment by such committee of one or more attorneys, accountants, or other agents, to represent or perform services for such committee [Section 1103(a)];

b. consult with the trustee or debtor in possession concerning the administration of the case;

c. investigate the acts, conduct, assets, liabilities and financial condition of the debtor, the operation of the debtor's business and the desirability of the continuance of such business, and any other matter relevant to the case or to the formulation of a plan;

d. participate in the formulation of a plan [of reorganization], advise those represented by such committee of such committee's recommendations as to any plan formulated, and collect and file with the court acceptances of a plan;

e. request the appointment of a trustee or examiner . . . if a trustee or examiner, as the case may be, has not previously been appointed . . .; and

f. perform such other services as are in the interest of those represented [Section 1103(c)].

4. **Plan of reorganization.** Under Chapter 11 of the 1978 act, a plan of reorganization may alter the legal, equitable, and contractual rights of any class of creditors' claims, secured or unsecured, or of equity interests. Such an alteration is known as **impairment** of a claim or an interest (Section 1124). In a common plan of reorganization, all unsecured creditors agree to accept payment at a percentage of their respective claims—for example, 25 cents on the dollar—with the remainder of the debt canceled.

The debtor has the exclusive right to propose a plan during the 120 days after the order for relief. At the end of this period, any party of interest—such as the trustee, committee, a creditor, or an equity security holder—may file a plan, provided certain conditions are met (Section 1121). The role of the Securities and Exchange Commission (SEC) is quite limited:

> The Securities and Exchange Commission may raise and may appear and be heard for any issue . . . but the SEC may not appeal from any judgment, order, or decree entered in the case [Section 1109].

5. **Disclosure statement.** Before acceptance of a plan of reorganization can be solicited, the debtor must furnish the plan or a summary of the plan to the various classes of creditors and equity interests, along with a written disclosure statement approved by the court as containing **adequate information** (Section 1125[b]). Adequate information is defined as "information of a kind, and in sufficient detail, as far as is reasonably practicable in light of the nature and history of the debtor and the condition of the debtor's books and records, that would enable

a hypothetical reasonable investor . . . to make an informed judgment about the plan" (Section 1125[a][1]). This is obviously determined on a case-by-case basis.

6. **Acceptance of plan.** Each class of creditors and equity interests then votes to accept or reject the plan of reorganization. The requirements for approval are as follows:

   a. **Creditor's claims.** "A class of claims has accepted a plan if such plan has been accepted by creditors . . . that hold at least **two-thirds in amount and more than one-half in number** of the allowed claims of such class . . ." (Section 1126[c]).

   b. **Equity interests.** "A class of interests has accepted a plan if such plan has been accepted by holders of such interests . . . that hold at least **two-thirds in amount** of the allowed interests of such class . . ." (Section 1126[d]).

7. **Confirmation of the plan by the court.** After the plan of reorganization has been submitted to the court, a hearing is held. A plan must meet eleven specific requirements to be approved by the court. The overriding requirement is that the debtor must be unlikely to be liquidated or have need for further financial reorganization after the plan is confirmed. In other words, the plan of reorganization must be feasible. Another major requirement is that each class of claims or equity interests must have accepted the plan or must not be impaired under the plan. However, a provision in the law (referred to in House Committee Reports as "cram down"), allows the court to confirm the plan (if requested by the proponent of the plan) even if each class of claims or equity interests has not accepted it. For this to occur, the plan must not discriminate unfairly and must be fair and equitable with respect to each class of claims or equity interests that is impaired or has not accepted the plan (Section 1129).

   If the court does not confirm the plan of reorganization, it may, on request of a party of interest and after notice and a hearing, either dismiss the case or convert it to a Chapter 7 case (whereby the debtor is forced out of business through liquidation). Such action depends on which course is in the best interest of creditors and the estate (Section 1112).

8. **Discharge of indebtedness.** After the court confirms the plan of reorganization, the debtor is discharged of certain indebtedness as set forth in the plan. However, if the debtor has committed certain acts, then discharge of indebtedness does not occur even though a plan has been confirmed (Section 1141[d]). In general, discharge of indebtedness is not granted if (a) the debtor has not fully cooperated with the court (for example, by not making all properties and records available to the court's representative, failing to explain losses satisfactorily, or refusing to obey court orders); and if (b) the debtor has

performed certain specified acts involving the debtor's properties and records to hinder, delay, or defraud creditors (for example, concealing property, destroying records, failing to keep or preserve records, or obtaining money or property fraudulently) (Section 727[a]). A discharge is not granted if the debtor was granted a discharge in a case commenced within six years before the filing date of the petition (Section 727[a]).

9. **Exceptions to discharge of indebtedness.** Certain types of indebtedness cannot be discharged under the bankruptcy statutes. These debts, which eventually must be paid if the debtor survives Chapter 11 proceedings, are as follows:

a. Taxes owed to the United States or any state, county, district, or municipality, and customs duties.

b. Debts incurred in obtaining money, property, services, an extension renewal, or refinance of credit by either:

   (1) false pretenses, a false representation, or actual fraud, other than a statement concerning the debtor's financial condition.

   (2) use of a written statement that is materially false with respect to the debtor's financial condition on which the creditor reasonably relied and that the debtor made or published with intent to deceive.

c. Debts that have not been duly scheduled in time for proof and allowance because a creditor had no notice or knowledge of bankruptcy proceedings.

d. Debts for fraud or defalcation while acting in a fiduciary capacity, or larceny.

e. Debts related to willful and malicious injury by the debtor to another entity or to the property of another entity.

f. Fines, penalties, and forfeitures payable to and for the benefit of a governmental unit (Section 523).

## Accounting Issues

The accounting issues in bankruptcy reorganizations are the same as those discussed earlier for troubled debt restructurings—that is, how to calculate and report the amount of debt forgiven. After some initial confusion about the application of *FASB Statement No. 15* to bankruptcy reorganizations, *FASB Technical Bulletin No. 81-6* was issued to clarify the matter. This bulletin states that *FASB Statement No. 15* does not apply to bankruptcy reorganizations that result in a "general restatement of the debtor's liabilities" (defined earlier as a restructuring of most of the amount of a company's liabilities). Because this usually occurs in bankruptcy reorganizations, *FASB Statement No. 15* will rarely apply. Consequently, the following questions must be addressed:

- What is meaningful accounting for a reorganized company?
- What, if any, guidance is contained in promulgated accounting standards?

We first address the calculation of the amount of debt forgiven and then the reporting of such forgiveness.

**Calculation of Forgiveness of Debt.**   In reorganizations in which unsecured creditors are paid immediately at so many cents on the dollar, there is only one way to calculate the forgiveness. However, unsecured creditors may also be given cash and notes payable (and often equity securities as well). Traditionally, accountants have compared the amount owed with the fair value (discounted present value, in the case of debt) of the consideration given to determine the amount of debt forgiven. This method usually results in a much larger reported forgiveness ("gain") than would result under the *FASB Statement No. 15* approach of comparing the carrying amount of the debt (essentially the amount owed) with the undiscounted total future payments. To illustrate the dramatic difference that can occur, we assume that a company in bankruptcy reorganization proceedings proposes to settle with its unsecured creditors (who are owed $10,000,000) by paying $2,000,000 cash and giving $5,000,000 of 14% (assumed market rate) notes payable due in five years. The amount of debt forgiven under each approach is calculated as follows:

| | Fair Value of Consideration Given Approach | Total Future Payments Approach of *FASB Statement No. 15* |
|---|---|---|
| Carrying amount of debt............ | $10,000,000 | $10,000,000 |
| Amounts to be compared with carrying amount of debt: | (fair value) | (total future payments) |
| Cash ........................ | $ 2,000,000 | $ 2,000,000 |
| Notes payable ............... | 5,000,000 | 5,000,000 |
| Interest ($5,000,000 × 14% × 5 years) .............. | n/a | 3,500,000 |
| | $ 7,000,000 | $10,500,000 |
| Post-reorganization carrying value of the debt................ | $ 7,000,000 | $10,000,000 |
| Amount of debt forgiven ("gain")......................... | $ 3,000,000 | None |
| Future interest expense............ | $700,000 per year for the next five years | $500,000 total over the next five years |

Most reorganization plans attempt to structure a positive stockholders' equity (though not necessarily positive retained earnings) to place the company on firmer ground for emerging from bankruptcy proceedings.

To measure and report this effect is exceedingly difficult under the approach of *FASB Statement No. 15*. The pronouncement itself, if applicable, might very well be counterproductive to obtaining an agreement with the unsecured creditors concerning necessary sacrifices. (If applicable, the pronouncement requires much greater sacrifices by creditors to achieve a positive net worth.) This possibility may have been part of the FASB's rationale for exempting bankruptcy reorganizations from *FASB Statement No. 15* guidance. Another possible reason for the exemption involves the "fresh start" purpose of reorganizations under Chapter 11. Future income statements should reflect a reasonable amount of interest expense on restructured debt. This occurs under the "fair value of consideration given" approach but rarely occurs under the *FASB Statement No. 15* approach.

**Imputing of Interest.**   The imputing of interest issue, discussed earlier in connection with troubled debt restructurings, also pertains to bankruptcy reorganizations. Unfortunately, the current accounting literature gives no explicit guidance concerning whether or not to impute interest in bankruptcy reorganizations.[7] Our inquiries to practicing accountants who are involved in bankruptcy reorganizations reveal that some companies are imputing interest under the principles of *APB Opinion No. 21*, "Interest on Receivables and Payables," and others are not.

**Reporting Forgiveness of Debt.**   Current accounting pronouncements also do not explicitly state how to report (classify) a forgiveness of debt in bankruptcy proceedings. Some practicing accountants perceive the forgiveness of debt as a "gain from extinguishment of debt" and report it as an extraordinary item, if material, pursuant to the requirements of *FASB Statement No. 4*, "Reporting Gains and Losses from Extinguishment of Debt," paragraph 8. Practicing accountants who perceive the forgiveness of debt as a capital contribution credit it directly to Paid-in Capital. The latter treatment is usually found when the common stockholder accounts are adjusted on reorganization to eliminate an accumulated deficit as in quasi-reorganization accounting.

## The Role of Accountants in Bankruptcy Reorganizations

Certified public accountants are commonly employed in varying capacities in bankruptcy proceedings. Many accounting firms can generate

---

[7]This guidance was clear prior to the issuance of *FASB Statement No. 15*, because *FASB Interpretation No. 2*, "Imputing Interest on Debt Arrangements Made under the Federal Bankruptcy Act," extended the principles of *APB Opinion No. 21*, "Interest on Receivables and Payables," to bankruptcy reorganizations. Unfortunately, *FASB Interpretation No. 2* was expunged from the literature on the issuance of *FASB Statement No. 15* (supporting accountants who thought *FASB Statement No. 15* applied to bankruptcy reorganizations), and *FASB Technical Bulletin No. 81-6* did not reinstate it. It is not known whether this was an oversight or purposeful.

substantial fees for their services in this area. (The new bankruptcy statutes eliminated the longstanding requirement that accountants set their fees in a "spirit of economy"; bankruptcy assistance is no longer considered charity work.) The most common capacity for outside accountants is that of rendering advice and assistance on financial projections used in developing a plan of reorganization. Both the distressed company and its creditors' committee commonly hire their own outside accountants. Occasionally, outside accountants are responsible for determining the quality of the distressed company's accounts receivable. If management is suspected of improper actions, bankruptcy judges may need to appoint outside accountants to investigate such charges. The creditors' committee often hires outside accountants to determine the following:

1. Has the debtor made any transfers of assets that would constitute preferences to certain creditors?
2. Has management committed any acts that would constitute fraud, deception, or bad faith?
3. Has management committed any acts that would bar it from obtaining a discharge of certain indebtedness?
4. In what condition are the company's books and records?
5. What would be obtained in liquidation? Answering this question requires the preparation of a statement of affairs, which is discussed and illustrated later in the chapter.

The creditors' accountants need not perform an audit of the debtor's financial statements to be of assistance in these areas; a limited special purpose examination is usually sufficient. Obviously the scope of any such limited examination must be worked out with the creditors' committee.

## LIQUIDATIONS

Large companies with common stock that is publicly traded on the New York Stock Exchange are seldom liquidated because they usually have adequate capital and managerial talent to deal with adverse developments. The growing trend toward diversification also works against liquidation. A large, diverse business is less apt to be affected overall by an adverse development resulting from poor management decisions in one of its industry segments. Furthermore, if management cannot deal effectively with such problems in one of its industry segments, that segment will most likely be disposed of through sale (or possibly abandonment), but the remainder of the business will continue. Consequently, liquidation is generally associated with small and moderately sized businesses. The smaller and more unseasoned a company is, the more likely it is to face liquidation.

## Liquidation Outside of the Bankruptcy Courts

In some instances, liquidation may take place outside of the bankruptcy courts. In these situations, a formal **general assignment for the benefit of creditors** usually is executed, whereby the debtor's property is transferred to a designated assignee or assignees (who are often the debtor's creditors) for the purpose of converting the assets into cash and making appropriate distributions of cash to the creditors. Any assets that remain after creditors have been paid in full are returned to the debtor for ultimate distribution to its stockholders. However, if the proceeds from the conversion of assets into cash are insufficient to pay creditors in full, then the creditors have no other recourse and the stockholders receive nothing.

There are three possible advantages of liquidating outside of the bankruptcy court:

1. Legal fees are usually lower.
2. The debtor can designate the assignee or assignees.
3. There is greater flexibility in the conversion of assets into cash.

Under an *involuntary* proceeding, a general assignment for the benefit of creditors is considered grounds for the bankruptcy court to enter an order for relief. Accordingly, to avoid liquidation through the bankruptcy court, a general assignment must be agreed to by all of the creditors for all practical purposes. If a sufficient number of qualified creditors subsequently file an involuntary petition of bankruptcy, the general assignment for the benefit of creditors is null and void, and the bankruptcy court then supervises and controls the liquidation of the company.

## Liquidation through Bankruptcy Court

After a company has filed for liquidation under Chapter 7, one of the court's first duties is to determine if the case should be dismissed. As we mentioned at the beginning of the chapter, the filing of a voluntary petition constitutes an order for relief. Dismissals of voluntary filings are infrequent. When the debtor does not dispute an involuntary petition, the court enters an order for relief against the debtor. Dismissals of uncontested involuntary filings are also infrequent. However, if the debtor disputes an involuntary petition, then a trial must be held to determine whether the case should be dismissed or an order for relief should be entered.

**The Role of the Trustee.**   After an order for relief has been entered, the bankruptcy court must promptly appoint an interim trustee (Section 701[a]). In an involuntary filing, the debtor may continue to operate the business from the filing date until an order for relief is entered, just as though the petition had not been filed (Section 303[f]). However, the court may appoint an interim trustee during this period, if necessary, to preserve the property of the estate or to prevent loss to the estate, providing certain procedures are followed (Section 303[g]).

After an order for relief has been entered, the court must also call a meeting of the debtor's creditors (Section 341). In this meeting, the creditors first vote for a trustee and then select a creditor's committee that consults with the trustee in connection with the administration of the estate. If the creditors are unable to select a trustee, then the interim trustee becomes the trustee (Section 702[d]). Trustees are usually professionals, mostly practicing lawyers, who specialize in this type of work. The following duties of trustees are set forth under Section 704:

1. Collect and reduce to money the property of the estate for which such trustee serves, and close up such estate as expeditiously as is compatible with the best interests of parties of interest.
2. Be accountable for all property received.
3. Investigate the financial affairs of the debtor.
4. If a purpose would be served, examine proofs of claims and object to the allowance of any claim that is improper. . . .
5. Unless the court orders otherwise, furnish such information concerning the estate and the estate's administration as is requested by a party of interest.
6. If the business of the debtor is authorized to be operated, file with the court and with any governmental unit charged with responsibility for collection or determination of any tax arising out of such operation, periodic reports and summaries of the operation of such business, including a statement of receipts and disbursements, and such other information as the court requires. (Under Section 721, "the court may authorize the trustee to operate the business of the debtor for a limited period, if such operation is in the best interest of the estate and consistent with the orderly liquidation of the estate.")
7. Make a final report and file a final account of the administration of the estate with the court.

Accounting by trustees is discussed in detail later in the chapter.

**Technical Aspects of the Duties of Trustees.**   The following technical aspects of the duties of the trustee should be noted:

1. **Employment of professionals.** With the court's approval, the trustee may employ attorneys, accountants, appraisers, auctioneers, or other professional persons to represent or assist the trustee in carrying out his or her duties (Section 327).

2. **Avoidance powers.** A trustee is authorized to void both **fraudulent** and **preferential** transfers made by the debtor within certain specified periods preceding the filing date. (Such transfers include the giving of a security interest in a property.) Creditors, therefore, may be required to return monies and/or properties recovered or may lose their security interest, or both. The section of the act dealing with preferences is intended to prevent a debtor from giving certain creditors preferential treatment over other creditors. The 1978 act sets forth the conditions that must exist for a trustee to void a property transfer to a creditor. The act also sets forth certain transfers that a trustee cannot void.

3. **Setoffs.** With respect to mutual debts between the debtor and allowable claims of a creditor, the amount owed the debtor by the creditors is subtracted from or offset against the amount owed to the creditor (Section 553). (There are certain technical exceptions to this rule that we need not deal with now.)

**Distribution of Cash to Creditors.** The sequence of payments to creditors is as follows:

1. The proceeds from the sale of assets that have been pledged to secured creditors are applied to satisfy those claims. Note that the bankruptcy proceedings do not alter the rights of the secured creditors to the assets that have been pledged to them; these rights are only temporarily suspended.

2. If the proceeds exceed the secured creditors' claims, then such excess is available for payment to creditors with priority and unsecured creditors.

3. If the proceeds are insufficient to satisfy the claims of the secured creditors, the secured creditors become unsecured creditors to the extent of the deficiency.

4. The proceeds from the sale of unpledged assets are used to pay creditors with priority.

5. After creditors with priority have been paid, payments are made to the unsecured creditors. Payments are always stated as a percentage of all allowed claims.

6. To the extent that any creditors are not paid in full, the deficiency represents a loss.

After the final payment has been made to the unsecured creditors, the corporation is a **shell** corporation without any assets or liabilities. In most instances, the corporation then ceases its legal existence. The bankruptcy court is not authorized to grant a formal discharge of indebtedness with respect to any unpaid claims when the debtor is other than an individual (Section 727[a][1]). According to House Bankruptcy committee reports, this change is intended to prevent trafficking in corporate shells and bankrupt partnerships.

The selling of assets and the payment of proceeds to the debtor's various creditors does not always conclude a liquidation. Trustees may file suit against former directors and officers, asking for monetary damages on the grounds of gross negligence in the management of certain aspects of the business. When a sudden collapse of a company occurs shortly after its outside auditors have issued an unqualified ("clean") audit report on the company's financial statements, serious questions may be raised concerning the performance of the audit. In such situations, the auditors may be sued for alleged breach of performance.

**The Role of the Accountant in Liquidations.**    Bankruptcy trustees often employ certified public accountants to assist them in preserving the assets of the bankrupt's estate. The extent of the accountant's services usually depend on the complexity of the estate. If the debtor's in-house accountants have not resigned before the bankruptcy petition is filed, they generally leave shortly thereafter. A certified public accountant can provide the following types of services to the bankruptcy trustee:

1. Determining what accounting books and records exist at the debtor's offices.
2. Determining the condition of the accounting records, including the filing status of all tax reports.
3. Updating the debtor's accounting records as necessary.
4. Preparing current-year tax reports and informational forms.
5. Comparing creditors' claims (as filed with the court) with the debtor's books and records and with the schedule of liabilities filed with the court by the debtor.
6. In certain instances, if fraud is suspected or known, the accountant may examine certain of the debtor's books and records in detail and submit a formal report to the trustee.

This list is not exhaustive—the accountant may be called upon to perform any service within the realm of accounting expertise.

## The Statement of Affairs

Regardless of whether liquidation takes place outside of or through bankruptcy court, a special **statement of affairs** is prepared showing the financial condition of the company. The statement of affairs is prepared on the basis that the company is going out of business. Because the company is not considered a going concern, the historical cost basis for carrying assets loses its significance, and the amount expected to be realized in liquidation is the relevant valuation basis.

The statement of affairs provides information concerning how much money each class of creditors can expect to receive on liquidation of the company, assuming assets are converted into cash at the estimated realizable values used in preparing the statements. Thus, conventional classifications such as current assets and current liabilities lose their significance. Instead, assets are classified as to whether they are pledged with creditors or not pledged with creditors; liabilities are classified by category of creditor—namely, creditors with priority, secured creditors, and unsecured creditors. Stockholders' equity also loses its significance because companies in the process of liquidation usually have a negative net worth. The specific categories of assets and liabilities in the statement of affairs are as follows:

### Assets

1. **Assets pledged with fully secured creditors** are expected to realize an amount at least sufficient to satisfy the related debt.
2. **Assets pledged with partially secured creditors** are expected to realize an amount below the related debt.
3. **Free assets** are not pledged and are available to satisfy the claims of creditors with priority, partially secured creditors, and unsecured creditors.

### Liabilities

1. **Liabilities with priority** have priority under the bankruptcy statutes (explained earlier in the chapter).
2. **Fully secured creditors** expect to be paid in full as a result of their having sufficient collateral (pledged assets) to satisfy the indebtedness.
3. **Partially secured creditors** have collateral (pledged assets), the proceeds of which are expected to be insufficient to satisfy the indebtedness.
4. **Unsecured creditors** have no collateral (pledged assets) relating to their indebtedness.

Contingent liabilities that are reasonably calculable and probable as to payment (the criteria under *FASB Statement No. 5*, "Accounting for Contingencies") are shown in the statement of affairs. Contingent liabilities that do not meet these criteria should be disclosed in a note to the statement of affairs.

ILLUSTRATION
## The Statement of Affairs

The balance sheet of Fold-up Company which filed a voluntary bankruptcy petition (for liquidation under Chapter 7) on September 23, 19X5, is shown in Illustration 19-3. Additional information regarding realization follows:

### ■ ILLUSTRATION 19-3
### A Balance Sheet for a Company in Chapter 11 Bankruptcy Proceedings

| FOLD-UP COMPANY<br>Balance Sheet<br>September 23, 19X5 | |
|---|---:|
| **Assets** | |
| **Current Assets** | |
| Cash......................................................... | $    2,000 |
| Notes receivable.......................................... | 5,000 |
| Accounts receivable, net................................. | 25,000 |
| Inventory: | |
| Finished goods........................................ | 40,000 |
| Work in process....................................... | 30,000 |
| Raw materials......................................... | 20,000 |
| Supplies .................................................. | 5,000 |
| Prepayments.............................................. | 8,000 |
| Total Current Assets ............................... | $135,000 |
| **Noncurrent Assets** | |
| Land....................................................... | 70,000 |
| Building, net ............................................. | 110,000 |
| Equipment, net........................................... | 60,000 |
| Deferred charges......................................... | 15,000 |
| Total Assets...................................... | $390,000 |
| **Liabilities and Stockholders' Deficiency** | |
| **Current Liabilities** | |
| 10% Notes payable to bank, secured by accounts receivable ... | $  35,000 |
| Accounts payable ......................................... | 246,000 |
| Accrued liabilities: | |
| Interest ($2,000 to bank, $6,000 to insurance company).... | 8,000 |
| Salaries and wages .................................... | 7,000 |
| Payroll taxes.......................................... | 2,000 |
| Total Current Liabilities............................ | $298,000 |
| **Long-term Debt** | |
| 8% Notes payable to insurance company, secured by land and building ............................................... | 175,000 |
| Total Liabilities ................................... | $473,000 |
| **Stockholders' Deficiency** | |
| Common stock, no par.................................... | $100,000 |
| Accumulated deficit...................................... | (183,000) |
| Total Stockholders' Deficiency........................ | $ (83,000) |
| Total Liabilities in Excess of Stockholders' Deficiency ..... | $390,000 |

1. **Receivables.** The notes and accounts receivable are considered to have been adequately provided for in preparing the balance sheet; thus, the company expects to realize the amounts shown.
2. **Finished goods.** The finished goods can be sold for $47,000; however, the company expects to incur $4,000 of direct selling and shipping costs.
3. **Work in process.** The work in process can be completed if $3,000 of direct costs are incurred for labor. On completion, this inventory can be sold for $37,000; however, the company expects to incur $2,000 of direct selling and shipping costs.
4. **Raw materials.** The raw materials can be converted into finished goods if $7,000 of direct costs are incurred for labor. On completion, this inventory can be sold for $19,000; however, the company expects to incur $1,000 of direct selling and shipping costs.
5. **Supplies.** The supplies will be substantially consumed in the completion of the work in process and the conversion of raw materials into finished goods. The estimated realizable value of the remaining supplies after completion and conversion is $1,000.
6. **Prepayments.** The prepayments are expected to expire during the liquidation period.
7. **Land.** The land has a current market value of $90,000.
8. **Building.** The building has a current market value of $135,000.
9. **Equipment.** The equipment can be sold in auction for an estimated $35,000.
10. **Deferred charges.** Deferred charges include organization costs, issuance expenses relating to the notes payable to the insurance company, and plant rearrangement costs.
11. **Salaries and wages.** All salaries and wages were earned within the last 90 days, and no employee is owed more than $2,000.
12. **Liquidation expenses.** The company estimates that $15,000 in court and filing fees, appraisal fees, and legal and accounting fees will be incurred in connection with the liquidation. No amounts have been provided in these expenses at September 23, 19X5.
13. **Accounts payable.** Accounts payable include $6,000 to the company's attorneys for legal work incurred in connection with patent research and collection efforts on certain accounts receivable that have been written off. Accounts payable also include $5,000 owed to the company's certified public accountants in connection with the December 31, 19X4, audit of the company's financial statements.

A statement of affairs prepared using the above information is shown in Illustration 19-4. The following points are important for understanding Illustration 19-4.

1. The book value column is shown only for purposes of tying into the September 23, 19X5, balance sheet, which was prepared in the conventional manner.
2. Each asset and liability is assigned to its appropriate descriptive category. The categories themselves are the key to producing the desired information—that is, how much money can the unsecured creditors expect to receive in liquidation?
3. Accrued interest payable is classified with the debt to which it relates, because the pledged assets are security for both the principal and the interest.
4. Although the company has not recorded the $15,000 of estimated liquidation expenses in its general ledger at September 23, 19X5, the statement of affairs should reflect this estimate so that it is as useful as possible.
5. Legal and accounting fees incurred in connection with matters not related to the bankruptcy are not considered debts with priority under the bankruptcy statutes.
6. The bank is an unsecured creditor to the extent of $12,000, the amount by which the $25,000 collateral is insufficient to satisfy its $37,000 claim.
7. The unsecured creditors are estimated to receive $149,000 of the $258,000 owed them. This figure is often expressed in terms of recovery per dollar owed. In this situation, it would be 58 cents on the dollar ($149,000 ÷ $258,000).

Once a liquidation has occurred, no accounting issues exist for the former company. An accountant performing services for a trustee in liquidation, however, should have a basic familiarity with the liquidation process.

## ACCOUNTING BY TRUSTEES

The accountability of trustees to the bankruptcy court was set forth earlier in the discussion of liquidations under Chapter 7 of the Bankruptcy Reform Act of 1978. The same accountability exists in reorganizations under Chapter 11 of the 1978 act in which a trustee is appointed to operate the debtor's business. The act sets forth specific requirements concerning the type of report or reports rendered to the courts by trustees only when the debtor's business is operated by a trustee. In most liquidation cases, normal operations cease immediately. Accordingly, we discuss accounting by trustees in liquidations separately from reorganizations (when normal operations continue).

## ■ ILLUSTRATION 19-4
### A Statement of Affairs for a Company in Bankruptcy Proceedings

**FOLD-UP COMPANY**
**Statement of Affairs**
**September 23, 19X5**

| Book Value | Assets | Estimated Current Value | Estimated Amount Available for Unsecured Creditors | Gain or Loss on Realization |
|---|---|---|---|---|
| | **Assets Pledged with Fully Secured Creditors** | | | |
| $ 70,000 | Land | $ 90,000 | | $ 20,000 |
| 110,000 | Building | 135,000 | | 25,000 |
| | | $225,000 | | |
| | Less—Fully secured claims (from liability side) | (181,000) | $ 44,000 | |
| | **Assets Pledged with Partially Secured Creditors** | | | |
| 25,000 | Accounts receivable | $ 25,000 | | |
| | (Deducted on liability side) | | | |
| | **Free Assets** | | | |
| 2,000 | Cash | $ 2,000 | 2,000 | |
| 5,000 | Notes receivable | 5,000 | 5,000 | |
| | Inventory: | | | |
| 40,000 | Finished goods | 43,000[a] | 43,000 | 3,000 |
| 30,000 | Work in process | 32,000[b] | 32,000 | 2,000 |
| 20,000 | Raw materials | 11,000[c] | 11,000 | (9,000) |
| 5,000 | Supplies | 1,000 | 1,000 | (4,000) |
| 8,000 | Prepayments | | | (8,000) |
| 60,000 | Equipment | 35,000 | 35,000 | (25,000) |
| 15,000 | Deferred charges | | | (15,000) |
| | Estimated amount available for unsecured creditors, including creditors with priority | | $173,000 | |
| | Less—Liabilities with priority (from liability side) | | (24,000) | |
| | Estimated amount available for unsecured creditors | | $149,000 | |
| | Estimated deficiency to unsecured creditors (plug) | | 109,000 | |
| $390,000 | | | | $(11,000) |
| | Total Unsecured Debt | | $258,000 | |

[a]Net of $4,000 of estimated disposal costs.
[b]Net of $3,000 of estimated labor to complete and $2,000 of disposal costs.
[c]Net of $7,000 of estimated labor to convert into finished goods and $1,000 of disposal costs.

## ■ ILLUSTRATION 19-4 (continued)

**FOLD-UP COMPANY**
**Statement of Affairs**
**September 23, 19X5**

| Book Value | Liabilities and Stockholders' Deficiency | | Amount Unsecured |
|---|---|---|---|
| | **Liabilities with Priority** | | |
| $  –0– | Estimated liquidation expenses...................... | $  15,000 | |
| 7,000 | Salaries and wages................................... | 7,000 | |
| 2,000 | Payroll taxes ........................................ | 2,000 | |
| | (deducted from amount available for unsecured creditors on asset side) ........................... | $  24,000 | |
| | **Fully Secured Creditors** | | |
| 175,000 | Notes payable to insurance company ................ | $175,000 | |
| 6,000 | Accrued interest on notes........................... | 6,000 | |
| | Total (deducted on asset side).................... | $181,000 | |
| | **Partially Secured Creditors** | | |
| 35,000 | Note payable to bank ............................... | $  35,000 | |
| 2,000 | Accrued interest on note............................ | 2,000 | |
| | | $  37,000 | |
| | Less—Pledged accounts receivable (from asset side) . | (25,000) | $  12,000 |
| | **Unsecured Creditors** | | |
| 246,000 | Accounts payable and accruals ...................... | | 246,000 |
| (83,000) | Stockholders' deficiency | | |
| $390,000 | | | |
| | Total Unsecured Debt ............................. | | $258,000 |

## Accounting in Liquidation

When normal operations immediately cease, the preparation of an operating statement for the period covering the trustee's administration of the estate is inappropriate. This holds true even when a trustee, with the court's permission, continues the operations necessary to convert work in process (and possibly raw materials) into finished goods. Such activities by themselves do not constitute normal operations; accordingly, costs incurred in this regard are treated as bankruptcy administration costs. Because the 1978 act does not prescribe the type of report or reports rendered by trustees when normal operations are not conducted (as was the case under the old law), each bankruptcy court establishes its own requirements. Most bankruptcy courts simply require a written explanation as to the disposition of the various assets and a statement of cash receipts and disbursements. Such a statement typically shows the following: (1) cash balances of the debtor that were turned over to the trustee at the trustee's appointment; (2) the proceeds from the conversion of non-cash assets into cash; (3) cash disbursements (which are usually limited to bankruptcy administration costs); (4) the remaining cash balance available for distribution to creditors; and (5) a summary of how the remaining cash balance should be distributed to the various classes of creditors (including creditors with priority). In most cases, only one report is rendered (called the *final report*). In some cases, cash is distributed to creditors on an interim basis, after an interim report proposing such a distribution is filed with and approved by the court. Some courts require the cash disbursements in summary form only; others require detail by check number, payee, and purpose of disbursement.

Most trustees find it expedient to (1) open a separate checking account for each estate they administer, and (2) use the related cash receipts and disbursements records to prepare the required statement of cash receipts and disbursements. Trustees usually do not use the debtor's general ledger or any of the debtor's journals to record transactions and events. If the court or creditors desire information that relates the trustee's activity with the book balances existing when the trustee was appointed, then a **statement of realization and liquidation** can be prepared. Such a statement for Fold-up Company is shown in Illustration 19-5. The beginning balances are taken from Illustration 19-3. The activity during the assumed period that the trustee administers the estate is consistent with the estimated amounts and information provided in the data used to prepare the statement of affairs in Illustration 19-4.

In some cases, a trustee may be authorized to operate the debtor's business. This is often done when a greater amount may be realized by selling the business in its entirety rather than in piecemeal, and when a greater amount may be realized by selling an active business rather than one that has been shut down. The accounting reports rendered during the time that a trustee operates the debtor's business are the same as those required in reorganizations, which are discussed in the following section.

## Accounting in Reorganization

When a trustee is appointed in a Chapter 11 reorganization, the new law requires trustees to submit

> periodic reports and summaries of the operation of such business, including a statement of receipts and disbursements, and such other information as the court requires [Sections 704 and 1106].

**■ ILLUSTRATION 19-5**
**A Statement of Realization and Liquidation**

**FOLD-UP COMPANY**
**Statement of Realization and Liquidation**
**For the Period September 23, 19X5, to May 18, 19X6**

| | Assets | | Liabilities | | | | Stockholders' |
| --- | --- | --- | --- | --- | --- | --- | --- |
| | Cash | Noncash | With Priority | Fully Secured | Partially Secured | Unsecured | Deficiency |
| Book Balances, September 23, 19X5 (from Illustration 19-4) | $ 2,000 | $388,000 | $ 9,000 | $181,000 | $37,000 | $246,000 | $ (83,000) |
| **Cash Receipts** | | | | | | | |
| Collection of note receivable and related interest | 5,200 | (5,000) | | | | | 200 |
| Proceeds from sale of inventory, net of $16,700 "actual" direct costs | 85,800[a] | (90,000) | | | | | (4,200) |
| Proceeds from sale of supplies | 1,100[a] | (5,000) | | | | | (3,900) |
| Proceeds from sale of equipment | 35,400[a] | (60,000) | | | | | (24,600) |
| Proceeds from sale of land and building, net of $181,000 withheld by title company to pay off fully secured creditor | 45,500[a] | (180,000) | | (181,000) | | | 46,500 |
| **Cash Disbursements** | | | | | | | |
| Payment of bankruptcy administration costs, net of $16,700 "actual" inventory conversion and selling costs shown above | (2,000) | | | | | | (2,000) |
| **Other** | | | | | | | |
| Amortization of prepaids | | (8,000) | | | | | (8,000) |
| Write-off of deferred charges | | (15,000) | | | | | (15,000) |
| Release of accounts receivable to partially secured creditor | | (25,000) | | | (25,000) | | |
| Reclassification of residual amount to unsecured status | | | | | (12,000) | 12,000 | |
| Accrual of bankruptcy administration costs | | | 12,600 | | | | (12,600) |
| Book Balances, May 18, 19X6 | $173,000 | $ -0- | $21,600 | $ -0- | $ -0- | $258,000 | $(106,600) |
| Proposed distribution | $173,000 | | $21,600 (100%) | | | $151,400 (58.7%) | |

[a]The actual proceeds here are purposely slightly different from the "estimated" current values shown in Illustration 19-4, inasmuch as it is highly unlikely that the actual proceeds would agree with the estimated proceeds in a real-world situation.

In addition to these items, the courts usually require that a balance sheet be presented whenever operating statements or summaries are furnished. In most cases, trustees find it practical to use the debtor's books and records to record transactions and events. However, the date the trustee was appointed is usually recorded so that the activity during the trustee's administration can be reported separately. Also, a distinction is usually made between (1) assets on hand and liabilities owed at the trustee's appointment, and (2) assets acquired and liabilities incurred during the trustee's administration. This distinction is necessary because trustees are responsible for the acquisition and realization of new assets as opposed to only the realization of old assets, and for the incurrence and liquidation of new liabilities as opposed to only the liquidation of old liabilities.

The preparation of required reports and statements presents no unusual problems when the trustee uses the debtor's books and records. In some cases a trustee may account for some or all of the debtor's assets and operations in a new set of books. In this case, the transfer of assets to the new set of books and the accounting for subsequent operations parallels the accounting for a home office and a branch. Accordingly, the balances and activity on each set of books must be combined to the extent necessary in preparing financial reports. Traditionally, advanced accounting textbooks have included a discussion and illustration of a somewhat involved statement of realization and liquidation encompassing assets, liabilities, and operations. However, current practice favors the use of the separate conventional financial statements, and we do not present a discussion and illustration of this single comprehensive statement.

## CONCLUDING COMMENTS

Most companies in serious financial difficulty never recover and must be liquidated. A company that can feasibly effect a successful recovery must show complete honesty and good faith with its creditors during this difficult period. Creditors should realize that often they can minimize their losses if a successful troubled debt restructuring can be achieved. The use of professionals in insolvency proceedings can minimize the procedural problems and help the company and its creditors to be realistic in arriving at an acceptable plan of recovery.

Not all proposed troubled debt restructurings succeed. Many are rejected as infeasible, with liquidation best serving the creditors' interests. Others are rejected as a result of evidence of management fraud, deception, or bad faith—again, liquidation best serves the creditors' interests. Consequently, an accountant furnishing assistance to a debtor or a creditors' committee must be skeptical, alert, and imaginative in carrying out this difficult assignment.

# END-OF-CHAPTER REVIEW

## Summary of Key Points

1. The accounting issues involved with troubled debt restructurings include how to calculate whether any debt has been forgiven and how to report a forgiveness of debt. *FASB Statement No. 15* does not allow the imputing of interest in making this calculation.
2. The total amount owed (the "carrying amount of the debt") is compared with the total amount to be paid back (the "total future payments").
3. If the total future payments exceed the carrying amount of the debt, the excess is reported as interest expense between the restructuring date and the maturity date. However, if the carrying amount of the debt exceeds the total future payments, a forgiveness of debt results. *FASB Statement No. 15* treats a forgiveness of debt as a gain reported as an extraordinary item, if material.
4. As a result of these procedures, the debtor's future income statements reflect either no interest expense (when a forgiveness of debt results) or unrealistically low interest expense (when no forgiveness of debt results) until the maturity date of the debt.
5. In most instances, *FASB Statement No. 15* does not apply to either quasi-reorganizations or formal bankruptcy reorganizations under Chapter 11 of the bankruptcy statutes. In these situations, the amount owed is compared with the consideration given in settlement.
6. Because the current accounting literature does not state specifically how to calculate and report a forgiveness of debt in formal reorganizations, some companies do not impute interest in making this calculation, whereas others do. Some companies treat the forgiveness of debt as a gain, while others treat it as a capital contribution.

## Glossary of New Terms

**Creditors with priority** A special class of creditors created by the bankruptcy statutes. These creditors are entitled to payment before a debtor's other unsecured creditors may be paid.

**Debtor** Under the bankruptcy statutes, a debtor is the party that is the subject of a bankruptcy proceeding.

**Estate** Under the bankruptcy statutes, all of a debtor's property.

**Impairment** The alteration of the rights of a creditor or equity holder in a bankruptcy reorganization case.

**Involuntary petition** The filing of a petition by the creditors of a company in financial distress to have the distressed company liquidated or financially reorganized under the control and supervision of the bankruptcy court.

**Liquidation** The process of converting a company's assets into cash, paying off creditors to the extent possible, and ceasing operations.

**Quasi-reorganization** A process outside of bankruptcy court for eliminating a deficit balance in Retained Earnings (properly called an accumulated deficit) to give the entity a "fresh start."

**Reorganization**   The altering of a distressed company's liability and/or equity structure under Chapter 11 of the bankruptcy statutes for purposes of financially rehabilitating the company to avoid liquidation.

**Restatement of liabilities generally**   Restructurings or modifications of debt that encompass most of the debtor's liabilities coincidentally with either a reorganization under Chapter 11 of the bankruptcy statutes or a quasi-reorganization.

**Setoffs**   In a bankruptcy proceeding, offsetting amounts owed to a debtor by a creditor against amounts owed to that creditor by the debtor.

**Troubled debt restructuring**   The granting of a concession by a creditor because of a debtor's financial difficulties.

**Voluntary petition**   The filing of a petition with the bankruptcy court by a company in financial distress to have the company liquidated or financially reorganized under the control and supervision of the bankruptcy court.

# Self-Study Questions
*(Answers are at the end of this chapter.)*

## I. BANKRUPTCY LAW: FILING THE PETITION AND DEBTS WITH PRIORITY

1. Which of the entities listed below are entitled to file a voluntary bankruptcy petition under Chapter 7 or 11?
   a. A banking corporation.
   b. A partnership.
   c. A corporation that manufactures consumer goods.
   d. A corporation that provides personal services.
   e. A municipal corporation.
   f. A railroad.
   g. An insurance corporation.

2. Select the entities in question 1 that may have an involuntary bankruptcy petition filed against them.

3. In which of the following situations could an involuntary bankruptcy petition be filed?
   a. The debtor has debts of at least $5,000.
   b. The appropriate number of creditors required to sign the petition are owed at least $5,000.
   c. The debtor has committed a fraudulent act.
   d. The debtor has recently appointed a custodian.
   e. The debtor has made asset transfers that constitute a preference to one or more creditors.
   f. Wages are owed to employees for more than 90 days.
   g. The debtor is not paying its debts as they mature.
   h. The debtor has entered into discussions with its creditors to restructure its debt.
   i. The debtor's net worth is negative as a result of operating losses.

4. Which of the following debts have priority under the bankruptcy statutes?
   a. Amounts owed to secured creditors.
   b. In an involuntary petition, amounts owed to the creditors who signed the petition.

   c. Costs of administering the bankruptcy proceedings.

   d. Debts incurred by issuing materially false statements as to financial condition.

   e. All wages owed to employees that were earned within 90 days prior to filing the bankruptcy petition.

   f. Wages of up to $2,000 per employee, no matter when earned.

   g. Taxes owed to the United States or any state or subdivision thereof.

## II. BANKRUPTCY LAW: REORGANIZATION UNDER CHAPTER 11

5. Each of the following statements is true except

   a. In a Chapter 11 reorganization, management usually continues to operate the business.

   b. The legal and contractual rights of any class of creditors may be altered or impaired under a plan of reorganization.

   c. A plan of reorganization must be approved by the Securities and Exchange Commission.

   d. A simple majority of creditors in a class of claims is required to approve a plan of reorganization.

   e. None of the above.

6. Each of the following statements is false except

   a. A simple majority in the amount of claims in a class of creditors is required to approve the dollar amount of claims in a plan of reorganization.

   b. The bankruptcy court usually imposes a plan of reorganization on the creditors.

   c. The rights of secured creditors are eliminated when a company files for reorganization under Chapter 11.

   d. In a reorganization under Chapter 11, the discharge provisions have no meaningful application.

   e. None of the above.

## III. BANKRUPTCY LAW: LIQUIDATION UNDER CHAPTER 7

7. Each of the following statements is false except

   a. In involuntary filings under Chapter 7, the case is dismissed if the debtor contests the filing.

   b. In a Chapter 7 filing, the bankruptcy court usually appoints a trustee.

   c. In a Chapter 7 filing, management usually continues to operate the business until the liquidation is completed.

   d. The primary function of a trustee in Chapter 7 filings is to settle disputes between the debtor and the debtors' creditors.

   e. None of the above.

8. Each of the following statements is true, except

   a. When a company is liquidated under Chapter 7, all unpaid debts (except those specified in the bankruptcy statutes) are discharged by the bankruptcy court.

   b. In a Chapter 7 filing, trustees have the authority to dispose of the debtor's assets.

c. Trustees are authorized to void preferential transfers made to certain creditors.

d. The concept of creditors with priority applies to both Chapter 7 and Chapter 11 filings.

e. None of the above.

# ASSIGNMENT MATERIAL

## Review Questions

1. Between what two broad categories are the bankruptcy statutes divided (as they pertain to business corporations)?
2. What fundamental objectives do the bankruptcy statutes accomplish?
3. Under what conditions may an involuntary petition be filed?
4. What is meant by the term *creditors with priority?*
5. List the order of priority of creditors with priority.
6. In an involuntary bankruptcy filing, do secured creditors lose their right to their security?
7. Why do companies try to restructure their debt outside of Chapter 11 of the bankruptcy statutes if at all possible?
8. What are the advantages of filing for reorganization under Chapter 11 of the bankruptcy statutes?
9. Summarize the general procedures for determining if a gain on the restructuring of debt exists as set forth in *FASB Statement No. 15.*
10. How are material gains on the restructuring of debt reported in the income statement?
11. To what extent are the present procedures discussed in *APB Opinion No. 21* used in determining a gain on the restructuring of debt under *FASB Statement No. 15?*
12. What is the essence of a composition agreement?
13. What is meant by a *discharge of indebtedness* in a bankruptcy reorganization?
14. Which debts cannot be discharged in a bankruptcy reorganization?
15. Is a discharge of indebtedness automatic in a liquidation proceeding? In a reorganization proceeding?
16. How is the statement of affairs different from the balance sheet?
17. State two purposes for which a statement of affairs may be used.
18. Contrast the statement of affairs with the balance sheet.
19. Give four classifications of liabilities that can appear in a statement of affairs.

## Discussion Cases

| DC 19-1 | **Troubled Debt Restructuring: Theory** |

Debtco Company has recently completed restructuring a substantial portion of its debt with one of its major lenders, which was owed $1,000,000 of principal and $100,000 of interest as of the date the restructuring was consummated. Under the terms of the restructured debt agreement, the accrued interest of $100,000 is forgiven and the principal of $1,000,000 is to be paid two years hence, with no interest to be paid for these two years.

Debtco Company's controller has indicated to you that the company intends to value the debt owed at $826,446, which is the present value of $1,000,000 using a discount rate of 10% (the interest rate before the restructuring). This valuation results in the reporting of (1) a gain on restructuring of debt of $273,554 in the current year, (2) interest expense of $82,645 in the first year following the restructuring, and (3) interest expense of $90,909 in the second year following the restructuring. The controller gives you the following reasons why this approach best reflects the economics of the restructuring:

1. The creditor's $1,000,000 note receivable is worth no more than what the note receivable can be sold for or discounted on a nonrecourse basis.
2. If the creditor sold the note receivable to a financial institution on a nonrecourse basis, it certainly could not sell it for more than its present value using an interest rate commensurate with the issuing company's risk.
3. Considering the poor financial condition of the company, a higher rate than 10% probably would be justified. However, the controller decided not to use a rate higher than 10% to be conservative in the computation of the gain on restructuring of the debt.
4. If the value of the note receivable on the creditor's books cannot be worth more than $826,446, the excess of the carrying amount of the note payable (including accrued interest) over this amount must represent the true value of the debt forgiveness.

### Required:

1. Disregarding the requirements of *FASB Statement No. 15*, evaluate the soundness of the controller's approach.
2. Is the controller's approach conservative? What other reason might have prompted the controller to use a low interest rate?
3. What impact will this approach have on retained earnings at the end of the two years? What impact will the approach set forth in *FASB Statement No. 15* have on retained earnings?

## DC 19-2 · Troubled Debt Restructuring: Theory

Assume that *FASB Statement No. 15* required that income statements of periods subsequent to a troubled debt restructuring reflect interest expense related to restructured debt based on an interest rate commensurate with the risk associated with the restructured debt.

### Required:

How would you determine an appropriate interest rate "commensurate with the risk"?

## DC 19-3 · Bankruptcy Reorganization: Theory

You are the controller of a company that has been attempting to work out a troubled debt restructuring at lengthy meetings with its major creditors. At the last meeting, the company's president told the creditors that if they did not agree to the restructuring plan proposed by the company, management would file for reorganization under Chapter 11 of the bankruptcy statutes.

**Required:**
1. How would the accounting change as a result of restructuring the debt through the bankruptcy courts versus outside of the bankruptcy courts?
2. What is the rationale for having different rules for the restructuring of debt in bankruptcy reorganizations?

| DC 19-4 |
|---|

## Bankruptcy Reorganization: Theory

Assume you are the controller for a company that, after several years of operating losses, filed for reorganization under Chapter 11 of the bankruptcy statutes. The company's plan of reorganization was confirmed 18 months after the filing, and unsecured creditors were paid 40 cents on the dollar ($30 million was owed to these creditors). You want to report the $18 million amount of debt canceled in the income statement.

**Required:**
1. Disregarding the accounting pronouncements, evaluate whether or not a company should report income from a bankruptcy reorganization. (Try to list arguments for and against this position.)
2. What other options does the company have?
3. Why might it not make much difference which way the company reports the $18 million canceled debt?

# Exercises

| E 19-1 |
|---|

## Troubled Debt Restructuring: Modification of Terms

A company having serious financial difficulty executed an agreement with its bank whereby the currently due $500,000 note payable to the bank was extended for five years. The old interest rate of 10% was lowered to 4%. Interest is to be paid annually in arrears. Accrued interest of $20,000 as of the restructuring date was canceled.

**Required:**
1. Determine if a gain on restructuring of debt has resulted.
2. Prepare the journal entry related to the restructuring.

| E 19-2 |
|---|

## Troubled Debt Restructuring: Modification of Terms

A company having serious financial difficulty executed an agreement with one of its major vendors whereby the $800,000 account payable to the vendor was converted into a $600,000 note payable, all due and payable in two years. The interest rate on the note is 10%, with interest payable annually in arrears. The remaining $200,000 of the original note payable was canceled.

#### Required:
1. Determine if a gain on restructuring of debt has resulted.
2. Prepare the journal entry related to the restructuring.
3. How would your answer be different if the due date of the note payable were four years from the restructuring date?

---

**E 19-3**

### Troubled Debt Restructuring: Modification of Terms—Use of Present Value Concepts

A company having serious financial difficulty has entered into a restructuring agreement with a creditor that is owed $1,000,000 of principal (now due and payable) and $28,000 of interest. In the restructuring agreement, the company agrees to pay the principal in three years, with interest paid annually in arrears at 4%. The accrued interest of $28,000 is canceled.

#### Required:
1. Determine if a gain on restructuring of debt has resulted.
2. Determine the total amount of interest expense reported over the next three years.
3. Using present value tables, calculate the approximate effective interest rate.
4. Prepare the journal entries made between the restructuring date and the maturity date, assuming all required payments are made on time.

---

**E 19-4**

### Troubled Debt Restructuring: Equity Interest Granted

A company having serious financial difficulty executed an agreement with one of its note holders whereby a $100,000 note payable was converted into 30,000 shares of the company's $1 par value common stock. The common stock was traded at $2 per share on the date of the agreement.

#### Required:
1. Determine if a gain on restructuring of debt has resulted.
2. Prepare the journal entry related to the restructuring.

---

**E 19-5**

### Troubled Debt Restructuring: Transfer of Noncash Assets

A company having serious financial difficulty executed an agreement with one of its creditors whereby a $200,000 note payable and the $25,000 related accrued interest was canceled in exchange for a parcel of land. The land had cost the company $100,000 and has a current appraised value of $150,000.

**Required:**
1. Determine the amount of "gain on restructuring" to be reported.
2. Prepare the required journal entry or entries.

## Bankruptcy Reorganization: Settlement for Cash and Stock

New Life Company's plan of reorganization under Chapter 11 of the bankruptcy statutes calls for a cash payment of $4,000,000 and the issuance of 800,000 shares of its $1 par value common stock to its unsecured creditors on a pro rata basis. These unsecured creditors are composed of vendors (owed $8,000,000) and a bank (owed $3,500,000 principal and $500,000 interest). New Life's common stock is currently trading at $1.25 per share.

**Required:**
Prepare the journal entry related to this settlement.

## Bankruptcy Reorganization: Settlement for Cash and Notes

Skiddex Company's plan of reorganization under Chapter 11 of the bankruptcy statutes calls for a cash payment of $1,500,000 and the issuance of $2,000,000 of 14% notes payable to its unsecured creditors on a pro rata basis. These unsecured creditors are composed of vendors (owed $2,300,000) and a bank (owed $3,300,000 principal and $400,000 interest). (The 14% interest rate on the notes is considered reasonable under the circumstances.) The notes are to be paid in full in three years.

**Required:**
Prepare the journal entry related to this settlement.

## Statement of Affairs: Calculating Expected Settlement Amounts

The statement of affairs for Defuncto Company reflects the following amounts:

|  | Book Value | Estimated Current Value |
|---|---|---|
| **Assets** | | |
| Assets pledged with fully secured creditors..... | $150,000 | $180,000 |
| Assets pledged with partially secured creditors . | 80,000 | 60,000 |
| Free assets ................................ | 220,000 | 150,000 |
|  | $450,000 | $390,000 |
| **Liabilities** | | |
| Liabilities with priority...................... | $ 20,000 | |
| Fully secured creditors....................... | 130,000 | |
| Partially secured creditors................... | 100,000 | |
| Unsecured creditors ........................ | 260,000 | |
|  | $510,000 | |

**Required:**

Compute the amount that each class of creditors can expect to receive if assets are converted into cash at their estimated current values.

(AICPA adapted)

## Problems

### Troubled Debt Restructuring: Modification of Terms

Stallex Company, which is having serious financial difficulty, entered into an agreement with its major lender on December 31, 19X4. The amount owed to the lender was restructured as follows:

1. Of the $2,000,000 of principal owed to the lender (all of which was currently due), 10% was canceled.
2. Accrued interest of $300,000 was canceled.
3. The due date on the remaining principal amount was extended to December 31, 19X8.
4. The interest rate on the remaining principal amount was reduced from 12% to 3% for 19X5 and 19X6. For 19X7 and 19X8, the interest rate is 6%. All interest at these new rates is to be paid annually in arrears.

**Required:**

1. Determine if a gain on restructuring of debt has resulted.
2. Prepare the journal entry to record the restructuring.
3. Calculate the total amount of interest expense, if any, reported from the restructuring date to the maturity date.

### Troubled Debt Restructuring: Combination of Equity Interest Granted and Modification of Terms

Ganes Company, which is having serious financial difficulty, entered into an agreement with holders of its notes payable on December 31, 19X5. The debt was restructured as follows:

1. Of the total $14,000,000 of notes payable (all of which was currently due), $7,000,000 of principal was canceled in exchange for 300,000 shares of the company's $1 par value common stock. (The common stock had a market value of $20 per share on December 31, 19X5.)
2. The remaining $7,000,000 of principal is to bear interest at 5%, payable annually in arrears. The maturity date of this $7,000,000 was extended to December 31, 19X8.
3. Accrued interest of $350,000 was canceled.

**Required:**

1. Determine if a gain on restructuring of debt has resulted.
2. Prepare the journal entry to record the restructuring.
3. Calculate the total amount of interest expense, if any, reported from the restructuring date to the maturity date.

### Troubled Debt Restructuring: Combination of Equity Interest Granted and Modification of Terms

Lossco Company, which is having serious financial difficulty, entered into an agreement with its bondholders on December 31, 19X1. The debt was restructured as follows:

1. Of the total $25,000,000 in face value of bonds outstanding (which bear interest at 12%), $5,000,000 was canceled in exchange for 50,000 shares of a new class of preferred stock having a par value of $100.
2. The maturity date of the remaining $20,000,000 of bonds was extended to December 31, 19X3.
3. The interest rate on the $20,000,000 is 3% until maturity.
4. Of the $2,000,000 interest payable accrued at December 31, 19X1, $1,500,000 was canceled. The remaining $500,000 was paid when the restructuring agreement was signed (at the close of business on December 31, 19X1).

#### Additional Information:
1. The bonds were issued at a $700,000 premium eight years ago. The straight-line method of amortization had been used.
2. The original life of the bonds was 10 years. The bonds were due in full during 19X1 as a result of a default in the interest payments.

#### Required:
1. Determine if a gain on restructuring of debt has resulted.
2. Prepare the journal entry to record the restructuring.
3. Calculate the total amount of interest expense, if any, reported from the restructuring date to the maturity date.

### Troubled Debt Restructuring: Combination of Equity Interest Granted and Modification of Terms Involving Contingent Interest

Futura Company, which is having serious financial difficulty, entered into an agreement with its major lender on December 31, 19X3. The amount owed to the lender was restructured as follows:

1. Of the $100,000,000 of principal owed to the lender (all of which was currently due), $40,000,000 was canceled in exchange for $400,000 shares of a new class of preferred stock, having a par value of $100 per share.
2. The maturity date of the remaining $60,000,000 of principal was extended to December 31, 19X8.
3. The interest rate on the $60,000,000 of principal was reduced to 4% from 8%, with interest payable annually in arrears.
4. If the company's cumulative earnings before interest expense and income taxes from January 1, 19X4, through December 31, 19X8, exceed $25,000,000, then the interest rate reverts to 8% retroactive to January 1, 19X4. (As of December 31, 19X3, it is not probable that cumulative earnings during this period will exceed $25,000,000.)

5. Accrued interest payable of $15,000,000 as of December 31, 19X3, was for-given.

### Required:
1. Determine if a gain on restructuring of debt has resulted.
2. Prepare the journal entry to record the restructuring.
3. Determine the total amount of interest expense, if any, reported during the next five years, assuming that the company's cumulative earnings before interest expense and income tax expense during that period
   a. Did not exceed $25,000,000.
   b. Did exceed $25,000,000 as of September 30, 19X7.

## Troubled Debt Restructuring: Modification of Terms—Use of Present Value Concepts

Defaulto Company, which is having serious financial difficulty, entered into a re-structuring agreement with a creditor that is owed $3,000,000 of principal (now due and payable) and $427,000 of interest. The terms of the restructuring agree-ment (dated January 1, 19X1) call for:

1. Cancellation of $277,000 of accrued interest, with payment of the remaining $150,000 on signing the agreement. (This payment was indeed made at that time.)
2. Principal payments of $1,000,000 per year beginning January 1, 19X2 (one year from now), until the loan is paid in full on January 1, 19X4.
3. Interest to be paid annually in arrears, beginning January 1, 19X2, at 10% on the unpaid balance. (The interest rate prior to the restructuring was 14%.)

### Required:
1. Determine if a gain on restructuring of debt has resulted.
2. Prepare the journal entry to record the restructuring.
3. Determine the total amount of interest expense reported over the next three years.
4. Using present value tables, calculate the approximate effective interest rate.
5. Prepare the journal entries made between the restructuring date and the ma-turity date, assuming all required payments are made on time.

## COMPREHENSIVE   Troubled Debt Restructuring

On July 1, 19X2, TDR Company entered into a troubled debt restructuring agree-ment with its creditors. Data pertaining to the various classes of creditors and equity interests prior to the restructuring are as follows:

| | |
|---|---|
| Accounts payable, unsecured . . . . . . . . . . . . . . . . . . . . . . . . . . . . . . . . . . . . | $1,800,000 |
| 10% Note payable to bank, currently due and payable . . . . . . . . . . . . . . | 3,000,000 |
| Accrued interest on note payable . . . . . . . . . . . . . . . . . . . . . . . . . . . . . . . . | 400,000 |
| 8% Debenture bonds (subordinated to bank loan) . . . . . . . . . . . . . . . . . | 2,000,000 |

*(continued)*

| | |
|---|---|
| Accrued interest on debenture bonds . . . . . . . . . . . . . . . . . . . . . . . . . . . . . | $100,000 |

6% Preferred stock, $100 par value, cumulative, dividends in
   arrears of $90,000; 5,000 shares outstanding
Common stock, no-par value, 200,000 shares outstanding

The terms of the restructuring are as follows:

1. Accounts payable of $400,000 are canceled outright. Accounts payable of $600,000 are canceled in exchange for 80,000 shares of common stock. Trading in the company's common stock was suspended on January 15, 19X2. Just before that time, the common stock was selling at $2 per share. Trading was resumed on July 2, 19X2, and the stock closed at 50 cents per share on that day. All remaining payables are to be paid within 180 days.
2. Principal of $500,000 on the bank note, along with all accrued interest, is canceled. The due date on the remaining principal is extended to July 1, 19X5. The interest rate is reduced to 5%. However, if TDR's cumulative earnings exceed $2,000,000 during the three years ended June 30, 19X5, then the interest rate reverts to 10% retroactively. (It appears unlikely that TDR's earnings will exceed $2,000,000 during this period.)
3. Principal of $1,000,000 on the debenture bonds is exchanged for a new class of 7% preferred stock. This new preferred stock, which is designated Series A, is senior to the existing preferred stock with respect to dividends and distributions in the event of liquidation. The existing preferred stock (which was issued at par) is designated Series B. All accrued interest on the debentures is canceled. The June 30, 19X7, due date is unchanged. The interest rate on the remaining $1,000,000 of principal is reduced to 5% until maturity.
4. The dividends in arrears on the existing preferred stock is canceled, and the future dividend rate is reduced to 3% for a period of five years.

**Required:**

1. Prepare the accounting entries related to the above restructurings, assuming July 1, 19X2, is the consummation date.
2. What entry, if any, would be made on June 30, 19X5, if TDR's earnings do not exceed $2,000,000 from July 1, 19X2, to June 30, 19X5?
3. Calculate the total amount of interest expense reported in the income statement for the next five years with respect to the debenture bonds.

## COMPREHENSIVE   Bankruptcy Reorganization

**P 19-7**

Assume that the information in Problem 19-6 pertains to a Chapter 11 bankruptcy reorganization rather than a troubled debt restructuring outside of the bankruptcy courts.

**Required:**

1. Prepare the journal entries related to this plan of reorganization. Assume that it is *not* necessary to apply the provisions of *APB Opinion No. 21*.

2. With respect to the bank note, what entry, if any, would be made on June 30, 19X5, if TDR's earnings do not exceed $2,000,000 from July 1, 19X2, to June 30, 19X5?

3. Calculate the total amount of interest expense reported in the income statement for the next five years with respect to the debenture bonds.

## Bankruptcy Reorganization: Settlement with Unsecured Creditors—Use of Present Value Concepts

Debtorex Corporation's plan of reorganization was confirmed by the bankruptcy court on June 30, 19X1. Under the plan, unsecured creditors (who are owed $850,000,000) are to receive the following:

| | |
|---|---|
| Cash. . . . . . . . . . . . . . . . . . . . . . . . . . . . . . . . . . . . . . . . . . . . . . . . . | $300,000,000 |
| 12% Unsecured notes. . . . . . . . . . . . . . . . . . . . . . . . . . . . . . . . | $300,000,000 |
| Common stock, $1 par value. . . . . . . . . . . . . . . . . . . . . . . . . . | 10,000,000 shares |

The company's investment bankers have determined that the 12% unsecured notes will trade at a discount on issuance to yield a return of approximately 15%. These notes are to be paid off at $60,000,000 per year beginning June 30, 19X2, until their maturity five years from now. Interest is to be paid annually in arrears each June 30.

The company's common stock (2,000,000 shares now outstanding) traded at $1.50 per share when the company's plan of reorganization was confirmed.

Assume that *APB Opinion No. 21* applies to the 12% unsecured notes. Selected present value factors follow:

| | Present Value Factors | |
|---|---|---|
| Periods | 12% | 15% |
| 1 | .89286 | .86957 |
| 2 | .79719 | .75614 |
| 3 | .71178 | .65752 |
| 4 | .63552 | .57175 |
| 5 | .56743 | .49718 |
| Five payments (annuity) | 3.60478 | 3.35216 |

### Required:

1. Prepare the journal entries related to the plan of reorganization.
2. Prepare the journal entries made for the first two years following confirmation of the plan, assuming all required payments are made on time. (Assume that the company has a June 30 fiscal year end.)

## Liquidation: Preparing a Statement of Affairs

As Die-hard Corp.'s CPA, you are aware that it is facing bankruptcy proceedings. Its balance sheet at June 30, 19X1, and supplementary data are as follows.

### Assets

| | |
|---|---:|
| Cash. . . . . . . . . . . . . . . . . . . . . . . . . . . . . . . . . . . . . . . . . . . . . . . . . . . . . . . . . . | $   2,000 |
| Accounts receivable, less allowance for | |
|    uncollectibles. . . . . . . . . . . . . . . . . . . . . . . . . . . . . . . . . . . . . . . . . . . . . . . | 70,000 |
| Inventory, raw materials. . . . . . . . . . . . . . . . . . . . . . . . . . . . . . . . . . . . . . . . | 40,000 |
| Inventory, finished goods. . . . . . . . . . . . . . . . . . . . . . . . . . . . . . . . . . . . . . . | 60,000 |
| Marketable securities. . . . . . . . . . . . . . . . . . . . . . . . . . . . . . . . . . . . . . . . . . . | 20,000 |
| Land. . . . . . . . . . . . . . . . . . . . . . . . . . . . . . . . . . . . . . . . . . . . . . . . . . . . . . . . . . | 13,000 |
| Buildings, net of accumulated depreciation . . . . . . . . . . . . . . . . . . . . . . | 90,000 |
| Machinery, net of accumulated depreciation . . . . . . . . . . . . . . . . . . . . . | 120,000 |
| Goodwill . . . . . . . . . . . . . . . . . . . . . . . . . . . . . . . . . . . . . . . . . . . . . . . . . . . . . | 20,000 |
| Prepaid expenses. . . . . . . . . . . . . . . . . . . . . . . . . . . . . . . . . . . . . . . . . . . . . . | 5,000 |
|    Total Assets . . . . . . . . . . . . . . . . . . . . . . . . . . . . . . . . . . . . . . . . . . . . . . . | $440,000 |

### Liabilities and Equity

| | |
|---|---:|
| Accounts payable. . . . . . . . . . . . . . . . . . . . . . . . . . . . . . . . . . . . . . . . . . . . . | $  80,000 |
| Notes payable. . . . . . . . . . . . . . . . . . . . . . . . . . . . . . . . . . . . . . . . . . . . . . . . | 135,000 |
| Accrued wages. . . . . . . . . . . . . . . . . . . . . . . . . . . . . . . . . . . . . . . . . . . . . . . | 15,000 |
| Mortgages payable. . . . . . . . . . . . . . . . . . . . . . . . . . . . . . . . . . . . . . . . . . . | 130,000 |
| Common stock. . . . . . . . . . . . . . . . . . . . . . . . . . . . . . . . . . . . . . . . . . . . . . . | 100,000 |
| Accumulated deficit . . . . . . . . . . . . . . . . . . . . . . . . . . . . . . . . . . . . . . . . . | (20,000) |
|    Total Liabilities and Equity . . . . . . . . . . . . . . . . . . . . . . . . . . . . . . . . . | $440,000 |

## Additional Information:

1. Cash includes a $500 travel advance that has been expended.
2. Accounts receivable of $40,000 have been pledged to bank loans of $30,000. Credit balances of $5,000 are netted in the accounts receivable total.
3. Marketable securities consist of government bonds costing $10,000 and 500 shares of Bumm Company stock. The market value of the bonds is $10,000 and the stock is $18 per share. The bonds have accrued interest due of $200. The securities are collateral for a $20,000 bank loan.
4. Appraised value of raw materials is $30,000 and of finished goods is $50,000. For an additional cost of $10,000, the raw materials would realize $70,000 as finished goods.
5. The appraised value of fixed assets is land, $25,000; buildings, $110,000; and machinery, $75,000.
6. Prepaid expenses will be exhausted during the liquidation period.
7. Accounts payable include $15,000 of withheld payroll taxes and $6,000 owed to creditors who had been reassured by Die-Hard's president that they would be paid. Unrecorded employer's payroll taxes total $500.
8. Wages payable are not subject to any limits under bankruptcy laws.
9. Mortgages payable consist of $100,000 on land and buildings and $30,000 chattel mortgage on machinery. Total unrecorded accrued interest for these mortgages amounts to $2,400.
10. Estimated legal fees and expenses connected with the liquidation are $10,000.
11. Probable judgment on a pending damage suit is $50,000.
12. You have not rendered a $5,000 invoice for last year's audit, and you estimate a $1,000 fee for liquidation work.

### Required:

1. Prepare a statement of affairs. (The book value column should reflect adjustments that properly should have been made at June 30, 19X1, in the normal course of business.)
2. Compute the estimated settlement per dollar of unsecured liabilities.

(AICPA adapted)

## Liquidation: Preparing a Statement of Affairs

Last-Legg Corporation is in financial difficulty because of low sales. Its stockholders and principal creditors want an estimate of the financial results of the liquidation of the assets and liabilities and the dissolution of the corporation.

**LAST-LEGG CORPORATION**
Postclosing Trial Balance
December 31, 19X3

|  | Debit | Credit |
|---|---:|---:|
| Cash. | $   5,000 | |
| Accounts Receivable. | 82,000 | |
| Allowance for Uncollectibles. | | $   3,000 |
| Inventories. | 160,000 | |
| Supplies Inventory. | 12,000 | |
| Investment in Hye-Flyer Company's 5% Bonds (at face value). | 20,000 | |
| Accrued Bond Interest Receivable. | 3,000 | |
| Advertising. | 24,000 | |
| Land. | 16,000 | |
| Building. | 120,000 | |
| Accumulated Depreciation—Building. | | 20,000 |
| Machinery and Equipment. | 184,000 | |
| Accumulated Depreciation—Machinery and Equipment. | | 32,000 |
| Accounts Payable. | | 104,000 |
| Notes Payable—Bank. | | 100,000 |
| Notes Payable—Officers. | | 80,000 |
| Payroll Taxes Payable. | | 3,000 |
| Wages Payable. | | 6,000 |
| Mortgage Payable. | | 168,000 |
| Mortgage Interest Payable. | | 2,000 |
| Capital Stock. | | 200,000 |
| Accumulated Deficit. | 117,000 | |
| Estimated Liability for Product Guarantees. | | 25,000 |
|  | $743,000 | $743,000 |

The following information has been collected for a meeting of the stockholders and principal creditors to be held on January 10, 19X4:

1. Cash includes a $2,000 protested check from a customer. The customer stated that funds to honor the check will be available in about two weeks.

2. Accounts receivable include accounts totaling $40,000 that are fully collectible and have been assigned to the bank in connection with the notes payable. Included in the unassigned receivables is an uncollectible account of $1,000. The Allowance for Uncollectibles account of $3,000 now on the books will adequately provide for other doubtful accounts.

3. Purchase orders totaling $36,000 are on hand for the corporation's products. Inventory with a book value of $24,000 can be processed at an additional cost of $2,000 to fill these orders. The balance of the inventory, which includes obsolete materials with a book value of $4,000, can be sold for $41,000.

4. In transit at December 31 but not recorded on the books is a shipment of defective merchandise being returned by a customer. The president of the corporation authorized the return and the refund of the $1,000 purchase price after the merchandise had been inspected. Other than this return, the president knows of no other defective merchandise that would affect the Estimated Liability for Product Guarantees account. The merchandise being returned has no salvage value.

5. The supplies inventory comprises advertising literature, brochures, and other sales aids, which could not be replaced for less than $14,000.

6. The investment in 10% bonds of Hye-Flyer Company is recorded at face value (two bonds each having a $10,000 face value). They were purchased in 19X1 for $8,500, and the adjustment to face value was credited to Retained Earnings. At December 31, 19X3, the bonds were quoted at 30.

7. The Advertising account represents the future benefits of a 19X3 advertising campaign. The account contains 10% of certain advertising expenditures. The president stated that this figure was too conservative and that 20% would be a more realistic measure of the market that was created.

8. The land and building are in a downtown area. A firm offer of $200,000 has been received for the land, which would be used as a parking lot; the building would be razed at a cost of $48,000 to the buyer. Another offer of $160,000 was received for the real estate, which the bidder stated would be used for manufacturing that would probably employ some employees of Last-Legg.

9. The highest offer received from used machinery dealers was $72,000 for all of the machinery and equipment.

10. One creditor, whose account for $16,000 is included in the accounts payable, confirmed in writing that he would accept 75 cents on the dollar if the corporation paid him by January 10.

11. Wages payable are for amounts earned within the last 30 days.

12. The mortgage payable is secured by the land and building. The last two monthly principal payments of $800 each were not made.

13. Estimated liquidation expenses amount to $13,000.

14. For income tax purposes the corporation has the following net operating loss carryovers (the combined federal and state tax rate is 40%): 19X1, $40,000; 19X2, $48,000; and 19X3, $32,000.

### Required:

1. Prepare a statement of affairs. (The book value column should reflect adjustments that should have been made at December 31, 19X3, in the normal course of business. Assume the company has a June 30 fiscal year-end.)

2. Prepare a schedule that computes the estimated settlement per dollar of unsecured liabilities.

(AICPA adapted)

## ANSWERS TO SELF-STUDY QUESTIONS

1. b, c, d, f     5. c
2. b, c, d, f     6. e
3. a, b, d, g     7. b
4. c, g         8. a

# IV

# GOVERNMENT AND NONPROFIT ORGANIZATIONS

■ ■ ■ ■ ■

# 20
**· · · · ·**

# GOVERNMENTAL ACCOUNTING: BASIC PRINCIPLES AND THE GENERAL FUND

## *TOPIC OUTLINE*

**A**ccounting for state and local governmental units could be the subject of an entire textbook. A major portion of this chapter, therefore, is devoted to introductory material, to give you an overall understanding of (1) the historical development and current status of accounting principles applicable to governmental units, (2) the nature of governmental operations, and (3) the current shortcomings of governmental financial reporting.

# ESTABLISHMENT OF ACCOUNTING PRINCIPLES

## The GFOA, *GAAFR*, and NCGA

Before 1978, the Financial Accounting Standards Board (FASB) and its predecessor organizations restricted their efforts to the establishment of accounting principles for the private sector of the economy—that is, to enterprises engaged in a trade or business for a profit. To fill the void that existed with respect to the accounting principles and practices peculiar to governmental units, the National Committee on Municipal Accounting was established in 1934 through the efforts of the Government Finance Officers Association of the United States and Canada (GFOA).[1] The committee was not a permanent one, but was reestablished periodically as necessary to upgrade standards and address current problems. In 1949, the committee's name was changed to the National Committee on Governmental Accounting (NCGA) to signify the expansion of its activities to encompass all governmental units except the federal government and its agencies. Over the years, the committee issued numerous publications dealing with principles, practices, and procedures of accounting, budgeting, auditing, and financial reporting for state and local governmental units. In 1968, it combined most of its publications issued up to that time under a single title, *Governmental Accounting, Auditing and Financial Reporting* (referred to and cited as *GAAFR*).[2] In 1974, the American Institute of Certified Public Accountants (AICPA) issued an audit guide, *Audits of State and Local Governmental Units* (referred to as the AICPA governmental audit guide and cited *ASLGU*). This audit guide (which was revised in 1986) not only acknowledged *GAAFR* as "an authoritative publication in the area of accounting for governmental units," but also considered the principles set forth therein to "constitute generally accepted accounting principles [GAAP]," except as modified in the audit guide.[3]

It was soon evident that major improvements in financial reporting were still needed. Accordingly, the National Council on Governmental

---

[1]Prior to 1984, the GFOA was called the Municipal Finance Officers Association. In this chapter we use its new name.

[2]National Committee on Governmental Accounting, *Governmental Accounting, Auditing and Financial Reporting* (Chicago: Government Finance Officers Association of the United States and Canada, 1968).

[3]Committee on Governmental Accounting and Auditing, *Audits of State and Local Governmental Units* (New York: American Institute of Certified Public Accountants, 1974), pp. 8–9.

Accounting was established in 1974 as the successor to the National Committee on Governmental Accounting. Certain structural changes were made and due-process procedures similar to those of the FASB were adopted.

**Major Improvements Made.**   In 1979, the NCGA issued *NCGA Statement 1*, "Governmental Accounting and Financial Reporting Principles." This major pronouncement substantially upgraded the basic principles set forth in *GAAFR*. The most important revisions pertained to the manner of financial reporting. Narrative explanations and financial statements illustrate the application of the basic principles (which include the manner of financial reporting) and incorporate accounting provisions of *ASLGU*. We discuss these basic principles (grouped into seven broad categories) in detail later in the chapter. (In 1980, the AICPA issued *Statement of Position 80-2*, which amended *ASLGU* as a result of the issuance of *NCGA Statement 1*.)

**_GAAFR_ Reissued but Becomes a Guide.**   In 1980, the GFOA published a revised, updated edition of *GAAFR* based on *NCGA Statement 1*. Unlike the 1968 edition of *GAAFR*, the 1980 edition was not an official pronouncement of the NCGA. It neither prescribed nor authoritatively interpreted generally accepted accounting principles for governmental units. Instead, it provided detailed guidance to apply the principles in *NCGA Statement 1* to the accounting and financial reporting activities of state and local governments. Thus, NCGA Statements and Interpretations replaced *GAAFR* as the official pronouncements dealing with GAAP. The 1980 edition of *GAAFR* was superseded in 1988 by the third edition of *GAAFR*, which was needed because of changes in governmental GAAP resulting from pronouncements issued subsequent to the issuance of *NCGA Statement 1* in 1979. With over 30,000 copies in print, *GAAFR* is widely used as a guide by state and local governmental accountants and to a lesser extent by certified public accountants.

**Additional Accomplishments of the NCGA.**   The NCGA issued six additional statements, one of which we discuss later in the chapter. The others either deal with special topics or are beyond the scope of this and the following chapter. The NCGA also issued eleven interpretations. In addition, it started a research project to develop a conceptual framework for governmental accounting and financial reporting standards. This resulted in the 1981 issuance of *Concepts Statement No. 1*, which provides guidance in the future establishment of accounting and financial reporting principles for state and local governments.

## FASB Involvement

Because of growing concern about the reliability and relevance of the financial reports of governmental units in the 1970s, many people urged the Financial Accounting Standards Board to become involved in the nonbusiness sector. In response to these requests, the FASB (1) sponsored a research study dealing with the conceptual issues of financial accounting in nonbusiness organizations; (2) issued a discussion memorandum in 1978 (based on the research study); (3) held public hearings on the issues set forth in the discussion memorandum; (4) decided in 1979 to develop one or more Statements of Financial Accounting Concepts on the objectives of financial reporting by nonbusiness organizations; (5) issued in 1980 *Statement of Financial Accounting Concepts No. 4*, "Objectives of Financial Reporting by Nonbusiness Organizations"; and (6) proposed in 1983 amendments to its *Statements of Financial Accounting Concepts No. 2* and *No. 3* to apply them to nonbusiness organizations as well as business enterprises. (These amendments were subsequently finalized in *Statement of Financial Accounting Concepts No. 6*).

*Statement of Financial Accounting Concepts No. 4* did not establish any new accounting standards, nor did it place the FASB in a standard-setting role for state and local governmental units. The statement outlined helpful objectives for developing improved standards for financial reporting.

## The Creation of the GASB

The NCGA operated under several handicaps. It never had adequate financing to build and retain a sufficient staff and to support an adequate system of due process. Furthermore, its close ties to the GFOA, which primarily constitutes preparers of financial statements, gave the appearance of a lack of independence. Because of these handicaps, it seemed logical that the NCGA should be disbanded and that the FASB should assume sole responsibility for issuing reporting standards for governmental units. This alternative was opposed by governmental accounting groups.

Much discussion and committee work led to the creation in 1984 of a new standard-setting body, the Governmental Accounting Standards Board (GASB) to succeed the NCGA, which was dissolved in June 1984. The Financial Accounting Foundation (FAF), which oversees the FASB, also oversees the GASB. Its five-member board (appointed for five-year terms) includes a full-time chairman and is located in the same Norwalk, Connecticut, headquarters as the FASB.

The first pronouncement of the GASB was *GASB Statement No. 1*, "Authoritative Status of NCGA Pronouncements and AICPA Audit Guide," which states that all NCGA pronouncements issued and currently in effect are considered to be generally accepted accounting principles until their status is changed by a subsequent GASB pronouncement. The financial status is changed by a subsequent GASB pronouncement. The financial reporting guidance contained in the audit guide (since revised) continues in force.

## The AICPA Recognizes the GASB

In 1986, the AICPA adopted a resolution that specified the GASB as the designated body to establish accounting principles for state and local governmental units, enforceable under Rule 203 of the AICPA's code of professional ethics. Under this rule, an auditor must communicate any departures from GAAP in his or her audit report.

## The GASB's Accomplishments to Date

Since its inception in 1984, the GASB has divided its efforts between long-term projects and current problems requiring immediate attention.

**Long-term Projects.**    The major long-term project involves a reexamination of accounting and financial reporting for government. In 1987, "Objectives of Financial Reporting," a major achievement in building a solid foundation for this financial reporting project was attained as a result of the issuance of *Concepts Statement No. 1.* In 1990, *GASB Statement No. 11* titled "Measurement Focus and Basis of Accounting—Governmental Fund Operating Statements" (MFBOA) was issued. This new standard requires the use of the accrual basis (currently a modified accrual basis, which we discuss later, is used). However, this new standard does not become effective until periods beginning after June 15, 1994. (More about this new standard shortly.)

**Current Issues Addressed.**    The GASB has addressed approximately fifteen current issues deemed to be pressing problems. As a result, twelve other GASB Statements of Governmental Accounting Standards, one GASB interpretation, and two GASB technical bulletins have been issued. (Some issues still have exposure drafts outstanding.) To the extent that these pronouncements are within the scope of this and the following two chapters, they are dealt with later.

**The GASB Codification of Governmental GAAP.**    In 1984, the GASB codified all existing governmental accounting and financial reporting standards in a joint effort with the GFOA. This book, *Codification of Governmental Accounting and Financial Reporting Standards,* is periodically updated for subsequent changes. The second (and most recent) update is as of June 15, 1987. The result is a useful and accessible reference previously not available. In referring to governmental GAAP, the AICPA's governmental audit guide cites the GASB codification rather than the various NCGA Statements, NCGA Interpretations, and GASB Statements in force at the time of the codification. This makes the most sense, and for this reason we do the same, citing the codification in the same manner as in the audit guide (for example, "GASB Cod. sec. xxx"), after first citing it in full.

## AN OVERVIEW: MAJOR DIFFERENCES BETWEEN GOVERNMENTAL AND PRIVATE-SECTOR REPORTING

As this section makes clear, governmental financial reporting is different from private-sector reporting in the following major respects:

- It contains no mechanism for enforcing compliance with GAAP.
- It has no uniform requirement for audited annual financial statements.
- It has several shortcomings compared with private-sector reporting.

### The Lack of a Mechanism for Enforcing 100% Compliance with GAAP

In the private sector, publicly owned corporations must follow accounting standards as a result of legal requirements imposed by the Securities and Exchange Commission. No comparable enforcement mechanism exists for the governmental sector. Instead, the 50 states have the sovereign right to impose accounting and financial reporting requirements on governmental units within their jurisdiction. Thus, the rule-making bodies to date, being private organizations, have had no power over state and local governmental units. The states have been inconsistent in requiring their local governmental units to follow generally accepted accounting principles. Fortunately, a majority of local governments are required by other levels of government to follow GAAP. For governmental units that legally are not required to follow GAAP, two major incentives to follow GAAP are that (1) bond-rating companies (Moody's and Standard and Poor's) will lower a governmental unit's bond rating if its financial statements are not in compliance with GAAP; and (2) independent public auditors of governmental units must address in their audit report whether GAAP has been followed. Thus, some minority percentage of governmental units issue financial statements that do not comply with GAAP in one or more respects.

### No Requirement for Audited Annual Financial Statements

Many governmental units are audited annually by certified public accountants or governmental audit agencies as a result of state laws, charter provisions, or voluntary action. In addition, the Single Audit Act of 1984 requires an independent audit of all recipients of general revenue-sharing funds of $100,000 or more in any fiscal year. (Special rules apply to amounts of less than $100,000.)

However, the financial statements of many state and local governmental units do not need to be audited annually. Such units may issue securities to the public without the public having the benefit of audited financial statements. In the private sector, a corporation that issues securities (stocks and bonds) to the public must (1) register the sale of such securities with the Securities and Exchange Commission (unless a statutory exemption is available), (2) maintain its books in accordance with generally accepted accounting principles, and (3) have its financial statements audited annually by a certified public accountant. The GFOA has issued a pronouncement, *Disclosure Guidelines for Offerings of Securities by State and Local Governments,* that it recommends be used when offering securities to investors. As with GASB Statements, however, compliance is voluntary.

## Financial Reporting Shortcomings

Prior to 1979, most annual financial reports served the needs of government officials more than the needs of bond investors and other outsiders. Such reports contained masses of detail and were therefore quite difficult for the average citizen to understand. It was almost impossible to obtain a clear picture of either the overall financial condition or the operations of governmental units. General Motors, for example, could issue an annual report having ten pages of financial statements and notes that presented an understandable picture of its financial condition and operations, whereas the city of Detroit would issue an extensive financial report having over a hundred pages of financial statements, notes, and supporting schedules that few people could understand.

**The First Giant Step Forward: General Purpose Financial Statements.**   This manner of governmental reporting was criticized in the 1970s, when several major cities and counties had widely publicized, severe, and seemingly sudden financial crises. In response to this serious shortcoming, the GASB Codification calls for the presentation of specified financial statements, formally called **general purpose financial statements,** in the annual financial reports of governmental units. Such statements give readers a summary overview of financial position and operations. Although the annual financial reports still contain masses of detail, the addition of the general purpose financial statements has been a giant step forward in financial reporting. The specific requirements pertaining to these financial statements are presented and discussed later.

**Still Substantial Room for Improvement.**   Despite these improvements, financial reporting by governmental units is far below the level of reporting for the private sector. In a survey in 1986 of nearly 500 governmental units (out of more than 80,000), 28% of the opinions rendered by auditors contained qualifications for departures from generally accepted accounting principles. The reasons for the qualified opinions varied; the most common ones were the improper accounting for fixed assets, revenues and expenditures, and pensions, in that order.[4]

Accounting for pension plans is without a doubt the biggest deficiency in financial reporting. Numerous governmental units use the "pay-as-you-go" system, which is the cash basis and not an acceptable actuarial funding method. The dollar amount of the unfunded liabilities pertaining to pension plans that use this system is staggering. Consequently, to the extent that the financial statements of these governmental units do not reflect liabilities for these unfunded future obligations, such financial statements are grossly misleading. For example, Massachusetts has an unfunded pension liability approaching $18 billion under its pay-as-you-go system while most other states, including New York and California, use actuarial funding assumptions under which state pension contributions are based on a determination of projected needs.

**On the Horizon.**   The GASB is currently addressing pension accounting. However, the implementation of an eventual standard on pensions is scheduled to coincide with the implementation of the Measurement Focus and Basis of Accounting (MFBOA)—Governmental Fund Operating Statement standard in 1994. This latter standard, briefly discussed earlier, will result in a massive change in financial reporting as indicated in the article on page 868. Underlying the new MFBOA standard is the concept that interperiod equity is an essential aspect of accountability. The concept of interperiod equity focuses on whether financial resources obtained during a period are sufficient to cover claims incurred during that period. Stated more simply, it focuses on whether current-year citizens received services for which future-year citizens will be required to pay—a major deficiency of current financial reporting by governmental units. A summary of the major changes in the new MFBOA standard is set forth at the end of this chapter.

# THE NATURE OF GOVERNMENTAL OPERATIONS

Governmental operations are unique for several reasons:

1. Their absence of a profit motive
2. Their extensive legal requirements
3. Their diversity
4. Their use of fund accounting

## The Absence of a Profit Motive: What to Measure?

The fundamental difference between the private sector and the governmental sector is that the former is organized and operated to make a profit

[4]Cornelius E. Tierney and Philip T. Calder of Arthur Young & Co., *Governmental Accounting Procedures and Practices* (New York: Elsevier Science Publishing Company, Inc., 1986), pp. 239, 252.

## PERSPECTIVE

### Accounting Plan Would Put Cities in Red

*States Join Dispute over Handling of Costs*

The bottom lines of many major cities and states—particularly New York City—would quickly turn red under a measure proposed by the Governmental Accounting Standards Board, the chief accounting rule-making body for local and state governments.

After digesting public comment on the proposal, the GASB will vote on the proposal later this year. If approved, the measure would take effect in early 1989. An indication of the measure's controversial nature was reflected in the board's narrow, 3-to-2 approval of the draft proposal last winter.

As city and state financial officers begin to recognize the impact of the proposal, made last December, opposition is mounting. If approved, the measure would force cities and states to deduct immediately from their surpluses a wide range of costs that the governments have deferred for as long as 40 years in the future.

Such costs include accrued vacation pay and earned sick leave for employees, court claims and judgments, certain pension liabilities and future lease obligations.

Taking an immediate hit for such costs in the general fund of cities and states could lower their debt ratings, force them to raise added funds in the bond market and eventually spur them to increase taxes, say accountants.

Many state and city officials agree that the costs should be given more current treatment, but argue that they should be phased in, over periods as long as 15 years, rather than absorbed all at once.

Under the proposal, New York City's current surplus of $51 million would be converted into a devastating deficit of $5.75 billion. Chicago would go from a $20 million surplus to a $50 million deficit. And Detroit would drop from a $14 million surplus to a $20 million deficit.

| SURPLUS TO DEFICIT: EFFECT OF GASB ACCOUNTING PROPOSAL ON SELECTED MUNICIPALITIES | | |
|---|---|---|
| | Current Surplus | Deficit under GASB Proposal* |
| New York City | $51 million | $5.75 billion |
| Los Angeles | $138 million | $375 million |
| Chicago | $20 million | $50 million |
| Cleveland | $6 million | $20 million |
| Detroit | $14 million | $20 million |
| Pittsburgh | $10 million | $100,000** |
| *Pro-forma estimates | **Surplus | |

The GASB proposal "would mean immediate and severe fund-balance reductions or deficits for many governments," says Edward M. Klasny, national director of governmental accounting and auditing at Cleveland-based Ernst & Whinney [now Ernst & Young as a result of a 1989 merger], the third biggest U.S. accounting firm. A political entity's general-fund balance is the surplus or deficit remaining after general operating expenses are deducted from revenues.

Adds Mr. Klasny: "In some cases, this may create illegal deficits requiring short-term financing. In government units forced to quickly fund the resulting deficits, it could force them to raise taxes."

GASB staff members say the proposal would show more accurately the current obligations of government bodies, and whether the obligations require current or future payment. Even some opponents of the proposal, such as Mr. Klasny, concede it would "provide a more accurate picture of a government's overall financial conditions."

The GASB has held five public hearings on the proposal this year and has 172 written

*(continued)*

comments from government bodies and accountants.

A study by the GASB of 27 large cities, states, counties and school districts shows that 18 would have decreases in their general-fund balances under the accounting proposal. While the entities surveyed were assured anonymity, the survey does show that fund-balance declines ranged from 4.6% to 27.6% of the political bodies' annual revenue, the GASB says.

The political bodies requested anonymity because they fear both the political and economic consequences of the GASB proposal. "Without understanding that this proposal is simply an accounting change and isn't really money out of our pockets, all hell could break loose with our citizens and our councilmen," says William Van Note, first deputy comptroller of New York City.

Mr. Van Note says he is particularly distressed because three members of the five-member GASB, based in Norwalk, Conn., want the accrued costs deducted immediately from general-fund balances. James Antonio, GASB chairman, and Martin Ives, vice chairman, voted against the proposal last December.

"The majority of the board may wish to put (the change) into place all at once, but without phasing it in over a period of time, a lot of governments will go from a healthy surplus to a deficit overnight," says Mr. Antonio, former state auditor of Missouri.

"It would be a political disaster to impose the proposal without a phase-in period," says Ronald Picur, comptroller of the city of Chicago. "It would force our mayor to wear a red jacket that says 'deficit' and would confuse our city council, which believes in a balanced budget."

Charles Brown, director of finance for Cleveland, cautions the GASB to move slowly on the proposal. "It's taken the public a while to understand how government bodies are moving to generally accepted accounting principles," he says. "Rushing into accruing expenses we haven't yet paid will cause financial statements to take big swings to the deficit side and could create big confusion."

Rollin Henderson, chief accounting officer for Detroit, would prefer to continue to account for such costs as they are paid out. "They are more properly reflected in long-term obligations, since they aren't paid out in the current year," he says.

New York City's Mr. Van Note says that if the GASB forces governments to reflect such costs in the current general-fund balance, he would prefer to see the charge as a "separate line that can be amortized or accounted for by future revenues." He says he'd prefer to call the big one-time adjustment "a negative fund balance" rather than a deficit.

To prevent any economic and political hardships resulting from the GASB proposal, Ernst & Whinney's Mr. Klasny recommends phasing in the costs over a period of as long as 15 years. In this way, he adds, "governments and their constituents could avoid the shock and consequences of 'big-bang' implementation."

Mr. Klasny also suggests that the GASB delay the proposed rule's implementation for two years to enable governments "to begin planning for changes in their financial reporting."

(Note: The GASB "proposal" referred to in this article was finalized in *GASB Statement No. 11* in 1990, as discussed on page 864.)

for its owners, whereas the latter exists to provide services to its citizens substantially on a nonprofit basis. In the private sector, profit measurement is possible because a causal relationship exists between expenses and revenues: costs and expenses are incurred to generate revenues. As a result, it is appropriate to compare these categories and determine profitability. The services of governmental units are not provided to generate revenues. Thus, revenues are not earned; they stand alone. This concept raises two key questions:

- Should revenues be compared with the costs of providing services?
- Is some other measurement base more appropriate?

The GASB Codification states that for most governmental activities revenues should not be compared with costs as in the private sector. Instead, it presumes that **the only appropriate measurement base is the flow of resources.** The source, or *inflow*, of resources (revenues and borrowings) is presented in a statement along with the use, or *outflow*, of resources (direct operating costs, payments for servicing debt, and payments for capital additions, all of which are referred to collectively as **expenditures**). Thus, this statement is a "flow" statement just as the statement of cash flows is a flow statement. The only difference between the two is that one deals only with cash flows, whereas the governmental one deals with the inflows and outflows of all assets (collectively referred to as resources). In governmental accounting, we call this statement a **statement of revenues, expenditures, and changes in fund balance.** The rationale for using the flow of resources as the measurement base is the presumption that the most meaningful question concerning a governmental unit's financial operations is: What resources were given to it and how were those resources used? The GASB Codification makes governmental units accountable in this respect.

Some accountants contend that in addition to measuring the flow of resources, a statement comparing revenues with the costs of providing services (including depreciation expense) should also be presented even though the costs do not generate revenues as in the private sector. Such a statement would provide additional information as to **whether sufficient tax revenues were raised to cover the current costs of providing services.** (In the 1970s, many governmental units had severe financial crises from providing services far beyond the tax revenues being raised, creating substantial liabilities to be borne by future taxpayers.)

Even though the concept of interperiod equity is dealt with in the proposed MFBOA standard, the new operating statement is still that of measuring the flow of resources—not an operating statement comparing revenues with the costs of providing services. Whether such an operating statement will be a reporting requirement in the future is conjecture; such a statement is a controversial issue. However, the improved financial reporting requirements contained in the GASB Codification (particularly the requirement to show borrowings separately from revenues in the statement of revenues, expenditures, and changes in fund balance) do provide a much better picture as to whether a governmental unit is spending beyond its means.

### Extensive Legal Requirements

Governmental units are regulated by constitutions, charters, and statutes. Many legal provisions pertain to financial accounting areas. For example, certain activities or specified revenues must frequently be accounted for separately from all other operations. The uses of certain revenues may be limited. In some instances, a certain method of accounting—such as the cash basis—may be stipulated. We discuss the accounting ramifications of these requirements later in the chapter.

## Diversity of Operations

Governmental operations are tremendously diverse. The GASB Codification classifies governmental operations in three broad categories:

1. **Governmental.** Operations that do not resemble commercial activities are classified in the governmental category. These operations provide primary services and are normally financed from tax revenues. Examples are education, public safety, the judicial system, social services, and administration.

2. **Proprietary.** Proprietary operations resemble commercial activities. Usually financed wholly or partially from user charges, these operations may be considered secondary services. Examples are utilities, public transportation, parking facilities, and recreational facilities. Proprietary operations usually have the objective of earning a profit or recovering a certain level of operating costs from fees charged the public for their use.

3. **Fiduciary.** Fiduciary operations pertain to accounting for assets held by a governmental unit as trustee or agent. The most common example is a pension fund for public employees.

## The Use of Fund Accounting

Because of the legal requirements pertaining to financial accounting areas and the diversity of governmental operations, the use of a single set of accounts to record and summarize all the financial transactions of a governmental unit is neither legally possible nor practical. As a result, **fund accounting,** whereby certain operations are accounted for separately from other operations, is predominant in governmental accounting. The GASB Codification defines a **fund** as follows:

> A fund is . . . a fiscal and accounting entity with a self-balancing set of accounts recording cash and other financial resources, together with all related liabilities and residual equities or balances, and changes therein,

which are segregated for the purpose of carrying on activities or attaining certain objectives in accordance with special regulations, restrictions, or limitations.[5]

Thus, from an accounting viewpoint, a governmental unit consists of all the individual funds used to account for the entity's various operations and activities.

**Fund Equity.**  The difference between a fund's assets and liabilities is called the fund equity (as compared to stockholders' equity for commercial enterprises). Different account descriptions are used within the fund equity section of the balance sheet for governmental and fiduciary type funds than for proprietary funds as shown below:

| Governmental and Fiduciary Type Funds | Proprietary Funds |
|:---:|:---:|
| Fund Balance | Contributed Capital |
| | Retained Earnings |

# BASIC PRINCIPLES OF THE GASB CODIFICATION

In reading the twelve basic principles of the GASB Codification, we must understand their relationship to the accounting principles that have been established by the FASB and its predecessor organizations. This relationship is expressed in the AICPA's governmental audit guide as follows:

> GASB pronouncements . . . constitute the primary source of GAAP for governmental units. GASB pronouncements take precedence over FASB pronouncements with regard to state and local governmental entities, but if the accounting treatment of a transaction or event is not specified in a GASB pronouncement, and the FASB has dealt with the subject, the FASB pronouncement is presumed to apply.[6]

We have grouped the twelve basic principles in the GASB Codification into the following seven broad categories:

Category
I.    Accounting and Reporting Capabilities (GAAP, Legal Provisions, and Conflicts)
II.   Types of Funds and Account Groups
III.  Basis of Accounting
IV.   Financial Reporting (presented in three subcategories)

---

[5]*Codification of Governmental Accounting and Financial Reporting Standards* (Stamford: Governmental Accounting Standards Board, 1987), sec. 1100.102.
[6]*ASLGU* (1986 revised edition), pars. 1.7, 1.8.

Category
- V.     Long-term Liabilities
- VI.    Fixed Assets
- VII.   Budgets and Budgetary Accounting

## Category I: Accounting and Reporting Capabilities (GAAP, Legal Provisions, and Conflicts)

The GASB Codification recommends the following:

> A governmental accounting system must make it possible both: (a) to present fairly and with full disclosure the financial position and results of financial operations of the funds and account groups of the governmental unit in conformity with generally accepted accounting principles; and (b) to determine and demonstrate compliance with finance-related legal and contractual provisions.[7]

In many cases, both objectives are satisfied through the use of a separate fund for a designated activity and the preparation of separate financial statements for the separate fund. In some cases, a legal provision may specify the use of a practice that is not in accordance with generally accepted accounting principles—for example, requiring that a certain fund maintain its books on the cash basis. In these cases, the books must be maintained according to the law. For financial reporting purposes, however, the cash basis trial balance must be adjusted (on a worksheet) to arrive at a presentation in accordance with GAAP. Financial statements would then be prepared and reported according to GAAP. The GASB Codification addresses such conflicts as follows:

> Where financial statements prepared in conformity with GAAP do not demonstrate finance-related legal and contractual compliance, the governmental unit should present such additional schedules and narrative explanations in the comprehensive annual financial report as may be necessary to report its legal compliance responsibilities and accountabilities. In extreme cases, preparation of a separate legal-basis special report may be necessary.[8]

The long-range solution to this problem is to eliminate any legal provisions that conflict with generally accepted accounting principles. Efforts are continuously made in this respect, but progress is slow.

## Category II: Types of Funds and Account Groups

The GASB Codification recognizes and recommends the use of seven major types of funds (categorized into three broad areas) and two account groups, as follows:

[7]GASB Cod. sec. 1100.101.
[8]GASB Cod. sec. 1200.113.

### Governmental Funds

1. *The General Fund*—to account for all financial resources except those required to be accounted for in another fund.
2. *Special Revenue Funds*—to account for the proceeds of specific revenue sources (other than expendable trusts or for major capital projects) that are legally restricted to expenditure for specified purposes.
3. *Capital Projects Funds*—to account for financial resources to be used for the acquisition or construction of major capital facilities (other than those financed by proprietary funds and Trust Funds).
4. *Debt Service Funds*—to account for the accumulation of resources for, and the payment of, general long-term debt principal and interest.

### Proprietary Funds

5. *Enterprise Funds*—to account for operations (a) that are financed and operated in a manner similar to private business enterprises—where the intent of the governing body is that the costs (expenses including depreciation) of providing goods or services to the general public on a continuing basis be financed or recovered primarily through user charges; or (b) where the governing body has decided that periodic determination of revenues earned, expenses incurred, and/or net income is appropriate for capital maintenance, public policy, management control, accountability, or other purposes.
6. *Internal Service Funds*—to account for the financing of goods or services provided by one department or agency to other departments or agencies of the governmental unit, on a cost-reimbursement basis.

### Fiduciary Funds

7. *Trust and Agency Funds*—to account for assets held by a governmental unit in a trustee capacity or as an agent for individuals, private organizations, other governmental units, and/or other funds. These include (a) Expendable Trust Funds (b) Nonexpendable Trust Funds, (c) Pension Trust Funds, and (d) Agency Funds.

### Account Groups

1. *General Fixed Assets Account Group*—to account for fixed assets other than those accounted for in the proprietary funds and trust funds.
2. *General Long-term Debt Account Group*—to account for all unmatured long-term debt that is not accounted for in the proprietary funds and trust funds.[9]

The number of funds used by a given governmental unit depends on legal requirements and what is practical in relation to the scope of opera-

[9]GASB Cod. sec. 1300.104.

tions. The General Fund, which usually accounts for the largest part of a governmental unit's total operations, is discussed and illustrated later in the chapter. The remaining types of funds and the two account groups are discussed and illustrated in Chapter 21.

## Category III: Basis of Accounting

*APB Statement No. 4*, "Basic Concepts and Accounting Principles Underlying Financial Statements of Businesses," defines the accrual basis of accounting as follows:

> The effects of transactions and other events on the assets and liabilities of a business enterprise are recognized and reported in the time period to which they relate rather than only when cash is received or paid.[10]

Thus, the difference between the accrual basis and the cash basis is merely one of **timing.** The private sector initially developed the accrual basis concept to determine net income and financial position properly. Even though the profit motive is absent from most public-sector operations, the concept of recording items in the period to which they relate can be applied. The GASB Codification recommends using the accrual basis "to the fullest extent practicable in the government environment."[11]

Certain activities in the public sector lend themselves to the use of the accrual basis of accounting. For most activities, however, the position is taken that it is not practicable to use the accrual basis. Instead, a combination of the accrual basis and the cash basis is more appropriate. As a result, certain items are not recorded in the period to which they relate. Although this accounting basis might be appropriately called the "combination accrual and cash basis," the GASB Codification chose to call it the **modified accrual basis.**

**Accrual Basis Funds.** Activities accounted for in Enterprise Funds and Internal Service Funds (proprietary funds) and Nonexpendable Trust Funds (fiduciary funds) have the objectives of profit measurement or capital maintenance. Thus, the accrual basis of accounting as conceived for private businesses is entirely suitable for these funds. Also, Pension Trust Funds (fiduciary funds) exhibit the same characteristics as pension funds established in the private sector. Thus, the accrual basis also lends itself to use with Pension Trust Funds. Accordingly, for each of these funds, revenues earned and expenses incurred may be accrued and recognized in the period to which they relate in essentially the same manner as in the private sector. For these reasons, the GASB Codification recommends the use of the accrual basis for these funds.

[10]*Accounting Principles Board Statement No. 4*, "Basic Concepts and Accounting Principles of Businesses" (New York: American Institute of Certified Public Accountants, 1970), par. 35.
[11]GASB Cod. sec. 1600.103.

**Modified Accrual Basis Funds.** For all remaining funds (the four governmental funds, Expendable Trust Funds, and Agency Funds), the GASB Codification recommends the use of the modified accrual basis of accounting, which is described as follows:

> Revenues should be recognized in the accounting period in which they become **available and measurable** [emphasis added]. Expenditures should be recognized in the accounting period in which the fund liability is incurred, if measurable, except for unmatured interest on general long-term debt, which should be recognized when due.[12]

The reason for using the modified accrual basis of accounting for these funds may be attributed to the nature of governmental revenue sources and activities. We discuss the modified accrual basis first concerning revenues and then expenditures.

**Revenues.** Fund revenues are not recognized when earned (as is done in the private sector); the "available and measurable" criterion is used because it is more appropriate. (Most governmental operations do not "earn" revenues.) Thus, revenues are recognized when they become **"susceptible to accrual."** The term **"available"** means that a revenue source is "collectible within the current period or soon enough thereafter to be used to pay liabilities of the current period."[13] For property tax revenues (discussed shortly), collection must occur within 60 days of the balance sheet date (barring unusual circumstances) to be reportable as revenues. Amounts expected to be collected after 60 days must be reported in the balance sheet as deferred revenues.

The application of these revenue-related criteria results in (1) certain revenues being recognized entirely on the accrual basis, (2) certain revenues being recognized entirely on the cash basis, and (3) certain revenues being recognized partially on the cash basis and partially on the accrual basis. We discuss each of these revenue categories more fully below.

1. **Accrual basis revenues.** Many revenue sources may be accrued in essentially the same manner as is done in the private sector. Some of the most common examples are property taxes, grants, and interfund transfers:

   a. **Property taxes.** Property taxes may be precisely determined for each specific property to which a legally enforceable lien attaches. Some governmental units bill property owners in advance of the fiscal year to which the property taxes relate. For control purposes, property taxes should be recorded at the time of billing. Property tax revenues, however, should be shown as deferred revenues until the start of the fiscal year to which they pertain, because the rev-

---

[12]GASB Cod. sec. 1100.108.
[13]GASB Cod. sec. 1600.106.

enues do not relate to the prior fiscal year (even though the assessment date may have been in that year.

b. **Grants and interfund transfers.** Most grants from other governmental units and interfund transfers within a governmental unit are susceptible to accrual in the period to which they relate because an irrevocable commitment exists.

2. **Cash basis revenues.** Many revenue sources may not be accrued, because governmental units cannot determine the tax receivable from individual taxpayers at each month-end. The two broad categories of such revenues are self-assessment basis revenues and such miscellaneous revenues as license and permit fees, and fines.

a. **Self-assessment basis revenues.** Self-assessment basis revenues include income taxes, sales taxes, and gross receipts taxes. The distinguishing feature of this type of revenue is that the governmental unit does not bill the taxpayer. The receivable for each revenue source at each month-end may only be estimated, because the actual amounts are unknown until taxpayer reports are received or payments are collected. It should be noted that the use of income tax withholding procedures often produces results that closely approximate the accrual basis of accounting in that tax revenues are received substantially in the period in which the income is earned by taxpayers. Even when income tax withholding procedures are used, however, the final amount to be paid to the government (or to be refunded to the taxpayer in the event of excess withholdings or estimated interim payments) is not known until several months after the year in which the taxpayer earns the income.

b. **Miscellaneous revenues.** Miscellaneous revenues include the following items:

(1) **Annual business licenses.** Licenses are usually issued for new businesses at the time of payment. Because a license may not be granted, a bona fide receivable does not exist when an application is filed. Although governmental units often bill taxpayers for renewals of their annual business licenses, this billing (whether prior to or at the start of the fiscal year to which the bill pertains) is usually not relevant. The governmental unit does not know if the taxpayer will renew the license until it receives payment.

(2) **Construction and home improvement permits.** Construction and home improvement permits are usually issued at the time of payment. The filing of an application does not create a bona fide receivable, because the permit may not be granted.

(3) **Fines.** Most fines are collected when they are levied, which is when the amount of the fine is determined.

3. **Partial cash and partial accrual basis revenues.** This category merely applies the accrual concept to portions of revenues normally

recognized on the cash basis. For example, sales taxes due from other governmental units or merchants that have not been received at the normal time of receipt should be accrued, providing the criteria of measurability and availability are met. Revenues received before their normal time of receipt that pertain to subsequent periods should be recorded as deferred revenues.

**Expenditures.**   The accrual basis is used by requiring expenditures to be recognized in the period in which the liability is incurred. (This is merely a different way of saying that items should be recorded and recognized in the period to which they relate.) In Chapter 21, we discuss the one specific exception to the use of the accrual basis—recognizing interest on general long-term debt when due rather than in the period in which the interest liability arises.

**The AICPA Position on the Modified Accrual Basis.**   The AICPA governmental audit guide accepts the modified accrual basis as being appropriate and in conformity with generally accepted accounting principles.[14]

## Category IV (A): Financial Reporting—The Basics

**The Balance Sheet.**   As discussed earlier, the accounts used within the fund equity section for the governmental funds are different than those used within the fund equity section of the proprietary funds. For the governmental funds, a unique aspect of the balance sheet is the manner of reporting the Fund Balance in the fund equity section. If no restrictions exist, the Fund Balance account may be viewed as a "surplus" (a term often used in newspapers) that is available for spending in the new fiscal year. In most cases, however, restrictions exist that earmark a portion of the fund balance for a specific purpose. These restrictions are reflected in the fund equity section as reservations of the fund balance. For example, a restriction pertaining to outstanding (unfilled) purchase orders of $33,000 at year-end would be presented as follows:

Fund Equity
Fund balance—
| | |
|---|---|
| Reserved | $  33,000 |
| Unreserved | 427,000 |
| | $460,000 |

Certain proprietary funds also have some unique balance sheet features; however, we delay their discussion until Chapter 21.

**The Operating Statement.**   In governmental accounting, the operating statement is the statement that presents the financial results of operations in

[14]*ASLGU* (1986 revised edition), p. 59.

conformity with GAAP. For proprietary funds and nonexpendable trust funds, the operating statement is an income statement (to which is appended an analysis of retained earnings). For governmental funds and expendable trust funds, income statements are not prepared, and the operating statement is that statement which presents the inflows and out-flows of resources (the measurement focus in these funds). Recall that although this statement is called the statement of revenues, expenditures, and changes in fund balance, substantively it is merely a statement of sources and uses of resources. Note that the format of this statement (shown in Illustration 20-1) includes the beginning and ending fund balance amounts, thereby requiring all changes in the fund balance for the period to be shown. This "all-inclusive" format makes it unnecessary to present a separate statement of changes in fund equity (similar to a statement of changes in stockholders' equity for a commercial enterprise). The statement format is modified slightly when (1) bond proceeds are recorded in a governmental fund and (2) a fund has certain types of transactions with other funds. These modifications are discussed and illustrated in the following section.

## Category IV (B): Financial Reporting of Bond Proceeds and Interfund Transactions

The GASB Codification recommends the following classification reporting practices:

> Interfund transfers and proceeds of general long-term debt issues [that are not recorded as fund liabilities] should be classified separately from fund revenues and expenditures or expenses.[15]

Classifying proceeds of general long-term debt separately from fund revenues is a substantial improvement over the former practice of show-ing such proceeds as revenues. Such proceeds must be shown under a separate section of the operating statement of the recipient fund. This

### ■ ILLUSTRATION 20-1

| Statement of Revenues, Expenditures, and Changes in Fund Balance | |
|---|---|
| Revenues (an inflow of resources)............................... | $550,000 |
| Expenditures (an outflow of resources)........................ | (450,000) |
| Excess of Revenues over Expenditures........................ | $100,000 |
| Fund Balance, January 1, 19X1................................ | 360,000 |
| Fund Balance, December 31, 19X1............................. | $460,000 |

[15]GASB Cod. sec. 1800.

section is called **Other Financing Sources and Uses.** Reporting interfund transfers separately from fund revenues and expenditures or expenses is also a substantial improvement over the former practice of showing these items as revenues and expenditures or expenses. Before showing the operating statement, as revised for the inclusion of the Other Financing Sources and Uses section, it is necessary to discuss the various types of interfund transactions.

### Types of Interfund Transactions.

In the GASB Codification, all interfund transactions fall into one of the following four categories:

1. Loans and advances
2. Quasi-external transactions
3. Residual equity transfers
4. Operating transfers

### Loans and Advances.

Often the General Fund makes a loan or advance to another fund. If the borrowing is to be repaid within a relatively short period (one year or less is commonly used), the borrowing is called a loan. For longer periods, the borrowing is called an advance. **Loans and advances affect only the balance sheet.** The lending fund reports a receivable, and the borrowing fund reports a liability. Special descriptive terminology is used for the accounts reported in the balance sheet as follows:

| Receivable Accounts | Liability Accounts |
|---|---|
| Interfund Receivable | Interfund Payable |
| Advance to XXXX Fund | Advance from XXXX Fund |

### Quasi-External Transactions.

Often one fund provides a service to another fund. An example would be when a city's water utility (which would be accounted for in an Enterprise Fund) supplies water to the city. The most meaningful form of reporting for such transactions is to report expenditures in the fund receiving the services and report revenues in the fund providing the services, because the fund receiving the services would have had to charge expenditures if it had obtained the services from an organization external to the governmental unit. Furthermore, recording revenues in the fund providing the services is essential to the proper determination of that fund's operating results when such fund is a proprietary fund. The entries that would be recorded in the General Fund and the Municipal Water Utility Enterprise Fund for supplying water to the city are as follows:

### General Fund

| | | |
|---|---|---|
| Expenditures | 45,000 | |
|     Due to Municipal Water Utility | | |
|       Enterprise Fund | | 45,000 |

### Municipal Water Utility Enterprise Fund

| | | |
|---|---|---|
| Due from General Fund | 45,000 | |
|     Revenues | | 45,000 |

These *Due to* and *Due from* accounts are used only for **interfund transactions that do not involve loans or advances,** such as in this case in which services are provided by an Enterprise Fund to the General Fund. (They may also be used in setting up liabilities and receivables involving residual equity transfers and operating transfers, which are discussed shortly.)

Other examples of quasi-external transactions are as follows:

1. Payments in lieu of taxes from an Enterprise Fund to the General Fund.
2. Internal Service Fund billings for services to departments of other funds.
3. Routine service charges for inspection, engineering, utility, or similar charges.
4. Routine employer contributions from the General Fund to a Pension Trust Fund.

Quasi-external transactions are the only type of interfund transactions that may be recorded as revenues, expenditures, or expenses.

### Residual Equity Transfers.

Residual equity transfers are **nonrecurring** or **nonroutine** transfers of equity between funds made in connection with the formation, expansion, contraction, or discontinuance of a fund (usually involving the General Fund and one of the Proprietary Funds). **Because such transfers are of a nonoperating nature, they are reported as direct additions to or subtractions from the fund equity accounts** (Fund Balance, Contributed Capital, or Retained Earnings, as appropriate). For example, assume the General Fund transferred $300,000 to a newly-established Municipal Golf Course Enterprise Fund as a capital contribution in its start-up period. The entries to be made by each fund are as follows:

### General Fund

| | | |
|---|---|---|
| Residual Equity Transfer Out | 300,000 | |
|     Cash | | 300,000 |

*(continued)*

**Municipal Golf Course Enterprise Fund**

| | | |
|---|---|---|
| Cash . . . . . . . . . . . . . . . . . . . . . . . . . . . . . . . . . . . . . . . . . . . . . | 300,000 | |
|     Contributed Capital—Government . . . . . . . | | 300,000 |

For the General Fund to make such a transfer, it must, of course, have an unreserved fund balance of at least $300,000.

Assume that 15 years later, the golf course is sold to a real estate developer. At the time the Municipal Golf Course Enterprise Fund is discontinued, assume it has $300,000 in its Contributed Capital account and $50,000 in its Retained Earnings account. The entries to record the transfer of the discontinued fund's residual equity to the General Fund would be recorded as follows:

**General Fund**

| | | |
|---|---|---|
| Cash . . . . . . . . . . . . . . . . . . . . . . . . . . . . . . . . . . . . . . . . | 350,000 | |
|     Residual Equity Transfer In . . . . . . . . . . . . . | | 350,000 |

**Municipal Golf Course Enterprise Fund**

| | | |
|---|---|---|
| Contributed Capital . . . . . . . . . . . . . . . . . . . . . . . . . | 300,000 | |
| Retained Earnings . . . . . . . . . . . . . . . . . . . . . . . . . . . | 50,000 | |
|     Cash . . . . . . . . . . . . . . . . . . . . . . . . . . . . . . . . . . . | | 350,000 |

---

### Comparative Practice Note

In showing the entries for the General Fund, we used a Residual Equity Transfer Out account and a Residual Equity Transfer In account. In practice, some governmental units shortcut the procedures slightly by debiting or crediting directly the Unreserved Fund Balance account (in the same manner that commercial enterprises charge dividends declared directly to retained earnings rather than to a separate Dividends Declared account, which must be later closed out to retained earnings).

---

### Operating Transfers.

Operating transfers are made in connection with the **normal operations of the recipient fund.** In comparison to residual equity transfers (which are made in connection with the formation and discontinuance of a fund), operating transfers are conceptually the opposite. An example of an operating transfer would be subsidizing of the operations of a Municipal Golf Course Enterprise Fund each year, as necessary, when expenses exceed revenues. Operating transfers are presented in the operating statements as a separate line item. The manner of presentation is slightly different for governmental funds than for proprietary funds as shown as follows:

| Governmental Funds | Proprietary Funds |
|---|---|
| REVENUES | REVENUES |
| EXPENDITURES | EXPENSES |
| OTHER FINANCING SOURCES AND USES: | OPERATING TRANSFERS IN |
|   Operating Transfers In | OPERATING TRANSFERS OUT |
|   Operating Transfers Out | |

The difference in presentation of these two types of funds is attributable to the difference in the nature of the operating statement used (an income statement for the proprietary funds and a source and use of resources statement for governmental funds). As a result, the description of the accounts used in the general ledgers is dictated by the presentation in the respective operating statements. The following entries assume the General Fund made an operating transfer to the Municipal Golf Course Enterprise Fund:

### General Fund

| | | |
|---|---|---|
| Other Financing Uses—Operating Transfers Out | 20,000 | |
|     Cash | | 20,000 |

### Municipal Golf Course Enterprise Fund

| | | |
|---|---|---|
| Cash | 20,000 | |
|     Operating Transfer In | | 20,000 |

Other examples of operating transfers are as follows:

1. Transfers of tax revenues from a Special Revenue Fund to a Debt Service Fund or the General Fund.
2. Transfers from the General Fund to a Capital Projects Fund to help pay for construction costs.
3. Transfers from the General Fund to a Debt Service Fund to enable interest and principle payments to be made on General Long-term Debt.
4. Transfers from an Enterprise Fund to the General Fund other than payments in lieu of taxes to finance General Fund expenditures.

### The Operating Statement for Governmental Funds—Modified for Reporting of Bond Proceeds and Interfund Transfers.

In Illustration 20-2, we present the statement of revenues, expenditures, and changes in fund balance used by governmental funds when bond proceeds have been received in such a fund and both residual equity transfers and operating transfers exist. To enhance understanding of this illustration, we used the amounts shown in Illustration 20-1 plus the following previously illustrated interfund transactions:

■ **ILLUSTRATION 20-2**

**Statement of Revenues, Expenditures and Changes in Fund Balance—Modified for Reporting Bond Proceeds and Interfund Transfers**

| GENERAL FUND<br>Statement of Revenues, Expenditures,<br>and Changes in Fund Balance<br>For the Year Ended December 31, 19X1 | |
|---|---:|
| Revenues | $550,000 |
| Expenditures | (495,000)[a] |
| Excess of Revenues over Expenditures | $ 55,000 |
| Other Financing Sources and Uses: | |
| Bond proceeds | –0– |
| Operating transfers in | –0– |
| Operating transfers out | (20,000) |
| Excess of Revenues and Other Financing Sources<br>over Expenditures and Other Financing Uses | $ 35,000 |
| Fund Balance, January 1, 19X1 | 360,000 |
| Residual equity transfer out to Municipal Golf Course<br>Enterprise Fund | (300,000) |
| Fund Balance, December 31, 19X1 | $ 95,000 |

[a]Includes $45,000 for purchase of water from Municipal Water Enterprise Fund (a quasi-external transaction).

1. Quasi-External Transaction: The purchase of water by the General Fund from the Municipal Water Utility Fund for $45,000.
2. Residual Equity Transfer: The transfer of $300,000 from the General Fund at the inception of the Municipal Golf Course Enterprise Fund.
3. Operating Transfer: The transfer of $20,000 from the General Fund to subsidize the day-to-day operations of the Municipal Golf Course Enterprise Fund.

Because the illustration is for the General Fund, no amount is shown on the bond proceeds line inasmuch as virtually all bond proceeds into governmental funds are into Capital Projects Funds. (Most governmental units are prohibited by law from issuing bonds to finance current operations; thus, it is rare for the General Fund to report bond proceeds.) We also omit an amount on the "Operating transfer in" line inasmuch as the General Fund rarely has operating transfers in—it usually has numerous operating transfers out.

**Additional Items to be Classified under the Other Financing Sources and Uses Category.** When a governmental unit sells some of its General Fixed Assets (discussed shortly), the proceeds are to be reported under the other financing sources and uses category. Also, when a governmental unit enters into a capital lease, the present value of the lease payments is deemed to be the equivalent of proceeds from a loan, which amount is to be reported under the other financing sources and uses category. Accordingly, this category of the operating statement could appear as follows if all types of transactions occur:

**Other Financing Sources and Uses**

| | |
|---|---|
| Bond Proceeds . . . . . . . . . . . . . . . . . . . . . . . . . . . . . . . . . . . . . . . . . . . . . . . | XXX |
| Operating Transfers In . . . . . . . . . . . . . . . . . . . . . . . . . . . . . . . . . . . . | XXX |
| Operating Transfers Out . . . . . . . . . . . . . . . . . . . . . . . . . . . . . . . . . . . | (XXX) |
| Proceeds from Sale of General Fixed Assets . . . . . . . . . . . . . . | XXX |
| Proceeds from Capital Lease . . . . . . . . . . . . . . . . . . . . . . . . . . . . . | XXX |

No other types of transactions are reportable under the other financing sources and uses category.

## Category IV (C): Financial Reporting—General Purpose Financial Statements and the Comprehensive Annual Financial Report (CAFR)

The annual financial report for governmental units is called "The Comprehensive Annual Financial Report" (CAFR). Three distinct types of financial statements are presented in the CAFR:

1. **Combined Financial Statements.** These are five specific financial statements that are collectively referred to as the **"General Purpose Financial Statements." They are designed to present an overview** much in the same manner as consolidated financial statements serve for corporations. The five specific financial statements are as follows:

   1. Combined Balance Sheet—All Fund Types and Account Groups.
   2. Combined Statement of Revenues, Expenditures, and Changes in Fund Balance—All Governmental Fund Types.
   3. Combined Statement of Revenues, Expenditures, and Changes in Fund Balances—Budget and Actual—General and Special Revenue Fund Types (and similar governmental fund types for which annual budgets have been legally adopted).
   4. Combined Statement of Revenues, Expenses, and Changes in Retained Earnings (or Equity)—All Proprietary Fund Types.
   5. Combined Statement of Cash Flows—All Proprietary Fund Types and Nonexpendable Trust Funds.

   (Illustrations of the first four of the five combined statements are shown in Chapter 21 on pages 975–79. At this point, we suggest you briefly review those illustrations before proceeding.)

2. **Combining Financial Statements—By Fund Type.** In these statements, all funds of a given type are shown individually, along with a

"combining" total. For example, if a government has three special revenue funds, the three special revenue funds are shown along with the combining total. (The combining total is presented in the combined financial statements.)

3. **Individual Fund and Account Group Statements.** The individual statements are presented whenever it is desirable to present additional detailed information not provided in the combining statements (such as budgetary or prior-year comparative data).

Although not normally subject to audit by outside auditors, the combining financial statements and the individual fund and account group statements are required by the GASB Codification to follow the identical format of the more significant combined financial statements (the general purpose financial statements) on which the outside auditors express an opinion. (The only exception to this is a utility operated as an Enterprise Fund, whereby the individual financial statements may be presented in the regulatory format.)

In discussing each of the seven funds and the two account groups, we will illustrate the individual financial statements. The combined financial statements (the general purpose financial statements) are discussed at the conclusion of the discussion of the seven funds and two account groups in Chapter 21.

## Category V: Long-term Liabilities

According to the GASB Codification, long-term debt should be accounted for as follows:

> Long-term liabilities of proprietary funds and trust funds should be accounted for through those funds. All other unmatured general long-term liabilities of the governmental unit, which includes special assessment debt for which the government is obligated in some manner, should be accounted for through the General Long-term Debt Account Group.[16]

**General long-term debt** (as opposed to liabilities of proprietary funds and trust funds) is the liability of the governmental unit as a whole and not that of any specific fund. As such, it is secured by the taxing powers of the governmental unit and not by the resources available in a specific fund.

The General Long-term Debt Account Group is a "self-balancing" set of accounts because the list of liabilities, maintained in account form, is balanced by accounts showing (1) amounts, if any, set aside in Debt Service Funds for repayment of the General Long-term Debt, and (2) amounts yet

---

[16]GASB Cod. sec. 1100.105.

to be provided for repayment of the General Long-term Debt. The General Long-term Debt Account Group is discussed in detail in Chapter 21.

## Category VI: Fixed Assets

**Accounting for Fixed Assets.** The nature of governmental operations is such that more meaningful financial reporting results if certain fixed assets are accounted for in fund accounts and all other fixed assets (referred to collectively as **general fixed assets**) are accounted for outside the funds in **account groups.** The GASB Codification recommends the following:

> Fixed assets related to specific proprietary funds or trust funds should be accounted for through those funds. All other fixed assets of a governmental unit should be accounted for through the General Fixed Assets Account Group.[17]

**Valuation of Fixed Assets.** With respect to the valuation of fixed assets, the GASB Codification specifies the following:

> Fixed assets should be accounted for at cost or, if the cost is not practicably determinable, at estimated cost. Donated fixed assets should be recorded at their estimated fair value at the time received.[18]

Fixed assets are excluded from the governmental funds because such assets do not constitute financial resources available for spending purposes. Because one of the reporting objectives of the governmental funds is to reflect the financial resources available for spending purposes, fixed assets must be excluded from governmental funds to accomplish this objective.

The General Fixed Assets Account Group is not a separate fund but merely a list of a governmental unit's general fixed assets, maintained in account form. These accounts are complemented by credit accounts showing the sources by which the assets are obtained. Because of the manner of making entries, the General Fixed Asset Account Group is also a "self-balancing" set of accounts. The General Fixed Assets Account Group is discussed in detail in Chapter 21.

**Depreciation of Fixed Assets.** With respect to depreciating fixed assets, the GASB Codification recommends the following:

> Depreciation of general fixed assets should not be recorded in the accounts of governmental funds. Depreciation of general fixed assets may

[17]GASB Cod. sec. 1100.105.
[18]GASB Cod. sec. 1100.106.

be recorded in cost accounting systems or calculated for cost finding analysis; and accumulated depreciation may be recorded in the General Fixed Assets Account Group [an optional treatment].

Depreciation of fixed assets accounted for in a proprietary fund should be recorded in the accounts of that fund. Depreciation is also recognized in those Trust Funds where expenses, net income, and/or capital maintenance are measured.[19]

Commercial businesses record depreciation expense to match revenues with expenses, so that net income may be properly determined. Fixed assets accounted for in proprietary funds and certain trust funds also have the objectives of profitability or capital maintenance (cost recovery). Accordingly, depreciation expense is properly recorded in these funds, because income statements are prepared.

For all other funds, income statements are not presented, nor is a statement presented comparing revenues with the costs of providing services (which would include depreciation expense). Instead, only a statement of revenues, expenditures, and changes in fund balance based on the "flow of resources" measurement base is presented. Accordingly, when a general fixed asset is acquired, it is reflected as an expenditure in the fund at the time of acquisition. Depreciation expense would not be recorded in this statement because it does not constitute a flow of resources.

The absence of depreciation expense in the statement of revenues, expenditures, and changes in fund balance should not be considered a departure from the accrual basis of accounting. The GASB Codification makes an important clarification regarding what is encompassed by the accrual basis of accounting:

> Unfortunately, the terms "accrual" and "accrual accounting" often are interpreted to mean "income determination accounting," and thus to connote the recognition of depreciation in the course of expense measurement. This misunderstanding likely has arisen because most literature centers on income determination and uses the terms "accrual" and "accrual accounting" in that context. It should be recognized, however, that depreciation and amortization are allocations, not accruals, and that "accrual" in a governmental fund accounting context does not mean that depreciation, amortization, and similar allocations should be recognized.[20]

This position is consistent with the AICPA's governmental audit guide, which does not state that the lack of depreciation expense in these funds is a departure from generally accepted accounting principles.

19GASB Cod. sec. 1100.107.
20GASB Cod. sec. 1600.104.

## Category VII: Budgets and Budgetary Accounting

**Budgets.**    Budgets are used in the public sector for planning, controlling, and evaluating operations just as they are used in the private sector. A **budget** is merely a plan of financial operations covering a specified period of time. For all governmental, proprietary, and fiduciary funds (other than Agency Funds), the GASB Codification recommends that "an annual budget(s) should be adopted by every governmental unit."[21]

Prepared under the direction of the governmental unit's chief executive officer, the **annual** budget is submitted to the legislative body for review, possible modification, and formal adoption. The significance of the budget for each of these funds is as follows:

| Fund Type | Significance |
|---|---|
| Governmental Funds and certain Fiduciary Funds | The statutory authorization for spending an estimated amount during the subsequent fiscal year. The authorization is referred to as an **appropriation.** |
| Proprietary Funds and certain Fiduciary Funds | The approval of a proposed operating plan (as distinct from a statutory authorization to spend a certain amount in dollars). |

A **long-term** budget covers a period of several years. Long-term budgets restricted to major capital additions and improvements are referred to as **capital** budgets.

**Budgetary Accounting.**    Because legal limitations are imposed on certain of the funds (primarily the governmental funds) as to the amount that may be spent during a fiscal year, it is exceedingly important to monitor and control spending, so that expenditures do not exceed this limitation. The GASB Codification recommends, "The accounting system should provide the basis for appropriate budgetary control."[22]

The GASB Codification specifies the following two areas in which budgetary accounts should be used to monitor and control spending: (1) recording the annual budget in the general ledger; and (2) recording purchase order commitments in the general ledger, which is referred to as *encumbrance accounting.*

To enhance the understanding of budgetary integration in the general ledger, we use the technique, illustrated in the 1988 edition of *GAAFR*, of **printing budgetary account descriptions in all capital letters.** As a result,

[21]GASB Cod. sec. 1100.109.
[22]GASB Cod. sec. 1100.109.

we can consider all budgetary accounts as a separate trial balance from the regular general ledger accounts. We also use the same account descriptions, for budgetary and actual accounts, used in the 1988 edition of *GAAFR*, because these descriptions are now used by both the AICPA (in its official solutions to the CPA examinations) and the CPA examination review courses (in their course materials).

### Recording the Annual Budget—Simplified Situation Involving No Interfund Transfers.

The budget for the General Fund and Special Revenue Funds is recorded in the general ledger. (The annual budget pertaining to Capital Projects Funds and Debt Service Funds is recorded in the general ledger only if it would serve a useful purpose, determined on a case-by-case basis.) Assuming a governmental unit expects its General Fund revenues to exceed its General Fund appropriations for the new fiscal year, the budget is recorded in the General Fund's general ledger as follows:

| | | |
|---|---:|---:|
| ESTIMATED REVENUES | 1,000,000 | |
| APPROPRIATIONS | | 980,000 |
| BUDGETARY FUND BALANCE | | 20,000 |

To record the legally adopted annual
operating budget.

The ESTIMATED REVENUES account is a control account. Actual revenues are usually recorded in individual subsidiary Revenue accounts (and in a Revenues Control Account). The detail making up the ESTIMATED REVENUES account is also recorded directly in the individual subsidiary Revenue accounts at the start of the year. As a result, estimated revenues may be readily compared with actual revenues throughout the year. Although revenues cannot be "controlled" in the manner that expenditures can be controlled, a governmental unit may be able to curtail spending if it appears that revenue inflows will not be reasonably close to estimated revenues.

Likewise, the APPROPRIATIONS account is a control account. Actual expenditures are usually recorded in individual subsidiary Expenditures accounts, (and in an Expenditures Control account). The detail making up the APPROPRIATIONS account is also recorded directly in the individual subsidiary Expenditures accounts at the start of the year. As a result, expenditures to date may be readily compared with the authorized spending limitation, revealing how much more may be spent.

A governmental unit's budget for the coming fiscal year may reflect an intention to increase (as in the above example) or decrease the fund balance amount existing at the beginning of the year. Most governmental units (with the notable exception of the federal government) try to accumulate a reasonable "surplus" in the Fund Balance account in case unforeseen adverse events occur. In recording the budget in the general ledger, the difference between the debit to ESTIMATED REVENUES and the credit to APPROPRIATIONS is credited (as in the above example) or debited to BUDGETARY FUND BALANCE.

Recording the budget in the general ledger does not affect the year-end balance in the Fund Balance account because the budget entry is reversed at year-end as part of the normal closing process.

### Recording the Annual Budget—Typical Situation Involving Interfund Transfers.

When interfund transfers exist, up to four additional budgetary accounts may be used to record the budget. The budgetary accounts can be classified as either those that pertain to inflows or those that pertain to outflows as shown below:

**Budgetary Accounts Pertaining to Estimated Inflows (recorded as debits)**
ESTIMATED REVENUES
ESTIMATED OPERATING TRANSFERS IN
ESTIMATED RESIDUAL EQUITY TRANSFERS IN

**Budgetary Accounts Pertaining to Legally Authorized Outflows (recorded as credits)**
APPROPRIATIONS (a general category)
APPROPRIATIONS—OPERATING TRANSFERS OUT
APPROPRIATIONS—RESIDUAL EQUITY TRANSFERS OUT

The budgetary account BUDGETARY FUND BALANCE is not listed in either of the above categories as it is merely used to balance the entry recording the budget. Later in the chapter, we illustrate the use of some of these additional budgetary accounts that pertain to interfund transfers.

---

#### Comparative Practice Note

The illustrative entries shown in the 1988 edition of *GAAFR* use the accounts ESTIMATED OTHER FINANCING SOURCES—OPERATING TRANSFERS IN and APPROPRIATIONS: OTHER FINANCING USES—OPERATING TRANSFERS OUT. The use of the additional descriptive terminology OTHER FINANCING SOURCES and OTHER FINANCING USES (the category in the operating statement under which operating transfers are to be reported) is unnecessary and cumbersome in our opinion. Inquiries to numerous cities and counties reveal that almost all governmental units bypass this additional descriptive terminology in recording their annual budgets.

---

### Encumbrance Accounting.

As stated earlier, expenditures are recognized when the fund liability is incurred, which is usually when goods are received or services are rendered. Many expenditures involve the issuance of purchase orders, whereby goods are received or services are rendered at a later date. Outstanding purchase orders are commitments for future expenditures. To monitor and control spending properly, governmental units must keep track of the amount of outstanding purchase orders. This is accomplished by recording the amount of each purchase order (including the amount of contracts entered into) in the general ledger at the time of issuance. For example, assuming a purchase order for $50,000 is issued, the following budgetary entry would be made:

ENCUMBRANCES............................ 50,000
    BUDGETARY FUND BALANCE
      RESERVED FOR ENCUMBRANCES....         50,000
  To record encumbrances for purchase
  orders issued.

The ENCUMBRANCES account may be thought of as an "expenditure-to-be" account. Likewise, the BUDGETARY FUND BALANCE RESERVED FOR ENCUMBRANCES account may be thought of as a "liability-to-be" account. At a later date, when the goods are received or services are rendered, the entry is reversed and the expenditure and liability are recorded. Assume in the preceding example tht the actual cost of the goods received under the purchase was $49,000. The following entries would be made:

BUDGETARY FUND BALANCE RESERVED FOR
  ENCUMBRANCES........................... 50,000
    ENCUMBRANCES.......................         50,000
  To cancel encumbrances of $50,000 upon
    receipt of materials and rendering of
    services totaling $49,000.
Expenditures.................................. 49,000
  Vouchers Payable.......................         49,000
  To record expenditures of $49,000 for goods
  and services which were previously
  encumbered for $50,000.

Like the APPROPRIATIONS account, the ENCUMBRANCES account is a control account. Each encumbrance is usually recorded in the individual subsidiary Expenditures accounts. As a result, the remaining amount that may be legally spent at a given time is readily determined by subtracting expenditures to date and encumbrances outstanding from appropriations. (Because an Expenditures Control account is also maintained, this calculation can be done at the control level or at the detail level using the individual subsidiary accounts.)

Illustration 20-3 shows what a subsidiary ledger might look like at the departmental level. Note that the format indicates the spendable amount

**■ ILLUSTRATION 20-3**
**Example of a Department's Subsidiary Ledger Account**

| Department No. 34 | | | | |
|---|---|---|---|---|
| Date | Appropriation | Expenditures | Encumbrances | Remaining Spendable Amount |
| July 1, 19X1......... | $100,000 | | | $100,000 |
| July 19X1 ......... | | $ 6,000 | $7,000 | (13,000) |
| July 31, 19X1........ | $100,000 | $ 6,000 | $7,000 | $ 87,000 |
| August 19X1........ | | 11,000 | (3,000) | (8,000) |
| August 31, 19X1..... | $100,000 | $17,000 | $4,000 | $ 79,000 |

remaining at the end of each month. (Only two months' activities are illustrated.) If an encumbrances column were not included, the department supervisor might erroneously conclude that $94,000 ($100,000 appropriations − $6,000 expenditures) was available for spending at July 31, 19X1. This figure is incorrect because purchase orders outstanding at July 31, 19X1, total $7,000. Thus, of the $94,000 not yet spent at July 31, 19X1, $7,000 is earmarked for the outstanding purchase orders. This leaves only $87,000 available for spending at July 31, 19X1. The objective of the procedure, of course, is to prevent spending more than has been authorized (appropriated).

From the preceding discussion and analysis, you should realize that only the debit entry recording the encumbrance is used in controlling spending. The credit to the BUDGETARY FUND BALANCE RESERVED FOR ENCUMBRANCES account serves no control function other than to provide a credit for double-entry bookkeeping. Thus, it is merely a contra account. The steps in the process of using financial resources may be summarized as follows:

1. **Appropriation** (legal authorization to spend by governing body).
2. **Encumbrances** (commitment to spend by issuing purchase orders or signing contracts).
3. **Expenditures** (liability incurred upon vendor or contractor performance).
4. **Disbursement** (actual payment of liability).

**Budgetary Comparisons.** A financial reporting requirement of the GASB Codification is the preparation of "budgetary comparison statements or schedules" (as appropriate) in which budgeted data are compared with actual data for the year. Under GAAP reporting, encumbrances outstanding at year-end are not reported in the statement of revenues, expenditures, and changes in fund balance. They would become expenditures in the following year and be reported as expenditures in that year. To present a meaningful comparison of actual expenditures with the budgeted expenditures, the budgeted expenditures must be prepared on a basis consistent with GAAP. To do this, amounts must be included in the following year's budget for encumbrances outstanding at the current year-end. Thus, it can be said that **encumbrances outstanding at the end of the current year "lapse," but then they are "rebudgeted" and "reappropriated" in the following year.** Without this procedure, the following year's expenditures would include amounts relating to the encumbrances outstanding at the end of the prior year, but no amount would appear in the following year's budget for these expenditures, resulting in a meaningless comparison.

To illustrate this comparison process, we assume the following data:

1. For 19X1, a governmental unit expects routine expenditures of $500,000 and also the purchase of a new fire truck for $30,000. Thus, it budgets $530,000 for 19X1 expenditures.
2. Actual spending occurs according to budget, except that the fire truck is received in early 19X2 rather than 19X1.
3. The governmental unit expects routine expenditures of $500,000 for 19X2. It also "reappropriates" or "rebudgets" an additional $30,000 to cover the fire truck for 19X2. Thus, the total budget for 19X2 expenditures is $530,000.
4. Actual spending for 19X2 occurs according to budget.

The budgetary comparison is as follows:

|  | Budget | Actual | Variance Favorable (Unfavorable) |
|---|---|---|---|
| 19X1: |  |  |  |
| Expenditures ......... | $530,000 | $500,000 | $30,000 |
| 19X2: |  |  |  |
| Expenditures ......... | 530,000 | 530,000 | –0– |

# THE GENERAL FUND

Recall that (1) the General Fund is a governmental fund, (2) governmental funds use the modified accrual basis of accounting, and (3) the measurement focus for governmental funds is the flow of resources.

## Nature and Scope of Activities

The **General Fund** accounts for all revenues and expenditures of a governmental unit that are not accounted for in one of the special purpose funds.

Because all other funds are special purpose funds, most activities and current operations of governmental units are financed from the General Fund. For instance, general government administration, public safety, judicial system, health, sanitation, welfare, and culture-recreation are usually accounted for in this fund.

Normally, more types of revenues flow into this fund than any other fund. For example, property taxes, sales taxes, income taxes, transfer taxes, licenses, permits, fines, penalties, and interest on delinquent taxes commonly flow into the General Fund. In addition, the General Fund may receive monies from other governmental units; such receipts are classified by the GASB Codification as follows:

> **Grant.** A contribution or gift of cash or other assets from another government to be used or expended for a specified purpose, activity, or facility.
> **Capital grant.** A contribution or gift of cash or other assets restricted by the grantor for the acquisition and/or construction of fixed (capital) assets [which would be accounted for in a Capital Projects Fund].
> **Operating grant.** Grants that are intended to finance operations or that may be used for either operations or capital outlays at the discretion of the grantee.
> **Entitlement.** The amount of payment to which a state or local government is entitled as determined by the federal government (e.g., the Director of the Office of Revenue Sharing) pursuant to an allocation formula contained in applicable statutes.
> **Shared revenue.** A revenue levied by one government but shared on a predetermined basis, often in proportion to the amount collected at the local level, with another government or class of government.[23]

**ILLUSTRATION**

## COMPREHENSIVE   Journal Entries and Financial Statements

The June 30, 19X1, balance sheet for Funn City's General Fund is shown in Illustration 20-4.

Before proceeding with assumed transactions for the subsequent fiscal year, the following points should be understood with regard to Illustration 20-4:

1. **Inventory.** The "consumption method" (discussed in more detail later) is used to account for the supplies inventory. Under this method, the inventory is viewed as a resource just as is cash and receivables. No reservation of the fund balance is made under the consumption method.
2. **Fund Balance—Unreserved.** The entire fund balance of $105,000 is designated as being "unreserved." This signifies that the fund has

---

[23]GASB Cod. sec. G60.501–505.

■ **ILLUSTRATION 20-4**

| FUNN CITY | |
|---|---|
| **Balance Sheet—General Fund** | |
| **June 30, 19X1** | |
| **Assets** | |
| Cash. . . . . . . . . . . . . . . . . . . . . . . . . . . . . . . . . . . . . . . . . . . . . . . . . . . . . . . | $ 90,000 |
| Property taxes receivable—delinquent . . . . . . . . . . . . . . . . . . . . . . | 43,000 |
| Less: Allowance for estimated uncollectible taxes—delinquent. . . | (3,000) |
| Inventory . . . . . . . . . . . . . . . . . . . . . . . . . . . . . . . . . . . . . . . . . . . . . . . | 10,000 |
| Total Assets. . . . . . . . . . . . . . . . . . . . . . . . . . . . . . . . . . . . . . . | $140,000 |
| **Liabilities and Fund Equity** | |
| Vouchers payable. . . . . . . . . . . . . . . . . . . . . . . . . . . . . . . . . . . . . . . . | $ 35,000 |
| Fund balance: | |
| Unreserved . . . . . . . . . . . . . . . . . . . . . . . . . . . . . . . . . . . . . . . . . . . . . | 105,000 |
| Total Liabilities and Fund Equity. . . . . . . . . . . . . . . . . . . . | $140,000 |

$105,000 of assets available for spending in the following fiscal year. Later in this illustration, we examine when a portion of the fund balance must be shown as being reserved.

Assumed transactions and related journal entries for the fiscal year July 1, 19X1, through June 30, 19X2, are discussed in the following paragraphs.

**1. Adoption of the Budget.** The city council approved and adopted the budget for the year. The budget contained the following amounts:

| | |
|---|---|
| Estimated revenues. . . . . . . . . . . . . . . . . . . . . . . . . . . . . . . . . . . . . | $700,000 |
| Authorized expenditures . . . . . . . . . . . . . . . . . . . . . . . . . . . . . . . . | 660,000 |
| Authorized operating transfer out to the Library Debt | |
| Service Fund. . . . . . . . . . . . . . . . . . . . . . . . . . . . . . . . . . . . . . . . . . | 30,000 |
| Authorized residual equity transfer out to establish a | |
| Central Motor Pool Internal Service Fund . . . . . . . . . . . . . . | 25,000 |

As explained earlier, the adoption of the budget for the General Fund involves the use of budgetary accounts, as follows:

| | Dr. | Cr. |
|---|---|---|
| ESTIMATED REVENUES. . . . . . . . . . . . . . . . . . . . . | 700,000 | |
| BUDGETARY FUND BALANCE . . . . . . . . . . . . . . . | 15,000 | |
| APPROPRIATIONS . . . . . . . . . . . . . . . . . . . . . . | | 660,000[a] |
| APPROPRIATIONS—OPERATING | | |
| TRANSFERS OUT . . . . . . . . . . . . . . . . . . . . | | 30,000 |

|  | Dr. | Cr. |
|---|---|---|
| APPROPRIATIONS—RESIDUAL EQUITY TRANSFER OUT |  | 25,000 |

To record the legally adopted annual
operating budget.

[a]In practice, this amount is often broken down by category, such as General Government, Public Safety, Sanitation, etc.

### 2. Property Taxes.

Property taxes for the period July 1, 19X1, through June 30, 19X2, were levied in the amount of $500,000. It was estimated that $5,000 of this amount would be uncollectible. During the year, $485,000 was collected ($41,000 of which pertained to delinquent taxes of the prior fiscal year), and $2,000 of prior-year delinquent balances was written off as uncollectible. A $9,000 allowance for uncollectibles was considered necessary as of June 30, 19X2. The net amount expected to be collected is expected to be collected within 60 days. Property taxes unpaid at the end of the fiscal year become delinquent.

As explained earlier, the accrual basis of accounting is usually appropriate for property taxes. In this case, the city's fiscal year coincides with the period to which the property taxes relate; accordingly, the property tax levy is appropriately recorded on the first day of the new fiscal year. In recording the property taxes, the estimated uncollectible amount is netted against the revenues, and the use of a Bad Debts Expense account is avoided. A Bad Debts Expense account would be inappropriate, because the General Fund has expenditures, not expenses. At the end of the fiscal year, remaining property tax receivables and the related allowance for uncollectible accounts are transferred to accounts that designate these items as relating to delinquent taxes. Thus, tax levies of the following fiscal year may be separated from the delinquent taxes.

| | Dr. | Cr. |
|---|---|---|
| Property Taxes Receivable—Current | 500,000 | |
|     Allowance for Uncollectibles—Current | | 5,000 |
|     Revenues | | 495,000 |
| To record the property tax levy. | | |
| Cash | 485,000 | |
|     Property Taxes Receivable—Current | | 444,000 |
|     Property Taxes Receivable—Delinquent | | 41,000 |
| To record the collection of property taxes. | | |
| Allowance for Uncollectibles—Delinquent | 2,000 | |
|     Property Taxes Receivable—Delinquent | | 2,000 |
| To write off accounts determined to be uncollectible. | | |
| Allowance for Uncollectibles—Delinquent | 1,000 | |
|     Revenues | | 1,000 |

*(continued)*

To eliminate the remaining balance in
the Allowance for Uncollectibles—
Delinquent account as a result of
collections of $41,000 being in excess
of the $40,000 net amount estimated
to be collected at the end of the prior
year.[a]

| | | |
|---|---|---|
| Revenues | 4,000 | |
|     Allowance for Uncollectibles—Current | | 4,000 |

To increase the allowance for
uncollectibles—current from $5,000
to $9,000.

| | | |
|---|---|---|
| Property Taxes Receivable—Delinquent | 56,000 | |
| Allowance for Uncollectibles—Current | 9,000 | |
|     Property Taxes Receivable—Current | | 56,000 |
|     Allowance for Uncollectibles—Delinquent | | 9,000 |

To transfer the fiscal year-end balances
to the delinquent accounts.

[a]The beginning of year balance in the Allowance for Uncollectibles—Delinquent account was $3,000.

### 3. Revenues Other Than Property Taxes.

The total estimated revenues for the year include an estimated **entitlement** from the federal government of $22,000. We assume these funds are used for purposes normally financed through the General Fund. The amount is assumed to be susceptible to accrual; the actual amount received midway through the year is $23,000. Revenues of $181,000 are collected from sales taxes, business licenses, permits, and miscellaneous sources. Because these revenues are not susceptible to accrual, they are accounted for on the cash basis.

| | | |
|---|---|---|
| Entitlement Receivable | 22,000 | |
|     Revenues | | 22,000 |

To record entitlement from the federal government.

| | | |
|---|---|---|
| Cash | 23,000 | |
|     Entitlement Receivable | | 22,000 |
|     Revenues | | 1,000 |

To record collection of entitlement.

| | | |
|---|---|---|
| Cash | 181,000 | |
|     Revenues | | 181,000 |

To record revenues accounted for on the cash basis.

### 4. Expenditures and Encumbrances for Items Other Than Inventory.

During the year, $115,000 of encumbrances on purchase orders (pertaining to other than inventory) and contracts were recorded. For $103,000 of these encumbrances, the city received billings of $102,000, which it approved for payment. Additional expenditures of $524,000 (which did not involve the use of purchase orders or contracts) were incurred.

| | | |
|---|---|---|
| ENCUMBRANCES | 115,000 | |
|     BUDGETARY FUND BALANCE | | |
|         RESERVED FOR ENCUMBRANCES | | 115,000 |
|     To record encumbrances on purchase | | |
|     orders issued. | | |
| | | |
| BUDGETARY FUND BALANCE RESERVED | | |
|     FOR ENCUMBRANCES | 103,000 | |
|         ENCUMBRANCES | | 103,000 |
|     To cancel encumbrances of $103,000 | | |
|     upon receipt of goods and services | | |
|     totaling $102,000. | | |
| | | |
| Expenditures | 102,000 | |
|     Vouchers Payable | | 102,000 |
|     To record expenditures of $102,000 for | | |
|     goods and services which were | | |
|     previously encumbered for $103,000. | | |
| | | |
| Expenditures | 524,000 | |
|     Vouchers Payable | | 524,000 |
|     To record expenditures for items not | | |
|     previously encumbered. | | |

### 5. Acquisition and Consumption of Inventory.
During the current year, purchase orders totaling $15,000 for supplies were issued. All of these purchase orders were filled by year-end, with billings of $15,000 having been received and approved. The government uses the "consumption" method of accounting for supplies inventories whereby the inventory account is charged upon acquisition. As the supplies are used, the inventory account is relieved and the Expenditures account is charged. (Note that this manner of accounting parallels the accounting for inventories for commercial enterprises). During the year, $11,000 of supplies were consumed.

| | | |
|---|---|---|
| ENCUMBRANCES | 15,000 | |
|     BUDGETARY FUND BALANCE | | |
|         RESERVED FOR ENCUMBRANCES | | 15,000 |
|     To record encumbrances on purchase | | |
|     orders issued for supplies. | | |
| | | |
| BUDGETARY FUND BALANCE | | |
|     RESERVED FOR ENCUMBRANCES | 15,000 | |
|         ENCUMBRANCES | | 15,000 |

*(continued)*

To cancel encumbrances of $15,000 upon
receipt of goods totaling $15,000

| | | |
|---|---|---|
| Inventory | 15,000 | |
|     Vouchers Payable | | 15,000 |
| To record acquisition of supplies received. | | |

| | | |
|---|---|---|
| Expenditures | 11,000 | |
|     Inventory | | 11,000 |
| To record consumption of supplies used during the year. | | |

---

### Comparative Practice Note

Some governmental units simplify the procedures under the consumption method by assuming throughout the year that the supplies received will always approximate the supplies used. Accordingly, they charged the Expenditures account as the supplies are received instead of charging the Inventory account. At year-end, a physical count is taken and the Inventory account is adjusted to its proper balance (the offsetting adjustment being to the Expenditures account).

---

If significant amounts of inventory exist at the balance sheet date, the GASB Codification requires such inventory to be reported in the balance sheet. This automatically occurs under the consumption method. Note that under the consumption method, the acquisition of inventory is viewed merely as **the conversion of resources (from cash to inventory)— not the use of resources.** The GASB Codification also sanctions the use of the "purchases" method, which takes the opposite position and, therefore, results in the charging of the Expenditures account upon acquisition of inventory. However, the purchases method is an outdated method that has lost much support in recent years. Under the GASB's new MFBOA standard (scheduled to become effective in 1994), the purchases method is prohibited. At the end of the chapter we discuss the purchases method in detail and show its procedures for reporting significant amounts of inventory in the balance sheet.

### 6. Disbursements (Other Than Interfund). Cash disbursements totaled $606,000.

| | | |
|---|---|---|
| Vouchers Payable | 606,000 | |
|     Cash | | 606,000 |
| To record cash disbursements other than interfund disbursements. | | |

### 7. Interfund Transactions. The city had the following interfund transactions:

## A. Quasi-External Transactions

During the year, the city's electric utility, which is operated as an Enterprise Fund, rendered billings for electricity supplied to the General Fund in the amount of $21,000. Of this amount, $19,000 was paid during the fiscal year. These billings qualify for treatment as **quasi-external transactions.** Accordingly, they are treated as expenditures in the General Fund (and as revenues in the Enterprise Fund).

| | | |
|---|---:|---:|
| Expenditures | 21,000 | |
| Due to Electric Utility Enterprise Fund | | 21,000 |
| To record as expenditures electricity acquired from the Electric Utility Enterprise Fund. | | |
| | | |
| Due to Electric Utility Enterprise Fund | 19,000 | |
| Cash | | 19,000 |
| To record payment made to Electric Utility Enterprise Fund. | | |

## B. Operating Transfer

The operating transfer of $30,000 to be made to the Library Debt Service Fund is recorded on the first day of the fiscal year, because the amount is susceptible to being accrued.

| | | |
|---|---:|---:|
| Other Financing Uses—Operating Transfers Out | 30,000 | |
| Due to Library Debt Service Fund | | 30,000 |
| To record operating transfer to be made to the Library Debt Service Fund. | | |

The following entry assumes the payment was made in accordance with the authorized amounts.

| | | |
|---|---:|---:|
| Due to Library Debt Service Fund | 30,000 | |
| Cash | | 30,000 |
| To record payment of operating transfer to the Library Debt Service Fund. | | |

## C. Residual Equity Transfer

The Central Motor Pool Internal Service Fund was established in September 19X1. A residual equity transfer was made from the General Fund.

| | | |
|---|---:|---:|
| Residual Equity Transfer Out | 25,000 | |
| Cash | | 25,000 |
| To record residual equity transfer to the newly-established Central Motor Pool Internal Service Fund. | | |

The General Fund preclosing trial balances after recording the preceding items are shown in Illustration 20-5.

### 8. Closing Entries (excluding Encumbrances).  The closing entries at June 30, 19X2 are as follows:

| | Dr. | Cr. |
|---|---|---|
| APPROPRIATIONS . . . . . . . . . . . . . . . . . . . . . . . . . . | 660,000 | |
| APPROPRIATIONS—OPERATING TRANSFER OUT . . . . . . . . . . . . . . . . . . . . . . . . | 30,000 | |
| APPROPRIATIONS—RESIDUAL EQUITY TRANSFER OUT . . . . . . . . . . . . . . . . . . . . . | 25,000 | |
| ESTIMATED REVENUES . . . . . . . . . . . . . . . | | 700,000 |

### ■ ILLUSTRATION 20-5

| FUNN CITY<br>Preclosing Trial Balances—General Fund<br>June 30, 19X2 | | |
|---|---|---|
| | **Debit** | **Credit** |
| **Actual (nonbudgetary) Accounts** | | |
| Cash. . . . . . . . . . . . . . . . . . . . . . . . . . . . . . . . | 99,000 | |
| Property taxes receivable—delinquent . . . . . . . . . . . | 56,000 | |
| Allowance for estimated uncollectibles— delinquent. . . . . . . . . . . . . . . . . . . . . . . . . . . . | | 9,000 |
| Inventory . . . . . . . . . . . . . . . . . . . . . . . . . . . . . | 14,000 | |
| Vouchers payable . . . . . . . . . . . . . . . . . . . . . . | | 70,000 |
| Due to Electric Utility Enterprise Fund. . . . . . . . | | 2,000 |
| Unreserved fund balance. . . . . . . . . . . . . . . . . . . | | 105,000 |
| Revenues . . . . . . . . . . . . . . . . . . . . . . . . . . . . . | | 696,000 |
| Expenditures . . . . . . . . . . . . . . . . . . . . . . . . . . . | 658,000 | |
| Other Financing Uses—Operating transfers out. . . | 30,000 | |
| Residual equity transfer out. . . . . . . . . . . . . . . . . | 25,000 | |
| Totals. . . . . . . . . . . . . . . . . . . . . . . . . . . . . . | 882,000 | 882,000 |
| **Budgetary Accounts** | | |
| ESTIMATED REVENUES. . . . . . . . . . . . . . . . . . . . . | 700,000 | |
| BUDGETARY FUND BALANCE . . . . . . . . . . . . . . . . . | 15,000 | |
| APPROPRIATIONS . . . . . . . . . . . . . . . . . . . . . . . | | 660,000 |
| APPROPRIATIONS—OPERATING TRANSFER OUT . . . . . . . . . . . . . . . . . . . . . . . . . . . . . | | 30,000 |
| APPROPRIATIONS—RESIDUAL EQUITY TRANSFER OUT. . . . . . . . . . . . . . . . . . . . . . . . . | | 25,000 |
| ENCUMBRANCES CONTROL . . . . . . . . . . . . . . . . . . | 12,000 | |
| BUDGETARY FUND BALANCE RESERVED FOR ENCUMBRANCES . . . . . . . . . . . . . . . . . . . | | 12,000 |
| Totals. . . . . . . . . . . . . . . . . . . . . . . . . . . . . . | 727,000 | 727,000 |

|  | Dr. | Cr. |
|---|---|---|
| BUDGETARY FUND BALANCE . . . . . . . . . . |  | 15,000 |

To reverse the entry previously made
to record the legally adopted annual
operating budget.

| Revenues . . . . . . . . . . . . . . . . . . . . . . . . . . . . . . . | 696,000 |  |
|---|---|---|
| Expenditures . . . . . . . . . . . . . . . . . . . . . . . |  | 658,000 |
| Other Financing Uses—Operating |  |  |
| Transfers Out. . . . . . . . . . . . . . . . . . . . . . |  | 30,000 |
| Unreserved Fund Balance . . . . . . . . . . . . . |  | 8,000 |

To close operating statement accounts.

| Unreserved Fund Balance . . . . . . . . . . . . . . . . . . . . | 25,000 |  |
|---|---|---|
| Residual Equity Transfer Out . . . . . . . . . . |  | 25,000 |

To close residual equity transfer out
(a nonoperating statement account to be
shown as a direct adjustment to the
beginning fund balance).

**9. Closing Entry Relating to Encumbrances.** When encumbrances are outstanding at year-end, the encumbrances budgetary accounts must be closed as follows:

| BUDGETARY FUND BALANCE RESERVED |  |  |
|---|---|---|
| FOR ENCUMBRANCES. . . . . . . . . . . . . . . . . . . . . . | 12,000 |  |
| ENCUMBRANCES. . . . . . . . . . . . . . . . . . . . . . . |  | 12,000 |

To close encumbrances outstanding at
year-end by reversing the entry that
previously recorded them.

**10. Adjusting Entry to Reserve a Portion of the Fund Balance.** If the governmental unit intends to honor purchase orders and commitments outstanding at year-end (the customary practice), the encumbrances outstanding must be disclosed as a reservation of the Fund Balance account (similar to an appropriation of retained earnings for a commercial corporation). This requires the following adjusting entry:

| Unreserved Fund Balance . . . . . . . . . . . . . . . . . . . . | 12,000 |  |
|---|---|---|
| Fund Balance Reserved for |  |  |
| Encumbrances . . . . . . . . . . . . . . . . . . . . . . . |  | 12,000 |

To record *actual* fund balance reserve
account to indicate the portion of the
year-end fund balance segregated for
expenditure upon vendor performance.

At the start of the new year, the preceding two $12,000 journal entries would be reversed to reestablish budgetary control over encumbrances outstanding in the normal manner. These reversing entries are as follows:

|  |  |  |
|---|---|---|
| Fund Balance Reserved for Encumbrances.... | 12,000 | |
| Unreserved Fund Balance ............... | | 12,000 |

To reverse appropriation of fund balance
made at the end of the prior year.

|  |  |  |
|---|---|---|
| ENCUMBRANCES......................... | 12,000 | |
| BUDGETARY FUND BALANCE | | |
| RESERVED FOR ENCUMBRANCES.... | | 12,000 |

To reestablish budgetary control over
encumbrances outstanding at the end of
the prior year which will be honored
during the current year.

The individual financial statements for the fiscal year ended June 30,
19X2, are shown in Illustrations 20-6 and 20-7.

## Manner of Classifying Expenditures

The operating statement for Funn City classifies expenditures by **character** and **function.** Character refers to the fiscal period that the expenditures are presumed to benefit. Virtually all of Funn City's expenditures

### ■ ILLUSTRATION 20-6

| **FUNN CITY** Balance Sheet—General Fund June 30, 19X2 |  |
|---|---|
| **Assets** | |
| Cash......................................................... | $ 99,000 |
| Property taxes receivable—delinquent ......................... | 56,000[a] |
| Less: Allowance for estimated uncollectible taxes—delinquent ... | (9,000) |
| Inventory.................................................... | 14,000 |
| Total Assets .......................................... | $160,000 |
| **Liabilities and Fund Equity** | |
| Vouchers payable............................................. | $ 70,000 |
| Due to Electric Utility Enterprise Fund ...................... | 2,000 |
| Total Liabilities ..................................... | $ 72,000 |
| Fund balance: | |
| Reserved for encumbrances................................. | $ 12,000 |
| Unreserved................................................ | 76,000 |
| Total Fund Balance ................................... | $ 88,000 |
| Total Liabilities and Fund Equity..................... | $160,000 |

[a]No Deferred Revenues are shown in the balance sheet. Thus, it was assumed that the $47,000 net
realizable amount of the property tax receivables ($56,000 − $9,000) is expected to be collected
within 60 days enabling such receipts to be "available to pay existing liabilities." If only $20,000
were expected to be collected within 60 days, then $27,000 of Deferred Revenues would have to
be reflected.

**■ ILLUSTRATION 20-7**

**FUNN CITY**
**Statement of Revenues, Expenditures, and**
**Changes in Fund Balance—Budget and Actual—General Fund**
**For the Fiscal Year Ended June 30, 19X2**

| Classified by | | Budget | Actual | Variance Favorable (Unfavorable) |
|---|---|---|---|---|
| | **Revenues** | | | |
| | Property taxes . . . . . . . . . . . . . . . . . . . . . . . . | $495,000 | $492,000 | $(3,000) |
| | Intergovernmental grant . . . . . . . . . . . . . . . . | 22,000 | 23,000 | 1,000 |
| Source | Sales taxes[a] . . . . . . . . . . . . . . . . . . . . . . . . . . | 130,000 | 124,000 | (6,000) |
| | Licenses and permits[a] . . . . . . . . . . . . . . . . . . | 45,000 | 38,000 | (7,000) |
| | Miscellaneous[a] . . . . . . . . . . . . . . . . . . . . . . . . | 8,000 | 19,000 | 11,000 |
| | Total Revenues . . . . . . . . . . . . . . . . . . . . . | $700,000 | $696,000 | $(4,000) |
| | **Expenditures** | | | |
| Character | Current: | | | |
| | General government[a] . . . . . . . . . . . . . . . . . . | $103,000 | $101,000 | $ 2,000 |
| | Public safety[a] . . . . . . . . . . . . . . . . . . . . . . . . | 215,000 | 220,000 | (5,000) |
| Function | Sanitation[a] . . . . . . . . . . . . . . . . . . . . . . . . . . | 50,000 | 49,500 | 500 |
| | Health[a] . . . . . . . . . . . . . . . . . . . . . . . . . . . . . | 40,000 | 41,500 | (1,500) |
| | Welfare[a] . . . . . . . . . . . . . . . . . . . . . . . . . . . . | 70,000 | 62,700 | 7,300 |
| | Education[a] . . . . . . . . . . . . . . . . . . . . . . . . . . | 175,000 | 176,300 | (1,300) |
| | Subtotal. . . . . . . . . . . . . . . . . . . . . . . . . . . | $653,000 | $651,000 | $ 2,000 |
| Character | Capital outlay. . . . . . . . . . . . . . . . . . . . . . . . . | 7,000 | 7,000 | — |
| | Total Expenditures . . . . . . . . . . . . . . . . . | $660,000 | $658,000 | $ 2,000 |
| | Excess of Revenues over Expenditures | $ 40,000 | $ 38,000 | $(2,000) |
| | **Other Financing Sources (Uses)** | | | |
| | Operating transfers out . . . . . . . . . . . . . . . . . | $ (30,000) | $ (30,000) | — |
| | Total Other Financing Sources (Uses) | $ (30,000) | $ (30,000) | — |
| | Excess of Revenues and Other Sources over Expenditures and Other Uses . . . . | $ 10,000 | $ 8,000 | $(2,000) |
| | **Fund Balance (in total)—July 1, 19X1** . . . . . | 105,000 | 105,000[b] | — |
| | Residual equity transfer out to establish Internal Service Fund . . . . . . . . . . . . . . . . | (25,000) | (25,000) | — |
| | **Fund Balance (in total)—June 30, 19X2** . . . | $ 90,000 | $ 88,000[b] | $(2,000) |

Note: Some governmental units use only the *Unreserved Fund Balance* rather than the *total* Fund Balance in the changes in fund balance section of the statement. Inquiries made to the GFOA revealed that only about 10% of the governmental units use this manner of reporting. However, the GFOA does deem this manner of reporting to be GAAP.

[a]These assumed amounts were not given in the transactions and journal entries.
[b]This is the total fund balance (reserved and unreserved portions).

were presumed to benefit the current fiscal year. Other major categories of character classification are *Capital Outlay* (which benefits primarily future periods) and *Debt Service* (which benefits the period encompassing the useful life of the related fixed assets acquired or constructed with the proceeds of the borrowing).

Note that the operating statement shows a minor amount for the Capital Outlay category and no Debt Service category. In Chapter 21, which covers the other types of funds, the capital outlay category is also encountered in Capital Projects Funds (in which the amounts are usually not minor); the debt service category is encountered in Debt Service Funds.

When desirable, the major functions may be subdivided into **activities** and **objects.** For example, the sanitation function could be subdivided into sewage treatment and disposal, garbage collection, garbage disposal, and street cleaning. Alternatively, the sanitation function could be subdivided into employee salaries, contracted services, materials, and supplies. These other ways of classifying expenditures may be presented in the financial statements, in supporting schedules to the financial statements, or in notes to the financial statements.

## Manner of Reporting Inventory under the Purchases Method

Recall that under the purchases method, inventory is charged to the Expenditures account upon acquisition, regardless of when actually consumed. Thus, the use of resources is deemed to occur upon the acquisition—not the consumption. To report significant amounts of inventory in the balance sheet when the purchases method is used, the following entry is used:

| | | |
|---|---|---|
| Inventory of Supplies......................... | xxx | |
|     Fund Balance Reserved for Inventory | | |
|       of Supplies ........................... | | xxx |
|    To report supplies inventory in the | | |
|     balance sheet. | | |

This entry, which is made only in the balance sheet, superimposes inventory into the balance sheet—no adjustment is made to the Expenditures account. If the amount of inventory on hand changes from the preceding balance sheet date, the above two accounts are adjusted accordingly. Note that the credit side of the entry is to Fund Balance Reserved for Inventory of Supplies and not to the Unreserved Fund Balance Account. The reason for this is that it would be improper to credit the Unreserved Fund Balance account because that would indicate an additional amount available for spending, when in fact the inventory has already been reported as an expenditure in the operating statement. Thus, it cannot be "spent" twice.

# SUMMARY OF MAJOR CHANGES IN NEW STANDARD ON MEASUREMENT FOCUS AND BASIS OF ACCOUNTING—GOVERNMENTAL FUND OPERATING STATEMENTS

(as set forth in *GASB Statement No. 11*, which was issued in 1990, but is not scheduled to become effective until 1994)

### I. MEASUREMENT FOCUS (WHAT SHOULD BE MEASURED AND REPORTED IN GOVERNMENTAL FUND OPERATING STATEMENTS?):

The **flow of financial resources** is retained as the measurement focus. Unlike current practice, however, **not all sources and uses of financial resources are to be reported in the operating statement—operating debt borrowings and repayments are to be excluded.** (If these items were not excluded, interperiod equity could not be measured inasmuch as governmental units could report having achieved interperiod equity merely by borrowing money to finance current operations.) The following are key definitions:

> **Financial resources.** Cash, claims to cash (such as accounts and taxes receivable and investments in debt securities of another entity), claims to goods or services (such as prepaid items), consumable goods (such as supplies inventories), and investments in equity securities of another entity.
> **Operating debt.** Debt incurred to finance operations (as opposed to **capital debt,** which is debt incurred to finance the construction or acquisition of capital assets).

Comment: This flow of financial resources measurement focus does not fully accomplish a measure of the cost of providing services (a charge for depreciation of capital assets is excluded). However, it is a step in that direction.

### II. BASIS OF ACCOUNTING (WHEN SHOULD TRANSACTIONS AND EVENTS BE RECOGNIZED IN GOVERNMENTAL FUND OPERATING STATEMENTS?):

The use of the accrual basis is mandated in the recognition of revenues and expenditures.

Comment: The occurrence of the underlying transaction or event as the basis for recognition is now the sole criterion—the timing of the inflow or outflow of cash or financial resources is no longer a consideration. Accordingly, the "availability" criterion used for revenue recognition would no longer be operative. Expenditure recognition would no longer be tied to the use of available expendable financial resources. (For supplies inventories and prepayments, the consumption method is mandated, with the currently allowable purchases method being prohibited.)

## Concluding Comments:

The effect on the balance sheet of all the changes in the new MFBOA standard will be dealt with separately, at a later date as part of the GASB's financial reporting project. Although the MFBOA project has a broad scope, it specifically does not establish recognition and measurement standards for the following items (all of which are being dealt with instead in other projects):

1. Pension expenditures.
2. Other post-employment benefits.
3. Special termination benefits.
4. Claims and judgments and related insurance transactions.
5. Intergovernmental grants, entitlements, and shared revenues.

## END-OF-CHAPTER REVIEW

## Summary of Key Points

1. The Governmental Accounting Standards Board (GASB) establishes accounting principles for state and local governments.
2. The major deficiency of current financial reporting by a high percentage of governmental units is the use of practices that result in the omission of substantial liabilities for pension costs and vested sick leave.
3. Fund accounting is used extensively in government.
4. Governmental funds are accounted for on the modified accrual basis (actually a combination of the accrual basis and the cash basis). For proprietary funds, the accrual basis is used inasmuch as activities accounted for in these funds resemble commercial activities.
5. The operating statement for governmental funds is a "flow" of resources (all assets) statement called the statement of revenues, expenditures, and changes in fund balance (an all-inclusive approach)—this is not an income statement. The operating statement for proprietary funds is an income statement.
6. Interfund transactions may be categorized as (a) loans and advances (shown as receivables and payables in the balance sheets), (b) quasi-external transactions (shown as revenues in the fund providing the service and shown as expenditures in the fund receiving the services), (c) residual equity transfers (shown as direct adjustments to the opening fund balance), and (d) operating transfers (shown as an other financing source or use in governmental funds).
7. Budgetary accounts are used to control spending. All budgetary accounts are closed at year-end.
8. Unfilled purchase orders and uncompleted contracts at year-end that are intended to be honored in the following year require a reservation of the fund balance in the balance sheet.

## Glossary of New Terms

**Appropriation** "A legal authorization granted by a legislative body to make expenditures and to incur obligations for specific purposes. An appropriation usually is limited in amount and as time it may be expended."*

**Budgetary accounts** "Accounts used to enter the formally adopted annual operating budget into the general ledger as part of the management control technique of formal budgetary integration."*

**Encumbrances** "Commitments related to unperformed (executory) contracts for goods or services. Used in budgeting, encumbrances are not GAAP expenditures or liabilities, but represent the estimated amount of expenditures ultimately to result if unperformed contracts in process are completed."*

**Expenditures** "Decreases in net financial resources. . . ."*

**Fund** "A fiscal and accounting entity with a self-balancing set of accounts in which cash and other financial resources, all related liabilities and residual equities, or balances, and changes therein, are recorded and segregated to carry on specific activities or attain certain objectives in accordance with special regulations, restrictions or limitations."*

**Fund balance** "The difference between fund assets and fund liabilities of governmental and similar trust funds."*

**General fixed assets** "Capital assets that are not assets of any fund, but of the government unit as a whole. Most often these assets arise from the expenditure of the financial resources of governmental funds."*

**General Fixed Assets Account Group (GFAAG)** "A self-balancing group of accounts established to account for fixed assets of a government not accounted for through specific proprietary funds or trust funds."*

**General Fund** "The fund used to account for all financial resources, except those required to be accounted for in another fund."*

**General long-term debt** "Long-term debt [including special assessment debt for which the governmental unit is obligated] expected to be repaid from governmental funds."*

**General Long-term Debt Account Group** "A self-balancing group of accounts established to account for the unmatured general long-term debt of a government . . ."*

**General purpose financial statements (GPFS).** "Five combined financial statements that, together with the accompanying notes, constitute the minimum financial reporting needed for fair presentation in conformity with GAAP."*

**Operating statement** "The financial statement disclosing the financial results of operations of an entity during an accounting period in conformity with GAAP. In governmental financial reporting, operating statements and statements of changes in fund equity are combined into "all-inclusive" operating statement formats."*

**Operating transfers** "All interfund transfers other than residual equity transfers (e.g., legally authorized transfers from a fund receiving revenue to the fund through which the resources are to be expended)."*

*GAAFR, 1988 edition, Appendix B.

**Other financing sources** "Governmental fund general long-term debt proceeds, amounts equal to the present value of minimum lease payments arising from capital leases, proceeds from the sale of general fixed assets, and operating transfers in. Such amounts are classified separately from revenues on the governmental operating statement."*

**Other financing uses** "Governmental fund operating transfers out and the amount of refunding bond proceeds deposited with the escrow agent. Such amounts are classified separately from expenditures on the governmental operating statement."*

**Quasi-external transactions** "Interfund transactions that would be treated as revenues, expenditures or expenses if they involved organizations external to the government unit (e.g., payments in lieu of taxes from an enterprise fund to the general fund; internal service fund billings to departments; routine employer contributions to a pension trust fund and routine service charges for inspection, engineering, utilities or similar services provided by a department financed from one fund to a department financed from another fund). These transactions should be accounted for as revenues, expenditures or expenses in the funds involved."*

**Residual equity transfers** "Nonrecurring or nonroutine transfers of equity between funds (e.g., contribution of enterprise fund or internal service fund capital by the general fund, subsequent return of all or part of such contribution to the general fund and transfers of residual balances of discontinued funds to the general fund or a debt service fund)."*

# Self-Study Questions

*(Answers are at the end of this chapter.)*

## I. THEORY AND BASIC PRINCIPLES

1. Each of the following is a fund type except
   a. Budgetary.
   b. Fiduciary.
   c. Governmental.
   d. Proprietary.
2. Which of the following is the appropriate basis of accounting for a governmental fund?
   a. Accrual basis.
   b. Cash basis.
   c. Modified accrual basis.
   d. Modified cash basis.
3. Which of the following is the appropriate basis of accounting for a proprietary fund?
   a. Accrual basis.
   b. Cash basis.
   c. Modified accrual basis.
   d. Modified cash basis.

4. Under the modified accrual basis, revenues are recognized in the accounting period in which they
   a. Are collected.
   b. Are measurable.
   c. Become available.
   d. Become available and measurable.

5. Under the modified accrual basis, expenditures are recognized in the accounting period in which the
   a. Liability becomes susceptible to accrual.
   b. Liability is paid.
   c. Liability is incurred.
   d. Liability becomes measurable.

6. The use of financial resources of a fund are broadly referred to as a(n)
   a. Encumbrance.
   b. Expenditure.
   c. Appropriation.
   d. Disbursement.

7. Commitments related to unperformed contracts and purchase orders are called
   a. Appropriations.
   b. Encumbrances.
   c. Expenditures.
   d. Reservations of the fund balance.

8. The statement of revenues, expenditures, and changes in fund balance could in substance be called any of the following except
   a. Statement of Where Got and Where Gone.
   b. Statement of Sources and Uses of Resources.
   c. Statement of Cash Flows.
   d. Statement of Changes in Financial Position.

9. Which of the following is not one of the four types of interfund transactions?
   a. All-inclusive external transactions.
   b. Residual equity transfers.
   c. Operating transfers.
   d. Loans and advances.

10. Indicate how each of the following interfund transactions are classified in the operating statement of a governmental fund:

| | Under Other Financing Sources and Uses | As an Increase to or a Subtraction from the Beginning Fund Balance |
|---|---|---|
| a. | Residual equity transfers | Operating transfers |
| b. | Quasi-external transactions | Residual equity transfers |
| c. | Operating transfers | Loans and Advances |
| d. | Operating transfers | Residual equity transfers |

11. Which of the following items is not reportable under the category "Other Financing Sources and Uses" in the operating statement of a governmental fund?
    a. Bond proceeds.
    b. Quasi-external transactions.
    c. Operating transfers.
    d. Proceeds from sale of general fixed assets.

12. Expenditures may be classified by each of the following categories except
    a. Character.
    b. Function.
    c. Activity.
    d. Object.
    e. Source.

13. Each of the following statements is incorrect except
    a. General long-term debt is a liability of the General Fund.
    b. General Fixed Assets refer to fixed assets that are recorded in the General Fund as assets.
    c. The practice of not recording depreciation in the governmental funds is a departure from the accrual basis of accounting.
    d. It is appropriate for a proprietary fund to report long-term debt.

## II. REVENUES

14. For the four governmental funds, revenues are recognized
    a. In the period to which they relate.
    b. When they become susceptible to accrual.
    c. When earned.
    d. When the related expenditures are recognized.
    e. None of the above.

15. For the four governmental funds, revenues are
    a. Matched against the cost of providing services.
    b. Generated by expenditures.
    c. Earned.
    d. Reported in a quasi-income statement.
    e. None of the above.

16. Under the modified accrual basis, which of the following would be a revenue susceptible to accrual?
    a. Income taxes.
    b. Business licenses.
    c. Sales taxes.
    d. Property taxes.
    e. Parking meter receipts.
    f. None of the above.

17. At the end of the fiscal year, a governmental unit increased its allowance for uncollectible accounts relating to property tax receivables. The entry resulted in a charge to
    a. Unreserved fund balance.
    b. ENCUMBRANCES.

c. Bad debts expense.

d. Revenues.

e. ESTIMATED REVENUES.

f. APPROPRIATIONS.

### III. EXPENDITURES AND ENCUMBRANCES

18. Under the modified accrual basis, expenditures (other than the exceptions) are recognized
    a. When the vendor or contractor submits a bill.
    b. When paid.
    c. When the related revenues are recognized.
    d. When the goods or services are ordered or contracted for.
    e. None of the above.

19. Expenditures are defined as
    a. The cost of providing services.
    b. Costs incurred to generate revenues.
    c. An outflow of resources.
    d. Amounts arising from encumbrances.
    e. None of the above.

20. When a fire truck is received by a governmental unit, it should be recorded in the General Fund as a(n)
    a. Appropriation.
    b. Encumbrance.
    c. Expenditure.
    d. Expense.
    e. Fixed asset.
    f. Transfer to the General Fixed Assets Account Group.

21. When supplies are ordered out of the General Fund, they should be recorded as a(n)
    a. Appropriation.
    b. Encumbrance.
    c. Expenditure.
    d. Estimated expenditure.
    e. Reduction of the fund balance.

22. Which of the following terms refers to an actual cost rather than an estimate in reporting for the four governmental funds?
    a. Appropriation.
    b. Encumbrance.
    c. Expenditure.
    d. Expense.
    e. None of the above.

23. Wages that have been earned by the employees of a governmental unit but not paid should be recorded in the General Fund as an
    a. Appropriation.
    b. Encumbrance.
    c. Expenditure.

d. Expense.

e. None of the above.

## IV. BUDGETARY ACCOUNTING

24. Which of the following is a budgetary account in governmental accounting?

    a. Fund balance reserved for encumbrances.

    b. Unreserved fund balance.

    c. APPROPRIATIONS.

    d. Estimated uncollectible property taxes.

    e. Expenditures.

25. Authority granted by a legislative body to make expenditures and to incur obligations during a fiscal year is the definition of an

    a. Appropriation.

    b. Authorization.

    c. Encumbrance.

    d. Expenditure.

    e. None of the above.

26. The actual general ledger account Fund Balance—Reserved for Encumbrances is a(n)

    a. Liability in substance.

    b. Budgetary account.

    c. Contra account.

    d. Appropriation of the fund balance.

    e. None of the above.

27. An encumbrance could not be thought of as a(n)

    a. Commitment.

    b. Contingent liability.

    c. Future expenditure.

    d. Eventual reduction of the fund balance.

    e. Liability of the period in which the encumbrance was created.

28. Which of the following General Fund accounts would be credited when a purchase order is issued?

    a. APPROPRIATIONS.

    b. ENCUMBRANCES.

    c. Estimated expenditures.

    d. Vouchers payable.

    e. Fund balance.

    f. None of the above.

29. At the end of 19X1, a governmental unit has unfilled purchase orders. In 19X2, these purchase orders are filled. In the 19X2 operating statement, which of the following is reported?

    a. Encumbrances.

    b. Expenditures.

    c. Neither encumbrances nor expenditures.

    d. Expenditures only if the items were rebudgeted for in the 19X2 budget.

## ASSIGNMENT MATERIAL

### Review Questions

1. Distinguish between the Governmental Finance Officers Association (GFOA), the National Council on Governmental Accounting (NCGA), and the Governmental Accounting Standards Board (GASB).
2. What has been the role of the FASB and its predecessor organizations in the development of generally accepted accounting principles peculiar to state and local governmental units?
3. For governmental units, explain the relationship between the pronouncements of GASB and FASB.
4. Must all state and local governmental units prepare their financial statements in accordance with GASB pronouncements?
5. What are some unique features of the governmental sector compared with the private sector?
6. Explain the relationship between revenues and expenditures.
7. What is meant by *fund accounting?*
8. Name the seven major types of funds.
9. Are general fixed assets and general long-term debt accounted for in funds? Explain.
10. When is it appropriate to depreciate fixed assets of a governmental unit?
11. Is the modified accrual basis of accounting in accordance with generally accepted accounting principles? Why or why not?
12. What is meant by *budgetary accounting?*
13. What are the two major types of interfund transfers? Explain the difference between the two.
14. How are operating transfers classified in the operating statement of governmental funds? In proprietary funds?
15. What is the difference between a quasi-external transaction and an operating transfer?
16. Explain the difference between an *expenditure* and an *encumbrance.*

### Discussion Cases

| DC 20-1 | **Modified Accrual Basis of Accounting** |

As an accountant for the city of Tulipville, you assist the city manager in answering questions raised at city council meetings. At one meeting, a taxpayer asks why the city (which has a June 30 fiscal year-end) uses the modified accrual basis of accounting for its General Fund rather than the accrual basis, which is required for public corporations in the private sector. Furthermore, the taxpayer would like to know "the magnitude of the misstatement at-the end of the recently concluded fiscal year as a result of not using the accrual basis." Assume that the city has an income tax, a sales tax, a property transfer tax, a property tax, and annual business licenses.

**Required:**

Respond to these questions.

## Comparison with Private Sector

DC
20-2

George Jones is executive vice-president of Bottle Industries, Inc., a publicly held industrial corporation. Jones has just been elected to the city council of Old York City. Before assuming office as a member of the city council, he asks you as his CPA to explain the major differences in accounting and financial reporting for a large city compared with a large industrial corporation.

**Required:**

1. Describe the major differences in the purposes of accounting and financial reporting and in the types of financial reports of a large city and a large industrial corporation.
2. Under what circumstances should depreciation be recognized in accounting for local governmental units? Explain.

(AICPA adapted)

# Exercises

## Revenue Recognition

E
20-1

The City of Potterville, which has a calendar year-end, was awarded a $300,000 federal job development grant on December 18, 19X1. The grant is expected to be disbursed by the federal government in May 19X2. In 19X1, the city levied property taxes of $800,000. At year-end, $100,000 remains uncollected, of which $75,000 is expected to be collected within 60 days. An allowance for uncollectibles of $10,000 is deemed adequate at year-end.

**Required:**

Determine the amount to be reported for revenues for 19X1 for the above items.

## Revenue Recognition

E
20-2

Wilbur Whoops mistakenly paid his tax bill for the fiscal year ended June 30, 19X4, twice. He noticed this in June 19X4 and contacted the governmental unit. Rather than requesting a refund, he told the governmental unit to apply the overpayment of $3,000 to his taxes for the fiscal year ended June 30, 19X5. The governmental unit (which had credited Accounts Receivable $6,000) agreed to do this.

**Required:**

Prepare the entry or entries required by the General Fund, if any, at June 30, 19X4, relating to the overpayment.

| E |
| 20-3 |

## Revenue Recognition

The city of Joy has the following tax assessment related accounts at its fiscal year-end, June 30, 19X7:

| | |
|---|---|
| Property taxes receivable—Delinquent . . . . . . . . . . . . . . . . . . . . . . . . . . . . . | $470,000 |
| Allowance for uncollectibles—Delinquent . . . . . . . . . . . . . . . . . . . . . . . . . | (20,000) |

The net amount expected to be collected at year-end is usually collected within 60 days of the fiscal year-end. At June 30, 19X7, however, only about $300,000 is expected to be collected within 60 days, with the remaining $150,000 expected to be collected after that time over many months. The reason for the delay is a severe recession in the city's economy. The total property tax assessment was $1,000,000. No property tax receivables existed at June 30, 19X6.

### Required:

1. Prepare the entry or entries required for the General Fund at June 30, 19X7, if any.
2. Determine the amount to be reported for property tax revenues for the year ended June 30, 19X7.

| E |
| 20-4 |

## Interfund Transactions—Preparing Journal Entries

The city of Mityville had the following interfund transactions during the year ended December 31, 19X5:

1. The General Fund received a billing of $11,000 from its city-owned Water Fund, which is accounted for in an Enterprise Fund.
2. The General Fund disbursed $22,000 to its Library Debt Service Fund, so that interest could be paid to bondholders.
3. The General Fund disbursed $33,000 to start up a central purchasing fund, which is accounted for in an Internal Service Fund.
4. The General Fund disbursed $44,000 to its Municipal Transit Fund (accounted for in a Special Revenue Fund) as its annual subsidy.
5. The General Fund disbursed $55,000 to its Convention Center Enterprise Fund. Repayment is to be made in three years.
6. The General Fund received $66,000 from its Library Capital Projects Fund in repayment of money the General Fund had advanced to the architectural firm designing the library. The General Fund had charged Expenditures when the advance was made.

### Required:

Prepare the entries required in the General Fund.

| E |
| 20-5 |

## Preparation of Statement of Revenues, Expenditures and Changes in Fund Balance from Year-end Trial Balance

Below are selected preclosing account balances at June 30, 19X2 of Borrowsville Township's General Fund:

|  | Dr. | Cr. |
|---|---|---|
| Expenditures . . . . . . . . . . . . . . . . . . . . . . . . . . . . . . . . . . . . . | 600,000 | |
| Residual equity transfers out . . . . . . . . . . . . . . . . . . . . . . | 70,000 | |
| Operating transfers out . . . . . . . . . . . . . . . . . . . . . . . . . . | 50,000 | |
| Subsidy to Airport Enterprise Fund. . . . . . . . . . . . . . . . | 80,000 | |
| Amount Paid to Internal Service Fund for | | |
|    Printing Services . . . . . . . . . . . . . . . . . . . . . . . . . . . . . . . . | 10,000 | |
| Advance to City Transit Enterprise Fund . . . . . . . . . . . . | 90,000 | |
|      Due to City Water Fund . . . . . . . . . . . . . . . . . . . . . | | 20,000 |
|      Bond Proceeds Received . . . . . . . . . . . . . . . . . . . . | | 100,000 |
|      Revenues. . . . . . . . . . . . . . . . . . . . . . . . . . . . . . . . . | | 650,000 |
|      Residual equity transfers in . . . . . . . . . . . . . . . . | | 15,000 |
|      Unreserved fund balance. . . . . . . . . . . . . . . . . . . | | 200,000 |

In some cases, the bookkeeper was not sure of the proper account to use and used a description of the transaction instead. Encumbrances of $25,000 are outstanding at June 30, 19X2, whereas there were no encumbrances outstanding at June 30, 19X1.

### Required:
Prepare a statement of revenues, expenditures, and changes in fund balance for the year ended June 30, 19X2.

---

| E 20-6 |
|---|

## Recording the Budget

A city's legislative body approved the budget for the coming fiscal year. The details of the budget follow:

1. Estimated revenues of $500,000.
2. Estimated expenditures of $450,000.
3. Authorized transfer of $30,000 to Debt Service Fund to pay interest on bond indebtedness.
4. Estimated receipt of $15,000 from closure of Municipal Swimming Pool Enterprise Fund.
5. Authorized transfer of $5,000 to Capital Projects Fund to pay for cost overrun on construction of new civic center.
6. Estimated receipt of $50,000 subsidy from Electric Utility Enterprise Fund to help finance General Fund expenditures (this is not a payment in lieu of taxes).

### Required:
Prepare the General Fund's entry to record the budget.

---

| E 20-7 |
|---|

## Budgetary Control

The following balances are included in the subsidiary records of Tylersville's fire department at May 31, 19X2:

| | |
|---|---|
| Appropriation—supplies | $33,000 |
| Expenditures—supplies | 27,000 |
| Encumbrances—supply orders | 2,000 |

**Required:**

Determine how much the fire department has available for additional purchases of supplies.

## Presentation of Financial Statements: Expenditures and Encumbrances

The city of Thrillsville has the following accounts in its preclosing trial balance at June 30, 19X5:

| | Amount | |
|---|---|---|
| Account | Dr. | Cr. |
| Expenditures—Current Year | 800,000 | |
| Expenditures—Prior Year | 60,000 | |
| ENCUMBRANCES | 28,000 | |
| APPROPRIATIONS | | 902,000 |
| BUDGETARY FUND BALANCE RESERVED FOR ENCUMBRANCES | | 28,000 |

The encumbrances outstanding at each year end ($62,000 at June 30, 19X4) are reappropriated in the following year's budget. The city council has requested that expenditures relating to such encumbrances be kept separate in the accounting records.

**Required:**

Prepare the applicable section of the budgetary comparison statement for the year ended June 30, 19X4.

## Preparing Budgetary Comparison Statements from Selected Data

The following information is given for the City of Budgetville:

| | |
|---|---|
| **Fund Balance at December 31, 19X1:** | |
| Reserved for encumbrances | $ 30,000 |
| Unreserved | 70,000 |
| Total Fund Balance | $100,000 |
| **Budgeted items for 19X2:** | |
| Estimated revenues | $500,000 |
| Appropriations (including $30,000 rebudgeted for encumbrances outstanding at December 31, 19X1) | 480,000 |
| **Actual amounts for 19X2:** | |
| Revenues | 503,000 |
| Expenditures (including $29,000 relating to encumbrances outstanding at December 31, 19X1) | 473,000 |
| Encumbrances outstanding at December 31, 19X2 | 5,000 |

E 20-8

E 20-9

**Required:**

Prepare a budgetary comparison statement of revenues, expenditures, and changes in fund balance for 19X2.

# Problems

## General Fund: Preparing Transaction and Closing Journal Entries— Fundamentals

The city of Smileyville had the following activities pertaining to its General Fund for the fiscal year ended June 30, 19X6:

1. **Adoption of the budget.** Revenues were estimated at $1,000,000, and authorized expenditures were $950,000. (Assume no encumbrances were outstanding at June 30, 19X5.)
2. **Property taxes.** Property taxes were billed in the amount of $800,000, of which $25,000 was expected to be uncollectible. Collections were $750,000. A $22,000 allowance for uncollectibles is deemed adequate at year-end. All uncollected property taxes at year-end are delinquent.
3. **Other revenues.** Cash collections of $210,000 were received from sales taxes, licenses, fees, and fines.
4. **Purchase orders.** Purchase orders totaling $300,000 were issued to vendors and contractors during the year. For $270,000 of these purchase orders and contracts, billings totaling $268,000 were received. Cash payments totaling $245,000 were made.
5. **Payroll and other operating costs.** Expenditures for payroll and other operating costs not requiring the use of purchase orders and contracts totaled $631,000. Cash payments of $590,000 were made on these items.

**Required:**

1. Prepare the journal entries relating to the above items.
2. Prepare the year-end closing entries assuming that encumbrances outstanding at year-end will be honored in the following year.
3. Prepare the entry or entries that must be made on the first day of the following fiscal year.

## General Fund: Preparing Financial Statements from Preclosing Trial Balance

Below is the trial balance of Ponder City at June 30, 19X2, prior to adjusting and closing entries. The bookkeeper was not certain of the exact account to use in some cases and merely used an account that was most descriptive of the nature of the transaction.

| | |
|---|---|
| Cash.............................................. | $ 550,000 |
| Taxes Receivable—Current.......................... | 80,000 |
| Allowance for Uncollectibles—Current ............. | (90,000) |

| | |
|---|---:|
| Inventory. . . . . . . . . . . . . . . . . . . . . . . . . . . . . . . . . . . . . . . . . . . . . . . . | 20,000[a] |
| BUDGETARY FUND BALANCE. . . . . . . . . . . . . . . . . . . . . . . . . . . . . . . . | 220,000 |
| ESTIMATED REVENUES . . . . . . . . . . . . . . . . . . . . . . . . . . . . . . . . . . . | 920,000 |
| ENCUMBRANCES . . . . . . . . . . . . . . . . . . . . . . . . . . . . . . . . . . . . . . . . | 80,000 |
| Expenditures . . . . . . . . . . . . . . . . . . . . . . . . . . . . . . . . . . . . . . . . . . . | 790,000 |
| Residual Equity Transfer Out to New Golf Course Enterprise Fund. . . . . . . . . . . . . . . . . . . . . . . . . . . . . . . . . . . . . . . . | 230,000 |
| Quasi-External Payment to City Utility Enterprise Fund. . . . . . . . . . . . . . . . . . . . . . . . . . . . . . . . . . . . . . . . . . . . . . . . . | 40,000 |
| Annual Subsidy to City Transit Enterprise Fund. . . . . . . . . . . . . . . | 60,000 |
| | $2,900,000 |

| | |
|---|---:|
| Vouchers Payable. . . . . . . . . . . . . . . . . . . . . . . . . . . . . . . . . . . . . . . . | $ 280,000 |
| Due to Internal Service Fund. . . . . . . . . . . . . . . . . . . . . . . . . . . . . . | 30,000 |
| APPROPRIATIONS. . . . . . . . . . . . . . . . . . . . . . . . . . . . . . . . . . . . . . | 840,000 |
| APPROPRIATIONS—OPERATING TRANSFERS OUT. . . . . . . . . . . . . . | 70,000 |
| APPROPRIATIONS—RESIDUAL EQUITY TRANSFER OUT. . . . . . . . . | 230,000 |
| Revenues. . . . . . . . . . . . . . . . . . . . . . . . . . . . . . . . . . . . . . . . . . . . . . | 870,000 |
| Unreserved Fund Balance . . . . . . . . . . . . . . . . . . . . . . . . . . . . . . . . | 300,000 |
| Bond Proceeds Received . . . . . . . . . . . . . . . . . . . . . . . . . . . . . . . . . | 200,000 |
| BUDGETARY FUND BALANCE RESERVED FOR ENCUMBRANCES . . | 80,000[b] |
| | $2,900,000 |

[a]The "consumption method" is used.
[b]At June 30, 19X1 (the end of the *prior* year), encumbrances outstanding totaled $25,000.

### Required:

1. Prepare a balance sheet and an operating statement (*no* comparison to budget required).
2. Prepare a "T" account analysis of the Unreserved Fund Balance account as it should have been posted for the year (inclusive of any year-end adjusting entries *and* the year-end closing entries).

## General Fund: Preparing Transaction and Closing Entries and a Statement of Revenues, Expenditures, and Changes in Fund Balance

Ledgerville had the following events and transactions for its fiscal year ended June 30, 19X2:

1. The budget for the year was approved. It provided for (a) $620,000 of estimated revenues; (b) $565,000 of expenditures; (c) $40,000 for servicing general long-term debt (principal and interest); and (d) $30,000 to establish a central printing department that will provide services to all city departments. (The $30,000 will not be repaid to the General Fund.)
2. Items (c) and (d) above were expended in accordance with authorizations.
3. Property taxes totaling $450,000 were levied, of which $8,000 was estimated to be uncollectible. Property tax collections totaled $405,000. At year-end, the estimated allowance for uncollectibles was increased from $8,000 to $12,000. Unpaid taxes at year-end become delinquent.
4. City income taxes, sales taxes, business licenses, and fines totaled $162,000.

5. Some equipment accounted for in the General Fixed Assets Account Group was sold for $11,000. This transaction was not included in the budget.

6. A Capital Projects Fund was short $3,000 as a result of changes to contracts issued in connection with certain street improvements being charged to certain property owners. Authorization was given during the year to transfer funds to this fund to make up the shortage. The amount was not budgeted and will not be repaid.

7. Purchase orders and contracts totaling $280,000 were entered into. For $255,000 of this amount, invoices for goods and services totaling $254,000 were rendered. (Assume that no encumbrances were outstanding at June 30, 19X1.)

8. Payroll and other operating costs not involving the use of purchase orders and contracts totaled $282,000.

9. Cash disbursements (other than to other funds) totaled $507,000.

**Required:**

1. Prepare the General Fund entries for these items.

2. Prepare the closing entries at June 30, 19X2, assuming that encumbrances outstanding at year-end will be honored in the following year.

3. Prepare a statement of revenues, expenditures, and changes in fund balance for the year ended June 30, 19X2, for the General Fund that compares budgeted amounts with actual amounts. (Assume that the General Fund had a total fund balance of $100,000 at June 30, 19X1.)

4. Prepare the fund equity section of the balance sheet at June 30, 19X2.

### COMPREHENSIVE   Preparing Transaction and Closing Journal Entries and a Budgetary Comparison Statement (Several Interfund Transactions)

The city of Postville had the following items and transactions pertaining to its General Fund for the fiscal year ended June 30, 19X3:

1. The budget for the year was as follows:

| | |
|---|---|
| Estimated revenues. . . . . . . . . . . . . . . . . . . . . . . . . . . . . . . . . . . . . . . . . . . . . . . . | $800,000 |
| Authorized expenditures (including $55,000 reappropriated for encumbrances outstanding at June 30, 19X2, which lapsed) . . . . . . . . . . . . . . . . . . . . . . . . . . . . . . . . . . . . . . . . . . . . . . | 725,000 |
| Authorized operating transfers to other funds . . . . . . . . . . . . . . . . . . . | 50,000 |
| Estimated inflow from discontinuance of Central Motor Pool Internal Service Fund . . . . . . . . . . . . . . . . . . . . . . . . . . . . . . . . . . . . . . . . | 25,000 |

2. Property taxes were levied totaling $550,000. Of this amount, $10,000 was estimated to be uncollectible. Collections during the year were $535,000, of which $12,000 pertained to property tax levies of the prior year that had been declared delinquent at the end of the prior year. All remaining property tax receivables at the beginning of the current year totaling $4,000 were written off as uncollectible.

3. The estimated revenues for the year include an entitlement from the federal government for $34,000. During the year, $36,000 was received.

4. City income taxes, sales taxes, licenses, permits, and miscellaneous revenues totaled $222,000.

5. Purchase orders and contracts totaling $370,000 were entered into during the year. For $330,000 of this amount, invoices totaling $326,000 for goods and services were rendered. Assume that the city generally allows encumbrances outstanding at year-end to lapse but reappropriates amounts in the following year to honor the encumbrances. Of the $326,000 amount, $76,000 was for the acquisition of supplies inventory. The city uses the consumption method of accounting for supplies.

6. Encumbrances outstanding at the beginning of the year totaled $55,000. The goods and services relating to these encumbrances were received along with invoices totaling $53,000.

7. Payroll and other items not involving the use of purchase orders and contracts totaled $280,000. (This amount excludes interfund billings.)

8. Cash disbursements (other than to other funds) totaled $740,000.

9. Interfund transactions consisted of the following:
   a. The Central Motor Pool Internal Service Fund was discontinued pursuant to authorization given by the legislative body at the beginning of the year. The actual amount disbursed to the General Fund during the year when the fund was discontinued was $17,000.
   b. A payment of $30,000 was made to the Electric Utility Enterprise Fund to make up its operating deficit, which was initially estimated to be $35,000.
   c. A payment of $15,000 was made to a Capital Projects Fund to finance a portion of certain street improvements. (This payment was equal to the amount budgeted.)
   d. The Electric Utility Enterprise Fund rendered billings to the city totaling $26,000 for electricity supplied to the city by the Enterprise Fund. Cash disbursements to this fund during the year in payment of such billings totaled $22,000.
   e. A disbursement of $80,000 was made to the City Center for Performing Arts Enterprise Fund. Repayment is expected in three years.

10. A physical inventory of supplies inventory at year-end shows that the supplies inventory decreased during the year from $44,000 to $42,000.

### Required:

1. Prepare General Fund journal entries only for the above items.
2. Prepare the closing entries at June 30, 19X3, for the General Fund.
3. Prepare a statement of revenues, expenditures, and changes in fund balance for the year ended June 30, 19X3, that compares budgeted amounts with actual amounts. (Assume the fund balance at the beginning of the year was $100,000.)
4. Prepare the fund equity section of the balance sheet at June 30, 19X3.

---

**P 20-5**

## COMPREHENSIVE    Preparing Transaction and Closing Journal Entries and a Budgetary Comparison Statement

The General Fund trial balance of the city of Solna at December 31, 19X2, was as follows:

| | Dr. | Cr. |
|---|---|---|
| Cash. . . . . . . . . . . . . . . . . . . . . . . . . . . . . . . . . | $ 62,000 | |
| Taxes receivable—delinquent . . . . . . . . . . . . . . . . . . | 46,000 | |
|    Allowance for uncollectible taxes—delinquent . . | | $ 8,000 |
| Stores inventory—program operations. . . . . . . . . . | 18,000 | |
|    Vouchers payable. . . . . . . . . . . . . . . . . . . . . . . | | 28,000 |
|    Fund balance reserved for encumbrances. . . . . . . | | 12,000 |
|    Unreserved fund balance . . . . . . . . . . . . . . . . . . . | | 78,000 |
| | $126,000 | $126,000 |

Collectible delinquent taxes are expected to be collected within 60 days after the end of the year. Solna uses the "consumption" method to account for stores inventory. The following data pertain to 19X3 General Fund operations:

1. Budget adopted (including reappropriation of 19X2 items):

   **Revenues and Other Financing Sources**

   | | |
   |---|---|
   | Taxes . . . . . . . . . . . . . . . . . . . . . . . . . . . . . . . . . . . . . . . . . . . . . . . . . . . . . . | $220,000 |
   | Fines, forfeits, and penalties . . . . . . . . . . . . . . . . . . . . . . . . . . . . . . . . . . | 80,000 |
   | Miscellaneous revenues . . . . . . . . . . . . . . . . . . . . . . . . . . . . . . . . . . . . . . . | 100,000 |
   | Share of bond issue proceeds . . . . . . . . . . . . . . . . . . . . . . . . . . . . . . . . . | 200,000 |
   | | $600,000 |

   **Expenditures and Other Financing Uses**

   | | |
   |---|---|
   | Program operations. . . . . . . . . . . . . . . . . . . . . . . . . . . . . . . . . . . . . . . . . . . | $312,000 |
   | General administration. . . . . . . . . . . . . . . . . . . . . . . . . . . . . . . . . . . . . . . . | 120,000 |
   | Stores—program operations . . . . . . . . . . . . . . . . . . . . . . . . . . . . . . . . . . | 60,000 |
   | Capital outlay . . . . . . . . . . . . . . . . . . . . . . . . . . . . . . . . . . . . . . . . . . . . . . . | 80,000 |
   | Periodic transfer to Special Revenue Fund . . . . . . . . . . . . . . . . . . . . . | 20,000 |
   | | $592,000 |

2. Taxes were assessed at an amount that would result in revenues of $220,800, after deduction of 4% of the tax levy as uncollectible.
3. Orders placed but not received:

   | | |
   |---|---|
   | Program operations. . . . . . . . . . . . . . . . . . . . . . . . . . . . . . . . . . . . . . . . . . . | $176,000 |
   | General administration. . . . . . . . . . . . . . . . . . . . . . . . . . . . . . . . . . . . . . . . | 80,000 |
   | Capital outlay. . . . . . . . . . . . . . . . . . . . . . . . . . . . . . . . . . . . . . . . . . . . . . . . | 60,000 |
   | | $316,000 |

4. The city council designated $20,000 of the unreserved fund balance for possible future appropriation for capital outlay.
5. Cash collections and transfer:

   | | |
   |---|---|
   | Delinquent taxes . . . . . . . . . . . . . . . . . . . . . . . . . . . . . . . . . . . . . . . . . . . . . | $ 38,000 |
   | Current taxes . . . . . . . . . . . . . . . . . . . . . . . . . . . . . . . . . . . . . . . . . . . . . . . . | 226,000 |
   | Refund of overpayment of invoice for purchase | |
   |    of equipment. . . . . . . . . . . . . . . . . . . . . . . . . . . . . . . . . . . . . . . . . . . . . . | 4,000 |

| | |
|---|---|
| Fines, forfeits, and penalties. . . . . . . . . . . . . . . . . . . . . . . . . . . . . . . . . . . | 88,000 |
| Miscellaneous revenues. . . . . . . . . . . . . . . . . . . . . . . . . . . . . . . . . . . . . | 90,000 |
| Share of bond issue proceeds . . . . . . . . . . . . . . . . . . . . . . . . . . . . . . . | 200,000 |
| Transfer of remaining fund balance of a | |
| discontinued fund . . . . . . . . . . . . . . . . . . . . . . . . . . . . . . . . . . . . . . . | 18,000 |
| | $664,000 |

6. Cancelled encumbrances:

| | Estimated | Actual |
|---|---|---|
| Program operations. . . . . . . . . . . . . . . . . . . . . . . . . . . . | $156,000 | $166,000 (1) |
| General administration. . . . . . . . . . . . . . . . . . . . . . . | 84,000 | 80,000 |
| Capital outlay. . . . . . . . . . . . . . . . . . . . . . . . . . . . . . . . | 62,000 | 62,000 |
| | $302,000 | $308,000 |

(1) Includes $36,000 of stores inventory purchases.

7. Additional vouchers:

| | |
|---|---|
| Program operations. . . . . . . . . . . . . . . . . . . . . . . . . . . . . . . . . . . . . . . . | $182,000 |
| General administration. . . . . . . . . . . . . . . . . . . . . . . . . . . . . . . . . . . . . . | 38,000 |
| Capital outlay. . . . . . . . . . . . . . . . . . . . . . . . . . . . . . . . . . . . . . . . . . . . . | 18,000 |
| Transfer to Special Revenue Fund . . . . . . . . . . . . . . . . . . . . . . . . . . . | 20,000 |
| | $258,000 |

8. Albert, a taxpayer, overpaid his 19X3 taxes by $2,000. He applied for a $2,000 credit against his 19X4 taxes. The city council granted his request.
9. Vouchers paid amounted to $580,000 (including $20,000 paid to the Special Revenue Fund).
10. Stores inventory on December 31, 19X3, amounted to $12,000.

### Required:
1. Prepare General Fund journal entries only for the above items.
2. Prepare any required year-end adjusting entries.
3. Prepare the closing entries at December 31, 19X3.
4. Prepare a balance sheet at December 31, 19X3.
5. Prepare a statement of revenues, expenditures, and changes in fund balance for 19X3 that compares budgeted amounts with actual amounts.
6. Qualitatively evaluate the city's financial statements.

(AICPA adapted)

### General Fund: Reconstructing Transaction and Closing Journal Entries; Preparing a Budgetary Comparison Statement

The following data were obtained from the general ledger for the General Fund of the City of Hope after the general ledger had been closed for the fiscal year ended June 30, 19X6:

| | Balances June 30, 19X5 | Fiscal 19X5–19X6 Charges | | Balances June 30, 19X6 |
|---|---|---|---|---|
| | | Debit | Credit | |
| Cash......................... | $180,000 | $ 955,000 | $ 880,000 | $255,000 |
| Taxes receivable................. | 20,000 | 809,000 | 781,000 | 48,000 |
| Allowance for uncollectible taxes... | (4,000) | 6,000 | 9,000 | (7,000) |
| | $196,000 | | | $296,000 |
| Vouchers payable................ | $ 44,000 | 813,000 | 822,000 | $ 53,000 |
| Due to Internal Service Fund....... | 2,000 | 7,000 | 10,000 | 5,000 |
| Due to Debt Service Fund......... | 10,000 | 60,000 | 100,000 | 50,000 |
| Fund balance reserved for encumbrances ................. | 40,000 | 40,000 | 47,000 | 47,000 |
| Unreserved fund balance ......... | 100,000 | 47,000 | 88,000 | 141,000 |
| | $196,000 | $2,737,000 | $2,737,000 | $296,000 |

### Additional Information:

1. The budget for fiscal 19X5–19X6 provided for estimated revenues of $1,000,000, appropriations of $905,000 (including $40,000 pertaining to encumbrances outstanding at June 30, 19X5), and $100,000 to be transferred to a debt service fund.
2. Expenditures totaled $832,000, of which $37,000 pertained to encumbrances outstanding at June 30, 19X5.
3. Purchase orders issued during 19X5–19X6 totaled $170,000.
4. The city does not use delinquent accounts for delinquent taxes.

### Required:

1. Using the given data, reconstruct the original detailed journal entries that were required to record all transactions for the fiscal year ended June 30, 19X6, including the recording of the current year's budget. (Hint: Use T-accounts.)
2. Prepare the year-end closing entries from the entries you have reconstructed.
3. Prepare a budgetary comparison statement of revenues, expenditures, and changes in fund balance for the current year.

(AICPA adapted)

**P 20-7**

### General Fund: Reconstructing Transactions, Preparing Closing Entries, and Preparing a Statement of Revenues, Expenditures, and Changes in Fund Balance

The following summary of transactions was taken from the accounts of the Good Times School District General Fund *before* the books had been closed for the fiscal year ended June 30, 19X5:

| | Postclosing Balances June 30, 19X4 | Preclosing Balances June 30, 19X5 |
|---|---|---|
| **Actual Accounts** | | |
| Cash..................................... | $400,000 | $ 630,000 |
| Property taxes receivable—delinquent ..... | 150,000 | 180,000 |

|  | Postclosing Balances June 30, 19X4 | Preclosing Balances June 30, 19X5 |
|---|---|---|
| Allowance for uncollectibles—delinquent... | (40,000) | (80,000) |
| Expenditures | — | 2,900,000 |
|  | $510,000 | $3,630,000 |
| Vouchers payable | $ 80,000 | $ 408,000 |
| Due to other funds | 210,000 | 62,000 |
| Fund balance reserved for encumbrances... | 60,000 | — |
| Unreserved fund balance | 160,000 | 220,000 |
| Revenues from property taxes | — | 2,800,000 |
| Miscellaneous revenues | — | 140,000 |
|  | $510,000 | $3,630,000 |

**Budgetary Accounts**

|  |  |
|---|---|
| ESTIMATED REVENUES | $3,000,000 |
| ENCUMBRANCES | 91,000 |
|  | $3,091,000 |
| APPROPRIATIONS | $2,980,000 |
| BUDGETARY FUND BALANCE | 20,000 |
| BUDGETARY FUND BALANCE RESERVED FOR ENCUMBRANCES | 91,000 |
|  | $3,091,000 |

## Additional Information:

1. The property tax levy for the year ended June 30, 19X5, was $2,870,000. Taxes collected during the year totaled $2,810,000, of which $100,000 pertained to delinquent balances as of June 30, 19X4. Of the June 30, 19X4, delinquent balances, $30,000 was written off as uncollectible. Unpaid taxes become delinquent at the end of the fiscal year.

2. Encumbrances outstanding at each year-end are always honored in the following year. The encumbrances are rebudgeted or reappropriated in the following year. During the current year, invoices totaling $58,000 were rendered on encumbrances outstanding at the beginning of the year. On May 2, 19X5, commitment documents were issued for the purchase of new textbooks at a cost of $91,000. Only this encumbrance is outstanding at June 30, 19X5. Other purchase orders issued during the year totaled $850,000, with invoices having been rendered for $847,000.

3. An analysis of the transactions in the Vouchers Payable account for the year ended June 30, 19X5, follows:

| | |
|---|---|
| Balance, June 30, 19X4 | $ 80,000 |
| Expenditures | 2,758,000 |
| Cash disbursements | (2,430,000) |
| Balance, June 30, 19X5 | $ 408,000 |

4. During the year, the General Fund was billed $142,000 for services performed on its behalf by other city funds.

**Required:**

1. Using the data presented above, reconstruct the original detailed journal entries that were required to record all transactions for the fiscal year ended June 30, 19X5, including the recording of the current year's budget. (Hint: Use T-accounts.)
2. Prepare the closing entries at June 30, 19X5.
3. Prepare a statement of revenues, expenditures, and changes in fund balance for fiscal 19X4–19X5.

(AICPA adapted)

| P 20-8 | **CHALLENGER   Preparing Adjusting and Closing Entries; Preparing Balance Sheet and Budgetary Comparison Statement—Non–General Fund Transactions Improperly Recorded in General Fund** |
|---|---|

The General Fund trial balances of the Blackboard School District at June 30, 19X7, are as follows:

**BLACKBOARD SCHOOL DISTRICT**
**General Fund Trial Balances**
**June 30, 19X7**

| | Dr. | Cr. |
|---|---|---|
| **Actual Accounts** | | |
| Cash | $    60,000 | |
| Taxes receivable—current year | 31,800 | |
| Allowance for uncollectibles—current-year taxes | | $      1,800 |
| Inventory of supplies | 10,000 | |
| Buildings | 1,300,000 | |
| Bonds payable | | 500,000 |
| Vouchers payable | | 12,000 |
| Operating expenses: | | |
| Administration | 25,000 | |
| Instruction | 602,000 | |
| Other | 221,000 | |
| Capital outlays (equipment) | 22,000 | |
| Debt service (interest) | 30,000 | |
| State grant revenue | | 300,000 |
| Revenues from tax levy, licenses, and fines | | 1,008,000 |
| Unreserved fund balance | | 480,000 |
| Totals | $2,301,800 | $2,301,800 |
| **Budgetary Accounts** | | |
| Estimated Revenues | $1,007,000 | |
| Appropriations | | $1,000,000 |
| Budgetary Fund Balance | | 7,000 |
| Totals | $1,007,000 | $1,007,000 |

**Additional Information:**

1. The recorded allowance for uncollectible current-year taxes is considered sufficient. Unpaid taxes become delinquent at year-end.

2. During the year, the local governmental unit gave the school district 20 acres of land for a new grade school and a community playground. The unrecorded estimated value of the land donated was $50,000. In addition, a state grant of $300,000 was received, and the full amount was used in payment of contracts pertaining to the construction of the grade school. Purchases of classroom and playground equipment costing $22,000 were paid from general funds of the school district.

3. On July 1, 19X2, a 5%, 10-year serial bond issue in the amount of $1,000,000 for constructing school buildings was issued. Principal payments of $100,000 must be made each June 30, along with interest for the year. All payments required through June 30, 19X7, have been made.

4. Outstanding purchase orders for operating expenses not recorded in the accounts at year-end were as follows:

| | |
|---|---:|
| Administration | $1,000 |
| Instruction | 1,400 |
| Other | 600 |
| Total | $3,000 |

The school district honors encumbrances outstanding at each year-end and reappropriates amounts in the following year's budget. No encumbrances were outstanding at June 30, 19X6.

5. Appropriations for the year consisted of the following:

**Current**

| | |
|---|---:|
| Administration | $ 25,000 |
| Instruction | 600,000 |
| Other | 222,000 |
| Capital outlay | 23,000 |

**Debt Service**

| | |
|---|---:|
| Principal | 100,000 |
| Interest | 30,000 |
| | $1,000,000 |

6. The consumption method is used for the supplies inventory (the balance at June 30, 19X6 was $9,000).

## Required:

1. Prepare the appropriate adjusting entry to eliminate the activities and accounts that the school district should be accounting for in separate funds or account groups outside the General Fund. (It is not necessary to prepare the entries that would be made in these other funds or account groups to account properly for these items.) (*Note: Problem 20-8 will be used in the requirement for Problem 21-9.*)

2. Prepare any adjusting entries to accounts that are properly part of the General Fund.

3. Prepare the closing entries relating to the General Fund.
4. Prepare a balance sheet at June 30, 19X7.
5. Prepare a statement of revenues, expenditures, and changes in fund balance for the year ended June 30, 19X7, comparing budgeted amounts with actual amounts. (The beginning fund balance amount must be "forced" as though a correcting entry had been made at June 30, 19X6.)

(AICPA adapted)

## ANSWERS TO SELF-STUDY QUESTIONS

| | | | | |
|---|---|---|---|---|
| 1. a | 7. b | 13. d | 19. c | 25. a |
| 2. c | 8. c | 14. b | 20. c | 26. d |
| 3. a | 9. a | 15. e | 21. b | 27. e |
| 4. d | 10. d | 16. d | 22. c | 28. f |
| 5. c | 11. b | 17. d | 23. c | 29. b |
| 6. b | 12. e | 18. e | 24. c | |

# 21
...

# GOVERNMENTAL ACCOUNTING: SPECIAL PURPOSE FUNDS AND ACCOUNT GROUPS

## TOPIC OUTLINE

**THE REMAINING GOVERNMENTAL FUNDS AND THE ACCOUNT GROUPS**

Special Revenue Funds

Preview of Interrelationship of Capital Projects Funds, Debt Service Funds, and Related Account Groups

Capital Projects Funds

General Fixed Assets Account Group

Debt Service Funds

General Long-term Debt Account Group

Special Assessments

**THE PROPRIETARY FUNDS**

Internal Service Funds

Enterprise Funds

**THE FIDUCIARY FUNDS**

Agency Funds

Trust Funds

**FINANCIAL REPORTING TO THE PUBLIC: GENERAL PURPOSE FINANCIAL STATEMENTS**

In Chapter 20, we discussed the General Fund. In this chapter, we discuss the remaining six types of funds used for governmental accounting, the General Fixed Asset Account Group, and the General Long-term Debt Account Group. Concerning the number of funds to be used by a governmental unit, the GASB Codification states:

> Only the minimum number of funds consistent with legal and operating requirements should be established . . . since unnecessary funds result in inflexibility, undue complexity and inefficient financial administration.[1]

Certain revenues, functions, or activities of government often must be accounted for in a designated fund separate from all others. In some situations, greater accounting control may be obtained through the use of a separate fund, even though it is not required by law. In most cases, the type of fund to be used to account for the specific revenues, functions, or activities is readily determinable. In a few instances, selecting the most appropriate type of fund requires greater scrutiny.

Certain transactions or events require entries in one or more funds or account groups. For example, the decision to build a new civic center to be financed through the issuance of general obligation bonds eventually results in entries being made in a Capital Projects Fund, a Debt Service Fund, the General Fixed Assets Account Group, the General Long-term Debt Account Group, and in some cases the General Fund.

## THE REMAINING GOVERNMENTAL FUNDS AND THE ACCOUNT GROUPS

## SPECIAL REVENUE FUNDS

Special Revenue Funds account for **"the proceeds of specific revenue sources (other than expendable trusts or for major capital projects) that are legally restricted to expenditure for specified purposes."**[2] Special Revenue Funds may be used for such small activities as the maintenance of a municipal swimming pool or such gigantic operations as a state highway system. The distinguishing feature of a Special Revenue Fund is that its revenues are obtained primarily from tax and nontax sources not directly related to services rendered or facilities provided for use. In other words, revenues are *not* obtained primarily from direct charges to the

---

[1]*Codification of Governmental Accounting and Financial Reporting Standards* (Stamford: Governmental Accounting Standards Board, 1987), sec. 1100.104.

[2]GASB Cod. sec. 1300.104.

users of the services or facilities. Conceptually, therefore, Special Revenue Funds are the opposite of *most* Enterprise Funds, which recover the majority of their operating costs from charges to users.

The GASB Codification requires the use of Enterprise Funds when the costs of providing goods or services are recovered primarily from user charges. In addition, **under certain circumstances,** which we discuss later, Enterprise Funds may be used for activities that do not recover their costs primarily from user charges. The following activities could be accounted for in either Special Revenue Funds or Enterprise Funds, depending on the individual facts, circumstances, and operating policies: off-street parking facilities, transportation systems, turnpikes, golf courses, swimming pools, libraries, and auditoriums.

Special Revenue Funds may derive their revenues from one or several sources, commonly (1) specified property tax levies, (2) state gasoline taxes, (3) licenses, (4) grants, and (5) shared taxes from other governmental units (including federal revenue sharing).

Unless legal provisions specify to the contrary, Special Revenue Funds are accounted for using the same accounting principles, procedures, and financial statements shown for the General Fund in Chapter 20. Accordingly, we do not illustrate any journal entries for Special Revenue Funds.

## PREVIEW OF INTERRELATIONSHIP OF CAPITAL PROJECTS FUNDS, DEBT SERVICE FUNDS, AND RELATED ACCOUNT GROUPS

Virtually all governmental buildings are constructed by the governmental units and are financed by bond offerings. In commercial accounting, all of this activity (the construction of the building, the subsequent capitalization and accounting for the building, and the servicing of the debt incurred to finance the construction of the building) is accounted for using one general ledger. In government, four general ledgers are used—two of which are funds and two of which are account groups.

This separation into four general ledgers results in the following arrangement:

1. **Capital Projects Fund.** Receives cash from bond offerings and uses cash to construct fixed assets (reporting the outflow of resources as expenditures).
2. **General Fixed Assets Account Group.** Accounts for fixed assets during and after construction.
3. **General Long-term Debt Account Group.** Accounts for unmatured general long-term debt. At the maturity date, the liability is transferred to a Debt Service Fund.
4. **Debt Service Fund.** Services general long-term debt, making both interest and principal payments using money obtained from tax levies or operating transfers from the General Fund.

This system is somewhat cumbersome and can be confusing when first trying to learn it. Accordingly, in Illustration 21-1, we present a simplified number of events and transactions. To highlight the effect on the asset and liability accounts (one of which is used in each journal entry), the other half of each entry is shown in a shaded format. These shaded portions of each entry involve either (1) a "flow" account (describing the nature of the inflow or the nature of the outflow) in the two funds, or (2) a "balancing" account in the two account groups. The flow accounts used in the two funds were discussed and illustrated in Chapter 20. The balancing accounts are discussed in detail later in this chapter.

# CAPITAL PROJECTS FUNDS

Capital Projects Funds account for

> financial resources to be used for the acquisition or construction of major capital facilities (other than those financed by proprietary funds and Trust Funds).[3]

Examples of major capital facilities are administration buildings, auditoriums, civic centers, and libraries. These funds do not account for the purchase of fixed assets having comparatively limited lives, such as vehicles, machinery, and office equipment, which are normally budgeted for and acquired through the General Fund or a Special Revenue Fund and recorded as expenditures.

Capital Projects Funds **do not account for the fixed assets acquired— only for the construction of the fixed assets.** The fixed assets constructed are accounted for in the General Fixed Asset Account Group, which we discuss later in the chapter. Furthermore, Capital Projects Funds do not account for the repayment and servicing of any debt obligations issued to raise money to finance the acquisition of capital facilities. Such debt and related servicing is accounted for in the Long-term Debt Account Group and a Debt Service Fund, both of which we discuss later in the chapter.

Capital Projects Funds are categorized as governmental funds. Recall that the measurement basis for governmental funds is sources and uses (and balances) of financial resources. Accordingly, the same financial statements that are used for the General Fund are used for Capital Projects Funds. Likewise, the modified accrual basis of accounting is used.

## Establishment and Operation

Capital Projects Funds are usually established on a project-by-project basis, because legal requirements may vary from one project to another.

---

3GASB Cod. sec. 1300.104.

**■ ILLUSTRATION 21-1**

**Overview of Interrelationship of Capital Projects Fund, Debt Service Fund, General Fixed Assets Account Group, and General Long-term Debt Account Group—Flow and Balancing Accounts Shown in Shaded Format**

| Event or Transaction | Capital Projects Fund Dr. | Capital Projects Fund Cr. | General Fixed Assets Account Group Dr. | General Fixed Assets Account Group Cr. | General Long-term Debt Account Group Dr. | General Long-term Debt Account Group Cr. | Debt Service Fund Dr. | Debt Service Fund Cr. |
|---|---|---|---|---|---|---|---|---|
| 1. Issue bonds. | Cash 50,000 Other Financing Sources— Bond Proceeds | 50,000 | | | Amount to Be Provided 50,000 Bonds Payable | 50,000 | | |
| 2. Construct new building. | Expenditures 50,000 Cash | 50,000 | Buildings 50,000 Investment in General Fixed Assets | 50,000 | | | | |
| 3. Bond matures. | | | | | Bonds Payable 50,000 Amount to Be Provided | 50,000 | Expenditures 50,000 Bonds Payable | 50,000 |
| 4. Operating transfer made from General Fund. | | | | | | | Cash 50,000 Other Financing Sources— Operating Transfer In | 50,000 |
| 5. Redeem bonds. | | | | | | | Bonds Payable 50,000 Cash | 50,000 |

(Some governmental units include annual capital budgets as part of their annual appropriated budget, in which case the annual capital budget is recorded in the general ledgers of the various Capital Projects Funds.) Most capital facilities are financed through the issuance of general obligation bonds, the liability for which is recorded in the General Long-term Debt Account Group. In many cases, some portion is financed by the General Fund or a Special Revenue Fund. Such transfers are **operating transfers,** which we discussed in the preceding chapter. Federal and state grants are another major source of funds.

Major capital facilities are usually constructed by contracted labor. Because encumbrance accounting procedures alone are usually deemed sufficient for control purposes, recording the budgeted amounts in the general ledger is usually considered unnecessary. Construction costs incurred are charged to expenditures. At the end of each year, expenditures are closed out to the Unreserved Fund Balance account, as are any amounts recorded in accounts pertaining to bond proceeds and operating transfers in for the year. Each Capital Project Fund is terminated upon completion of the project for which it was created.

At the completion of the project, the cost of the facility is recorded as a fixed asset in the General Fixed Assets Account Group. Until then, any costs incurred are shown as Construction Work in Progress in the General Fixed Assets Account Group. Generally, the year-end closing entry in the Capital Projects Fund triggers the recording of an amount in the General Fixed Assets Account Group equal to the credit to the Expenditures account. (We explain more fully later in the chapter that the GASB Codification makes optional the recording in the General Fixed Assets Account Group of certain types of improvements constructed through Capital Projects Funds.)

**Issuance of Bonds at a Premium.**  Bond premiums (and discounts, which are discussed shortly) arise because of adjustments to the interest rate. The bond indenture agreements usually specify that any bond premium is to be set aside in the related Debt Service Fund. This is desirable because it removes the incentive to spend more on a project than is authorized merely by raising additional cash by increasing the interest rate. In the Capital Projects Fund, the proceeds of the bond offering—including the premium—is reported as an Other Financing Source—Bond Proceeds in the operating statement. The transfer of the premium to the Debt Service Fund is reported as an operating transfer out in the Capital Projects Fund and an operating transfer in the Debt Service Fund. Regardless of whether the bonds are issued at a premium (or a discount), the bond issue is recorded at its face amount in the General Long-term Debt Account Group.

**Issuance of Bonds at a Discount.** Bond discounts are rare because the stated interest rate is usually set high enough so that no discount results. (Many governmental units are legally prohibited from issuing bonds at a discount.) If a discount does result, theoretically there should be a transfer from the related Debt Service Fund to the Capital Projects Fund to cover the shortfall. In practice, such a transfer may not be possible because money may not be available in the related Debt Service Fund or because of legal restraints. In such cases, the size of the project may be curtailed or the shortage may be covered by an operating transfer from the General Fund.

**Investing Excess Cash until Needed.** All the money necessary to pay for the capital project is usually raised at or near the inception of the project, but contractors are paid as work progresses. Excess cash, therefore, may be temporarily invested in high-quality, interest-bearing securities. In such cases, the interest income on the investments is credited to revenues in the Capital Projects Fund. This inflow of resources may be spent on the project or transferred to the related Debt Service Fund (an operating transfer) depending on legal requirements.

**Cash Remaining at Completion Date.** Any cash remaining at the completion date is disposed of in accordance with legal requirements. In most cases, the remaining cash is transferred to the related Debt Service Fund, with the transfer reported as a residual equity transfer.

**Cost Overruns.** The source of additional money to pay for cost overruns is specified by legal requirements or operating policy. In most cases, an operating transfer is made from the General Fund to pay for the cost overrun.

## ILLUSTRATION  Journal Entries and Financial Statements

Assume that Funn City established a Capital Projects Fund during the fiscal year ended June 30, 19X2, for the construction of a new city hall. Assumed transactions pertaining to the establishment and operation of the fund, along with the related journal entries, are as follows:

1. **Establishment of the fund.** The new city hall is expected to cost $5,000,000. The city obtained a **capital grant** from the state government of $1,500,000, of which $600,000 was contributed at the inception of the project. The remaining $900,000 is deemed to be susceptible to accrual. The General Fund contributes $500,000, of which $200,000 was contributed at the inception of the project.

| | | |
|---|---|---|
| Cash | 600,000 | |
| Grant Receivable from State Government | 900,000 | |
| Revenues | | 1,500,000 |

*(continued)*

To record amounts received and due
from the state government.

| | | |
|---|---|---|
| Cash | 200,000 | |
| Due from General Fund | 300,000 | |
|    Other Financing Sources—Operating | | |
|      Transfer In | | 500,000 |
| To record amounts received and due from | | |
| the General Fund. | | |

2. **Sale of bonds.** The remaining $3,000,000 was obtained from the sale of general obligation bonds at 101. The bond indenture agreement requires any premium to be set aside in the related Debt Service Fund.

| | | |
|---|---|---|
| Cash | 3,030,000 | |
|    Other Financing Sources—Bond | | |
|      Proceeds | | 3,030,000 |
| To record the sale of general obligation | | |
| bonds. | | |

| | | |
|---|---|---|
| Other Financing Uses—Operating | | |
|    Transfers Out | 30,000 | |
|      Cash | | 30,000 |
| To transfer bond premium to Debt | | |
| Service Fund. | | |

Recall that the bond liability must also be recorded in the General Long-term Debt Account Group. That entry would be:

| | | |
|---|---|---|
| Amount to Be Provided for: | | |
|    Payment of Bonds | 3,000,000 | |
|      Bonds Payable | | 3,000,000 |

3. **Construction-related activity.** A construction contract for $4,600,000 is authorized and signed. During the year ended June 30, 19X2, billings of $2,700,000 were rendered, and payments totaling $2,200,000 were made.

| | | |
|---|---|---|
| ENCUMBRANCES | 4,600,000 | |
|    BUDGETARY FUND BALANCE | | |
|      RESERVED FOR ENCUMBRANCES | | 4,600,000 |
| To record encumbrance on | | |
| construction contract. | | |

| | | |
|---|---|---|
| BUDGETARY FUND BALANCE RESERVED | | |
|    FOR ENCUMBRANCES | 2,700,000 | |
|      ENCUMBRANCES | | 2,700,000 |

To cancel part of encumbrance for
project contract with general
contractor for completions to date.

| | | |
|---|---|---|
| Expenditures | 2,700,000 | |
|     Contracts Payable | | 2,700,000 |

To record actual expenditures to date on
contract with general contractor
for completions to date.

| | | |
|---|---|---|
| Contracts Payable | 2,200,000 | |
|     Cash | | 2,200,000 |

To record payments to contractor.

In addition to the preceding construction contract, $390,000 was incurred for the services of architects and engineers. Of this amount, $310,000 was paid. (For simplicity, we assume that encumbrance accounting procedures were not used.)

| | | |
|---|---|---|
| Expenditures | 390,000 | |
|     Vouchers Payable | | 390,000 |

To record fees for architects and
engineers.

| | | |
|---|---|---|
| Vouchers Payable | 310,000 | |
|     Cash | | 310,000 |

To record payment of architect and
engineering fees.

4. **Closing entries.** The appropriate closing entries at June 30, 19X2, are as follows:

| | | |
|---|---|---|
| Revenues | 1,500,000 | |
| Other Financing Sources—Bond Proceeds | 3,030,000 | |
| Other Financing Sources—Operating Transfer In | 500,000 | |
|     Expenditures ($2,700,000 + $390,000) | | 3,090,000 |
|     Other Financing Uses—Operating Transfers Out | | 30,000 |
|     Unreserved Fund Balance | | 1,910,000 |

To close out actual revenues, other
financing sources and uses, and
expenditures into unreserved
fund balance.

| | | |
|---|---|---|
| BUDGETARY FUND BALANCE RESERVED FOR ENCUMBRANCES | 1,900,000 | |
|     ENCUMBRANCES | | 1,900,000 |

*(continued)*

To close encumbrances outstanding at
year-end by reversing the entry that
previously recorded them.

| | | |
|---|---|---|
| Unreserved Fund Balance | 1,900,000 | |
| Fund Balance Reserved for Encumbrances | | 1,900,000 |

To record *actual* fund balance reserve
account to indicate the portion of year-
end balance segregated for expenditure
upon contractor performance.

In addition to the preceding closing entries, the partially completed capital facility must be reflected in the General Fixed Assets Account Group at June 30, 19X2. These accounts are discussed in detail later in the chapter. For now, you should know that the following entry would be made:

| | | |
|---|---|---|
| Construction Work in Progress | 3,090,000 | |
| Investment in General Fixed Assets from Capital Projects | | 3,090,000 |

To record city hall construction in
progress.

**Financial Statements.**   The financial statements that would be prepared for the fiscal year ended June 30, 19X2, as a result of the preceding journal entries are shown in Illustrations 21-2 and 21-3.

**Completion of Project in Following Year.**   Assume the project is completed in the following fiscal year. The journal entries that would be made during the fiscal year ended June 30, 19X3, follow.

1. **Reestablishment of budgetary control over outstanding encumbrances.** Budgetary control must be reestablished over outstanding encumbrances on July 1, 19X2. This is done by reversing the prior year-end closing entries related to encumbrances.

| | | |
|---|---|---|
| EMCUMBRANCES | 1,900,000 | |
| BUDGETARY FUND BALANCE RESERVED FOR ENCUMBRANCES | | 1,900,000 |

To reestablish budgetary control on
remainder of construction contract.

| | | |
|---|---|---|
| Fund Balance Reserved for Encumbrances | 1,900,000 | |
| Unreserved Fund Balance | | 1,900,000 |

To reverse appropriation of fund
balance made at June 30, 19X2,
relating to encumbrances
outstanding at June 30, 19X2, that
will be honored during the current year.

■ **ILLUSTRATION 21-2**

| FUNN CITY<br>Capital Projects Fund—City Hall<br>Balance Sheet<br>June 30, 19X2 | |
| --- | --- |
| **Assets** | |
| Cash. | $1,290,000 |
| Grant receivable | 900,000 |
| Due from general fund | 300,000 |
| Total Assets. | $2,490,000 |
| **Liabilities and Fund Equity** | |
| Vouchers payable. | $ 80,000 |
| Contracts payable. | 500,000 |
| Total Liabilities | $ 580,000 |
| Fund balance: | |
| Reserved for encumbrances | $1,900,000 |
| Unreserved | 10,000 |
| Total Fund Balance | $1,910,000 |
| Total Liabilities and Fund Equity. | $2,490,000 |

■ **ILLUSTRATION 21-3**

| FUNN CITY<br>Capital Projects Fund—City Hall<br>Statement of Revenues, Expenditures,<br>and Changes in Fund Balance<br>For the Fiscal Year Ended June 30, 19X2 | |
| --- | --- |
| **Revenues** | |
| Intergovernmental—state grant | $ 1,500,000 |
| **Expenditures** | |
| Capital outlay. | (3,090,000) |
| Revenues under Expenditures. | $(1,590,000) |
| **Other Financing Sources (Uses)** | |
| Proceeds of general obligation bonds | $ 3,030,000 |
| Operating transfer in from general fund. | 500,000 |
| Operating transfer out to debt service fund. | (30,000) |
| Total Other Financing Sources (Uses) | $ 3,500,000 |
| Excess of Revenues and Other Sources over Expenditures and Other Uses | $ 1,910,000 |
| Fund Balance, July 1, 19X1. | –0– |
| Fund Balance, June 30, 19X2. | $ 1,910,000 |

2. **Cash receipts.** All receivables were collected.

| | | |
|---|---:|---:|
| Cash | 900,000 | |
|     Grant Receivable | | 900,000 |
|     To record collection of grant receivable. | | |
| | | |
| Cash | 300,000 | |
|     Due from General Fund | | 300,000 |
|     To record collection of amounts received from the General Fund. | | |

3. **Construction-related activity.** The contractor submitted bills for the remainder of the contract. Additional engineering services totaled $6,000. All liabilities were paid.

| | | |
|---|---:|---:|
| BUDGETARY FUND BALANCE RESERVED FOR ENCUMBRANCES | 1,900,000 | |
|     ENCUMBRANCES | | 1,900,000 |
|     To cancel remainder of encumbrance for project contract with general contractor upon completion of contract. | | |
| | | |
| Expenditures | 1,900,000 | |
|     Contracts Payable | | 1,900,000 |
|     To record expenditures relating to billings on remainder of contract. | | |
| | | |
| Contracts Payable | 2,400,000 | |
|     Cash | | 2,400,000 |
|     To record payments to contractor. | | |
| | | |
| Expenditures | 6,000 | |
|     Vouchers Payable | | 6,000 |
|     To record fees for engineering services. | | |
| | | |
| Vouchers Payable | 86,000 | |
|     Cash | | 86,000 |
|     To record payment of engineering fees. ($6,000 + $80,000 owed at June 30, 19X2). | | |

4. **Disposition of Remaining Cash.** After payment of all liabilities, $4,000 of remaining cash was transferred to the Debt Service Fund.

| | | |
|---|---:|---:|
| Residual Equity Transfer Out | 4,000 | |
|     Cash | | 4,000 |
|     To record transfer of remaining cash to Debt Service Fund. | | |

5. **Closing entry.** The appropriate closing entry at June 30, 19X3, is as follows:

| | | |
|---|---:|---:|
| Unreserved Fund Balance | 1,910,000 | |
| Expenditures | | 1,906,000 |
| Residual Equity Transfer Out | | 4,000 |
| To close out expenditures and residual equity transfer out into Unreserved Fund Balance. | | |

In addition to the preceding closing entry, the fully completed capital facility would be reflected in the General Fixed Assets Account Group at June 30, 19X3, as a result of the following entry in these accounts:

| | | |
|---|---:|---:|
| Buildings | 4,996,000 | |
| Construction Work in progress | | 3,090,000 |
| Investment in General Fixed Assets from Capital projects | | 1,906,000 |
| To record completed city hall in the General Fixed Assets Account Group. | | |

**Financial Statements for Year Ended June 30, 19X3.** Because all liabilities were paid by June 30, 19X3, and no assets remained, a balance sheet at June 30, 19X3, is not necessary. The operating statement for the year ended June 30, 19X3, is shown in Illustration 21-4.

## GENERAL FIXED ASSETS ACCOUNT GROUP

The General Fixed Assets Account Group is created to account for a governmental unit's fixed assets that are not accounted for in an Enterprise Fund,

### ■ ILLUSTRATION 21-4

| FUNN CITY<br>Capital Projects Fund—City Hall<br>Statement of Revenues, Expenditures and<br>Changes in Fund Balance<br>For the Fiscal Year Ended June 30, 19X3 | |
|---|---:|
| Revenues | $ —0— |
| Expenditures: | |
| Capital outlay | (1,906,000) |
| Excess of Expenditures over Revenues | $(1,906,000) |
| Fund Balance, July 1, 19X2 | 1,910,000 |
| Residual equity transfer out to debt service fund | (4,000) |
| Fund Balance, June 30, 19X3 | $ —0— |

an Internal Service Fund, or a Trust Fund. This group of accounts is not a fund, but rather a self-balancing group of accounts. For each asset recorded in the group of accounts, there is a corresponding offsetting credit descriptive of the source of the asset. The following are the five asset accounts generally used:

1. Land.
2. Buildings.
3. Improvements other than buildings.
4. Equipment.
5. Construction work in progress.

A statement of general fixed assets classified by type of asset is the basic financial statement for this group of accounts. This statement may be supplemented with: (1) a statement showing these assets broken down by function, activity, or department; and (2) a statement showing the changes in the account balances for the year. A typical statement of general fixed assets classified by type of account and source is shown in Illustration 21-5.

As mentioned previously, not all improvements constructed through Capital Projects Funds must be recorded in the General Fixed Assets Account Group. According to the GASB Codification:

> Reporting public domain or "infrastructure" fixed assets—roads, bridges, curbs and gutters, streets and sidewalks, drainage systems, lighting systems, and similar assets that are immovable and of value only to the governmental unit—is optional.[4]

In practice, only a small percentage of governmental units capitalize and report "infrastructure" fixed assets in the General Fixed Assets Account Group.

## Accounting Procedures

Most high-dollar general fixed assets originate from Capital Projects Funds. Most of the equipment shown in this account group originates from expenditures made through the General Fund and Special Revenue Funds. When such assets are constructed or acquired, each of these three funds debits Expenditures. At the same time or at the end of the fiscal year, entries are made in the General Fixed Assets Account Group debiting the appropriate asset category and crediting the appropriate source investment accounts.

Entries relating to the construction of a new city hall that would be made in the General Fixed Assets Account Group were shown earlier, in

[4]GASB Cod. sec. 1400.109.

the discussion of the Capital Projects Funds. A typical entry pertaining to the acquisition of equipment by the General Fund is as follows:

| | | |
|---|---|---|
| Equipment...................................... | 47,000 | |
|     Investment in General Fixed Assets from | | |
|       General Fund Revenues .............. | | 47,000 |
|     To record equipment purchased through | | |
|     the General Fund. | | |

General fixed assets acquired through purchase or construction are recorded at cost. Assets arising from gifts or donations are recorded at their estimated current fair values at the time of donation. On abandonment, the entry is reversed. On sale, the entry is reversed, and the sales proceeds are recorded as an inflow of resources in the General Fund (typically) using the account Other Financing Sources—Proceeds from Sale of Fixed Assets. As discussed in Chapter 20, accumulated depreciation may be reflected for general fixed assets in the General Fixed Assets Account Group at the option of the governmental unit. Depreciation expense, however, may not be reported in the operating statements of the governmental funds.

## ■ ILLUSTRATION 21-5

| FUNN CITY<br>Statement of General Fixed Assets<br>June 30, 19X2 | |
|---|---|
| **General Fixed Assets** | |
| Land............................................... | $ 1,300,000 |
| Buildings......................................... | 12,900,000 |
| Improvements other than buildings...................... | 1,100,000 |
| Equipment......................................... | 450,000 |
| Construction work in progress........................... | 3,600,000[a] |
|     Total General Fixed Assets........................... | $19,350,000 |
| **Investment in General Fixed Assets from:** | |
| Capital Projects Funds— | |
|     General obligation bonds............................... | $15,300,000 |
|     Federal grants ..................................... | 1,000,000 |
|     State grants........................................ | 800,000 |
|     County grants ..................................... | 600,000 |
| General Fund Revenues ................................. | 560,000 |
| Special Revenue Fund Revenues......................... | 310,000 |
| Gifts.............................................. | 180,000 |
| Special Assessments .................................. | 600,000 |
|     Total Investment in General Fixed Assets.............. | $19,350,000 |

[a]This is work in progress in the Capital Projects Funds.

The GASB Codification covers accounting for lease agreements and requires that *FASB Statement No. 13*, "Accounting for Leases," be followed.

## DEBT SERVICE FUNDS

For discussion purposes, long-term debt of governmental units may be categorized as follows:

1. **Revenue bonds.** Revenue bonds are issued to finance the establishment or expansion of activities accounted for in Enterprise Funds. These bonds are shown as liabilities of the Enterprise Funds, because their repayment and servicing can only come from money generated from the operations of those funds.
2. **General obligation bonds serviced from Enterprise Funds.** General obligation bonds also are issued to finance establishment or expansion of activities accounted for in Enterprise Funds. They bear the full faith and credit of the governmental unit. When such bonds are to be repaid and serviced from money generated from the operations of an Enterprise Fund, the bonds should be shown as liabilities of the Enterprise Fund and as a contingent liability of the General Long-term Debt Account Group. (We discuss these bonds more fully later in the chapter.)
3. **All other long-term debt.** All long-term debt not fitting into one of the two preceding categories is shown as a liability of the General Long-term Debt Account Group.

Debt Service Funds **are created for long-term debt that is shown as a liability of the General Long-term Debt Account Group.** Remember that the General Long-term Debt Account Group is not a fund but merely a self-balancing group of accounts that keep track of all unmatured long-term debt in category 3 above. Debt Service Funds account for the **matured portion of and the payment of principal and interest on such long-term debt.** Although notes payable are occasionally encountered, substantially all long-term debt of governmental units consists of one of the following two major types of bonds:

1. **Term bonds** are bonds whose principal is repaid in a lump sum at their maturity date. Such a lump-sum payment is usually made possible through the accumulation of money in the Debt Service Fund on an actuarial basis over the life of the bond issue ("sinking fund"). Term bonds are less prevalent than they used to be.
2. The principal of **serial bonds** is repaid at various predetermined dates over the life of the issue. **Regular** serial bonds are repaid in equal annual installments. The **deferred** serial bonds are also repaid in equal annual installments, but the first serial payment is delayed a specified number of years. **Irregular** serial bonds are repaid in other than equal principal repayments.

On the date that a principal payment relating to general long-term debt is to be made, a liability is established in the Debt Service Fund for the amount of the payment. Simultaneously, the amount of the debt as recorded in the General Long-term Debt Account Group is reduced by a like amount. Thus, liabilities recorded in this group are effectively transferred at their maturity dates to a Debt Service Fund for their liquidation.

**An Unusual Feature.**   The only unusual feature of Debt Service Funds is the method of accounting for interest on the general long-term debt. **Interest is not reflected as a liability in the Debt Service Fund until the date it is due and payable.** This use of the cash basis of accounting is the major exception to the accrual of expenditures in the period to which they relate. As a result, interest for the period from the last payment date to the end of the fiscal year is not reflected as a liability at the end of the fiscal year. This is because governmental units generally budget for interest on the cash basis instead of the accrual basis.

Debt Service Funds are categorized as governmental funds. Accordingly, the modified accrual basis of accounting is used, and the financial statements used for the General Fund are also used for Debt Service Funds.

## Establishment and Operation

The legal provisions of a specific debt issue may require the establishment of a separate Debt Service Fund solely for that debt issue. In other cases, several debt issues may be accounted for using a single Debt Service Fund. Concerning the appropriateness of recording budgeted amounts in the general ledger, the GASB Codification states:

> it would not be necessary [to record the budget] in controlling most Debt Service Funds, where the amounts required to be received and expended are set forth in bond indentures or sinking fund provisions and few transactions occur each year.[5]

Encumbrance accounting is not appropriate because contracts are not entered into and purchase orders are not issued.

**Sources of Revenues.**   Debt Service Funds may obtain their revenues from one or several sources. The most common is property taxes. A separate rate is levied for each bond issue or group of bond issues. In these situations, the revenues are recognized on the accrual basis. (The accounting procedures are identical to those used by the General Fund in accounting for property taxes.) Revenues obtained from sources such as shared sales

[5]GASB Cod. sec. 1700.119

taxes are customarily recorded at the time of receipt. When money is to be transferred from the General Fund, a receivable from the General Fund may be recorded at the start of the fiscal year for the amount authorized to be transferred to the Debt Service Fund.

Recall from Chapter 20 that an interfund transfer made in connection with the routine operation of the recipient fund is an operating transfer. In this case, the General Fund debits the outflow account, Other Financing Uses—Operating Transfers Out; the Debt Service Fund credits the inflow account, Other Financing Sources—Operating Transfers In. Payments made for principal and interest are recorded as expenditures.

Governmental units commonly use designated fiscal agents to make the payments to the bondholders. In such cases, money is transferred from the Debt Service Funds to the fiscal agents, who submit reports and canceled coupons (if used) to the governmental unit. The fee charged for such services is recorded as an expenditure of the Debt Service Fund.

The operation of Debt Service Funds pertaining to issues of **regular** serial bonds essentially involves collecting revenues and transferring monies to the fiscal agent. Significant accumulations of money requiring investment do not occur. In these cases, the journal entries to record the revenues, the expenditures, and the closing of the books parallel those used in the General Fund. Accordingly, an illustration of journal entries and financial statements for this type of Debt Service Fund is not presented.

The operation of Debt Service Funds is more complex when **deferred** serial bonds and **term** bonds are involved. Accumulated money must be invested, and bond premiums and discounts may exist on such investments. Actuarial computations are used to determine additions and earnings. The journal entries and financial statements for a Debt Service Fund pertaining to term bonds are illustrated in the following section.

## ILLUSTRATION    Journal Entries and Financial Statements: Term Bonds

Assume that Funn City established a Debt Service Fund on October 1, 19X1, for an 8%, $400,000 general obligation bond issue due in 20 years (the proceeds of which will be used to construct a new civic center). Interest is to be paid seminannually on March 31 and September 30. We assume that all required additions to the fund will come from the General Fund and a specific tax levy. Assumed transactions pertaining to the operation of the fund for the fiscal year ended June 30, 19X2; along with related journal entries, are as follows:

| Transaction or Event | Journal Entry | | |
|---|---|---|---|
| The required fund transfer from the General Fund is recorded on October 1, 19X1. | Due from General Fund.... Other Financing Sources—Operating Transfer In ........... | 5,000 | 5,000 |

| Transaction or Event | Journal Entry | | |
|---|---|---|---|
| The required fund transfer is received from the General Fund. | Cash . . . . . . . . . . . . . . . . . . . .  Due from General    Fund . . . . . . . . . . . . . . | 5,000 | 5,000 |
| Property taxes are levied. | Property Tax Receivables . .  Allowance for    Uncollectibles . . . . . . .  Revenues . . . . . . . . . . . . | 23,000 | 1,000  22,000 |
| Property taxes are collected.[a] | Cash . . . . . . . . . . . . . . . . . . . .  Property Tax    Receivables . . . . . . . . . . | 20,000 | 20,000 |
| An investment of $8,500 is made. | Investment . . . . . . . . . . . . . . .  Cash . . . . . . . . . . . . . . . . | 8,500 | 8,500 |
| Cash is transferred to the fiscal agent for the March 31, 19X2, interest payment. | Cash with Fiscal Agent . . . .  Cash . . . . . . . . . . . . . . . . | 16,000 | 16,000 |
| Interest of $16,000 and the fiscal agent's fee of $100 is charged as an expenditure on the interest due date (March 31, 19X2). | Expenditures . . . . . . . . . . . . .  Interest Payable . . . . . . .  Accrued Liability . . . . . . | 16,100 | 16,000  100 |
| Interest is paid by the fiscal agent, and the fiscal agent's fee is paid. | Interest Payable . . . . . . . . . .  Accrued Liability . . . . . . . . .  Cash with Fiscal Agent  Cash . . . . . . . . . . . . . . . .  Interest Receivable . . . . . . . . | 16,000  100 | 16,000  100 |
| Interest earned on investments is accrued at June 30, 19X2. | Revenues . . . . . . . . . . . . | 500 | 500 |
| The fiscal year-end closing entry is made. | Other Financing Sources—  Operating Transfer In . . . . .  Revenues . . . . . . . . . . . . . . .  Expenditures . . . . . . . . .  Fund Balance Reserved    for Debt Service . . . . . . | 5,000  22,500 | 16,100  11,400 |

[a]For simplicity, we ignore the establishment of delinquent accounts at year-end.

**Financial Statements.**    The financial statements that would be prepared for the fiscal year ended June 30, 19X2 as a result of the preceding journal entries are shown in Illustrations 21-6 and 21-7.

The following points are important for understanding the financial statements:

1. A liability for interest for the period April 1, 19X2, through June 30, 19X2, is not reflected in the balance sheet at June 30, 19X2, in accordance with the modified accrual basis of accounting. This interest will be shown as an expenditure in the following year when the September 30, 19X2, interest payment is due and payable.

■ **ILLUSTRATION 21-6**

| FUNN CITY<br>Debt Service Fund—Civic Center<br>Balance Sheet<br>June 30, 19X2 | |
|---|---:|
| **Assets** | |
| Cash. | $    400 |
| Property tax receivables. | 3,000 |
| Less: Allowance for uncollectible taxes | (1,000) |
| Investments. | 8,500 |
| Interest receivable. | 500 |
| Total Assets. | $11,400 |
| **Fund Equity** | |
| Fund balance reserved for debt service | $11,400[a] |

[a]The actuarial requirement at June 30, 19X2, is $10,200.

■ **ILLUSTRATION 21-7**

| FUNN CITY<br>Debt Service Fund—Civic Center<br>Statement of Revenues, Expenditures,<br>and Changes in Fund Balance<br>For the Fiscal Year Ended June 30, 19X2 | |
|---|---:|
| **Revenues** | |
| Property taxes | $22,000 |
| Interest on investments | 500 |
| Total Revenues. | $22,500 |
| **Expenditures** | |
| Interest on bonds | $16,000 |
| Fiscal agent's fees. | 100 |
| Total Expenditures. | $16,100 |
| Revenues over Expenditures | $ 6,400 |
| **Other Financing Sources** | |
| Operating transfer in from general fund. | 5,000 |
| Excess of Revenues and Other Sources over Expenditures. | $11,400[a] |
| Fund Balance, July 1, 19X1. | –0– |
| Fund Balance, June 30, 19X2. | $11,400 |

[a]The actuarial requirement for the year was $9,300.

2. If all required additions are made on time and earnings on investments earn the rate assumed in the actuarial calculations, then $400,000 will be accumulated in the Debt Service Fund by the maturity date of the bonds ($19\frac{1}{4}$ years from June 30, 19X2).
3. At the maturity date of the bonds, the entire $400,000 is recorded as a liability in the Debt Service Fund by debiting the Expenditures account and crediting Bonds Payable. Simultaneously, this debt is removed from the General Long-term Debt Account Group.
4. Making all required additions and earning interest at rates at least equal to the actuarially assumed interest rate is critical to the accumulation of the $400,000 required to redeem the bonds. If a lower interest rate is actually earned, then additional money must be contributed to the fund to make up the shortage. To the extent that earnings exceed the actuarially assumed rate, future contributions may be reduced accordingly.
5. The following essential disclosures for Debt Service Funds pertain to term bonds: (a) the actuarially computed amount that should exist in the Fund Balance account as of the statement of financial position date, and (b) the actuarially computed amount of earnings that should have been earned during the current fiscal year.

## GENERAL LONG-TERM DEBT ACCOUNT GROUP

The General Long-Term Debt Account Group presents a governmental unit's debt that (1) has a maturity date of more than one year at the time of issuance and (2) is not properly shown in proprietary funds (Enterprise Funds and Internal Service Funds), or Trust Funds. Such debt is shown as a liability in this account group until its maturity date, when the liability is effectively transferred to the appropriate Debt Service Fund. For governmental purposes, "long-term debt" includes the portion of long-term debt that is due and payable in the coming fiscal year.

As previously discussed, the General Long-term Debt Account Group does not include the following types of long-term debt:

1. **Revenue bonds of Enterprise Funds,** which are recorded as liabilities of the applicable Enterprise Funds.
2. **General Obligation Bonds to be repaid and serviced from Enterprise Fund operations,** which are recorded as liabilities of the applicable Enterprise Funds. (The contingent liability must be disclosed in a footnote.)

When general long-term debt is created, an entry is made in the General Long-term Debt Account Group crediting a descriptive liability account—

for example, Serial Bonds Payable—and debiting an offsetting account called Amount to Be Provided for Payment of Bonds (Serial or Term). As money accumulates in the Debt Service Fund, the Amount to Be Provided for Payment of Bonds account is reduced to that extent, and an account called Amount Available for Payment of Bonds is debited to signify the availability of these monies. (The proceeds are recorded in the appropriate fund authorized to use the borrowings.) For financial reporting purposes, a statement of general long-term debt is used. A typical statement of general long-term debt is shown in Illustration 21-8.

## Accounting Procedures

Typical entries that would be made in the General Long-term Debt Account Group are as follows:

| | | |
|---|---|---|
| Amount to Be Provided for Payment of Bonds (serial or term) | 3,500,000 | |
| Bonds Payable (serial or term) | | 3,500,000 |
| To record the issuance of bonds for the new community center. | | |
| Amount Available in Debt Service Fund | 100,000 | |
| Amount to Be Provided for Repayment of Serial Bonds | | 100,000 |
| To record increase in assets available for retirement of serial bonds. | | |
| Serial Bonds Payable | 100,000 | |
| Amount Available in Debt Service Fund | | 100,000 |
| To transfer liability to Debt Service Fund. | | |

## SPECIAL ASSESSMENTS

Some government activities involve constructing **public improvements that benefit a specific geographical area rather than the community as a whole.** The most common examples are residential streets, sidewalks, street lighting, and sewer lines. In these cases, governmental units usually charge all or most of the costs of the improvements directly to the owners of the properties benefited. In most cases, money is collected from the appropriate property owners in installments over a period of years. In some cases, the General Fund contributes monies for part of the improvements. Such transfers are **operating transfers.**

Although construction may be started after all the necessary money has been collected, it is more common to: (1) borrow money (usually by issuing bonds); (2) use the borrowed funds to pay for the improvements; (3) collect money in installments from property owners in succeeding years;

**■ ILLUSTRATION 21-8**

| FUNN CITY<br>Statement of General Long-term Debt<br>June 30, 19X2 | | | |
|---|---|---|---|
| Amount Available and to Be Provided for<br>the Payment of General Long-term Debt: | | | |
| Term Bonds— | | | |
| Amount available in Debt Service Fund... | $ | 11,400[a] | |
| Amount to be provided.................. | | 388,600 | |
| | | | $   400,000 |
| Serial Bonds— | | | |
| Amount available in Debt Service Funds . | $ | 14,000 | |
| Amount to be provided.................. | | 2,386,000 | |
| | | | 2,400,000 |
| Total Amount Available and to Be<br>Provided...'..................... | | | $2,800,000 |
| General Long-term Debt Payable: | | | |
| Term Bonds payable...................... | | | $   400,000 |
| Serial Bonds payable..................... | | | 2,400,000 |
| Total General Long-term Debt Payable.. | | | $2,800,000 |

[a]This amount agrees with the amount in the fund balance account of the Civic Center Debt Service Fund balance sheet in Illustration 21-6. Thus, it was assumed that no other Debt Service Funds involving term bonds exist.

Note: Footnote disclosure is required for the contingent liability that exists for general obligation bonds recorded in Enterprise Funds.

and (4) use the collected money to make principal and interest payments on the borrowings. In these cases, the borrowings are generally serial bonds, which may be either special assessment bonds or general obligation bonds. The former may be repaid only from assessments made against the applicable properties benefited, whereas the latter bear the full faith and credit of the governmental unit. To pay for the interest on outstanding bonds, the assessment payers are charged interest in installments.

## Manner of Accounting

Prior to the issuance of *GASB Statement No. 6*, "Accounting and Financial Reporting for Special Assessments" in 1987, special assessments were accounted for in Special Assessment Funds. *GASB Statement No. 6* eliminated this type of fund because a much criticized nonsensical reporting result occurred with them and it was felt that the other fund types could readily accommodate special assessments.

**Construction Activity.** Under *GASB Statement No. 6*, **all construction activity is to be accounted for and reported like any other capital improvement—**

**in a Capital Projects Fund.** No illustrations of entries are provided here inasmuch as they would be identical to those shown earier for Capital Projects Funds. The capital improvements (depending on their nature) may have to be reported in the General Fixed Assets Account Group.

### Financing Activity: The Critical Determinant Is the Government's Obligation to Assume the Debt.

The manner of accounting for Special Assessment Receivables from the property owners and the Special Assessment Bonds depends on whether or not the governmental unit is "obligated in some manner" to make good the repayment of the special assessment bonds in the event of default by the assessed property owners. According to *GASB Statement No. 6:*

> The phrase *obligated in some manner* as used in this Statement is intended to include all situations *other than* those in which (a) the government is *prohibited* (by constitution, charter, statute, ordinance, or contract) from assuming the debt in the event of default by the property owner or (b) the government is not legally liable for assuming the debt and makes no statement, or gives no indication, that it will, or may, honor the debt in the event of default.[6]

In the vast majority of cases, the governmental unit is obligated in some manner. We discuss these situations in the following paragraphs. In the section on Agency Funds, later in the chapter, we discuss the situation in which the governmental unit is not obligated in any manner (and, consequently, the financing activity must be accounted for in an Agency Fund).

### When the Government Is Obligated in Some Manner.

In situations in which the governmental unit is obligated in some manner, *GASB Statement No. 6* requires that a Debt Service Fund be used to account for the servicing of any Special Assessment debt and the collection of Special Assessment Receivables. The Special Assessment debt is initially recorded in the General Long-term Debt Account Group. To the extent that such debt is to be repaid from Special Assessment Receivables, a special classification, "Special Assessment Debt with Governmental Commitment," is to be used in the General Long-term Debt Account Group. Other than this special designation, accounting and reporting for this debt is the same as for general obligation debt recorded in the General Long-term Debt Account Group and serviced through a Debt Service Fund.

The accounting procedures for Special Assessment Receivables in a Debt Service Fund are nearly the same as for other property tax receivables accounted for in Debt Service Funds (illustrated earlier). **The one sig-**

---

[6]*GASB Statement No. 6,* par. 16.

nificant difference is that the deferred portion of the assessment cannot be recognized as revenues until later periods because the amounts are not "available to pay current-period liabilities" (the revenue-recognition criteria discussed in Chapter 20). To illustrate, assume a street lighting project has an estimated cost of $500,000. On July 1, 19X1, certain property owners are assessed $500,000, which is to be collected in five equal installments of $100,000 per year beginning April 1, 19X2. Interest at 12% is to be charged on the deferred portion of the assessment ($400,000). Also on July 1, 19X1, special assessment bonds having a face value of $500,000 are issued at par, with interest at 8% to be paid annually. The entries pertaining to the assessment (but not the bonds) for the years ended June 30, 19X2, and June 30, 19X3, follow.

For the year ended June 30, 19X2:

| | | |
|---|---:|---:|
| Special Assessment Receivables—Current.... | 100,000 | |
| Special Assessment Receivables—Deferred... | 400,000 | |
| Revenues | | 100,000 |
| Deferred Revenues | | 400,000 |
| To record levy of assessments on July 1, 19X1. | | |
| | | |
| Cash | 100,000[a] | |
| Special Assessment Receivables—Current | | 100,000 |
| To record collection of current assessment receivables due on April 1, 19X2. | | |

[a]These proceeds would be used to retire a portion of the special assessment bonds.

For the year ended June 30, 19X3:

| | | |
|---|---:|---:|
| Special Assessment Receivables—Current.... | 100,000 | |
| Special Assessment Receivables—Deferred | | 100,000 |
| To reflect the current portion at July 1, 19X2. | | |
| | | |
| Deferred Revenues | 100,000 | |
| Revenues | | 100,000 |
| To recognize revenues. | | |
| | | |
| Cash | 148,000[a] | |
| Special Assessment Receivables—Current | | 100,000 |
| Revenues | | 48,000 |
| To record collection of current assessment receivables due on April 1, 19X3, along with interest of $48,000 ($400,000 × 12%). | | |

[a]These proceeds would be used to retire a portion of the special assessment bonds and pay related interest.

**Manner of Recording Interest.**    Recall from the discussion of Debt Service Funds that: (1) Debt Service Funds are used to service debt recorded in the General Long-term Debt Account Group; and (2) interest is recognized when due rather than in the period to which the interest relates. Because of this manner of accounting for interest, *GASB Statement No. 6* allows interest on Special Assessment Receivables to be recognized when due, inasmuch as the amounts will usually offset each other approximately. If the amounts do not, interest is to be recognized in the period to which it relates.

## Service-type Special Assessments

Governmental units provide many routine services that are financed from general revenues, such as street cleaning and snow plowing. Sometimes these services are provided at more frequent intervals or provided outside the normal service area. In these cases, the affected property owners may be assessed for the incremental services. Under *GASB Statement No. 6*, such assessment revenues and the related expenditures (expenses) for which the assessments were levied are to be accounted for and reported

> in the fund type that best reflects the nature of the transactions, usually the general fund, a special revenue fund, or an enterprise fund, giving consideration to the "number of funds" principle . . .[7]

# THE PROPRIETARY FUNDS

# INTERNAL SERVICE FUNDS

In this section and the next, we discuss the two proprietary types of funds—Internal Service Funds and Enterprise Funds, the accounting for which parallels that of commercial businesses. The primary distinction between an Internal Service Fund and an Enterprise Fund is that **the former provides services to departments within a governmental unit or to related governmental units, whereas the latter provides services primarily to the general public.**

Various departments of a governmental unit usually require common services. Each department may hire people to perform these services or it may contract with outside vendors. It is usually cheaper, however, for the governmental unit to establish one or more separate operations to provide

---

[7]*GASB Statement No. 6*, par. 14.

these services to its various departments. Internal Service Funds account for each of these separate operations in a manner that charges the total cost of an operation to the various user departments. Internal Service Funds commonly are established for motor pool operations, central purchasing and stores, maintenance services, printing and reproduction services, and data-processing services.

The objective of an Internal Service Fund is to recover the total cost of an operation from billings to the various user departments. Generally, billings are not set at levels intended to generate significant profits—only to recover costs or generate a slight profit. The accounting principles and procedures used in private industry also lend themselves to use with Internal Service Funds, even though billings are not made to independent parties. Accordingly, the accrual basis of accounting is used, depreciation expense is recorded, and any earnings are closed out at year-end to a Retained Earnings account. The following financial statements are used:

1. A balance sheet.
2. A statement of revenues, expenses, and changes in retained earnings (or equity).
3. A statement of cash flows.

Simply because all costs are recovered through billings, it does not automatically follow that the services are being provided at a lower cost than would be incurred if the Internal Service Fund were not used. This determination may only be made by comparing the total cost incurred with amounts that would have been incurred if the Internal Service Fund had not been established.

## Establishment and Operation of Internal Service Funds

Internal Service Funds are normally established by contributions or advances from the General Fund. Contributions are credited to a Contributed Capital account (which is considered the equivalent of a private corporation's capital stock accounts). Recall from Chapter 20 that this type of interfund transfer is a residual equity transfer. Recall also from Chapter 20 that if an advance is made by the General Fund (rather than a contribution), the General Fund would record a receivable (Advance to Internal Service Fund) and the Internal Service Fund would record a liability (Advance from General Fund). Cash is then used to purchase materials, parts, supplies, and equipment as needed to fulfill the objectives of the fund.

A significant managerial accounting issue is that of developing a cost accounting system for charging the various user departments for the costs of the operation as reflected in the statement of revenues and expenses. When billings exceed costs, some or all of the retained earnings may need to be transferred to the General Fund. When billings are below cost, an accumulated deficit may be made up through additional charges to the user departments or a transfer from the General Fund. These inter-fund transfers must be substantively evaluated as to whether they are **operating transfers** or **residual equity transfers.** As discussed in the pre-ceding chapter, **nonrecurring** or **nonroutine** transfers are considered **residual equity transfers,** and all other transfers are treated as **operating transfers.**

| ILLUSTRATION | ## Journal Entries and Financial Statements |

Assume Funn City established a Central Printing and Reproduction Fund during the fiscal year ended June 30, 19X2. Assumed transactions per-taining to the establishment and operation of the fund, along with related journal entries, are as follows:

1. **Establishment of the fund.** The fund was established by a contribu-tion of $40,000 from the General Fund. The operation is conducted in a facility leased on a month-to-month basis from a privately owned company.

| | | |
|---|---|---|
| Cash............................................ | 40,000 | |
|     Contributed Capital—General Fund..... | | 40,000 |
|   To record contribution from the | | |
|   General Fund. | | |

2. **Purchase and depreciation of equipment.** Equipment costing $30,000 was acquired on July 3, 19X1. The equipment is assigned a 10-year life and no salvage value.

| | | |
|---|---|---|
| Equipment...................................... | 30,000 | |
|     Vouchers Payable........................ | | 30,000 |
|   To record purchase of equipment. | | |

| | | |
|---|---|---|
| Operating Expenses............................ | 3,000 | |
|     Accumulated Depreciation ............. | | 3,000 |
|   To record depreciation expense. | | |

3. **Purchase and use of supplies inventory.** Supplies costing $65,000 were acquired. A physical inventory taken on June 30, 19X2, was val-ued at $11,000.

| | | |
|---|---|---|
| Inventory of Supplies.......................... | 65,000 | |
|     Vouchers Payable........................ | | 65,000 |
|   To record purchase of supplies. | | |

| | | |
|---|---|---|
| Operating Expenses | 54,000 | |
|     Inventory of Supplies | | 54,000 |
|     To record cost of supplies used. | | |

Note that inventories are accounted for in the same manner as in a private corporation.

4. **Incurrence of operating expenses and payment of liabilities.** Various operating expenses were incurred. Of these expenses, $7,000 represented charges from the city's electric utility (an Enterprise Fund).

| | | |
|---|---|---|
| Operating Expenses | 67,000 | |
|     Vouchers Payable | | 60,000 |
|     Due to Electric Utility Fund | | 7,000 |
|     To record operating expenses. | | |

| | | |
|---|---|---|
| Vouchers Payable | 138,000 | |
| Due to Electric Utility Fund | 5,000 | |
|     Cash | | 143,000 |
|     To record partial payment of liabilities. | | |

5. **Billings and collections.** Total billings to the city's various departments were $125,000. Of this amount, $9,000 pertained to services performed for the city's electric utility and $5,000 pertained to services performed for the city's central garage (an Internal Service Fund).

| | | |
|---|---|---|
| Due from General Fund | 111,000 | |
| Due from Electric Utility Fund | 9,000 | |
| Due from Central Garage Fund | 5,000 | |
|     Operating Revenues | | 125,000 |
|     To record billing to departments for<br>    services rendered. | | |

| | | |
|---|---|---|
| Cash | 110,000 | |
|     Due from General Fund | | 102,000 |
|     Due from Electric Utility Fund | | 5,000 |
|     Due from Central Garage Fund | | 3,000 |
|     To record partial collection of amounts<br>    due from other funds. | | |

Because closing entries would be identical to those made for a private enterprise, they are not shown.

**Financial Statements.** The balance sheet and operating statement that would be prepared for the fiscal year ended June 30, 19X2, are shown in Illustrations 21-9 and 21-10.

■ **ILLUSTRATION 21-9**

| FUNN CITY | |
|---|---|
| **Central Printing and Reproduction Fund** | |
| **Balance Sheet** | |
| **June 30, 19X2** | |

**Assets**

| | |
|---|---|
| Cash | $  7,000 |
| Due from general fund | 9,000 |
| Due from electric utility fund | 4,000 |
| Due from central garage fund | 2,000 |
| Inventory of supplies | 11,000 |
| Equipment | 30,000 |
| Accumulated depreciation | (3,000) |
| Total Assets | $60,000 |

**Liabilities and Fund Equity**

| | |
|---|---|
| Vouchers payable | $17,000 |
| Due to electric utility fund | 2,000 |
| Total Liabilities | $19,000 |
| Contributed capital | $40,000 |
| Retained earnings: | |
| Unreserved | 1,000 |
| Total Fund Equity | $41,000 |
| Total Liabilities and Fund Equity | $60,000 |

■ **ILLUSTRATION 21-10**

| FUNN CITY | | |
|---|---|---|
| **Central Printing and Reproduction Fund** | | |
| **Statement of Revenues, Expenses, and** | | |
| **Changes in Retained Earnings** | | |
| **For the Year Ended June 30, 19X2** | | |

| | | |
|---|---|---|
| Operating revenues: | | |
| Charges for services | | $125,000 |
| Operating expenses: | | |
| Supplies | $54,000 | |
| Salaries and wages | 42,000 | |
| Lease expense | 18,000 | |
| Utilities | 7,000 | |
| Depreciation | 3,000 | 124,000 |
| Net Income | | $    1,000 |
| Retained Earnings, July 1, 19X1 | | –0– |
| Retained Earnings, June 30, 19X2 | | $    1,000 |

Note: A statement of cash flows would also be prepared.

## ENTERPRISE FUNDS

According to the GASB Codification, Enterprise Funds account for

> operations (a) that are financed and operated in a manner similar to private business enterprises—where the intent of the governing body is that the costs (expenses, including depreciation) of providing goods or services to the general public on a continuing basis be financed or recovered primarily through user charges; or (b) where the governing body has decided that periodic determination of revenues earned, expenses incurred, and/or net income is appropriate for capital maintenance, public policy, management control, accountability, or other purposes.[8]

The most common type of activity accounted for in an Enterprise Fund is the public utility providing water services, electricity, or natural gas. Other activities commonly accounted for in Enterprise Funds are off-street parking facilities, recreational facilities (principally golf courses and swimming pools), airports, hospitals, and public transit systems. The language of the GASB Codification is so broad that a governmental unit may establish an Enterprise Fund for almost any activity regardless of the extent of financing obtained from user charges. In practice, however, only a small percentage of governmental units use Enterprise Funds for activities that recover less than 50% of their costs from user charges, with public transit systems probably being the most common.

Because Enterprise Funds evaluate operations from a profit-and-loss perspective, the results of operations are reported in an income statement (using the accrual basis of accounting), which includes depreciation expense. At year-end, earnings are closed out to a Retained Earnings account. The following financial statements are prepared:

1. A balance sheet (which includes all the fund's assets and liabilities).
2. A statement of revenues, expenses, and changes in retained earnings (or equity).
3. A statement of cash flows.

Although evaluated from a profit-and-loss perspective, the activities accounted for in Enterprise Funds are not engaged in to maximize profits, as in the private sector. Instead, the intent is to raise sufficient revenues to either (1) recover costs to break even, or (2) generate profits so that capital is effectively raised to finance expansion of operations.

### Establishment and Expansion

Some of the more common ways of establishing an operation to be accounted for as an Enterprise Fund or expanding the operations of an existing Enterprise Fund are as follows:

[8]GASB Cod. sec. 1300.104.

1. **Contribution from the General Fund.** An interfund transfer from the General Fund is categorized as a **residual equity transfer.** Accordingly, the Enterprise Fund debits cash and credits an account called Contributed Capital. Contributed Capital accounts are similar to the capital stock accounts used by private corporations in that both reflect the value of assets contributed. Thus, Enterprise Funds do not use a Fund Balance account. Contributed Capital accounts are normally shown by the source of the contribution—for example, Contributed Capital from Municipality.

2. **Loan from the General Fund.** When the General Fund makes a loan, it debits an account called Advance to Enterprise Fund and credits Cash. The Enterprise Fund debits Cash and credits Advance from General Fund (a liability account). If interest is paid on the advance, then the Enterprise Fund has interest expense and the General Fund has interest revenue.

3. **Issuance of revenue bonds.** Revenue bonds are issued by an Enterprise Fund and are repayable, with interest, only from the earnings of the operations accounted for in the Enterprise Fund. (If the bonds also have a security interest in the fixed assets of the Enterprise Fund, then they are called mortgage revenue bonds.) Revenue bonds require accounting entries only in the Enterprise Fund. Bond indenture agreements frequently restrict the use of bond proceeds to specific capital projects; therefore, the bond proceeds are deposited in a separate checking account called, for example, Construction Cash. Using a separate account provides greater accounting control to ensure that the proceeds are spent only on authorized projects. The offsetting credit is to Revenue Bonds Payable.

4. **Issuance of general obligation bonds.** General obligation bonds are issued by a governmental unit with its full faith and backing. The proceeds are transferred to the Enterprise Fund, which uses the cash in accordance with the bond indenture agreement. General obligation bonds fall into the following two categories, based on the source of their repayment and payment of related interest:

   a. **Repayable from earnings of the enterprise.** When the governmental unit intends to repay the principal and related interest from Enterprise Fund earnings, the GASB Codification recommends that such debt be reflected as a liability in the Enterprise Fund.

   b. **Repayable from taxes and general revenues.** When the bonds and related interest are to be repaid from taxes and general revenues of the governmental unit, the bond liability is shown as a liability of the General Long-term Debt Account Group. The Enterprise Fund treats the money received as a contribution and credits the Contributed Capital from Municipality account. Thus, a liability is not reflected in the Enterprise Fund.

## Unique Features of Financial Statements

Because the financial statements of Enterprise Funds are similar to those of private enterprises engaged in comparable activities, typical transactions, related journal entries, and a complete set of illustrative financial statements are not presented. Instead, we discuss the unique features of Enterprise Fund financial statements and then illustrate the balance sheet for a water utility. (The balance sheet has certain unique classification features.)

1. **Contributed capital accounts.** As mentioned previously, Enterprise Funds use Contributed Capital accounts rather than capital stock accounts.
2. **Restricted assets.** Assets that are restricted as to use are shown separately. The most common examples are:
   a. **Construction cash.** Construction cash is not available for normal operating purposes and must be identified as usable only for its designated purpose—for example, expansion of plant.
   b. **Customer deposits.** For public utilities that require their customers to make deposits to ensure payment of final statements, the deposits constitute restricted assets that are not available for normal operations. When such deposits are invested in allowable investments, the investments should also be shown as restricted assets.
   c. **Debt-related accumulations.** Some bond indenture agreements require that certain amounts of cash provided from operations be set aside in separate accounts for retirement and servicing of bonds. In some cases, monies must be set aside to cover potential future losses.
3. **Appropriation of retained earnings.** When money relating to debt retirement and servicing of bonds has been set aside pursuant to bond indenture agreements, it may be necessary to appropriate a portion of retained earnings. The appropriation indicates that a portion of the retained earnings is not available for normal operations, internal expansion, or cash transfers to the General Fund; that is, cash that might otherwise be used for such purposes has been set aside for other purposes. This practice is at variance with customary practice in private industry, where showing the restricted assets separately is deemed sufficient disclosure.

   Technically, at any balance sheet date, the appropriation should equal only the amounts set aside to cover (a) future interest expense, (b) future principal payments (above and beyond amounts deemed to have been generated from operations to date), and (c) potential future losses.
4. **Depreciation expense.** For public utilities, depreciation expense is usually a major expense because of the large capital investment required. Depreciation expense is customarily shown on a separate line of the income statement.

5. **Income taxes.** Because governmental units do not pay income taxes, no income tax expense is shown in the statement of revenues and expenses.

6. **Payments to the General Fund.** Payments to the General Fund in lieu of taxes are **quasi-external transactions,** which we discussed in Chapter 20. Accordingly, such payments are recorded as **expenses in the Enterprise Fund** and as **revenues in the General Fund.** Payments to the General Fund not in lieu of taxes but for the purpose of financing General Fund expenditures are **operating transfers.**

7. **Inverted balance sheet format.** Some governmental utilities use an inverted format for their balance sheets. (For many states, this is a requirement of the state's Public Utilities Commission.) Under this presentation, fixed assets, long-term debt, and capital balances are shown before current items to emphasize the relative importance of the investment in fixed assets and the related financing sources. However, the conventional format, which places current items first, is still more prevalent than the inverted format. A utility fund balance sheet using the conventional format is shown in Illustration 21-11.

# THE FIDUCIARY FUNDS

Agency Funds and Trust Funds are created to account for money and property received but not owned.

# AGENCY FUNDS

Agency Funds act as conduits for the transfer of money. Thus, they are purely custodial in nature. Money deposited with such a fund is generally disbursed shortly after receipt to authorized recipients, such as other governmental funds, other governmental units, and private corporations. Common examples of Agency Funds are tax collection funds and employee benefit funds.

1. **Tax collection funds:** When overlapping governmental units collect tax revenues from the same source, it is usually more practical and economical for only one of the governmental units to collect the taxes and then distribute the taxes collected to the various taxing authorities. Counties commonly collect all property taxes and then distribute amounts collected to the various cities, school districts, water districts, and any other special districts.

2. **Employee benefit funds:** When governmental employees have premiums on medical and dental insurance plans withheld from their paychecks, withholdings are deposited in such funds. Periodically, the governmental unit makes a lump-sum payment from these funds to an insurance company. (The alternative to using employee benefit funds is to set up liabilities in the appropriate funds.)

Agency Funds have no unusual operating characteristics or unique accounting issues. Usually, cash is the only asset, which is completely offset by liabilities to the authorized recipients. Thus, it has no Fund Balance account. Because cash disbursements are made frequently, on many occasions throughout the year these funds have no assets or liabilities at all.

**Basis of Accounting and Financial Statements.**   Agency funds do not report operations. A balance sheet is presented, the assets and liabilities of which are recognized using the modified accrual basis. Because no operating statement is presented, a **statement of changes in assets and liabilities** (a statement unique to this fund) is presented to report the changes in the governmental unit's custodial responsibilities. In light of their simplicity, we do not illustrate journal entries and financial statements for Agency Funds beyond the journal entries shown in the following discussion of special assessment debt for which the governmental unit is not obligated in any manner.

**Special Assessment Debt for Which the Government Is Not Obligated in Any Manner.**   In situations in which the governmental unit is not obligated in any manner to pay off special assessment debt in the event of a default by the property owners, *GASB Statement No. 6* requires that the collection activity pertaining to the special assessment receivables and the debt service activity pertaining to the special assessment debt be accounted for in an Agency Fund. The rationale here is that the governmental unit is acting merely as an agent for the assessed property owners and the debtholders. Accordingly, the special assessment debt is not reflected as a liability in the financial statements of the governmental unit. Nor is the special assessment levy accrued as a receivable in the governmental unit's financial statements. Only the cash collections of the levy and the disbursement of this money to the debtholders is recorded in the Agency Fund.

To illustrate, the entries relating to the collection of the first annual installment of $100,000 due April 1, 19X2 from the property owners (the same information used earlier in the chapter in the discussion and illustration of special assessments) are as follows:

| | | |
|---|---|---|
| Cash . . . . . . . . . . . . . . . . . . . . . . . . . . . . . . . . . . . . . . . . . . . . . . . . . . . . . | 100,000 | |
|     Due to Special Assessment Bondholders | | 100,000 |

*(continued)*

■ **ILLUSTRATION 21-11**

**FUNN CITY**
**Water Fund**
**Balance Sheet**
**June 30, 19X2**

### Assets

**Current Assets**

| | | |
|---|---:|---:|
| Cash . . . . . . . . . . . . . . . . . . . . . . . . . . . . . . . . . | $ 330,000 | |
| Customers' accounts receivable, less $185,000 allowance for uncollectible accounts . . . . . . . . . . | 2,490,000 | |
| Due from other funds . . . . . . . . . . . . . . . . . . . . . . | 55,000 | |
| Unbilled accounts receivable . . . . . . . . . . . . . . . . . | 670,000 | |
| Inventories of materials and supplies . . . . . . . . . . . | 240,000 | |
| Prepaid expenses . . . . . . . . . . . . . . . . . . . . . . . . . . | 34,000 | |
| Total Current Assets . . . . . . . . . . . . . . . . . . . . . | | $ 3,819,000 |

**Restricted Assets**

| | | | |
|---|---:|---:|---:|
| Customers' deposits: | | | |
| Cash . . . . . . . . . . . . . . . . . . . . . . . . . . . . . . . . . | $ 23,000 | | |
| Investments . . . . . . . . . . . . . . . . . . . . . . . . . . . | 512,000 | $ 535,000 | |
| Revenue bond construction account: | | | |
| Cash . . . . . . . . . . . . . . . . . . . . . . . . . . . . . . . . . | | 188,000 | |
| Revenue bond current debt service account: | | | |
| Cash . . . . . . . . . . . . . . . . . . . . . . . . . . . . . . . . . | $ 10,000 | | |
| Investments . . . . . . . . . . . . . . . . . . . . . . . . . . . | 1,130,000 | 1,140,000 | |
| Revenue bond future debt service reserve account: | | | |
| Cash . . . . . . . . . . . . . . . . . . . . . . . . . . . . . . . . . | $ 70,000 | | |
| Investments . . . . . . . . . . . . . . . . . . . . . . . . . . . | 1,200,000 | 1,270,000 | |
| Total Restricted Assets . . . . . . . . . . . . . . . . . . . | | | 3,133,000 |

**Property, Plant, and Equipment**

| | | |
|---|---:|---:|
| Land . . . . . . . . . . . . . . . . . . . . . . . . . . . . . . . . . . . | $ 1,511,000 | |
| Buildings . . . . . . . . . . . . . . . . . . . . . . . . . . . . . . . | 4,477,000 | |
| Improvements other than buildings . . . . . . . . . . . . . | 38,870,000 | |
| Machinery and equipment . . . . . . . . . . . . . . . . . . . | 18,440,000 | |
| Construction in process . . . . . . . . . . . . . . . . . . . . . | 2,900,000 | |
| | $66,198,000 | |
| Less: Accumulated depreciation . . . . . . . . . . . . . . . | (12,450,000) | 53,748,000 |
| Total Assets . . . . . . . . . . . . . . . . . . . . . . . . . . . | | $60,700,000 |

To record collection of first annual
installment from property owners.

| | | |
|---|---:|---:|
| Due to Special Assessment Bondholders . . . . . . | 100,000 | |
| Cash . . . . . . . . . . . . . . . . . . . . . . . . . . . . . . . . . . . | | 100,000 |

To distribute money to bondholders.

## ■ ILLUSTRATION 21-11 (continued)

**FUNN CITY**
**Water Fund**
**Balance Sheet**
**June 30, 19X2**

### Liabilities and Fund Equity

**Current Liabilities (payable from current assets)**

| | | |
|---|---:|---:|
| Vouchers payable | $ 1,347,000 | |
| Accrued wages and taxes | 73,000 | |
| Accrued interest payable on advance from municipality | 26,000 | |
| Advance from municipality | 50,000 | |
| Total | | $ 1,496,000 |

**Current Liabilities (payable from restricted assets)**

| | | |
|---|---:|---:|
| Customer deposits | $ 535,000 | |
| Construction contracts payable | 172,000 | |
| Accrued revenue bond interest payable | 400,000 | |
| Revenue bonds payable | 1,000,000 | |
| Total | | 2,107,000 |
| Total Current Liabilities | | $ 3,603,000 |

**Liabilities Payable after One Year**

| | | |
|---|---:|---:|
| Revenue bonds payable | $28,000,000 | |
| Advance from municipality | 650,000 | |
| Total | | 28,650,000 |
| Total Liabilities | | $32,253,000 |

**Fund Equity**

| | | |
|---|---:|---:|
| Contributions: | | |
| Contributions from municipality | $ 5,000,000 | |
| Contributions from subdividers | 7,880,000 | |
| Total Contributions | | $12,880,000 |
| Retained Earnings: | | |
| Reserved for revenue bond future debt service reserve account | $ 1,270,000 | |
| Unreserved | 14,297,000 | |
| Total Retained Earnings | | 15,567,000 |
| Total Fund Equity | | $28,447,000 |
| Total Liabilities and Fund Equity | | $60,700,000 |

Because the bonds are not reported as a liability in the governmental unit's financial statements, *GASB Statement No. 6* requires:

> The source of funds in the capital projects fund should be identified by a description other than "bond proceeds," such as "contribution from property owners."[9]

[9]*GASB Statement No. 6*, par. 19.

# TRUST FUNDS

Most Trust Funds involve investing and using money in accordance with stipulated provisions of trust indenture agreements or statutes. Common examples of Trust Funds include the following:

1. **Public employee pension and retirement systems:** These Trust Funds account for employer and employee retirement contributions, the investment of such contributions, and the payments to retired employees.
2. **Nonexpendable Trust Funds:** These funds account for **endowments,** the money and property given to a governmental unit. The principal must be preserved intact; only the Trust Fund income may be expended or completely used in the course of operations.
3. **Expendable Trust Funds:** These funds also account for endowments. However, the principal does not have to be preserved intact; the trust principal and income may be expended or completely used in the course of operations. State and federal grant programs that establish a continuing trustee relationship are to be accounted for in this type of fund under the requirements of the GASB Codification.

**Classification for Accounting Measurement Purposes.** The GASB Codification states:

> Each Trust Fund is classified for accounting measurement purposes as either a governmental fund or a proprietary fund. Expendable Trust Funds are accounted for in essentially the same manner as governmental funds. Nonexpendable Trust Funds and Pension Trust Funds are accounted for in essentially the same manner as proprietary funds.[10]

Because the nature of the activities accounted for in Expendable Trust Funds resemble the nature of the activities accounted for in the governmental funds, operations are reported in a statement of revenues, expenditures, and changes in fund balance (using the modified accrual basis of accounting). Because the nature of the activities accounted for in Nonexpendable Trust Funds and Pension Trust Funds resemble the nature of the activities accounted for in the proprietary funds, operations are reported in a statement of revenues, expenses, and changes in retained earnings (using the accrual basis of accounting).

**Establishment and Operation.** Public employee pension and retirement trust funds have the same operating characteristics and accounting issues as

---

[10]GASB Cod. sec. 1300.102.

private pension and retirement plans that are funded with a trustee. Accordingly, journal entries and financial statements for these funds are not illustrated. As mentioned in the preceding chapter, a major shortcoming of many such trust funds is the lack of a sound actuarial basis in accounting for contributions to meet retirement payments.

No significant accounting issues exist for state and federal grant programs accounted for in **expendable Trust Funds.** As the creators of trusts, donors of **nonexpendable Trust Funds** have the right to specify in the trust agreement the accounting treatment to be accorded specific items. Such instructions prevail over generally accepted accounting principles. In the absence of specific accounting instructions, the governing authority is state statutes, which usually confict with GAAP in several respects. For example, most state statutes require gains and losses on the sale of trust investments to be credited or charged, respectively, to trust principal rather than to trust income. For nonexpendable trusts, separate trust funds may be established for the principal and for the income generated by the principal. (The latter fund is essentially treated as a Special Revenue Fund.) We illustrate journal entries and financial statements for this type of fund next.

**ILLUSTRATION**

## Journal Entries and Financial Statements

Assume that Funn City received $100,000 from a citizen, who specifies that the principal amount should remain intact. Earnings on the principal are to be used for park beautification projects. Assumed transactions pertaining to the establishment and operation of these funds, along with related journal entries, are as follows:

### Endowment Principal
### Nonexpendable Trust Fund

| Transaction or Event | Journal Entry | | |
|---|---|---|---|
| The endowment principal fund is established. | Cash . . . . . . . . . . . . . . . . . . . . . . . . | 100,000 | |
| | Operating Revenues . . . . . . | | 100,000 |
| Investment of cash. | Investments . . . . . . . . . . . . . . . . . | 96,000 | |
| | Cash . . . . . . . . . . . . . . . . . . . . | | 96,000 |
| Accrual of interest on investments. | Interest Receivable. . . . . . . . . . . | 8,000 | |
| | Operating Revenues . . . . . . | | 8,000 |
| Amortization of bond discount on investments. | Investments . . . . . . . . . . . . . . . . . | 700 | |
| | Operating Revenues . . . . . . | | 700 |
| Collection of interest on investments. | Cash . . . . . . . . . . . . . . . . . . . . . . . . | 4,500 | |
| | Interest Receivable. . . . . . . . | | 4,500 |
| To reflect liability to Endowment Revenues Fund. | Operating Transfers Out | 8,700 | |
| | Due to Endowment Revenues Fund . . . . . . . . . . | | 8,700 |

*(continued)*

| To close operating revenues and operating transfer out accounts. | Operating Revenues . . . . . . . . . | 108,700 | |
| --- | --- | --- | --- |
| | Operating Transfers Out . . | | 8,700 |
| | Fund Balance Reserved for Endowments . . . . . . . . | | 100,000 |
| Payment of part of amount due to Endowment Revenues Fund. | Due to Endowment Revenues Fund . . . . . . . . . . . . | 7,500 | |
| | Cash . . . . . . . . . . . . . . . . | | 7,500 |

**Endowment Revenues
Expendable Trust Fund**

| Transaction or Event | Journal Entry | | |
| --- | --- | --- | --- |
| To reflect revenues earned by and payable from Endowment Principal Fund. | Due from Endowment Principal Fund . . . . . . . . . . . . . | 8,700 | |
| | Other Financing Sources— Operating Transfer In . . . . | | 8,700 |
| Receipt of part of amount due from Endowment Principal Fund. | Cash . . . . . . . . . . . . . . . . . . . . | 7,500 | |
| | Due from Endowment Principal Fund . . . . . . . . . . | | 7,500 |
| Payment of administrative expenses. | Expenditures . . . . . . . . . . . . . . . . | 300 | |
| | Cash . . . . . . . . . . . . . . . | | 300 |
| Costs incurred on park beautification projects are paid. | Expenditures . . . . . . . . . . . . . . . . | 6,300 | |
| | Cash . . . . . . . . . . . . . . . | | 6,300 |
| To close other financing sources and expenditures into Fund Balance Reserved for Endowments. | Other Financing Sources— Operating Transfer In . . . . . . . . | 8,700 | |
| | Expenditures . . . . . . . . . . . . | | 6,600 |
| | Fund Balance Reserved for Endowments . . . . . . . . | | 2,100 |

**Financial Statements.**  The balance sheets and operating statements that would be prepared at June 30, 19X2, for each of these funds are shown in Illustrations 21-12, 21-13, and 21-14. (Nonexpendable Trust Funds must also present a statement of cash flows).

## FINANCIAL REPORTING TO THE PUBLIC: GENERAL PURPOSE FINANCIAL STATEMENTS

The annual financial report for governmental units is called "The Comprehensive Annual Financial Report" (CAFR). The GASB Codification requires that financial statements be presented using a "reporting pyramid" concept. The "reporting pyramid" consists of four levels of financial information, each of which provide more detailed information than the previous level. Illustration 21-15 shows how this reporting pyramid might appear.

■ **ILLUSTRATION 21-12**

### FUNN CITY
### Endowment Trust Funds
### Balance Sheet
### June 30, 19X2

|  | Principal Fund (Nonexpendable) | Revenue Fund (Expendable) |
|---|---|---|
| **Assets** | | |
| Cash . . . . . . . . . . . . . . . . . . . . . . . . . . . . . . . . . . . . . . . . | $ 1,000 | $ 900 |
| Due from endowment principal fund . . . . . . . . . . . . | | 1,200 |
| Investments . . . . . . . . . . . . . . . . . . . . . . . . . . . . . . . . | 96,700 | |
| Interest receivable . . . . . . . . . . . . . . . . . . . . . . . . . . | 3,500 | |
| Total Assets . . . . . . . . . . . . . . . . . . . . . . . . . | $101,200 | $2,100 |
| **Liabilities and Fund Equity** | | |
| Due to endowment revenues fund . . . . . . . . . . . . . . . | $ 1,200 | |
| Fund balances: | | |
| Reserved for endowments . . . . . . . . . . . . . . . . . . . . | $100,000 | $2,100 |
| Total Fund Balance . . . . . . . . . . . . . . . . . . . . . . . | $100,000 | $2,100 |
| Total Liabilities and Fund Equity . . . . . . . . . . | $101,200 | $2,100 |

■ **ILLUSTRATION 21-13**

### FUNN CITY
### Endowment Principal Fund (Nonexpendable)
### Statement of Revenues, Expenses,
### and Changes in Fund Balance
### For the Year Ended June 30, 19X2

| | |
|---|---|
| Operating revenues: | |
| Gifts . . . . . . . . . . . . . . . . . . . . . . . . . . . . . . . . . . . . . . . . . . . . . . . . . . . . . . . . . . . . . | $100,000 |
| Interest income . . . . . . . . . . . . . . . . . . . . . . . . . . . . . . . . . . . . . . . . . . . . . . . . . . | 8,700 |
| Total Revenues . . . . . . . . . . . . . . . . . . . . . . . . . . . . . . . . . . . . . . . . . . . . . | $108,700 |
| Operating expenses . . . . . . . . . . . . . . . . . . . . . . . . . . . . . . . . . . . . . . . . . . . . . . . | –0– |
| Income before Operating Transfers . . . . . . . . . . . . . . . . . . . . . . . . . . . | $108,700 |
| Operating transfers out . . . . . . . . . . . . . . . . . . . . . . . . . . . . . . . . . . . . . . . . . . . | (8,700) |
| Net Income . . . . . . . . . . . . . . . . . . . . . . . . . . . . . . . . . . . . . . . . . . . . . . . . . | $100,000 |
| Fund Balance, July 1, 19X1 . . . . . . . . . . . . . . . . . . . . . . . . . . . . . . . . . . . . . . | –0– |
| Fund Balance, June 30, 19X2 . . . . . . . . . . . . . . . . . . . . . . . . . . . . . . . . . . . . . | $100,000 |

■ **ILLUSTRATION 21-14**

| FUNN CITY<br>Endowment Revenues Fund (Expendable)<br>Statement of Revenues, Expenditures,<br>and Changes in Fund Balance<br>For the Year Ended June 30, 19X2 | |
|---|---:|
| Revenues. . . . . . . . . . . . . . . . . . . . . . . . . . . . . . . . . . . . . . . . . . . . . . . . . . . . . . . . | $ –0– |
| Expenditures: | |
| Park beautification. . . . . . . . . . . . . . . . . . . . . . . . . . . . . . . . . . . . . . . . . . . . | $ 6,300 |
| Administrative. . . . . . . . . . . . . . . . . . . . . . . . . . . . . . . . . . . . . . . . . . . . . . . . | 300 |
| Total Expenditures. . . . . . . . . . . . . . . . . . . . . . . . . . . . . . . . . . . . . . . . . | $ 6,600 |
| Revenues under expenditures. . . . . . . . . . . . . . . . . . . . . . . . . . . . . . . . . . . . | $(6,600) |
| Other Financing Sources: | |
| Operating transfer in. . . . . . . . . . . . . . . . . . . . . . . . . . . . . . . . . . . . . . . . . . | 8,700 |
| Excess of Revenues and Other Financing Sources over | |
| Expenditures. . . . . . . . . . . . . . . . . . . . . . . . . . . . . . . . . . . . . . . . . . . . . . . | $ 2,100 |
| Fund Balance, July 1, 19X1. . . . . . . . . . . . . . . . . . . . . . . . . . . . . . . . . . . . . . . | –0– |
| Fund Balance, June 30, 19X2. . . . . . . . . . . . . . . . . . . . . . . . . . . . . . . . . . . . . . | $ 2,100 |

The reporting pyramid includes the following levels of financial information:

**Level 1: Combined financial statements—Overview (General purpose financial statements).** The financial statements in the first level present the overall financial position and operating results of a governmental unit as a whole. They are referred to as the "General Purpose Financial Statements." Level 1 contains

1. Combined Balance Sheet—All Fund Types and Account Groups.
2. Combined Statement of Revenues, Expenditures, and Changes in Fund Balances—All Governmental Fund Types.
3. Combined Statement of Revenues, Expenditures, and Changes in Fund Balances—Budget and Actual—General and Special Revenue Fund Types (and similar governmental fund types for which annual budgets have been legally adopted).
4. Combined Statement of Revenues, Expenses, and Changes in Retained Earnings (or Equity)—All Proprietary Fund Types. [Segment financial information for major nonhomogeneous Enterprise Funds must also be presented.]
5. Combined Statement of Cash Flows—All Proprietary Fund Types and Nonexpendable Trust Funds.
6. Notes to the financial statements.
Trust Fund operations may be reported in (2), (4), and (5), as appropriate, or separately.)[11]

[11]GASB Cod. sec. 1900.113.

**■ ILLUSTRATION 21-15**
**The "Financial Reporting Pyramid"**

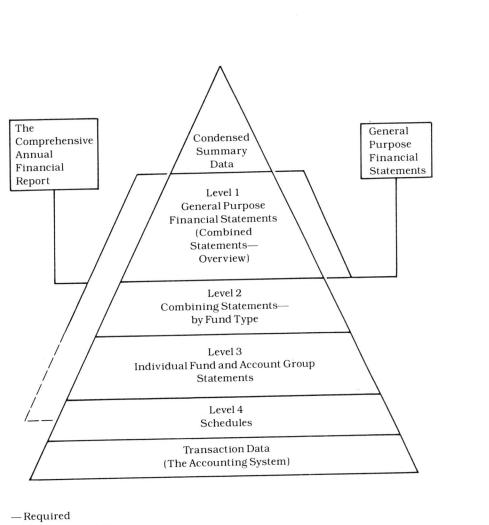

—Required
- - May be necessary
() Refers to "The Financial Section 'Pyramid'" discussion

Source: GASB Cod. sec. 1900.114

The combined balance sheet in 1 shows data for each fund type and account group in columnar format. The combined statement in 2 shows data only for each fund type. Both statements may present a total column, which may or may not reflect interfund and similar eliminations. If a total column is presented, it is described as "memorandum only." For the combined statements in 3, 4, and 5, a total "memorandum only" column is used. Illustrations of the first four of these five general purpose financial statements are presented in Illustrations 21-16 through 21-19. (A general familiarity with these statements is required by CPA candidates.) The fifth statement (the statement of cash flows) is not illustrated. However, you should note that the following classifications of cash receipts and cash payments are to be used (per the requirements of *GASB Statement No. 9*, "Reporting Cash Flows of Proprietary and Nonexpendable Trust Funds and Governmental Entities That Use Proprietary Fund Accounting," which was issued in 1989 in response to *FASB Statement No. 95*, "Statement of Cash Flows"):

a. **Cash flows from operating activities** (operations).
b. **Cash flows from noncapital financing activities** (borrowings for working capital purposes and related repayments, including interest).
c. **Cash flows from capital and related financing activities** (acquiring capital assets, borrowing money to acquire capital assets and related repayments, including interest).
d. **Cash flows from investing activities** (including interest and dividends on investments).

**Level 2: Combining statements by fund type.** In preparing combined financial statements for the first reporting level, individual funds of a given type must be combined. The financial statements in level 2 present the individual funds that have been combined, along with a total column that ties into the appropriate column of the combined financial statements in level 1. (Note that this level would be completely bypassed if a governmental unit had no more than one fund for each type of fund.)

**Level 3: Individual fund and account group statements.** Level 3 presents data for (a) individual funds not shown in level 2, and (b) individual funds for which additional detailed information is provided—such as budgetary and prior-year comparative data. Illustrations of individual fund and account group financial statements were presented earlier in the chapter and in Chapter 20. (Recall from Chapter 20, that the individual financial statements must follow the same format as the combined financial statements.)

**Level 4: Schedules.** Level 4 primarily presents data in connection with demonstrating legal compliance for finance-related matters. Other useful information may also be presented at this level.

■ **ILLUSTRATION 21-16**
**The First of the Five General Purpose Financial Statements**

**NAME OF GOVERNMENT**
**COMBINED BALANCE SHEET—ALL FUND TYPES AND ACCOUNT GROUPS**
**December 31, 19X2**
**With Comparative Totals for December 31, 19X1**
**(amounts expressed in thousands)**

| | Governmental Fund Types | | | | Proprietary Fund Types | | Fiduciary Fund Type | Account Groups | | Totals (Memorandum Only) | |
|---|---|---|---|---|---|---|---|---|---|---|---|
| | General | Special Revenue | Debt Service | Capital Projects | Enterprise | Internal Service | Trust and Agency | General Fixed Assets | General Long-term Debt | 19X2 | 19X1 |
| **Assets and Other Debits** | | | | | | | | | | | |
| Assets: | | | | | | | | | | | |
| Cash | $1,369 | $ 211 | $ 10 | $ 552 | $ 1,164 | $ 100 | $ 293 | $ — | $ — | $ 3,699 | $ 1,893 |
| Investments | 2,091 | 1,577 | 1,513 | 11,051 | 15,523 | 50 | 17,327 | — | — | 49,132 | 36,301 |
| Receivables (net of allowances for uncollectibles): | | | | | | | | | | | |
| Interest | 92 | 2 | 30 | 411 | 420 | 2 | 434 | — | — | 1,391 | 1,014 |
| Taxes | 952 | — | 10 | — | — | — | — | — | — | 962 | 897 |
| Accounts | 72 | — | — | — | 2,622 | — | — | — | — | 2,694 | 2,386 |
| Special assessments | — | — | 4,230 | — | — | — | — | — | — | 4,230 | — |
| Intergovernmental | 215 | — | — | 199 | — | 4 | — | — | — | 418 | 422 |
| Due from other funds | 105 | — | — | 335 | 39 | 126 | — | — | — | 605 | 382 |
| Inventories | 39 | — | — | — | 308 | 23 | — | — | — | 370 | 498 |
| Prepaid items | — | — | — | — | — | 38 | — | — | — | 38 | — |
| Advances to other funds | 78 | — | — | — | — | — | — | — | — | 78 | 50 |
| Restricted assets | — | — | — | — | 27,454 | — | — | — | — | 27,454 | 5,290 |
| Deferred charges | — | — | — | — | 651 | — | — | — | — | 651 | 581 |
| Fixed assets (net, where applicable, of accumulated depreciation) | — | — | — | — | 120,053 | 2,904 | — | $58,912 | — | 181,869 | 167,074 |
| Other Debits: | | | | | | | | | | | |
| Amount available in debt service fund | — | — | — | — | — | — | — | — | $ 1,384 | 1,384 | 10 |
| Amount to be provided for retirement of general long-term debt | — | — | — | — | — | — | — | — | 41,473 | 41,473 | 39,256 |
| Total Assets and Other Debits | $5,013 | $1,790 | $5,793 | $12,548 | $168,234 | $3,247 | $18,054 | $58,912 | $42,857 | $316,448 | $256,054 |

**■ ILLUSTRATION 21-16 (continued)**

| | Governmental Fund Types | | | | Proprietary Fund Types | | Fiduciary Fund Type | Account Groups | | Totals (Memorandum Only) | |
|---|---|---|---|---|---|---|---|---|---|---|---|
| | General | Special Revenue | Debt Service | Capital Projects | Enterprise | Internal Service | Trust and Agency | General Fixed Assets | General Long-term Debt | 19X2 | 19X1 |
| **Liabilities, Equity and Other Credits** | | | | | | | | | | | |
| **Liabilities:** | | | | | | | | | | | |
| Vouchers payable | $ 772 | $ 340 | $ — | $ — | $ 1,469 | $ — | $ — | | $ — | $ 2,581 | $ 1,378 |
| Accounts payable | 165 | 76 | — | 784 | 336 | 242 | 38 | | — | 1,641 | 1,001 |
| Compensated absences payable | 225 | — | — | — | 390 | 28 | — | | 2,242 | 2,885 | 2,414 |
| Intergovernmental payable | — | — | — | — | — | — | — | | — | — | 11 |
| Due to other funds | 476 | — | — | — | 87 | 42 | — | | — | 605 | 382 |
| Matured bonds payable | — | — | $ 8 | — | 123 | — | — | | — | 131 | — |
| Accrued interest payable | — | — | — | — | 1,201 | — | — | | — | 1,201 | 1,261 |
| Deferred revenue | 240 | — | 4,240 | — | — | — | — | | — | 4,480 | 230 |
| General obligation bonds payable—current | — | — | — | — | 1,641 | — | — | | — | 1,641 | 1,523 |
| Capital leases—current | — | — | — | — | 23 | — | — | | — | 23 | — |
| Liabilities payable from restricted assets | — | — | — | — | 4,358 | — | — | | — | 4,358 | 2,177 |
| Advances from other funds | — | — | — | — | — | 78 | — | | — | 78 | 50 |
| General obligation bonds payable | — | — | — | — | 32,934 | — | — | | 35,790 | 68,724 | 65,000 |
| Special assessment debt with government commitment | — | — | — | — | — | — | — | | 4,700 | 4,700 | — |
| Revenue bonds payable | — | — | — | — | 32,828 | — | — | | 125 | 32,828 | 8,580 |
| Capital leases payable | — | — | — | — | 78 | — | — | | | 203 | — |
| Deferred compensation benefits payable | — | — | — | — | — | — | 1,216 | | — | 1,216 | 900 |
| Total Liabilities | $1,878 | $ 416 | 4,248 | 784 | $ 75,468 | $ 390 | 1,254 | $ — | $42,857 | $127,295 | $ 85,069 |
| **Equity and Other Credits:** | | | | | | | | | | | |
| Investment in general fixed assets | | | | | | | | $58,912 | — | $ 58,912 | 59,377 |
| Contributed capital | | | | | 59,395 | 2,486 | | | — | 61,881 | 52,152 |
| Retained earnings: | | | | | | | | | | | |
| Reserved | | | | | 3,817 | — | | | — | 3,817 | 2,590 |
| Unreserved | | | | | 29,554 | 371 | | | — | 29,925 | 28,252 |
| Fund balances: | | | | | | | | | | | |
| Reserved for encumbrances | 320 | 361 | — | 6,563 | | | | | — | 7,244 | 840 |
| Reserved for advances | 78 | — | — | — | | | | | — | 78 | 50 |
| Reserved for debt service | — | — | 1,545 | — | | | | | — | 1,545 | 10 |
| Reserved for perpetual care | — | — | — | — | | | 1,193 | | — | 1,193 | 1,102 |
| Reserved for employees' retirement system | — | — | — | — | | | 16,670 | | — | 16,670 | 14,248 |
| Unreserved, undesignated | 2,737 | 1,013 | — | 5,201 | | | (1,063) | | — | 7,888 | 12,364 |
| Total Equity and Other Credits | $3,135 | $1,374 | $1,545 | $11,764 | $ 92,766 | $2,857 | $16,800 | $58,912 | $ — | $189,153 | $170,985 |
| Total Liabilities, Equity and Other Credits | $5,013 | $1,790 | $5,793 | $12,548 | $168,234 | $3,247 | $18,054 | $58,912 | $42,857 | $316,448 | $256,054 |

Source: Adapted from *Governmental Accounting, Auditing and Financial Reporting* (Chicago: Government Finance Officers Association, 1988). pp. 246–47.

## ■ ILLUSTRATION 21-17
### The Second of the Five General Purpose Financial Statements

**NAME OF GOVERNMENT**
**COMBINED STATEMENT OF REVENUES, EXPENDITURES, AND CHANGES IN FUND BALANCES—ALL GOVERNMENT FUND TYPES AND EXPENDABLE TRUST FUNDS**
For the Fiscal Year Ended December 31, 19X2
With Comparative Totals for the Fiscal Year Ended December 31, 19X1 (amounts expressed in thousands)

| | Governmental Fund Types | | | | Fiduciary Fund Type | Totals (Memorandum Only) | |
| --- | --- | --- | --- | --- | --- | --- | --- |
| | General | Special Revenue | Debt Service | Capital Projects | Expendable Trust | 19X2 | 19X1 |
| **Revenues** | | | | | | | |
| Taxes | $25,068 | $1,528 | $1,650 | $ — | $ — | $28,246 | $24,271 |
| Licenses and permits | 2,041 | — | — | — | — | 2,041 | 1,820 |
| Intergovernmental | 5,770 | 100 | — | 462 | — | 6,332 | 5,674 |
| Charges for services | 2,300 | — | — | — | — | 2,300 | 2,335 |
| Fines | 808 | — | — | — | — | 808 | 521 |
| Special assessments | — | — | 470 | — | — | 470 | — |
| Interest | 623 | 116 | 280 | 844 | 6 | 1,869 | 807 |
| Miscellaneous | 345 | 149 | — | — | 82 | 576 | 605 |
| Total Revenues | $36,955 | $1,893 | $2,400 | $ 1,306 | $88 | $42,642 | $36,033 |
| **Expenditures** | | | | | | | |
| Current: | | | | | | | |
| General government | $ 4,244 | $ — | $ — | $ — | $86 | $ 4,330 | $ 3,850 |
| Public safety | 13,438 | — | — | — | — | 13,438 | 12,150 |
| Highways and streets | 3,735 | 742 | — | — | — | 4,477 | 3,389 |
| Sanitation | 3,726 | — | — | — | — | 3,726 | 3,404 |
| Culture and recreation | 5,882 | 1,001 | — | — | — | 6,883 | 5,972 |
| Capital outlay | — | — | — | 5,461 | — | 5,461 | 2,501 |
| Debt service: | | | | | | | |
| Principal | 15 | — | 2,045 | — | — | 2,060 | 1,470 |
| Interest and fiscal charges | 150 | — | 2,993 | — | — | 3,143 | 1,865 |
| Total Expenditures | $31,190 | $1,743 | $5,038 | $ 5,461 | $86 | $43,518 | $34,601 |
| Excess (Deficiency) of Revenues Over (Under) Expenditures | $ 5,765 | $ 150 | $(2,638) | $(4,155) | $ 2 | $ (876) | $ 1,432 |
| **Other Financing Sources (Uses)** | | | | | | | |
| Operating transfers in | $ — | $ — | $4,173 | $ 1,210 | $ — | $ 5,383 | $ 6,154 |
| Operating transfers out | (4,537) | — | — | (846) | — | (5,383) | (6,154) |
| General obligation bond proceeds | — | — | — | — | — | — | 7,500 |
| Special assessment bond proceeds | — | — | — | 4,690 | — | 4,690 | — |
| Sale of general fixed assets | 145 | — | — | — | — | 145 | — |
| Total Other Financing Sources (Uses) | $(4,392) | $ — | $4,173 | $ 5,054 | $ — | $ 4,835 | $ 7,500 |
| Excess of Revenues and Other Financing Sources Over Expenditures and Other Financing Uses | $ 1,373 | $ 150 | $1,535 | $ 899 | $ 2 | $ 3,959 | $ 8,932 |
| Fund Balances, January 1 | 1,807 | 1,224 | 10 | 10,865 | 49 | 13,955 | 5,023 |
| Residual equity transfers out | (45) | — | — | — | — | (45) | — |
| Fund Balances, December 31 | $ 3,135 | $1,374 | $ 1,545 | $11,764 | $51 | $17,869 | $13,955 |

Source: Adapted from *Governmental Accounting, Auditing and Financial Reporting* (Chicago: Government Finance Officers Association 1988), p. 248.

# ■ ILLUSTRATION 21-18
## The Third of the Five General Purpose Financial Statements

**NAME OF GOVERNMENT**
**COMBINED STATEMENT OF REVENUES, EXPENDITURES AND CHANGES IN FUND BALANCES—BUDGET AND ACTUAL—GENERAL, SPECIAL REVENUE AND DEBT SERVICE FUNDS**
For the fiscal year ended December 31, 19X2 (amounts expressed in thousands)

| | General Fund | | | Special Revenue Funds | | | Debt Service Fund | | |
|---|---|---|---|---|---|---|---|---|---|
| | Budget | Actual | Variance Favorable (Unfavorable) | Budget | Actual | Variance Favorable (Unfavorable) | Budget | Actual | Variance Favorable (Unfavorable) |
| **Revenues** | | | | | | | | | |
| Taxes | $25,566 | $25,068 | $ (498) | $ 1,307 | $1,528 | $ 221 | $ 1,500 | $ 1,650 | $ 85 |
| Licenses and permits | 1,827 | 2,041 | 214 | 100 | 100 | -0- | | | — |
| Intergovernmental | 5,661 | 5,770 | 109 | | | — | | | — |
| Charges for services | 2,158 | 2,300 | 142 | | | — | | | — |
| Fines | 810 | 808 | (2) | | | — | | | -0- |
| Special assessments | | | | 73 | 116 | 43 | 470 | 470 | -0- |
| Interest | 555 | 623 | 68 | 23 | 149 | 126 | 220 | 280 | 60 |
| Miscellaneous | 345 | 345 | -0- | | | — | | | — |
| Total Revenues | $36,922 | $36,955 | $ 33 | $ 1,503 | $1,893 | $ 390 | $ 2,190 | $ 2,400 | $ 145 |
| **Expenditures** | | | | | | | | | |
| Current: | | | | | | | | | |
| General government | $ 4,628 | $ 4,244 | $ 384 | $ — | $ — | $ — | $ — | $ — | $ — |
| Public safety | 13,645 | 13,453 | 192 | | | | | | |
| Highways and streets | 3,866 | 3,735 | 131 | 1,437 | 742 | 695 | | | |
| Sanitation | 3,848 | 3,726 | 122 | | | | | | |
| Culture and recreation | 5,950 | 5,882 | 68 | 1,095 | 1,001 | 94 | | | |
| Capital outlay | | | | | | | | | |
| Debt service: | | | | | | | | | |
| Principal | | | | | | | 2,054 | 2,045 | 24 |
| Interest and fiscal charges | 150 | 150 | -0- | | | | 3,006 | 2,993 | 13 |
| Total Expenditures | $32,087 | $31,190 | $ 897 | $ 2,532 | $1,743 | $ 789 | $ 5,075 | $ 5,038 | $ 37 |
| Excess (Deficiency) of Revenues Over (Under) Expenditures | $ 4,835 | $ 5,765 | $ 930 | $(1,029) | $ 150 | $1,179 | $(2,885) | $(2,638) | $ 182 |
| **Other Financing Sources (Uses)** | | | | | | | | | |
| Operating transfers in | $ — | $ — | $ — | $ — | $ — | $ — | $ 3,500 | $ 4,173 | $ 673 |
| Operating transfers out | (4,700) | (4,537) | 163 | | | | | | |
| Other | 34 | 145 | 111 | | | | | | |
| Total Other Financing Sources (Uses) | $(4,666) | $(4,392) | $ 274 | $ — | $ — | $ — | $ 3,565 | $ 4,173 | $ 673 |
| Excess (Deficiency) of Revenues and Other Financing Sources Over (Under) Expenditures and Other Financing Uses | $ 169 | $ 1,373 | $1,204 | $(1,029) | $ 150 | $1,179 | $ 680 | $ 1,535 | $ 855 |
| Fund Balances, January 1 | 1,807 | 1,807 | -0- | 1,224 | 1,224 | -0- | 10 | 10 | -0- |
| Residual equity transfers out | (60) | (45) | 15 | | | | | | |
| Fund Balances, December 31 | $ 1,916 | $ 3,135 | $1,219 | $ 195 | $1,374 | $1,179 | $ 690 | $ 1,545 | $ 855 |

Source: Adapted from *Governmental Accounting, Auditing and Financial Reporting* (Chicago: Government Finance Officers Association. 1988). p. 249.

■ **ILLUSTRATION 21-19**
**The Fourth of the Five General Purpose Financial Statements**

**NAME OF GOVERNMENT**
**COMBINED STATEMENT OF REVENUES, EXPENSES AND CHANGES IN RETAINED EARNINGS/FUND BALANCES**
**ALL PROPRIETARY FUND TYPES AND SIMILAR TRUST FUNDS**
For the fiscal year ended December 31, 19X2
With Comparative Totals for the Fiscal Year Ended December 31, 19X1
(amounts expressed in thousands)

| | Proprietary Fund Types | | Fiduciary Fund Types | | Totals (Memorandum Only) | |
| --- | --- | --- | --- | --- | --- | --- |
| | Enterprise | Internal Service | Non-expendable Trust | Pension Trust | 19X2 | 19X1 |
| **Operating Revenues** | | | | | | |
| Charges for sales and service . . . . . . . . . . . . . . | $17,676 | $1,857 | $ — | $ — | $19,533 | $14,729 |
| Interest. . . . . . . . . . . . . . . . . . . . . . . . . . . . . . . . | — | — | 41 | 774 | 815 | 867 |
| Employer contributions. . . . . . . . . . . . . . . . . . . | — | — | — | 1,051 | 1,051 | 1,047 |
| Employee contributions . . . . . . . . . . . . . . . . . . | — | — | — | 729 | 729 | 511 |
| Total Operating Revenues . . . . . . . . . . . . | $17,676 | $1,857 | $ 41 | $ 2,554 | $22,128 | $17,154 |
| **Operating Expenses** | | | | | | |
| Costs of sales and services . . . . . . . . . . . . . . . | $ 7,797 | $1,145 | $ 13 | $ — | $ 8,955 | $ 7,127 |
| Administration . . . . . . . . . . . . . . . . . . . . . . . . . | 3,148 | 134 | — | 160 | 3,442 | 3,048 |
| Benefits . . . . . . . . . . . . . . . . . . . . . . . . . . . . . . | — | — | — | 455 | 455 | 380 |
| Refunds . . . . . . . . . . . . . . . . . . . . . . . . . . . . . . | — | — | — | 15 | 15 | 34 |
| Depreciation. . . . . . . . . . . . . . . . . . . . . . . . . . . | 2,507 | 511 | — | — | 3,018 | 2,415 |
| Total Operating Expenses . . . . . . . . . . . . | $13,452 | $1,790 | $ 13 | $ 630 | $15,885 | $13,004 |
| Operating Income . . . . . . . . . . . . . . . . . | $ 4,224 | $ 67 | $ 28 | $ 1,924 | $ 6,243 | $ 4,150 |
| **Nonoperating Revenues (Expenses)** | | | | | | |
| Interest revenue . . . . . . . . . . . . . . . . . . . . . . . . | $ 1,823 | $ 8 | $ — | $ — | $ 1,831 | $ 1,944 |
| Interest expense . . . . . . . . . . . . . . . . . . . . . . . . | (3,734) | — | — | — | (3,734) | (3,098) |
| Other . . . . . . . . . . . . . . . . . . . . . . . . . . . . . . . . | (35) | — | 138 | — | 103 | 47 |
| Total Nonoperating Revenues (Expenses) . . | $ (1,946) | $ 8 | $ 138 | $ — | $ (1,800) | $ (1,107) |
| Net Income before Extraordinary Items . . | $ 2,278 | $ 75 | $ 168 | $ 1,924 | $ 4,443 | $ 3,043 |
| Extraordinary Gain (Loss) on Advance Refunding . . . . . . . . . . . . . . . . . . . | 547 | — | — | — | 547 | (76) |
| Net Income. . . . . . . . . . . . . . . . . . . . . . . . . . . . | $ 2,825 | $ 75 | $ 166 | $ 1,924 | $ 4,990 | $ 2,967 |
| Retained Earnings/Fund Balances, January 1 . . | 30,546 | 296 | 1,887 | 12,772 | 45,501 | 42,534 |
| Retained Earnings/Fund Balances, December 31 | $33,371 | $ 371 | $2,053 | $14,696 | $50,491 | $45,501 |

Source: Adapted from *Governmental Accounting, Auditing and Financial Reporting* (Chicago: Government Finance Officers Association, 1988), p. 250.

In presenting operating statements at any level in the reporting pyramid and for any fund or fund type, the GASB Codification recommends that such statements incorporate changes in fund balance or retained earnings (as appropriate).

In addition to financial statements and notes required for adequate disclosure, governmental units generally include in their annual reports substantial statistical tables and data covering such items as population, number of employees, assessed values, and principal taxpayers.

# END-OF-CHAPTER REVIEW

## Summary of Key Points

Illustrations 21-20 and 21-21 summarize the major key points of this chapter.

## ■ ILLUSTRATION 21-20

### Summary Comparison of All Funds and Account Groups

| Fund Type or Account Group | Basis of Accounting | Records Annual Budget in General Ledger | Uses Encumbrances Accounting | Reports Fixed Assets and Long-term Debt in Its Own Balance Sheet | Does Not Have a Fund Equity |
|---|---|---|---|---|---|
| **Governmental Funds** | | | | | |
| General Fund . . . . . . . . . . . | M-A | X | X | | |
| Special Revenue Funds. . . . | M-A | X | X | | |
| Capital Projects Funds . . . . | M-A | (1) | X | | |
| Debt Service Funds . . . . . . . | M-A | (1) | | | |
| **Fiduciary Funds** | | | | | |
| Agency Funds. . . . . . . . . . . . | M-A | | | | X |
| Trust Funds— | | | | | |
| Expendable. . . . . . . . . . . . | M-A | | | | |
| Nonexpendable . . . . . . . . . | A | | | X | |
| Pension trusts . . . . . . . . . . | A | | | X | |
| **Proprietary Funds** | | | | | |
| Internal Service Funds . . . . | A | | | X | |
| Enterprise Funds . . . . . . . . . | A | | | X | |
| **Account Groups** | | | | | |
| General Fixed Assets . . . . . . | n/a | | | (2) | n/a |
| General Long-term Debt . . | n/a | | | (3) | n/a |

(1) This depends on whether the governmental unit has legally adopted an annual budget for this fund—some governmental units do and some do not.

(2) General Fixed Assets are reported in a Statement of General Fixed Assets (Level 3 of the financial reporting pyramid) and in the Combined Balance Sheet—All Fund Types and Account Groups (Level 1 of the financial reporting pyramid).

(3) General Long-term Debt is reported in a Statement of General Long-term Debt (Level 3 of the financial reporting pyramid) and in the Combined Balance Sheet—All Fund Types and Account Groups (Level 1 of the financial reporting pyramid).

**■ ILLUSTRATION 21-21**
**Summary of Required General Purpose Financial Statements (Level 1 of the "Financial Reporting Pyramid")**

| Fund Type or Account Group | Combined Balance Sheet | Combined Statement of | | | |
|---|---|---|---|---|---|
| | | Revenues, Expenditures, and Changes in Fund Balances | Revenues, Expenditures, and Changes in Fund Balances— Budget versus Actual | Revenues, Expenses, and Changes in Retained Earnings | Cash Flows |
| **Governmental Funds** | | | | | |
| General Fund . . . . . . . . . . . . . | X | X | X | | |
| Special Revenue Funds. . . . . | X | X | X | | |
| Capital Projects Funds . . . . . | X | X | (1) | | |
| Debt Service Funds . . . . . . . . | X | X | (1) | | |
| **Fiduciary Funds** | | | | | |
| Agency Funds. . . . . . . . . . . . . | X | | | | |
| Trust Funds— | | | | | |
| Expendable. . . . . . . . . . . . . | X | X | | | |
| Nonexpendable . . . . . . . . . | X | | | X | X |
| Pension trusts. . . . . . . . . . | X | | | X | X |
| **Proprietary Funds** | | | | | |
| Internal Service Funds . . . . . | X | | | X | X |
| Enterprise Funds . . . . . . . . . | X | | | X | X |
| **Account Groups** | | | | | |
| General Fixed Assets . . . . . . . | X | | | | |
| General Long-term Debt . . . | X | | | | |

(1) This depends on whether the governmental unit has legally adopted an annual budget for this fund.

## Self-Study Questions
*(Answers are at the end of this chapter.)*

### I. DIFFERENTIATION OF TYPES OF FUNDS: ACTIVITIES

1. Recreational facilities run by a governmental unit and financed on a user-charge basis most likely would be accounted for in which fund?
   a. General Fund.
   b. Trust Fund.
   c. Enterprise Fund.
   d. Capital Projects Fund.
   e. Special Revenue Fund.

2. The activities of a municipal golf course that receives most of its revenues from a special tax levy should be accounted for in which fund?
   a. Capital Projects Fund.
   b. Internal Service Fund.

    c. Special Revenue Fund.

    d. General Fund.

    e. Enterprise Fund.

3. A data-processing center established by a governmental unit to service all agencies within the unit should be accounted for in which fund?

    a. Capital Projects Fund.

    b. Internal Service Fund.

    c. Agency Fund.

    d. Trust Fund.

    e. Enterprise Fund.

4. The activities of a municipal employees' retirement and pension system should be recorded in which fund?

    a. General Fund.

    b. Special Revenue Fund.

    c. Debt Service Fund.

    d. Agency Fund.

    e. Trust Fund.

5. Receipts from taxes levied in connection with a special assessment for sidewalk improvements (involving a bond issuance for which the governmental unit has guaranteed repayment) would be accounted for in which fund?

    a. Special Revenue Fund.

    b. General Fund.

    c. Internal Service Fund.

    d. Capital Projects Fund.

    e. Debt Service Fund.

6. A city collects property taxes for the benefit of the local sanitary, park, and school districts and periodically remits collections to these units. This activity should be accounted for in a(n)

    a. Agency Fund.

    b. General Fund.

    c. Internal Service Fund.

    d. Special Revenue Fund.

    e. None of the above.

7. The operations of a public library receiving the majority of its support from property taxes levied for that purpose should be accounted for in a(n)

    a. General Fund.

    b. Special Revenue Fund.

    c. Enterprise Fund.

    d. Internal Service Fund.

    e. None of the above.

8. The proceeds of a federal grant to help finance the future construction of an adult training center should be recorded in a(n)

    a. General Fund.

    b. Special Revenue Fund.

    c. Capital Projects Fund.

    d. Internal Service Fund.

    e. None of the above.

9. The receipts from a special tax levy to retire and pay interest on general obligation bonds issued to finance the construction of a new city hall should be recorded in a
   a. Debt Service Fund.
   b. Capital Projects Fund.
   c. General Fund.
   d. Special Revenue Fund.
   e. None of the above.

10. The lump-sum monthly remittance to an insurance company for hospital-surgical insurance premiums collected as payroll deductions from employees should be recorded in a(n)
    a. General Fund.
    b. Agency Fund.
    c. Special Revenue Fund.
    d. Internal Service Fund.
    e. None of the above.

11. The activities of a central motor pool that supplies and services vehicles for the use of municipal employees on official business should be accounted for in a(n)
    a. Agency Fund.
    b. General Fund.
    c. Internal Service Fund.
    d. Special Revenue Fund.
    e. None of the above.

12. To provide for the retirement of general obligation bonds, a city invests a portion of its general revenue receipts in marketable securities. This investment activity should be accounted for in a(n)
    a. Trust Fund.
    b. Enterprise Fund.
    c. General Long-term Debt Account Group.
    d. Special Revenue Fund.
    e. None of the above.

(AICPA adapted, nos. 1–12)

## II. UNDERSTANDING THE INTERRELATIONSHIP AMONG THE FUNDS AND ACCOUNT GROUPS FOR FIXED ASSETS

13. A new fire truck was purchased out of a city's General Fund. An entry is also required in a(n)
    a. Internal Service Fund.
    b. Capital Projects Fund.
    c. Special Revenue Fund.
    d. General Fixed Assets Account Group.
    e. None of the above.

14. A city sells an unused fire station that previously was accounted for in its General Fixed Assets Account Group. An entry is also required in a
    a. General Fund.
    b. Special Revenue Fund.

    c. Trust Fund.

    d. Debt Service Fund.

    e. None of the above.

15. A city built a new city hall, the construction of which was accounted for in a Capital Projects Fund. Entries relating to the new building are also required in a(n)

    a. General Fixed Assets Account Group.

    b. Enterprise Fund.

    c. Internal Service Fund.

    d. General Fund.

    e. None of the above.

16. A city made certain public improvements from a special assessment. Entries relating to the improvements are optional in a(n)

    a. General Fixed Assets Account Group.

    b. Internal Service Fund.

    c. Enterprise Fund.

    d. Capital Projects Fund.

    e. None of the above.

17. A city's water utility, which is accounted for in an Enterprise Fund, acquired some new fixed assets. An entry is also required in a(n)

    a. General Fixed Assets Account Group.

    b. Internal Service Fund.

    c. General Fund.

    d. Agency Fund.

    e. None of the above.

18. A city's central purchasing and stores department is properly accounted for in an Internal Service Fund. When fixed assets are acquired for this department, accounting entries are required in a(n)

    a. General Fixed Assets Accounting Group.

    b. Internal Service Fund.

    c. General Fixed Assets Account Group and an Internal Service Fund.

    d. General Fund and the General Fixed Assets Account Group.

    e. Enterprise Fund.

    f. Enterprise Fund and the General Fixed Assets Account Group.

### III. UNDERSTANDING THE INTERRELATIONSHIP OF THE FUNDS AND ACCOUNT GROUPS FOR LONG-TERM DEBT

19. A transaction in which a municipal electric utility issues bonds (to be repaid from its own operations) requires accounting recognition in a(n)

    a. Enterprise Fund.

    b. Debt Service Fund.

    c. Enterprise and Debt Service Funds.

    d. Enterprise Fund, a Debt Service Fund, and the General Long-term Debt Account Group.

    e. None of the above.

20. The liability for general obligation bonds issued for the benefit of a municipal electric company and serviced by its earnings should be recorded in
a(n)
   a. Enterprise Fund.
   b. General Fund.
   c. Enterprise Fund and the General Long-term Debt Account Group.
   d. Enterprise Fund and disclosed in a footnote in the statement of General
   Long-term Debt.
   e. None of the above.
21. The liability for special assessment bonds that carry a secondary pledge of a
municipality's general credit should be recorded in a(n)
   a. Debt Service Fund.
   b. General Long-term Debt Account Group.
   c. Agency Fund.
   d. Only disclosure would be made in a footnote in the statement of General
   Long-term Debt.
   e. None of the above.
22. The liability for special assessment bonds where the municipality is not obligated in any manner in the event of default by the property owners should
be recorded in a(n)
   a. Debt Service Fund.
   b. General Long-term Debt Account Group.
   c. Agency Fund.
   d. Only disclosures would be made in a footnote in the statement of General
   Long-term debt.
   e. None of the above.
23. A transaction in which a municipality issues general obligation serial
bonds to finance the construction of a fire station requires accounting
recognition in the
   a. General Fund.
   b. Capital Projects and General Funds.
   c. Capital Projects Fund and the General Long-term Debt Account Group.
   d. General Fund and the General Long-term Debt Account Group.
   e. None of the above.
24. Several years ago, a city established a sinking fund to retire an issue of general obligation bonds. This year, the city made a $50,000 contribution to
the sinking fund from general revenues and realized $15,000 in revenue
from sinking fund securities. The bonds due this year were retired. These
transactions require accounting recognition in the
   a. General Fund.
   b. Debt Service Fund and the General Long-term Debt Account Group.
   c. Debt Service Fund, the General Fund, and the General Long-term Debt
   Account Group.
   d. Capital Projects Fund, a Debt Service Fund, the General Fund, and the
   General Long-term Debt Account Group.
   e. None of the above.

(AICPA adapted, nos. 19–24)

## IV. FAMILIARITY WITH GENERAL PURPOSE FINANCIAL STATEMENTS

25. In the comprehensive annual financial report (CAFR), the combined balance sheet should include all of the

| | Governmental Funds | Proprietary Funds | Account Groups |
|---|---|---|---|
| a. | Yes | Yes | Yes |
| b. | Yes | Yes | No |
| c. | Yes | No | Yes |
| d. | Yes | No | No |
| e. | No | Yes | Yes |

26. The comprehensive annual financial report (CAFR) should include a combined statement of revenues, expenses, and changes in retained earnings (or equity) for

| | Governmental Funds | Proprietary Funds | Account Groups |
|---|---|---|---|
| a. | Yes | Yes | Yes |
| b. | Yes | Yes | No |
| c. | Yes | No | Yes |
| d. | No | Yes | Yes |
| e. | No | Yes | No |

27. The comprehensive annual financial report (CAFR) should include a combined statement of revenues, expenditures, and changes in retained earnings (or equity) for

| | Governmental Funds | Proprietary Funds | Account Groups |
|---|---|---|---|
| a. | Yes | Yes | Yes |
| b. | No | No | No |
| c. | Yes | No | No |
| d. | No | Yes | No |
| e. | Yes | Yes | No |

28. The comprehensive annual financial report (CAFR) should include a combined statement of cash flows for

| | Governmental Funds | Proprietary Funds | Account Groups |
|---|---|---|---|
| a. | No | Yes | Yes |
| b. | Yes | Yes | No |
| c. | No | Yes | No |
| d. | Yes | No | No |
| e. | Yes | No | Yes |

29. Which financial statement is not one of the five general purpose financial statements?
    a. A combined balance sheet—all funds and account groups.
    b. A combined statement of revenues, expenditures, and changes in fund balances—all governmental fund types.

c. A combined statement of revenues, expenses, and changes in retained earnings—all proprietary fund types.
d. A combined statement of cash flows—all fund types.
e. None of the above.

30. The comprehensive annual financial report (CAFR) is required to include a statement of cash flows for which of the following?
a. Agency Fund.
b. General Fixed Assets Account Group.
c. General Long-term Debt Account Group.
d. Expendable Trust Fund.
e. Pension Trust Fund.
f. None of the above.

# ASSIGNMENT MATERIAL

## Review Questions

1. When would a Special Revenue Fund be used instead of the General Fund?
2. What is the relationship between a Capital Projects Fund and the General Fixed Assets Account Group?
3. Does the General Fixed Assets Account Group include all fixed assets of a governmental unit? Why or why not?
4. What is the relationship between the Debt Service Funds and the General Long-term Debt Account Group?
5. What is the difference in meaning of the term *long-term debt* as used in the General Long-term Debt Account Group and as used in private industry?
6. Does the General Long-term Debt Account Group include all long-term debt? Why or why not?
7. What determines whether Special Assessment Receivables are recorded in a Debt Service Fund or in an Agency Fund?
8. Which fund would be used to account for construction activity to be financed from a special assessment to certain property owners?
9. What is the distinction between an Agency Fund and a Trust Fund?
10. What are the two types of Trust Funds?
11. In what way are Enterprise Funds and Internal Service Funds similar to commercial operations?
12. What significance may be attributed to the fact that the billings of an Internal Service Fund exceed its costs and expenses?

## Discussion Cases

| DC 21-1 |
|---|

### Expenditure Recognition on Construction Contract

On January 1, 19X1, the city council of Centersville approved the construction of a new civic center. It immediately signed a construction contract having a fixed price of $10,000,000. The terms of the contract follow:

1. A payment of $2,000,000 is to be made to the contractor at the time of the signing. (The city made the payment.)
2. Progress billings are to be made each December 20 based on the percentage of completion times $7,000,000.
3. Progress payments are to be made within ten days after bills are submitted.
4. Upon completion of the project, the final payment of $1,000,000 is to be made.

On December 20, 19X1, the contractor submitted a progress billing for $2,800,000 (40% of $7,000,000). The city paid this billing on December 30, 19X1.

### Required:
1. What amount should the city report for expenditures in its Capital Projects Fund for 19X1?
2. Assuming the contractor uses the percentage of completion method of accounting, what amount should the contractor report for sales for 19X1?
3. Explain the disparity between requirements 1 and 2.

---

| DC |
| 21-2 |

## Accounting for General Fund Overhead Allocation to an Enterprise Fund

Crystal City has an Electric Utility Enterprise Fund. The city feels that some of the general overhead of the city (that is accounted for in the General Fund) should be allocated to the Electric Utility Enterprise Fund, inasmuch as it obtains benefits in this respect. If the utility were a private corporation, its overhead would be greater than it is now. A cash payment will be made from the Electric Utility Enterprise Fund to the General Fund for the amount of the overhead allocation.

### Required:
How should the overhead allocation and cash payment be reported in each fund's financial statements?

---

# Exercises

| E |
| 21-1 |

## General Long-term Debt: Preparing Journal Entries

The following transactions occurred during Bondsville County's fiscal year ended June 30, 19X2:

1. On October 1, 19X1, general obligation term bonds having a face value of $1,000,000 and an interest rate of 8% were issued. Interest is payable semi-annually on April 1 and October 1. The $980,000 proceeds were used for the construction of a new courthouse.
2. On January 1, 19X2, the county transferred $16,000 from the General Fund to a Debt Service Fund for sinking fund purposes.
3. The Debt Service Fund immediately invested this money, and by June 30, 19X2, the county's fiscal year-end, $1,000 of interest had been earned on these investments.

4. On March 27, 19X2, $40,000 was transferred from the General Fund to the Debt Service Fund to meet the first interest payment.
5. On April 1, 19X2, the Debt Service Fund made the required interest payment of $40,000. (A fiscal agent is not used.)

### Required:

Prepare the journal entries that would be made in all of the appropriate funds and account groups for these transactions.

## Debt Service Fund and General Long-term Debt Account Group: Preparing Journal Entries

The city of Promises had the following transactions during its fiscal year ended June 30, 19X4.

1. General obligation serial bonds having a face value of $100,000 matured during the year and were redeemed. (Money was transferred from the General Fund to the Debt Service Fund to redeem this debt.)
2. Total interest paid on serial bonds during the year was $80,000. (Money was transferred from the General Fund to the Debt Service Fund to pay this interest.)
3. General obligation term bonds having a face value of $500,000 were issued for $505,000. The proceeds are for construction of a new fire station, which is expected to cost $500,000. The $5,000 premium, which will not be used for construction purposes, was properly transferred to the Debt Service Fund.
4. A cash transfer of $10,000 was made from the General Fund to a Debt Service Fund in connection with a sinking fund requirement pertaining to general obligation term bonds.
5. Special assessment bonds having a face value of $400,000 were issued at par. The proceeds are for construction of residential street improvements. (The city is liable for this debt in the event of default by the assessed property owners.)
6. General obligation serial bonds having a face value of $800,000 were issued at par. The proceeds will provide working capital for the General Fund.

### Required:

Prepare journal entries for each of the above transactions in all appropriate funds or account groups. Use the following headings for your workpaper:

| Transaction Number | Account Titles and Explanations | Amount Dr. | Cr. | Fund or Account Group |
|---|---|---|---|---|

## Problems

## Capital Projects Fund: Preparing Journal Entries and Financial Statements

On August 1, 19X2, the city of Atlantis authorized the issuance of 6% general obligation serial bonds having a face value of $8,000,000. The proceeds will be used to construct a new convention center that is estimated to cost $8,300,000. Over the last several years, the Unreserved Fund Balance account in the city's General Fund has been approximately $300,000 greater than is prudently needed. Accordingly, this excess accumulation will be used to pay for the remainder of the construction cost. A Capital Projects Fund, designated the Convention Center Construction Fund, was established to account for this project.

The following transactions occurred during the fiscal year ended June 30, 19X3:

1. On August 4, 19X2, a payment of $180,000 was made out of the General Fund to Ace Architectural Company. This payment was for the design of the convention center. (This $180,000 for architect's fees was part of the $8,300,000 total estimated cost of the Convention Center.) The Expenditures account was charged on the books of the General Fund.
2. On September 5, 19X2, a construction contract was entered into with Nautilus Construction Company in the amount of $8,100,000.
3. On October 2, 19X2, the city deposited $120,000 ($300,000 − $180,000 paid to the architect) into the Convention Center Construction Fund.
4. On December 1, 19X1, one-half of the authorized bond issue was sold at 101. The bond premium was properly transferred to a Debt Service Fund.
5. On April 30, 19X3, Nautilus submitted a billing of $2,100,000 for work completed to date. Only $1,900,000 was paid.
6. On June 1, 19X3, the first semiannual interest payment on the bonds was made. (Principal payments are deferred until December 1, 19X4.)
7. On June 20, 19X3, the city was awarded an irrevocable federal grant totaling $1,000,000 to help finance the cost of the convention center. Payment will be received within 60 days. The city had applied for this grant in May 19X1, with slight expectation of receiving it. Accordingly, it obtained authorization for a bond issue of $8,000,000 instead of $7,000,000.

### Additional Information:

1. The city intends to use a Special Revenue Fund to account for the operations of the convention center upon completion of the project.
2. The city does not record budgets for capital projects in Capital Projects Funds.

### Required:

1. For the above transactions, prepare the entries that should be made in the Convention Center Construction Fund for the year ended June 30, 19X3. (Also, show the appropriate General Fund entry for items 1 and 3.)
2. Prepare the appropriate closing entries at June 30, 19X3.
3. Prepare a balance sheet at June 30, 19X3.
4. Prepare a Statement of Revenues, Expenditures, and Changes in Fund Balance for the year ended June 30, 19X3.

### Debt Service Fund: Preparing a Statement of Revenues, Expenditures, and Changes in Fund Balance from Selected Information—No Journal Entries Involved

The following information relating to the city of Debtville's Debt Service Fund is provided for the year ended December 31, 19X2:

### Interest

| | |
|---|---|
| Interest owed at December 31, 19X1 (none past due) . . . . . . . . . . . . . | $ 160,000 |
| Interest payments made at due dates during 19X2 . . . . . . . . . . . . . . | 700,000 |
| Interest owed at December 31, 19X2 (none past due) . . . . . . . . . . . . | 130,000 |
| Cash received from the General Fund to pay interest . . . . . . . . . . . . | 700,000 |

### Property Taxes

| | |
|---|---|
| Property tax assessments made in 19X2 (to be collected by the Debt Service Fund) . . . . . . . . . . . . . . . . . . . . . . . . . . . . . . . . . | 566,000 |
| Property tax collections by the Debt Service Fund . . . . . . . . . . . . . . | 550,000 |
| Allowance for uncollectible accounts: | |
| December 31, 19X1 . . . . . . . . . . . . . . . . . . . . . . . . . . . . . . . . . . . | 4,000 |
| December 31, 19X2 . . . . . . . . . . . . . . . . . . . . . . . . . . . . . . . . . . . | 5,000 |
| Accounts written off during 19X2 (from 19X1 assessments) . . . . . . . | 2,000 |
| Property tax receivables: | |
| December 31, 19X1 . . . . . . . . . . . . . . . . . . . . . . . . . . . . . . . . . . . | 26,000[a] |
| December 31, 19X2 . . . . . . . . . . . . . . . . . . . . . . . . . . . . . . . . . . . | 40,000[b] |

### Long-term Debt

| | |
|---|---|
| Cash received from the General Fund to pay for the retirement of debt principal . . . . . . . . . . . . . . . . . . . . . . . . . . . . . . . . . . . . | 400,000 |
| General long-term debt that matured during 19X2 and was paid off . . . . . . . . . . . . . . . . . . . . . . . . . . . . . . . . . . . . . . . . . . | 1,000,000 |

### Miscellaneous

| | |
|---|---|
| Gain on sale of investments . . . . . . . . . . . . . . . . . . . . . . . . . . . . . . . | 11,000 |
| Interest on investments . . . . . . . . . . . . . . . . . . . . . . . . . . . . . . . . . | 75,000 |
| Fund balance, December 31, 19X1 (all reserved for debt service) . . . | 621,000 |

[a]At December 31, 19X1, the entire net realizable amount of the property tax receivables was expected to be collected within 60 days, the time period the city uses in determining whether revenues are "available."

[b]At December 31, 19X2, $25,000 of the net realizable amount of the property tax receivables are expected to be collected after 60 days.

### Required:

Prepare a Statement of Revenues, Expenditures, and Changes in Fund Balance for 19X2. (Hint: Use T-accounts for calculations pertaining to property tax revenues.)

## Special Assessments: Preparing Journal Entries and Combined Financial Statements

Sunn City had the following transactions pertaining to street improvements for which a special assessment was made:

1. On September 1, 19X1, a special assessment levy of $200,000 was made against properties on Main Street for street improvements. The $200,000 is to be paid in four annual installments beginning March 1, 19X2. No uncollectible accounts are expected. Concurrently, a $200,000 bond issue was authorized, which carries a secondary pledge by the city. The proceeds can be used only on the project.

2. On October 1, 19X1, $203,000 was received from the sale of 10% special assessment serial bonds. The bond indenture requires any premium to be set aside for servicing the bonds.

3. On October 5, 19X1, a construction contract for $195,000 was signed with a general contractor who is to be paid at the completion of the work.
4. On December 5, 19X1, the contractor's work was completed. The city paid the contractor in full.
5. In February 19X2, the first installment of the special assessment levy was collected in full.
6. On March 31, 19X2, the city retired $50,000 of the special assessment bonds and made the semiannual interest payment of $10,000. The city council has authorized all interest payments on the bonds to be the responsibility of the General Fund.

### Required:
1. Prepare the journal entries that would be made in all of the appropriate funds and account groups for these transactions.
2. Prepare any appropriate year-end adjusting entries.
3. Prepare a combined statement of revenues, expenditures, and changes in fund balance for the fiscal year ended June 30, 19X2—omit the General Fund.
4. Prepare a combined balance sheet at June 30, 19X2 for all funds and account groups—omit the General Fund. (Assume the city follows customary practice in reporting street improvements.)

### Capital Projects Fund and Debt Service Fund: Preparing Journal Entries and Combined Financial Statements

River City, whose citizens were troubled by the lack of recreational facilities for its youths, entered into the following transactions during its fiscal year ended December 31, 19X1:

1. On January 3, 19X1, a $600,000 serial bond issue having a stated interest rate of 8% was authorized for the acquisition of land and the construction of a youth recreation center thereon. The bonds are to be redeemed in 10 equal annual installments beginning February 1, 19X2.
2. On January 10, 19X1, the city made a $50,000 nonrefundable deposit on the purchase of land, which is to be the site of the youth recreation center. The contracted price for the land is $150,000, which is $40,000 below what the city estimated it would have to spend to acquire a site.
3. On March 1, 19X1, the city issued serial bonds having a $450,000 face value at 102. The bond indenture requires any premium to be set aside for servicing bond indebtedness.
4. On March 10, 19X1, the city paid the remaining amount on the land contract and took title to the land.
5. On March 17, 19X1, the city signed a $400,000 construction contract with Rover Construction Company.
6. On July 10, 19X1, the contractor was paid $200,000 based on work completed to date.
7. On September 1, 19X1, a semiannual interest payment was made on the outstanding bonds. (The source of the money was the General Fund.)

8. On December 1, 19X1, the city issued serial bonds having a $100,000 face value at par.

9. On December 2, 19X1, the contractor completed the recreation center and submitted a final billing of $210,000, which includes $10,000 of additional work authorized by the city in October 19X1. The $210,000 was paid to the contractor on December 12, 19X1.

10. Through December 10, 19X1, the city had invested excess cash (from the bond offering) in short-term certificates of deposit. The amount collected on these investments totaled $12,000.

### Required:

1. Prepare the journal entries for the preceding transactions.
2. Prepare any appropriate year-end adjusting entries.
3. Prepare a combined statement of revenues, expenditures, and changes in fund balance for 19X1—omit the General Fund.
4. Prepare a combined balance sheet for all funds and account groups at December 31, 19X1—omit the General Fund.

## Internal Service Funds: Preparing Journal Entries and Financial Statements

The city of Paradise had the following transactions relating to its newly established Central Printing Internal Service Fund during the fiscal year ended June 30, 19X1:

1. A contribution of $100,000 was received from the General Fund to establish the Internal Service Fund.

2. Machinery and equipment costing $80,000 was purchased and paid for by the Internal Service Fund. These items were placed in service on January 4, 19X1, and have an estimated useful life of 10 years. (All machinery and equipment in the General Fixed Assets Account Group is depreciated using a 10-year life.)

3. Materials and supplies of $18,000 were ordered using purchase orders. For $14,000 of these purchase orders, the materials and supplies were received at a cost of $14,300. Payments totaling $9,500 were made on these billings.

4. Total billings for the year were $60,000. Of this amount, $7,000 was billed to the city's water utility, which is operated in an Enterprise Fund. The remaining amount was billed to various departments in the General Fund. Of these billings, $32,000 was collected from the General Fund and $5,500 was collected from the water utility.

5. Salaries and wages totaling $49,000 were paid.

6. The city's electric utility, which is operated as an Enterprise Fund, billed the Internal Service Fund $900. Of this amount, $700 was paid.

7. Materials and supplies on hand at June 30, 19X1, were counted and costed at $3,800.

8. A subsidy of $5,000 was received from the General Fund near the end of the fiscal year in recognition of the fact that the first year of operations was a start-up year at a loss. In addition, $10,000 was received from the General Fund near the end of the fiscal year as a temporary advance to be repaid (without interest) during the following fiscal year.

**Required:**

1. Prepare the appropriate journal entries for the above transactions in the Internal Service Fund.
2. Prepare the year-end closing entry.
3. Prepare a balance sheet at June 30, 19X1.
4. Prepare a Statement of Revenues, Expenses, and Changes in Retained Earnings for the year ended June 30, 19X1.

| P 21-6 |
|---|

## Enterprise Fund: Preparing Journal Entries

The following activities pertain to Enterprise Funds:

1. City A contributed $1,000,000 to a newly established Enterprise Fund formed to provide off-street parking facilities.
2. City B established an Enterprise Fund to account for its municipal golf course, which would be built using the proceeds of $3,000,000 of general obligation bonds and be repaid from golf course earnings. The bonds were issued at a premium of $50,000.
3. City C established an Enterprise Fund to account for its municipal swimming pools to be built using the proceeds of $2,000,000 of general obligation serial bonds to be repaid from taxes and general revenues. The bonds were issued at a discount of $25,000.
4. City D operates a water utility in an Enterprise Fund. To expand operations, the city issued $5,000,000 of revenue bonds at a premium of $40,000.
5. City E operates an electric utility in an Enterprise Fund, which made a $500,000 payment in lieu of taxes to the city's General Fund.
6. City F operates an airport in an Enterprise Fund, which made a $600,000 payment to the city to finance General Fund expenditures.
7. City G discontinued its municipal golf course, which was accounted for in an Enterprise Fund. The land was sold to a residential home developer. All outstanding liabilities were paid, and the remaining $750,000 cash was disbursed to the General Fund. (The Enterprise Fund had $300,000 in its Capital Contribution from Municipality account and $450,000 in its Retained Earnings account just before the disbursement.)
8. City H operates a public transit system in an Enterprise Fund. The transit system usually recovers approximately 60% of its costs and expenses from user charges. During the current year, the Enterprise Fund received an $800,000 subsidy from the General Fund.
9. City I operates an electric utility in an Enterprise Fund. During the year, the city redeemed $500,000 of its electric utility's revenue bonds.
10. City J operates a gas utility in an Enterprise Fund. During the year, the city redeemed $1,000,000 of its general obligation serial bonds, which were issued many years ago to finance expansion of the gas utility. The bonds were to be repaid from taxes and general revenues.

**Required:**

For each transaction, prepare the necessary journal entries for all the funds and account groups involved. Use the following headings for your workpaper:

| Transaction Number | Account Titles and Explanations | Amount Dr. | Cr. | Fund or Account Group |
|---|---|---|---|---|

## Agency Fund (Resulting from a Special Assessment)

On January 2, 19X1, the city council of Walkerville approved a six-year special assessment project for a sidewalk improvement program. Transactions during 19X1 and other information pertaining to this project follow:

1. January 2, 19X1: 10% serial bonds having a face amount of $500,000 were issued at their face amount. (The city is not obligated in any manner in the event of default.)
2. January 2, 19X1: A construction contract having a fixed price of $600,000 was signed.
3. January 2, 19X1: Special assessments were levied totaling $660,000, of which $60,000 is expected to be uncollectible. Beginning July 1, 19X1, interest at 10% is to be charged on the deferred installments of $550,000, of which $110,000 is due annually each July 1 beginning July 1, 19X2, along with accrued interest.
4. July 1, 19X1: The current portion of the assessment ($110,000) became due and collections of $101,000 were made.
5. July 1, 19X1: A disbursement of $100,000 was made to the Capital Projects Fund.

### Required:
Prepare the entries required in the Agency Fund for 19X1.

## COMPREHENSIVE   (All Funds and Account Groups) Preparing Journal Entries for Typical Transactions

The village of Starville had the following transactions for the year ended December 31, 19X3.

1. Property taxes were levied in the amount of $500,000. Of this amount, $100,000 was a special levy for the servicing and retirement of serial bonds issued 15 years/ago for the construction of a fire station. It was estimated that 2% of the total amount levied would be uncollectible. An Agency Fund was used.
2. The village received its share of state sales taxes on gasoline. The $33,000 share can be used only for street improvements and maintenance. During the year, the village spent $31,000 for this purpose. (The village used its own work force.)
3. On March 31, 19X3, general obligation bonds bearing interest at 6% were issued in the face amount of $500,000. The proceeds were $503,000, of which $500,000 was authorized to be spent on a new library. The remaining $3,000 was set aside for the eventual retirement of the debt. The bonds are due in 20 years, with interest to be paid on March 31 and September 30 of each year.

4. A construction contract in the amount of $490,000 was entered into with Booker Construction Company to build the new library. Billings of $240,000 were submitted, of which $216,000 was paid.

5. On September 30, 19X3, the interest due on the library bonds was paid using the money from the General Fund.

6. On November 30, 19X3, the fire station serial bonds referred to in (1) above were paid off ($60,000), along with interest due at that time ($36,000).

7. On July 31, 19X1, 8% special assessment bonds having a face value of $90,000 were issued at par; the proceeds will be used for a street lighting project. Interest is paid annually each July 31. (The village has pledged to pay off these bonds in the event the assessed property owners default.)

8. Assessments were levied totaling $100,000 for the residual street lighting project; the village contributed $7,000 out of the General Fund as its share. Of the $100,000 assessed, $10,000 was collected, with the remaining $90,000 to be collected in succeeding years.

9. A General Fund transfer of $8,000 was made to establish an Internal Service Fund to provide for a central purchasing and stores function.

10. During the year, the Internal Service Fund purchased various supplies at a cost of $6,500. Of this amount, $4,400 was billed to the city's various departments at $5,500.

11. A Capital Projects Fund having a fund balance of $2,000 was terminated. The cash was sent to the General Fund as required.

12. A local resident donated marketable securities with a market value of $80,000 (the resident's cost was $44,000) under the terms of a trust agreement. The principal is to remain intact. Earnings on the principal are to be used for college scholarships to the needy students. Revenues earned during 19X3 totaled $7,500, of which $7,000 was disbursed for scholarships.

13. The village water utility billed the General Fund $6,600.

14. A new fire truck costing $22,000 was ordered, received, and paid for. The old fire truck (which cost $8,000) was sold for $1,500.

**Required:**

For each transaction, prepare the necessary journal entries for all of the appropriate funds and account groups involved. Use the following headings for your workpaper:

| Transaction Number | Account Titles and Explanations | Amount Dr. | Cr. | Fund or Account Group |
|---|---|---|---|---|

## Additional Requirement for Problem 20-8

**P 21-9**

**Required:**

Prepare the entries that would be made in the other funds and account groups in Problem 20-8 to account properly for the items that should not be accounted for in the General Fund.

| P 21-10 |
|---------|

## COMPREHENSIVE    Preparing a Combined Balance Sheet from Trial Balances

Below is the trial balance of all of the funds and account groups for Nerf City at June 30, 19X6, just *prior* to the adjusting and closing entries. All depreciation adjustments have been made.

### GENERAL FUND

| | | | |
|---|--:|---|--:|
| Cash | $ 150,000 | Vouchers Payable | $ 75,000 |
| Taxes Receivable—Current | 130,000 | Due to Internal Service Fund | 15,000 |
| Inventory | 20,000 | BUDGETARY FUND BALANCE | |
| ESTIMATED REVENUES | 900,000 | RESERVED FOR | |
| ENCUMBRANCES | 30,000 | ENCUMBRANCES | 30,000 |
| Expenditures | 770,000 | **Budgetary Fund Balance** | 100,000 |
| | | Unreserved Fund Balance | 50,000 |
| | | APPROPRIATIONS | 800,000 |
| | | Revenues | 930,000 |
| | $2,000,000 | | $2,000,000 |

### NEW FIRE STATION CAPITAL PROJECTS FUND[a]

| | | | |
|---|--:|---|--:|
| Cash | $ 10,000 | Unreserved Fund Balance | $100,000 |
| Expenditures | 90,000 | | |
| | $100,000 | | $100,000 |

[a]This project was completed by year-end. The money raised can be spent only on the fire station.

### NEW FIRE STATION DEBT SERVICE FUND

| | | | |
|---|--:|---|--:|
| Cash | $22,000 | Revenues | $ 2,000 |
| Investments | 20,000 | Unreserved Fund Balances | 40,000 |
| | $42,000 | | $42,000 |

### INTERNAL SERVICE FUND

| | | | |
|---|--:|---|--:|
| Cash | $ 85,000 | Revenues | $ 90,000 |
| Due from General Fund | 15,000 | Accumulated Depreciation | 50,000 |
| Equipment | 200,000 | Retained Earnings | 260,000 |
| Expenses | 100,000 | | |
| | $400,000 | | $400,000 |

### TRUST AND AGENCY FUNDS

| | | | |
|---|--:|---|--:|
| Cash | $ 80,000 | Accumulated Depreciation | $ 30,000 |
| Office Building | 300,000 | Revenues | 30,000 |
| Expenses | 10,000 | Liability to Federal Government | 14,000 |
| | | Liability to State Government | 6,000 |
| | | Unreserved Fund Balance | 310,000 |
| | $390,000 | | $390,000 |

*(continued)*

## GENERAL FIXED ASSETS ACCOUNT GROUP

| | | | |
|---|---|---|---|
| Buildings..................... | $390,000 | Investment in GFA-CPF ...... | $430,000 |
| Equipment.................... | 50,000 | Investment in GFA-GF ....... | 70,000 |
| Construction W.I.P............ | 60,000 | | |
| | $500,000 | | $500,000 |

## GENERAL LONG-TERM DEBT ACCOUNT GROUP

| | | | |
|---|---|---|---|
| Amount Available in Debt | | Bonds Payable.............. | $350,000 |
| Service Fund............... | $ 40,000 | | |
| Amount To Be Provided ....... | 310,000 | | |
| | $350,000 | | $350,000 |

### Required:

Prepare a Combined Balance Sheet for all funds and account groups.

### ANSWERS TO SELF-STUDY QUESTIONS

| | | | | |
|---|---|---|---|---|
| 1. c | 7. b | 13. d | 19. a | 25. a |
| 2. c | 8. c | 14. a | 20. d | 26. e |
| 3. b | 9. a | 15. a | 21. b | 27. b |
| 4. e | 10. b | 16. a | 22. e | 28. c |
| 5. e | 11. c | 17. e | 23. c | 29. d |
| 6. a | 12. e | 18. b | 24. c | 30. f |

# 22
**· · · · ·**

# ACCOUNTING FOR NONPROFIT ORGANIZATIONS

## *TOPIC OUTLINE*

An Overview of Accounting for Nonprofit Organizations

The Development of Generally Accepted Accounting Principles

The Characteristics of Nonprofit Organizations

Framework of Accounting

Accounting for Colleges and Universities

Accounting for Health Care Providers

Voluntary Health and Welfare Organizations

Accounting for Other Nonprofit Organizations

APPENDIX A: Illustrated Current Funds Group Transactions: Colleges and Universities

APPENDIX B: Illustrated Plant Funds Group Transactions: Colleges and Universities

APPENDIX C: Illustrated General Funds Transactions: Hospitals

APPENDIX D: Illustrated Transactions for Endowment and Similar Funds, Agency Funds, Annuity Funds, Life Income Funds, and Loan Funds

APPENDIX E: Investment Pools

# AN OVERVIEW OF ACCOUNTING FOR NONPROFIT ORGANIZATIONS

In Chapters 20 and 21 we examined one type of nonprofit organization—governmental units. In this chapter we focus on the remaining types of nonprofit organizations, which increasingly represent a significant segment of the U.S. economy. Billions of dollars, representing voluntary financial contributions, and millions of hours of donated services, flow into these organizations annually. In this chapter we consider the following organizations:

1. Colleges and universities
2. Health care providers (for example, hospitals, nursing homes, health maintenance organizations)
3. Voluntary health and welfare organizations (for example, United Way and the American Heart Association)
4. Other nonprofit organizations (for example, labor unions, political parties, private foundations, professional and religious organizations)

Except for certain health care providers, we do not include in our discussion the types of entities that operate essentially as commercial enterprises for the direct economic benefit of members or shareholders—for example, employee benefit and pension plans, mutual insurance companies, mutual banks, credit unions, trusts, and farm cooperatives.

Many nonprofit organizations have grown in size and influence and have developed from individually operated entities to organizations of national and international scope. Along with this growth has come an increasing awareness of the nature and importance of the roles of nonprofit organizations and the need for improved accounting standards and reporting practices. Many constituencies need full knowledge of an organization's activities and financial information showing how well the organization is meeting its goals. Constituencies include governing boards, creditors, donors and prospective donors, granting agencies, oversight committees of federal, state, and local legislative bodies, federal and state health care cost reimbursement agencies, insurance companies, regulatory governmental agencies, national headquarters of organizations with local chapters, and accrediting agencies.

In this chapter, we introduce the generally accepted accounting principles that apply specifically to nonprofit organizations. In addition to the individual treatment of selected types of nonprofit organizations, we compare the various types of nonprofit organizations, emphasizing differences in fund structure, revenue recognition practices, investment valuation, and the content and format of financial statements.

# THE DEVELOPMENT OF GENERALLY ACCEPTED ACCOUNTING PRINCIPLES

## Early Development

Statements of generally accepted accounting principles promulgated by the Financial Accounting Standards Board (FASB) and its predecessor bodies generally have applied only to business enterprises. For example, *Accounting Research Bulletin No. 43*, which is a 1953 restatement and revision of all Accounting Research Bulletins issued up to that time and which is still in force, states that

> except where there is a specific statement of a different intent by the committee, its opinions and recommendations are directed primarily to the business enterprises organized for profit.[1]

The early development of accounting principles specifically for non-profit organizations was largely undertaken by nonprofit industry groups outside the accounting profession. Accounting manuals representing a codification of industry practices and the delineation of reporting problems were developed by colleges and universities, religious organizations, hospitals, country clubs, museums, and voluntary health and welfare organizations. The manuals provided guidance in accounting for specific types of nonprofit organizations. Not surprisingly, this piecemeal process, representing a compilation of practices, resulted in inconsistencies.[2]

## Development of the Audit Guides

Increased public awareness of the nonprofit sector of our economy in the 1960s largely brought on the increased recognition by the accounting profession of the shortcomings of the industry-developed manuals. The American Institute of Certified Public Accountants (AICPA) developed and issued the following four audit guides in the early 1970s through the early 1980s: *Audit Guide for Voluntary Health and Welfare Organizations*, *Hospital Audit Guide*, *Audits of Colleges and Universities*, and *Audits of Certain Nonprofit Organizations*. These guides, and subsequent amendments in the form of Statements of Position (SOPs), provided the substantial authoritative support required for all generally accepted accounting principles for nonprofit organizations. The fifth edition of the *Hospital Audit Guide* states:

[1]*Accounting Research and Terminology Bulletins*, final ed. (New York: American Institute of Certified Public Accountants, 1961), Intro., par. 5.
[2]Malvern J. Gross, Jr., "Nonprofit Accounting: The Continuing Revolution," *Journal of Accountancy*, June 1977, p. 67.

This audit guide is published for the guidance of members of the Institute in examining and reporting on financial statements of hospitals. It represents the considered opinion of the Committee on Health Care Institutions and as such contains the best thought of the profession as to the best practices in this area of reporting. Members should be aware that they may be called upon to justify departures from the Committee's recommendations.[3]

## GAAP for Nonprofit Organizations and the FASB

In 1979, the FASB announced plans to extract the specialized accounting principles and practices set forth in these guides and Statements of Position and issue them as FASB statements, after appropriate study. As an interim measure, in 1979 it issued *FASB Statement No. 32*, "Specialized Accounting and Reporting Principles and Practices in AICPA Statements of Position and Guides on Accounting and Auditing Matters." *FASB Statement No. 32* accorded the status of "preferable accounting principles" to the special accounting and reporting practices set forth in the guides and Statements of Position when applying *APB Opinion No. 20*, "Accounting Changes" (that is, when justifying a change in accounting principle).[4]

## On the Horizon

The development of a set of uniform, generally accepted accounting principles for nonprofit organizations based on a logical conceptual framework is apparently gaining momentum. In the late 1970s, the FASB published a research report, *Financial Accounting in Nonbusiness Organizations: An Exploratory Study of Conceptual Issues.* Under the broad scope of the study, government is considered a type of nonbusiness organization. The report's author, Robert N. Anthony, states its purpose as follows:

This study attempts to identify the problems that would be involved in arriving at one or more statements of objectives and basic concepts of financial reporting for nonbusiness organizations. It identifies certain issues that need to be addressed in arriving at such statements and the principal arguments, pro and con, that are advanced in connection with each issue. It does not recommend how any of these issues should be resolved.[5]

---

[3]*Hospital Audit Guide*, 5th ed. (New York: American Institute of Certified Public Accountants, 1985), inside cover.

[4]*Statement of Financial Accounting Standards. No. 32*, "Specialized Accounting and Reporting Principles and Practices of AICPA Statements of Position and Guides on Accounting and Auditing Matters" (Stamford: Financial Accounting Standards Board, 1979), pars. 2, 10.

[5]Robert N. Anthony, *Financial Accounting in Nonbusiness Organizations: An Exploratory Study of Conceptual Issues* (Stamford: Financial Accounting Standards Board, 1978), p. 7.

In 1980, the FASB issued such a statement of concepts, "Objectives of Financial Reporting by Nonbusiness Organizations."[6] Although the statement did not establish any new accounting standards, its purpose was to set forth objectives for financial reporting to help in the development of improved standards.

In 1985, the FASB issued *Concepts Statement No. 6*, "Elements of Financial Statements," which replaced *Concepts Statement No. 3*, "Elements of Financial Statements of Business Enterprises," and extended definitions to nonprofit organizations. *Concepts Statement No. 6*

> confirms conclusions in paragraph 2 of *Concepts Statement No. 3* that (a) assets and liabilities are common to all organizations and can be defined the same for business and not-for-profit organizations, (b) the definitions of equity (net assets), revenues, expenses, gains, and losses fit both business and not-for-profit organizations, and (c) not-for-profit organizations have no need for elements such as investments by owners, distributions to owners, and comprehensive income. Thus, this Statement continues unchanged the elements defined in *Concepts Statement No. 3*, although it contains added explanations stemming from characteristics of not-for-profit organizations and their operations. It also defines three classes of net assets of not-for-profit organizations, distinguished by the presence or absence of donor-imposed restrictions and the changes in those classes during a period-change in permanently restricted, temporarily restricted, and unrestricted net assets.[7]

Looking beyond the statement of concepts stage in the future, it is likely that the FASB will impose more aggregated financial reporting on nonprofit organizations. The focus will be on meeting the needs for financial information of external providers of resources, emphasizing information for assessing financial viability and cost of service.

## A New Audit Guide

In 1990, a new audit guide, *Audits of Providers of Health Care Services* was issued to replace the *Hospital Audit Guide* and five of the six Statements of Position which amended it. The new guide covers entities, both for profit and nonprofit organizations, whose principal operations involve providing health care services to individuals. The guide incorporates the ideas discussed in *Concept Statements No. 3* and *No. 6* of the FASB.

---

[6]*Statement of Financial Accounting Concepts, No. 4*, "Objectives of Financial Reporting by Nonbusiness Organizations" (Stamford: Financial Accounting Standards Board, December 1980).

[7]*Statement of Financial Accounting Concepts, No. 6*, "Elements of Financial Statements" (Stamford: Financial Accounting Standards Board, December 1985), p. 240.

# THE CHARACTERISTICS OF NONPROFIT ORGANIZATIONS

Nonprofit organizations vary in their size, scope, geographical influence, and objectives. Most of them, however, share certain common characteristics. We consider these characteristics now to provide an important frame of reference within which to explain their current and prospective accounting and reporting practices.

## Objective

The objective of nonprofit organizations is to provide various types of services to their membership or to society as a whole. Often, the fees charged to the users of their services are less than the expenditure incurred to provide the services. For example, many hospitals and private colleges and universities cannot meet operating expenditures through patient fees and student tuition alone. The difference must be provided by such private and public funding as federal and state governments, philanthropic organizations, and individuals. These *external providers* perceive the nonprofit organization as a public-service agency accomplishing goals for the public good.

In contrast, an important objective of a business enterprise is to generate a satisfactory amount of income in relation to its resource or equity base. The emphasis is on income, and success is generally measured by the ability of the business enterprise to achieve acceptable rates of profitability, the benefits from which accrue to specific equity interests. Nonprofit organizations are not owned by an individual proprietor or investor but by the organization's membership or the general public.

The financial viability of a business organization is judged by its ability to meet its maturing obligations and to retain and attract new capital through earnings. The nonprofit organization is also judged by its ability to meet its commitments and obligations, but unlike business, the second concern is with the nature of the resource inflows and any restrictions on their use. Nonprofit organizations that generate their resources principally from services as opposed to gifts are considered more financially viable. They are less vulnerable to changes in donor attitudes and other external factors beyond their control. The greater the restrictions as to use that providers place on their donations, the more difficult it is for the organization to meet new objectives.

The traditional matching concept used to determine net income does not apply to a nonprofit organization as it does to a business enterprise. For many of the activities of nonprofit organizations, no essential causal relationship exists between the incurrence of an expense and the generation of revenue. For example, generally there is no direct relationship between contributions, grants and governmental appropriations, and the services provided by the nonprofit organization. Such resource inflows are not *earned,* in the general definition of the term. The difference, then, between revenue and expense does not have the same meaning to the nonprofit organization as it does to the business enterprise.

## Reporting Emphasis

The financial statements of nonprofit organizations disclose information about the flows of funds, solvency, and liquidity, like that of business enterprises. Nonprofit organizations, however, place greater emphasis on the nature of resource inflows and the degree of resource transferability. Anthony states:

> An important distinction in some [nonprofit] organizations is between hard money (e.g., revenues from services rendered) and soft money (e.g., annual gifts); the higher the proportion of hard money, the firmer the financial foundation.[8]

Regarding the transferability of resources he states

> Resource transferability refers to the organization's freedom to use resources for various purposes; the greater the proportion of resources that is restricted to specified uses, the more difficult it is to change direction or to meet new needs.[9]

Financial statements for nonprofit organizations must also disclose compliance with a number of *spending mandates,* such as conditions of grants, gifts, and bequests. The organization must provide assurance that the resources have been used for the intended purposes. **Externally imposed spending mandates provide the rationale for fund accounting and reporting.**

# FRAMEWORK OF ACCOUNTING

## Organizational Objectives and User Needs

The accounting and financial reporting for nonprofit organizations must be adapted to the objectives of each organization and the needs of the users of the financial information. Clearly, the organization's accounting system must ensure compliance with all external restrictions and all internal designations by the governing board (for example, funds designated

[8]*Financial Accounting in Nonbusiness Organizations,* p. 49.
[9]*Financial Accounting in Nonbusiness Organizations,* p. 49.

for student loans, construction, and future equipment acquisitions). As mentioned earlier, the necessity to comply with spending mandates is the rationale for fund accounting. *Fund accounting* permits financial resources to be classified for accounting and reporting purposes in accordance with their intended use, as directed either by the externally imposed restrictions or by the governing board.

An essential accounting differentiation exists between externally imposed spending mandates and designations imposed internally by the governing board. External restrictions are long-term, usually irrevocable restraints on the uses of resources, but the governing board may change the designation of unrestricted funds at a later date. Knowing which funds are restricted is important to a user assessing the transferability of the organization's resources.

## A Comparative Overview of the Fund Groups

The assets, liabilities, fund balances, and changes in the fund balances of a nonprofit organization may be classified into the following six basic self-balancing fund groups:

1. Current Funds (unrestricted and restricted)
2. Plant Funds
3. Endowment and Similar Funds
4. Agency Funds
5. Annuity of Life Income Funds
6. Loan Funds

Illustration 22-1 compares the types of funds used in nonprofit organizations as recommended by the audit guides. The rest of this section introduces these funds:

1. **Funds in support of current operations:**

■ **Current Unrestricted Fund** (for health care providers, General Funds) accounts for all resources over which the governing board has discretionary control to use in carrying on the operations of the organization, except for unrestricted amounts for investments in plant that may be accounted for in a separate fund. For example, colleges and universities account for investment in plant in a Plant Funds Group, whereas voluntary health and welfare organizations generally account for investment in plant in a separate fund, Land, Building, and Equipment. Note that the governing board may designate portions of the Current Unrestricted Fund for specific purposes. As part of this type of action, it may set up separate accounts for such designations within this fund and thus segregate portions of it within the Fund Balance section of the Unrestricted Fund balance sheet. Because the

■ **ILLUSTRATION 22-1**
**Overview of Funds Used in Nonprofit Organizations**

| Purpose of Fund | Colleges and Universities | Health Care Providers | Voluntary Health and Welfare Organizations[a] |
|---|---|---|---|
| 1. Funds in support of current operations | Current Unrestricted Fund | General Funds (includes investment in plant and long-term debt) | Current Unrestricted Fund |
| | Current Restricted Fund | Specific Purpose Funds | Current Restricted Fund |
| 2. Funds with resources in support of fixed asset renewal, replacement, and expansion | Plant Funds Group:[b] Investment in Plant | | Land, Building, and Equipment Funds |
| | Plant Funds Group:[b] Unexpended For Renewals and Replacement For Retirement of Indebtedness | Plant Replacement and Expansion Funds | |
| 3. Funds providing accountability for fiduciary responsibilities | Endowment and Similar Funds | Endowment Funds | Endowment Funds |
| | Annuity and Life Income Funds | Annuity Funds | Loan and Annuity Funds |
| | Loan Funds | Loan Funds | |
| | Agency Funds | Agency Funds | Custodian Funds |

[a]The audit guide for certain nonprofit organizations does not specify a fund structure. However, illustrations included in the guide's financial statements do show the use of funds similar to voluntary health and welfare organizations for complex operations.
[b]All funds in this group are considered one fund.

board has the power to reverse its actions, these funds are never included in a restricted fund.

■ **Current Restricted Fund** (for health care providers, **Specific Purpose Fund**) accounts for those resources currently available for use, but expendable only for purposes specified by a donor or grantor. Resources received by this fund are credited initially to a Fund Balance. When the funds are expended for the intended use as designated by the donor, the Fund Balance is reduced and an appropriate revenue account is credited.

- **Investment in Plant:** There is considerable diversity in accounting for plant assets. Colleges and universities account for investment in plant through a Plant Funds Group. Hospitals account for investment in plant as part of their General Funds, and voluntary health and welfare organizations generally use a separate fund for plant assets.

2. **Funds with resources in support of renewal, replacement, and expansion of fixed assets:**

- For colleges and universities, **Plant Funds Group** accounts for unexpended funds to be used for acquisition of fixed assets; funds set aside for renewal and replacement of those assets; funds designated for debt service charges and for the retirement of indebtedness; and funds expended for fixed assets. These funds will be addressed in more detail later in the chapter.
- For health care providers, **Plant Replacement and Expansion Fund** accounts for resources committed to future expansion and replacement of a health care providers' fixed assets. Amounts received are credited directly to the Fund Balance. When appropriate expenditures are made in accordance with a donor's wishes, the amount is transferred to the General Funds.

3. **Funds providing accountability for fiduciary responsibilities of the organization:**

- **Endowment, Annuity, Loan, and Agency Funds** are treated similarly in all nonprofit organizations. Appropriate illustrations are provided later in Appendix D to the chapter.

## ACCOUNTING FOR COLLEGES AND UNIVERSITIES

Colleges and universities provide educational services, including teaching and research. They may be public, profit-oriented, and private nonprofit institutions. Financial statements for public institutions reflect generally accepted accounting principles used for governmental units and those specified by *Audits of Colleges and Universities.* Financial statements for profit-oriented institutions reflect generally accepted accounting principles for businesses and also those specified in the audit guide. Our study focuses primarily on nonprofit institutions, and we give primary attention to these organizations.

### Overview

Colleges and universities should generally include three basic types of financial statements:

- A balance sheet
- A statement of current funds revenues, expenditures, and other changes
- A statement of changes in fund balances

The balance sheet is usually presented in "pancake" form as in Illustration 22-2 in which each fund appears stacked on one another. (This illustration is discussed more fully later.) The major funds groups discussed earlier are arranged on the balance sheet in the following manner:

**Current Funds**
    Current Unrestricted Fund
    Current Restricted Fund

**Plant Funds**
    Unexpended Plant Funds
    Renewals and Replacement Funds
    Retirement of Indebtedness Funds
    Investment in Plant

**Loan Funds**

**Endowment and Similar Funds**
    Endowment Funds
    Term Endowment Funds
    Quasi-Endowment Funds

**Annuity and Life Income Funds**
    Annuity Funds
    Life Income Funds

**Agency Fund**

The **Current Funds Group,** consisting of resources expendable for operating purposes, includes the asset, liability, and activity accounts necessary to record daily operations. For example, expenditures for instruction, research, extension programs, and auxiliary enterprise activities would be accounted for in the Current Funds Group. In many ways, this group operates in the same manner as the general fund of a city.

Within the group, unrestricted funds that have not been designated by the governing board for loan, investment, or plant purposes may be expended for operating purposes. For example, the governing board may transfer unrestricted funds to a **Quasi-Endowment Fund,** in which such funds serve as endowments until some other more suitable purpose is determined. The board may decide to transfer funds to Loan Funds for supplemental governmental appropriations, to Plant Funds for expansion or rehabilitation, or use them for debt retirement. In such cases, the receiving fund would credit the unrestricted fund's balance for these board-designated transfers. Board-designated funds should be accounted for as unrestricted, since the distinction between the balances that are externally restricted and those that are internally designated should be

■ ILLUSTRATION 22-2

**PARKMOOR COLLEGE**
**Balance Sheet**
**June 30, 19X1**
**with Comparative Figures at June 30, 19X0**

| Assets | 19X1 | 19X0 |
|---|---|---|
| **Current funds:** | | |
| Unrestricted: | | |
| Cash | $ 210,000 | $ 110,000 |
| Investments | 450,000 | 360,000 |
| Accounts receivable, less allowance of $18,000 both years | 228,000 | 175,000 |
| Inventories, at lower of cost (first-in, first-out basis) or market | 90,000 | 80,000 |
| Prepaid expenses and deferred charges | 28,000 | 20,000 |
| Total Unrestricted | 1,006,000 | 745,000 |
| Restricted: | | |
| Cash | 145,000 | 101,000 |
| Investments | 175,000 | 165,000 |
| Accounts receivable, less allowance of $8,000 both years | 68,000 | 160,000 |
| Unbilled charges | 72,000 | –0– |
| Total Restricted | 460,000 | 426,000 |
| Total Current Funds | $ 1,466,000 | $ 1,171,000 |
| **Loan funds:** | | |
| Cash | $ 30,000 | $ 20,000 |
| Investments | 100,000 | 100,000 |
| Loans to students, faculty, and staff, less allowance of $10,000 current year and $9,000 prior year | 550,000 | 382,000 |
| Due from unrestricted funds | 3,000 | –0– |
| Total Loan Funds | $ 683,000 | $ 502,000 |
| **Endowment and similar funds:** | | |
| Cash | $ 100,000 | $ 101,000 |
| Investments | 13,900,000 | 11,800,000 |
| Total Endowment and Similar Funds | $14,000,000 | $11,901,000 |
| **Annuity and life income funds:** | | |
| Annuity funds: | | |
| Cash | $ 55,000 | $ 45,000 |
| Investments | 3,260,000 | 3,010,000 |
| Total Annuity Funds | 3,315,000 | 3,055,000 |

| Liabilities and Fund Balances | 19X1 | 19X0 |
|---|---|---|
| **Current funds:** | | |
| Unrestricted: | | |
| Accounts payable | $ 125,000 | $ 100,000 |
| Accrued liabilities | 20,000 | 15,000 |
| Students' deposits | 30,000 | 35,000 |
| Due to other funds | 158,000 | 120,000 |
| Deferred credits | 30,000 | 20,000 |
| Fund balance | 643,000 | 455,000 |
| Total Unrestricted | 1,006,000 | 745,000 |
| Restricted: | | |
| Accounts payable | 14,000 | 5,000 |
| Fund balances | 446,000 | 421,000 |
| Total Restricted | 460,000 | 426,000 |
| Total Current Funds | $ 1,466,000 | $ 1,171,000 |
| **Loan funds:** | | |
| Fund balances: | | |
| U.S. government grants refundable | $ 50,000 | $ 33,000 |
| University funds: | | |
| Restricted | 483,000 | 369,000 |
| Unrestricted | 150,000 | 100,000 |
| Total Loan Funds | $ 683,000 | $ 502,000 |
| **Endowment and similar funds:** | | |
| Fund balances: | | |
| Endowment | $ 7,800,000 | $ 6,740,000 |
| Term endowment | 3,840,000 | 3,420,000 |
| Quasi-endowment—unrestricted | 1,000,000 | 800,000 |
| Quasi-endowment—restricted | 1,360,000 | 941,000 |
| Total Endowment and Similar Funds | $14,000,000 | $11,901,000 |
| **Annuity and life income funds:** | | |
| Annuity funds: | | |
| Annuities payable | $ 2,150,000 | $ 2,300,000 |
| Fund balances | 1,165,000 | 755,000 |
| Total Annuity Funds | 3,315,000 | 3,055,000 |

**Assets**

| | | |
|---|---:|---:|
| **Life income funds:** | | |
| Cash | 15,000 | |
| Investments | 2,045,000 | |
| Total Life Income Funds | | 2,060,000 |
| Total Annuity and Life Income Funds | | $ 5,375,000 |
| **Plant funds:** | | |
| Unexpended: | | |
| Cash | $ 275,000 | |
| Investments | 1,285,000 | |
| Due from unrestricted current funds | 150,000 | |
| Total Unexpended | | 1,710,000 |
| Renewals and replacements: | | |
| Cash | 5,000 | |
| Investments | 150,000 | |
| Deposits with trustees | 100,000 | |
| Due from unrestricted current funds | 5,000 | |
| Total Renewals and Replacements | | 260,000 |
| Retirement of indebtedness: | | |
| Cash | 50,000 | |
| Deposits with trustees | 250,000 | |
| Total Retirement of Indebtedness | | 300,000 |
| Investment in plant: | | |
| Land | 500,000 | |
| Land improvements | 1,000,000 | |
| Buildings | 25,000,000 | |
| Equipment | 15,000,000 | |
| Library books | 100,000 | |
| | 41,600,000 | |
| Accumulated depreciation | 4,000,000 | |
| | | 37,600,000 |
| Total Plant Funds | | $39,870,000 |
| **Agency funds:** | | |
| Cash | $ 50,000 | |
| Investments | 60,000 | |
| Total Agency Funds | | $ 110,000 |

**Liabilities and Fund Balances**

| | | |
|---|---:|---:|
| **Life income funds:** | | |
| Income payable | 5,000 | |
| Fund balances | 2,055,000 | |
| Total Life Income Funds | | 2,060,000 |
| Total Annuity and Life Income Funds | | $ 4,810,000 |
| **Plant funds:** | | |
| Unexpended: | | |
| Accounts payable | $ 10,000 | –0– |
| Notes payable | 100,000 | –0– |
| Bonds payable | 400,000 | –0– |
| Fund balances: | | |
| Restricted | 1,000,000 | 1,860,000 |
| Unrestricted | 200,000 | 260,000 |
| Total Unexpended | | 2,120,000 |
| Renewals and replacements: | | |
| Fund balances: | | |
| Restricted | 25,000 | 180,000 |
| Unrestricted | 235,000 | 200,000 |
| Total Renewals and Replacements | | 380,000 |
| Retirement of indebtedness: | | |
| Fund balances: | | |
| Restricted | 185,000 | 125,000 |
| Unrestricted | 115,000 | 168,000 |
| Total Retirement of Indebtedness | | 293,000 |
| Investment in plant: | | |
| Notes payable | 790,000 | 810,000 |
| Bonds payable | 2,200,000 | 2,400,000 |
| Mortgages payable | 400,000 | 200,000 |
| Net investment in plant | 38,210,000 | 36,540,000 |
| Total Investment in Plant | 41,600,000 | 39,950,000 |
| Total Plant Funds | $39,870,000 | $40,743,000 |
| **Agency funds:** | | |
| Deposits held in custody for others | $ 110,000 | 90,000 |
| Total Agency Funds | $ 110,000 | 90,000 |

Source: Adapted from *Audits of Colleges and Universities*, 2nd ed. (New York: American Institute of Certified Public Accountants, 1975), Exh. 1, pp. 108–110. The illustration was further modified to include the provisions of *FASB Statement No. 93* requiring recognition of depreciation expense by private colleges and universities.

maintained in the accounts and disclosed in the financial statements. This disclosure is clearly important to the balance sheet user who attempts to assess transferability.

Restricted current funds are also available for operating purposes, but they are restricted by donors or other outside agencies as to the specific purpose for which they may be expended. Restricted current funds are augmented through gifts, endowment income, contracts, grants and appropriations received from private organizations or governments (for research, public service, or other restricted purposes), and income and gains from investments of restricted current funds. Earnings and contributions are not recognized as revenue until expended for the intended purpose. The amounts of earnings or contributions are credited to a Fund Balance account.

A second primary financial statement, the statement of current funds, revenues, expenditures, and other changes, shows the flow of funds only through the Current Funds Group. Illustration 22-3 shows such a statement. Two points are important for understanding this illustration:

1. Revenues for restricted current funds are recognized only to the extent that they were expended for the intended purpose. (In contrast, revenue earned by unrestricted or board-designated funds should be recognized when earned.)
2. Because the emphasis is on the flow of funds, the term "expenditure" is used rather than "expenses."
3. Unrestricted resources that had previously been transferred to Plant Funds or Quasi-Endowment Funds and are now being returned should be reported as transfers and not as revenues.
4. All student tuition and fees are recognized as revenues. To the extent that students are granted fee remission, generally in connection with scholarships, the waived amounts are recorded as expenditures for scholarships.
5. Financial accounting and reporting standards require private colleges and universities to reflect depreciation of long-lived assets in general purpose external financial statements.

**Loan Funds** are usually established to provide loans to students, faculty and staff of colleges and universities. Loan Funds are generally revolving; that is, repayments of principal and interest are loaned to other individuals. Illustration 22-4 shows their sources and uses.

Notes receivable are carried at face value, less an allowance for doubtful notes. Provisions for doubtful notes are charged directly to the Loan Fund's Equity account. All other transactions that affect this fund's Equity account are also credited or charged directly to that account.

The college is simply a fiscal agent for assets that are not actually its property. An **Agency Fund** accounts for these assets. For example, a college may act as fiscal agent for the assets of student government and of

### ■ ILLUSTRATION 22-3

**PARKMOOR COLLEGE**
**Statement of Current Funds Revenues, Expenditures, and Other Changes**
**For the Year Ended June 30, 19X1 with Comparative Figures for 19X0**

| | 19X1 | | | 19X0 |
| --- | --- | --- | --- | --- |
| | Unrestricted | Restricted | Total | Year Total |
| **Revenues** | | | | |
| Educational and general: | | | | |
| Student tuition and fees . . . . . . . . . . . . . . . . . . . . . . . . . | $2,600,000 | | $2,600,000 | $2,300,000 |
| Governmental appropriations . . . . . . . . . . . . . . . . . . . . . | 1,300,000 | | 1,300,000 | 1,300,000 |
| Governmental grants and contracts. . . . . . . . . . . . . . . . | 35,000 | $ 425,000 | 460,000 | 595,000 |
| Gifts and private grants. . . . . . . . . . . . . . . . . . . . . . . . . | 850,000 | 380,000 | 1,230,000 | 1,190,000 |
| Endowment income. . . . . . . . . . . . . . . . . . . . . . . . . . . | 325,000 | 209,000 | 534,000 | 500,000 |
| Sales and services of educational departments . . . . . . . . | 90,000 | | 90,000 | 95,000 |
| Organized activities related to educational departments | 100,000 | | 100,000 | 100,000 |
| Other sources (if any) . . . . . . . . . . . . . . . . . . . . . . . . . | | | | |
| Total Educational and General . . . . . . . . . . . . . . . . | 5,300,000 | 1,014,000 | 6,314,000 | 6,080,000 |
| Auxiliary enterprises . . . . . . . . . . . . . . . . . . . . . . . . . . . | 2,200,000 | | 2,200,000 | 2,100,000 |
| Expired term endowment . . . . . . . . . . . . . . . . . . . . . . . . | 40,000 | | 40,000 | |
| Total Revenues . . . . . . . . . . . . . . . . . . . . . . . . . . . | 7,540,000 | 1,014,000 | 8,554,000 | 8,180,000 |
| **Expenditures and Mandatory Transfers** | | | | |
| Educational and general: | | | | |
| Instruction and departmental research. . . . . . . . . . . . . . | 2,820,000 | 300,000 | 3,120,000 | 2,950,000 |
| Organized activities related to educational departments | 140,000 | 189,000 | 329,000 | 350,000 |
| Sponsored research . . . . . . . . . . . . . . . . . . . . . . . . . . | | 400,000 | 400,000 | 500,000 |
| Other separately budgeted research . . . . . . . . . . . . . . . | 100,000 | | 100,000 | 150,000 |
| Other sponsored programs . . . . . . . . . . . . . . . . . . . . . . | | 25,000 | 25,000 | 50,000 |
| Extension and public service . . . . . . . . . . . . . . . . . . . . | 130,000 | | 130,000 | 125,000 |
| Libraries. . . . . . . . . . . . . . . . . . . . . . . . . . . . . . . . . . | 250,000 | | 250,000 | 225,000 |
| Student services . . . . . . . . . . . . . . . . . . . . . . . . . . . . | 200,000 | | 200,000 | 195,000 |
| Operation and maintenance of plant . . . . . . . . . . . . . . . | 220,000 | | 220,000 | 200,000 |
| General administration . . . . . . . . . . . . . . . . . . . . . . . . | 200,000 | | 200,000 | 195,000 |
| General institutional expense . . . . . . . . . . . . . . . . . . . . | 250,000 | | 250,000 | 250,000 |
| Student aid . . . . . . . . . . . . . . . . . . . . . . . . . . . . . . . . | 90,000 | 100,000 | 190,000 | 180,000 |
| Depreciation expense . . . . . . . . . . . . . . . . . . . . . . . . . | | 2,000,000 | 2,000,000 | |
| Educational and General Expenditures . . . . . . . . . . . . | 4,400,000 | 3,014,000 | 7,414,000 | 5,370,000 |
| Mandatory transfers for: | | | | |
| Principal and interest . . . . . . . . . . . . . . . . . . . . . . . . . | 90,000 | | 90,000 | 50,000 |
| Renewals and replacements. . . . . . . . . . . . . . . . . . . . . | 100,000 | | 100,000 | 80,000 |
| Loan fund matching grant. . . . . . . . . . . . . . . . . . . . . . . | 2,000 | | 2,000 | |
| Total Education and General . . . . . . . . . . . . . . . . . . | 4,592,000 | 3,014,000 | 7,606,000 | 5,500,000 |
| Auxiliary enterprises: | | | | |
| Expenditures. . . . . . . . . . . . . . . . . . . . . . . . . . . . . . . | 1,830,000 | | 1,830,000 | 1,730,000 |
| Mandatory transfers for: | | | | |
| Principal and interest . . . . . . . . . . . . . . . . . . . . . . . . . | 250,000 | | 250,000 | 250,000 |
| Renewals and replacements. . . . . . . . . . . . . . . . . . . . . | 70,000 | | 70,000 | 70,000 |
| Total Auxiliary Enterprises . . . . . . . . . . . . . . . . . . . . | 2,150,000 | | 2,150,000 | 2,050,000 |
| Total Expenditures and Mandatory Transfers. . . . . . . . | 6,742,000 | 3,014,000 | 9,756,000 | 7,550,000 |
| **Other Transfers and Additions/(Deductions)** | | | | |
| Excess of restricted receipts over transfers to revenues . . . . . | | 45,000 | 45,000 | 40,000 |
| Refunded to grantors . . . . . . . . . . . . . . . . . . . . . . . . . . | | (20,000) | (20,000) | |
| Unrestricted gifts allocated to other funds . . . . . . . . . . . . | (650,000) | | (650,000) | (510,000) |
| Portion of quasi-endowment gains appropriated. . . . . . . . . | 40,000 | | 40,000 | |
| Net Increase in Fund Balances . . . . . . . . . . . . . . . . . . | $ 188,000 | $ 25,000 | $ 213,000 | $ 160,000 |

Source: Adapted from *Audits of Colleges and Universities.* 2nd ed. (New York: American Institute of Certified Public Accountants, 1975), Exh. 3, pp. 114–115. The illustration was further modified to include the provisions of *FASB Statement No. 93* requiring recognition of depreciation expense by private colleges and universities.

■ **ILLUSTRATION 22-4**
**Sources and Uses of Loan Funds**

| Sources | Uses |
|---|---|
| Gifts, bequests, and government advances | Loans written off |
| | Deductions to provide appropriate allowances for uncollectible loans |
| Interest on loan notes | |
| Income from endowment funds | Interfund transfers |
| Interfund transfers | Refunds to grantors |
| Income, gains, and losses on investment of Loan Funds | Administrative and collection costs |

faculty and staff organizations. The net assets of such a fund would appear as a **liability,** because the college has no equity in the fund.

For most nonprofit organizations, the **Endowment Funds Group** includes funds for endowments and for term endowments. College and university boards also designate Quasi-Endowment Funds, and, therefore, the title of this funds group is Endowment and Similar Funds.

Endowment Funds are established by donors that have stipulated that the principal is nonexpendable. The income generated from the endowment usually may be expended by current operating funds. Term Endowment Fund principal becomes expendable at some specified time or after a designated event. These funds are then available for operating needs. Quasi-Endowment Funds are internally designated by the board rather than externally restricted. The board may expend the principal at any time.

Legal restrictions in the endowment instrument determine the accounting for each fund's principal, income, and investments. Each endowment is accounted for as a separate fund, but the resources are generally pooled for investment purposes unless restrictive convenants limit investments to certain types of securities.

**Annuity and Life Income Funds** of a college consists of assets contributed to it with the stipulation that the college, in turn, promises to pay a certain sum periodically to a designated individual, usually for the remainder of his or her life. On the death of that person, the unexpended assets of the Annuity Fund are transferred to the college's Current Unrestricted Fund, Current Restricted Fund, or Endowment Fund, as specified by the donor.

At the date of the contribution, the assets are accounted for at their fair market value, an Annuities Payable account is credited for the current value of the liability (based on life expectancy tables), and the balance is credited to the annuity's Fund Balance account.

Investment income and gains or losses are credited or charged to the Liability account. Annuity payments are also charged to Liability. The liability and the fund balance are periodically adjusted to record the actuarial gain or loss due to recomputation of the liability based on revised life expectancy of the donor.

The essential difference between Annuity Funds and Life Income Funds is that for the latter the principal remains intact, and all income is distributed to the beneficiary. Annuity Fund distributions are fixed, whereas distributions of Life Income Funds reflect all fund earnings.

Colleges and universities include investment in plant within a **Plant Funds Group,** which accounts for both unexpended and expended resources. This group consists of:

> (1) funds to be used for the acquisition of physical properties for institutional purposes but unexpended at the date of reporting; (2) funds set aside for the renewal and replacement of institutional properties; (3) funds set aside for debt service charges and for the retirement of indebtedness on institutional properties; and (4) funds expended for and thus invested in institutional properties.[10]

Illustration 22-5 discloses in more detail the nature of the funds flows for the accounts in the Plant Funds Group.

## Depreciation

Up to fiscal years beginning before May 16, 1988, colleges and universities, public and private, were not required to recognize depreciation on their long-lived assets. However, in August 1987, the FASB issued *FASB Statement No. 93,* "Recognition of Depreciation by Not-for-Profit Organizations," which required all nonprofit entities, including colleges and universities, to record depreciation. This new statement became effective for fiscal years beginning on or after May 16, 1988.

In January 1988, the GASB issued *Statement No. 8,* "Applicability of SFAS 93 Recognition of Depreciation by Not-for-Profit Organizations to Certain State and Local Governmental Entities." In effect, the GASB's *Statement No. 8* provides that nonprofit units that are governmental entities need not charge depreciation as a result of *FASB Statement No. 93.*

Most recently, the FASB passed *FASB Statement No. 99* extending the effective date of *FASB Statement No. 93* to fiscal years beginning on or after January 1, 1990. Therefore, for fiscal years beginning on or after January 1, 1990, **financial accounting and reporting standards require private colleges and universities to reflect depreciation of long-lived assets in general purpose external financial statements.**

---

[10]*Audits of Colleges and Universities,* p. 44.

■ **ILLUSTRATION 22-5**
**Plant Funds Group for Colleges and Universities: Subgroup Funds Flows**

| Unexpended Plant Funds | |
|---|---|
| **Inflows** | **Outflows** |
| Bond sales proceeds | Disbursements |
| Private donations | Investment losses |
| Restricted government appropriations | Return of unrestricted amounts to |
| Income and gains from the investment | unrestricted current funds |
| of unexpended funds | Transfers: Investment in plant |
| Transfers from other fund groups | |

| Renewals and Replacement Funds | |
|---|---|
| **Inflows** | **Outflows** |
| Mandatory and voluntary transfers | Investment losses |
| from current funds | Return of unrestricted amounts to |
| Income and gains from the | unrestricted current funds |
| investment of funds | Expenditures not capitalized |
| | Capitalized expenditures for renewals |
| | and replacements |

| Retirement of Indebtedness Funds | |
|---|---|
| **Inflows** | **Outflows** |
| Transfers from current funds for | Payments on principal and interest |
| principal and interest payments | Trustees' fees and expenses |
| Income and gains from the | Investment losses |
| investment of funds | |
| Gifts, grants, and government | |
| appropriations restricted to debt | |
| retirement | |
| Transfers from other fund groups as | |
| directed by donors (such as expired | |
| term endowments, annuity, and life | |
| income funds) | |

| Investment in Plant | |
|---|---|
| **Inflows** | **Outflows** |
| Current fund equipment | Disposal |
| replacements | Abandonment |
| Gifts of plant assets | Sale of plant assets |
| Transfers from unexpended plant and | Depreciation |
| renewals and replacement funds | |
| Debt retirement | |

The illustrated balance sheet in Illustration 22-6 shows how a college's Plant Funds Group is presented. The following points are important for understanding Illustration 22-6:

1. The first two funds are, in effect, unexpended plant funds. Frequently, they are summarized or combined and disclosed as Unexpended Funds for financial reporting purposes.
2. Unexpended plant funds include both externally restricted and internally designated funds.
3. The Investment in Plant is, in effect, the Expended Plant Fund. The resources are carried at cost, less accumulated depreciation. This fund's residual equity is referred to as Net Investment in Plant, not Fund Balance.

Illustrated transaction entries for the various funds are presented and explained in the appendices to this chapter.

## Pledge Disclosure and Accounting

**Gifts and bequests** can represent a significant source of funds to a college or university. **Pledges** of gifts may be disclosed in the notes to the financial statements or they may be reported within the financial statements. If the latter approach is used, they should be accounted for at their net realizable value and credited to Unrestricted Revenues, Deferred Income, Current Restricted Funds, or Plant Funds. The pledge receivable should be presented net of an appropriate allowance for uncollectible pledges.

ILLUSTRATION

## Pledge Disclosure and Accounting for a Pledge Collected over Several Years

Pledge revenue should be recognized in the year in which the pledge or installment of the pledge is received. The donor's intention determines its future accounting. For example, beginning this year, several donors have agreed to give a total of $25,000 a year for four years for normal operating expenses. Therefore, only $22,500 should be recorded as revenue in the current year, as shown in the following entry:

| | | |
|---|---|---|
| Pledges Receivable | 100,000 | |
|     Allowance for Uncollectible Pledges | | 10,000 |
|     Pledge Revenue | | 22,500 |
|     Deferred Pledge Revenue | | 67,500 |

## Donated Services

Colleges and universities operated by religious groups generally account for the value of **donated services** provided by members of the religious

■ ILLUSTRATION 22-6

## PARKMOOR COLLEGE
### Statement of Changes in Fund Balances
### For the Year Ended June 30, 19X1

| | Current Funds | | Loan Funds | Endowment and Similar Funds | Annuity and Life Income Funds | Plant Funds | | | |
| --- | --- | --- | --- | --- | --- | --- | --- | --- | --- |
| | Unrestricted | Restricted | | | | Unexpended | Renewal and Replacement | Retirement of Indebtedness | Investment in Plant |
| **Revenues and Other Additions** | | | | | | | | | |
| Educational and general revenues | $5,300,000 | | | | | | | | |
| Auxiliary enterprises revenues | 2,200,000 | | | | | | | | |
| Expired term endowment revenues | 40,000 | | | | | | | | |
| Expired term endowment—restricted | | | | | | $ 50,000 | | | |
| Gifts and bequests—restricted | | $ 370,000 | $100,000 | $ 1,500,000 | $ 800,000 | 115,000 | | $ 65,000 | $ 15,000 |
| Grants and contracts—restricted | | 500,000 | | | | | | | |
| Governmental appropriations—restricted | | | | | | 50,000 | | | |
| Investment income—restricted | | 224,000 | 12,000 | 10,000 | | 5,000 | $ 5,000 | 5,000 | |
| Realized gains on investments—unrestricted | | | | 109,000 | | | | | |
| Realized gains on investments—restricted | | | 4,000 | 50,000 | | 10,000 | 5,000 | 5,000 | |
| Interest on loans receivable | | | 7,000 | | | | | | |
| U.S. government advances | | | 18,000 | | | | | | |
| Expended for plant facilities (including $100,000 charged to current funds expenditures) | | | | | | | | | 1,550,000 |
| Retirement of indebtedness | | | | | | | | | 220,000 |
| Accrued interest on sale of bonds | | | | | | | | 3,000 | |
| Matured annuity and life income funds restricted to endowment | | | | 10,000 | | | | | |
| Total Revenues and Other Additions | 7,540,000 | 1,094,000 | 141,000 | 1,679,000 | 800,000 | 230,000 | 10,000 | 78,000 | 1,785,000 |

**Expenditures and Other Deductions**

|  |  |  |  |  |  |  |  |  |  |
|---|--:|--:|--:|--:|--:|--:|--:|--:|--:|
| Educational and general expenditures | 4,400,000 | 1,014,000 |  |  |  |  |  |  |  |
| Auxiliary enterprises expenditures | 1,830,000 |  |  |  |  |  |  |  |  |
| Indirect costs recovered |  | 35,000 |  |  |  |  |  |  |  |
| Refunded to grantors |  | 20,000 | 10,000 |  |  |  |  |  |  |
| Loan cancellations and write-offs |  |  | 1,000 |  |  |  |  |  |  |
| Administrative and collection costs |  |  | 1,000 |  |  |  |  |  |  |
| Adjustment of actuarial liability for annuities payable |  |  |  |  | 75,000 |  |  |  |  |
| Expended for plant facilities (including noncapitalized expenditures of $50,000) |  |  |  |  |  | 1,200,000 | 300,000 |  |  |
| Retirement of indebtedness |  |  |  |  |  |  |  | 220,000 |  |
| Interest on indebtedness |  |  |  |  |  |  |  | 190,000 |  |
| Disposal of plant facilities |  |  |  |  |  |  |  |  | 115,000 |
| Expired term endowments ($40,000 unrestricted, $50,000 restricted to plant) |  |  |  | 90,000 |  |  |  |  |  |
| Matured annuity and life income funds restricted to endowment |  |  |  |  | 10,000 |  |  |  |  |
| Depreciation |  |  |  |  |  |  |  |  | 2,000,000 |
| Total Expenditures and Other Deductions | 6,230,000 | 1,069,000 | 12,000 | 90,000 | 85,000 | 1,200,000 | 300,000 | 411,000 | 2,115,000 |

**Transfers Among Funds—Additions/(Deductions)**

Mandatory:

|  |  |  |  |  |  |  |  |  |  |
|---|--:|--:|--:|--:|--:|--:|--:|--:|--:|
| Principal and interest | (340,000) |  |  |  |  |  |  | 340,000 |  |
| Renewals and replacements | (170,000) |  |  |  |  |  | 170,000 |  |  |
| Loan fund matching grant | (2,000) |  | 2,000 |  |  |  |  |  |  |
| Unrestricted gifts allocated | (650,000) |  | 50,000 | 550,000 | 50,000 |  |  |  |  |
| Portion of unrestricted quasi-endowment funds investment gains appropriated | 40,000 |  |  | (40,000) |  |  |  |  |  |
| Total Transfers | (1,122,000) |  | 52,000 | 510,000 | 50,000 |  | 170,000 | 340,000 |  |
| Net increase/(decrease) for the year | 188,000 | 25,000 | 181,000 | 2,099,000 | 715,000 | (920,000) | (120,000) | 7,000 | (330,000) |
| Fund balance at beginning of year | 455,000 | 421,000 | 502,000 | 11,901,000 | 2,505,000 | 2,120,000 | 380,000 | 293,000 | 36,540,000 |
| Fund Balance at End of Year | $ 643,000 | $ 446,000 | $683,000 | $14,000,000 | $3,220,000 | $1,200,000 | $260,000 | $300,000 | $36,210,000 |

Source: Adapted from Audits of Colleges and Universities, 2nd ed. (New York: American Institute of Certified Public Accounts, 1975), pp. 112–13.

group. The value of services performed (perhaps by comparison with lay salaries) are recorded as an expenditure with an equivalent credit to gift revenues.

## Investments

Colleges and universities generally account for **investments** (exclusive of investments in physical plant) at cost or at market value if they are received as gifts; the *Audits of Colleges and Universities* provides an alternative. The investments may also be reported in the financial statements at market value, if this valuation basis is used by all funds. Unrealized gains and losses measured using this alternative basis should be reported in the same manner as realized gains and losses.

## ACCOUNTING FOR HEALTH CARE PROVIDERS

The AICPA issued a new audit and accounting guide, *Audits of Providers of Health Care Services*, in 1990. It supersedes *Hospital Audit Guide*, including five of the six AICPA Statements of Position that subsequently amended it.

The new guide reflects the massive changes in the structure of the health care industry brought about by rapidly increasing costs for providing health care. Among the early events that precipitated change was the implementation by the federal government and health insurance carriers of prospective payment systems that limit payments to health care providers to a predetermined fixed amount. Driven by rapidly increasing costs and reimbursement limit, the industry has experienced a major shift from inpatient to outpatient services. With this change has come new organizations such as outpatient surgery centers, wellness centers, continuing-care retirement communities (CCRCs), and home health care agencies. We have also seen the development of prepaid health care plans such as health maintenance organizations (HMOs) and preferred provider organizations (PPOs).

The new guide excludes government health care providers from its scope with the exception of hospitals. However, in the case of government hospitals, it defers to any future GASB pronouncements for authoritative guidance.

## Overview

*Audits of Providers of Health Care Services* applies to both profit and non-profit health care entities excluding, with the exception of hospitals, governmental units. These entities include:

Hospitals (includes governmental units)
Nursing homes
Health maintenance organizations and other providers of prepaid care
Continuing-care retirement communities
Home health agencies
Medical group practices
Clinics
Other ambulatory care organizations

Nonprofit health care providers and governmental hospitals should present the following financial statements:

- A balance sheet
- A statement of revenues and expenses of general funds
- A statement of changes in fund balances
- A statement of cash flows of general funds

The financial reporting requirements for profit-oriented entities are similar to those of other proprietary entities.

Unlike the other guides, this guide explicitly makes fund accounting and reporting optional. The guide refers to *Concepts Statement No. 6,* "Elements of Financial Statements," in support of this position. Therefore, for example, the balance sheet format is optional: either aggregated (single or combined fund) or disaggregated (layered funds) balance sheets can be used. Examples of balance sheets for aggregated and disaggregated funds are shown in Illustrations 22-7 and 22-8.

If fund accounting is used, then the guide would embrace the following funds structure:

**Unrestricted**
    General Funds
    Agency Fund

**Restricted (donor-restricted)**
    Specific Purpose Funds
    Plant Replacement and Expansion Funds
    Term Endowment Funds
    Endowment Funds (permanently restricted)
    Other donor-restricted funds (Annuity and Life Income Funds)

Unlike colleges and universities, health care providers do not use a Current Funds Group. For operating purposes, they use General Funds that comprise all assets and liabilities not recorded in donor-restricted funds, including assets whose use is limited, Agency Funds, and property and equipment related to the general operations of the entity.

Limited-use assets include (1) assets set aside by the governing board for identified purposes [not donor-restricted], (2) proceeds of debt issues and

# ILLUSTRATION 22-7
## Disaggregated Comparative Balance Sheets

**BRENMARR HOSPITAL**
**Balance Sheets**
**December 31, 19X1 and 19X0**

**GENERAL FUNDS**

| Assets | 19X1 | 19X0 |
|---|---:|---:|
| Current assets: | | |
| Cash and cash equivalents | $ 3,103,000 | $ 4,525,000 |
| Assets whose use is limited—required for current liabilities | 970,000 | 1,300,000 |
| Patient accounts receivable, net of estimated uncollectibles of $2,500,000 in19X1 and $2,400,000 in 19X0 | 15,100,000 | 14,194,000 |
| Estimated third-party payer settlements—Medicare | 441,000 | 600,000 |
| Supplies, at lower of cost (first-in, first-out) or market | 1,163,000 | 938,000 |
| Other current assets | 321,000 | 403,000 |
| Due from donor-restricted funds, net | –0– | 500,000 |
| Total Current Assets | 21,098,000 | 22,460,000 |
| Assets whose use is limited: | | |
| By board for capital improvements | 11,000,000 | 10,000,000 |
| By agreements with third-party payers for funded depreciation | 9,234,000 | 6,151,000 |
| Under malpractice funding arrangement—held by trustee | 3,007,000 | 2,682,000 |
| Under indenture agreement—held by trustee | 11,708,000 | 11,008,000 |
| Total Assets Whose Use Is Limited | 34,949,000 | 29,841,000 |
| Less assets whose use is limited and that are required for current liabilities | 970,000 | 1,300,000 |
| Noncurrent assets whose use is limited | 33,979,000 | 28,541,000 |
| Property and equipment, net | 51,038,000 | 50,492,000 |

| Liabilities and Fund Balances | 19X1 | 19X0 |
|---|---:|---:|
| Current liabilities: | | |
| Current installments of long-term debt | $ 970,000 | $ 1,200,000 |
| Current portion of capital lease obligations | 500,000 | 550,000 |
| Accounts payable | 2,217,000 | 2,085,000 |
| Accrued expenses | 3,396,000 | 3,225,000 |
| Estimated third-party payer settlements—Medicaid | 2,143,000 | 1,942,000 |
| Deferred third-party reimbursement | 200,000 | 210,000 |
| Advances from third-party payers | 122,000 | 632,000 |
| Current portion of estimated malpractice costs | 600,000 | 500,000 |
| Retainage and construction accounts payable | 955,000 | 772,000 |
| Due to donor-restricted funds | 300,000 | –0– |
| Total Current Liabilities | 11,403,000 | 11,116,000 |
| Deferred third-party reimbursement | 746,000 | 984,000 |
| Estimated malpractice costs, net of current portion | 3,207,000 | 2,182,000 |
| Long-term debt, excluding current installments | 22,644,000 | 23,614,000 |
| Capital lease obligations, excluding current installments | 500,000 | 400,000 |
| Fund balance | 69,310,000 | 64,567,000 |

### Other assets:

| | | |
|---|---:|---:|
| Prepaid pension cost | 85,000 | 35,000 |
| Deferred financing costs | 693,000 | 759,000 |
| Investment in affiliated company | 917,000 | 576,000 |
| | 1,695,000 | 1,370,000 |
| **Total Other Assets** | **$107,810,000** | **$102,863,000** |

| | | |
|---|---:|---:|
| Commitments and contingent liabilities | –0– | –0– |
| | $107,810,000 | $102,863,000 |

## DONOR-RESTRICTED FUNDS
### Specific-Purpose Funds

**Assets**

| | | |
|---|---:|---:|
| Cash | $ 378,000 | $ 378,000 |
| Investments, at cost which approximates market | 728,000 | 455,000 |
| Grants receivable | 613,000 | 535,000 |
| | $ 1,719,000 | $ 1,368,000 |

**Liabilities and Fund Balance**

| | | |
|---|---:|---:|
| Accounts payable | $ 205,000 | $ 72,000 |
| Deferred grant revenue | 92,000 | –0– |
| Due to general funds | –0– | 255,000 |
| Fund balance | 1,422,000 | 1,041,000 |
| | $ 1,719,000 | $ 1,368,000 |

### Plant Replacement and Expansion Funds

**Assets**

| | | |
|---|---:|---:|
| Cash | $ 24,000 | $ 321,000 |
| Investments, at cost which approximates market | 252,000 | 165,000 |
| Pledges receivable, net of estimated uncollectibles of $60,000 in 19X1 and $120,000 in 19X0 | 132,000 | 380,000 |
| Due from general funds | 150,000 | –0– |
| | $ 558,000 | $ 866,000 |

**Liabilities and Fund Balance**

| | | |
|---|---:|---:|
| Due to general funds | $ –0– | $ 345,000 |
| Fund balance | 558,000 | 521,000 |
| | $ 558,000 | $ 866,000 |

### Endowment Funds

**Assets**

| | | |
|---|---:|---:|
| Cash | $ 1,253,000 | $ 653,000 |
| Investments, net of $175,000 valuation allowance in 19X1 market value $3,798,000 in 19X1 and $5,013,000 in 19X0 | 3,856,000 | 5,320,000 |
| Due from general funds | 150,000 | 100,000 |
| | $ 5,259,000 | $ 6,073,000 |

**Fund Balance**

| | | |
|---|---:|---:|
| Fund balance | $ 5,259,000 | $ 6,073,000 |
| | $ 5,259,000 | $ 6,073,000 |

Source: Adapted from Audits of Providers of Health Care Services (New York: American Institute of Certified Public Accountants, 1990), App. A, pp. 147–49.

# ILLUSTRATION 22-8
## Aggregated Comparative Balance Sheets

**BRENMARR HOSPITAL**
**Balance Sheets**
**December 31, 19X1 and 19X0**

| Assets | 19X1 | 19X0 |
|---|---|---|
| Current assets: | | |
| Cash and cash equivalents | $ 2,803,000 | $ 5,025,000 |
| Assets whose use is limited—required for current liabilities | 1,267,000 | 1,372,000 |
| Patient accounts receivable, net of estimated uncollectibles of $2,500,000 in 19X1 and $2,400,000 in 19X0 | 15,100,000 | 14,194,000 |
| Estimated third-party payer settlements—Medicare | 441,000 | 600,000 |
| Supplies, at lower of cost (first-in, first-out) or market | 1,163,000 | 938,000 |
| Other current assets | 321,000 | 403,000 |
| Total Current Assets | 21,095,000 | 22,532,000 |
| Assets whose use is limited or restricted: | | |
| By board for capital improvements | 11,000,000 | 10,000,000 |
| By agreements with third-party payers for funded depreciation | 9,234,000 | 6,151,000 |
| Under malpractice funding arrangement—held by trustee | 3,007,000 | 2,682,000 |
| Under indenture agreement—held by trustee | 11,708,000 | 11,008,000 |
| By donors or grantors for specific purposes | 2,277,000 | 1,634,000 |
| By donors for permanent endowment funds | 5,259,000 | 6,073,000 |
| Total Assets Whose Use Is Limited or Restricted | 42,485,000 | 37,548,000 |

| Liabilities and Fund Balances | 19X1 | 19X0 |
|---|---|---|
| Current liabilities: | | |
| Current installments of long-term debt | $ 970,000 | $ 1,200,000 |
| Current portion of capital lease obligations | 500,000 | 550,000 |
| Accounts payable | 2,422,000 | 2,157,000 |
| Accrued expensese | 3,396,000 | 3,225,000 |
| Estimated third-party payer settlements—Medicaid | 2,143,000 | 1,942,000 |
| Deferred third-party reimbursement | 200,000 | 210,000 |
| Advances from third-party payers | 122,000 | 632,000 |
| Current portion of estimated malpractice costs | 600,000 | 500,000 |
| Retainage and construction accounts payable | 955,000 | 772,000 |
| Advances and deferred revenue | 92,000 | –0– |
| Total Current Liabilities | 11,400,000 | 11,188,000 |
| Deferred third-party reimbursement | 746,000 | 984,000 |
| Estimated malpractice costs, net of current portion | 3,207,000 | 2,182,000 |
| Long-term debt, excluding current installments | 22,644,000 | 23,614,000 |
| Capital lease obligations, excluding current installments | 500,000 | 400,000 |
| Total Liabilities | $ 38,497,000 | $ 38,368,000 |

| | | | | | |
|---|---|---|---|---|---|
| Less assets whose use is limited and that are required for current liabilities | 1,267,000 | 1,372,000 | Net assets: | | |
| | | | Unrestricted | 69,310,000 | 64,567,000 |
| Noncurrent assets whose use is limited or restricted | 41,218,000 | 36,176,000 | Temporarily restricted by donors/grantors | 1,980,000 | 1,562,000 |
| | | | Permanently restricted by donors | 5,259,000 | 6,073,000 |
| Property and equipment, net | 51,038,000 | 50,492,000 | Total Net Assets | $ 76,549,000 | $ 72,202,000 |
| Other assets: | | | | | |
| Prepaid pension cost | 85,000 | 35,000 | | | |
| Deferred financing costs | 693,000 | 759,000 | | | |
| Investment in affiliated company | 917,000 | 576,000 | | | |
| Total Other Assets | 1,695,000 | 1,370,000 | | | |
| | $115,046,000 | $110,570,000 | | $115,046,000 | $110,570,000 |

Source: Adapted from *Audits of Providers of Health Care Services* (New York: American Institute of Certified Public Accountants, 1990). App. A, pp. 168–69.

funds deposited with a trustee and limited in use in accordance with the requirements of an indenture or a similar agreement, (3) other assets limited for use for identified purposes through an agreement between the health care entity and an outside party other than a donor or grantor. Examples of the last include assets set aside under agreements with third-party payors to meet depreciation funding requirements and assets set aside under self-insurance funding arrangements.[11]

One of the essential differences between accounting for colleges and universities and accounting for health care providers is in how fixed assets are handled. Colleges and universities have a complex set of funds called the Plant Funds Group, which includes funds for plant in service, unexpended funds for plant, renewals and replacement funds, and the debt which relates to the fixed assets. In contrast, health care providers account for their investment in plant and equipment and related long-term debt in the General Funds. Property and equipment and related liabilities which are unrestricted but not used for general operations, are presented separately in the General Funds. Externally restricted resources for plant and equipment replacement and expansion are accounted for separately in a restricted fund—Plant Replacement and Expansion Fund.

Health care providers also use a Specific Purpose Fund, which is similar to the Current Restricted Funds subgroup used by colleges and universities in that it accounts for resources temporarily restricted by external donors or other outside agencies as to the specific purpose for which they may be expended. It differs from the Current Restricted Funds subgroup in that it does not ultimately expend the resources for the specific purpose. The spending unit is the General Funds. Like Current Restricted Funds of colleges and universities, earnings and contributions to the Specific Purpose Fund are credited to Fund Balance and not to revenue. Interfund transfers occur between the Specific Purpose Fund to the General Funds as the resources are expended. Also, similar treatment may be found in accounting for Plant Replacement and Expansion Funds and Endowment Funds; the expending fund is the General Funds.

The statement of revenue and expenses resembles a performance statement for a profit-oriented firm more than a nonprofit entity. Hospitals have historically been viewed more as businesses than nonprofit organizations. The focus has been on their viability as going concerns and the maintenance of their capital. Illustrations 22-9, 22-10, and 22-11 show revenue and expense statements for a hospital, a health maintenance organization, and a continuing care retirement community, respectively. (The shaded portion of Illustration 22-11 will be discussed later.)

The statement of revenue and expenses for the hospital shows that the primary source of revenue are end-users: the patients. The patient service

---

[11]*Audits of Providers of Health Care Services*, p. 18.

■ **ILLUSTRATION 22-9**
**Comparative Statements of Revenue and Expenses for a Hospital**

| BRENMARR HOSPITAL<br>Statements of Revenue and Expenses of General Funds<br>For the Years Ended December 31, 19X1 and 19X0 | | |
|---|---|---|
| | **19X1** | **19X0** |
| Net patient service revenue | $92,656,000 | $88,942,000 |
| Other revenue | 6,010,000 | 5,380,000 |
|     Total Revenue | 98,666,000 | 94,322,000 |
| Operating expenses: | | |
|   Professional care of patients | 53,016,000 | 48,342,000 |
|   Dietary services | 4,407,000 | 4,087,000 |
|   General services | 10,888,000 | 9,973,000 |
|   Administrative services | 11,075,000 | 10,145,000 |
|   Employee health and welfare | 10,000,000 | 9,335,000 |
|   Medical malpractice costs | 1,125,000 | 200,000 |
|   Depreciation and amortization | 4,782,000 | 4,280,000 |
|   Interest | 1,752,000 | 1,825,000 |
|   Provision for bad debts | 1,010,000 | 1,103,000 |
|     Total Operating Expenses | 98,055,000 | 89,290,000 |
|     Income from operations | 611,000 | 5,032,000 |
| Nonoperating gains (losses): | | |
|   Unrestricted gifts and bequests | 822,000 | 926,000 |
|   Loss on investment in affiliated company | (37,000) | (16,000) |
|   Income on investments of endowment funds | 750,000 | 650,000 |
|   Income on investments whose use is limited: | | |
|     By board for capital improvements | 1,120,000 | 1,050,000 |
|     Under indenture agreement | 100,000 | 90,000 |
|     By agreements with third-party payers | | |
|       for funded depreciation | 850,000 | 675,000 |
|   Other investment income | 284,000 | 226,000 |
| Nonoperating gains, net | 3,889,000 | 3,601,000 |
| Revenues and gains in excess of<br>  expenses and losses | $ 4,500,000 | $ 8,633,000 |

Source: Adapted from *Audits of Providers of Health Care Services* (New York: American Institute of Certified Public Accountants, 1990), App. A, p. 150.

revenue is shown at net. It reflects adjustments for charity services, and contractual adjustments. The contractual adjustments relate to third-party payer agreements (such as Blue Cross, Medicare, and Medicaid), and they include estimated retroactive adjustments under reimbursement agreements. Retroactive adjustments are accrued on an estimated basis in the period the related services are rendered and adjusted in future periods as final settlements are determined.

■ **ILLUSTRATION 22-10**
**Comparative Statements of Revenue and Expenses for a Health Maintenance Organization**

| APPLE HEALTH CARE (HMO) Statements of Revenue and Expenses and Changes in Fund Balance For the Years Ended June 30, 19X5 and 19X4 | | |
|---|---|---|
| | **19X5** | **19X4** |
| Revenue: | | |
| Premiums earned | $27,682,000 | $22,500,000 |
| Coinsurance | 689,000 | 500,000 |
| Interest and other income | 242,000 | 100,000 |
| Total Revenue | 28,613,000 | 23,100,000 |
| Expenses: | | |
| Contracted hospital, physician, and other services | 12,749,000 | 9,734,000 |
| Health centers—medical services | 10,116,000 | 8,786,000 |
| Health centers—administration | 1,556,000 | 1,530,000 |
| General administration | 1,695,000 | 1,309,000 |
| Membership services | 527,000 | 440,000 |
| Interest | 385,000 | 375,000 |
| Depreciation and amortization | 367,000 | 336,000 |
| Total Expenses | 27,395,000 | 22,510,000 |
| Income from operations | 1,218,000 | 590,000 |
| Fund balance at beginning of year | 900,000 | 310,000 |
| Fund balance at end of year | $ 2,118,000 | $ 900,000 |

Source: Adapted from *Audits of Providers of Health Care Services* (New York: American Institute of Certified Public Accountants, 1990), App. A, p. 193.

The primary income of prepaid health care plans, such as health maintenance organizations and preferred provider organizations, are "premiums." In return for accepting a fixed, predetermined amount, the organization agrees to provide services to a specified group. Illustration 22-10 shows such income as "premiums" earned. Hospitals also enter into what are called "capitation agreements" with prepaid health care plans and earn this type of revenue. Hospitals may report this income from capitation fees as a separate line in the statement of revenues and expenses if it is material.

In order to promote consistency from various health care entities, the new guide draws from *Concepts Statement No. 6* for guidance in assigning income to operating and nonoperating classifications. Under the provisions of this statement, entities should draw this distinction based on

■ **ILLUSTRATION 22-11**
**Comparative Statements of Revenue and Expenses for a Continuing-care Retirement Community**

| | | |
|---|---|---|
| **PRUNE DALE**<br>**Statements of Revenue and Expenses**<br>**and Changes in Fund Balance**<br>**For the Years Ended December 31, 19X5 and 19X4** | | |
| | **19X5** | **19X4** |
| Revenue: | | |
| Resident services, including amortization | | |
| of advance fees of $935,000 and $915,000 | $3,946,000 | $ 3,152,000 |
| Patient revenue from nonresidents | 249,000 | 275,000 |
| Investment income | 107,000 | 78,000 |
| Other | 75,000 | 68,000 |
| Total Revenue | 4,377,000 | 3,573,000 |
| Operating expenses: | | |
| Resident care | 649,000 | 566,000 |
| Dietary | 781,000 | 701,000 |
| Housekeeping | 185,000 | 170,000 |
| Plant | 491,000 | 421,000 |
| General and administrative | 436,000 | 445,000 |
| Depreciation | 452,000 | 447,000 |
| Interest | 967,000 | 955,000 |
| Total Operating Expenses | 3,961,000 | 3,705,000 |
| | 416,000 | (132,000) |
| Change in obligation to provide future services<br>and use of facilities to current residents | 12,000 | (82,000) |
| Income (loss) from operations | 428,000 | (214,000) |
| Nonoperating revenue—Contributions | 109,000 | 73,000 |
| Excess (deficiency) of revenue over<br>expenses | 537,000 | (141,000) |
| Fund balance (deficit), beginning of year | (1,489,000) | (1,348,000) |
| Fund balance (deficit), end of year | $ (952,000) | $(1,489,000) |

Source: Adapted from *Audits of Providers of Health Care Services* (New York: American Institute of Certified Public Accountants, 1990), App. A, p. 180.

whether the income results from activities that are major and central to ongoing operations ("operating") or activities that are peripheral and incidental ("nonoperating"). Therefore, items such as investment income and donations may be reported differently among health care entities.

Activities directly associated with providing health care services constitute the ongoing major or central operations of providers of health care services. Therefore, revenue, expenses, gains, and losses arising from these activities are classified as operating revenue or expense. Revenue, expenses, gains, and losses arising from activities that are peripheral or incidental to providing health care services are classified as nonoperating revenue or expense. Nonoperating revenue would include unrestricted contributions or grants, unrestricted income from Endowment Funds, tax support, and other subsidies, as well as income and gains (losses) from investments of General Funds.

Other operating revenue normally includes revenues from services other than health care provided to patients and residents, as well as sales and services to nonpatients. Such revenue arises from the normal day-to-day operations of most health care entities and is accounted for separately from health care service revenue. Other operating revenue may include revenue from educational programs, research and other specific-purpose gifts and grants, proceeds from the sale of cafeteria meals, revenue from gift shops, parking lots, etc.

Health care providers are also expected to include a statement of cash flows as in Illustration 22-12. Note that this statement follows the direct method format and only presents cash flows of the General Funds, the funds under the management of the governing board of the entity. The mechanics for the construction of a cash flow statement can be reviewed in any intermediate accounting text. The fourth primary statement is the statement of changes in funds balances, an example of which is shown in Illustration 22-13.

## Donated Services, Medicines, and Supplies

The nature and extent of donated services received by nonprofit health care providers range from fund-raising activities to direct participation in the entity's service programs. Generally, the value of these services is not reflected because it is often difficult to measure. However, the guide provides that if certain conditions are met, the estimated value of donated services may be reported as an expense with a corresponding amount reported as contributions. The conditions are as follows:

    a. The services are significant and form an integral part of the efforts of the entity as it is presently constituted; the services would be performed by salaried personnel if donated services were not available for the entity to accomplish its purpose; and the entity would continue this program or activity.

    b. The entity controls the employment and duties of the service donors, and is able to influence their activities in a way comparable to the control it would exercise over employees with similar responsibilities.

    c. The entity has a clearly measurable basis for the amount to be recorded.[12]

---

[12]*Audits of Providers of Health Care Services,* p. 15.

■ **ILLUSTRATION 22-12**

**BRENMARR HOSPITAL**
**Statement of Cash Flows of General Funds**
**For the Years Ended December 31, 19X1 and 19X0**

|  | 19X1 | 19X0 |
|---|---|---|
| Cash flows from operating activities and gains and losses: |  |  |
| Cash received from patients and third-party payers | $90,342,000 | $85,619,000 |
| Cash paid to employees and suppliers | (89,214,000) | (81,510,000) |
| Other receipts from operations | 6,042,000 | 5,563,000 |
| Receipts from unrestricted gifts and bequests | 1,122,000 | 905,000 |
| Interest and dividends received | 2,510,000 | 2,330,000 |
| Interest paid (net of amount capitalized) | (1,780,000) | (1,856,000) |
| Net Cash Provided by Operating Activities | 9,022,000 | 11,051,000 |
| Cash flows from investing activities: |  |  |
| Purchase of property and equipment | (4,728,000) | (5,012,000) |
| Transfer from donor-restricted fund for purchase of property and equipment | 243,000 | 255,000 |
| Investment in affiliated company | (394,000) | (425,000) |
| Capital contribution to Accorn Health System | –0– | (1,000,000) |
| Cash invested in assets whose use is limited | (4,798,000) | (855,000) |
| Net Cash Used by Investing Activities | (9,677,000) | (7,037,000) |
| Cash flows from financing activities: |  |  |
| Increase in retainage and construction accounts payable | 183,000 | 175,000 |
| Repayment of long-term debt | (1,200,000) | (1,630,000) |
| Payments from donor-restricted funds related to temporary loans | 500,000 | –0– |
| Payments on capital lease obligations | (550,000) | (600,000) |
| Temporary loans from (to) donor-restricted funds | 300,000 | (193,000) |
| Net Cash Used by Financing Activities | (767,000) | (2,248,000) |
| Net increase (decrease) in cash and cash equivalents | (1,422,000) | 1,766,000 |
| Cash and cash equivalents at beginning of year | 4,525,000 | 2,759,000 |
| Cash and cash equivalents at end of year | $ 3,103,000 | $ 4,525,000 |

Source: Adapted from *Audits of Providers of Health Care Services* (New York: American Institute of Certified Public Accountants, 1990), App. A, p. 153.

# ILLUSTRATION 22-13

**BRENMARR HOSPITAL**
**Statement of Changes in Fund Balances for the Years Ended December 31, 19X1 and 19X0**

| | 19X1 | | | | 19X0 | | | |
| | | Donor-Restricted Funds | | | | Donor-Restricted Funds | | |
| | General Funds | Specific-Purpose Funds | Plant Replacement and Expansion Funds | Endowment Funds | General Funds | Specific-Purpose Funds | Plant Replacement and Expansion Funds | Endowment Funds |
|---|---|---|---|---|---|---|---|---|
| Balances at beginning of year | $64,567,000 | $1,041,000 | $521,000 | $6,073,000 | $56,679,000 | $ 933,000 | $501,000 | $5,973,000 |
| **Additions:** | | | | | | | | |
| Revenues and gains in excess of expenses and losses | 4,500,000 | –0– | –0– | –0– | 8,633,000 | –0– | –0– | –0– |
| Gifts, grants, and bequests | –0– | 869,000 | 220,000 | –0– | –0– | 558,000 | 290,000 | –0– |
| Investment income | –0– | 62,000 | 20,000 | –0– | –0– | 50,000 | 15,000 | –0– |
| Net realized gain on sale of investments | –0– | –0– | 100,000 | –0– | –0– | –0– | 20,000 | 100,000 |
| Transfer to finance property and equipment additions | 243,000 | –0– | (243,000) | –0– | 255,000 | –0– | (255,000) | –0– |
| | 4,743,000 | 931,000 | 97,000 | –0– | 8,888,000 | 608,000 | 70,000 | 100,000 |
| **Deductions:** | | | | | | | | |
| Provision for uncollectible pledges | –0– | –0– | (60,000) | –0– | –0– | –0– | (50,000) | –0– |
| Capital contribution to Accorn Health System | –0– | –0– | –0– | –0– | (1,000,000) | –0– | –0– | –0– |
| Net realized loss on sale of investments | –0– | –0– | –0– | (639,000) | –0– | –0– | –0– | –0– |
| Unrealized loss on marketable equity securities | –0– | –0– | –0– | (175,000) | –0– | –0– | –0– | –0– |
| Transfer to other revenue | –0– | (550,000) | –0– | –0– | –0– | (500,000) | –0– | –0– |
| | –0– | (550,000) | (60,000) | (814,000) | (1,000,000) | (500,000) | (50,000) | –0– |
| Balances at end of year | $69,310,000 | $1,422,000 | $558,000 | $5,259,000 | $64,567,000 | $1,041,000 | $521,000 | $6,073,000 |

Source: Adapted from *Audits of Providers of Health Care Services* (New York: American Institute of Certified Public Accountants, 1990). App. A. p. 151–52.

Donated medicines and supplies that normally would be purchased by the entity and unrestricted as to use are reported as operating or nonoperating revenue depending on whether the donations constitute the entity's ongoing major or central operations or are peripheral and incidental to the entity's operations. If the donations are restricted, they would be accounted for as additions to the appropriate fund balance.

## Pledge Disclosure and Accounting

Pledges are reported in the period in which they are made to the entity, net of an allowance for uncollectible amounts. Pledges are classified as unrestricted (General Funds) or donor-restricted (restricted funds). Unrestricted pledges are reported in the statement of revenue and expenses. If part of the pledge is to be applied during some future period, that part is reported in the General Fund in the period in which it is received as deferred revenue or, if restricted, as an addition to donor-restricted funds. If pledges are restricted in any other way, they are reported as additions to donor-restricted funds.

## Investments

In 1978, *Statement of Position 78-1* on accounting by hospitals for certain marketable equity securities was issued by the Accounting Standards Division of the AICPA. *Statement of Position 78-1* amended the *Hospital Audit Guide* to recommend that nonprofit hospitals apply the provisions of *FASB Statement No. 12*, which states that marketable securities should be carried at the lower of aggregate cost or market. The *Audits for Providers of Health Care Services* is consistent with *Statement of Position 78-1* concerning marketable equity securities. Debt securities are reported at amortized cost if there is the intent and ability to hold them to maturity, or at the lower of cost or market value if they are not intended to be held to maturity. Investments in other than debt or equity securities (for example, real estate or oil and gas interests) are reported at amortized cost, or at market value if an impairment in value is deemed to be other than temporary.

The accounting for investment income, gains, and losses varies depending on the funds that are involved. Income and gains (losses) from investments of General Funds which ordinarily includes interest, dividends, and rents, as well as net gains or losses resulting from increases and decreases in the value of investments, would generally be accounted for as nonoperating revenue in the statement of revenue and expense. However, if investment income is directly related to the ongoing major or central operations of the health care entity, it would be classified as operating income. For example, investment income of HMOs and CCRCs is most likely to be classified as operating revenue, because investment income earned on general investments is likely to be central to the operation of the HMO or CCRC; for a hospital, such income is more likely to be peripheral or nonoperating.

Endowment Funds account for realized gains and losses on the sale of investments through Endowment Funds principal unless such amounts are legally available for other use or are chargeable against other funds. The investment income of the Endowment Funds is accounted for in accordance with the donor's instructions.

Income and net realized gains or losses on investments of restricted funds other than Endowment Funds are added to, or deducted from, the respective fund balance unless such amounts are legally available for other use or chargeable against other funds. If such amounts are legally available for unrestricted purposes, they are reported in the statement of revenue and expenses.

## Obligations under Continuing-care Contracts

**Continuing-care retirement communities (CCRCs)** use various methods for charging residents for services and use of facilities. Three dominant methods include Advance Fees, a combination of Advance Fees and Periodic Fees, and simply Periodic Fees. The Advance Fee scheme requires a resident to pay "up front" upon entering into a continuing-care contract. These Advance Fees, net of a refundable portion are recorded as deferred revenue and are amortized into income using the straight-line method over the estimated remaining life expectancy of the resident.

If Advance Fees and Periodic Fees are insufficient to meet the costs of providing future services and the use of facilities by current residents, the CCRC's obligation to provide the future services and the use of the facilities should be accrued and reported in the financial statements.

Referring to the statement of revenues and expenses and changes in fund balance for a CCRC (Illustration 22-11) and the balance sheet for a CCRC (Illustration 22-14) look at the shaded portions of these statements, which disclose in part the nature of the financial reporting of these long-term obligations. How this liability is measured is as follows:

> CCRC annually calculates the present value of the net cost of future services and use of facilities to be provided to current residents and compares that amount with the balance of deferred revenue from advance fees. If the present value of the net cost of future services and use of facilities exceeds the deferred revenue from advance fees, a liability is recorded (obligation to provide future services and use of facilities) with the corresponding charge to income. The obligation is discounted . . . based on the expected long-term rate of return on government obligations.[13]

[13]*Audits of Providers of Health Care Services*, p. 183.

# ILLUSTRATION 22-14
## Comparative Balance Sheets for a Continuing-care Retirement Community

**PRUNE DALE**
**Balance Sheets**
**December 31, 19X5 and 19X4**

| Assets | 19X5 | 19X4 |
|---|---:|---:|
| Current assets: | | |
| Cash | $ 375,000 | $ 330,000 |
| Accounts receivable (net of allowance for doubtful accounts of $4,000 and $5,000) | 187,000 | 197,000 |
| Supplies | 40,000 | 21,000 |
| Prepaid expenses | 15,000 | 8,000 |
| Total Current Assets | 617,000 | 556,000 |
| Assets whose use is limited: | | |
| Under note agreement—investments | 2,130,00 | 1,753,000 |
| By Board for capital improvements—investments | 100,000 | 65,000 |
| | 2,230,000 | 1,818,000 |
| Property and equipment: | | |
| Land | 557,000 | 557,000 |
| Land improvements | 205,000 | 203,000 |
| Buildings and improvements | 14,573,000 | 14,564,000 |
| Furniture and equipment | 752,000 | 698,000 |
| | 16,087,000 | 16,022,000 |
| Accumulated depreciation | (1,194,000) | (742,000) |
| Total Property and Equipment | 14,893,000 | 15,280,000 |
| Deferred financing costs (net of accumulated amortization of $28,000 and $21,000) | 83,000 | 90,000 |
| Total Assets | $17,823,000 | $17,744,000 |

| Liabilities and Fund Balance (Deficit) | 19X5 | 19X4 |
|---|---:|---:|
| Current liabilities: | | |
| Current maturities of long-term debt | $ 90,000 | $ 77,000 |
| Accounts payable | 180,000 | 174,000 |
| Accrued expenses | 161,000 | 178,000 |
| Deposits on unoccupied units | 22,000 | 40,000 |
| Total Current Liabilities | 453,000 | 469,000 |
| Long-term debt, less current maturities | 8,871,000 | 8,935,000 |
| Refundable fees | 59,000 | 144,000 |
| Estimated obligation to provide future services, in excess of amounts received or to be received | 88,000 | 100,000 |
| Deferred revenue from advance fees | 9,304,000 | 9,585,000 |
| Fund balance (deficit) | (952,000) | (1,489,000) |
| Total Liabilities and Fund Balance (deficit) | $17,823,000 | $17,744,000 |

Source: Adapted from *Audits of Providers of Health Care Services* (New York: American Institute of Certified Public Accountants, 1990), App. A, p. 178–79.

A proposed Statement of Position, "Accounting and Reporting by Continuing-Care Retirement Communities for Fees and the Obligation to Provide Future Services and the Use of Facilities, and for Initial Direct Cost of Acquiring Continuing-Care Contracts," will provide the needed guidance in this area.

# VOLUNTARY HEALTH AND WELFARE ORGANIZATIONS

Voluntary health and welfare organizations provide a broad scope of public services in the areas of health, social welfare, and community services. Such organizations include the American Red Cross, the American Heart Association, Goodwill Industries, the Cancer Society, Planned Parenthood, United Way, and many others dedicated to serving human needs and the public good.

## Overview

The financial statements usually provided by voluntary health and welfare organizations include:

- A balance sheet
- A statement of support, revenues and expenses, and changes in fund balances
- A statement of functional expenses

The principal sources of revenue for voluntary health and welfare organizations are public contributions made either directly or through the United Way, and government grants. The following funds structure for these organizations is based on the example in *Audit Guide for Voluntary Health and Welfare Organizations* and includes extensions reflecting other purposes for which resources may be restricted:

> **Current Unrestricted Fund**
> **Current Restricted Fund**
> **Land, Building, and Equipment Fund**
> **Endowment Funds**
> **Loan and Annuity Funds**
> **Custodian Funds**

The balance sheet in Illustration 22-15 shows the content of these funds for a voluntary health and welfare organization. The first two funds, the Current Unrestricted Fund and the Current Restricted Fund, are comparable to the Current Funds Group for colleges and universities and the Unrestricted Fund/Specific Purpose Fund for hospitals.

# ILLUSTRATION 22-15

## THE CHAMANAUDE FOUNDATION
### Balance Sheets, December 31, 19X1 and 19X0

#### CURRENT FUNDS
#### Unrestricted

| Assets | 19X1 | 19X0 | Liabilities & Fund Balance | 19X1 | 19X0 |
|---|---|---|---|---|---|
| Cash | $2,207,000 | $2,530,000 | Accounts payable | $ 148,000 | $ 139,000 |
| Investments: | | | Research grants payable | 596,000 | 616,000 |
| For long-term purposes | 2,727,000 | 2,245,000 | Contributions designated for future | | |
| Other | 1,075,000 | 950,000 | periods | 245,000 | 219,000 |
| Pledges receivable less allowance for uncollectibles of $105,000 and $92,000 | 475,000 | 363,000 | Total Liabilities and Deferred Revenues | 989,000 | 974,000 |
| Inventories of educational materials, at cost | 70,000 | 61,000 | Fund balances: Designated by the governing board for: Long-term investments | 2,800,000 | 2,300,000 |
| Accrued interest, other receivables and prepaid expenses | 286,000 | 186,000 | Purchases of new equipment | 100,000 | –0– |
| | | | Research purposes | 1,152,000 | 1,748,000 |
| | | | Undesignated, available for general activities | 1,799,000 | 1,313,000 |
| | | | Total Fund Balance | 5,851,000 | 5,361,000 |
| Total | $6,840,000 | $6,335,000 | Total | $6,840,000 | $6,335,000 |

#### Restricted

| Assets | 19X1 | 19X0 | Liabilities & Fund Balance | 19X1 | 19X0 |
|---|---|---|---|---|---|
| Cash | $ 3,000 | $ 5,000 | Fund balances: | | |
| Investments | 71,000 | 72,000 | Professional education | $ 84,000 | $ –0– |
| Grants receivable | 58,000 | 46,000 | Research grants | 48,000 | 123,000 |
| Total | $ 132,000 | $ 123,000 | Total | $ 132,000 | $ 123,000 |

#### LAND, BUILDING, AND EQUIPMENT FUND

| Assets | 19X1 | 19X0 | Liabilities & Fund Balance | 19X1 | 19X0 |
|---|---|---|---|---|---|
| Cash | $ 3,000 | $ 2,000 | Mortgage payable, 8% due 19XX | $ 32,000 | $ 36,000 |
| Investments | 177,000 | 145,000 | Fund balances: | | |
| Pledges receivable less allowance for uncollectibles of $7,500 and $5,000 | 32,000 | 25,000 | Expended | 484,000 | 477,000 |
| | | | Unexpended—restricted | 212,000 | 172,000 |
| Land, buildings, and equipment, at cost less accumulated depreciation of $296,000 and $262,000 | 516,000 | 513,000 | Total Fund Balance | 696,000 | 649,000 |
| Total | $ 728,000 | $ 685,000 | Total | $ 728,000 | $ 685,000 |

#### ENDOWMENT FUNDS

| Assets | 19X1 | 19X0 | Liabilities & Fund Balance | 19X1 | 19X0 |
|---|---|---|---|---|---|
| Cash | $ 4,000 | $ 10,000 | Fund balance | $1,948,000 | $2,017,000 |
| Investments | 1,944,000 | 2,007,000 | | | |
| Total | $1,948,000 | $2,017,000 | Total | $1,948,000 | $2,017,000 |

Source: *Audit Guide for Voluntary Health and Welfare Organizations* (New York: American Institute of Certified Public Accountants, 1974), Exh. C, pp. 46–47.

Pledges are reported net of an allowance for uncollectibles. Pledges that relate to a future period are reported in the Contributions Designated for Future Periods account in the Current Unrestricted Fund.

Custodian Funds are equivalent to Agency Funds of colleges and universities and hospitals. They account for assets received by an organization to be held or disbursed only on instructions of the person or organization from whom they were received.

Although the statement of support, revenue, and expenses and changes in fund balances, shown in Illustration 22-16, does not include the value of donated services, many voluntary health and welfare organizations require extensive use of volunteers in providing the organization's program services. However, because of the difficulty of measuring the value of volunteer services, donated services are often not recorded as revenue and expense. The fair market value of donated materials and facilities use should be listed as support when they are received and as expenses when they are used.

The statement of functional expenses, as in Illustration 22-17, provides further detail of the expenses included in Illustration 22-16. Another important attribute of this statement is that the expenses are identified with particular programs and supporting services.

Restricted contributions of voluntary health and welfare organizations are given recognition as revenue immediately upon receipt of the contribution. The recognition of revenue is required without regard to whether the contribution had been used or the restrictions met. This approach implies that the critical event for revenue recognition is the donation and not the expenditure.

The Land, Building, and Equipment Fund (Plant Fund) accounts for expended and unexpended funds and the Fund Balances separate the unrestricted from the restricted amounts. Land, buildings, and equipment are carried at cost and buildings and equipment are depreciated.

## Investments

Investments are recorded at cost (or at market value, if donated) and reduced to market value if market is below cost. The determination of a decline in market value is computed on a portfolio basis and is generally accomplished through the use of a contra asset Allowance for Decline in Market Value account.

Investments may also be carried at market value. If they are, however, the unrealized gains or losses are included in revenues or other expenses of the appropriate fund and presented in the statement of support, revenue, and expenses and changes in fund balances.

The disposition of investment income, including realized (or unrealized, if carried at market value) gains and losses depends on the fund involved. If the investment income was earned on investments of unrestricted funds, then it should simply be reported as unrestricted revenue. If the income and net realized gains is earned on investments of restricted funds, (other than Endowment Funds), then it should be reported as revenue of the restricted funds. However, if it is available for unrestricted purposes, the income should be included in the Current Unrestricted Fund.

Realized losses on investments in restricted funds in excess of gains should be reported as a loss in the statement of support, revenue, and expenses and changes in fund balance of the restricted fund unless legal restrictions require otherwise.

Investment income from Endowment Funds, unless restricted to a specific purpose by the donor, is available for unrestricted purposes and should be included in the revenues of the Current Unrestricted Fund.

## Comparison of Accounting Practices

Accounting for voluntary health and welfare organizations can be compared to accounting for colleges and universities and health care providers as follows:

1. **Funds structure:** The funds structure of all three types of nonprofit organizations is similar. However, voluntary health and welfare organizations account for investment in plant in a separate fund called Land, Buildings, and Equipment. These organizations also use a Custodian Fund, which is similar to the Agency Funds of the other organizations.
2. **Restricted and unrestricted distinction:** Like the other types of nonprofit organizations, a clear distinction is made between restricted funds and unrestricted funds.
3. **Donated services:** The value of donated services, materials and facilities may be recognized by all three types of nonprofit organizations.
4. **Depreciation of fixed assets:** Like all other nonprofit organizations, voluntary health and welfare organizations depreciate their fixed assets.
5. **Restricted contributions:** Unlike the other two types of nonprofit organizations, voluntary health and welfare organizations recognize restricted contributions as revenue immediately upon receipt.

## ACCOUNTING FOR OTHER NONPROFIT ORGANIZATIONS

**Other nonprofit organizations** are those nonprofit units other than colleges and universities, voluntary health and welfare organizations, hospitals, and state and local governments. They include:

■ ILLUSTRATION 22-16

**THE CHAMANAUDE FOUNDATION**
**Statement of Support, Revenue and Expenses, and Changes in Fund Balances**
**For the Year Ended December 31, 19X1, with Comparative Total for 19X0**

| | 19X1 | | | | Total All Funds | |
| | Current Funds | | Land, Building, and Equipment Fund | Endowment Fund | | |
| | Unrestricted | Restricted | | | 19X1 | 19X0 |
|---|---|---|---|---|---|---|
| Public support and revenue: | | | | | | |
| Public support: | | | | | | |
| Contributions (net of estimated uncollectible pledges of $195,000 in 19X1 and $150,000 in 19X0) | $3,764,000 | $162,000 | $ –0– | $ 2,000 | $3,928,000 | $3,976,000 |
| Contributions to building fund | –0– | –0– | 72,000 | –0– | 72,000 | 150,000 |
| Special events (net of direct costs of $181,000 in 19X1 and $163,000 in 19X0) | 104,000 | –0– | –0– | –0– | 104,000 | 92,000 |
| Legacies and bequests | 92,000 | –0– | –0– | 4,000 | 96,000 | 129,000 |
| Received from federated and nonfederated campaigns (which incurred related fund-raising expenses of $38,000 in 19X1 and $29,000 in 19X0) | 275,000 | –0– | –0– | –0– | 275,000 | 308,000 |
| Total Public Support | 4,235,000 | 162,000 | 72,000 | 6,000 | 4,475,000 | 4,655,000 |
| Revenue: | | | | | | |
| Membership dues | 17,000 | –0– | –0– | –0– | 17,000 | 12,000 |
| Investment income | 98,000 | 10,000 | –0– | –0– | 108,000 | 94,000 |
| Realized gain on investment transactions | 200,000 | –0– | –0– | 25,000 | 225,000 | 275,000 |
| Miscellaneous | 42,000 | –0– | –0– | –0– | 42,000 | 47,000 |
| Total Revenue | 357,000 | 10,000 | –0– | 25,000 | 392,000 | 428,000 |
| Total Support and Revenue | 4,592,000 | 172,000 | 72,000 | 31,000 | $4,867,000 | $5,083,000 |

| Expenses: | | | | | | |
|---|---|---|---|---|---|---|
| Program services: | | | | | | |
| Research | 1,257,000 | 155,000 | 2,000 | –0– | $1,414,000 | $1,365,000 |
| Public health education | 539,000 | –0– | 5,000 | –0– | 544,000 | 485,000 |
| Professional education and training | 612,000 | –0– | 6,000 | –0– | 618,000 | 516,000 |
| Community services | 568,000 | –0– | 10,000 | –0– | 578,000 | 486,000 |
| Total Program Services | 2,976,000 | 155,000 | 23,000 | –0– | 3,154,000 | 2,852,000 |
| Supporting services: | | | | | | |
| Management and general | 567,000 | –0– | 7,000 | –0– | 574,000 | 633,000 |
| Fund raising | 642,000 | –0– | 12,000 | –0– | 654,000 | 546,000 |
| Total Supporting Services | 1,209,000 | –0– | 19,000 | –0– | 1,228,000 | 1,184,000 |
| Total Expenses | 4,185,000 | 155,000 | 42,000 | –0– | $4,382,000 | $4,036,000 |
| Excess (deficiency) of Public Support and Revenue over Expenses | 407,000 | 17,000 | 30,000 | 31,000 | | |
| Other changes in fund balances: | | | | | | |
| Property and equipment acquisitions from unrestricted funds | (17,000) | –0– | 17,000 | –0– | | |
| Transfer of realized endowment fund appreciation | 100,000 | –0– | –0– | (100,000) | | |
| Returned to donor | –0– | (8,000) | –0– | –0– | | |
| Fund Balances, beginning of year | 5,361,000 | 123,000 | 649,000 | 2,017,000 | | |
| Fund Balances, end of year | $5,851,000 | $132,000 | $696,000 | $1,948,000 | | |

Source: Adapted from *Audit Guide for Voluntary Health and Welfare Organizations* (New York: American Institute of Certified Public Accountants, 1974), Exh. A, pp. 42–43.

**THE CHAMANAUDE FOUNDATION**
**Statement of Functional Expenses**
**For the Year Ended December 31, 19X1**
**with Comparative Totals for 19X0**

| | Program Services | | | | | Supporting Services | | | Total Expenses | |
| --- | --- | --- | --- | --- | --- | --- | --- | --- | --- | --- |
| | Research | Public Health Education | Professional Education and Training | Community Services | Total | Management and General | Fund Raising | Total | 19X1 | 19X0 |
| Salaries | $ 45,000 | $291,000 | $251,000 | $269,000 | $ 856,000 | $331,000 | $368,000 | $ 699,000 | $1,555,000 | $1,433,000 |
| Employee health and retirement benefits | 4,000 | 14,000 | 14,000 | 14,000 | 46,000 | 22,000 | 15,000 | 37,000 | 83,000 | 75,000 |
| Payroll taxes, etc. | 2,000 | 16,000 | 13,000 | 14,000 | 45,000 | 18,000 | 18,000 | 36,000 | 81,000 | 75,000 |
| Total Salaries and Related Expenses | 51,000 | 321,000 | 278,000 | 297,000 | 947,000 | 371,000 | 401,000 | 772,000 | 1,719,000 | 1,583,000 |
| Professional fees and contract service payments | 1,000 | 10,000 | 3,000 | 8,000 | 22,000 | 26,000 | 8,000 | 34,000 | 56,000 | 53,000 |
| Supplies | 2,000 | 13,000 | 13,000 | 13,000 | 41,000 | 18,000 | 17,000 | 35,000 | 76,000 | 71,000 |
| Telephone and telegraph | 2,000 | 13,000 | 10,000 | 11,000 | 36,000 | 15,000 | 23,000 | 38,000 | 74,000 | 68,000 |
| Postage and shipping | 2,000 | 17,000 | 13,000 | 9,000 | 41,000 | 13,000 | 30,000 | 43,000 | 84,000 | 80,000 |
| Occupancy | 5,000 | 26,000 | 22,000 | 25,000 | 78,000 | 30,000 | 27,000 | 57,000 | 135,000 | 126,000 |
| Rental of equipment | 1,000 | 24,000 | 14,000 | 4,000 | 43,000 | 3,000 | 16,000 | 19,000 | 62,000 | 58,000 |
| Local transportation | 3,000 | 22,000 | 20,000 | 22,000 | 67,000 | 23,000 | 30,000 | 53,000 | 120,000 | 113,000 |
| Conferences, conventions, meetings | 8,000 | 19,000 | 71,000 | 20,000 | 118,000 | 38,000 | 13,000 | 51,000 | 169,000 | 156,000 |
| Printing and publications | 4,000 | 56,000 | 43,000 | 11,000 | 114,000 | 14,000 | 64,000 | 78,000 | 192,000 | 184,000 |
| Awards and grants | 1,332,000 | 14,000 | 119,000 | 144,000 | 1,609,000 | –0– | –0– | –0– | 1,609,000 | 1,448,000 |
| Miscellaneous | 1,000 | 4,000 | 6,000 | 4,000 | 15,000 | 16,000 | 21,000 | 37,000 | 52,000 | 64,000 |
| Total Expenses before Depreciation | 1,412,000 | 539,000 | 612,000 | 568,000 | 3,131,000 | 567,000 | 650,000 | 1,217,000 | 4,348,000 | 4,004,000 |
| Depreciation of buildings and equipment | 2,000 | 5,000 | 6,000 | 10,000 | 23,000 | 7,000 | 4,000 | 11,000 | 34,000 | 32,000 |
| Total Expenses | $1,414,000 | $544,000 | $618,000 | $578,000 | $3,154,000 | $574,000 | $654,000 | $1,228,000 | $4,382,000 | $4,036,000 |

Source: Adapted from *Audit Guide for Voluntary Health and Welfare Organizations* (New York: American Institute of Certified Public Accounts, 1974), Exh. B, p. 44–45.

| | |
|---|---|
| Cemetery organizations | Private elementary and secondary |
| Civic organizations | schools |
| Fraternal organizations | Professional associations |
| Labor unions | Public broadcasting stations |
| Libraries | Religious organizations |
| Museums | Research and scientific |
| Other cultural institutions | organizations |
| Performing arts organizations | Social and country clubs |
| Political parties | Trade associations |
| Private and community foundations | Zoological and botanical societies |

An authoritative guide, *Audits of Certain Nonprofit Organizations,* including *Statement of Position 78-10,* was issued by the AICPA in 1981. Like the other guides, extensive illustrations of financial statements are provided in its index.

## Overview

Nonprofit organizations in this group should generally provide three basic types of financial statements:

- A balance sheet
- A statement of activity
- A statement of changes in financial position

The presentation formats vary depending on the complexity of the organization and the need to distinguish between externally restricted and unrestricted assets, liabilities, and fund balances.

As with the *Audits of Health Care Providers,* the guide for other nonprofit organizations does not specify a funds structure; but a review of its illustrative financial statements shows that a typical funds structure would include the following funds:

> **Current Unrestricted Fund**
> **Current Restricted Fund**
> **Plant Funds (Land, Building, and Equipment)**
> **Endowment**
> **Loan and Annuity**

The extent to which the various funds are used depends on the complexity of the organization and the requirements imposed by external donors and grantors.

The financial statements of three types of other nonprofit organizations are illustrated: a country club, a performing arts organization, and a research and scientific group. The financial statements of the country club clearly resemble those of a profit-oriented organization. With some exceptions the terminology and format of the balance sheet (shown as

Illustration 22-18) could be used for that of a profit-oriented entity. What distinguishes the unit as nonprofit is the terminology in the equity section, in which the phrase "Cumulative Excess of Revenue over Expenses" is used rather than "Retained Earnings." The country club's statement of revenue, expenses, and changes in cumulative excess of revenue over expenses, shown in Illustration 22-19, closely resembles that of a statement of income and retained earnings. Although not apparent, depreciation is included in the various expenses. It is also important to note that **accrual basis accounting** is used. The statement of changes in financial position, shown in Illustration 22-20, reflects the same format as that used for profit-oriented firms.

The financial statements of the performing arts organization also reflect accrual basis accounting and depreciation is reflected in its activity statement. However, unlike the country club, the equity section of its balance sheet, in Illustration 22-21, shows how externally imposed restrictions on funds are presented for plant funds and endowment funds. The statement of activity in Illustration 22-22 closely resembles the statement of revenues and expenses of a hospital; revenues derived from sources other than operations are presented separately. The performing arts organization also includes a statement that delineates expenses by function, Illustration 22-24, which is similar to the one presented by voluntary health and welfare organizations.

The third illustrated unit is a research and scientific group. Like the performing arts organization, it uses fund accounting for its restricted funds, but it combines all the assets and liabilities and simply discloses the restrictions in the fund balance, shown in Illustration 22-26, much like an appropriations-of-fund balance. The statements also show that accrual basis accounting is used and depreciation expense is taken. And, again, the statement of changes in financial position, shown in Illustration 22-24, is very much like all of the others presented earlier.

## Pledge Disclosure and Accounting

Pledges that are legally enforceable represent a significant source of revenue for many other nonprofit organizations. Measurement and disclosure requirements are the same as colleges and universities.

## Donated Services

Donated services represent a significant resource that allows many nonprofit organizations to carry on their activities. However, accounting recognition is seldom given to the imputed value of these services. The principal problem is measuring their value. *Audits of Certain Nonprofit Organizations* suggests that donated services should be reported as an expense (and of course, as revenue) when all the following circumstances exist:

■ **ILLUSTRATION 22-18**

### DRY CREEK COUNTRY CLUB
### Balance Sheet
### March 1, 19X1 and 19X0

| | 19X1 | 19X0 |
|---|---|---|
| **Assets** | | |
| Current assets: | | |
| Cash. . . . . . . . . . . . . . . . . . . . . . . . . . . . . . . . . . | $ 44,413 | $ 37,812 |
| Investments. . . . . . . . . . . . . . . . . . . . . . . . . . . | 289,554 | 388,007 |
| Accounts receivable, less allowances of | | |
| $5,000 in 19X1, and $6,000 in 19X0. . . . | 71,831 | 45,898 |
| Inventories, at lower of cost (FIFO) or | | |
| market. . . . . . . . . . . . . . . . . . . . . . . . . . . . . . . | 27,930 | 28,137 |
| Prepaid expenses. . . . . . . . . . . . . . . . . . . . . . . | 19,154 | 13,948 |
| Total Current Assets . . . . . . . . . . . . . . . . . . | 452,882 | 513,802 |
| Property and equipment, at cost: | | |
| Land and land improvements. . . . . . . . . . . . | 1,085,319 | 1,098,828 |
| Buildings . . . . . . . . . . . . . . . . . . . . . . . . . . . . | 1,331,590 | 1,200,585 |
| Furniture, fixtures, and equipment . . . . . . . | 274,761 | 254,540 |
| | 2,691,670 | 2,553,953 |
| Less accumulated depreciation . . . . . . . . . . | 864,564 | 824,088 |
| | 1,827,106 | 1,729,865 |
| Other assets: | | |
| Deferred charges. . . . . . . . . . . . . . . . . . . . . . | 15,077 | 16,524 |
| Beverage license. . . . . . . . . . . . . . . . . . . . . . | 10,500 | 10,500 |
| | 25,577 | 27,024 |
| | $2,305,565 | $2,270,691 |
| **Liabilities and Membership Equity** | | |
| Current liabilities: | | |
| Accounts payable and accrued expenses . . . | $ 61,426 | $ 63,000 |
| Deferred revenues—initiation fees. . . . . . . . | 15,677 | 7,755 |
| Due to resigned members . . . . . . . . . . . . . . . | 16,400 | 12,900 |
| Taxes . . . . . . . . . . . . . . . . . . . . . . . . . . . . . . . | 20,330 | 23,668 |
| Total Current Liabilities. . . . . . . . . . . . . . | 113,833 | 107,923 |
| Membership equity: | | |
| Proprietary certificates, 500 at $1,500 | | |
| each—no change during the years. . . . . | 750,000 | 750,000 |
| Cumulative excess of revenue over expenses | 1,441,732 | 1,412,768 |
| | 2,191,732 | 2,162,768 |
| | $2,305,565 | $2,270,691 |

Source: Adapted from *Audits of Certain Nonprofit Organizations* (New York: American Institute of Certified Public Accountants, 1981), Exh. 3, p. 114.

■ **ILLUSTRATION 22-19**

| DRY CREEK COUNTRY CLUB<br>Statement of Revenue, Expenses, and Changes in<br>Cumulative Excess of Revenue over Expenses<br>For the Years Ended March 1, 19X1 and 19X0 | | |
|---|---|---|
| | **19X1** | **19X0** |
| Revenue: | | |
| Dues | $ 590,000 | $ 600,000 |
| Restaurant and bar charges | 270,412 | 265,042 |
| Greens fees | 171,509 | 163,200 |
| Tennis and swimming fees | 83,829 | 67,675 |
| Initiation fees | 61,475 | 95,220 |
| Locker and room rentals | 49,759 | 49,954 |
| Interest and discounts | 28,860 | 28,831 |
| Golf cart rentals | 26,584 | 24,999 |
| Other—net | 4,011 | 3,893 |
| Total Revenue | 1,286,439 | 1,298,814 |
| Expenses: | | |
| Greens | 241,867 | 244,823 |
| House | 212,880 | 210,952 |
| Restaurant and bar | 153,035 | 136,707 |
| Tennis and swimming | 67,402 | 48,726 |
| General and administrative | 533,838 | 690,551 |
| Net (gains) losses on investments | 98,453 | (95,813) |
| Total Expenses | 1,307,475 | 1,232,946 |
| Excess (deficiency) of Revenue over<br>Expenses before Capital Additions | (21,036) | 65,868 |
| Capital additions: | | |
| Assessments for capital improvements | 50,000 | –0– |
| Excess (deficiency) of Revenue over<br>Expenses after Capital Additions | 28,964 | 65,868 |
| Cumulative excess of revenue over expenses—<br>beginning of year | 1,412,768 | 1,346,900 |
| Cumulative Excess of Revenue over<br>Expenses—End of Year | $1,441,732 | $1,412,768 |

Source: Adapted from *Audits of Certain Nonprofit Organizations* (New York: American Institute of Certified Public Accountants, 1981), Exh. 3B, p.115.

1. The services performed are significant and essential to the organization and would be performed by salaried personnel if volunteers were not available. The organization would continue this program or activity if volunteers were not available.
2. The organization controls the utilization and duties of the donors of the services. It can influence the activities of the volunteers (including

■ **ILLUSTRATION 22-20**

| DRY CREEK COUNTRY CLUB<br>Statement of Changes in Financial Position<br>For the Years Ended March 31, 19X1 and 19X0 | | |
| --- | --- | --- |
| | **19X1** | **19X0** |
| Sources of funds: | | |
| Excess (deficiency) of revenue over expenses before capital additions..................... | $ (21,036) | $ 65,868 |
| Capital additions............................ | 50,000 | –0– |
| Excess (Deficiency) of Revenue over Expenses after Capital Additions .................... | 28,964 | 65,868 |
| Add-back provision for depreciation, which does not affect working capital ............ | 40,476 | 61,618 |
| Total from Operations................... | 69,440 | 127,486 |
| Decrease in deferred charges—net........... | 1,447 | –0– |
| Total Sources ......................... | 70,887 | 127,486 |
| Applications of funds: | | |
| Purchases of property and equipment ....... | 137,717 | 84,377 |
| Increase in deferred charges—net .......... | –0– | 8,909 |
| Total applications ..................... | 137,717 | 93,286 |
| Increase (Decrease) in Working Capital .. | $ (66,830) | $ 34,200 |
| Changes in the components of working capital are summarized as follows: | | |
| Increase (decrease) in current assets | | |
| Cash..................................... | $   6,601 | $ (70,928) |
| Investments.............................. | (98,453) | 98,813 |
| Accounts receivable ...................... | 25,933 | 5,000 |
| Inventories............................... | (207) | 8,112 |
| Prepaid expenses......................... | 5,206 | 2,056 |
| | (60,920) | 43,053 |
| (Increase) decrease in current liabilities | | |
| Accounts payable and accrued expenses ... | 2,174 | (5,597) |
| Deferred revenues—initiation fees ......... | (7,922) | (3,517) |
| Due to resigned members ................ | (3,500) | (2,700) |
| Taxes ................................... | 3,338 | 2,961 |
| | (5,910) | (8,853) |
| Increase (Decrease) in Working Capital .. | $ (66,830) | $ 34,200 |

Source: Adapted from *Audits of Certain Nonprofit Organizations* (New York: American Institute of Certified Public Accountants, 1981), Exh. 3C, p. 116.

■ **ILLUSTRATION 22-21**

### GARDEN VALLEY BALLET
### Balance Sheet
### June 30, 19X1 and 19X0

| | 19X1 | 19X0 |
|---|---|---|
| **Assets** | | |
| Current assets: | | |
| Cash.................................... | $216,074 | $169,466 |
| Marketable securities ..................... | 266,330 | 50,967 |
| Accounts receivable, net of allowance for | | |
| doubtful accounts...................... | 70,051 | 26,685 |
| Grants receivable ........................ | –0– | 6,100 |
| Other.................................... | 39,378 | 13,441 |
| Total Current Assets ................. | 591,833 | 266,659 |
| Noncurrent assets: | | |
| Investments and endowment funds cash... | 267,869 | 256,648 |
| Property and equipment at cost, net of | | |
| accumulated depreciation.............. | 55,061 | 40,226 |
| Rent and other deposits .................. | 3,839 | 9,130 |
| | $918,602 | $572,663 |
| | | |
| **Liabilities and Entity Capital** | | |
| Current liabilities: | | |
| Accounts payable and accrued expenses ... | $111,150 | $166,351 |
| Deferred revenues—subscriptions ......... | 297,430 | 193,042 |
| Deferred revenues—grants ................ | 42,562 | –0– |
| Current portion of long-term debt ......... | 50,000 | 50,000 |
| Total Current Liabilities.............. | 501,142 | 409,393 |
| Long-term debt .......................... | 32,000 | 69,740 |
| Contingencies | | |
| Entity capital: | | |
| Plant fund .............................. | 33,061 | 38,594 |
| Endowment funds........................ | 267,869 | 256,648 |
| Unrestricted funds....................... | 84,530 | (201,712) |
| | $918,602 | $572,663 |

Source: Adapted from *Audits of Certain Nonprofit Organizations* (New York: American Institute of Certified Public Accountants, 1981), Exh. 6A, p. 132.

control over the volunteers' time, location, duties, and performance) in a way comparable to the control it would exercise over paid employees with similar responsibilities.

3. The organization has a clearly measurable basis for the amount to be recorded.

4. The program services of the reporting organization are not principally intended for the benefit of the organization's members.

**■ ILLUSTRATION 22-22**

| GARDEN VALLEY BALLET<br>Statement of Activity<br>For the Years Ended June 30, 19X1 and 19X0 | | |
|---|---|---|
| | **19X1** | **19X0** |
| Revenue and support from operations: | | |
| Admissions | $1,557,567 | $1,287,564 |
| Dividends and interest | 21,555 | 2,430 |
| Net realized gains and losses | 54,700 | 18,300 |
| Tuition | 242,926 | 130,723 |
| Concessions and other support | 103,582 | 68,754 |
| | 1,980,330 | 1,507,771 |
| Production costs | 476,982 | 427,754 |
| Operating expenses | 797,044 | 685,522 |
| Ballet school | 473,658 | 301,722 |
| Neighborhood productions | 378,454 | 81,326 |
| General and administrative expense | 390,487 | 469,891 |
| | 2,516,625 | 1,966,215 |
| Deficiency from operations | (536,295) | (458,444) |
| Donated services, materials, and facilities | — | 8,000 |
| Annual giving | 150,379 | 78,469 |
| Grants | 702,368 | 678,322 |
| Fund-raising costs | (35,743) | (50,454) |
| | 817,004 | 714,337 |
| Excess from current endeavors | 280,709 | 255,893 |
| Capital additions | 11,221 | 18,250 |
| Total Increase in Entity Capital | $ 291,930 | $ 274,143 |

Source: Adapted from *Audits of Certain Nonprofit Organizations* (New York: American Institute of Certified Public Accountants, 1981), Exh. 6B, p. 133.

Essentially, an employee–employer relationship must exist between the organization and its volunteers, and objective measurement or valuation of the services must be possible. These circumstances are most often met only by organizations operated by religious groups. In such cases, the value of the services is determined by subtracting the amounts paid to or on behalf of the religious personnel from the amount of compensation that would be paid to lay persons.

Accounting for restricted contributions by other nonprofit organizations uses an approach whereby revenue is recognized upon expenditure of restricted or unrestricted funds, and unexpended amounts are credited to deferred revenue and not to a Fund Balance account. *Audits of Certain Nonprofit Organizations* states:

■ **ILLUSTRATION 22-23**

| | Endowment Funds | Plant Fund | Unrestricted Funds | Total |
|---|---|---|---|---|
| **GARDEN VALLEY BALLET** | | | | |
| **Statement of Changes in Entity Capital** | | | | |
| **For the Years Ended June 30, 19X1 and 19X0** | | | | |
| Entity capital— June 30, 19X9 ....... | $238,398 | $43,214 | $(462,225) | $(180,613) |
| Excess from current endeavors ............ | –0– | (4,620) | 260,513 | 255,893 |
| Capital additions ....... | 18,250 | –0– | –0– | 18,250 |
| Entity capital— June 30, 19X0 ....... | 256,648 | 38,594 | (201,712) | 93,530 |
| Excess from current endeavors ............ | –0– | (5,533) | 286,242 | 280,709 |
| Capital additions ....... | 11,221 | –0– | –0– | 11,221 |
| Entity capital— June 30, 19X1 ....... | $267,869 | $33,061 | $ 84,530 | $ 385,460 |

Source: Adapted from *Audits of Certain Nonprofit Organizations* (New York: American Institute of Certified Public Accountants, 1981), Exh. 6B, p. 133.

If a donor restricted a contribution . . . to be used for a specific program service, and the organization subsequently . . . incurred expenses for that particular program service, the . . . obligation imposed by the restriction should be deemed to have been met even if unrestricted funds were used. Management should not avoid recognizing the restricted contribution as support in that period simply because it chose to use dollars attributed to unrestricted funds at the time the expense was incurred. . . . Current restricted gifts, grants, bequests, and other income should be accounted for as revenue and support in the statement of activity to the extent that expenses have been incurred for the purpose specified by the donor or grantor during the period. The balances should be accounted for as deferred revenue or support in the balance sheet outside the fund balance section until the restrictions are met.[14]

## Investments

Unlike colleges and universities, hospitals, and voluntary health and welfare organizations, other nonprofit organizations establish a valuation practice that depends on the nature of the security and the ability and intention to hold the securities to maturity. *Statement of Position 78-10*, included within the audit guide, provides that investments should be reported as follows:

[14]*Audits of Certain Nonprofit Organizations* (New York: American Institute of Certified Public Accountants), p. 76.

**■ ILLUSTRATION 22-24**

**GARDEN VALLEY BALLET**
**Schedule of Functional Expenses—Supplementary Schedule**
**For the Year Ended June 30, 19X1, with Comparative Totals for 19X0**

| Item of Expense | Program Services | | | | | Support Services | | Total Year Ended 19X1 | Total Year Ended 19X0 |
|---|---|---|---|---|---|---|---|---|---|
| | Production Costs | Operating Expenses | Ballet School | Neighborhood Productions | Total Program Services | General and Administrative | Fund Raising | | |
| Salaries, payroll taxes, and employee benefits | $219,370 | $464,570 | $388,113 | $306,026 | $1,378,079 | $260,755 | $15,782 | $1,654,616 | $1,312,504 |
| Professional fees | 7,864 | –0– | 2,785 | –0– | 10,649 | 15,624 | –0– | 26,273 | 21,722 |
| Supplies | 15,628 | 17,128 | –0– | 3,728 | 36,484 | 25,823 | –0– | 62,307 | 43,784 |
| Telephone | –0– | –0– | –0– | –0– | –0– | 10,725 | 1,211 | 11,936 | 10,783 |
| Postage and shipping | –0– | –0– | –0– | –0– | –0– | 3,816 | 14,439 | 18,255 | 15,622 |
| Occupancy | –0– | 258,622 | 82,760 | 5,478 | 346,860 | 41,540 | 1,527 | 389,927 | 322,147 |
| Rental and maintenance of equipment | –0– | 56,724 | –0– | –0– | 56,724 | 6,927 | 2,784 | 66,435 | 52,764 |
| Printing and publications | –0– | –0– | –0– | –0– | –0– | 10,381 | –0– | 10,381 | 10,078 |
| Travel | –0– | –0– | –0– | –0– | –0– | 5,824 | –0– | 5,824 | 4,728 |
| Conferences, conventions, and meetings | –0– | –0– | –0– | –0– | –0– | 2,783 | –0– | 2,783 | 1,568 |
| Membership dues | –0– | –0– | –0– | –0– | –0– | 756 | –0– | 756 | 2,064 |
| Scenery | 154,682 | –0– | –0– | 35,540 | 190,222 | –0– | –0– | 190,222 | 143,523 |
| Costumes | 79,438 | –0– | –0– | 27,682 | 107,120 | –0– | –0– | 107,120 | 70,762 |
| Depreciation and amortization | –0– | –0– | –0– | –0– | –0– | 5,533 | –0– | 5,533 | 4,620 |
| Total, year ended June 30, 19X1 | $476,982 | $797,044 | $473,658 | $378,454 | $2,126,138 | $390,487 | $35,743 | $2,552,368 | |
| Total, year ended June 30, 19X0 | $427,754 | $685,522 | $301,722 | $81,326 | $1,496,324 | $469,891 | $50,454 | | $2,016,669 |

Source: Adapted from *Audits of Certain Nonprofit Organizations* (New York: American Institute of Certified Public Accountants, 1981), Exh. 8F, p. 137.

■ **ILLUSTRATION 22-25**

| | | |
|---|---|---|
| **GARDEN VALLEY BALLET** | | |
| **Statement of Changes in Financial Position** | | |
| **For the Years Ended June 30, 19X1 and 19X0** | | |
| | **19X1** | **19X0** |
| Funds provided by: | | |
| Excess from current endeavors................ | $280,709 | $255,893 |
| Add expenses not requiring outlay of working capital in current period | | |
| Depreciation............................. | 5,533 | 4,620 |
| Other deferred charges .................... | –0– | 7,500 |
| Funds Provided from Current Endeavors | 286,242 | 268,013 |
| Increase in long-term debt .................. | 12,260 | –0– |
| Other ....................................... | 5,291 | –0– |
| Capital additions............................ | 11,221 | 18,250 |
| Total Funds Provided .................. | 315,014 | 286,263 |
| Funds applied: | | |
| Increase in noncurrent investments and cash . | 11,221 | –0– |
| Acquisition of property, plant, and equipment . | 20,368 | 4,362 |
| Reduction of long-term debt................. | 50,000 | 25,280 |
| Total Funds Applied .................. | 81,589 | 29,642 |
| Increase in Working Capital............ | $233,425 | $256,621 |
| Changes in the components of working capital | | |
| Increase (decrease) in current assets: | | |
| Cash........................................ | $ 46,608 | $220,342 |
| Marketable securities...................... | 215,363 | 42,312 |
| Accounts receivable ....................... | 43,366 | 21,269 |
| Grants receivable.......................... | (6,100) | –0– |
| Other ...................................... | 25,937 | 15,413 |
| Increase in Current Assets.............. | 325,174 | 299,336 |
| (Increase) decrease in current liabilities: | | |
| Accounts payable and accrued expenses....... | 55,201 | 36,149 |
| Deferred revenues—subscriptions ........... | (104,388) | (78,864) |
| Deferred revenues—grants ................. | (42,562) | –0– |
| (Increase) in Current Liabilities......... | (91,749) | (42,715) |
| Increase in Working Capital............ | $233,425 | $256,621 |

Source: Adapted from *Audits of Certain Nonprofit Organizations* (New York: American Institute of Certified Public Accountants, 1981), Exh. 6D, p. 135.

■ ILLUSTRATION 22-26

## SDI RESEARCH GROUP
### Balance Sheet
### June 30, 19X1 and 19X0

| Assets | 19X1 | 19X0 |
|---|---|---|
| Current assets: | | |
| Cash | $ 125,000 | $ 115,000 |
| Certificates of deposit | 200,000 | 210,000 |
| Accounts receivable | 372,000 | 346,000 |
| Unbilled contract revenues and reimbursable grant expenses | 488,000 | 390,000 |
| Prepaid expenses and other current assets | 40,000 | 38,000 |
| Total Current Assets | 1,225,000 | 1,099,000 |
| Property, plant, and equipment: | | |
| Land and building | 220,000 | 220,000 |
| Furniture and equipment | 167,000 | 156,000 |
| Leased property under capital leases | 479,000 | 479,000 |
| | 866,000 | 855,000 |
| Less—accumulated depreciation and amortization | 259,000 | 185,000 |
| | 607,000 | 670,000 |
| | $1,832,000 | $1,769,000 |

| Liabilities and Fund Balance | 19X1 | 19X0 |
|---|---|---|
| Current liabilities: | | |
| Accounts payable and accrued expenses | $ 418,000 | $ 388,000 |
| Restricted grant advances | 261,000 | 210,000 |
| Obligations under capital leases | 88,000 | 82,000 |
| Total Current Liabilities | 767,000 | 680,000 |
| Noncurrent capital lease obligations | 309,000 | 397,000 |
| | 1,076,000 | 1,077,000 |
| Fund balance: | | |
| Unrestricted | 458,000 | 419,000 |
| Net equity in fixed assets | 298,000 | 273,000 |
| Total Fund Balance | 756,000 | 692,000 |
| | $1,832,000 | $1,769,000 |

Source: Adapted from *Audits of Certain Nonprofit Organizations* (New York: American Institute of Certified Public Accountants, 1981), Exh. 10A, p. 153.

■ **ILLUSTRATION 22-27**

| SDI RESEARCH GROUP Statement of Revenues, Expenses and Changes in Fund Balance For the Years Ended June 30, 19X1 and 19X0 | | |
|---|---|---|
| | **19X1** | **19X0** |
| Revenues: | | |
| Contract revenues—U.S. government....... | $ 5,958,000 | $5,578,000 |
| Restricted grants—foundations and individuals............................ | 4,752,000 | 4,172,000 |
| Other, including interest .................. | 43,000 | 41,000 |
| | 10,753,000 | 9,791,000 |
| Expenses: | | |
| Research and development | | |
| Environmental........................... | 5,263,000 | 4,997,000 |
| Health ................................ | 2,992,000 | 2,766,000 |
| National defense ..................... | 1,166,000 | 938,000 |
| Management and general.................. | 1,103,000 | 985,000 |
| Contract and grant procurement ........... | 165,000 | 151,000 |
| | 10,689,000 | 9,837,000 |
| Excess (deficiency) of Revenues over Expenses ........................ | 64,000 | (46,000) |
| Fund Balance, beginning of year ............. | 692,000 | 738,000 |
| Fund Balance, end of year ................... | $ 756,000 | $ 692,000 |

Source: Adapted from *Audits of Certain Nonprofit Organizations* (New York: American Institute of Certified Public Accountants, 1981), Exh. 10B, p. 154.

- Marketable debt securities, when there is both the ability and intention to hold the securities to maturity, should be reported at amortized cost, market value, or the lower of amortized cost or market value.
- Marketable equity securities and marketable debt securities that are not expected to be held to maturity should be reported at either market value or the lower of cost or market value.
- Other types of investments, for example, real estate or oil and gas interests, should be reported at either fair value or the lower of cost or fair value.

The application of a particular valuation method should be based on each of the three groups identified above.

When the lower of cost or market valuation basis is used, and the investment is classified as noncurrent, adjustments should be charged or credited directly to Fund Balance. If the investment is classified as current, then adjustments should be reflected in the statement of activity in the same manner as realized gains or losses. Investments held in Current Restricted Funds should normally be considered current investments.

Accounting for investment income or loss depends on the nature of the fund. Unrestricted investment income from all funds should be reported as revenue in the statement of activity. This includes unrestricted gains and losses on investments of unrestricted and restricted funds.

Restricted income, including gains and losses, from investments of Current Restricted Funds and restricted Plant Funds should be reported as **deferred** amounts in the balance sheet. Restricted expendable income from investments of endowment funds should also be deferred on the balance sheet.

Investment income of endowment funds that must be added to the principal as stipulated by the donor should be reported as capital additions. Gains and losses should also be reported as capital additions or deductions.

## Accounting for Fixed Assets

The accounting for fixed assets of other nonprofit organizations is similar to that for hospitals and voluntary health and welfare organizations. Purchased fixed assets are recorded at cost and at fair value if acquired through donation. However, inexhaustible collections owned by museums, art galleries, botanical gardens, libraries, and similar entities need not be capitalized. If historical cost is not available or if alternative valuation methods outlined in *Statement of Position 78-10* cannot be used, then the term "collections" should appear on the balance sheet, referenced to a note that describes the collections.

Although fixed assets are depreciated, only exhaustible fixed assets are depreciated. Landmarks, monuments, cathedrals, historical treasures, and structures used for worship need not be depreciated.

## END-OF-CHAPTER REVIEW

## Summary of Key Points

1. **Funds Structure.** The nature of the accounting system for nonprofit organizations depends on the complexity of each organization and its external mandates. Many of the nonprofit organizations use some form of fund accounting system in order to ensure compliance with all external restrictions and all internal designations by the governing board. In some cases, nonfund accounting is used when there are not externally imposed restrictions or when the external donor will permit a simple "appropriation" of Fund Balance disclosing the restrictions. Illustration 22-29 shows the funds structures of all nonprofit organizations.

■ **ILLUSTRATION 22-28**

| | | |
|---|---|---|
| **SDI RESEARCH GROUP** | | |
| **Statement of Changes in Financial Position** | | |
| **For The Years Ended June 30, 19X1 and 19X0** | | |
| | **19X1** | **19X0** |
| Financial resources were provided by: | | |
| Excess (deficiency) of revenues over expenses. | $ 64,000 | $ (46,000) |
| Add—expenses not requiring current outlay of working capital—depreciation and amortization. . . . . . . . . . . . . . . . . . . . . . . . . . . . | 74,000 | 26,000 |
| Working Capital Provided by (used in) Operations. . . . . . . . . . . . . . . . . . . . . . . . | 138,000 | (20,000) |
| Financing of fixed asset additions through capital leases. . . . . . . . . . . . . . . . . . . . . . . . . . | –0– | 397,000 |
| Total Resources Provided. . . . . . . . . . . . | 138,000 | 377,000 |
| Financial resources were used for: | | |
| Acquisition of property, plant and equipment. | 11,000 | 481,000 |
| Reduction of noncurrent capital lease obligations. . . . . . . . . . . . . . . . . . . . . . . . . . . | 88,000 | –0– |
| Total Resources Used. . . . . . . . . . . . . . . | 99,000 | 481,000 |
| Increase (Decrease) in Working Capital. . . . . . . . . | $ 39,000 | $(104,000) |
| | | |
| Changes in working capital were represented by: | | |
| Increase (decrease) in current assets— | | |
| Cash. . . . . . . . . . . . . . . . . . . . . . . . . . . . . . . | $ 10,000 | $ (14,000) |
| Certificates of deposit. . . . . . . . . . . . . . . . . . | (10,000) | (40,000) |
| Accounts receivable . . . . . . . . . . . . . . . . . . . . | 26,000 | 10,000 |
| Unbilled contract revenues and reimbursable grant expenses . . . . . . . . . . . . | 98,000 | 42,000 |
| Other . . . . . . . . . . . . . . . . . . . . . . . . . . . . . . . | 2,000 | (1,000) |
| | 126,000 | (3,000) |
| (Increase) decrease in current liabilities— | | |
| Accounts payable and accrued expenses. . . . | (30,000) | (23,000) |
| Restricted grant advances . . . . . . . . . . . . . . . | (51,000) | 4,000 |
| Obligations under capital leases. . . . . . . . . . . | (6,000) | (82,000) |
| | (87,000) | (101,000) |
| Increase (Decrease) in Working Capital. . . . . . . . . | $ 39,000 | $(104,000) |

Source: Adapted from *Audits of Certain Nonprofit Organizations* (New York: American Institute of Certified Public Accountants, 1981), Exh. 10C, p. 155.

2. **Basis of Accounting.** All nonprofit organizations must use accrual basis accounting for financial reporting purposes. However, this does not preclude organizations from using cash basis accounting throughout the period if it is cost-effective. The system need only be adjusted to accrual basis when preparing the financial statements.

Some nonprofit organizations use an encumbrance system for outstanding purchase orders and other commitments. However, the encumbrances should not be reported as expenses nor included as liabilities in the financial statements. However, like governmental units, the nonprofit organization may designate a portion of Fund Balance that is committed.

3. **Financial Statements.** All nonprofit organizations require a balance sheet, as well as a statement or statements that show revenues, expense (or expenditures), and changes in Fund Balance for the reporting period. Health care providers and other nonprofit organizations also require a statement of cash flow and changes in financial position, respectively. Voluntary health and welfare organizations also require a very specialized statement which delineates functional expenses.

4. **Pledges.** Pledge receivables and related revenue, deferred income, or increases in Fund Balance are generally recorded by all nonprofit organizations. A valuation reserve—an allowance for uncollectible pledges—must also be estimated and offset against the receivable. As an exception, colleges and universities permit disclosure of the pledge receivable in the footnotes as an alternative to its recording. Other nonprofit organizations require recording the pledge receivable only if it is legally enforceable.

5. **Donated Services.** The value of donated services are generally recognized in the financial statements of nonprofit organizations but only if there is an equivalent of an employer–employee relationship and there is an objective basis for valuation. Other nonprofit organizations impose a further restriction that the services must be essential and would be performed by salaried personnel if volunteers were not available.

6. **Investments.** As Illustration 22-29 shows, the valuation practices for investments are diverse among the various types of nonprofit organizations. However, the principal methods are (1) lower of cost or market and (2) market value. If the latter method is used, unrealized gains or losses must be recognized in the financial statements.

7. **Restricted Contributions.** There are many methods for accounting for restricted contributions. One method, currently used by voluntary health and welfare organizations, recognizes the restricted contribution as revenue immediately upon receipt. A second method, used by colleges and hospitals, requires a credit to Fund Balance until the restrictions are met, at which time the Fund Balance is charged and Revenue is credited. A third method, used by all other nonprofit organizations, requires an initial credit to Deferred Revenue and subsequently to Revenue when restrictions have been met. Health care providers use a number of methods, depending on the fund involved.

8. **Fixed Assets.** As Illustration 22-29 shows, fixed assets are generally recorded at cost. However, other nonprofit organizations provide an exception for inexhaustible assets. Also, depreciation is recognized by all of the nonprofit organizations.

## Glossary of New Terms

**Agency Fund**   "Funds received and held by an organization as fiscal agent for others."*

*Statement of Position 78-10.*

■ **ILLUSTRATION 22-29**
**Comparative Summary of All Nonprofit Organizations**

| Colleges and Universities | Health Care Providers | Voluntary Health and Welfare Organizations | Other Nonprofit Organizations |
|---|---|---|---|
| **Funds Structures** | | | |
| Current Unrestricted Fund Current Restricted Fund Plant Funds Group Endowment and Similar Funds Annuity and Life Income Funds Loan Funds Agency Funds | Fund accounting and reporting is optional. If fund accounting is used, then the Guide recommends the following funds structure: General Funds (Includes Agency Funds) Restricted Funds: Specific Purpose Funds Plant Replacement and Expansion Funds Endowment Funds Term Endowment Funds Other Restricted Funds (annuity and life income) | Current Unrestricted Fund Current Restricted Fund Land, Buildings, and Equipment Fund Endowment Funds Loan and Annuity Funds Custodian Funds | Depending on complexity, could be similar to voluntary health and welfare organizations, although not specified by the audit guide |
| **Basis of Accounting** | | | |
| **Full accrual method for all types of nonprofit organizations** | | | |
| **Financial Statements** | | | |
| Balance sheet Statement of changes in fund balances Statement of current funds revenues, expenditures, and other changes | The financial statement requirements for profit-oriented healthcare institutions are similar to those of other proprietary entities. Nonprofit health care providers should present the following set of financial statements: Balance Sheet Statement of revenues and expenses of general funds Statement of changes in fund balances Statement of cash flows of general funds | Balance sheet Statement of support, revenues and expenses, and changes in fund balance Statement of functional expenses | Balance sheet Statement of activity Statement of changes in financial position |
| **Pledges** | | | |
| Recorded, net of allowance for uncollectible pledges, or Disclosed in notes to financial statements | Recorded, net of allowance for uncollectible amounts | Recorded, net of allowance for uncollectible pledges | Recorded if legally enforceable, net of allowance for uncollectible pledges |

| Colleges and Universities | Health Care Providers | Voluntary Health and Welfare Organizations | Other Nonprofit Organizations |
|---|---|---|---|
| **Donated Services** | | | |
| Generally recognized by colleges and universities operated by religious groups Generally record the difference between the fair value and the amount paid for the services of members of the order as donated services. The difference is recorded as expenditures with the credit to gift revenues. | Usually not recorded because they are difficult to measure. However, it may be reported as an expense and a corresponding amount reported as contributions, if the services are significant, would be covered by paid personnel if uncovered by volunteers, are measurable and the entity controls the employment and duties of the service donors. | Same as health care providers The difference is recorded as expense with the credit to support. | Same as hospitals but with the additional requirements that services must be essential and would be performed by salaried personnel if volunteers were not available. Same as for voluntary health and welfare organizations The difference is recorded as expense with the credit to support. |
| **Investments** | | | |
| At acquisition cost (at market value at donation) or at market value | Initially recorded at acquisition cost or, at fair market value if received as a donation or gift.<br><br>Equity securities are reported at the lower of aggregate cost or market; debt securities are reported at amortized cost if there is the intent and ability to hold to maturity, or at the lower of cost or market if not intended to be held to maturity. | At acquisition, cost adjusted for market decline or at market value | Marketable debt securities held to maturity:<br>• amortized cost<br>• market value<br>• lower of amortized cost or market value<br>Marketable equity securities and marketable debt securities not held to maturity:<br>• market value<br>• lower of cost or market<br>Other types:<br>• fair value<br>• lower of cost or fair value |

■ **ILLUSTRATION 22-29 (continued)**
**Comparative Summary of All Nonprofit Organizations**

| Colleges and Universities | Health Care Providers | Voluntary Health and Welfare Organizations | Other Nonprofit Organizations |
|---|---|---|---|
| | **Restricted Contributions** | | |
| Contributions are credited to an appropriate Fund Balance account. When the restrictions are met or lapse, the amount is transferred to current restricted fund revenue for colleges and universities. | Contributions restricted by donors and grantors for specific operating purposes are recorded as additions to the restricted fund balance when received and are reclassified as revenue of general funds when expenditures are incurred for the purpose intended by the donor or grantor. | Contributions are recognized as revenue immediately upon receipt. The recognition of revenue is required without regard to whether the contributions had been used or the restrictions met. | Revenue is recognized upon expenditure of restricted funds, and unexpended amounts are credited to deferred revenue and not to a Fund Balance account. |
| | Contributions restricted by donors for additions to property and equipment are considered to be capital contributions and are reported in restricted plant replacement and expansion funds. A reclassification of the contributions from the plant replacement and expansion fund balance to the general funds balance is reported in statement of change in fund balances when expenditures are incurred for the purpose intended by the donor. | | |
| | When term endowment funds become available for unrestricted purposes, they are reported as revenue in the statement of revenues and expenses. If they are further restricted under the provisions of the term endowment, they are shown as a reclassification to the appropriate donor-restricted funding the statement of changes in fund balances. | | |

| Colleges and Universities | Health Care Providers | Voluntary Health and Welfare Organizations | Other Nonprofit Organizations |
|---|---|---|---|
| **Fixed Assets** | | | |
| Recorded at cost or fair value if donated | Recorded at cost or fair value if donated. | Recorded at cost or fair value if donated | Recorded at cost or fair value if donated, except for inexhaustible assets, which may be simply listed in the footnotes. |
| Depreciation taken | Depreciation taken | Depreciation taken | Depreciation taken on exhaustible fixed assets only. Excludes landmarks, monuments, cathedrals, or historical treasures. |
| Use a Plant Funds Group of funds including: Investment in Plant, Unexpended Plant Funds, Renewals and Replacement Funds and Retirement of Indebtedness Funds. | 1. Property and equipment used for general operations and related liabilities are accounted for in the general funds. | Fixed assets used in operations are accounted for in a Plant Fund, unless donor restrictions require unexpended funds in a restricted fund. | Same as voluntary health and welfare organizations |
| | 2. Contributions restricted by donors for additions to property and equipment are accounted for in restricted plant replacement and expansion funds. | | |
| | 3. Property, plant and equipment not related to operations are reported separately as part of general funds. If donor-restricted, report in donor-restricted fund. | | |

**Annuity Fund** A fund that includes gifts of money or other property given to an organization on the condition that the organization bind itself to make periodic stipulated payments that terminate at a specified time to the donor or other designated individuals.

**Capitation fee** "A fixed amount per individual that is paid periodically to a provider as compensation for providing comprehensive health care services for the period. The fee is set by contract between a prepaid health care plan and the provider. These contracts are generally with a medical group or independent practice association, but may also be with hospitals and other providers. Capitation fees may be actuarially determined or negotiated based on expected costs to be incurred."**

**Continuing-care retirement community (CCRC)** "A legal entity sponsoring and/ or guaranteeing residential facilities, meals and health care services for a community of retired persons who may reside in apartments, other living units, or in some cases, a nursing center."**

**Contractual adjustments** "Differences between revenue at established rates and amounts realizable from third-party payors under contractual agreements."**

**Custodian Funds** Funds received and held by an organization as fiscal agent for others.

**Deferred revenue and support** "Revenue or support received or recorded before it is earned, that is, before the conditions are met, in whole or in part, for which the revenue or support is received or is to be received."*

**Designated Funds** Unrestricted funds set aside for specific purposes by action of the governing board.

**Endowment Funds** "The fund in which a donor has stipulated in the donative instrument that the principal is to be maintained inviolate and in perpetuity and only the income from the investments of the fund may be expended."*

**Fund** "An accounting entity established for the purpose of accounting for resources used for specific activities or objectives in accordance with special regulations."*

**Funds Group** "A group of funds of similar character for example, operating funds, endowment funds, annuity funds, and life income funds."*

**Health maintenance organization (HMO)** "A generic set of medical care organizations organized to deliver the finance health care services. An HMO provides comprehensive health care services to enrolled members for fixed, prepaid fees (premiums)."**

**Investment pool** "Assets of several funds pooled or consolidated for investment purposes."*

**Loan Funds** "Resources restricted for loans. When both principal and interest on the loan funds received by an organization are loanable, they are included in the loan fund group. If only the income from a fund is loanable, the principal is included in endowment funds, while the cumulative income constitutes the loan fund."*

**Market value unit method** A method of allocating realized and unrealized gains (or losses) and income to participating funds in an investment pool.

*\*\*Audits of Providers of Health Care Services.*

**Pledge**   "A promise to make a contribution to an organization in the amount and form stipulated."*

**Premiums (or subscriber's fee)**   "The consideration paid for providing contract coverage."**

**Prepaid health care plan**   "A plan in which the provider is compensated in advance by the sponsoring organization. The sponsoring organization pays or compensates the provider based on either a fixed sum or a per enrollee amount. Prepaid health care plans include health maintenance organizations, preferred provider organizations, eye care plans, dental care plans, and similar plans. Under such plans, the financial risk of delivering the health care has transferred to the provider of services."**

**Quasi-Endowment Funds**   "Funds that the governing board of an organization, rather than a donor or other outside agency, has determined are to be retained and invested. The governing board has the right to decide at any time to expend the principal of such funds."* Also called designated funds.

**Renewal and Replacement Funds**   A fund within the Plant Fund Group of colleges and universities that represents unexpended resources held for renewal and replacement of plant assets.

**Resource transferability**   The nonprofit organization's freedom to use resources for various purposes.

**Restricted Funds**   "Funds for which use is restricted by outside agencies or persons as contrasted with funds over which the organization has complete control and discretion."*

**Revenues**   "Gross increases in assets, gross decreases in liabilities, or a combination of both from delivering or producing goods, rendering services, or other earning activities of an organization during a period, for example, dues, sale of services, ticket sales, fees, interest, dividends and rent."*

**Support**   "The conveyance of property from one person or organization to another without consideration, for example, donations, gifts, grants, or bequests."*

**Term endowment**   "A fund that has all the characteristics of an endowment fund except that at some future date or event it will no longer be required to be maintained as an endowment fund."*

**Third-party payer**   "Any agency (such as Blue Cross, the Medicare program, or commercial insurance companies) that contracts with health care entities and patients to pay for the care of covered patients."**

**Unexpended Plant Fund**   A fund within the Plant Funds Group of colleges and universities that represents unexpended resources for the acquisition of plant assets.

**Unrestricted Funds**   "Funds that have no external restrictions on their use or purpose—that is, funds that can be used for any purpose designated by the governing board, distinguished from funds restricted externally for specific purposes (for example, for operations, plant or endowment)."*

# Self-Study Questions
*(Answers are at the end of this chapter, preceding the appendices.)*

1. Sunnyvale College is sponsored by a religious group. Volunteers from this religious group regularly contribute their services to Sunnyvale and are paid

nominal amounts to cover their commuting costs. During 19X1, the aggregated total paid to these volunteers was $12,000. The gross value of services performed by the volunteers determined by reference to lay-equivalent salaries was $300,000. What amount should Sunnyvale record as expenditures in 19X1 for these volunteers' services?

a. $312,000
b. $300,000
c. $ 12,000
d. $–0–

Would your response be different if the organization was a hospital or extended care facility and the volunteers distributed books and flowers to the patients?

2. Street Wise, a voluntary health and welfare organization funded by contributions from the general public, received unrestricted pledges of $500,000 during 19X1. It was estimated that 12% of these pledges would be uncollectible. By the end of 19X1, $400,000 of the pledges had been collected, and it was expected that $40,000 more would be collected in 19X2, with the balance of $60,000 to be written off as uncollectible. Donors did not specify any periods during which the donations were to be used. What amount should Street Wise include under public support in 19X1 for net contributions?

a. $500,000
b. $450,000
c. $440,000
d. $400,000

Would your answer be different if the donors specified use over a period of three years? What essential differences exist in accounting for pledges among the various nonprofit organizations?

3. On January 2, 19X1, a nonprofit botanical society received a gift of an exhaustible fixed asset with an estimated useful life of ten years and no salvage value. The donor's cost of this asset was $20,000; its fair market value at the date of the gift was $30,000. What amount of depreciation of this asset should the society recognize in its 19X1 financial statements?

a. $3,000
b. $2,500
c. $2,000
d. $–0–

What if the organization was a hospital and the fixed asset was donor-restricted. Assuming that a funds structure was used, how would it be accounted for?

4. In 19X1, Knox Hospital received a $250,000 pure endowment fund grant. Also in 19X1, Knox's governing board designated $300,000, which had originated from unrestricted gifts, for special uses. What amount of these resources should be accounted for as part of general funds?

a. $–0–
b. $250,000
c. $300,000
d. $550,000

Why is the separation between unrestricted and restricted funds important for nonprofit organizations? How do hospitals account for restricted contributions restricted by donors for specific operating purposes?

# ASSIGNMENT MATERIAL

## Review Questions

1. Compare the objectives of nonprofit organizations with those of business organizations.
2. Discuss why nonprofit organizations place greater emphasis on the nature of resource inflows and the degree of resource transferability.
3. Financial statements of nonprofit organizations distinguish between restricted and unrestricted funds. Why is this separation important?
4. Nonprofit organizations recognize depreciation expense even though income is not a stated objective. What are some arguments in support of this practice?
5. How do nonprofit organizations account for pledges?
6. Compare the accounting and reporting of fixed assets by health care providers and colleges and universities.
7. Explain why the contributed services are generally not given accounting recognition.
8. What common characteristics are shared by governmental units and the nonprofit organizations discussed in this chapter?
9. Outline the historical development of generally accepted accounting principles for nonprofit organizations.
10. Identify the differences in the content of current operating funds that exist among the various nonprofit organizations.
11. Describe the differences in accounting for restricted revenue among colleges, health care providers, voluntary health and welfare organizations, and other nonprofit organizations.
12. Why do voluntary health and welfare organizations use a financial statement that discloses their functional expenses?
13. *Audit Guide for Health Care Providers* draws from the FASB *Concepts Statement No. 6* for guidance in assigning income to operating and nonoperating classifications. What is the nature of this guidance, and why is it important?
14. What are the accounting issues related to continuing-care contracts for continuing-care retirement communities?
15. Under what conditions may health care providers reflect the value of donated services in the financial statements?
16. What is the nature of limited-use assets, and how are they shown in the balance sheet of a health care provider?
17. How are investment incomes of HMOs and CCRCs likely to be shown on the statement of revenue and expenses?
18. Patient service revenue of hospitals is reported "net." What is deducted from gross fees to arrive at net patient service revenue?

## Discussion Cases

| DC 22-1 | **Defining User Needs and Meaningful Financial Statements** |
|---------|-------------------------------------------------------------|

The Stecca Foundation is a nonprofit health and welfare organization concerned with public nutrition. Its program services include research, public education, and professional education and training.

The governing board has asked certain public accounting firms to submit proposals to review the foundation's accounting system—including its internal controls—and to perform an audit of its financial statements for the current year. The organization has never been audited. The governing board is acting in compliance with new state legislation that requires audits of all health and welfare organizations by public accountants.

Your accounting firm is submitting a proposal. In reviewing the foundation's most recent financial statements, you discover that they were prepared on a cash basis and that the activity statement is simply a cash receipts and disbursements statement. The balance sheet discloses only one asset—cash—and a Fund Balance. The organization owns a significant amount of fixed assets, including a large office building and other real properties.

### Required:

Prepare the part of the proposal that sets forth your recommended changes in the organization's financial reporting system. Your recommendations should represent a careful delineation of user needs, internal and external, and how the statements and system should be designed to meet these particular needs.

| |
|---|
| **DC 22-2** |

## Responding to the Issue of Depreciation Expense

The board of the Stecca Foundation has reviewed your proposals concerning the organization's financial reporting system and has asked you to expand on certain proposal recommendations.

The recommendation that generated the most concern from the board members concerned the accounting for depreciation expense. Arguments centered on the belief that income is not an objective and no causal relationship exists between depreciation and revenue.

### Required:

Defend your recommendation that depreciation expense be recognized in the accounts and included in the financial statements.

| |
|---|
| **DC 22-3** |

## Accounting for Donated Services

Andersson Medical Services is a voluntary medical service organization that renders limited medical assistance to the elderly residing in several cities in the western United States. The organization receives funding from United Way, other philanthropic organizations, and various government agencies. The medical and lay staff—including doctors, registered nurses, medical technicians, and lay persons who assist the medical staff—are all volunteers.

Peter Karppinen, the organization's director, wishes to consult with you concerning the possible inclusion of the value of donated services in his organization's financial statements. Apparently, his current accountant feels that "it simply cannot be done."

During the conversation, Karppinen develops several points that he believes represent sufficient support for including donated services in the financial statements. First, he argues that the fair value of the services of the doctors, nurses, and medical technicians is readily determinable. Second, the inclusion of the donated services would show more accurately the amount of services rendered to its various programs, which, in his opinion, would assist him in obtaining additional funding, especially from philanthropic organizations. He also argues that the inclusion of the value of donated services may assist him in competing more effectively for matching grants, because he can argue that the organization's matching contribution is the value of its human resources.

### Required:
Respond to Karppinen in writing, outlining current accounting practices concerning accounting for donated services and carefully develop the essential rationale for the current accounting practice.

## Exercises

E 22-1

## Voluntary Health and Welfare Organizations: Accounting for Revenue and Expense

Delta House is a voluntary welfare organization funded by contributions from the general public. During 19X3, unrestricted pledges of $900,000 were received, half of which were payable in 19X3, with the other half payable in 19X4 for use in 19X4. It was estimated that 10% of these pledges would be uncollectible. In addition, Tom Walker, a social worker on Delta's permanent staff, earning $20,000 annually for a normal workload of 2,000 hours, contributed an additional 800 hours of his time to Delta House at no charge.

### Required:
How much should Delta House report as net contribution revenue for 19X3 with respect to the pledges?

a. $–0–
b. $405,000
c. $810,000
d. $900,000

How much should Delta House record in 19X3 for contributed service expense?

a. $8,000
b. $4,000
c. $800
d. $–0–

(AICPA adapted)

E 22-2

## Voluntary Health and Welfare Organizations: Accounting for Expenses

Revere Foundation, a voluntary health and welfare organization supported by contributions from the general public, included the following costs in its statement of functional expenses for the year ended December 31, 19X3:

| Fund-raising | $500,000 |
|---|---|
| Administrative (including data processing) | 300,000 |
| Research | 100,000 |

### Required:

Revere's functional expenses for 19X3 program services included:

a. $900,000
b. $500,000
c. $300,000
d. $100,000

(AICPA adapted)

---

**E 22-3**

## Voluntary Health and Welfare Organizations: Accounting for Contributions

Helping Hand Center, a voluntary health and welfare organization, received a cash donation in 19X3 from a donor specifying that the amount donated was to be used in 19X5.

### Required:

The cash donation should be accounted for as:

a. Support in 19X3.
b. Support for 19X3, 19X4, and 19X5, and as a deferred credit in the balance sheet at the end of 19X3 and 19X4.
c. Support in 19X5, and no deferred credit in the balance sheet at the end of 19X3 and 19X4.
d. Support in 19X5, and as a deferred credit in the balance sheet at the end of 19X3 and 19X4.

(AICPA adapted)

---

**E 22-4**

## Colleges and Universities: Accounting for Tuition and Fees

For the fall semester of 19X1, Westmoor College assessed its students $2,300,000 for tuition and fees. The net amount realized was only $2,100,000 because of the following revenue reductions:

| Refunds occasioned by class cancellations and student withdrawals | $ 50,000 |
|---|---|
| Tuition remissions granted to faculty members' families | 10,000 |
| Scholarships and fellowships | 140,000 |

### Required:

How much should Westmoor report for the period for unrestricted current funds revenues from tuition and fees?

a. $2,100,000
b. $2,150,000
c. $2,250,000
d. $2,300,000

(AICPA adapted)

E
22-5

## Colleges and Universities: Accounting for Revenues

During the years ended June 30, 19X4 and 19X5, Cabrillo University conducted a major scientific research project. During 19X5 the university received a corporate gift of $1,500,000, the use of which was left to the discretion of the university's governing board. The governing board restricted this gift to the major research project. During the two-year research period, expenditures for the scientific research projects were as follows:

|  | Year Ended June 30 | |
| --- | --- | --- |
|  | 19X4 | 19X5 |
| Gift receipts . . . . . . . . . . . . . . . . . . . . . . . . . . . . . . . . . . . . . . | $700,000 | $1,000,000 |

### Required:

How much gift revenue should Cabrillo report in the restricted column of its statement of current funds revenues, expenditures, and other changes for the year ended June 30, 19X5?

a. $–0–
b. $700,000
c. $1,000,000
d. $1,700,000

E
22-6

## Hospitals: Accounting for Contributions and Fund Classifications

On July 1, 19X4, Good Shepherd Hospital's governing board designated $200,000 for expansion of out-patient facilities. The $200,000 will be expended in the fiscal year ended June 30, 19X7.

### Required:

In Good Shepherd's June 30, 19X5, balance sheet, this cash should be classified as a $200,000

a. Restricted current asset.
b. Restricted noncurrent asset.
c. Unrestricted current asset.
d. Unrestricted noncurrent asset.

(AICPA adapted)

E
22-7

## Universities: Accounting for Unrestricted Current Funds

For the summer session of 19X1, Aptos University assessed its students $1,700,000 (net of refunds), covering tuition and fees for educational and general purposes. However, only $1,500,000 was expected to be realized because scholarships totaling $150,000 were granted to students, and tuition remissions of $50,000 were allowed to faculty members' children attending Aptos.

**Required:**
What amount should Aptos include in the unrestricted current funds as revenues from student tuition and fees?

a. $1,500,000
b. $1,550,000
c. $1,650,000
d. $1,700,000

(AICPA adapted)

| E 22-8 |
|---|

## Universities: Accounting for Unrestricted Current Funds

Los Gatos University's unrestricted current funds comprised the following:

| | |
|---|---|
| Assets ........................................................ | $5,000,000 |
| Liabilities (including deferred revenues of $100,000) .............. | $3,000,000 |

**Required:**
The fund balance of Los Gatos University's unrestricted current funds was

a. $1,900,000
b. $2,000,000
c. $2,100,000
d. $5,000,000

| E 22-9 |
|---|

## Universities: Current Funds Revenues

The following receipts were among those recorded by Touche College during 19X1:

| | |
|---|---|
| Unrestricted gifts ........................................... | $500,000 |
| Restricted current funds (expended for current operating purposes) . | $200,000 |
| Restricted current funds (not yet expended) ..................... | $100,000 |

**Required:**
The amount that should be included in current funds revenue is

a. $800,000
b. $700,000
c. $600,000
d. $500,000

| E 22-10 |
|---|

## Universities: Accounting for Endowment Income

The following information pertains to interest received by Winchester University from Endowment Fund investments for the year ended June 30, 19X1:

|  | Received | Expended for Current operations |
|---|---|---|
| Unrestricted | $300,000 | $100,000 |
| Restricted | 500,000 | 75,000 |

### Required:

What amount should be credited to endowment income for the year ended June 30, 19X1?

a. $800,000
b. $375,000
c. $175,000
d. $100,000

## Universities: Accounting for Gift Revenue

**E 22-11**

During the years ended June 30, 19X0 and 19X1, Santa Cruz University conducted a cancer research project financed by a $2,000,000 gift from an alumnus. This entire amount was pledged by the donor on July 10, 19X9, although he paid only $500,000 at that date. The gift was restricted to the financing of this particular research project. During the two-year research period, the university's related gift receipts and research expenditures were as follows:

|  | Year Ended June 30 | |
|---|---|---|
|  | 19X0 | 19X1 |
| Gift receipts | $1,200,000 | $ 800,000 |
| Cancer research expenditures | 900,000 | 1,100,000 |

### Required:

How much gift revenue should Santa Cruz University report in the Restricted column of its statement of current funds revenues, expenditures, and other changes for the year ended June 30, 19X1?

a. $–0–
b. $800,000
c. $1,100,000
d. $2,000,000

## Hospitals: Accounting for Contributions and Fund Classifications

**E 22-12**

El Camino Hospital's property, plant, and equipment (net of depreciation) consist of the following:

| | |
|---|---|
| Land | $ 500,000 |
| Buildings | 10,000,000 |
| Movable equipment | 2,000,000 |

**Required:**

What amount should be included in the donor-restricted funds?

a. $–0–
b. $2,000,000
c. $10,500,000
d. $12,500,000

(AICPA adapted)

---

## Hospitals: Accounting for Contributions and Donated Services

During the year ended December 31, 19X1, Middlefield Hospital received the following donations stated at their respective fair values:

| | |
|---|---|
| Employee services from members of a religious group . . . . . . . . . . . . . | $100,000 |
| Medical supplies from an association of physicians (these supplies were restricted for indigent care and were used for such purpose in 19X1) . . . . . . . . . . . . . . . . . . . . . . . . . . . . . . . . . . . . . | 30,000 |

**Required:**

How much revenue (both operating and nonoperating) from donations should Middlefield report in its 19X1 statement of revenue and expenses?

a. $–0–
b. $30,000
c. $100,000
d. $130,000

---

## Hospitals: Accounting for Revenues

Under Homestead Hospital's established rate structure, the hospital would have earned patient service revenue of $6,000,000 for the year ended December 31, 19X3. However, Homestead did not expect to collect this amount because of charity allowances of $1,000,000 and discounts of $500,000 to third-party payers. In May, 19X3, Homestead purchased bandages from Loredo Supply Co. at a cost of $1,000. However, Loredo notified Homestead that the invoice was being cancelled and that the bandages were being donated to Homestead. At December 31, 19X3, Homestead had board-designated assets consisting of cash $40,000 and investments $700,000.

**Required:**

For the year ended December 31, 19X3, how much should Homestead record as patient service revenue?

a. $6,000,000
b. $6,500,000
c. $5,000,000
d. $4,500,000

For the year ended December 31, 19X3, Homestead should record the donation of bandages as

a. A $1,000 reduction in operating expenses.
b. Nonoperating revenue of $1,000.
c. Other operating revenue of $1,000.
d. A memorandum entry only.

How much of Homestead's board-designated assets should be included in General Funds?

a. $–0–
b. $40,000
c. $700,000
d. $740,000

E
22-15

## Hospitals: Accounting for Restricted Funds

Ocamura Hospital's property, plant and equipment, net of depreciation, amounted to $10,000,000, with related mortgage liabilities of $1,000,000.

### Required:

What amount should be included in the donor-restricted funds?

a. $–0–
b. $1,000,000
c. $9,000,000
d. $10,000,000

E
22-16

## Hospitals: Patient Service Revenues

Parma Hospital's patient service revenues for services provided in 19X1, at established rates, amounted to $8,000,000 on the accrual basis. For internal reporting, Parma uses the discharge method. Under this method, patient service revenues are recognized only when patients are discharged, with no recognition given to revenues accruing for services to patients not yet discharged. Patient service revenues at established rates using the discharge method amounted to $7,000,000 for 19X1.

### Required:

According to generally accepted accounting principles, Parma should report patient service revenues for 19X1 of

a. Either $8,000,000 or $7,000,000, at the option of the hospital.
b. $8,000,000
c. $7,500,000
d. $7,000,000

## Hospitals: Accounting for Contributions

**E 22-17**

During 19X1, Davenport Hospital purchased medicines for hospital use totaling $800,000. Included in this $800,000 was an invoice of $10,000 that was canceled in 19X1 by the vendor because the vendor wished to donate this medicine to Davenport.

### Required:

This donation of medicine should be recorded as

a. A $10,000 reduction of medicine expense.
b. An increase in other operating revenue of $10,000.
c. A direct $10,000 credit to the General (unrestricted) Funds balance.
d. A $10,000 credit to the restricted funds balance.

## Hospitals: Accounting for Nonoperating Revenue

**E 22-18**

An organization of high school seniors performs services for patients at Soquel Hospital. These students are volunteers and perform services that the hospital would not otherwise provide, such as wheeling patients in the park and reading to patients. Soquel has no employer–employee relationship with these volunteers, who donated 5,000 hours of service in 19X1. At the minimum wage rate, these services would amount to $18,750, while it is estimated that the fair value of these services was $25,000.

### Required:

In Soquel's 19X1 statement of revenues and expenses, what amount should be reported as nonoperating revenue?

a. $25,000
b. $18,750
c. $6,250
d. $–0–

## Other Nonprofit Organizations: Accounting for Fund-Raising Costs

**E 22-19**

The following expenditures were among those incurred by a nonprofit botanical society during 19X1:

| | |
|---|---|
| Printing of annual report. . . . . . . . . . . . . . . . . . . . . . . . . . . . . . . . . . . . . . . . | $10,000 |
| Unsolicited merchandise sent to encourage contributions . . . . . . . . . . | $20,000 |

### Required:

What amount should be classified as fund-raising costs in the society's activity statement?

a. $–0–
b. $10,000
c. $20,000
d. $30,000

# Problems

| P |
|---|
| **22-1** |

## Sports Clubs: Transactions and Preparation of Activity Statement

In 19X0, a group of merchants in Sunnyview City organized the Committee of 100 to establish the Bay View Sports Club, a nonprofit sports organization for the city's youth. Each of the committee's 100 members contributed $1,000 toward the club's capital and in turn received a participation certificate. In addition, each partici- pant agreed to pay dues of $200 per year for the club's operations. All dues have been collected in full for the fiscal year ended March 31. Members who have dis- continued their participation have been replaced by an equal number of new mem- bers through a transfer of the participation certificates. The club's April 1, 19X4, trial balance follows:

|  | Debit | Credit |
|---|---|---|
| Cash. . . . . . . . . . . . . . . . . . . . . . . . . . . . . . . . . . . . . . . . . . . . . . . | $  9,000 | |
| Investments (market value equals cost) . . . . . . . . . . . . . . | 58,000 | |
| Inventories . . . . . . . . . . . . . . . . . . . . . . . . . . . . . . . . . . . . | 5,000 | |
| Land. . . . . . . . . . . . . . . . . . . . . . . . . . . . . . . . . . . . . . . . . . | 10,000 | |
| Building. . . . . . . . . . . . . . . . . . . . . . . . . . . . . . . . . . . . . . . | 164,000 | |
| Accumulated Depreciation—Building . . . . . . . . . . . . . . . | | $130,000 |
| Furniture and Equipment. . . . . . . . . . . . . . . . . . . . . . . . . | 54,000 | |
| Accumulated Depreciation—Furniture and Equipment . | | 46,000 |
| Accounts Payable . . . . . . . . . . . . . . . . . . . . . . . . . . . . . . . | | 12,000 |
| Participation Certificates (100 at $1,000 each) . . . . . . . . | | 100,000 |
| Cumulative Excess of Revenue over Expenses. . . . . . . . . | | 12,000 |
| | $300,000 | $300,000 |

Club transactions for the year ended March 31, 19X5, were as follows:

1. Collections of dues from participants amounted to $20,000.
2. Snack bar and soda fountain sales receipts totaled $28,000.
3. Interest and dividends received were $6,000.
4. Additions to the voucher register were as follows:

| House expenses. . . . . . . . . . . . . . . . . . . . . . . . . . . . . . . . . . . . . . . . . . . . . . . . | $17,000 |
|---|---|
| Snack bar and soda fountain expenses. . . . . . . . . . . . . . . . . . . . . . . . . . . . | 26,000 |
| General and administrative expenses . . . . . . . . . . . . . . . . . . . . . . . . . . . | 11,000 |

5. Vouchers paid totaled $55,000.
6. Assessments for capital improvements not yet incurred, $10,000 (assessed on March 20, 19X5; none collected by March 31, 19X5; deemed 100% collectible during the year ended March 31, 19X6).
7. Unrestricted bequests received amounted to $5,000.

### Additional Information:

1. Investments are valued at market, which amounted to $65,000 at March 31, 19X5. No investment transactions were made during the year.

2. Depreciation for the year was as follows:

| | |
|---|---:|
| Building | $4,000 |
| Furniture and equipment | 8,000 |

This depreciation was allocated as follows:

| | |
|---|---:|
| House expenses | $9,000 |
| Snack bar and soda fountain expenses | 2,000 |
| General and administrative expenses | 1,000 |

3. A physical inventory at March 31, 19X5, revealed that $1,000 worth of supplies remained in the snack bar and soda fountain.

### Required:
1. Prepare journal entries for the above transactions.
2. Prepare the appropriate activity statement for the year ended March 31, 19X5.

(AICPA adapted)

## P 22-2

## University Current Funds: Transactions Analysis and Preparation of Statement of Changes in Fund Balances

A partial balance sheet for St. Juliann University at the end of its fiscal year (July 31, 19X4) is as follows:

**ST. JULIANN UNIVERSITY**
**Balance Sheet—Current Funds**
**July 31, 19X4**

**Assets**

Current Funds:
Unrestricted:

| | |
|---|---:|
| Cash | $200,000 |
| Accounts receivable—student tuition and fees, less $15,000 allowance for doubtful accounts | 360,000 |
| Prepaid expenses | 40,000 |
| Total Unrestricted | $600,000 |
| Restricted: | |
| Cash | $ 10,000 |
| Investments | 210,000 |
| Total Restricted | $220,000 |
| Total Current Funds | $820,000 |

**Liabilities and Fund Balances**

Current Funds:
Unrestricted:

| | |
|---|---:|
| Accounts payable | $100,000 |
| Due to other funds | 40,000 |

| | | |
|---|---|---|
| Deferred revenue—tuition and fees | | 25,000 |
| Fund balance | | 435,000 |
| Total Unrestricted | | $600,000 |
| Restricted: | | |
| Accounts payable | | $ 5,000 |
| Fund balance | | 215,000 |
| Total Restricted | | $220,000 |
| Total Current Funds | | $820,000 |

The following financial events and transactions occurred during the fiscal year ended July 31, 19X5:

1. Cash collected from student tuition totaled $3,000,000. Of this amount, $362,000 was outstanding at July 31, 19X4; $2,500,000 was for current-year tuition, and $138,000 was for tuition applicable to the semester beginning in August 19X5.
2. Deferred revenue at July 31, 19X4, was earned during the year ended July 31, 19X5.
3. July 31, 19X4, accounts receivable that were not collected during the year ended July 31, 19X5, were declared uncollectible and were written off against the allowance account. At July 31, 19X5, the Allowance for Doubtful Accounts was an estimated $10,000.
4. During the year, an unrestricted grant of $60,000 was awarded by the state. This state grant was payable to St. Juliann sometime in August 19X5.
5. During the year, unrestricted cash gifts of $80,000 were received from alumni. St. Juliann's board of trustees allocated $30,000 of these gifts to the student loan fund.
6. During the year, investments costing $25,000 were sold for $31,000. Restricted fund investments were purchased for $40,000. Investment income of $18,000 was earned and collected during the year.
7. Unrestricted general expenses of $2,500,000 were recorded in the voucher register. At July 31, 19X5, the unrestricted Accounts Payable balance was $75,000.
8. The restricted Accounts Payable balance at July 31, 19X4, was paid.
9. The $40,000 due to other funds at July 31, 19X4, was paid to the Plant Fund as required.
10. One-quarter of the prepaid expenses at July 31, 19X4, which pertain to general education expenses, expired during the current year. No additions to prepaid expenses were made during the year.

### Required:

1. Prepare general journal entries for the foregoing transactions for the year ended July 31, 19X5. Number each entry to correspond with the indicated transaction number. Organize your answer as follows:

| | | Current Funds | | | |
|---|---|---|---|---|---|
| Entry | | Unrestricted | | Restricted | |
| No. | Account | Dr. | Cr. | Dr. | Cr. |

2. Prepare a statement of changes in fund balances for the year ended July 31, 19X5.

(AICPA adapted)

---

**P 22-3**

## Hospitals: Preparation of an Aggregated Balance Sheet; Distinguishing Characteristics of the Equity of a Business Enterprise and That of a Nonprofit Entity; The Importance of Disclosure of the Classes of Net Assets of a Nonprofit Entity

Foggy Meadows Hospital's balance sheet format is viewed as disaggregated, meaning that it discloses the assets and liabilities classified by the various funds.

### Required:
1. Recast Foggy Meadows Hospital's balance sheet, which is shown in Illustration 22-30, into the aggregated format.
2. The equity or net assets of both a business enterprise and a nonprofit entity is the difference between the entity's assets and its liabilities. The change in net assets of both types of organizations occur from the entity's operations and other events and circumstances affecting the entity. What, then, are the distinguishing characteristics of the equity of a business enterprise and that of a nonprofit organization?
3. Net assets on the aggregated balance sheet is divided into three mutually exclusive classes: unrestricted net assets, temporarily restricted net assets, and permanently restricted net assets. Why is it important to disclose these net asset classes? (Hint: capital maintenance.)

---

**P 22-4**

## Hospitals: Preparation of Statement of Revenues and Expenses and Writing Appropriate Disclosures

The following selected information was taken from the books and records of Merrcy Hospital (a voluntary hospital) as of and for the year ended June 30, 19X2:

1. Patient service revenue totaled $16,000,000, with allowances and uncollectible accounts amounting to $3,400,000. Other operating revenue aggregated $346,000, and included $160,000 from specific purpose funds. Revenue of $6,000,000 recognized under cost-reimbursement agreements is subject to audit and retroactive adjustment by third-party payers. Estimated retroactive adjustments under these agreements have been included in allowances.
2. Unrestricted gifts and bequests of $410,000 were received.
3. Unrestricted income from Endowment Funds totaled $160,000.
4. Income from board-designated funds aggregated $82,000.
5. Operating expenses totaled $13,370,000, and included $500,000 for depreciation computed on the straight-line basis. However, accelerated depreciation is used to determine reimbursable costs under certain third-party reimbursement agreements. Net cost reimbursement revenue amounting to $220,000, resulting from the difference in depreciation methods, was deferred to future years.

6. Also included in operating expenses are pension costs of $100,000, in connection with a noncontributory pension plan covering substantially all of Merrcy's employees. Accrued pension costs are funded currently. Prior service cost is being amortized over a period of 20 years. The actuarially computed value of vested and nonvested benefits at year-end amounted to $3,000,000 and $350,000, respectively. The assumed rate of return used in determining the actuarial present value of accumulated plan benefits was 8%. The plan's net assets available for benefits at year-end was $3,050,000.
7. Gifts and bequests are recorded at fair market values when received.
8. Patient service revenue is accounted for at established rates on the accrual basis.

### Required:
1. Prepare a formal statement of revenues and expenses for Merrcy Hospital for the year ended June 30, 19X2.
2. Draft the appropriate disclosures in separate notes accompanying the statement of revenues and expenses, referencing each note to its respective item in the statement.

(AICPA adapted)

### P 22-5 Voluntary Health and Welfare Organizations: Preparation of a Statement of Support, Revenues, and Expenses and Changes in Fund Balances and a Balance Sheet

Following are the adjusted current funds trial balances of Westwinds Association for Handicapped Children, at June 30, 19X4:

### WESTWINDS ASSOCIATION FOR HANDICAPPED CHILDREN
### ADJUSTED CURRENT FUNDS TRIAL BALANCE, JUNE 30, 19X4

|  | Unrestricted | | Restricted | |
| --- | --- | --- | --- | --- |
|  | Dr. | Cr. | Dr. | Cr. |
| Cash | $ 40,000 |  | $ 9,000 |  |
| Bequest receivable |  |  | 5,000 |  |
| Pledges receivable | 12,000 |  |  |  |
| Accrued interest receivable | 1,000 |  |  |  |
| Investments (at cost, which approximates market) | 100,000 |  |  |  |
| Accounts payable and accrued expenses |  | 50,000 |  | 1,000 |
| Deferred revenue |  | 2,000 |  |  |
| Allowance for uncollectible pledges |  | 3,000 |  |  |
| Fund balances, July 1, 19X3: |  |  |  |  |
| Designated |  | 12,000 |  |  |
| Undesignated |  | 26,000 |  |  |
| Restricted |  |  |  | 3,000 |
| Transfers of endowment fund income |  | 20,000 |  |  |

*(continued)*

**■ ILLUSTRATION 22-30**
**Foggy Meadows Hospital Balance Sheet December 31, 19X7**

## GENERAL FUNDS

| Assets | 19X7 |
|---|---:|
| Current assets: | |
| Cash and cash equivalents | $ 2,000,000 |
| Assets whose use is limited—required for current liabilities | 950,000 |
| Patient accounts receivable, net of estimated uncollectibles of $2,500,000 | 12,000,000 |
| Estimated third-party payer settlements—Medicare | 500,000 |
| Supplies, at lower of cost or market | 1,200,000 |
| Other current assets | 200,000 |
| Total Current Assets | 16,850,000 |
| Assets whose use is limited: | |
| By board for capital improvements | 10,000,000 |
| By agreements with third-party payers for funded depreciation | 6,000,000 |
| Under malpractice funding arrangement—held by trustee | 2,400,000 |
| Under indenture agreement—held by trustee | 13,500,000 |
| Total Assets Whose Use Is Limited | 31,900,000 |
| Less assets whose use is limited and that are required for current liabilities | 950,000 |
| Noncurrent assets whose use is limited | 30,950,000 |
| Property and equipment, net | 80,000,000 |

| Liabilities and Fund Balances | 19X7 |
|---|---:|
| Current liabilities: | |
| Current installments of long-term debt | $ 950,000 |
| Current portion of capital lease obligations | 500,000 |
| Accounts payable | 2,000,000 |
| Accrued expenses | 1,200,000 |
| Estimated third-party payer settlements—Medicaid | 1,800,000 |
| Deferred third-party reimbursement | 200,000 |
| Current portion of estimated malpractice costs | 300,000 |
| Due to donor-restricted funds | 400,000 |
| Total Current Liabilities | 7,150,000 |
| Deferred third-party reimbursement | 450,000 |
| Estimated malpractice costs, net of current portion | 2,300,000 |
| Long-term debt, excluding current installments | 25,500,000 |
| Capital lease obligations, excluding current installments | 1,500,000 |
| Fund balance | 92,560,000 |

| | | | |
|---|---|---|---|
| Other assets: | | | |
| Prepaid pension cost | 60,000 | | |
| Deferred financing costs | 650,000 | | |
| Investment in affiliated company | 950,000 | Commitments and contingent liabilities | |
| Total Other Assets | 1,660,000 | | |
| | $129,460,000 | | $129,460,000 |

## DONOR-RESTRICTED FUNDS
### Specific-Purpose Funds

| | | | |
|---|---|---|---|
| Cash | $ 400,000 | Accounts payable | $ 200,000 |
| Investments, at cost which approximates market | 700,000 | Deferred grant revenue | 90,000 |
| Grants receivable | 600,000 | Fund balance | 1,410,000 |
| | $ 1,700,000 | | $ 1,700,000 |

### Fixed Asset Replacement and Expansion Funds

| | | | |
|---|---|---|---|
| Cash | $ 25,000 | | |
| Investments, at cost which approximates market | 260,000 | | |
| Pledges receivable, net of estimated uncollectibles of $60,000. | 140,000 | Fund balance | 675,000 |
| Due from general funds | 250,000 | | |
| | $ 675,000 | | $ 675,000 |

### Endowment Funds

| | | | |
|---|---|---|---|
| Cash | $ 1,300,000 | Fund balance | $ 4,950,000 |
| Investments, net of $175,000 valuation allowance | 3,500,000 | | |
| Due from general funds | 150,000 | | |
| | $ 4,950,000 | | $ 4,950,000 |

## WESTWINDS ASSOCIATION FOR HANDICAPPED CHILDREN
## ADJUSTED CURRENT FUNDS TRIAL BALANCE, JUNE 30, 19X4

| | Unrestricted | | Restricted | |
| --- | --- | --- | --- | --- |
| | Dr. | Cr. | Dr. | Cr. |
| Contributions.................... | | 300,000 | | 15,000 |
| Membership dues ............... | | 25,000 | | |
| Program service fees ............. | | 30,000 | | |
| Investment income .............. | | 10,000 | | |
| Deaf children's program........... | 120,000 | | | |
| Blind children's program.......... | 150,000 | | | |
| Management and general services.. | 45,000 | | 4,000 | |
| Fund-raising services............. | 8,000 | | 1,000 | |
| Provision for uncollectible pledges . | 2,000 | | | |
| | $478,000 | $478,000 | $19,000 | $19,000 |

**Required:**

1. Prepare a statement of support, revenue, and expenses and changes in fund balances, presenting each current fund separately, for the year ended June 30, 19X4.
2. Prepare a balance sheet, presenting each current fund separately as of June 30, 19X4.

(AICPA adapted)

<table><tr><td>

**P
22-6**

</td><td>

## Preparation of a Statement of Changes in Financial Position

The following are the June 30, 19X5 and 19X4, balance sheets of Discovery Foundation, a nonprofit research and scientific organization:

</td></tr></table>

## DISCOVERY FOUNDATION
## BALANCE SHEETS, JUNE 30, 19X5 AND 19X4

**Assets**

| | | |
| --- | --- | --- |
| Current assets: | | |
| Cash...................................... | $  650,000 | $  630,000 |
| Accounts receivable........................ | 744,000 | 712,000 |
| Unbilled contract revenues and reimbursement | | |
| grant expenses............................ | 976,000 | 780,000 |
| Prepaid expenses.......................... | 80,000 | 76,000 |
| Total Current Assets ................... | 2,450,000 | 2,198,000 |
| Investments and endowment fund cash .......... | 840,000 | 780,000 |
| Property, plant, and equipment | | |
| Land and building ......................... | 440,000 | 40,000 |
| Furniture and equipment .................... | 334,000 | 312,000 |
| Leased property under capital leases .......... | 958,000 | 958,000 |
| Total Property, Plant, and Equipment..... | 1,732,000 | 1,710,000 |
| Less accumulated depreciation and amortization | 518,000 | 370,000 |
| Net Property, Plant, and Equipment ...... | 1,214,000 | 1,340,000 |
| Total Assets ............................. | $4,504,000 | $4,318,000 |

**Liabilities and Fund Balances**
Current liabilities:

| | | |
|---|---:|---:|
| Accounts payable | $ 836,000 | $ 776,000 |
| Restricted grant advances | 522,000 | 420,000 |
| Obligations under capital leases | 176,000 | 164,000 |
| Total Current Liabilities | 1,534,000 | 1,360,000 |
| Noncurrent capital lease obligations | 618,000 | 794,000 |
| Total Liabilities | 2,152,000 | 2,154,000 |

Fund balances:

| | | |
|---|---:|---:|
| Unrestricted | 916,000 | 838,000 |
| Net equity in property, plant, and equipment | 596,000 | 546,000 |
| Endowment | 840,000 | 780,000 |
| Total Fund Balances | 2,352,000 | 2,164,000 |
| Total Liabilities and Fund Balances | $4,504,000 | $4,318,000 |

## Excerpts from Discovery Foundation's Notes to Financial Statements:

**Revenue Recognition:** Substantially all of the organization's revenue is derived from restricted grants and cost-plus-fixed-fee contracts. Revenue is recognized based on the proportion of project expenses incurred to total anticipated project expenses (percentage-of-completion method). Losses on contracts are recognized when identified.

**Fund Balance:** Of the $188,000 increase in fund balances from 19X4 to 19X5, $128,000 represents the results of current operating activities, and $60,000 represents capital additions from interest earned in Endowment Fund investments. The Endowment Fund, in the principal amount of $700,000, was received in 19X2. The donor of this fund specified that principal and accumulated interest not be expended until 19X0, at which time the fund, including accumulated interest, will be used for environmental research projects. Net equity in property, plant, and equipment is the carrying value of all property, plant, and equipment less related noncurrent liabilities to finance their acquisition. There were no dispositions of property, plant, and equipment during the year.

**Lease Commitments:** The organization uses scientific equipment under capital leases expiring in 19X1 that provide for the transfer of ownership of the equipment at the end of the lease term. The related future minimum lease payments as of June 30, 19X5, for subsequent fiscal years, are as follows:

| | |
|---|---:|
| 19X6 | $188,000 |
| 19X7 | 188,000 |
| 19X8 | 188,000 |
| 19X9 | 188,000 |
| 19X0 | 188,000 |
| 19X1 | 20,000 |
| Total | 960,000 |
| Less amount representing interest | (166,000) |
| Present value of minimum lease payments | $794,000 |

## Required:

Prepare the statement of changes in financial position, including the schedule of changes in working capital, for the year ended June 30, 19X5.

(AICPA adapted)

**P 22-7**

## Voluntary Health and Welfare Organizations: Preparation of Balance Sheets

The LollyPop Foundation, a voluntary health and welfare organization committed to funding research and education for certain childhood diseases, presents the following account listing for its current funds as of December 31, 19X1:

| | |
|---|---:|
| Cash | $1,200,000 |
| Cash—Restricted | 400,000 |
| Investments—Donor Restricted | 1,000,000 |
| Investments—Board Designated | 3,000,000 |
| Accounts Payable | 500,000 |
| Research Grants Payable | 600,000 |
| Fund Balance: Restricted for Research Grants | 500,000 |
| Contributions Designated for Future Periods | 400,000 |
| Pledges Receivable | 700,000 |
| Inventories of Educational Materials | 200,000 |
| Fund balance: Designated for Long-Term Investments | 2,000,000 |
| Prepaid Expenses | 100,000 |
| Allowance for Pledges | 100,000 |
| Fund balance: Restricted for Professional Education | 1,500,000 |
| Grants receivable—Restricted | 600,000 |
| Fund Balance: Undesignated | 1,600,000 |

### Required:

Prepare in good form balance sheets for the Current Unrestricted Fund and for the Current Restricted Fund as of December 31, 19X1.

**P 22-8**

## Symphony: Comments on Presentation Deficiencies, Preparation of Balance Sheet, and Comparisons with Other Nonprofit Organizations

### WASHINGTON SQUARE SYMPHONY
### BALANCE SHEET, FOR THE YEAR ENDED JUNE 30, 19X1

**Assets**

| | |
|---|---:|
| Cash | $ 200,000 |
| Marketable securities | 200,000 |
| Rent and other deposits | 100,000 |
| Investments and endowment funds cash | 500,000 |
| Grants receivable | 150,000 |
| Accounts receivable | 300,000 |
| Other | 100,000 |
| Property and equipment, at cost | 1,000,000 |
| | $2,550,000 |

**Liabilities and Fund Balance**

| | |
|---|---:|
| Long-term debt | $ 500,000 |
| Deferred revenues | 1,000,000 |
| Accounts payable and accrued expenses | 200,000 |
| Fund Balance | 850,000 |
| | $2,550,000 |

### Required:

1. Review the Washington Square Symphony balance sheet and comment on any observed deficiencies.
2. Recast the balance sheet in conformity with the *Audit Guide for Certain Non-profit Organizations.*
3. Compare the accounting practices of other nonprofit organizations with those of colleges and universities and voluntary health and welfare organizations in the following areas:
   a. Pledges
   b. Investments
   c. Fixed assets

---

**P 22-9** | **Continuing-care Retirement Community: Preparation of Statement of Revenue and Expenses and Changes in Fund Balance; Responding to Questions by the Governing Board.**

### SPREADING OAKS
### (A CONTINUING-CARE RETIREMENT COMMUNITY)
### STATEMENT OF REVENUE AND EXPENSES
### FOR THE YEAR ENDED DECEMBER 31, 19X1

**Revenue**

| | |
|---|---:|
| Resident services | $4,000,000 |
| Patient revenue from nonresidents | 250,000 |
| Contributions | 100,000 |
| Investment income | 110,000 |
| Change in obligation to provide future services and use of facilities to current residents | 15,000 |
| Total Revenue | $4,475,000 |

**Expenses**

| | |
|---|---:|
| Resident care | $ 650,000 |
| Dietary | 800,000 |
| Housekeeping | 200,000 |
| Plant | 500,000 |
| General and administrative | 400,000 |
| Depreciation | 450,000 |
| Interest | 300,000 |
| Total Expenses | $3,300,000 |
| Excess of revenue/expense | $1,175,000 |
| Fund balance beginning of year | 1,625,000 |
| Fund balance end of year | 2,800,000 |

### Required:

1. Recast the Spreading Oaks statement in accordance with *Audits of Providers of Health Care Services.*
2. As the accountant for Spreading Oaks, you have been asked to appear at a board meeting to answer questions from members of the board. Respond to the following in a manner that would be clear to a nonaccountant:

a. How is Revenue—Resident Services measured?

b. How is the distinction made between operating and nonoperating revenue? Why is it important?

c. What does the change in obligation to provide future services and use of facilities to current residents represent?

d. Does the excess of revenue/expense represent a useful stand-in for cash flow? Why not?

e. Does depreciation provide a "fund" for replacement of plant and equipment?

### ANSWERS TO SELF-STUDY QUESTIONS

1. b  Generally, hospitals do not record donated services because they are difficult to measure. However, they may be reported as an expense with a corresponding amount reported as contributions if (1) the services were significant, (2) they would be covered by paid personnel if uncovered by volunteers, (3) they are measurable, and (4) the entity controls the employment and duties of the volunteers.

2. c  ($500,000 − $60,000 = $440,000)   No; all of the pledge would be recognized in 19X1.

     Generally, all of the nonprofit organizations record the pledge, net of allowance for uncollectibles, except that colleges may elect to disclose the information in footnotes and other nonprofit organizations covered by *Statement of Position 78-10* can only record them if legally enforceable.

3. a  The fixed asset would be accounted for in donor-restricted funds.

4. c  Separation of restricted and unrestricted is important when assessing the organization's transferability and capital maintenance.

     They're recorded as additions to the Restricted Fund balance when received and are reclassified as revenues of general funds when expenditures are incurred for the purpose intended by the donor.

---

## Appendix A | ILLUSTRATED CURRENT FUNDS GROUP TRANSACTIONS: COLLEGES AND UNIVERSITIES

The following sections illustrate the accounting for Current Funds Group transactions.

**ILLUSTRATION**

### Unrestricted Current Funds Subgroup Transactions

The following journal entries pertain to financial events and transactions of Andover University's Unrestricted Current Funds for the year ended June 30, 19X2.

1. Student tuition and fees billed for the year were $8,000,000, which was used for educational and general purposes. Prior experience shows that $100,000 of this billing will be uncollectible. At year-end, $800,000 remains uncollected.

| | | |
|---|---:|---:|
| Cash | 7,200,000 | |
| Accounts Receivable | 800,000 | |
| Expenditures—Instruction | 100,000 | |
| Revenue—Student Tuition and Fees | | 8,000,000 |
| Allowance for Bad Debts | | 100,000 |

2. Unrestricted government appropriations for the year amounted to $5,000,000, all of which have been collected.

| | | |
|---|---:|---:|
| Cash | 5,000,000 | |
| Revenue—Government Appropriations | | 5,000,000 |

3. Unrestricted gifts and private grants received during the period amounted to $50,000.

| | | |
|---|---:|---:|
| Cash | 50,000 | |
| Revenue—Gifts and Private Grants | | 50,000 |

4. Unrestricted income from endowment and similar funds amounted to $185,000.

| | | |
|---|---:|---:|
| Cash | 185,000 | |
| Revenue—Endowment Income | | 185,000 |

5. Auxiliary enterprise included $175,000 from student residence halls; $200,000 from cafeterias; and $750,000 from the college store sales. All billed amounts have been collected except for $50,000 in student residence fees. Of this amount, an estimated $5,000 will be uncollectible.

| | | |
|---|---:|---:|
| Cash | 1,075,000 | |
| Accounts Receivable | 50,000 | |
| Expenditures—Auxiliary Enterprises | 5,000 | |
| Revenue—Auxiliary Enterprises | | 1,125,000 |
| Allowance for Bad Debts | | 5,000 |

6. Term endowment funds that are now available for unrestricted use amount to $300,000.

| | | |
|---|---:|---:|
| Cash | 300,000 | |
| Revenue—Endowment Income | | 300,000 |

7. Purchases of materials and supplies amounted to $800,000 for the year. A perpetual inventory is used. Purchases of $150,000 remain unpaid at year-end.

| Materials and Supplies Inventory | 800,000 | |
| Cash | | 650,000 |
| Vouchers Payable | | 150,000 |

8. Operating expenditures are incurred and assigned as shown in the following journal entry. Note that $2,250,000 of these expenditures are unpaid vouchers payable at year-end.

| Expenditures—Instruction | 3,500,000 | |
| Expenditures—Research | 1,200,000 | |
| Expenditures—Academic Support | 3,000,000 | |
| Expenditures—Student Services | 380,000 | |
| Expenditures—Operation and Maintenance of Plant | 1,120,000 | |
| Expenditures—Institutional Support | 500,000 | |
| Cash | | 7,450,000 |
| Vouchers Payable | | 2,250,000 |

9. Use of materials and supplies is assigned as shown in the following journal entry:

| Expenditures—Instruction | 300,000 | |
| Expenditures—Research | 150,000 | |
| Expenditures—Academic Support | 50,000 | |
| Expenditures—Student Services | 25,000 | |
| Expenditures—Institutional Support | 120,000 | |
| Materials and Supplies Inventory | | 645,000 |

10. The university's student aid committee granted student tuition and fee reductions of $200,000.

| Expenditures—Student Aid | 200,000 | |
| Accounts Receivable | | 200,000 |

11. The trustees have specified that certain Current Fund revenues must be transferred to meet the debt service provisions relating to the university's institutional properties, including amounts set aside for debt retirement, interest, and required provisions for renewal and replacement. For this year, these mandatory transfers total $550,000.

| Transfers—Plant Funds | 550,000 | |
| Cash | | 550,000 |

12. Auxiliary enterprises expenditures amount to $650,000.

| Expenditures—Auxiliary Enterprises | 650,000 | |
| Vouchers Payable (Cash) | | 650,000 |

13. Closing entries are not illustrated. Revenues, expenditures, and transfers are merely closed to the Fund Balance account.

**ILLUSTRATION** ## Restricted Current Funds Subgroup Transactions

The following journal entries pertain to financial events and transactions of Andover University's Restricted Current Funds for the year ended June 30, 19X2.

1. Restricted gifts in the amount of $100,000 were received from the Wollaston Foundation to be used for student aid.

| | | |
|---|---|---|
| Cash | 100,000 | |
|     Fund Balance[15] | | 100,000 |

2. A $750,000 federal government grant was received for library acquisitions in science and engineering.

| | | |
|---|---|---|
| Cash | 750,000 | |
|     Fund Balance | | 750,000 |

3. Federal government contracts were awarded to certain academic departments to develop training programs and instructional institutes for child care and development. These contracts amounted to $1,500,000 and included a provision for reimbursement to the university of indirect costs of $75,000. The contract payments were collected.

| | | |
|---|---|---|
| Cash | 1,500,000 | |
|     Fund Balance | | 1,500,000 |
| Fund Balance | 75,000 | |
|     Cash | | 75,000 |

The latter entry transfers the indirect cost recovery to the Unrestricted Current Fund, which would acknowledge receipt of the payment with the following entry:

| | | |
|---|---|---|
| Cash | 75,000 | |
|     Revenue—General | | 75,000 |

4. Expenditures incurred were for: student aid, $85,000; instruction (library acquisitions), $700,000; training programs and instructional institutes, $1,425,000. At year-end, 10% of the expenditures remain unpaid.

---

[15]Subsidiary accounts would usually show the sources, purposes, and applications of restricted resources.

| Expenditures—Student Aid | 85,000 | |
| Expenditures—Instruction | 700,000 | |
| Expenditures—Instruction | 1,425,000 | |
| Cash | | 1,989,000 |
| Vouchers Payable | | 221,000 |
| Fund Balance | 2,210,000 | |
| Revenue—Student Aid | | 85,000 |
| Revenue—Instruction | | 2,125,000 |

5. Closing entries are not illustrated. (Because total revenues equal total expenditures, these accounts offset each other in the closing entry.)

## Appendix B ILLUSTRATED PLANT FUNDS GROUP TRANSACTIONS: COLLEGES AND UNIVERSITIES

The following sections illustrate accounting for Plant Funds Group transactions.

ILLUSTRATION

### Plant Funds Group Transactions

The following journal entries pertain to transactions of Andover University's Plant Funds Group for the year ended June 30, 19X2. First we illustrate Unexpended Plant Fund activities.

1. A major fund-raising drive for new laboratory equipment generated $300,000 cash and $250,000 in marketable securities.

| Cash | 300,000 | |
| Marketable Securities | 250,000 | |
| Fund Balance—Restricted | | 550,000 |

2. The university received a federal grant of $1,000,000 for the construction of a new classroom wing for the science department. The grant requires the university to match the government appropriation.

| Cash | 1,000,000 | |
| Fund Balance—Restricted | | 1,000,000 |

3. The university's governing board directed a transfer from Unrestricted Current Funds for the construction of the new classroom wing for the science department. The $1,000,000 transfer complied with the government's building grant.

| Cash | 1,000,000 | |
| Fund Balance—Restricted | | 1,000,000 |

4. The addition to the science department building was completed during the year and cost the university $2,500,000. A mortgage was signed for $500,000.

| | | |
|---|---:|---:|
| Cash | 500,000 | |
|     Mortgage Payable | | 500,000 |
| Construction in Progress | 2,500,000 | |
|     Cash | | 2,500,000 |
| Mortgage Payable[16] | 500,000 | |
| Fund Balance—Restricted | 2,000,000 | |
|     Construction in Progress | | 2,500,000 |

5. Income from pooled investments totaled $25,000.

| | | |
|---|---:|---:|
| Cash | 25,000 | |
|     Fund Balance—Unrestricted | | 25,000 |

6. A planned expansion of the university's sports stadium was abandoned because of cutbacks in available federal funds. The governing board directed the return of $400,000 to Unrestricted Current Funds.

| | | |
|---|---:|---:|
| Fund Balance—Unrestricted | 400,000 | |
|     Cash[17] | | 400,000 |

7. Expenses of $20,000 were incurred in connection with fund-raising activities for the new science department classroom wing and laboratory equipment.

| | | |
|---|---:|---:|
| Fund Balance—Unrestricted | 20,000 | |
|     Cash | | 20,000 |

Now we cover Renewals and Replacement Fund activities.

1. Income from pooled investments totaled $15,000.

| | | |
|---|---:|---:|
| Cash | 15,000 | |
|     Fund Balance—Unrestricted | | 15,000 |

2. The governing board transferred cash to the Renewals and Replacements Fund for equipment replacement in the science department, $80,000.

---

[16]This entry transfers the building cost and mortgage to the investment in Plant Fund account.
[17]The Unrestricted Current Fund would credit the Transfers—Unexpended Plant Fund account.

| Cash[18] | 80,000 | |
|---|---|---|
| Fund Balance—Unrestricted | | 80,000 |

3. Replacement equipment was purchased for the science department for $78,000.

| Fund Balance—Unrestricted[19] | 78,000 | |
|---|---|---|
| Cash | | 78,000 |

The Retirement of Indebtedness Fund has the following activity:

1. Income earned from pooled investments amounts to $10,000.

| Cash | 10,000 | |
|---|---|---|
| Fund Balance—Unrestricted | | 10,000 |

2. The governing board transferred $250,000 to the Retirement of Indebtedness Fund for interest and principal payments on debt. The debt payments were made.

| Cash | 250,000 | |
|---|---|---|
| Fund Balance—Unrestricted | | 250,000 |

| Fund Balance—Unrestricted | 250,000 | |
|---|---|---|
| Cash | | 250,000 |

The Investment in Plant Fund has the following activity:

1. Completed science building is transferred from Unexpended Plant Fund (see transaction 4, Unexpended Plant Fund).

| Building (science) | 2,500,000 | |
|---|---|---|
| Mortgage Payable | | 500,000 |
| Net Investment in Plant | | 2,000,000 |

2. Replacement equipment is transferred from the Renewals and Replacement Fund (see transaction 3, Renewals and Replacement Fund).

| Equipment (science) | 78,000 | |
|---|---|---|
| Net Investment in Plant | | 78,000 |

3. Mortgage payable is reduced (see transaction 2, Retirement of Indebtedness Fund).

---

[18]The Unrestricted Current Fund would charge the Transfers—Plant Funds Renewals and Replacements account.

[19]This entry transfers the equipment cost to the Investment in Plant Fund account.

| Mortgage Payable | 250,000 | |
| Net Investment in Plant | | 250,000 |

4. The university received an art collection and several rare books for its library. The appraised values were $325,000 for the art collection and $200,000 for the rare books.

| Valued Collections—Art | 325,000 | |
| Valued Collections—Rare Books | 200,000 | |
| Net Investment in Plant | | 525,000 |

5. The laboratory equipment that was replaced was sold for $30,000. The recorded value of the equipment was $55,000.

| Net Investment in Plant[20] | 55,000 | |
| Equipment (science) | | 55,000 |

6. Assuming Andover University is a private university, under the provisions of *FASB Statement No. 93*, it would be required to recognize depreciation of long-lived assets in general purpose financial statements. Although *FASB Statement No. 93* does not provide specific guidance where or how depreciation should be charged, generally universities would make the following entry in the Investment in Plant Fund:

| Depreciation Expense | xxxxxx | |
| Accumulated Depreciation | | xxxxxx |

## Appendix C    ILLUSTRATED GENERAL FUNDS TRANSACTIONS: HOSPITALS

ILLUSTRATION

### General Funds Transactions

The following journal entries pertain to the financial events and transactions of Charleston Memorial Hospital's General Funds for the year ended June 30, 19X1:

1. Gross billings to patients for the year were assigned as shown in the following entry:

| Patient Accounts Receivable | 4,050,000 | |
| Patient Service Revenue | | 4,050,000 |

[20]The sales proceeds could be accounted for by the Unrestricted Current Fund or by the Unexpended Plant Funds, depending on the disposition of the funds.

Typically, more detailed revenue accounts are maintained by specific revenue producing segments (for example, Daily Patient Services: cardiac unit).

2. Adjustments made to gross revenue include contractual adjustments of $500,000 with third-party payers and ~~approved charity~~ adjustments of $200,000.

| | | |
|---|---|---|
| Patient Service Revenue..................... | 700,000 | |
|     Patient Accounts Receivable ............ | | 700,000 |

3. Collection of accounts receivable totaled $3,350,000.

| | | |
|---|---|---|
| Cash......................................... | 3,350,000 | |
|     Patient Accounts Receivable ............ | | 3,350,000 |

4. Inventory acquisitions, including materials and supplies, amounted to $700,000. One-fourth of the approved invoices remain unpaid at year-end.

| | | |
|---|---|---|
| Materials and Supplies Inventory ............ | 700,000 | |
|     Cash...................................... | | 525,000 |
|     Vouchers Payable........................ | | 175,000 |

5. Use of the materials and supplies inventory is assigned as shown in the following entry:

| | | |
|---|---|---|
| Expense—Professional Care of Patients[21]..... | 190,000 | |
| Expense—Dietary Services .................. | 75,000 | |
| Expense—General Services.................. | 300,000 | |
| Expense—Administrative Services........... | 15,000 | |
|     Materials and Supplies Inventory ....... | | 580,000 |

6. Salaries and wage expenses incurred for the year total $2,200,000. Of this amount, $176,000 is accrued at year-end.

| | | |
|---|---|---|
| Expense—Professional Care of Patients ...... | 1,000,000 | |
| Expense—Dietary Services .................. | 700,000 | |
| Expense—General Services.................. | 300,000 | |
| Expense—Administrative Services........... | 200,000 | |
|     Cash...................................... | | 2,204,000 |
|     Accrued Salaries and Wages ............ | | 176,000 |

7. Other operating expenses processed through the voucher system are assigned as shown, including $18,000 of approved but unpaid vouchers at year-end.

---

[21]In practice, hospitals maintain detailed expense control accounts and even more detailed subsidiary accounts for managerial control purposes.

| | | |
|---|---|---|
| Expense—Professional Care of Patients . . . . . . | 75,000 | |
| Expense—Dietary Services . . . . . . . . . . . . . . . . . | 50,000 | |
| Expense—General Services . . . . . . . . . . . . . . . . | 30,000 | |
| Expense—Administrative Services. . . . . . . . . . . | 45,000 | |
| Cash. . . . . . . . . . . . . . . . . . . . . . . . . . . . . . . . . . . | | 182,000 |
| Vouchers Payable. . . . . . . . . . . . . . . . . . . . . . | | 18,000 |

8. The provision for estimated uncollectible accounts is $125,000.

| | | |
|---|---|---|
| Provision for Uncollectible Accounts . . . . . . . . | 125,000 | |
| Allowance for Uncollectible Accounts. . . | | 125,000 |

9. Depreciation expense for the year is $350,000. This provision is based on historical cost, which conforms with generally accepted accounting principles. Hospitals may compute depreciation expense based on replacement cost for internal management purposes.

| | | |
|---|---|---|
| Expense—Depreciation[22]. . . . . . . . . . . . . . . . . . . . | 350,000 | |
| Accumulated Depreciation . . . . . . . . . . . . . | | 350,000 |

10. Estimated malpractice costs for the year were $1,125,000.

| | | |
|---|---|---|
| Medical Malpractice Costs . . . . . . . . . . . . . . . . . | 1,125,000 | |
| Estimated Malpractice Costs Pay. . . . . . . | | 1,125,000 |

11. Interfunds transfers for the year to the General Funds are recorded as shown.[23]

| | | |
|---|---|---|
| Cash. . . . . . . . . . . . . . . . . . . . . . . . . . . . . . . . . . . . . | 945,000 | |
| Revenue—[24]Transfers from Specific | | |
| Purpose Fund . . . . . . . . . . . . . . . . . . . . . . | | 320,000 |

*(continued)*

[22]Generally, for reporting purposes, depreciation is not charged to the functional areas (for example, Expenses—Nursing Services). For internal management purposes, depreciation is charged to subsidiary expense accounts by cost center.

[23]Receipts of restricted resources by the Specific Purpose, Plant Renewal and Replacement, and Endowment funds are credited directly to the respective Fund Balance. All subsequent earnings from investments of these resources are also credited to Fund Balance. When the General Funds expend resources for the designated purpose, the affected restricted fund charges Fund Balance and credits Cash or an interfund payable. The Unrestricted Fund acknowledges receipt of the transfer by a charge to Cash and a credit to Other Revenue—Transfers.

[24]The following entries would be recorded by the other funds reflecting transfers to the Unrestricted Fund.

| | | |
|---|---|---|
| Specific Purpose Fund: | | |
| Fund Balance . . . . . . . . . . . . . . . . . . . . . . . . . . . . . . | 320,000 | |
| Cash. . . . . . . . . . . . . . . . . . . . . . . . . . . . . . . . . . . . | | 320,000 |
| Plant Renewal and Replacement Fund: | | |
| Fund Balance . . . . . . . . . . . . . . . . . . . . . . . . . . . . . . | 500,000 | |
| Cash. . . . . . . . . . . . . . . . . . . . . . . . . . . . . . . . . . . . | | 500,000 |
| Endowment Fund: | | |
| Fund Balance . . . . . . . . . . . . . . . . . . . . . . . . . . . . . . | 125,000 | |
| Cash. . . . . . . . . . . . . . . . . . . . . . . . . . . . . . . . . . . . | | 125,000 |

|  |  |  |
|---|---|---|
| Revenue—Transfers from Endowment Fund | 125,000 |  |
| Fund Balance—General Funds: Transfers from Plant Replacement and Expansion Funds | 500,000 |  |

12. Closing entries are not shown. Revenues, expenses, charity services, contractual adjustments, and the provision for uncollectibles are merely closed to Fund Balance.

<br>

**Appendix D**

# ILLUSTRATED TRANSACTIONS FOR ENDOWMENT AND SIMILAR FUNDS, AGENCY FUNDS, ANNUITY FUNDS, LIFE INCOME FUNDS, AND LOAN FUNDS

## Endowment and Similar Funds

ILLUSTRATION

### Endowment and Similar Funds Group Transactions

The following journal entries pertain to transactions of Andover University's Endowment and Similar Funds Group.

1. The Quincy family established an Endowment Fund, the income from which should be used to maintain the university's rare books collection. This permanent endowment does not restrict the investment of the funds.

|  |  |  |
|---|---|---|
| Cash | 350,000 |  |
| Fund Balance—Endowment | | 350,000 |

2. The university's board of trustees directed the accounting officer to establish a Quasi-Endowment Fund of $200,000. The income is to be used to maintain the campus theater. No restrictions were imposed on the investment of the funds. The transfer was made from Unrestricted Current Fund.

|  |  |  |
|---|---|---|
| Cash | 200,000 |  |
| Fund Balance—Endowment[25] | | 200,000 |

3. Coulomb Corporation established an Endowment Fund in the amount of $150,000, the income from which will augment a professorial chair in electrical engineering. The endowment instrument stipulates that

---

[25]Unrestricted Current Fund:

|  |  |  |
|---|---|---|
| Transfers—Endowment and Similar Funds | 200,000 |  |
| Cash | | 200,000 |

all income and investment gains are expendable for salary augmentation for five years. At the end of the fifth year, the principal is to be used to replace equipment in the engineering laboratories.

| | | |
|---|---|---|
| Cash. . . . . . . . . . . . . . . . . . . . . . . . . . . . . . . . . . . . . | 150,000 | |
| Fund Balance—Term Endowment . . . . . . . | | 150,000 |

4. Investment earnings from pooled investments totaled $19,500, received as shown:

| | | |
|---|---|---|
| Cash. . . . . . . . . . . . . . . . . . . . . . . . . . . . . . . . . . . . . | 19,500 | |
| Fund Balance—Endowment . . . . . . . . . . . . | | 6,500 |
| Fund Balance—Term Endowment . . . . . . . | | 8,000 |
| Fund Balance—Quasi-Endowment . . . . . . | | 5,000 |

5. Salary augmentation payments for the professorial chair in electrical engineering amount to $6,500.

| | | |
|---|---|---|
| Fund Balance—Term Endowment[26]. . . . . . . . . . | 6,500 | |
| Cash . . . . . . . . . . . . . . . . . . . . . . . . . . . . . . . . . . | | 6,500 |

## Agency Funds

## Agency Fund Transactions

The following journal entries pertain to Andover University's Agency Fund transactions.

1. Student government fees collected during the registration process are deposited in the student government fund.

| | | |
|---|---|---|
| Cash. . . . . . . . . . . . . . . . . . . . . . . . . . . . . . . . . . . . . | 25,000 | |
| Fund Balance—Agency (liability). . . . . . . . | | 25,000 |

2. Income earned from student government fund investments amounted to $2,000.

| | | |
|---|---|---|
| Cash. . . . . . . . . . . . . . . . . . . . . . . . . . . . . . . . . . . . . | 2,000 | |
| Fund Balance—Agency . . . . . . . . . . . . . . . . . | | 2,000 |

---

[26]Restricted Current Fund:

| | | |
|---|---|---|
| Cash . . . . . . . . . . . . . . . . . . . . . . . . . . . . . . . . . . . . | 6,500 | |
| Fund Balance—Endowment Fund . . . . . . . . . . . . . . . . . . . | | 6,500 |
| Then, as expended: | | |
| Fund Balance—Endowment Fund . . . . . . . . . . . . . . . . . . . . . | 6,500 | |
| Revenue—Instruction . . . . . . . . . . . . . . . . . . . . . . . . . | | 6,500 |

3. Authorized disbursements for the period amounted to $7,500.

| | | |
|---|---|---|
| Fund Balance—Agency | 7,500 | |
| Cash | | 7,500 |

4. Fund maintenance charges were $350.

| | | |
|---|---|---|
| Fund Balance—Agency | 350 | |
| Cash | | 350 |

## Annuity Funds

### Annuity Funds Group Transactions

The following journal entries show Andover University's Annuity Funds Group transactions.

1. Phyllis Sims donated $250,000 to the university with the stipulation that she receive $20,000 per year for the rest of her life. Thereafter, the principal should be used to provide student aid. The acturial value of the annuity is $85,000.

| | | |
|---|---|---|
| Cash | 250,000 | |
|     Annuities Payable | | 85,000 |
|     Fund Balance—Annuity | | 165,000 |

2. Net investment gains for the period were $24,000, and investment income was $14,000.

| | | |
|---|---|---|
| Cash | 38,000 | |
|     Annuities Payable | | 38,000 |

3. Payments to annuitant Phyllis Sims were $20,000.

| | | |
|---|---|---|
| Annuities Payable | 20,000 | |
|     Cash | | 20,000 |

4. There was a periodic adjustment for the actuarial gain due to recomputation of the liability based on the revised life expectancies of all annuitants.

| | | |
|---|---|---|
| Annuities Payable | 53,500 | |
|     Fund Balance—Annuity | | 53,500 |

5. Annuitant Josh Gaylord died. The annuity was transferred to the Endowment Funds Group according to the provisions of the gift instrument.

| | | |
|---|---|---|
| Annuities Payable | 1,500 | |
| Fund Balance—Annuity | 23,000 | |
| Cash | | 24,500 |

## Life Income Funds

 ### Life Income Funds Group Transactions

The following journal entries show Andover University's Life Income Fund Group transactions.

1. Gerald Baumann established a Life Income Fund, which specified that at his death the principal is to be transferred to the Unrestricted Current Fund group and used at the discretion of the board of trustees.

| | | |
|---|---|---|
| Cash | 50,000 | |
| Investments | 150,000 | |
| Fund Balance—Life Income | | 200,000 |

2. Income earned on investments amounted to $15,000.

| | | |
|---|---|---|
| Cash | 15,000 | |
| Income Payable | | 15,000 |

3. Life Income Fund distributions amounted to $15,000.

| | | |
|---|---|---|
| Income Payable | 15,000 | |
| Cash | | 15,000 |

4. The Erika Meagher Life Income Fund was transferred to Endowment Funds in accordance with the provisions of the gift instrument.

| | | |
|---|---|---|
| Fund Balance—Life Income | 100,000 | |
| Cash | | 100,000 |

## Loan Funds

### Loan Fund Transactions

The following journal entries show Andover University's Loan Fund transactions.

1. A fund-raising drive for student loan funds generated $750,000.

| | | |
|---|---|---|
| Cash | 750,000 | |
| Fund Balance—Loan | | 750,000 |

2. The board of trustees directed the use of $200,000 of Unrestricted Current Funds for low interest real estate loans to the faculty.

| | | |
|---|---|---|
| Cash[27] | 200,000 | |
| Fund Balance—Loan | | 200,000 |

3. Loans to students and faculty totaled $500,000. An allowance for uncollectible loans was established for 1% of this amount.

| | | |
|---|---|---|
| Notes Receivable | 500,000 | |
| Cash | | 500,000 |
| Fund Balance—Loan | 5,000 | |
| Allowance for Doubtful Loans | | 5,000 |

4. Excess cash of $400,000 was invested in marketable securities.

| | | |
|---|---|---|
| Investments | 400,000 | |
| Cash | | 400,000 |

5. Investment income earned amounted to $8,000.

| | | |
|---|---|---|
| Cash | 8,000 | |
| Fund Balance—Loan | | 8,000 |

6. Certain notes having a face amount of $25,000 proved to be uncollectible and were written off.

| | | |
|---|---|---|
| Allowance for Doubtful Loans | 25,000 | |
| Notes Receivable | | 25,000 |

7. Administrative and collection costs for the period amounted to $4,000.

| | | |
|---|---|---|
| Fund Balance—Loan | 4,000 | |
| Cash | | 4,000 |

[27]Unrestricted Current Funds:

| | | |
|---|---|---|
| Transfer—Endowment Fund | 200,000 | |
| Cash | | 200,000 |

## Appendix E  INVESTMENT POOLS

Nonprofit organizations frequently pool the investments of their various funds. Pooling provides several advantages, including increased investment flexibility, enhanced protection of fund principal through broad diversification, and, in some cases, lower investment costs.

Nonprofit organizations commonly use both pooled and nonpooled investments. Provisions in a gift instrument may prohibit participation in pooled investment schemes. In some cases, several pools are used so that different investment objectives may be accommodated. For example, certain endowment funds may be invested in one investment pool to obtain a high rate of investment income and protection of principal. Other funds could be placed in investment pools with a goal of capital appreciation.

The use of investment pooling requires careful attention to an accounting system that ensures equitable determination of principal, allocation of realized and unrealized gains or losses, and income. The method most generally in use and one specified in the audit guides is the market value unit method.

The **market value unit method** assigns units in the investment pool to individual participating funds. The number of units assigned to a participating fund is calculated on the basis of the market value of the total assets of the pool when the specific fund enters the pool. This method is similar to the method used with open-end investment trusts or mutual funds.

ILLUSTRATION  ### Investment Pool Transactions

1. Four funds of Andover University form an investment pool and contribute cash as shown in the following schedule:

| | |
|---|---:|
| Quasi-Endowment Fund | $ 20,000 |
| Endowment Fund | 30,000 |
| Unrestricted Fund | 40,000 |
| Plant Fund Group | 10,000 |
| | $100,000 |

An arbitrarily determined value per unit is selected. Subsequently, value per unit is determined by dividing the current market value of all net assets in the investment pool by the number of outstanding units.

| Fund | Unit Value | Units | Market Value |
|---|---:|---:|---:|
| Quasi-Endowment Fund | $10 | 2,000 | $20,000 |
| Endowment Fund | 10 | 3,000 | 30,000 |

(continued)

| Fund | Unit Value | Units | Market Value |
|---|---|---|---|
| Unrestricted Fund . . . . . . . . . . . . . . . . . . | 10 | 4,000 | 40,000 |
| Plant Fund Group. . . . . . . . . . . . . . . . . . | 10 | 4,000 | 10,000 |
| | | 10,000 | $100,000 |

2. During the first quarter, the board of trustees authorizes the withdrawal of $10,000 of the Quasi-Endowment Fund's investment in the pool. Calculation of the number of units withdrawn is as follows:

$$\text{units withdrawn} = \frac{\text{amount withdrawn}}{\text{market value per unit}} = \frac{\$10,000}{\$10} = 1,000 \text{ units}$$

Market value per unit is from the previous valuation date. After the withdrawal, the investment pool contains the following funds:

| Fund | Unit Value | Units | Market Value |
|---|---|---|---|
| Quasi-Endowment Fund . . . . . . . . . . . . | $10 | 1,000 | $10,000 |
| Endowment Fund . . . . . . . . . . . . . . . . . . | 10 | 3,000 | 30,000 |
| Unrestricted Fund . . . . . . . . . . . . . . . . . | 10 | 4,000 | 40,000 |
| Plant Fund Group. . . . . . . . . . . . . . . . . . | 10 | 1,000 | 10,000 |
| | | 9,000 | $90,000 |

The following funds made additional investments to the investment pool during the second quarter:

| | |
|---|---|
| Plant Fund Group. . . . . . . . . . . . . . . . . . . . . . . . . . . . . . . . . . . . . . . . | $15,000 |
| Life Income Funds Group. . . . . . . . . . . . . . . . . . . . . . . . . . . . . . . . | 30,000 |

The value per unit of funds currently in the investment pool is calculated as follows:

$$\text{Market Value per Unit} = \frac{\text{Total Market Value}}{\text{Units Outstanding}} = \frac{\$108,000}{9,000} = \$12$$

The units allocated to each additional investment are determined by dividing the amount of each additional investment by the corresponding current unit value:

| Fund | Addition | Units |
|---|---|---|
| Plant Funds Group. . . . . . . . . . . . . . . . . . . . . . . . | $15,000 | 1,250 |
| Life Income Funds Group . . . . . . . . . . . . . . . . . . . . | 30,000 | 2,500 |

Immediately after this transaction, the fund includes the following:

| Fund | Unit Value | Units | Market Value |
|---|---|---|---|
| Quasi-Endowment Fund . . . . . . . . . . . . | $12 | 1,000 | $12,000 |
| Endowment Fund . . . . . . . . . . . . . . . . . . | 12 | 3,000 | 36,000 |
| Unrestricted Fund . . . . . . . . . . . . . . . . | 12 | 4,000 | 48,000 |
| Plant Fund Group . . . . . . . . . . . . . . . . . | 12 | 2,250 | 27,000 |
| Life Income Funds Group . . . . . . . . . . | 12 | 2,500 | 30,000 |
| | | 12,750 | $153,000 |

Income distributions, including gains or losses on sales of investments, is allocated by dividing the total income available by the total units.

# PARTNERSHIPS

■ ■ ■ ■ ■

# 23
**. . . . .**

# PARTNERSHIPS: FORMATION AND OPERATION

## TOPIC OUTLINE

# CHAPTER OVERVIEW

**A** **partnership** is an association of two or more persons who contribute money, property, or services to carry on as co-owners of a business, the profits and losses of which are shared in an agreed-upon manner. The term **person** refers to individuals, corporations, and even other partnerships. Indeed, most partners are individuals. Partnerships that comprise one or more partnerships or corporations usually are formed to combine managerial talent and financial resources to conduct a specific undertaking—for example, the design and development of a large shopping center. Such partnerships are commonly referred to as *joint ventures*. Regardless of whether the partners are individuals, other partnerships, or corporations, the accounting and tax issues are the same.

Chapters 23 to 25 deal with **general partnerships**—that is, partnerships in which each partner is personally liable to the partnership's creditors if partnership assets are insufficient to pay such creditors. In Appendix A of this chapter we briefly discuss **limited partnerships,** in which certain partners (called *limited partners*) are not personally liable to the partnership's creditors if partnership assets are insufficient to pay such creditors.

## Introduction to the Professional Corporation

**Why They Were Created.**    Traditionally, the partnership form of organization has been used by small retail establishments and businesses that are considered the professions—for example, public accounting, law, and medicine. Such professions could not incorporate under the existing laws. In the late 1960s, more and more professionals recognized that much greater tax benefits were available with the corporate form of organization, primarily with respect to pension, profit-sharing, medical, and insurance plans. Consequently, many professional people made considerable efforts to urge legislation that would allow professional businesses to incorporate. Their efforts were so successful that each of the 50 states now has some form of legislation on the books, under the broad category of **professional corporations,** enabling professional businesses to incorporate.

**Their Explosive Growth.**    Initially, the Internal Revenue Service (IRS) did not recognize professional corporations as corporations for federal income tax reporting purposes. In 1969, however, after a continuous series of court defeats, the IRS issued regulations recognizing the professional corporation as a corporation for federal tax purposes. As a result of this change, many existing partnerships (as well as many sole proprietorships) have incorporated. Furthermore, substantial numbers of new businesses, which would have been conducted as either partnerships or sole proprietorships, have chosen the professional corporation form of business. Even one of the "Big 6" public accounting firms had plans in 1982 to change from a partnership to a professional corporation. In 1984, tax legislation designed to achieve parity became effective, enabling partnerships and sole proprietorships to obtain almost the same tax benefits available to professional corporations. Thus, a great deal of the advantage of incorporating was eliminated. As a result, the mushrooming growth of the professional corporation form of business ended, and some shift (although not explosive) away from the professional corporation form has occurred.

Because an accountant rendering services to a professional can expect to encounter a professional corporation as often as a partnership, a limited discussion of professional corporations is included at the end of this chapter. The advantages and disadvantages of professional incorporation must be carefully weighed against the advantages and disadvantages of either the partnership or sole proprietorship form of organization. Furthermore, the accountant can expect to be a key consultant in choosing the form of organization. (According to the latest IRS publications, over 1.5 million partnerships exist, which is over a 50% increase in the last 20 years.)

## MAJOR FEATURES OF THE PARTNERSHIP FORM OF BUSINESS

**Ease of Formation.**   Forming a partnership is a relatively simple process. The partners merely put their agreement into writing concerning who contributes assets or services, who performs which functions in the business, and how profits and losses are shared. The written document is called the **partnership agreement.**

Thus, compared with the corporation form of business, a partnership need not prepare articles of incorporation, write bylaws, print stock certificates, prepare minutes of the first meeting of the board of directors, pay state incorporation fees, or register stocks.

**Potential Noncontinuity of Existence.**   Historically, the possibility that the operations of a partnership could not continue after the death or withdrawal of a partner (with the business subsequently liquidated) was considered a major disadvantage of the partnership form of organization. In practice, this problem occurs only for small partnerships. Even then, some steps can be taken to minimize the impact of the loss of a partner. For example, life insurance proceeds on the death of a partner can be used to settle with the deceased partner's estate, thus conserving the assets of the business so that the remaining partners can continue the operation. For larger partnerships, this feature usually is not significant.

Some of the largest partnerships have more than 1,000 partners. Obviously, the loss of one or even several partners in a partnership of such size has minimal impact on the day-to-day operations of the business.

**Difficulty in Disposing of Interest.** An ownership interest in a partnership is a personal asset, as is the ownership of stock in a corporation. No formal established marketplace exists for the sale of a partnership interest, however, as for the sale of stock in a publicly owned corporation. Accordingly, a partner who wishes to sell or assign his or her partnership interest will have more difficulty finding a buyer than a shareholder who wishes to sell stock in a publicly owned corporation. To make this process even more difficult, the person buying a partnership interest does not have the automatic right to participate in the management of the business—the consent of the remaining partners is necessary.

**Unlimited Liability.** If a partnership's assets are insufficient to pay its creditors, the creditors have recourse to the personal assets of any and all general partners of the partnership. This characteristic contrasts sharply with the corporate form of organization, in which the personal assets of the shareholders are insulated from the corporation's creditors. This is undoubtedly the major disadvantage of the partnership form of organization.

**Mutual Agency.** The partnership is bound by each partner acting within the scope of partnership activities. Thus, each partner acts as an agent for the partnership in dealing with persons outside the partnership.

**Sharing of Profits and Losses.** Profits and losses are shared among the partners in any manner to which the partners agree.

**Nontaxable Status.** Unlike a corporation, a partnership does not pay income taxes. Instead, partnerships must file with the IRS an information return on Form 1065, which shows the partnership's taxable income and each partner's share of such income. Each partner then reports and pays taxes on his or her share of the partnership's taxable income. These procedures eliminate the undesirable "double taxation," which is a feature of corporations. That is, the earnings of the corporation are taxed and then the dividends of the corporations are also taxed—whereas partnership income is taxed only once, at the individual partner level.

**Concluding Comments.** For professionals, the form of organization of a partnership is simple and flexible compared with that of a professional corporation, which is generally considered complex and cumbersome. The partnership form is still common largely because it is "a more effective way to relate to each other."

Partnerships often begin with great enthusiasm and rosy expectations. Keeping the partnership going is much harder. In many cases, the partners must seek help of a professional business therapist (often a psychologist) because they cannot work together harmoniously.

## Incorporating a Partnership

Many corporations began as partnerships. Then at some point in the enterprise's existence, the advantages of incorporation outweighed the advantages of the partnership form of organization. When a partnership incorporates, its assets are transferred to the corporation, which assumes the partnership's liabilities. One technical point should be noted: The corporation's board of directors is responsible for placing a value on the assets transferred to the corporation. In theory, the assets can be revalued to their current values, and this is often done. However, if the corporation ever decides to register its common stock with the Securities and Exchange Commission, the SEC will insist that assets transferred to the corporation be carried at the partnership's historical cost, adjusted for depreciation and amortization. In other words, no upward revaluation of assets on incorporation is allowed. (Presumably, a downward revaluation would be permitted if appropriate.)

# FORMATION OF A PARTNERSHIP

## The Uniform Partnership Act

Before discussing the partnership agreement in detail, some understanding of the laws that govern partnerships is necessary. Although each of the 50 states has laws pertaining to partnerships, most states have adopted the Uniform Partnership Act (UPA) or a variation thereof as a means of governing partnerships. In this text, we consider the UPA the governing statute.

The UPA is reasonably comprehensive in defining the consequences of a partnership relationship. For our purposes, its more relevant sections pertain to:

1. Relations of partners to one another.
2. Relations of partners to persons dealing with the partnership.
3. Dissolution and winding up of the partnership.

Some sections of the UPA cannot be circumvented merely by contrary provisions or omissions in the partnership agreement. For example, Section 15 imposes joint liability on all general partners for partnership debts. If a partnership agreement contained a provision excusing certain general partners from joint liability, then that provision of the agreement would be inoperable, and creditors could seek recourse from any partner.

Other sections of the UPA apply only when a partnership agreement is silent. For example, suppose a partnership agreement is silent with respect to remuneration for partners who are active in the management of the business. If one of the active partners should claim subsequently to be entitled to remuneration for services, then the dispute would be settled against that partner in a court of law. Section 18 expressly provides that unless otherwise stated in the partnership agreement, "no partner is entitled to remuneration for acting in the partnership interest." A partner's remuneration for managerial services would have to be provided for in the partnership agreement.

On the other hand, the UPA is not so comprehensive that it provides for every possible provision that otherwise could be included in a partnership agreement. For example, Section 27 discusses certain consequences of the sale by a partner of his or her partnership interest. Although a partner need not give the remaining partners the first opportunity to acquire the partnership interest, neither does the UPA prevent a partnership agreement from containing a clause to the effect that if a partner desires to sell any or all of his or her interest, the remaining partners must be given the right of first refusal.

Selected sections of the Uniform Partnership Act appear in Appendix B of this chapter.

## The Partnership Agreement

The partnership agreement is merely a written expression of what the partners have agreed to. Because state laws govern the consequences of partnership relationships, however, the partnership agreement should be prepared by an attorney who is experienced in partnership law. This is essential for the following reasons:

1. Mandatory provisions of the UPA may be included or referred to, so that the partners are aware of and somewhat familiar with partnership law.
2. Provisions that conflict with the UPA can be avoided.
3. Optional provisions that do not conflict with the UPA can be considered for possible inclusion.

A well-written partnership agreement should be a guide to the partners' relationship and any allowable variations from the UPA to which they have agreed. It should also minimize potential disputes among the partners.

In addition to essential legal provisions, the partnership agreement should include the following:

1. The partnership's exact name and designated place of business.
2. The names and personal addresses of each partner.

3. The date on which the partnership was formed.
4. The business purpose of the partnership.
5. The duration of the partnership.
6. A list of the assets contributed by each partner and the related agreed-upon valuation of those assets to the partnership.
7. The basis of accounting to be used (for example, the accrual basis, the cash basis, or some variation of either of these methods).
8. The partnership's accounting year-end for purposes of closing the books and dividing the profits and losses.
9. The specific procedures for sharing profits and losses.
10. The amounts that partners can periodically withdraw from the business and any related conditions for such withdrawals (for example, a certain amount per month or an amount up to a percentage of current-period earnings).
11. Provisions for settling with a partner (or a partner's estate) who withdraws from the partnership throough choice, retirement, or death.

An accountant can assist persons who are in the preliminary stages of forming a partnership in the following ways:

1. By explaining the cash basis and accrual basis of accounting.
2. By explaining and illustrating the numerous alternative methods available for sharing profits and losses and the appropriateness of each method. (A significant portion of this chapter is devoted to this subject.)
3. By discussing the tax ramifications compared with other methods of organizing the business. (This subject is also discussed later in the chapter.)

## The Partnership as an Entity

The business of the partnership should logically be accounted for separately from the personal transactions of the partners. Although partnerships are not separate legal entities with unlimited lives, as is the case for corporations, this does not prevent partnerships from being accounted for as separate, operating, business entities.

Although partners legally must contribute additional cash or property to the partnership to satisfy the claims of creditors, this does not mean that the partnership is inseparable from the partners. It is a common banking practice for certain top officers of corporations to guarantee personally loans made to the corporation. Thus, the fact that additional collateral for creditors exists is irrelevant.

Income tax laws do not determine sound accounting theory. They do treat partnerships as separate reporting entities, although not as separate tax-paying entities. Most partnerships are considered separate business entities in that they prepare monthly financial statements for internal use. Some of the large public accounting firms even publish annual reports, complete with financial statements, for use by their partners, employees, and other interested parties.

## Applicability of Generally Accepted Accounting Principles

To study partnerships, we must make an important transition from corporate accounting (in which generally accepted accounting principles are almost always followed) to partnership accounting (in which generally accepted accounting principles need not be and often are not followed). The professional pronouncements of the American Institute of Certified Public Accountants (AICPA) and the Financial Accounting Standards Board (FASB) apply to businesses that present their financial statements in accordance with generally accepted accounting principles. Such businesses include: (1) publicly held corporations, which must present their financial statements in accordance with generally accepted accounting principles; (2) nonpublicly held corporations, which usually present their financial statements in accordance with generally accepted accounting principles (often pursuant to requirements of loan agreements with financial institutions); and (3) partnerships and sole proprietorships that choose to present their financial statements in accordance with generally accepted accounting principles.

When a partnership does not maintain its books in accordance with generally accepted accounting principles, such a departure usually falls into one of the following categories:

1. **Cash basis instead of accrual basis.** The cash basis of recording receipts and expenses is often more efficient and economical than the accrual basis.
2. **Prior-period adjustments.** To achieve greater equity among the partners, prior-period adjustments are often made even though the items do not qualify as such under *FASB Statement No. 16*, "Prior Period Adjustments."
3. **Current values instead of historical cost.** When the ownership of the partnership changes, it is sometimes more expedient to reflect assets at their current values than to continue to reflect them at their historical cost.
4. **Recognition of goodwill.** To accommodate a partner's wishes, goodwill may be recognized on the admission or retirement of a partner, even though a business combination has not occurred.

Categories 3 and 4 are discussed and illustrated in Chapter 24 on changes in ownership.

## Partners' Accounts

**Capital Accounts.**   Each partner has a **capital account,** which is created when the partner contributes assets to the partnership. The account is increased for subsequent capital contributions and decreased for withdrawals. In addition, the account is increased for the partner's share of earnings and decreased for the partner's share of losses.

Traditionally, accountants have not attempted to maintain a balance sheet distinction between contributed capital and earnings that have been retained in the partnership, as is customary for corporations. This is primarily because the partnership's earnings do not reflect any salary expense for the partners (they are owners, not employees), and therefore they must be evaluated carefully. If the corporate form of business were used rather than the partnership form, the corporation's earnings would be lower than those reported by the partnership, because the services performed by the partners would be performed by salaried officers and employees of the corporation. Earnings under the corporate form of business would also be lower because of income tax. To avoid the implication that the earnings retained in the partnership are comparable to the retained earnings of a corporation, a Retained Earnings account is considered inappropriate for partnerships. Accordingly, the earnings or losses of a partnership are added or subtracted, respectively, to the capital accounts of the individual partners.

**Drawing Accounts.**   Typically, partners do not wait until the end of the year to determine how much of the profits they wish to withdraw from the partnership. To meet personal living expenses, partners customarily withdraw money on a periodic basis throughout the year. Such withdrawals could be charged directly to the capital accounts of the individual partners. However, a special account called the **drawing account** is used to charge current-year withdrawals. In substance, the drawing accounts are contra capital accounts. At year-end, each partner's drawing account is closed to that partner's capital account. The maximum amount partners may withdraw during the year is usually specified in the partnership agreement.

**Loan Accounts.**   Partners may make loans to the partnership in excess of their required capital contributions. Section 18 of the UPA provides that unless otherwise agreed to by the partners, "a partner, who in aid of the partnership makes any payment or advance beyond the amount of capital which he agreed to contribute, shall be paid interest from the date of the payment or advance." Interest on partners' loans to the partnership is a bona fide borrowing expense of the business, is treated as interest expense in the general ledger, and enters into the determination of the profit or loss.

If a partnership loans money on an interest-bearing basis to a partner, the interest is recorded as interest income in the general ledger. It also enters into the determination of the profit or loss.

## Recording the Initial Capital Contributions

The following two fundamental principles are deeply rooted in partnership accounting:

1. Noncash assets contributed to a partnership should be valued at their current values.
2. Liabilities assumed by a partnership should be valued at their current values.

These principles achieve equity among the partners, an objective that is repeatedly stressed in partnership accounting. If these principles were not followed, the subsequent operations would not reflect the true earnings of the partnerships, and certain partners would be treated inequitably.

For example, assume a partner contributed to a partnership marketable securities with a current market value of $10,000 and a cost basis to the individual partner of $7,000. If the marketable securities were later sold by the partnership for $12,000, the recorded gain on the partnership's books would be $2,000, which is the amount of appreciation that occurred during the period that the partnership held the asset. However, if the marketable securities had been valued on the partnership's books at the partner's cost basis of $7,000, the recorded gain would be $5,000. This would result in the other partner's sharing in an additional $3,000 of profit, the appreciation that occurred before the asset was contributed to the partnership. Current values must be used to prevent such inequities. The partnership agreement normally indicates the agreed-upon valuation assigned to noncash assets contributed and liabilities assumed.

The entry to record initial capital contributions for an assumed two-person partnership is shown below using the following assumed facts:

| Assets Contributed and Liabilities Assumed | Adjusted Basis[a] | Current Value |
|---|---|---|
| **By Partner A** | | |
| Cash | $23,000 | $23,000 |
| Marketable securities | 7,000 | 10,000 |
| | $30,000 | $33,000 |
| **By Partner B** | | |
| Cash | $ 5,000 | $ 5,000 |
| Land | 15,000 | 20,000 |
| Building, net | 25,000 | 35,000 |

*(continued)*

| Assets Contributed and Liabilities Assumed | Adjusted Basis[a] | Current Value |
|---|---|---|
| Note payable, secured by land and building | (20,000) | (20,000) |
| | $25,000 | $40,000 |

Entry to Record Initial Contributions

| | | |
|---|---|---|
| Cash . . . . . . . . . . . . . . . . . . . . . . . . . . . . . . . . . . . . . . . . . . | 28,000 | |
| Marketable Securities . . . . . . . . . . . . . . . . . . . . | 10,000 | |
| Land . . . . . . . . . . . . . . . . . . . . . . . . . . . . . . . . . . . . . . . . . | 20,000 | |
| Building. . . . . . . . . . . . . . . . . . . . . . . . . . . . . . . . . . . . . | 35,000 | |
| Notes Payable . . . . . . . . . . . . . . . . . . . . . . . | | 20,000 |
| Capital, Partner A . . . . . . . . . . . . . . . . . . . . | | 33,000 |
| Capital, Partner B . . . . . . . . . . . . . . . . . . . | | 40,000 |

[a]"Adjusted Basis" means each partner's historical cost, as adjusted for depreciation and amortization previously allowed (or allowable) for income tax reporting purposes.

The adjusted basis column is completely irrelevant for purposes of recording the initial capital contributions in the general ledger, but it is significant for income tax reporting. Income tax aspects are discussed later in the chapter.

## METHODS OF SHARING PROFITS AND LOSSES

Section 18 of the UPA specifies that profits and losses are shared equally unless otherwise provided for in the partnership agreement. Because the sharing of profits and losses is such an important aspect of a partnership relationship, it would be rare to find a partnership agreement that did not spell out the divisions of profits and losses in detail. The formula that is used to divide profits and losses is arrived at through negotiations among the partners. Whether or not it is fair does not concern the accountant.

Profits and losses can be shared in many ways. Partners should select a formula that is sensible, practical, and equitable. Most profit and loss sharing formulas include one or more of the following features or techniques:

1. Sharing equally or in some other agreed-upon ratio.
2. Imputed salary allowances to acknowledge time devoted to business.
3. Imputed interest on capital investments to recognize capital invested.
4. Expense sharing arrangements.
5. Performance criteria to recognize above- or below-average performance.

Note that the computations to determine the allocation of profit and loss among the partners are made on worksheets. The only journal entry that results from this process is to close the Profit and Loss Summary account to the capital accounts of the partners, using the amounts determined from the worksheet computations.

## Ratios

Under the *ratio method*, each partner is allocated a percentage of the profits and losses. For example, partner A is to receive 60% and partner B is to receive 40% of the profits and losses. These percentages are then expressed as a ratio. Thus, profits and losses are shared between A and B in the ratio 3:2, respectively. If the partnership of A and B had profits of $100,000, the entry to record the division of the profits would be as follows:

| | | |
|---|---|---|
| Profit and Loss Summary | 100,000 | |
| Capital, Partner A | | 60,000 |
| Capital, Partner B | | 40,000 |

An infrequently used variation of this method is to specify one ratio for profits and a different ratio for losses. Because profit and loss years may alternate, it is extremely important that profit or loss for each year be determined accurately in all material respects whenever this variation is used.

## Salary Allowances and Ratios

Sometimes certain partners devote more time to the business than other partners. In these cases, a frequently used method for sharing profits and losses is to provide for salary allowances, with any residual profit or loss allocated in an agreed-upon ratio. For example, assume partner A devotes all of her time to the business, and partner B devotes only one-third of his time to the business. The partners could agree to provide for salary allowances in relation to the time devoted to the business—for example, $30,000 to partner A and $10,000 to partner B. All remaining profits or losses could then be divided in the agreed-upon ratio—that is, 3:2, respectively.

Using these salary allowances and a residual sharing ratio of 3:2 for partner A and partner B, respectively, the partnership would divide $100,000 in profits in the following way:

| | Total | Allocated to | |
|---|---|---|---|
| | | Partner A | Partner B |
| Total profit | $100,000 | | |
| Salary allowances | (40,000) | $30,000 | $10,000 |
| Residual profit | $ 60,000 | | |
| Allocate 3:2 | (60,000) | 36,000 | 24,000 |
| | $ –0– | $66,000 | $34,000 |

The general ledger entry to divide the profits would be as follows:

| | | |
|---|---|---|
| Profit and Loss Summary | 100,000 | |
| Capital, Partner A | | 66,000 |
| Capital, Partner B | | 34,000 |

Remember that partners are owners, not employees. Accordingly, it is not appropriate to charge a Salary Expense account and credit Accrued Salary Payable. However, some partnerships do record salary allowances in this manner. Although not technically correct, it does not affect the final profit and loss allocations. In these cases, cash distributions that relate to salary allowances are charged to Accrued Salary Payable. Any remaining credit balance in a partner's Accrued Salary Payable account at year-end is then transferred to that partner's capital account.

In the above example, the total profit was greater than the total salary allowances of $40,000. What if that were not the case? Profit of only $25,000 would be shared as follows:

| | | Allocated to | |
|---|---|---|---|
| | Total | Partner A | Partner B |
| Total profit | $ 25,000 | | |
| Salary allowances | (40,000) | $30,000 | $10,000 |
| Residual loss | $(15,000) | | |
| Allocate 3:2 | 15,000 | (9,000) | (6,000) |
| | $ –0– | $21,000 | $ 4,000 |

The general ledger entry to divide the profits would be as follows:

| | | |
|---|---|---|
| Profit and Loss Summary | 25,000 | |
| Capital, Partner A | | 21,000 |
| Capital, Partner B | | 4,000 |

Another way of handling this situation would be if the partners agreed not to use a residual sharing ratio in the event profits were less than the total salary allowances. In this case, the first $40,000 of profit would be divided in the ratio of the salary allowances. Using the above example, a profit of $25,000 would be divided as follows:

| | | Allocated to | |
|---|---|---|---|
| | Total | Partner A | Partner B |
| Total profit | $ 25,000 | | |
| Salary allowances—up to $40,000 in a 3:1 ratio | (25,000) | $18,750 | $6,250 |
| | $ –0– | $18,750 | $6,250 |

Large and moderately sized partnerships usually function with an administrative hierarchy. Partnership positions within such a hierarchy have greater responsibilities than positions outside the hierarchy. To compensate the partners who assume these greater responsibilities, salary allowances commonly are used and their amounts are correlated to the various levels of responsibility within the hierarchy.

## Imputed Interest on Capital, Salary Allowances, and Ratios

When partners' capital investments are not equal, the profit sharing formula frequently includes a feature that recognizes the greater capital investment of certain partners. Accordingly, interest is imputed on each partner's capital investment. For example, a profit and loss sharing formula could specify that interest be imputed at 10% of each partner's average capital investment. To illustrate how this procedure is applied, assume the following profit sharing formula and average capital investments:

|  | Partner A | Partner B |
| --- | --- | --- |
| Profit sharing formula: | | |
| Salary allowances | $30,000 | $10,000 |
| Interest on average capital balance | 10% | 10% |
| Residual profit or loss (3:2) | 60% | 40% |
| Average capital investments | $10,000 | $40,000 |

Profits of $100,000 would be divided as follows:

|  | Total | Allocated to | |
| --- | --- | --- | --- |
|  |  | Partner A | Partner B |
| Total profit | $100,000 | | |
| Salary allowances | (40,000) | $30,000 | $10,000 |
| Interest on average capital investments | (5,000) | 1,000 | 4,000 |
| Residual profit | $ 55,000 | | |
| Allocate 3:2 | (55,000) | 33,000 | 22,000 |
|  | $ –0– | $64,000 | $36,000 |

The general ledger entry to divide the profits would be as follows:

| Profit and Loss Summary | 100,000 | |
| --- | --- | --- |
| Capital, Partner A | | 64,000 |
| Capital, Partner B | | 36,000 |

Remember that the partner's capital investments are just that—they are not loans to the partnership. Accordingly, it is not appropriate to charge an Interest Expense account and an Accrued Interest Payable account. However, some partnerships do record imputed interest in this manner. This procedure is not technically correct, but it does not affect the final profit and loss allocations. In these cases, cash distributions that relate to imputed interest are charged to Accrued Interest Payable. Any remaining credit balance in a partner's Accrued Interest Payable account at year-end is then transferred to that partner's capital account.

In the above example the profit was greater than both the total of the salary allowances of $40,000 and the total of imputed interest of $5,000. A profit of only $25,000 would be divided as follows:

|  | Total | Allocated to | |
|---|---|---|---|
|  |  | Partner A | Partner B |
| Total profit. | $ 25,000 |  |  |
| Salary allowances | (40,000) | $30,000 | $10,000 |
| Interest on average capital investments | (5,000) | 1,000 | 4,000 |
| Residual loss | $(20,000) |  |  |
| Allocate 3:2 | 20,000 | (12,000) | (8,000) |
|  | $ –0– | $19,000 | $ 6,000 |

The general ledger entry to divide the profits would be as follows:

| Profit and Loss Summary | 25,000 | |
|---|---|---|
| Capital, Partner A | | 19,000 |
| Capital, Partner B | | 6,000 |

**Order of Priority Provision.** Alternatively, the partners could agree not to use a residual sharing ratio in the event profits did not exceed the total of the salary allowances and the imputed interest on average capital balances. In this case, the partners must agree on **the priority of the various features.** If the partnership agreement gives salary allowances priority over imputed interest on capital balances, the first $40,000 of profit would be divided in the ratio of the salary allowances, and the next $5,000 would be divided in the ratio of the imputed interest amounts. Using the profit sharing formula and data given in the preceding example, a profit of only $42,000 would be divided as follows:

|  | Total | Allocated to | |
|---|---|---|---|
|  |  | Partner A | Partner B |
| Total profit. | $ 42,000 |  |  |
| Salary allowances | (40,000) | $30,000 | $10,000 |
| Available for interest on capital | $ 2,000 |  |  |

| | Total | Allocated to | |
| | | Partner A | Partner B |
| --- | --- | --- | --- |
| Interest on average capital investment 1:4 .............. | (2,000) | 400 | 1,600 |
| | $ –0– | $30,400 | $11,600 |

Note: If interest on capital had priority over salary allowances, the division of the $42,000 profit would result in Partner A being allocated $28,750 ($1,000 for interest and $27,750 for salary) and Partner B being allocated $13,250 ($4,000 for interest and $9,250 for salary).

In the preceding examples, interest was imputed on the average capital investments. Although this is apparently the most equitable method, using the beginning or ending capital investments are other options. Whenever this imputed interest on capital feature is used, the partnership agreement should specify whether the beginning, average, or ending capital balances should be used. Furthermore, if the partnership agreement calls for using average or ending capital investments, it should define specifically how the average or ending capital investments are determined. Only the capital account or the capital account and the drawing account of each partner may be used. For the average capital balance method, the method of computing the average must be selected—that is, using daily balances, beginning of month balances, or end of month balances.

The following assumptions and capital account activities illustrate the computation of an average capital investment.

1. The drawing account activity is considered in arriving at the average capital investment for the year.
2. An average capital investment for each month is used to arrive at the average capital investment for the year.

| Capital, Partner X | | Drawings, Partner X | |
| --- | --- | --- | --- |
| 50,000 | 1/1/X5 | 6/30/X5 | 6,000 |
| 10,000 | 4/1/X5 | 9/15/X5 | 6,000 |
| 2,000 | 11/15/X5 | 12/31/X5 | 6,000 |

| Computation Month | Monthly Averages |
| --- | --- |
| January . . . . . . . . . . . . . . . . . . . . . . . . . . . | $ 50,000 |
| February . . . . . . . . . . . . . . . . . . . . . . . . . . | 50,000 |
| March . . . . . . . . . . . . . . . . . . . . . . . . . . . . | 50,000 |
| April . . . . . . . . . . . . . . . . . . . . . . . . . . . . | 60,000 |
| May . . . . . . . . . . . . . . . . . . . . . . . . . . . . . | 60,000 |
| June . . . . . . . . . . . . . . . . . . . . . . . . . . . . | 60,000 |
| July . . . . . . . . . . . . . . . . . . . . . . . . . . . . . | 54,000 |
| August . . . . . . . . . . . . . . . . . . . . . . . . . . . | 54,000 |

*(continued)*

| Computation<br>Month | Monthly<br>Averages |
|---|---:|
| September .................................................. | 51,000 |
| October .................................................. | 48,000 |
| November .................................................. | 49,000 |
| December .................................................. | 50,000 |
| | $636,000 |
| Average capital investment for 19X5<br>($636,000 ÷ 12) .................................... | $ 53,000 |

## Capital Balances Only

Many international accounting firms allocate profits and losses *solely* on the basis of capital balances. In these cases, each partner must maintain a specified capital balance, which is correlated to the level of responsibility assumed in the partnership. This method is not only easy to apply, but it can prevent certain inequities from occurring among partners if the partnership is liquidated. These potential inequities are discussed in Chapter 25, which deals with partnership liquidations.

## Expense-sharing Arrangements

Sometimes a small partnership operates as a confederation of sole proprietorships, in that the profit sharing formula entitles each partner to all net billings generated by that partner. Expenses are then allocated to partners on the basis of total floor space, amount of billings, or some other arbitrary method. This arrangement is common when two or two more sole proprietorships form a partnership, with each partner maintaining former clients. Any net billings from clients obtained after the formation of the partnership may be assigned either to the partner responsible for obtaining the client or to a common pool to be allocated to all partners on some arbitrary basis.

## Performance Methods

Many partnerships use profit and loss sharing formulas that give some weight to the specific performance of each partner, to provide incentives to perform well. Some examples of areas in which performance criteria may be used are listed below:

1. **Chargeable hours.** Chargeable hours are the total number of hours that a partner incurred on client-related assignments. Weight may be given to hours in excess of a norm.
2. **Total billings.** The total amount billed to clients for work performed and supervised by a partner constitutes total billings. Weight may be given to billings in excess of a norm.

3. **Write-offs.** Write-offs consist of the amount of uncollectible billings. Weight may be given to a write-off percentage below a norm.
4. **Promotional and civic activities.** Time devoted to the development of future business and to the development of the partnership name in the community is considered promotional and civic activity. Weight may be given to time spent in excess of a norm or to specific accomplishments resulting in new clients.
5. **Profits in excess of specified levels.** Designated partners commonly receive a certain percentage of profits in excess of a specified level of earnings.

An additional allocation of profits to a partner on the basis of performance is frequently referred to as a **bonus.** As with salary allowances and imputed interest, a bonus should not be charged to an expense account in the general ledger, although some partnerships improperly do this.

## Subsequent Changes in Methods of Sharing Profits and Losses

If the partners subsequently agree to change the method of sharing profits and losses, equity dictates that assets be revalued to their current values at the time of the change. To illustrate, assume partners A and B shared profits and losses equally, and at a later date they agree to share profits and losses in a 3:2 ratio, respectively. Suppose also that the partnership holds a parcel of land that is carried on the books at $60,000 but now has a current value of $80,000. Partner A would receive a greater share of the profit on the land (when it is later sold) than if the land were sold before the method of sharing profits and losses was changed. This is not equitable because the land appreciated $20,000 while the profits and losses were shared equally.

An alternative to revaluing the land to its current value would be to stipulate in the new profit sharing formula that the first $20,000 of profit on the sale of that parcel of land is to be shared in the old profit and loss sharing ratio. Under this method, the partnership avoids making an entry that would be at variance with generally accepted accounting principles. However, this is not a major reason for selecting this alternative if revaluing assets is more practical.

When the profit and loss sharing formula is revised, the new formula should contain a provision specifying that the old formula applies to certain types of subsequent adjustments arising out of activities that took place before the revision date. Examples are:

1. Unrecorded liabilities existing at the revision date.
2. Settlements on lawsuits not provided for at the revision date, even though the liability may not have been probable as to payment or reasonably estimable at that time.
3. Write-offs of accounts receivable existing as of the revision date.

Regardless of the fact that some of these items would not qualify as prior-period adjustments under *FASB Statement No. 16,* "Prior Period Adjustments," greater equity usually would be achieved among the partners by using the old sharing formula. Because partnerships need not follow generally accepted accounting principles, the will of the partners may prevail.

## FINANCIAL REPORTING

Because partnerships are not publicly owned, their financial statements are prepared primarily for internal use. Such statements normally include all of those that a corporation prepares, except for the statement of changes in stockholders' equity, for which a statement of changes in partners' equity is substituted.

One common reason for making partnership financial statements available to outside parties is to borrow money from financial institutions. (Under the Uniform Partnership Act, partnerships can hold debt in the partnership name rather than in the names of its individual partners.) Financial statements made available to outside parties should be converted to the accrual basis if the cash basis is used for book purposes. (Most partnerships use the cash basis as a matter of convenience.) Because partnership earnings are not comparable to what they would have been had the business been organized as a corporation, an indication to this effect should be made in the footnotes to the financial statements.

Some accountants have suggested that a partnership's income statement should reflect an imputed amount for salaries that would have been paid to the partners had the corporate form of business been used. Presumably, such an approach would state the "true earnings" of the partnership. In our opinion, this is a somewhat futile exercise involving substantial subjectivity. Furthermore, from a technical standpoint, consideration should also be given to (1) additional payroll taxes; (2) deductions for fringe benefits (primarily pension and profit sharing plans), which are not available to partners; and (3) income taxes. It would seem sufficient to state in a footnote that, because the partnership form of organization is used, the earnings must be evaluated carefully because, conceptually, earnings should provide for equivalent salary compensation, return on capital invested in the partnership, retirement, and payroll-type fringe benefits.

Virtually all partnerships maintain strict confidentiality of their financial statements. International public accounting partnerships that do issue financial statements to interested parties commonly show the following:

1. The financial statements are converted from the cash basis to the accrual basis of accounting.

2. An imputed amount for salaries is not reflected in the income statement.
3. A footnote to the financial statements indicates that the firm's earnings are not comparable to those of a corporation.
4. The financial statements are prepared in accordance with generally accepted accounting principles, and the notes to the financial statements are complete as to required disclosures—for example, disclosures of accounting policies, lease commitments, and segment information.

The income statement of small partnerships commonly shows how the profit or loss is divided. The allocation can be shown immediately below net income, as follows:

### A & B PARTNERSHIP
### INCOME STATEMENT FOR THE YEAR ENDED DECEMBER 31, 19X1

| | |
|---|---:|
| Revenues | $1,000,000 |
| Expenses | (900,000) |
| Net Income | $ 100,000 |

Allocation of net income to partners:

| | Partner A | Partner B |
|---|---:|---:|
| Salary allowances | $30,000 | $10,000 |
| Imputed interest on capital | 1,000 | 4,000 |
| Residual (3:2) | 33,000 | 22,000 |
| Total | $64,000 | $36,000 |

Furthermore, a small partnership's statement of changes in partners' equity is often shown *by partner* as follows:

### A & B PARTNERSHIP
### STATEMENT OF CHANGES IN PARTNERS' EQUITY
### FOR THE YEAR ENDED DECEMBER 31, 19X1

| | Partner A | Partner B | Total |
|---|---:|---:|---:|
| Beginning capital | $25,000 | $ 85,000 | $110,000 |
| Contributions | 5,000 | –0– | 5,000 |
| Drawings | (10,000) | (15,000) | (25,000) |
| Net income | 64,000 | 36,000 | 100,000 |
| Ending capital | $84,000 | $106,000 | $190,000 |

## INCOME TAX ASPECTS

Other than dividing the profits and losses among the partners in accordance with the profit sharing formula, accounting for the operations of a partnership presents no unusual problems. The income tax aspects of partnerships, however, are much more involved. An accountant providing services to a partnership must have a solid grasp of partnership tax concepts to serve his or her clients adequately. The following discussion will not make you an expert in partnership taxation; it will only provide a basic understanding of partnership taxation.

## Equity versus Tax Basis

A partner's interest in a partnership is a personal, capital asset that can be sold, exchanged, assigned, or otherwise disposed of. From a financial accounting viewpoint, a partner's equity in the partnership is the balance in his or her capital account net of any balance in his or her drawing account. If a partner were to sell his or her interest in the partnership, the gain or loss from a partnership accounting viewpoint would be determined by comparing the proceeds to his or her equity at the time of sale. The gain or loss from an accounting viewpoint, however, is not important. The sale is a personal transaction; therefore, any gain or loss is not reflected in the partnership's general ledger. In this respect, it is similar to the sale of stock by a shareholder of a corporation—it does not enter into the operations of the business entity. From the selling partner's viewpoint, the relevant objective is to determine the amount of the taxable gain or loss.

**Contributing Assets.** The tax laws are not structured around a partner's equity as recorded in the partnership general ledger. Thus, to determine the amount of gain or loss for tax purposes on the sale of a partner's interest in a partnership, we must be familiar with the concept of tax basis. For tax purposes, a partner's interest in a partnership is referred to as that partner's **tax basis.** Tax basis is an asset-related concept; if a partner contributed $5,000 cash to a partnership, his or her tax basis in the partnership is $5,000. (Coincidentally, this would be the amount credited to his or her capital account in the general ledger, but this fact is irrelevant from a tax standpoint.) If a partner contributes equipment to a partnership, then that partner's tax basis in the partnership increases by the adjusted tax basis of the equipment immediately before the contribution or transfer. The adjusted tax basis of the equipment is the partner's historical cost less (1) any depreciation previously allowed (deducted) for income tax reporting purposes, or (2) any depreciation allowable for income tax reporting purposes if no previous depreciation deduction was taken. Thus, if equipment that cost the partner $10,000 had been depreciated $2,000 in the partner's business before the contribution or transfer, the adjusted tax basis would be $8,000. Accordingly, the partner's tax basis in the partnership would increase by $8,000.

If the equipment was completely paid for at the time of the contribution or transfer to the partnership, the amount credited to the partner's capital account in the general ledger would depend on the current value assigned to the equipment and agreed to by the partners. This current value could be more or less than the $8,000 adjusted tax basis. Thus, it would only be a coincidence that the credit to the partner's capital account increases by the amount of the adjusted tax basis at the time of the contribution or transfer.

**No Step-up or Step-down in Tax Basis.** For tax purposes, any difference between the current value and the adjusted tax basis at the time of the contribution or transfer to a partnership is not recognized. In other words, no gain or loss must be reported. The adjusted tax basis of the asset (in the hands of the partner immediately before the contribution or transfer) is not stepped up or stepped down on transfer to the partnership. Accordingly, the adjusted tax basis of each asset contributed to a partnership merely carries over to the partnership for tax reporting purposes. To the extent that future depreciation and amortization expenses are different for book (general ledger) reporting purposes than for tax reporting purposes, the book income or loss must be adjusted (on a worksheet) to arrive at taxable income.

**Contributing Liabilities.** This concept of tax basis is slightly more involved if the contributed asset has a debt attached to it that is assumed by the partnership. Suppose the equipment had a $3,000 installment note payable attached to it, for which the partnership assumed responsibility. The contributing partner's tax basis still increases by $8,000 (the amount of the adjusted tax basis of the asset at the time of the contribution or transfer). The fact that the partnership has assumed responsibility for payment of the debt, however, is significant from a tax viewpoint. The tax law says the other partners (by becoming jointly responsible for the payment of this debt), in substance, have given money to this partner. Accordingly, their tax bases should be increased and the tax basis of the partner who contributed the liability should be decreased by the amount of money deemed to have been given constructively to the partner. The profit and loss sharing ratio is used to determine this deemed amount. For example, if a three-person partnership shared profits equally, then the tax basis of the partner contributing the equipment and the related $3,000 liability would be reduced from $8,000 to $6,000 (two-thirds of $3,000) and the tax basis of each of the other partners would be increased by $1,000 (one-third of $3,000). This procedure is used even though the creditor could seek personal recourse from the partner who contributes the liability to the partnership.

**Keeping Track of Each Partner's Basis.**    Because a **partner's tax basis cannot be determined by using the amounts recorded in the general ledger capital accounts,** each partner must determine his or her own individual tax basis in the partnership on a memorandum tax basis outside the general ledger. In summary, each partner's tax basis can be determined when the partnership is formed by adding the first three of the following categories and subtracting the fourth category.

- Cash contributed to the partnership by a partner.
- Add—A partner's adjusted tax basis in any noncash property contributed or transferred to the partnership.
- Add—A partner's share of any liabilities assumed by the partnership that were contributed by other partners.
- Less—The other partners' share of any liabilities assumed by the partnership that the partner contributed to the partnership.

**Comprehensive Illustration.**    To further demonstrate the application of these procedures for determining a basis, we assume the same facts related to the formation of a partnership as in the example on page 1115. In addition, we assume that partners A and B share profits and losses in a 3:2 ratio, respectively. The adjusted tax basis of each partner is as follows:

|  | Adjusted Basis | | |
|  | Partner A | Partner B | Total |
| --- | --- | --- | --- |
| Cash contributed | $23,000 | $ 5,000 | $28,000 |
| Noncash assets contributed: | | | |
|    Marketable securities | 7,000 | | 7,000 |
|    Land | | 15,000 | 15,000 |
|    Building | | 25,000 | 25,000 |
| | $30,000 | $45,000 | $75,000 |
| Adjustments to **tax** basis for liabilities of $20,000 assumed by the partnership[a] | 12,000 | (12,000) | |
| Basis | $42,000 | $33,000 | $75,000 |

[a]The adjustment to each partner's tax basis is 60% of $20,000, because partner A assumes a 60% responsibility for the $20,000 liability contributed by partner B.

In reviewing the above illustration, one major point should be understood. Partner A's $42,000 tax basis plus partner B's $33,000 tax basis equals the partnership's tax basis in the assets of $75,000 for tax reporting purposes. This equality always exists. Note also that the sum of the tax bases of the assets immediately before the transfer ($30,000 for partner A's assets and $45,000 for partner B's assets) also equals the partnership's tax basis in the assets for tax reporting purposes.

## Subsequent Adjustments to Each Partner's Tax Basis

The personal tax basis of each partner's interest in the partnership is adjusted as subsequent partnership activity takes place. Such activities can be grouped as follows:

1. **Contributions and distributions (withdrawals).** If a partner subsequently contributes additional assets to the partnership, the tax basis of that partner's interest in the partnership increases. If the partner withdraws assets from the partnership, the tax basis of that partner's interest in the partnership decreases. (It can never be less than zero.)
2. **Profits and losses.** To the extent that there are profits, each partner's tax basis in the partnership increases by that partner's share of the partnership's taxable income. To the extent that there are losses, each partner's tax basis in the partnership decreases by that partner's share of the partnership's loss for tax reporting purposes.
3. **Changes in partnership liabilities.** Tax laws effectively treat partnership liabilities as personal liabilities of the partners. For example, if a partnership borrowed $1,000 from a financial institution, the partnership's assets would increase by $1,000. The same result could be produced if one of the partners were personally to borrow the $1,000 from the financial institution and then make an additional capital contribution of $1,000. The form of each transaction is different, but the substance is the same.

Thus, an increase in a partnership's liabilities is treated as an additional capital contribution by the partners. This increase is shared among the partners, and each partner's tax basis in the partnership increases.[1] A decrease in a partnership's liabilities is treated as a distribution of partnership assets to its partners. This decrease also is shared among the partners, and each partner's tax basis in the partnership decreases.

In the example given in the preceding illustration we showed a $12,000 adjustment to the tax bases of partners A and B as a result of partner B's contributing a $20,000 liability to the partnership. In a different approach to this adjustment, we assume that (1) instead of partner B's contributing the $20,000 liability to the partnership, the partnership borrowed $20,000 from a financial institution, and (2) the partnership then distributed that $20,000 to partner B, who paid off his personal loan of $20,000. The adjustments to the tax basis of each of the partners are as follows:

---

[1] If one ratio exists for profits and a different ratio exists for losses, the IRS uses the loss ratio (unless the debt is nonrecourse debt in which case the IRS uses the profit ratio). The rationale for using the loss ratio for recourse debt is that if the partnership were unable to repay the debt, it would be because of operating losses.

|  | Adjustments to Basis ||
|  | Partner A | Partner B |
|---|---|---|
| Borrowing of $20,000 by the partnership (60% to partner A and 40% to partner B) . . . . . . . . . . . . . . . . . . . . | $12,000 | $ 8,000 |
| Distribution of $20,000 to partner B . . . . . . . . |  | (20,000) |
| Net change to basis . . . . . . . . . . . . . . . . . . . . | $12,000 | $(12,000) |

Note that the net effect on each partner's tax basis is still $12,000.

The determination of a partner's tax basis in a partnership is relevant when a partner disposes of some or all of his or her partnership interest. This situation is discussed more fully in Chapter 24 on ownership changes.

## Net Operating Loss Carrybacks and Carryforwards

Because partnerships are not taxable entities, they do not have net operating loss carrybacks or carryforwards. However, when a partner's share of a partnership's loss for a given year exceeds the excess of the partner's nonbusiness income over nonbusiness deductions (excluding personal exemptions as deductions), this net amount is a net operating loss that can be carried back three years and then forward seven years on the partner's individual income tax return. The excess of nonbusiness deductions (excluding personal exemptions as deductions) over nonbusiness income does not increase the net operating loss because it is not business related.

## THE PROFESSIONAL CORPORATION

A complete discussion of the legal aspects and tax laws related to professional corporations is beyond the scope of this book. In general, the professional corporation form of business is available to professionals who render personal service—for example, accountants, architects, attorneys, dentists, optometrists, physicians, real estate brokers, and veterinarians. A professional corporation must act like a corporation and maintain a corporate appearance throughout its existence. For example, shareholders' and directors' meetings must be held and minutes of these meetings must be maintained. From a tax standpoint, the professional corporation is subject to tax laws that apply to corporations, including provisions related to (1) the reasonableness of compensation paid to shareholder-employees, (2) the reasonableness of accumulated earnings, and (3) the restrictions on amounts that can be deducted for pension and profit sharing plans.

## Tax Advantages to Incorporation

Under the partnership form of organization, only employees of the partnership can participate in fringe benefits such as pension, profit sharing, medical, and insurance plans. Because partners are not employees, they cannot participate in these plans. The tax laws do allow professionals to provide for their retirement through the use of H.R. 10 (Keogh) plans. A self-employed professional operating as a sole proprietor or a member of a partnership may take a deduction for contributions to a qualified Keogh plan. The earnings on funds invested in a qualified Keogh plan are not taxed currently. As funds from the plan are distributed during retirement years, the distributions are reported for income tax purposes.

By having the partnership become a professional corporation, the partners become employees of the corporation, even though they are also its shareholders. They can then participate in pension, profit sharing, medical, and insurance plans. (Pension and profit sharing plans are the major fringe benefits by far.)

**Pre-1984 Tax Advantages.** Prior to 1984, the contributions allowed under Keogh plans were substantially below the maximum contributions allowed to corporate employees. Thus, in a professional corporation, more pretax dollars could be set aside to earn money that is not currently taxable, enabling a professional to provide much more generously for retirement than through the partnership or sole proprietorship forms of organization. These tax advantages were the major impetus for the explosive shift to the professional corporation.

**Parity Achieved in 1984.** Such disparities were inequitable, and many individuals and organizations (notably the tax section of the New York State Bar Association) worked to achieve parity so that deductions for profit sharing and pension plans would be the same for all people who work, regardless of whether they are self-employed or work for a corporation. As a result, beginning in 1984, the maximum annual Keogh plan deductions were made the same as deductions for profit sharing and pension plans allowed for corporate employees. (For profit sharing plans, the maximum annual deduction is $30,000; for pension plans, the maximum annual benefit is $90,000.)[2] As a further effort to achieve parity, the new law eliminated or changed many of the special limitations affecting Keogh plans. Thus, the major reasons for using a professional corporation have been eliminated.

**The Remaining Tax Advantages.** The only remaining significant tax advantages associated with professional corporations are medical and insurance plan deductions. Even though the major advantages for using professional corporations were eliminated, only a slight shift away from the professional corporation form of business has occurred. Nontax factors favoring incorporation (discussed shortly) largely account for this.

**The Double Tax Disadvantage Is Easily Avoided.** Recall that one disadvantage of the corporate form of business is the double taxation of earnings—that

---

[2]The $102,770 is for 1990 and is adjusted annually for inflation. The $30,000 is not adjusted for inflation until the $102,770 reaches $120,000.

is, the corporation's earnings are taxed and then corporate dividends are taxed. This disadvantage is usually of little significance to a professional corporation, which can enter into employment contracts with its shareholder-employees and adopt bonus plans, applying primarily to shareholder-employees, whereby salaries and bonuses can be paid to the extent necessary to eliminate any income that would be taxable at the corporate level. (Such compensation must still pass the IRS's tests of reasonableness to be allowed as a tax deduction and must not be deemed dividends rather than compensation.) In this way, the professional corporation form avoids or substantially mitigates the double tax.

## Nontax Advantages to Incorporation

### Unlimited versus Limited Liability.

The incorporation of a partnership does not automatically insulate the former partners' personal assets from the corporation's creditors. Shareholder-employees are still responsible for liabilities that arise out of acts they perform (or acts that are performed under their supervision) while rendering professional services as employees of the professional corporation. Certain states impose joint and several liability on all shareholders for professional services rendered by the professional corporation or its employees. Other states require personal participation for a shareholder of a professional corporation to be held individually liable. Note that shareholder-employees are not individually responsible (in most states) for liabilities that arise out of acts not involving rendering professional services (such as an automobile accident incurred in delivering an audit report to a client). In summary, some limited liability protection is obtainable by incorporating.

## Impracticality of Accountants Incorporating

Accounting firms that operate on a multistate basis find it impractical to incorporate because of licensing and qualification requirements. For example, many of the states' professional corporation statutes and corresponding accounting regulations require that all shareholders be licensed to practice in the state of incorporation. Primarily for this reason, virtually all of the national, multistate, and regional public accounting firms have retained the partnership form of organization.

## END-OF-CHAPTER REVIEW

## Summary of Key Points

1. In general partnerships, each partner is personally liable to the partnership's creditors if partnership assets are insufficient to pay such creditors. (In limited partnerships, the limited partners have limited liability.)

2. The partnership agreement governs the manner of operating the partnership, including the manner of dividing profits and losses and withdrawing earnings and capital.
3. Partnerships are accounted for as separate business entities, with the primary accounting objective being to achieve equity among the partners.
4. Partnership accounting often deviates from GAAP to achieve equity.
5. Upon formation of a partnership, assets and liabilities contributed into the partnership are recorded at their current values, which usually results in a new basis of accounting for financial reporting purposes. (For tax purposes, no change in basis occurs.)
6. Each partner must keep track of his or her tax basis in the partnership. (In almost all cases, a partner's capital balance in the general ledger differs from the tax basis.)

## Glossary of New Terms

**Drawing account**   A contra capital account used to keep track of amounts withdrawn during the year by a partner.

**General partnerships**   Partnerships in which all of the partners are personally liable to the partnership's creditors.

**Limited partnerships**   Partnerships in which certain partners (called limited partners) are not personally liable to the partnership creditors (there must be at least one general partner).

## Self-Study Questions
*(Answers are at the end of this chapter, preceding the appendices.)*

1. Don Doss and Kim Keyes form a partnership. Doss contributes into the partnership a personal computer that he has used at home in nonbusiness-related activities. Doss paid $10,000 for the computer two years ago. The replacement cost of the computer is $9,000. The partners, after reviewing IRS rules, assigned the computer a remaining life of six years. For financial reporting purposes, at what amount should the computer be recorded in the partnership's general ledger?
   a. $10,000
   b. $9,000
   c. $7,500
   d. $6,750

2. For income tax reporting purposes, at what amount should the computer in question 1 be accounted for by the partnership?
   a. $10,000
   b. $9,000
   c. $7,500
   d. $6,750

3. Partners Harry and Sally share profits and losses of their business equally after (1) annual salary allowances of $25,000 for Harry and $20,000 for Sally, and (2) 10% interest is provided on average capital balances. During 19X1, the partnership had earnings of $50,000; Harry's average capital balance was

$60,000, and Sally's average capital balance was $90,000. How should the $50,000 of earnings be divided?

| Harry | Sally |
|-------|-------|
| a. $26,000 | $24,000 |
| b. $27,000 | $23,000 |
| c. $25,000 | $25,000 |
| d. $27,500 | $22,500 |

4. Assume the same information in question 3 but also assume an order of priority is specified whereby salary allowances have a higher priority than interest on capital.

5. Kelly, a partner in the Kelly and Green partnership, is entitled to 40% of the profits and losses. During 19X1, Kelly contributed land to the partnership that cost her $50,000 but had a current value of $60,000. Also during 19X1, Kelly had drawings of $80,000. The balance in Kelly's capital account was $120,000 at the beginning of the year and $150,000 at the end of the year. Determine the partnership's earnings for 19X1.
   a. $(75,000)
   b. $(50,000)
   c. $150,000
   d. $125,000

6. Contrera and Badgez have just formed a partnership. Contrera contributed cash of $50,000 and some equipment that cost him $45,000. The equipment had been used in his sole proprietorship and had been depreciated $20,000. The replacement cost of the equipment is $30,000. Contrera also contributed a note payable of $10,000. Contrera is to receive 60% of the profits and losses. Badgez contributed only $90,000 cash. Determine the following items for Contreras:

| | Capital Account Balance | Tax Basis |
|---|---|---|
| a. | $80,000 | $69,000 |
| b. | $80,000 | $71,000 |
| c. | $70,000 | $71,000 |
| d. | $70,000 | $69,000 |
| e. | $70,000 | $79,000 |

# ASSIGNMENT MATERIAL

## Review Questions

1. Define *general partnership*.
2. How is a partnership defined?
3. Why is it advisable to use an attorney's services in preparing a partnership agreement?
4. What is the function of the partnership agreement?

# ILLUSTRATION 22-14
## Comparative Balance Sheets for a Continuing-care Retirement Community

**PRUNE DALE**
**Balance Sheets**
**December 31, 19X5 and 19X4**

| Assets | 19X5 | 19X4 |
|---|---|---|
| Current assets: | | |
| Cash | $ 375,000 | $ 330,000 |
| Accounts receivable (net of allowance for doubtful accounts of $4,000 and $5,000) | 187,000 | 197,000 |
| Supplies | 40,000 | 21,000 |
| Prepaid expenses | 15,000 | 8,000 |
| Total Current Assets | 617,000 | 556,000 |
| Assets whose use is limited: | | |
| Under note agreement—investments | 2,130,00 | 1,753,000 |
| By Board for capital improvements—investments | 100,000 | 65,000 |
| | 2,230,000 | 1,818,000 |
| Property and equipment: | | |
| Land | 557,000 | 557,000 |
| Land improvements | 205,000 | 203,000 |
| Buildings and improvements | 14,573,000 | 14,564,000 |
| Furniture and equipment | 752,000 | 698,000 |
| | 16,087,000 | 16,022,000 |
| Accumulated depreciation | (1,194,000) | (742,000) |
| Total Property and Equipment | 14,893,000 | 15,280,000 |
| Deferred financing costs (net of accumulated amortization of $28,000 and $21,000) | 83,000 | 90,000 |
| Total Assets | $17,823,000 | $17,744,000 |

| Liabilities and Fund Balance (Deficit) | 19X5 | 19X4 |
|---|---|---|
| Current liabilities: | | |
| Current maturities of long-term debt | $ 90,000 | $ 77,000 |
| Accounts payable | 180,000 | 174,000 |
| Accrued expenses | 161,000 | 178,000 |
| Deposits on unoccupied units | 22,000 | 40,000 |
| Total Current Liabilities | 453,000 | 469,000 |
| Long-term debt, less current maturities | 8,871,000 | 8,935,000 |
| Refundable fees | 59,000 | 144,000 |
| Estimated obligation to provide future services, in excess of amounts received or to be received | 88,000 | 100,000 |
| Deferred revenue from advance fees | 9,304,000 | 9,585,000 |
| Fund balance (deficit) | (952,000) | (1,489,000) |
| Total Liabilities and Fund Balance (deficit) | $17,823,000 | $17,744,000 |

Source: Adapted from *Audits of Providers of Health Care Services* (New York: American Institute of Certified Public Accountants, 1990), App. A, p. 178–79.

| DC |
|---|
| 23-3 |

## Dividing Profits and Losses

Barr and Courtner, both lawyers, have decided to form a partnership. They have asked your advice on how the profits and losses should be divided and have provided you with the following information:

1. Initial capital contributions:

| | |
|---|---|
| Barr | $20,000 |
| Courtner | 80,000 |

2. Time devoted to the business:

| | |
|---|---|
| Barr | 75% |
| Courtner | 100% |

3. Personal facts:

    Barr has an excellent reputation in the community. Substantially all new clients will come from her efforts.

    Courtner is strong technically and is an excellent supervisor of staff lawyers who are expected to do most of the detailed legal research and initial preparation of legal documents.

### Required:

How would you advise the partners to share profits and losses?

| DC |
|---|
| 23-4 |

## Recording the Initial Capital Contributions

High and Lowe have agreed to form a partnership in which profits are divided equally. High contributes $100,000 cash, and Lowe contributes a parcel of land, which the partnership intends to subdivide into residential lots on which to build custom homes for sale. Data regarding the parcel of land are as follows:

| | |
|---|---|
| Cost of land to Lowe (acquired three years ago) | $100,000 |
| Current market value, based on most recent county property tax assessment notice | 120,000 |
| Appraised value, based on recent appraisal by independent appraiser | 150,000 |

Lowe feels the land should be recorded on the partnership books at $120,000. High feels the land should be recorded at $100,000 so that the tax basis to Lowe carries over to the partnership. Neither feels the current appraised value is appropriate because an objective, verifiable transaction has not occurred. They have asked your advice on how to record the land.

### Required:

1. How would you respond?
2. Assuming the land is sold two years later for $140,000 (the land having been overappraised by $10,000), would this change your answer in requirement 1?

| DC |
|---|
| 23-5 |

## Selecting the Form of Business Organization

Sam Seeker has invested $600,000 in a new business venture, in which two, possibly three, former business associates will join him. He has purchased the patent rights to a revolutionary adhesive substance known as "sticko." He is considering the various forms of business organization he might use in establishing the business. You have been engaged to study the accounting and business problems he should consider in choosing either a general partnership or a corporation. Seeker requests specific advice on the following aspects as they relate to one of these two forms of business organization.

1. Personal liability if the venture is a disaster.
2. The borrowing capacity of the entity.
3. Requirements for operating a multistate business.
4. The recognition of the entity for income tax reporting purposes and major income tax considerations in selecting one of these forms of business organization.

### Required:
Discuss the legal implications of each above-mentioned form of organization for each specific aspect on which Seeker requests advice.

(AICPA adapted)

## Exercises

| E |
| 23-1 |

## Dividing the Profit or Loss: Partnership Agreement Is Silent

The partnership of Hatter and Widden had earnings of $40,000 for the year. Hatter devotes all of her time to the business, and Widden devotes 50% of his time to the business. Hatter's average capital balance was $60,000, and Widden's average capital balance was $30,000. The partnership agreement is silent regarding the distribution of profits.

### Required:
1. Prepare a schedule showing how the profit should be divided.
2. Prepare the entry to divide the profit.

| E |
| 23-2 |

## Dividing the Profit or Loss: Performance Features and Ratio

The partnership of Maxe and Lisle has the following provisions in its partnership agreement:

1. Maxe, who is primarily responsible for obtaining new clients, is to receive a 30% bonus on revenues in excess of $200,000.
2. Lisle, who is primarily responsible for administration is to receive a 30% bonus on profits in excess of 50% of revenues, as reflected in the general ledger.
3. All remaining profits or losses are to be divided equally.

### Additional Information:

| | |
|---|---|
| Revenues for the year . . . . . . . . . . . . . . . . . . . . . . . . . . . . . . . . . . . . . . . . . . . . . . . | $280,000 |
| Operating Expenses . . . . . . . . . . . . . . . . . . . . . . . . . . . . . . . . . . . . . . . . . . . . . . . . . | 120,000 |

**Required:**
1. Prepare a schedule showing how the profit or loss should be divided for the year.
2. Prepare the entry to divide the profit or loss for the year.

| E |
|:-:|
| 23-3 |

## Dividing the Profit or Loss: Ratio and Salary Allowances

The partnership of Darden and Louis shares profits and losses in a ratio of 7:3, respectively, after Louis receives a $10,000 salary allowance.

**Required:**
1. Prepare a schedule showing how the profit or loss should be divided, assuming the profit or loss for the year is
   a. $30,000.
   b. $6,000.
   c. $(10,000).
2. Prepare the entry to divide the profit or loss in situations (a) to (c) of requirement 1.

| E |
|:-:|
| 23-4 |

## Dividing the Profit or Loss: Ratio, Salary Allowances, and Imputed Interest on Capital

The partnership of Eddy and MacDonald has the following provisions in the partnership agreement:

1. Eddy and MacDonald receive salary allowances of $19,000 and $11,000, respectively.
2. Interest is imputed at 10% of the average capital investments.
3. Any remaining profit or loss is shared between Eddy and MacDonald in a 3:2 ratio, respectively.

**Additional Information:**

| Average capital investments: | |
|---|---|
| Eddy . . . . . . . . . . . . . . . . . . . . . . . . . . . . . . . . . . . . . . . . . . . . . . . . . . . . . . . . . . . . | $ 60,000 |
| MacDonald . . . . . . . . . . . . . . . . . . . . . . . . . . . . . . . . . . . . . . . . . . . . . . . . . . . . | 100,000 |

**Required:**
1. Prepare a schedule showing how the profit would be divided, assuming the partnership profit or loss is
   a. $76,000.
   b. $42,000.
   c. $(14,000).
2. Prepare the entry to divide the profit or loss in situations (a) to (c) of requirement 1.

## E 23-5

## Dividing the Profit or Loss: Ratio, Salary Allowances, and Imputed Interest on Capital—Order of Priority Specified

Assume the information provided in Exercise 23-4, except that the partnership agreement stipulates the following **order of priority** in the distribution of profits:

1. Salary allowances (only to the extent available).
2. Imputed interest on average capital investments (only to the extent available).
3. Any remaining profit in a 3:2 ratio. (No mention is made regarding losses.)

### Required:

The requirements are the same as for Exercise 23-4.

## E 23-6

## Recording Initial Capital Contributions

On May 1, 19X7, Booker and Page formed a partnership. Each contributed assets with the following agreed-upon valuations:

|  | Booker | Page |
|---|---|---|
| Cash | $80,000 | $ 20,000 |
| Machinery and equipment | 50,000 | 60,000 |
| Building | –0– | 240,000 |

The building is subject to a mortgage loan of $100,000, which is assumed by the partnership. The partnership agreement provides that Booker and Page share profits and losses 40% and 60%, respectively.

### Required:

1. Prepare the journal entry to record the capital contributions of each partner.
2. *Optional:* Assuming that no difference exists between the agreed-upon valuation of each asset contributed and its related adjusted basis, determine the tax basis of each partner on May 1, 19X7.

## E 23-7

## Determination of Tax Basis of Each Partner

Evers, Glade, and Marsh have formed a partnership by combining their respective sole proprietorships. The profit and loss sharing ratio is 4:3:3, respectively. The assets and liabilities contributed to the partnership are as follows:

|  | Adjusted Basis | Current Value |
|---|---|---|
| Evers: | | |
| Cash | $50,000 | $50,000 |
| Accounts receivable | 20,000 | 20,000 |
| Glade: | | |
| Land | 30,000 | 40,000 |

*(continued)*

| | Adjusted Basis | Current Value |
|---|---|---|
| **Marsh:** | | |
| Equipment...................................... | 20,000[a] | 25,000 |
| Equipment note payable........................ | 10,000 | 10,000 |

[a]Original cost of $27,000 minus $7,000 of depreciation taken to date.

## Required:

1. Determine the tax basis of each partner's interest in the partnership.
2. What is the tax basis of each noncash asset in the hands of the partnership?
3. Prepare the general ledger entry to record these contributions.
4. Assume that Glade decided to quit the partnership one day after it was formed and received cash in full satisfaction of his capital account balance. What gain or loss, if any, should Glade report for tax purposes?

---

| E |
|---|
| **23-8** |

## Subsequent Changes in Tax Basis of Each Partner

The tax basis of Reed, Storey, and Teller at the beginning of their partnership year was $50,000, $35,000, and $65,000, respectively. Profits and losses are shared equally.

## Additional Information:

| | |
|---|---|
| Additional cash capital contributions: | |
| Reed............................................ | $18,000 |
| Storey.......................................... | 10,000 |
| Teller.......................................... | 4,000 |
| Withdrawals during the year: | |
| Reed............................................ | 6,000 |
| Storey.......................................... | 12,000 |
| Teller.......................................... | 5,000 |
| Profits for the year: | |
| From the general ledger......................... | 30,000 |
| From the tax return............................. | 33,000 |

## Required:

1. Determine the tax basis of each partner at year-end, assuming no change in partnership liabilities.
2. Determine the tax basis of each partner at year-end, assuming that the only change in liabilities during the year was a $24,000 bank loan obtained at year-end. (The $24,000 borrowed, along with $6,000 cash on hand, was used to purchase equipment costing $30,000.)

# Problems

---

| P |
|---|
| **23-1** |

## Dividing Profits: Interest on Capital, Bonuses, and Salary Allowances

Horn and Sax are in partnership. The activity in each partner's capital account for 19X1 is as follows:

|  | Horn |  |  |  | Sax |  |
|---|---|---|---|---|---|---|
|  | 20,000 | 1/1 |  |  | 30,000 | 1/1 |
|  | 8,000 | 2/12 | 3/23 | 5,000 |  |  |
| 5/25 4,000 |  |  | 7/10 | 5,000 |  |  |
|  | 7,000 | 10/19 | 9/30 | 5,000 |  |  |
| 12/10 2,000 |  |  |  |  | 18,000 | 12/5 |
|  | 1,000 | 12/30 | 12/30 | 23,000 |  |  |
|  | 30,000 | 12/31 |  |  | 10,000 | 12/31 |

A drawings account is not used. The profit for 19X1 is $200,000.

### Required:

Divide the profit for the year between the partners using each of the following formulas:

a. Beginning capital balances.
b. Average capital balances. (Investments and withdrawals are assumed to have been made as of the beginning of the month if made before the middle of the month, and assumed to have been made as of the beginning of the following month if made after the middle of the month.)
c. Ending capital balances.
d. Bonus to Horn equal to 20% of profit in excess of $150,000; remaining profit divided equally.
e. Salary allowances of $45,000 and $35,000 to Horn and Sax, respectively; interest on average capital balances imputed at 10%; any residual balance divided equally. (Investments and withdrawals are treated as explained in part b.)

**P 23-2**

## Dividing Profits: Revision of Profit Sharing Agreement—Prior Period Adjustments

The partnership of Browne, Silvers, and Tanner was formed in 19X5. The partnership agreement specified that profits and losses were determined on the accrual basis and were divided as follows:

|  | Browne | Silvers | Tanner |
|---|---|---|---|
| Salary allowances . . . . . . . . . . . . . . . . . . . . . . . . . | $15,000 | $15,000 | $5,000 |
| Bonuses (percentage of profits in excess of $90,000) . . . . . . . . . . . . . . . . . . . . . . . . . . | 20% | 20% |  |
| Residual profit or loss . . . . . . . . . . . . . . . . . . . . . | 40% | 40% | 20% |

On January 1, 19X9, the partnership agreement was revised to provide for the sharing of profits and losses in the following manner:

|  | Brown | Silvers | Tanner |
|---|---|---|---|
| Salary allowances . . . . . . . . . . . . . . . . . . . . . . . . . | $20,000 | $20,000 | $15,000 |
| Bonuses (percentage of profits in excess of $110,000). . . . . . . . . . . . . . . . . . . . . . . . . . | 20% | 20% | 10% |
| Residual profit or loss . . . . . . . . . . . . . . . . . . . . . | 35% | 35% | 30% |

The partnership books show a profit of $145,000 for 19X9 before the following errors were discovered:

1. Inventory at December 31, 19X7, was overstated by $7,000.
2. Inventory at December 31, 19X8, was understated by $8,000.

3. Inventory at December 31, 19X9, was understated by $18,000.
4. Depreciation expense for 19X9 was understated by $5,000.

### Required:

1. Divide the profit among the partners for 19X9, assuming the partnership agreement calls for any prior years' errors to be treated as prior-period adjustments.
2. Assuming the reported profits for 19X7 and 19X8 were $85,000 and $110,000, respectively, prepare the proper adjusting entry to correct the capital balances as of January 1, 19X9. The old profit sharing agreement is used for these items.

## P 23-3 Combining Two Partnerships: Recording the Initial Capital Contributions

The partnerships of Hill & Mounds and Flatt & Level began business on July 1, 19X1; each partnership owns one retail appliance store. The two partnerships agree to combine as of July 1, 19X4, to form a new partnership known as Four Partners Discount Stores.

The following additional information is available:

1. **Profit and loss ratios.** The profit and loss sharing ratios for the former partnerships were 40% to Hill and 60% to Mounds, and 30% to Flatt and 70% to Level. The profit and loss sharing ratio for the new partnership is Hill, 20%; Mounds, 30%; Flatt, 15%; and Level, 35%.
2. **Capital investments.** The opening capital investments for the new partnership are to be in the same ratio as the profit and loss sharing ratios for the new partnership. If necessary, certain partners may have to contribute additional cash and others may have to withdraw cash to bring the capital investments into the proper ratio.
3. **Accounts receivable.** The partners agreed that the new partnership's allowance for bad debts is to be 5% of the accounts receivable contributed by Hill & Mounds, and 10% of the accounts receivable contributed by Flatt & Level.
4. **Inventory.** The opening inventory of the new partnership is to be valued by the FIFO method. Hill & Mounds used the FIFO method to value inventory (which approximates its current value), and Flatt & Level used the LIFO method. The LIFO inventory represents 85% of its FIFO value.
5. **Property and equipment.** The partners agree that the land's current value is approximately 20% more than its historical cost, as recorded on each partnership's books.

   The depreciable assets of each partnership were acquired on July 1, 19X1. Hill & Mounds used straight-line depreciation and a 10-year life. Flatt & Level used double-declining balance depreciation and a 10-year life. The partners agree that the current value of these assets is approximately 80% of their historical cost, as recorded on each partnership's books.

6. **Unrecorded liability.** After each partnership's books were closed on June 30, 19X4, an unrecorded merchandise purchase of $4,000 by Flatt & Level was discovered. The merchandise had been sold by June 30, 19X4.
7. **Accrued vacation.** The accounts of Hill & Mounds include a vacation pay accrual. The four partners agree that Flatt & Level should make a similar accrual for their five employees, who will receive a one-week vacation at $200 per employee per week.

The June 30, 19X4, postclosing trial balances of the partnerships appear below:

| | Hill & Mounds Trial Balance June 30, 19X4 | | Flatt and Level Trial Balance June 30, 19X4 | |
|---|---|---|---|---|
| Cash | $ 20,000 | | $ 15,000 | |
| Accounts receivable | 100,000 | | 150,000 | |
| Allowance for doubtful accounts | | $ 2,000 | | $ 6,000 |
| Merchandise inventory | 175,000 | | 119,000 | |
| Land | 25,000 | | 35,000 | |
| Buildings and equipment | 80,000 | | 125,000 | |
| Accumulated depreciation | | 24,000 | | 61,000 |
| Prepaid expenses | 5,000 | | 7,000 | |
| Accounts payable | | 40,000 | | 60,000 |
| Notes payable | | 70,000 | | 75,000 |
| Accrued expenses | | 30,000 | | 45,000 |
| Hill, capital | | 95,000 | | |
| Mounds, capital | | 144,000 | | |
| Flatt, capital | | | | 65,000 |
| Level, capital | | | | 139,000 |
| Totals | $405,000 | $405,000 | $451,000 | $451,000 |

## Required:

1. Prepare the journal entries to record the initial capital contribution after considering the effect of the above information. Use separate entries for each of the combining partnerships.
2. Prepare a schedule computing the cash contributed or withdrawn by each partner to bring the initial capital account balances into the profit and loss sharing ratio.

(AICPA adapted)

P
23-4

## Combining Three Sole Proprietorships: Dividing the Profit for the First Year of Operations

Arby, Bobb, and Carlos, who are attorneys, agree to consolidate their individual practices as of January 1, 19X3. The partnership agreement includes the following features:

1. Each partner's capital contribution is the net amount of the assets and liabilities assumed by the partnership, which are as follows:

|                              | Arby      | Bobb      | Carlos    |
| ---------------------------- | --------- | --------- | --------- |
| Cash.....................    | $ 5,000   | $ 5,000   | $ 5,000   |
| Accounts receivable .....    | 14,000    | 6,000     | 16,000    |
| Furniture and library ...    | 4,300     | 2,500     | 6,200     |
|                              | $23,300   | $13,500   | $27,200   |
| Allowance for depreciation . | $ 2,400   | $ 1,500   | $ 4,700   |
| Accounts payable.........    | 300       | 1,400     | $ 700     |
|                              | $ 2,700   | $ 2,900   | $ 5,400   |
| Capital contribution ....    | $20,600   | $10,600   | $21,800   |

Each partner guaranteed the collectibility of receivables.

2. Carlos had leased office space and was bound by the lease until June 30, 19X3. The monthly rental was $600. The partners agree to occupy Carlos's office space until the expiration of the lease and to pay the rent. The partners concur that the rent is too high for the space and that a fair rental value would be $450 per month. The excess rent is charged to Carlos at year-end. On July 1, the partners move to new quarters with a monthly rental of $500.

3. No salaries are paid to the partners. The individual partners receive 20% of the gross fees billed to their respective clients during the first year of the partnership. After deducting operating expenses (excluding the excess rent), the balance of the fees billed is credited to the partners' capital accounts in the following ratios: Arby, 40%; Bobb, 35%; and Carlos, 25%.

   On April 1, 19X3, Mack is admitted to the partnership; Mack receives 20% of the fees from new business obtained after April 1, after deducting expenses applicable to that new business. Expenses (excluding the excess rent) are apportioned to the new business in the same ratio that total expenses, other than bad debt losses, bear to total gross fees.

4. The following information pertains to the partnership's activities in 19X3:
   a. Fees are billed as follows:

| | |
| --- | --- |
| Arby's clients ........................................... | $ 44,000 |
| Bobb's clients........................................... | 24,000 |
| Carlos's clients ......................................... | 22,000 |
| New business: | |
|    Prior to April 1......................................... | 6,000 |
|    After April 1 ........................................... | 24,000 |
|      Total ............................................. | $120,000 |

   b. Total expenses, excluding depreciation and bad debt expenses, are $29,350 including the total amount paid for rent. Depreciation is computed at the rate of 10% on original cost. Depreciable assets purchased during 19X3, on which one-half year's depreciation is taken, total $5,000.

   c. Cash charges to the partners' accounts during the year are as follows:

| | |
| --- | --- |
| Arby................................................... | $ 5,200 |
| Bobb.................................................. | 4,400 |

| | |
|---|---:|
| Carlos | 5,800 |
| Mack | 2,500 |
| | $17,900 |

d. Of Arby's and Bobb's receivables, $1,200 and $450, respectively, proved to be uncollectible. A new client billed in March for $1,600 went bankrupt, and a settlement of 50 cents on the dollar was made.

### Required:

1. Determine the profit for 19X3.
2. Prepare a schedule showing how the profit for 19X3 is to be divided.
3. Prepare a statement of the partners' capital accounts for the year ended December 31, 19X3.

(AICPA adapted)

| P 23-5 |
|---|

## Computation of Billings and Determination of Profits

Funn and Kidd, architectural designers and interior decorators, combined May 1, 19X8, agreeing to share profits as follows: Kidd, two-thirds; and Funn, one-third. Funn contributed furniture and fixtures, $3,000, and cash, $2,000; Kidd contributed cash, $500.

They plan to submit monthly bills and make the following arrangements with their clients:

1. The firm employs draftspersons who are paid on an hourly basis. Time spent on client assignments is billed to clients at their hourly rate plus 125% for overhead and profit.
2. Partners' time on jobs is billed at $10 an hour.
3. A 10% service fee is charged on purchases of furniture, drapes, and so on, installed on the jobs. (As an accommodation to their clients, Funn and Kidd pay the vendors and charge their clients for these purchases; however, they would like the amounts paid to vendors excluded from their revenues in their operating statements.)
4. No service fee is charged on taxis, telephone, and other expenses identifiable to jobs and charged to clients.

Voucher register totals for May are given below:

Credits:

| | |
|---|---:|
| Vouchers payable | $3,469 |
| Taxes withheld—Federal income | 93 |
| Taxes withheld—FICA | 27 |
| Total | $3,589 |

Debits:

| | |
|---|---:|
| Purchases and expenses chargeable to clients | $1,615 |
| Partners' drawings (Funn, $100; Kidd, $125) | 225 |
| General expenses | 549 |
| Salaries | 1,200 |
| Total | $3,589 |

The first debit column is analyzed in the voucher register as follows:

Purchases subject to 10% fee:

| | | |
|---|---:|---:|
| Client M, Job 51 | $1,210 | |
| Client H, Job 52 | 320 | $1,530 |

Expenses chargeable to clients:

| | | |
|---|---:|---:|
| Client M, Job 51 | $   23 | |
| Client M, Job 54 | 7 | |
| Client H, Job 52 | 19 | |
| Client L, Job 53 | 36 | 85 |
| | | $1,615 |

Client M has not yet authorized Funn and Kidd to do job 54. The partners are confident, however, that the job will be authorized, and the above expenses, as well as charges for time spent by a draftsperson and Funn on preliminary designs, will be billed and collected. Assume it is proper to consider this an unbilled account receivable.

The payroll analysis is summaried below. Partners' time on jobs, charged to the jobs at $10 an hour, is summarized in the payroll analysis for convenience in posting costs to job sheets, although the partners are not paid for direct time on jobs.

| Job | Secretary | Draftspersons | Funn | Kidd |
|---|---:|---:|---:|---:|
| 51 | | $   312 | $240 | $300 |
| 52 | | 276 | 120 | 230 |
| 53 | | 304 | 130 | 320 |
| 54 | | 48 | 240 | |
| | | $   940 | $730 | $850 |
| | | | | |
| **Nonbillable** | | | | |
| General office | $160 | 40 | | |
| Idle time | | 60 | | |
| Total payroll | $160 | $1,040 | | |

Journal entries recorded $25 depreciation on furniture and fixtures and the $54 employer's share of federal and state taxes.

There were no cash receipts other than the original investment. The cash disbursements journal shows the following totals:

Debit:

| | |
|---|---:|
| Vouchers Payable | $2,373 |

Credit:

| | |
|---|---:|
| Cash | $2,358 |
| Discount on purchases | 15 |

## Required:

1. Compute the billings to clients for May.
2. Prepare a worksheet for the month, showing the opening balances, the transactions for the month, and an adjustment trial balance at month-end.

3. Divide the profit for the month.

4. Prepare a statement of changes in partners' capital for the month.

(AICPA adapted)

**P
23-6***

## Converting from Cash to Accrual Basis

The partnership of Green, Redd, and White engaged you to adjust its accounting records and convert them uniformly to the accrual basis in anticipation of admitting Frost as a new partner. Some accounts are on the accrual basis and others are on the cash basis. The partnership's books were closed at December 31, 19X6, by the bookkeeper, who prepared the following trial balance:

### GREEN, REDD, AND WHITE
### TRIAL BALANCE, DECEMBER 31, 19X6

|  | Debit | Credit |
|---|---|---|
| Cash | $ 10,000 | |
| Accounts Receivable | 40,000 | |
| Inventory | 26,000 | |
| Land | 9,000 | |
| Buildings | 50,000 | |
| Accumulated Depreciation—Buildings | | $ 2,000 |
| Equipment | 56,000 | |
| Accumulated Depreciation—Equipment | | 6,000 |
| Goodwill | 5,000 | |
| Accounts Payable | | 55,000 |
| Allowance for Future Inventory Losses | | 3,000 |
| Green, Capital | | 40,000 |
| Redd, Capital | | 60,000 |
| White, Capital | | 30,000 |
| Totals | $196,000 | $196,000 |

Your inquiries disclosed the following:

1. The partnership was organized on January 1, 19X5, with no provision in the partnership agreement for the distribution of partnership profits and losses. During 19X5, profits were distributed equally among the partners. The partnership was amended effective January 1, 19X6, to provide for the following profit and loss ratio: Green, 50%; Redd, 30%; and White, 20%. The amended partnership agreement also stated that the accounting records should be maintained on the accrual basis and that any adjustments necessary for 19X5 should be allocated according to the 19X5 distribution of profits.

2. The following amounts were not recorded as prepayments or accruals.

*The financial statement information presented for problems accompanied by asterisks is provided on Model 23 (filename: Model23) of the software disk that is available for use with the text, enabling the problem to be worked on the computer.

|  | December 31 | |
| --- | --- | --- |
|  | 19X6 | 19X5 |
| Prepaid insurance | $700 | $ 650 |
| Advances from customers | 200 | 1,100 |
| Accrued interest expense | | 450 |

The advances from customers were recorded as sales in the year the cash was received.

3. In 19X6, the partnership recorded a $3,000 provision for anticipated declines in inventory prices. You convinced the partners that the provision was unnecessary and should be removed from the books.

4. The partnership charged equipment purchased for $4,400 on January 3, 19X6, to expense. This equipment has an estimated life of 10 years. The partnership depreciates its capitalized equipment under the double-declining balance method at twice the straight-line depreciation rate.

5. The partners established an allowance for doubtful accounts at 2% of current accounts receivable and 5% of past due accounts. At December 31, 19X5, the partnership had $54,000 of accounts receivable, of which only $4,000 was past due. At December 31, 19X6, 15% of accounts receivable were past due, of which $4,000 represented sales made in 19X5 that were generally considered collectible. The partnership had written off uncollectible accounts in the year the accounts became worthless, as follows:

|  | Account Written Off in | |
| --- | --- | --- |
|  | 19X6 | 19X5 |
| 19X6 accounts | $ 800 | |
| 19X5 accounts | 1,000 | $250 |

6. Goodwill was recorded on the books in 19X6 and credited to the partners' capital accounts in the profit and loss ratio in recognition of an increase in the value of the business resulting from improved sales volume. The partners agreed to write off the goodwill before admitting the new partner.

### Required:

Prepare a worksheet showing the adjustments and the adjusted trial balance for the partnership on the accrual basis at December 31, 19X6. All adjustments affecting income should be made directly to partners' capital accounts. Number your adjusting entries. (Prepare formal journal entries and show supporting computations.)

(AICPA adapted)

P
23-7*

### Preparing Worksheets to Arrive at Current Trial Balance

The Joker & Laffer Company is a partnership that has not maintained adequate accounting records because it has been unable to employ a competent bookkeeper. The company sells hardware items to the retail trade and also sells wholesale to builders and contractors. As Joker & Laffer's CPA, you prepare the company's financial statements as of June 30, 19X2.

The company's records provide the following postclosing trial balance at December 31, 19X1:

### THE JOKER & LAFFER COMPANY
### POSTCLOSING TRIAL BALANCE, DECEMBER 31, 19X1

| | Debit | Credit |
|---|---|---|
| Cash | $10,000 | |
| Accounts Receivable | 8,000 | |
| Allowance for Bad Debts | | $ 600 |
| Merchandise Inventory | 35,000 | |
| Prepaid Insurance | 150 | |
| Automobiles | 7,800 | |
| Accumulated Depreciation—Automobiles | | 4,250 |
| Furniture and Fixtures | 2,200 | |
| Accumulated Depreciation—Furniture and Fixtures | | 650 |
| Accounts Payable | | 13,800 |
| Bank Loan Payable (due January 2, 19X2) | | 8,000 |
| Accrued Liabilities | | 200 |
| Joker, Capital | | 17,500 |
| Laffer, Capital | | 18,150 |
| Totals | $63,150 | $63,150 |

You collect the following information at June 30, 19X2:

1. Your analysis of cash transactions, derived from the company's bank statements and checkbook stubs, is as follows:

| Deposits: | |
|---|---|
| Cash receipts from customers | $65,000 |
| ($40,000 of this amount represents collections on receivables including redeposited protested checks totaling $600) | |
| Bank loan, January 2, 19X2 (due May 1, 19X2, 5%) | 7,867 |
| Bank loan, May 1, 19X2 (due September 1, 19X2, 5%) | 8,850 |
| Sale of old automobile | 20 |
| Total Deposits | $81,737 |

| Disbursements: | |
|---|---|
| Payments to merchandise creditors | $45,000 |
| Payment to Internal Revenue Service on Laffer's 19X2 declaration of estimated income taxes | 3,000 |
| General expenses | 7,000 |
| Bank loan, January 2, 19X2 | 8,000 |
| Bank loan, May 2, 19X2 | 8,000 |
| Payment for new automobile | 7,200 |
| Protested checks | 900 |
| Joker, withdrawals | 5,000 |
| Laffer, withdrawals | 2,500 |
| Total Disbursements | $86,600 |

2. The protested checks include customers' checks totaling $600 that were redeposited and an employee's check for $300 that was redeposited.

3. At June 30, 19X2, accounts receivable from customers for merchandise sales amount to $18,000 and include accounts totaling $800 that have been placed with an attorney for collection. Correspondence with the client's attorney reveals that one of the accounts for $175 is uncollectible. Experience indicates that 1% of credit sales will prove uncollectible.

4. On April 1, 19X2, a new automobile was purchased. The list price of the automobile was $7,500, and $300 was allowed for the trade-in of an old automobile, even though the dealer stated that its condition was so poor that he did not want it. The client sold the old automobile, which cost $1,800 and was fully depreciated at December 31, 19X1, to an auto wrecker for $20. The old automobile was in use up to the date of its sale.

5. Depreciation is recorded by the straight-line method and is computed on acquisitions to the nearest full month. The estimated life for furniture and fixtures is 10 years and for automobiles is three years. (Salvage value is ignored in computing depreciation. No asset other than the car in item 4 was fully depreciated prior to June 30, 19X2.)

6. Other data as of June 30, 19X2, are the following:

| | |
|---|---:|
| Merchandise inventory | $37,500 |
| Prepaid insurance | 80 |
| Accrued expenses | 166 |

7. Accounts payable to merchandise vendors total $18,750. A $750 credit memorandum was received from a merchandise vendor for returned merchandise; the company will apply the credit to July merchandise purchases. Neither the credit memorandum nor the return of the merchandise had been recorded on the books.

8. Profits and losses are divided equally between the partners.

### Required:

Prepare a worksheet that provides, on the accrual basis, information regarding transactions for the six months ended June 30, 19X2, the results of the partnership operations for the period, and the financial position of the partnership at June 30, 19X2. (Do not prepare formal financial statements or formal journal entries, but show supporting computations when necessary.)

(AICPA adapted)

### ANSWERS TO SELF-STUDY QUESTIONS

1. b    3. a    5. d.
2. c    4. b    6. c

---

## Appendix A   LIMITED PARTNERSHIPS

An explosive increase in the use of limited partnerships has occurred in recent years. Such partnerships are used as investment vehicles by passive investors. A **limited partnership** consists of a general partner and limited partners. Unlike the general partner, a limited partner's liability is limited to his or her cash investments. Furthermore, a limited partner plays no role in the management of the partnership, this being the complete responsibility of the general partner.

### Historical Use of Limited Partnerships.

Limited partnerships have been used primarily in the oil and gas exploration field and in real estate. Shortly, we will discuss real estate limited partnerships in some detail. We will also discuss a relatively new type of limited partnership, the master limited partnership, which has certain similarities to a corporation. For the historical record, we now briefly mention another type of limited partnership that became immensely popular in the late 1970s and early 1980s: the research and development partnerships. Used for start-up businesses, the limited partner investors could write off, for tax purposes, their share of the money spent each year on research and development (that is, their share of the partnership's loss). Thus, they obtained immediate tax deductions. If the investors had invested directly in the start-up company, the research and development expenses would not flow through to them. Instead, such expenses would just give the start-up company a net operating loss carryforward, which might not be utilized for several years.

In addition, the partners received research and development tax credits that were used to reduce income taxes on any remaining taxable income—this was an extremely attractive feature. In the 1980s, three specific pieces of tax legislation resulted in the rapid decline in the use of these partnerships: (1) disallowance of the use of the tax credits against other income, (2) making the research and development deductions a tax preference item for alternative minimum tax (AMT) purposes (90% having to be added back leaving only 10% deductible), and (3) enacting passive activity limitations. Also, a high percentage of these research and development partnerships did not bear fruit, further contributing to their rapid decline. (An example was the $26 million invested in John DeLorean's automobile development venture in which the limited partners lost their entire investment.) In the late 1980s, many Wall Street brokerage firms formed limited partnerships that took an equity stake in leveraged buyouts.

## Real Estate Limited Partnerships

**Real estate limited partnerships** (RELPs) are formed by companies that package real estate investments. Such companies, which generally have real estate experience, are commonly referred to as *sponsors* or *syndicators.* These companies employ securities brokers to sell interests in the limited partnerships to individual investors. The sponsor or an affiliated company is usually the general partner. The partnership then acquires rental apartments, shopping centers, or office buildings (the most common investments). Sponsors generally receive an up-front fee, an annual management fee, and a share of the income and appreciation. The general partner controls when the property is sold. (The average life of such partnerships is seven to twelve years.) It is difficult for limited partners to get their money out of the partnership until liquidation, because they cannot readily sell their interests. They must personally find a buyer. This is a major drawback for many investors. However, such investments appear to be ideal for persons with little or no real estate experience or who do not want the headaches associated with property management.

Although real estate investment packages can take any form of ownership (such as a corporation, a general partnership, or a real estate investment trust), limited partnerships have the unique advantage of limited liability (to the limited partners) and the ability to pass through the partnership income or loss to the partners.

**Investing in RELPs.**   There are two types of syndications: public and private. Public partnerships must be registered with the SEC, which reviews the registration statement (as opposed to approving the offering) before interests may be sold to investors. In addition, each state has investor-eligibility requirements. Generally, an investor needs either a net worth of $75,000 (excluding one's home) or a gross income of $30,000 and a net worth of $30,000 (excluding one's home). Private partnerships (which are not registered with the SEC) account for a much bigger portion of real estate partnerships and require much wealthier investors. In public partnerships, the minimum required investment is generally $5,000, but may be as low as $2,000 (to accommodate Individual Retirement Account investments). The minimum investments in private partnerships generally range from $30,000 to $150,000. As a result, small investors who otherwise are unable to invest individually in real estate are able to pool their resources and invest in shopping centers and large apartment complexes.

**Unique Tax Feature.**   Special tax laws apply to real estate. Typically, real estate partnerships borrow from a financial institution most of the money needed to acquire the real estate. This increase in liabilities may be added to the bases of all partners (including the limited partners), even though the limited partners are not personally obligated to repay the loan if the partnership cannot repay the loan (as might happen if the project is not properly managed or the real estate declines in value). As a result, the limited partners can write off for tax purposes more than their cash investments. (However, the Tax Reform Act of 1986 did impose some limited restrictions in this respect.) Such partnerships are commonly considered the only "true" tax shelter, because the depreciation write-off is considered a paper loss, not an economic loss.

**Popularity from 1981 to 1986.** During the period 1981 to 1986, highly leveraged real estate limited partnerships were immensely popular because of the combination of short depreciable lives (15 to 19 years) allowable during these years under the Internal Revenue Code and the taxation of capital gains at rates 60% less than ordinary income tax rates. In fact, so much money poured into these investments that the three most important things to look for in real estate were no longer "location, location, and location." Instead, they became "tax benefit, tax benefit, and tax benefit." However, the Tax Reform Act of 1986 lengthened depreciable lives on real estate approximately 50% and eliminated the favorable tax treatment on capital gains. In addition, the right to shield other income using partnership losses was severely limited. As a result, these types of investments lost much of their appeal, and unleveraged (or "income-oriented") partnerships became more attractive. In these partnerships, sound property management and good cost control are important, inasmuch as healthy returns cannot be obtained merely by having favorable tax laws.

**Potential Pitfalls.** In addition to the business risks of the syndicator buying an undesirable property, paying too much for a property, having an insufficient cash flow from operations to service debt (in a highly leveraged partnership), and not properly managing the property, there are several other risks that are unique to this form of organization. In a limited partnership, controls over the general partner are quite limited in comparison to controls over management in the corporate form of business, which has a board of directors, an audit committee, and corporate officers. Many unscrupulous general partners have enriched themselves at the expense of the limited partners. Attempting to obtain information from a limited partnership in financial difficulty can be exasperating. Trying to replace a general partner for inadequate performance can sometimes be difficult.

## Master Limited Partnerships

**Master limited partnerships** (MLPs) are unique in that their ownership units (commonly called *shares*) are traded on the stock exchanges, usually the New York Stock Exchange or the American Stock Exchange. Thus, the limited partners can readily dispose of their shares, and this ability gives them liquidity not available in other limited partnerships. Introduced by the oil and gas industry in the early 1980s, the concept has spread to real estate and other industries.

Many types of incorporated businesses took steps in 1986 to disincorporate into MLPs, mainly in an attempt to avoid the double taxation of corporate income taxes; MLPs are taxed only once—at the individual partner level.

A burdensome problem for accountants of such partnerships is allocating the partnership's income or loss to each of the limited partners, who may have purchased their shares at different times.

<hr>

**Appendix B   THE UNIFORM PARTNERSHIP ACT**

<hr>

The Uniform Partnership Act has 45 sections that are separated into the following seven parts:

Part    I    Preliminary provisions
Part   II    Nature of partnership
Part  III    Relations of partners to persons dealing with the partnership
Part  IV    Relations of partners to one another
Part   V    Property rights of a partner
Part  VI    Dissolution and winding up
Part VII    Miscellanous provisions

The UPA is approximately 14 pages long and can be found in law library books that contain all of the various uniform acts. Because of its length, the UPA is not set forth here in its entirety. However, two of the sections are presented here to give you an idea of the content of the UPA.

## Part III: Relations of Partners to Persons Dealing with the Partnership

**Sec. 15. (Nature of Partner's Liability.)**
All partners are liable:

a. Jointly and severally for everything chargeable to the partnership under sections 13 and 14.
b. Jointly for all other debts and obligations of the partnership; but any partner may enter into a separate obligation to perform a partnership contract.

## Part IV: Relations of Partners to One Another

**Sec. 18. (Rules Determining Rights and Duties of Partners.)**
The rights and duties of the partners in relation to the partnership shall be determined by the following rules:

a. Each partner shall be repaid his contributions, whether by way of capital or advances to the partnership property and share equally in the profits and surplus remaining after all liabilities, including those to partners, are satisfied; and must contribute toward the losses, whether of capital or otherwise, sustained by the partnership according to his share in the profits.

b. The partnership must indemnify every partner in respect of payments made and personal liabilities reasonably incurred by him in the ordinary and proper conduct of its business, or for the preservation of its business or property.

c. A partner, who in aid of the partnership makes any payment or advance beyond the amount of capital which he agreed to contribute, shall be paid interest from the date of the payment or advance.

d. A partner shall receive interest on the capital contributed by him only from the date when repayment should be made.

e. All partners have equal rights in the management and conduct of the partnership business.

f. No partner is entitled to remuneration for acting in the partnership business, except that a surviving partner is entitled to reasonable compensation for his services in winding up the partnership affairs.

g. No person can become a member of a partnership without the consent of all the partners.

h. Any difference arising as to ordinary matters connected with the partnership business may be decided by a majority of the partners; but no act in contravention of any agreement between the partners may be done rightfully without the consent of all the partners.

# 24
.....

# PARTNERSHIPS: CHANGES IN OWNERSHIP

## TOPIC OUTLINE

# CHAPTER OVERVIEW

A business conducted as a partnership usually has changes in ownership during its existence. In this chapter, we discuss the changes in ownership that do not result in the termination of the partnership's business activities. Such changes in ownership may be categorized as follows:

1. **An increase in the number of partners.**
   a. **Admission of a new partner.** More partners may be needed to serve clients properly, or additional capital may be required above and beyond the personal resources of existing partners.
   b. **Business combinations.** Two partnerships may combine in such a manner that a pooling of interests occurs—that is, the partners of each individual partnership become partners in a larger, combined business.
2. **A decrease in the number of partners.**
   a. **Willful or forced withdrawal.** A partner may withdraw from a partnership in order to (1) engage in another line of work; (2) continue in the same line of work but as a sole proprietor; (3) retire. In addition, a partner may be forced out of a partnership for economic reasons or for not having performed adequately the responsibilities entrusted to him or her.
   b. **Death or incapacity.** Aside from death, a partner may become so seriously ill that he or she cannot continue partnership duties.
3. **Purchase of an existing partnership interest.** A partner may decide to sell his or her partnership interest to someone outside the partnership.

The first two categories may generate issues of how to treat each partner equitably when (1) tangible assets have current values different from book values, and (2) intangible elements exist. For simplicity, we discuss these issues separately. The third category consists entirely of personal transactions conducted outside the partnership. Because no partnership accounting issues are associated with this category, we discuss it only briefly at this point, before discussing the first two categories.

## Purchase of an Existing Partner's Interest

The purchase of an interest from one or more of a partnership's existing partners is a personal transaction between the incoming partner and the selling partners. No additional money or properties are invested in the partnership. In this respect, it is similar to the sale of a corporation's stock by individuals. The only entry that is made on the partnership's books is an entry to transfer an amount from the selling partner's Capital account to the new partner's Capital account. For example, assume the following information:

1. A and B are in partnership and share profits and losses equally.
2. A and B have Capital account balances of $30,000 each.
3. C purchases B's partnership interest for $37,500, making payment directly to B.

The entry to record the transaction on the books of the partnership is as follows:

| | | |
|---|---:|---:|
| Capital, Partner B | 30,000 | |
|     Capital, Partner C | | 30,000 |

The purchase price paid by C is completely irrelevant to the entry recorded on the books, regardless of why C paid more than the book value of the partnership interest. The fact that the partnership may have undervalued tangible assets or possible superior earnings power is not relevant to the accounting issues. A personal transaction has occurred, which is independent of accounting for the business of the partnership.

Alternatively, C could purchase a portion of each existing partner's interest in the partnership. For example, assume that C purchased one-third of A's interest for $12,500 and one-third of B's interest for $12,500, making payments directly to A and B. The entry to record the transaction on the books is as follows:

| | | |
|---|---:|---:|
| Capital, Partner A | 10,000 | |
| Capital, Partner B | 10,000 | |
|     Capital, Partner C | | 20,000 |

Again, the purchase of an existing partnership interest is a personal transaction between the old and the new partners.

## An Increase or Decrease in the Number of Partners: Methods to Prevent Inequities

The number of partners in a partnership may increase or decrease without the purchase of an existing partner's interest. Recall that in Chapter 23 we stated that to prevent partners from being treated inequitably as a result of revisions to the profit and loss sharing formula, either the partnership assets should be revalued to their current values or the new profit and loss sharing formula should include a special provision whereby the old profit and loss sharing formula would be used in specified instances. Because a change in ownership of a partnership produces a new profit and loss sharing formula, the same techniques to prevent inequities may be applied to situations of changes in ownership. In addition, we introduce a new method—the **bonus method**—that also may be used to prevent inequities.

The determination of the journal entry to reflect a change in the ownership of a partnership is to some extent an after-the-fact mechanical process using the terms and methods selected by the partners. A far more important role for the accountant when a change in ownership is contemplated is explaining and illustrating the various methods (and their ramifications) of dealing with situations in which assets have current values different from book values and/or intangible elements exist. The accountant may even assist partners in determining the amount of any goodwill by demonstrating some of the common methods that may be used to calculate goodwill. Remember that in these situations the accountant is only an advisor. It is not his or her role to select a method for determining the amount of goodwill or to select one of the three methods available for achieving equity among the partners.

## TANGIBLE ASSETS HAVING CURRENT VALUES DIFFERENT FROM BOOK VALUES

### Admission of a New Partner

In most cases, a partner is admitted into a partnership by making a capital contribution to the partnership. In accounting and attorney partnerships, virtually all the partners admitted make substantial contributions after spending years in lower levels of the business obtaining the necessary training and experience. A capital contribution creates a new partner's interest. In substance, this is similar to a corporation issuing additional shares of its stock to new stockholders.

One of the three available methods of preventing an inequity must be applied when a new partner is admitted. Each method, although different procedurally, produces the same result. To illustrate how each method would be applied to a situation in which a new partner is admitted into a partnership by making a capital contribution, assume the following facts:

1. The partnership of A and B desires to admit C.
2. The Capital accounts of A and B are $25,000 each.
3. Profits and losses are shared equally between A and B. On admission of C, profits and losses are shared equally among the three partners.
4. All the partnership's assets have carrying values equal to their current values, except for a parcel of land that is worth $12,000 more than its book value of $100,000.
5. Because the current value of the existing partner's equity is $62,000 ($25,000 + $25,000 + $12,000), A and B agree to admit C into the partnership on contribution of $31,000 cash.

The credit to be made to the new partner's Capital account regarding the $31,000 capital contribution may be determined only after the partners agree on one of the following three methods.

**Revaluing of Assets Method.** Under the **revaluing of assets method,** the parcel of land merely is written up to its current value using the following entry:

| | | |
|---|---|---|
| Land | 12,000 | |
| Capital, Partner A | | 6,000 |
| Capital, Partner B | | 6,000 |

Because the old partners shared profits and losses equally until C was admitted, each of their Capital accounts is increased by 50% of the upward revaluation. The entry to record C's contribution is as follows:

| | | |
|---|---|---|
| Cash | 31,000 | |
| Capital, Partner C | | 31,000 |

The revaluing of assets method is the simplest of the three methods. Although it is not in accordance with generally accepted accounting principles, this disadvantage is usually not important to the partnership form of business. If the partners agree to this method, the new partnership agreement should specify that the new partner is to receive a one-third interest in the new net assets of the partnership **after the land has been written up by $12,000,** thus receiving a full credit to his Capital account for the $31,000 capital contribution.

**Special Profit and Loss Sharing Provision Method.** Under the **special profit and loss sharing provision** approach, the land is carried at its historical cost. However, the new profit and loss sharing formula contains a provision that (a) acknowledges that the land's current value is $12,000 in excess of its book value at the time of C's admission, and (b) specifies that the old partners are entitled to share equally in the first $12,000 profit on the sale of the land. Assuming the land is sold for a $15,000 profit several years after C is admitted to the partnership, the profit on the sale would be divided as follows:

| | Total | Partner A | Partner B | Partner C |
|---|---|---|---|---|
| First $12,000 | $12,000 | $6,000 | $6,000 | |
| Excess over $12,000 | 3,000 | 1,000 | 1,000 | $1,000 |
| | $15,000 | $7,000 | $7,000 | $1,000 |

The entry to record C's contribution is the same as shown in the preceding method. If the partners agree to this method, the new partnership agreement should state that the new partner is to receive a full credit to his Capital account for the $31,000 capital contribution, **with no revaluation made to the assets of the partnership.**

**The Bonus Method.**   Under the **bonus method,** no adjustment is made to the carrying amount of the land, nor is any special provision included in the new profit and loss sharing formula because the land is worth more than its book value. When the land subsequently is sold, C will receive one-third of the *entire* profit. From an equity viewpoint, C is not entitled to one-third of the first $12,000 profit; therefore, C's Capital account is reduced at his admission by the amount that will be credited to his Capital account in the event the land is sold for $12,000 in excess of its current book value. Thus, one-third of $12,000, or $4,000, of C's $31,000 initial capital contribution is not credited to his Capital account. Instead, the $4,000 is credited to the old partners' Capital accounts. The $4,000 is shared by partners A and B in the old profit and loss sharing ratio. The entry to record C's admission into the partnership is as follows:

| | | |
|---|---|---|
| Cash | 31,000 | |
| Capital, Partner A | | 2,000 |
| Capital, Partner B | | 2,000 |
| Capital, Partner C | | 27,000 |

Assuming the land is sold for a $15,000 profit several years after C is admitted to the partnership, the profit on the sale would be divided as follows:

| | Total | Partner A | Partner B | Partner C |
|---|---|---|---|---|
| Total profit | $15,000 | $5,000 | $5,000 | $5,000 |

In this situation, C initially gives up part of his capital contribution, only to recover at a later date the amount given up. The old partners initially receive a bonus, but on the subsequent sale of the land, they would not be allocated all of the first $12,000 profit. In this sense, "bonus" is a misnomer because it is not permanent. If the partners agree to the bonus method, the new partnership agreement should state that the new partner is to receive a one-third interest in the new assets of the partnership of $81,000 ($50,000 + $31,000), **with no revaluation to be made to the partnership assets.**

**Review Points Regarding the Three Methods.**   Note the following:

1. If the land subsequently is sold for $112,000 (which is $12,000 more than its $100,000 book value immediately before C was admitted into

the partnership), the individual Capital account balances will be identical under each method. Thus, each method ensures that partners A and B share equally in the first $12,000 of profit on the sale of the land. Furthermore, each method ensures that partners A, B, and C share equally on any profit on the sale of the land in excess of $12,000.

2. The exact method chosen depends on the personal whims of the partners. Often an incoming partner desires to have the full amount of his or her capital contribution credited to his or her Capital account, if only for psychological reasons. The method agreed upon by the partners should be specified in the new partnership agreement.

3. If the new profit and loss sharing formula includes a feature providing for imputed interest on capital investments, then the second method would result in an inequity to the old partners, because their individual Capital accounts would be less than that of the new partner.

4. The key to achieving the same result with each method is the assumption that the partnership assets actually are worth the agreed-upon amounts. If they are not, then these methods do not always prevent inequities from occurring. We discuss this situation more fully next.

**What if Agreed-upon Current Values Are Erroneous?**  Because the determination of the current values of assets is so subjective, the possibility exists that the land is not really worth $12,000 more than its book value. What if shortly after C is admitted into the partnership the land is sold for only $9,000 more than its book value immediately before C was admitted? Would each method still treat each partner equitably? The answer is no. Partner C would not be treated equitably under the revaluation of assets method because he would be allocated one-third of the book loss of $3,000; he would effectively lose $1,000 of his initial $31,000 capital contribution. Partner C would not be treated equitably under the bonus method because he would not recoup all of the $4,000 bonus he initially gave to the old partners. He would recoup only $3,000 (one-third of the $9,000 book profit) and, therefore, lose $1,000 of his initial $31,000 capital contribution. However, under the special provision in the new profit and loss sharing method, C cannot lose any of his initial capital contribution; he is best protected under this method.

The land may actually have a current value $12,000 more than its book value immediately before C is admitted into the partnership, but then subsequently decline in value after C is admitted. The same question must be asked: Would each method treat each partner equitably? Under the special provision in the new profit and loss sharing formula, partners A and B would be treated inequitably because they would share the entire loss of value that occurred after C was admitted. From an equity viewpoint, C should share in this loss of value, and he does so only under the revaluation of assets method and the bonus method.

Obviously, each partner strives to select the method that best protects his or her personal interest. Often there is a conflict between an incoming partner and the old partners concerning which method to use. The ultimate resolution takes place through negotiation. In large partnerships—such as the national accounting firms—differences between current values and book values usually are ignored for the sake of simplicity. Of course, such partnerships usually do not have significant amounts of land and depreciable assets, which are most likely to have current values different from book values.

## Business Combinations

Historically, business combinations are thought of as occurring only between corporations. However, a large number of business combinations involve partnerships, especially public accounting partnerships. Business combinations in the public accounting sector range from a two-person partnership combining with a sole proprietorship to a large international firm combining with another large international firm (as occurred in 1989 when Arthur Young & Company, the sixth largest accounting firm, combined with Ernst & Whinney, the third largest accounting firm, to form Ernst & Young, the largest accounting firm). Although *APB Opinion No. 16*, "Accounting for Business Combinations," was intended primarily for combinations among corporations, paragraph 5 of that pronouncement states that "its provisions should be applied as a general guide" when two or more unincorporated businesses combine.[1] Accordingly, business combinations among unincorporated accounting entities may be classified as either purchases or pooling of interests. Whether the substance of a combination is one or the other depends on whether or not the owners of the combining businesses continue as owners in the new, enlarged business.

If the owners of one business do not continue as owners of the enlarged business, a **purchase** has occurred. Purchases do not increase the number of partners. Thus, no change in ownership of the acquiring partnership occurs, and such transactions do not concern us here. The acquiring firm merely applies the provisions of *APB Opinion No. 16* with respect to the assets acquired. The assets of the acquiring business are not revalued to their current values.

If the owners of both businesses continue as owners of the enlarged business, a **pooling of interests** has occurred. Pooling of interests results in an increase in the number of partners; thus, the issues associated with changes in ownership exist. If the assets of either or both of the combining firms have current values different from their book values, then one of the methods of preventing inequities from occurring must be used

---

[1]*Accounting Principles Board Opinion No. 16*, "Accounting for Business Combinations" (New York: American Institute of Certified Public Accountants, 1970), par. 5.

(revaluing the assets, using a special provision in the new profit and loss sharing formula, or the bonus method). A strict application of the pooling of interests procedures does not permit the revaluing of assets of either combining firm. If the partners revalue the assets, however, they may do so and depart from generally accepted accounting principles. These three methods are procedurally the same as when a new partner is admitted, other than through a business combination.

## Decrease in Number of Partners

If a partnership's assets have current values different from their book values when a partner withdraws from a partnership, the partners are not treated equitably unless this difference in value is considered in settling with the withdrawing partner or his estate. In these situations, each method of preventing an inequity is available. To illustrate how each method would be applied in such a situation, we assume the following facts:

1. A, B, and C are in partnership.
2. The Capital accounts of all three partners are $25,000 each.
3. Carrying values of the partnership's tangible assets equal their current values, except for a parcel of land that is worth $12,000 more than its book value.
4. Profits and losses are shared equally.
5. C decides to withdraw from the partnership.

**Revaluing of Assets Method.**   Under the revaluing of assets method, the land is merely written up to its current value using the following entry:

| | | |
|---|---|---|
| Land | 12,000 | |
| Capital, Partner A | | 4,000 |
| Capital, Partner B | | 4,000 |
| Capital, Partner C | | 4,000 |

Each of the partners' Capital accounts is increased by one-third of the upward revaluation, because the partners shared profits and losses equally until C decided to withdraw from the partnership. The entry to record C's withdrawal from the partnership is as follows:

| | | |
|---|---|---|
| Capital, Partner C | 29,000 | |
| Payable to Partner C | | 29,000 |

As indicated previously, this is the simplest of the three methods. The fact that it departs from generally accepted accounting principles may be of little concern to the partnership.

**Special Profit and Loss Sharing Provision Method.** Under the special profit and loss sharing provision approach, the land is carried at its historical cost. However, the new profit and loss sharing formula contains a provision that (a) acknowledges that the land's estimated current value is $12,000 in excess of its current book value and (b) specifies that the withdrawing partner is entitled to one-third of the first $12,000 profit on the sale of the land. The entry to record C's withdrawal from the partnership is as follows:

| | | |
|---|---|---|
| Capital, Partner C | 25,000 | |
|     Payable to Partner C | | 25,000 |

Effectively, there is a contingent liability with respect to the amount that is to be paid to C upon sale of the land. This method has limited application in situations involving withdrawing partners. If different appraisals of current value of partnership assets exist, this method may be a practical alternative to the other two methods, especially if such assets are expected to be sold within a relatively short period of time. Normally, however, this method is impractical, because a withdrawing partner does not want to wait until such assets are disposed of to obtain his or her final settlement from the partnership.

**The Bonus Method.** Under the bonus method, no adjustment is made to the carrying amount of the land, nor is any special provision included in the new profit and loss sharing formula because the land is worth more than its book value. Consequently, when the land is later sold, A and B share all the profit. From an equity viewpoint, A and B are not entitled to one-third of the first $12,000 profit; therefore, their Capital accounts are reduced at C's withdrawal by the amount that represents C's share of the $12,000 of unrealized profit. Thus one-third of $12,000, or $4,000, is charged to the Capital accounts of A and B in their respective profit and loss sharing ratio. A and B will recoup this bonus to C later if the land is sold for $12,000 in excess of its current book value. The entry to record the bonus and C's withdrawal from the partnership is as follows:

| | | |
|---|---|---|
| Capital, Partner A | 2,000 | |
| Capital, Partner B | 2,000 | |
|     Capital, Partner C | | 4,000 |
|     To record the bonus to the withdrawing partner. | | |
| Capital, Partner C | 29,000 | |
|     Payable to Partner C | | 29,000 |
|     To record the withdrawal of Partner C. | | |

In this situation, A and B gave up part of their Capital account balances, expecting to recover at a later date the amounts given up. Thus, the bonus is not permanent, because it will be recovered later.

**Review Points Regarding the Three Methods.** Note the following:

1. If the land is later sold for $112,000 ($12,000 more than its $100,000 book value immediately before C withdrew from the partnership), the settlement to C is the same under each method. Also, the Capital account balances of A and B are identical under each method. Thus, each method ensures that the withdrawing partner receives one-third of the first $12,000 profit on the sale of the land. Furthermore, each method ensures that C does not share in any of the profit on the sale of the land in excess of $12,000.

2. The real problem is obtaining reasonable assurance of the current values of partnership assets. If the agreed-upon values are overstated, then the revaluing the asset method and the bonus method result in an excess settlement to the withdrawing partner. However, under the special profit and loss sharing provision method, no such excess payment is possible; thus, A and B are best protected under this method. If the agreed-upon values are understated, then one of the methods protects the withdrawing partner. The remaining partners share the entire increase above the agreed-upon value.

3. If the land declined in value after C withdrew, then C would not be treated equitably under the special profit and loss sharing provision method, because he would be sharing in a loss that occurred after he withdrew.

In all the preceding examples, the partnership's tangible assets were undervalued. When tangible assets have current values less than their book values, the first method—whereby the assets are written down—makes the most sense. (This procedure would be in accordance with generally accepted accounting principles.) The second choice would be the bonus method. The use of the special profit and loss sharing provision method would usually be impractical.

# INTANGIBLE ELEMENT EXISTS

We restricted our discussion in the preceding section to situations in which a partnership's tangible assets have current values different from their book values. In the next section, we discuss situations in which either the existing partnership or an income partner possesses an intangible element. In discussing these situations, we assume that all partnership tangible assets have current values equal to their book values. Although this assumption is not necessarily realistic, it allows us to concentrate on the issue of accounting for this intangible element.

The discussion of intangible elements usually has wider application than the earlier discussion of tangible assets, because most partnerships—other than those engaged in real estate development—do not have substantial investments in the types of assets that appreciate or depreciate, such as inventory, land, buildings, and equipment. The largest asset for such partnerships is usually accounts receivable.

Intangible elements are usually associated with an existing partnership. The most common intangible element is a partnership's superior earnings. Obviously, a partner's interest in such a partnership is worth more than its book value. Even when a partnership has only average earnings, a partner's interest may be worth more than its book value to an incoming partner merely because the organization already has clients and the potential to develop superior earnings.

An incoming partner may also possess intangible elements. For example, the incoming partner may have a successful sole proprietorship business with superior earnings power. He or she may have individual potential that the existing partners are willing to pay for. This is similar to situations in which corporations pay one-time bonuses to executives to induce them to work for them, or in professional sports in which a rookie may receive a one-time bonus just for signing with a particular team.

In these situations, whether the existing partnership or an incoming partner possesses the intangible element, the intangible element is referred to as **goodwill.** The accounting issue is to how to compensate the partner or partners who have created or possess the goodwill. If there is no compensation, the other partner or partners share unfairly in a portion of the partnership's future earnings.

The general approach to compensating the appropriate partners parallels that for situations in which tangible assets have current values different from book values—that is, we may apply the same three methods that we discussed and illustrated in the preceding section of the chapter. However, the first method is called **recording the goodwill** rather than revaluing of assets. Other than this descriptive change, the three methods are procedurally the same.

In the following material on the treatment of intangibles, note that the larger the partnership, the less the partners are inclined to compute the value of goodwill. For example, in the interest of simplicity, most national public accounting firms completely ignore goodwill for all changes in ownership situations. Instead, a simpler approach is adopted whereby an incoming partner initially accepts a lower than normal profit and loss sharing percentage; that percentage is increased on a sliding scale over a period of years until the incoming partner eventually shares profits and losses equally with other partners. Such an approach has the same overall effect as the three mechanical methods of dealing with goodwill, although the exact effect on each partner would be different.

## Admission of a New Partner: Existing Partnership Possesses Goodwill

Traditionally, advanced accounting textbooks have approached the issue of goodwill by presenting a set of assumed facts regarding (1) the capital contribution made by the incoming partner, (2) the percentage interest the incoming partner receives in the partnership's net assets, and (3) whether the net assets in that percentage interest include or exclude the value of the goodwill. Given all this information, we can determine (as if trying to solve a puzzle) which method the partners have used to compensate the partner or partners who have created or possess the goodwill. Under the valuing of the goodwill method, the value of the goodwill may then be determined and recorded on the books of the partnership. Under the bonus method, the amount of the bonus given to the old partners or their new partner may then be determined and recorded on the books of the partnership. This approach implies that (1) the value of the goodwill and the amount of the bonus given are derivatives of these given amounts and percentages, and (2) the partners arrive at the ownership percentages without agreeing to the value of the goodwill. This implication is completely misleading.

Although the goodwill and the amount of the bonus, or both, may be determined using this approach, the normal procedure when a partner is admitted into a partnership is obscured. The normal process, the sequence of which may vary, is as follows:

1. The value of the existing goodwill is agreed upon between the old partners and the new partner.
2. One of the available accounting methods designed to compensate the partner or partners who have created or possess the goodwill is selected.
3. The profit and loss ratio is agreed upon.
4. The capital contribution of the incoming partner is agreed upon.

Once these items are agreed upon, each partner's Capital account balance may be computed (using the appropriate accounting method selected). After determining each partner's Capital account balance, we may then express each partner's interest as a percentage of the partnership's net assets (as defined). Thus, the ownership percentage of each partner in the partnership's net assets is a *derived* amount—not the agreed-upon value of the goodwill. Accordingly, in the following illustrations, the value of the goodwill will be given.

In the first illustration, the partnership possesses the goodwill. To illustrate the application of the three methods of compensating the old partners for the goodwill they have created, we assume the following information:

1. A and B are in partnership, sharing profits equally.
2. C is to be admitted into the partnership.
3. A, B, and C agreed that the existing partnership will generate superior earnings of $10,000 for one year after C's admission.

4. C contributes $30,000 cash to the partnership.
5. Profits and losses are to be shared among A, B, and C in a ratio of 4:4:2, respectively. (Thus, the old partners are to receive 80% of the profits and losses and the new partner is to receive 20%.)
6. A and B have capital account balances of $45,000 and $15,000, respectively (for a total of $60,000), immediately before admitting C.

**Recording the Goodwill Method.**    Under the recording the goodwill method, C's admission into the partnership results in the recording of the entire amount of the agreed-upon goodwill in the partnership's books, as follows:

| | | |
|---|---|---|
| Goodwill. . . . . . . . . . . . . . . . . . . . . . . . . . . . . . . . . . . . | 10,000 | |
| Capital, Partner A . . . . . . . . . . . . . . . . . . . . . . | | 5,000 |
| Capital, Partner B . . . . . . . . . . . . . . . . . . . . . . | | 5,000 |
| To record the agreed-upon value of the goodwill, shared equally between the old partners using their old profit and loss sharing ratio. | | |

The entry to record C's capital contribution of $30,000 is as follows:

| | | |
|---|---|---|
| Cash . . . . . . . . . . . . . . . . . . . . . . . . . . . . . . . . . . . . . | 30,000 | |
| Capital, Partner C . . . . . . . . . . . . . . . . . . . . . . | | 30,000 |
| To record C's capital contribution. | | |

The following points are important for understanding the preceding entries:

1. It can be stated that C has a 30% interest in the net assets of the partnership ($30,000 ÷ $100,000 total of the capital accounts).
2. The recording of goodwill in this manner is not in accordance with generally accepted accounting principles, because the goodwill did not result from the purchase of a business.
3. The goodwill will be amortized over a one-year period, because the partnership is expected to produce superior earnings only for one year.
4. Because of the goodwill amortization in the year after C's admission, earnings will be $10,000 lower than if goodwill had not been recorded on the books.
5. Effectively, $10,000 of future profits have been capitalized into the Capital accounts of the old partners. In this respect, the partners have guaranteed that they alone will receive the first $10,000 of future earnings (determined without regard to the goodwill amortization expense).

6. If $10,000 of superior earnings result in the following year, then such superior earnings completely absorb the goodwill amortization of $10,000.

7. If the superior earnings in the following year are less than $10,000, then C effectively loses a portion of his initial capital contribution of $30,000. This is because the normal earnings of the partnership must absorb a portion of the goodwill amortization, and C cannot share in a portion of the normal earnings.

To illustrate how this method may favor the old partners over the new partner if the entire amount of the superior earnings does not materialize, assume that during the year after C's admission, only $8,000 of superior earnings materialized. These superior earnings would absorb only $8,000 of goodwill amortization. The remaining $2,000 of goodwill amortization would be absorbed by normal earnings. Thus, C would not share in $2,000 of normal earnings. Because C's profit and loss sharing percentage is 20%, he effectively loses $400 (20% of $2,000) of his $30,000 initial capital contribution.

**Special Profit and Loss Sharing Provision Method.** Under the special profit and loss sharing provision method, no entry is made on the partnership's books with respect to the goodwill. As under the previous method, C's Capital account is credited with the full amount of his capital contribution of $30,000. It can be stated that C has a one-third interest in the partnership's net assets ($30,000 ÷ $90,000 total of the Capital accounts). The new profit and loss sharing formula would stipulate that the old partners are entitled to share (in accordance with their old profit and loss sharing ratio) in the first $10,000 of earnings in excess of a specified amount, the specified amount being the expected normal earnings for the year after C's admission into the partnership.

If the superior earnings of $10,000 do not materialize during this year, then the old partners will have credited to their Capital accounts only the superior earnings that do materialize. Of course, the normal earnings and any earnings above the $10,000 of superior earnings during the next year would be shared in accordance with the new profit and loss sharing ratio. This method protects the new partner's initial capital contribution of $30,000 in the event superior earnings of $10,000 do not materialize. Obviously, the old partners would prefer the previous method, under which they are assured of the first $10,000 of earnings, regardless of whether such earnings are superior earnings.

**The Bonus Method.** Under the bonus method, no entry is made on the partnership's books with respect to goodwill. Unlike the previous two methods, C does not receive a full credit to his Capital account for his capital contribution of $30,000, because he must give a bonus to the old partners. The amount of the bonus given to the old partners is C's profit and loss sharing percentage of 20% times the agreed-upon value of the goodwill of $10,000. Thus, the bonus given the old partners is $2,000, which they share in their old profit and loss sharing ratio as follows:

| | | |
|---|---|---|
| Cash | 30,000 | |
|     Capital, Partner A | | 1,000 |
|     Capital, Partner B | | 1,000 |
|     Capital, Partner C | | 28,000 |
|   To record C's capital contribution and to | | |
|   record the bonus to the old partners. | | |

The following points are important for understanding the above entry:

1. It can be stated that C has a 31.11% interest in the partnership's net assets ($28,000 ÷ $90,000 total of the Capital accounts).
2. Generally accepted accounting principles are followed by not recording goodwill on the books.
3. If superior earnings of $10,000 materialize in the year following C's admission, then C shares in these superior earnings. His share is $2,000 (20% of $10,000). Consequently, he recoups the bonus he initially gave to the old partners.
4. The bonus method compensates the old partners currently for the portion of the superior earnings that will later be credited to the new partner's Capital account. Thus, if all the superior earnings materialize, the bonus is temporary.
5. If the superior earnings in the year following C's admission are less than $10,000, then C effectively loses a portion of his initial capital contribution of $30,000. This is because he does not share in the amount of superior earnings that he thought would materialize, for which he was willing to give a bonus to the old partners.

To illustrate how the bonus method may favor the old partners over the new partner if the entire amount of superior earnings does not materialize, assume that during the year following C's admission, only $8,000 of superior earnings materialized. C's share of the $8,000 of superior earnings that did materialize would be $1,600 (20% of $8,000). Because he gave a bonus of $2,000, he only recouped $1,600 of the bonus, effectively losing $400 of his initial capital contribution of $30,000.

**Approach if the Value of Goodwill Is Not Given.** Assume that the partners in their negotiations agree upon an amount for the goodwill, but that they do not state this amount in the new partnership agreement. Instead, knowing the amount of agreed-upon goodwill, they merely calculate the percentage that the incoming partner has in the partnership's net assets.

In these situations, the accountant may determine the goodwill using the available information regarding the individual ownership percentage the new partner has in the partnership's net assets. We demonstrate the general approach using the information in our example.

If the value of the goodwill is to be recorded on the partnership's books and the new partner has a 30% interest in the net assets (tangible and intangible) of the partnership, the goodwill implicit in the transaction could be determined as follows:

1. Divide C's $30,000 capital contribution by his 30% interest in the net assets to arrive at $100,000.
2. Subtract from the amount determined in step 1 the sum of the Capital account balances of the old partners immediately before C is admitted ($60,000) plus C's capital contribution ($30,000). Thus, the goodwill would be $10,000 ($100,000 − $90,000).

Alternatively, if goodwill is not to be recorded on the partnership's books and the new partner has a 31.11% interest in the net assets (tangible assets only) of the partnership, the bonus to be given and the related goodwill implicit in the transaction could be determined as follows:

1. Determine the total tangible net assets of the partnership including C's contribution ($60,000 + $30,000).
2. Multiply the amount determined in step 1, $90,000, by C's given ownership percentage in the partnership's net assets ($90,000 × 31.11% = $28,000).
3. Subtract the $28,000 determined in step 2 from C's $30,000 capital contribution to determine the $2,000 bonus that is to be given to the old partners.
4. Divide the $2,000 bonus by C's profit and loss sharing percentage of 20% to obtain the value of the goodwill implicit in the transaction, or $10,000.

## Admission of a New Partner: New Partner Possesses Goodwill

Although in most situations the existing partnership has created the goodwill, an incoming partner may possess goodwill. To illustrate the three methods of compensating an incoming partner for goodwill, assume the following information:

1. A and B are in partnership, sharing profits equally.
2. C is to be admitted into the partnership.
3. A, B, and C agree that C is expected to generate superior earnings of $10,000 for one year following his admission.
4. C contributes $30,000 cash to the partnership.
5. Profits and losses are to be shared among A, B, and C in a ratio of 4:4:2, respectively.

6. A and B have Capital account balances of $45,000 and $15,000, respectively (a total of $60,000), immediately before admitting C.

**Recording the Goodwill Method.** Under the recording the goodwill method, the entire amount of the agreed-upon value of the goodwill is credited to C's Capital account, along with his capital contribution of $30,000, as follows:

| | | |
|---|---|---|
| Goodwill. . . . . . . . . . . . . . . . . . . . . . . . . . . . . . . . . . . . . | 10,000 | |
| Cash . . . . . . . . . . . . . . . . . . . . . . . . . . . . . . . . . . . . . . . | 30,000 | |
| Capital, Partner C . . . . . . . . . . . . . . . . . . . . . | | 40,000 |
| To record the agreed upon value of the | | |
| goodwill and C's capital contribution. | | |

Compared with the situation in which the old partners created the goodwill, the roles are now reversed. The new partner will receive the first $10,000 of future earnings (determined without regard to the goodwill amortization expense), even if superior earnings do not materialize. If the superior earnings of $10,000 do not materialize, then the old partners will lose the subsequent increases to their Capital accounts that they would have received. In this situation, it can be stated that C has a 40% interest in the partnership's net assets ($40,000 ÷ $100,000 total of the Capital accounts).

**Special Profit and Loss Sharing Provision Method.** Under the special profit and loss sharing provision method, no entry is made on the partnership's books with respect to the goodwill. C would receive a credit to his Capital account equal to his capital contribution of $30,000. It can be stated that C has a one-third interest in the partnership's net assets ($30,000 ÷ $90,000 total of the Capital accounts). The new profit and loss sharing formula would stipulate that the new partner is entitled to receive the first $10,000 of earnings in excess of a specified amount. That amount would be the expected normal earnings for the year after C's admission into the partnership. If superior earnings of $10,000 do not materialize during this year, then the new partner will have credited to his Capital account only the superior earnings that do materialize. In this situation, this method protects the old partners' capital balances that existed when C was admitted into the partnership.

**The Bonus Method.** Under the bonus method, no entry is made on the partnership's books with respect to goodwill. Because the new partner possesses the goodwill, the old partners give a bonus to him. The amount of the bonus given to the new partner is the total of the old partners' profit and loss sharing percentage of 80% times the agreed-upon value of the goodwill, which is $10,000. Thus, the bonus given the new partner is $8,000, recorded as follows:

| | | |
|---|---:|---:|
| Cash . . . . . . . . . . . . . . . . . . . . . . . . . . . . . . . . . . . . . . . . . . | 30,000 | |
| Capital, Partner A . . . . . . . . . . . . . . . . . . . . . . . . . . . | 4,000 | |
| Capital, Partner B . . . . . . . . . . . . . . . . . . . . . . . . . . . | 4,000 | |
| Capital, Partner C . . . . . . . . . . . . . . . . . . . . | | 38,000 |
| To record C's capital contribution and to record the bonus given to him. | | |

It can be stated that C has a 42.22% interest in the partnership's net assets ($38,000 ÷ $90,000). Compared with the situation in which the old partners created the goodwill, the roles now are reversed. The old partners will recoup the bonus they gave to the new partner only if superior earnings of $10,000 materialize. To the extent that the superior earnings are less than $10,000, then the old partners will lose a portion of the balances that existed in their Capital accounts immediately before C was admitted.

**Approach if the Value of Goodwill Is Not Given.**  If the agreed-upon value of the goodwill is not available (an unusual situation), the accountant may determine this amount so long as information is available regarding the individual ownership percentage the new partner has in the partnership's net assets. We demonstrate the general approach using the information in our example.

If the value of the goodwill is to be recorded on the partnership's books and the new partner has a 40% interest in the net assets (tangible and intangible) of the partnership, the goodwill implicit in the transaction could be determined as follows:

1. Divide the total of the old partners' Capital accounts by their total interest in the net assets ($60,000 ÷ 60%) to arrive at $100,000.
2. Subtract from the amount determined in step 1 the sum of the Capital account balances of the old partners immediately before C is admitted ($60,000) plus C's tangible capital contribution of $30,000. Thus, the goodwill would be $10,000 ($100,000 − $90,000).

Alternatively, if goodwill is not to be recorded on the partnership's books and the new partner has a 42.22% interest in the net assets (tangible assets only), the bonus to be given by the old partners and the goodwill implicit in the transaction could be determined as follows:

1. Determine the total net assets of the partnership, including C's tangible contribution ($60,000 + $30,000).
2. Multiply the amount determined in step 1, $90,000, by C's given ownership percentage in the partnership's net assets ($90,000 × 42.22% = $38,000).

3. Subtract from the $38,000 amount determined in step 2 C's tangible capital contribution of $30,000 to arrive at the $8,000 bonus that C receives from the old partners.
4. Divide the $8,000 bonus by the old partners' combined profit and loss sharing percentage of 80% to obtain the value of the goodwill implicit in the transaction, or $10,000. (Recall that the profit and loss sharing ratio is 4:4:2.)

## Formula Approach if the Value of Goodwill Is Not Given and It Is Unknown Whether the Old Partners or New Partner(s) Possess Goodwill

If the value of the goodwill is not given and it is not known whether the old partners or the new partner(s) possess goodwill, the following steps are performed to calculate the goodwill and determine which partner(s) possesses goodwill:

1. Divide the new partner's tangible capital contribution by his or her ownership percentage in the net assets of the partnership (for example, $35,000 ÷ 20% = $175,000).
2. Divide the total recorded capital balances of the old partners by their total ownership interest in the net assets of the partnership (for example, $120,000 ÷ 80% = $150,000).
3. Add together the numerators used in steps 1 and 2 ($35,000 + $120,000 = $155,000) to arrive at the total recorded net assets of the new partnership excluding goodwill.
4. Select the larger of the amounts calculated in steps 1 and 2 ($175,000). From this amount, subtract the total calculated in step 3 ($155,000) to obtain the goodwill ($20,000). (If the amount in step 1 is selected, the old partners possess goodwill; if the amount in step 2 is selected, the new partner possesses goodwill.)

## Business Combinations

When two businesses combine in such a manner that the owners of each separate business continue as owners in the enlarged business (substantively, a pooling of interests) and when one of the businesses possesses goodwill, then we may apply the same three methods that have been illustrated in this section to compensate the partners of the business possessing the goodwill. Procedurally, these three methods are the same as in situations in which a new partner is admitted other than through a business combination. The mechanics are more involved, however, as the number of combining partners increases.

## A Decrease in the Number of Partners

If a partnership possesses unrecorded goodwill when a partner withdraws from the partnership, the withdrawing partner is not treated equitably unless this difference in value is considered in settling with the withdrawing partner or his estate. In these situations, each of the methods of compensating the partner is available—the recording the goodwill method, the special profit and loss sharing provision method, and the bonus method. To illustrate how each of these methods would be applied in such a situation, assume the following facts:

1. A, B, and C are in partnership, sharing profits equally.
2. The Capital accounts of A, B, and C are $40,000, $30,000, and $20,000, respectively.
3. All the partnership's tangible assets have carrying values equal to their current values.
4. C withdraws from the partnership.
5. The partners agree that the partnership currently has unrecorded goodwill of $15,000.

**Recording the Goodwill Method.**   Under the recording the goodwill method, goodwill is recorded on the books and shared among the partners in their profit and loss ratio, as follows:

| | | |
|---|---|---|
| Goodwill. . . . . . . . . . . . . . . . . . . . . . . . . . . . . . . . . . . . . | 15,000 | |
| Capital, Partner A . . . . . . . . . . . . . . . . . . . . . | | 5,000 |
| Capital, Partner B . . . . . . . . . . . . . . . . . . . . . | | 5,000 |
| Capital, Partner C . . . . . . . . . . . . . . . . . . . . . | | 5,000 |
| To record the agreed-upon value of goodwill existing at the time of C's withdrawal from the partnership. | | |

The entry to record C's withdrawal is as follows:

| | | |
|---|---|---|
| Capital, Partner C . . . . . . . . . . . . . . . . . . . . . . . . . . . | 25,000 | |
| Payable to Partner C. . . . . . . . . . . . . . . . . . . . | | 25,000 |

An alternative to recording all the goodwill is to record only C's share of the goodwill, which is $5,000. The entry is as follows:

| | | |
|---|---|---|
| Goodwill. . . . . . . . . . . . . . . . . . . . . . . . . . . . . . . . . . . . | 5,000 | |
| Capital, Partner C . . . . . . . . . . . . . . . . . . . . . | | 5,000 |

Whether all or a portion of the goodwill is recorded is irrelevant from an equity standpoint—both methods produce the same result with respect to the withdrawing partner. As previously indicated, the goodwill method is not in accordance with generally accepted accounting principles, but the partners need not follow generally accepted accounting principles. If superior earnings of $15,000 do not materialize after C's withdrawal, the remaining partners lose a portion of their capital balances that existed at the time of C's withdrawal as a result of writing off the goodwill.

### Special Profit and Loss Sharing Provision Method.

Under the special profit and loss sharing provision method, goodwill is not recorded on the books. Instead, C's withdrawal is conditional on the new profit and loss sharing formula between A and B, which contains a provision that C is to share in one-third of future earnings in excess of a specified level for a certain period of time. If past superior earnings have been largely dependent on C's efforts, the partnership may not be able to generate superior earnings after C withdraws. Accordingly, this method best protects the remaining partners in the event superior earnings do not materialize during the stipulated period of time after C's withdrawal.

### The Bonus Method.

Under the bonus method, the old partners give a bonus to the withdrawing partner. The bonus equals C's share of the agreed-upon value of the goodwill, which is one-third of $15,000, or $5,000. The bonus is shared between the remaining partners in their respective profit and loss sharing ratio as follows:

| | | |
|---|---|---|
| Capital, Partner A | 2,500 | |
| Capital, Partner B | 2,500 | |
| Capital, Partner C | | 5,000 |
| To record the bonus to C on his withdrawal from the partnership. | | |

This method does not deviate from generally accepted accounting principles. If $15,000 of above-normal earnings do not materialize during the stipulated period of time after C withdraws, however, then the remaining partners do not recoup all of the bonus they gave to C.

### Spin-off Situations.

A partner may withdraw from a partnership and then immediately commence business in the same line of work as a sole proprietor. In such a situation, the withdrawing partner often requests the partnership's clients and customers that he or she personally has been serving to give their future business to the newly formed sole proprietorship. When this happens, the method selected for equitably treating the withdrawing partner should be accompanied by provisions that protect the remaining partners from any loss of clients and customers as a result of the withdrawing partner forming a sole proprietorship. In other words, the remaining partners must guard against recording goodwill or paying a bonus and also losing clients or customers to the newly formed sole proprietorship.

# LEGAL AND TAX ASPECTS OF CHANGES IN OWNERSHIP

## Legal Aspects

Although a thorough discussion of the legal aspects of a change in ownership of a partnership is properly the subject of an upper-division course on business law, a brief discussion of the major legal aspects is appropriate at this point.

Section 29 of the Uniform Partnership Act (UPA) states that "the dissolution of a partnership is the change in the relation of the partners caused by any partner ceasing to be associated in the carrying on as distinguished from the winding up of the business." This definition implies that dissolution occurs only when a partner withdraws from a partnership. Section 41(1) of the UPA (which also is concerned with dissolution) refers to a partnership that admits a partner as being the "first or dissolved partnership." Accordingly, any change in ownership (whether by withdrawal of a partner, admission of a new partner, or a business combination that is in substance a pooling of interests) legally dissolves the existing partnership. Because we are dealing with changes in ownership that do not terminate the business activities of the partnership, a new partnership must be formed immediately to continue the business of the dissolved partnership.

The fact that a legal dissolution has occurred is meaningless in terms of continuity of existence; the business continues to operate just as though no change in ownership had occurred. However a legal dissolution does have personal significance to new partners, withdrawing partners, continuing partners, and creditors of the dissolved partnership.

**Admission of a Partner.** With respect to an incoming partner, Section 17 of the UPA provides that "a person admitted as a partner into an existing partnership is liable for all the obligations of the partnership arising before his admission as though he had been a partner when such obligations were incurred, except that his liability shall be satisfied only out of partnership property." This provision insulates the personal assets of the new partner from creditors' claims existing at the new partner's admission.

In practice, the existing partners usually insist that an incoming partner be jointly responsible for all such preexisting partnership debts. If the new partner agrees to this, Section 17 of the UPA may be circumvented by including a provision in the new partnership agreement to that effect. Because of the possibility of undisclosed liabilities (actual or contingent), the new partner in these situations should limit his or her responsibilities to the liabilities that are set forth in a scheduled exhibit to the partnership agreement.

**Withdrawal of a Partner.** With respect to a withdrawing partner, Section 36(1) of the UPA provides that "the dissolution of the partnership does not of itself discharge the existing liability of any partner." Section 36(2), however, provides that a withdrawing partner may be relieved of his or her responsibility for such debt if and only if the creditor expressly releases the partner from this responsibility by entering into an agreement to that effect between the withdrawing partner and the person or partnership continuing the business. Some court cases have held that a withdrawing partner may be liable for debts incurred after his or her withdrawal unless prior notice was given of that withdrawal. Notice usually must be given directly to persons who have dealt with the partnership. For persons who have not dealt with the partnership, a notice usually may be given by publication in a newspaper or some other appropriate manner.

## Tax Aspects

The general ledger entries to the Capital accounts of the partners in connection with the revaluation of assets, recording the goodwill, or the bonus method are not significant from a tax viewpoint. The only tax significance of such entries is the existence of unrealized gains (when partners' Capital accounts increase) and unrealized losses (when partners' Capital accounts decrease). In general, until the partnership interest is disposed of, such gains and losses are not reportable for tax purposes.

**Withdrawal of a Partner.** When a withdrawing partner receives cash from either the partnership or persons to whom his or her partnership interest was sold, the determination of the withdrawing partner's gain or loss for income tax reporting purposes is made by comparing the proceeds to his or her tax basis. The *proceeds* are the sum of cash received plus the share of existing partnership liabilities for which he or she is relieved of responsibility. (The assumption of the partner's share of the liabilities by the remaining partners is treated as a distribution of money to the withdrawing partner.) To illustrate, we assume the following:

1. The withdrawing partner has a capital balance of $20,000.
2. The withdrawing partner is to receive a $5,000 bonus.
3. The partnership has liabilities of $24,000.
4. The partnership shares profits and losses equally (three partners).
5. The withdrawing partner's tax basis is $27,000.

The withdrawing partner's taxable gain is calculated as follows:

Proceeds:
    **Cash distribution ($20,000 + $5,000 bonus)** .............. $25,000

*(continued)*

| Relief of partnership liabilities ($\frac{1}{3} \times$ \$24,000) | 8,000 |
| Total Proceeds | \$33,000 |
| Withdrawing partner's tax basis | 27,000 |
| Taxable Gain | \$ 6,000 |

When a withdrawing partner receives noncash consideration, the tax laws are complex; a discussion of these laws is beyond the scope of this chapter.

**Admission of a Partner.** The procedures for determining an incoming partner's tax basis are the same as those illustrated in the preceding chapter on the formation of partnerships. The incoming partner's tax basis equals the sum of (1) the amount of cash contributed, (2) the adjusted basis of any noncash assets contributed, and (3) the share of any partnership liabilities for which he or she is jointly responsible, (4) less the old partners' share of any liabilities the new partner contributes to the partnership. As when a partnership is formed, the profit and loss sharing ratios are used to adjust each partner's tax basis for any liabilities relieved of or assumed.

When a partner is admitted by directly purchasing a partner's interest, the incoming partner's tax basis is the sum of the cash paid plus the share of any partnership liabilities for which he or she is jointly responsible. The incoming partner's tax basis need not coincide with the selling partner's tax basis, because the amount paid is a negotiated amount. The partnership may elect to adjust the tax basis of the partnership assets to reflect the difference between the tax basis of the incoming partner and that of the selling partner. (No entries are made in the general ledger—the difference is kept on a memorandum basis.)

The amount of the increase or decrease in tax basis affects only the incoming partner. For example, assume that an incoming partner's tax basis exceeds that of the selling partner and this difference is allocable to merchandise inventory, a building, unrealized receivables, and goodwill. In future years, the incoming partner's share of earnings is adjusted by (1) treating the amount allocable to inventory as additional cost of goods sold (as the inventory is sold), (2) treating the amount allocable to the building as additional depreciation expense, and (3) treating the amount allocable to the unrealized receivables as a reduction of revenues (as the accounts receivable are collected). Although the goodwill is assigned a tax basis, the incoming partner's share of the earnings would not be adjusted for the amount allocable to goodwill, because goodwill is not deductible for income tax reporting purposes.

This election to adjust the tax basis of the assets is much more common in small partnerships than in large partnerships because the partnership—not the individual incoming partner—must do the record keeping, and most large partnerships do not bother with this record-keeping function. If the election is made to adjust the tax basis of the partnership assets, the sum of the tax bases of each partner will equal the partnership's tax basis in its assets. If the election is not made, this equality will not exist, and the difference will exist until the partner disposes of his or her interest.

# END-OF-CHAPTER REVIEW

## Summary of Key Points

1. The bonus method may be applied when:

| New Partnership Capital | = | Old Partners' Capital | + | New Partner's Asset Investment |
|---|---|---|---|---|

2. The goodwill method is applied when:

| New Partnership Capital | > | Old Partners' Capital | + | New Partner's Asset Investment |
|---|---|---|---|---|

3. Both methods are designed to achieve equity among the partners; however, both methods will result in an inequity to one or more partners if the goodwill does not materialize.

## Glossary of New Terms

**Bonus method** A method designed to achieve equity among partners upon a change in the number of partners when partnership assets are undervalued or goodwill exists. Adjustments are made within the partners' equity accounts to the extent of the undervaluation or the agreed-upon value of goodwill, thereby neither changing the recorded amounts of the partnership assets nor recording goodwill as an asset.

**Goodwill method** A method designed to achieve equity among partners upon a change in the number of partners when goodwill is deemed to exist. Goodwill is recorded on the books of the partnership with an offsetting credit made to the partner(s) who possesses or created the goodwill.

## Self-Study Questions

*(Answers are at the end of this chapter.)*

1. Flutie and Harper are partners with capital balances of $90,000 and $60,000, respectively. They share profits and losses in a 2:1 ratio, respectively. Tuba is admitted into the partnership for a cash contribution of $50,000. Tuba

receives a 20% capital interest and a 20% interest in profits and losses. Determine the implied goodwill in the transaction and whether the old partners or the new partner possesses the goodwill:

a. $10,000.      a. New partner.
b. $12,500.      b. Old partners.
c. $40,000.
d. $50,000.

2. Horne and Picolo are partners with capital balances of $140,000 and $100,000, respectively. They share profits and losses in a 2:1 ratio, respectively. Sax is admitted into the partnership for a cash contribution of $60,000. Sax shares in 25% of the profits and losses and is to have a 25% capital interest. Assuming goodwill is recorded, how much should be credited to Sax's capital account?

a. $60,000.
b. $75,000.
c. $80,000.
d. $100,000.

3. Use the data in the preceding question, but assume goodwill is not recorded. How much should be credited to Sax's capital account under the bonus method?

a. $60,000.
b. $75,000.
c. $80,000.
d. $100,000.

4. Bell, Ring, and Toner are partners having capital balances of $72,000, $48,000 and $40,000, respectively. Their profit and loss sharing ratio is 5:3:2, respectively. Toner is withdrawing from the partnership. The partners agree that the partnership possesses goodwill of $50,000 which is not to be recorded. The total cash payment to Toner in full settlement of Toner's partnership interest is

a. $40,000.
b. $50,000.
c. $52,500.
d. $53,333.

5. Use the information in the preceding question and determine the capital balance of Bell assuming all of the goodwill is recorded.

a. $72,000
b. $88,667
c. $94,500
d. $97,000

6. Use the information in question 4, and determine the capital balance of Bell assuming the bonus method is used.

a. $65,750
b. $66,000
c. $67,000
d. $72,000

7. Drummer decides to retire from a partnership in which she has 20% of the profits and losses and a 25% capital interest. Just prior to this decision, her

capital balance was $60,000. The partnership agrees she should receive a cash bonus of $7,000 upon retirement. The partnership has liabilities of $150,000 at the retirement date. Drummer's tax basis just prior to retirement is $85,000. Drummer's taxable gain or loss is
a. $18,000 loss.
b. $25,000 loss.
c. $5,000 gain.
d. $12,000 gain.

# ASSIGNMENT MATERIAL

## Review Questions

1. What is the primary objective of accounting for changes in the ownership of a partnership?
2. What three methods are available for achieving equity among partners when a change in ownership occurs?
3. Does each method of achieving equity always treat each partner equitably in every situation?
4. Under the bonus method, is the bonus temporary or permanent?
5. Is recognizing goodwill on the admission of a partner into a partnership considered to be in accord with generally accepted accounting principles?
6. Describe a business combination of two partnerships that would be, in substance, a pooling of interests.
7. Is a business combination that is in substance a purchase (as opposed to a pooling of interest) deemed a change in ownership with respect to the acquiring partnership?
8. How does an accountant know whether the bonus method, the special profit and loss sharing provision method, or the recording the goodwill method should be used to reflect a change in ownership?
9. Under the recording the goodwill method, substantively, what has occurred?
10. Under the bonus method, substantively, what has occurred?
11. What is the significance of a legal dissolution when a partner is admitted into a partnership? When a partner withdraws?
12. When a partner withdraws from a partnership after many years as a partner and such partner has a gain on the liquidation of his or her interest, is such gain treated as a capital gain for income tax reporting purposes?

## Discussion Cases

### DC 24-1

### Admission of a Partner: Evaluation of the Bonus Method

Gentry and Royals are in partnership, and they are contemplating the admission of Squires into the partnership. Gentry and Royals have proposed that Squires give a $20,000 bonus to them as a condition of admittance. Squires feels that this bonus is ridiculous considering that: (1) all tangible assets have fair market values equal to their book values; (2) all partners will be devoting 100% of their time to the partnership business; (3) future profits and losses are to be shared equally; (4) Squires' capital contribution is to be 50% of the existing partnership capital of $100,000 immediately before his admission; and (5) his tax basis would be reduced by $20,000. Squires has asked you as his accountant to counsel him on this matter.

**Required:**

How would you respond to this request?

| DC 24-2 | ### Admission of a Partner: Adherence to Generally Accepted Accounting Principles |
|---|---|

Castle and Hurst are partners in the process of negotiating with Randolph regarding his admission into the partnership. Agreement has been reached regarding the value of goodwill that the existing partnership possesses. However, the partners disagree as to whether the goodwill should be recorded on the books. Castle and Hurst feel goodwill should be recognized and recorded on the books at Randolph's admission. Randolph feels it is improper to record goodwill, because it was not bought and paid for. Furthermore, Randolph contends that it is senseless to record goodwill, because it is not deductible for income tax purposes. They have asked you as the partnership's accountant to settle this disagreement.

**Required:**

How would you respond to this request?

| DC 24-3 | ### Admission of a Partner: Role of the Accountant |
|---|---|

Disnee and Walters are partners contemplating the admission of Duckett as a partner. They have requested that you, the partnership's accountant, determine how this should be done.

**Required:**

How would you respond to this request? Be specific about the advice you would give to the partners.

| DC 24-4 | ### Admission of a Partner: Role of the Accountant |
|---|---|

Berry and Knott are partners contemplating the admission of Farmer into the partnership. Berry and Knott believe the partnership possesses goodwill of $60,000, whereas Farmer believes the partnership possesses goodwill of only $20,000. As the partnership's accountant, you have been asked to determine the amount of goodwill that the partnership possesses.

**Required:**

How would you respond to this request?

# Exercises

### E 24-1

## Admission of a Partner: Calculation of Required Contribution

Partners Angel, Bird, and Crow share profits and losses 50:30:20, respectively. The April 30, 19X5, balance sheet is as follows:

| | |
|---|---|
| Cash. | $ 40,000 |
| Other assets. | 360,000 |
| | $400,000 |
| | |
| Accounts payable. | $100,000 |
| Capital, Angel. | 74,000 |
| Capital, Bird. | 130,000 |
| Capital, Crow | 96,000 |
| | $400,000 |

The assets and liabilities are recorded and presented at their respective fair values. Dove is to be admitted as a new partner with a 20% capital interest and a 20% share of profits and losses in exchange for a cash contribution. No goodwill or bonus is to be recorded.

### Required:
1. Determine how much cash Dove should contribute.
2. Prepare the entry to record Dove's admission.

(AICPA adapted)

### E 24-2

## Admission of a Partner: Recording the Goodwill Method

Abbey and Landly are partners with capital balances of $80,000 and $40,000, and they share profits and losses in the ratio of 2:1, respectively. Deere invests $36,000 cash for a one-fifth interest in the capital and profits of the new partnership. The partners agree that the implied partnership goodwill is to be recorded simultaneously with the admission of Deere.

### Required:
1. Calculate the total implied goodwill of the firm.
2. Prepare the entry or entries to record the admission of Deere.

(AICPA adapted)

### E 24-3

## Admission of a Partner: The Bonus Method

Cord and Stringer are partners who share profits and losses in the ratio of 3:2, respectively. On August 31, 19X4, their Capital accounts were as follows:

| | |
|---|---|
| Cord. | $ 70,000 |
| Stringer. | 60,000 |
| | $130,000 |

On that date, they agreed to admit Twiner as a partner with a one-third interest in the capital and profits and losses, for an investment of $50,000. The new partnership will begin with a total capital of $180,000.

**Required:**
Prepare the entry or entries to record the admission of Twiner.

(AICPA adapted)

**E 24-4**

## Admission of a Partner: Recording the Goodwill Method and the Bonus Method

Waters is admitted into the partnership of Dunes, Kamel, and Sanders for a total cash investment of $40,000. The capital Accounts and respective percentage interests in profits and losses immediately before Waters' admission are as follows:

|  | Capital Accounts | Percentage Interests in Profits and Losses |
|---|---|---|
| Dunes | $ 80,000 | 60 |
| Kamel | 40,000 | 30 |
| Sanders | 20,000 | 10 |
|  | $140,000 | 100 |

All tangible assets and liabilities are fairly valued. Waters receives a one-fifth interest in profits and losses and a 20% interest in the partnership's net assets.

**Required:**
1. Prepare the entry to record Waters' admission into the partnership, assuming goodwill is to be recorded.
2. Prepare the entry to record Waters' admission into the partnership, assuming no goodwill is to be recorded.

**E 24-5**

## Admission of a Partner: Determining Bonus and Goodwill from Interest in Net Assets

Ball and Batt are partners, share profits and losses equally, and have capital balances of $30,000 and $20,000, respectively. All tangible assets have current values equal to book values. Glover is admitted into the partnership. Determine the entry to record Glover's admission in each of the following independent situations:

1. Glover contributes $10,000 cash for a 10% interest in the new net assets of the partnership of $60,000.
2. Glover contributes $10,000 cash for a 10% interest in the new net assets of the partnership, with Glover to receive a credit to his Capital account equal to his full cash contribution.
3. Glover contributes $10,000 for a one-sixth interest in the new net assets of the partnership of $60,000.

4. Glover purchases 10% of each existing partner's interest for a total cash payment of $10,000 to the existing partners.
5. Glover contributes $10,000 cash for a 20% interest in the new net assets of the partnership of $60,000.
6. Glover contributes $10,000 cash for a 20% interest in the new net assets of the partnership, with the old partners not to have any decrease made to their Capital accounts.

## E 24-6 Retirement of a Partner

On June 30, 19X1, the balance sheet for the partnership of Oakley, Pine, and Woods, together with their respective profit and loss ratios, were as follows:

| | |
|---|---:|
| Assets, at cost | $180,000 |
| Oakley, loan | $ 9,000 |
| Oakley, Capital (20%) | 42,000 |
| Pine, Capital (20%) | 39,000 |
| Woods, Capital (60%) | 90,000 |
| | $180,000 |

Oakley has decided to retire from the partnership. By mutual agreement, the assets are to be adjusted to their current value of $216,000. It was agreed that the partnership would pay Oakley $61,200 for his partnership interest, including his loan, which is to be repaid in full.

### Required:

1. Prepare the required entries assuming goodwill is to be recorded on the partnership's books. (Note: Two alternative amounts may be recorded for goodwill. Prepare entries under each alternative.)
2. Prepare the entries assuming that goodwill is not to be recorded on the partnership's books.

(AICPA adapted)

## E 24-7 Calculation of Gain on Sale of Partnership Interests

The Capital accounts of the partnership of Fender, Hood, and Shields on May 31, 19X5, are presented below with their respective profit and loss ratios:

| | | |
|---|---:|---:|
| Fender | $200,000 | 1/2 |
| Hood | 150,000 | 1/3 |
| Shields | 100,000 | 1/6 |
| | $450,000 | |

On May 31, 19X5, Wheeler was admitted into the partnership when she purchased for $120,000 an interest from Fender in the net assets and profits of the partnership. As a result of this transaction, Wheeler acquired a one-fifth interest in the net assets and profits of the firm. Assume that implied goodwill is not to be recorded. Fender's tax basis just prior to the sale was $180,000.

**Required:**
1. What is the gain realized by Fender on the sale of a portion of this interest in the partnership to Wheeler?
2. Is the gain calculated in requirement 1 a gain for book purposes, a gain for tax purposes, or both?
3. Prepare the entry required on the partnership's books.
4. What is Fender's taxable gain or loss if he retires on June 1, 19X5, and receives cash equal to the balance in his capital account at this date? (Assume the partnership had no liabilities at this date.)

# Problems

|  | **Admission of a Partner: Tangible Assets Undervalued and Goodwill Exists** |
|---|---|
| P<br>24-1 | Fields and Hill are in partnership, share profits and losses in the ratio 4:1, respectively, and have capital balances of $22,500 each. Tangible assets of the partnership have a fair value of $15,000 in excess of book value. Mounds is admitted into the partnership for a cash contribution of $30,000. The new profit and loss sharing formula is Fields, 56%; Hill, 14%; and Mounds, 30%. The value of the partnership's existing goodwill is agreed to be $10,000. |

**Required:**
1. Prepare the required entries assuming the tangible assets are to be revalued and the goodwill is to be recorded on the partnership's books.
2. Prepare the required entries assuming that the bonus method is to be used with respect to the undervalued tangible assets and the goodwill.

|  | **Retirement of a Partner: Tangible Assets Undervalued and Goodwill Exists** |
|---|---|
| P<br>24-2 | The April 30, 19X5, balance sheet of the partnership of Arbee, Karl, and MacDonald is as follows. The partners share profits and losses in the ratio 2:2:6, respectively. |

| | |
|---|---|
| Assets, at cost . . . . . . . . . . . . . . . . . . . . . . . . . . . . . . . . . . . . . . . . . . . . . . . . . . . | $100,000 |
| Arbee, loan . . . . . . . . . . . . . . . . . . . . . . . . . . . . . . . . . . . . . . . . . . . . . . . . . . . . . . | $  9,000 |
| Capital, Arbee . . . . . . . . . . . . . . . . . . . . . . . . . . . . . . . . . . . . . . . . . . . . . . . . . . . . | 15,000 |
| Capital, Karl . . . . . . . . . . . . . . . . . . . . . . . . . . . . . . . . . . . . . . . . . . . . . . . . . . . . . | 31,000 |
| Capital, MacDonald . . . . . . . . . . . . . . . . . . . . . . . . . . . . . . . . . . . . . . . . . . . . . . . | 45,000 |
| | $100,000 |

Arbee retires from the partnership. By mutual agreement, the assets are to be adjusted to their fair value of $130,000 at April 30, 19X5. Karl and MacDonald agree that the partnership will pay Arbee $37,000 cash for his partnership interest, exclusive of his loan, which is to be paid in full. No goodwill is to be recorded.

**Required:**
1. Prepare the entry to record the revaluation of assets to their fair value.
2. Prepare the entry to record Arbee's retirement.
3. What is the implicit goodwill?

(AICPA adapted)

---

| P 24-3 |
|---|

### Business Combination: Each Partnership Has Undervalued Tangible Assets and Goodwill

The partnership of A, B, C, and D has agreed to combine with the partnership of X and Y. The individual Capital accounts and profit and loss sharing percentage of each partner are shown below:

| | Capital Accounts | Profit and Loss Sharing Percentages | |
|---|---|---|---|
| | | Now | Proposed |
| A | $ 50,000 | 40 | 28 |
| B | 35,000 | 30 | 21 |
| C | 40,000 | 20 | 14 |
| D | 25,000 | 10 | 7 |
| | $150,000 | 100 | 70 |
| X | $ 60,000 | 50 | 15 |
| Y | 40,000 | 50 | 15 |
| | $100,000 | 100 | 30 |

The partnership of A, B, C, and D has undervalued tangible assets of $20,000, and the partnership of X and Y has undervalued tangible assets of $8,000. All the partners agree that (1) the partnership of A, B, C, and D possesses goodwill of $30,000, and (2) the partnership of X and Y possesses goodwill of $10,000. (Assume that the combined businesses will continue to use the general ledger of A, B, C, and D.)

**Required:**
1. Prepare the entries required to reflect the combination, assuming tangible assets are to be revalued and goodwill is to be recorded.
2. Prepare the entries required to reflect the combination, assuming the bonus method is to be used with respect to the undervalued tangible assets and the goodwill.

---

| P 24-4 |
|---|

### Calculation of Tax Basis of New Partner and Adjustment to Old Partners' Tax Bases: Admission by Capital Contribution into the Partnership

Bishop and Knight are in partnership; share profits and losses in the ratio 5:3, respectively; and have capital balances of $80,000 and $60,000, respectively. They admit Rook into the partnership for a cash contribution of $50,000, of which

$16,000 is to be credited to the Capital accounts of the old partners as a bonus. The new profit and loss sharing percentages are Bishop, 50%; Knight, 30%; and Rook, 20%. The partnership has $120,000 of liabilities at Rook's admission. Rook became jointly responsible for these liabilities at his admission pursuant to a provision in the new partnership agreement. Bishop's tax basis just prior to Rook's admission was $138,000.

**Required:**
1. Prepare the entry required on the partnership's books.
2. Calculate the tax basis of Rook's interest in the partnership.
3. Calculate the required adjustment to the tax basis of each of the old partners as a result of Rook's admission.
4. What is Bishop's tax basis after Rook's admission?
5. What is the tax significance of the bonus received by Bishop and Knight?
6. Calculate Bishop's taxable gain or loss assuming (1) he quits the partnership one day after Rook is admitted and (2) Bishop receives cash in full liquidation of his capital interest equal to the balance in his capital account.

**P 24-5**

### Calculation of Tax Basis of New Partner and Determination of Old Partner's Proceeds and Taxable Gain: Admission by Purchase of Existing Partner's Interest

Board and Checker are in partnership, share profits and losses equally, and have capital balances of $60,000 and $40,000, respectively. Kingmee purchases all of Checker's interest for $50,000 and agrees to be jointly responsible for all existing partnership liabilities, which total $14,000.

**Required:**
1. Prepare the entry required on the partnership's books.
2. Calculate the tax basis of Kingmee's interest in the partnership.
3. Calculate the adjustment, if any, to Board's tax basis as a result of Kingmee's purchase of Checker's interest.
4. Assuming Checker's tax basis was $47,000 when he sold his interest, determine the proceeds he received on the sale of his interest and his taxable gain, if any.

**P 24-6**

### COMPREHENSIVE Admission of New Partners: Withdrawal of Old Partner and Division of Profits

You have been engaged to prepare the June 30, 19X2, financial statements for the partnership of Ash, Cherry, and Douglas. You have obtained the following information from the partnership agreement, as amended, and from the accounting records.

1. The partnership was formed originally by Ash and Burch on July 1, 19X1. At that date:
   a. Burch contributed $400,000 cash.
   b. Ash contributed land, a building, and equipment with fair market values of $110,000, $520,000, and $185,000, respectively. The land and buildings

were subject to a mortgage securing an 8% per annum note (interest rate of similar notes at July 1, 19X1). The note is due in quarterly payments of $5,000 plus interest on January 1, April 1, July 1, and October 1 of each year. Ash made the July 1, 19X1, principal and interest payment personally. The partnership then assumed the obligation of the remaining $300,000 balance.

c. The agreement further provided that Ash had contributed a certain intangible benefit to the partnership because of her many years of business activity in the area serviced by the new partnership. The assigned value of this intangible asset plus the net tangible assets she contributed gave Ash a 60% initial capital interest in the partnership.

d. Ash was designated the only active partner, at an annual salary of $24,000 plus an annual bonus of 5% of net income after deducting her salary but before deducting interest on partners' capital investments (see below). Both the salary and the bonus are to be recorded as operating expenses of the partnership.

e. Each partner is to receive a 10% return on average capital investment; such interest is to be an expense of the partnership.

f. All remaining profits or losses are to be shared equally.

2. On October 1, 19X1, Burch sold his partnership interest and rights as of July 1, 19X1, to Cherry for $370,000. Ash agreed to accept Cherry as a partner if he would contribute sufficient cash to meet the October 1, 19X1, principal and interest payment on the mortgage note. Cherry made the payment from personal funds.

3. On January 1, 19X2, Ash and Cherry admitted a new partner, Douglas. Douglas invested $150,000 cash for a 10% capital interest based on the initial investments (tangible and intangible) at July 1, 19X1, of Ash and Burch, plus Douglas' capital contribution of $150,000. At January 1, 19X2, the book values of the partnership's assets and liabilities approximated their fair market values. Douglas contributed no intangible benefit to the partnership.

Similar to the other partners, Douglas is to receive a 10% return on his average capital investment. His investment also entitled him to 20% of the partnership's profits or losses as defined above. For the year ended June 30, 19X2, however, Douglas would receive one-half his pro rata share of the profits or losses.

4. The accounting records show that on February 1, 19X2, the Other Miscellaneous Expenses account had been charged $3,600 for hospital expenses incurred by Ash's eight-year-old daughter, Fern.

5. All salary payments to Ash have been charged to her drawing account. On June 1, 19X2, Cherry made a $33,000 withdrawal. These are the only transactions recorded in the partners' drawing accounts.

6. Presented below is a trial balance, which summarizes the partnership's general ledger balances at June 30, 19X2. The general ledger has not been closed.

|  | Debit | Credit |
|---|---|---|
| Current Assets | $ 307,000 | |
| Fixed Assets | 1,285,000 | |
| Current Liabilities | | $ 104,100 |
| 8% Mortgage Note Payable | | 285,000 |

*(continued)*

|  | Debit | Credit |
|---|---|---|
| Ash, Capital | | 515,000 |
| Cherry, Capital | | 400,000 |
| Douglas, Capital | | 150,000 |
| Ash, Drawing | 24,000 | |
| Cherry, Drawing | 33,000 | |
| Douglas, Drawing | –0– | |
| Sales | | 946,900 |
| Cost of Sales | 695,600 | |
| Administrative Expenses | 28,000 | |
| Other Miscellaneous Expenses | 11,000 | |
| Interest Expense | 17,400 | |
| Totals | $2,401,000 | $2,401,000 |

## Required:

Prepare a worksheet to adjust the net income (loss) and partners' Capital accounts for the year ended June 30, 19X2, and to close the net income (loss) to the partners' Capital accounts at June 30, 19X2. Supporting schedules should be in good form. Amortization of goodwill, if any, is to be over a 10-year period. (Ignore all tax considerations.) Use the following column headings and begin with balances from the books as shown:

| Description | Net Income (Loss) (Dr.) Cr. | Partners' Capital | | | Other Accounts | |
|---|---|---|---|---|---|---|
| | | Ash (Dr.) Cr. | Cherry (Dr.) Cr. | Douglas (Dr.) Cr. | Amount Dr. (Cr.) | Name |
| Book balances at June 30, 19X2 | $194,900 | $515,000 | $400,000 | $150,000 | | |

(AICPA adapted)

## ANSWERS TO SELF-STUDY QUESTIONS

1. d, b    3. b    5. d    7. d
2. c       4. b    6. a

# 25

# PARTNERSHIPS: LIQUIDATIONS

## CHAPTER OVERVIEW

The termination of a partnership's business activities is known as **liquidation.** A partnership may be liquidated for many reasons—for example, the original agreed-upon term of existence has expired, the business is not as successful as expected, or the partnership is in serious financial difficulty. Although a partnership in serious financial difficulty may attempt rehabilitation either by filing under Chapter 11 of the Bankruptcy Reform Act of 1978 or through a troubled debt restructuring outside of bankruptcy court, such courses of action for partnerships do not entail any significant special problems not already discussed for corporations. Consequently, we restrict our discussion in this chapter to the process of liquidation.

The liquidation process for partnerships is in several respects identical to the liquidation process for corporations. Over a period of time, the noncash assets of the business are converted into cash (the realization process), creditors are paid to the extent possible, and remaining funds, if any, are distributed to the owners (partners). Partnership liquidations, however, are different from corporate liquidations in the following respects:

1. Because partners have unlimited liability, any partner may be called upon to contribute additional funds to the partnership if partnership assets are insufficient to satisfy creditors' claims.
2. To the extent that a partner does not make good a deficit balance in his or her Capital account, the remaining partners must absorb such deficit balance. Absorption of a partner's deficit balance gives the absorbing partners legal recourse against the partner.

The special problems created by these two situations are discussed throughout this chapter.

Liquidations may be categorized broadly as lump-sum liquidations and installment liquidations.

1. In *lump-sum liquidations,* no distributions are made to the partners until the realization process is completed, when the full amount of the realization gain or loss is known.
2. In *installment liquidations,* distributions are made to some or all of the partners as cash becomes available. Thus, cash distributions are made to partners before the full amount of the realization gain or loss is known.

Within each category, a variety of situations may arise concerning the ability of the partnership and the individual partners to satisfy the claims of partnership creditors. Before discussing each situation in detail, we discuss some general aspects of liquidations.

# FUNDAMENTAL PROCEDURES IN LIQUIDATIONS

## Procedures for Minimizing Inequities among Partners

**Sharing of Gains and Losses.** Gains and losses incurred on the realization of assets may be allocated among the partners in the manner they have agreed to in the partnership agreement. If the partnership agreement is silent with respect to the sharing of gains and losses during liquidation, then the Uniform Partnership Act (UPA) treats such gains and losses in the same way as preliquidation profits and losses—that is, gains and losses are allocated in accordance with the profit and loss sharing formula. Most partnerships follow the profit and loss sharing formula in distributing gains and losses incurred during liquidation. This is the most equitable manner for the following reasons:

1. The cumulative profit and loss of a partnership during its existence is the difference between total capital contributions and total capital withdrawals. Accordingly, the cumulative profit or loss of a partnership during its existence should include start-up periods, normal operating periods, and wind-down periods.
2. Certain gains and losses recognized during the liquidation process actually may have occurred during normal operating periods. This would be the case when (a) land or buildings have been held for several years and appreciated in value prior to the liquidation, and (b) certain accounts receivable should have been written off as uncollectible before liquidation. The use of a method other than the profit and loss sharing formula would result in inequities among the partners.

If a partner's Capital account is not sufficient to absorb his or her share of the losses incurred in liquidation, Section 18 of the UPA provides that "each partner . . . must contribute toward the losses . . . sustained by the partnership according to his share in the profits." In other words, a partner must contribute additional funds to the partnership to eliminate any deficit balance in his or her Capital account created by losses incurred through normal operations or in the liquidation process. If such a partner does not have the personal resources to eliminate this deficit, the remaining partners must absorb the capital deficit, resulting in inequities to them. A basic procedure that may minimize such potential inequities is discussed in the next section.

**Advance Planning when the Partnership Is Formed.** Although every partnership commences business under the "going concern" concept, it would be unrealistic if the partners did not acknowledge the possibility that the partnership may have to be liquidated at some time. It is in the interest of each partner, therefore, to take prudent steps to minimize the possibility of inequities occurring in liquidation. Inequities among partners may arise during liquidation if a deficit balance is created in a partner's Capital account (as a result of losses incurred during the conversion of non-cash assets into cash), and that partner cannot contribute capital to eliminate the deficit. The partners who do not have deficit balances in their Capital accounts must absorb the deficit balance of the partner who does. In other words, they must absorb losses greater than their agreed-upon profit and loss sharing percentage.

Because a partnership has no control over its partners' personal affairs, it has no assurance that its partners will have sufficient personal funds to contribute if a deficit balance is created during liquidation. Accordingly, the partnership should be operated in a manner that minimizes the possibility of a deficit balance occurring. If the partnership agreement specifies that all partners' capital balances are to be maintained in the profit and loss sharing ratio, then a partnership may incur losses on the conversion of noncash assets into cash up to the total equity of the partnership, without creating a deficit balance in any partner's Capital account. This safeguard is so important that many partnerships (including most of the international accounting partnerships) require Capital accounts to be maintained in the profit and loss sharing ratio. Furthermore, as cash is available for distribution to the partners (a situation that occurs only if losses during liquidation are less than the total partnership equity), such cash may be distributed to the partners in the profit and loss sharing ratio with complete assurance that no inequities will result. In such situations, the liquidation process is quite simple. Unfortunately, not all partnerships use such a provision. Partners in such partnerships needlessly expose themselves to potential inequities in the event of liquidation, making the liquidation process much more complex.

Although the potential for inequities occurring during liquidation cannot be completely eliminated, a partnership that requires Capital accounts to be maintained in the profit and loss sharing ratio has taken a big step toward minimizing any potential inequities that may arise.

**Rule of Setoff.** When a partnership has a loan outstanding **to a partner,** the partnership receivable should be subtracted, or *set off,* from the partner's Capital account. It would not be equitable to assume that the receivable is uncollectible (even though the partner may not have sufficient personal assets to repay the loan) and thereby allocate the loss among all the partners. The partner's Capital account less the receivable represents the partner's true capital investment.

When a partner has a loan outstanding **to the partnership,** the loan does not rank on an equal level with other partnership liabilities. Section 40 of the UPA states that the *order of payment* to creditors and partners during liquidation is as follows:

(I) Those owing to creditors other than partners.
(II) Those owing to partners other than for capital and profits [loans].
(III) Those owing to partners in respect of capital.
(IV) Those owing to partners in respect of profit.

When profits and losses are closed in the partners' Capital accounts at each year-end, the last two categories may be considered one amount, which is the balance in each partner's Capital account. Although this section of the UPA implies that partners' loans are paid off before any cash distributions are made to partners in liquidation of their capital balances, a strict application of this order of payment could result in inequities among the partners. For example, a partner with a loan to a partnership could be repaid the loan, a deficit balance could be created in his or her Capital account at a later date because of losses on the realization of assets, and the partner might not be able to make a capital contribution to eliminate that deficit balance. The other partners would have to absorb such partner's deficit balance and thus incur a greater portion of the losses during liquidation than they originally agreed to. The legal doctrine of **setoff**—whereby a deficit balance in a partner's Capital account may be set off against any balance existing in his or her loan account—has been incorporated into accountants' procedures for determining which partners should receive cash as it becomes available. These procedures effectively treat the loan as an additional capital investment. The mechanical procedures, which are different in lump-sum liquidations and installment liquidations, are discussed and illustrated later in the chapter.

## The Statement of Realization and Liquidation

Because normal operations do not take place during the liquidation period, traditional financial statements are not appropriate. Instead, the partners prefer to have a statement that provides information on the following:

1. Gains and losses on the realization of assets, including the impact of such gains and losses on the partners' Capital accounts.
2. Payments that have been made to creditors and partners.
3. The noncash assets still to be converted into cash.

Accordingly, accountants have devised a statement called the **statement of realization and liquidation** to provide this information. The statement is entirely historical; it reflects only the actual transactions that have occurred during the liquidation period up to the date of the statement. If the liquidation process takes place over several months, the statement is updated periodically as noncash assets are converted into cash and payments are made to creditors, partners, or both. Other than the allocation of realization gains and losses among the partners and the exercising of the right of setoff, the statement is essentially a summary of cash inflows and outflows.

## Liquidation Expenses

Certain costs incurred during the liquidation process should be treated as a reduction of the proceeds from the sale of noncash assets—for example, costs to complete inventory, sales commissions and shipping costs related to the disposal of inventory, escrow and title transfer fees associated with the sale of real property, and costs of removing equipment. Other liquidation costs should be treated as expenses. It is preferable to make a reasonable estimate of these expenses at the beginning of the liquidation process and record an estimated liability in the general ledger at that time, adjusting the liability as necessary during the liquidation process. Recording the estimated liability at the inception of the liquidation process minimizes the possibility of making excess cash distributions to partners. Any cash available for distribution to partners should be set aside in an amount equal to the remaining estimated liability so that it is not distributed to partners.

## LUMP-SUM LIQUIDATIONS

In a **lump-sum liquidation,** all noncash assets are converted to cash and outside creditors are paid in full before cash is distributed to the partners. Thus, the full amount of the gain or loss on realization of assets is known before the partners receive any cash distributions. Lump-sum liquidations are rare or nonexistent, because partners liquidate their loan and Capital accounts as cash becomes available for distribution. Usually, partners have personal needs for cash, and there is no sound business reason for waiting until the very last asset is converted to cash before distributing any cash to the partners. We illustrate several lump-sum liquidations for instructional purposes only.

### Partnership Is Solvent and All Partners Are Personally Solvent

In the first three illustrations in this section, (1) the partnership is solvent (the fair value of partnership assets is sufficient to satisfy outside creditors' claims), and (2) all partners who must make capital contributions have either sufficient loans to the partnership (for purposes of exercising the right of setoff) or are personally solvent, so that the capital deficit from losses incurred during the realization process is eliminated by contributions.

| ILLUSTRATION | ### Loss on Realization Does Not Create a Deficit Balance in Any Partner's Capital Account |

To illustrate how the statement of realization and liquidation is prepared in a lump-sum liquidation, assume partners A and B share profits and losses in the ratio 3:2, respectively, and the balance sheet of the partnership is as follows:

### A AND B PARTNERSHIP
### BALANCE SHEET, MAY 31, 19X5

| | | | |
|---|---|---|---|
| Cash . . . . . . . . . . . . . . . | $ 5,000 | Liabilities . . . . . . . . . . . | $20,000 |
| Noncash assets . . . . . | 70,000 | Loan, Partner B . . . . . . | 3,000 |
| | | Capital: | |
| | | Partner A . . . . . . . . . . | 37,000 |
| | | Partner B . . . . . . . . . . | 15,000 |
| | $75,000 | | $75,000 |

Also, assume during June 19X5 that (1) the noncash assets of $70,000 are converted into $40,000 cash, resulting in a $30,000 loss, which is distributed 60% to partner A ($18,000) and 40% to partner B ($12,000); (2) outside creditors are paid in full; and (3) the remaining cash is distributed to the partners. The statement of realization and liquidation covering the entire liquidation period would be prepared as in Illustration 25-1.

### ■ ILLUSTRATION 25-1

| A AND B PARTNERSHIP | | | | | | |
|---|---|---|---|---|---|---|
| Statement of Realization and Liquidation | | | | | | |
| June 19X5 | | | | | | |
| | **Assets** | | **Outside** | **Loan** | **Partners' Capital** | |
| | Cash | Noncash | Liabilities | B | A(60%)[a] | B (40%)[a] |
| Preliquidation balances . . . . | $ 5,000 | $70,000 | $20,000 | $ 3,000 | $37,000 | $ 15,000 |
| Realization of assets and | | | | | | |
|   allocation of loss . . . . . . . | 40,000 | (70,000) | | | (18,000) | (12,000) |
|   Subtotal . . . . . . . . . . . . . . | $45,000 | $ –0– | $20,000 | $ 3,000 | $19,000 | $ 3,000 |
| Cash distributions: | | | | | | |
|   Outside creditors . . . . . . . | (20,000) | | (20,000) | | | |
|   Partner's loan . . . . . . . . . . | (3,000) | | | (3,000) | | |
|   Partner's capital . . . . . . . . | (22,000) | | | | (19,000) | (3,000) |
| Postliquidation balances . . . | $ –0– | | $ –0– | $ –0– | $ –0– | $ –0– |

[a]Denotes profit and loss sharing percentage.

**Review Points for Illustration 25-1.** Note the following:

1. The format of the statement does not combine the loan account of partner B with his Capital account. The loan is a bona fide loan and not a capital investment.
2. Cash distributions were made in accordance with the priority set forth in Section 40 of the UPA.

ILLUSTRATION
### Loss on Realization Creates a Deficit Balance in One Partner's Capital Account: Right of Setoff Exercised

Assume the information in the preceding illustration, except that partner B's loan account is $10,000 instead of $3,000 and his Capital account is $8,000 instead of $15,000. The statement of realization and liquidation would be prepared as shown in Illustration 25-2.

**Review Points for Illustration 25-2.** Note the following:

1. The fact that partners' loans are assigned a higher priority for repayment than partnership Capital accounts under Section 40 of the UPA is not significant if a partner with a loan account also has a deficit balance in his or her Capital account—that is, the full amount of the loan is not paid before payments are made to partners in liquidation of their Capital accounts.

■ **ILLUSTRATION 25-2**

<table>
<tr><td colspan="7" align="center">**A AND B PARTNERSHIP**<br>**Statement of Realization and Liquidation**<br>**June 19X5**</td></tr>
<tr><td></td><td colspan="2" align="center">Assets</td><td>Outside</td><td>Loan</td><td colspan="2" align="center">Partners' Capital</td></tr>
<tr><td></td><td>Cash</td><td>Noncash</td><td>Liabilities</td><td>B</td><td>A(60%)[a]</td><td>B (40%)[a]</td></tr>
<tr><td>Preliquidation balances....</td><td>$ 5,000</td><td>$70,000</td><td>$20,000</td><td>$10,000</td><td>$37,000</td><td>$ 8,000</td></tr>
<tr><td>Realization of assets and allocation of loss.........</td><td>40,000</td><td>(70,000)</td><td></td><td></td><td>(18,000)</td><td>(12,000)</td></tr>
<tr><td>Subtotal............</td><td>$45,000</td><td>$ –0–</td><td>$20,000</td><td>$10,000</td><td>$19,000</td><td>$ (4,000)</td></tr>
<tr><td>Right of setoff exercised....</td><td></td><td></td><td></td><td>(4,000)</td><td></td><td>4,000</td></tr>
<tr><td>Subtotal............</td><td>$45,000</td><td></td><td>$20,000</td><td>$ 6,000</td><td>$19,000</td><td>$ –0–</td></tr>
<tr><td>Cash distributions:</td><td></td><td></td><td></td><td></td><td></td><td></td></tr>
<tr><td>Outside creditors........</td><td>(20,000)</td><td></td><td>(20,000)</td><td></td><td></td><td></td></tr>
<tr><td>Partner's loan...........</td><td>(6,000)</td><td></td><td></td><td>(6,000)</td><td></td><td></td></tr>
<tr><td>Partners' capital........</td><td>(19,000)</td><td></td><td></td><td></td><td>(19,000)</td><td></td></tr>
<tr><td>Postliquidation balances...</td><td>$ –0–</td><td></td><td>$ –0–</td><td>$ –0–</td><td>$ –0–</td><td></td></tr>
</table>

[a]Denotes profit and loss sharing percentage.

2. The $4,000 deficit in partner B's Capital account after the realization loss of $30,000 on the noncash assets means that partner B must contribute $4,000 to the partnership, so that he can fully absorb his share of the loss on realization.

3. Partner B did not contribute $4,000 to the partnership to eliminate his Capital account deficit, because he could exercise the right of set-off whereby $4,000 was transferred from his loan account to his Capital account.

4. Each partner received the same amount of cash in Illustration 25-1 and 25-2. For all practical purposes, partner B's loan account is the equivalent of an additional capital investment for liquidation purposes.

ILLUSTRATION ### Loss on Realization Creates a Deficit Balance in One Partner's Capital Account: Right of Setoff Exercised and Additional Capital Contribution Is Required and Made

Assume the information in the preceding illustration, except that the loss on the realization of the noncash assets is $50,000 rather than $30,000. This additional $20,000 loss will result in partner B's having a capital deficit, which is not completely eliminated on his exercising the right of setoff. Assume that partner B is personally solvent and makes the required capital contribution to eliminate the remainder of his capital deficit. The statement of realization and liquidation would be prepared as shown in Illustration 25-3.

## Partnership Is Solvent and at Least One Partner Is Personally Insolvent

In the next two illustrations, at least one partner is personally insolvent and unable to make a capital contribution to eliminate his or her capital deficit. In such circumstances, the remaining partners must absorb the capital deficit of the insolvent partner in their respective profit and loss sharing ratio. If this, in turn, causes a capital deficit for an absorbing partner, then that partner must make a capital contribution to eliminate the deficit. If such partner also is personally insolvent, then his or her capital deficit must be absorbed by the remaining partners, using their respective profit and loss sharing ratio.

The absorption of a partner's deficit capital balance by other partners is a violation of the UPA, in that the partner who cannot eliminate his or her deficit capital balance has broken the terms of the partnership agreement. The other partners have legal recourse against the personal assets of the defaulting partner. This situation raises the question of how such claims against the personal assets of the defaulting partner are treated in relation to claims of personal creditors of the defaulting partner. In the

■ **ILLUSTRATION 25-3**

| | | | | | | |
|---|---|---|---|---|---|---|
| **A AND B PARTNERSHIP**<br>**Statement of Realization and Liquidation**<br>**June 19X5** | | | | | | |
| | **Assets** | | **Outside<br>Liabilities** | **Loan<br>B** | **Partners' Capital** | |
| | **Cash** | **Noncash** | | | **A(60%)[a]** | **B (40%)[a]** |
| Preliquidation balances.... | $ 5,000 | $70,000 | $20,000 | $10,000 | $37,000 | $ 8,000 |
| Realization of assets and<br>allocation of loss........ | 20,000 | (70,000) | | | (30,000) | (20,000) |
| Subtotal............. | $25,000 | $ –0– | $20,000 | $10,000 | $ 7,000 | $(12,000) |
| Right of setoff exercised.... | | | | (10,000) | | 10,000 |
| Subtotal............. | $25,000 | | $20,000 | $ –0– | $ 7,000 | $ (2,000) |
| Cash contribution by B .... | 2,000 | | | | | 2,000 |
| Subtotal............. | $27,000 | | $20,000 | | $ 7,000 | $ –0– |
| Cash distributions<br>  Outside creditors........ | (20,000) | | (20,000) | | | |
| Partner's capital........ | (7,000) | | | | (7,000) | |
| Postliquidation balances... | $ –0– | | $ –0– | | $ –0– | |

[a]Denotes profit and loss sharing percentage.

next section of the chapter, we answer this question and discuss situations in which the **partnership is insolvent** and at least one partner is personally insolvent.

ILLUSTRATION

## Loss on Realization Creates a Deficit Balance in One Partner's Capital Account: Right of Setoff Exercised and Additional Capital Contribution Is Required but Not Made

Assume partners A, B, C, and D share profits in the ratio 4:2:2:2, respectively. The partnership's balance sheet at the beginning of the liquidation process is as follows:

### A, B, C AND D PARTNERSHIP
### BALANCE SHEET, JUNE 30, 19X5

| | | | |
|---|---|---|---|
| Cash ............... | $ 10,000 | Liabilities ........... | $157,000 |
| Noncash assets ..... | 290,000 | Loan: | |
| | | Partner B.......... | 10,000 |
| | | Partner C.......... | 5,000 |
| | | Partner D ......... | 2,000 |
| | | Capital: | |
| | | Partner A.......... | 70,000 |

## A, B, C AND D PARTNERSHIP
## BALANCE SHEET, JUNE 30, 19X5

|  |  |  |  |
|---|---|---|---|
|  |  | Partner B. . . . . . . . . . | 30,000 |
|  |  | Partner C. . . . . . . . . . | 20,000 |
|  |  | Partner D . . . . . . . . . | 6,000 |
|  | $300,000 |  | $300,000 |

Assume also that during July 19X5 the noncash assets realize $210,000 cash, resulting in a realization loss of $80,000, which is shared among the partners (using the profit and loss sharing ratio 4:2:2:2) as follows: A, $32,000; B, $16,000; C, $16,000; and D, $16,000. The realization loss creates a deficit in D's Capital account, which is not completely eliminated through his exercising the right of setoff. D must make an additional capital contribution of $8,000 but is unable to do so. As a result, his $8,000 capital deficit must be allocated to partners A, B, and C in their profit and loss sharing ratio of 4:2:2, respectively. Assuming all cash was distributed in July 19X5, the statement of realization and liquidation would be prepared as shown in Illustration 25-4.

**Review Points for Illustration 25-4.** Note the following:

1. Because partner D was unable to eliminate the deficit balance in his Capital account, the remaining partners had to bear a greater percentage of the realization loss than their individual profit and loss sharing percentages. For example, partner A suffered a total loss of $36,000 ($32,000 + $4,000). This represents 45% of the $80,000 total realization loss, which is greater than her stipulated profit and loss sharing percentage of 40%. Partners A, B, and C needlessly exposed themselves to this additional $8,000 loss by not employing the fundamental safeguard provision of maintaining Capital accounts in the profit and loss sharing ratio.

2. The illustration assumes that partner D was unable to make any of the required contribution. If a partner contribution had been made, then a smaller deficit balance would have had to be absorbed by the remaining partners.

3. A partner with a deficit balance may indicate that he is unable to eliminate completely the deficit balance when it is created but that he might be able to make a capital contribution at a later date (which may or may not be specified). If partner D had indicated this, the available $220,000 cash could have been distributed to the outside creditors and the remaining partners. The partnership books then could be kept open until partner D makes a capital contribution or it subsequently is determined that he cannot make a payment after all. This

## ■ ILLUSTRATION 25-4

### A, B, C, and D PARTNERSHIP
### Statement of Realization and Liquidation
### July 19X5

| | Assets | | Outside Liabilities | Partners' Loans | | | Partners' Capital | | | |
| --- | --- | --- | --- | --- | --- | --- | --- | --- | --- | --- |
| | Cash | Noncash | | B | C | D | A (40%)[a] | B (20%)[a] | C (20%)[a] | D (20%)[a] |
| Preliquidation balances | $ 10,000 | $290,000 | $157,000 | $10,000 | $5,000 | $2,000 | $70,000 | $30,000 | $20,000 | $ 6,000 |
| Realization of assets and allocation of loss | 210,000 | (290,000) | | | | | (32,000) | (16,000) | (16,000) | (16,000) |
| Subtotal | $220,000 | $ –0– | $157,000 | $10,000 | $5,000 | $2,000 | $38,000 | $14,000 | $ 4,000 | $(10,000) |
| Right of setoff exercised | | | | | | (2,000) | | | | 2,000 |
| Subtotal | $220,000 | | $157,000 | $10,000 | $5,000 | $ –0– | $38,000 | $14,000 | $ 4,000 | $ (8,000) |
| Absorption of D's capital deficit | | | | | | | (4,000) | (2,000) | (2,000) | 8,000 |
| Subtotal | $220,000 | | $157,000 | $10,000 | $5,000 | | $34,000 | $12,000 | $ 2,000 | $ –0– |
| Cash distributions: | | | | | | | | | | |
| Outside creditors | (157,000) | | (157,000) | | | | | | | |
| Partners' loans | (15,000) | | | (10,000) | (5,000) | | | | | |
| Partners' capital | (48,000) | | | | | | (34,000) | (12,000) | (2,000) | |
| Postliquidation balances | $ –0– | | $ –0– | $ –0– | $ –0– | $ –0– | $ –0– | $ –0– | $ –0– | $ –0– |

[a]Denotes profit and loss sharing percentage.

procedure could result in a lengthy delay in completing the partnership liquidation. There is no sound reason for keeping the partnership books open indefinitely, thereby delaying the completion of the liquidation process, merely because of partner D's uncertain financial situation. When partner D's Capital account deficit was created (and not completely eliminated through exercising the right of setoff), he became liable for his deficit to the other partners. Accordingly, if partner D later makes a capital contribution, he makes the payment directly to the other partners. Consequently, in situations involving lump-sum liquidations in which a partner cannot immediately eliminate his or her capital deficit, the accountant should complete the liquidation process by transferring the capital deficit to the Capital accounts of the remaining partners (using their respective profit and loss sharing ratios). The partnership books may then be closed, and the liquidation process can be completed.

**ILLUSTRATION** ### Loss on Realization Creates a Deficit Balance in One Partner's Capital Account—Absorption by Other Partners Creates a Deficit Balance in Another Partner's Capital Account

Assume the information in the preceding illustration, except that the noncash assets are sold for only $170,000. This results in a realization loss of $120,000 rather than $80,000. The $120,000 realization loss is allocated among the partners (using the profit and loss sharing ratio 4:2:2:2) as follows: A, $48,000; B, $24,000; C, $24,000; and D, $24,000. In addition to the previously described consequences to partner D, the greater loss results in partner C being unable to absorb fully his share of partner D's deficit balance. Thus, partner C has a deficit balance that he cannot eliminate through setoff or contribution. His capital deficit, in turn, must be allocated to partners A and B in their respective profit and loss sharing ratio of 4:2. (Partners A and B have legal recourse against the personal assets of partners C and D—such recourse is discussed in the next section of this chapter.) Assuming all cash was distributed in July 19X5, the statement of realization and liquidation would be prepared as shown in Illustration 25-5.

## Partnership Is Insolvent and at Least One Partner Is Personally Solvent

In the next two illustrations, the partnership is insolvent—that is, the loss on the realization of noncash assets is greater than the total of the partners' capital (including their loan accounts). Because unlimited liability is a feature of the partnership form of organization, creditors may seek payment from any or all of the partners as individuals.

■ ILLUSTRATION 25-5

## A, B, C, and D PARTNERSHIP
### Statement of Realization and Liquidation
### July 19X5

| | Assets | | Outside Liabilities | Partners' Loans | | | Partners' Capital | | | |
|---|---|---|---|---|---|---|---|---|---|---|
| | Cash | Noncash | | B | C | D | A (40%)[a] | B (20%)[a] | C (20%)[a] | D (20%)[a] |
| Preliquidation balances | $ 10,000 | $290,000 | $157,000 | $10,000 | $ 5,000 | $2,000 | $70,000 | $30,000 | $20,000 | $ 6,000 |
| Realization of assets and allocation of loss | 170,000 | (290,000) | | | | | (48,000) | (24,000) | (24,000) | (24,000) |
| Subtotal | $180,000 | $ -0- | $157,000 | $10,000 | $ 5,000 | $2,000 | $22,000 | $ 6,000 | $ (4,000) | $(18,000) |
| Right of setoff exercised | | | | | (4,000) | (2,000) | | | 4,000 | 2,000 |
| Subtotal | $180,000 | | $157,000 | $10,000 | $ 1,000 | $ -0- | $22,000 | $ 6,000 | $ -0- | $(16,000) |
| Absorption of D's capital deficit | | | | | | | (8,000) | (4,000) | (4,000) | 16,000 |
| Subtotal | $180,000 | | $157,000 | $10,000 | $ 1,000 | | $14,000 | $ 2,000 | $ (4,000) | $ -0- |
| Right of setoff exercised | | | | | (1,000) | | | | 1,000 | |
| Subtotal | $180,000 | | $157,000 | $10,000 | $ -0- | | $14,000 | $ 2,000 | $ (3,000) | |
| Absorption of C's capital deficit | | | | | | | (2,000) | (1,000) | 3,000 | |
| Subtotal | $180,000 | | $157,000 | $10,000 | | | $12,000 | $ 1,000 | $ -0- | |
| Cash distributions: | | | | | | | | | | |
| Outside creditors | (157,000) | | (157,000) | | | | | | | |
| Partner's loan | (10,000) | | | (10,000) | | | | | | |
| Partners' capital | (13,000) | | | | | | (12,000) | (1,000) | | |
| Postliquidation balances | $ -0- | | $ -0- | $ -0- | | | $ -0- | $ -0- | | |

[a]Denotes profit and loss sharing percentage.

## Loss on Realization Creates a Deficit Balance in Certain Partners' Capital Accounts—All Partners Are Personally Solvent

In this situation, all the partners are personally solvent, and the partners with deficit capital balances contribute funds to the partnership to eliminate their capital deficits, enabling creditors to be paid in full by the partnership. Using the same preliquidation balances that are given for Illustration 25-5, assume the noncash assets of $290,000 are sold for $130,000, resulting in a realization loss of $160,000. The realization loss is shared among the partners (using the profit and loss sharing ratio 4:2:2:2) as follows: A, $64,000; B, $32,000; C, $32,000; and D, $32,000. After exercising the right of setoff, partner A has a capital balance of $6,000; partner B has a loan balance of $8,000; and partners C and D have capital deficits of $7,000 and $24,000, respectively. At this point, the available $140,000 cash may be distributed to outside creditors. Assuming partners C and D contribute funds to the partnership to eliminate their capital deficits, the $31,000 cash then may be distributed to outside creditors and partners A and B. The statement of realization and liquidation would be prepared as shown in Illustration 25-6.

In this Illustration we assume that partners C and D made additional cash contributions to the partnership, thereby eliminating their capital deficits. Thus, the partnership could make the remaining $17,000 payment to the outside creditors. Creditors occasionally take legal action against some or all of the partners as individuals when the creditors do not receive full satisfaction from the partnership. As a result, a partner personally may make payments to partnership creditors. Such payments should be reflected in the general ledger and on the statement of realization and liquidation as a reduction of partnership liabilities and an additional capital contribution by that partner. A partner's personal payments to creditors are in substance the equivalent of a cash contribution to the partnership that the partnership then distributes to the creditors.

## Loss on Realization Creates a Deficit Balance in Certain Partners' Capital Accounts—Certain Partners Are Personally Insolvent

Before illustrating in detail a situation in which a partnership is insolvent and certain of its partners are personally insolvent, we discuss the following legal questions raised in such circumstances:

1. If partnership creditors initiate legal proceedings against a partner who is personally insolvent, what would be the legal status (priority of payment) of such claims in relation to the claims of that partner's personal creditors?

2. If a partner is personally insolvent and unable to eliminate the deficit balance in his or her Capital account, thereby causing other partners

■ ILLUSTRATION 25-6

**A, B, C, and D PARTNERSHIP**
**Statement of Realization and Liquidation**
**July 19X5**

| | Assets | | Outside | Partners' Loans | | | Partners' Capital | | | |
| --- | --- | --- | --- | --- | --- | --- | --- | --- | --- | --- |
| | Cash | Noncash | Liabilities | B | C | D | A (40%)[a] | B (20%)[a] | C (20%)[a] | D (20%)[a] |
| Preliquidation balances | $ 10,000 | $290,000 | $157,000 | $10,000 | $5,000 | $2,000 | $70,000 | $30,000 | $20,000 | $ 6,000 |
| Realization of assets and allocation of loss | 130,000 | (290,000) | | | | | (64,000) | (32,000) | (32,000) | (32,000) |
| Subtotal | $140,000 | $ –0– | $157,000 | $10,000 | $5,000 | $2,000 | $ 6,000 | $ (2,000) | $(12,000) | $(26,000) |
| Exercise right of setoff | | | | (2,000) | (5,000) | (2,000) | | 2,000 | 5,000 | 2,000 |
| Subtotal | $140,000 | | $157,000 | $ 8,000 | $ –0– | $ –0– | $ 6,000 | $ –0– | $ (7,000) | $(24,000) |
| Distribution to outside creditors | (140,000) | | (140,000) | | | | | | | |
| Subtotal | $ –0– | | $ 17,000 | $ 8,000 | | | $ 6,000 | | $ (7,000) | $(24,000) |
| Contributions by C and D | 31,000 | | | | | | | | 7,000 | 24,000 |
| Subtotal | $ 31,000 | | $ 17,000 | $ 8,000 | | | $ 6,000 | | $ –0– | $ –0– |
| Cash distributions: | | | | | | | | | | |
| Outside creditors | (17,000) | | (17,000) | | | | | | | |
| Partner's loan | (8,000) | | | (8,000) | | | | | | |
| Partner's capital | (6,000) | | | | | | (6,000) | | | |
| Postliquidation balances | $ –0– | | $ –0– | $ –0– | | | $ –0– | | | |

[a]Denotes profit and loss sharing percentage.

to absorb that deficit balance (which is a breach of the partnership agreement entitling the wronged partners to legal recourse against the defaulting partner), what is the legal status of such claims in relation to the claims of that partner's personal creditors?
3. If a partner is personally insolvent, to what extent may such partner's personal creditors obtain payments from the partnership?

The answers to the first two questions are found in Section 40(i) of the UPA:

> Where a partner has become bankrupt or his estate is insolvent, the claims against his separate property shall rank in the following order:
> (I) Those owing to separate creditors.
> (II) Those owing to partnership creditors.
> (III) Those owing to partners by way of contribution.

The answer to the third question is found in Section 40(b) of the UPA, which specifies that partnership creditors have first claim on partnership assets. Consequently, these two sections of the UPA are consistent with the longstanding court procedure of **marshalling of assets,** which is summarized as follows: Partnership creditors have first priority as to partnership assets, and personal creditors of an insolvent partner have first priority as to the personal assets of such partner. However, the Bankruptcy Reform Act of 1978 (which applies only in bankruptcy proceedings) modified this doctrine so that partnership creditors now share on a pro rata basis with personal creditors of an insolvent partner in the distribution of the personal assets of such partner.

**Application of Marshalling of Assets.**    To illustrate how the marshalling of assets procedure is applied, assume the information in Illustration 25-6 with respect to partners' balances after (1) the realization loss of $160,000 is distributed, (2) the right of setoff is exercised, and (3) payment of $140,000 is made to outside creditors, leaving $17,000 owed to such creditors. At this point, the partners' accounts are as follows:

| Partner | Loan Balance | Capital Balance |
|---------|--------------|-----------------|
| A       |              | $6,000          |
| B       | $8,000       |                 |
| C       |              | (7,000)         |
| D       |              | (24,000)        |

Assume the personal status of each partner (exclusive of interest in or obligation to the partnership) is as follows:

| Partner | Personal Assets | Personal Liabilities | Personal Net Worth (Deficit) |
|---------|-----------------|----------------------|------------------------------|
| A | $50,000 | $25,000 | $25,000 |
| B | 4,000 | 15,000 | (11,000) |
| C | 16,000 | 6,000 | 10,000 |
| D | 20,000 | 33,000 | (13,000) |

1. Partner D has a capital deficit and is personally insolvent. Thus, none of his personal assets is available for contribution to the partnership, because his personal creditors are entitled to all his personal assets. Consequently, his $24,000 capital deficit must be absorbed by partners A, B, and C in their respective profit and loss sharing ratio, 4:2:2. Partner A's share is $12,000; partner B's share is $6,000; and partner C's share is $6,000.

2. Partner C had a $7,000 capital deficit, which increased to $13,000 when he absorbed his share of partner D's capital deficit. Partner C has a personal net worth of $10,000. Thus, he can contribute $10,000 to the partnership, leaving a $3,000 deficit, which must be absorbed by partners A and B in their respective profit and loss sharing ratio of 4:2. Partner A's share is $2,000 and Partner B's share is $1,000.

3. Partner B had a loan balance of $8,000. However, his Capital account was charged with $6,000 when partner D's capital deficit was written off and $1,000 when partner C's capital deficit was written off. Thus, $7,000 must be transferred from his loan account under the right of setoff to eliminate his capital deficit. This leaves $1,000 in his loan account, which, when distributed to him, is available to his personal creditors because he is personally insolvent.

4. Because partner A has the largest personal net worth, let us assume that partnership creditors took legal action against her (as opposed to proceeding against partner C, who is the only other personally solvent partner from whom they could collect anything). The creditors collected the $17,000 owed them from partner A personally. Partner A had a capital balance of $6,000, which was reduced by $12,000 for her share of partner D's capital deficit and $2,000 for her share of partner C's capital deficit. This gives her a capital deficit of $8,000. Her $17,000 payment to the partnership creditors, however, is the equivalent of a capital contribution. Thus, her Capital account deficit is eliminated, and she now has a positive capital balance of $9,000.

5. This leaves the partnership with $10,000 cash, which is distributed to partner B ($1,000 in payment of his loan) and partner A ($9,000 in liquidation of her capital balance).

Illustration 25-7 summarizes the preceding sequence of events in a statement of realization and liquidation.

**■ ILLUSTRATION 25-7**

### A, B, C, and D PARTNERSHIP
### Statement of Realization and Liquidation
### July 19X5

| | Assets Cash | Assets Noncash | Outside Liabilities | Loans B | Loans C | Loans D | Capital A (40%)[a] | Capital B (20%)[a] | Capital C (20%)[a] | Capital D (20%)[a] |
|---|---|---|---|---|---|---|---|---|---|---|
| Preliquidation balances | $ 10,000 | $290,000 | $157,000 | $10,000 | $5,000 | $2,000 | $70,000 | $30,000 | $ 20,000 | $ 6,000 |
| Realization of assets and allocation of loss | 130,000 | (290,000) | | | | | (64,000) | (32,000) | (32,000) | (32,000) |
| Subtotal | $140,000 | $ –0– | $157,000 | $10,000 | $5,000 | $2,000 | $ 6,000 | $ (2,000) | $(12,000) | $(26,000) |
| Exercise right of setoff | | | | (2,000) | (5,000) | (2,000) | | 2,000 | 5,000 | 2,000 |
| Subtotal | $140,000 | | $157,000 | $ 8,000 | $ –0– | $ –0– | $ 6,000 | $ –0– | $ (7,000) | $(24,000) |
| Distribution to outside creditors | (140,000) | | (140,000) | | | | | | | |
| Subtotal | $ –0– | | $ 17,000 | $ 8,000 | | | $ 6,000 | | $ (7,000) | $(24,000) |
| Absorption of D's deficit | | | | | | | (12,000) | (6,000) | (6,000) | 24,000 |
| Subtotal | $ –0– | | $ 17,000 | $ 8,000 | | | $ (6,000) | $ (6,000) | $(13,000) | $ –0– |
| Capital contribution by C | 10,000 | | | | | | | | 10,000 | |
| Subtotal | $ 10,000 | | $ 17,000 | $ 8,000 | | | $ (6,000) | $ (6,000) | $ (3,000) | |
| Absorption of C's deficit | | | | | | | (2,000) | (1,000) | 3,000 | |
| Subtotal | $ 10,000 | | $ 17,000 | $ 8,000 | | | $ (8,000) | $ (7,000) | $ –0– | |
| Exercise right of setoff | | | | (7,000) | | | | 7,000 | | |
| Subtotal | $ 10,000 | | $ 17,000 | $ 1,000 | | | $ (8,000) | $ –0– | | |
| Capital contribution by A | | | (17,000) | | | | 17,000 | | | |
| Subtotal | $ 10,000 | | $ –0– | $ 1,000 | | | $ 9,000 | | | |
| Cash distributions: Partner's loans | (1,000) | | | (1,000) | | | | | | |
| Partner's capital | (9,000) | | | | | | (9,000) | | | |
| Postliquidation balances | $ –0– | | $ –0– | $ –0– | | | $ –0– | | | |

[a] Denotes profit and loss sharing percentage.

# INSTALLMENT LIQUIDATIONS

In an **installment liquidation,** the conversion of noncash assets into cash takes place over a period of time. As a result, the partnership realizes greater proceeds than would be possible in a quick liquidation. Because of the lengthier conversion period, cash may become available for distribution to partners long before the last noncash asset is sold. In such situations, the partners usually want cash distributed as it becomes available.

## The Two Worst-case Assumptions

If Capital accounts are not maintained in the profit and loss sharing ratio, cash may not be distributed to the partners on some arbitrary basis such as the profit and loss sharing ratio, the capital balances ratio, or personal needs. Such a distribution might result in later inequities to certain partners. For example, cash may be distributed to a partner who may not be able to return such cash to the partnership if a deficit balance subsequently is created in his or her Capital account as a result of future losses on the conversion of noncash assets into cash. Such partner's deficit balance would have to be allocated to partners who have credit balances, and those partners would have to bear a greater portion of the loss than their profit and loss sharing percentages. To prevent this potential inequity accountants use two worst-case assumptions to determine which partners should receive available cash at any particular time. These assumptions are as follows:

1. **First worst-case assumption:** All noncash assets are assumed to be completely worthless. Thus, a hypothetical loss equal to the carrying values of noncash assets is assumed to have occurred. On a worksheet, the hypothetical loss is allocated to the partners' Capital account balances existing at that time.

2. **Second worst-case assumption:** If, as a result of the first worst-case assumption, a partner's Capital account is in a deficit position (on the worksheet only), we assume that such partner is not able to make contributions to the partnership to eliminate the hypothetical deficit. (This assumption is made regardless of the partner's personal financial status.) Accordingly, the hypothetical deficit balance is allocated to the partners who have credit balances, using their respective profit and loss sharing ratio. If, in turn, this process creates a hypothetical deficit balance in another partner's Capital account, then such hypothetical deficit balance is allocated (on the worksheet only) to the remaining partners who still have credit balances. This process is repeated until only partners with credit balances remain on the worksheet. Cash may then be distributed to the partners who have credit balances on the worksheet.

The result of these two assumptions is that cash is distributed only to the partners who have capital balances sufficient to absorb their share of (1) the maximum potential loss on noncash assets, and (2) any capital deficiencies that may result to other partners as a result of a maximum loss on noncash assets. In other words, payments may safely be made to such partners with full assurance that the money will not have to be returned to the partnership at some later date in the event of future realization losses.

Under this method of distributing cash to the partners, the Capital accounts are brought into the profit and loss sharing ratio. This is usually accomplished only after several cash distributions have been made. Once the capital accounts have been brought into the profit and loss sharing ratio, cash distributions may be made in the profit and loss sharing ratio. The two worst-case assumptions need not be used for any future cash distributions, because their use would produce the same result as the profit and loss sharing ratio.

Applying the two worst-case assumptions shows that a partner's Capital account (on the worksheet) is reduced for any loans the partnership has outstanding to the partner. Also, a partner's Capital account (on the worksheet) is increased for any loan the partner may have outstanding to the partnership; this automatically provides for the hypothetical exercising of the right of setoff.

ILLUSTRATION

## Loss on Realization Creates a Deficit Balance in Certain Partners' Capital Accounts: One Partner Is Personally Insolvent

To illustrate how these two worst-case assumptions are applied to an installment liquidation, assume the following:

1. The partnership of A, B, C, and D has the same preliquidation balances as shown in Illustration 25-7.
2. The noncash assets of $290,000 are sold as follows:

| Date | Book Value | Proceeds | Loss |
|------|-----------|----------|------|
| July 14, 19X5 | $183,000 | $168,000 | $(15,000) |
| August 12, 19X5 | 70,000 | 25,000 | (45,000) |
| September 21, 19X5 | 37,000 | 27,000 | (10,000) |
| | $290,000 | $220,000 | $(70,000) |

3. Cash was distributed to outside creditors and partners as it became available.
4. Partner D could contribute only $4,000 to the partnership during the liquidation proceedings. His remaining $2,000 Capital account deficit had to be absorbed by the other partners.

The statement of realization and liquidation would be prepared as shown in Illustration 25-8. The cash distributions to partners were determined from the **schedule of safe payments** shown in Illustration 25-9, which is a supporting schedule to Illustration 25-8. The schedule of safe payments shows the cash distributions that may be made safely to individual partners in light of the objectives of minimizing potential inequities and limiting the legal exposure of the accountant.

**Review Points for Illustrations 25-8 and 25-9.** Note the following:

1. The statement of realization and liquidation reflects only the historical transactions as recorded in the general ledger. Although the statement covers the entire liquidation period, it was started when the liquidation process began and then periodically updated as noncash assets were sold and cash distributions were made.
2. The schedule of safe payments to partners reflects the assumptions that were made at those dates when cash was available for distribution to partners. The purpose of the schedule is to determine which partners should receive the cash that is available at those dates.
3. The payments that may be made to partners, as shown on the schedule of safe payments, are first applied as a reduction of a partner's loan and then as a reduction of his or her capital in the statement of realization and liquidation.
4. After the first cash distribution to partners on July 14, 19X5, the Capital accounts of partners A and B are in their respective profit and loss sharing ratio of 4:2. All future cash distributions to these two partners are in this 2:1 ratio.
5. After the second cash distribution to partners on August 12, 19X5, the Capital accounts of partners A, B, and C (which includes partner C's loan account balance) are in their respective profit and loss sharing ratio of 4:2:2. All future cash distributions to these three partners are in this 4:2:2 ratio.
6. Obviously, the schedule of safe payments is prepared only after cash is available for distribution to partners. Thus, it may be used only when the partnership is solvent.

## Cash Distribution Plan

When cash is available for distribution to partners, a schedule of safe payments to partners must be prepared using the two worst-case assumptions (except for the final payment, of course). The result of distributing cash to partners in the sequence resulting from the use of the two worst-case assumptions is to bring the Capital accounts into the profit and loss sharing ratio. (As determined earlier in the chapter, a partner's loan to

■ **ILLUSTRATION 25-8**

### A, B, C, and D PARTNERSHIP
### Statement of Realization and Liquidation
### July 1, 19X5, through September 21, 19X5

| | Assets Cash | Assets Noncash | Outside Liabilities | Partners' Loans B | Partners' Loans C | Partners' Loans D | Partners' Capital A (40%)[a] | Partners' Capital B (20%)[a] | Partners' Capital C (20%)[a] | Partners' Capital D (20%)[a] |
|---|---|---|---|---|---|---|---|---|---|---|
| Preliquidation balances | $ 10,000 | $290,000 | $157,000 | $10,000 | $5,000 | $2,000 | $70,000 | $30,000 | $20,000 | $ 6,000 |
| Realization of assets and allocation of loss | 168,000 | (183,000) | | | | | (6,000) | (3,000) | (3,000) | (3,000) |
| Subtotal | $178,000 | $107,000 | $157,000 | $10,000 | $5,000 | $2,000 | $64,000 | $27,000 | $17,000 | $ 3,000 |
| July cash distribution: | | | | | | | | | | |
| Outside creditors | (157,000) | | (157,000) | | | | | | | |
| Partner's loan | (10,000)[b] | | | (10,000)[b] | | | | | | |
| Partners' capital | (11,000)[b] | | | | | | (10,667)[b] | (333)[b] | | |
| Subtotal | $ –0– | $107,000 | $ –0– | $ –0– | $5,000 | $2,000 | $53,333 | $26,667 | $17,000 | $ 3,000 |
| Realization of assets and allocation of loss | 25,000 | (70,000) | | | | | (18,000) | (9,000) | (9,000) | (9,000) |
| Subtotal | $ 25,000 | $ 37,000 | | | $5,000 | $2,000 | $35,333 | $17,667 | $ 8,000 | $ (6,000) |
| Exercise right of setoff | | | | | | (2,000) | | | | 2,000 |
| Subtotal | $ 25,000 | $ 37,000 | | | $5,000 | $ –0– | $35,333 | $17,667 | $ 8,000 | $ (4,000) |
| Cash contribution by D | 4,000 | | | | | | | | | 4,000 |
| Subtotal | $ 29,000 | | | | $5,000 | | $35,333 | $17,667 | $ 8,000 | $ –0– |
| August cash distribution: | | | | | | | | | | |
| Partner's loan | (3,750)[b] | | | | (3,750)[b] | | | | | |
| Partners' capital | (25,250)[b] | | | | | | (16,833)[b] | (8,417)[b] | | |
| Subtotal | $ –0– | | | | $1,250 | | $18,500 | $ 9,250 | $ 8,000 | |
| Realization of assets and allocation of loss | 27,000 | (37,000) | | | | | (4,000) | (2,000) | (2,000) | (2,000) |
| Subtotal | $ 27,000 | $ –0– | | | $1,250 | | $14,500 | $ 7,250 | $ 6,000 | $ (2,000) |
| Write-off of D's deficit | | | | | | | (1,000) | (500) | (500) | 2,000 |
| Subtotal | $ 27,000 | | | | $1,250 | | $13,500 | $ 6,750 | $ 5,500 | $ –0– |
| Final cash distribution: | | | | | | | | | | |
| Partner's loan | (1,250) | | | | (1,250) | | | | | |
| Partner's capital | (25,750) | | | | | | (13,500) | (6,750) | (5,500) | |
| Postliquidation balances | $ –0– | | $ –0– | $ –0– | $ –0– | $ –0– | $ –0– | $ –0– | $ –0– | $ –0– |

[a]Denotes profit and loss sharing percentage.
[b]See Illustration 25-9.

■ **ILLUSTRATION 25-9**
Supporting Schedule to Illustration 25-8

| | A (40%)[a] | B (20%)[a] | C (20%)[a] | D (20%)[a] |
|---|---|---|---|---|
| **A, B, C, AND D PARTNERSHIP** Schedule of Safe Payments to Partners | | | | |
| | **Partner** | | | |
| **Computation to Determine How Available Cash on July 14, 19X5, Should Be Distributed** | | | | |
| Capital and loan balances at cash distribution (from Illustration 25-8)— | | | | |
| Capital . . . . . . . . . . . . . . . . . . . . . . . . . . . . . . . . | $64,000 | $27,000 | $17,000 | $ 3,000 |
| Loan . . . . . . . . . . . . . . . . . . . . . . . . . . . . . . . . . | | 10,000 | 5,000 | 2,000 |
| Total . . . . . . . . . . . . . . . . . . . . . . . . . . . . . . . | $64,000 | $37,000 | $22,000 | $ 5,000 |
| First worst-case assumption—Assume full loss on noncash assets of $107,000 . . . . . . . . . . . . . | (42,800) | (21,400) | (21,400) | (21,400) |
| Subtotal . . . . . . . . . . . . . . . . . . . . . . . . . . . . . | $21,200 | $15,600 | $ 600 | $(16,400) |
| Second worst-case assumption—Assume D's deficit must be absorbed by A, B, and C . . . . | (8,200) | (4,100) | (4,100) | 16,400 |
| Subtotal . . . . . . . . . . . . . . . . . . . . . . . . . . . . . | $13,000 | $11,500 | $ (3,500) | $ –0– |
| Repeat second worst-case assumption— Assume C's deficit must be absorbed by A and B . . . . . . . . . . . . . . . . . . . . . . . . . . . | (2,333) | (1,167) | 3,500 | |
| Cash to be distributed to each partner . . . . . . . | $10,667 | $10,333[b] | $ –0– | |
| **Computation to Determine How Available Cash on August 12, 19X5, Should Be Distributed** | | | | |
| Capital and loan balances at cash distribution (from Illustration 25-8)— | | | | |
| Capital . . . . . . . . . . . . . . . . . . . . . . . . . . . . . . . . | $35,333 | $17,667 | $ 8,000 | |
| Loan . . . . . . . . . . . . . . . . . . . . . . . . . . . . . . . . . | | | 5,000 | |
| Total . . . . . . . . . . . . . . . . . . . . . . . . . . . . . . . | $35,333 | $17,667 | $13,000 | $ –0– |
| First worst-case assumption—Assume full loss on noncash assets of $37,000 . . . . . . . . . . . . . | (14,800) | (7,400) | (7,400) | (7,400) |
| Subtotal . . . . . . . . . . . . . . . . . . . . . . . . . . . . . | $20,533 | $10,267 | $ 5,600 | $ (7,400) |
| Second worst-case assumption—Assume D's deficit must be absorbed by A, B, and C . . . . | (3,700) | (1,850) | (1,850) | 7,400 |
| Cash to be distributed to each partner . . . . . . . | $16,833 | $ 8,417 | $ 3,750[c] | $ –0– |

[a]Denotes profit and loss sharing percentage.
[b]Of this amount, $10,000 is deemed a repayment of the loan.
[c]All of this amount is deemed a repayment of the loan.

the partnership is, in substance, part of that partner's capital investment.) Once the Capital accounts are in this ratio, all future cash distributions to partners are made in the profit and loss sharing ratio.

By understanding the result of this process, we may analyze the relationship of the Capital accounts at the beginning of liquidation to determine which partners receive cash as it becomes available. The analysis results in a **cash distribution plan.** A cash distribution plan has the advantage of informing partners at **the beginning of the liquidation process** when they will receive cash **in relation to the other partners.**

Understanding the methodology underlying the preparation of a cash distribution plan requires an intuitive understanding of the fact that when the capital accounts are not in the profit and loss sharing ratio, one or more partners have capital balances sufficient to absorb his, her, or their share of losses that exceed the partnership's net worth, whereas one or more other partners have capital balances sufficient to absorb only his, her, or their share of losses that are less than the partnership's net worth. To illustrate this fact, we present the following comparative analysis:

| | Total | Partner | | | |
|---|---|---|---|---|---|
| | | W (40%) | X (30%) | Y (20%) | Z (10%) |
| Actual preliquidation capital and loan balances ............ | $100,000 | $48,000 | $33,000 | $11,000 | $ 8,000 |
| Hypothetical capital and loan balances in the profit and loss sharing ratio of 4:3:2:1 ............ | $100,000 | $40,000 | $30,000 | $20,000 | $10,000 |
| Percentage relationship of actual balances to hypothetical balances.... | | 120% | 110% | 55% | 80% |

Only partners W and X (because their actual balances exceed the balances that would exist if balances were kept in the profit and loss sharing ratio) could absorb their share of losses greater than the partnership capital of $100,000. On the other hand, partners Y and Z (because their actual balances are less than the balances that would exist if balances were kept in the profit and loss sharing ratio) could absorb only their share of losses that are less than the partnership capital of $100,000.

**Ranking the Partners.** The percentage line of the analysis above ranks the partners in terms of which partner could absorb the largest loss to which partner could absorb the smallest loss. The ranking in this example is W, X, Z, and Y—that is, partner W (who has the highest percentage) can absorb the largest loss, and partner Y (who has the lowest percentage) can absorb the smallest loss. This ranking can be readily proved by calculating the exact loss needed to eliminate each partner's capital and loan balance. We divide each partners' capital and loan balance by his or her profit and loss sharing percentage. Continuing with our example, this calculation is as follows:

| | Partner | | | |
|---|---|---|---|---|
| | W | X | Y | Z |
| Actual preliquidation capital balances .......... | $ 48,000 | $ 33,000 | $11,000 | $ 8,000 |
| Profit and loss sharing percentage................ | 40% | 30% | 20% | 10% |
| Loss absorption potential | $120,000 | $110,000 | $55,000 | $80,000 |
| Ranking .................... | 1 | 2 | 4 | 3 |

Note that a loss of $120,000 would eliminate the capital and loan balance of partner W (the highest ranking partner), whereas for partner Y (the lowest ranking partner) a loss of only $55,000 would eliminate his capital and loan balance.

Ranking the partners in this manner reveals the order in which cash should be distributed to the partners as it becomes available. Distributing cash in this order brings the capital balances into the profit and loss sharing ratio on a step-by-step basis, as follows:

1. **Distribution to highest ranking partner:** Distribute sufficient cash to partner W so that his capital balance is brought into the profit and loss sharing ratio with the next highest ranking partner (partner X).
2. **Distribution to two highest ranking partners:** Distribute sufficient cash to partners W and X in their respective profit and loss sharing ratio of 4:3 so that their capital balances are brought into the profit and loss sharing ratio with the next highest ranking partner (partner Z).
3. **Distribution to three highest ranking partners:** Distribute sufficient cash to partners W, X, and Z in their respective profit and loss sharing ratio of 4:3:1 so that their capital balances are brought into the profit and loss sharing ratio with the next highest ranking partner (partner Y).

Only the exact amount of cash distributed at each stage in this sequence needs to be determined. The calculations are shown in Illustration 25-10.

## Review Points for Illustration 25-10.   Note the following:

1. The cash distribution plan is operable only after outside creditors have been paid in full.
2. The schedule reflects only the order in which cash distributions to the partners will be made *if* cash is available for distribution to the partners.
3. The sequence of distributing cash in the cash distribution plan coincides with the sequence that would result if cash were distributed using the schedule of safe payments.

■ **ILLUSTRATION 25-10**

| | | | | |
|---|---|---|---|---|
| **W, X, Y, AND Z PARTNERSHIP** | | | | |
| **Schedule of Cash Distribution to Partners** | | | | |
| | Partner | | | |
| | **W** | **X** | **Y** | **Z** |
| Preliquidation capital and loan balances.............. | $48,000 | $33,000 | $11,000 | $8,000 |
| Ranking ............................................... | 1 | 2 | 4 | 3 |
| Step 1: Cash to be distributed to W: | | | | |
| Balances, per above ............................ | $48,000 | $33,000 | | |
| Balances in profit and loss ratio of 4:3 using | | | | |
| X's actual balance as the base .................. | 44,000[a] | $33,000 | | |
| | $ 4,000 | | | |
| Step 2: Cash to be distributed to W and X: | | | | |
| Balances, per above ............................ | $44,000 | $33,000 | | $8,000 |
| Balances in profit and loss ratio of 4:3:1 using | | | | |
| Z's actual balance as the base ................. | 32,000[b] | 24,000[c] | | $8,000 |
| | $12,000 | $ 9,000 | | |
| Step 3: Cash to be distributed to W, X, and Z: | | | | |
| Balances, per above ............................ | $32,000 | $24,000 | $11,000 | $8,000 |
| Balances in profit-and-loss ratio of 4:3:2:1 using | | | | |
| Y's actual balance as the base ................. | 22,000 | 16,500 | $11,000 | 5,500 |
| | $10,000 | $ 7,500 | | $2,500 |

After this distribution, all Capital accounts would be in the profit and loss sharing ratio of 4:3:2:1. Accordingly, all future cash distributions would be made in this ratio.

**Summary of Cash Distribution Plan**

| | W | X | Y | Z |
|---|---|---|---|---|
| First $4,000......................................... | $ 4,000 | | | |
| Next $21,000 (4:3) .................................. | 12,000 | $ 9,000 | | |
| Next $20,000 (4:3:1) ................................ | 10,000 | 7,500 | | $2,500 |
| Any additional amounts (4:3:2:1).................... | 40% | 30% | 20% | 10% |

[a]$33,000 × 4/3.
[b]$8,000 × 4/1.
[c]$8,000 × 3/1.

# END-OF-CHAPTER REVIEW

## Summary of Key Points

1. Partners may greatly minimize the possibility of having to absorb another partner's deficit balance by specifying in the partnership agreement that capital balances are to be maintained in the profit and loss sharing ratio.

2. To the extent that a partner must absorb some or all of another partner's capital account deficit, the absorbing partner has legal recourse against the

personal assets of the partner who could not make good the deficit balance through setoff or contribution.

3. In lump-sum liquidations, no distributions are made to the partners until the realization process is completed, when the full amount of the gain or loss on realization of the partnership assets is known. In these cases, cash is distributed to the partners who have credit balances in their capital and loan accounts.

4. In installment liquidations, distributions are made to some or all of the partners as cash becomes available; thus, cash is distributed to partners before the full amount of the gain or loss on realization of the partnership assets is known. In these cases, cash distributions are made to partners in such a manner that the capital and loan balances of the individual partners are brought into line with the profit and loss sharing ratio.

5. The settlement of claims pursuant to legal recourse is governed by the marshalling of assets principle.

## Glossary of New Terms

**Rule of setoff**    The subtraction of a partner's deficit balance in his or her Capital account from the balance of any loan outstanding to the partnership. Also, the subtraction of a partnership's loan to a partner from the partner's capital account.

**Marshalling of assets**    A legal doctrine whereby a partnership's creditors are given first claim on partnership assets, and personal creditors of an insolvent partner are given first claim on such partner's personal assets.

## Self-Study Questions
*(Answers are at the end of this chapter.)*

1. Under the rule of setoff
   a. A partnership's loan to a partner is deemed the equivalent of partnership capital.
   b. A deficit in a partner's capital account may be eliminated against a partner's loan account to the partnership.
   c. Partnership assets must be set aside to pay off personal creditors of an insolvent partner before any cash distributions may be made to that partner.
   d. Partnership creditors have first priority against partnership assets.
   e. None of the above.

2. In the installment liquidation of a partnership, cash is distributed to partners
   a. Equally.
   b. In their normal profit and loss sharing ratio.
   c. Using the ratio of the partners' capital balances.
   d. Using the marshalling of assets procedure.
   e. None of the above.

3. Under the marshalling of assets principle (and disregarding the Bankruptcy Reform Act of 1978),
   a. The capital and loan balances of the partners are combined.
   b. The two worst-case assumptions are used.

c. A cash distribution plan is prepared.

d. Cash is distributed to the partner having the highest capital balance.

e. None of the above.

4. The following condensed balance sheet is presented for the partnership of Acres, Farmer, and Tillman, who share profits and losses in the ratio of 3:2:1, respectively:

| | |
|---|---|
| Cash | $ 60,000 |
| Other assets | 440,000 |
| | $500,000 |
| | |
| Liabilities | $200,000 |
| Capital, Acres | 30,000 |
| Capital, Farmer | 100,000 |
| Capital, Tillman | 170,000 |
| | $500,000 |

The partners decided to liquidate the partnership. The other assets are sold for $320,000. How should the available cash be distributed?

a. Acres, –0–; Farmer, $40,000; Tillman, $140,000.

b. Acres, $60,000; Farmer, $60,000; Tillman, $60,000.

c. Acres, –0–; Farmer, $45,000; Tillman, $135,000.

d. Acres, –0–, Farmer, $53,333; Tillman, $127,667.

e. None of the above.

5. The following condensed balance sheet is presented as of July 1, 19X1, for the partnership of Rane, Waters, and Wells, who share profits and losses in the ratio of 5:3:2, respectively:

| | |
|---|---|
| Cash | $ 20,000 |
| Other assets | 380,000 |
| | $400,000 |
| | |
| Liabilities | $100,000 |
| Capital, Rane | 210,000 |
| Capital, Waters | 43,000 |
| Capital, Wells | 47,000 |
| | $400,000 |

The partners decided to liquidate the partnership. On July 3, 19X1, the first cash sale of other assets with a carrying amount of $240,000 realized $190,000. Safe installment payments to the partners were made on the same date. How should the available cash be distributed to the partners?

a. Rane, $55,000; Waters, $33,000; Wells, $22,000.

b. Rane, $108,000; Waters, –0–; Wells, $2,000.

c. Rane, $105,000; Waters, –0–; Wells, $5,000.

d. Rane, $115,000; Waters, –0–; Wells, $9,000.

e. None of the above.

# ASSIGNMENT MATERIAL

## Review Questions

1. How are partnership liquidations different from corporate liquidations?
2. What is the significance of maintaining partners' Capital accounts in the profit and loss sharing ratio?
3. How is a deficit balance in a partner's Capital account disposed of if that partner is unable to eliminate the deficit through setoff or contribution?
4. In what ratio should realization gains and losses during liquidation be shared among the partners? Why?
5. Explain how the rule of setoff is applied.
6. What is the function of the statement of realization and liquidation?
7. In what order does the UPA specify that cash distributions are to be made to creditors and partners during liquidation?
8. Is the order in question 7 strictly followed in all situations? Why or why not?
9. Explain the marshalling of assets doctrine.
10. Under what conditions may cash be distributed to partners on the installment basis rather than in a lump sum?
11. When a partnership is insolvent and some partners have positive Capital account balances, whereas other partners have deficit balances, against which partners may creditors proceed personally to obtain full payment of their claims?
12. How is a partner's personal payment to partnership creditors treated on the partnership's books?

## Discussion Cases

| DC 25-1 |
|---|

### Manner of Sharing Realization Losses during Liquidation

Jennings and Nelson recently formed a partnership under the following terms:

|  | Jennings | Nelson |
|---|---|---|
| Capital contributions . . . . . . . . . . . . . . . . . . . . . . . . . . . . . | $80,000 | $20,000 |
| Time devoted to the business . . . . . . . . . . . . . . . . . . . . . . . | 100% | 100% |
| Profit and loss sharing formula— |  |  |
| Interest rate on capital over $20,000 . . . . . . . . . . . . . . . | 10% | 10% |
| Residual profit and loss . . . . . . . . . . . . . . . . . . . . . . . . . | 50% | 50% |

You have been hired as the partnership's accountant. While closing the partnership books for the first month of operations, Jennings casually mentions to you that he feels a "good and equitable" partnership agreement was negotiated between himself and Nelson.

**Required:**

How would you respond to this comment?

## DC 25-2

## Manner of Sharing Realization Losses during Liquidation

Harper, McCord, and Stringer are attempting to form a partnership in which profits and losses are shared in the ratio 4:4:2, respectively. They cannot agree on terms of the partnership agreement relating to potential liquidation. Harper feels it is a waste of time to have any provisions relating to liquidation, because the prospective partners firmly believe that the business will be successful. McCord feels that in the event of liquidation, any realization losses should be shared in the ratio of the capital balances, because this method allows each partner to absorb losses in relation to his or her capacity to absorb such losses. Stringer feels any liquidation losses should be shared equally, because if the business is not successful it will most likely be the fault of each partner. As the accountant who will be keeping the partnership's books, you have been asked to settle this dispute.

### Required:

How would you respond to this request?

## DC 25-3

## Procedures for Distributing Available Cash to Partners

The partnership of Dials and Winder is in the process of liquidation, which is expected to take several months. Dials, who is in need of cash, wants cash distributed to the partners as it is available. Winder feels that no cash should be distributed to either partner until all the assets are sold and the total realization gain or loss is known. Thus, the partnership would not distribute cash to a partner and later request a capital contribution to absorb any capital deficits created by realization losses.

### Required:

Evaluate the positions of each partner.

## DC 25-4

## Procedures for Distributing Available Cash to Partners

The partnership of Jurnell, Ledgley, and Post is in the process of being liquidated. The trial balance immediately after the sale of a portion of the noncash assets and full payment to outside creditors is as follows:

| | | |
|---|---|---|
| Cash | $20,000 | |
| Note Receivable from Ledgley | 14,000 | |
| Other Assets | 36,000 | |
| Loan, Jurnell | | $ 5,000 |
| Capital: | | |
| Jurnell | | 11,000 |
| Ledgley | | 20,000 |
| Post | | 34,000 |
| | $70,000 | $70,000 |

Jurnell wants the available cash distributed to her to pay off her loan—she cites Section 40(b) of the UPA, which states that partners' loans have priority over partners' capital. Post wants the cash distributed to him, because he has the largest capital investment. Ledgley feels it should be distributed equally, which is how profits and losses are shared.

**Required:**

1. Evaluate the positions of each partner.
2. Who should receive the $20,000 available cash?

## Exercises

**E 25-1**

### Lump-sum Liquidation: Solvent Partnership Having Partners' Loans—All Partners Personally Solvent

Partners Hall, Lane, and Tower share profits and losses in the ratio 3:2:1, respectively. The partners voted to liquidate the partnership when its assets, liabilities, and capital were as follows:

| | | | |
|---|---:|---|---:|
| Cash | $ 2,000 | Liabilities | $20,000 |
| Noncash assets | 78,000 | Loans: | |
| | | Hall | 5,000 |
| | | Tower | 10,000 |
| | | Capital: | |
| | | Hall | 20,000 |
| | | Lane | 15,000 |
| | | Tower | 10,000 |
| | $80,000 | | $80,000 |

Assume that all the noncash assets were sold for $36,000, and all cash was distributed to outside creditors and partners.

**Required:**

Prepare a statement of liquidation and realization.

**E 25-2**

### Lump-sum Liquidation: Insolvent Partnership Having Loans to and from Partners—All Partners Personally Insolvent

Partners Bass, Singer, and Tennor share profits and losses equally. The partners voted to liquidate the partnership when its assets, liabilities, and capital were as follows:

| | | | |
|---|---:|---|---:|
| Cash | $ 14,000 | Liabilities | $ 80,000 |
| Note receivable from | | Loans: | |
| Tennor | 11,000 | Bass | 4,000 |
| Other noncash assets | 120,000 | Singer | 16,000 |
| | | Capital: | |
| | | Bass | 15,000 |
| | | Singer | 15,000 |
| | | Tennor | 15,000 |
| | $145,000 | | $145,000 |

Assume the following:

1. All the noncash assets of $120,000 were sold for $54,000.
2. Tennor instructed the partnership to write off the $11,000 he borrowed from the partnership inasmuch as he has no liquid personal assets at this time (even though he is personally solvent).
3. All partners could eliminate any deficits in their Capital accounts through set-off or contribution, or both.
4. All cash was distributed to outside creditors and partners.

### Required:
Prepare a statement of realization and liquidation.

## E 25-3   Lump-sum Liquidation: Solvent Partnership Having Loans to and from Partners—Certain Partners Personally Insolvent

Partners Criss, Kross, and Zigge share profits and losses in the ratio 3:3:2, respectively. The partners voted to liquidate the partnership when its assets, liabilities, and capital were as follows:

| | | | |
|---|---:|---|---:|
| Cash | $ 1,000 | Liabilities | $34,000 |
| Note receivable from Zigge | 9,000 | Loans: | |
| Other noncash assets | 75,000 |   Kross | 15,000 |
| | | Capital: | |
| | |   Criss | 11,000 |
| | |   Kross | 10,000 |
| | |   Zigge | 15,000 |
| | $85,000 | | $85,000 |

Assume the following:

1. All the noncash assets of $75,000 were sold for $43,000.
2. Zigge was personally insolvent and unable to contribute any cash to the partnership.
3. Criss and Kross were both personally solvent and able to eliminate any deficits in their Capital accounts through setoff or contribution.
4. All cash was distributed to outside creditors and partners.

### Required:
Prepare a statement of realization and liquidation.

## E 25-4   Lump-sum Liquidation: Insolvent Partnership Having Loans from Partners—Certain Partners Personally Insolvent

Partners Cattie, Deere, Fox, and O'Hare share profits and losses in the ratio 5:2:2:1, respectively. The partners voted to liquidate the partnership when its assets and liabilities were as follows:

| | | | |
|---|---|---|---|
| Cash | $ 15,000 | Liabilities | $165,000 |
| Noncash assets | 235,000 | Loans: | |
| | | Deere | 7,000 |
| | | Fox | 5,000 |
| | | O'Hare | 3,000 |
| | | Capital: | |
| | | Cattie | 40,000 |
| | | Deere | 16,000 |
| | | Fox | 10,000 |
| | | O'Hare | 4,000 |
| | $250,000 | | $250,000 |

Assume the following:

1. All the noncash assets were sold for $135,000.
2. Cattie contributed $5,000 to the partnership after the noncash assets were sold. He has no additional funds above and beyond what is needed to satisfy personal creditors.
3. All other partners were personally solvent and made capital contributions as necessary to eliminate deficits in their Capital accounts.
4. All cash was distributed to outside creditors and partners.

**Required:**
Prepare a statement of realization and liquidation.

## Insolvent Partnership and Insolvent Partners—Theory

Q, R, S, and T are partners sharing profits and losses equally. The partnership is insolvent and is therefore being liquidated; the status of the partnership and each partner is as follows:

| Partner | Partnership Capital Balance | Personal Assets (Exclusive of Partnership Interest) | Personal Liabilities (Exclusive of Partnership Interest) |
|---|---|---|---|
| Q | $ 15,000 | $100,000 | $40,000 |
| R | 10,000 | 30,000 | 60,000 |
| S | (20,000) | 80,000 | 5,000 |
| T | (30,000) | 1,000 | 28,000 |
| | $(25,000) | | |

**Required:**
Select the correct response to the question below.
Assuming the Uniform Partnership Act applies, the partnership creditors:

a. Must first seek recovery against S because she is personally solvent and has a negative capital balance.

b. Will not be paid in full regardless of how they proceed legally because the partnership assets are less than the partnership liabilities.

c. Must share R's interest in the partnership on a pro rata basis with R's personal creditors.

d. Have first claim to the partnership assets before any partner's personal creditors have rights to the partnership assets.

(AICPA adapted)

## E 25-6 Installment Liquidation: Solvent Partnership Having Partner's Loan—First Cash Distribution to Partners

Partners Deeds, Grant, and Trusty share profits and losses in the ratio 6:3:1, respectively. The partners voted to liquidate the partnership when its assets, liabilities, and capital were as follows:

| | | | |
|---|---|---|---|
| Cash | $ 1,000 | Liabilities | $35,000 |
| Noncash assets | 94,000 | Loan: | |
| | | Trusty | 10,000 |
| | | Capital: | |
| | | Deeds | 30,000 |
| | | Grant | 15,000 |
| | | Trusty | 5,000 |
| | $95,000 | | $95,000 |

Assume that noncash assets with a book value of $74,000 were sold for $54,000.

**Required:**
Determine how the cash available after this sale should be distributed.

## E 25-7 Installment Liquidation: Solvent Partnership—First Cash Distribution to Partners

Partners Springer, Sumner, and Winters share profits and losses in the ratio 5:3:2, respectively. The partners voted to liquidate the partnership when its assets, liabilities, and capital were as follows:

| | | |
|---|---|---|
| Cash | $ 40,000 | |
| Other assets | 210,000 | |
| Liabilities | | $ 60,000 |
| Capital: | | |
| Springer | | 48,000 |
| Sumner | | 72,000 |
| Winters | | 70,000 |
| | $250,000 | $250,000 |

The partnership will be liquidated over a long period of time. Cash is to be distributed to the partners as it becomes available. The first sale of noncash assets having a book value of $120,000 realized $90,000.

**Required:**

Determine how the available cash should be distributed to the partners after this first sale.

(AICPA adapted)

---

### Installment Liquidation: Solvent Partnership with Partnership's and Partner's Loans—First Cash Distribution to Partners

**E 25-8**

Partners Castle, King, and Queen share profits and losses in the ratio 4:4:2, respectively. The partners voted to liquidate the partnership when its assets, liabilities, and capital were as follows:

| | | |
|---|---:|---:|
| Cash | $ 20,000 | |
| Note Receivable from Castle | 10,000 | |
| Other Assets | 170,000 | |
| Liabilities | | $ 50,000 |
| Loan from King | | 30,000 |
| Capital: | | |
| Castle | | 37,000 |
| King | | 15,000 |
| Queen | | 68,000 |
| | $200,000 | $200,000 |

The partnership will be liquidated over a long period of time. Cash will be distributed to the partners as it becomes available. The first sale of noncash assets having a book value of $90,000 realized $50,000.

**Required:**

Determine how the available cash should be distributed to the partners after this first sale.

(AICPA adapted)

## Problems

### Lump-sum Liquidation: Solvent Partnership Having Partner's Loan—All Partners Personally Solvent

**P 25-1***

Partners Rockne and Stone share profits in the ratio 3:2, respectively. The partners agreed to liquidate the partnership when the assets, liabilities, and capital were as follows:

---

*The financial statement information presented for problems accompanied by asterisks is also provided on Model 25 (filename: Model25) of the software disk that is available for use with the text, enabling the problem to be worked on the computer.

| Cash | $ 6,000 | Liabilities | $27,000 |
| Noncash assets | 44,000 | Loan: | |
| | | Stone | 6,000 |
| | | Capital: | |
| | | Rockne | 14,000 |
| | | Stone | 3,000 |
| | $50,000 | | $50,000 |

Assume the following:

1. Rockne agreed personally to take certain equipment having a book value of $5,000. (The partners estimated the current value of this equipment at $6,500.)
2. Stone agreed personally to take certain office furniture having a book value of $3,000. (The partners estimated the current value of this at $2,000.)
3. All other noncash assets were sold for $25,000.
4. Liquidation expenses of $1,000 were incurred.
5. Cash was distributed to outside creditors and partners.

### Required:

Prepare a statement of realization and liquidation.

## Lump-sum Liquidation: Solvent Partnership Having Partners' Loans— Certain Partners Personally Insolvent

Partners Duke, Lord, Noble, and Prince share profits and losses in the ratio 4:3:2:1, respectively. The partners agreed to liquidate the partnership when it had assets, liabilities, and capital as follows:

| Cash | $ 10,000 | Liabilities | $ 78,000 |
| Noncash assets | 140,000 | Loans: | |
| | | Duke | 4,000 |
| | | Lord | 3,000 |
| | | Capital: | |
| | | Duke | 10,000 |
| | | Lord | 10,000 |
| | | Noble | 30,000 |
| | | Prince | 15,000 |
| | $150,000 | | $150,000 |

Assume the following:

1. The noncash assets were sold for $90,000.
2. Duke is personally insolvent.
3. Lord contributed $2,000 cash to the partnership; he had no other available funds in excess of amounts needed to satisfy personal creditors.
4. All cash was distributed to outside creditors and partners.

**Required:** .
Prepare a statement of realization and liquidation.

### Lump-sum Liquidation: Insolvent Partnership Having Partners' Loans—Certain Partners Personally Insolvent

Partners Oates, Ryley, and Wheatman share profits and losses in the ratio 3:3:2, respectively. The partners agreed to liquidate the partnership when assets, liabilities, and capital were as follows:

| | | | |
|---|---|---|---|
| Cash | $ 5,000 | Liabilities | $48,000 |
| Noncash assets | 85,000 | Loans: | |
| | | Oates | 10,000 |
| | | Ryley | 3,000 |
| | | Capital: | |
| | | Oates | 11,000 |
| | | Ryley | 10,000 |
| | | Wheatman | 8,000 |
| | $90,000 | | $90,000 |

Assume the following:

1. The noncash assets were sold for $29,000.
2. Outside creditors of the partnership proceeded against Wheatman and collected from her $14,000 that the partnership was unable to pay.
3. The partnership incurred liquidation expenses of $4,000, which were paid personally by Ryley.
4. Oates is personally insolvent.
5. Ryley and Wheatman (who are both personally solvent) make a personal settlement between themselves.

### Required:
Prepare a statement of realization and liquidation.

### Installment Liquidation: Schedule of Safe Payments—First Cash Distribution to Partners

On January 1, 19X2, the partners of Allen, Brown, and Cox, who share profits and losses in the ratio of 5:3:2, respectively, decide to liquidate their partnership. The partnership trial balance at this date is as follows:

| | Debit | Credit |
|---|---|---|
| Cash | $ 18,000 | |
| Accounts Receivable | 66,000 | |
| Inventory | 52,000 | |
| Machinery and Equipment | 249,000 | |

|  | Debit | Credit |
|---|---|---|
| Accumulated Depreciation. . . . . . . . . . . . . . . . . . . . . . . |  | $ 60,000 |
| Allen, Loan . . . . . . . . . . . . . . . . . . . . . . . . . . . . . . . . . . . | 30,000 |  |
| Accounts Payable . . . . . . . . . . . . . . . . . . . . . . . . . . . |  | 53,000 |
| Brown, Loan. . . . . . . . . . . . . . . . . . . . . . . . . . . . . . . . . |  | 20,000 |
| Allen, Capital . . . . . . . . . . . . . . . . . . . . . . . . . . . . . . . . |  | 118,000 |
| Brown, Capital . . . . . . . . . . . . . . . . . . . . . . . . . . . . . . . |  | 90,000 |
| Cox, Capital . . . . . . . . . . . . . . . . . . . . . . . . . . . . . . . . . |  | 74,000 |
|  | $415,000 | $415,000 |

The partners plan a program of piecemeal conversion of assets in order to minimize liquidation losses. All available cash, less an amount retained to provide for future expenses, is to be distributed to the partners at the end of each month. The liquidation transactions for January 19X2 follow:

1. $51,000 was collected on accounts receivable; the balance is uncollectible.
2. $38,000 was received for the entire inventory.
3. $2,000 of liquidation expenses were paid.
4. $50,000 was paid to outside creditors, after offset of a $3,000 credit memorandum received on January 11, 19X2.
5. $10,000 cash was retained in the business at the end of the month for potential unrecorded liabilities and anticipated expenses.

### Required:

Prepare a schedule of safe payments showing how cash was distributed to the partners as of January 31, 19X2.

(AICPA adapted)

## Installment Liquidation: Schedule of Safe Payments and Statement of Realization and Liquidation

Partners Barley, Flax, and Rice share profits and losses in the ratio 6:3:1, respectively. The partners decided to liquidate the partnership on June 30, 19X5, when its assets, liabilities, and capital were as follows:

| | | | | |
|---|---|---|---|---|
| Cash. . . . . . . . . . . . . . . . . . . . | $ 10,000 | Liabilities . . . . . . . . . . . . . . . | $ 42,000 |
| Noncash assets . . . . . . . . . . . | 130,000 | Loans: | |
| | | Barley. . . . . . . . . . . . . . . . . | 4,000 |
| | | Flax. . . . . . . . . . . . . . . . . | 1,000 |
| | | Capital: | |
| | | Barley. . . . . . . . . . . . . . . . . | 84,000 |
| | | Flax. . . . . . . . . . . . . . . . . | 5,000 |
| | | Rice. . . . . . . . . . . . . . . . . | 4,000 |
| | $140,000 | | $140,000 |

Assume the following:

1. On July 1, 19X5, liquidation expenses were estimated at approximately $3,000. Actual liquidation expenses totaled only $2,500 and were paid as follows:

| | |
|---|---:|
| July 31, 19X5 | $1,000 |
| August 31, 19X5 | 1,000 |
| September 30, 19X5 | 500 |
| | $2,500 |

2. Noncash assets were sold as follows:

| Date | Book Value | Proceeds |
|---|---:|---:|
| July 11, 19X5 | $ 30,000 | $ 36,000 |
| August 14, 19X5 | 40,000 | 28,000 |
| September 27, 19X5 | 60,000 | 44,000 |
| | $130,000 | $108,000 |

3. Partners were able to eliminate any deficits in their Capital accounts through setoff or contribution as deficit balances occurred.
4. Cash was distributed to outside creditors and partners as it was available.

### Required:

Prepare a statement of realization and liquidation, including supporting schedules showing how cash was distributed to creditors and partners as it was available.

## Installment Liquidation: Schedule of Cash Distribution

**P 25-6**

Partners Brickley, Glass, Steele, and Woods decide to dissolve their partnership. They plan to sell the assets gradually to minimize losses. They share profits and losses as follows: Brickley, 40%; Glass, 35%; Steele, 15%; and Woods, 10%. The partnership's trial balance as of October 1, 19X0, the date on which liquidation begins, is shown below.

| | Debit | Credit |
|---|---:|---:|
| Cash | $ 200 | |
| Receivables | 25,900 | |
| Inventory, October 1, 19X0 | 42,600 | |
| Equipment (net) | 19,800 | |
| Accounts payable | | $ 3,000 |
| Brickley, Loan | | 6,000 |
| Glass, Loan | | 10,000 |
| Brickley, Capital | | 20,000 |
| Glass, Capital | | 21,500 |
| Steele, Capital | | 18,000 |
| Woods, Capital | | 10,000 |
| | $88,500 | $88,500 |

**Required:**

1. Prepare a statement as of October 1, 19X0, showing how cash will be distributed among partners by installments as it becomes available.
2. On October 31, 19X0, $12,700 cash was available to partners. How should it be distributed?

(AICPA adapted)

## Installment Liquidation: Schedule of Cash Distribution

Partners Arbuckle, Beltmore, and Tanner want you to assist them in winding up the affairs of their partnership. You gather the following information:

1. The June 30, 19X2, trial balance of the partnership is as follows:

|  | Debit | Credit |
|---|---|---|
| Cash. . . . . . . . . . . . . . . . . . . . . . . . . . . . . . . . . . . . . . . . . . . . | $ 6,000 | |
| Accounts Receivable. . . . . . . . . . . . . . . . . . . . . . . . . . . . . . . | 22,000 | |
| Inventory. . . . . . . . . . . . . . . . . . . . . . . . . . . . . . . . . . . . . . . . | 14,000 | |
| Plant and Equipment (net). . . . . . . . . . . . . . . . . . . . . . . . . | 99,000 | |
| Note Receivable—Arbuckle . . . . . . . . . . . . . . . . . . . . . . . . | 12,000 | |
| Note Receivable—Tanner . . . . . . . . . . . . . . . . . . . . . . . . . . | 7,500 | |
| Accounts Payable . . . . . . . . . . . . . . . . . . . . . . . . . . . . . . . . | | $ 17,000 |
| Arbuckle, Capital. . . . . . . . . . . . . . . . . . . . . . . . . . . . . . . . . | | 67,000 |
| Beltmore, Capital. . . . . . . . . . . . . . . . . . . . . . . . . . . . . . . . . | | 45,000 |
| Tanner, Capital. . . . . . . . . . . . . . . . . . . . . . . . . . . . . . . . . . | | 31,500 |
| | $160,500 | $160,500 |

2. The partners share profits and losses as follows: Arbuckle, 50%; Beltmore, 30%; and Tanner, 20%.

The partners are considering an offer of $100,000 for the accounts receivable inventory and for plant and equipment as of June 30. The $100,000 would be paid to the partners in installments, the number and amounts of which are to be negotiated.

**Required:**

Prepare a cash distribution schedule as of June 30, 19X2, showing how the $100,000 would be distributed as it is available.

(AICPA adapted)

## Installment Liquidation: Schedule of Cash Distribution and Statement of Realization and Liquidation

Assume the facts in Problem 25-7, except that the partners decide to liquidate their partnership instead of accepting the offer of $100,000. Cash is distributed to the partners at the end of the month.

A summary of the liquidation transactions follows:

*July*
1. Collected $16,500 on accounts receivable; the balance is uncollectible.
2. Received $10,000 for the entire inventory.
3. Paid $1,000 liquidation expenses.
4. Retained $8,000 cash in the business at month-end.

*August*
1. Paid $1,500 liquidation expenses. As part payment of his capital, Tanner accepted a piece of special equipment that he developed that had a book value of $4,000. The partners agreed that a value of $10,000 should be placed on the machine for liquidation purposes.
2. Retained $2,500 cash in the business at month-end.

*September*
1. Received $75,000 on sale of remaining plant and equipment.
2. Paid $1,000 liquidation expenses.
3. No cash retained in the business.

### Required:
Prepare a statement of realization and liquidation.

(AICPA adapted)

### ANSWERS TO SELF-STUDY QUESTIONS
1. b    4. a
2. e    5. c
3. e

# 26

## ESTATES
## AND TRUSTS

## CHAPTER OVERVIEW

I n this chapter, we consider the role accountants play in the administration of estates and trusts. Before proceeding into this subject, however, we discuss briefly the role accountants may play in estate planning, which takes place before an individual dies.

### Estate Planning

People commonly make plans for the orderly transfer of their property upon death to relatives, other persons, organizations, or trusts to be set up for the benefit of relatives. Such forethought is known as **estate planning** and is done under the guidance of attorneys, often working closely with accountants. The attorney's role centers around preparing wills and, in many cases, trust agreements (discussed in detail later in the chapter). The accountant's role consists of suggesting planning techniques consistent with the objective of minimizing *transfer costs* (federal estate taxes, state inheritance taxes, and fees and expenses). In this capacity, an accountant often determines expected transfer costs under various options. An accountant may also play an important role in advising his or her client on accounting matters pertaining to trusts that are to be established.

Participation by accountants in estate planning is usually limited to cases in which individuals are wealthy or moderately wealthy. The Tax Reform Act of 1976 substantially overhauled the federal state and gift tax laws, and an estimated 98% of all estates became exempt from estate and gift tax laws. However, inflation was lowering this percentage. Furthermore, certain inequities were perceived to exist still. To address these two areas, further changes were enacted in the Economic Recovery Tax Act of 1981, and an estimated 99.5% of all estates are now exempt from estate and gift tax laws. An accountant participating in estate planning must have substantial expertise in estate and gift taxes—a complex area of the tax laws. A detailed discussion of these laws and the use of planning techniques to minimize transfer costs is properly the subject matter of a tax course. However, a brief discussion of the estate and gift tax laws is included later in the chapter.

### The Trust Feature of Estate Planning

Frequently a will contains a provision for the establishment of a trust, whereby certain designated property of the decedent's estate is to be transferred to a **trustee** when the person dies. The trustee holds legal title to the property and administers it for the benefit of one or more other persons, who are called **beneficiaries.** Thus, the trustee serves in a position of trust with respect to the beneficiaries. This is a fiduciary relationship, and the trustee is commonly referred to as a **fiduciary.** (Recall another type of fiduciary relationship discussed in Chapter 19 in connection with companies in bankruptcy proceedings.) The person creating the trust is referred to as the **trustor** (also known as the **grantor, donor, creator,** and **settlor**). The legal document creating the trust is the **trust agreement.** Trust beneficiaries are of the following two classes:

1. **Income beneficiary.** An income beneficiary is entitled to the income earned by the trust's assets, which are referred to as the trust **principal,** or **corpus.**
2. **Principal beneficiary.** A principal beneficiary is entitled to the principal, or *corpus,* of the trust, which is distributed according to the terms of the trust agreement (usually at the specified termination date of the trust). A principal beneficiary is also known as a **residuary beneficiary** or **remainderman.**

The income and principal beneficiaries may or may not be the same person. A common arrangement is to name one's spouse as the income beneficiary for his or her remaining life and name one's children as the principal beneficiaries. Another common arrangement is to name one's minor children as both income and principal beneficiaries, with some or all of the income to be used for their support and the principal to be distributed to them when they reach a specified age.

## The Basic Accounting Problem

Regardless of whether the income and principal beneficiaries of a trust are the same person or persons, **it is necessary to account for the separate interests of each class.** The manner of accomplishing this task is the subject of this chapter. The requirement of correct separate accounting for the interests of each class is the reason for the special theories and techniques for accounting for the administration of estates and trusts by fiduciaries. Otherwise, quite simple record-keeping procedures would be adequate.

Accounting for the separate interests of each class of beneficiaries is even more difficult because there is a built-in clash of interests between the two classes. When the principal and income beneficiaries are not the same person or persons, the clash revolves around who gets what. When the principal and income beneficiaries are the same person or persons, the clash concerns the timing of distributions. Frequently, disputes between these interests lead to litigation.

Although a trust may be established by a transfer of property to the trustee during the transferor's lifetime (known as an **inter vivos** trust), we deal solely with trusts that are created by a gift made in the will of a decedent (known as a **testamentary trust**). Thus, we must consider the administration of a decedent's estate in connection with the establishment of a trust.

## Relationship between an Estate and a Testamentary Trust

All the states have enacted some form of legislation concerning the administration of trusts. State statues pertaining to trusts are operative, in most cases, only to the extent that they do not conflict with the terms of a trust agreement. Twenty states have adopted the Revised Uniform Principal and Income Act (of 1962) either in its entirety or with modifications; accordingly, we base our discussion on this act. Under this act, testamentary trusts are deemed to be created at the time of a person's death, even though the property to be placed in trust usually is not actually distributed to the trustee until some time after the person dies.[1] Property to be placed in trust becomes subject to the trust at the time of death; the rights of the income beneficiary are also established at the time of death. Therefore, the interests of the income beneficiary of the trust must be accounted for separately from the interests of the principal beneficiary of the trust **during the period of the estate administration,** as well as after the property is actually transferred to the trustee. (Some trust agreements simplify matters by specifying that the rights of the income beneficiary do not begin until the assets are actually transferred to the trustee.)

For accounting purposes, we treat the estate and the trust as separate accounting entities. (Conceptually, we view each of these entities as comprising two accounting entities—a "principal entity" and an "income entity.") For tax-reporting purposes, estates and trusts both are treated as taxable entities. However, they are not legal entities in the sense that corporations are legal entities.

## PRINCIPAL VERSUS INCOME

When a testamentary trust is established, every transaction must be analyzed to determine if it relates to principal or income. An incorrect determination has important legal consequences to a fiduciary. If it is later determined that income has been overstated and the fiduciary cannot recover the amount of an overpayment from the income beneficiary, then the fiduciary must make up the deficiency. In turn, if the error was made by the accountant or was based on the bad advice of the fiduciary's legal counsel, then these persons may be professionally responsible to the fiduciary.

[1]Revised Uniform Principal and Income Act, U.L.A. Volume 7A, Section 4 (St. Paul: West Publishing Co.).

## Manner of Analyzing Transactions

**Reference to the Trust Agreement.** In determining whether a transaction pertains to principal or income, **generally accepted accounting principles are not the point of reference.** The trustor may create his or her own definition of income. In other words, the trustor may specify the receipts that are to be income and the receipts that are to be principal. Likewise, the trustor may specify disbursements that are to be treated as charges against income and disbursements that are to be treated as reductions of the principal. Accordingly, all transactions must be analyzed as to the decedent's intent.

Because the decedent is not available, the first step is to determine if the decedent's intent is expressed in the trust agreement. Unfortunately, a common shortcoming of estate planning is that trust agreements usually do not explain in detail the treatment to be accorded specific types of receipts and disbursements. Many potential problems can be avoided if the decedent's personal accountant, who should have a knowledge of his or her client's properties, participates in the preparation of the trust agreement sections that pertain to accounting matters.

**Reference to State Law.** If the treatment of an item cannot be resolved by referring to the trust agreement, the second step is to find out what the state law is on the subject. Again, generally accepted accounting principles are not the point of reference. The Revised Uniform Principal and Income Act specifically addresses the principal versus income treatment of several items. Much of the impetus for revising the original Uniform Principal and Income Act (of 1931) resulted from the development of new forms of investment property, the treatment of which was not specified in state statutes. The treatment accorded many items specifically dealt with in the act produces income results that would be obtained if generally accepted accounting principles were applied. For numerous other items, however, the treatment produces results that are quite contrary to generally accepted accounting principles. For example, the act provides that the following items be treated as increases and decreases, respectively, to the trust principal instead of to income:

1. Gains and losses on the sale of corporate securities.
2. Gains and losses on the sale of rental property.
3. Bond discounts (with certain exceptions) and bond premiums.

We present the general thrust of the act's accounting requirements later in the chapter. Section 5 of the act calls for income during the administration of an estate to be determined in the same manner that income is to be determined by a trustee in administering a trust. Thus, the act applies to estates as well as trusts.

### Reference to Case Law.

If the treatment of an item is not covered in state law, the third step is to determine if the courts have encountered and ruled on the same problem. If so, the answer is found in case law. If the answer cannot be found there, then the fiduciary may petition the court for a determination.

### The Accountant's Role in Analyzing Transactions.

When the treatment to be accorded an item is not clearly set forth in the trust agreement or state statutes, the accountant does not determine whether an item pertains to principal or income. This is the function of the fiduciary, the fiduciary's legal counsel, or the courts. The accountant's role would be expanded, of course, when the trust agreement specifies that income is to be determined in accordance with generally accepted accounting principles. Such cases are the exception and not the rule.

## Manner of Record Keeping

Because the interests of the principal beneficiary and the income beneficiary must be accounted for separately, it is necessary to identify the assets and transactions pertaining to principal and those pertaining to income. Conceptually, we may view the assets and transactions pertaining to principal as belonging to a separate accounting entity and do likewise for the assets and transactions pertaining to income. Thus, a trust may be viewed as comprising two entities, each with a self-balancing set of books.

One method of record keeping is physically to maintain separate journals and general ledgers for each conceptual entity. An alternate method is to use one set of books for both entities but to use separately identified columns in the journals and separately identified accounts in the general ledger for principal and income. This technique allows separate trial balances to be prepared for each conceptual entity, just as though two general ledgers were used. In practice, this technique is quite simple to work with, largely because cash is usually the only type of asset common to both principal and income. Regardless of which method is used, it is not necessary to use one bank account for cash pertaining to principal and another bank account for cash pertaining to income, unless the trust agreement requires it. When only one set of books is used, the separation of the total cash balance is reflected in the general ledger through a Principal Cash ledger account and an Income Cash ledger account. One set of books is generally used in practice. We illustrate this manner of record keeping later in the chapter.

## Cash Basis versus Accrual Basis

### At the Beginning and the End of the Income Beneficiary's Rights.

In most respects, the Revised Uniform Principal and Income Act provides for the use of the accrual basis in determining at the time of the person's death the assets that are to be treated as part of the trust principal. The purpose, of course, is to establish a reasonably fair and practical starting point to determine income for the income beneficiary. Specifically, the following items are to be included as part of the trust principal at the time of death:

1. Amounts due but not paid at the time of death (Section 4[a]).
2. Prorations of amounts not due at the time of death that pertain to periodic payments, including rents, interest, and annuities (Section 4[b]).
3. Corporate distributions declared for which the date of record precedes the person's death (Section 4[e]).

The cash basis is specified for all other items (Section 4[c]). In a somewhat parallel manner, the act provides in most respects for the use of the accrual basis on termination of an income interest, to effect a reasonably fair and practical cutoff of the income beneficiary's interest (Sections 4[d] and [e]).

### Accounting Periods between the Beginning and the End of the Income Beneficiary's Rights.

For accounting periods between the beginning and the end of the income beneficiary's rights, the accrual basis in most respects does not fit in with the underlying objective of the fiduciary, which is to account for the **flow of assets in and out of his or her control.** Accordingly, with one major exception, the cash basis is considered more appropriate for such accounting periods. However, the accrual basis offers much better measuring results when determining the income of a business in which principal is invested.

### At the End of the Estate Administration.

When the income rights of the income beneficiary are established at the time of the person's death, the end of the estate administration is not relevant to the income and principal beneficiaries. Using the accrual basis is therefore unnecessary at the end of probate administration. Of course, if the trust agreement provides that income rights do not start until the end of the estate administration, then accrual techniques would be appropriate.

# ACCOUNTING FOR ESTATES

## Probate Administration

When a person dies, his or her property and liabilities (collectively referred to as the **estate**) must be administered, regardless of whether the person died with a will (referred to as having died **testate**) or without a will (referred to as having died **intestate**). Each state has laws concerning the affairs of decedents, commonly known as **probate law** or the **law of decedent estates.** A Uniform Probate Code exists, but only two states have adopted it. Accordingly, uniformity among the states in this area is negligible. The objectives of probate laws are to (1) discover and make effective the decedent's intent in the distribution of his or her property, (2) gather and preserve the decedent's property, and (3) provide for an efficient and orderly system of making payments of estate debts and distributions in the course of liquidating estates. If the decedent does not have a will, property is distributed according to state inheritance tax laws.

Under the probate laws, the affairs of decedents must be administered by fiduciaries who are subject to the control of the state **probate courts** (referred to in a few of the states as **surrogate courts** or **orphans' courts**). The following two terms are used for estate fiduciaries:

1. An **executor** is named in the decedent's will to serve as the decedent's personal representative in administering his or her estate and is appointed by the court to serve in that capacity.
2. An **administrator** is appointed by the court when (a) a person dies intestate, (b) a person does not name anyone in his or her will, (c) the person named in the decedent's will refuses to serve as executor, or (d) the court refuses to appoint the person named in the will.

The title to a decedent's property is subject to the possession of the fiduciary and the control of the court, even though title passes at the time of death to the person or persons to whom the property is to be distributed. In short, the probate court serves as guardian of the estate. If a person dies testate, his or her will has no legal effect until it has been "probated." **Probate** is the act by which the court determines if the will submitted to it meets the statutory requirements concerning wills. If the court so determines, then it issues a certificate or decree that enables the terms of the will to be carried out. The will is said to have been "admitted to probate."

Basically, an estate fiduciary must (1) take an inventory of the decedent's assets, (2) settle the claims of the decedent's creditors, (3) prepare and file the applicable income, estate, and inheritance tax returns, (4) distribute the remaining assets as gifts as provided for in the will, and (5) make the appropriate accountings to the court.

# Gift Terminology

A gift of personal property by means of a will is called a **legacy.** The recipient of a legacy is called a **legatee.** Legacies are classified as follows:

1. A **specific legacy** is a gift of specified noncash items. For example, "my automobile to my son, Harvey."
2. A **demonstrative legacy** is a gift of cash for which a particular fund or source is designated from which payment is to be made. For example, "$1,000 to my sister, Christine, out of my savings account."
3. A **general legacy** is a gift of cash for which no particular fund or source is designated from which payment is to be made. For example, "$2,000 to my brother Chad."
4. A **residual legacy** is a gift of all personal property remaining after distribution of specific, demonstrative, and general legacies. For example, "the balance of my personal property to my wife, Ann Marie."

If the balance of the estate assets after payment of estate liabilities, taxes, and administrative expenses is insufficient to make good all of various types of legacies, then the legacies are deemed to be null and inoperative in the reverse of the above order (referred to as the process of **abatement**).

A gift of real property by means of a will is called a **devise.** The recipient of a devise is called a **devisee.** Devises are classified as specific, general, or residual devises. Estate assets to be transferred to a trustee pursuant to the establishment of a testamentary trust may be any type of legacy or devise. The most common type of legacy given to a trustee is a residual legacy, which we illustrate later in the chapter.

# Inventory of Decedent's Property

The estate fiduciary's first major task in administering the estate is to take an inventory of the decedent's property. Each item must then be valued at its current market value for federal estate and state inheritance tax purposes (using state inheritance tax or private appraisers, as required), and the appropriate tax forms must be filed. (We discuss these in more detail in the following section.) In addition, the estate fiduciary must submit to the probate court an inventory of the decedent's property that is subject to probate administration. Not all items included for estate tax and state inheritance tax purposes are subject to probate administration. Many states allow real property to pass directly to the beneficiaries (or to the trustee, in the case of real property placed in trust), bypassing probate administration. Likewise, many states allow certain types of personal property—such as personal effects, clothing, household items, and a limited amount of cash—to pass directly to beneficiaries outside of probate. State probate law must be consulted to determine which items are subject to probate administration; an attorney's services are usually used for this. Although required only by some states, a separate schedule should list the items not subject to probate administration, if only for the record.

In general, the following items are subject to probate administration:

1. Cash in checking and savings accounts, cash in a safety deposit box, and cash on hand.
2. Investments in stocks and bonds.
3. Interest accrued on bonds through the date of the person's death.
4. Dividends declared on stocks prior to the person's death.
5. Investments in businesses and partnerships.
6. Life insurance proceeds that name the estate as the beneficiary.
7. Notes and accounts receivable, including interest accrued through the date of the person's death.
8. Accrued rents and royalties receivable.
9. Advances to those named in the will as beneficiaries, including interest accrued through the date of death.
10. Unpaid wages, salaries, and commissions.
11. Valuables such as jewelry and coin collections.
12. Real estate not specifically exempted (the most common exemption is property held in joint tenancy, because all rights in such property immediately pass to the surviving tenant at the time of death).

Even though other items may be includible for federal estate tax and state inheritance tax purposes, the fiduciary's accountability to the probate court includes only the items subject to probate administration. The fiduciary must take control of these items for estate preservation purposes.

## Payment of Estate Liabilities

The liabilities of the estate must be paid before any distributions are made to beneficiaries. Probate laws usually require the estate fiduciary to publish promptly notices in newspapers for a certain period of time calling for persons having claims against the decedent to file them within a specified period of time or be barred forever. The estate fiduciary is responsible for determining the validity of claims filed. If the estate assets are insufficient to pay all liabilities, payment must be made in accordance with the priority provided for in state law. This general order of priority is as follows:

1. Funeral expenses.
2. Estate administration expenses.
3. Allowances for support of the decedent's spouse and dependent children for a specified period of time.
4. Expenses of the deceased's last illness.
5. Wages owed to employees of the decedent.

6. Debts owed to the federal, state, or local government that have priority under federal or state law.
7. Lien claims.
8. All other debts.

## Tax Matters

The estate fiduciary is responsible for preparing and filing tax returns for the decedent and the decedent's estate.

**Decedent's Final Income Tax Return.**    A final income tax return must be filed for the decedent, covering the period from the date of the decedent's last income tax return to the date of death. Any taxes owed are paid from estate assets.

**Taxation of Estate Income.**    An estate is a taxable entity, which comes into being at the time of the person's death. Estate income taxes must be filed annually on federal Form 1041 (U.S. Fiduciary Income Tax Return) until the estate is terminated upon discharge of the fiduciary by the probate court. The gross income of an estate is computed in the same manner as that of an individual. In addition to deductions for expenses relating to the generation of income, a deduction is allowed for net income currently distributable to beneficiaries. As a result, the estate is taxed only on the remaining net income not currently distributable. The beneficiaries, in turn, are taxed on the currently distributable net income. The tax rates that apply to estates are those that apply to trusts:

| Taxable Income | Tax Rate |
|---|---|
| First $5,000 | 15% |
| Over $5,000 | 28% |

The concept of estate income for tax reporting purposes differs in many respects from the concept of estate income for fiduciary reporting purposes. Accordingly, working paper adjustments to fiduciary book income amounts are usually necessary to arrive at gross income and deductions for income tax reporting purposes.

**State Inheritance Taxes.**    Most states impose an inheritance tax on the value of property to be distributed to each individual heir. This tax is based on the **right to receive or inherit** property; thus, the burden of taxation falls on the recipient of the property. Although the taxes are paid to the state out of the estate assets, the estate fiduciary either seeks reimbursement from the individual heirs (when noncash assets are distributed) or reduces proportionately the amount to be distributed to each individual heir (when cash is distributed). The tax rates and allowable exemptions are based on the relationship of the heir to the decedent, with tax rates increasing and exemptions decreasing as the relationship becomes more distant. It is quite common, however, for wills to provide specifically that state inheritance taxes be paid out of the residue of the estate, so that the entire burden of taxation falls on the heirs who receive the residue.

**Federal Estate Taxes.** Unlike state inheritance taxes, the federal estate tax is based on the **right to give** property. The burden of taxation, therefore, falls entirely on the estate and not on each individual heir. Of course, this merely reduces the amount of the residue of the estate that otherwise would be distributed to heirs. (Some state probate codes require the federal estate tax to be borne by each heir, as with the state inheritance taxes.) Assuming a decedent has made no gifts during his or her lifetime, estate taxes are calculated in the following manner:

1. The total value, or **gross estate,** of the decedent's property is determined at the time of death or, if the estate fiduciary elects, at a date six months after death. Property sold within six months of the person's death is valued at its selling price. (Recall that the gross estate for federal estate tax purposes is usually greater than the probate estate.)
2. The taxable estate is determined by making the following deductions from the gross estate determined in step 1:
   a. Liabilities of the estate.
   b. Administrative expenses, including funeral expenses, court costs, and attorney fees.
   c. Casualty and theft losses during the administration of the estate.
   d. A **marital deduction** (a term used to describe **a transfer between spouses** that is exempt from transfer taxes). The marital deduction is unlimited; thus, any amount may be used.
   e. Charitable contributions.
3. The estate tax rates are then applied to the taxable estate to arrive at the **gross estate tax.** The estate tax rates are graduated from 18% on taxable estates in excess of $10,000 to a maximum of 50% on taxable estates in excess of $2,500,000.
4. Certain specified tax credits—such as state death taxes (with limitations) and the unified transfer tax credit—are subtracted from the gross estate tax to arrive at the **net estate tax.**

The *unified transfer tax credit* is the equivalent of an exemption. The following table shows the amount of the unified transfer tax credit and the related exemption equivalent:

| Unified Transfer Tax Credit | Exemption Equivalent |
| --- | --- |
| $192,800 | $600,000 |

Accordingly, a single individual may transfer a taxable estate of $600,000 and incur no federal estate tax.

Because a surviving spouse may take a marital deduction for any amount, all federal estate taxes otherwise payable can be deferred until the death of that surviving spouse. Thus, the tax law treats a married couple as a single economic unit.

To use the unified credit fully, the marital deduction amount chosen generally is small enough to leave a taxable estate equal to the $600,000 exemption equivalent of the unified transfer tax credit. (The taxable estate of $600,000 is then placed in a trust for the decedent's children.) For example, assume that (1) Henry Steele passed away, (2) his gross estate is $3,700,000, and (3) all deductions other than the marital deduction are $100,000. With a marital deduction amount of $3,000,000, the taxable estate is $600,000, resulting in a gross estate tax of $192,800. However, because of the unified transfer tax credit of $192,800, no net estate tax is payable. The unified transfer tax credit can also be used on the death of Steele's surviving spouse (who was transferred $3,000,000). Thus, the exemption equivalent of $600,000 is really $1,200,000 for a married couple.

The calculation of estate taxes is substantially more complicated when the decedent has made gifts during his or her lifetime. One of the major changes in the Tax Reform Act of 1976 was to unify the previously separate estate and gift tax rate schedules into a combined transfer tax system, so that lifetime transfers and transfers at death are no longer taxed at different rates. The unified transfer tax credit is labeled as such because it also may be applied against gift taxes due on lifetime gifts. The amount of any unused credit is then applied against the gross estate tax.

## The Opening Entry

Once an inventory of the decedent's property that is subject to probate administration has been compiled, the opening entry for the "principal entity" of the estate is made. The entry consists of debits to the various assets and a credit to an Estate Principal account. This account is merely a balancing account that facilitates the double-entry bookkeeping system. It does not reflect the "net worth" of the estate, inasmuch as the decedent's liabilities are not recorded as part of the opening entry. Liabilities are recorded in the books when they are paid, and such payments are eventually reflected as reductions to the Estate Principal account. This manner of accounting reflects the fiduciary's role, which is to **administer the decedent's assets,** rather than attempting to establish and account for the net worth of the estate. As expected, no opening entry pertains to the "income entity."

## Transactions Pertaining to Principal

Transactions pertaining to principal are recorded by debiting or crediting the appropriate asset account and crediting or debiting, respectively, an account that is descriptive of the transaction. Transactions pertaining to principal may be grouped as follows:

1. **Transactions that increase principal:**
   a. Assets subsequently discovered
   b. Gains on disposition of principal assets
2. **Transactions that decrease principal:**
   a. Losses on disposition of principal assets
   b. Payments of debts and certain taxes
   c. Payment of funeral expenses
   d. Payment of administrative expenses
   e. Distributions of gifts
3. **Transactions that do not affect principal:**
   a. Disposition of principal assets at their carrying values
   b. Receipts of amounts to be given to legatees (which are reflected as liabilities until paid)
   c. Disbursements of amounts held by legatees, as described in category (3)b
   d. Payments of amounts chargeable to a beneficiary (which are reflected as receivables until collected)

The nonasset accounts that are debited or credited in categories 1 and 2 are nominal or temporary accounts that are eventually closed to the Estate Principal account. (Some finer points concerning principal transactions are discussed later in the chapter.)

## Transactions Pertaining to Income

The accounting techniques used for the principal entity are also used for the income entity. An income asset account is debited or credited, and the other half of the entry is to an account that substantively explains the transaction. Initially, the income entity has no assets. Revenues, expenses, and distributions to income beneficiaries are closed periodically to an Estate Income account, which accumulates undistributed earnings.

A detailed discussion of the various types of income transactions and charges made against income is delayed until after the illustration of estate accounting. For simplicity, the illustration limits income transactions to interest on savings and bond investments, cash dividends on corporate stock investments, and interest on a partnership investment.

 ## The Opening Entry and Subsequent Transactions

David Diamond died testate on March 27, 19X1, with the following provisions in his will:

1. The decedent's residence and household items are left to his wife, Krystal Diamond, who assumes the mortgage on the residence.
2. Cash of $150,000 is to be given to Krystal Diamond.
3. All the corporate stocks are to be given to the decedent's alma mater, Krebitsville University, to be used for scholarships in accounting.
4. The decedent's automobile is to be given to Ruby Diamond, the decedent's sister.
5. The residual balance of the estate is to be placed in trust with the following terms:
   a. *Trustee:* Coral Point Bank
   b. *Income beneficiary:* Krystal Diamond, wife of the decedent, for the remainder of her natural life.
   c. *Principal beneficiaries:* Jade and Opal Diamond, the only two children of the decedent. The principal is to be distributed at the later of: (a) the date of death of Krystal Diamond, or (b) when both Jade and Opal Diamond reach the age of 25. (If Krystal Diamond dies before both children reach the age of 25, then the children succeed her as income beneficiaries until they both reach the age of 25.)
   d. The accrual basis is to be used in determining principal at the time of death.
6. State inheritance taxes are to be paid out of the residue of the estate and not by the individual heirs, except for the case of the automobile given to Ruby Diamond.
7. The decedent's personal financial advisor, Jack Cass, is named executor of the estate.

The estate of David Diamond consists of the following items, each listed at its current value:

**Assets Subject to Probate Administration**

| | | |
|---|---:|---:|
| Cash (including checking and savings accounts) | | $   70,000 |
| U.S. government and corporate bonds—face value, | | |
| $350,000; cost, $341,000 | | 337,000 |
| Corporate stocks—cost, $38,000 | | 63,000 |
| Life insurance (payable to the estate) | | 100,000 |
| Investment in partnership of Diamond, Ring, | | |
| and Stone: | | |
| Capital account balance at date | | |
| of death, net of drawings | $84,000 | |
| Share of profits from close of | | |
| preceding partnership accounting | | |
| period to date of death | 14,000 | |
| Share of partnership goodwill deemed | | |
| to exist at date of death (calculated | | |
| according to the terms of the | | |
| partnership agreement) | 22,000 | 120,000 |

*(continued)*

| | |
|---|---|
| Accrued interest receivable on bonds ............... | 10,000 |
| Accrued interest receivable on savings accounts..... | 2,000 |
| Dividends declared on corporate stocks............ | 1,000 |
| Automobile ...................................... | 7,000 |
| Total...................................... | $  710,000 |

**Assets Not Subject to Probate Administration**

| | |
|---|---|
| Residence and household items .................... | 240,000 |
| Duplex rental unit (cost, $75,000) subject to secured loan of $55,000 ................................. | 110,000 |
| Total Estate Assets ......................... | $1,060,000 |

**Liabilities to Be Paid Out of Probate Estate**

| | |
|---|---|
| Outstanding balance on credit cards ............... | $    1,100 |
| Medical expenses pertaining to illness............. | 3,700 |
| State and federal income taxes for the period January 1, 19X1 to March 27, 19X1 ......................... | 5,500 |
| Total....................................... | $   10,300 |

**Liabilities Not to Be Paid Out of Probate Estate**

| | |
|---|---|
| Mortgage on residence.......................... | 30,000 |
| Mortgage on duplex rental unit..................... | 55,000 |
| Total Estate Liabilities ...................... | $   95,300 |

In reviewing the items making up the estate, note that we have assumed that the decedent's residence, household items, and the duplex rental unit are not subject to probate administration of the state probate law. Consequently, the residence and household items pass immediately to the decedent's surviving spouse outside probate, and the duplex rental unit passes immediately to the trustee outside of probate. None of these items is accounted for in the administration of the estate. Accounting for the depreciable assets of a trust (such as the duplex rental unit used in this illustration) is discussed and illustrated later in the chapter.

The opening entry in the estate books follows.

| | | |
|---|---|---|
| Principal Cash.................................... | 70,000 | |
| Investment in Bonds.............................. | 337,000 | |
| Investment in Stocks............................. | 63,000 | |
| Life Insurance Receivable ........................ | 100,000 | |
| Investment in Partnership of Diamond, Ring, and Stone ......................................... | 120,000 | |
| Accrued Interest Receivable on Bonds ........... | 10,000 | |
| Accrued Interest Receivable on Savings Accounts | 2,000 | |
| Dividends Declared on Corporate Stocks......... | 1,000 | |
| Automobile ...................................... | 7,000 | |
| Estate Principal ............................ | | 710,000 |

No liabilities are recorded, because the accounting concerns the administration of estate assets.

Assumed transactions and related journal entries pertaining to activities completed by the executor during the administration of the estate from March 27, 19X1, to June 30, 19X2, are as follows:

| Transaction | Entry | | |
|---|---|---|---|
| 1. Subsequent discovery of a checking account. | Principal Cash . . . . . . . . . . . . . Asset Subsequently Discovered . . . . . . . . . . . . | 700 | 700 |
| 2. Receipt of life insurance proceeds. | Principal Cash . . . . . . . . . . . . Life Insurance Receivable . . . . . . . . . . . | 100,000 | 100,000 |
| 3. Receipt of proceeds from liquidation of investment in partnership, along with interest to date of receipt. | Principal Cash . . . . . . . . . . . . . Income Cash . . . . . . . . . . . . . . Investment in Partnership . . . . . . . . . . Interest Income . . . . . . . . | 120,000 4,000 | 120,000 4,000 |
| 4. Receipt of interest on bonds. | Principal Cash . . . . . . . . . . . . . Income Cash . . . . . . . . . . . . . . Accrued Bond Interest Receivable . . . . . . . . . . . Interest Income . . . . . . . . | 10,000 18,000 | 10,000 18,000 |
| 5. Receipt of interest on savings accounts. | Principal Cash . . . . . . . . . . . . . Income Cash . . . . . . . . . . . . . Accrued Interest Receivable on Savings Accounts . . . . . Interest Income . . . . . . . . | 2,000 6,000 | 2,000 6,000 |
| 6. Receipt of cash dividends on corporate stocks. (Receipts pertaining to dividends declared during the estate administration accrue to the legatee.) | Principal Cash . . . . . . . . . . . . Accrued Dividends Receivable . . . . . . . . . . Liability to Krebitsville University . . . . . . . . . . . . | 4,000 | 1,000 3,000 |
| 7. Payment of credit card, medical, and income tax liabilities. | Debts of Decedent . . . . . . . . . Principal Cash . . . . . . . . | 10,300 | 10,300 |
| 8. Payment of funeral and administrative expenses. | Funeral and Administrative Expenses . . . . . . . . . . . . . . . . Principal Cash . . . . . . . . | 11,000 | 11,000 |

*(continued)*

| | | | |
|---|---|---|---|
| 9. Payment of $49,300 inheritance taxes, $300 of which is to be borne by Ruby Diamond, who received the decedent's automobile. | Inheritance Taxes . . . . . . . . . .<br>Receivable from Legatee,<br>  Ruby Diamond . . . . . . . . . . .<br>    Principal Cash . . . . . . . . . | 49,000<br><br>300 | <br><br><br>49,300 |
| 10. Distribution of automobile as gift (a specific legacy) and collection of related inheritance taxes from legatee. | Principal Cash . . . . . . . . . . . .<br>Legacies Distributed . . . . . . .<br>  Receivable from<br>  Legatee, Ruby<br>  Diamond . . . . . . . . . . . . .<br>  Automobile . . . . . . . . . . . | 300<br>7,000 | <br><br><br><br>300<br>7,000 |
| 11. Distribution of corporate stocks as gift (specific legacy) to Krebitsville University, along with dividend receipts pertaining to dividends declared and received during the estate administration. | Legacies Distributed . . . . . . .<br>Liability to Krebitsville<br>  University . . . . . . . . . . . . . . . .<br>    Investment in Stocks . . .<br>    Principal Cash . . . . . . . . . | 63,000<br><br>3,000 | <br><br><br>63,000<br>3,000 |
| 12. Sale of a portion of the bonds to raise cash. (Current value at Diamond's death was $9,600.) | Principal Cash . . . . . . . . . . . .<br>  Investment in Bonds . . .<br>  Gain on Sale of Principal<br>    Asset . . . . . . . . . . . . . . . . | 9,800 | <br>9,600<br><br>200 |
| 13. Distribution of cash (general legacy) to Krystal Diamond. | Legacies Distributed . . . . . . .<br>  Principal Cash . . . . . . . . . | 150,000 | <br>150,000 |
| 14. Payment of income taxes relating to estate income. | Estate Income Tax Expense.<br>  Income Cash . . . . . . . . . . | 4,600 | <br>4,600 |
| 15. Payment of administration expenses pertaining to income. | Administration Expenses . .<br>  Income Cash . . . . . . . . . . | 300 | <br>300 |
| 16. Distributions to income beneficiary of trust. | Distributions to Income<br>  Beneficiary . . . . . . . . . . . . . .<br>    Income Cash . . . . . . . . . . | <br>18,000 | <br><br>18,000 |

We assume that no estate taxes are owed because of the use of the unlimited marital deduction. If estate taxes had been paid, the entry would appear as follows:

| | | |
|---|---|---|
| Estate Taxes | xxx | |
| Principal Cash | | xxx |

## Charge and Discharge Statements

Continuing with our illustration, the only remaining task for the estate fiduciary is to submit an accounting to the probate court with a request to distribute the residual balance of the estate to the trustee, Coral Point Bank. Trial balances for the principal entity and the income entity as of June 30, 19X2, are presented in Illustration 26-1. Charge and discharge statements, which portray the activity of these entities through June 30, 19X2, are shown in Illustration 26-2. The charge and discharge statements are usually accompanied by supporting schedules—such as the detail of the decedent's debts paid and the detail of legacies distributed. Because they are quite simple, such schedules are not presented.

### ■ ILLUSTRATION 26-1

**ESTATE OF DAVID DIAMOND**
**Trial Balance—Principal**
**June 30, 19X2**

| | Debit | Credit |
|---|---|---|
| Cash | $ 93,200 | |
| Investments in bonds | 327,400 | |
| Estate principal | | $710,000 |
| Asset subsequently discovered | | 700 |
| Gain on sale of principal asset | | 200 |
| Debts of decedent | 10,300 | |
| Funeral and administrative expenses | 11,000 | |
| Inheritance taxes | 49,000 | |
| Legacies distributed | 220,000 | |
| Totals | $710,900 | $710,900 |

**ESTATE OF DAVID DIAMOND**
**Trial Balance—Income**
**June 30, 19X2**

| | Debit | Credit |
|---|---|---|
| Cash | $ 5,100 | |
| Interest income | | $ 28,000 |
| Estate income tax expense | 4,600 | |
| Administrative expenses | 300 | |
| Distributions to income beneficiary | 18,000 | |
| Totals | $ 28,000 | $ 28,000 |

■ ILLUSTRATION 26-2

| ESTATE OF DAVID DIAMOND<br>Jack Cass, Executor of the Estate<br>Charge and Discharge Statements<br>March 27, 19X1–June 30, 19X2 | | |
|---|---|---|
| First, as to Principal: | | |
| I charge myself as follows: | | |
| Assets per inventory......................... | $710,000 | |
| Assets discovered ........................... | 700 | |
| Gain on asset realization.................... | 200 | $710,900 |
| I credit myself as follows: | | |
| Debts of decedent paid...................... | $ 10,300 | |
| Funeral and administrative expenses paid.... | 11,000 | |
| Inheritance taxes paid ...................... | 49,000 | |
| Legacies distributed......................... | 220,000 | (290,300) |
| Balance of the estate: | | |
| Principal cash ............................. | $ 93,200 | |
| Investment in bonds ........................ | 327,400 | $420,600 |
| Second, as to Income: | | |
| I charge myself as follows: | | |
| Interest received on bonds.................... | $ 18,000 | |
| Interest received on savings accounts ........ | 6,000 | |
| Interest received on partnership investment.. | 4,000 | $ 28,000 |
| I credit myself as follows: | | |
| Estate income taxes paid.................... | $ 4,600 | |
| Administrative expenses paid ................ | 300 | |
| Distributions made to income beneficiary .... | 18,000 | (22,900) |
| Balance of the estate: | | |
| Income cash ................................ | | $ 5,100 |

<table>
<tr><td>ILLUSTRATION</td></tr>
</table>

## Closing Entries for the Estate

Assuming the probate court authorizes the distribution of the residual Diamond estate assets to the trustee, the entries to record the distributions and close the estate books are as follows:

| Transaction | Entry | | |
|---|---|---|---|
| 1. Distribution of residual estate assets of principal entity to Coral Point Bank, trustee. | Legacies Distributed....... Principal Cash ......... Investment in Bonds ... | 420,600 | 93,200 327,400 |
| 2. Distribution of residual estate assets of income entity to Coral Point Bank, trustee. | Distribution to Trustee for Income Beneficiary ....... Income Cash ........... | 5,100 | 5,100 |

3. Closing of nominal accounts of principal entity into estate principal.

| | | |
|---|---:|---:|
| Asset Subsequently Discovered | 700 | |
| Gain on Sale of Principal Asset | 200 | |
| Estate Principal | 710,000 | |
| Debts of Decedent | | 10,300 |
| Funeral and Administrative Expenses | | 11,000 |
| Inheritance Taxes | | 49,000 |
| Legacies Distributed | | 640,600 |

4. Closing of nominal accounts of income entity.

| | | |
|---|---:|---:|
| Interest Income | 28,000 | |
| Estate Income Tax Expense | | 4,600 |
| Administrative Expenses | | 300 |
| Distributions to Income Beneficiary | | 18,000 |
| Distribution to Trustee for Income Beneficiary | | 5,100 |

## ACCOUNTING FOR TRUSTS

Accounting for trusts is identical to accounting for estates, except that a Trust Principal account is used rather than Estate Principal for the principal entity, and a Trust Income account is used rather than Estate Income for the income entity to accumulate undistributed earnings. The nature of the transactions is also different. An estate fiduciary is concerned primarily with cleaning up the affairs of a decedent and making proper distributions of estate property. A trustee, on the other hand, is concerned primarily with prudently managing a pool of assets in accordance with the powers granted to him or her by the trust agreement. This task usually involves buying and selling trust assets. Trustees must make periodic accountings to the principal and income beneficiaries and the probate court. A charge and discharge statement similar to the one illustrated for estates is used. Upon termination of the life of the trust, the trustee distributes the assets of the trust principal to the remainderman, makes a final accounting to the court, and requests to be discharged.

Using the illustration from the preceding section, the entries to record the receipt of the gifts from the estate of David Diamond are as follows. This is the principal entity:

| | | |
|---|---:|---:|
| Principal Cash | 93,200 | |
| Investment in Bonds | 327,400 | |
| Trust Principal | | 420,600 |

This is the income entity:

| | | |
|---|---:|---:|
| Income Cash | 5,100 | |
| Trust Income | | 5,100 |

## Transactions Pertaining to Principal

Early in the chapter we summarized the general thrust of the accounting requirements of the Revised Uniform Principal and Income Act regarding principal transactions. Some finer points of principal transactions are as follows:

1. The costs of investing and reinvesting principal assets are charged against principal.
2. The costs of preparing property for rental or sale are charged against principal.
3. Taxes levied on gains or profits allocated to principal are charged against principal.
4. The costs incurred in maintaining or defending any action to protect the trust or trust property or ensure title to any trust property are charged against principal.
5. Extraordinary repairs or costs incurred in making capital improvements paid for out of principal may be recouped from income through depreciation charges.
6. Trustee's fees and costs relating to the periodic accounting to the court of jurisdiction (court costs, attorney fees, and accounting fees, for example) are shared equally between principal and income.
7. Liquidating dividends are considered to be principal.
8. Stock dividends go to principal, not income.

## Transactions Pertaining to Income

As mentioned earlier, under the Revised Uniform Principal and Income Act, interest and cash dividends are considered income transactions. The act also includes the following as income: rents, loan repayment penalties, lease cancellation charges, lease renewal fees, and the net profits of any business in which principal is invested. Losses of any business in which principal is invested are charged to principal, because no provision exists for loss carryforward or carryback into any other calendar or fiscal year for purposes of calculating net income. Profits and losses of such businesses are to be determined using generally accepted accounting principles.

Among other things, the act includes as charges against income the interest expense on trust liabilities (such as a mortgage on a trust rental property), property taxes, insurance premiums, ordinary repairs, depreciation expenses (including depreciation charges pertaining to extraordinary repairs), income taxes attributable to trust income, a share of trustee fees and costs relating to periodic accounting to the court, and any other ordinary expense incurred in connection with the administration, management, or preservation of trust property. (Depreciation and unusual charges are discussed in detail in the following paragraphs because of the unique manner in which journal entries are recorded.)

**Depreciation.** Under the act, depreciation is mandatory and results in preserving the estate principal for the principal beneficiaries. However, under many state statutes, depreciation is provided at the discretion of the trustee. When depreciation is to be provided, a portion of the income entity's revenue flow must go to the principal entity. Because we view the trust as comprising two entities, the accounting entries to record depreciation produce results as if the principal entity had sent a bill to the income entity for the use or consumption of the depreciable asset. The entries are as follows:

1. To record depreciation:

| | Income Entity | | Principal Entity | |
|---|---|---|---|---|
| Depreciation Expense | 1,000 | | | |
| Due to Principal | | 1,000 | | |
| Due from Income | | | 1,000 | |
| Accumulated Depreciation | | | | 1,000 |

2. To record payment:

| | Income Entity | | Principal Entity | |
|---|---|---|---|---|
| Due to Principal | 1,000 | | | |
| Income Cash | | 1,000 | | |
| Principal Cash | | | 1,000 | |
| Due from Income | | | | 1,000 |

Whether or not to provide depreciation should be thoroughly explored in estate planning. Depreciation charges may deprive an income beneficiary of income necessary to maintain the standard of living intended by the decedent. Depreciation makes no sense if the properties are appreciating in value, as is the case with many rental properties. If depreciation is to be provided, it should be computed based on the current value of the property when it becomes subject to the trust.

**Unusual Charges against Income.** The Revised Uniform Principal and Income Act states:

If charges against income are of unusual amount, the trustee may by means of reserves or other reasonable means charge them over a reasonable period of time and withhold from distribution sufficient sums to regularize distributions [Section 13(b)].

The provision is somewhat ambiguous and open-ended. Under the "by means of reserves" approach, the trustee must anticipate and estimate expected unusual charges before they are incurred. Charges are then made against income over a reasonable period of time prior to their incurrence, resulting in the buildup of a "reserve," or estimated liability. The cash distributable to the income beneficiary during these periods is limited; thus, funds accumulate from which to make the expenditure when it actually arises. Under the "by other reasonable means" option, the trustee can possibly have the principal entity make the expenditure when it arises but record the expenditure as a deferred charge, which is subsequently amortized against income.

The entries under each approach for an unusually large expenditure, such as the painting of an apartment building exterior, are as follows:

1. **Accumulation Method:**
   a. Periodic charge.

|  | Income Entity | | Principal Entity | |
|---|---|---|---|---|
| Estimated Painting Expense... | 1,000 | | (no entry) | |
| Estimated Future Liability | | 1,000 | | |

   b. Actual payment.

|  | Income Entity | | Principal Entity | |
|---|---|---|---|---|
| Estimated Future Liability..... | 5,000 | | (no entry) | |
| Income Cash .............. | | 5,000 | | |

2. **Amortization Method:**
   a. Actual payment.

|  | Income Entity | | Principal Entity | |
|---|---|---|---|---|
| Painting of Building........... | (no entry) | | 5,000 | |
| Principal Cash ............ | | | | 5,000 |

   b. Periodic amortization.

|  | Income Entity | | Principal Entity | |
|---|---|---|---|---|
| Painting Expense.............. | 1,000 | | | |
| Due to Principal.......... | | 1,000 | | |
| Due from Income.............. | | | 1,000 | |
| Painting of Building....... | | | | 1,000 |

# END-OF-CHAPTER REVIEW

## Summary of Key Points

1. The fundamental function of estate and trust fiduciaries is to administer assets under their control rather than attempting to determine the net worth of an estate or trust. Accordingly, accounting for estates and trusts involves accounting for assets rather than accounting for net worth. As a result, special bookkeeping practices and accountability statements are used for estates and trusts that are quite unlike those found in commercial enterprises. Furthermore, the cash basis of accounting suffices in most instances.
2. Generally accepted accounting principles have virtually no application to estates and trusts. Trust income (including trust income during the administration of an estate) is determined according to the terms and provisions of the trust agreement. If the trust agreement is silent on the treatment to be accorded an item, then state statutes control.
3. An accountant rendering services to a trust must recognize that his or her role is a passive one when it comes to determining the treatment to be accorded items that are not clearly set forth in the trust agreement or state statutes. Decisions on such matters should be referred to legal counsel or the courts. In most cases, an accountant rendering services to an estate or trust must also have expertise in estate, inheritance, and trust taxation.

## Glossary of New Terms

**Administrator**  A person appointed by the court to administer the affairs of a decedent when an executor is not appointed.

**Demonstrative legacy**  A gift of cash for which a particular fund or source is designated from which payment is to be made.

**Devise**  A gift of real property.

**Devisee**  The recipient of a devise.

**Estate**  The property of a decedent.

**Estate planning**  The making of plans for the orderly transfer of one's property on death as desired, with a view toward minimizing transfer costs.

**Executor**  A person who is named in a will to serve as the decedent's personal representative in administering the estate and who is appointed by the court to serve in that capacity.

**General legacy**  Gifts of cash for which no particular fund or source is designated.

**Income beneficiary**  The party to a trust who is entitled to the income earned on trust assets.

**Inter vivos trust**  A trust created during a person's life.

**Intestate**  A term used to refer to having died without a will.

**Legacy**  A gift of personal property.

**Legatee**  The recipient of a legacy.

**Principal beneficiary**  The party to a trust who is entitled to the trust principal.

**Probate**  The act by which a probate court determines if a decedent's will meets the statutory requirements concerning wills.

**Probate court**   Courts in the state court system that have jurisdiction over the affairs of decedents.

**Remainderman**   The party to a trust who is entitled to the trust principal.

**Residual legacy**   A gift of all personal property remaining after distribution of specific, demonstrative, and general legacies.

**Specific legacy**   A gift of specified noncash items.

**Testamentary trust**   A trust that comes into being on a person's death, pursuant to provisions in the decedent's will.

**Testate**   A term used to refer to having died with a will.

**Trust**   An arrangement in which property is transferred to a person, called a trustee, who holds title to the property but administers the property for the benefit of other parties, who are called the beneficiaries.

**Trustee**   That party to a trust who takes title to trust property and administers the property for the benefit of others.

**Trustor**   The party to a trust agreement who created the trust. (Also referred to as a settlor, grantor, donor, or creator.)

## Self-Study Questions
*(Answers are at the end of this chapter.)*

1. In determining whether a transaction pertains to principal or income, which of the following is *not* a point of reference, unless specified?
   a. Case law.
   b. Generally accepted accounting principles.
   c. State law.
   d. The trust agreement.
   e. None of the above.

2. Under the Revised Uniform Principal and Income Act (of 1962), the rights of the income beneficiary are established at the
   a. Time of death of the deceased person.
   b. Completion of probate proceedings.
   c. Time the property is physically transferred to the trustee.
   d. Time the trust agreement is drawn up.
   e. None of the above.

3. Which of the following statements concerning tax matters is *not* correct?
   a. Federal estate tax is based on the right to give property.
   b. State inheritance taxes are based on the right to receive or inherit property.
   c. The marital deduction is unlimited in amount.
   d. The tax rates that apply to estate income are different from those that apply to trust income.
   e. None of the above.

4. Under the Revised Uniform Principal and Income Act (of 1962), which of the following does *not* hold true?
   a. Gains on disposition of principal assets increase principal.
   b. Costs of investing and reinvesting principal assets are to be charged against principal.
   c. Depreciation is mandatory.
   d. Insurance premiums on principal assets are chargeable against income.
   e. None of the above.

# ASSIGNMENT MATERIAL

## Review Questions

1. What role do generally accepted accounting principles play in determining trust income? Explain.
2. How do we determine whether a transaction pertains to principal or income?
3. What is the nature of the relationship between a trust income beneficiary and a trust principal beneficiary?
4. What are legacies and devises?
5. Are estate liabilities recorded in the opening entry for an estate? Explain why or why not.
6. An estate fiduciary may have to deal with what four types of taxes?
7. Under the Revised Uniform Principal and Income Act, when do the rights of income beneficiaries begin?
8. When is the accrual method used in accounting for estates and trusts?
9. What is the function of probate administration?
10. State the major tasks of an estate fiduciary.
11. Describe the accountant's role with respect to distinguishing between principal and income transactions.
12. Must assets and transactions pertaining to income be accounted for in separate general ledgers? Explain.

## Discussion Cases

### DC 26-1

### Estate Planning

Your client, Jan Landers, has asked your advice on accounting matters with respect to her attorney's preparation of a testamentary trust agreement. Jan wants all her residential rental property holdings placed in trust for the benefit of her husband (as income beneficiary) and her children (as principal beneficiaries).

**Required:**

On what points should you advise your client? (Assume you are located in a state that has adopted the Revised Uniform Principal and Income Act without modification.)

### DC 26-2

### Role of the Accountant

An attorney who is an acquaintance of yours has suggested that you attend a meeting that may lead to some work for you. At the meeting, you are informed that (1) Ken Dall died approximately one year ago; (2) the attorney is serving as the executor of the estate; (3) the residual balance of the estate is to be placed in trust; and (4) the trustee is Barbara Dall, Ken's widow. Mrs. Dall describes the nature of the trust assets as bonds, residential rental properties, and the stock of a wholly owned corporation, which continues to operate. She requests that you become the accountant for the trust and, in that capacity, do the following:

1. Maintain the books and records.
2. Make all accounting decisions.
3. Prepare the fiduciary income tax returns.
4. Prepare the annual financial statements.

### Required:

How would you respond to this request? Elaborate on the points you should discuss with Mrs. Dall.

## Exercises

| E |
|---|
| 26-1 |

### Estates: True or False

Indicate whether the following statements are true or false. Explain any false answers.

1. An estate is a taxable entity.
2. An estate is a legal entity.
3. The probate estate is usually smaller than the estate for federal estate tax purposes.
4. One function of an estate fiduciary is to account for the estate in a manner that continually reflects the estate's net worth.
5. Federal estate taxes are effectively borne by the residual beneficiaries of the estate.
6. State inheritance taxes are based on the right to give away one's property.
7. The Estate Principal account reflects the net worth of the estate at a given point in time.
8. Accounting for estates revolves around the administration of the decedent's assets.
9. The probate court essentially serves as the guardian of the estate.
10. A legacy is a gift of real property.

| E |
|---|
| 26-2 |

### Estates: Fill-in Statements

Fill in the missing words for the following items.

1. An estate fiduciary who is named in a decedent's will is called a(n) _____.

2. An estate fiduciary who is appointed by the probate court when no person is named in a decedent's will is called a(n) _____.
3. A gift of personal property is called a _____.
4. A gift of real property is called a _____.
5. The four types of legacies are _____, _____, _____, and _____.

6. A person who dies without a will is said to have died _____.
7. A person who dies with a will is said to have died _____.
8. State laws dealing with the affairs of decedents are commonly known as _____ _____.

9. Federal estate taxes are based on the right to _____ property.

10. State inheritance taxes are based on the right to _____ property.

## Trusts: True or False

**E
26-3**

Indicate whether the following statements are true or false. Explain any false answers.

1. When the income beneficiary and the principal beneficiary are the same person, no built-in clash of interests exists as in trusts in which these beneficiaries are not the same person.

2. The rights of an income beneficiary begin when assets are actually transferred to the trustee.

3. In trust accounting matters, the terms of the trust agreement prevail over generally accepted accounting principles.

4. When the accounting treatment of an item is not clearly specified in the trust agreement, reference is made to generally accepted accounting principles.

5. The Revised Uniform Principal and Income Act of 1962 is somewhat outdated because it is based on generally accepted accounting principles in effect at that time.

6. When reference must be made to state laws to distinguish trust principal from trust income, it is the accountant's role to interpret those laws concerning accounting matters.

7. The Revised Uniform Principal and Income Act specifies the use of the accrual basis for many items at the commencement of a trust.

8. Accounts and transactions pertaining to trust income must be accounted for in a separate ledger to prevent commingling of accounts and transactions with that of trust principal.

9. If the answer to an accounting question cannot be found by referring to the trust agreement, state law, or case law, then reference is made to generally accepted accounting principles.

10. Trustors may specify their own definition of net income, even if this definition is contrary to state law pertaining to trust principal and income.

## Trusts: Fill-in Statements

**E
26-4**

Fill in the missing words for the following items.

1. The person creating a trust is commonly called the _____.

2. Trusts established pursuant to the provisions of a will are called _____ trusts.

3. Trusts established during a person's life are called _____ trusts.

4. The party taking title to trust assets is called the _____.

5. The two classes of trust beneficiaries are the _____ beneficiaries and the _____ beneficiaries.

6. Another term for trust principal is trust _____.

7. The basis of accounting that is used in most respects when an income beneficiary's rights are established is the _____ basis.

8. Depreciation is _____ under the Revised Uniform Principal and Income Act.

9. When the accounting treatment of an item is in doubt, the first place to look is the _____ _____.

10. The _____ basis of accounting is used during the administration of a trust but not at the beginning and end of an income beneficiary's rights.

## Estates: Preparing Journal Entries

**E 26-5**

Emory Feldspar died on May 12, 19X1, with a provision in his will for the establishment of a testamentary trust. His estate had the following assets subject to probate administration:

| | Current Value |
|---|---|
| Cash in checking and savings accounts | $ 42,000 |
| Investment in U.S. government bonds | 387,000 |
| Coin collection | 11,000 |
| Bond interest receivable | 6,500 |
| Total | $446,500 |

The estate fiduciary had the following receipts and disbursements from May 12, 19X1, to January 20, 19X2:

1. Personal liabilities totaling $2,200 were paid.
2. Funeral expenses of $1,800 were paid.
3. Federal estate taxes of $37,000 were paid.
4. State inheritance taxes of $14,000 were paid. Of this amount, $400 is to be borne by the legatee receiving the coin collection, and $1,100 is to be borne by the legatee (Children's Hospital) that is to receive $25,000 cash.
5. Administrative expenses of $3,300 were paid.
6. A note receivable of $2,000 was discovered in September 19X1.
7. The note receivable in item 6 was collected in December 19X1, along with $150 interest.
8. Interest on bonds was received totaling $22,000.
9. Bonds having a current value of $60,500 at Feldspar's death were sold for $58,800.
10. The coin collection was distributed to the specified legatee, and the legatee reimbursed the estate for the inheritance taxes at that time.
11. Cash of $23,900 was distributed to Children's Hospital ($25,000 specified in the will—$1,100 state inheritance taxes).
12. Estate income taxes for the period May 12, 19X1, to December 31, 19X1, totaling $3,800 were paid.
13. Cash of $10,000 was distributed to the income beneficiary of the trust, Pearl Feldspar.

**Required:**

1. Prepare the opening and subsequent transaction journal entries for the estate.
2. Prepare closing journal entries as of January 20, 19X2.

---

**E
26-6**

## Trusts: Preparing Journal Entries

Following are the 19X3 transactions of a trust that has investments in corporate bonds and an apartment house:

1. Rental receipts totaled $38,500.
2. Property taxes of $1,400 were paid.
3. Mortgage payments of $15,500 were made. Of this amount, $14,900 pertained to interest and $600 pertained to principal. (Assume that the mortgage liability is reflected as a liability in the trust general ledger only on a memorandum basis.)
4. Normal operating costs of the apartment totaling $7,300 were paid.
5. The exterior of the apartment building was painted in January 19X3 for $2,100, and payment was made at that time. The apartment exterior is painted approximately every seven years. (Assume that this qualifies as an "unusual amount," as that term is used in Section 13[b] of the Revised Uniform Principal and Income Act.)
6. The annual depreciation charge on the apartment is $4,500.
7. Bond investments having a face value of $50,000 matured during the year and were redeemed. (These bonds had a current value of $48,800 when they became subject to the trust.)
8. Federal trust income taxes pertaining to the prior year were paid totaling $450.
9. Estimated federal trust income tax payments for the current year were paid totaling $1,850.
10. The $2,200 trustee's fee for the year was paid.
11. Interest receipts on bond investments totaled $14,400.
12. Cash distributions totaling $9,000 were made to the income beneficiary.

**Required:**

1. Prepare the trust transaction journal entries for the year.
2. Prepare the year-end closing entries.

# Problems

---

**P
26-1**

## Estates: Preparing Charge and Discharge Statements

The will of Tom Ford, deceased, directed that his executor, Wayne Pilgrim, liquidate the entire estate within two years of the date of Ford's death and pay the net proceeds and income, if any, to the Children's Town Orphanage. Ford, who never married, died February 1, 19X4, after a brief illness.

An inventory of the decedent's property subject to probate administration was prepared, and the fair market value of each item was determined. The preliminary inventory, before the computation of any appropriate income accruals on inventory items, follows:

| | Fair Market Value |
|---|---:|
| Monument Valley Bank checking account . . . . . . . . . . . . . . . . . . . . . | $ 6,000 |
| $60,000 of 8% Bootville City school bonds, payable January 1 and July 1, maturity date of July 1, 19X8 . . . . . . . . . . . . . . . . . . . | 59,000 |
| 2,,000 shares of Rider Corporation capital stock . . . . . . . . . . . . . . | 220,000 |
| Term life insurance, beneficiary—estate of Tom Ford . . . . . . . . . . | 20,000 |
| Personal residence ($75,000) and furnishings ($15,000). . . . . . . . . | 90,000 |

The following transactions occurred during 19X4:

1. The interest on the Bootville City bonds was collected. The bonds were sold on July 1 for $59,000, and the proceeds and interest were paid to the orphanage.
2. The Rider Corporation paid cash dividends of $1 per share on March 1 and December 1, as well a 10% stock dividend on July 1. All dividends were declared 45 days before each payment date and were payable to stockholders of record as of 40 days before each payment date. On September 2, Pilgrim sold 1,000 shares at $105 per share, and paid the proceeds to the orphanage.
3. Because of a depressed real estate market, the personal residence was rented furnished at $300 per month commencing April 1. The rent is paid monthly, in advance. Real estate taxes of $900 for calendar year 19X4 were paid. The house and furnishings have estimated lives of 45 and 10 years, respectively. The part-time caretaker was paid four months' wages totaling $500 on April 30 for services performed, and he was released.
4. The Monument Valley Bank checking account was closed; the $6,000 balance was transferred to an estate bank account.
5. The term life insurance was paid on March 1 and deposited in the estate bank account.
6. The following disbursements were made:
   a. Funeral expenses, $2,000.
   b. Final illness expenses, $1,500.
   c. April 15 income tax remittance, $700.
   d. Attorney's and accountant's fees, $12,000.
7. On December 31, the balance of the undistributed income, except for $1,000, was paid to the orphanage. The balance of the cash on hand derived from the estate principal was also paid to the orphanage on December 31.

### Required:

Prepare Charge and Discharge Statements, separating principal and income, together with supporting schedules, on behalf of the executor for the period February 1, 19X4, through December 31, 19X4. The following supporting schedules should be included:

1. Original Principal of Estate
2. Gain or Loss on Disposal of Estate Assets
3. Funeral, Administration, and Other Expenses
4. Debts of Decedent Paid
5. Legacies Paid or Delivered
6. Assets (Corpus) on Hand, December 31, 19X4

7. Income Collected
8. Expenses Chargeable to Income
9. Distributions of Income

(AICPA adapted)

## P 26-2 Estates: Preparing Charge and Discharge Statements

Ron Ho died in an accident on May 31, 19X1. His will, dated February 28, 19X0, provided that all just debts and expenses be paid and that his property be disposed of as follows:

1. Personal residence is devised to Donna Ho, widow. (Real property is not subject to probate administration in the state in which the deceased resided.)
2. U.S. Treasury bonds and Bubb Company stock is to be placed in trust. All income to go to Donna Ho during her lifetime, with right of appointment on her death.
3. Happe Company mortgage notes are bequeathed to Lulu Ho Waters, daughter.
4. A bequest of $10,000 cash goes to Dave Ho, son.
5. Remainder of estate is to be divided equally between the two children.

The will further provided that during the administration period, Donna Ho was to be paid $800 a month out of estate income. Estate and inheritance taxes are to be borne by the residue. Dave Ho was named executor and trustee.

An inventory of the decedent's property was prepared. The fair market value of all items as of Ho's death was determined. The preliminary inventory, before the computation of any appropriate income accruals on inventory items, is as follows:

| | |
|---|---:|
| Personal residence property | $145,000 |
| Jewelry—diamond ring | 9,600 |
| Oahu Life Insurance Company—term life insurance policy on life of Ron Ho; beneficiary, Donna Ho, widow | 120,000 |
| Marble Trust Company—8% savings account, Ron Ho, in trust for Lelani Waters (grandchild), interest credited January 1 and July 1; balance May 31, 19X1 | 400 |
| Hilo National Bank—checking account; balance May 31, 19X1 | 141,750 |
| $200,000 U.S. Treasury bonds, 10%; interest payable March 1 and September 1 | 200,000 |
| $10,000 Happe Company first mortgage notes, 12%, 19X5; interest payable June 30 and December 31 | 9,900 |
| 800 shares Bubb Company common stock | 64,000 |
| 700 shares Maui Manufacturing Company common stock | 70,000 |

The executor opened an estate bank account, to which he transferred the decedent's checking account balance. Other deposits, through July 1, 19X2, were as follows:

| | |
|---|---:|
| Interest collected on bonds: | |
| $200,000 U.S. Treasury— | |
| September 1, 19X1 | $10,000 |
| March 1, 19X2 | 10,000 |

Dividends received on stock:

|  |  |
|---|---:|
| 800 shares Bubb Company— | |
| June 15, 19X1, declared May 7, 19X1, payable to holders of | |
| record May 27, 19X1 .......................................... | 800 |
| September 15, 19X1 ........................................... | 800 |
| December 15, 19X1 ............................................ | 1,200 |
| March 15, 19X2 ............................................... | 800 |
| June 15, 19X2................................................. | 800 |
| Net Proceeds of June 19, 19X1, sale of 700 shares of Maui | |
| Manufacturing Company ...................................... | 68,810 |
| Interest collected on Happe Company first mortgage notes— | |
| June 30, 19X1................................................. | 600 |

Payments were made from the estate's checking account through July 1, 19X2, for the following items:

|  |  |
|---|---:|
| Funeral expenses........................................... | $ 2,000 |
| Assessments for additional 19X0 federal and state income tax | |
| ($1,700) plus interests ($110) to May 31, 19X1 ................ | 1,810 |
| 19X1 income taxes of Ron Ho for the period January 1, 19X1, | |
| through May 31, 19X1, in excess of estimated taxes paid by the | |
| decedent ..................................................... | 9,100 |
| Federal and state fiduciary income taxes, fiscal year ended | |
| June 30, 19X1 ($75), and June 30, 19X2 ($1,400) .............. | 1,475 |
| State inheritance taxes....................................... | 28,000 |
| Monthly payments to Donna Ho: 13 payments of $800 ............ | 10,400 |
| Attorney's and accountant's fees ............................ | 25,000 |
| Payment of interest collected on Happe Company mortgage notes | |
| that accrues to legatee ...................................... | 600 |

The executor waived his commission. However, he wanted his father's diamond ring in lieu of the $10,000 specific legacy. All parties agreed to this in writing, and the court's approval was secured. All other specific legacies were delivered by July 15, 19X1.

## Required:

Prepare Charge and Discharge Statements for principal and income, and supporting schedules, to accompany the attorney's formal court accounting on behalf of the executor of the Estate of Ron Ho for the period May 31, 19X1, through July 1, 19X2. The following supporting schedules should be included:

1. Original Capital of Estate
2. Gain on Disposal of Estate Assets
3. Loss on Disposal of Estate Assets
4. Funeral, Administration, and Other Expenses
5. Debts of Decedent Paid
6. Legacies Paid or Delivered
7. Assets (Corpus) on Hand, July 1, 19X2
8. Proposed Plan of Distribution of Estate Assets
9. Income Collected
10. Distribution of Income

(AICPA adapted)

| P |
|---|
| **26-3** |

## Trusts: Treatment of Disputed Items

You have been assigned by a CPA firm to work with the trustees of a large trust in the preparation of the first annual accounting to the court. The income beneficiaries and the remaindermen cannot agree on the proper allocation of the following items on which the trust agreement is silent:

1. Costs incurred in expanding the garage facilities of an apartment house owned by the trust and held for rental income.
2. Real estate taxes on the apartment house.
3. Cost of casualty insurance premiums on the apartment house.
4. A 2-for-1 stock split of common stock held by the trust for investment.
5. Insurance proceeds received as the result of a partial destruction of an office building that the trust owned and held for rental income.
6. Costs incurred by the trust in the sale of a tract of land.
7. Costs incurred to defend title to real property held by the trust.

### Required:

Locate a copy of the Revised Uniform Principal and Income Act in your library. Indicate the allocations between principal and income to be made for each item, using the act as the point of reference. Be sure to quote the applicable section of the act. (The purpose of this problem is to force you to search out items in the act, a task that is necessary in actual practice.)

| P |
|---|
| **26-4** |

## Trusts: Preparing Journal Entries and Charge and Discharge Statements

The postclosing combined trial balance for the principal entity and the income entity of a trust as of December 31, 19X3, is as follows:

|  | Debit | Credit |
|---|---|---|
| Principal Cash | $ 3,500 | |
| Income Cash | 800 | |
| Investments in Bonds | 123,400 | |
| Investment in E & T Corporation Common Stock | 86,200 | |
| Duplex Rental Unit | 95,000 | |
| Accumulated Depreciation on Duplex Rental Unit | | $ 12,000 |
| Trust Principal | | 296,100 |
| Trust Income | | 800 |
| Totals | $308,900 | $308,900 |

Following are the 19X4 trust transactions:

1. Rental receipts were $11,500.
2. Property taxes of $1,000 were paid.
3. Mortgage payments of $6,500 were made. Of this amount, $5,800 pertained to interest and $700 pertained to principal. (The mortgage liability of $57,500 on the duplex at December 31, 19X3, is recorded in the trust general ledger on a memorandum basis.)

4. Normal operating costs of the duplex rental unit totaling $600 were paid.

5. New carpeting was installed in both units of the duplex in January, 19X4, at a cost of $1,800, with payment being made at that time. (New carpeting is installed approximately every ten years.)

6. The annual depreciation charge on the duplex is $2,000. (Of the $95,000 value assigned to the duplex when it became subject to the trust, $15,000 was assigned to land, and $80,000 was assigned to the building, carpets, and drapes. The $80,000 is depreciated over 40 years.)

7. Bonds investments having a face value of $25,000 matured during the year and were redeemed. (These bonds had a $25,500 current value when they became subject to the trust.)

8. Bonds having a face value of $20,000 were purchased in the open market for $19,000 on July 1, 19X4. The maturity date of the bonds is June 30, 19X9.

9. Interest receipts on bond investments totaled $9,800.

10. E & T Corporation declared a 10% stock dividend on April 1, 19X4. The trust held 200 shares of E & T's common stock prior to this declaration. (The market price of E & T's common stock increased $30 per share during 19X4.)

11. Cash dividends of $3,300 on E & T Corporation's common stock were received.

12. The $1,500 trustee's fee for the year was paid.

13. Attorney's and accountant's fees for periodic judicial accounting totaling $1,200 were paid.

14. Cash distributions totaling $8,000 were made to the income beneficiary.

15. "Due to" and "due from" accounts are settled at year-end.

### Required:

1. Prepare the trust transaction journal entries for the year.
2. Prepare the year-end closing entries.
3. Prepare Charge and Discharge Statements for the year for trust principal and trust income.

### ANSWERS TO SELF-STUDY QUESTIONS

1. b
2. a
3. d
4. e

# APPENDIX

■ ■ ■ ■ ■

# STUDENT MANUAL FOR ELECTRONIC SPREADSHEET TEMPLATES

## *TOPIC OUTLINE*

## GENERAL MATTERS

### Introduction

Almost all companies with subsidiaries (and the outside independent auditors of these companies) now use software programs to perform both consolidation of financial statements and translation of foreign currency financial statements. Although some companies and some auditors use an internally developed software program, the common practice is to use one of the more popular, commercially developed electronic spreadsheet software packages. Accordingly, accounting majors need to obtain some hands-on experience in performing consolidations and translations using an electronic spreadsheet software package to be prepared for their future work environment.

### What Is an Electronic Spreadsheet?

An **electronic spreadsheet** is merely an accountant's working paper on a video screen (called a **monitor**). Amounts and account descriptions are entered on the screen through a keyboard (very similar to a typewriter keyboard), just as a pencil is used to enter these items onto a working paper. To have ready control over entering data on the screen, it is necessary to divide the screen into columns and rows. Thus, the screen can be thought of as a matrix or grid system. Each column and row is labeled alphabetically or numerically. The intersection of a given column and a given row is referred to as a **cell.** For example, Cell A7 refers to the intersection (or the coordinate) of Column A and Row 7. For most accounting applications, column widths are designed so that nine to twelve characters can be entered into a cell.

**The Cursor.** The location of the **cursor** (also called a pointer or a highlighter) on the screen determines which cell is the **active cell.** Data can be entered into (or erased from) only the active cell. Most of the time, the cursor is moved around on the video screen using the four arrow keys (up, down, left, or right) located in the lower right corner of the keyboard. (Some other ways to move the cursor more quickly are explained later.)

### The Template Approach

Companies using a spreadsheet package usually design spreadsheets to be used for specific applications (such as budgeting and consolidating financial statements). A spreadsheet configured for a specific application is called a **template.** Typically, the template is stored on a diskette (or on the hard disk within the computer) and loaded into the computer's memory when the application is to be performed. The user then merely enters data into the computer and completes the applicable task. Thus, the templates are used over and over again, making it unnecessary for the user to set up the design and configuration of the spreadsheet each time the task is to be performed. Since designing and programming a template is an involved and time-consuming task, the software industry now offers templates to be used with spreadsheet packages. With templates available, users need only a minimal understanding of an electronic spreadsheet software package. Although a thorough understanding of spreadsheet software is desirable, that is beyond the scope of this appendix.

## Using Templates but with Some Programming Required

The *Electronic Spreadsheet Templates* diskette available for use with this text was designed to be used with version 2.0 or higher of Lotus 1-2-3® spreadsheet software on an IBM PC, XT, AT, or fully compatible computer. (See Page 1304 for system requirements.) The diskette contains templates for these chapters:

| Chapter | File Name | Description |
|---------|-----------|-------------|
| 1 | MODEL1 | Combining statement worksheet |
| 3 | MODEL3 | Consolidating statement worksheet |
| 4 | MODEL4 | Consolidating statement worksheet |
| 5 | MODEL5 | Consolidating statement worksheet |
| 6 | MODEL6 | Consolidating statement worksheet |
| 7 | MODEL7 | Consolidating statement worksheet |
| 8 | MODEL8 | Consolidating statement worksheet |
| 9–10 | MODEL9 | Consolidating statement worksheet |
| 16 | MODEL16T | Foreign currency translation worksheet |
| 16 | MODEL16R | Foreign currency remeasurement worksheet |
| 23 | MODEL23 | Partnership trial balance worksheet |
| 25 | MODEL25 | Partnership statement of realization and liquidation |

Templates for all the chapters are purposely not 100 percent complete (partly to give students some limited "programming" experience and partly because of the variations in assignment material). For the consolidation templates, for example, you will need to add from one to five asset or liability accounts in the space provided for these additional accounts, all depending on the problem selected. In the early consolidation models, you must insert formulas at certain locations in order that these added accounts cross-total on the spreadsheet. (Instructions for writing formulas and entering data appear on pages 1290–93.)

## Creating a Template from Scratch

Employers expect their accountants not only to be able to use templates but also to create templates from scratch. Accordingly, we have included an assignment in Chapter 5 (Advanced Problem 5-3) that requires you to create a consolidation template from scratch. For this assignment, only a basic knowledge of Lotus 1-2-3 is needed, most of which can be obtained from this appendix. The student should refer to a Lotus 1-2-3 reference book for the following "basics" not covered in this appendix: the Copy command, the Move command, the Format command, the Insert and Delete commands, and the use of the edit function ⟨F2⟩ key. This assignment also includes a requirement to create two **keystroke macros** (stored instructions) that are very useful in reviewing a newly created template for programming errors in formulas used in the template. Detailed specific instructions are provided in this problem regarding how to program these macros.

## Purchasing Two Personal Diskettes

A master templates diskette is available to students from the instructor. However, you will have to purchase two personal diskettes: one on which to copy this master and one on which to save your work. This arrangement is used for several reasons. First, it is more convenient to have your own copy of the master templates diskette than to share the master with classmates. Second, when working a problem on the computer you may have to stop the session before you have completed the problem, and unless you wish to begin the problem all over again from scratch, you must save your work from that session. By saving your work on your second personal diskette, you avoid the possibility of unintentionally erasing a model from your master templates diskette (as could happen if you used an improper file name). Third, the master templates take up nearly all of the disk space on a $5\frac{1}{4}$-inch, double-sided, double-density 360KB diskette (only about 9 KB of storage space remains).

Before making your personal copy of the master or saving your recent work on your second personal diskette, first make sure that both of your personal diskettes are formatted for the IBM PC, AT, XT, or fully compatible computer. If it is, no formatting is necessary. If it is not, read and perform the steps that follow. Remember that formatting a diskette erases all previous files on that diskette, if there were any, so be sure to copy files you wish to save to another diskette first. For this reason, do **not** attempt to format the master diskette obtained from your instructor.

**Double-density versus High-density Diskettes.** Regardless of which type of diskette you buy, it must be double-sided. Determine whether your workstation computers have double-density disk drives (360 KB of storage) or high-density disk drives (1.2 MB of storage) and buy accordingly. Some workstation computers will have both, in which case you could buy either type.

## Formatting Your Personal Diskettes

The procedures for formatting a diskette depend on whether or not your workstation computer has a hard disk (or is served by a computer having a hard disk). Formatting a diskette is done using the MS-DOS or PC-DOS operating system. The DOS operating system is ready to accept a valid DOS command when the A⟩ prompt (or usually the C⟩ prompt if you are using a hard disk) appears on your computer screen.

**Formatting on a Computer Not Having a Hard Disk and Not Served by a Computer Having a Hard Disk.**   To format your personal diskettes, perform the following steps:

1. Put the MS-DOS or PC-DOS operating system diskette in Drive A. (In almost all cases, this will be on a separate diskette from the Lotus 1-2-3 diskette.)
2. Turn on the computer (the unit that has the disk drives).
3. Time and date prompts will appear. To bypass them, press ⟨**ENTER**⟩ twice. ⟨**ENTER**⟩ is discussed more fully on page 1279.)
4. When the A⟩ prompt appears, put the diskette you wish to format in Drive B and close the flap.
5. Type the following:

    **FORMAT B: ⟨ENTER⟩**

    **Caution:**   Be sure to insert a space after **FORMAT.**

6. After formatting, the computer will ask you whether you want to format another disk. If yes, follow the instructions on the screen. If no, press **N.**

**Formatting on a Computer Having a Hard Disk or Served by a Computer Having a Hard Disk.**   In almost all cases, the MS-DOS or PC-DOS operating system is stored on the hard disk (usually called Drive C). To format your personal diskettes, perform the following steps:

1. Put the diskette you wish to format in either Drive A or Drive B (depending on the type of diskette).
2. Turn on the computer (the unit that has the disk drives).
3. In most cases, a menu of options will appear (all depending on the configuration used by your school's computer center). If one of the options listed is to format a diskette in Drive A or Drive B, select that option by using the arrow keys and the ⟨ENTER⟩ key. By selecting that option by itself you will accomplish the formatting of a diskette. If a formatting option does not appear, then you should select that option

that calls up DOS. You are in DOS when the C⟩ prompt appears (the C Drive is usually the default drive). When you see the C⟩ prompt, type one of the following depending on whether you placed the diskette to be formatted in Drive A or Drive B:

**FORMAT A: ⟨ENTER⟩ or FORMAT B: ⟨ENTER⟩**

**Caution:**    Be sure to insert a space after **FORMAT.**

4. After formatting, the computer will ask you whether you want to format another disk. If yes, follow the instructions on the screen. If no, press **N.**

## Copying the Master Templates Diskette

The master templates diskette has been made **available to your instructor on a double-density, 5$\frac{1}{4}$-inch floppy diskette.** However, your instructor may have had your computer center store the master templates on a hard disk as a more convenient way of making them available to you. If your workstation computers have hard disks, the master templates could be stored on each workstation computer. Alternatively, if your computer center has a file-server computer in a local area network (commonly referred to as an LAN) arrangement, then the master templates would most likely be stored on the hard disk of the file-server computer. A file-server computer is a computer designed to serve a number of workstation computers by (1) providing software (such as the MS-DOS or PC-DOS operating system, the Lotus 1-2-3 applications system, and the master templates data files), and (2) managing the printer. An advantage to having the master templates on the hard disk of a file-server computer versus the hard disk of a workstation computer is that a user cannot accidentally make changes to the master templates data files. This could occur if the master templates data files were stored on the hard disk of a workstation computer.

### Significance of the Type of Workstation Computer.    The procedures for copying the master templates are also dependent on the type of workstation computer. The most common possibilities are as follows:

1. **Two double-density disk drives and no hard disk.** This is the IBM XT type. (Some of the newer IBM XTs have a hard disk.)
2. **One high-density disk drive and a hard disk.** This is the IBM AT type, which now may be the most common configuration in use.
3. **One double-density disk drive, one high-density disk drive, and a hard disk.**

The configuration of your workstation computer will determine whether you should copy the master templates to a $5\frac{1}{4}$-inch, double-density diskette or a $5\frac{1}{4}$-inch, high-density diskette. Also, you should understand that **a high-density disk drive can read files from a double-density diskette.** However, a high-density disk drive can save files to a double-density diskette only if the double-density diskette has been formatted on a high-density disk drive. **A double-density disk drive cannot read files from a high-density diskette or save files to a high-density diskette.** Consult your computer center personnel as to the appropriate means of copying the master templates to a personal diskette.

**Displaying a Directory Listing after Copying the Master Templates.**   You can readily determine whether your personal diskette contains all of the master templates by calling for a display of the files on your personal diskette. The steps are as follows:

1. Call up DOS. (When the DOS prompt for your particular installation appears, typically C⟩ or A⟩, DOS is ready to accept a command.)
2. If your personal diskette is in Drive B, type the following:

   **DIR B: ⟨ENTER⟩**

   **Caution:**   Be sure to leave a space before **B:**

   If your personal diskette is in Drive A, type the following:

   **DIR A: ⟨ENTER⟩**

   **Caution:**   Be sure to leave a space before **A:**

## Accounting Instructions

Before working your first problem on the computer, do the following:

1. Work the problem manually. This should be unnecessary for subsequent problems. If your first problem is a consolidations problem, you most likely will perform the following steps:
   a. Make any necessary adjustments to the parent's and subsidiary's financial statements.
   b. Prepare any required analyses for purposes of developing elimination entries.
   c. Prepare all elimination entries.
2. Make sure the elimination entries you prepare balance as to debit and credit totals.

By working the first problem manually before working the problem on the computer, you will be able to concentrate solely on how to use the computer once you start using it. This will make your initial learning process go much more smoothly.

## Computer-related Aspects of the Assignments

For most problems, working a problem using the computer consists of the following steps:

1. Loading the operating system and the Lotus 1-2-3 electronic spreadsheet software program into the computer's memory.

   **Note:** If your computer has a hard disk (such as on the IBM AT) or is served by a file-server computer, the DOS operating system and the Lotus 1-2-3 program are most likely stored on a hard disk. Accordingly, it is not necessary for you to insert a disk containing Lotus 1-2-3 (or a disk containing the operating system program) for loading purposes. **Be sure to inquire about this.**

2. Loading the desired template into the computer's memory.
3. Entering your name on the spreadsheet in the space provided.
4. Entering the problem number on the spreadsheet in the space provided.
5. Entering the appropriate company name or names and year-end date in the heading section of the worksheet (spaces are provided).
6. Entering the appropriate company name or names in certain columns (spaces are provided).
7. Determining whether additional asset and liability accounts need to be added to the worksheet section of the templates.
8. Adding the appropriate additional asset and liability accounts.
9. Entering formulas in certain columns of the worksheet of any accounts in step 8 that you added, so that amounts will cross-total.

   **Caution:** You do not have to enter or modify any formulas for vertical totals as a result of adding one or more accounts. (Ignore all accounts that you do not need for your particular problem.)

10. Entering financial statement amounts in certain columns of the worksheet (either manually or using macros).
11. Entering elimination entries in the appropriate elimination columns (either manually or using a macro) for consolidation problems.
12. Making a hard-copy printout of the completed problem.

The following sections explain how to do each of the preceding tasks in a step-by-step manner. However, you will be much more comfortable and efficient in using the computer if you first read this material once or twice thoroughly *before* proceeding to work on the computer.

## USING LOTUS 1-2-3

### The ⟨ENTER⟩ Key

Using an electronic spreadsheet requires the entering of data and commands into the computer's memory. The keyboard key that performs this function is labeled ↵ and is called the ⟨**RETURN**⟩ key in some manuals and the ⟨**ENTER**⟩ key in others. Because the latter term describes the exact function of the key, this key is called the ⟨**ENTER**⟩ key in this appendix. Before we can enter data and commands, it is necessary to load Lotus 1-2-3 into the computer's memory.

### Loading the Lotus 1-2-3 Spreadsheet Software Program

The procedures for loading Lotus 1-2-3 depend on whether or not Lotus 1-2-3 is stored on a hard disk. Follow the appropriate loading procedures that apply to your situation:

#### A. Loading Procedures If Stored on a Hard Disk:

In this situation, you most likely have a menu of software application options to choose from (such as Lotus 1-2-3, Wordstar, WordPerfect, Database).

1. Select the Lotus 1-2-3 option. After selecting this option, the following will appear on the control panel:

   **ENTER 1-2-3—Lotus Worksheet/Graphics/Database program**
   **1-2-3  View  Printgraph  Install  Translate  Exit** (1-2-3 should be highlighted on the second line of the control panel.)

2. Select the 1-2-3 option by pressing the ⟨**ENTER**⟩ key. This loads the 1-2-3 program into the computer's memory (takes about 30 seconds). After 1-2-3 has been loaded, the Lotus copyright information will appear.
3. Press any key, and within five seconds, column titles (labeled alphabetically) and row titles (labeled numerically) will appear on the screen. During this step, 1-2-3 also reads Drive A to see what 1-2-3 files are stored there.

### B.  Loading Procedures If Not Stored on a Hard Disk:

In this situation, you most likely have two double-density disk drives.

1. Obtain the MS-DOS or PC-DOS operating system diskette (version 2.00 or greater) for the IBM PC, AT, XT, or fully compatible computer. Insert this diskette into Drive A and close the flap.
2. Turn on the computer. (It may take about a minute for the computer to check its circuits before Drive A begins to operate.) After checking its circuits, the computer will automatically search Drive A and load the computer's operating system. (This step will take about 20 to 30 seconds.)

   **Caution:**  When the computer is accessing either disk drive, the appropriate red light comes on. Never attempt to remove or replace a diskette when either of these lights is on.

   After the operating system has been loaded, time and date prompts will appear. To bypass them, press ⟨**ENTER**⟩ twice. Remove the DOS diskette from Drive A.
3. Obtain the Lotus 1-2-3 software diskette. Insert this diskette in Drive A and close the flap.
4. Type 123 and press the ⟨**ENTER**⟩ key to load the 1-2-3 program. (Loading 1-2-3 takes about 30 seconds.) After 1-2-3 has been loaded, the Lotus copyright information will appear. Then press any key, and within five seconds, column titles (labeled alphabetically) and row titles (labeled numerically) will appear on the screen. During this step, 1-2-3 also reads Drive B to see what 1-2-3 files are there.

## Building Commands

You build a command by stringing together subcommands in the proper order. Each subcommand has a name, consisting of one or more command keywords, such as **Copy, Erase, File,** and **Print.** These command keywords (approximately 200 of them) are organized into a logical multi-level hierarchy called a **menu system.** Generally, each level of the menu system has several command keywords from which a choice is to be made. To indicate to the computer that you wish to build a command, press the / (slash) key. At this point, the top-level menu would be displayed in the upper left corner of the monitor (called the control panel). You would then make a choice from this top-level menu, after which the second-level menu would appear. You would then proceed through this level and lower levels as necessary to complete your command. For example, the command

/ **Worksheet** (1st level)    **Global** (2nd level)

**Format** (3rd level)    **Currency** (4th level)

would be used to specify the use of dollar signs and commas when amounts are entered into the spreadsheet. In creating the templates, the Comma format (which specifies the use of commas and the display of negative values in parentheses) with zero decimal places was used.

> **Caution:** If you experiment with the command shown above while having a model loaded, you could unintentionally change the format to Currency (with two decimal places, which is the default setting). You should always use the ⟨**ESCAPE**⟩ key to back out of a command step-by-step.

**Making Command Keyword Choices.** There are two ways to select a command keyword from any level of the command menu:

a. **"Point and pick" method.** To minimize errors and to make building commands as "user-friendly" as possible, 1-2-3 uses a cursor (or highlighter) within the control panel. For simplicity, we refer to this cursor as the **menu pointer.** (It should not be confused with the cell cursor, which is used later in entering labels, values [amounts], and formulas.) Using the arrow keys (on the numeric keypad to the right of the alphabetic keyboard), move the menu pointer to the command keyword of your choice. You have *pointed to* a command keyword when you see that command keyword highlighted on the monitor. To *pick* that option, press the ⟨**ENTER**⟩ key.

b. **"First-letter-only" method.** At each level of the command menu, press the first letter of the command keyword of your choice. (The chosen command keyword does not have to be highlighted in the menu line— but you must be able to see that command keyword in the menu line.)

> **Comparative Note:** The "first-letter-only" method of selecting command keywords is much quicker than the "point and pick" method because it is not necessary to either move the menu pointer or use the ⟨**ENTER**⟩ key. However, it is easier to make a typing mistake.

We shall present both "point and pick" and "first-letter-only" explanations for a few critical 1-2-3 commands.

> **Caution:** When using the keyboard, press and release the keys quickly. Pressing a key slowly or holding it down produces multiple entries for the key.

If you make a mistake using the keyboard, go to page 1284, which explains how to correct such mistakes.

## Determining the Default Drive

In installing and customizing Lotus 1-2-3 for the computers in your computer center, one of the disk drives was assigned the one from which 1-2-3 will automatically use to retrieve data files and save data files. This disk drive is referred to as the default drive. Before loading any of the templates, we must identify the default drive. Press the following keys: **/FR** (This is the File Retrieve command discussed more fully shortly.) At this point, the control panel will show:

**Name of file to retrieve: A: or B: or C: \LOTUS**

If **A:** appears, place your personal diskette containing the templates in Drive A. If **B:** appears, place your personal diskette containing the templates in Drive B. If **C: \LOTUS** appears, place your personal diskette containing the templates in Drive A or Drive B, as appropriate. Later, in loading the templates you will have to (1) use the backspace key to erase **C: \LOTUS;** (2) type in **A:** or **B:** depending on which disk drive you have placed your personal templates diskette, and (3) press the ⟨**ENTER**⟩ key to get the computer to read a file from that disk drive. (Alternately, you could change the default drive for your current session only by changing the default drive temporarily by pressing **/FD** [the File Directory command, which allows you to view or change the default drive], typing in **A:** or **B:** as appropriate, and pressing the ⟨**ENTER**⟩ key.) Regardless of whether **A:** or **B:,** or **C:** appears on the screen, press the ⟨**Escape**⟩ key five times to back fully out of this command.

**The Default Directory.**   In addition to being programmed to retrieve or save data files using an assigned disk drive, the computer can be instructed to do so using a specific location of the hard disk or the floppy diskette. Although rarely done for nonhard disk systems, this is virtually always done for hard disk systems because of their much bigger capacity. For hard disk systems, the hard disk is partitioned for organizational purposes in a hierarchy system. Each partitioned portion of a hard disk is called a directory or a subdirectory. If your computer has a hard disk, you normally will not be storing your data files (the templates and problem solutions) on the hard disk. In dealing with the default drive and the default directory, the Lotus 1-2-3 command structure uses the term **default directory.** This term encompasses the default drive as well as the specific location (directory) within the hard disk.

## Loading Templates

The templates are loaded into the computer's memory by pressing the following keys:

| Keys to Be Pressed | Explanation and Guidance |
|---|---|

/ 

By pressing the / (slash) key, you are telling 1-2-3 that you want to build up a command, using command keywords. After pressing /, see on the screen the top-level menu of command keywords:

**Worksheet Range Copy Move File Print Graph Data System Quit**

→ ← ↑ ↓

Use the four arrow keys on the numeric keypad to point to your next menu choice, which is to be the command keyword File. (Use the right and left arrows for moving across a single line of menu choices to highlight an option; use the up and down arrows on a multi-line menu.) Or press the single letter F.

F

By pressing the F key or by pressing ⟨ENTER⟩ after pointing to File on the menu, you are telling 1-2-3 to access the File command. You want to load the consolidation template that is stored on the diskette in Drive A or Drive B. After selecting File, the following menu choices appear on the prompt line of the monitor:

**Retrieve Save Combine Xtract Erase List Import Directory**

The Retrieve command should appear highlighted on the screen. If it is not, you can point to it by pressing the left and right arrow keys to move the menu pointer. Or you can just press the single letter R.

R

By selecting the Retrieve command, you are telling 1-2-3 to load a 1-2-3 file from a diskette into the computer's memory. Next, you will see the prompt:

**Enter name of file to retrieve   A: or B: or C:**

**Reminder:** If your default drive is the C Drive, it is at this point that you must: (1) use the backspace key to erase **C:**, (2) type in **A:** or **B:** as appropriate, and (3) press the ⟨**ENTER**⟩ key.

Notice that the file name **MODEL1** is highlighted under the prompt. Assume, however, that you want to load Model 4 (the file name is MODEL4).

| Keys to Be Pressed | Explanation and Guidance |
|---|---|
| **MODEL4** and/or ⟨**ENTER**⟩ | Typing MODEL4 (the file name under which the template for Chapter 4 is stored on the data diskette) and then pressing ⟨**ENTER**⟩ loads that file into the computer's memory. If instead you use the arrow keys so that MODEL4 becomes highlighted under the file name prompt, you only need to press ⟨**ENTER**⟩. (Loading a template takes 10–20 seconds.) |
| | After 1-2-3 has retrieved the desired template from the diskette, it will appear on the screen. Note that the cell cursor is positioned in cell A1 and that the contents of that cell (TEMPLATE:) is displayed on the cursor coordinate line (the top line in the upper left corner of the screen). Note also that the contents is preceded by ', an apostrophe. The apostrophe signifies that a **label** (text string) is stored in this cell. |

**Summary:**  Here, you loaded one of the templates by building and entering a command. If you used the "point and pick" method, which requires the use of the arrow keys and the ⟨**ENTER**⟩ key for each step in building the complete command, your process was as follows:

**/ File ⟨ENTER⟩ Retrieve ⟨ENTER⟩ MODEL4 ⟨ENTER⟩**

If you used the "first-letter-only" method, which requires typing only the first letter of each command keyword, your process was as follows:

**/FR MODEL4 ⟨ENTER⟩**

## Correcting Keyboard Mistakes

The manner of making corrections depends on whether you: (a) are building commands; (b) typing labels, values, or formulas **to be entered** into a cell; or (c) **have entered** an incorrect label, value, or formula into a cell.

a. **Making corrections when building commands:**

| Keys to Be Used | Location on Alphabetic Keyboard | How They Work |
|---|---|---|
| ⟨**ESCAPE**⟩ | Labeled **Esc** in upper left corner. | Cancels the last command keyword choice that you selected. Repeated pressing takes you backward through the main command menus, **one subcommand at a time.** |

| Keys to Be Used | Location on Alphabetic Keyboard | How They Work |
|---|---|---|
| ⟨CONTROL⟩ and ⟨BREAK⟩ | Labeled **Ctrl** above left shift key. Labeled **Break** (on front) and **Scroll Lock** (on top) in upper right corner. | Cancels with one stroke the **entire command sequence constructed to this point.** To execute, first hold down the ⟨CONTROL⟩ key and *then* press the ⟨BREAK⟩ key. |

b. **Making corrections when typing labels, values, or formulas that have not yet been entered into a cell:**

| Keys to Be Used | Location on Alphabetic Keyboard | How They Work |
|---|---|---|
| ⟨BACKSPACE⟩ | Labeled ← in upper right corner (a very large key) to left of the ⟨NUM LOCK⟩ key. | Erases the last character typed. Repeated pressing erases other characters in the line, one character at a time, in right-to-left (LIFO) order. |
| ⟨ESCAPE⟩ | Labeled **Esc** in upper left corner. | Cancels the entire text line that you have typed, allowing you to begin that line again. |

c. **Erasing labels, values, or formulas that have been entered into a cell:**

| Command | Explanation and Guidance |
|---|---|
| **/ Range** ⟨ENTER⟩ **Erase** ⟨ENTER⟩ ⟨ENTER⟩ or **/RE** ⟨ENTER⟩ | Erases the contents of a cell. (Cell cursor must first be moved to that cell.) Note: Lotus 1-2-3 assumes here that the range (the extent of data to be erased) is just the cell to which you have moved the cell cursor. A range is expanded using the arrow keys, enabling multiple cells to be erased simultaneously. |

## Printing a Hard Copy of the Template

At this point, it will be useful to instruct the computer to print out a hard copy of a template in model form. This takes from one to five minutes depending on the type of printer. You can then study the entire template before entering any data relating to the assigned problem. If the cell cursor is not already in cell A1, use the arrow keys to move it there now.

Jump ahead to page 1294, which gives instructions for printing a hard copy of solutions. Then come back to this section and proceed from here.

In reviewing the hard copy of the template, note the following items:

a. **General instructions and cautions** are located in the upper left corner of each template. Read them carefully.

b. For models for Chapters 3–10 and 16, an **analysis of the investment account section** (along with the related **primary elimination entry section**) follows the general instructions and cautions.

c. Next comes **the worksheet section.** In reviewing the worksheet, note that whenever a zero **(O)** shows, there is a formula stored in the cell at that location. **Formulas** are used to arrive at subtotals, totals, and cross-totals. (How to write formulas is explained later.) Everything printed except the zeros are called **labels.** At this point, there are no **values** (amounts) in the worksheet section of the template. If there were, the worksheet would not be a model but a finished document.

d. The **macros** (stored instructions) are located at the bottom portion of the template, as it is customary to store them in an out of the way location. You should review these macros to see how their use will save you time.

e. The **problem data** (which you need not have printed out) is stored to the right of the worksheet in columns U through AN. (For Model 4, macros \A through \I are for loading problem data into the parent and subsidiary columns of the worksheet.)

## Moving the Cell Cursor

Note that Lotus 1-2-3 displays only a small portion of the template at one time on the monitor, even though the entire template is stored in the computer's memory. Any section of the template can be displayed merely by moving the cell cursor to the desired section. Familiarize yourself with cursor movement by doing the following:

1. If the cell cursor is not at cell A1, then use the directional arrow keys (in the numeric keypad) to move it there.

2. Press the down arrow key and hold it down until you reach cell A112. Note that the contents of cell A112 are displayed on the cursor coordinate line (the top line in the upper left corner of the screen).

3. Using the right arrow key, move the cell cursor to B112. Note that this cell is blank and that the cursor coordinate line is blank except for the coordinate of the cell cursor (B112). Later in this assignment, you will have to enter a value in this and many other cells. (Instructions are provided on p. 1291.)

4. Using the right arrow key, move the cell cursor to cell F112. Note that the contents of this cell is a zero but that the cell cursor coordinate line displays the following:

**F112: (B112 + C112 + D112 − E112)**

This means that the above formula (which produces a value) is stored in this cell. Thus as values (amounts) are entered in cells B112, C112, D112, and E112, the cross-total of these four cells will appear in cell F112. Cross-totaling and totaling are done automatically by the computer wherever formulas are stored.

**The GOTO Key.** When you need to pass over a great number of rows or columns to get to a particular cell, it is more efficient to use the **GOTO** key. Here is how to operate the GOTO feature:

The GOTO key is labeled **F5,** one of the keys located to the left of the alphabetic keyboard. After pressing the GOTO key, the prompt line (the second line from the top in the upper left corner) displays the following:

**ENTER address to go to: (your current position)**

This means that 1-2-3 is prompting you to enter the coordinate to which you want to move the cell cursor. Assume that you want to position the cell cursor at coordinate A25. Press the following:

**A25 ⟨ENTER⟩**

The cell cursor is now positioned at cell A25.

**Other Cell Cursor Movement Keys.** The following keys (some of which are located on the numeric keypad) are other convenient and time-saving ways to move the cell cursor (or the worksheet):

| Key | What It Does |
| --- | --- |
| Moving Page by Page: | |
| **PgUp** | Moves the cell cursor up one screen (20 rows). |
| **PgDn** | Moves the cell cursor down one screen (20 rows). |
| **Ctrl** $\rightarrow$ | Moves the cell cursor to the right one screen (70 characters). |
| **Ctrl** $\leftarrow$ | Moves the cell cursor to the left one screen (70 characters). |
| Moving to a Margin-in the Active Area: | |
| **Ctrl-PgUp** | Moves cell cursor to top margin. |
| **Ctrl-PgDn** | Moves cell cursor to bottom margin. |
| **Ctrl-Home** | Moves cell cursor to left margin. |
| **Ctrl-End** | Moves cell cursor to right margin. |

*(continued)*

| Key | What It Does |
|---|---|
| Miscellaneous: | |
| **Home** | Moves the cell cursor to cell A1. |
| **End-Home** | Moves the cell cursor to bottom right section of active (or used) portion of the spreadsheet. |
| **End-(and an arrow key)** | Locates either the first or last occupied cell in a row (when using the right or left arrow keys) or a column (when using the up or down arrow keys). |
| **Scroll lock- (and an arrow key)** | Moves the worksheet: (1) up or down one row when using the up or down arrow keys, and (2) right or left one column when using the right or left arrow keys. |

**Note:** When more than one key is used, the first key must by typed **and held down while the other key is typed.**

## Cell Protection

To prevent the accidental altering or erasing of labels and formulas, each of the models has been **cell protected.** When a cell is protected, the user is prevented from: (a) altering or erasing the contents of a cell, and (b) entering a label, formula, or value into an empty cell. Trying to do so causes the computer to beep and display the error message "Protected cell." Of course, those cells that you need to use in preparing your solution have been **unprotected.** You can readily determine if a cell is protected by referring to the first line of the control panel. If a cell is protected, the abbreviation **PR** is shown preceding the display of the cell's literal contents. If the cell is unprotected, the abbreviation **U** is shown preceding the display of the cell's literal contents. If you have a color monitor, the unprotected cells are displayed in a different color.

**Cell Protection Using the Range Command.** Once the cell protection option has been activated for an entire model (or template), as has been done for each of the models on the templates diskette and your copy of it, individual cells may have their protection removed or added using the Range command as follows:

| Command | Explanation |
|---|---|
| **/RU** | To unprotect a cell. |
| **/RP** | To protect a cell. |

For either command, the cell cursor must be in the cell you wish to unprotect or protect.

## Entering Labels

The templates for most chapters have been designed so that columns B through F are each 11 characters wide. Each cell can be programmed to contain: (1) a label (such as a column heading, an account description, an instruction, your name, or a problem number); (2) a value (such as 500), or (3) a formula (such as a listing of cells whose values are to be totaled or cross-totaled). Note that the number of characters needed for a formula in a cell is not restricted by the width of that cell. We first cover labels.

For these templates you must enter several labels—your name, the problem number, the name of the company or companies, and in most cases several account descriptions. To perform these tasks, it is first necessary to understand (1) how to enter labels into a cell, and (2) when to use the ' (apostrophe) symbol so that 1-2-3 knows you are entering a label. Without the apostrophe, 1-2-3 might interpret your string of characters as a value (an amount).

1. Move the cell cursor to cell A118. This is a blank line to be used for entering an additional asset account to the balance sheet. Assume that we want to add the account Installment Receivables on this row. The caption "Installment Receivables" contains 23 characters and is to be indented one space from the left boundary of cell A118. Because column A has been designed to hold only 17 characters, the caption must be abbreviated: for example, "Installment Rec." With one space for indenting and one period at the end, there are 17 characters. (Use the **space bar** for indenting.)

   As you press the letter keys (remember to indent one space), the letters appear on the third line from the top in the upper left corner of the screen. This line is called the **edit line,** and its purpose is to allow you to see what you have typed. (If you make any typing mistakes, use the ⟨**BACKSPACE**⟩ or ⟨**ESCAPE**⟩ keys.)

2. Press the ⟨**ENTER**⟩ key and "Installment Rec." appears in two places: the cursor coordinate line and cell A118.

3. If you made a mistake, try it again. (It is not necessary to erase your mistake from the cell to try again; but if you desire to do so, press /**RE** ⟨**ENTER**⟩ which you should recall is the erase command.)

4. After you have entered the label correctly, erase the contents of cell A118.

5. Move the cell cursor to cell E81, where the year-end of the company is to be inserted.

   Whenever you write a label whose first character in the cell is not a letter of the alphabet or a blank space as a result of using the space bar, you must begin that string of characters with an apostrophe ('). In this way, 1-2-3 knows you are entering a label rather than a value. So to enter 12/31/X1 in cell E81, type:

**'12/31/X1 ⟨ENTER⟩**

6. **Specific labels.** The following labels would have to be entered for MODEL4:
   a. Your name (cells A25 and B25).
   b. The problem assignment number (cell B28).

**Caution:**   Assume you are working Problem 4-1 in Chapter 4. If you try to enter 4-1, Lotus 1-2-3 will think you are trying to enter a value and will enter 3. It is necessary to alert 1-2-3 that you intend to enter a label instead of a value. Accordingly, you must begin with ' (an apostrophe); then type 4-2.

   c. Your class time (cell B29).
   d. The parent company's name (cells C79 and D79).
   e. The parent company's year-end (cell E81).
   f. The parent company's name and the subsidiary company's name (cells B84 and C84).
   g. Account descriptions for assets (rows 117 to 120).
   h. Account descriptions for liabilities (row 125).

The labels to be entered vary depending on the particular template.

**Note:**   When working a problem on the computer and you cannot complete the problem at one sitting, you can store the partially completed solution (at any stage of completion) on your personal diskette and then return to the computer at a later time to complete the assignment. Refer to page 1301 for instructions on saving a partially completed solution on a diskette.

## Entering Formulas

For any asset or liability account that you add to the balance sheet in the early consolidation models (Models 1 through 4), you must enter a formula in column F, so that amounts on these rows will cross-total. You do not need to write any formulas for subtotals and totals. Before entering any formulas, move the cell cursor to cell F110, the intersection of the column labeled "Consolidated" and the row labeled "Cash." The formula for this cell is displayed in the upper left corner of the screen. For accounts that you add, you must write formulas such as these. Assume that you have added the account Goodwill to row 120. You would write the formulas for cell F120 as follows:

| Position Cell Cursor at | Press These Keys |
| --- | --- |
| F120 | (B120 + C120 + D120 − E120) ⟨ENTER⟩ |

At this point, you would enter formulas for any balance sheet accounts that you had to add to the template.

**Caution:**   When writing formulas, be sure to (1) use no space characters within the formulas and (2) either enclose the formulas within parentheses or begin with an "operator" such as the plus sign.

**Note:**   You may use either upper- or lowercase letters when you enter formulas. But if you enter lowercase letters, 1-2-3 will automatically convert them and store them as uppercase.

## Entering Values

Continuing with Model 4 as an example, you would enter values only in columns B through E. No values would be entered into column F, since the appropriate cells in this column contain formulas to make the amounts cross-total automatically. Also, no values need be entered at any total or subtotal, since these cells already contain formulas so that amounts will automatically total. **You can readily see on the screen where formulas have been placed, since a zero (0) is displayed there. (Entering values at these locations would destroy the formulas.)**

With column widths of 11 characters in columns B through F in Model 4, Lotus 1-2-3 will accept up to eight numeric characters for a value. (Two positions are required for commas, automatically inserted by 1-2-3, and one space must be left blank for spacing between columns.) Because negative amounts are shown in parentheses and space must be provided for the left parenthesis, only seven numeric characters can be accepted when entering negative amounts. Enter values by pressing the numeric keys and then the ⟨**ENTER**⟩ key. For example, move the cell cursor to cell B92 and enter the value **500** using the numeric keyboard, and then press ⟨**ENTER**⟩.

**Caution:**   Because the numeric keyboard is used both for moving the cell cursor and entering values, it is necessary to press the **NUM LOCK** key (located directly above the numeric keyboard) when you want to enter values.

The disadvantage of this arrangement is that when you want to move the cell cursor to another cell (after having entered a value in your present cell), it is necessary to: (a) press the **NUM LOCK** key again (to go back to the "moving the cell cursor" mode); (b) press the appropriate arrow keys to move the cell cursor to your desired cell, and (c) press the **NUM LOCK** key to go to the "entering values" mode. **For most of the templates, a special purpose macro (/N) is available to circumvent this advantage.**

Using the arrow keys, note how this value is totaled and cross-totaled in the income statement and also carried forward to the analysis of retained earnings, and then to the retained earnings account in the balance sheet. Now move the cursor to cell B92 and press **/RE ⟨ENTER⟩**, which erases the 500 value.

### Key Points in Entering Values.   Note the following:

1. **Enter values as you would on a calculator.** Thus, enter **8700,** not $8,700. Lotus 1-2-3 will automatically insert commas when it displays your values, and display the values right-justified (as would a calculator).

   #### Summary caution for entering values:
   a. **Never** enter commas.
   b. **Never** enter dollar signs.
   c. **Never** enter spaces (via the space bar).

2. **Entering negative values.** Use a minus sign when entering a negative value (as you would on a calculator). A negative amount of $3,200 would be entered as **– 3200** (the minus sign must be entered first); Lotus 1-2-3 will automatically display the negative value as (3,200). Thus, you *never* need to enter parentheses.

   **Caution:**   For Models 1 through 9 and 16T, only certain accounts in columns B and C (the parent and subsidiary company columns) require the use of negative values:

   | | |
   |---|---|
   | Income Statement and Statement of Retained Earnings: | All debit balances. |
   | Balance Sheet—Assets: | All credit balances (such as Accumulated Depreciation). |
   | Balance Sheet—Liabilities and Equity: | All debit balances (such as Bond Discount). |

   Accordingly, you would *not* use a minus sign in any column other than columns B and C.

3. **For values containing the number 1** (6100, for example). Be sure to use the 1 in the numeric keyboard—not the lowercase letter *l* next to the letter *k*.

4. **Entering elimination entries.** Enter only the values; do *not* try to code the values. Thus, enter **300000**—not 300,000(1). Lotus 1-2-3 has no facility to allow the coding of entries in a worksheet. After you have obtained a hard copy printout of a completed problem, you can *manually* code elimination entires.

In working a problem using Model 4, values in columns B through E would be entered manually. This is best done by entering all required values in column B and then proceeding to the next column (making sure the balance sheet balances in column B before proceeding to the next column). As each value is entered, the computer automatically subtotals, totals, and cross-totals the values. If you have entered labels, formulas, and values properly, the balance sheet should balance in column F. Also, the debit and credit postings in the two elimination columns (at the bottom of the worksheet section of the spreadsheet) should agree. You would then make a printout of the appropriate sections of the spreadsheet, as explained starting on page 1294.

**Reminder:** You can save substantial time by using macros to enter data in columns B and C (and for templates for Chapters 3–10, columns D and E, as well).

**Reminder:** Be sure to use only those income statement and balance sheet accounts that you need for working your particular problem. Ignore all other accounts.

## Using Macros

A **macro** is a stored instruction. By invoking (using) a macro, you can execute a complex and involved instruction by typing only a few keys. The templates for Chapters 1 through 16 contain several macros. By using them you can perform several operations quickly, and easily:

1. Load problem data (stored to the right of the worksheets in most of the models) into the worksheet portion of the template (thus not having to enter this data manually).

   **Caution:** Amounts for retained earnings and dividends must be entered **manually.**

2. Automatically post the primary elimination entry to the worksheet. (For models 3 through 16T, space is provided in a section of the worksheet for preparing this elimination entry.)
3. Simplify the entering of data in columns.
4. Erasing selected portions of a worksheet.
5. "Freeze" or lock in column titles or row descriptions along the top or left edge of the screen in order to scroll.

   **Caution:** Use this macro only after you no longer need access to the frozen area. Otherwise, you must undo the macro (using the command **/Worksheet ⟨ENTER⟩ Title ⟨ENTER⟩ Clear ⟨ENTER⟩** or **/WTC**) to gain access.

Each template's macros are stored (along with instructions for using the macros and a description of each macro) at the bottom of the template. Macros are easy to use. Each macro is assigned a letter of the alphabet. To invoke the macro stored in letter E, for example, merely press and hold down the ALT key (located below the left shift key). While holding this key down, press the letter E. (Some of the more involved macros take about ten seconds to be executed.)

As you proceed to use one template and then the next, it is recommended that you make a hard-copy printout of each template before using it on the computer. This will enable you to review the template in its entirety and readily see which macros are available to you on a particular template.

## Printing a Hard Copy of the Solution

**Overview.** You can print (or file on a diskette) all or any portion of the electronic spreadsheet. To obtain a general familiarity with a particular template, first print the entire template. In printing the solution to a specific problem, however, it usually would not be necessary to print the **macro information** (stored in the lower section of each template) or the **problem data** (stored to the right of each worksheet in an out of the way location). Accordingly, print only the worksheet portion of the template and any supporting information. For Models 3–9 and 16T, you also should print out the conceptual analysis section that precedes the consolidation worksheet. Below are the widths of the various sections in characters per line (excluding the problem data) of each of the templates, along with the letters of the columns used for each section:

|  | Section of Template | | |
| Model | Conceptual Analysis | Worksheet | Macros |
| --- | --- | --- | --- |
| 1 | n/a | 72 (A-F) | 72 (A-F) |
| 3 | 149 (A-M) | 72 (A-F) | 72 (A-F) |
| 4 | 160 (A-N) | 72 (A-F) | 72 (A-F) |
| 5 | 171 (A-O) | 72 (A-F) | 72 (A-F) |
| 6 | 94 (A-H) | 72 (A-F) | 72 (A-F) |
| 7 | 149 (A-M) | 72 (A-F) | 72 (A-F) |
| 8 | 149 (A-M) | 72 (A-F) | 72 (A-F) |
| 9 | 171 (A-O) | 72 (A-F) | 72 (A-F) |
| 16T | 94 (A-H) | 72 (A-F) | 72 (A-F) |
| 16R | n/a | 72 (A-F) | 72 (A-F) |
| 23 | n/a | 88 (A-H) | 72 (A-F) |
| 25 | n/a | 120 (A-J) | 72 (A-F) |

**The area to be printed must be designated as a rectangle.** The rectangle is defined by indicating: (a) the cell in the upper left corner of the rectangle, and (b) the cell in the lower right corner of the rectangle. How to enter the coordinates that define this rectangular area is explained on page 1297.

**Printer Capabilities.** Printers that use only $8\frac{1}{2}'' \times 11''$ paper (which for convenience we refer to as **regular printers**) output either 80 or 85 characters per row when using the normal pica pitch of 10 characters per inch (cpi), all depending on the printer model. For our purposes, we will assume that all regular printers have 80-character print heads. Printers that can accommodate 14″ paper (which for convenience we refer to as **wide-carriage printers**) output 132 characters per row when using the normal pica pitch of 10 cpi. (Technically, this paper is actually 15″ wide; however, it is commonly referred to as 14″ paper inasmuch as approximately $\frac{5}{8}$ inch is reserved on each side for the punched holes used for feeding the paper into the printer, leaving a print area of approximately $13\frac{1}{2}$ inches.) For models through Chapter 16, **the worksheet section of each model can be printed in one step using either type of printer,** inasmuch as the worksheets are all less than 80 characters wide (each worksheet being only 72 characters wide). **To print the conceptual analysis, however, two or three steps are required,** all depending on the type of printer and the length of the conceptual analysis section of the model (which may be from 94 characters to 171 characters wide). For example, for Model 4 (with a conceptual analysis section that is 160 characters wide), two steps would be required using a wide-carriage printer. These two steps might be to print out, for example, columns A through G (83 characters) and then print out columns G through N (77 characters).

The use of the **compressed printing option,** however, which uses a very small typesize of 16.5 cpi (this is smaller than elite typesize, which is 12 cpi) **enables 132 characters** ($8'' \times 16.5$ cpi) **to be printed per row on a regular printer and approximately 230 characters to be printed per row on a wide-carriage printer.** (Some printers use 17 cpi instead of 16.5 cpi.) Accordingly, the entire conceptual analysis section could be printed in one step on a wide-carriage printer (and in two steps instead of three steps on a regular printer). This option is explained on page 1299. We strongly suggest you use it (it saves paper as well as time), but only after you have mastered the basics of printing a hard copy.

**Left and Right Margin Settings Reduce Horizontal Printing Output.** The Lotus 1-2-3 left and right margin default settings and the resulting available horizontal printing output are as follows:

|  | Maximum Printing Capability (in characters) | Left and Right Margin Default Settings | Remaining Printing Capability (in characters) |
|---|---|---|---|
| **Regular printers:** |  |  |  |
| Pica type............ | 80 | 4 and 76 | 72 |

*(continued)*

| | Maximum Printing Capability (in characters) | Left and Right Margin Default Settings | Remaining Printing Capability (in characters) |
|---|---|---|---|
| Compressed type . . . . . . . | 132 | 4 and 128 | 124 |
| **Wide-carriage printers:** | | | |
| Pica type . . . . . . . . . . . . . . | 132 | 4 and 128 | 124 |
| Compressed type . . . . . . . | 230[a] | 4 and 226[a] | 222[a] |

[a]Approximately.

You will have to keep this in mind when determining your print ranges. The margin settings can be changed using the **/Printer Print Options Margin Left (or Right)** command as is illustrated later in the discussion of the compressed printing option.

**You can determine your margin default settings using one of the following two commands:**

1. **/Worksheet Global Default Status** (or **/WGDS**)
2. **/Printer Print Options Margin Left** (or Right) (or **/PPOML** or **R**) (At this point, the default setting will be displayed on the control panel.)

For each of these commands, use the escape key as many times as is necessary to fully back out of the command.

**Connecting the Printer to the Computer.**   There are various ways to connect the printer to the computer. Determine which arrangement is in use at your computer center.

**Printing Instructions.**   Follow these steps in proper sequence:

1. Connect the printer to the computer.
2. Position the paper properly in the printer.
3. Turn on the printer. If the "ready" or "on-line" indicator on the printer is not on, then press the printer button that will turn it on.
4. Press the following keys in the sequence indicated:

| Keys to Be Pressed | Explanation and Guidance |
|---|---|
| / | Tells 1-2-3 to display the top-level menu. |
| P | To select the "Print" command. After the letter *P* is pressed, the prompt line displays the following menu choices: |
| | **Printer File** |

| Keys to Be Pressed | Explanation and Guidance |
|---|---|
| | 1-2-3 is prompting you to select one of the above subcommands. Pressing the F key selects the File subcommand; pressing the P key selects the Printer subcommand. |
| **P** | Since you want to print, press the P key. The prompt line then displays the following menu choices:<br><br>**Range Line Page Options Clear Align Go Quit**<br><br>Each of these menu choices stands for a possible printing suboption. Unlike other menu displays, this is a "sticky" menu—after you make a choice, **the menu reappears to see if you want to select additional printing suboptions.** (We will eventually press Go to start printing; the Quit option is the only other way to get out of this menu.) |
| **R** | To specify the Print Range, the upper left and lower right coordinates of the print area. The first coordinate of the Print Range then appears:<br><br>**Enter Print range: A1**<br><br>A1 identifies the current location of the cell cursor. For our purposes, ignore this cell location and type over it.<br><br>The remaining illustrative steps assume we want to print the entire template (excluding the problem data stored in cells U81-AN137) for Model 4 (which has 160 characters per row in its widest section, which is the conceptual analysis). **We also assume the use of a wide-carriage (132 characters) printer in the pica type mode**—not the compressed printing mode. Accordingly, the printing process takes two steps rather than one step as in the compressed printing mode. |
| **A1.G245**<br>**⟨ENTER⟩** | Cell A1 is the upper left corner of the spreadsheet. Cell G245 is a convenient place to set the lower right corner of the rectangular print area. (This Print Range will allow you to print the first seven columns that comprise 83 characters.) Then proceed to step 5; when you are finished with step 5, return to this place in step 4.<br><br>While the computer is printing the first portion of the spreadsheet, as soon as the flashing WAIT message |

*(continued)*

| Keys to Be Pressed | Explanation and Guidance |
|---|---|
| | in the upper right corner of the screen stops, you can prepare the commands for printing the remainder of the spreadsheet. The remaining portion to be printed is in the right half of the conceptual analysis located in columns H through N (rows 30 through 55). |
| | The menu will list a series of options (beginning with Range). Press R for Range and specify the Print Range as follows: |
| **H30..N55** ⟨ENTER⟩ | Cell H30 is the upper left corner of the unprinted portion of the spreadsheet. Cell N55 is the lower right corner of that portion. (This print range will allow you to print the remaining seven columns comprising the remaining 77 characters.) |

5. Once you have entered the print range, the previous higher-level menu choices (beginning with Range) reappear. (The range you entered has been remembered, however.) You could now select Go, and the spreadsheet would be sent to the printer. However, to print a spreadsheet that is longer than one page in a **continuous format,** that is without any margin at the bottom of each page and without any margin at the top of each new page (referred to as page breaks), it is first necessary to override the top and bottom of page default margin settings of 5 each. (Otherwise, the worksheet would be split for no good reason.) To do so, press the following keys:

| Keys to Be Pressed | Explanation and Guidance |
|---|---|
| O | Press the letter O to request one of the special printing Options. |
| O | Press the letter O to request one of the special print options grouped under the command keyword Other. |
| U | Pressing U specifies that the format should be Unformatted (no top and bottom margins to be inserted). Then the previous higher-level menu containing the command keyword Other reappears to allow you to select additional print options. |
| Q | Because no additional print options are needed, tell the computer that you are finished selecting print options by pressing Q for Quit. Then the previous higher-level menu (beginning with the option Range) reappears. You are now ready to select Go. |
| G | This command sends the spreadsheet to the printer. |

Naturally, you can always use the "point and pick" method of building the command: moving the menu cursor to each option **and pressing ⟨ENTER⟩ for each selection:**

**/ Print Printer Range A1..H245 Option Other Unformatted Quit Go**

**Caution:**  If you are printing more than one copy of a solution or model, you may have to include the **Align** command, which resets the line counter within the printer to zero. If you do not do this, you may get page breaks where you do not want them to appear. This all depends on the printer you are using. Of course, you should always be sure the paper is properly positioned in the printer each time you print.

**Note:**  If you had used a **regular (80 characters) printer,** the printing process would take three steps using the following coordinates:

Step 1: A1..F245 (six columns comprising 72 characters on 245 rows)

Step 2: G30..L55 (six columns comprising 66 characters on 26 rows)

Step 3: M30..N55 (two columns comprising 22 characters on 26 rows)

**Designating a Print Range Wider than Your Printer's Capability.**  In the previous example, we showed you the safest way to print the template (using two print ranges resulting in two printing passes). If you had designated your print range to be Al..N245 (the full 160 characters wide and 245 rows), Lotus 1-2-3 would have recognized that the width of the print range at 160 characters exceeds the 132 character output of the wide-carriage printer. Accordingly, it automatically would have printed through column K (127 characters) and printed on later pages the remaining columns L through N (33 characters). For this feature to work as you would want it to, the right margin default setting cannot exceed the printer's output capability as specified in the printer's manual.

## Using Setup Codes to Change to Compressed Printing Mode

Although some printers have a button, which when pressed puts the printer into the compressed printing mode, this is not that common. Accordingly, it will be necessary in most cases to use one of the printing options available in Lotus 1-2-3. In the printer's manual that accompanies your printer, look up the decimal digit code applicable to your printer. (The manual probably will also list the ASCII and hexadecimal codes as well—ignore them.) Use the decimal codes to enter a setup string. Each string is prefaced by a (reverse backslash), with all two-digit numbers also prefaced with a zero. For example, if your manual lists the codes to use as 27 and 80, you would enter them as \027\080. If your manual lists the code to use as 15 (the code for certain IBM, Epson, and Hewlett-Packard printers), you would enter it as \015. The command for selecting the compressed printing option **assuming the digit code is 15** is as follows:

/ **Printer Print Options Setup** \015 ⟨**ENTER**⟩ (or /**PPOS 015** ⟨**ENTER**⟩)

The above command changes the **default** setting in the printer's memory—not the computer's memory. Note that you must be connected to the printer to execute this command. The printer will stay in this new setting until someone changes it back to its original default setting (10-pitch type). This is usually done for most printers by turning the printer off and then back on again.

**Changing the Right Margin Setting.**   You must also change the right margin setting from its default setting so that additional characters in columns to the right of the default setting can be printed (otherwise you lose the benefit of using compressed printing). In most cases, you merely need to set the right margin setting at its maximum allowable setting as listed below:

|  | Right Margin Default Setting for Pica Printing | Right Margin Maximum Allowable Setting for Compressed Printing |
| --- | --- | --- |
| Regular printers | 76 | 132 |
| Wide-carriage printers | 128 | 240 |

However, some printers have an output that is slightly different from the above listed maximum allowable settings. If you set your right margin at greater than the printer's printing output capability, and you then specify a print range greater than this output capability, you have effectively "lied" to 1-2-3 as to the printer's capability. Accordingly, it will get confused and will wind up printing the extra characters from the column that straddles the output capability on the next row in Column A, resulting in a confusing looking printout. This situation should never occur if you have a wide-carriage printer, inasmuch as the widest section of any of the templates (excluding the problem data that you will not be printing) is 171 characters (far below the output capability of these printers. However, it could occur for the regular printers. Accordingly, **you should inquire regarding the exact maximum printing output of your printer for the compressed printing mode and use that output capability in changing the right margin setting.**

## Saving a Completed or Partially Completed Solution

Recall that earlier we suggested that you buy two personal diskettes—one for copying the templates to and one for saving solutions to problems. By having a separate diskette for solutions, you minimize the possibility of unintentionally destroying a template. As a further precaution, in saving a completed or partially completed problem on your second diskette, we advise assigning a specific file name to that problem, such as PROB42 if you are working Problem 4-2 in Chapter 4.

**Caution:** Never save your solution under a file name beginning with MODEL—you might destroy the model on your templates diskette (if you happen to have the wrong disk inserted in the disk drive). This would prevent you from using that template for working a different problem. To prevent accidental destruction of any of your templates, follow carefully the following instructions for assigning file names and for filing solutions.

**File Names.** File names in Lotus 1-2-3 can be up to eight characters long. However, the characters can consist only of letters of the alphabet (A through Z) and numbers (0 through 9). Accordingly, you **cannot use dashes, periods, other forms of punctuation, or blank spaces;** the computer will reject these as improper file names by beeping. Note that previously we suggested using PROB42 as an example—not an improper file name such as PROBLEM 4-2 or PROB. 4-2 (both of which have three rule infractions—see whether you can identify them). If you type in lowercase letters in assigning a file name, Lotus 1-2-3 will automatically convert them to upper case.

**Instructions for Saving Your Work.** To save a completed or partially completed solution on your personal diskette, do the following:

| Keys to Be Pressed | Explanation and Guidance |
|:---:|:---|
| / | To display the top-level menu. |
| **F** | To select the File command. |
| **S** | To select the subcommand Save within the File command. |
| | At this point, 1-2-3 tries to be helpful by displaying on the monitor the names of any of the files already on your personal diskette. For example, assume you previously have saved problems 1-3 and 3-5. The display should be: **PROB13.WK1 PROB35.WK1** with PROB13.WK1 highlighted. (Lotus automatically appends the file extension .WK1 to each worksheet file name |

*(continued)*

| Keys to Be Pressed | Explanation and Guidance |
|---|---|
| | you create, so as to distinguish them from other types of files, such as graph files and print files). |
| | Assuming you select PROB42 as your file name; proceed as follows: |
| **PROB42** | To indicate the file name you wish to assign to your solution. |
| ⟨**ENTER**⟩ | To begin the filing process (takes about 10–20 seconds). Watch for the blinking WAIT in the upper right corner of the screen to return to READY. |

Using the "point and pick" method of building the command, the sequence is as follows: / **File** ⟨**ENTER**⟩ **Save** ⟨**ENTER**⟩ **PROB42** ⟨**ENTER**⟩.

To terminate your session with 1-2-3, call for the main menu by pressing /. Then select Quit (or press **Q**). When 1-2-3 asks for a confirmation, select Yes (or type **Y**). **Be sure to save your work from your current session before quitting.**

**Starting Again Where You Previously Stopped.** Assume you later return to the computer to finish Problem 4-2, which you filed in its partially completed stage as previously instructed. Load the PROB42 file from your personal diskette (rather than the original MODEL4 file from the templates diskette), thereby enabling you to begin where you left off earlier. The command would be: /**FR PROB42** ⟨**ENTER**⟩.

**Filing a Solution a Second (or Third) Time.** Suppose you are either unable to complete Problem 4-2 at the end of the second session or you have completed it and want to file your completed solution. Again, it will be necessary to file the solution on your personal diskette. This time, however, you will be **replacing** the existing PROB42 file with the file from your latest session, rather than creating it. In replacing an existing file, an additional step is added to the previously shown filing instructions. The complete process is as follows:

| Keys to Be Pressed | Explanation and Guidance |
|---|---|
| /**FS PROB42** ⟨**ENTER**⟩ | Same explanation as previously shown. After pressing these keys, the prompt line shows: |
| | **Cancel Replace** |
| | 1-2-3 is merely checking to see if you want to update (replace) the PROB42 file. If you really do not want to replace PROB42, abort (Cancel) this command. |

| Keys to Be Pressed | Explanation and Guidance |
|---|---|
| **R** | By pressing R, you are confirming that you want the file replaced. The old PROB42 file is destroyed and is replaced by the new PROB42 file. |

**Other Technical Points Concerning Files.** Some other technical points that may be of interest are as follows:

| Commands | Explanation and Guidance |
|---|---|
| **/ Worksheet** ⟨**ENTER**⟩ **Erase** ⟨**ENTER**⟩ **Yes** (or **/WEY**) | This command erases only the screen—it does not erase any files on the diskette. |
| **/File** ⟨**ENTER**⟩ **Erase** ⟨**ENTER**⟩ **Worksheet** (file name) ⟨**ENTER**⟩ **Yes** (or **/FEW** file name **Y**) | This command erases a file on the diskette. After Worksheet (or W) is selected, it is necessary to "point" to the file name to be erased—all file names on the diskette are displayed (or can be displayed) to allow a choice to be made. By using the right arrow key to move the menu pointer all the way to the right, file names not initially displayed become displayed. |

## Using Range Names

For illustrative purposes, load Model 4 into the computer's memory. Then go to cell D160, which is the first row of macro \A. This macro was created to copy the problem data for Problem 4-1, which is stored in columns W and X of the spreadsheet, into the parent and subsidiary company columns of the consolidation worksheet (columns B and C respectively). The first line of the macro copies the income statement accounts. The second line copies the assets. The third and fourth lines are for the liabilities and equity accounts. The range name P/L—#1 was assigned to the income statement accounts in columns W and X. The range name P/L—P&S was assigned to the corresponding income statement accounts in columns B and C of the worksheet.

By using range names in this manner (as opposed to the alternative of using cell coordinates), the location of the problem data and worksheet can be changed without having to revise the macro (as would be necessary if cell coordinates were used). The use of range names in spreadsheets is quite common in practice, and you should obtain some familiarity with them. A display of all the range names used in this model can be easily obtained by executing the command:

**/Range Name Create** (and then pressing the F3 function key)

You should then use the escape key to back out of this command after reviewing the display.

## SYSTEM REQUIREMENTS

- IBM PC (or IBM XT or IBM AT with 360 KB drive)
- Two double-sided, double-density or high-density disk drives for IBM PC; one floppy disk drive for IBM XT or IBM AT
- 256 K RAM of memory
- Lotus 1-2-3 System disk, version 2 or later
- 80-column, parallel printer (if worksheets are to be printed)

# INDEX

| | | |
|---|---|---|
| **P10-1** | | Carrying value of investment, $1,430,000 |
| **P10-2** | 1. | Decrease in parent's equity interest, $360,000 |
| | 2. | Goodwill element at Jan. 1, 19X6, $165,000 |
| **P10-3** | 1. | Goodwill element at Jan. 1, 19X6, $190,000 |
| **P10-4** | 1. | Carrying value of investment at Dec. 31, 19X4, $1,411,500; Gain on sale of shares, $32,000 |
| **P10-5** | 1. | Carrying value of investment at Dec. 31, 19X7, $292,667; Gain on disposal, $26,500 |
| **P10-6** | 1. | Parent's dilution, $225,000 |
| **P10-7** | 1. | Parent's accretion, $40,000 |
| **P10-8** | 1. | Dec. 31, 19X5 investment balance: MODULE 1, $709,000; MODULE 2, $699,000; MODULE 3, $705,000 |
| | 5. | Gain on extinguishment of debt, $9,000; Minority interest, income statement, $69,000; Consolidated net income, $872,000; Consolidated assets, $4,680,000; Consolidated retained earnings, $2,620,000; Minority interest, balance sheet, $233,000 |
| **P10-9** | 2. | Minority interest at Dec. 31, 19X2, $329,000 |
| **P10-10** | 2. | Minority interest at Dec. 31, 19X1, $157,000 |
| **P10-11** | 2. | Minority interest at Dec. 31, 19X1, $44,000 |
| | 5. | Consolidated net income, $178,000 Consolidated assets, $1,030,000 |
| **E11-1** | 2. | $38,000 |
| **E11-2** | 2. | $207,000 |
| **E11-3** | 2. | $31,000 |
| **E11-4** | 1. | $9,977,480 |
| | 2. | $1,132,520 |
| **E11-5** | 1. | $580,000 and $20,000 |
| | 2. | $567,391 and $32,609 |
| **P11-1** | 1. | $584,000 |
| | 2. | $30,000 |
| **P11-2** | 1. | $1,080,700 |
| | 2. | $21,800 |
| **P11-3** | 1. | $687,600 |
| | 2. | $21,400 |
| **P11-4** | 1. | $878,000 and $10,000 |
| | 2. | $868,352 and $19,648 |
| **P11-5** | 1. | $450,000 and $40,000 |
| | 3. | $430,851 and $59,149 |
| | 4. | Controlling interest balance at Dec. 31, 19X1, $1,157,533; Minority interest balance at Dec. 31, 19X1; $205,447 |
| **P11-6** | 2. | $223,000 |
| **E12-1** | 1. | Goodwill, $55,000 |
| **E12-2** | | Income tax expense, $12,000 |
| **E12-3** | | Income tax expense, $−0− |
| **E12-4** | | Income tax expense, $−0− |
| **E12-5** | | 1a. $2.80; 1b. $2.82 |
| **E12-6** | | 1a. $13.75; 1b. $14.25 |

| | | |
|---|---|---|
| **E12-7** | | 1a. $2.24; 1b. $2.42 |
| **P12-1** | 1. | Goodwill, $82,000 |
| **P12-2** | | Income tax expense, $20,000 |
| **P12-3** | 1. | Income tax expense, $20,000 plus $30,000 |
| **P12-4** | 1. | Income tax expense, $90,000 plus $30,000 |
| **P12-5** | 1. | Parent's income tax expense, $278,400; Subsidiary's income tax expense, $60,000 |
| | 3. | Consolidated net income, $481,600 |
| **P12-6** | 1. | Parent's income tax expense, $698,000; Subsidiary's income tax expense, $100,000 |
| | 3. | Consolidated net income, $797,000 |
| **P12-7** | | 1a. $1.62; 1b. $1.65 |
| **P12-8** | | 1a. $.81; 1b. $.83 |
| **P12-9** | | 1a. $1.62 and $1.40 |
| | | 1b. $1.67 and $1.43 |
| **P12-10** | | Consolidated cash flow from: Operations, $138,000; Investing, $(90,000); Financing, $2,000 |
| **P12-11** | | Cash flow from: Operations, $86,000; Investing, $(77,000); Financing, $6,000 |
| **E13-1** | | Operating profit, $320,000 |
| **E13-2** | 1. | Segments A, B, D, and G |
| | 2. | 75% test is not satisfied |
| **E13-3** | | S. America, Australia, Middle East |
| **E13-4** | | 19X6 loss from discontinued operations, $150,000; 19X7 gain on disposal of discontinued operations, $78,000 |
| **E13-5** | | Loss from operations, $180,000; Loss on disposal, $750,000 |
| **P13-1** | 1. | Segments B, D, E, and G |
| **P13-2** | | Consolidated operating profit, $99,200 |
| **P13-3** | | Segment A's operating profit, $290,000; Consolidated operating profit, $350,000 |
| **P13-4** | 1. | Consolidated operating profit, $444,000; Segment A's operating profit, $196,000 |
| | 2. | Segement A's operating profit, $206,000; Consolidated operating profit, $455,600 |
| **P13-5** | | U.S. operating profit, $587,600; Consolidated operating profit, $717,600 |
| **P13-6** | | Segment G, $200, $200, and $500 Segment H, $200, $100, and $200 |
| **P13-7** | | Loss from discontinued operations, $(810,000); Net income, $270,000 |
| **E14-1** | 1. | Direct rate at Dec. 31, 19X1, 1 peso equals $0.005 |
| **E14-4** | | Foreign currency transaction loss: Dec. 31, 19X1, $57 and $126; Jan. 5, 19X2, $156 and $66 |
| **P14-1** | | Vendor A: $200 transaction gain at July 31, 19X1; Customer A: $125 transaction loss at July 30, 19X1 |
| **P14-2** | | Vendor A: $1,000 transaction gain at June 30, 19X1; Customer A: $300 transaction loss at June 30, 19X1 |
| **P14-3** | | Dec. 31, 19X1: Offsetting $2,400 gain and loss; Jan. 15, 19X2: Offsetting $800 gain and loss |

(continued on back endpapers)

| | |
|---|---|
| | June 30, 19X3, two $1,500 adjustments; July 30, 19X3, two $500 adjustments |
| P14-5 | Capitalized cost of equipment, $481,000 |
| | |
| E15-1 | Credit retained earnings, $160,000 |
| E15-2 | 3. Decrease in cash of $100,000 |
| E15-3 | a. $10,000—Adverse |
| | b. $25,000—Favorable |
| E15-4 | Brazil, Net monetary liability position; Mexico, Net monetary asset position; Belgium, Net liability position; Ireland, Net asset position |
| E15-5 | $.44 |
| | |
| E16-3 | 2a. $30,000 |
| | 2b. $63,000 |
| E16-4 | a. $8,000; b. $(40,000) |
| E16-5 | a. $180,000; b. $200,000 |
| E16-6 | 1. Parent records $9,000 loss |
| | 2. Subsidiary records $100,000 loss in widgettas |
| E16-7 | 1. Dividend receivable, $1,500,000 |
| | 2. F.C. transaction gain, $78,930 |
| P16-1 | 1a. $42,000 1b. $13,000—Favorable 2a. $70,000 2b. $10,000 gain |
| P16-2 | 1. Translation adjustment, $(157,000) |
| | 2. Net income, $72,000 |
| P16-3 | 1. Gain from remeasurement, $211,000 |
| | 2. Net income, $195,000 |
| P16-4 | 1. Translation adjustment, $195,000 |
| | 2. Net income, $420,000 |
| P16-5 | 1. Loss from remeasurement, $(286,000) |
| | 2. Net income, $329,000 |
| P16-6 | 1. Parent records $160,000 loss |
| | 2. Subsidiary records 133,333 loss in pounds |
| | 3. $25,000 |
| | 6. $1,000 |
| P16-7 | 1. F.C. transaction gain of $50,000 |
| P16-9 | 1. Current year translation adjustment, $(79,000) |
| | 2. Ending retained earnings, $514,000 |
| | 3. Parent records $22,000 transaction loss |
| | 4. Defer $62,000 of intercompany profit |
| | 8. Consolidated net income, $1,436,000; Total assets, $5,007,000 |
| | |
| E17-3 | $60,000 each quarter |
| E17-4 | $1,100,000 |
| E17-5 | Expense in second quarter |
| P17-1 | First quarter income tax expense, $200,000; Second quarter income tax expense, $220,000 |
| P17-2 | First quarter bonus expense, $14,000 or $8,000; Second quarter bonus expense, $5,000 or $4,000 |
| P17-3 | 3. Revised estimated annual tax rate, 42.36%; Second quarter income tax expense, $170,160 |

There are no key figures for Chapter 18

| | |
|---|---|
| E19-1 | 1. No gain on restructuring |
| E19-2 | 1. Gain on restructuring, $80,000 |
| | 3. No gain on restructuring |

| | |
|---|---|
| E19-3 | 1. No gain on restructuring |
| | 2. $92,000 |
| | 3. 3% |
| E19-4 | 1. Gain on restructuring, $40,000 |
| E19-5 | 1. Gain on restructuring, $75,000 |
| E19-6 | Gain on restructuring, $7,000,000 |
| E19-7 | Gain on restructuring, $2,500,000 |
| E19-8 | $156,000 available to unsecured creditors |
| P19-1 | 1. Gain on restructuring, $176,000 |
| P19-2 | 1. Gain on restructuring, $300,000 |
| P19-3 | 1. Gain on restructuring, $440,000 |
| P19-4 | 3a. Future interest expense, $-0- |
| | 3b. Future interest expense, $9,000,000 |
| P19-5 | 3. Future interest expense, $323,000 |
| | 4. Approx. effective interest rate, 5% |
| | 5. 19X1 interest expense, $163,850 |
| P19-6 | 2. Gain on restructuring, $375,000 |
| | 3. Future interest expense, $150,000 |
| P19-7 | 2. No entry required |
| | 3. 5% of the face amount |
| P19-8 | 1. Discount, $19,773,720 Gain on restructuring, $254,773,720 |
| | 2. First-year interest expense, $42,033,942 |
| P19-9 | 1. Deficiency to unsecured creditors, $18,200 |
| P19-10 | 1. Deficiency to unsecured creditors, $41,000 |
| | |
| E20-1 | $775,000 |
| E20-2 | Credit deferred revenues, $3,000 |
| E20-3 | Credit deferred revenues, $150,000 |
| E20-4 | 6. Credit Expenditures, $66,000 |
| E20-5 | Fund balance at June 30, 19X2, $155,000 |
| E20-6 | Credit Budgetary Fund Balance, $80,000 |
| E20-7 | $4,000 |
| E20-8 | $42,000 favorable variance |
| E20-9 | $10,000 favorable variance |
| P20-1 | 2. Total expenditures, $899,000; Total revenues, $988,000 |
| P20-2 | 1. Revenues, $880,000; Expenditures, $830,000 Total fund balance at June 30, 19X2, $260,000 |
| | 2. Unreserved fund balance at June 30, 19X2, $180,000 |
| P20-3 | 2. Credit unreserved fund balance, $32,000 |
| | 3. June 30, 19X2 fund balance, $102,000 |
| P20-4 | 2. Credit unreserved fund balance, $66,000 |
| | 3. June 30, 19X3 fund balance, $183,000 |
| P20-5 | 3. Credit unreserved fund balance, $34,000 |
| | 4. Total assets, $158,000; Total fund balance, $142,000 |
| P20-6 | 3. Total expenditures, $832,000; June 20, 19X6 fund balance, $188,000 |
| P20-7 | 3. Excess of revenues over expenditures, $40,000; June 30, 19X5 fund balance, $260,000 |
| P20-8 | 5. July 1, 19X6 fund balance (corrected retroactively), $80,000; June 30, 19X7 fund balance (corrected), $88,000 |
| | |
| P21-1 | 3. June 30, 19X3 fund balance, $3,020,000 |
| P21-2 | Revenues (under) expenditures, $(1,076,000) |
| P21-3 | 3. Fund Balance at June 30, 19X2: Capital |